Ex Líbrís

Randy Manning

SHERMAN'S HORSEMEN

SHERMAN'S
HORSEMEN

Union Cavalry Operations
in the Atlanta Campaign

David Evans

INDIANA UNIVERSITY PRESS ✦ BLOOMINGTON AND INDIANAPOLIS

The paper used in this publication meets the minimum requirements of American National Standard for Information Sciences—Permanence of Paper for Printed Library Materials, ANSI Z39.48–1984.

MANUFACTURED IN THE UNITED STATES OF AMERICA

Library of Congress Cataloging-in-Publication Data

Evans, David, date
    Sherman's horsemen: Union cavalry operations in the Atlanta campaign / David Evans.
       p.   cm.
    Includes bibliographical references and index.
    ISBN 0–253–32963–9 (alk. paper)
    1. Atlanta Campaign, 1864—Cavalry operations. I. Title.
E476.7.E93   1996
973.7'37—dc20   95–47981

1   2   3   4   5   01   00   99   98   97   96

For Mary . . .
who made all the long marches.

CONTENTS

ILLUSTRATIONS

MAPS

ORDER OF BATTLE
JULY 1–SEPTEMBER 2, 1864

CAVALRY CORPS, ARMY OF THE CUMBERLAND
Brigadier General Washington Lafayette Elliott

Escort
4th Ohio, Company D, Capt. Phillip H. Warner

1st Division
Brigadier General Edward Moody McCook[1,2]

1st Brigade
Colonel Joseph B. Dorr
Colonel John T. Croxton[3]
Colonel Joseph B. Dorr[4]
Colonel James P. Brownlow[5]
Brigadier General John T.
   Croxton

8th Iowa Cavalry
   Major Richard Root
   Colonel Joseph B. Dorr[6]
   Major Richard Root
4th Kentucky Mounted Infantry[7]
   Colonel John T. Croxton
   Lt. Col. Robert M. Kelly[6]
   Capt. James H. West[4,8]
   Lt. Granville C. West
   Capt. James I. Hudnall
1st Tennessee Cavalry
   Colonel James P. Brownlow

2nd Brigade
Lt. Col. Horace P. Lamson
Lt. Col. William H. Torrey[9]
Lt. Col. Horace P. Lamson

2nd Indiana Cavalry
   Major David A. Briggs
4th Indiana Cavalry[10]
   Capt. Albert J. Morley[11]
   Capt. John Austin[12]
   Capt. Albert J. Morley
   Lt. Col. Horace P. Lamson
   Major George H. Purdy
1st Wisconsin Cavalry
   Major Nathan Paine
   Lt. Col. W. H. Torrey[13]
   Major Nathan Paine[14]
   Capt. Lewis M. B. Smith

Artillery
18th Indiana Battery
Lt. William B. Rippetoe

[1]The Senate confirmed McCook's promotion to brigadier general on April 27, but he apparently was not notified until sometime later and continued to sign his correspondence as Colonel McCook until June 12. [2]McCook's escort consisted of men detailed from several different regiments. [3]Assumed command July 20. [4]Assumed command July 30. [5]In command July 31–August 12. [6]Captured July 30. [7]Joined the division on July 18. [8]Captured July 31. [9]Assumed command July 20, mortally wounded July 30. [10]Company C on detached duty in the Department of the Gulf, serving as escort to Major General A. J. Smith. [11]In command July 6. [12]In command July 10. [13]Assumed command July 12. [14]Mortally wounded July 29.

2nd Division
Brigadier General Kenner Dudley Garrard

Escort
Company D, 7th Pennsylvania, Capt. John T. Newcomer

1st Brigade
Colonel Robert H. G. Minty

4th Michigan Cavalry
Major Frank Mix[1]
Capt. L. Briggs Eldridge
7th Pennsylvania Cavalry
Major William H. Jennings
4th United States Cavalry
Capt. James B. McIntyre

2nd Brigade
Colonel Eli Long[1]
Colonel Beroth B. Eggleston

1st Ohio Cavalry[2]
Colonel Beroth B. Eggleston
Lt. Col. Thomas J. Patten
3rd Ohio Cavalry
Colonel Charles B. Seidel
4th Ohio Cavalry[3]
Lt. Col. Oliver P. Robie

3rd Brigade
Colonel Abram O. Miller

17th Indiana Mounted Infantry
Major Jacob G. Vail

98th Illinois Mounted Infantry
Lt. Col. Edward C. Kitchell

72nd Indiana Mounted Infantry
Capt. Adam Pinkerton
Lt. Col. Samuel C. Kirkpatrick[4]

123rd Illinois Mounted Infantry
Lt. Col. Jonathan Biggs

Artillery
Chicago Board of Trade Battery
Lt. George I. Robinson

[1]Wounded August 20. [2]Companies A and C on detached duty at Nashville, Tennessee. Company L serving as escort to Major General George H. Thomas. Company B serving as escort to Major General James B. McPherson. [3]Company D serving as escort to Brigadier General Washington L. Elliott. [4]Assumed command on July 19.

3rd Division
Colonel William W. Lowe[1]
Brigadier General Judson Kilpatrick[2]
Colonel Eli Murray[3]
Brigadier General Judson Kilpatrick

1st Brigade
Lt. Col. Robert Klein[4]
Major J. Morris Young[5]

3rd Indiana Cavalry[6]
  Major Alfred Gaddis
5th Iowa Cavalry[7]
  Major Harlon Baird
  Lt. Col. Matthewson T. Patrick[8]
  Major J. Morris Young[9]
  Capt. Martin Choumee[5]

2nd Brigade
Lt. Col. Robert Klein
Lt. Col. Fielder A. Jones[10]

8th Indiana Cavalry
  Major Thomas Herring[10]
  Major Thomas Graham
2nd Kentucky Cavalry
  Major Owen Star
10th Ohio Cavalry
  Lt. Col. Thomas W. Sanderson

3rd Brigade
Colonel Eli H. Murray
Lt. Col. Robert H. King[3]
Colonel Eli H. Murray

92nd Illinois Mounted Infantry
Colonel Smith D. Atkins[11]
Major Albert Woodcock
Colonel Smith D. Atkins[12]
3rd Kentucky Cavalry
Lt. Col. Robert H. King
Major Lewis Wolfley[13]
5th Kentucky Cavalry
Colonel Oliver L. Baldwin[14]
Major Christopher L. Cheek[13]

Artillery
10th Wisconsin Battery
Capt. Yates V. Beebe

---

[1]In command from May 21 to July 22. Ordered to Nashville, August 1, to take command of dismounted cavalry of the Department of the Cumberland. [2]Resumed command July 22. [3]In command August 18–22. [4]Commanded 2nd Brigade until August 6. [5]Assumed command August 29. [6]Assigned to 2nd Brigade until August 6. [7]Joined the 1st Brigade August 6. [8]Commanding 1st Brigade dismounted men. [9]Assumed command August 17. [10]Assumed command August 6, disabled August 31. [11]Relieved of command July 19. [12]Resumed command September 2. [13]Probably in command August 18–22. [14]Absent with leave August 4–26.

ROUSSEAU'S DIVISION[1]
Major General Lovell Harrison Rousseau

Escort
Two companies of the 2nd Kentucky Cavalry

Companies E and G, 9th Ohio[2]
Lt. St. Clair J. Fechner and Lt. Thomas W. Fanning

1st Brigade
Colonel Thomas Joshua Harrison

2nd Kentucky Cavalry
Lt. Col. Elijah S. Watts
8th Indiana Cavalry
Lt. Col. Fielder A. Jones
5th Iowa Cavalry[3]
Lt. Col. Matthewson T. Patrick
Major Harlon Baird[4]

2nd Brigade
Colonel William D. Hamilton
Lt. Col. Matthewson T. Patrick[4]

9th Ohio Cavalry[5]
Capt. William Stough
Colonel William D. Hamilton[4]
4th Tennessee Cavalry
Major Meshack Stephens

Artillery
One section, Battery E, 1st Michigan Light Artillery
Lt. Leonard Wightman

[1]Rousseau's command was an expeditionary force assembled from elements of the 3rd Cavalry Division of the Army of the Cumberland and garrison troops from the District of Northern Alabama. [2]Assigned to replace the two companies of the 2nd Kentucky Cavalry on July 20. [3]Transferred to 2nd Brigade July 13. [4]Assumed command July 13. [5]Transferred to 1st Brigade July 13.

CAVALRY CORPS, ARMY OF THE OHIO[1]
Major General George Stoneman, Jr.[2]
Colonel Horace Capron[3]
Colonel Israel Garrard[4]

Escort
Company D, 7th Ohio Cavalry, Lt. Washington W. Manning[2]

Adams's Brigade
Colonel Silas Adams

1st Kentucky Cavalry
Major Francis N. Helveti[5]
11th Kentucky Cavalry
Major William O. Boyle

Capron's (Third) Brigade[8]
Colonel Horace Capron

14th Illinois Cavalry
Lt. Col. David P. Jenkins
8th Michigan Cavalry
Lt. Col. Elisha Mix[2]
Major William L. Buck[7]
Major Edward L. Coates
McLaughlin's Ohio Squadron
Major Richard Rice

Biddle's (Second) Brigade
Colonel James Biddle
Colonel Thomas H. Butler
Colonel James Biddle[2,6]

5th Indiana Cavalry
Major Moses D. Leeson
Colonel Thomas H. Butler[2,6]
6th Indiana Cavalry
Lt. Col. Courtland C. Matson[7]
Major William W. Carter

Garrard's (First) Brigade
Colonel Israel Garrard

7th Ohio Cavalry[9]
Lt. Col. George G. Miner
9th Michigan Cavalry[10]
Colonel George S. Acker

Artillery
24th Indiana Battery[11]
Capt. Alexander Hardy[2]

---

[1]Reorganized August 11 into mounted and dismounted contingents under the command of Colonel Israel Garrard. The mounted brigade, led by Colonel George S. Acker, except from August 16 to 23, when Colonel William D. Hamilton was in command, consisted of the 9th Michigan Cavalry, Lt. Col. William B. Way; 7th Ohio Cavalry, Lt. Col. George G. Miner; a detachment of the 9th Ohio Cavalry, Capt. Lewis H. Bollus; McLaughlin's Ohio Squadron, Major Richard Rice; and a section of the 24th Indiana Battery, Lt. William Allen. The dismounted brigade, led by Colonel Horace Capron, consisted of the 14th and 16th Illinois, 5th and 6th Indiana, and 12th Kentucky Cavalry. The 6th Indiana was ordered to Nashville on August 23 to remount. [2]Captured July 31. [3]In command from August 1. [4]In command from August 11. [5]Promoted to lieutenant colonel July 15. [6]Assumed command on or about July 10. [7]Captured August 3. [8]Joined the division in the field, June 30. [9]Joined the division in the field, July 27. [10]Joined the division in the field, August 8. [11]Transferred from 1st Division, XXIII Army Corps, on July 6.

PREFACE

Shortly after the turn of the century, a young man stood on a crowded sidewalk in a large Southern city. A brass band was playing and throngs of cheering spectators pressed close to the curb as a group of old Confederate soldiers marched down the street. As the proud veterans of Antietam, Gettysburg, and a score of other battles paraded past, the young man noticed their ranks, now gray and stooped with age, were thinner than the year before, their step a little slower. With tears welling up in his eyes, he clenched his fists and vowed, "If someone doesn't write the story of these men, it will be lost forever, and I'm go'n' to do it!"

The young man's name was Douglas Southall Freeman and his award-winning studies *R. E. Lee* and *Lee's Lieutenants* inspired a whole generation of Civil War historians. Most of them followed Freeman's example, focusing their attention on the campaigns and battles in Virginia. Only recently have events in the western theater, like Shiloh, Vicksburg, and Chickamauga, come under close scrutiny.

Despite this changing emphasis in Civil War historiography, there is still a tendency to describe campaigns and battles solely in terms of bloody clashes between rival armies of massed infantry. This is understandable. Foot soldiers did most of the fighting and decided the outcome of the war. But by 1864, more than one out of every ten Civil War soldiers was a cavalryman. They, too, have a story to tell, and nowhere did horse soldiers play a more important role than in William Tecumseh Sherman's Atlanta campaign.

Six times during July and August of 1864, Sherman sent mounted columns to cut the railroads supplying the besieged city. These raids, Sherman's motives for launching them, and their impact on the course of the campaign are among the least known and less understood aspects of one of the most interesting and most important chapters of our Civil War.

I became fascinated with the cavalry operations around Atlanta because this was history that had happened right where I lived. The more I learned the more I wanted to know, but the few articles and even fewer books focusing on these raids rarely delved beyond the reports in the *Official Records* and a handful of regimental histories. Sherman's cavalry commanders seemed lifeless in comparison to their colorful counterparts in Virginia, like Phil Sheridan and George Armstrong Custer. The marches they made, the battles they fought, had all faded into obscurity. I became convinced if someone did not tell their story of leadership and courage, incompetence and cowardice, cruelty and compassion, it was going to be lost forever. The result is this book about generals and privates, hardtack and horse sweat, fluttering guidons and cavalry charges.

I hope I have done the story justice, but anyone claiming to have authored a book is a lot like the terrapin two little barefoot boys found sitting on top of a six-foot fence post. "Wow!" one of them exclaimed, craning his neck to get a better look. "How'd he get up there?" "Don't know," said the other, "but I'll bet he didn't do it by hisself."

I want to thank my mom and dad, Kitty and Ebb Evans, for their unfailing support and encouragement. I know they must have gotten tired of answering the question, "Has your son finished his book yet?" My thanks also go out to my in-laws, William and Helen Thrasher, for their patient faith and interest. Drs. Emory M. Thomas, Carl Vipperman, Nash Boney, and Phinizy Spalding of the University of Georgia sagely guided me through the initial stages of my research, while university vice-president Dr. Robert C. Anderson made funds available when no one else would. I also relied heavily on the expertise and assistance of dozens of librarians, archivists, and administrators I met during my research at the institutions listed in the bibliography. Elaine Everly, Mike Musick, Dale Floyd, Charles Shaughnessy, Bob Matchette, Mike Pilgrim, Stuart Butler, Mike Meier, DeAnne Blanton, William F. Sherman, Mary Walton Livingston, Jeff Kushkowski, Ann C. Gray, George Perros, Dr. Harold D. Williams, and L. E. Smith of the National Archives; Archie Motley of the Chicago Historical Society; Cheryl Pence of the Illinois State Historical Library; Leona T. Alig of the Indiana Historical Society; Ann C. Altemose and Pamela Wasmer of the Indiana State Library; Mary Jo Pugh of the Bentley Historical Library; Dr. Josephine Harper and Joanne Hohler of the State Historical Society of Wisconsin; Phyllis E. McLaughlin of the State Historical Society of Iowa; Kenneth Vinsel of the Filson Club; Mimi C. Jones and Dr. Norwood Kerr of the Alabama Department of Archives and History; Bill Sumners of the Auburn University Department of Archives; Bill Hanna of the Mississippi Department of Archives and History; Lynn Wolfe of the Wisconsin Veterans Museum; LeRoy Barnett of Michigan State Archives; Mary Ellen Brooks of the Hargrett Library; Charlotte Ray, Sally Moseley, and Gail Miller DeLoach of the Georgia Department of Archives and History; Alan C. Aimone of the United States Military Academy; and Dr. Richard Sommers of the U.S. Army Military History Institute all went out of their way to be helpful. Barbara Snedden, James D. Walker, Melissa Kilpatrick, Betty Bush, Dr. Linda McCurdy, Milton D. Thompson, William D. Matter, Elizabeth Baldwin, and Denis C. Bateman did wonderful work as surrogate researchers, while Marie Ellis, Bertie Herbert, Barbara Rystrom, and Susan Morris of the University of Georgia Library and Sara McGee, Betty Belanger, and Prudence Taylor of the Athens Regional Library cheerfully hunted down every obscure title I could throw at them. Lurlene Richardson and Mary Shaw of the Georgia Department of Transportation and Tom Hardaway of the University of Georgia Library rooted out old maps that were a tremendous help in retracing the routes the raiders took. A. C. Jones, Jr., Peter Silcox, and Paul Carine patiently answered my questions about railroads, while Franklin Garrett was always just a phone call away, ready to pinpoint some obscure Atlanta locale.

I also want to thank Maja Keech of the Library of Congress, Michael Winey and Randy Hackenburg of the U.S. Army Military History Institute, Rebecca Rose and Cory Hudgins of the Museum of the Confederacy, Ted Ryan and Helen Mathews of the Atlanta History Center, Milton Kaplan, Bruce Erion, Tracy Miller, Darlene Walsh, Roger Hunt, Jim Barnett, Bill Rasp, Gary Kross, and Robert Parham for their help in locating elusive photographs and illustrations. Jim Ingram and Xueling Hu of the Cartographic Services Laboratory at the University of Georgia put long hours, good humor, and considerable ingenuity into drawing the maps I needed.

I also had the assistance of some wonderful people, like Margaret M. Beecher, Stanley E. Butcher, Judge Jack Camp, Ruth Crump, Dr. Barbara C. Dickey, Dick Dickson, Mrs. Dean R. Giles, Douglas G. Hoskins, Robert Houghtalen, Mildred

Kilen, Jim Kegel, Willard McBurney, Michael and Kitty Morehead, James K. Scott, Jr., Ann Rippetoe Shafer, Katharine B. Simpson, and Juliet Powell Turner, who all graciously gave me access to treasured family letters, diaries, and photographs. More than anyone else, they helped put a human face on the events of the summer of 1864.

But writing history takes more than just sitting in the confines of a musty room surrounded by piles of aging manuscripts. Sometimes you have to go out and literally beat the bushes for information. On those occasions, I was glad I knew avid relic hunters and knowledgeable amateur historians like Drs. Roger R. Rowell, Edgar V. Howell, and Kerry Elliott. My Coweta County kin, Uncles John and Ralph Evans and Cousin Weyman C. Evans, explained a lot of the local lore about McCook's raid. My grandfather, Ealie L. Shivers, a former police chief, taught me some simple but lasting lessons about research as he squired "his boy" on field trips through western Georgia on hot summer days when I know it must have hurt his arthritic old joints just to walk. James O. Wilson, Mrs. W. P. Williamson, Brian McDowell, John Philpot, Will Sledge, Tommy Lynch, Thomas L. French, Jr., Lynda Eller, Dennis Sauls, Tom King, Fred Ingram, and M. E. Whisenant all took time to answer a stranger's questions about local history and long-ago landmarks. Gerald R. Smith, Monroe M. King, and Jim Watterson unselfishly shared their interest and insights into the raids and showed me places where the Yankees had been. My brother, Danny, my friends Marshall Rice, Doug Thrasher, and Jon Lanier helped me explore the old roads, cross the muddy rivers, and occasionally dig the pickup truck out of the mire.

I also want to thank Lauren Bryant for convincing Indiana University Press to undertake this project, Bob Sloan, Cindy Ballard, and Terry Cagle for having the patience to see it through, and Dr. Richard McMurry, Wiley Sword, and Ken Goodall for constructive critiques and criticism along the way. I am also indebted to Don Troiani and the folks at the Arts & Entertainment Network for repeatedly advertising the impending publication of this book. To these and countless others I have written, called, questioned, and pestered over the years, my deepest, most heartfelt thanks for showing me the letters, diaries, and documents, places, relics, and tangible pieces of the past which I hope will convey some sense of what it was like to ride with Sherman's horsemen and to fight against them.

DAVID EVANS

INTRODUCTION

Speed, audacity, even recklessness were what
he wanted, not meticulous advances from one
set point to another. Shake up the enemy,
rough him up, tear the campaign wide open.
"To hell with compromises."

—Martin Blumenson,
The Patton Papers, 1940–1945

They marched into Marietta that bright Sunday morning with the confident, swinging stride of conquerors. They were the proud veterans of the Federal XV Corps, lean, shaggy-haired men, each shouldering a rifle and forty rounds.

Sergeant Ben Magee watched as their unbroken ranks tramped past the brick courthouse, the deserted hotel, and the ransacked storefronts, their hats pulled low against the hot Georgia sun. Magee belonged to Company I, 72nd Indiana Mounted Infantry. His company and three others, A, D, and F, the advance guard for Brigadier General Kenner Dudley Garrard's 2nd Cavalry Division, had ridden into town a few moments earlier, crowding south on Main Street just as the bristling, bluecoated column of Federal infantry filed in from the west. Halting to give the foot soldiers the right-of-way, Magee and his comrades were lounging in their saddles when a gilt-edged group of horsemen descended upon them like a thunderbolt.

"Where's Gar'd? Where's Gar'd? Where'n the hell's Gar'd?" a red-bearded officer in a low-crowned felt hat demanded angrily.

The Hoosiers shifted uncomfortably in their stirrups, trying to avoid the withering glare of William Tecumseh Sherman.

When Garrard rode up a few moments later, Sherman waded into him with "a perfect storm of abuse." The cavalryman suffered silently for awhile, then, "very mildly and meekly," tried to explain his division had been delayed because some of his pickets had to walk almost four miles to rejoin their regiments. Then there was a delay while his division drew rations.

But Sherman was in no mood to listen to excuses. During the night, Confederate General Joseph E. Johnston had abandoned the formidable defenses on Kennesaw Mountain and retreated southward through Marietta. Sherman had sent his whole army in pursuit at daylight and ridden into town at 8:30 A.M., fully expecting to find Garrard's cavalry snapping at the heels of the Rebel rear guard.

Instead, he found only a few stragglers roaming the empty streets. There was no sign of Garrard's cavalry and for two and a half hours, he waited with growing impatience. By the time the first Federal troopers finally arrived at 11:00 A.M., he was absolutely livid. A golden opportunity to destroy the whole Rebel army was fast slipping through his fingers, and the more Garrard tried to explain, the madder Sherman got.

"Git out of here, quick!" he exploded. Garrard naively inquired which way he should go. "Don't make a damned bit of difference," Sherman snarled, "so you get out of here and go for the rebels."

The words snapped like a whip, sending Garrard and his men down Main Street at a prudent trot. Turning to the left, they soon overtook the infantrymen toiling eastward on the Roswell Road. Undeterred, the horse soldiers ploughed into their midst, bumping, jostling, crowding them off the road as loud curses chorused above the jangle of sabers and the metallic clatter of tin cups and canteens.[1]

It was July 3, 1864, the third summer of civil war between North and South. The naive, flag-waving enthusiasm that had answered the call to arms in 1861 had been bled white on the fatal, flaming fields of Antietam, Gettysburg, Chickamauga, and scores of lesser battles. Both sides longed for an end to the carnage; neither was willing to yield, and the war raged on with insatiable fury.

A war-weary North had pinned its hopes and the three stars of a lieutenant general on the stooped shoulders of a cigar-smoking soldier named Ulysses Simpson Grant. Critics whispered he drank too much, but Grant had one undeniable virtue. He won battles. His victories at Forts Henry and Donelson, at Shiloh, Vicksburg, and Chattanooga had reclaimed much of Tennessee, Alabama, and Mississippi for the Union and reopened the Mississippi River to navigation, effectively cutting the Southern Confederacy in two.

A plain, straightforward man, Grant had an approach to war that was equally simple: "Find out where your enemy is. Get at him as soon as you can. Strike at him as hard as you can, and keep moving on."[2]

As the newly commissioned general-in-chief of all the Union armies, he planned to marshal the North's preponderance of manpower and munitions into a series of coordinated offensives that would batter the beleaguered South into submission. He would go east to personally lead the ill-starred Army of the Potomac against Confederate General Robert E. Lee's vaunted Army of Northern Virginia, leaving Major General William Tecumseh Sherman to command three smaller Federal armies in the west.

"General Sherman was then in the prime of life," noted a subordinate, "—a tall, brisk, wiry man; with dark reddish hair, inclining to baldness; sharp blue eyes, kindly as a rule, but cold and hard as steel sometimes; an aggressive, fighting nose and mouth; considerable of jaw; and a face a mass of wrinkles. . . . He impressed you at once as a keen, wide-awake man of affairs, with a mind and will of his own; bookish, but greater than his books; a master of his profession; alert, decided, farsighted; knowing well what was needed, and resolute to do it, and also resolved everybody about and under him should know and do the same."[3]

"Uncle Billy," as his soldiers called him, usually campaigned in a faded private's coat, with nothing to signify his rank but a pair of shoulder straps. "He can live on hard bread and water," wrote Albert D. Richardson of the *New York Tribune*, "and fancies any one else can do so." He wore low shoes and high shirt collars, and was noted for what one officer called "his 'gamey' qualities at all times and everywhere."

But what men remembered most about Sherman was his speech. "He talks with great rapidity," noted correspondent William F. G. Shanks of the *New York Herald*, and punctuated his remarks with "strange, quick, and ungraceful gestures." The relentless rush of words reminded one listener of a drum sounding the long roll.

"He never hesitates at interrupting any one," Shanks added, "but can not bear to be interrupted himself." Once he had the gist of what someone was trying to say, he launched into his own orders and instructions, taking a subordinate by the shoulder and steering him toward the door, "all the time talking and urging him off."

He was never quiet. He was never still. Whenever he was deep in thought or events seemed to be hanging by a thread, he folded his arms behind him and began pacing, wreathed in a haze of blue cigar smoke. Unlike Grant, who smoked leisurely and thoughtfully, Sherman was a steam engine in britches. He puffed furiously, frequently snatching the cigar from his lips and carelessly thumping away the ashes with the little finger of his left hand. He rarely finished half of one before lighting another. When he did stop long enough to sit down, he would cross and uncross his legs, fidget nervously with the buttons on his coat, drum his lean fingers on the table, or comb them through his hair and closely cropped beard. Soon he was back on his feet, an unruly shock of red hair keeping time with his relentless pacing, pacing, pacing.

His restive, razor-sharp mind never slept through the night. He habitually rose hours before dawn, but made up the deficit by pulling a battered felt hat over his eyes and stealing short naps during the day. He could be impatient, irritable, and abrupt to the point of rudeness.[4]

"Who are you, sir?" he once demanded of a frock-coated civilian who offered him a pair of field glasses on a hotly contested battlefield.

"My name is Lovejoy," came the reply, "and I'm a member of Congress."

"What are you doing here?" Sherman growled. "Get out of my lines, sir! Get out of my lines!"

Not long afterward, a disgruntled subordinate approached President Abraham Lincoln, complaining Sherman had threatened to shoot him if he tried to leave camp. "Well," the President said in a stage whisper, "if I were you and he threatened to shoot, I would not trust him, for I believe he would do it."

Sherman disliked politicians. He loathed newspaper reporters. When a correspondent disparaged his manners as those of a Pawnee Indian, Sherman demanded a retraction. The reporter apologized to the Pawnees.[5]

"He is by far our most brilliant general," wrote Shanks, "but not by any means the most reliable; the most fascinating, but not the most elegant; the quickest, but not the safest; the first to resolve, but not the most resolute. As a man he is always generous, but not uniformly just; affectionate by nature, but not at all times kind in demonstration; confiding, and yet suspicious; obstinate, yet vacillating; decided, but not tenacious—a mass of contradictions so loosely and yet so happily thrown together as to produce the most interesting combination imaginable."[6]

His wrinkled, careworn face was that of a man whose journey through life had been filled with detours, deadends, and disappointments. Born in Lancaster, Ohio, on February 8, 1820, he was nine years old when his father died, leaving his mother to raise eleven children on a legacy of $250 per year, a sum so inadequate several of the younger Shermans had to be parceled out among sympathetic neighbors and kin.

"I want one of them," insisted Thomas W. Ewing, a close family friend. "You must give me the brightest of the lot, and I will make a man of him." Mrs. Sherman summoned Tecumseh, or Cump as he was called, and sent him with the big man who lived two doors up the street.[7]

The devoutly Catholic Ewings raised Cump as if he were one of their own. Thomas Ewing was elected to the Senate, and in 1836 he appointed his redheaded young ward to the United States Military Academy at West Point. Sherman excelled in the classroom during his four years at the Academy, but he also accumulated 380 demerits, mostly for slovenly appearance, and never rose above the rank of private. Graduating sixth in the class of 1840, he was assigned to the 3rd U.S. Artillery.[8]

He spent most of the next six years in the South, serving in the coastal forts of Florida, Alabama, and South Carolina. Unlike other officers who turned to whisky and cards to relieve the monotony of garrison life, Sherman found other diversions. "I have great love for painting," he confided to Thomas Ewing's oldest daughter, Ellen, "and find that sometimes I am so fascinated that it amounts to pain to lay down the brush. . . ."[9]

When the United States declared war on Mexico in May 1846, Sherman immediately requested duty in the field. Ordered to New York City, he embarked for California with a detachment of the 3rd Artillery and Lieutenant Henry W. Halleck of the Corps of Engineers. After a storm-tossed, six-month voyage around Cape Horn, he arrived too late to participate in the conquest of California, but a report he authored and sent to Washington in 1848 with samples from placer mines on the Sacramento River helped precipitate the California gold rush.

After three years of watching other men get rich, Sherman was sent to Washington to deliver dispatches to the War Department. Thomas Ewing, now the Secretary of the Interior, was living in the famous Blair House on Pennsylvania Avenue, and here, in an impressive ceremony attended by President Zachary Taylor, John C. Calhoun, Daniel Webster, Henry Clay, and most of the political luminaries of the day, Cump and Ellen were married on May 1, 1850.

Promoted to captain, Sherman served briefly at St. Louis and New Orleans, but by September 1853 it had become painfully apparent his army pay could not support a fashionable wife and two infant daughters. At the urging of Ellen and his father-in-law, Sherman resigned his commission to accept a job directing the San Francisco office of Lucas, Turner & Company, a St. Louis banking firm.

For two years he prospered. Then, in February 1855, the California bubble suddenly burst with a wild run on the banks. Sherman's management stemmed the flood of anxious depositors, but several overextended banks failed. Businesses closed, commerce dried up, and the resulting recession forced Lucas, Turner & Company to close its doors.

To complicate matters, Sherman had established a trust fund for several old army friends, investing heavily in municipal bonds. When the city of San Francisco defaulted on its debt, much of this money was lost. While not legally responsible, Sherman felt a moral obligation to his friends and quietly began reimbursing $20,000 out of his own pocket.

Destitute and discouraged, he had to borrow money from his father-in-law to move his family back to Ohio. Leaving them in Lancaster, he went to New York City to open a Wall Street branch of his bank. Once again, Sherman's management was sound, but the financial malaise gripping California followed him eastward. Less than three months after opening for business, the Panic of 1857 forced Lucas, Turner & Company into bankruptcy. "I ought to have had sense enough to keep out of such disreputable business," he wrote. "Banking and gambling are synonymous."[10]

Sherman spent an uncomfortable Christmas in Lancaster. He was thirty-seven years old. He had no job, no prospects, and no roof to put over his family's head.

Thomas Ewing tried to get his luckless son-in-law to settle in Lancaster and superintend the family salt works. Sherman bristled at the idea of charity, but his declining fortunes soon forced him to relent. "All I stipulate is that I don't want to live in Lancaster," he wrote to his father-in-law. "You can understand what Ellen does not—that a man needs consciousness of position among his peers. In the army I know my place . . . at Lancaster I can only be Cump Sherman."[11]

Ewing agreed to let him manage the family's extensive properties in Kansas, and in the fall of 1858 Sherman moved his family to Leavenworth. He was admitted to the bar "on the ground of general intelligence," but lost the only case he ever took to trial. A speculation in corn went sour, and in the spring of 1859, a pregnant, homesick Ellen took her brood back to Lancaster. "I am doomed to be a vagabond, and shall no longer struggle against my fate," Sherman wrote. "I look upon myself as a dead cock in the pit."[12]

Before quitting Leavenworth, he sent a letter to the War Department, asking for a job as an army paymaster or "anything." Learning a new military school in Louisiana was looking for a commandant, he submitted an application, and in August 1859 he received the welcome news he had been selected superintendent and professor of engineering, architecture, and drawing at the State Seminary of Learning and Military Academy in Alexandria, Louisiana.

During the next few months, Sherman laid the foundations for the school that eventually became Louisiana State University, but his tenure was a short one. The debate over slavery had come to color every aspect of national politics, and while Sherman abhorred abolition, he had no sympathy for secession. "If Louisiana withdraw[s] from the Union . . . ," he wrote to Governor Thomas O. Moore in January 1861, "I beg you to take immediate steps to relieve me as superintendent . . . for on no earthly account will I do any act or think any thought hostile to or in defiance of the old Government of the United States."

Eight days later, Louisiana left the Union. Convinced that war was inevitable, Sherman bid his faculty and cadets an emotional farewell. "You are all here," he said tearfully, putting his hand over his heart.[13]

After squaring his accounts with state officials, he went to Washington, hoping his brother, John, now an influential Republican senator, could get him a job in the Treasury Department. When this failed, he asked for a place in the army. President Abraham Lincoln politely brushed him aside. Spurning a Confederate commission, Sherman accepted the presidency of a St. Louis street car company.

Friends in Washington persuaded the Lincoln administration to offer him the chief clerkship of the War Department, promising to make him Assistant Secretary of War when Congress convened, but Sherman shied away from such a responsible position, lamely protesting he could not forsake his obligations in St. Louis. When Southern gunners fired on the Federal garrison at Fort Sumter, South Carolina, compelling President Lincoln to call for 75,000 men to put down the rebellion, John Sherman urged his brother to return to Ohio and raise a regiment of volunteers. "I cannot and will not mix myself in this present call . . . ," Cump insisted. "The first movements of the government will fail and the leaders will be cast aside. A second or third set will rise, and among them I may be, but at present I will not volunteer as a soldier or anything else."

Tempered by past failures, tortured by self-doubt, he remained "a chip on the whirling tide." When friends lobbied to have him replace recently resigned Joseph E. Johnston as the army's quartermaster general, Sherman replied, "I do not conceive myself qualified. . . ."[14]

He was a proud man, unwilling to run the risk of failing again. When the government finally offered him a prominent but not overly responsible position as colonel of the 13th U.S. Infantry, he accepted. He led a brigade into the first big battle of the war at Bull Run, Virginia, only to see the whole Union army swept off the field in a disgraceful rout. Fully expecting to be cashiered, Sherman was surprised to learn he had been promoted to brigadier general of volunteers. "This will still keep me where I want," he confided to Ellen, "in a modest position till time and circumstance show us daylight."[15]

Sent to Kentucky with the understanding his role would be a subordinate one, Sherman was catapulted into command when illness forced the senior Union general to resign. Plagued by incompetent officers, raw recruits, and shortages of all kinds, he grew increasingly despondent and may have suffered a nervous breakdown. He banned newspaper reporters from his camps, fearing they would advertise his weaknesses to the enemy. When they disobeyed his orders, he summarily expelled them from his lines or threw them in jail. He grossly overestimated the strength of the opposing Rebel forces and badgered Washington for reinforcements. None came. Finally, in a celebrated interview in Louisville with Secretary of War Simon Cameron, he excitedly poured out his troubles, insisting he needed 60,000 men to secure Kentucky and 200,000 to carry the war into Tennessee.

Cameron ignored the "insane" request, and Sherman, overwhelmed with real and imagined burdens, asked to be relieved. He was ordered to Missouri, where his old shipmate, Major General Henry W. Halleck, concluded, "General S[herman's] physical and mental system is so completely broken by labor and care . . . that in his present condition it would be dangerous to give him a command here."

Once again, Sherman returned to Lancaster. There, on December 12, 1861, he picked up a copy of the *Cincinnati Daily Commercial* and read, "General W. T. Sherman, late commander of the Department of the Cumberland, *is insane*. It appears that he was at times when commanding in Kentucky, stark mad. . . ."

Other newspapers parroted the vicious libel. Sherman, by his own admission, sank "into a perfect 'slough of despond,'" and even contemplated suicide.[16]

When his leave expired, he dutifully returned to Missouri, where he was given the menial task of drilling recruits. By March 1862 he had improved enough for Halleck to entrust him with command of a division when Major General Ulysses S. Grant's army began moving south.

Determined not to repeat the mistakes he had made in Kentucky and Missouri, Sherman scoffed at a skittish colonel who sent him reports early on April 6, 1862, warning that the woods near a little Methodist meetinghouse called Shiloh were full of Rebels. Then the morning erupted with crashing volleys and wild yells as the Confederates came charging into his camps. Raw recruits panicked; whole regiments fled in terror. Sherman had three horses shot out from under him. A piece of buckshot pierced his right hand; a spent bullet tore at one of his shoulder straps, but Shiloh was Sherman's salvation. His nervous energy evaporated in the heat of battle. He became quiet, resolute, almost serene, and his coolness under fire helped Grant turn almost certain defeat into an important Union victory.[17]

Sherman was promoted to major general of volunteers, but the old allegations of insanity and incompetence would not die. He had been "surprised" at Shiloh. When his troops were bloodily repulsed at Chickasaw Bluff, Mississippi, in December 1862 during Grant's first attempt to capture the citadel city of Vicksburg, newspapers howled for his dismissal. An easy victory two weeks later at Fort Hindman, Arkansas, silenced most of the critics, but the consequences of failure still weighed so heavily on Sherman's mind that one of Grant's aides characterized him as "a timid leader, who could not be depended upon to push home an advantage."[18]

When Grant proposed to break the Vicksburg impasse in April 1863 by cutting the army loose from its supply line on the Mississippi and moving fifty miles inland to take the high ground east of the city, Sherman argued it was too risky. "This whole plan of attack will fail, must fail and the fault will be on us all of course . . . ," he asserted. Then he worked night and day to make it succeed. "He could not have done more if the plan had been his own," Grant later wrote.[19]

Vicksburg surrendered on July 4, 1863, and its capture marked what Sherman called "the first gleam of daylight in this war."

At his urging, Ellen brought Minnie, Lizzie, Willy, and Tommy, the oldest of their six children, to visit his camp on Mississippi's Big Black River. Sherman took particular pride in his namesake, nine-year-old Willy. Soldiers in his old regiment, the 13th U.S. Infantry, taught the boy the manual of arms and made him an honorary sergeant, complete with a little uniform.

At summer's end, Sherman received orders to relieve the besieged Union army at Chattanooga. He loaded his family aboard a troop transport for the first leg of the trip up the Mississippi, but as the boat ploughed upstream, he noticed the usually rambunctious Willy standing listlessly against the rail. One touch of the boy's pallid brow convinced Mrs. Sherman to put him to bed and summon an army surgeon. The diagnosis was grim. Willy had typhoid fever. He was rushed ashore as soon as the boat reached Memphis, but there was nothing the doctors could do. Within twenty-four hours, Willy was dead.

Sherman tried to focus on the pressing demands of outfitting his XV Corps for the long march to Chattanooga, but it was no use. "Sleeping—waking—everywhere I see poor Little Willy," he wrote. He berated himself for "taking my family to so fatal a climate at so critical [a] period of the year," and vowed to "make Poor Willy's memory the cure for the defects which have sullied my character."[20]

He was shepherding his troops eastward when a courier overtook him on October 24. Grant had been given command of all the Union armies in the west, and he directed Sherman to take the reins of the Army of the Tennessee. This was followed by orders to hurry to Chattanooga. "Spite of my efforts," Sherman wrote Ellen, "I am pushed into complicated places that others aspire to and which I wish they had."[21]

Hampered by bad weather, miserable roads, and a cumbersome wagon train, Sherman was slow getting to Chattanooga. His troops floundered at the foot of Missionary Ridge on November 25 while the rest of Grant's men triumphantly stormed up the slope, driving the Rebel defenders into Georgia. "He will never be successful," Major General Joseph Hooker wrote. "Please remember what I tell you."[22]

Grant, however, did not share these misgivings. When he was promoted to lieutenant general in March 1864, he named Sherman to succeed him as commander of the sprawling Military Division of the Mississippi, embracing all the Union armies east of the Mississippi River and west of the Appalachian Mountains.[23]

It was an awesome responsibility, and Sherman realized the upcoming campaign would make or break his reputation as a man and as a soldier. Failure would resurrect all the old talk of insanity and incompetence. He would be relieved and sent home in disgrace, a spectre too horrible for a man of Sherman's fragile ego to contemplate. He had to succeed.[24]

Meeting in Nashville on March 17, Grant and Sherman boarded a train for Cincinnati and began mapping out their strategy. Grant would continue eastward to direct operations in Virginia. Sherman would go south to carry the war into Georgia, where the Confederate Army of Tennessee, now led by General Joseph E. Johnston, had wintered at Dalton after the humiliating defeat at Missionary Ridge.

"You I propose to move against Johnston's army," Grant summarized in a letter on April 4, "to break it up and to get into the interior of the enemy's country as far as you can, inflicting all the damage you can against their war resources."

"I will not let side issues draw me off . . . ," Sherman replied from Nashville on April 10. "I am to knock Joe Johnston, and do as much damage to the resources of the enemy as possible." He proposed to send most of his army straight against Johnston, "fighting him cautiously, persistently, and to the best advantage," while flanking columns struck at Confederate communications with Atlanta, the railroad hub of the South. If Johnston sought refuge behind the precipitous banks of the Chattahoochee River, just north of Atlanta, Sherman intended to feint to the right, but move left, cutting the railroad east of the city while his cavalry rode downstream to threaten rail connections to the west and south. "This," he concluded, "is about as far ahead as I feel disposed to look. . . ."[25]

Sherman spent the next three weeks wrestling with what he called "the troublesome question of transportation and supplies." The railroad linking Nashville's bulging depots with his advance base at Chattanooga was barely delivering enough food and forage to meet the army's daily demands when he ordered his quartermaster and commissary officers to stockpile a two months' surplus in Chattanooga and do it in thirty days. When the superintendent of his military railroad protested he did not have enough rolling stock, Sherman ordered him to commandeer every freight car and locomotive south of the Ohio River. He forced beef and livestock contractors to move their herds southward on the hoof, ordered soldiers returning from furlough to march to Chattanooga instead of ride, and banned all civilian passengers and freight south of Nashville.

Seething with righteous indignation, officials of the Christian Commission demanded an exemption for the Bibles and religious tracts they distributed to the troops. "Rations and ammunition are much better," Sherman snapped. When President Lincoln appealed to him to carry supplies to east Tennessee's suffering civilian population, Sherman respectfully refused. "To make war we must and will harden our hearts," he wrote Assistant Secretary of War Charles A. Dana. "Therefore, when preachers clamor and the sanitaries wail, don't join in, but know that war, like the thunderbolt, follows its laws, and turns not aside even if the beautiful, the virtuous, and the charitable stand in its path."

Food, clothing, ammunition, and equipment poured into Chattanooga, but it soon became apparent the single-tracked railroad simply could not supply 100,000 men and 35,000 horses and mules. Sherman suspended shipments of hay and limited grain rations to five pounds of corn or oats per animal per day. "I was willing to risk the question of forage in part," he explained, "because I expected to find wheat and corn fields, and a good deal of grass, as we advanced into Georgia at that season of the year."

Within a month, deliveries to Chattanooga jumped from an average 79 carloads a day to as many as 193. "I am going to move on Joe Johnston the day General Grant telegraphs me he is going to hit Bobby Lee," Sherman told a harried quartermaster as he prepared to leave Nashville on April 28; "and if you don't have my army supplied, and keep it supplied, we'll eat your mules up, sir—eat your mules up!"[26]

By May 1, Sherman had assembled three veteran armies commanded by Major Generals George Henry Thomas, James Birdseye McPherson, and John McAllister Schofield, "three generals of education and experience," he later wrote, "admirably qualified for the work before us."

The work, however, was unequally divided. Schofield's Army of the Ohio consisted of a single corps, numbering 13,559 men and 28 guns. McPherson's Army of the Tennessee was almost twice as large, with 24,465 men and 96 guns, while Thomas's Army of the Cumberland, with 60,773 men and 130 guns, was larger than the other two combined. On May 5, 1864, Sherman ordered them all forward. "Joe Johnston is my objective," he announced; "where he goes, I will follow."[27]

From Red Clay, from Ringgold, from Lee and Gordon's Mills, the blue columns funneled south, down the winding green valleys that led to Dalton, where Sherman's spies estimated Johnston had an army of 45,000 to 60,000 men dug in on Rocky Face Ridge, an abrupt, 800-foot elevation straddling the Western & Atlantic Railroad. A deep gorge, Mill Creek Gap, carried the railroad and the main wagon road through the ridge at a heavily fortified notch known as Buzzard's Roost, but Sherman had no intention of attacking this "terrible door of death."

Six weeks earlier, George Thomas had proposed bypassing the Rebel stronghold, taking the Army of the Cumberland through Snake Creek Gap, a narrow, unguarded defile skirting the southern shoulder of Rocky Face. While McPherson and Schofield kept Johnston busy in front of Dalton, Thomas planned to push eastward to Resaca, a little town perched on the north bank of the Oostenaula River, overlooking the railroad and wagon bridges that brought the Rebels all their supplies. Faced with the loss of this railroad, Johnston would have no choice but to quit Rocky Face and retreat southward, only to find Thomas's men planted squarely across his front and McPherson and Schofield closing in from behind.

Sherman had adopted the plan as his own, with one important modification. Instead of sending Thomas's 60,000 men through Snake Creek Gap, he substituted McPherson's much smaller Army of the Tennessee. McPherson was to force the gap, cut the railroad at Resaca, then fall back to the mouth of the gap, ready to ravage the Rebel right flank when Johnston hurried out of Dalton. Strike hard, Sherman admonished McPherson on May 5, "as it may save us what we have most reason to apprehend—a slow pursuit, in which he gains strength as we lose it."[28]

For the next four days, Sherman watched and waited anxiously while Thomas and Schofield sparred with the Rebel defenders on Rocky Face. He was just sitting down to supper on the evening of May 9 when a courier delivered a note from McPherson. His XVI Corps had driven a small Rebel cavalry detachment from Snake Creek Gap

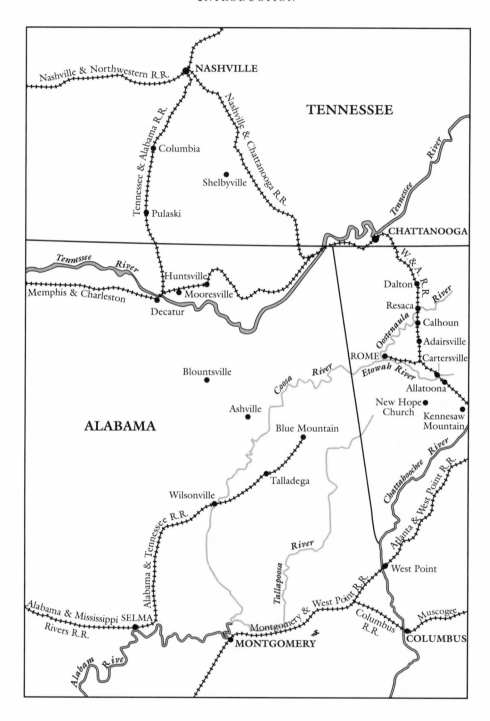

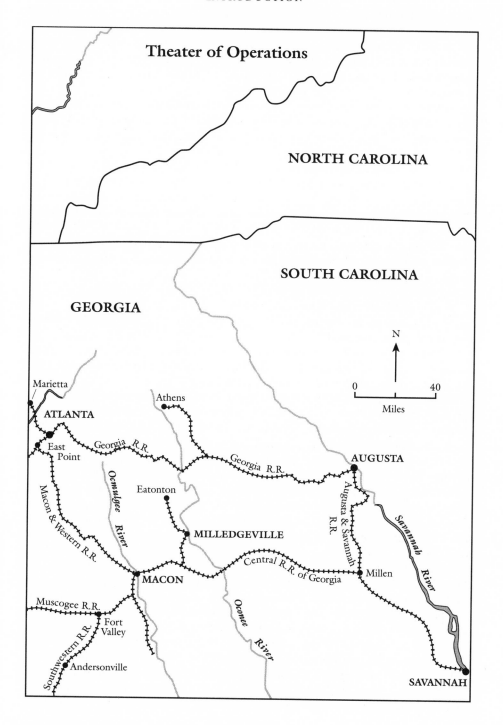

and was within two miles of the railroad at Resaca. "I've got Joe Johnston dead!" Sherman exclaimed, pounding the table with a fist that made the dinner dishes dance.

The next morning, another message arrived. McPherson had encountered unexpectedly heavy resistance on the outskirts of Resaca. After suffering fewer than fifty casualties, he had fallen back to the mouth of Snake Creek Gap to wait for reinforcements.

Seething with disappointment, Sherman left Thomas's IV Corps to keep up the ruse in front of Rocky Face and sent the rest of his troops marching south to Snake Creek Gap. "Well, Mac," he remarked upon overtaking McPherson on the morning of May 12, "you have missed the opportunity of a lifetime."[29]

Sherman wanted to interpose his armies between Johnston and Resaca, but the Rebel general reacted too quickly. By May 13 it was clear Johnston had abandoned Rocky Face and was falling back on Resaca, where Lieutenant General Leonidas Polk, the white-haired Episcopal bishop turned soldier, had arrived with heavy reinforcements from Mississippi and Alabama.

As Sherman's columns converged on Resaca from the north and west on the morning of May 14, a Federal foot soldier noticed a bluecoated officer sprawled beside the road with his hat pulled over his eyes.

"Is that a general?" he asked.

"Yes," replied an orderly who stood nearby.

"A pretty way we are commanded," the soldier groused, "when our generals are lying drunk beside the road!"

Sherman was on his feet in an instant. "Stop, my man. Stop, my man. I am not drunk. While you were sleeping last night, I was planning for you, sir; and now I was taking a nap. General Sherman never gets drunk, sir."[30]

That afternoon, the battle for Resaca began in earnest. Attack and counterattack seesawed back and forth, but on the evening of May 15 Sherman succeeded in planting his artillery on the high ground commanding the bridges over the Oostenaula and putting one of McPherson's divisions across the river at Lay's Ferry, three miles downstream, to threaten the Rebel left. That night, Johnston quietly abandoned his trenches and retreated across the river, burning the bridges behind him.

Sherman surveyed the smoldering wreckage early the next morning. The wagon bridge was still passable, but the railroad trestle was a blackened ruin. How long, Sherman asked one of his engineers, would it take to repair? About four days was the reply. "Sir," Sherman said pointedly, "I give you forty-eight hours, or a position in the front ranks."[31]

Bridging the Oostenaula at three widely separated points, Sherman pushed the stubborn Rebel rear guard southward through Calhoun and Adairsville. On May 19, his far-flung columns found Johnston waiting on the hills south of Cassville, seemingly ready for battle. But the next morning, the Rebels were gone, retreating across the Etowah River to dig in again at Allatoona Pass.

Sherman remembered the rugged approaches to Allatoona from a visit he had made twenty years earlier as a young lieutenant of artillery. Sitting in a small cottage near the railroad depot in Kingston, drumming a pencil on the window sill, he pondered his next move. He would outflank Allatoona, just like Rocky Face Ridge. Abandoning his communications with Chattanooga, he loaded his wagons with twenty days' rations and struck off into the wilderness on May 23, confidently predicting his armies would "swarm along the Chattahoochee in five days."[32]

Rebel cavalry soon spotted Sherman's ponderous columns, and when the Federal advance guard reached the important road junction at New Hope Church on May 25, they found Johnston's infantry dug in and waiting for them. Neither side could gain an advantage in the six days of savage fighting that followed, and on June 1 Sherman began sliding east toward the railroad. The Chattahoochee was still twenty miles away.

Then the rains came, three weeks of mist, drizzle, shower, and storm. Roads mired and teamsters swore as both armies sank axle-deep in the mud. Riding the front lines during a rare break in the weather on the morning of June 14, Sherman noticed a group of Rebel officers peering at him with their field glasses from the crest of Pine Mountain, 800 yards away. "How saucy they are!" he exclaimed, and ordered a nearby battery to "touch them up; teach those fellows to keep cover." The first shot scattered the men in gray. The second ranged too high. The third tore Confederate General Polk in half.[33]

As the rains continued, Sherman's mood turned as foul as the weather. "My chief source of trouble is with the Army of the Cumberland, which is dreadfully slow," he wrote to Grant on June 18. "A fresh furrow in a plowed field will stop the whole column, and all begin to intrench . . . and yet it seems that the whole Army of the Cumberland is so habituated to be on the defensive that, from its commander down to its lowest private, I cannot get it out of their heads."[34]

The arrival of McPherson's XVII Corps on June 8 and a steady influx of men returning from sick leave and furlough had kept the Federal ranks full. Knowing Johnston had been unable to recoup his losses, Sherman took a calculated risk. On the morning of June 27, he hurled eight brigades at the Confederate trenches girdling Kennesaw Mountain. These were the same troops who had stormed the besieging heights at Chattanooga only seven months earlier, but the miracle of Missionary Ridge would not be repeated on the fiery slopes of Kennesaw. The attackers were shot down, bayoneted, and hurled back, leaving 3,000 casualties in their wake.

"The assault I made was no mistake," Sherman insisted; "I had to do it. The enemy and our own army and officers had settled down into the conviction that the assault of lines formed no part of my game, and the moment the enemy was found behind anything like a parapet, why everybody would deploy, throw up counter-works and take it easy, leaving it to the 'old man' to turn the position."

Casualties had been high, but not excessive. In fact, he wrote Ellen on June 30, "I begin to regard the death and mangling of a couple thousand men as a small affair, a kind of morning dash. . . ."[35]

The fearful slaughter did, however, convince Sherman of the futility of any more frontal assaults. Resorting to the old flanking tactics that had served him so well, on the night of July 2 he pulled McPherson's troops out of the trenches north and east of Kennesaw and circled them behind Thomas and Schofield to threaten the crossings over the Chattahoochee. The maneuver forced Johnston to beat a hasty retreat, and at daylight on July 3, Sherman peered through a telescope and saw Federal skirmishers cavorting on the coveted crest of Kennesaw.

Convinced he could have captured "3,000 or 4,000 prisoners and many wagons" if his cavalry had been handled properly, he was, by his own admission, "terribly angry" when Garrard finally came mincing into Marietta. Despite his outburst, the pursuit continued at a plodding pace and shortly before dark Thomas sent word his infantry had run up against a formidable line of Rebel breastworks at Smyrna Church, six miles farther south.

Sherman was surprised. He had assumed Johnston would not stop until his army was safely across the Chattahoochee. "The more I reflect," he wrote to Thomas, "the more I know Johnston's halt is to save time to cross his men and material. No general, such as he, would invite battle with the Chattahoochee behind him."

Exhorting Thomas to press the Rebel lines all night and early the next morning, "at any cost of life and material," he ordered McPherson and Schofield to bend every effort to drive Johnston's left into the river. "We will never have such a chance again," he wrote.[36]

Early on July 4, Sherman rode to the front, trying to prod Thomas's IV Corps forward. "Sherman swears there is no Rebel artillery this side of the Chattahoochee River," an Illinois lieutenant noted in his diary. "Will give any man $50 if there is a single piece of artillery in our front, and the old man is right here among us looking for it."

Perturbed by the seemingly cautious pursuit, Sherman rode to a grove of trees where the commanding general of the IV Corps, one-armed Oliver Otis Howard, was conferring with some of his officers. "Howard," Sherman demanded with evident impatience, "what are you waiting for? Why don't you go ahead?"

"The enemy is strongly intrenched yonder in the edge of the thick wood," Howard replied; "we have come upon his skirmish-line."

"Oh, nonsense, Howard," Sherman shot back; "he is laughing at you. You ought to move straight ahead. Johnston's main force must be across the river."

"You shall see, general," Howard said. After giving his artillery a few minutes to soften up the opposing earthworks, he sent his skirmishers charging across an intervening cornfield. Rebel rifle pits at the edge of the woods erupted with a roar. A shell hurtled through the treetops in the grove where Sherman stood, striking an old chimney and scattering bricks and staff officers in every direction. "Howard," Sherman called out after watching for a few minutes, "your report was correct. Our Confederate opponents were undoubtedly there."[37]

Thomas's probing attacks that noisy Fourth of July failed to find any weak spots in Johnston's defenses, but McPherson and Schofield drove the Rebel left back for more than a mile. The next morning, the Rebel trenches at Smyrna Church were empty.

Sherman was back in the saddle early on July 5, following close behind skirmishers from the Army of the Cumberland's XIV Corps as they advanced down the main road toward Atlanta. Late that morning, he caught up with his old friend George Thomas. They had been roommates at West Point and together they climbed the shaded slopes of McRae's Hill, just west of the railroad, Sherman lean, red-haired, and mercurial, Thomas thickset, grizzled, and deliberate.

Looking south from this commanding height, they got their first glimpse of what Sherman later described as "one of the strongest pieces of field-fortification I ever saw," an unbroken line of earthen redoubts stretching from just above the railroad bridge over the Chattahoochee toward Turner's Ferry, five miles downstream. But what arrested their attention lay across the river, where a few church spires poked

Major General William Tecumseh Sherman astride Duke, one of the horses that carried him through the Atlanta campaign. A "superb" bay Thoroughbred who pranced gaily at the sound of his name, Duke was "particular about his meals," and refused to drink out of creeks or mud holes. "He was a City Gent," Sherman noted, and seemed "to like getting into town again." Reproduced from the Collections of the Library of Congress.

above the Georgia pines. Atlanta, the Gate City of the South, the crossroads of the Confederacy, stood glistening in the morning sun, only nine miles away.

"Mine eyes have beheld the promised land!" wrote a staff officer who stood nearby.[38]

Quitting the crest of McRae's Hill, Sherman mounted his horse and rode westward, eager to hurry the ragged Rebel columns across the Chattahoochee. "General Sherman was a nervous and somewhat careless rider," according to one observer. "He wore his stirrup leathers very long, seeming to be, almost all the time, standing in the irons. This appearance was intensified by his habit of rising in his stirrups on reaching a turn in the road or some advantageous point of observation . . . and his eye seemed to be everywhere except where his horse was treading."

Thinking Thomas's men held a continuous line just north of the Chattahoochee, Sherman rode into a thicket, seemingly unconcerned by the absence of any bluecoated troops. A moment later, he found himself face to face with a Rebel cavalry patrol. The course of history hung in the balance as he wheeled and spurred his long-legged Thoroughbred into a gallop.

Not far away, one of Thomas's regiments, the 15th U.S. Infantry, halted on the edge of the main road running west from Vining's Station. "Directly in front of our company," noted Private William A. Gilday, "a road branched off nearly at right angles, and at about 300 yards from us turned to the right, nearly parallel to the one in front of us."

As they waited they heard hoofbeats pounding toward them. A moment later, Sherman and a brigade staff officer, Captain Will Lyster, swept around the bend at a dead run, with a squad of Confederate cavalry in hot pursuit. Seeing the blue uniforms, Sherman slowed down. His pursuers saw them too, and piled up in the road behind him before they wheeled around and fled.

"Sherman looked confused," noted Private Gilday, "and we just smiled as he rode by."

Undeterred by his narrow escape, Sherman continued his tour of Thomas's lines before returning to his headquarters near Vining's Station, where he spent the evening of July 5 reading and answering dispatches. "We have a nice game of war," he wrote, "and must make no mistakes."[39]

That first tantalizing glimpse of Atlanta marked a turning point in the campaign. For two months, Sherman's chief aim had been the destruction of Johnston's army. He had failed. Johnston had skillfully parried every thrust, answered every riposte, at Snake Creek Gap, at Resaca, at New Hope Church, and at Kennesaw Mountain. Outnumbered and outgunned, the Rebel general had grudgingly given ground, but the army he brought to the north bank of the Chattahoochee was still a potent fighting force, ready to defend every bridge, ford, and ferry. Even if Sherman shouldered his way across the river, Johnston would find ready refuge a half-day's march to the south, inside the formidable earthworks already ringing Atlanta.

Sherman would have few options then. A frontal assault offered scant hope of success; Kennesaw Mountain had proved that. Conventional wisdom suggested laying siege to the city, but Sherman had already rejected that idea.[40] He did not have enough troops to encircle the city, and even if he did, siegecraft took time, time that might enable the Confederate government to send enough troops from Virginia and the Carolinas to turn the tide of battle against him. He wanted a quick victory, before some cruel twist of fate snatched Atlanta from his grasp.

A quick victory—that elusive end prompted a subtle shift in Sherman's priorities during the first week of July. The Rebel army that had so often eluded his grasp during the past two months seemed to slip out of focus. Now Atlanta became the glittering prize that must be won. But to take Atlanta, he first had to cross the Chattahoochee.

SHERMAN'S
HORSEMEN

1

CROSSING THE CHATTAHOOCHEE

JULY 3–JULY 10, 1864

I shall treat neutrality as equivalent
to a declaration of war against me.

—Gustavus Adolphus

Napoleon once said, "The secret of war lies in the communications."[1] The advent of the railroad and telegraph had changed things considerably since the Emperor's day, but the basic principle was still the same: an army marched on its stomach. Sherman reasoned if he could effectively cut the Rebel communications, or more specifically the railroads that fed them, clothed them, and equipped them, he could bring Atlanta to its knees.

There were four railroads radiating out of Atlanta in the summer of 1864: the Western & Atlantic, the Georgia Railroad, the Macon & Western, and the Atlanta & West Point. The state-owned Western & Atlantic snaked through the north Georgia mountains for 138 miles, linking Atlanta and Chattanooga. It had been heavily damaged as Johnston's army retreated southward during May and June, but Sherman's section gangs had repaired the track almost as fast as the Rebels could tear it up. Already, the shrill whistle of Yankee locomotives could be heard as far south as Big Shanty, and the slender ribbon of rails that once succored Johnston's ragged columns was now Sherman's sole source of supply.

Johnston had to rely on the extensive rail network south of the Chattahoochee. The Georgia Railroad stretched eastward from Atlanta, 171 miles, to Augusta, the site of an important arsenal and the Confederacy's largest gunpowder works. It supplied Johnston with munitions, and rail connections with Richmond and Charleston made it the most direct route for any reinforcements coming from Virginia and the Carolinas.

However, the Georgia Railroad was not vital to Johnston's defense of Atlanta. Even if it were cut, the Macon & Western offered a roundabout way to Augusta and the Atlantic seaboard. This route followed a convoluted 102-mile course from Atlanta south to Macon, the site of another large Confederate arsenal and the junction for two other important roads, one diverging southeast toward Savannah and the coastal routes out of Augusta, the other west, toward the Georgia-Alabama border and the vast workshops and arsenal at Columbus.

The Macon & Western shared a common track with the Atlanta & West Point route as it left Atlanta. Six miles south of the city, at East Point, the A. & W.P. diverged toward its terminus at West Point, 81 miles to the southwest, where it met the Montgomery & West Point Railroad, with its river and rail connections into central Alabama and Mississippi.

But instead of joining, the two tracks ran parallel to each other and thirty-one feet apart, because, unlike practically every other railroad in the deep South, the Montgomery & West Point measured four feet, eight-and-one-half inches between the rails. This was three-and-a-half inches narrower than the Atlanta & West Point's standard five-foot gauge, making it impossible to transfer rolling stock from one line to the other. All freight, eastbound or west, had to be unloaded when it got to West Point, manhandled across a thirty-foot platform, and loaded on another train before it could reach its final destination. It was awkward, slow, and inefficient, but since the hard-pressed Confederate Commissary Department had earmarked the crops in central and southern Georgia for Lee's Army of Northern Virginia, Johnston depended on this route for the bulk of his supplies. That made the Atlanta and Montgomery route perhaps the most important railroad south of the Chattahoochee. It was also the most vulnerable, and Sherman knew it.[2]

As early as April 10, 1864, a month before the campaign had even begun, he had written to General Grant, proposing to send his cavalry "straight for Opelika, West Point, Columbus, or Wetumpka, to break up the road between Montgomery and Georgia," the moment Johnston retreated across the Chattahoochee. This would compel Johnston to abandon Atlanta and retreat farther south, or risk everything on the outcome of a pitched battle against seemingly impossible odds. In either event, Sherman felt confident of success, provided, of course, his horsemen did their part.[3]

Like their comrades in the eastern theatre of the war, Yankee cavalrymen in the western armies had been hastily recruited, indifferently armed, and often miserably mounted. Most regiments arrived at the front with little or no training and were scattered among the infantry brigades and divisions as couriers, scouts, and escorts. These small detachments had played insignificant roles in the early battles at Shiloh, Perryville, and Stone's River, and usually came out second best when pitted against Confederate cavalry. It was not until the middle of 1862, when orders began reuniting companies and battalions with their regiments and organizing these regiments into brigades and divisions, that the Yankee troopers began to show promise.

They had achieved some notable successes. In what Sherman called "the most brilliant raid of the war," Colonel Benjamin H. Grierson had led two regiments down the length of Mississippi in April 1863, diverting Confederate attention away from Grant's army at a critical stage of the Vicksburg campaign. The following September, on the first day of the battle of Chickamauga, Colonel Robert H. G. Minty's little brigade had held up the advance of 7,000 Rebel infantry for ten hours, foiling a determined attempt to turn the Federal left flank.

There had also been some conspicuous defeats. During a raid into northern Alabama in May 1863, Colonel Abel D. Streight had been overtaken and tricked into surrendering by an embarrassingly inferior force of Confederate cavalry commanded by Nathan Bedford Forrest. Sherman had seen Forrest frustrate his own plans in February 1864, when the wily Rebel leader routed Brigadier General William Sooy Smith and a raiding column of 7,000 Federals at Okolona, Mississippi.

Old troopers said it took at least a year to make a man into a good horse soldier. By the spring of 1864, most regiments had seen that much service. They were "better armed and equipped, and better drilled than ever before," but Sherman remained "mistrustful of cavalry," a strange admission from a man who was about to mount one of the largest cavalry offensives of the war.[4]

He had started the campaign with four cavalry divisions numbering 11,714 officers and men. Each division was composed of two or three brigades; each brigade consisted of three or four regiments of cavalry or mounted infantry. Only one regiment of Sherman's horsemen, the 4th U.S. Cavalry, was part of the regular army. The others were volunteers, designated by a number and the state they hailed from, such as the 5th Indiana, the 4th Michigan, or the 8th Iowa. Regulations divided cavalry regiments into twelve companies, lettered A through M, and mounted infantry regiments into ten companies lettered A through K. A long-standing army tradition did not provide for a Company J, although the unorthodox 1st Kentucky Cavalry was an exception to this rule.

At full strength, a cavalry company consisted of a captain, a first lieutenant, second lieutenant, first sergeant, quartermaster sergeant, commissary sergeant, five sergeants, eight corporals, two buglers, two farriers or blacksmiths, one saddler, two wagoneers, and at least sixty, but no more than seventy-eight, privates. Mounted infantry companies were organized along similar lines, but after three years of war, it was a rare company that could muster even forty officers and men.

The average trooper was about twenty-five years old. Most were volunteers. They came from cities and towns, factories and fields: farmers, shopkeepers, and teachers; carpenters, bricklayers, and smiths; lumberjacks, miners, millers, mechanics, shoemakers, tailors, printers, butchers, and bakers. Man for man, they were as good as any horse soldiers in the Union army.[5]

For the most part, however, they were led by an ill-starred collection of cast-offs; generals who, for one reason or another, had failed to measure up in the Army of the Potomac. Senior among them was Major General George Stoneman, Jr., who commanded a small division generously styled the Cavalry Corps of the Army of the Ohio. Another eastern expatriate, Brigadier General Washington Lafayette Elliott, directed the three divisions that were the Cavalry Corps of the Army of the Cumberland. "An old cavalryman of high character," Elliott rarely ventured far from his headquarters and never accompanied his troops in the field.

Sherman usually ignored him and issued orders directly to Elliott's division commanders, Brigadier Generals Edward Moody McCook, Kenner Dudley Garrard, and Hugh Judson Kilpatrick. Be bold, he prodded them; "measure your fighting qualities with the enemy's cavalry" and intimidate them, so as to be "a moral force to you in after operations."[6]

There had been few opportunities to do that. During the first two months of the campaign the cavalry's main responsibility had been the decidedly unglamorous task of protecting the flanks of Sherman's advancing armies. "The Yankee cavalry . . . do not leave their infantry," a Confederate cavalry officer reassured his anxious wife, "hence we have no running fights of late."

"The enemy's Cavalry . . . is visible at any time from our outpost, but seldom make any demonstration against us . . . ," agreed a Mississippi cavalryman. "They fight very shy and . . . we very seldom come to close quarters."[7]

Ambitious Yankee officers like Ed McCook, commanding Elliott's 1st Cavalry Division, chafed at being tied to the infantry's apron strings. "This thing of covering the flank of the infantry seems to be a one-sided affair," he complained; "if they are attacked I am to pitch in, while, if I was attacked by a superior force I can expect no assistance."

North Georgia, he added, was "utterly unfit for cavalry operations." Densely wooded hills and valleys, laced with high-banked rivers and streams, confined troopers to narrow wilderness roads or compelled them to dismount and fight on foot. Farms were small and scattered, and Confederate cavalry had often already emptied the barns and corncribs. Sherman had seriously underestimated the availability of forage, and his horses suffered terribly. "They ate dry leaves," recounted a Pennsylvania cavalryman. "They chewed the bridle reins and the picket lines." By June 2, things had gotten so bad McCook felt compelled to advise General Elliott, "my horses are absolutely dying from starvation; five from one company dropped on picket this morning, totally exhausted for want of something to eat." Stoneman's division, having marched from Kentucky, was scarcely in any better shape, and hundreds of otherwise healthy troopers had to be sent to the rear or reassigned to infantry commands because their horses had died of hunger, disease, wounds, or neglect.[8]

"Our cavalry is dwindling away," Sherman lamented in a letter to General Grant. "We cannot get full forage and have to graze, so that the cavalry is always unable to attempt anything." Stoneman was "lazy," Garrard was "over-cautious," and Kilpatrick had gone home with a crippling wound, leaving his division scattered all the way back to Dalton, guarding bridges and supply depots.[9]

By the first week of July, Sherman seemed more concerned about the safety of his own supply line than sending his cavalry to cut the railroad between Atlanta and Montgomery. He was 130 miles deep in Confederate territory and absolutely dependent on the single-track railroad stretching back to Chattanooga. "A spider swinging from the ceiling by a single fibre of his web is not an inapt illustration of the situation . . . ," noted the *Macon Telegraph*.

"Let Sherman's rations be cut off for a week, and even less," declared the editor of the *Mobile Advertiser and Register*, "and his fate is sealed."

"All that we have to do," echoed the *Augusta Chronicle & Sentinel*, "is to fall upon the enemy's rear, and sweep his line of communication with blazing destruction. That vast army of invaders, now in the heart of our State, depends upon a single line of railroad for its supplies—that is its sole dependence for existence—upon that brittle thread hangs its hope of conquest—cut that, and it is gone. Surely there is enterprise, there is daring, there is determination, there is fury enough in the Southern heart, to destroy that line of railroad, to burn every bridge, to tear up every rail, to annihilate every tie, and to blow up every tunnel between Atlanta and Louisville."[10]

Prompted by two Rebel deserters who warned of just such a raid on the Western & Atlantic Railroad, late on July 4 Sherman sent one of his aides, Major James C. McCoy, with orders for Kenner Garrard's 2nd Cavalry Division to move to Roswell, sixteen miles northeast of Marietta. Garrard was to capture the covered bridge spanning the Chattahoochee and prevent the Rebel cavalry from crossing the river and cutting the vital rail artery that was the army's lifeline . "You may draw out at once . . . ," Sherman wrote; "report to me frequently and use your cavalry as though you were preparing to cross yourself or were waiting only for the waters to subside and make the ford practicable."[11]

Sherman had been at odds with the commander of his biggest and best-equipped cavalry division since the start of the campaign, and made little or no effort to hide his feelings. "Garrard has moved so slow that I doubt if he has the dash we need in a cavalry officer," he had written on May 10. He repeatedly prodded Garrard to "strike boldly," but soon began belittling him as "over-cautious" and timid. On June 20, as part of a plan to turn the right flank of Johnston's Kennesaw Mountain line, Sherman had ordered Garrard to cross Noonday Creek, pointedly adding that if Confederate cavalrymen could cross rain-swollen streams like the Etowah and the Oostenaula, surely his own troopers could cross "the little Noonday."

The normally reticent Garrard bristled at Sherman's insulting tone. "I regret exceedingly that on several occasions the major-general commanding has seen fit to write as if he were dissatisfied with my activity and zeal . . . ," he wrote on June 21. "My service with the cavalry this campaign has been very unsatisfactory, for I have been made to feel more than once that it was not equal to the occasion. . . . Should the commanding general desire a change in the command of this division, I will most cheerfully yield it and take command of a brigade of infantry."[12]

Sherman apparently did not bother to reply, but the enmity between the two men festered until matters came to a head on the streets of Marietta on July 3. It was more than just a clash of tempers; it was a fundamental difference in style. Unlike Sherman, Garrard was reserved and modest, and he waged war with a kid-glove gentility. Born on or about September 13, 1827, at Fairfield, the Kentucky plantation of his paternal grandfather, a twice-elected governor of the Bluegrass State, he was the son of Jeptha Dudley Garrard, a respected Cincinnati attorney. His stepfather, Judge John McLean, was an associate justice of the United States Supreme Court.[13]

Garrard may have had aspirations of a law career himself, but after four years of study at Virginia's Bethany College and two more at Harvard, he suddenly decided to become a soldier. Accepting an at-large appointment to West Point, he excelled in mathematics and engineering, and learned cavalry tactics from George Thomas, or "Old Slow Trot" as the cadets called him, because that was the gait he always called for whenever they tried to spur one of the Academy's few horses into a gallop.

Graduating eighth in the class of 1851, Garrard served briefly in the 4th U.S. Artillery and the 1st U.S. Dragoons before being promoted to first lieutenant and assigned to the 2nd U.S. Cavalry early in 1855. This elite regiment, officered by a handpicked cadre that included Lieutenant Colonel Robert E. Lee, Major George Thomas, Captain George Stoneman, and Lieutenant John Bell Hood, spent the next five years fighting fierce Comanche and Kiowa Indians on the Texas plains, but Garrard did most of his soldiering behind a desk as the regimental and departmental adjutant. Attended by a French servant, he apparently did not depend on his meagre army pay.

When Texas left the Union, the 2nd Cavalry received instructions to withdraw, but special orders detained Garrard at San Antonio, where insurgent Texas troops arrested him and several other officers on April 12, 1861. Paroled and released pending his exchange as a prisoner of war, Garrard made his way to Washington, where he turned in $20,000 in government funds he had somehow hidden from his captors.

He was promoted to captain, but the terms of his parole restricted him to noncombat duties. When friends urged him to ignore these limitations, arguing he had been taken prisoner by "an irresponsible armed force," Garrard insisted on settling the

Reticent and retiring Brigadier General Kenner Dudley
Garrard (seen here as a lieutenant colonel) commanded the
2nd Cavalry Division. Sherman condemned him as "over-
cautious." Garrard regarded Sherman as "unjust and ungener-
ous." After the war, Garrard retired to Cincinnati, where he
was an active member of the Music Festival Association.
Reproduced from the Collections of the Library of Congress.

matter in accordance with the articles of war. He worked quietly in the Commissary
General's office until September 1861, when the War Department assigned him to
West Point, first as an assistant instructor of cavalry, then as commandant of cadets
and instructor of artillery, cavalry, and infantry tactics with the unofficial rank of
lieutenant colonel.[14]

During his tenure at the Academy, Garrard authored *Nolan's System for Training
Cavalry Horses*. Actually, he put his name on a book a British officer, Captain S. E.
Nolan, had written in 1852, but he did add two new chapters, "Rarey's Method of
Taming Horses" and "Horseshoeing," which he also copied from other texts. "Cap-
tain Nolan's work is now out of print," he explained in a brief introduction acknowl-
edging his debt to the other authors, and he sought only to "preserve to the Cavalry
Service so valuable a system" for training horses.[15]

Garrard's parole might have dragged on indefinitely if Cassius Clay, the flamboyant

Kentucky abolitionist, had not written to President Lincoln on August 19, 1862, urging his appointment as a brigadier general of volunteers. Lincoln forwarded the recommendation to General-in-Chief Henry Halleck, adding Garrard was "the son of Mrs. Judge McLean, whom I would like to oblige if consistent with law & the public service."

Halleck promptly arranged an exchange, but the coveted brigadier general's commission was not immediately forthcoming. On Halleck's advice, Garrard resigned his post at the Academy to accept the colonelcy of the 146th New York Infantry.

"At first, we were all inclined to believe that he was a martinet," the regimental historian later wrote, "and it was not until we had had an opportunity of witnessing his sterling courage on the field of battle, and associating with him during miles of heavy marching, that we came to love and respect him. We soon found that he always had uppermost in his mind the welfare of the men under his command . . . knew the name of every man in the regiment, and it was no unusual thing to have him call out of the ranks by name some man who had been delinquent, or . . . to commend someone who might be worthy of praise."

The "Royal Tiger," as the New Yorkers dubbed their aristocratic colonel, led his men into battle at Fredericksburg and Chancellorsville. His "gallant and meritorious services" during the fight for Little Round Top at the battle of Gettysburg earned him his promotion to brigadier general in July 1863 and command of a brigade. Recalled to Washington in December, he served a brief apprenticeship in the Cavalry Bureau before replacing an old acquaintance, Major General George Stoneman, as chief of that troubled office on January 2, 1864. Despairing at the graft and corruption he found, he resigned on January 26, telling Secretary of War Edwin M. Stanton, "I cannot hope to surpass the efforts of Stoneman."

An officer who shirked an important and difficult duty ordinarily would have been shelved, but Garrard had powerful friends. Within a week, George Thomas had agreed to give his erstwhile cadet command of the 2nd Cavalry Division of the Army of the Cumberland.

Garrard was a strict disciplinarian, and a few days after joining his division, he directed his troopers to walk their horses to a nearby stream. Then he hid by the roadside to see that his orders were obeyed. Most of the men approached at the prescribed walk, but Private Daniel D. Walker thundered past at a gallop.

"Halt," Garrard barked, emerging from his hiding place. "Dismount." "Do you see that tree?" he demanded, pointing to a distant landmark about 400 yards down the road. "Well, double-quick to it and back, and be lively about it."

"Double-quick, Dan; double-quick and be lively about it," Walker's comrades jeered as the embarrassed trooper jogged away. When he returned, red-faced and panting, Garrard asked him how he enjoyed his little gallop. Walker got the point and sheepishly remounted, urging his horse forward at a more leisurely pace.

A few minutes later, Garrard punished Private Tom Holsenbee for the same offense. After Holsenbee had double-quicked to the tree and back, Garrard asked him if he thought hard running would tire a horse. Holsenbee naively replied he did not know; it did not tire him. "Try it again," Garrard suggested sternly.

A tall, sandy-haired, slightly balding bachelor with a full beard and piercing gray eyes, Garrard shunned the plumes and pretense affected by many cavaliers. "His

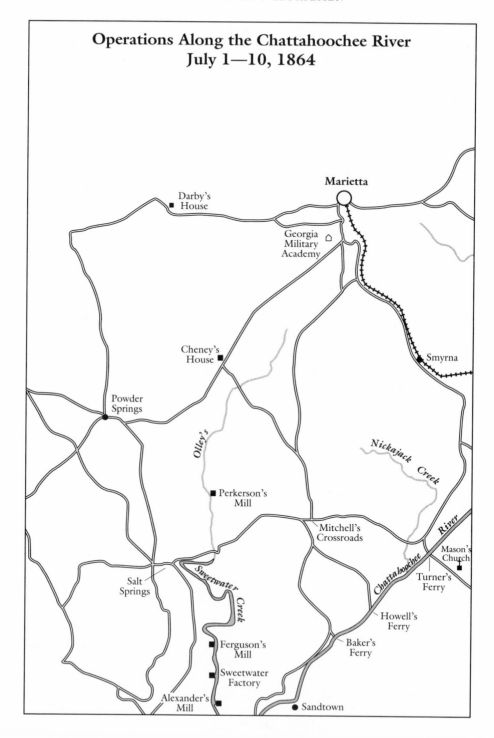

Operations Along the Chattahoochee River
July 1—10, 1864

Marietta

Darby's
House

Georgia
Military
Academy

Cheney's
House

Smyrna

Powder
Springs

Olley's

Nickajack

Creek

Perkerson's
Mill

Mitchell's
Crossroads

River

Mason's
Church

Turner's
Ferry

Salt
Springs

Sweetwater Creek

Chattahoochee

Howell's
Ferry

Ferguson's
Mill

Baker's
Ferry

Sweetwater
Factory

Alexander's
Mill

Sandtown

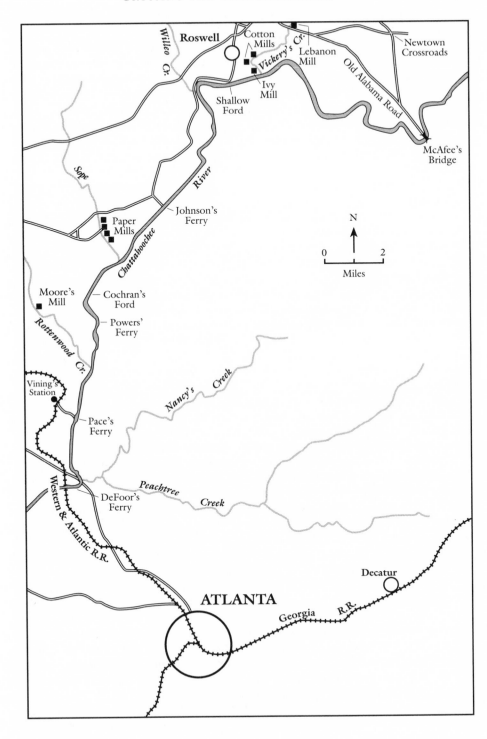

intimacies were few and his tastes simple, ..." wrote a fellow officer. "It required long intercourse, because of his retiring nature, to understand his character."[16]

Darkness had already fallen by the time Sherman's aide, Major McCoy, rode into Garrard's bivouac on the north side of Rottenwood Creek, five miles southeast of Marietta, on July 4. The meandering little stream and the ridge beyond it had been the scene of some sharp skirmishing on July 3 and 4 when Garrard's three brigades encountered dismounted cavalry screening the right flank of the Rebel army. A half dozen Yankee troopers had been wounded or captured in the indecisive clashes, but pickets peering into the darkness that night heard Rebel officers giving commands and the creak and groan of artillery limbers and caissons. Johnston's army was retreating south again, toward the Chattahoochee. However, the orders McCoy delivered directed Garrard to move his division north and east, to capture the bridge at Roswell.[17]

Buglers sounded the brassy notes of "Reveille" at 2:00 A.M., rousting tired troopers from their bedrolls. Yawning, stretching, hitching up their trousers, the men stumbled into line in the predawn darkness to stand for roll call. Sergeants droned down the long list of names, issued orders for the day, then dismissed the companies to feed and groom their horses.

The division wagon trains, escorted by the 1st Ohio Cavalry, had trundled into camp during the night with rations and forage, and once the animals had been fed, the dark woods began to glow with the pale light of hundreds of cooking fires. Breakfast was usually a meager affair in the cavalry. Three or four men, sharing a sheet-iron frying pan, a two-quart pail, and maybe a small kettle, huddled around a flickering blaze. Blinking the smoke from their eyes, they fished greasy slabs of bacon onto battered tin plates with knives and forks, filled their blackened cups with scalding hot coffee, and rounded out the bill of fare with a couple of pieces of hardtack, plain or fried in bacon grease. Once they had eaten, the men gave their dishes a perfunctory swipe with a handful of leaves or a quick rinse in a nearby stream and hurried to get everything packed away before the bugles sounded "Boots and Saddles."[18]

This morning, however, there was a brief pause in the busy camp routine. Corporal David C. Fields of the 3rd Ohio Cavalry, shot through the lungs the previous day, had died during the night. As his body was laid to rest in a shallow grave, the 1st Brigade band played the somber tones of the funeral dirge. "A corporals guard only served as excort [sic]," noted Private John A. Nourse of the Chicago Board of Trade Battery, "his regiment following. 'Tis not often we get time to even give our comrades this little attention but coming back to camp the band played, 'We are coming father Abraham three hundred thousand more,' very appropriate."[19]

As the red sun rose in the eastern sky, the division formed ranks. Private Thomas A. Simpson of the 7th Pennsylvania Cavalry swung into his saddle and waited for his comrade, Private Isaac Schloss, to mount. Before lifting his foot in the stirrup, Schloss carelessly threw the Spencer carbine slung at his side over his right shoulder. The gun fired, the loud blast echoing through the surrounding forest. Startled, Schloss wheeled around and was horrified to see Simpson clutching his left hand, his little finger dangling from a bloody shred of skin. "Py Got tamm it to hell, Tom," Schloss entreated in his thick German accent, "I didn't go to do it!"[20]

While a regimental surgeon amputated Simpson's finger, the column began moving forward. Garrard commanded three brigades, led by Colonels Robert H. G.

Minty, Eli Long, and Abram O. Miller, three officers of intelligence and ability. The 7th Pennsylvania, 4th Michigan, and 4th U.S. Cavalry of Bob Minty's 1st Brigade led the way north on the Pace's Ferry Road, accompanied by the 1st section of the Chicago Board of Trade Battery. The other two sections of the six-gun battery followed with Long and Miller's 2nd and 3rd Brigades.

Two miles east of Marietta, Minty's advance guard turned to the right on the Roswell Road. The morning air was already hot and oppressive, but it was caution, not the heat, that compelled Garrard to call a midmorning halt after an easy six-mile march to Sope Creek. While the 2nd battalion of the 4th Michigan moved a mile ahead to picket the road in front of the column, he sent Major Jacob Vail's 17th Indiana Mounted Infantry and Major William H. Jennings's 7th Pennsylvania Cavalry riding south and east with orders to converge on Roswell.

Major Vail's regiment and a few companies of the 72nd Indiana Mounted Infantry ranged down the west side of Sope Creek until they came to a paper mill belonging to William R. Phillips. An ardent secessionist, at the outbreak of the war Phillips had raised a regiment of infantry, cavalry, and artillery known as Phillips' Legion. The loss of an eye had forced him to retire from active duty in 1862 but had done nothing to lessen his hatred of Yankees. Watching from the south side of the Chattahoochee when Major Vail and his men arrived on July 5, he sent them a message which declared, "The mill belonged to a man who had fought them from the beginning of the war, and who could continue to fight them to the bitter end; that he had been taught to hate them as enemies to him and his, and that he would die hating them; that he did not ask any favor from them; and they might burn to their heart's content."[21]

It is uncertain whether Vail actually received this fiery epistle, but his Hoosiers put the paper mill and neighboring flour mills and machine shops to the torch. Continuing up the road that followed the north bank of the Chattahoochee, they took several prisoners before meeting pickets from Major Jennings's 7th Pennsylvania on the outskirts of Roswell early that afternoon and turning back to rejoin the rest of the command at Sope Creek.

Roswell was a thriving little town once described as "three miles long, a quarter of a mile wide and three feet deep." About twenty "commodious dwellings," surrounded by carefully groomed lawns and gardens, fronted the village green. A steeple crowning the whitewashed Presbyterian church peaked through the trees shading dusty streets lined with neat little cottages. There was also a red-brick Methodist church, a slave chapel, and a schoolhouse, but for a small Southern town, Roswell had an uncommon amount of industry, including a machine shop, a cotton gin, a grist mill, a tannery, two shoe factories, two smithies, and three stores. On the east side of town, three sprawling factories perched on the banks of Vickery's Creek, where spindles whirled and looms shuttled, eleven hours a day, six days a week, weaving osnaburg, kersey, cotton, and wool. "It was altogether perhaps the neatest and prettiest manufacturing town in the country," noted a Yankee lieutenant.

Water power was what attracted the first settler, Roswell King, back in 1837. A Connecticut Yankee and low-country planter, King, along with his son, Barrington, and several wealthy investors, incorporated the Roswell Manufacturing Company in 1839. The elder King died in 1844, but his son and grandsons expanded the original mill into a four-story brick building, supervised the construction of the Ivy Woolen Mill near the mouth of Vickery's Creek, and converted a large grist mill, a mile and a half above town, into a second cotton mill. Each mill employed 300 or 400 people, most of them nimble-fingered women and girls. They lived in company houses, obeyed the company temperance rule, and took their pay in company scrip redeemable only at the company store.

When the war began, King's Georgia-born grandsons, Thomas Edward and James Roswell King, owners of the Ivy Mill, contracted with the Confederate government to furnish a monthly quota of woolen cloth. Despite wartime shortages of lubricants and spare parts, the King brothers managed to produce about 15,000 yards of high-quality woolens every month, and thousands of eager young Confederate volunteers marched to war clad in uniforms of "Roswell grey."

Thomas Edward King was killed in September 1863, while serving as a volunteer aide at the battle of Chickamauga. The following March, his brother, James, made an unusual decision. Convinced it was only a matter of time before war came to Roswell, he consigned a $50,000 interest in the Ivy Mill to Theophile Roche, a journeyman weaver who had come to work in the cotton mills. Roche was a Frenchman, a citizen of a neutral power, and by making him a partner, King hoped the mill would share his neutral status, rendering it inviolable in the eyes of international law. However, King stipulated Roche's interest was conditional and temporary and, if necessary, he must protect the mill at the risk of his life. Roche, in turn, signed a disclaimer, relieving King of any further obligations in the event the mill was destroyed.

When Sherman invaded Georgia, most of the King clan fled south to safer locales. Among the last to leave was James Roswell King. He crossed the covered bridge over the Chattahoochee on the evening of July 4.[22]

Captain Will Clark's Roswell Battalion, three home guard companies of infantry, artillery, and cavalry composed largely of mill hands, followed early the next morning, leaving a detachment of the 4th Tennessee Cavalry to patrol the Roswell Road. About 11:00 A.M., these Tennessee troopers collided with the advance guard of Major Jennings's 7th Pennsylvania two or three miles west of town.[23]

Outnumbered and outgunned, the Rebel horsemen fled through Roswell at a gallop. When they tried to make a stand at the south end of town, the pursuing Pennsylvanians drew sabers and charged. The glimmer of cold steel sent the Tennesseans flying, but not before they set fire to the covered bridge over the Chattahoochee.

Fed by bundles of cotton and straw, the flames spread quickly, turning the bridge into a tunnel of fire. Jennings and his men could only watch as the span sagged off its stone pilings and crashed into the muddy water fourteen feet below. After rounding up a few prisoners, Jennings sent a courier to give Garrard the bad news. The bridge was gone.

Roswell seemed strangely indifferent to the calamity. Someone had pulled furiously on a bellrope, ringing the alarm as the Yankee troopers dashed into town, but all three factories kept humming along as if nothing had happened. The only thing that looked out of place was a pair of French flags, one flying over the Ivy Mill and the other over Mrs. Thomas Edward King's residence at Bulloch Hall.

The reason for the red, white, and blue tricolors soon became apparent when Theophile Roche sauntered up, pipe in hand, and introduced himself as the proprietor of the Ivy Mill. As a French citizen, he demanded protection for himself and his property. Major Jennings apparently had no orders regarding the mills and directed Roche up the chain of command.[24]

Garrard was still waiting on the Roswell Road at Sope Creek when Jennings's courier brought word the Rebels had destroyed the bridge over the Chattahoochee. Without even waiting to call in his pickets, he hurried Minty's and Long's brigades forward at 3:00 P.M., leaving Abe Miller with orders to concentrate the 3rd Brigade on the east side of Sope Creek.

The rest of the division halted two and a half miles short of Roswell, at Willeo Creek, the only stream capable of watering all their thirsty horses. The 1st and 2nd Brigades were making camp on the west bank when Theophile Roche and a group of concerned citizens sought out Colonel Bob Minty and repeated their demand for protection. Minty promptly escorted the group to Garrard's headquarters.

Garrard received Roche and his companions courteously, but the Frenchman's demand for protection obviously took him by surprise. Earlier that evening, Garrard had sent a note advising Sherman his division was camped near Roswell Factory and would "destroy all buildings." This was possibly not so much a declaration of intent as an acknowledgment of verbal instructions Sherman's aide, Major McCoy, may have delivered the previous evening. Before the campaign began, Sherman had studied the 1860 census returns from Georgia and a statistical abstract describing the industrial output of every county in the state. He knew about the mills at Sope Creek and Roswell, and when he sent orders to Garrard on July 4, it seems likely his courier, Major McCoy, intimated that Sherman wanted them destroyed.

However, Roche's appeals to international law apparently shook Garrard's resolve. After listening to the Frenchman's story, he assured him no orders had been issued to burn the mills. He gave Roche and each of his followers a pass to travel freely within the Union lines, but warned them against mingling with the troops, especially at night. Seemingly satisfied, Roche returned to Bulloch Hall, where he had promised Thomas King's widow he would look after things.[25]

Sometime that evening or early the next morning, Garrard sent Captain Darius E. Livermore's Company B of the 3rd Ohio and an unidentified company of the 4th Ohio to garrison Roswell. Livermore persuaded Roche to make him a present of the flags flying over Bulloch Hall and the Ivy Mill, and in return, he gave the Frenchman a receipt stating:

> Provost Marshall [*sic*] Hd. Qrs.
> Roswell, Ga. July 6, 1864

> This will certify that the bearer Mr. Theophile Roche has voluntarily given the undersigned two French flags. His property will receive the same protection as though the flags still remained on his premises.

> (sgd) D. E. Livermore
> Capt. 3rd Post Commander[26]

That afternoon, Garrard rode into town, accompanied by several members of his staff, Colonels Minty, Miller, perhaps Colonel Long, and an escort of "considerable force." Whether he harbored some lingering doubt about the alleged neutrality of the mills or simply acted out of natural curiosity is uncertain. Dismounting, he and his officers entered the cotton mill closest to the town square at street level.

They found themselves on the fourth floor. This was where the picking and packing

The cotton mills at Roswell, Georgia, as they appeared during the war. Garrard and his staff visited the large building in the left foreground. Used by permission of the Atlanta History Center, the Atlanta Historical Society, Inc.

work was done, the obliging mill superintendent explained. The cotton was then carded on the third floor, spun into thread on the second floor, and woven into cloth in the basement. The mill boss estimated the building and all its machinery were worth at least a million Yankee dollars. Garrard made a thorough inspection, and the letters "C.S.A." he found woven into every bolt of cloth he examined soon convinced him Roche's claim of neutrality was a farce.

Among the officers accompanying Garrard was an aide whom Garrard's clerk, Private Silas Stevens, later identified as "McCloud." There was, however, no one by that name on Garrard's staff, and it seems likely "McCloud" was actually Sherman's aide, Major McCoy.

About 4:30 P.M., this "McCloud" approached the mill superintendent and, "with the greatest politeness and civility," asked him to turn off the machinery and evacuate the building. At the same time, Garrard directed Captain Livermore to remove any cloth that might be of use to the Federal field hospitals in Marietta before putting all three mills to the torch.

When Roche heard this order, he reacted with Gallic fury, warning of dire consequences if anyone so much as laid a finger on property belonging to a citizen of France. His ranting fell on deaf ears. Captain Livermore gave the women and children working the mills a half hour to take all the yard goods they wanted. Then he and his men went to work, assisted by small detachments from the 17th Indiana, the 7th Pennsylvania, and some of Garrard's staff.

"The entire machinery, running to its full capacity when we entered the building

. . . came suddenly to a full stop," wrote Silas Stevens. "The women and children filed out of the structure at once and stood in quiet wonder on the banks of the stream, watching our preparations for the destruction of the mills."

While some troopers bustled in and out of the building, gathering armloads of cloth for Sherman's hospitals, others roamed up and down the aisles with sledge hammers, smashing looms, spindles, and carding machinery. At the company warehouse, Silas Stevens and two other men doused raw cotton with oil and liberally distributed it throughout the building, starting on the top floor. Then, as "a matter of courtesy," Stevens waited until "McCloud" had set fire to the adjacent cotton mill before putting the warehouse to the torch.

"My idea," Stevens later explained, "was not to endanger the buildings of the residents of the place, whose houses were in the immediate vicinity, and if my fire was communicated by floors, from the top downward, there would possibly be less danger from flying sparks, and each floor would fall quickly as [it] burned, into the basement and the waters of the stream. The walls which were very stout would probably remain standing, but the contents of the entire edifice would be consumed."

The storehouse burned exactly as Stevens had planned, each floor collapsing on the one beneath it until only the charred walls remained. The nearby cotton mill, fired from the basement, burned more slowly. These two buildings and thirteen others were still in flames when "McCloud" ordered Stevens and another man to return to headquarters to tell Garrard the mills had been destroyed. Most of the other troops also drifted away, but Captain Livermore's two companies waited until the last fire burned itself out before starting back to camp about 10:30 P.M.

Garrard had returned to his headquarters on the west bank of Willeo Creek well before dark. At 7:00 P.M., he penned a lengthy dispatch to Sherman, describing the mills. He also included a map he had drawn of the Roswell area. On the righthand side of the sheet he had written, "Roswell is a very pretty factory town of about four thousand inhabitants. Mills & private property not injured by me." Now he took a pencil and scratched out the word "Mills."[27]

The rest of Garrard's report dealt with roads and terrain. Roswell would be hard to defend, he argued:

> There is a good ford at this place, so I am informed (the shallow ford) but as the opposite banks command this one, and pickets lie on the other side, I have not crossed any of my men. The approach to Roswell from Marietta can be made on two roads—one, as it approaches within two miles of Roswell, is by a crooked, hilly road that could be easily defended; the other, the river road, passes so close to the river as to come under fire of the enemy's rifles. I had one man [a 7th Pennsylvania trooper] shot on this road from the other side.

Garrard wanted to concentrate his division on the Roswell Road near the 3rd Brigade's bivouac at Sope Creek, where he could "watch all this country." Discounting Sherman's fears of an impending Rebel raid on his railroad, he opined "that Johnston will make no attempt on this flank," because he had shifted most of his cavalry to his left to "keep his communications with the source of his supplies westward." But then, having outlined all the reasons for moving back to Sope Creek, Garrard suddenly changed his mind. "I may not take up the position first proposed in this letter," he concluded.[28]

The apparent reason for this abrupt about-face was the belated arrival of a message Sherman had dispatched shortly after 8:00 A.M. on July 6:

> I have just received your note [of July 5th] announcing that you have possession of Roswell. This is important; watch well the crossing there, but not in force; keep your main force concealed somewhat. General McCook has just started for some point between Rottenwood and Soap [Sope] Creek, where he will be near you. I propose to throw Schofield over on that flank the moment I propose to attempt a crossing; fords are much better than bridges, and therefore have the river examined well as to fords. I am on the main road at the point where a branch goes to Vining's on the railroad. . . . Atlanta is in plain view. Stoneman threatens the river down to Sweet Water. I will soon have a telegraph at Vining's and you can communicate by Marietta. You will have rest for a few days and should take advantage of all grain fields.[29]

Ed McCook's sudden appearance at Sope Creek was not the result of hard fighting or hell-for-leather charges. His 1st Cavalry Division, the smallest in Sherman's army, had spent the first four days of July in reserve, supporting George Stoneman's sweep down Sweetwater Creek. Relieved from this do-nothing duty late on July 4, the division had moved northward to the crossroads at Darby's plantation, where the men drew three days' rations of raw bacon, salt, coffee, sugar, and hardtack from the supply trains.

Early the next morning, McCook had received orders to march eastward to be within supporting distance of Garrard's division as it moved toward Roswell. Leaving Darby's at 10:00 A.M, McCook's little command rode past the southern shoulder of Kennesaw Mountain to the Georgia Military Institute on the outskirts of Marietta. Turning to the right, the column followed the Western & Atlantic Railroad southward for another five or six miles before halting at 6:00 P.M. to camp behind Thomas's XIV Corps.

This was not far from Sherman's headquarters at Vining's Station, and sometime that night or early the next morning, McCook conferred briefly with the commanding general. Sherman directed him to move his small division to Power's Ferry, about halfway between Vining's Station and Roswell. Schofield's XXIII Corps would follow and take up positions along the Chattahoochee on McCook's left. Early the next morning, July 6, McCook received written orders to that effect from General Elliott, directing him to "proceed with your command to Powers' Ferry and hold that position, communicating with General Garrard."

Forming ranks at 8:00 A.M, McCook's troopers crossed the railroad at Smyrna Station. A three-mile ride carried them over the Moore's Mill bridge at Rottenwood Creek to Asbury Hargrove's house, where the road branched northeast, south, and east toward Roswell, Pace's Ferry, and Powers' Ferry. While the 8th Iowa and 1st Tennessee Cavalry of Colonel Joseph B. Dorr's 1st Brigade continued east toward Powers' Ferry, McCook rode northeast with the 2nd and 4th Indiana and 1st Wisconsin Cavalry of Lieutenant Colonel Horace P. Lamson's 2nd Brigade until he came to the ruins of the paper mill Garrard's men had burned on July 5. A nearby bridge also lay in ruins, barring any further progress toward Roswell. Turning south, McCook steered Lamson's column down the right side of Sope Creek.

They had gone about a mile when a lone Rebel cannon barked on the other side of the river. Lamson's advance guard quickly backed out of range and waited while scouts fanned out along the riverbank. After an hour or two, McCook left a few men to picket the mouth of Sope Creek and Johnson's Ferry, a mile and a half upstream, and withdrew to make his headquarters at the Hargrove house.

The scene was repeated three miles downstream, where Dorr's 1st Brigade caught only a brief glimpse of Powers' Ferry before two Rebel guns perched on a hill on the south side of the river drove them back. Leaving a small detachment to watch the riverbank above and below the ferry, the rest of Dorr's brigade also retraced their steps to the Hargrove house.

Patrols contacted Abe Miller's brigade, camped at Sope Creek, and after sifting through bits and pieces of information brought in by his officers and scouts, McCook wrote to Elliott, explaining there was a ferry at the mouth of Sope Creek, and a bad ford, which local residents considered "almost impracticable." Downstream, there was a small boat attached to a cable stretched across the river at Powers' Ferry. "Artillery was opened from the other side of the river on my men at both points . . . ," he added, "killing 3 horses." McCook suggested he could get his 18th Indiana Battery within range of the Rebel guns at Powers' Ferry, but warned, "This ferry is well watched and guarded."

As night drew near, he wrote Elliott again, asking permission to move his camp closer to the river. "General Schofield's infantry have got to my left and I am crowded by them," he complained. "I think that I could drive away the enemy's artillery and take up a much better position on the river bank five or six miles to the left. Please notify me early in the morning if I am allowed to do so. The smoke from the infantry camp fires is almost stifling."[30]

Elliott apparently rejected his request and, for the time being, McCook's division remained wedged between the left flank of Thomas's IV Corps and the right flank of Schofield's XXIII Corps. However, his scouts and patrols prowled about the countryside freely and sometime that evening four or five enterprising troopers from Joseph Dorr's 1st Brigade slipped across the river near Powers' Ferry, becoming, in all probability, the first Yankee soldiers to reach the south side of the Chattahoochee. Just above the ferry, they discovered a large island from which Rebel movements could easily be observed. Early the next day, McCook directed Dorr to occupy the island and, if possible, establish a small bridgehead on the south side of the river. Dorr assigned this ambitious undertaking to Colonel James Patton Brownlow of the 1st Tennessee Cavalry.

At age twenty-two, Brownlow was already a legend. The youngest son of the famed Tennessee Unionist "Parson" Brownlow, he had once sent a note challenging a Rebel commander to battle, promising to whip him "like hell." On another occasion, after his men drove some Confederate pickets into camp, Brownlow had his buglers blow "Boots and Saddles," taunting them to come out and fight. One of the youngest colonels in the Union army, he was "tall and well-proportioned," wrote one of his men, "with keen, penetrating gray eyes . . . a soldier of fine ability, full of enterprise, energy and courage. He was never heard to say 'Go, boys,' but always, 'Come on, boys!'"

As Dorr had ordered, Brownlow took possession of the heavily wooded island above Powers' Ferry early on July 7. "A consultation of officers was held," recounted

Sergeant William R. Carter of the 1st Tennessee, "and it was decided to find a native who knew the ford and to show its course. Meanwhile . . . carbines were kept busy, and as the day wore on, Colonel Dorr . . . made his appearance and seemed as mad as a hornet because the boys were not in possession of the opposite side. Dissatisfied with the explanations made, he gave Brownlow peremptory orders to move at once on the enemy, and uttering an unnecessary threat that would be executed in case his order was not promptly obeyed."

With the sun almost directly overhead, there was no hope of taking the Rebels by surprise, but orders were orders, and several of Brownlow's men valiantly urged their horses into the swift, rock-strewn channel. They were halfway across when Rebel cavalrymen lying in wait on the south bank stood up and opened fire. Caught like ducks on a pond, Brownlow's boys churned the muddy water white with foam trying to beat a hasty retreat. All of them made it back safely, but their ardor, to say nothing of their clothing and ammunition, had been considerably dampened. "As the ford was ascertained to be very rocky," Dorr observed laconically in a note to McCook, "I did not think it best to renew the attempt."[31]

Later that afternoon, McCook sent some of his officers six or seven miles upstream to examine Isham's Ford at the mouth of Sope Creek. Finding Schofield was already there laying plans to cross his XXIII Corps, they soon returned. The rest of the day passed quietly until shortly before sundown, when the Rebel battery overlooking Powers' Ferry hurled a few shells across the river. The salvo did no damage, and as twilight cast its long shadows, the guns fell silent.

Nightfall found Brownlow's Tennesseans picketing the north bank of the Chatta-hoochee from Powers' Ferry up to Cochran's Ford. "The river here is very shallow," Brownlow wrote, "and we have to be on the alert night and day. I was glad to have the position, from the fact that it was a locality where no soldiers had ever been, and we consequently could live on the 'fat of the land.' We have potatoes, berries, honey, and chickens for nearly every meal. There are five large fish-traps in this ford and the river furnishes an abundance of fish. However, we can only get them by visiting the trap under cover of night."

In contrast, troopers camped near McCook's headquarters at the Hargrove house and Moore's Mill on Rottenwood Creek found little relief from a steady diet of hardtack and sowbelly. Confederate foragers had already picked the countryside clean, and Private Stanley Lathrop of the 1st Wisconsin Cavalry complained he could find nothing more appetizing than a peck of dried beans someone had hidden in an outhouse.[32]

Garrard's division fared much better in the splendid isolation of Roswell. Horses had their fill of corn and wheat, and the men feasted on blackberries, wild cherries, apples, potatoes, and assorted vegetables. Of course, there was duty on the picket lines, and Garrard's troopers manned outposts from the Ivy Mill all the way down to the mouth of Sope Creek, while patrols ranged upriver, looking for fords and ferries.

Garrard spent most of July 7 scouting the hills north of Roswell. Returning to his headquarters at Willeo Creek, he wrote to Sherman at 5:00 P.M.:

> I . . . find I can take position to advantage north of Roswell and about two miles
> from the town. . . . I think I will move early to-morrow. I have not seen nor heard of
> any of the enemy this side of McAfee's Bridge, eight miles up the river. The only
> good ford I can hear of is just at this point. The Island ford, three miles above, is good

for footmen, but no roads lead to it or from it. . . . I can hear of no practicable fords except these within fifteen miles of this place. McAfee's Bridge is not burnt and the rebels hold it.

He had barely finished writing when Captain Joseph C. Audenried rode up at 5:30 P.M. and delivered a lengthy letter from Sherman. "Your report is received and most acceptable," Sherman wrote, acknowledging Garrard's July 6 dispatch:

> I had no idea that the factories at Roswell remained in operation, but supposed the machinery had all been removed. Their utter destruction is right and meets my entire approval, and to make the matter complete you will arrest the owners and employees and send them, under guard, charged with treason, to Marietta, and I will see as to any man in America hoisting the French flag and then devoting his labor and capital in supplying armies in open hostility to our Government and claiming the benefit of his neutral flag. Should you, under the impulse of anger, natural at contemplating such perfidy, hang the wretch, I approve the act before hand.[33]

Sherman was in high spirits. The left and right wings of his army had drawn abreast of the Chattahoochee. Johnston still held a shallow enclave covering the railroad trestle and the wagon bridge on the main road to Atlanta, but a Federal lodgment anywhere on the south side of the river would make the whole Rebel line untenable. Sherman was already massing McPherson's XV, XVI, and XVII Corps at Turner's Ferry, as if intending to turn the Rebel left, just as he had done at Dalton, Resaca, Allatoona, and Kennesaw, but this was merely a ruse to draw Johnston's cavalry downstream. Sherman's real objective, as he had intimated to Grant back on April 10, was the Rebel right.

"I want a lodgment made on the other bank as soon as possible anywhere from Roswell down to the vicinity of Soap [Sope] Creek," Sherman continued in his letter to Garrard. "I have no doubt the opposite bank is picketed, but, as you say, the main [Rebel] cavalry force . . . has moved to the other flank, and we should take advantage of it."

Sherman suggested Garrard select a ford, "say the second or third below the mouth of Willeyo [Willeo] Creek, on your sketch," and cover it with a brigade and a battery while detachments from his other two brigades crossed at the nearest fords above and below, "at night . . . and, without firing a gun." Once a bridgehead had been secured, the remaining brigade should cross with its artillery and dig in on a commanding hill. "I will see that the cavalry is relieved by General Schofield at once," Sherman promised. "I merely suggest this plan and its execution about daylight to-morrow, and I prefer you should do it."

To this Sherman added an apology, a small one, but an apology nonetheless, for the tongue-lashing he had given Garrard at Marietta. "I assure you," he wrote, "[de]spite of any little disappointment I may have expressed, I feel for you personally not only respect but affection, and wish for your unmeasured success and reputation, but I do wish to inspire all cavalry with my conviction that caution and prudence should be but a very small element in their characters."

Having salved his conscience, Sherman then reiterated:

> I repeat my orders that you arrest all people, male and female, connected with those factories, no matter what the clamor, and let them foot it, under guard, to Marietta, whence I will send them by cars to the North. Destroy and make the same

disposition of all mills save small flouring mills manifestly for local use, but all saw-mills and factories dispose of effectually, and useful laborers, excused by reason of their skill as manufacturers from conscription, are as much prisoners as if armed. The poor women will make a howl. Let them take along their children and clothing, providing they have the means of hauling or you can spare them. We will retain them until they can reach a country where they can live in peace and security.[34]

With Sherman's aide, Captain Audenried, looking over his shoulder, Garrard did not waste any time. That evening, a Yankee captain strode up to the white-pillared portico of Bulloch Hall and informed Theophile Roche that Garrard wanted to see him. Roche accompanied the officer to the town square, where four bluecoated cavalrymen promptly arrested him and marched him off to Garrard's headquarters at Willeo Creek with about forty-four other male civilians. Officers told the other residents to pack their belongings. The army would take them North or they could go South, but they could not stay in Roswell.

In the meantime, Garrard conferred with his brigade commanders, and about 10:00 P.M. he advised Audenried his division could not even attempt to cross the Chattahoochee until July 9, a day later than Sherman had planned. Audenried promptly sent a note advising Sherman of Garrard's delay and added, "I will accompany him in the morning and will join you during the day with such information as I may gather."[35]

Garrard began his preparations by ordering a thorough inspection of the entire command. Early on July 8, the 2nd Brigade's Eli Long directed his regimental commanders to form their troops in line at 9:00 A.M. and "count every *officer* and *man* present." Companies on picket duty were also to be mustered and tallied.

At the appointed hour, Long's 1st, 3rd, and 4th Ohio assembled and counted off 1,569 officers and men present and equipped for duty. It was the largest cavalry brigade in Sherman's command, and would have been even larger, except for the absence of five full companies, almost half a regiment. Companies A and C of the 1st Ohio were on detached duty at Nashville. Company L was General Thomas's escort, Company D of the 4th Ohio was General Elliott's escort, and on July 2, Captain George F. Conn and Company B of the 1st Ohio had suddenly been assigned as General McPherson's escort. Long wanted that company back, and after the inspection he wrote the colonel of the 1st Ohio demanding to know who had given Captain Conn permission to offer his services to the Army of the Tennessee.

Even with the absence of these five companies, the 2nd Cavalry Division still mustered about 4,200 officers and men. Anticipating the bloody work that lay ahead, Garrard had Dr. William C. Cole of the 72nd Indiana convert Roswell's Presbyterian church into a field hospital. "I . . . am prepared for the contest," Cole confided in his diary.[36]

Sometime that morning, Abe Miller rode up from the 3rd Brigade's bivouac at Sope Creek to see where Garrard intended to cross the river. He was shown an unlikely looking spot called Shallow Ford, half a mile below the ruins of the Roswell bridge. The river was 200 yards wide, rain swollen, and swift. A steep ridge, terraced with Rebel rifle pits, loomed up on the other side, but if Miller had any misgivings, he kept them to himself.

A big, quiet, unassuming man, he had been a country doctor before the war began.

A country doctor before the war, Colonel Abram O. Miller commanded the 3rd Brigade of the 2nd Cavalry Division. His four regiments of mounted infantry, armed with Spencer repeating rifles and carbines, were known as the "Lightning Brigade" because of the tremendous firepower they brought into battle. Reproduced from the Collections of the Library of Congress.

Three years of soldiering had honed him into a fine officer, commanding four regiments of mounted infantry, the 17th and 72nd Indiana and the 98th and 123rd Illinois of the famous "Lightning Brigade," or "Wilder's Brigade" as it was sometimes called, in honor of its first colonel, John T. Wilder. Early in 1863, Wilder had persuaded the army to mount four otherwise ordinary infantry regiments on captured horses and convinced bankers in his hometown of Greensburg, Indiana, to put up enough money to arm them with the then-untried Spencer rifle. The gun could be fired seven times without reloading, and the men eagerly signed promissory notes to have the $35 cost of each weapon deducted from their pay.

A spring-tensioned tubular magazine in the Spencer's stock held seven copper-cased .52 caliber rimfire cartridges. Pushing the gun's loading lever down lowered the breechblock, ejecting a spent cartridge. Pulling the lever back up raised the breechblock and chambered a fresh round. The hammer was cocked by hand like a regular musket, but a practiced marksman could empty the magazine in as little as ten seconds. Wilder's men soon learned they could keep up a withering fire by moving the loading lever just enough to unseat the spent casing and reloading from their cartridge boxes. That way, a good trooper always had seven rounds in reserve.

Ill health had forced Wilder's resignation in June 1864, but Miller had proved himself an able successor. "Steady as a clock and intrepid as the best grenadier of them all," declared an admiring superior, "Miller was equal to any undertaking that might fall his lot. . . . His brigade . . . was a model of efficiency. Whether mounted or on foot as skirmishers, it was invincible." That was why Garrard wanted him to lead the charge across the Chattahoochee.[37]

Garrard's meticulous preparations took most of the day, but the main obstacle to the swift execution of Sherman's orders seems to have been several hundred despairing women and girls suddenly at loose ends after the destruction of the Roswell mills. Left to wrestle with the logistics of moving them sixteen miles to the railhead at Marietta, Garrard decided the most practical solution was to cart them off in his empty supply wagons, then bring back a load of hardtack, bacon, and coffee on the return trip.

At 4:00 P.M., Yankee troopers herded Roche and the other civilian prisoners back to town and told them they had one hour to gather up their belongings. Roche, still clinging defiantly to his French neutrality, demanded an exemption from the order, but to no avail. Returning to his lodgings, he stuffed a few things in an old carpetbag and then joined 400 or 500 other villagers queuing up in the town square behind 110 canvas-topped army wagons.

Most of those electing to go North were women and young girls. "Think of it!" wrote a correspondent for the *Cincinnati Daily Commercial.* "Four hundred weeping and terrified Ellens, Susans, and Maggies transported, in springless and seatless army wagons, away from their lovers and brothers of the sunny South, and all for the offense of weaving tent-cloth and spinning stocking yarn!" Escorted by Company L of the 7th Pennsylvania, Company H of the 3rd Ohio, and presumably a company from the 3rd Brigade, the wagons began rolling out of Roswell about 7:00 P.M.[38]

About an hour later, the deserted streets again echoed with the clatter of hooves, as Eli Long's 2nd Brigade rode into town, followed by Bob Minty's 1st Brigade and the Chicago Board of Trade Battery. While the artillerymen parked their big black guns on the village green and troopers unsaddled their horses, Garrard set up headquarters at Barrington King's imposing home, Barrington Hall.[39]

He issued orders directing Long's 1st and 3rd Ohio to remain in Roswell as a mounted reserve while Lieutenant Colonel Oliver P. Robie's 4th Ohio rode eight miles upstream to capture McAfee's Bridge, if it could be done "without too much loss or risk." In any event, after arriving at the bridge, "or as near to it as he can get," Robie was to take up enough planks "to prevent the enemy from coming on him in force," and hold the bridge until further orders, "neither destroying it himself or permitting the enemy to do so," while making a noisy demonstration to divert Rebel attention from Shallow Ford, where the 1st and 3rd Brigades would begin crossing the Chattahoochee at daylight.[40]

Anxious to conceal his preparations from prying Rebel eyes on the south side of the river, Garrard would not allow his men to build fires. The need for secrecy may also have compelled him to keep Abe Miller's mounted infantry at Sope Creek until sundown. It was 11:00 P.M. by the time they rode into Roswell and bedded down on the outskirts of town.

Miller's rear guard had scarcely gotten to sleep when "Reveille" sounded at 2:00 A.M., July 9. There were no campfires, no breakfast, no hot coffee to take the chill off the night air. At 3:00 A.M., Robie's 4th Ohio mounted their horses and rode out of Roswell, following one of the division scouts, Corporal Henry Cook, who led the way east toward McAfee's Bridge. A few moments later, Abe Miller's Lightning Brigade trudged into town and turned south. The moon had set and it was so dark the men could scarcely see beyond the rank in front of them. They had no inkling of where they were going or what they were supposed to do, but about three-quarters of a mile below Roswell officers steered Miller's 72nd Indiana and 123rd Illinois to the left on a road paralleling the river. His other two regiments, the 17th Indiana and 98th Illinois, continued south until they reached the bluff overlooking Shallow Ford. While Captain John J. Weiler secreted two companies of the 17th Indiana in the bushes along the riverbank, the 72nd Indiana and the 123rd Illinois quietly deployed about 200 yards upstream, where Companies D and I of the 72nd Indiana formed on Weiler's left.

Garrard watched with Sherman's aide, Major McCoy, as the rest of Miller's brigade lined up on top of the bluff. McCoy had arrived sometime during the night to relieve Captain Audenried and deliver a message from Sherman, promising Garrard, "The moment I hear you have made a lodgment on the south bank I will send a division up to re-enforce you, . . . followed by one of McPherson's corps from the extreme right. . . . Schofield will cross below you near the mouth of Soap [Sope] Creek. . . . Send word the instant you get a good foothold and the troops will start. Audenried can guide them."[41]

Once Miller's brigade had deployed on top of the bluff, Bob Minty's 1st Brigade came up on foot and formed ranks behind them. The 1st and 2nd sections of the Board of Trade Battery quietly wheeled into position, unlimbered, and sent their teams to the rear.

A dense white fog hung over the river, obscuring the four companies crouched at the water's edge, where troopers speculated in hushed tones about what they were supposed to do. Captain Chester G. Thomson, the officer in charge of the skirmish line, was no better informed than the lowliest private. He surmised the brigade had been sent to cover pontoniers laying a bridge across the river, but all he knew for sure was he was supposed to report to Colonel Miller once his men were in position. After examining his line, he started the steep climb up the bluff. Halfway to the top, he paused to look over his shoulder. The eastern sky was just beginning to pale; the fog was starting to lift. Across the river, he could see a big white house where a bunch of sleeping Rebel soldiers lay sprawled on the porch. He also noted a line of sentries posted at regular intervals along the riverbank. The river itself was wide and deep, and Thomson shuddered to think how difficult it would be to cross in the face of a determined foe. He scrambled to the top of the bluff and reported to Miller.

"Well," Miller said, "as soon as the artillery opens, move your men right across."

Thomson stared at his colonel in disbelief. "You don't mean to say we are expected to wade that river?" he asked incredulously.

"Yes," Miller replied matter-of-factly, "that is what we have been sent here for, and we expect to do it."

Thomson's first impulse was to tell him it was impossible, but he checked himself. "If you order it, we will try it," he said simply. Then he turned and started back down the bluff.

Thomson was not alone with his doubts. Several nearby enlisted men were discussing the situation, and Miller overheard one exclaim, "By God, I'll not believe it till Miller says so!"

The men on the skirmish line were equally skeptical. "We'll never cross it," asserted one as Thomson reached the bottom of the bluff.

"If they order us to, we'll do it," prompted another, "but I don't believe Colonel Miller will ever order us to."

Just then, as if to dispel their doubts, the battery on the bluff roared, sending four 10-pounder Parrott shells shrieking across the river. "Forward!" yelled Thomson. With a lusty cheer, 200 men plunged into the water. At the same time, Garrard spurred his horse to the edge of the bluff, waving his hat and shouting, "Bully boys! Bully boys! *Whisky in the morning!*"[42]

This brought Miller's whole brigade to their feet, cheering wildly over the roar of the artillery. About fifty Rebel riflemen answered with a scattering of shots that sent tiny geysers spewing up around the men floundering waist deep in the water. Thomson's troopers crouched lower, trying to present the smallest possible target, but the current was swift and they slipped and stumbled on the rocky bottom, occasionally disappearing completely, only to bob to the surface, sputtering for breath.

The four guns booming on the bluff had hurled about twenty-five shells across the river when they were ordered to cease fire,[43] but Miller had detailed two companies of the 17th Indiana and one from the 72nd to make the Rebel pickets keep their heads down and they kept up a rapid fusillade. Some of their bullets began splashing uncomfortably close to the men in the water, who turned and motioned frantically for their friends on the heights to raise their sights. Thomson's own troopers got off a few rounds whenever they could find firm footing, levering a metallic cartridge into their Spencers, pouring the water out of the barrel, and standing up to squeeze off a quick shot before dropping shoulder deep in the water again. "Look at them Yankee sons of bitches, loading their guns under water!" marveled a Rebel defender.[44]

The sight caused utter consternation among his comrades. Most of those who had not already panicked under the weight of the artillery barrage now fled as Thomson's men stormed into the shallows with a wild yell. Sergeant James A. Mount of the 72nd Indiana (a future governor of the Hoosier state), was the first to clamber ashore. Private David Frazier followed close behind. Soon, all four companies were across, without a single casualty.[45]

For a few moments the exhausted troopers hugged the riverbank, uncertain what to do next. Then Private Eugenius B. Dunwoody of the 72nd Indiana suggested if they stayed hemmed up between the bluff and the river, the Rebels could come back and cut them to pieces. Captain Thomson replied the only order he had was to cross the river. Dunwoody countered that his grandmother was ninety-five years old, but even she would have more sense than to stay here. Thomson agreed, and the order passed down the line: take the high ground.

As the Hoosiers scrambled up the slope, they encountered a few Rebels, seemingly mesmerized by the sight of armed men boiling up out of the river. The Johnnies surrendered meekly, almost eagerly in some cases, telling their captors they were the "God-damndest fellas they ever seed," loading their guns under water like that.[46]

When questioned, these prisoners volunteered that Brigadier General John H. Kelly's division of Rebel cavalry was camped nearby. This sent Thomson's men double-quicking to the top of the ridge. In their haste, some of them slipped and slid down the slope. By the time they regained their footing, their wet uniforms were so muddy they were barely distinguishable from the butternut brown their prisoners wore. But they clambered to the crest, 300 yards beyond the river, and raised a triumphant shout. In less than thirty minutes, they had done the impossible.

Now they had to hold what they had won, and Thomson put them to work building breastworks of logs, rocks, fence rails, anything that would stop a Rebel bullet. The rest of Miller's brigade waded across the river to join them. Minty's brigade followed, some troopers cutting long sticks to help them feel their way across the rocky riverbottom, and formed on Miller's left.

By 7:00 A.M., Garrard had 2,500 dismounted men manning a semicircular line nearly a mile long. "I have the ridge on the south bank of the river," he wrote Sherman. "The infantry should come up at once. I see no reason why I cannot hold it, but cannot tell what may occur before long."[47]

While couriers relayed this note to the telegraph office at Marietta, Garrard sent riders down to the mouth of Sope Creek to communicate with John Schofield's XXIII Corps, which had splashed across the Chattahoochee late the previous afternoon at Isham's Ford. He also summoned the 3rd section of the Board of Trade Battery from Roswell with the caissons carrying extra ammunition and posted these two guns on a hilltop half a mile east of the rest of the battery to cover the approaches to the charred ruins of the Roswell bridge and the left flank of the hastily built breastworks on the other side of the river.[48]

As the morning wore on, Garrard received a report from Lieutenant Colonel Robie at McAfee's Bridge. This was followed at 10:00 A.M. by a telegram from Sherman, impatiently demanding, "What news? Have you crossed? You know that Schofield is across."

Realizing his first dispatch must have passed Sherman's message somewhere en route, Garrard replied:

> At 7 o'clock I sent you word that I was over the river and had the ridge. I have now a good position, and hold the Roswell and Atlanta road, which passes over the bridge. The ford is a little rough, but not deep. All is quiet in my front; but the regiment I sent to take the bridge, eight miles above, failed, and find some considerable force there. They can keep the enemy from burning the bridge, but cannot get possession of it. Prisoners report Kelly's division, Wheeler's corps, near that bridge.

Early that afternoon, couriers delivered a second telegram from Sherman acknowledging receipt of Garrard's first dispatch. "One division of Thomas' moved for Roswell last night by the river road," he added. "Two divisions of McPherson, Dodge's [XVI] corps, are now moving for Roswell via Marietta. Hold fast all you have made and fortify until re-enforced."

Later, in a third telegram, Sherman advised Garrard, "I have your second dispatch. Dodge was here en route for Roswell, and will come to you to-morrow; but in the mean time a division of Thomas' should be near there now. . . ."

The vanguard of these promised reinforcements, Brigadier General John Newton's division of Thomas's IV Corps, had halted a half mile west of Roswell at 1:00

P.M. after marching sixteen miles in the sweltering heat. Many of the men were on the verge of collapse, and it was nearly dark before they began crossing Shallow Ford to relieve the dismounted cavalry on the south bank.[49]

Leaving a few companies to picket the front of Newton's infantry, Miller's and Minty's brigades began withdrawing at 8:00 P.M. Some of the men looked more like ditch diggers than soldiers as they approached the river in their stiff, mudcaked clothes, but as Private Jerome B. Quinn of the 123rd Illinois Mounted Infantry noted, "When we got across we were boys in blue again."[50]

Not relishing the idea of spending the night in wet clothes, Captain Thomson and several of his men shucked their muddy uniforms and hoisted the bundles over their heads before wading into the ford. Thomson, a strapping six-footer, was halfway across when he stepped into a pothole and plunged out of sight. His men bent double with laughter as the captain thrashed to the surface, desperately trying to grab his precious bundle before it floated away.

A little farther upstream, Bob Minty's 4th Michigan Cavalry tried to keep their feet dry by picking their way across the half-submerged ruins of the Roswell bridge. The 1st and 2nd battalions were making good progress when the middle section of wreckage suddenly gave way, taking the two rearmost companies, G and M, with it. Swept up by the current, the ungainly craft floated downstream for more than 200 yards before snagging on a pile of driftwood. Alert troopers on the north side of the river built bonfires to illuminate the scene, and with the help of boards, sticks, and long poles, the castaways used some nearby boulders like giant stepping stones to disembark with the loss of nothing more than a few carbines.

This, however, left the 4th Michigan's 3rd battalion stranded on the south bank. Groping their way back to Shallow Ford, these troopers waded across and marched back to Roswell, "weary, hungry, *wet and thirsty.*"[51]

The arrival of Sherman's infantry coincided with the retreat of the Rebel cavalry who had stymied Lieutenant Colonel Robie's efforts to capture McAfee's Bridge. Hurrying his regiment across the 220-foot span, Robie had just thrown out a strong skirmish line when a courier brought orders to return to Roswell. Abandoning the bridge, Robie's men retrieved their mounts and climbed into the saddle. Private Moses McClure of the 4th Ohio had suffered a slight head wound during the day's skirmishing, but he was the only casualty the Yankees had suffered in storming the last great natural barrier between Sherman and Atlanta.[52]

Garrard returned to his headquarters at Barrington Hall well ahead of his troops and wrote to Sherman at 9:00 P.M., acknowledging the arrival of Newton's infantry. "My cavalry pickets are about two miles from the river, on the Atlanta road," he added. "There has been but slight opposition to-day, though my cavalry pickets stand opposite those of the enemy, and have had some skirmishing. No sign of large force of the enemy's infantry. . . ."[53]

Garrard's troopers were not the only Yankee cavalrymen to cross the Chattahoochee on July 9. That afternoon, McCook had sent Colonel Dorr and a small detachment over one of two pontoon bridges Schofield had strung across the river at the mouth of Sope Creek. Ordered to scout the roads toward Atlanta, they soon returned with disturbing news. Joe Wheeler's Confederate cavalry had not been drawn downstream by McPherson's noisy demonstrations at Turner's Ferry as Sherman had assumed. They were right in front of Schofield, in strength.

In what may have been an attempt to create a diversion for Dorr, McCook also ordered Jim Brownlow's 1st Tennessee to cross the river at Cochran's Ford, a few hundred yards below Sope Creek. Still smarting from his repulse at Powers' Ferry on July 7, Brownlow decided against another frontal assault. Calling aside Captain Moses Wiley, he ordered two companies of the 1st Tennessee to strip to the skin and charge the ford. This would divert the Rebel pickets' attention long enough for Brownlow and another detachment to cross upstream and surprise them from the rear.

Leaving an astonished Wiley to carry out these bizarre orders, Brownlow selected ten of his best swimmers. "Boys," he said, "we are going to cross that river. It is plain we can't ford it here, and as we have no pontoons, and can't very well make a swimming charge, we'll find another way or break the breeching."

Leading his men through the woods and around a narrow bend in the river, Brownlow halted about 400 yards upstream and commandeered a small canoe. After a few hurried instructions, he and his men peeled off their blue uniforms and piled their guns and cartridge boxes aboard.

Taking a firm grip on the gunwales, they eased into the current. Sometimes wading, sometimes swimming, they were almost to the southern shore when Captain Wiley's naked troopers burst from the bushes at Cochran's Ford and charged into the water. Unfortunately, someone had misjudged the location of the ford, and both companies rushed headlong into the deepest part of the river. The commotion quickly attracted the attention of the Rebel pickets, who opened fire on the floundering white figures. Unable to advance or retreat, Wiley and his men took cover behind some large rocks jutting out of the water, leaving Brownlow's little band stranded on the south side of the river.

Undaunted, Brownlow outlined his plan of attack in hushed tones.

"I'll be durned if this ain't baring our breasts to the foe for a fact," observed one trooper.

"I reckon the rebs will climb them trees when they find out we're a lot of East Tennessee bear hunters," punned another.

"Talk low, talk low!" Brownlow cautioned, "for the success of this attack depends upon our quietness until we close in with the game, and then you may yell like hell."

Leaving one man to guard the canoe, the young colonel led the way into the woods. Pricked by pine needles, bedeviled with briars, and assailed by swarms of blood-thirsty insects, Brownlow soon found it necessary to turn to his followers and admonish, "cuss low, cuss low."

After what seemed like an eternity, the Tennesseans finally reached the road about 400 yards behind the Rebel outpost firing on Captain Wiley's men. Subsequent Confederate accounts said nine pickets were present; Brownlow put the number at twelve. In any event, he figured the odds were about even. Forming in a line roughly parallel with the river, he and his companions crept within forty or fifty yards of their quarry and charged.

The sight of ten screaming men bursting out of the woods wearing nothing but cartridge boxes so unnerved the unsuspecting Rebels that most of them ran away under "a very heavy fire." Three chagrined Confederates—Sergeant Warren Johnson, and Privates Hiram Pollard and Henry Immen of the 5th Georgia Cavalry—were captured. "'Taint fair to come at us that way," they complained bitterly. Brownlow's boys simply grinned. Anxious to get back across the river, they herded their prisoners aboard a flat-bottomed ferry boat and charted a course for the friendly shore, where they rejoined Captain Wiley's men, who had managed to extricate themselves without any losses.[54]

"Brownlow performed one of his characteristic feats to-day," Ed McCook wrote to General Elliott that night, describing how his Tennessee boys had captured the Rebel pickets. "They would have got more," he added, "but the rebels had the advantage in running through the bushes with clothes on." McCook called it "one of the funniest sights of the war." Others simply referred to it as "raw courage."[55]

The next day, July 10, a Rebel sentry hollered across the Chattahoochee, "Hello, Yank!"

"What do you want, Johnny?" answered a bluecoated soldier.

"Can't talk to you'uns any more!"

"How is that?"

"Orders to dry up!"

"What for, Johnny?"

"Oh, Jim Brownlow, with his damned Tennessee Yankees swam over upon the left last night and stormed our rifle pits naked, captured sixty of our boys and made 'em swim back with him. We'uns have got to keep you'uns on your side of the river now."[56]

2

"AN ASS OF EMINENT GIFTS"

Old troopers and old horses are good, and
recruits of either are absolutely useless.

—Maurice de Saxe, *Mes Reveries*

Three months earlier, Sherman had resolved to send his cavalry to cut the railroad between Atlanta and Montgomery as soon as his armies got to the Chattahoochee. Reaching the river had taken a lot longer than he expected, and fierce Rebel resistance, combined with an undisguised lack of confidence in his cavalry commanders, had left him little time and less inclination to elaborate on the plan. It took a letter from another Union officer to breathe new life into the idea.

Major General Lovell Harrison Rousseau had been following the course of the campaign from his desk in Nashville, where he commanded the District of Tennessee. Early in June, he had learned Bedford Forrest's Confederate cavalry had struck again, routing a much larger Union column led by Brigadier General Samuel D. Sturgis at Brice's Crossroads, Mississippi. Convinced that Forrest's victorious troopers would soon descend on middle Tennessee and play havoc with the railroad connecting Louisville and Chattanooga, Rousseau had written George Thomas's headquarters on June 16, suggesting, "the most certain and effective mode of keeping the enemy off our lines of communication would be to place a portion of this [district's] Cavalry on the other side of the Tennessee River, and operate offensively from Decatur [Alabama], and falling back on that place when hard pressed. In this way the enemy would find employment in defending himself."[1]

Rousseau also sent a copy of this letter to Sherman and two days later, on June 18, he had ordered Lieutenant Colonel D. G. Thornburgh's brigade of Tennessee cavalry and two artillery batteries southward to Decatur. "Offensive operations from that point will give the enemy something else to do than plot and execute raids against our lines of communication," Rousseau explained, "while it will increase the courage and prowess of our own men and intimidate the enemy."

Rousseau, however, had something more ambitious in mind than just intimidating the enemy. For months, he had been toying with the idea of assembling a small cavalry force at Guntersville, Alabama, and striking deep into Dixie to destroy the railroads and vast ordnance works at Selma. Shortly after Sturgis's humiliating defeat at Brice's Crossroads, he learned Major General A. J. Smith and 12,000 Union troops were preparing to leave Memphis for another foray into Mississippi. Rousseau reasoned Smith's powerful column would undoubtedly keep Forrest busy, and might even draw Brigadier General Philip D. Roddey's Rebel horsemen out of northern Alabama, leaving the road to Selma wide open.

Confiding only with his adjutant, Major Burr H. Polk, and Sherman's Nashville chief-of-staff, Brigadier General Joseph D. Webster, Rousseau hastily drew up the broad outlines of his plan and petitioned General Thomas for permission to present them. Thomas readily allowed him to bypass the normal chain of command, and on June 19, Rousseau wrote directly to Sherman, declaring, "With 3,000 men I could go down and destroy fifty to one hundred millions' worth of property belonging to the rebel government, including a portion of the important road between Selma and Atlanta."

This was not the idle boast of a brass-button soldier. Rousseau had been gathering bits and pieces of information from spies and refugees filtering through his Nashville headquarters, and he assured Sherman:

> There are several long trestles on that [rail]road within twenty-five miles of Selma, and at that place there are important manufacturing establishments far more extensive and important than they have in Atlanta, while between here and Selma there are five or six of the most important iron-works there are in the Southern Confederacy. With Thornburgh's brigade, now on its way to Decatur, and Colonel Harrison's Eighth Indiana Cavalry, . . . and the Second Kentucky Cavalry, I could . . . quietly take a position on this side of the Tennessee [River] in the vicinity of Guntersville, and upon a sudden cross there and set off for Selma. I could have at least three days the start of the enemy, and to avoid being intercepted on my return could strike off eastwardly to Montevallo through Ashville, Gadsden, and on up to Ringgold. At Ringgold we could take the return empty cars and come back to the district. A blow like this now would be of great service to the cause, and might effect materially your own immediate position. I have a guide here who knows every foot of the way. . . . I hope you will think of it and allow me to try it.

The plan was very similar to the one Sherman had outlined on April 10, calling for a cavalry division to break up the railroad between Atlanta and Montgomery. However, Rousseau's letter arrived at a time when Sherman was bogged down in front of Kennesaw Mountain. It was June 24 before his adjutant, Captain Lewis M. Dayton, wrote to Thomas acknowledging Sherman was favorably impressed with Rousseau's plan and intended to implement it just as soon as he drove Johnston across the Chattahoochee. In the meantime, Thomas was to order Rousseau to gather all his available cavalry and infantry at Athens and Decatur, Alabama, and Pulaski, Tennessee, ostensibly to protect Sherman's supply lines from Forrest, but in reality to make preparations to "strike as proposed."

The wheels of bureaucracy turned too slowly to suit Rousseau. Before receiving word of the plan's acceptance, he petitioned Sherman again on June 27, reminding him:

> I wrote to you some days ago and asked to be allowed to go to Selma. I now beg leave to renew my request, and that I be allowed to go when it is understood the force of the enemy in that direction is not too large to be overcome by such force as I can prudently take from here. I send a reliable man to talk with you and General Thomas on the subject. He is known to General Thomas and myself to be loyal and reliable in every way. Indeed, General, I think there is nothing in the way, provided only that Forrest be entertained. . . . Hoping for a favorable reply I shall go on and prepare for the trip as well as I can, in a quiet way, and be ready as soon as may be. I have conversed freely with General Webster and he agrees fully with me on the subject. On looking over the copy of my letter, not carefully read at the time, I find Selma

instead of Montgomery is named as the point between which and Atlanta there are important bridges and trestles that could be destroyed. The bearer will explain fully all I could say on this as on other matters. If Forrest be kept engaged . . . I could with prudence take from this district enough men to do the work. There are about 800 armed men in Selma, nearly all of whom are workmen, the balance boy militia. But I need not say more.

Rousseau's emissary, James Carroll McBurney, reached Sherman's headquarters on June 29, two days after the army's bloody repulse at Kennesaw Mountain. McBurney found a receptive audience and at 8:00 P.M., Sherman wired Rousseau, acknowledging:

> I have yours of the 27th. Of course go on and make all the preparations but do not start till we know something definite of A. J. Smith, and until I have pushed Johnston across the Chattahoochee. The points of importance are Montgomery, Opelika, and Columbus, Ga.; Selma is secondary. I have had forage placed at Pensacola in case of the party having to go there. Don't move until I give specific orders.

The next day, he wired coded instructions to Nashville, advising Rousseau:

> The movement that I want you to study and be prepared for is contingent on the fact that General A. J. Smith defeats Forrest or holds him well in check, and after I succeed in making Johnston pass the Chattahoochee with his army, when I want you in person, or to send some good officer with 2,500 good cavalry, well armed, and with sufficient number of pack-mules, loaded with ammunition, salt, sugar, and coffee, and some bread or flour, depending on the country for forage, meat, and corn meal. The party might take two light Rodman guns, with orders, in case of very rapid movements, to cut the wheels, burn the carriages, taking sledges along to break off the trunnions and wedging them in the muzzle. The expedition should start from Decatur, move slowly to Blountsville and Ashville, and if the way is clear, to cross the Coosa at the Ten Islands or the railroad bridge, destroying it after their passage, then move rapidly for Talladega or Oxford, and then for the nearest ford or bridge over the Tallapoosa. That passed, the expedition should move with rapidity on the railroad between Tuskegee and Opelika, breaking up the road and twisting the bars of iron. They should work on that road night and day, doing all the damage toward and including Opelika. If no serious opposition offers, they should threaten Columbus, Ga., and then turn up the Chattahoochee to join me between Marietta and Atlanta, doing all the mischief possible. No infantry or position should be attacked, and the party should avoid all fighting possible, bearing in mind for their own safety that Pensacola, Rome, and Etowah and my army are all in our hands. If compelled to make Pensacola, they should leave their horses, embark for New Orleans, and come round to Nashville again.
>
> Study this well, and be prepared to act on order when the time comes. Selma, though important, is more easily defended than the route I have named.[2]

Sherman said nothing more about the expedition until the evening of July 2, when George Thomas sent him some captured Rebel newspapers indicating Forrest's cavalry was concentrating at Tupelo, Mississippi, to oppose A. J. Smith, just as Rousseau had anticipated. "Now will be a good time for the raid from Decatur on Opelika," Sherman mused in a field telegram to Thomas that night. "If you agree with me I will order it now."

Thomas agreed the time was right if a good officer could be placed in command. "I have heard that Roddey also had moved west of Tuscumbia," he added, "evidently attracted in that direction by the movements of Smith." This meant northern Alabama was virtually defenseless.

"Now is the time for the raid on Opelika," Sherman wired Rousseau later on July 2. "Telegraph me whether you go yourself or who will command."

"I shall go in person . . . ," Rousseau replied on July 3. "A little preparation will be required. I will announce to you when I am ready to go."[3]

Rousseau had always been a man who could get things done. One of twelve children, he was born on a hardscrabble farm near Stanford, Kentucky, on August 4, 1818. Before he was ten years old, he had quit school to help his family make ends meet. By the time he was fourteen, he was earning a few cents a day, breaking up rocks for construction of the Lexington Turnpike. He also taught himself French. Writing out the conjugations at night and putting the paper on the ground in front of him each morning, he committed the lessons to memory while he swung his hammer.

Moving to Louisville, he studied law with the same fierce determination, reading Blackstone and other legal commentaries for fourteen hours a day and history for two. Admitted to the bar in Bloomfield, Indiana, he married, joined the Whig Party, and in 1844 his traditionally Democratic district elected him to the Indiana House of Representatives.[4]

Reelected in 1845, he resigned his seat at the outbreak of the Mexican War to raise a company of volunteers. Like French or law or anything else he set out to do, soldiering came to him easily. In his first battle, at Buena Vista, his regiment was caught in a murderous Mexican crossfire. Most of the men fled in panic, but Rousseau calmly rallied four companies and was "present and very active" in repelling a charge of Mexican lancers that threatened to turn the left flank of the American army.[5]

Returning to a hero's welcome in Indiana, he was overwhelmingly elected to the state Senate. After serving a year of his term he announced he was stepping down to practice law in Louisville, but his constituents flatly refused to accept his resignation. Bowing to their wishes, Rousseau commuted across the Ohio River to represent them, much to the chagrin of his Democratic colleagues, who disdainfully referred to him as "the member from Louisville."

In partnership with his older brother, Richard, Rousseau earned a reputation as one of the best criminal lawyers in Kentucky. Cheerful and unpretentious, he championed the rights of the poor, often representing clients who could neither hope nor promise to pay. An outspoken critic of the anti-Catholic, anti-immigrant philosophies of the Know-Nothing party that dominated Louisville politics, he was shot through the abdomen when he gallantly sprang to the defense of a harassed German voter in the election of 1856.

Returning to the political arena in 1860, Rousseau ran unopposed for the state Senate. He railed against secession, and after the firing on Fort Sumter he resigned his seat and secured an authorization to raise twenty companies of volunteers. When faint-hearted Unionists enjoined him from raising troops on Kentucky soil for fear it would precipitate a Confederate invasion, Rousseau used his own money to establish Camp Jo Holt on the Indiana side of the Ohio River, where he recruited a force of infantry, cavalry, and artillery known as the Louisville Legion.[6]

In recognition of his pivotal role in keeping Kentucky in the Union, the War

A Southern newspaper described Major General Lovell Harrison Rousseau as "tall . . . bulky . . . can drink as much *good* whiskey as the next best man . . . a fair third rate lawyer about forty years old." A gifted, self-taught soldier, he was elected to Congress in 1865, censured for caning a rival representative, and then overwhelmingly reelected. Used by permission of the Chicago Historical Society. From the Ezra Warner collection.

Department made him a brigadier general of volunteers. He led a brigade at Shiloh and a division at Perryville. Praised as "one of the most conspicuous lights of the war" and promoted to major general, he commanded the Army of the Cumberland's reserve at the battle of Stone's River, Tennessee. When a furious assault hurled back the Federal right flank like a gate swinging on its hinges, he planted his troops in front of the onrushing Rebel tide and vowed he "would not budge a step—not a damned inch, Sir." The Union lines held.[7]

"When he showed himself on the battle-field," noted an admiring officer, "with his hat raised on the point of his sword, encouraging or urging them into the fight, his influence over them was unbounded. He was their Murat, their Ajax, and at all times, in season and out of season, they recognized him with cheers. . . . His fine physique, noble bearing, his thoroughbred horse and gorgeous trappings caught their eyes and aroused their enthusiasm. With all this splendor he was without ostentation, and he was easily approached."

Rousseau had no military training and this same officer acknowledged, "if by reading the tactics and army regulations once over he could have been assured that ever afterward he would have known their contents, it is very doubtful whether he would have taken so much pains. But the men thought he knew it all." He was one of the most popular generals in the Army of the Cumberland, and it became a standard joke, whenever any commotion erupted in camp, that the men were after either "Rousseau or a rabbit."

He rarely studied maps and often handed them to his aides unopened. If an order had to be given, he galloped across the field and delivered it personally. When his troops marched into battle, he led the way. Unlike most politicians who wore general's stars, Rousseau was a born soldier.[8]

He was also an ambitious one, and late in July 1863 he went to Washington, seeking permission to create an elite corps of 2,000 cavalry and 10,000 mounted infantry to suppress guerrilla activity in Tennessee and disrupt Rebel rail traffic in Georgia and Alabama. General-in-Chief Henry Halleck saw "no advantages in this project" and dismissed it as a scheme for "a special organization for a special purpose and with a special commander." Undaunted, Rousseau took his case directly to President Lincoln, who directed Secretary of War Edwin M. Stanton to see Rousseau "at once." Stanton directed the Quartermaster General to study the feasibility of mounting Rousseau's division on mules.

So many mules and horses starved to death during the ensuing Rebel siege of Chattanooga that the plan was dropped. A sweeping reorganization of the Army of the Cumberland followed, putting George Thomas of the XIV Corps in command. Rousseau, the XIV Corps' senior major general, seemed like Thomas's logical successor, but Charles A. Dana, the Assistant Secretary of War who had been traveling with the army since August, had formed an intense dislike for the popular Kentuckian. Referring to Rousseau as "an ass of eminent gifts," he disparaged him as "so unfit he cannot be considered."[9]

Command of the XIV Corps went to a junior officer and Rousseau was reassigned to the District of Tennessee, a thankless, rear-echelon post headquartered in Nashville. "He does not like the way in which he has been treated," wrote a sympathetic subordinate; "thinks there is a disposition on the part of those in authority to shelve him and that his assignment to Nashville is for the purpose of letting him down easily."[10]

Since then, Rousseau had been behind a desk, deploying small detachments to guard railroads and chase down guerrillas. But he had never given up his dream of leading a mounted column into the very heart of the Confederacy, and now that fortune smiled on him, he threw all his considerable energy into the project, knowing this might well be his last chance to get back into the war.

Rousseau had originally intended to use the 8th Indiana and 2nd Kentucky Cavalry, garrisoned at Nashville, and Lieutenant Colonel Duff G. Thornburgh's Tennessee brigade, stationed at Decatur, Alabama, but he soon had second thoughts. While Thornburgh's 4th Tennessee had been cited for "coolness and courage and discipline" at the battle of Okolona, Mississippi, on February 22, the rest of the brigade had performed poorly. "On so hazardous an undertaking," Rousseau wrote, "I greatly desired to have with me officers and men whom I knew to be of tried courage and efficiency to insure the success of the expedition." With this in mind, he decided to replace Thornburgh's 2nd and 3rd Tennessee with the 5th Iowa and 9th Ohio Cavalry.[11]

The 5th Iowa, composed of companies from Nebraska and Missouri as well as

Iowa, had been mustered into service in February 1862. Most of the men had reenlisted as veteran volunteers in December 1863, turned in their arms and equipment, and gone home on furlough. Since returning to duty, they had encountered difficulty in getting remounted and reequipped. Major Harlon Baird, commanding Companies A, B, C, H, L, and M, stationed sixty-five miles south of Nashville near Pulaski, Tennessee, had procured enough Sharps carbines and .44 caliber Colt revolvers to arm his men, but no horses. Conversely, Lieutenant Colonel Matthewson T. Patrick, posted at Nashville with Companies D, E, F, G, I, and K, had 360 horses and enough saddles and bridles for the whole regiment, but only a few carbines.

Perhaps because they were armed, Major Baird's troopers were the first to be summoned. On July 4, Rousseau telegraphed Brigadier General John C. Starkweather at Pulaski and directed him to "relieve the detachment of the 5th Iowa Cavalry under your command, ordering it to Decatur at once." A southbound freight was leaving Nashville at 6:00 that evening; Baird's men could catch a ride on the top of the cars when it stopped at Pulaski.

Starkweather ordered Baird to have his troopers ready to move at midnight, promising, "Your detailed men at block houses will be relieved on the sixth (6th) Inst., and will report to you at Decatur."

Baird and his men were waiting when the train chugged into Pulaski. Climbing aboard the tops of the cars, they hung on as the locomotive gave a convulsive lurch and began rolling south through the starry summer night. They reached Decatur the next morning, July 5, and waited there until the rest of the detachment arrived from Pulaski on July 7.[12]

The 1st battalion of the 9th Ohio Cavalry was already in Decatur, and this was probably why Rousseau chose them to replace Thornburgh's Tennesseans. Other than that, the regiment had little to recommend it. While the other units Rousseau had selected for the raid were veterans with two or three years' service, the 9th Ohio had done very little campaigning. The 1st battalion, Companies A, B, C, and D, had seen some action in Kentucky and Tennessee, but the rest of the regiment had not even been mustered in until December 1863. Their performance since then had not been impressive. Morale was low, discipline poor, and the commanding officer, Colonel William Douglas Hamilton, a Scottish-born Ohio attorney, was constantly laying down the law to his men.

Noting several soldiers had rendered themselves unfit for duty by "the contractions of certain vineral [sic] diseases," on June 18 Hamilton had ordered all noncommissioned officers suffering from such illnesses, "the result of their own licentiousness," stripped of rank. Henceforth, he warned, "the contractions of any of the diseases referred to" would result in immediate demotion, and he enjoined his officers to see that no one "shall hold a position of trust anywhere in this command who would thus forfeit his claims to the respect of his comrades and bring shame upon his family at home."

Hamilton also deplored "the playing of cards for money" and ordered all gambling stopped "as a protection to the young and those who be honest and as a check to the designing and unscrupulous men of this command." Any commissioned officers "found guilty of the crime" would be subject to dismissal. Any noncommissioned officer would be "immediately reduced to the ranks."

This was followed by orders on June 27 addressing the "frequent accidents that have been occuring [*sic*] in this command from careless handling of loaded arms." Henceforth, Hamilton ordered, no one in the regiment would carry a loaded gun, "either while in camp or on the march, not even when marching to meet the enemy." While on the march, the men were to carry their carbines capped, but cartridges would be inserted only at the command of company officers. "The advanced guards *alone* will form an exception to this rule and will march with their arms loaded," Hamilton decreed, and company commanders were to take "stringent measures" to see that the order was "strictly enforced."

These constant edicts did nothing to endear Hamilton to his men, and some of his officers were preparing charges against him. But this unhappy regiment was one of the largest in the district and Rousseau needed it. Early on July 5, about the same time Major Baird's Iowans were climbing off the cars, he wired General Starkweather to order the 9th Ohio's 2nd battalion to "march to Decatur and await further orders."

Companies E, F, G, and H of the 2nd battalion were bivouacked at Athens, Alabama, near the Nashville and Decatur Railroad. Upon receipt of Rousseau's orders, officers directed the men to be ready to march at 8:00 A.M., July 6, but it was 9:30 before the last troopers left camp. Heading southeast, they rode all day under a blistering sun, covering thirty-five miles before halting at 5:00 P.M. at the 3rd battalion's bivouac at Mooresville, just across the Tennessee River from Decatur.[13]

While the Ohioans marched for Mooresville, Sherman was keeping the telegraph wires hot. Uncertain where Rousseau's preparations might have taken him, he wired both Nashville and Decatur on July 6, insisting:

> That cavalry expedition must now be off, and must proceed with the utmost energy and confidence. Everything here is favorable, and I have official information that General A. J. Smith is out from Memphis with force enough to give Forrest full occupation. Expeditions inland are also out from Vicksburg and Baton Rouge, as well as against Mobile. If managed with secrecy and rapidity the expedition cannot fail of success and will accomplish much good.

When neither of these ciphered messages elicited a response, Sherman fired off another telegram, demanding in plain English, "Has that expedition started?"[14]

This telegram also went unanswered, at least for awhile. Rousseau was beset with problems, not the least of which was a critical shortage of horses. On June 29, one of his staff officers, Captain A. E. Magill, had written Colonel Thomas Joshua Harrison of the 8th Indiana Cavalry, asking him to report "how many horses you have in your regiment and how many you are likely to have ten days hence."

The answer was not encouraging. The 8th Indiana had neither horses nor saddles. Neither did the 2nd Kentucky. This prompted Rousseau's adjutant, Major Polk, to wire the Union garrison at Huntsville, Alabama, on July 6, asking, "Are the horse equipments of the 7th Ill. mounted infantry at Huntsville, and if so how many sets are there?"

That same day, Rousseau had another telegram sent to Franklin, Kentucky, directing the 9th Pennsylvania Cavalry to dismount and send all their horses, saddles, and bridles on the next train to Nashville.[15]

He also alerted the 8th Indiana's Colonel Harrison to have his troops ready in twenty-four hours for an extensive raid in which Harrison would command a brigade. A similar message went to Decatur, summoning the 9th Ohio's Colonel Hamilton to Nashville.

Crossing the quarter-mile-long pontoon bridge spanning the Tennessee River, Hamilton boarded a northbound freight that night and reported to Rousseau's headquarters at the Felix DeMoville house on Vine Street early on July 7. There Rousseau showed him a copy of Sherman's June 30 telegram, outlining plans for the raid.

"This will require a march of about three hundred miles," Rousseau explained. "How many good men and horses can you furnish?"

Hamilton calculated he could provide 500 officers and men. Rousseau directed him to hurry back to Decatur and prepare his troops to march. "I will be at Decatur on the ninth with two thousand men besides," he added, "and will organize the force so as to be ready to start on the tenth."[16]

Sometime during those hectic first days of July, Rousseau also brought Brigadier General Robert S. Granger up from Decatur to discuss preparations for the raid. Granger commanded the District of Northern Alabama, and his cooperation was essential if Rousseau was going to assemble all the men and horses he needed.

"Have had a good deal of trouble organizing an efficient force," Rousseau wired Sherman at 10:00 A.M., July 7. "Shall go to Decatur to-morrow, and leave Decatur on the 9th at daylight."

He did not mention that of the five regiments earmarked for the raid, only the 4th Tennessee, the 9th Ohio, and six companies of the 5th Iowa were anywhere near Decatur. That left less than forty-eight hours to load the 8th Indiana, the 2nd Kentucky, and the rest of the 5th Iowa on freight cars, move them 115 miles, and provide them with horses, saddles, bridles, blankets, food, clothing, and ammunition.

To make matters worse, Rousseau was not quite as familiar with the lay of the land as he had led Sherman to believe. On July 7, he sent a ciphered telegram to Major General Grenville M. Dodge, commanding the XVI Corps of McPherson's Army of the Tennessee. "Please see *R. T. Smith* an Alabamian and ask him to report to me at Decatur at once, to give information touching the country below," he implored. "This is all important."[17]

That afternoon, Rousseau sent a second telegram to Sherman. Somehow he had concluded he was supposed to cross the Coosa River at the railroad trestle at Ten Islands. The problem was there was no trestle at Ten Islands. "There is one at Wilsonville and plenty of supplies along below [that] route," Rousseau wired at 4:00 P.M.; "also a pretty good ford just at that bridge," but there was no bridge at Ten Islands.

Perhaps a little perturbed at this last-minute misunderstanding, Sherman clarified his orders later that evening. "My instructions were to cross the Coosa at the Ten Islands or the railroad bridge," he explained; "those points are well apart and you can best choose between them after you are well out."

Unsure of Rousseau's whereabouts, at 9:00 P.M. Sherman sent another coded message to both Nashville and Decatur. "I have no new instructions or information to convey to you, but expect you to leave Decatur on the 9th," he said firmly. Adding that he was "convinced A. J. Smith will give full employment to Forrest," he advised Rousseau:

> When you reach the road do your work well, burn the ties in piles, heat the iron in the middle, and when red hot let the men pull the ends so as to give a twist to the rails. If simply bent, the rails may be used, but if they are twisted or wrenched they cannot

be used again. In returning you should take the back track, and if pursued, turn for me or for Rome or Kingston or Allatoona. Be sure to take no wagons, but pack some led horses. Travel early and late in the day, but rest at midday and midnight. Spare your horses for the first week, and keep the horses ready for the return trip. I think the only force in your route is Pillow's, about Oxford or Jacksonville or Gadsden. . . .[18]

While Sherman was prodding Rousseau to get started, Harrison's 8th Indiana Cavalry was still at Camp Graham, "a very nice open piece of woods," two and a half miles south of Nashville. The regiment had drawn new boots and clothing on July 6, but it was 10:00 A.M., July 7, before orders came to prepare to march. Each man was to pack five days' rations and 250 rounds of ammunition, except for Companies L and M. Rousseau wanted only veteran troopers on this expedition, and these two newly recruited companies, commanded by Captain Alfred J. Fortner, were to be left behind.

Originally mustered into service as the 39th Indiana Infantry, Harrison's Hoosiers had fought at Shiloh and Stone's River before being outfitted with horses and Spencer rifles in April 1863. They had acquitted themselves as mounted infantry at the battle of Chickamauga, and when two new companies, L and M, joined the ranks in October 1863, the War Department had redesignated the regiment as the 8th Indiana Cavalry. Their prowess with their seven-shot Spencers was well known, and Rousseau knew such men might well mean the difference between failure and success in the days that lay ahead.

At 4:00 P.M., July 7, the 1st battalion of the 8th Indiana got orders to proceed immediately to the railroad depot. As the evening shadows lengthened into night, Major Thomas Herring led Companies A, B, C, and D out of Camp Graham and up the road toward Nashville. They reached the depot at dark, only to discover the train that was supposed to take them south had already left or railroad officials were having trouble procuring enough cars. Learning it would be at least 4:00 A.M. before they could leave, Herring ordered his men to bivouac on the Nashville common.

They did not get much sleep. After a restless night punctuated by bells and alarms as a large fire raged somewhere in the city, buglers sounded "Reveille" well before daylight. All four companies breakfasted from the cold contents of their haversacks and then marched back to the rail yards, where they climbed aboard a string of waiting freight cars. At 4:30 A.M., an engine snatched the slack out of the couplings and the train started south.

The trip was uneventful, except for a torrential thunderstorm that drenched everyone who had taken passage on top of the cars. Soon there was not a dry stitch of clothing among them, and they gratefully piled off what they called "the hurricane deck" when the train braked to a halt at the Huntsville junction, three miles north of Decatur, sometime between 4:00 and 5:00 that afternoon. After unloading their baggage, the battalion marched down to the pontoon bridge spanning the Tennessee River and crossed into Decatur, "a small, poor looking town," long since stripped of most of its houses and all its civilian population.

The 8th Indiana's 2nd and 3rd battalions, minus Companies L and M, left Camp Graham at 3:00 A.M., July 8, and reached the depot at 4:30 A.M., just about the same time the train carrying Major Herring's men was leaving. It took several hours to assemble another train, and it was noon before Companies E, F, G, H, I, and K scrambled aboard the cars. The men had no idea where they were going, but it was not long before they realized they must be heading for Huntsville or Decatur. During the afternoon, they ran into the same showers the 1st battalion had weathered and the men riding on the rain-swept roofs were soaked to the skin by the time they reached the end of the line at Huntsville junction at 10:00 P.M. Rather than cross the pontoon bridge in the dark, the Hoosiers camped on the north side of the Tennessee River, with orders to march at 4:00 A.M. to join Major Herring's battalion in Decatur.[19]

The rest of Lieutenant Colonel Patrick's 5th Iowa also left Nashville on July 8. His six companies, bivouacked at Camp Patrick, a mile and a half south of the city, were awakened at 1:00 A.M. by buglers sounding "The General," the call to prepare to march. Instructed to take only veteran troopers, Patrick detailed Quartermaster Sergeant Josiah Conzett and the regimental adjutant, Lieutenant William Aston, to stay behind with Companies G, I, and K, composed mainly of recruits. The rest of the men were ordered to draw three days' rations and break camp immediately. They were still gathering their equipment when "Boots and Saddles" sounded at 1:30 A.M. Heaving saddles into place, pulling the cinches tight, and buckling bridles, the Iowans mounted, formed into a column of fours, and followed Patrick up the Murfreesboro Pike toward Nashville.

"The boys are pretty much all glad of the change," noted Private Oscar Reese, "as Nashville is a very dull place anyhow and camp life is very monotonous."

There was plenty to do when they reached the depot. Loading 300 or 400 skittish horses and all their saddles and equipment on boxcars required a considerable amount of coaxing, yelling, and cussing. Darkness soon melted into dawn, and the sun was high overhead before everything was ready. At 1:00 P.M., just an hour behind the 2nd and 3rd battalions of the 8th Indiana, the train carrying Lieutenant Colonel Patrick and Companies D, E, and F of the 5th Iowa Cavalry pulled out of the switching yard. For the next thirteen hours, the Iowans clung to the tops of the cars as the engine belched clouds of black smoke and cinders overhead. It was 2:00 A.M., July 9, before the brakes squealed and the train lurched to a stop just short of the Tennessee River. Tired and hungry after the long trip, Patrick and his men spent the next twelve hours getting their horses unloaded and saddled. Once everything was sorted out, they led their mounts across the pontoon bridge into Decatur at 2:00 P.M., July 9, to join Major Baird and Companies A, B, C, H, L, and M.[20]

Lieutenant Colonel Elijah S. Watts and nine companies of the 2nd Kentucky Cavalry also started south on July 8. Most of these men were part of the old Louisville Legion Rousseau had recruited at Camp Jo Holt back in 1861. In March 1864, they had reenlisted as veteran volunteers and screened the right wing of Sherman's advance into Georgia as part of the 3rd Cavalry Division of the Army of the Cumberland before being sent back to Nashville to rest and remount.

Most of the 2nd Kentucky was stationed southwest of the city along a stretch of the Nashville and Northwestern Railroad, but Company L and a detachment of about sixty-five unassigned recruits, commanded by Major William H. Eifort, were stationed at Shelbyville, fifty miles to the southeast. At 7:20 A.M., July 4, Rousseau had telegraphed Eifort from Nashville directing him to "move your command to this place without delay. Those of your command that are mounted [can] march up. The dismounted portion will come by railroad." He repeated these instructions in a letter to Eifort the next day, adding, "Let there be no delay."

Eifort reached Nashville on July 7 or 8 with about 130 men, mostly recruits. Rousseau had no use for raw levies and ordered Company L of the 2nd Kentucky and all the regiment's unassigned troopers left behind, directing Lieutenant Colonel Watts to "relieve Co. 'G' of your command, now in Fort Negley, with recruits, leaving Capt. [Lovell H.] Thickston [of Company I] in command. . . ." He also gave verbal orders for Major Eifort to remain in Nashville with this detachment.

In the meantime, Companies A, B, C, D, E, F, G, H, and I (there were no companies K and M) began drawing rations and supplementing their single-shot Merrill and Sharps carbines with about 130 Spencer repeaters collected from the two companies the 8th Indiana had left behind. Late that afternoon or early that evening, Lieutenant Colonel Watts marched his nine companies to the depot to board a train for the trip south.[21]

With the last of his regiments finally en route to Decatur, Rousseau prepared to follow. Knowing there was a good chance of being killed or captured, he and his staff arranged their affairs accordingly. An old friend of Rousseau's, *New York Herald* correspondent William F. G. Shanks, witnessed what he called "quite an amusing scene . . . at headquarters in the closing and balancing of accounts, writing farewell letters and giving directions for the disposition of private property." Nashville's provost marshal, Major Rigney, provided Rousseau and each of his staff with about $2,000 in Confederate money; "not *fac simile*," noted Shanks, "but the genuine article, which is said to be nearly as valuable as the imitation, though not equalling it in engraving and printing."

Before leaving Nashville, someone, possibly Rousseau himself, took Shanks aside and described the proposed raid in great detail, recounting the number of troops involved, the officers and regiments accompanying the expedition, and how they were brigaded. Shanks's informant also traced the column's route through Alabama, explaining they would move via Blountsville and Ashville, cross the Coosa River near Ten Islands, and proceed to Talladega. From Talladega, they would take a southeasterly course, fording the Tallapoosa River in the vicinity of Tehopeka, and passing through Dadeville before striking the Montgomery & West Point Railroad somewhere between Montgomery and Opelika. After destroying the road, the column would march up the west bank of the Chattahoochee to join Sherman's army near Marietta or, if this proved impractical, turn south toward the Gulf coast and Union-occupied Pensacola. Trusting Shanks not to reveal any of this information until they were safely back inside Union lines, Rousseau and his staff left Nashville shortly before 7:00 P.M., July 8, "very confident of success."[22]

Among the officers accompanying Rousseau was his aide-de-camp, Captain Thomas A. Elkin of the 5th Kentucky Cavalry. Captain Thomas C. Williams of the 19th U.S. Infantry went along as acting assistant adjutant general to handle the paper work and draft written orders. The inspector general, Captain S. E. McConnell of the 71st Ohio Infantry, was responsible for seeing that the troops were properly equipped and only the fittest men and horses accompanied the expedition. Captain Edward M. Ruger, a topographical engineer from the 13th Wisconsin Infantry, was the pathfinder in the group. He had been interrogating refugees and preparing maps of northern Alabama for months.[23]

Rousseau's entourage also included the mysterious Irishman, James Carroll McBurney. Born in Tullenearly, near Castle Blarney, on June 20, 1826, McBurney had emigrated to New York City in 1844, saved his money, and invested in a small stock of Irish linens, silks, tablecloths, and crepe shawls, which he peddled in the small towns between New York and Philadelphia. His business prospered, he married, and in 1856 he bought a two-story house on Summit Avenue in Bergen, New Jersey. He also made several trips through South Carolina, Georgia, and Alabama, and was so impressed with the opportunities there he sold the house in Bergen to his father-in-law in November 1858 and moved south.

Settling in Macon, Georgia, he opened an auction and commission house on Cherry Street. "I did a large business there," he recalled in later years, "and sold everything from a mule to a negro."

When the war began, McBurney took his wife and three young children to live with her parents in Ithaca, New York, but he returned to Macon and made no secret of his Union sympathies. He boycotted Presbyterian worship services because of "disloyal" sentiments spouted from the pulpit, helped several Union men flee north, and even took blankets and other little luxuries to relieve the suffering of Union soldiers interned at Macon's Camp Oglethorpe.

Confederate authorities were either blind or amazingly tolerant of him. When he traveled to Alabama in March 1863 to settle an uncle's estate, he carried a letter of introduction signed by fifteen of Macon's leading citizens, who swore the affable Irishman enjoyed "the confidence of all who know him."

McBurney frequently peddled merchandise along the stagecoach and rail lines linking Macon with Columbus, Montgomery, and points farther west, and in the spring of 1863 he made a trip to the Mississippi Valley. In a memoir written nearly forty years later, he made a vague reference to using his itinerary to spy for the Union army besieging Vicksburg. Military records tend to support his claim. Writing to General Grant on June 14, 1863, Major General Cadwallader C. Washburn introduced "Mr. McBirney [sic] a Spy that I sent five days ago to Yazoo City." Washburn added he had "assured McBirney that if he would make this trip he should receive big pay . . . in proportion to the hazard incurred." Ten days later, Washburn advised Grant, "McBirney arrived this morning from an Exploration in rear of Greenville."

If this was indeed McBurney, he did not wait to witness the surrender of Vicksburg. Returning to Macon, he announced he was going to Europe to recover from the effects of a chronic case of typhoid fever. Never one to put patriotism ahead of profit, he extended the post commander over a thousand dollars in credit and rented his store to the Rebel government.

McBurney left Macon in December 1863, but instead of heading across the Atlantic, he got a pass through the Confederate lines and apparently went to Nashville en route to rejoining his family in Ithaca. During this trip, he probably ingratiated himself with Rousseau, but his activities for the next six months are a mystery. In June 1864 he was in New York City and Newark, conferring with three former Macon residents who shared his Union sympathies, and family tradition insists a raid was planned in the attic of the house on Summit Avenue. It may have been coincidence, but McBurney's arrival in Nashville closely coincided with Rousseau's first letter proposing an expedition to Selma, and he was the man Rousseau sent to Sherman's headquarters on June 27 to explain his plans.

After meeting with Sherman, McBurney had returned to Nashville, where

Rousseau commissioned him as a volunteer aide-de-camp on July 8 with the rank of captain. If he were captured, this would hopefully keep the Rebels from hanging him as a spy.[24]

After a restless night on the cars, Rousseau and his aides reached the Huntsville junction early Saturday morning, July 9. Met by a host of last-minute details demanding immediate attention, Rousseau waded in, adding Dr. Luther D. Waterman of the 8th Indiana to his staff as chief surgeon, Lieutenant John Frey of the 9th Ohio and Lieutenant Charles A. B. Langdon of the 5th Iowa as quartermaster and assistant quartermaster, and Private Jacob Shreiner of the 5th Iowa as orderly. He also appointed Captain Alfred Matthias of Company C, 5th Iowa, as his provost marshal and detailed the captain's men as the provost guard.

Rousseau had promised Sherman he would leave Decatur at daylight on July 9, but this was obviously impossible. There was even some doubt he would be ready by July 10. The 2nd and 3rd battalions of the 9th Ohio and all of the 4th Tennessee were still at Mooresville, on the north side of the Tennessee River, and the 5th Iowa, 8th Indiana, and 2nd Kentucky were scrambling madly for horses and equipment.[25]

The 8th Indiana's experiences were typical. After breaking camp near the Huntsville junction at 4:00 A.M., July 9, the 2nd and 3rd battalions crossed the pontoon bridge over the tawny Tennessee to join Major Herring's 1st battalion, bivouacked on the common near the edge of Decatur. They had just settled in and were beginning preparations for their midday meal when orders came at 9:00 A.M. to pack up and move back across the river. Grousing and grumbling, the men doused their cook fires and trooped back across the pontoon bridge to a stand of timber on the north bank.

While most of the regiment began setting up a new camp, a small detail from each company marched up to the Hunstville junction and put their backs into pushing three baggage-laden freight cars down to the end of the track near the river's edge. Once this was done, these same troopers went to some nearby government corrals to draw two pack mules for each of the regiment's ten companies. The mules were mostly green stock, and more than one red-faced trooper went sprawling in the dirt trying to halter a half-crazed animal and strap a pack on its back. Once saddled, the mules were turned loose in another corral, where they kicked and bucked furiously, trying to shed their unaccustomed burdens. With the hot sun bearing down, it was not long before they wore themselves out, and once they had quieted, troopers led them back to camp.

By this time, it was obvious that the horses Rousseau had commandeered from the 9th Pennsylvania Cavalry would not be enough to mount the 8th Indiana. Colonel Harrison sent another detail to the south side of the river to requisition horses and saddles from the 2nd Tennessee Cavalry and Battery A of the 1st Tennessee Artillery. The Hoosiers led their acquisitions back to camp about 5:00 P.M., and the cry of "Horses!" that greeted their arrival brought every trooper to his feet, eager to pick out a good mount. Amid shouts and yells and nickers and smells, officers assigned animals to the different companies. Men thronged around the three railroad cars grabbing saddles, blankets, and bridles, but even with the equipment they got from Thornburgh's Tennesseans, there was still not enough to go around. General Granger had to order Patrick's 5th Iowa to turn over all their surplus saddles and bridles to the Hoosiers.[26]

It was the same story on the south side of the river. Lieutenant Colonel Patrick had brought enough horses from Nashville for only about two-thirds of his men. Thornburgh's 2nd Tennessee Cavalry and Battery A, 1st Tennessee Artillery, were ordered to supply the rest and give whatever horses, saddles, and bridles they had left to the 2nd Kentucky.[27]

The pace was not quite so frantic in the camp of the 1st battalion of the 9th Ohio. The Ohioans were pretty well mounted, and Colonel Hamilton's main concern on July 9 seemed to be his troops' flagging efficiency and morale. In hopes of "promoting the interest of the service and inspiring a laudable ambition upon the part of officers and men," he directed each of his company commanders to nominate one sergeant, one corporal, and ten privates who had "performed some particular act of courage or conduct," for membership in the "Field Guards of the 9th Ohio Cavalry." This elite unit would act as the advance guard when the regiment was on the march and be distinguished by a special badge to be awarded at some future date.

Just how much of this plan Hamilton was able to implement is uncertain. His 2nd and 3rd battalions were still at Mooresville and did not get orders to join the rest of the regiment until late that afternoon. Leaving their baggage and unserviceable horses behind, these eight companies began crossing the Tennessee at 9:00 P.M. Acting on similar orders, Major Meshack Stephens's 4th Tennessee Cavalry, except for the newly recruited Company M, also left Mooresville about sundown and moved down to the river to bivouac at the northern end of the pontoon bridge.[28]

With the last of his cavalry finally in place, albeit a day late, Rousseau issued marching orders for early the next morning and distributed a circular dividing his five regiments into two brigades according to a plan he had worked out before leaving Nashville. Colonel Harrison of the 8th Indiana would take charge of the 1st Brigade, composed of Lieutenant Colonel Watts's 2nd Kentucky, Lieutenant Colonel Patrick's 5th Iowa, and Harrison's own 8th Indiana, now led by Lieutenant Colonel Fielder A. Jones. Colonel Hamilton would command the 2nd Brigade, composed of the 9th Ohio, Captain William Stough commanding, and Major Stephens's 4th Tennessee.

Rousseau made no mention of artillery in this circular, probably because he was still waiting for Lieutenant Leonard Wightman and a pair of 10-pounder Parrott guns from Battery E, 1st Michigan Light Artillery. The train carrying Wightman's section did not even leave Nashville until July 9, and it was late that night before they reached Decatur and took their place with Hamilton's 2nd Brigade.[29]

Meanwhile, the incessant clang of the blacksmith's hammer echoed hour after hour as each horse was fitted for two extra shoes to replace any that might be lost on the march. "The boys are now drawing their rations and everything is in a regular bustle," twenty-two-year-old Private George W. Healey of the 5th Iowa wrote to his mother. "I understand we have to leave tomorrow morning at six o'clock. . . . The boys are all anxious for a fight and ready to go."

Sergeant Tom Jackson of the 8th Indiana went to sleep that night with orders to be ready to march at 4:00 A.M. Private Williamson D. Ward, also of the 8th Indiana, understood the march would begin at 10:00 A.M., but sunrise on July 10 found several of Rousseau's regiments still trying to requisition mules, horses, saddles, bridles, rations, and ammunition.

In some parts of Decatur, anything but a Sabbathlike calm prevailed. During the night, the pack mules had busted out of the corral and about a hundred had escaped

This pontoon bridge, 1,650 feet long, crossed the Tennessee River at Decatur, Alabama. Three of Rousseau's regiments, camped on the far bank, led their horses and pack mules across the swaying span to join the rest of the column in Decatur on July 10. Courtesy of Decatur, Alabama, Public Library. Used by permission.

into the countryside. Loading packsaddles on those that remained, many of them barely even halterbroken, took longer than anyone had anticipated, and more than one trooper damned their stubborn, jackassed ways.

Troopers in the 8th Indiana enjoyed a leisurely breakfast while they waited for orders to march. By the time they had finished and fed and watered their horses, it was apparent the rest of Rousseau's column was nowhere near ready and many of the men took advantage of the delay to go swimming in the Tennessee River. About mid-morning, the blare of "Boots and Saddles," interrupted their frolicking and there was a mad rush back to camp to saddle the horses. Each trooper folded a large indigo-blue saddle blanket into six layers and smoothed it on the horse's back with the folded edge toward the front. Then he hoisted his rawhide-covered McClellan saddle into place and pulled the woven girth tight. Practiced hands slipped a single-reined black leather bridle over the horse's halter and coaxed a curb bit into his mouth.

Soon everything was ready, and the regiment stepped smartly into line, except for the pack mule carrying Company E's ammunition. Defying all manner of prodding and pleading, the animal steadfastly refused to budge. Finally the company commander, Captain John E. Boyer, ordered the packs unloaded and the extra ammunition distributed among his troopers. This done, the 8th Indiana's 613 officers and men led their horses across the pontoon bridge and into Decatur at 11:00 A.M.[30]

They had to wait while the other regiments moved from their bivouacs, and many of the men took this opportunity to write a last-minute letter or two. Rousseau addressed a note to Lieutenant Colonel Thornburgh. Except for the 4th Tennessee, Thornburgh's brigade had been excluded from the expedition and stripped of its horses and equipment. Perhaps sensing that Thornburgh, who had tendered his resignation in June, might interpret this as a reflection on him and the character of his brigade, Rousseau wrote:

> Colonel: —I cannot permit you to leave the service without rendering you my thanks for the promptitude and energy you have always displayed while serving under my command. It affords me pleasure to bear testimony to your character as an efficient and gallant soldier and courteous gentleman.[31]

Rousseau also sent a telegram advising Sherman:

> I am off to-day after all sorts of petty annoyances composing delays. I hope to accomplish fully what you desire, and shall do my best. I go sixteen (16) miles to-day, and hope to reach the point in seven (7) to eight (8) days.[32]

Most of the letters scribbled in Decatur that bright Sunday morning were of a more personal nature. "I [leave] this point . . . in 5 minutes," the 1st Brigade's Colonel Tom Harrison wrote to his wife. "I have the finest command of its size in the world. I have with me the veterans of three of the finest Regts. in the army. We have 1800 men. There is another Brigade making a veteran command of 3000 all under Genl. Rousseau with a battery. We will go from here direct for Montgomery and likely to the Gulf at Fort Pickens. I am in great haste. My love to all. . . . Good-bye."[33]

After what General Granger called "much confusion and embarrasment [sic]," the bugles sounded "Forward," and at 1:00 p.m. Rousseau's raiders, some 2,700 strong, filed out of Decatur in a column of fours, led by Hamilton's 2nd Brigade.

A typical trooper wore a black leather waist belt, two inches wide, clasped by a rectangular brass belt plate embossed with an eagle and wreath. This supported a cavalry saber slung on his left side, usually counterbalanced by a .36 or .44 caliber Colt revolver cradled butt first in a black leather holster on his right hip. Troopers in the 8th Indiana and the 9th Ohio had not been issued revolvers, but most of the enlisted men wore a broad black leather belt slung over the left shoulder, suspending a steel snaphook attached to a Spencer repeating carbine or a breechloading Gallagher, Smith, Merrill, or Sharps. To keep the gun handy, the barrel was thrust through a short, cylindrical leather socket strapped to the saddle D-ring behind the trooper's right leg, although some of the men in the 8th Indiana and the 2nd Kentucky, armed with long-barreled Spencers, carried them hung from the shoulder by a regulation rifle sling.

Each individual make of rifle and carbine, regardless of caliber, required its own peculiar type of ammunition. A trooper usually carried twenty rounds in a cartridge box attached to his waist belt or hung over his shoulder, with additional cartridges in the pockets of his haversack or in his saddlebags. The number varied greatly. Troopers in the 9th Ohio were carrying 120 rounds apiece; some companies of the 8th Indiana had drawn as much as 250 rounds per man.

Fifteen days' rations of sugar, salt, and coffee, a five-day supply of hardtack, and one of bacon or sowbelly commingled in a tarred haversack slung over the trooper's right shoulder or tied to a corner of his saddle along with a tin cup, canteen, and perhaps a small kettle or skillet. A pair of black leather saddlebags rode behind him, bulging with paper-jacketed pistol cartridges, two extra horseshoes and the nails to attach them, and personal items such as a razor, eating utensils, and a few extra clothes. "We are only allowed to take 2 shirts, 2 pair drawers, 2 pair socks and a rubber blanket," Private Healey explained in a letter to his mother. "This order is to keep the boys from loading down the horses." All tents, extra baggage, and even blankets were to be left behind.[34]

A few wagons accompanied the column, carrying a day's supply of hardtack and forage, but Rousseau planned to send them back to Decatur after the first day's march, leaving only the artillery limbers and caissons and five regimental ambulances to encumber the column. The extra ammunition and rations, as well as spades, picks, axes, and crowbars, were strapped on the backs of perhaps a hundred pack mules, two or three for each of the fifty-one cavalry companies.

Getting the mules to stand still long enough to be loaded had already delayed Rousseau's departure for several hours, and at the first crack of the drover's whip, some of them charged to the left, others to the right, and a few made a determined effort to overtake the head of the column. The sight of packsaddles and panniers bouncing wildly against their heaving flanks reminded one trooper of "the wings of some huge bird whose speed was not sufficient to raise him into aerial flight, yet not quite willing to give up the attempt."

With a clash and clatter reminiscent of a gigantic shivaree, the mules charged through Rousseau's neatly ordered ranks, strewing supplies and equipment in their wake. Frightened cavalry horses reared and plunged. Unwary riders sprawled in the dirt. Eventually the runaways were rounded up, order was restored, and the column headed southeast on what Private Healey confidently predicted would be "one of the biggest raids ever known."[35]

3

TO MOORE'S BRIDGE AND BACK

JULY 1–JULY 18, 1864

Hesitation and half measures lose all in war.

—Napoleon,
Maxims of War

Sherman seemed more skeptical about the raid's chances of success. On July 7, the same day Rousseau telegraphed asking for clarification about where to cross the Coosa River, he sent the much-traveled Major McCoy riding down to Turner's Ferry with a message for McPherson. "If you see Stoneman," Sherman wrote, "feel him [out] and see how he would like to work down the river, say thirty miles, and also make a dash for Opelika, swinging back to us or to Rome for safety. A break of twenty miles from Opelika westward is perfectly practicable and would be a good blow."

Whether Sherman harbored doubts about Rousseau's ability to reach the railroad at Opelika or his resolve to wreck it once he got there is uncertain, but early on July 8 he rode over to the right flank to talk with Stoneman and McPherson. He explained he wanted McPherson's XV and XVII Corps to keep up the illusion the Army of the Tennessee was going to cross the Chattahoochee at Turner's Ferry. This would compel the Confederates to shift more troops downstream, while McPherson's XVI Corps marched upstream, through Marietta, to reinforce Garrard and the real effort at Roswell. A foray down the river by Stoneman's cavalry would misdirect even more Confederate cavalry and further disguise Sherman's strategy.[1]

Like Garrard, George Stoneman was "old Army," a regular. "He lived as a soldier," noted a Kentucky cavalryman. "During this campaign one mule carried all his baggage. He despised *style* in the army. I never saw a General so familiar with the minutiae of a cavalry command."

The oldest and most experienced of Sherman's cavalry generals, Stoneman had graduated thirty-third in the West Point class of 1846, sixteen places behind his roommate, a quiet Virginian named Thomas Jonathan Jackson. He had served in the 1st U.S. Dragoons during the Mexican War and afterwards saw action in frontier clashes with hostile Indians in California, Oregon, and Arizona. "Lieutenant Stoneman was an universal favorite with all the officers, and likewise beloved by the private soldiers . . . ," wrote one of his contemporaries; "when a detachment was ordered out for scouting or other purposes, the men all wanted to go if Lieutenant Stoneman was in command."

Promoted to captain in 1855, he was one of the army's best and brightest, selected to officer the elite 2nd U.S. Cavalry. "He was a fine soldier, strict in discipline and exemplary in habits . . . ," noted a fellow officer. "When he went out on expeditions against . . . [the Indians] he showed great activity, and was very generally successful in overtaking and punishing them. He took great interest in his Company, and strived to make it the most efficient one in the Regiment."[2]

On the night of March 15, 1860, he was ordered across the Rio Grande with two companies of the 2nd Cavalry and about seventy-five Texas Rangers in pursuit of the notorious Mexican bandit Juan Cortina. A lookout sounded the alarm while the column was still half a mile from the bandit's suspected hideout, but Stoneman sent his men charging in from three sides, killing and wounding several Mexicans in a wild melee and capturing 300 more. Only then did daylight reveal he had attacked a very surprised and very angry garrison of Mexican soldiers.

Stoneman apologized profusely, but when confronted by an even larger force of Mexicans demanding his return to the Texas side of the border, he stubbornly refused. For the next five days, he and his troopers boldly scoured the Mexican countryside for twenty miles in every direction until orders compelled them to withdraw.[3]

In February 1861, Stoneman defied instructions from his commanding general to surrender his troops to Texas secessionists. Boasting he could "march all over Texas" with two companies of cavalry, he proposed uniting several small detachments and striking northward for Kansas or Missouri. When other officers convinced him the idea was impractical, he loaded his men and all the equipment they could carry aboard a steamer and sailed for New York City. Ordered to Washington, he was promoted to major in the 1st U.S. Cavalry and assigned to the staff of an old classmate, Major General George B. McClellan. A successful summer campaign in the mountains of western Virginia earned McClellan command of the Army of the Potomac and made Stoneman his chief of cavalry with the rank of brigadier general.

When McClellan began his ponderous advance up the Virginia peninsula in May 1862, Stoneman led the way. He made a bold aerial reconnaissance of the Richmond defenses with the famed balloonist Professor Thaddeus S. C. Lowe, but his scattered units could not prevent Confederate cavalryman Jeb Stuart from literally riding circles around McClellan's army. Hobbled by infirmities one subordinate asserted "would have kept a man of less fortitude in the hospital," Stoneman embarked for Baltimore in the midst of the bloody Seven Days' battles.[4]

Still in poor health when he returned to duty, he accepted a less rigorous assignment in the infantry, commanding the III Corps at the mismanaged battle of Fredericksburg. A horse soldier at heart, he eagerly accepted when Major General Joseph Hooker assumed command of the Army of the Potomac and offered to make him chief of cavalry again in February 1863.

Promoted to major general of volunteers, Stoneman supervised a much-needed reorganization of Hooker's cavalry, consolidating the scattered regiments and brigades into a cohesive corps. In mid-April, as part of a concerted plan to crush Robert E. Lee's Army of Northern Virginia, Hooker ordered him to cross the Rapidan River and throw his command between Lee and the Confederate capital at Richmond, "isolating him from his supplies, checking his retreat, and inflicting on him every possible injury which will tend to his discomfiture and defeat."

"Bear in mind," Hooker added, "that celerity, audacity, and resolution are everything in war, and especially is it the case with the command you have and the enterprise upon which you are about to embark."

Plagued by a chronic case of hemorrhoids, Stoneman was slow getting started. Heavy rains made the Rapidan unfordable and it took almost two weeks to get his troops across. Meeting only feeble opposition, he closed to within a few miles of

A gruff, by-the-book West Pointer, Major General George Stoneman commanded the Cavalry Corps of the Army of the Ohio. Sherman complained that he was "lazy," but Stoneman's seeming lack of initiative may have stemmed from a chronic physical complaint. In 1882 he was elected governor of California. Reproduced from the Collections of the Library of Congress.

Richmond and summoned his regimental commanders. "I gave them to understand that we had dropped in that region of country like a shell," he recounted, "and that I intended to burst it in every direction, expecting each piece or fragment would do as much harm and create nearly as much terror as would result from sending the whole shell, and thus magnify our small force into overwhelming numbers. . . ."

His detachments played havoc on Rebel railroad and telegraph lines, causing considerable consternation in the Confederate capital. They might have ridden into the defenseless city and liberated thousands of Union soldiers confined at Libby Prison and Belle Isle, but when a staff officer urged him to make the attempt, Stoneman replied irritably, "I know damn well we can do it, but my orders are not to go to Richmond."

"Stoneman was too much of a Regular of the old school to disobey orders," a trooper concluded, "even if he knew it would result in great good to his cause."

To make matters worse, the absence of Stoneman's cavalry enabled his old roommate, Confederate General "Stonewall" Jackson, to slip past Hooker's exposed right flank and smash the Union army at the battle of Chancellorsville. Casting about for a scapegoat, Hooker charged Stoneman had "almost destroyed one-half of my serviceable cavalry force."[5]

Some of Stoneman's subordinates chimed in, citing his lack of initiative during the Richmond raid. A few even whispered doubts about his loyalty, citing his recent marriage to Mary Oliver Hardisty, the daughter of a prominent pro-Southern family in Baltimore. Relieved of his command, Stoneman was transferred to the War Department, where he became the first chief of the newly created Cavalry Bureau. He was not an energetic administrator, and when his efforts failed to reform the army's graft-riddled horse-buying procedures, he was replaced by Kenner Garrard.

Exiled to the west, Stoneman became chief of cavalry for John Schofield's Army of the Ohio. Late in April, he began assembling his regiments at Nicholasville, Kentucky, for the spring campaign. Most of his troopers were seasoned veterans from Indiana, Illinois, and Kentucky, a swaggering, boisterous lot who did not bend easily to authority.

Stoneman, on the other hand, was a no-nonsense officer, a tall, thin man, whose melancholy round eyes peered from behind a gray-tinged beard and mustache with "an air of habitual sadness." Possessing what one trooper called "an austere, dignified bearing that was somewhat repellant," his brusque disposition had already earned him the nickname "Dyspepsia."

A clash of wills was inevitable, and the trouble started on April 28, when Stoneman issued orders prohibiting straggling, foraging, or leaving the ranks for any purpose during the march south. "No excuse will be received for neglect of duty or ignorance of orders," he warned.

But Stoneman's line of march passed near the homes of many of the men in his 1st Kentucky Cavalry, and the temptation to pay one last visit to wives, sweethearts, and loved ones was simply too much to resist. Officers and men alike began quitting the ranks, discreetly at first, dropping out of the column in ones and twos, but on April 30 four companies deserted en masse, compounding the offense by riding over Stoneman's escort. Livid with rage, Stoneman ordered the roll called two days later and found the 1st Kentucky could muster only two lieutenants and seventy-one enlisted men out of more than 800 who had left Nicholasville.

Stoneman had the absentee officers arrested when they rejoined the ranks. Most of the enlisted men also returned before the column caught up with Sherman's armies near Dalton on May 10. Circumstances soon compelled Stoneman to release the arrested officers, but the incident engendered quite a bit of bad feeling.

"One great difficulty I have to contend against is the utter incompetency of subordinate officers," he complained to Sherman on May 20. "I have to post and put in every regiment myself and send out every party. I know that my movements appear tardy, but I can't help it; it is next to impossible to get up a trot even on the field."[6]

Obviously, this was not the bold dragoon who had led a handful of men into Mexico, defied an order to surrender, and ascended in a balloon to get a better look at the Confederate capital. Perhaps because he distrusted his unruly westerners, perhaps because his hemorrhoids made long hours in the saddle almost unbearable, he had grown increasingly cautious and conservative, and he was not enthusiastic when Sherman broached the idea of sending the Cavalry Corps of the Army of the Ohio to meet Rousseau at Opelika. A corps in name only, Stoneman's three brigades could barely muster 2,600 officers and men. Horses had become so scarce that on June 27 two whole regiments, the 16th Illinois and 12th Kentucky, had been dismounted and reassigned to one of Schofield's infantry divisions, but even this left 500 of Stoneman's troopers on foot.

Posted on the right flank of McPherson's Army of the Tennessee, Stoneman's cavalry occupied a triangular swath of countryside bisected by Sweetwater Creek. On the east side of the creek, Colonel Thomas H. Butler's Indiana brigade, Stoneman's four-gun battery, and his dismounted men fronted the Chattahoochee opposite Sandtown. Colonel Silas Adams's Kentucky brigade bivouacked on the west side of the creek and patrolled as far as the Campbellton Ferry, ten miles downstream, while Colonel Horace Capron's brigade camped at the apex of the triangle near the Sweetwater Bridge at Sweetwater Town, scouting westward toward Villa Rica and Powder Springs. These patrols had convinced Stoneman there was a sizable force of Rebel cavalry lurking somewhere west of the Sweetwater.[7]

This seemed to confirm a similar report Sherman had received from Garrard on July 6. Sending Stoneman all the way to Opelika, he reasoned, when the Rebels seemed to be shifting their cavalry downriver to counter the Federal buildup at Turner's Ferry might unnecessarily expose McPherson's right flank. It would be less risky, and perhaps just as effective, if Stoneman struck the railroad somewhere closer to Atlanta. That would afford McPherson at least some protection for his flank and allow Stoneman to fall back on friendly infantry if he got into trouble. Anxious for news of Garrard's and Schofield's pending crossings at Roswell and Sope Creek, Sherman apparently sketched only the broad outlines of this plan before hurrying back to his headquarters at Vining's Station.

In the wee, restless hours of July 9, he wrote to Stoneman:

> In pursuance of our conversation of this day, I have to request that you proceed with your command to Campbellton to-morrow night, appearing suddenly before the place and securing if possible the boats there, or forcing the enemy to destroy them. If you can possibly do it[,] get possession of those boats and also of the other bank. I am very anxious that an attack or demonstration be made against the railroad below Atlanta, and . . . I am satisfied that the crossing of Schofield and Garrard above will draw in that direction Johnston's chief army, and that what troops are left south of Atlanta will be strung out as far as West Point, where he will keep the chief force. The point where the road would be easiest reached will be, say, half way from Atlanta and West Point, but it would not be safe for you to pass Campbellton unless the ferry was well destroyed. The bridge at Franklin is almost too far down, but still it too might be reached by you and either used or destroyed. A ford but little known or used below Campbellton and this side of Franklin bridge will be the best if such exists, and you may incur any risk sure of my approval, for whether you make a break of the road or merely cause a diversion you will do good. Don't be absent more than four or five days, and keep me advised on all possible occasions.[8]

There were also some verbal instructions. Somewhere in the course of his conversation with Stoneman on July 8, Sherman repeated the orders he had sent to Garrard: destroy all sawmills, factories, and large gristmills and send the employees to Marietta as prisoners of war.

Early on July 9, Stoneman's provost marshal, Major Haviland Tompkins, led a detail of eight men to the Sweetwater Factory, a huge cotton mill perched on the west bank of Sweetwater Creek. Chartered in 1849 as the New Manchester Manufacturing Company, the mill towered five stories above the roaring, rock-strewn rapids, taller than any building in Atlanta. Troopers from Silas Adams's Kentucky brigade had shut down production about 10:00 A.M. on July 2 during Stoneman's initial sweep down the west side of the creek. Returning the next day, they had pulled the belting out of the machinery and ripped cotton cloth and thread from the looms and spindles.

Adams's brigade spent the next week picketing and scouting in the neighborhood, so no one was particularly alarmed when Major Tompkins and his men rode up. Calling the workers together, Tompkins told them he had orders from General Sherman to burn the mill down. He gave them fifteen minutes to gather up their personal belongings and as much cloth as they could carry. As the crowd of mostly women and girls scurried away, he and his men began wetting down several nearby houses to keep them from catching fire. Then they strode purposefully into the mill, carrying large cans of kerosene. A curl of smoke appeared at the windows and yellow tongues of flame soon began licking at the roof.

The Yankees then turned their attention to the company store, a two-story brick building a few hundred feet away. Once it was primed, Tompkins threw the doors open, telling the workers to help themselves to whatever they wanted. When the stampede subsided, he put the building to the torch. A mile upstream, some of Stoneman's men also set fire to Ferguson's gristmill over the vigorous protests of the owner. Farther north, a small detachment from the 14th Illinois Cavalry burned another large gristmill near Powder Springs.

The ashes were still smoldering when Tompkins assembled the mill hands at Sweetwater and told them they could stay in their company-owned homes or move farther south if they would sign a parole promising not to work for the Confederacy in any capacity. Otherwise the army intended to send them north of the Ohio River and turn them loose to shift for themselves.

"There really wasn't much choice in the matter, . . ." recalled S. H. Causey, a seventeen-year-old boy working in the spinning room, "as long as we were to be allowed to earn a livelihood we would not starve. Nearly all our neighbors were women with large families of small children dependent upon them for support, and most of them did the same as we did. The Federals faithfully carried out their part of the agreement, and treated us kindly as long as we were in their charge."

About a hundred of Causey's friends and neighbors loaded themselves and a few precious belongings into Stoneman's supply wagons. A jolting, sixteen-mile ride carried them to Marietta, where guards herded them into the abandoned classrooms and barracks of the Georgia Military Institute, along with workers from the Roswell factories.

"The most of them are women," George Thomas cautioned Sherman on July 10. "I can only order them transportation to Nashville, where it seems hard to turn them adrift. What had best be done with them?"

"They will be sent to Indiana," Sherman replied in a field telegram, but it took several days to ready the trains to take them north. In the meantime, the proximity of so many females aroused considerable interest among Sherman's battle-hardened veterans.

"Some of them are tough," Sergeant Theodore F. Upson of the 100th Indiana Infantry noted after being assigned to guard the calicoed captives on July 11, "and its [sic] a hard job to keep them straight and the men away from them. General Sherman says he would rather try to gaurd [sic] the whole Confederate army, and I guess he is right about it."[9]

The ruins of the New Manchester Manufacturing Company on Sweetwater Creek. A detachment of George Stoneman's cavalry burned the mill on July 9, 1864. At that time, the huge five-story brick structure was taller than any building in Atlanta. Courtesy of Bruce Erion and Tracy Miller, WXIA-TV Atlanta.

As the pillars of thick, black smoke boiled into the sky above Sweetwater Creek, George Stoneman quietly began abandoning his outposts on the Chattahoochee in preparation for moving downstream. Major William W. Carter's detachment of 500 dismounted men left Sandtown Ferry at 10:00 A.M. on July 9 and trudged northward to Mitchell's Crossroads. Colonel Tom Butler's 5th and 6th Indiana Cavalry and Captain Alexander Hardy's 24th Indiana Battery remained at the ferry, where they had arranged a fragile ceasefire with the Rebels across the river, but that evening, shells suddenly came crashing through the treetops, bursting uncomfortably close by. The Hoosiers scurried out of range before any damage was done, but the unexpected barrage made it clear the Rebels still had a firm grip on Sandtown.

Anxious to learn just how far the Confederate lines extended downriver, Stoneman ordered Tom Butler to send a patrol down the north bank of the Chattahoochee. That night, a large detachment, consisting of Companies B and D of the 5th Indiana Cavalry and perhaps the regiment's entire 1st battalion, splashed across the ford at the mouth of Sweetwater Creek and cautiously probed down to Campbellton Ferry. They found no Rebels, and slaves and reluctant civilians told them there were no fords or bridges anywhere between Campbellton and Franklin, forty miles downstream. A courier took this information back to Stoneman, while the Hoosiers hunkered down to wait for the rest of the division.

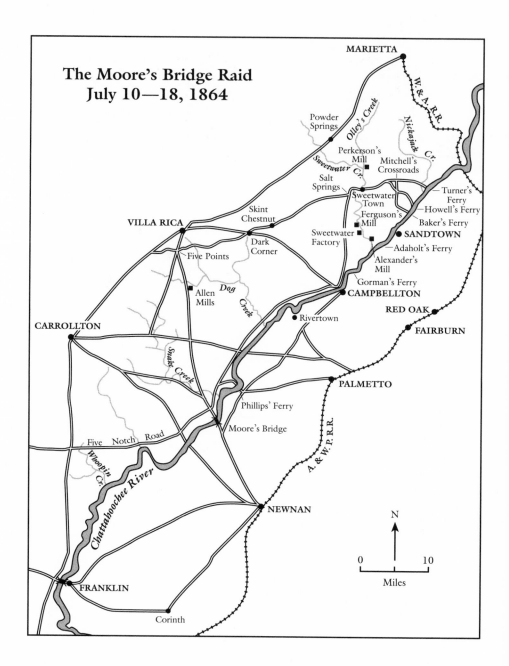

The Moore's Bridge Raid
July 10—18, 1864

As the night wore on, the Rebel guns along the Chattahoochee fell silent. The next morning, sleepless Yankee pickets from Turner's Ferry to Vining's Station peered through the pale gray light and blinked their tired eyes in disbelief. Joe Johnston's army was gone. Threatened by Schofield's bridgehead at Sope Creek and Garrard's crossing at Shallow Ford, the Confederate commander had slipped all his infantry, wagons, and artillery across the Chattahoochee during the night, burning the railroad trestle, wagon bridge, and three pontoon bridges behind him. The furious pounding Rebel batteries had laid on Stoneman's pickets at Sandtown Ferry and other Union positions on the evening of July 9 had merely been a parting shot, a final flurry to cover the retreat.[10]

As long lines of bluecoated skirmishers began filing past the once formidable Rebel breastworks, George Stoneman rode eastward on July 10 under a dark and lowering sky to confer with McPherson near Turner's Ferry. He had left his troopers with orders to be ready to march at 2:00 P.M., but after learning the results of the 5th Indiana's reconnaissance to Campbellton, he wanted to know if the Rebels' sudden retreat had changed the instructions Sherman had sent him the previous day. McPherson posed the question in a message he dispatched to Sherman at noon, just as thunder pealed across the leaden skies, unleashing a torrential downpour.

Sherman spent much of July 10 inspecting his new lines as his troops drew abreast of the Chattahoochee, and it was late that afternoon before he got back to his headquarters at Vining's Station. As a result, several hours passed before McPherson's courier returned to Turner's Ferry with instructions for Stoneman to proceed as planned. Stoneman asked McPherson to send an infantry brigade down to Sandtown Ferry to relieve Tom Butler's cavalry and issued orders for his troopers to be ready to march at 8:00 P.M. with five days' rations.

It was still raining when Butler got his marching orders late that afternoon. His men drew the necessary rations and ammunition and culled their unserviceable horses. Shortly before dark, the rain stopped. Companies called in their pickets and by 8:00 P.M., the Indiana brigade was ready to ride.

At Sweetwater Bridge, Horace Capron's troopers also stood to horse at 8:00 P.M. They had been standing in a muddy cornfield for about an hour, waiting for orders to mount, when Capron received a message from Stoneman's headquarters, directing him to have his brigade "at the *Salt Spring Cross roads at day light in the morning.* Be on hand punctually."[11]

Stoneman's other brigade commanders probably got similar instructions, but the reason for the delay is unclear. Returning to camp, Capron's officers redeployed their pickets; the men left their horses saddled and spent a disagreeable night trying to sleep in the mud. "Reveille" sounded at 3:00 A.M., July 11, but before anyone could eat breakfast, the bugles began blowing "To Horse."

Capron and his men, the 14th Illinois Cavalry, 8th Michigan Cavalry, and McLaughlin's Ohio Squadron, were newcomers to Stoneman's command. Joining the division on June 30 after a 350-mile march from Kentucky, they had arrived just in time to see action in the daily skirmishes with dismounted Rebel cavalry during Sherman's advance from Kennesaw Mountain to the Chattahoochee. As daylight began to filter through the broken clouds on July 11, they climbed into the saddle and turned their horses down the west side of Sweetwater Creek toward the rendezvous at Salt Springs. Most likely, Stoneman met them there with orders to move south to join Silas Adams's Kentucky brigade near the ruins of the Sweetwater Factory. Following the narrow, rutted road for about two miles, the mud-spattered column halted just short of Adams's bivouac. After pausing long enough for the men to eat a little breakfast and feed their mounts, Capron started a detachment back to Mitchell's Crossroads with his led horses and mules. The rest of his brigade mounted and filed into the road behind Adams's 1st and 11th Kentucky Cavalry and Captain Hardy's 24th Indiana Battery.[12]

Taking a southwesterly course, the head of Stoneman's column reached the Campbellton Ferry about noon. The detachment from the 5th Indiana had been waiting there since July 9, and the rest of Tom Butler's brigade, having forded rain-swollen Sweetwater Creek early that morning, was three miles upstream, at Gorman's Ferry, where Butler's advance guard had captured two Rebel soldiers.

More Confederates were dug in on the east side of the river at both Gorman's Ferry and Campbellton, and the usual desultory skirmishing began almost immediately. The sharp crack of carbines was soon drowned out by the roar of artillery, as Captain Hardy trained his four Rodman guns on the Rebel pickets in front of Campbellton. "They skedaddled," assistant surgeon Samuel D. Tobey of the 8th Michigan noted approvingly, "and the citizens hung out white flags."

Nonetheless, Hardy's guns kept pounding away until it was too dark to see, setting fire to a large factory in the town. By that time, Stoneman had concluded there were 8,000 Confederates, with artillery, dug in at Campbellton. Clearly it was no use trying to cross here. If he was going to strike the railroad as Sherman wanted, he had to move farther south. According to the information the 5th Indiana's scouts had brought him on July 10, the next likely spot was the bridge at Franklin, forty miles downstream. It would be a long ride, but if his men could capture the bridge intact, they might be able to outflank the Rebel pickets and cut the Atlanta & West Point Railroad.

Convinced this was his only alternative, Stoneman ordered Colonel James Biddle, who had resumed command of the Indiana brigade from Tom Butler after a brief absence, to bring his two regiments downstream at daylight to relieve the two brigades opposite Campbellton. At the same time, he directed Silas Adams and Horace Capron to have their commands ready to march as soon as Biddle's men relieved their pickets. Until then, he advised his officers to post extra sentries and be especially vigilant.

Biddle's 5th and 6th Indiana arrived on schedule early on July 12. Leaving them and a section of artillery to keep the Rebels at Campbellton busy, Stoneman sent a note advising Sherman of his plans and marched at 10:00 A.M. with Capron, Adams, and the rest of Captain Hardy's battery. Capron's troopers led the column almost due west, toward Dark Corner, well out of sight of Rebel eyes on the other side of the Chattahoochee. The sparsely populated countryside was rough and heavily wooded, and Stoneman's men and horses plodded up one hill and down another for twenty-five taxing miles before halting for the night at Reece Watkins's farm on the banks of Dog Creek.

About the same time, one of Stoneman's scouts, dressed in civilian clothes, stopped at John M. Strickland's house and inquired if there was any place to cross the river without going all the way down to Franklin. Strickland, a prosperous farmer who professed to oppose the war, replied that Moore's Bridge, a covered span twenty-five miles below Campbellton, was just down the road. The two men talked over supper and far into the night. The next morning, after a hearty breakfast, the scout thanked his host and went on his way.

Just when he reported to Stoneman is uncertain. The Yankee horsemen were on the road at daylight on July 13, still moving toward Franklin, but four or five miles beyond Dog Creek the head of the column suddenly turned sharply to the southeast at Five Points and headed straight for Moore's Bridge. The steep, wooded hillsides, much like those they had encountered the previous day, gradually became fewer and farther apart and the road stretched out straight and shimmering in the summer heat. Moving ahead rapidly, the advance guard surprised and captured several Rebel scouts and riders, including a courier with a message warning the lieutenant commanding the Rebel picket at Moore's Bridge that a large force of Yankee cavalry was moving downriver and he must hold the bridge at all costs until reinforcements arrived.

This reference to reinforcements bothered Stoneman. If they got to the bridge before he did, they could keep him from getting across the river. Determined to get there first, he ordered Silas Adams to hurry a detachment to Moore's Bridge.

Never one to miss a good fight, the twenty-four-year-old Adams personally led his 11th Kentucky toward the river at a fast clip. Shortly before noon, nine of his men, dressed in captured Confederate uniforms, rode up to the bridge and coolly leveled their carbines at the Rebel pickets skinny-dipping in the shallows. Literally caught with their pants down, some of the surprised bathers immodestly clambered up the opposite bank and sprinted across the fields as fast as bare feet could carry them. Others tried to get to their guns, but Adams's men opened fire, wounding a Rebel lieutenant and capturing sixteen to twenty others, including the bridge's owner, James D. Moore.[13]

The prisoners identified themselves as a squadron of the 1st Tennessee Cavalry. They had mined the walls of the bridge with pine knots and straw, ready for burning at the first sign of trouble, but Adams's clever ruse had thwarted that scheme. Except for a few pried-up planks and sleepers, the 480-foot span was intact and the West Point railroad lay only nine miles away.

On the west bank of the river, right by the bridge, stood Horace King's house. A master carpenter, King had built Moore's Bridge about 1855 or 1856 in exchange for forty shares of stock in the venture. Currently employed by the Confederate navy yard at Columbus, Georgia, he was not at home when the flurry of gunshots sounded and his wife and children saw the bluecoated Kentuckians spilling into their yard, chasing down chickens and ransacking the house and outbuildings. Approaching an officer, Mrs. King inquired if there was a Mason among them. Yes, he said, what of it? Well, she replied, her husband was a Mason, so was her father, and she thought her family ought to be protected. The officer had his men put back two sacks of flour, but these soldiers who ostensibly were fighting to break the chains of bondage took almost everything else this prosperous free black family owned: 200 pounds of sugar, 400 pounds of bacon, 1,500 pounds of flour, 100 bushels of corn, a brand new wagon, two mules, a saddle, and all the clothing, bedding, cooking utensils, and tableware they could carry.

Horace King's white neighbors fared a little better, at least at first. William Chasteen, an elderly farmer who lived on the main road from Five Points to Moore's Bridge, watched as Horace Capron's brigade passed his house about 2:00 P.M. Swarming into his yard, bluecoated troopers took his two dapple-gray mules and were about to go to work on his barn and smokehouse when Capron rode up to the gate, introduced himself, and politely asked for a drink of water. Chasteen acquiesced, then asked if Capron was going to let the soldiers carry off his mules. Capron said he had to because so many of his horses had given out, leaving their riders on foot. He did write Chasteen's name in a little book, however, and assured him the government would eventually reimburse him. He ordered his men not to bother Chasteen's property and threatened to punish anyone who disobeyed.

A little farther up the road, Bluegrass boys from Silas Adams's brigade stopped at the Strickland place, where Stoneman's scout had found food and shelter the previous night. As the soldiers rode into the yard, Mrs. Strickland bustled out of the house, pleading with them not to take her favorite buggy horse, a gentle sorrel. How old was the horse, a trooper asked? About nine years, Mrs. Strickland answered. Was he blind? Yes, she said hopefully, the horse was blind in one eye. The Kentuckians decided they did not have any use for him, but they warned her to hide the horse if she wanted to keep him. They would just take that fine pair of mules standing in the feed lot.

Mr. Strickland was working in the fields and did not get back to the house until the mules were gone. Proclaiming his Union sympathies, he welcomed his unexpected guests. When asked where he kept his corn, he led them to his crib and had some of his slaves fill up seven or eight sacks. When they asked for meat, Mrs. Strickland unlocked the smokehouse door and told them to help themselves. The soldiers offered to pay for the bacon they took, but Mrs. Strickland said she did not want their money. They advised her to hide what was left, but she refused, saying she did not care if they took it all. She did, however, hide her prized sorrel in the bushes a short distance from the house.

When the spoils-laden column finally reached Moore's Bridge that afternoon, Stoneman directed Captain Hardy to unlimber his two Rodman guns to cover the eastern approaches to the bridge while work details began replacing the missing planks and timbers. He also sent detachments ranging down both sides of the river to collect all the boats they could find. Troopers soon assembled a motley armada of dugouts, skiffs, and a large ferryboat and began shuttling men and horses across the Chattahoochee.[14]

Two hours' work made the bridge passable, but at the decisive moment, Stoneman hesitated. The captured dispatch, announcing the approach of Rebel reinforcements, still nagged at him. Instead of boldly pushing across the river to strike the Atlanta & West Point Railroad, he sent Major William L. Buck's battalion of the 8th Michigan Cavalry seven miles upstream to Phillips' Ferry to cover his flank. He ordered the rest of his troops to bivouac on the banks of nearby Snake Creek and build enough campfires to convince the Rebels his cavalry was screening the advance of a large force of Sherman's infantry.

As night came on, campfires glimmered along Snake Creek, mimicking the stars overhead, but they did not reflect any optimism from Stoneman. "We will try what we can do to-morrow morning as soon as it is light," he gloomily wrote to Sherman, ". . . but if we do nothing to the [rail] road it will create a diversion."[15]

Panic might have been a better choice of words. One of the Rebel pickets who had escaped the embarrassment at Moore's Bridge had ridden hell-for-leather to nearby Newnan to spread the alarm.

An important stop on the Atlanta & West Point Railroad, Newnan was the site of four large Confederate military hospitals: Bragg, Buckner, Foard, and Gamble. Its churches, schools, hotels, stores, and even some private residences were crowded with hundreds of haggard, glassy-eyed men in tattered, bloodstained uniforms, and every day the train from Atlanta brought more. The stench of festering wounds, the quiet murmur of ebbing voices, and the scrape of the gravedigger's shovel in the cemetery on the north side of town had become almost commonplace, but the war was only a distant reality until that lone Rebel rider skidded his foam-flecked steed to a stop on the courthouse square shortly before 1:00 P.M., July 13, and blurted out the unbelievable news. The Yankees were coming!

People boiled into the streets, wringing their hands and talking excitedly. Colonel Thomas M. Griffin, the post commander, hurried down to the depot and sent a telegram to Atlanta, urgently requesting reinforcements. But Griffin knew it would be hours before a troop train could arrive. Fearing the Yankees might use that time to capture a locomotive and turn it loose on a collision course with anything coming down the track, he had railroad officials wire Atlanta and LaGrange, suspending all north- and southbound traffic. Then, in the vain hope he could hold the Yankees at bay until help arrived, he rounded up as many walking wounded as he could find and sent them marching toward Moore's Bridge under the command of a Kentucky captain.

News of the Yankees' approach had a tonic effect on the 1,500 patients in Newnan's four hospitals. Wards emptied out like a schoolroom at recess. Most of the doctors, nurses, and attendants fled, too. The few stalwarts who stayed behind divided their time between caring for patients too sick to move and packing precious stocks of medical supplies and provisions into wagons. These included a large quantity of whisky, which was spirited away for fear of what would happen if it fell into the hands of thirsty Yankees.

The all too rapid onset of darkness and the arrival of a wounded soldier from Moore's Bridge only tightened the icy grip of terror. Frightened nurses cast anxious glances out the windows as they made their rounds, half expecting to see Yankee faces leering back at them. Instead, they saw wagons, carts, buggies, and vehicles of every description crowding the narrow streets. Lamps and lanterns bobbed up and down, casting a yellow pallor on the features of frightened townspeople scurrying past with baskets, boxes, bundles, and carpetbags, while knots of bewildered slaves and a veritable menagerie of livestock and poultry only added to the confusion as frantic owners herded them out of town.

The steady exodus continued far into the night, and hardly a soul among those who stayed behind dared close their eyes for fear of being murdered in their sleep. Rumors ran rampant, and there were repeated alarms the Yankees were on the outskirts of town. Hope flickered briefly around 10:00 P.M., when the shrill whistle of a locomotive sounded at the depot down at the foot of Broad Street, but instead of the eagerly awaited reinforcements, it was the night train from West Point, which had somehow gotten past LaGrange despite the ban on traffic. The engine paused briefly at the depot before chugging up the track toward Atlanta, apparently preferring to run the gauntlet instead of waiting to be captured.

Disheartened, the remaining townsfolk resumed their anxious vigil. As the dark, endless hours dragged on, the tension became almost unbearable. Many of those who had not fled began having second thoughts. Others cast repeated nervous glances at the clock, and watched and waited and hoped and prayed. Eventually a man brought word the Yankees were just down the road, waiting for daylight before they charged into town.[16]

But help was closer than anyone dared hope. Elements of Brigadier General Frank Crawford Armstrong's brigade of Mississippi cavalry had left Sandtown on Monday, July 11, and moved down the east side of the Chattahoochee, paralleling the 5th and 6th Indiana's line of march. These troopers and a handful of Georgia militia, perhaps 1,000 men in all, had duped Stoneman into believing there were 8,000 Confederates defending Campbellton. Another cavalry regiment or two left Sandtown at 2:00 P.M., July 12, to reinforce Armstrong, and that evening a pair of Rebel guns in each of the twin redoubts at Campbellton had "made it quite warm" for the Indiana regiments on the other side of the river.

The two Rodman guns Stoneman had left with Biddle returned the fire, but with seemingly little effect. Intermittent artillery duels continued the next day, and Rebel sharpshooters made it impossible for Biddle's men to venture anywhere near the river without drawing fire. But Stoneman's sudden disappearance and Biddle's continued presence opposite Campbellton confused the Confederate command until someone surmised the Yankees must be trying to slip around Johnston's left to cut the West Point railroad. Unfortunately, this valuable insight was wasted when the courier sent to warn the pickets at Moore's Bridge blundered into Stoneman's men.

Shortly before sundown on the 13th, Brigadier General William H. "Red" Jackson, commanding all the Confederate cavalry on Johnston's left, ordered Frank Armstrong to intercept the Yankee column before it reached the railroad. Leaving Campbellton just after dark, Armstrong headed downstream with parts of the 1st and 2nd Mississippi Cavalry, Ballentine's Regiment, and the left section of Captain Houston King's Missouri battery.

Born on the Choctaw Agency in Indian Territory in 1835 and educated at Holy Cross, Armstrong had the unusual distinction of commanding troops on both sides in this war. Spurning a Confederate commission in the spring of 1861, he had captained a company of the 2nd U.S. Dragoons at the first battle of Bull Run before resigning to swear allegiance to the South. His route on this July evening lay a mile or two east of the Chattahoochee, but by the time his advance guard reached the bridge over White Oak Creek, eight miles below Rivertown, the river was less than a quarter mile to the right.[17]

The pounding of hooves on the bridge's stout wooden floor echoed in the darkness, startling Major Buck's pickets on the other side of the river at Phillips' Ferry. They listened closely. The unmistakable clatter of cavalry, lots of it, seemed to be coming from somewhere upstream, moving directly toward their rear. Thinking his little battalion was about to be overwhelmed, Buck ordered his men to fall back and sent a courier racing to tell Stoneman the Rebels were crossing the river above him.

Stoneman alerted his command, but was a little skeptical. According to his scouts and all the civilians he had talked to, there was no bridge between Phillips' Ferry and Campbellton. Buck and his men had obviously heard something, but shortly before daylight Stoneman concluded the major must have spooked at the sound of a Rebel column crossing a bridge over the creek nearly opposite Phillips' Ferry. Satisfied his flanks were secure, Stoneman prepared to start for Newnan.

But it was too late. Seemingly oblivious to the consternation his passing had caused on the other side of the river, Armstrong had continued downstream and halted at 4:00 A.M., July 14, at an intersection just two miles east of Moore's Bridge. Sending a few men ahead to scout the Yankee positions, he ordered the rest of his sleepless troopers to dismount and form a line of battle. A short time later, his scouts returned and reported a few Federals were on the east side of the river, but the road to the bridge was clear. Encouraged, Armstrong ordered his men to mount up.

Dawn was just beginning to chase the shadows away when the long gray line of horsemen filed into the road. As they turned toward the bridge, the piney woods closed in on either side, screening their advance. Unchallenged, the Mississippians rode to within half a mile of the bridge before orders came back from the head of the column to count off by fours and prepare to fight on foot.

While the number fours led the horses to the rear, the rest of Armstrong's troopers disappeared into the woods on either side of the road and formed into line. Artillerymen unlimbered Captain King's pair of three-inch rifled guns in the edge of the timber. They had scarcely gotten into position when a column of Yankee horsemen appeared on the other side of the river and started toward the bridge as if there was not a Rebel within twenty miles. Captain King's "Missouri daredevils" quickly disabused them of that notion. Supported by dismounted troopers from the 2nd Mississippi Cavalry, the Rebel gunners sent two shells screaming across the river, scattering bluejacketed troopers in every direction. At the same time, another of Armstrong's regiments burst from the woods and rushed the rifle pits at the river's edge.

Seeing they were about to be overrun, the Yankee pickets sprinted across the bridge to take cover behind some breastworks their comrades had improvised during the night. Throwing their carbines to their shoulders, they aimed a volley at their pursuers. Hardy's two Rodman guns added their thunder to the din, but many of the Yankee shells failed to explode and plowed harmlessly into the ground. The Rebels returned the fire, winging Lieutenant Tilford N. Bruner of the 1st Kentucky in his left arm and severely wounding Sergeant James T. Byrum of the 11th Kentucky in his left thigh.[18]

As the chorus of battle swelled to a roar, Armstrong sent a courier to Newnan with a message to be telegraphed to General Johnston:

> I arrived here at 4:00 a.m. Found the enemy in possession of the bridge. . . . I have a small portion of my brigade; ordered the remainder to follow. I think I can hold them in check until my troops get up. They are working on the bridge. The abutment was knocked down. They have an excellent position and have made breastworks. It is a division of cavalry, with artillery. I have heard of no infantry. Scouts report a cavalry column gone below.[19]

The cavalry column Armstrong's scouts had seen moving downstream was merely a patrol. Stoneman had never shown any real enthusiasm for crossing the river or striking the railroad, and Armstrong's sudden appearance gave him just the excuse he needed. "Deeming it inexpedient to push our endeavors further," he later explained, "and knowing that it was easier to retain the men long enough to burn the bridge than to get them back again after they had been driven off, I ordered the bridge burned and the boats that had been collected there for security destroyed."

The dangerous task of setting the fire fell to Lieutenant William P. Ballard of the 1st

Kentucky Cavalry. Braving a hail of bullets, he dashed toward the bridge with a flaming torch and thrust it into the dry pine knots and straw the Rebels had stuffed into the walls. Arms pumping, legs flying, he ran the gauntlet again and rejoined his comrades just as smoke began billowing from the cavernous mouth of the span. Flames burst through the roof. Timbers cracked and groaned, and after a few minutes the bridge slid off its piling and plunged into the river.

Stoneman then ordered both his brigades to fall back a short distance while he awaited the return of the patrol he had sent downriver. While he waited, his men looted nearby farms and plantations.[20] They chased down chickens, broke open beehives, broiled bacon over smoky little fires of fence rails, and grazed their horses on fields of freshly shocked oats. Reneging on earlier promises, they even took Mrs. Strickland's little one-eyed sorrel. Few, if any, families were spared.

From an hour past sunrise until 4:00 that afternoon, Yankee troopers prowled up and down the Five Notch Road, paralleling the river. Some ventured as far south as the vicinity of Whooping Creek, only thirteen miles above Franklin. Upon returning, these wide-ranging patrols assured Stoneman there were no practicable fords, ferries, or bridges anywhere along this stretch of the Chattahoochee. Satisfied he had fulfilled the letter if not the spirit of Sherman's instructions, late that afternoon Stoneman ordered his troopers into the saddle and retraced his steps northward. A twenty-mile march under starry skies brought him back to his old camp at Dog Creek, where he called a halt at 2:00 A.M., July 15.[21]

He left Major Buck, his reputation somewhat tarnished after the false alarm at Phillips' Ferry, and a small detachment of the 8th Michigan to keep an eye on the Rebels across the river and scout as far west as Carrollton before rejoining the rest of the command. Quitting the river about 3:00 P.M. on July 14, Buck and his men apparently marched leisurely. It was daylight the next morning before they covered the fifteen miles to Carrollton.

The townspeople had little or no warning of their approach. Some bolted for the woods. Others simply stood and gawked at the dust-covered horsemen plodding down the street.

"It was really pitiful to watch the terrified countenances of the women when our boys went into their houses to procure water or food," noted a Michigan soldier. "They seemed to think that we were ferocious wild beasts seeking whom we might devour. But a few polite gentlemanly remarks from our boys, or a few winning smiles would dispell [sic] the illusion and before they left the house, the dear chivalrous ladies would become quite sociable and acknowledge that they had been deceived by their own men in regard to our ferociousness." A spontaneous, if somewhat forced, effusion of Southern hospitality followed and soon Major Buck and his men were feasting on the best Carrollton had to offer. "I have heard a great deal about Southern beauties," added the Michigan trooper, "but have been unable to find them when compared with our own Northern girls. What they call beauty here would be considered North as very commonplace."

After eating their fill, Buck's men strolled into several stores, where they discovered "heaps of tobacco." It had been a long time between chaws for most of them, and after appropriating all the tobacco they could carry, they destroyed what was left and took whatever else struck their fancy. "The town, except those houses which were still inhabited, was completely sacked," noted Samuel Tobey, the 8th Michigan's assistant surgeon.[22]

About noon, a small detachment of the 14th Illinois rode into town with orders for Major Buck to remain in Carrollton until the next morning, then catch up with the rest of the command at Sweetwater Town. Their message delivered, the Illinois boys rode on, part of a larger force Stoneman had sent out that morning with instructions to sweep the roads to the southwest, confiscating all the horses and mules they could find.

A column of 300 Federals was moving north on the main road between Carrollton and Villa Rica when about fifty Illinois troopers stopped at P. H. Hesterly's house at 11:00 A.M. Swinging down from their saddles, two soldiers approached the fifty-four-year-old farmer and announced they were going to take a matched pair of sorrel mules grazing in his pasture. Hesterly, an avowed Union man, said he would be grateful if they would leave him at least one, but the troopers shook their heads. Several of their horses had been killed or crippled at Moore's Bridge and they had orders to bring in all the serviceable mounts they could find. Resigning himself to the inevitable, Hesterly led his visitors into the pasture. As he came back, he saw two or three soldiers taking his gray mule, his saddle, and harness. Others were emptying his smokehouse and ransacking his home. "There was an officer along," Hesterly recounted. "He ordered them not to break up my things, told them not to pillage. He told the men to wait, that I would open the door for them. He said his men would not take anything they did not need." But these Yankees seemed to need everything. During the next two hours, they relieved Hesterly of his silver watch, all his knives and forks, a miscellaneous assortment of clothing and tinware, a shotgun, fifty pounds of tobacco, and two quart bottles of castor oil.

While these detachments looted and plundered, most of Stoneman's troopers idled away July 15 on the banks of Dog Creek. According to Sherman's original timetable, they should have rejoined the main army by now, but food was short, horses were worn out, and Stoneman had no desire to add to the ranks of the dismounted men he had left at Mitchell's Crossroads.

"We shall remain here and graze during the day," he wrote to Sherman, "and in the evening move to the vicinity of Sweet Water Town, or within eight miles of it." He added:

> We get plenty of forage for the horses, beef and blackberries and some bacon for the men, and are getting on finely. We want horseshoes and nails, and a little time where we can avail ourselves of a blacksmith shop to fit the shoes, to complete the cavalry and make it ready for any service. The artillery, however, want better horses and better ammunition, as the horses they have would be unable to make long consecutive marches, and the ammunition is but little better than solid shot.

Trying to put his failure to cut the Atlanta & West Point route in the best possible perspective, he insisted he was

> very anxious to strike the railroad, from personal as well as other considerations, but I became convinced that to attempt it would incur risks inadequate to the results, and unless we could hold the bridge, as well as penetrate into the country, the risk of capture or dispersion . . . was almost certain. It is impossible to move without every

step we take being known, women as well as men acting as scouts and messengers. I have sent to the rear about 40 prisoners, 1 of them the commander of the picket at the bridge on this side, and 16 or 17 of them pickets and scouts in the vicinity of the bridge. I am unable to say how much force is opposite us, but from what I can see and hear, I am convinced it is no inconsiderable one.

That afternoon, the details and detachments Stoneman had sent out began returning to camp, bringing with them what one Illinois trooper called "a fine lot of stock," assorted plunder, and at least three civilian prisoners. Officers supervised the distribution of captured horses and mules among the enlisted men, and that evening the column began moving back toward Campbellton. They had gone only twelve miles when Stoneman called a halt at Dark Corner.[23]

Sherman, in the meantime, was anxiously awaiting Stoneman's return before setting his armies in motion again. He had originally intended to leave McPherson's XV and XVII Corps on the right flank to "demonstrate as though intending to cross at Turner's [Ferry] or below," but at 7:45 P.M., July 11, McPherson had sent word the Rebels seemed to be pulling troops away from the lower ferries. Realizing Johnston had forfeited all hope of attacking across the Chattahoochee when he burned his pontoon bridges, Sherman decided the Army of the Tennessee could be put to better use reinforcing the shallow bridgeheads at Roswell and Sope Creek. At 2:00 A.M., July 12, he had sent orders directing McPherson to proceed to Roswell with the XV Corps "at once." The XVII Corps would follow "when General Stoneman does get back or is heard from."

Sherman had heard nothing from Stoneman since July 12, when the cavalryman sent word he was leaving Biddle's brigade in front of Campbellton and moving the rest of the division downstream to capture the bridge at Franklin. The only other clue to Stoneman's progress, or lack of it, came from Major General Frank P. Blair, commanding McPherson's XVII Corps, who reported long columns of Rebel cavalry moving down the east side of the Chattahoochee on the night of July 13–14. Sherman directed Blair to have Biddle forward any news from Stoneman at once, and was greatly relieved when a courier arrived on July 15, delivering the dispatch Stoneman had penned two days earlier at Moore's Bridge. Stoneman's subsequent report from Dog Creek arrived later that same day.

"I have just received your note of [the] 15th," Sherman acknowledged, "and wish you to hasten to your old position to relieve General Blair. I want you to cover and watch Turner's Ferry and [the] mouth of Nickajack [Creek] whilst we cross above and move out. You will have plenty of time to shoe and fix up. General Blair has your orders."[24]

He advised Blair, "I have just heard from General Stoneman, *who says he will be over at Sweet Water Town to-night* [author's italics]. I have ordered him to hurry and relieve you. Haul out of sight all your guns to-night ready in the morning to move to Roswell."[25]

Believing Stoneman's cavalry was only three or four miles away, Blair called in his pickets at sunrise on July 16, and sent his XVII Corps marching toward Marietta. But Stoneman had not promised to be at Sweetwater Town at daylight, only that he would "move to the vicinity" or "within eight miles of it." Sherman had misquoted him, and the result was Blair unwittingly left the north side of the Chattahoochee unguarded from Nickajack Creek all the way down to the mouth of the Sweetwater.[26]

Stoneman apparently did not even receive orders to relieve Blair's corps until that afternoon, and it was 4:00 P.M. before Silas Adams's brigade left Dark Corner. Crossing the bridge at Sweetwater Town shortly before sundown, the Kentuckians turned south to picket and patrol the riverbank between Sandtown Ferry and the mouth of Sweetwater Creek. Horace Capron's troopers followed as far as Mitchell's Crossroads, where they met Stoneman's wagon trains and halted for the night to replenish their supplies.

James Biddle's brigade began moving back upstream at sundown. As night came on, a pelting rain began to fall and the Hoosiers plodded north, heads down, hat brims dripping, until 1:00 A.M., July 17, when the column halted at Salt Springs Crossroads. The next morning, supply wagons delivered rations and clothing. After refilling their haversacks, at least one detachment, Company I of the 6th Indiana, crossed the heavily trafficked bridge at Sweetwater Town and followed the Old Alabama Road east and south for another ten miles to cover the left flank of Major Carter's dismounted men, who had moved from Mitchell's Crossroads to picket the river from the mouth of Nickajack Creek up to Turner's Ferry.

Major Buck's battalion of the 8th Michigan also moved east on July 16. After spending the night bivouacked in a vacant lot in the center of Carrollton that would later become the site of the Carroll County courthouse, they broke open a few boxes of tobacco they had previously overlooked and then rode out of town, taking at least one unhappy Confederate with them. Traveling leisurely on the Old Alabama Road, they halted for the night about six miles west of the bridge at Sweetwater Town. The next afternoon, they caught up with Horace Capron's brigade, which had left Mitchell's Crossroads about 1:00 P.M. with orders to picket the Chattahoochee from Nickajack Creek down to Howell's Ferry.

It was July 18 before Stoneman got the last of his troopers realigned on the riverbank. Early that morning, Biddle's brigade filed across the bridge at Sweetwater Town to occupy the position Capron had vacated at Mitchell's Crossroads the previous day. From there, the Hoosiers patrolled the area west of Sweetwater Creek, guarded Stoneman's communications with the supply depots at Marietta, and acted as a mounted reserve for the brigades picketing the banks of the Chattahoochee.

In eight days, Stoneman's men had ridden 120 miles. They had captured 200 or 300 horses and mules and at least forty prisoners. Their own casualties were two wounded, one mortally, during the skirmish at Moore's Bridge, and eight captured, mostly while out foraging.[27]

There were also some casualties among the dismounted men Stoneman had left at Mitchell's Crossroads. One trooper had shot himself through the foot on July 13 while trying to clean a loaded revolver. Two others had been captured. Then there was the strange case of Captain Loomis.[28]

Captain Ruell B. Loomis was one of the 5th Indiana's older officers. Intending to catch up on a backlog of quartermaster and ordnance reports, he and his company clerk, Private David S. Whitenack, had occupied a farmhouse near Mitchell's Crossroads. About July 15, they had received word, presumably from Major Carter, that the dismounted portion of the division was moving camp about a mile farther north, leaving the farmhouse in a rather isolated position. Loomis knew Rebel scouts had been seen in the neighborhood but was loath to give up his comfortable quarters.

A couple of nights later, the air hung hot and muggy, threatening rain. Private Whitenack bedded down inside the house, but Loomis decided he would be more comfortable outside. Taking off his hat, coat, and boots, he stretched out on the porch, placing a pair of pistols within easy reach. About midnight, he was awakened by the yelping and baying of the pack of mongrel hounds that every Southern family seemed to keep around the yard. Peering into the darkness, Loomis saw six or eight shadowy figures coming toward him. Thinking he was about to be captured, he jumped off the porch and ran for the woods. A voice ordered him to halt.

Hearing the commotion, Private Whitenack looked out the window just in time to see Loomis sprint past with a soldier in hot pursuit. As Whitenack watched, the soldier leveled his carbine and fired. A streak of flame stabbed at the darkness. A second shot rang out as Loomis disappeared into the shadows. In the momentary confusion that followed, Whitenack slipped out the window unnoticed. From the edge of the woods, he saw the captain's pursuers mount the porch steps and ask the lady of the house who was the man that ran away. She told them it was Captain Loomis of the 5th Indiana.

"My God, boys," exclaimed one of the intruders, "I believe that I shot him."

Whitenack waited until they had left before creeping back to the house. The woman told him the men belonged to the 6th Indiana Cavalry and had come to arrest her husband. Fearing the worst, Whitenack hurried outside and spent two or three hours calling Loomis's name. There was no answer. The next morning, he sent a hostler to see if the captain had turned up at headquarters. The hostler returned with sad news. Captain Loomis had been mortally wounded. He died that afternoon.[29]

On this tragic note, the Moore's Bridge raid came to an end. From their hilltop bivouac overlooking Nickajack Creek, Capron's men could see Atlanta's distant spires, but they were no closer than they had been when the raid began. Stoneman had not cut the West Point railroad; nor had he diverted any sizable bodies of Confederate cavalry from Sherman's front. There was something else, too, something that was already being whispered through the ranks. Stoneman had lost his nerve.[30]

4

TO THE GATES OF ATLANTA

JULY 10–JULY 20, 1864

*The passage of great rivers in the presence
of the enemy is one of the most delicate
operations in war.*

—Frederick the Great

If Sherman seemed remarkably unruffled by Stoneman's feeble effort to reach the West Point railroad, it was because all the reports he had received convinced him the expedition had drawn the Rebel cavalry downriver, away from Roswell. "I have now fulfilled the first part of the grand plan," he wrote to Grant on July 12. "Our lines are up to the Chattahoochee, and the enemy is beyond. . . . As soon as I hear from Stoneman I will shift all of McPherson to Roswell and cross Thomas about three miles above the railroad bridge and move against Atlanta, my left well to the east, to get possession of the Augusta road about Decatur or Stone Mountain. I think all will be ready in three days. I will have nearly 100,000 men."[1]

Sherman knew the biggest battles, the ones that would decide the fate of Atlanta, would likely be fought on the south side of the Chattahoochee, and while he waited for Stoneman's return, he gave his weary infantry a week to rest and resupply. Literally itching for a chance to wash off two months of sweat and grime, Federal foot soldiers quickly negotiated temporary truces with their Rebel counterparts and hundreds of them were soon frolicking along the riverbank, swimming, bathing, or just basking in the hot summer sun. Even Sherman shucked his worries long enough to take a dip in the river below Vining's Station.

"Water is cold, eh?" queried a teamster watching from the bank.

"Not very, sir," the commanding general replied crisply.

Sherman's soldiers frequently struck up conversations with the Southern sentries watching from the opposite shore, and it was not long before they were offering to swap Yankee newspapers, coffee, blankets, pocketknives, canteens, and greenback dollars for plugs of Rebel tobacco. After the customary haggling over price, representatives from each side waded or swam out to midstream, holding the proffered goods high overhead or clenched in their teeth. At night, when darkness and the swift current made such exchanges impractical, Federal bands entertained the troops with patriotic, humorous, and sentimental airs, readily accepting requests voiced from the south-bank shadows. If no musicians were available, Northerners sometimes serenaded their foes with song. Southerners returned the favor and each side would compliment the other's fine voices. Officers tried to keep their men from fraternizing with the enemy, but to no avail. "There was never before a civil war in which there was so little personal animosity," wrote a Union soldier.[2]

While his infantry enjoyed this brief respite, Sherman kept his cavalry busy.

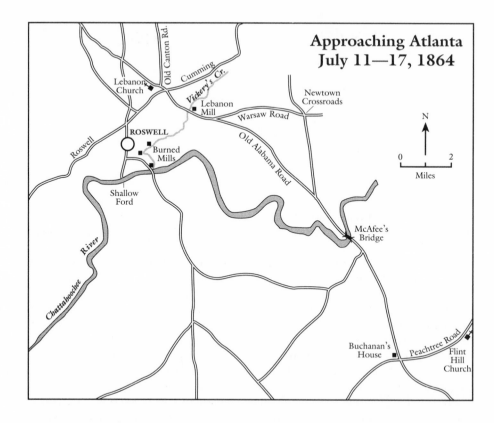

Alarmed by a report from Acworth that a regiment of 500 Texans threatened the railroad he depended on for supplies, at 9:40 P.M., July 9, he sent Kenner Garrard orders to strengthen his forces at McAfee's Bridge to prevent the raiders from using it to get back across the Chattahoochee. This, he asserted, was why the Rebels had defended that bridge so stubbornly while the rest of Garrard's division was crossing at Shallow Ford.

Sherman's courier did not reach Roswell until early on July 10. "I will make full investigation to-day in regard to what force the enemy have north of the river," Garrard promised, and right after breakfast he sent Eli Long's 2nd Brigade scouting the roads to the north and east. He also dispatched Bob Minty's 4th U.S. Cavalry to McAfee's Bridge to block the retreat of the Texans reportedly threatening the railroad. The rest of Minty's 1st Brigade remained in camp near the fire-blackened ruins of the woolen mill, not far from where the Board of Trade Battery's six Parrott guns frowned silently from the bluffs overlooking Shallow Ford.[3]

Abe Miller's 3rd Brigade was bivouacked on the town square. At 10:00 A.M., Chaplain Isaac De La Matyr of the 72nd Indiana rang the bell at the Presbyterian church and a goodly number of Miller's men filed into the sanctuary to hear the sermon. "The services were unusually impressive, . . ." noted Sergeant Ben Magee, "and could the *common people* of the South have been permitted to look upon our devotions, they must have been convinced that we Yankees were not the vandals their leaders had pictured us to be."

But not everyone went to church that Sunday morning. Several 72nd Indiana troopers were rambling through the Roswell cemetery when one of them sniffed the air and declared he could smell meat. A quick investigation revealed telltale grease stains on a large, flat stone covering one of the graves. The sharp-scented trooper nosed about some more and then pointed to a nearby burial vault. His comrades knocked a hole through one of the masonry walls and were resurrecting a cache of ham, bacon, and molasses when an old woman took them to task. "I've allus hearn tell o' you'uns robbin' the cradle and the grave to fight we'uns," she screeched, "and now I know you'uns will rob the grave."

Garrard only made matters worse when he redeemed the promise he had made to the 1st and 3rd Brigades at Shallow Ford the previous day and had his commissary officers issue each man a gill of whisky. Ordinarily, a quarter of a pint was not enough to do any harm, but there were temperance advocates in every regiment who refused their ration, leaving that much more for their less abstemious comrades. Others gambled for drinks in Sunday morning card and dice games, and it was not long before several troopers were "foolishly drunk."

Some of the factory girls who had elected not to go North were still around town, but the records are a little reticent about what happened next. "It is not within my power, nor do I desire, either to prove or disprove the stories which are still told . . . concerning the treatment of some of these women by Northern soldiers," wrote one Cobb County historian. Sergeant Magee was more explicit. "Upon this occasion," he wrote of his drunken comrades, "their delirium took the form of making love to the women."

By midmorning, the situation was rapidly getting out of hand. Private James Eldridge of the 4th Michigan Cavalry staggered out into the road in a drunken haze and tried to stampede the first horseman he saw. The rider was Major General Grenville M. Dodge, commanding McPherson's XVI Corps and, according to one eyewitness, "Jimmy barely escaped being cut down."[4]

These excesses of drunkenness, debauchery, and desecration and the arrival of two divisions of Dodge's infantry soon led Garrard to send some of his troops out of town. At 1:00 P.M., Abe Miller's 3rd Brigade moved two miles north of Roswell to bivouac in the shade of the tall pines on the Canton Road. The Board of Trade Battery trundled back into town about 4:00 P.M. and parked on the square in front of Garrard's headquarters at Barrington Hall about the same time Eli Long's patrols began returning from a fruitless search for elusive Texans.

"I can learn of no large force of cavalry on this side of the river," Garrard wrote to Sherman that night. There were small parties of five to ten roaming the countryside who had captured nearly a dozen of his men during the day, but most of the Rebel cavalry appeared to have crossed the Chattahoochee and fallen back toward Cross Keys. "The bridge [McAfee's] to-day eight miles above was crossed by my troops and is in good order," Garrard added. "Shall I send a force to keep it from being destroyed?"

"Certainly," Sherman replied in a telegram delivered the next day, "by all means save the bridge above Roswell, and get me information of the lay of the country from it toward Stone Mountain."[5]

These orders sent Company I of the 72nd Indiana across the river on July 11. The Hoosiers did not encounter any Rebels, but they did find a small building crammed full of medical supplies, including a half-ton of cornstarch neatly bundled in four-pound packages. On the advice of a trooper well-versed in the culinary arts, each man stuffed a couple of packages into his saddlebags and tied three or four more to his saddle. Blackberries were abundant in this part of Georgia, and when the Hoosiers returned to camp that evening, they experimented mixing a few ounces of cornstarch with a gallon of freshly cooked berries. Sergeant Ben Magee pronounced the results as "the most delicate pudding we have ever tasted."

Not everyone's camp cuisine was such an unqualified success. Two Signal Corps-men attached to Garrard's headquarters, Lieutenants Isaiah C. Worley and William W. Allen, found a sack of flour at Barrington Hall and decided to try their hand at making biscuits. Measuring out the ingredients, they carefully mixed and kneaded the dough, put it in an oven and eagerly awaited the results. Only when the biscuits were done did they learn the hard truth; their "flour" was really plaster of paris.[6]

Garrard spent July 11 redeploying his division to cover the roads north and east of Roswell. The 4th Michigan and 7th Pennsylvania of Bob Minty's 1st Brigade marched through town that morning on their way to Lebanon Mill, two miles to the northeast on the Old Alabama Road. Eli Long left a few companies to picket the roads in front of Dodge's infantry on the south side of the Chattahoochee and moved the balance of his 2nd Brigade due north of Roswell to the intersection of the Old Alabama and Cumming roads at Lebanon Church. By nightfall only Garrard's headquarters and the Board of Trade Battery remained in Roswell itself.

"I have nothing new to report," Garrard wrote to Sherman at 8:00 P.M. "All is quiet to-day. Parties have been in every direction and no evidence of any considerable force on this side of the river."[7]

Armed with these assurances, at daylight the next morning, the 1st Division of Oliver Otis Howard's IV Corps of the Army of the Cumberland began crossing one of the twin pontoon bridges Schofield had strung across the Chattahoochee at the mouth of Sope Creek. Brushing aside a few contentious Rebel cavalrymen, Howard's infantry moved three miles downstream and began digging in on the high ground overlooking Powers' Ferry. As soon as Howard's column had crossed, pontoniers from Colonel George P. Buell's 58th Indiana Infantry quickly dismantled one of the floating bridges at Sope Creek, loaded it into wagons, and moved down the north side of the river to Powers' Ferry, where the 3rd Division of Howard's corps was waiting. Working feverishly, Buell's men had a bridge laid shortly after noon and the 3rd Division began crossing at 1:00 P.M. Howard's 2nd Division, previously sent to Roswell to relieve Garrard's cavalry at Shallow Ford, arrived that evening after being replaced by Dodge's XVI Corps, and began crossing at 9:00 A.M., July 13. This put three Federal infantry corps, the IV, the XXIII, and the XVI, on the south side of the Chattahoochee.[8]

More were on the way. Late that afternoon, the vanguard of McPherson's XV Corps trudged into Roswell. Sweating and footsore after a hurried march from Turner's Ferry, they halted on the riverbank where Grenville Dodge was rebuilding the bridge the Rebels had burned on July 5. Dodge had put a foot bridge across Shallow Ford within ten hours of his arrival on July 10. Since then, he had kept 1,000 men working day and night, measuring, sawing, hammering, and pulling down nearby buildings for lumber to span the scorched stone piers rising out of the Chattahoochee. In a prodigious feat of engineering, by nightfall on July 13, they had finished a sturdy, double-tracked trestle bridge, eighteen feet wide and 710 feet long.

The Signal Corps had been busy, too, and by the time McPherson rode into town later that night, they had strung over twenty miles of telegraph wire connecting Roswell with Sherman's headquarters at Vining's Station. "The bridge is finished," McPherson wired Sherman early on July 14, "and the Fifteenth Army Corps will cross the river this afternoon. . . ."[9]

To make room for this influx of infantry, Garrard pulled the last of his units out of Roswell. The Board of Trade Battery rolled out of town at 8:00 A.M. on July 14, moving at a leisurely walk to keep their horses from sweating in their freshly oiled harness. About noon, they joined two of Bob Minty's regiments, the 4th Michigan and 7th Pennsylvania, comfortably camped at Lebanon Mill on Vickery's Creek.

Garrard also moved his headquarters to Lebanon Mill that day. It was a pastoral scene: horses grazing contentedly, swarthy troopers splashing and swimming in the mill pond, others prying timbers out of the mill to shore up the rickety bridge Abe Miller's mounted infantry had crossed earlier that morning.

Miller's men had left their camps in the tall pines, two miles north of Roswell, at 8:00 A.M., and crossed Vickery's Creek with orders to extend Garrard's picket line east of Lebanon Mill. After traveling about three miles east on the Warsaw Road, Miller halted his brigade at Newtown Crossroads. It was a bountiful place compared to the timbered wastes of northwest Georgia. Golden fields of grain lay cut, cured, and shocked, ready for harvest, and bluecoated squads, details, and detachments swarmed over the countryside like locusts. When a distraught farmer came to Miller complaining that soldiers were stealing his oats and robbing his corncrib, Miller tersely told him his men were going to take it all.

About noon, one of Miller's detachments reached McAfee's Bridge and relieved the 4th U.S. Cavalry, which had been on picket duty since July 10, occasionally probing the roads south of the river. Saddling their horses, the Regulars moved north, presumably to join the 4th Michigan, which left Lebanon Mill at 2:00 P.M. and moved two or three miles east to camp in some woods on the Warsaw Road.[10]

While Garrard jockeyed his cavalry north and east of Roswell, Sherman issued the orders that would carry his armies across the Chattahoochee. His Special Field Orders Number 35 directed Thomas to have the XIV and XX Corps of the Army of the Cumberland ready to cross the river at Pace's and Powers' ferries as soon as "he hears that General Stoneman is back from his present expedition." Schofield and McPherson would move south from Sope Creek and Shallow Ford "on the return of Major-General Stoneman." Stoneman's and McCook's cavalry would remain on the north side of the river, guarding supplies and communications, but Garrard's powerful division would cross at McAfee's Bridge and scout as far east as Pinckneyville, aligning on McPherson's left "about Buchanan's," if no Rebels were found.

"A week's work after crossing the Chattahoochee should determine the first object aimed at," Sherman concluded, "viz, the possession of the Atlanta and Augusta road east of Decatur, or of Atlanta itself."

Preliminary to this movement, Sherman wanted a reconnaissance in force toward the Georgia Railroad. According to a report he had received from Turner's Ferry, Rebel cavalry had been seen moving downstream during the night, undoubtedly drawn away, Sherman reasoned, by the movements of Stoneman and Rousseau. He directed McPherson to have Garrard "feel out strong and disturb those that are left."

McPherson urged something more ambitious. If Rebel cavalry was indeed being drawn downstream, he telegraphed Sherman at 5:00 P.M.:

> Would it not be a good move for Garrard to cross his division at McAfee's Bridge, push one of his brigades out toward Cross Keys, and engage the cavalry there; and send his other brigade[s] rapidly via Lawrenceville down to Covington on the railroad, and burn the bridge across Yellow River and other streams in the vicinity, and do all the damage they can? The distance is forty miles.

Sherman rejected the idea. "The bridge over Yellow River is too well guarded by men and redoubts to be carried by our cavalry," he telegraphed McPherson that night:

> but General Garrard might dash at the road east of the Stone Mountain. See him, and [sic] it is useless to attempt anything unless he be willing, for until our infantry is out as far as the railroad he may encounter most of Wheeler's cavalry, but I have no doubt most of Johnston's cavalry is gone to the south toward West Point, drawn there by Generals Stoneman and Rousseau. . . .[11]

If McPherson approached Garrard about making a "dash" at the railroad east of Stone Mountain, nothing came of the idea. Late that afternoon, scouts reported 200 or 300 Rebels at Cumming, a small town eighteen miles northeast of Roswell, poised to play havoc with Sherman's tenuous supply line. Garrard ordered his largest regiment, Colonel Charles B. Seidel's 3rd Ohio, to intercept them.

Seidel's entire 3rd battalion, Companies C, G, I, and K, had left Roswell on July 13, escorting Garrard's supply wagons to Marietta. Other troopers were out foraging when the bugles sounded "To Horse," but there was no time to wait for them. Garrard's orders were imperative. Leaving word for his absent troopers to follow as soon as they could, Seidel set out shortly before dark with 400 or 500 men.[12]

All night long, the column plodded northward. Day was just beginning to dawn when they rode into Cumming at 4:00 A.M., July 15. A small place nestled at the foot of an abrupt 760-foot elevation known as Sawnee Mountain, Cumming had a population of about 400 and most of them were still asleep when the Yankees arrived. There was no sign of any Rebels. Convinced the reports Garrard had received were greatly exaggerated, Seidel divided his command into several detachments and sent them looking for livestock and provisions.

Baylis Nichols and his daughter were gathering stove wood when two troopers rode into the yard. "Eh, Uncle," one of the soldiers asked, "where are your horses?"

"I told them a lie," Baylis later admitted. "I said . . . we hadn't got but one."

"God damn you," the soldier snarled, "if you don't tell us where they are, we will put daylight through you."

Thoroughly frightened, Baylis confessed there was a mare and a colt in the barn. He watched the Yankees break open the barn door, then ran into the house to tell his master.

Dr. Frank H. Nichols and his wife, Minerva, were still asleep when Baylis burst into their bedroom shouting the town was "right full of blue people."

"It is that old secesh gang of Wheeler's men," Dr. Nichols declared, leaping out of bed.

No sir, Baylis insisted. These looked like Yankees. Nichols lifted the curtain and looked outside. "Lord, Baylis," he exclaimed, "they are!"

Just then, the front door shook under a rain of heavy blows; a voice bellowed for someone to open up. Baylis scurried to the hallway and was fumbling with the latch when one of Seidel's soldiers shouldered the door open, sending him sprawling across the floor. A squad of bluecoated troopers barged in and began ransacking Dr. Nichols's office.

"They took everything out of the house that was fitten [sic] to be taken," Baylis lamented, "poured out all his medicines, took all the bottles and everything they could get, and me there begging all the time.

"A captain asked me if I didn't want to go with them and I told them I was living with a Yankee and a good Republican man and he was as good a man as I wanted to live with."

The soldiers scoffed. They had already found two pistols and a double-barreled shotgun in the house, and to their way of thinking, the doctor was nothing but a "damned reb," and a well-heeled one at that.

While some troopers carried off bacon from a storeroom filled with provisions, others broke open several boxes of tobacco, each man filling a sack to tie to his saddle. They loaded the rest of the tobacco, lard, flour, and some corn into two wagons taken from Nichols's neighbors.

The storeroom was also piled high with coffeepots, covered buckets, milk pails, tin cups, and sprinkling cans Dr. Nichols had taken to settle a debt. The Yankees filled the larger vessels with syrup, honey, and butter and used the tin cups to sample a five-gallon keg of brandy.

Baylis saw a good many troopers get "drunk enough to be fools though they knew very well what they were doing." They flung open the smokehouse door, expecting to find ham and bacon hanging from the rafters. Instead they were met by the inquisitive gaze of a mouse-colored mule Nichols had hidden inside to save it from roving bands of Confederate cavalry.

This brought the doctor and his wife running out of the house. Mrs. Nichols pleaded so fervently for the mule one trooper threatened to shoot her if she did not get out of the way. Another brought the doctor's saddle out of the house, strapped it on the mule, hoisted a Negro boy aboard, and told him to ride the animal out the gate.

Dr. Nichols complained to a Yankee major, explaining he was born in New York, educated in Buffalo and Philadelphia. He had been run out of the county once for his Union sympathies and then arrested. Friends and neighbors had posted a $100,000 bond to secure his release, and he had been forced to swear allegiance to the Confederacy, but he was still a good Union man. The major and his men were welcome to anything he had if they would just give him a receipt. Ask anyone, Nichols pleaded, pointing to a man passing the front gate. They would confirm everything he had said.

Something in the doctor's earnest manner convinced the major to question the man at the gate. Soon he returned with an agitated look on his face. He gruffly ordered his men to finish loading the wagons and put a guard at the front door of the house with instructions not to let anyone else inside.

Turning to Nichols, the major said, "Doctor, this is all wrong, but if we had not done this and taken your property from you, when we left your neighbors would have turned right around and have shot you or burnt you out." If he would come to Marietta, he could get a proper receipt for his property. Nichols shook his head. He had a sick wife and baby to take care of and he was under oath not to do anything hostile to the Confederate cause. He dared not leave home.

Nichols's neighbors suffered similarly. On the east side of town, two troopers reined up at the gate in front of Judge John G. Lott's house. "Old man," one of the troopers called out, "do you know what this means?"

"I guess I do," Lott replied, eyeing their blue uniforms carefully.

Some sixty or seventy Yankees rode into the yard, but Lott's slaves had somehow gotten wind of their approach and hidden the judge's mules in a nearby cornfield. Finding nothing on the hoof, the troopers took rations of bacon and hardtack out of their haversacks and sat down to eat.

Judge Lott circulated freely among them. A kindly, mild-mannered man who "seemed to want the world to know his views religiously and politically," he avowed his loyalty to the Union. Several troopers patted him on the back and told him he was "all right."

They were preparing to leave when a slave told them where to find the judge's stock. A few troopers went down to the cornfield and came back leading three mules. Lott begged the soldiers not to take them.

"You keep your mules too fat," a trooper grinned, "we cannot leave them."

As the Yankee column started back toward Cumming, one young soldier lingered behind, watching the doleful expressions of Judge Lott and his wife, Mary. Perhaps the gray-haired old couple reminded him of his own parents back in Ohio. Tears streamed down his cheeks as he stammered an apology, mounted his horse, and rode away.

At 3:00 P.M. Seidel's men started south with two wagonloads of tobacco and tinware and a "considerable number" of horses and mules. More than one trooper rode with his reins in one hand and a cup of brandy in the other, and many were in exceptionally high spirits by the time they reached their bivouac at Lebanon Church that night.[13]

Sherman's orders to "disturb" whatever Rebel cavalry was south of McAfee's Bridge also set another column in motion on July 15. At 5:00 A.M., about the same time Seidel reached Cumming, Lieutenant Colonel Jonathan Biggs, a "stalwart farmer" from Westfield, Illinois, led his 123rd Illinois Mounted Infantry and most of Captain Adam Pinkerton's 72nd Indiana south from Newtown Crossroads. Major William Jennings's 7th Pennsylvania followed from Lebanon Mill and joined the column somewhere near the Chattahoochee, swelling Biggs's ranks to perhaps 1,000 strong.

Crossing McAfee's Bridge, passing through the 3rd Brigade's picket lines on the south side of the river, their route took them within hailing distance of a log cabin, where a wizened old man stood by the fence, watching. When some 72nd Indiana boys asked how far it was to Atlanta, he said he had never been there but reckoned it was about sixteen miles.

Never been to Atlanta? The Hoosiers exchanged quizzical glances. "How long have you lived here?" one of them asked.

"Ever sense I kin ric'lick," the man answered.

"How far is it to Cross Keys?"

"I don't know," was the gruff reply.

A short time later these troopers passed a large chestnut tree with two crossed keys carved in the trunk where some of the bark had been peeled back. Three notches were cut underneath, indicating it was three miles to Cross Keys. Upon reaching the little crossroads settlement, Biggs's advance guard was greeted with a ragged burst of firing.

Swinging down from their saddles, the 72nd Indiana and the 123rd Illinois quickly formed a line of battle while the number fours led the horses to the rear. Like the rest of the Lightning Brigade, both regiments had long since abandoned the cumbersome two-rank formation where men armed with muzzle-loaders stood elbow to elbow to maximize their firepower. The rapid rate of fire of their Spencer rifles allowed them to spread out, taking advantage of whatever cover was available. Together with the 7th Pennsylvania, armed with shorter Spencer carbines, Biggs's skirmishers pushed the Rebel pickets back on their reserves at Prospect Church. Here resistance stiffened, and Biggs learned from prisoners he was facing Colonel George G. Dibrell's brigade of Tennessee cavalry.

For the next two or three hours, the fighting seesawed back and forth, with neither side gaining any real advantage. Fearing Dibrell might be maneuvering to turn his flank and cut his line of retreat back to McAfee's Bridge, Biggs ordered his three regiments to withdraw about midafternoon. Casualties were light. Only one Federal trooper had been wounded.

Just south of the Chattahoochee, Biggs steered his column into a ten-acre field, where each man paused long enough to tie four to six shocks of freshly bundled oats to his saddle. Leaving nothing behind but stubble, the blue ranks filed back across McAfee's Bridge and divided, the 123rd Illinois and 72nd Indiana taking the road north to Newtown Crossroads while the 7th Pennsylvania followed the Old Alabama Road west to Lebanon Mill. The Pennsylvania boys had ransacked the Cross Keys post office, and as they rode back to camp, they snickered over letters addressed to "My dear Honie," "My Sweet Duckie," or "My own dear Lassie."[14]

Eli Long was not as amused with his mail. The previous day, he had again written to General Thomas's headquarters, pointing out that General McPherson had asked for Company B of the 1st Ohio Cavalry to serve as his escort, "provided the Regimental, Brigade, and Division Commanders were willing for the detail to be made." Long reiterated that neither he nor Garrard had given their permission. "I would also further state," he added pointedly, ". . . that this now makes the fourth company (one third) of this regiment that is on Detached Service away from the Regiment."

On July 15, Long received a letter from Garrard's headquarters, advising him that Company A of the 1st Ohio "yesterday went beyond Alpharetta, and beyond Cumming, very much further than there was any necessity of going for the purpose of obtaining forage and while absent committed shameful depredating." Garrard ordered him to "have the matter investigated" and "forward the report of the investigation with the name of the Lieutenant commanding to these Hd. Qrs."

Long must have thrown up his hands in frustration. Did anyone understand? Company A was in Nashville and had not served with the 1st Ohio since the war began.[15]

While Long fumed, Garrard made plans for another foray across the Chattahoochee. He ordered the 4th Michigan to be ready to march at 8:00 A.M., July 16, and directed the Board of Trade Battery, parked near his headquarters at Lebanon Mill, to have two guns ready to roll without their caissons. As instructed, the battery's 1st section had their teams hitched up at 7:00 the next morning and the 4th Michigan waited for the bugles to sound "To Horse."

When no orders came, Private Dennis Falby, a young recruit in the 4th Michigan, sat down on a log near his tent to clean his carbine. "Careless," "quick tempered," and "insubordinate," Falby did not have many friends. No one was paying him much attention until a gunshot shattered the stillness. Startled troopers who hurried to the scene found Falby clutching his left foot. Blood was streaming from a wound between his second and third toes, and he gave the age-old excuse, "I didn't know it was loaded." A wounded comrade was usually the object of tenderest concern, but Falby's comrades immediately suspected him of trying to get a medical discharge. "By God," muttered one onlooker, "he done that a purpose." "He did not get much sympathy," noted another.

As the sun climbed higher in the summer sky, the 4th Michigan remained rooted in the shade near Newtown Crossroads. The Board of Trade battery lolled at Lebanon Mill, their orders countermanded by a telegram from Vining's Station.[16]

"I have heard from General Stoneman . . . ," Sherman had wired McPherson late on July 15. "He will be in to-night [sic], and I have ordered General Blair [and his XVII Corps] to move for Roswell to-morrow. You may, therefore, make all preparation to move out toward the Stone Mountain the day after to-morrow. Notify General Garrard to move in connection with you, sending his trains to yours. That Augusta [rail]road must be destroyed and occupied between Decatur and Stone Mountain by you and General Garrard."

McPherson accordingly issued orders on July 16 for his XV and XVI Corps to leave the fortified bluffs opposite Roswell at 5:30 the next morning and take the Shallow Ford Road south to Nancy's Creek. Blair's XVII Corps, still en route from Turner's Ferry, would cross the Chattahoochee on the rebuilt bridge at Roswell and catch up as soon as possible.

As for Garrard, McPherson sent him orders to move his command across McAfee's Bridge at 5:30 A.M., July 17, and push out to the vicinity of Nancy's Creek, picketing the roads to his left and front and opening communication with the infantry on his right. "He will also leave a sufficient guard for McAfee's Bridge," McPherson ordered, "and one regiment to be stationed near Roswell to form part of the guard for trains and to patrol the country in the vicinity."[17]

Garrard's own supply train, escorted by the 3rd battalion of the 3rd Ohio, had returned from Marietta on July 15. Understandably reluctant to assign a full regiment to this duty, Garrard, upon receipt of McPherson's orders, directed the eight remaining companies of the oft-depleted 1st Ohio to stay behind "in connection with (3) three Regiments of Infantry detailed from [the] Army [of] Tennessee to guard the trains" and "picket the roads as Col. Long has picketed them."

He designated Long's other regiments, the 3rd and 4th Ohio, as the "sufficient force" McPherson wanted to guard McAfee's Bridge. Long ordered them to draw six days' rations, 100 rounds of ammunition for each man, and all the forage their horses could carry. "The trains will be found about one mile this side of Roswell and everything needed from the wagons must be obtained at once," he warned. "All the wagons will be returned to the trains this evening."

After replenishing their supplies, both regiments broke camp at Lebanon Church and headed east on the Old Alabama Road. Crossing the Chattahoochee at McAfee's Bridge, they bivouacked a mile south of the river, relieving Abe Miller's pickets, who presumably returned to the camps at Newtown Crossroads, where troopers from the 1st and 3rd Brigades spent the afternoon of July 16 drawing shirts, pants, socks, hardtack, bacon, coffee, and ammunition. That evening, after all the haversacks and cartridge boxes were full, the wagons began rolling back to Roswell.[18]

At daylight on July 17, the Federal armies began to stir. As Sherman had directed, Brigadier General Thomas J. Wood's division of Thomas's IV Corps left their breastworks on the hills on the south side of the Chattahoochee at Powers' Ferry and slipped three miles downstream to cover the laying of two pontoon bridges at Pace's Ferry. "Gen. Wood give [sic] the Pioneers one hour to lay the pontoons down," noted an Ohio soldier. "They did it in one hour and 8 minutes."

Before the last boat was even in position, George Thomas came tiptoeing across the stringers, accompanied by three of his staff. The XIV Corps followed at 11:00 A.M., then the XX Corps. In a masterpiece of maneuver, Sherman had engineered an almost bloodless triumph, crossing the Chattahoochee in the face of over 50,000 Confederate defenders. From Pace's Ferry and Powers' Ferry, from Sope Creek and Shallow Ford, all roads led to Atlanta, and his armies began pushing forward, almost 100,000 strong.[19]

The cavalry, however, was late getting started. Kenner Garrard left his headquarters at Lebanon Mill at 5:00 A.M. and headed for McAfee's Bridge with the 7th Pennsylvania and the Chicago Board of Trade Battery. The rest of Bob Minty's brigade, the 4th Michigan and 4th Regulars, camped near Newtown Crossroads with Abe Miller's four regiments of mounted infantry, waited until 6:00 A.M. to call in their pickets. "Boots and Saddles" did not sound until 7:00 A.M., and another hour or hour and a half elapsed before the last of Garrard's troopers got started, two hours behind the schedule McPherson had outlined.[20]

About 9:00 A.M., Miller's mounted infantry led Garrard's converging columns across McAfee's Bridge, followed by the Board of Trade Battery and Minty's 1st Brigade. A mile beyond the bridge, they passed through Eli Long's picket lines and turned to the right, moving south in a pall of heat and dust. Taking the same road Lieutenant Colonel Biggs had traveled two days earlier, the column crossed Nancy's Creek and threaded past a few scattered farmhouses until fifteen or twenty shots brought the advance guard up short at Cross Keys.

Garrard's orders were to maintain contact with the infantry on his right, and rather than press the issue, he recalled Miller's brigade and made camp about 3:00 P.M. Later that evening, he wrote to Major General John A. Logan, commanding McPherson's XV Corps:

> I am in camp about a mile on the left of your line. I left Colonel Long with two regiments of his brigade at the bridge to picket the Stone Mountain and Pinckney[ville] road, and to guard the bridge. Colonel Minty's left rests near Buchanan's, and the Peach Tree road, and all roads leading from the Peach Tree road toward the river on the left are picketed. Patrols have been out well to the front, and

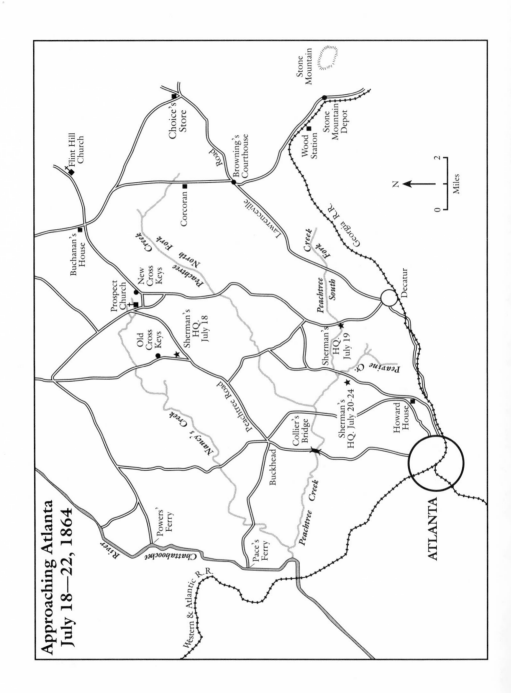

Approaching Atlanta
July 18–22, 1864

find but few rebels, and most of their tracks lead toward Atlanta or Buck Head. I learn since being here that there are two Cross Keys. The one on the maps is the old one, where there was a post-office some years since, but the name and the post-office were transferred to the present position, some four miles to the east. This will account for the fact that both you and I are so near Cross Keys. We are some four or five miles east of the point laid down on the map as Cross Keys, and about where we were ordered. Buchanan's is only one house. Please send this to General McPherson.[21]

Logan and McPherson forwarded this note to Sherman, who had crossed the Chattahoochee either on the pontoons at Powers' Ferry or the trestle bridge the 36th Indiana Infantry had completed on July 16. He had spent the day at the headquarters of Howard's IV Corps on land lot number 165, three-quarters of a mile south of the river, and all the reports he received told the same story. Resistance was light, mostly dismounted cavalry; all three armies would be astride Nancy's Creek by nightfall. Pleased with the progress his troops were making, shortly before noon Sherman drafted orders for the next day, directing Thomas's Army of the Cumberland to continue south toward Buckhead, occupying the ridge separating Nancy's and Peachtree creeks. Schofield's Army of the Ohio was to move past Old Cross Keys, aligning with Thomas's left, while McPherson's Army of the Tennessee crossed Nancy's Creek and moved southeast toward Stone Mountain to "secure strong ground within four miles of Schofield's position."

Leaving a four-mile gap in the center of the line between Schofield's left and McPherson's right was an open invitation to disaster, but it was a risk Sherman was willing to take in order to cut the railroad to Augusta. Convinced that Johnston would not interfere, he ordered McPherson to "push" Garrard's cavalrymen to the vicinity of Stone Mountain and have them disable the Georgia Railroad before retiring to a position on the front and left flank of the XV Corps.

McPherson issued detailed instructions that evening, directing Garrard to "move his command at 5:00 A.M. by the most practicable road or roads in his front to the railroad, and do what damage he can to it by burning bridges and culverts, piling rails on the track and setting them on fire so as to heat and warp the iron, tearing up the ties, piling them up, putting the iron rails on top, and setting the ties on fire."

In a closing paragraph addressed to all his commanders but obviously meant for Garrard, McPherson added, "The importance of making a break in the railroad cannot be overestimated, and the general commanding trusts that all will act with that spirit and determination which is the best guarantee of success."[22]

Garrard roused his troopers at 3:30 A.M. on July 18. He sent Lieutenant Trumbull D. Griffin and the 1st and 3rd sections of the Board of Trade Battery back to join Long's 2nd Brigade at McAfee's Bridge and corralled the sick and dismounted men and the 1st Brigade band to stay in camp with the pack mules and led horses. The rest of the command swung into the saddle at 5:00 A.M., carrying two days' rations.

Companies A, E, and I of the 1st battalion of the 7th Pennsylvania Cavalry led Bob Minty's 1st Brigade and the 2nd section of the Board of Trade Battery east on the Peachtree Road.[23] Abe Miller's Lightning Brigade followed at 5:40 A.M., bringing up the rear. At J. W. Buchanan's house, where the column turned to the right on the road to Stone Mountain, scores of slaves flocked to the roadside, eager to "see dem Yankees."

"Among the number was the funniest creature of the human species we ever saw," wrote Sergeant Ben Magee of the 72nd Indiana. "She was just about as thick as she was high, and the laughing surface of her face was simply extensive. She would weigh 300 pounds, and came waddling right out into the road, frightening our horses, and began immediately to talk and chatter like a parrot: 'Where all you'uns gwine to?' We told her we were going down here to tear up the railroad. 'What yu'uns want to tar up de railroad fo'?' 'To keep the rebels from using it.' This puzzled her, and for a second she was silent, when some one told her we were Yankees. She was the very picture of astonishment, and said 'No!' We told her we were, for a fact; when she raised her hands and said, 'Dey dun tole us you all had horns!'"

Leaving the slaves gaping in awe, Garrard's column continued south. Six miles below Buchanan's, the three Pennsylvania companies in the advance guard reached Browning's Courthouse, where they encountered forty or fifty Rebel horsemen. Drawing their Spencers, the Pennsylvanians dismounted, fully expecting to find Wheeler's cavalry ready and waiting for them. But the fierce resistance they anticipated never materialized and about 1:00 P.M. Garrard's skirmishers struck the Georgia Railroad a mile west of the Stone Mountain depot. While Captain Benjamin S. Dartt's 2nd battalion of the 7th Pennsylvania came up on foot to begin tearing up rails and ties, the advance guard followed the track eastward toward Stone Mountain, accompanied by Lieutenant Samuel Edge of the Signal Corps.[24]

Garrard dismounted the rest of the command a couple of miles to the rear, near Browning's Courthouse. Leaving a sizable reserve (probably the 98th and 123rd Illinois) and both pieces of artillery to guard the horses, he sent five regiments double-quicking toward the railroad. Huffing, red-faced troopers from Bob Minty's 7th Pennsylvania, 4th Regulars, and 4th Michigan lined up on the left of Dartt's battalion, while two of Abe Miller's regiments, the 17th and 72nd Indiana, formed on the right.

"When we got to the road we were told that a heavy force of the enemy were near and that we should destroy as much as possible before they came upon us," noted Sergeant Ben Magee.[25]

Laying down their carbines, Minty's 1st Brigade lined up shoulder to shoulder along one side of the track. At an officer's command, the men grabbed the near rail with both hands, and heaved rails, crossties, and all over to one side. Prying the crossties loose, they piled them up with any other wood they could find, balanced rails across the top of the heap, and set it on fire. "The boys engaged in [the] destruction resemble *fiends*," declared Private John Lemmon of the 4th Michigan.

This railroad business was new to Miller's 17th and 72nd Indiana, and they milled around, not quite sure what to do, until Garrard rode up and had them build fires at the ends of each rail. The Hoosiers were skeptical at first, but they tore down sections of a board fence on each side of the right-of-way and soon had a hundred fires kindled up and down the track. As the fires burned hotter, the iron rails began to expand. Animated by the intense heat, they writhed like serpents, hurling spikes and crossties in every direction. Fascinated with these results, the men hurried off to find more wood. Sweat poured down their faces as they furiously stoked the fires in the glare of the searing summer sun. "It was fun for us," said Sergeant Magee, "and we worked nearly hard enough to kill ourselves."[26]

They had been toiling for about an hour when Brigadier General Joseph A. Lightburn's brigade of the XV Corps came up on their right at 3:00 P.M. Stacking arms, the foot soldiers began overturning the track in the direction of Decatur.[27]

By this time, the three Pennsylvania companies Garrard had sent toward the Stone Mountain depot had returned and reported they had run into Rebel cavalry. Eager to learn just how many Confederates were massing on his left, about 5:00 P.M. Bob Minty sent Captain Levi T. Griffin's Company I of the 4th Michigan Cavalry to reconnoiter. The rest of the regiment soon followed, but a half mile west of the depot they met Griffin's company coming back.

Griffin reported he had charged into town only to find the Rebel cavalry "pretty strongly posted." Deeming it "expedient to fall back," he had extricated his little command without loss. Someone relayed this information to Minty, and in a few minutes orders came back announcing Garrard would withdraw before dark. The 4th Michigan was to cover the retreat.

Lightburn's infantry had already pulled back, after tearing up a mile and a half of track, and the rest of Garrard's men fell in behind them as they trudged toward Browning's Courthouse. Turning left at the courthouse, the foot soldiers continued west to rejoin the rest of the XV Corps at Henderson's Mill, while tired cavalrymen stopped to reclaim their horses. After watering their thirsty mounts in a nearby branch of Peachtree Creek, they made camp about three miles north of the railroad.

The 4th Michigan followed at dusk. "We done a good thing—and easily too," a weary Lieutenant Albert Potter wrote in his diary.

Garrard agreed and reported to McPherson that night:

> In obedience to orders, I left my camp at 5:00 a.m., this morning to break the railroad between Stone Mountain and Decatur. At Browning's Court-House I struck the rebel pickets, and skirmished for three miles to the railroad which I effectually destroyed for more than two miles, including several culverts [a wood yard] and the water tank at Stone Mountain depot. The only force I had opposed to me, as well as I can learn, was one brigade. I sent a force into Stone Mountain, and found the rebels there about 5:00 p.m., but not in force. The depot was not burned.[28]

A courier delivered this message to McPherson's headquarters at Blake's Mill on Peachtree Creek about 9:30 P.M., just as McPherson was completing his own account of the day's events. He enclosed it with his report and sent both documents to Sherman.

Darkness found Sherman quartered at the Samuel House residence, a large brick mansion at the intersection of the Peachtree and Old Cross Keys roads. He had spent most of July 18 with Schofield's column, watching the XXIII Corps advance against feeble opposition. By nightfall, all three of his armies were poised along the north bank of Peachtree Creek, just ten miles short of Atlanta. "It is hard to realize," he wrote to Thomas that night, "that Johnston will give up Atlanta without a fight, but it may be so. Let us develop the truth."

With that in mind, he had already issued orders directing Thomas to "press down from the north on Atlanta, holding in strength the line of Peach Tree [Creek], but crossing and threatening the enemy at all accessible points." Schofield was to continue south and cut the Georgia Railroad again at Decatur, while McPherson brought his three corps eastward along the railroad, linking up with Schofield if he heard guns booming around Decatur. Otherwise, he was to keep every soldier in his command "tearing up track, burning the ties and iron, and twisting the bars when hot." Garrard's cavalry would work in the opposite direction, toward Stone Mountain, destroying the railroad "as far as deemed prudent."

Just bending the rails was not good enough, Sherman stressed; the Rebels would simply straighten them out again. He wanted the track obliterated. "Pile the ties into shape for a bonfire," he urged, "put the rails across, and when red hot in the middle, let a man at each end twist the bar so that its surface become[s] spiral."

Couriers hastened copies of these orders to Thomas, Schofield, and McPherson, who each prepared detailed instructions for their corps commanders. McPherson had nothing to add to Sherman's plans for the cavalry, and simply directed Garrard to move his division eastward at 5:00 A.M., "along the line of the railroad, in the vicinity of Stone Mountain, continuing its destruction as far as possible."[29]

Garrard marched at the appointed hour, but not toward the railroad. During the night, some of his pickets had been driven in and reports of 2,000 Rebel horsemen in the vicinity had most of Abe Miller's mounted infantry scouting the roads to the north. Fears for the safety of the wagon train, pack mules, and led horses left at Nancy's Creek sent Bob Minty's 4th Michigan back to Buchanan's and then a couple of miles east to picket the Peachtree Road at Flint Hill Church. Garrard also ordered his smallest regiment, Lieutenant Colonel Edward Kitchell's 98th Illinois Mounted Infantry, back to McAfee's Bridge to relieve Long's 2nd Brigade and the 1st and 3rd sections of the Board of Trade Battery for duty with the rest of the division. "I did not feel justified in moving forward until all was secure," Garrard explained.

While he waited for Eli Long's two regiments at his headquarters at the Cochran (or Corcoran) house, a mile and a half north of Browning's Courthouse, he issued his Special Field Orders Number 1:

> The Division is ordered to move towards Stone Mountain and destroy the Rail Road eastward as far as possible. The movement will commence as soon as Col. Long's Command reaches here, which should be about 10 1/2 o'clock this A.M.
>
> Order of March—2nd Brigade, Artillery—3rd Brigade—The 1st Brigade will furnish at once one regiment to picket the road at Brannan's [Browning's] Court House and open communication with [the] infantry on the right. The other Regiments of that Brigade will remain in camp to guard the camp and all pack animals which will be also in camp with packs unloaded.[30]

Long received Garrard's summons before 8:00 A.M., presumably about the same time Kitchell's 98th Illinois reached McAfee's Bridge. He gave orders to march at 9:00, but many of his men had already left camp that morning, looking for wheat, oats, potatoes, apples, and blackberries. Recalling the organized foraging parties was difficult enough; rounding up enterprising individuals who had gone out on their own took even longer. It was 10:00 A.M. before Long and his two regiments started south. Even then, he had to leave behind the two sections of the Board of Trade Battery because several artillerymen were still missing. It was 1:00 P.M. before the last of these absentees finally straggled into camp.

By that time, Garrard had decided he could not dally any longer. Abandoning the order of march outlined that morning, he sent Abe Miller's three remaining regiments, the 17th and 72nd Indiana and the 123rd Illinois, toward Stone Mountain at noon with Lieutenant George Robinson's 2nd section of the Board of Trade Battery.

The advance guard, Captain Adam Pinkerton's 72nd Indiana, barely got beyond the picket lines at Browning's Courthouse when the surrounding woods erupted with the crack of rifles and carbines. Pinkerton's men dismounted, deployed a skirmish line, and soon drove the Rebels back to where the 4th Michigan had quit work on the railroad the day before, but more and more Confederate cavalrymen pitched into the fight. Soon Pinkerton was calling for help. The 17th Indiana and the 123rd Illinois dismounted and came running, accompanied by Lieutenant Robinson's two Parrott guns. About the same time, Garrard arrived with Long's 3rd and 4th Ohio and began wrecking the railroad just as fast as Miller's men could push the stubborn Southerners out of the way.

"The rebel force was said to be Dibrell's Mounted Infantry Brigade," noted Adjutant William E. Doyle of the 17th Indiana, "and they fought well on foot."[31]

Outnumbered and outgunned, the Tennesseans gave Miller's redoubtable Lightning Brigade all they could handle for the next hour or two. Bullets were flying thick and fast when Lieutenant Colonel Samuel C. Kirkpatrick of the 72nd Indiana arrived on the scene, fresh from detached duty with the 2nd Division's dismounted camp at Columbia, Tennessee. "We cheered him loud and long and went for the rebels bold and strong," Sergeant Magee waxed poetically.

Seemingly inspired by Kirkpatrick's presence, the Hoosiers fought their way into the outskirts of Stone Mountain, a picturesque little village framed against the largest mass of exposed granite in the world. The Yankees marveled at the huge gray dome towering 686 feet above the pine-studded plain, but there was no time for sightseeing. Rebel riflemen had taken refuge in and around the houses on the edge of town, where, Sergeant Magee said, "they annoyed us considerably." Sharpshooters firing from the upstairs windows of one house finally compelled Miller to send for one of Lieutenant Robinson's Parrott guns.

Taking careful aim, the artillerymen put their first shot through the upper story. The shell crashed into the front room about six inches above the floor, knocking a chair out from under the terrified owner and dumping him on the floor, unhurt, before exiting through the far wall.

Robinson's other gun also opened fire, and as Rebel sharpshooters came piling out of doors and windows, Miller's brigade charged. The Rebels broke and ran, but not before setting fire to 200 bales of cotton stacked in the railroad depot, three freight cars loaded with commissary stores, and three or four thousand bushels of corn.[32]

"This only saved us the trouble," shrugged Private Alva C. Griest, a fighting Quaker in the ranks of the 72nd Indiana, "so we did not grieve much." Still, it seemed a shame to let all those good things go to waste, and Griest and his comrades laid aside their rifles long enough to snatch hams, tobacco, and forage from the flames.

"My boys did some splendid skirmishing," Abe Miller noted proudly.[33] They had killed several Rebels without incurring a single casualty and captured a battle flag Dibrell's men dropped during their hasty retreat.

Deeming the dense woods around the base of the mountain unsuitable for mounting a pursuit, Garrard contented himself with tearing up the railroad as far as the depot and destroying the supplies not already appropriated by his men. Then, owing to the onset of darkness and reports of a fresh Rebel brigade in the vicinity, he ordered his men to fall back.

Mounting their horses, Miller's and Long's brigades and Robinson's artillery retraced their steps past Browning's Courthouse. The front ranks halted near Coch-ran's house about 8:00 P.M. and found the surrounding woods and fields crowded with the wagons and teams of the division trains and the tardy 1st and 3rd sections of the Board of Trade Battery, which had arrived from McAfee's Bridge during the afternoon.

Garrard immediately penned a report to McPherson, explaining his division's late start that morning. "We fought two brigades," he added, "but . . . I could only spare five regiments for this duty, and if I am to guard such an extended flank it will be impossible for me to do anything else. I would suggest the destruction of McAfee's Bridge, and that my line be contracted. I then can be of assistance to you and guard the left."[34]

Since crossing the Chattahoochee, Garrard had suffered only two casualties, one wounded, the other captured. He had cut the Georgia Railroad with surprising ease and the three Federal armies converging on Atlanta were meeting such feeble resistance Sherman thought "the enemy intended to evacuate the place."[35]

If Sherman could not understand Joe Johnston's seeming reluctance to fight, neither could officials in Richmond. Increasingly disturbed by the downhill spiral of events in Georgia, Confederate President Jefferson Davis had sent his chief military advisor, General Braxton Bragg, to confer with Johnston. Bragg's train reached Atlanta about 9:00 A.M. on July 13.

"Have just arrived without detention," he wired Davis. "Our army all south of the Chattahoochee, and indications seem to favor an entire evacuation of this place. Shall see General Johnston immediately."

Boarding a carriage, Bragg headed out on the Marietta Road. He found Johnston headquartered at the Dexter Niles residence, a roomy, white frame house three miles from Atlanta. Johnston greeted him cordially, and the two men spent several hours together. "We had no other conversation concerning the Army of Tennessee than such as I introduced," Johnston later wrote. "He asked me no questions concerning its operations, past or future, made no comments upon the one or suggestions for the other. . . . Supposing he had been sent by the President to learn and report upon the condition of military affairs here, I . . . proposed to send for the lieutenant-generals, that he might obtain from them such minute information as he desired. He replied that he would be glad to see those officers as friends, but only in that way, as his visit was unofficial."

But Bragg's visit was anything but unofficial. Before leaving Richmond, he and Davis had discussed the possibility of relieving Johnston from his command. Davis was reluctant to take such a drastic step at a crucial point in the campaign and apparently sent Bragg to determine if Johnston intended to fight for Atlanta. "I find but little encouraging," Bragg wired Richmond that afternoon.[36]

The next morning, he returned to the Niles house to meet with Johnston; his three corps commanders, Lieutenant Generals William Joseph Hardee, John Bell Hood, and Alexander P. Stewart; cavalryman Joseph Wheeler; and Major General Gustavus W. Smith and Brigadier General Robert A. Toombs of the Georgia militia. It was an interesting cast of characters. Bragg, who had commanded the Army of Tennessee until his stunning defeat at the battle of Missionary Ridge had forced his resignation, seemed to be nursing a growing resentment against Johnston, who had succeeded him. Johnston, in turn, despised Jefferson Davis and may have regarded Bragg as the

President's spy. To complicate matters, Bragg and Hardee were barely on speaking terms, while Hood and Wheeler had written several letters to Davis and Bragg criticizing Johnston's generalship. None of the participants recorded what transpired during the meeting, and that afternoon Bragg rode out to see the troops and visit the corps commanders at their headquarters.

Returning to Atlanta, he wired Davis on July 15 that after two meetings with Johnston, "I cannot learn that he has any more plans for the future than he has had in the past." In a long letter to Davis, he elaborated that Johnston apparently had no plans except to await the approach of the enemy. Valuable supplies and machinery were already being moved out of Atlanta and civilians were crowding the trains to Columbus, Macon, and Augusta. "There is but one remedy," Bragg declared, "—offensive action." While stopping short of recommending Johnston's removal, he suggested if any changes were made General Hood would give "unlimited satisfaction."

"Do not understand me as proposing him as a man of genius, or a great general," Bragg concluded, "but far better in the present emergency than any one else we have available."[37]

Before this letter could reach its destination, Johnston received a telegram from President Davis on July 16, asking him to explain the military situation in front of Atlanta and "your plans of operation so specifically as will enable me to anticipate events."

Johnston either had no plans to offer or did not feel obligated to share them with the President. "As the enemy has double our number," he telegraphed later that day, "we must be on the defensive. My plan of operations must, therefore, depend upon that of the enemy. It is mainly to watch for an opportunity to fight to advantage. We are trying to put Atlanta in condition to be held a day or two by the Georgia militia, that army movements may be freer and wider."

Johnston was at the Niles house, conferring with his chief engineer, when an officer handed him a telegram about 10:00 P.M., July 17. The words he read on the little slip of paper stung him like a slap in the face: "as you have failed to arrest the advance of the enemy to the vicinity of Atlanta, far in the interior of Georgia, and express no confidence that you can defeat or repel him, you are hereby relieved of command of the Army and Department of Tennessee, which you will immediately turn over to General Hood."

Johnston accepted the news stoically and sent Hood his congratulations. Early the next morning, Hood appeared at the Niles house with Hardee and Stewart, begging him to pocket the telegram and lead the army until the outcome of the impending battle for Atlanta had been decided.

"Gentlemen," Johnston said gravely, "I am a soldier. A soldier's first duty is to obey—I turn over the command of the army to-night!"

The three corps commanders then drafted a joint telegram, imploring Davis to suspend the order relieving Johnston. At Hood's "earnest request," Johnston agreed to remain at headquarters while they waited for a reply. At 5:20 P.M., Davis's response arrived from Richmond. The order relieving Johnston would stand.

"I returned to General Johnston's room alone," Hood recounted, "and urged him, for the good of the country, to pocket the correspondence, remain in command, and fight for Atlanta. . . ." When Johnston refused, Hood pleaded with him to stay with the army and at least give the benefit of his advice. "My earnest manner must have impressed him," Hood recalled, "since with tears of emotion gathering in his eyes, he finally made me the promise that after riding into Atlanta, he would return that evening."

If Johnston made such a promise, he soon reneged on it. With little or no fanfare, he mounted his horse at sunset and rode into Atlanta. The next evening, he and his wife boarded a freight train for Macon.[38]

The Yankees did not learn of Johnston's dismissal until July 19. John Schofield had crossed the south fork of Peachtree Creek and was shepherding his XXIII Corps toward Decatur when his advance guard sent him a day-old Atlanta newspaper. A bulletin on the front page announced Johnston had been relieved and replaced by Hood. Knowing Sherman would be along shortly, Schofield waited by the roadside.

When Sherman rode up about 10:00 A.M., Schofield handed him the paper, indicating a paragraph on the front page. Settling in the shade of a persimmon tree, Sherman hurriedly scanned a few lines. "Schofield," he asked, "do you know Hood? What sort of fellow is he?"

"Yes, I know him well," Schofield replied, "and I will tell you the sort of man he is. He'll hit you like hell now, before you know it."[39]

All three of Sherman's army commanders knew Hood. McPherson and Schofield had been his classmates at West Point, graduating first and seventh in the class of 1853 while Hood finished forty-fourth and might not have graduated at all if Schofield had not tutored him in mathematics.

George Thomas had been one of Hood's instructors at the academy and soldiered with him in the 2nd U.S. Cavalry. Even Sherman had met Hood once before, although he probably did not remember the lanky young lieutenant who made a draft on his San Francisco bank in 1855.

Hood's appearance had changed drastically since then. An outstanding brigade and division commander with Lee's Army of Northern Virginia, he had been badly wounded at the battle of Gettysburg when shell fragments riddled his left arm, leaving it limp and paralyzed. Less than three months later, at Chickamauga, a bullet shattered his right leg, forcing amputation at the thigh. It was an operation most men did not survive, but Hood did. Fitted with a cork prosthesis, the thirty-three-year-old Kentuckian now hobbled around on a single crutch, his withered left arm cradled in a sling.[40]

After listening to Schofield, Sherman concluded his new opponent was "bold even to rashness, and courageous in the extreme." Obviously the change in Confederate commanders meant "fight," but Sherman professed to be pleased. "This is just what we wanted . . . ," he later wrote, "to fight on open ground, on any thing like equal terms, instead of being forced to run up against prepared intrenchments. . . ."

Sherman and Schofield were still discussing this dramatic development when Grenville Dodge of the XVI Corps rode up. "Dodge, Dodge," Sherman greeted him with childlike enthusiasm, "glorious news—Joe Johnston is relieved and Hood is in command, and we will butt his brains out before to-morrow morning."

As Dodge dismounted, Schofield reiterated his belief Hood would attack within twenty-four hours. The three officers talked a bit longer, then, as Dodge remembered it, Sherman "sat down on a stump and issued his orders that concentrated his armies and . . . closed us all in on Thomas, showing he fully comprehended the situation."[41]

The orders Sherman issued directed each of his army commanders to "move on

Atlanta by the most direct roads to-morrow, July 20, beginning at 5 a.m.," and urged them to "accept battle on anything like fair terms." These instructions prompted McPherson to order Garrard's cavalry to break camp at Cochran's house and cover the left flank and rear as the army moved toward Atlanta.[42]

Bob Minty's 4th Regulars and the 7th Pennsylvania were in the saddle at 6:00 A.M. on July 20, heading north with the 1st section of the Board of Trade Battery to picket the Peachtree Road at Buchanan's. Eli Long's 3rd and 4th Ohio and the rest of the battery went west, threading past long columns of McPherson's infantry already crowding the road between Browning's Courthouse and Decatur. Abe Miller's 17th Indiana and 123rd Illinois followed at 7:00 A.M. with the division wagon trains, leaving the 72nd Indiana to bring up the rear.

Garrard was with the column approaching Decatur when he received orders, apparently verbal, approving the request he had made the previous evening to burn McAfee's Bridge and shorten his lines. Anxious to regroup his scattered detachments, he issued his Special Field Orders Number 2, directing Minty to move his entire 1st Brigade to New Cross Keys and cover the roads to the south and east, and north to the Roswell Bridge. These same orders instructed Ed Kitchell's 98th Illinois to destroy McAfee's Bridge and join the rest of the division at Decatur "by the most direct road from Cross Keys."[43]

Garrard's summons sent one of Minty's couriers riding east on the Peachtree Road to fetch the 4th Michigan. He delivered his message to the lonely outpost at Flint Hill Church (present-day Norcross) about noon. Calling in its pickets, the regiment marched at 2:00 or 2:30 P.M., joining the rest of the brigade at Buchanan's at 4:00 P.M. There was a brief halt while the Regulars and Pennsylvania troopers dozing by the roadside stirred from the shade and the artillerymen rehearsed their horses. Forming ranks, Minty's three regiments followed the Peachtree Road westward for another seven miles before halting at 8:00 P.M. to picket the roads converging at New Cross Keys. "The country is thinly settled," noted John Nourse of the Board of Trade Battery as the brigade made camp on the banks of Nancy's Creek, "poor soil, sandy, rolling ground, covered with small pine and black jack trees, a very poor place to live in."

While Minty marched to New Cross Keys, Garrard's 2nd and 3rd Brigades reached Decatur after several aggravating hours of jockeying past plodding columns of infantry and miles of stalled wagons. Thirty-six-year-old Mary Gay watched apprehensively as the Yankee troopers and then scores of teamsters from the XV, XVII, and XXIII Corps overran her yard, about a block north of the Decatur square.

"In less than two hours," she wrote, "our barn was demolished and converted into tents, which were occupied by privates and non-commissioned officers, and to the balusters of our portico and other portions of the house were tied a number of large ropes, which, the other ends being secured to trees and shrubbery, answered as a railing to which at short intervals apart smaller ropes were tied, and to these were attached horses and mules, which were eating corn and oats out of troughs improvised for the occasion out of bureau, washstand, and wardrobe drawers.

"Men in groups were playing cards on tables of every size and shape; and whisky and profanity held high carnival. Thus surrounded, we could but be apprehensive of danger; and, to assure ourselves of as much safety as possible, we barricaded the doors and windows, and arranged to sit up all night, . . . my mother and myself."[44]

Garrard and his staff made their headquarters in the parlor on the other side of those locked doors, while Eli Long's 3rd and 4th Ohio camped just north of Decatur and Abe Miller's 17th and 72nd Indiana and the 123rd Illinois bivouacked a half mile beyond the high railroad embankment on the south side of town. Pickets from both brigades watched the roads to the east and south and listened to the muted thunder of a furious cannonade.

It was just as Schofield had predicted. At 3:00 P.M., Hood had hurled five divisions of Rebel infantry at George Thomas's Army of the Cumberland. The headlong assault caught Thomas in an awkward position, with his back to Peachtree Creek and his troops halted in a disjointed line running along the crest of two parallel ridges. Heavy fighting erupted in front of the 2nd Division of the IV Corps and quickly spread to the right, engulfing the XX and XIV Corps. Thomas's men had not had time to dig in, and unlike previous encounters in the Atlanta campaign, this was a stand-up fight in the fields and woods. Yankee artillery hurled lethal loads of canister at point-blank range, and in some places dead and dying Rebels piled up only ten feet in front of the thin blue lines. But the howling gray ranks kept coming, driving a wedge between the IV and the XX Corps.

George Thomas watched from the north side of Peachtree Creek as the fate of his army trembled in the balance. Galloping up alongside two artillery batteries, "Old Slow Trot" urged the horses forward with the flat of his sword. "He is always working at his short, thick whiskers," noted an officer who saw him a few minutes later. "When satisfied he smooths them down, when troubled, he works them all out of shape . . . and it was at that moment, when our right and left, fighting in the woods, seemed ready to give way, he had his whiskers all out of shape. . . . But when he saw the rebels running, with us after them, he took off his hat and slung it on the ground and shouted, 'Hurrah! Look at the Third Division! They're driving them!' His whiskers were soon in good shape again."[45]

Thomas's lines held, but at a cost of 1,800 killed, wounded, and missing. Confederate casualties numbered between 2,500 and 5,000. That night, an exhausted Indiana infantryman sat on an empty ammunition box. "Atlanta," he mused silently as he gazed up at the Southern sky, "so near and yet so far. . . ."[46]

5

A COSTLY MISTAKE

JULY 21–JULY 22, 1864

Do not take counsel of your fears.

—George S. Patton, Jr.

Four days earlier, Sherman had talked about being in Atlanta within a week. Now, as the sun set over the carnage at Peachtree Creek, his optimism began to fade. "I think our only chance of entering Atlanta by a quick move . . . is lost," he wrote to McPherson that night.

Hood obviously meant to fight for the city and this only added to Sherman's load of worries. His wife, Ellen, had fallen grievously ill after giving birth to their seventh child on June 11. None of his anxious letters and telegrams about her condition had received a reply. "I should not be kept uneasy whilst charged with so high a responsibility," he complained.[1]

That responsibility was beginning to weigh heavily on him. On July 16, just as his army was preparing to strike across the Chattahoochee, he had received a telegram from Grant, warning that recent events around Richmond made it likely an entire corps from Lee's Army of Northern Virginia would soon arrive by rail to reinforce the Confederate troops defending Atlanta.

"I do not fear Johnston with re-enforcements of 20,000 if he will take the offensive," Sherman had responded cheerfully, but that was before Hood took command. Unlike Johnston, whom Sherman regarded as "a sensible man" who "only did sensible things," Hood was "eccentric," unpredictable, and dangerous. Peachtree Creek had proven that. The prospect of what Hood might do with several thousand fresh troops from Virginia suddenly loomed very large in Sherman's thinking.

"I am a damn sight smarter man than Grant," Sherman later confided to one of his officers; "I know a great deal more about war, military history, strategy, and grand tactics than he does; I know more about organization, supply, and administration and about everything else than he does; but I'll tell you where he beats me and where he beats the world. He don't care a damn for what the enemy does out of his sight, but it scares me like hell!"[2]

Determined to prevent troop trains from delivering thousands of Lee's battle-hardened veterans within ten miles of his left flank and rear, Sherman resolved to disable Atlanta's primary rail link with Virginia once and for all. Garrard and McPherson had already torn up several miles of the Georgia Railroad between Stone Mountain and Decatur, but Sherman wanted to disrupt traffic farther east by burning the trestles spanning the Yellow and Alcovy rivers. McPherson had proposed just such an expedition on July 14, but at the time Sherman had rejected the idea as too risky. Now, in the waning hours of July 20, he wrote to Kenner Garrard:

> After destroying the bridge at McAfee's, which I suppose is already done, you will send to General McPherson's guard at the bridge at Roswell your wagons, led

horses, and baggage, and proceed rapidly to Covington, on the main wagon and rail road east[,] distance about thirty miles from Decatur. Take the road by Latimar's [Latimer's], touching the railroad at or beyond Lithonia, and thence substantially along the railroad, destroying it effectually all the way, especially the Yellow River bridge this side of Covington, as well as the road bridge over Yellow River, after you have passed. From Covington send detachments to destroy the rail and road bridges east of Covington over the Ulcofauhachee [Alcovy]. Try and capture and destroy some locomotives and cars, and the depots and stores at Covington, but of private property take only what is necessary for your own use, except horses and mules, of which you will take all that are fit for service, exercising, of course, some judgment as to the animals belonging to the poor and needy. On your return select your own route, but I would suggest that by way of Sheffield, Rock Bridge, and Stone Mountain, or even further north if you prefer. I want you to put your whole strength at this, and do it quick and well. I know it can be done. . . . I believe that the cavalry is mostly withdrawn from that flank of the enemy, and that you can ride rough-shod over any force there; at all events, it is a matter of vital importance and must be attempted with great vigor. *The importance of it will justify the loss of [a] quarter of your command* [author's italics]. Be prepared with axes, hatchets, and bars to tear up sections of track and make bonfires. When the rails are red hot they must be twisted. Burning will do for bridges and culverts, but not for ordinary track. Let the work be well done. The whole thing should be done in two days, including to-morrow. . . .

If the McAfee Bridge is not already burned you can send a messenger to the guard already there to do it and move to Roswell. This need not delay your departure for Covington at once.

A courier delivered these orders to Mary Gay's parlor at 1:30 A.M., July 21. Garrard immediately sent riders to recall his scattered units, but the next morning, in a message acknowledging receipt of Sherman's instructions, he insisted he could not get ready to march on such short notice. Minty's brigade was at New Cross Keys, he explained, "with pickets in every direction from three to four miles." The 98th Illinois was still at McAfee's Bridge, and the 1st Ohio remained at Roswell guarding wagons. This left him with only five regiments and they were all picketing the roads around Decatur. "I desire to succeed, as you place so much importance in having it done," Garrard wrote, "and . . . I would have started with my five regiments here, but my force would have been too weak to tear up the railroad." He promised to march as soon as the troops arrived from New Cross Keys and McAfee's Bridge, "and by traveling to-night make up for the time lost in concentration." His pickets were constantly exchanging shots with Rebel horsemen on the roads to the south and east, he added, and a patrol sent down the Covington Road had captured two prisoners who belonged to a cavalry brigade they said was camped at Latimer's Crossroads. This would compel him to take a more roundabout route than the one Sherman had indicated, but, "If no misfortune happens I will burn the bridge east of Covington by 12 m. to-morrow. . . ."[3]

Colonel John W. Sprague's brigade of the XVI Corps marched into Decatur about noon to begin relieving Garrard's pickets. Ed Kitchell's 98th Illinois also arrived, having burned McAfee's Bridge the previous day.[4] Bob Minty's 1st Brigade left New Cross Keys sometime between 9:00 A.M. and noon, and although they took "a good sand road" south, herding the division's pack mules and led horses apparently hindered their progress and they did not reach Decatur until late that afternoon.[5]

While Garrard awaited their arrival, he issued Special Field Orders Number 3, directing the division to "hold itself in readiness to move at 4 o'clock this P.M." with "the entire effective force possible," including pioneers, one section of artillery "without caissons," and one ambulance for each regiment and brigade. The men were to carry enough rations, coffee, sugar, and salt to last for four days, and plenty of ammunition. All bands, wagons, pack animals, and led horses were to be left behind, guarded by one officer and a small detachment from each brigade, all under the general direction of Captain Henry B. Jeeter, the division provost marshal. Colonel Sprague's infantry, already posted on the roads in the rear of Garrard's outposts, would relieve the men on picket duty, but brigade commanders were to leave enough officers and vedettes behind, subject to Sprague's orders, to cover the division's withdrawal and "keep up [the] appearance of a Cavalry Camp."

After issuing these orders, Garrard delayed his departure, apparently waiting for Minty to arrive. It was 5:00 P.M. before Eli Long's 3rd and 4th Ohio, the center section of the Board of Trade Battery, and Abe Miller's four regiments of mounted infantry left Decatur, taking the familiar road back to Browning's Courthouse.

Minty's troopers, already weary after the ten-mile march from New Cross Keys, were left behind with orders to be ready to ride in two hours. Drawing the last of the rations from the division pack train, they ate a hasty supper and climbed back into the saddle at 7:30 P.M., ready for what one trooper anticipated would be a "long march, hard work, and perhaps heavy fighting."[6]

As ordered, members of the 1st Brigade band and the sick and dismounted men reported to Captain Jeeter, the division provost marshal, who had them move the pack mules and led horses to a ridge a mile north of town. Jeeter also instructed Lieutenant Trumbull D. Griffin, commanding the four Parrott guns and six caissons Garrard had left behind, to report to the infantry's Colonel Sprague.

In the gathering twilight of July 21, Sprague posted Griffin's guns on a hill near the Decatur jail, just below the courthouse square. From this vantage point, the artillery-men could see campfires flickering in a broad arc to the east, south, and west. Two 10-pounder Parrott guns from Battery C, 1st Michigan Artillery, were parked with their limbers and caissons near the railroad embankment on the south side of town. Sprague's 35th New Jersey and 25th Wisconsin Infantry bivouacked to the left and right of these guns, while the 63rd Ohio Infantry camped just west of the jail.

Earlier that afternoon, Sprague had sent six companies of infantry, two from each of his three regiments, to picket the roads to the east and south. Cavalry vedettes were posted well beyond the picket line. Together with Sprague's men, they were responsible not only for patrolling the roads but also for protecting an immense train of supply and ordnance wagons parked in and around the old cemetery on the east side of Decatur.

The town itself was largely deserted. Most of its 600 inhabitants had either fled or were cowering behind locked doors. "The rebs burnt the depot, warehouses, trains, & forage when they left here," noted John Nourse of the Board of Trade Battery. "Poor people here are short of food. Always the same old story."

Nourse and his comrades slept late on July 22 before getting up to feed their horses.

Since most of the battery's forage had gone with the two guns that went with Garrard, the animals had to be content with nibbling what little grass grew at their feet. The men busied themselves with washing clothes and cleaning harness. "We have to improve every 'half chance' we get," wrote Nourse, "or suffer by neglect."

The artillerymen were preparing their noon meal when some straggling foot soldiers wandered into camp and told them Rebel cavalry was probing the picket line. Looking southward from the jail, the Board of Trade boys saw the Michigan battery and its supporting infantry forming in line of battle. Concerned, Lieutenant Griffin hurried down to the railroad, where he found Colonel Sprague and asked what was happening. Sprague said it probably did not amount to much, just some Rebel cavalry. As a precaution, he had sent four companies of the 63rd Ohio and four companies of the 25th Wisconsin across the track to reconnoiter.

Convinced Sprague had the situation well in hand, Griffin started back up the hill. He could plainly hear the sporadic reports of rifles echoing in the distance, and upon reaching the jail, he ordered his men to harness the horses and hitch up the guns, just in case there was more to this than Sprague realized.

Griffin's men were adjusting buckles and taking the slack out of the trace chains when a Rebel shell burst with a roar in the road immediately to their left. There was another and another, all exploding deafeningly, dangerously near. Simultaneously, orders from Sprague directed Griffin to move two of his guns forward to support the infantry. Griffin started his 3rd section down the hill but had scarcely gone a hundred yards when a second order from Sprague directed him to fall back to his original position at the jail.

Looking southward, Griffin saw the Michigan battery come bounding over the railroad, closely followed by the confused remnants of the pickets and patrols Sprague had sent out earlier. They all came running up the hill toward the courthouse, where a company of the 63rd Ohio had raised the Stars and Stripes.

As Sprague and his officers dashed about, trying to form these fugitives into line, Griffin wheeled his two guns alongside Lieutenant Henry Bennett's 1st section. Together, at a range of 300 or 400 yards, the four breech-banded Parrotts began hurling canister into the oncoming gray ranks, while the Michigan battery unlimbered on the left to duel with the opposing artillery. The hail of canister and shells checked the Rebel advance just long enough for Sprague to rally his three regiments around the courthouse, but soon the long, gray lines started forward again.

Swarming over the railroad embankment, five brigades of dismounted Rebel cavalry, three ranks deep, struck Sprague's line obliquely, overlapping his right. Griffin's gunners raked them with canister. Sprague's riflemen blazed away from behind doorways, windows, buildings, and fences on three sides of the public square, but it was no use. The Yankees were hopelessly outnumbered. Some of them were already out of ammunition. The Michigan battery hitched up and moved fifty yards to the right and rear to meet a Rebel charge on the east side of the square. No sooner had they beat back this attack than they had to swing around to confront another assault from the west.

Griffin's men stood their ground near the jail until an officer ordered them to fall back. Hurriedly limbering up their guns, they started for the square, but at this crucial moment one of their teams got tangled up in a pile of scrap metal. Two of the horses stumbled and fell, and all the artillerymen could do was watch helplessly as both animals thrashed frantically in their harness, desperately trying to struggle to their feet. Seeing the battery's predicament, two companies of the 63rd Ohio fixed bayonets and waded into the advancing Rebels with cold steel, buying enough time for the guns to escape.

While the infantry and artillery fought to stem these relentless, repeated assaults, teamsters from the XV, XVII, and XXIII Corps and Garrard's division hitched up their wagons and urged their mules up the Shallow Ford Road at breakneck speed. "It was wonderful to see the men drive," noted John Nourse, "and they can thank their stars the road was wide and all the fences down. They drove at a tearing gallop three or four abreast, no stop[ping] for any obstruction."

The first inkling Captain Jeeter's stay-behinds had of the attack came when several Rebel shells ploughed into their camp on the north side of town. "We then went to work saddling for life," wrote Corporal William H. Records of the 72nd Indiana. Before they could finish, frightened pack mules, braying in terror, came stampeding into their midst. Records saw "horses . . . left tied to trees . . . the riders having run away on foot. Packs, cooking utensils were left laying & even *tents* were left standing & many that had got started with their packs rushed against trees in the jam, tore off the load and left it."

A few troopers, like Private Henry Heiney of the 72nd Indiana, took places in the ranks alongside Sprague's foot soldiers. "His Spencer was a great curiosity to the infantry regiment he fell in with," wrote one of Heiney's comrades; "he knew they were hard pressed and needed his help, and as he had plenty of ammunition and there were plenty of rebels to shoot, he entirely satisfied their curiosity," firing one hundred rounds before the afternoon was over.

Under cover of these raking volleys, Lieutenant Griffin redeployed his four guns, moving the 3rd section a short distance to the rear, while Lieutenant Bennett and the 1st section unlimbered on the south side of the square. Bennett and his men were still getting into position when Rebel batteries began lobbing shells at them, trying to find the range. Seemingly oblivious to the bullets and shell fragments whistling past, Bennett carefully sighted his twin Parrotts and quickly silenced the Rebel guns with a few well-placed rounds.

"His conduct with his section at the court house, as well as during the whole engagement was such as to deserve the highest praise and entitle him to the warmest regard of all who witnessed it," Griffin wrote. "Did he not exhibit something more than ordinary coolness and courage on this occasion, I should not under the circumstances have noticed his bravery."

No sooner had Bennett's shells done their deadly work than the Rebels charged again, this time from the front and both flanks. Leaving one gun facing the railroad, Bennett swung his other piece around to sweep the street on the south side of the square. His gunner yanked the lanyard, and the big Parrott rebounded violently, belching fire and smoke as it hurled a double charge of canister right into the Rebels' faces. The round had scarcely cleared the muzzle before Bennett's men swarmed over the gun. While one man held his thumb over the vent hole at the breech, others swabbed the bore to douse any lingering embers, reversed the sponge staff, and rammed home a bag of black powder and another tin of canister. As the loaders stepped aside, the man at the vent hole pierced the powder bag with a priming wire. Another hooked the end of the lanyard into a wire loop on the end of a friction primer, inserted the primer into the vent, and jerked the lanyard when Bennett gave the order to fire.

Swab, load, ram, and fire. Swab, load, ram, and fire. Again and again the gunners rammed their lethal charges home. The ground trembled underfoot with each ear-splitting blast, and the hot, smoke-filled air hummed with death. But there were just too many Rebels. The battery's infantry support began melting into the back streets and alleys.

"The rebs came up on both sides of us," lamented John Nourse, "through lots, behind fences, houses, etc., and shot our men like dogs, dropping them all round the guns, with not a soldier to help us, and not a shot from the Mich. battery, which had gone to the rear."

Private Edward C. Fields crumpled with a bullet in his bowels. Another bullet shattered Private Tom McClelland's left arm between the wrist and elbow. Corporal A. J. Close was shot through the jaw, Corporal Charles Holyland hobbled with a wound in his big toe, and Privates James B. Appleton, George Guckenheimer, William H. Tinsley, and John D. Toomey all went down. "We stood it for about three minutes," wrote John Nourse, "then moved back. . . ."

They found Griffin and the 3rd section about 400 yards to the rear, vainly trying to beat back the Rebel onslaught. Realizing it was hopeless to try to hold his position without infantry support, Griffin ordered both sections to withdraw. His men quickly limbered up their guns, collected their wounded, and trundled up the Shallow Ford Road.

Sprague moved quickly to cover their retreat. Riding up to what was left of the 63rd Ohio, he ordered Major John W. Fouts to form a line west of the road and keep the Rebels at bay until he got specific orders to withdraw. "We will hold until the last man falls," Fouts replied grimly.

Assisted by three companies of the 9th Illinois Mounted Infantry who had heard the firing while escorting a supply train down the Shallow Ford Road, Sprague's men held off the Rebels until the last of Griffin's guns passed safely to the rear.

"It was the hottest place I have ever been in for over 1/2 hour," declared Private John C. Fleming, a Board of Trade veteran of the bloody battles at Stone's River and Chickamauga. In thirty minutes, the battery had expended 125 rounds of shell and canister, one about every fifteen seconds. Of the 32 men present for duty, 8 were now casualties. The losses in Sprague's infantry were equally heavy, 18 killed, 118 wounded, and 118 missing out of approximately 900 officers and men engaged, and at least 17 of Garrard's pickets and vedettes were captured.

Estimates of Confederate casualties ranged anywhere from 100 to 600, and although Rebel General Joe Wheeler made much of driving the Federals from the field, he had failed to accomplish his larger objective, capturing the supply trains belonging to the XV, XVI, XVII, and XXIII Corps. The loss of these wagons would have virtually immobilized two of Sherman's armies, and the heroic stand that saved them earned Sprague a promotion to brigadier general and the Congressional Medal of Honor. But the fight for the wagons paled before the sound and fury of the epic struggle raging in front of Atlanta.[7]

About 2:00 that morning, Yankee pickets posted in front of Schofield's XXIII

Corps had made a startling discovery. The Rebel trenches were empty. Schofield immediately relayed this information to Sherman, who quickly came to a conclusion. Hood had abandoned Atlanta.

Hurrying to the front to direct the pursuit, Sherman reached the Howard house, a two-story dwelling near the center of the Union line. Looking across an intervening swale, he saw Rebel infantry cutting and trimming small trees to use for abatis and realized the truth. Hood had not abandoned Atlanta. He had merely contracted his lines, falling back to a new ring of works only two miles from the center of the city.

Joe Johnston had alluded to doing something similar to this in his vague response to Jefferson Davis's inquiry on July 16, but Hood preferred to think he drew his inspiration from what he called "the Lee and Jackson school." In a daring night march reminiscent of "Stonewall" Jackson's famous flanking maneuver at the battle of Chancellorsville, Hood took advantage of the absence of Garrard's cavalry to slip Hardee's entire corps past the unprotected left flank of the Army of the Tennessee. Shortly after noon on July 22, the mottled lines of butternut and gray burst from the woods, three and four ranks deep, expecting to fall on the unsuspecting Federals from the rear.

Instead, they found Dodge's XVI Corps halted for dinner, their arms stacked at a right angle with the rest of the Federal line. Grabbing their guns, Dodge's troops faced left and opened fire on the advancing Confederates. The crash of musketry and the roar of artillery brought McPherson at a gallop. He watched the XVI Corps beat back one assault and then another. Realizing there was still a half-mile gap between the head of Dodge's column and the left flank of the XVII Corps, he sent his staff officers to hurry up reinforcements, then spurred his big black horse into the woods, accompanied by a single orderly. Moments later, he blundered into some Rebel skirmishers who shot him dead.[8]

Sherman was anxiously pacing up and down the front porch of the Howard house when McPherson's adjutant, Lieutenant Colonel William T. Clark, galloped up and gasped McPherson was either "killed or a prisoner."[9]

Sherman was skeptical, but then another of McPherson's aides rode up and confirmed the worst. McPherson was dead.

"McPherson dead!" Sherman groaned incredulously. "Can it be?"

Quickly regaining his composure, he ordered Clark to go find McPherson's senior major general, John Logan, "and tell him that he has both the ability and the men that can stay Hood where he is, and I expect him to do it."

"Gen'l. Sherman was not much addicted to drinking," recounted an officer who witnessed the scene, ". . . but he always carried an extra large pair of saddle bags behind him on his saddle, and in one of these he had an extra large canteen made to fit the pocket. This canteen contained the best the Country or Medical Stores afforded and was always supposed to be well filled. After dispatching [his staff] . . . he went to his saddle bags, took out his big canteen and swallowed a full allopathic dose."[10]

In the meantime, Rebel brigades, following hard on the heels of the skirmishers who had killed McPherson, swept past Dodge's exposed right, striking Frank Blair's XVII Corps from front, flank, and rear. Blair's troops manfully stood their ground, scrambling from one side of their breastworks to the other to meet each new assault, but when Hood hurled three fresh divisions into the fight at 3:30 P.M., the XV Corps, on Blair's right, suddenly split wide open.

The calamity went unnoticed at the Howard house, where some of McPherson's staff arrived with the ambulance bearing the body of their beloved commander. Sherman had the stretcher carried inside, where a door was ripped off its hinges and laid across two chairs to form a crude bier. As Schofield and a few others looked on, Sherman wept over the lifeless features of his friend and subordinate, vowing that "the whole of the Confederacy could not atone for the sacrifice of one such life."

Tenderly drawing a flag over McPherson's handsome bearded face, he directed two aides to escort the body to Marietta. "Better start at once and drive carefully," he said in a voice choked with emotion.[11]

As Sherman emerged on the porch, Brigadier General Charles R. Woods, commanding the 1st Division of the XV Corps, galloped up and reported the Rebels had broken through on his left. Sherman could not believe it and sent him back to make sure. Soon another officer reported Confederate infantry swarming through the railroad cut in the center of the Union line. A few moments later, Woods returned and confirmed Hood's men had routed the 2nd Division of the XV Corps, capturing two batteries.

Sherman rattled off orders. Woods was to wheel his division to the left and strike the advancing Rebel column in flank. Schofield was to bring up all the batteries he could find, and Sherman personally directed them to some high ground in front of the Howard house. As the gunners hurriedly unlimbered their pieces and began lobbing shells and spherical case shot, Sherman sat astride his horse in front of the Howard house, watching intently. "I had never till then seen Sherman with such a look on his face," noted one-armed Oliver Otis Howard of the IV Corps. "His eyes flashed. He did not speak. He only watched the front. There appeared not only in his face, but in his whole pose, a concentrated fierceness."

His expression softened when he saw Logan leading the charge that plugged the breach in the Union line and retook most of the captured guns. This led Schofield to suggest hurling his XXIII Corps and Thomas's troops into the retreating Rebels before they could hole up in their trenches.

"Let the Army of the Tennessee fight it out!" Sherman snapped.[12]

What followed was some of the fiercest fighting of the war, as farm boys, shop clerks, mechanics, and lumberjacks from Iowa, Tennessee, Arkansas, Wisconsin, and a half dozen other states lunged across the parapets, grappling with swords, bayonets, clubbed muskets, and fists. The appalling bloodletting left 3,722 Federals and fully 5,000 Confederates killed, wounded, or captured, but by sundown the Army of the Tennessee had won its greatest victory and suffered its most grievous loss. The gallant McPherson was dead.

The tragedy might have been averted if Sherman had made better use of his cavalry. Instead, he had left McCook and Stoneman doing little or nothing on the north side of the Chattahoochee and impulsively sent away Garrard's watchdog pickets and patrols that would almost certainly have discovered Hood's flanking maneuver and given McPherson ample warning of his approach. It was a costly mistake.

"The army and the country have sustained a great loss by the death of McPherson," Sherman confided to Lieutenant Colonel Willard Warner as he rode back to his headquarters that night. "I had expected him to finish the war. Grant and I are likely to be killed, or set aside after some failure to meet popular expectation, and

McPherson would have come into chief command at the right time to end the war. He had no enemies."

Sherman recalled how circumstances had compelled him to cancel McPherson's plans to go to Baltimore that April to marry his fiancee. "He seemed to regret not having let him go," Warner noted. "He talked about it with tears."[13]

But soldiers have little time for grief. When Sherman got back to his headquarters at the intersection of the North Decatur and Durand's Mill roads that night, there was a telegram waiting for him. It was from Rousseau.[14]

6

ROUSSEAU'S RAID
DECATUR TO EASTABOGA

JULY 10–JULY 15, 1864

Over the mountains of the moon,
Down the valley of the Shadow
Ride, boldly ride . . .

—Edgar Allan Poe, "Eldorado"

It had been difficult, but Rousseau had done it. Despite serious shortages of men, horses, and materiel, he had assembled 2,700 cavalry on the south bank of the Tennessee River and marched them out of Decatur, Alabama, at 1:00 P.M., July 10. Delayed by a flurry of last-minute details, he and his staff followed two hours later, escorted by two companies of the 2nd Kentucky Cavalry.[1] By this time, the head of the column was already approaching the Flint River, a small tributary of the Tennessee, seven miles to the southeast. Fording this stream, the advance guard followed the rocky, undulating ribbon of road into the dense forest that crowded in on either side, leaving barely enough room in some places for riders to pass two abreast. Two miles beyond the Flint, bushwhackers fired a few shots at them. No one was hurt, and about 9:00 P.M. the Yankee troopers rode quietly into Somerville.[2]

Turning south, they rode on for another mile before halting near the West Fork of Cotaco Creek. Colonel William Hamilton's 2nd Brigade, the artillery, and the 1st Brigade's 5th Iowa and 2nd Kentucky wheeled to the right and camped near a plantation house, where Rousseau and his staff, having overtaken the column, made their headquarters. Presumably for want of space, the 8th Indiana moved to the left of the road and bivouacked on a little ridge so thickly overgrown with jack-oak trees that one trooper complained he could scarcely stick a knife blade between them.

While officers posted pickets for the night, the rest of the troops unsaddled and watered their horses. The column had covered seventeen miles since 1:00 P.M., and after feeding the animals from the supply of corn Rousseau had brought along in the wagons, more than one tired trooper fell asleep without waiting for supper. Others talked quietly over mouthfuls of hardtack and bacon, speculating about where they were going.[3]

Except for a few officers, no one seemed to know. Rousseau's adjutant, Captain Thomas C. Williams, noted that "all, however, felt that the expedition was of more than ordinary importance, and that it was intended to penetrate farther into the interior of the Confederacy than any similar expedition had reached. Hazardous it might be, but there was a smack of daring and dash about it, which was captivating, and gave to officers and men an inspiriting feeling different from that of an ordinary march."

Typical of the high spirits pervading the command at the end of this first day was

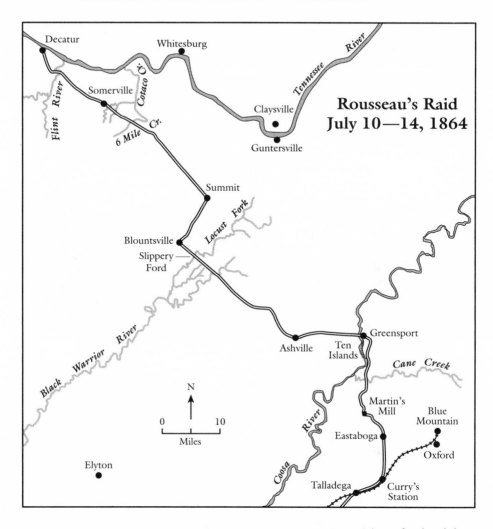

Rousseau's Raid
July 10—14, 1864

Company E of the 8th Indiana. The Hoosiers were preparing to bed down for the night when a trooper glanced about and asked, "I wonder what has become of Brantlinger and his mule?" Private Jack Brantlinger had been assigned to lead the pack mule carrying the company's extra ammunition, a task no one envied, and with good reason. It was Brantlinger's mule that had balked before leaving Decatur, forcing Captain John Boyer to unload much of the precious cargo and distribute an extra box of forty-two Spencer cartridges to each of his men. Even then, the mule had stubbornly insisted on setting his own pace, and despite Brantlinger's best efforts, the pair soon fell far behind the rest of the column.

Now it was pitch dark and there was no sign of man nor mule. The boys in Company E were just about to go to sleep when they heard someone rustling among the jack-oak trees where they had tied their horses. Soon they recognized Brantlinger swearing at the mule, the trees, the darkness. He stumbled about for awhile and then called out in a loud voice, "Cap Boyer, what will I do with this mule?" There was no answer, so again he hollered, "Cap Boyer, what will I do with this mule?"

Somewhere up on the ridge, a booming voice offered a novel suggestion. Brantlinger, his patience already at a low ebb, replied with some equally colorful remarks of his own. This brought peals of raucous laughter and catcalls cascading down the slope. Neighboring companies took up the hallowing and began cheering. Soon the other regiments joined in, and in the words of Private Eli Heaton of the 8th Indiana, "we just made those jack-oak bushes tremble with our noise."

A regimental band encamped near Rousseau's headquarters brought out their instruments and played with unbridled enthusiasm until the somber notes of "Taps" sounded late that night and the men finally settled down to sleep.[4]

The next morning, buglers woke the camps well before daylight with the rousing strains of "Reveille." Rubbing the sleep from their eyes, the men set about their morning chores. While quartermaster and commissary officers doled out the last of the corn and hardtack from the supply wagons, Rousseau and his staff scrutinized the breakfasting multitude of men and horses, looking for nonessential equipment and supplies. Most of the excess baggage consisted of tents and blankets, things Rousseau had ordered left in Decatur, but the 8th Indiana was actually overburdened with ammunition. Some companies had brought as many as 250 rounds per man. In obedience to orders Lieutenant Colonel Fielder Jones had issued the previous evening, the Hoosiers divested themselves of everything in excess of 120 rounds. Troopers loaded this and the other surplus property into the wagons returning to Decatur. Then, with Company A of the 8th Indiana in the advance, Rousseau's five regiments moved out at 5:30 A.M., accompanied by five ambulances, the pack mules, and Lieutenant Leonard Wightman's two Parrott guns.

Everything proceeded quietly until the advance vedettes flushed a couple of Rebel scouts out of the brush about 8:00 A.M. "Shot at them four times," Private Uriah W. Oblinger of the 8th Indiana noted in his diary.[5]

The rest of the morning passed uneventfully, and the column, no longer hampered by the cumbersome supply train, made good progress to the southeast, across Six Mile and Cotaco creeks, past Peach Grove to Sand Mountain, a broad, flat-topped plateau rimming the southern edge of the Tennessee Valley. Here the road became steeper as it climbed the abrupt face of the mountain, at one point rising over 200 feet in just a quarter of a mile. It was afternoon before the long file of horsemen struggled to the top. After a brief rest, they continued southeast, confiscating horses, mules, and bacon from the bewildered farmers along their route.[6]

Sergeant John N. Hurst, Corporal Ralph H. Jones, and Privates John N. Jones, James W. Larkin, and Uriah Oblinger of Company A, 8th Indiana, rode a quarter mile ahead of the rest of the column. Sometime that afternoon, they captured an uncomprehending Rebel soldier who, thinking he was about to be arrested by a Confederate provost guard, eagerly produced furlough papers to prove he was not a deserter. Knowing Rousseau probably had some questions to ask, Private John Jones waited beside the road with the prisoner while the rest of the advance guard rode ahead. It was not long before Rousseau and another officer wheeled up in a handsome carriage. Jones saluted and made a brief report.[7]

Rousseau studied the prisoner closely and then said gruffly, "I presume you are a spy; you intended to get behind a tree and count every man I have in my command as they passed, and then report to your rebel commander. We'll just hang you and save further trouble. Major, where's that rope?"

Protesting his innocence, the terrified Rebel pleaded for his life. After some intense negotiating, Rousseau agreed to let him go, on one condition. He must turn his back on the column passing down the road and run for the woods as fast as he could. If he slowed down or looked back even once, Rousseau would have him shot.

Scarcely in a position to argue, the Rebel sprinted for tall timber, his arms and legs pumping furiously. "Faster! Faster! Faster!" yelled Rousseau. The Rebel's speed increased with every word.

"He seemed to dodge the trees," noted Private Jones, "but overlooked the smaller growth of brush, which he swept down with the force of a cyclone. The scene was ludicrous to a laughable degree and yet pathetic; a man running for his life, or at least thinking he is, should not be laughed at." After all, they might all have to do some running before this raid was over.

Continuing toward the southeast, the column crossed Little Warrior Creek and Price Creek without meeting any opposition. At dusk, Rousseau's aide-de-camp, Captain Thomas A. Elkin, and forty troopers from the 8th Indiana charged into a small mountaintop village appropriately named Summit. They found nothing of any real value, except for some stale plug tobacco, which they promptly appropriated. After sifting through the post office, the Hoosiers professed great disappointment that their mail had not caught up with them.

They also captured a handful of prisoners, including at least two or three furloughed Rebel soldiers. Among the latter was a redheaded fellow who cried like a baby. Between sobs, he blubbered he was about to marry one of the local belles until the Yankees "tuk" him. He cursed his captors bitterly, but much to his surprise, an officer paroled him and his comrades almost immediately. Rousseau had no intention of burdening his column with captives.[8]

As darkness slowly drew its folds over the mountain, the rest of the command filed into town. They had ridden thirty miles since daylight, almost twice as far as the day before, and their gaunt, thin-lipped faces spoke eloquently of fatigue. Steering their horses into some open woods on the right of the road, they swung down stiffly from their saddles and bivouacked around an old mill near a Mr. Britton's place. The men dined on meagre rations of hardtack and coffee, but forage was scarce in this heavily wooded country, and most of the horses went hungry.

At 5:00 the next morning, the troopers climbed back into the saddle after a scanty breakfast that did little to fill all the hollow places in their bellies. As usual, the previous day's order of march was reversed. Major Meshack Stephens's 4th Tennessee, formerly the rear guard, now took the advance, followed by Lieutenant Wightman's artillery, the 9th Ohio, and Tom Harrison's 1st Brigade. The 8th Indiana brought up the rear, but the Hoosiers had not even gotten out of camp when shots rang out at the head of the column. Major Stephens's troopers had ridden into a carefully laid ambush just beyond the picket line. The Tennesseans returned the fire, the bushwhackers fled, and the column soon moved forward again.

This morning their route lay southwest, along the southern flank of Sand Mountain. Major Stephens's advance guard was wide awake after their early morning encounter, and before riding very far, they surprised and captured a Rebel quartermaster and eighteen enlisted men escorting four wagons. After questioning the prisoners and taking their parole, the Tennesseans pressed on, leaving the wagons for the rear guard to burn.[9]

About 9:00 A.M., vedettes at the head of the column spotted two Negro men and a boy riding down an intersecting country lane. Spurring after them, a few troopers confronted the trio and led them back to a house about a quarter mile up the road, where Rousseau and his staff had dismounted.

Rousseau was telling the men piling into the yard to get whatever they needed in the way of supplies and directing his officers to keep a close tally of what was taken. Turning to the owner, Thomas Nation, he introduced himself and explained his men were on a forced march. This was the first plantation they had passed that day, and they needed supplies.

By this time, bluecoated soldiers had broken down the door to the smokehouse and were carrying sides of bacon out to the road. Rousseau called to some of his officers, asking how much meat there was. About 300 pounds, came the reply. Rousseau directed them to see that it was properly distributed, and each regiment passing the house stopped long enough to pick up fifty or sixty pounds of meat. Troopers also took about 200 shocks of oats out of the barn and dumped it in the road for the horses to eat. Others wrestled two 150-pound sacks of salt down to the road and hoisted them on the back of a sturdy pack mule.

Nation managed to unlock the door to his storehouse before the marauders could break it down and inside someone discovered a barrel of molasses. Several troopers were clustered around the spout, filling their canteens with the sweet stuff, when Rousseau admonished them to leave enough for Nation and his family.

"They did not go around plundering," Nation admitted, "but only took what the general said they needed on the force[d] march, and after they had taken these things they came and reported it to one of their officers [presumably Rousseau's chief quartermaster, Lieutenant Frey] right near me." Other officers "pulled their little books out of their pockets and appeared to be putting it down."

Unaccustomed to spending all day on horseback, Rousseau had some of his men take a silver-mounted harness out of the buggy house and put it on one of Nation's mules. They were hitching up the planter's buggy for their general when Nation told them it was broken. Very well, Rousseau replied, he would leave it. He would, however, take Nation's fine set of harness, since there was sure to be another buggy somewhere down the road. "He appeared to be in an awful hurry," Nation observed ruefully, "as he hurried them up constantly."[10]

Within a few minutes, Rousseau's men were back in the saddle, trying to make up for lost time. But the ambush that morning, the captured wagons, and the stop at Thomas Nation's place had slowed them considerably. It was 10:00 A.M. before they covered the ten miles to Blountsville.

Blountsville was a dilapidated little town of 300 or 400 inhabitants. Finding little of military value, some of the men rifled the post office, while Rousseau and a few others visited the county jail, where they found three whites and four Negroes behind bars. When questioned, all four blacks admitted they were runaway slaves, while two of the whites claimed to be deserters from Johnston's army. The third, chained to the jailhouse floor, said he was being held for "mobbing" a man. Rousseau asked the jailer if this were true. The jailer assured him it was; the prisoner was awaiting trial for his role in lynching a wealthy citizen accused of raping two of his own daughters. Rousseau, with all his years of legal practice, had no sympathy for mob rule. Any man who tried to take the law into his own hands would have to face his day in court, but runaways and Confederate deserters had not broken any laws he felt bound to observe, and he ordered them released. The jailer blinked in disbelief. When he refused to open the cell door, Rousseau ordered his men to break it down. Realizing the Yankee general was dead serious, the jailer hastily produced a key and grudgingly set six of his prisoners free.[11]

After burning some cotton, Rousseau steered his horsemen southeast to begin the long, twisting descent into Brown's Valley. Six miles beyond Blountsville, his serpentine column splashed across the Locust Fork of the Black Warrior River at Slippery Ford and then wound past the knobby hills guarding the western approaches to Murphree's Valley, a long, shallow furrow flanked by two parallel ridges running northeast to southwest. Here the piney woods gave way to a few farms and pastures, and during the afternoon, Rousseau ordered the 8th Indiana's acting quartermaster, Lieutenant John W. Norvell, to take a small detail and round up some of the rangy beeves warily eyeing the column from the roadside.

The rest of Rousseau's dust-covered command trailed across the valley floor toward a low range of hills in the east. Early that afternoon, the advance guard reached James Brown's 280-acre farm, about ten miles east of Blountsville. Brown had a bay mule, a claybank mare, and a sorrel gelding standing in a lot next to the road, and an officer riding at the head of the column ordered his men to get them. Several Tennesseans dismounted and pulled back the draw bars that served as a gate. They were bridling the animals when Brown came running down from his house, complaining loudly to anyone who would listen. He needed those horses. They were the only ones he had. The troopers insisted they had to take them. Climbing into their saddles, they led his stock away, but a passing officer told Brown he was welcome to any of the broken-down animals the command left behind.

Brown did not particularly care about the war one way or the other. He was a farmer, and all he wanted was to be left alone. Until now, it had promised to be a pretty good year. He had oats curing in the field. Some of the wheat crop was already in the barn, waiting for threshing. But as his eyes darted over the harvest he and his sons had worked so hard for, the anger boiled up inside him. Those damn Yankees were taking it all.

Rousseau gave some orders to take forage and provisions and then hurried on after the advance guard without speaking to Brown. Troopers tied their horses to a roadside fence and began gathering bundles of wheat and oats from the fields. Without Rousseau looking over their shoulders, they were not as well-behaved as they had been earlier that day. Crowding into the yard "as thick as black birds," they used Brown's smithy to reset the shoes on some of their horses, then deliberately busted his bellows and took his hoof rasps and shoeing hammer. They looted his kitchen and demanded the key to the smokehouse.

About this time, Lieutenant Colonel Fielder Jones of the 8th Indiana rode into the yard and dismounted. Putting his horse in Brown's stable to feed, he walked up to the house, where Brown and his family stood on the porch watching. Brown's elderly mother-in-law, Mrs. Harris, railed at the troopers crowding into the smokehouse. She was eighty-five years old, she said, and she did not want to be starved to death in her old age. Jones looked at her and then stepped in front of the smokehouse. No more, he said to the soldiers trying to get inside. Locking the door, he took the key to where the defiant old lady was sitting. He introduced himself and tried to apologize for his men, explaining they had not had much to eat since leaving Decatur. In the awkward conversation that followed, Mrs. Harris mentioned she had a son, Peyton, who lived in Indiana.

"Good God," exclaimed Jones, "is that Peyton Harris, mother." He knew him well. Peyton Harris was "no secess."

At this point, James Brown spoke up bitterly and said if Jones ever saw Peyton Harris again, tell him how the Yankees treated his Alabama kin. Jones offered to arrange for Brown's family to get provisions at Decatur, but Brown shook his head. It would go hard on him if his neighbors found out he was drawing Yankee rations.

As the last of the 8th Indiana began passing the house, bringing up the rear of Rousseau's column, Jones handed the smokehouse key to Brown's daughter. Fetching his horse from the stable, he rode off to rejoin his regiment.[12]

The farms became fewer and farther apart as Rousseau and his men approached Raccoon Mountain late that afternoon. Threading their way through Allgood's Gap, they emerged atop a broad, heavily wooded plateau. At the head of the column, two 4th Tennessee troopers dropped out of the ranks and asked a white woman standing in the doorway of a rude cabin nestled among the trees about twenty yards from the road if they could have a drink of water. When this was supplied, they asked for something to eat. The woman brought them a corn pone. The two Tennesseans wolfed it down hungrily and were turning to leave when the woman asked, "And who mout you'ns be?"

Both troopers admitted they were Yankees.

"You'ns ain't no Yankees," the woman said.

The men insisted they were, but the woman shook her head.

"I know you'ns ain't no Yankees," she said, "for you'ns haint got no horns."

"Oh," replied one of her guests, "we are young Yankees, our horns haven't sprouted yet. The horned Yankees are in the rear and will be up directly." Leaving the woman looking anxiously down the road, the two troopers set out to catch up with their company.[13]

Sundown found the weary raiders still plodding eastward. They rode with their chins down, letting the reins go slack between their fingers as they swayed wearily on stiff, aching legs. The high-spiritedness so much in evidence when they left Decatur was gone now. They had been on the road for two days, or was it three? Places and events were beginning to blur against the grueling routine of walk, trot, dismount, and lead, but they kept moving, halting every fifty minutes or so for ten minutes' rest before starting again.

It was dark by the time they reached the eastern edge of the plateau at Blount Mountain. Here the road dropped through Aughtry's Gap and careened crazily down the mountainside, plummeting 600 feet in less than a mile. With only the faint light of a thin sliver of silver moon to guide them, the riders gamely urged their tired mounts over the crest and started down. It was treacherously steep. "At times my saddle would almost be on the ears of my horse," a 9th Ohio cavalryman declared with only slight exaggeration.

Most of the troopers soon dismounted and led their horses to keep them from pitching head over heels down the slope. Brakes squealed as teamsters tried to slow the ambulances, but limbers and gun carriages did not have brakes. Lieutenant Wightman and his artillerymen had to unhitch the guns, tie ropes around the axles, and carefully belay them down the slope.[14]

Private Edward W. Morris of the 8th Indiana was badly bruised when his horse collided with a tree, but everyone else made it safely down the mountain. After pausing to readjust their saddle girths, they mounted and rode on for another mile or so until the head of the column reached the Neely plantation on Gin Creek at 11:00 P.M. Here the order to halt echoed down the line, and Rousseau's exhausted troopers filed to the left and right of the road and slid to the ground without even bothering to unsaddle their horses. During the last eighteen hours, they had covered forty miles of some of the roughest terrain in Alabama, fought a minor skirmish, crossed three mountains, and forded a major river. But for some, there would be no sleep that night.

Calling aside Major Stephens of the 4th Tennessee, Rousseau explained rations were running short. The men were down to a few hard crackers, a little coffee and sugar, and whatever else they had scrounged from roadside farms. Rousseau wanted Stephens to take his tired Tennesseans and go with Captain Elkin to capture whatever supplies the Rebels had stockpiled at Ashville, five miles farther down the road. The rest of the command would join them as soon as it was light.

While Elkin and Stephens's 4th Tennessee set out for Ashville, the foragers Rousseau had sent with Lieutenant Norvell were trying to overtake the column with a sizable herd of cattle they had collected during the afternoon. Everything had gone smoothly at first, but as night came on, the beeves tired of the sport and began heading for home. Rounding up these strays before they disappeared into the darkness proved next to impossible, and more than one trooper, muttering something about not joining the army to become a cowboy, hurried to rejoin his regiment as soon as he got the chance. "I don't know which got away faster," chuckled John Jones of the 8th Indiana, "the detail or the cattle."

By 11:00 P.M., Private Jones and Lieutenant Norvell were all that was left of the detail. Between them, they had charge of a lone, white-faced Rebel steer, who became increasingly restless as the night wore on. Shortly before midnight, he darted past his captors and disappeared up the road, "with head and tail in a position that denoted top speed." Lieutenant Norvell angrily hurled a few choice invectives after him, then, turning to Jones, he suggested they catch up with the column and try to get a little sleep before sunrise. Jones nodded in agreement, and they rode on until the wee hours of the morning before they finally found the 8th Indiana sprawled along the roadside. By that time, even the hungriest trooper was fast asleep.

The raiders were back in the saddle again at 6:00 A.M., July 13. Stiff and sore after the previous day's grueling march, they moved along at an easy walk, occasionally stopping to load up bundles of oats curing in the fields along the roadside. The mountains lay behind them now; up ahead a broad, fertile valley glistened with dew. Seemingly in no hurry, the long column of men and horses took four hours to cover the five miles to Ashville.

They might have moved faster if they had known what was waiting for them. Captain Elkin, Major Stephens, and his Tennesseans had charged into Ashville about midnight, routing the small garrison without firing a shot. A Rebel cavalry patrol had brought word of the Yankees' approach some four hours earlier, and most of the townspeople had already fled, leaving the raiders in undisputed possession of a considerable quantity of Confederate flour, bacon, and corn. This was indeed a welcome sight, and when Rousseau arrived he immediately put his quartermasters, Lieutenants Frey and Langdon, to work distributing these badly needed supplies to his hungry men.

Rousseau then turned his thoughts to other concerns. Perhaps his inspector general, Captain McConnell, brought it to his attention, or perhaps he recalled the words Benjamin Franklin had penned in 1751:

> For want of a nail the shoe was lost;
> for want of a shoe the horse was lost;
> and for want of a horse the rider was lost;
> being overtaken and slain by the enemy,
> all for want of care about a horse-shoe nail.[15]

In any event, it was clear the rough, mountainous terrain had exacted a heavy toll in loose and missing horseshoes. Knowing a lot of hard marching still lay ahead, Rousseau instructed his officers to have the men check their horses' hooves and make sure they were properly shod. Regimental farriers were soon hard at work with hammer and rasp, nailing on the extra horseshoes each trooper carried in his saddlebags.

The rest of the raiders dozed fitfully after eating their fill or wandered around town taking in the sights. Private John Matz of the 8th Indiana donned a Rebel lieutenant's hat he found. The original owner, like most of the townspeople, had either fled or was cowering somewhere indoors. Undaunted by the apparent lack of Southern hospitality, the raiders treated Ashville just like any other town along their route, ransacking the post office with their customary diligence and visiting the county jail. Among the six or seven inmates, they were surprised to find a young woman of eighteen or twenty. She said she was a Union sympathizer and had been in jail for three months just for stealing some sewing thread. The boys agreed her sentence seemed unnecessarily harsh. Using a fence rail for a key, they pried the cell doors open, setting her and her companions free.

Despite their proclivity for opening jails and other people's mail, Rousseau's men generally respected private property. Seeking news of the war on other fronts, they did invade the offices of the town's weekly newspaper, the *Ashville Vidette*, and found the latest edition just as the printers had left it, the type set, the forms locked in place. The front page contained a speech former Congressman Clement L. Vallandigham had recently made in Hamilton, Ohio, bitterly criticizing the Lincoln administration. An adjacent editorial praised the notorious Copperhead leader as "a gifted statesman, orator, and patriotic exile."[16]

Rousseau thought the press could be put to better use. Culling several ex-printers from his ranks, he sent them with his adjutant, Captain Williams, to work up copies of the forms and circulars he had been unable to requisition before leaving Decatur. Under Williams's direction, the Yankee pressmen also set the type for a general order governing the conduct of the march:

HEADQUARTERS CAVALRY FORCES
In the Field, July 13th., 1864.

The Major General commanding calls the attention of officers and men to the absolute necessity of better attention to the stock of the command. It will never do as it is. Better care must be taken of the horses, or the rider will be afoot. Hereafter officers will see that every horse in their command is properly groomed and cared for; and will be held responsible for the same. There shall be no straggling under any pretext. Private houses will not be entered by soldiers on any pretext whatever—being a prolific cause of straggling. Such entries are generally made by those who maraud and rob. Such acts are denounced as unworthy a soldier, and will be summarily punished. Disgraceful excesses are reported to have occurred on yesterday, which will be investigated and attended to.

The Major General commanding tenders his thanks to the command generally for their good conduct and soldierly bearing, and hopes that such deportment will continue.

> By Order of
> Gen. Rousseau.
> Thomas C. Williams,
> A.A.A.G.[17]

Once a sufficient number of these had been printed, Williams's detail decided to remake the front page of the *Vidette*. Deleting some of the editors' secessionist sentiments, they inserted an article entitled "Distinguished Arrival," announcing:

> Maj. Gen. L. H. Rousseau, of [the] U.S. Army, paid our town the honor of a visit this morning, accompanied by many of his friends and admirers. The General looks well and hearty. It is not known at present how long he will sojourn in our midst. He expressed himself much pleased with the hospitality and kindness of the citizens of Ashville and the vicinity, and was apparently well satisfied with the manner in which he was entertained.
>
> The Staff of Maj. Gen. L. H. Rousseau, U.S.A., paid our office a visit this morning and kindly assisted us to issue our paper for to-day. . . .

Captain Williams and his men also inserted what one trooper described as "a most withering satire of Jeff. Davis and his Cabinet, denouncing them all as repudiators, scoundrels, devils and malefactors, the offscouring of Goths and Vandals." Adding a brief summary of recent Union victories, they printed a thousand copies, confident this latest issue would raise a few eyebrows among the *Vidette*'s regular subscribers.[18]

While his printers amused themselves, Rousseau was busy reshuffling his regiments. His appointment of Colonel William Hamilton to command the 2nd Brigade on July 9 had left the ill-disciplined 9th Ohio without a single officer above the rank of captain. Hamilton's successor, Captain William Stough, was described as "a fine infantry officer," but he had allowed his men to straggle badly during the march over the mountains. Hoping to restore some semblance of discipline, Rousseau ordered the younger, more energetic Hamilton to resume command of the 9th Ohio and relinquish the 2nd Brigade to Lieutenant Colonel Matthewson T. Patrick of the 5th Iowa. To help facilitate the change, Rousseau transferred Patrick's own 5th Iowa to the 2nd Brigade and assigned the 9th Ohio to Tom Harrison's 1st Brigade, perhaps hoping the 8th Indiana and the 2nd Kentucky would set a good example for some of Hamilton's miscreants.

Reorganized, refreshed, and reshod, Rousseau's men burned all the Confederate commissary supplies they could not eat and rode out of Ashville about 2:00 P.M. The 8th Indiana led the way, paralleling Beaver Creek as it coursed eastward through a narrow, sparsely cultivated valley. Flanked by the Beaver Creek Mountains on the right and Hines Mountain on the left, the bluecoated cavaliers rode all afternoon, the hot summer sun beating down on their backs. At 8:00 P.M., just as daylight was beginning to fade, Captain Elkin and a handful of Hoosiers struck the Coosa River at Greensport, fifteen miles east of Ashville. To their left, they could see two steamboats slowly churning upstream, too far away to consider giving chase. The Montgomery & West Point Railroad lay another hundred miles beyond the murky water eddying at their feet, and Rousseau knew he had to move fast if he was going to get there. Any delay in crossing the Coosa might well spell the difference between victory and defeat.

But getting 2,700 cavalrymen across the river was not going to be easy. The Coosa ran deep and slow here, and Green's ferryboat was moored on the opposite shore, 300 yards away. To complicate matters, Rousseau had already received reports that Rebel horsemen were waiting on the east bank, and he fully expected them do to everything in their power to stop him.

The first order of business was retrieving the ferryboat, a task Rousseau entrusted to Captain Elkin while the head of the column swung off the road to bivouac in a big cornfield bordering the riverbank. The two rearmost units, Companies D and E of the 5th Iowa, were still a couple of miles west of the river, lagging about 300 yards behind the regimental mule train. Halfway between the Iowans and the pack mules, Company D's commander, Captain William Curl, rode alongside the 2nd Brigade's foraging officer, Captain Jeremiah C. Wilcox.

A thirty-year-old native of Princeton, Indiana, Curl had been his widowed mother's sole source of support since he was sixteen. He worked the farm she rented, then leased another after moving her to more comfortable lodgings in town. Seeking out odd jobs when his own chores were done, he took his wages in flour and groceries.

Intent on buying his mother a home of her own, he had moved to the Nebraska Territory, but then the war intervened. Curl helped raise Company D of the Nebraska Battalion, which later became part of the 5th Iowa Cavalry, and had served with the regiment during all its marches and skirmishes. Between July 1862 and November 1863, he sent his mother $1,700, no small accomplishment for a man whose army pay was only $70 a month. Returning to Princeton on veteran furlough in February 1864, Curl found his mother sharing a house with another widow. Find a place of your own, he had told her; he would pay the rent.

But this was one promise Curl would not be able to keep. He and Wilcox were riding just ahead of the rear guard when six or seven armed men sprang from the dense underbrush, demanding their surrender. Both officers dug in their spurs and reined their horses toward the rear. A ragged volley erupted behind them, lifting Curl out of the saddle before his horse could take a single stride. Wilcox went down too, his right thigh horribly mangled by a large caliber ball and seven buckshot, while an eighth lodged in his right calf.

The shots brought the rear guard racing to the scene. A few troopers slid from their saddles to assist the two crumpled figures lying in the road. Others dashed into the underbrush, vainly trying to flush out the attackers. Someone summoned an ambulance and the Iowans gingerly lifted the painfully wounded Wilcox aboard, but Captain Curl was dead before he hit the ground. His men loaded his bullet-riddled body alongside Wilcox. Reaching Greensport about 9:00 that night, they buried him in a shallow grave in the cornfield. He was the expedition's first casualty, a grim reminder of what might be waiting for them on the other side of the river.[19]

The Coosa was Rousseau's Rubicon, the point of no return. Once across, there could be no hesitation, no thought of turning back. Any horse or trooper incapable of going the rest of the way had to be winnowed out now, and Rousseau ordered a thorough inspection of the entire command. The effects of three days of heat, hard marching, and short rations were all too apparent. Rousseau's inspector general, Captain McConnell, reported about 300 horses unfit for further service. There was an even larger number of sick and disabled men. Rousseau grouped them together in a special battalion and assigned Captain Joseph B. Daniels of the 9th Ohio to command. Coming from a regiment already short of officers, Daniels seemed like an odd choice, but he may have been sick, too. In any event, Rousseau ordered him to have the invalids ready to march at daylight, escorting the ambulance carrying the wounded Captain Wilcox and any men too sick to ride to the Union garrison at Claysville, forty miles to the north.

In the midst of these preparations, Jacob McElroy blundered into some of Rousseau's pickets about a half mile west of Greensport. Co-owner of the Dallas Iron Works in Selma, the thirty-four-year-old McElroy was returning from a business trip to St. Clair County, driving a pair of good-looking horses he had hired in Talladega. Troopers promptly replaced them with a couple of worn-out cavalry mounts and escorted him to headquarters, where Rousseau received the Canadian-born engineer with "the utmost courtesy and consideration."[20]

While Rousseau plied his prisoner with questions about the roads east of the Coosa, troopers led strings of horses and mules to water and feed. After caring for their mounts, they began preparing the evening meal and the quiet, comforting murmur of camp routine soon mingled with the scratchy chorusing of crickets along the riverbank. At the edge of the cornfield, Private John Jones and Captain Horace S. Foote of the 8th Indiana picked and ate blackberries in the pale light of the first quarter moon. Other Hoosiers squatted around smoky campfires, eagerly awaiting steaming cups of hot coffee. The water in the coffeepots was just coming to a boil when orders arrived at 10:00 P.M., directing Major Thomas Graham's battalion to saddle up and move out at once. Rousseau wanted them to hold the eastern approaches to Green's Ferry until daylight, then move four miles downstream to cover the crossing of the rest of the command at Ten Islands.

Grumbling and cursing, Companies E, F, G, and H of the 8th Indiana doused their cooking fires and saddled their horses. Forming ranks, they rode down to the landing, where the ubiquitous Captain Elkin and two thoroughly soaked scouts were waiting with the recently retrieved ferryboat. The squat, square-ended craft, commonly called a "flat," probably measured about forty feet long and perhaps twenty feet wide. Solidly built of beams and planks nailed or pegged together, the seams caulked watertight, the vessel's flat bottom curved up at both ends, allowing it to beach directly on the shore. A rope stretched across the river by a windlass passed through guides on one of the gunwales. By seizing the rope near the bow and walking to the stern, the ferryman and his assistant pushed the boat forward, repeating the laborious process over and over again until they reached the other side of the river.

Because of its low freeboard, the ferry could carry only ten or twelve men and horses at a time. First aboard was Sergeant Oliver J. Pursell's squad of Company E.

After landing on the opposite shore, they learned from some of Elkin's scouts that Rebels were already close by. Moving down the main road, Pursell posted pairs of vedettes across his front, holding the rest of his squad in reserve about a quarter mile beyond the ferry. Sergeant Tom Jackson's squad of Company E soon came up on their left and made similar dispositions in a cornfield, while Sergeant Milton Johnson's squad deployed in some brush on the right. Closer to the river, Company F quietly took cover in and around some old cotton warehouses, flanked by Companies G and H. Lieutenant Wightman and his two Parrott guns joined them, while other troopers ferried the pack mules and four remaining ambulances across in the darkness to avoid delaying the column the next morning.

By midnight, the last of Graham's men were safely across the river. Leaving their horses saddled, those not on picket slept on their arms. There were no fires, no loud talk. The only sound was the quiet rustling of cornstalks and branches as sergeants made their rounds along the picket lines, checking on their men. Pickets were usually relieved at two-hour intervals, but the late hour and the proximity of the enemy made this impractical. Graham's tired sentries stood watch all night, peering intently into the darkness.[21]

The object of the Hoosiers' sleepless vigil was Brigadier General James Holt Clanton's brigade of Alabama cavalry. Clanton had learned of the raid earlier that afternoon when a messenger brought word that 1,200 Yankee cavalrymen had spent the afternoon at Ashville, thirty miles northwest of his headquarters at Blue Mountain. Convinced this force was moving east toward the important iron works at Oxford, Clanton alerted Major William T. Walthall, the post commander at nearby Talladega. Then he rode out of Blue Mountain with 200 men from the 6th and 8th Alabama Cavalry, determined to keep the "blue bellies," as he called them, from crossing the Coosa.[22]

The son of "an opulent planter," Clanton was raised near Callebee Creek, Alabama. Like Rousseau, he had volunteered for duty in the Mexican War, practiced law, joined the Whig party, and served in the state legislature. He opposed secession, but when the war began he cast his lot with the Confederacy, raised a company at his own expense, and was elected colonel of the 1st Alabama Cavalry.

A tall, powerfully built man, with reddish-brown hair and beard framing a deep-set pair of flashing blue eyes, a hawklike nose, and high cheekbones, Clanton was "gallant to rashness," and "a perfect demon in appearance when aroused." He was fond of his liquor, and like Rousseau, his impulsive and sometimes outspoken behavior did not always sit well with his superiors. After a quarrel with Confederate General Braxton Bragg, he had resigned his commission and requested a transfer to the Army of Northern Virginia.

Instead, he was sent to northern Alabama, where he enrolled and equipped a brigade of infantry, cavalry, and artillery and was promoted to brigadier general. Many of his men were conscripts with little or no sympathy for the Southern cause. They formed a "Peace Society" and planned to desert at the earliest opportunity, but the plot was discovered and the ringleaders arrested in December 1863. Although a military court absolved Clanton of any involvement and commended his "zeal and efficiency in having the guilty parties properly prosecuted," his brigade was broken up and scattered among more loyal units.

Since then, his superiors had been reluctant to entrust him with another command.

"Gallant to rashness," Brigadier General James Holt Clanton commanded 200 Confederate cavalrymen who tried to keep Rousseau from crossing the Coosa River. A Mexican War veteran, lawyer, and Alabama legislator, Clanton was shot and killed by a former Union army officer in Knoxville, Tennessee, in 1871. Courtesy of Bill Rasp. Used by permission.

Most recently, he had served on Lieutenant General Leonidas Polk's staff, winning praise for skillfully evacuating artillery and supplies across the Etowah River. When Polk was killed on June 14, Joe Johnston wasted no time in transferring Clanton, whom he regarded as incompetent after the "Peace" mutiny, to Blue Mountain, an inconsequential post at the northern terminus of the Alabama and Tennessee Rivers Railroad. Arriving there on or about July 7 with the 6th Alabama Cavalry, Clanton had settled quietly into his new duties.[23]

Like Rousseau, he was eager to get back into the war, and twenty miles of hard riding brought him opposite Greensport by 1:00 A.M., July 14. What looked like a whole Yankee regiment had already crossed the Coosa at the ferry. Others were obviously preparing to ford at Ten Islands, four miles downstream. Clanton estimated his 200 men were outnumbered at least six to one. Undaunted, he decided to attack at dawn.

Dividing his small force in half, he deployed a hundred troopers from Lieutenant Colonel Washington T. Lary's 6th Alabama near Whisenant's Mill on the Green's Ferry road and sent Colonel Henry J. Livingston downstream with a hundred men from the 8th Alabama Cavalry to defend the ford at Ten Islands. He also dispatched a courier to Talladega, advising the post commander, Major Walthall, of his plans and urging him to send every available man to Blue Mountain at once.[24]

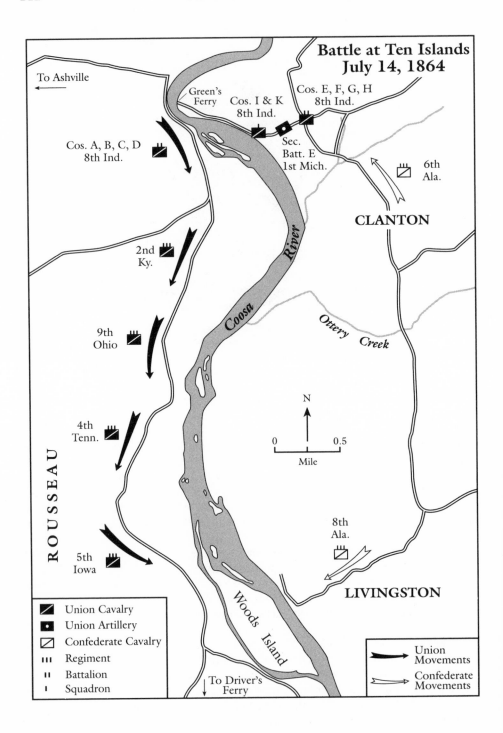

**Battle at Ten Islands
July 14, 1864**

To Ashville

Green's
Ferry

Cos. I & K
8th Ind.

Cos. E, F, G, H
8th Ind.

Cos. A, B, C, D
8th Ind.

Sec.
Batt. E
1st Mich.

6th
Ala.

CLANTON

2nd
Ky.

Coosa River

9th
Ohio

Ottery Creek

N

0   0.5

Mile

4th
Tenn.

ROUSSEAU

8th
Ala.

5th
Iowa

LIVINGSTON

Woods Island

To Driver's
Ferry

Union Cavalry
Union Artillery
Confederate Cavalry
Regiment
Battalion
Squadron

Union
Movements
Confederate
Movements

The Yankee camps began stirring well before daylight. At 5:00 A.M., Major Graham's battalion of the 8th Indiana started down the east side of the Coosa to secure the ford at Ten Islands. On the west bank, Captain Daniels's invalid battalion started northward with the ambulance carrying the grievously wounded Captain Wilcox.[25]

The rest of Rousseau's command was still lingering over morning coffee and a few mouthfuls of hardtack when the distant echo of gunfire came rolling across the river. Buglers sounded "Boots and Saddles," instantly transforming the tranquil cornfield into a milling mass of men and horses. Rousseau sent one hundred troopers, probably Companies I and K of the 8th Indiana, across the ferry to reinforce Major Graham's battalion. Then he hurried the rest of his column downstream, the 5th Iowa in the advance and the 1st battalion of the 8th Indiana bringing up the rear.

The fighting on the east side of the river had started when some of Clanton's men fired on the bluecoated cavalrymen picketing the approaches to Green's Ferry. The Hoosiers promptly replied with their seven-shot Spencers, and soon the sharp crack of rifles and carbines echoed up and down the length of the picket line. As the bullets droned overhead, Captain John Boyer and the reserve portion of Company E sprang into their saddles and hurried toward the sound of the guns. Forming a line behind a rail fence separating the cornfield from the woods, they sat astride their horses listening to the discordant notes of battle. One trooper, perhaps a little more apprehensive than the others, rested the butt of his Spencer on his thigh, his forefinger carelessly curled around the trigger. Suddenly the gun went off with a roar. Trying to make the best of an embarrassing situation, the red-faced trooper smiled weakly and said, "I'll bet you that came close to them Johnnies."

"Yes," scoffed one of his comrades, "if they had been in the moon."

This gave everyone a good laugh, but soon Captain Boyer was barking orders: dismount, prepare to fight on foot. Swinging down from their saddles, every three men handed their reins to the number four and climbed over the fence with their Spencers loaded and ready.[26]

By this time, Graham's pickets had advanced about half a mile and it took Boyer and his men several minutes to overtake them. Together they formed a strong skirmish line across the Green's Ferry road, near Whisenant's Mill. Major Graham brought up the rest of the battalion, deploying one company on Boyer's right and another on his left, apparently keeping Company H and the artillery in reserve.

Graham scarcely had time to perfect these arrangements before Clanton came charging around a bend in the road, pistol in hand, leading the 6th Alabama on foot. He was only twenty paces away when Captain Boyer's men leveled their Spencers and aimed a hail of lead at the Confederate general and his staff. Clanton was unscathed, but his clothes were riddled with bullet holes. His acting aide-de-camp, Lieutenant William Thomas Judkins, was killed. Another aide, Willie Seals, was hit in the arm. Clanton's kinsman and acting adjutant, Captain Robert S. Abercrombie, stood nearby, calmly emptying his revolver into the smoke-shrouded blue ranks. As he squeezed off his last shot, he toppled over, killed by a Yankee bullet.

The thin gray line behind him answered feebly with a scattering of shots, but no one could stand before those deadly Spencers. Clanton's chief of ordnance, Captain Batt Smith, was trying to rally a company when he staggered drunkenly and fell flat on his face, his leg broken by a .52 caliber slug. Captain James McRae, commanding

Company D of the 6th Alabama, was hit in the side, but he was luckier than most; his canteen deflected the bullet.

Clanton was standing a few yards to the rear when a tall, muscular black named Griffin approached him. "General," the youth asked, "where is Marse Batt?"

"There," Clanton pointed, "near the enemy's line dead."

Without a moment's hesitation, Griffin charged into the noise and smoke. Heedless of the bullets whistling past his head and Clanton's entreaties to come back, he searched among the figures sprawled in the road until he found Captain Smith lying on his back. Scooping his young master up in his sinewy arms, Griffin turned and dodged into the woods. A moment later he emerged from the trees near where Clanton was standing.

"Is he dead, Griffin?" Clanton asked apprehensively.

"I don't know, sir," the slave replied. "Mammy was his nurse, and I am the older. I promised mammy to take care of him and to bring him to her, and I am going to carry him home."

This withering fire was more than the rest of Clanton's men could stand and they broke and ran. The Hoosiers surged after them, capturing at least three and perhaps as many as eleven privates, as well as Lieutenant Colonel Lary and Major Eliphalet A. McWhorter of the 6th Alabama, and another of Clanton's aides, Lieutenant Albert Hyer, as he knelt over the body of his friend, Captain Abercrombie.[27]

Graham halted the pursuit after a quarter of a mile and sent for the number fours to bring up the horses. The men on the skirmish line, their faces flush with excitement, stood at ease, waiting for orders. It had been an almost bloodless triumph on their part. One member of Company E had been grazed in the hip, and the only serious casualty occurred in Company H when Private John Matz started through the brush wearing that Rebel lieutenant's hat he had picked up in Ashville. Seeing the old white hat, one of his comrades took aim and fired. The bullet struck Matz in the right side of his upper lip, knocking out all his upper teeth except for two right molars, fracturing the hard palate, and shattering his upper jaw before exiting the left side of his face.

News of the grievous mishap spread quickly through the ranks. The men were sympathetic, but there seemed to be a subtle undercurrent of thought chiding Matz for wearing that hat in the first place. After all, with the woods full of real Rebels, a man just naturally shot first and asked questions later.[28]

Conversation soon turned to other aspects of that morning's fighting. One Yankee sergeant even had the effrontery to ask Lieutenant Colonel Lary how many men he had. "Enough to whip you fellows if we had got them to do as I wanted them to," snapped the captured Confederate. He did not elaborate. Perhaps it was too painful. During the last two hours he had seen seventeen of his men killed and several wounded.[29]

Graham's men were still waiting for their horses when they heard approaching hoofbeats. A moment later, a lone horseman sped around a wooded bend in the road. A trooper in Company E yelled for him to halt and fired at almost the same instant. The rider's face mirrored the pain as the bullet smashed into his right knee, shattering bone and cartilage. Signifying his willingness to surrender, he reined his horse to a stop in the midst of the bluecoated cavalrymen blocking his path. When questioned, he proved to be a courier with important dispatches for General Clanton. The Hoosiers promptly turned the papers over to Major Graham and hustled their prisoner to the rear. Just what the papers said or who they were from is unclear, but they may have been what prompted Graham to send a rider racing after Rousseau.

Spearheaded by the 5th Iowa, Rousseau's column had reached the ford at Ten Islands at 6:30 A.M. Scattered along two and a half miles of river between the mouth of Shoal Creek and old Fort Strother, most of the islands were only a few yards across, but Woods Island, the largest and lowermost of the ten, was almost a mile and a half long and over a third of a mile wide. Guides said Andrew Jackson had crossed here during his campaign against the Creek Indians in 1813, and from the look of things, no one in his right mind had used the ford since then. The normally placid Coosa swelled to a churning, quarter-mile expanse of roaring white water as it shoaled past the islands. A single misstep in the rock-strewn rapids could easily sweep a horse and rider to their death, but this unlikely looking spot was the shallowest stretch of river for miles around and Rousseau's only hope of effecting a speedy junction with Major Graham.

The 5th Iowa, led by Major Harlon Baird since Lieutenant Colonel Patrick took command of the 2nd Brigade, plunged their horses belly-deep into the narrow channel separating Woods Island from the riverbank. Splashing across to the upper end of the island, they filed into the main current and carefully felt their way past a small, tree-covered isle on their left. They were about two-thirds of the way across the river when Livingston's 8th Alabama Cavalry sprang up on the opposite shore and loosed a terrific volley. Errant balls threw up tiny geysers all around Baird's floundering troopers. Two horses in Company C screamed in agony and fell, dumping their riders into the swirling water. The rest of the Iowans turned and scrambled for cover behind the little island on their left.

Hearing the shots and seeing the confusion at the head of the column, Lieutenant Colonel Patrick hurried the 4th Tennessee across the channel and deployed them on Woods Island, one hundred yards to the right and rear of the marooned Iowans. Sharpshooters from both regiments dismounted and took cover in the tangled maze of driftwood, trees, and boulders. Squinting down their sights, they fired at anything that moved on the distant shore. The Rebels made a spirited reply, and a spent ball flattened Private James Key of the 4th Tennessee, leaving him temporarily stunned. Another bullet plucked a stick out of Rousseau's hand.

Realizing the Rebels had the ford plugged tighter than a cork in a bottle, Rousseau sent two companies, probably E and G of the 9th Ohio, looking for another crossing rumored to be a couple of miles downstream. While awaiting their return, Fielder Jones begged for permission to take the rest of his 8th Indiana back to Greensport and ferry them to Graham's assistance. Rousseau rejected the idea, saying it would take too long. When the two companies he had sent downstream returned without finding any sign of another ford, he reluctantly ordered Tom Harrison to bring the 1st Brigade over to Woods Island and deploy on the right of the 4th Tennessee, sending Jones's four companies of the 8th Indiana to root out any Rebels lurking on the lower end of the island.

A thorough search failed to turn up even one Confederate soldier and along about midmorning Jones's buglers sounded "Recall." Regrouping at the head of the island, the Hoosiers waited in a column of fours while Jones and Rousseau conferred quietly on horseback. By now, both men had heard a brief account of the fighting on the other side of the river from Major Graham's courier, who, with the help of a friendly Negro, had forded the Coosa farther upstream. Clearly concerned about the six companies with Graham, Jones was determined to get reinforcements across the river as soon as possible. If moving the main column back to Greensport would take too much time, he argued, then there was only one alternative. Like it or not, they would have to attack here, at Ten Islands, straight into the teeth of those Rebel guns.

Rousseau hesitated. "Colonel," he asked, "who will lead this charge?"

"I will," Jones replied.

"But you are too valuable a man," Rousseau protested, "I can't spare you."

"My life is worth no more than any private of my regiment," Jones answered calmly.

"But as an officer, you're worth more to me," Rousseau insisted.

Jones shrugged. "Where my men go into danger, I go with them."[30]

This was no brag. A graduate of Pennsylvania's Allegheny College, he had answered Lincoln's first call for volunteers by enlisting in the 6th Indiana Infantry. Severely wounded at the battle of Carrick's Ford, Virginia, he was honorably discharged when his ninety-day enlistment expired. A lesser man, shot through the liver, arm, and thigh, would have gone home and rested on his laurels, but Jones cut short his convalescence to accept the lieutenant colonelcy of the 39th Indiana Infantry. Still troubled by old wounds, he had dueled hand-to-hand with the Rebels at Stone's River, cutting down several opponents with his sword and pistol. By the time the regiment was mounted and redesignated as the 8th Indiana Cavalry in the fall of 1863, he had earned a well-deserved reputation as "a gallant and intrepid officer."[31]

Rousseau was familiar with his record, and as he looked into the intense, deep-set eyes in that bearded, hound-dog face, he realized Jones would not rest until Graham's battalion had been relieved.

"How will you conduct this charge?" Rousseau asked.

"I will proceed to the second island and form," Jones answered; "then with A and B of the 2nd Kentucky to cover, I will make the charge with A and B of the 8th Indiana."

"If the opposite bank is mirey?" queried Rousseau.

"Dismount and go out with the carbine."

"If not mirey?"

"Ride out and give them the saber."

Rousseau mulled over the possibilities. "Colonel," he said, "I hate to lose so brave a man as you; I wish I had let you go back to the ferry when you proposed it. How long will it be before you can reinforce Graham by doing so now?"

"Two hours," Jones said flatly.

"Go," Rousseau said, gesturing toward the ferry.[32]

Jones saluted and urged his horse into the shallow waters of the strait. Companies A, B, C, and D of the 8th Indiana followed in a shower of foam and spray. Clambering up the west bank of the river, they turned to the right and hurried north toward Greensport. They had not gone far when Jones stopped a Negro man on the road and asked if there was a ford anywhere between Ten Islands and the ferry. Fortune smiled on him that morning, for this was the same man who had guided Major Graham's courier across the river. Pressed into service again, he led Jones and his men to some shoals about a half mile below Greensport.

Within an hour, all four of Jones's companies were safely across the river, but they were too late. Having shouldered Clanton and the 6th Alabama aside, Graham's men

Although troubled by three wounds he had suffered early in the war, Lieutenant Colonel Fielder Alsor Jones of the 8th Indiana would ride more miles and see more combat in the summer of 1864 than any other cavalry commander in Sherman's army. Courtesy of the Indiana State Library. Used by permission.

had mounted and moved downstream to threaten the right flank and rear of the Rebel force at Ten Islands. Far from needing help, their sudden appearance caused Livingston's 8th Alabama to beat a hasty retreat about 11:30 A.M., leaving behind the bodies of Captain John Moor and several privates killed during the exchange with Rousseau's sharpshooters.

From his vantage point on Woods Island, Lieutenant Colonel Patrick watched as the Rebel fire slackened and died. Sensing an opportunity, he ordered Major Stephens's troopers to charge. Mounting their horses, the Tennesseans pushed boldly into the raging current. A few stalwart Rebels, their ammunition almost exhausted, tried to discourage them, but their bullets either passed high overhead or fell harmlessly into the water. Half wading, half swimming, stumbling over rocks and disappearing into potholes, Stephens and his men steadily pressed forward. Wet and breathless, they struggled up the east bank and dashed after the retreating Rebels, taking a few prisoners.[33]

The rest of Rousseau's command began crossing about ten minutes later. "The passage of the river was a beautiful sight," wrote Rousseau's adjutant, Captain Thomas C. Williams. "The long array of horsemen winding between the green islands and taking a serpentine course across the ford—their arms flashing back the rays of the burning sun, and guidons gaily fluttering along the column, formed a bright picture, recalling the days of romance, and contrasting strongly with the stern hardships of the every-day life on the duty march."

It took a couple of hours before the last of the raiders were safely ashore. Those already on the east bank found various ways to pass the time. Lieutenant Thomas W. Fanning, commanding Company G of the 9th Ohio, pocketed a Masonic emblem he found on the body of the 8th Alabama's Captain Moor. Fielder Jones worked at reuniting the scattered elements of the 8th Indiana, while Lieutenant Wightman brought his two Parrott guns down from Green's Ferry along with the command's four ambulances. Private Matz rode in one of these, his horrible face wound swathed in bandages.

Anxious to learn something about the size and composition of Clanton's force, Rousseau alternately cajoled, cross-examined, and conciliated the captured Confederates, heartily assuring them they were of "fighting stock." With the possible exception of Lieutenant Colonel Lary, Major McWhorter, and the other Rebel officers, he then paroled his prisoners, including Jacob McElroy, the captured engineer, and told them to take a message to the Rebel commander. If Clanton persisted in following him, Rousseau warned, he would "turn and thrash him soundly."[34]

Early that afternoon the 5th Iowa formed ranks and led the column down the east bank of the Coosa. Five miles south of Ten Islands, they came to the Cane Creek Furnace, the second oldest smelter in Alabama. Built in 1840, it had provided pig iron for the government ordnance works at Mobile during the Mexican War. More recently, Cane Creek castings had been going to the Confederate arsenal at Selma, where they were used to manufacture everything from camp kettles to cannonballs. Rousseau ordered his engineer officer, Captain Edward Ruger, to take a few men and burn the place to the ground. Within minutes, the Cane Creek Furnace and its outlying buildings were engulfed in flames.

As pillars of black smoke boiled into the blue sky, Rousseau's column moved down the Jackson Trace, occasionally sending out small detachments to burn cotton stored in nearby barns and gin houses. Not a breeze was stirring among the long-needled pines that afternoon, and great clouds of dust, kicked up by the passing of ten thousand hooves, soon covered everyone and everything with a fine gray powder. Breathing became difficult, and the men peered into the shimmering haze with irritated, red-rimmed eyes. Runnels of sweat coursed down their dirty faces, and when they tried to swallow, their thick, coated tongues rasped dryly against gritty teeth. But they plodded on, mile after weary mile, with nothing to break the sullen monotony of discomfort.[35]

Late that afternoon, the column met an elderly woman and a barefoot girl of perhaps fifteen heading northward with a one-horse wagon. Both were poorly dressed. A pick and two shovels rattled around in the back of the wagon, the woman trudging stoically alongside while the girl rode astride the horse. A trooper playfully asked where they were going. To Ten Islands, the old woman said, to bury their dead. "I shall never forget the look of those poor distressed creatures," wrote Private Williamson Ward of the 8th Indiana.

Obviously, news of the fighting at Whisenant's Mill and Ten Islands had already outdistanced the raiders. The element of surprise was lost. Now everything depended on speed, and for the rest of the afternoon Rousseau pushed his men and horses to the limits of their endurance, trying to make up for the time lost crossing the Coosa. The column covered fifteen hot, dusty miles before he finally called a halt at sundown to rest and feed at Martin's Mill.

By that time, some of his men could barely lift themselves out of the saddle. Troopers in Major Graham's battalion of the 8th Indiana had eaten little or nothing since leaving Ashville the previous day. Those who had stood picket during the night had not slept in almost forty hours. The artillery horses stood in harness, heads hung low, their lathered flanks heaving up and down with each labored breath. Hampered by heat and the miserable condition of the roads, they had fallen farther and farther behind during the long, hot afternoon, impeding the progress of the four rearmost regiments. They were on the verge of collapse, and unless something was done, they would only slow down the column when the march resumed.

Knowing he could ill afford to lose any more time, Rousseau ordered Lieutenant Wightman to abandon one of his guns and harness both teams to the remaining piece so it could keep pace with the cavalry. Unpinning the cap squares, Wightman's men heaved the heavy cannon to the ground. While some hacked away at the limber and carriage with axes, others wielded the sledge hammers Sherman had ordered brought along for just such an occasion, and disabled the gun by breaking off the trunnions.

The extra team was hitched up, and at 10:00 P.M. the raiders wearily climbed back into the saddle. The cool night air was a welcome respite from the searing heat of the day, and a waxing yellow moon floated serenely overhead, bathing the woods and fields in a soft, pale light. Just beyond Martin's Mill, Major Baird's 5th Iowa led the column down a left-hand road, hoping to bypass any bushwhackers lying in wait on the Jackson Trace.

Almost immediately, the advance guard ran into Captain Joseph Hardie and six or eight Rebel riders scouting the northern approaches to Talladega. Shots rang out in the darkness, but Hardie's horsemen quickly melted into the shadows. After a brief halt Rousseau's column pressed forward again.

The next ten miles passed uneventfully, and the deceptive tranquillity of the soft summer night lulled more than one tired, stiff-legged trooper to sleep in the saddle. About 2:00 A.M., the column reached a little place called Eastaboga, and it was probably there that Baird's Iowans captured a Rebel paymaster carrying an estimated $160,000 to $170,000 in Confederate currency and shinplasters.

By this time, the moon had dipped below the western horizon, making it too dark to see. Only then did the seemingly tireless Rousseau give the order to halt and dismount. Sliding to the ground, looping the reins around their arms, his exhausted troopers sprawled in the road beside their weary mounts and were soon sound asleep.[36]

7

ROUSSEAU'S RAID
EASTABOGA TO LOACHAPOKA

July 15–July 17, 1864

My captain went a-scoutin'
And took my brother Jim;
He went to catch the Yankees,
But the Yankees they catched him.

—"I'll Lay Ten Dollars Down"

Major William T. Walthall, the Confederate commander at Talladega, had first learned of the raiders' approach at 10:30 P.M., July 13, when he received a hastily scrawled message from Clanton's headquarters at Blue Mountain. According to Clanton, 1,200 Yankee cavalrymen had passed through Ashville, probably on their way to the railroad terminus at Blue Mountain and the extensive iron works at Oxford. Walthall immediately relayed this information to Captain Andrew W. Bowie, who led a small cavalry detachment stationed at Talladega, and to Captain Jonathan George Ryan, who was in town with a few troopers nursing some convalescent horses belonging to Brigadier General Gideon J. Pillow's command. There was no telegraph at Talladega, so he dispatched an urgent request for ammunition to the Confederate arsenal at Selma by train, along with a message alerting Captain John W. Pitts, commanding a company of teenaged boys guarding the trestle spanning the Coosa River at Wilsonville, twenty miles to the west.

At 10:30 the next morning, a courier arrived from Green's Ferry with Clanton's note urging Walthall to send all available troops to Blue Mountain. Clanton had no authority over Walthall, and the major seriously questioned the wisdom of sending anyone to Blue Mountain. Talladega, situated halfway between the Oxford iron works and the equally important railroad bridge at Wilsonville, seemed like a more logical rendezvous. However, Walthall also realized the importance of concerted action and dutifully sent a train Wilsonville to fetch Captain Pitts and his boy militia.

At the same time, he ordered every conscript at Talladega's Camp Buckner to report to the railroad depot. Assisted by Major Alexander M. Haskell, who was in town mustering men for the state reserves, he also called upon all able-bodied citizens to shoulder arms. To his disgust, he soon discovered members of the local militia companies had simply vanished. A stockholders' convention of Alabama and Tennessee Rivers Railroad abruptly adjourned. Wagons, buggies, and carts piled high with household goods rattled down the dusty streets. Even Confederate Congressman William P. Chilton mounted a horse and, despite his fifty-three years, "did not make slow time towards a place of concealment."

By early afternoon, Walthall had mustered fewer than 200 men. They included Captain Pitts's boys, the conscripts from Camp Buckner, a squad of disabled veterans from the quartermaster and commissary offices, less than twenty members of Captain Joseph Hardie's company of mounted reserves, and sixty dismounted cavalrymen

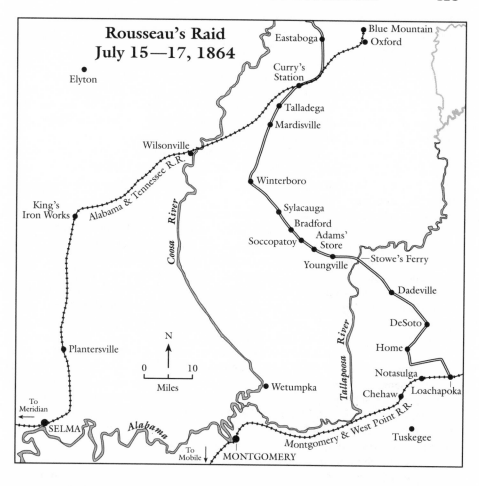

Rousseau's Raid
July 15—17, 1864

from Captain Ryan's command. Most, if not all, of Ryan's men were unarmed, but Walthall managed to provide them with Mississippi rifles, only to discover there was not a single round of .58 caliber ammunition on the post.

Ammunition was not the only thing in short supply. Three serviceable 6-pounders sat uselessly at Camp Buckner because Walthall did not have horses to pull them or any artillerymen to fire them. There were not enough field officers either, and Walthall found himself swamped with scores of menial chores that could have been done by a competent subordinate. It was midafternoon before everything was ready. Leaving a few men to help Major Haskell and the assistant quartermaster, Captain John Maguire, move badly needed war supplies out of town, Walthall sent Captain Hardie's horsemen northward to reinforce Clanton and herded the rest of his troops aboard a freight train for the twenty-five-mile trip to Blue Mountain.

Swaying and jostling along the track at only ten or twelve miles per hour, the cars did not reach Blue Mountain until 5:00 P.M. Learning Clanton had not yet returned from Green's Ferry, Walthall sent a courier to report his arrival and waited.

Clanton rode into town about 9:00 P.M., his broad shoulders stooped with fatigue.

Briefly, he described his frightful encounter with the Yankees, adding that rather than risk being outflanked and possibly cut off from his base of operations, he had gradually withdrawn the shattered remnants of his command eastward toward Alexandria and Blue Mountain.

Clanton's seeming fixation with Blue Mountain irritated Walthall. Convinced the Yankees were heading south, not east, he insisted on taking his troops back to the Coosa River bridge at Wilsonville, or at least as far as Talladega. Clanton reluctantly acquiesced and promised to move his own troops in that direction if the Yankees had not appeared at Blue Mountain by daylight.

Walthall had to wait until well after midnight before a train could be readied for his men. Arriving in Talladega between 2:00 and 3:00 A.M., July 15, he learned his worst fears were true. The Yankees were coming. Captain Hardie's men had met them just nine miles northeast of town.

Walthall wanted to send a patrol to reconnoiter, but at this critical juncture, there was not a single horseman to be found. Knowing how badly Clanton had been mauled at Green's Ferry and Ten Islands, he realized the hopelessness of pitting his ill-prepared, ill-equipped levies against several hundred Yankee cavalrymen. Reluctantly, he decided to abandon Talladega and move to the more easily defended trestle at Wilsonville. Ordering his men to stay on the cars, he hurried into town to save a few supplies and round up the troops he had left with Major Haskell and Captain Maguire. An hour later, after a hasty good-bye to his wife and children, he was back on board and the train chugged off into the darkness.

Haskell, Maguire, and a few teamsters stayed behind to haul off as many quartermaster and commissary supplies as they could, but by daylight they had scarcely made a dent in the mountain of materiel stockpiled at Talladega. Knowing the Yankees would soon be upon them, Maguire sent the last of his wagons rolling toward Wilsonville. Then he and Major Haskell hurried to Camp Buckner, a mile north of town, to set fire to the buildings housing the three small cannon Walthall had left behind. They scarcely had time to apply the torch before the vanguard of the Yankee column came charging into the courthouse square.[1]

Rousseau's raiders had left Eastaboga at 4:30 A.M., July 15, with perhaps two hours' sleep and no breakfast. Led by the 8th Indiana, they had crossed Choccolocco Creek and ridden eight miles due south, striking the Alabama and Tennessee Rivers Railroad at Curry's Station, eight miles above Talladega. As the column turned southwest and followed the winding country road that crossed and recrossed the railroad, three furloughed Confederate cavalrymen—Alva Hardie, William Stockdale, and Tom Childerson—fired a few shots, vainly trying to slow Rousseau's relentless advance.[2]

Pushing these bushwhackers aside, the 8th Indiana spurred ahead of the rest of the column and swept into Talladega about 8:00 A.M. Captain Joseph Hardie lingered long enough to snap a couple of errant shots at them and then fled before a veritable flood of bluecoated cavalrymen. Spilling into the shaded side streets, Yankee troopers swiftly dismounted and tied their horses to hitching rails and prim, whitewashed picket fences. While some led their thirsty mounts to drink from a natural spring pooled behind a twelve-by-seventy-foot stone enclosure in the center of town, others began to rifle, ransack, and burn.

Talladega was the largest town the raiders had encountered since leaving Decatur.

The county seat of Talladega County, it boasted a hotel, a pharmacy, the usual array of dry goods stores, smithies, and stables, as well as two weekly newspapers, *The Democratic Watchtower* and *The Alabama Reporter.* A three-story courthouse dominated the town square, ringed by what one chronicler described as "a collection of odd-sized wooden buildings, with one brick building on the north side, two on the east, none on the south and two on the west."

Most of these buildings had been appropriated by various Confederate agencies. The Exchange Hotel, for example, a large, three-story brick building on the northwest corner of Court and North streets, housed the Wayside Hospital. The raiders quickly made prisoners of 143 Confederate convalescents in its wards, but, as usual, Rousseau's provost marshal, Captain Matthias, paroled them all.[3]

Talladega normally had a population of about 800, but most of the white inhabitants had fled. The majority of those who remained were the wives and children of men serving with the Confederate armies in Virginia and Georgia. "We saw plenty of those who couldn't run away at our 'terrible approach,'" noted the 9th Ohio's Colonel Hamilton, "but they were so terror stricken that they could scarcely give an answer to any question propounded. Such misconceived impression[s] of the Yankee character have been taught them by their papers, that they expected us to burn their houses, kill their men and insult their women, and some of them seemed to be *awaiting, resigned, and expecting to be insulted.*"

The stubble-faced troopers who strolled into yards and parlors, unannounced except for the clank of a saber or the tread of heavy boots, did nothing to allay these fears. Many of the women, gathering up their skirts and their courage, bustled into the streets, appealing to passing Union officers for protection. Rousseau graciously provided guards to all who asked for them and assured one petitioner he was a "Kentucky gentleman" who did not come to make war on innocent women and children.[4]

For the most part, these guards did a good job of protecting private homes and property. However, they did not interfere with hungry comrades opening smokehouse doors or troopers coming out of barns and stables with armloads of corn and grain to feed their horses.

As was their custom, the raiders broke open the county jail and released a handful of Confederate deserters. They also ransacked the post office on the west side of the square, scattering letters everywhere. Several troopers rummaged through the East Street offices of the Conscript Bureau and the post quartermaster, while others looted the tax-in-kind warehouse, where Southern farmers were required to contribute one-tenth of their crop to the Confederate government. But the biggest crowd gathered around the railroad depot and the commissary warehouse on East Street. A hurried inventory of the depot tallied 100 sacks of flour, 300 bushels of wheat, 500 barrels of salt, mounds of cotton, piles of shoes, leather, empty sacks, nitre, all kinds of private property, and four platform scales. The nearby commissary warehouse contained 100,000 rations of sugar and salt, 20,000 rations of flour and bacon, and several boxes of tobacco. Rousseau ordered both buildings stripped of whatever supplies the command needed, then put to the torch.[5]

Exuberant troopers wrestled boxes, bags, and barrels into the street. Others destroyed a nearby water tank or hammered at railroad switching equipment. The railroad itself, a short line dead-ending at Blue Mountain, had little strategic value, and the raiders did not even bother to tear up the track. After removing needed supplies and much of the freight consigned to private individuals, they set fire to the depot and two nearby boxcars. The commissary warehouse would have suffered a similar fate had not Dr. Charles Smith, an assistant surgeon at Wayside Hospital, protested that the blaze would endanger the rest of the town, including the hospital.

The doctor made his point. Rescinding his original order, Rousseau invited Talladega's civilian population, both black and white, to help themselves to whatever was left in the warehouse. Dignity and class consciousness were cast aside, noted Private Jack Wilson of the 8th Indiana, as Southern ladies "joined and even vied with the soldiers and negroes in trying to obtain a supply of the rebel stores being distributed so lavishly."[6]

Rousseau had two hogsheads of sugar set aside for the patients at Wayside Hospital, perhaps hoping this gesture of goodwill would help ensure proper treatment for Private Matz. The young, German-born trooper, shot in the face at Green's Ferry, needed better care than the regimental surgeons could give him. Unable to speak or eat, he was going to be left behind, a prisoner of war for the second time in eighteen months.

Confinement in a Rebel prison camp was one of the grim possibilities most of Rousseau's men preferred not to contemplate. They were already sixty miles deep in Rebel territory. The death of Captain Curl and the wounding of Captain Wilcox were still fresh in their minds, and they made no secret of their dread of bushwhackers. According to one Talladegan, they "could talk of nothing else."[7]

This fear of ambush may have been what kept them from destroying Camp Buckner, nestled in the thick woods a mile north of town. More likely, however, they saw the smoke from the fires Captain Maguire and Major Haskell had set and simply assumed the camp was already ablaze. In any event, they did not even venture in that direction; nor did they bother the nitre sheds, 300 yards northeast of the depot.[8]

A few tents, some corn, and other items belonging to the quartermaster's department also went untouched, but these were the exceptions. For the most part, the raiders did a thorough job of destroying anything likely to be of use to the Confederacy.

Rousseau did spare Lewis G. Sturdivant's factory on North Street, a two-story brick building facing the courthouse square, where guns were repaired for the Confederate army. Fearing flames would spread to adjacent buildings, he had his men simply smash all the machinery. He gave similar instructions regarding a larger gun factory on the outskirts of town (probably Porter's Hall at the corner of Court and Battle streets), but the Rebels had obligingly wrecked the machinery before their hurried departure. In their haste, however, they had overlooked some munitions. Rousseau's men found a case or two of Mississippi rifles hidden in a stable and destroyed them along with a small lot of captured ammunition and accoutrements.[9]

About 10:00 A.M., the raiders mounted their horses and rode out of town on Battle Street, taking two or three Negroes and a few horses with them. In exchange, they left behind some worn-out stock, including "a fine horse" belonging to Rousseau's adjutant, Captain Williams.

A few stragglers also stayed behind, doubtlessly intending to catch up with the column later in the day. Some of them were sick. Others were no better than common thieves and robbed and plundered "in a most outrageous manner" before taking their leave. For one reason or another, at least three Yankee troopers lingered a little too long and were taken prisoner by Lieutenant Wilbur Duncan of Bowie's company of Rebel cavalry.

Just south of Talladega, the raiders burned Alex White's gin house and one hundred bales of cotton. There is a story, perhaps apocryphal, that as the Yankee column continued down the Mardisville road, Rousseau's adjutant, Captain Williams, found the 9th Ohio's regimental bugler, James Doran, blocking his path. Doran was roaring drunk on whisky he had confiscated in Talladega and Williams, perhaps already in a bad humor after losing his horse, brusquely ordered him out of the way, adding he had no time to bother with such a "fellow." The bugler quickly took exception to the adjutant's tone.

"I'll be damned if I'm any more of a *fellow* than you," he snarled, "and I can prove this to you mighty soon, if you think it needs to be proved."

Heated words followed. Both men began throwing punches, with Williams getting the worst of it. News of the incident quickly reached Rousseau. Realizing he could not allow this flagrant contempt for authority to go unchallenged, especially in front of the 9th Ohio, the burly six-foot-two Kentuckian ordered Doran to strip off his blouse and fight him, man to man. The five-foot-nine-inch Doran happily obliged, only to be flattened by one of Rousseau's meaty fists.

The point was not lost on the 9th Ohio. "The general must be a fighting man [in] every way," Lieutenant Thomas W. Fanning wrote admiringly, "as Doran, whom he whipped so easily, is equal in the science of fisticuffs to any prize fighter of his weight and size in the American roped arena."[10]

Three miles south of Talladega, Rousseau called a halt at Thornhill, a 1,700-acre plantation belonging to Captain Joseph Hardie's widowed mother. Whether Rousseau recognized the connection between Mrs. Hardie and the Rebel partisan who fired on his column earlier that morning is unclear, but his 8th Indiana advance guard emptied her barns and smokehouse in short order. While several companies of Hoosiers dismounted in Mrs. Hardie's front yard in the shade of some stately oaks, other units sought refuge from the noonday sun in a wet-weather swamp bordering nearby Talladega Creek. Sheltered by the trees, tired, hungry troopers pulled the saddles off their sweaty mounts for the first time since leaving Greensport. They opened saddlebags and greasy haversacks bulging with meat, grain, and other savory morsels, built fires, put coffee on to boil, and soon both men and animals were feasting sumptuously on the supplies taken from Talledega.[11]

While his troopers enjoyed this much-needed rest, Rousseau contemplated his next move. He was sorely tempted to make a dash for the Coosa River and destroy the bridge at Wilsonville and several nearby iron works. The bridge was only twenty miles away and lightly defended, from what he could learn. He could easily be there by midnight, and any move in that direction was sure to send Confederate troops rushing to the defense of Montgomery and the extensive arsenal at Selma. This would allow Rousseau to swing back to the southeast and march unopposed to his real objective, the Montgomery & West Point Railroad.

On the other hand, a detour to Wilsonville would require an extra day's effort from men and horses already showing signs of exhaustion. To use them up for the sake of creating a diversion when they would need all their strength just to reach the railroad was a risk Rousseau was unwilling to take. "Adhering to a determination, formed before starting, to proceed as rapidly as possible to the accomplishment of the main object of the expedition, and not deeming it prudent to detach any portion of my small command," he later explained, "I decided to proceed without delay."

Having "tuck a little for the iner man and fed our noble steeds," as Sergeant Tom Jackson phrased it, the raiders saddled up and moved out about 4:00 P.M. Hoping to give the impression he was indeed heading for the Coosa River, Rousseau aimed the head of the column toward Mardisville.

"Our road . . . lay through the most beautiful and fertile portion of Alabama I have yet seen," wrote Private Jack Wilson of the 8th Indiana, "many splendid, commodious and tastefully decorated dwellings studding the road on either side. At each house we passed, we were greeted by pantomiame gestures of pleasure, of the most expressive kind, from large numbers of Africa's sable daughters, and who also asked us some very pertinent questions, such as: 'Where *all* youns come from?' 'Hes all *youns* got names?' . . . 'How des *all* youns manage to get out of the weather, when it rains?'"

"We found the niggers everywhere to be our friends," added Colonel Hamilton of the 9th Ohio, "they all have an instinctive idea that some how or other they are to be set free in spite of the terrible teachings of their masters to the contrary. We are frequently met by the anxious question are you coming to murder us black folks, and when told that on the contrary we came to set them all free, they would clap their hands and say 'Bress the Lord, we thought so.'

"Colored men would frequently leave their families and everything and come with us. If we had dared to go slower we could have brought almost everyone we saw."

"The slaves along the route were exceedingly anxious to follow the Yankees," agreed Rousseau's adjutant, Captain Williams, "but the rate of marching was too rapid for them to keep along on foot, and all the horses and mules to be found were needed for remounts for the men whose horses were daily giving out. Nevertheless a number succeeded in making their way. They would trudge along uncomplainingly, riding when they could get an animal, and walking at other times, and if asked where they were going, the invariable answer was, '*Gwine wid you all.*'"

Late that afternoon, the raiders reached Mardisville, a sleepy little village straddling the fork where the road branched south to Montgomery and southwest toward the railroad bridge at Wilsonville. The head of the column veered to the left, leading the men, who still had no idea of where they were going, to speculate they were bound for the Alabama capital. This sudden change of direction also produced dramatic evidence of just how successful Rousseau's efforts to disguise his intentions had been. Several Southern families, thinking the Yankees were heading for Wilsonville, had fled down the Montgomery road in wagons and buggies hastily loaded with household treasures. Now they found themselves and their belongings squarely in the path of the bluecoated troopers they had so assiduously tried to avoid. They watched helplessly, according to one account, as "most of their effects were captured." While some looting probably did occur, the raiders, badly in need of remounts after five grueling days on the road, were more interested in the refugees' horses and mules.[12]

The Yankees' sudden appearance on the Montgomery road caught many of the local planters equally unprepared, leaving them with little or no time to hide their valuables. "We frequently found large amounts of silver ware in trunks or boxes hid out in the weeds, in fence corners and other places," wrote Colonel Hamilton, "in which cases we would notify the owners if we could find them, (which was not hard to do) to come and get their things and keep them in the house or some of the Yankees might be tempted to appropriate them, which indication of honesty surprised them exceedingly. Considerable gold and silver coin was found in the same way, which I believe was generally kept quiet by the finder."

Rousseau's men invariably emptied barns and corrals of whatever riding stock they found. Just beyond Mardisville, they took several mules, horses, and Negroes from Orange Vale, a 3,000-acre plantation belonging to Levi W. Lawler. A little farther down the road, at a palatial estate called Mt. Ida, they relieved Walker Reynolds of thirty mules and eight Negroes, and took another thirteen mules and other valuables from his son, Thomas. A neighboring planter, Judge Nathan Cook, lost several mules, five Negroes, and all his Thoroughbred horses.

Continuing southward through Winterboro, the raiders were still several miles north of Sylacauga when darkness overtook them. Guided by the light of the nearly full moon, they pressed on, riding into Sylacauga about 11:00 P.M. Confederate newspapers later accused the Yankees of stealing a bag containing $200 in silver from a poor woman who lived there, but the town had little else of value.[13]

It was, however, an important road junction. Leaving the Montgomery road, Rousseau took a southeasterly course through Deep Cut Gap. Two hours later, he finally called a halt in the hills overlooking the headwaters of Weogufka Creek, seven miles beyond Sylacauga. Ordinarily, he might have kept going, as there were still a couple of hours of moonlight left, but his troops had ridden thirty-nine miles since leaving Eastaboga that morning. The column was strung out almost all the way back to Sylacauga, and as Captain Williams explained, "having had but two or three hours' sleep the previous night, and a wearisome march through the day, the men were nearly overcome with fatigue and drowsiness, and as soon as the halt was made dropped themselves on the ground to seek repose."

The rearmost regiment, Major Baird's 5th Iowa, did not catch up until 2:00 or 3:00 A.M. and barely had time to lie down before the bugles sounded "To Horse" about 4:00 A.M., July 16. Wiping the sleep from their eyes, the men rose dazedly to their feet to begin another day without breakfast. Within a half hour, they were back in the saddle, with Baird's weary Iowans leading the way. The whole column moved as if in a dream. Sleep-starved troopers slumped over the pommels of their saddles or stared fixedly ahead out of half-closed, expressionless eyes. Fatigue had silenced the lively banter of the first day's march. Except for the creak of saddle leather and the rattling clatter of sabers and canteens, the only sound was the steady clip-clop of horses' hooves on the hard-packed earth. The rocky, narrow road led through what the 8th Indiana's Jack Wilson described as "a very barren, and almost deserted tract of country, presenting a wide contrast with yesterday's route. . . ."

Despite the heat, hunger, and fatigue, there was no complaining. Somehow, Rousseau had instilled a sense of purpose, even anticipation, in these men. They did not know where they were going or why, but they knew they were doing something important, and they pressed on, past Mt. Olive Church and across Hatchet Creek. By 9:00 A.M., they had covered twelve or fifteen miles when, in the words of Jack Wilson, "descending abruptly from a ridge upon which we had hitherto been marching, we suddenly came to a cosy little village, (perhaps it is a town) in which was a splendid manufactory, driven by water power, in full operation, the dusky hued operatives grinned and displayed their ivories with much evident delight at our appearance, a pleasure not shared by their blue-eyed, flaxen-haired co-workers, who were glancing at us very uneasily from the upper windows as we rode past."

The "cosy little village" was Bradford, named for Joseph H. Bradford, who owned the cotton mill situated on the banks of Soccopatoy Creek. The stout stone structure, currently leased to a Mr. Simpson and a Colonel Moore, employed 110 women and girls. Learning the mill was "the only source of support of poor and needy citizens," Rousseau ordered it spared.[14]

Continuing to the road junction at nearby Soccopatoy, he called a halt to give his tired troopers a rest. The surrounding countryside was more fertile than the barren wastes they had traveled earlier that day, and well-stocked farms and plantations gave promise of providing sustenance for man and beast. One of the larger plantations belonged to Patrick McKinney, and perhaps it was here an incident occurred which Rousseau later related to Sherman with evident relish.

According to Rousseau, the bluecoated column had halted in the road "below Talladega" when he and his staff dismounted and strode up to the home of a well-to-do planter. Cordially greeted by the owner, Rousseau asked if he and his officers might have a drink of water. After quenching their thirst, he and his aides sat down on the porch, chatting amiably with their host.

As they talked, Rousseau noticed "quite a number of good mules" standing in a lot across the road. Turning to the planter, he said, "My good sir, I fear I must take some of your mules."

Surprised at this sudden turn of events, the planter objected strenuously, insisting he had already contributed quite liberally to the "good cause." Why, only the week before he had supplied Confederate General Philip D. Roddey's command with ten mules.

"Well," said Rousseau, "in this war you should at least be neutral—that is, you should be as liberal to us as to Roddey."

The planter eyed Rousseau's uniform, now gray with dust, a bit closer. "Well, ain't you on our side?" he asked.

"No," replied Rousseau, "I am General Rousseau and all these men you see are Yanks."

"Great God!" exclaimed the thunderstruck Southerner. "Is it possible? Are these Yanks? Who ever supposed they would come away down here in Alabama?"

Needless to say, Rousseau got his mules, and if this incident did indeed take place at McKinney's, his hapless host also lost "a considerable quantity of gold, all his horses and . . . a quantity of provisions, besides other things."[15]

McKinney's neighbors also suffered at the hands of hungry Yankees who raided their barns, corncribs, and smokehouses. Rousseau's men apparently had a sweet tooth and robbed many of the beehives in the neighborhood. Sergeant Tom Jackson of the 8th Indiana breakfasted on a hearty meal of ham and honey, and it was not unusual to see a trooper riding along with his reins in one hand and a gourd full of honey in the other.

Once they had eaten, many of the weary raiders curled up in the shade and went to sleep. Others conjectured quietly about where they were going or found various forms of amusement. Some 9th Ohio soldiers pitted a black ant they dubbed Jeff Davis against a red one called Abe Lincoln and huddled around to watch the fight. Abe eventually prevailed over Jeff, a good omen if nothing else.

Slaves flocking around from nearby plantations told the Yankees a horrifying tale of crime and punishment, which, according to Captain Williams, "would be incredible, were it not supported by the testimony of eye-witnesses, and had not slavery and secession together turned men into fiends." Some citizens had recently arrested a Negro accused of murdering his master, tied him to a tree, and burned him to death. "His torture was, no doubt, to some extent, mitigated by the very means used to make it severe," Williams recounted. "Dry pitch-pine was piled up around him, which burned so rapidly, and poured out such a dense smoke, that he was almost instantly suffocated. A witness stated he never screamed or groaned, but seemed to suffocate at once."

As morning lengthened into afternoon, several detachments were sent out in search of horses and mules. A remount detail from Company I of the 9th Ohio was returning with several animals in tow when the horse Private George E. Heilman was leading spooked at something and began to plunge and rear. As Heilman struggled to hold on and keep his own mount under control, his rope got entangled with the .50 caliber Smith carbine hanging at his side. Colonel Hamilton's June 27 edict about loaded guns had either been rescinded or ignored, because Heilman's weapon fired, putting a bullet through his right foot. The wound was not serious, but Heilman had the painful distinction of being shot by a horse.

Another remount detail, a sergeant and four privates from Company K of the 9th Ohio, simply disappeared. Four other 9th Ohio troopers were also captured on July 16, but Rousseau could not waste any time looking for them. He had to keep moving.[16]

After six or seven hours' rest at Soccopatoy, the command saddled up about 4:00 P.M., but instead of turning south, as many of his troopers expected, Rousseau kept to the southeast, leaving Montgomery fifty miles to his right and rear. The Tallapoosa River was only fifteen miles away, and he intended to get there by sundown.

For the rest of the afternoon, Rousseau's five regiments kept up a steady pace. Plodding past Adams' Store with scarcely a pause, at 6:00 P.M. Captain Elkin and the advance guard rode into Youngville. Here they found four large tax-in-kind warehouses stockpiled with cornmeal, grain, and bacon collected from the surrounding countryside. The raiders took what they needed; the rest went up in flames.

Two hours later, Elkin and his men reached the Tallapoosa River at Stowe's Ferry. A swift, treacherous stream, the Tallapoosa was fordable in only a few places and most of these were unsuitable for artillery and ambulances. Elkin found the ferryboat conveniently moored on his side of the river, but Rousseau could not afford his 2,300 men the luxury of shuttling them across ten or twelve at a time. They were going to have to cross at a little-used ford Rousseau's scouts had located a half mile upstream, while Company H of the 5th Iowa stayed behind to ferry over the artillery, ambulances, and pack mules.

Following Rousseau's instructions, Lieutenant Colonel Patrick's 2nd Brigade turned to the left and led the column past a plantation house and down a wooded country lane scarcely wider than a bridle path. Emerging in a cornfield at the edge of the river, they found what passed for a ford in these parts, not as wide as the one at Ten Islands but still "a very difficult and dangerous looking place," where the water roiled knee-deep to a man on horseback.

Patrick's Iowans and Tennesseans managed to get across in the waning minutes of twilight, but for some unexplained reason, Tom Harrison's 1st Brigade was slow coming up. It was dark by the time his advance guard, Captain William Henderson's

Colonel William Douglas Hamilton commanded the 9th Ohio
Cavalry and briefly led Rousseau's 2nd Brigade. A straitlaced
Scotsman who was constantly issuing edicts to his men, he
enjoined his rowdy regiment from playing cards or carrying
loaded guns while on the march. Used by permission of the
Massachusetts Commandery, Military Order of the Loyal Legion, and the U.S. Army Military History Institute.

Company D of the 9th Ohio, filed out of the woods and into the cornfield. Even then,
they milled about on the riverbank, scarcely believing Rousseau meant for them to
cross here.

Puzzled by the delay, Colonel Hamilton rode to the head of the column, where he
met Captain Henderson, who explained it was too dark to see the ford, the 4th
Tennessee apparently having neglected to leave behind any guides to show the way.
Undaunted, Hamilton rode to a nearby cabin, where he roused a Negro and demanded
to be taken to the ford. The black man was "terribly frightened," Hamilton recalled,
"and said he could not tell where it was. I ordered him to put on his clothes and come
quickly or it would be the worse for him."

The slave grudgingly got dressed and came outside. Hamilton put him astride a
strong horse and told him to lead the way, promising to stay close behind him. "He
begged piteously," Hamilton recounted, "but I told him the boys would shoot him if
he did not go." This seemed to have the desired effect, and Hamilton instructed
Captain Henderson to follow them, stationing men at fifty-foot intervals to mark the
ford for the rest of the regiment. Then he ordered his reluctant guide forward. The
slave glanced nervously at the dark river in front of him, then at the gleam of the
Yankee colonel's pistol. Preferring the risk of drowning to the seeming certainty of
being shot in the back of the head, he urged his horse over the steep bank and into the
water. Hamilton plunged in after him.

The river ran deep near the bank, and the slave swam his horse about ten rods downstream before turning squarely to the left. Continuing toward the middle of the river, with Hamilton mimicking his every move, he turned his horse's head directly upstream. The animal struggled against the swift current until they were even with the spot where they had first slid down the bank. Turning to the right, the black man carefully felt his way among the rocks until he reached the far shore, wet and frightened, but none the worse for wear.[17]

In the meantime, Captain Henderson had ordered his men to take off their sabers and strap them to their saddles so they would have a better chance of saving themselves if their horses lost their footing. Turning to Private Samuel N. Cook, he said, "There are some of our boys yonder in the woods, go and tell them that we are ready to cross."

Cook prodded his weary mount across the cornfield, but when he reached the spot Henderson had indicated, he could not find anyone. Continuing down the narrow country lane, he was almost back to the big house near the main road when a pack of baying hounds challenged his approach. Cook prudently retraced his steps as quickly as the darkness and his tired horse would allow, but upon reaching the ford, he was dismayed to find his company, indeed his whole regiment, had disappeared. Peering across the river, he could barely discern the tail end of the column clambering up the far bank. Not wanting to be left behind, he plunged in after them.

Sometimes wading, sometimes swimming, horse and rider floundered over rocks and potholes. They were about a third of the way across when the horse slipped. The swift current swept Cook out of the saddle. Water closed in all around. He could not breathe. "This is the end," he thought. Panic swelled in his chest as he kicked and flailed wildly. The next thing he knew, he was clinging to a slippery, river-worn boulder, his head just above the water. Looking around, he saw his horse struggle to its feet a short distance downstream, then disappear into the darkness.

"Then it was," Cook recalled, "that I reviewed the less than 18 years of my life, thinking of the evil and the good, and wondering if there was enough of the latter for the recording angel to strike a fair balance when I went over. . . . I thought of home, thought of all the loved ones in the little quiet village in Ohio where I was born. Out from the mists of the night on the banks of the river came phantoms—the men in gray—the avenging pursuers. I wondered if they'd shoot me when daylight come, or would I grow numb and faint and be swept down the river to be heard of no more."

Wet and frightened, Cook was brooding over his "inglorious end" when he heard a voice on the east side of the river call out, "Whose horse is this?"

"Mine," Cook yelled.

"And who are you?" the voice called back.

"Cook of the 9th Ohio," the half-drowned trooper shouted.

"Where are you?"

"Down the river, clinging to a rock."

"Then hold on," the voice answered, "the 2nd Kentucky Cavalry is coming; they will bring you over."

Cook soon saw a file of horsemen coming toward him, but they all passed several yards upstream. When an errant trooper finally came within reach, Cook grabbed at the horse's tail. Sensing something was wrong, the rider turned in the saddle. "Let go that horse," he demanded angrily.

"Well, I won't," Cook resolutely replied.

"If I get off you will," the Kentuckian growled.

"You won't get off," Cook assured his reluctant rescuer, and grimly hung on until he reached shallow water. Dragging himself ashore, he took his horse's reins from a waiting lieutenant and rejoined his regiment, feeling fortunate that the only thing he had lost was his saber.[18]

Once the 2nd Kentucky was safely across, it was the 8th Indiana's turn. The rear guard, Company D, lost their way two or three times after leaving the main road at Stowe's Ferry, but they soon reached the riverbank and lined up across the cornfield with the rest of the regiment. Reversing their previous order of march, the Hoosiers advanced by the right flank, so that Company D filed over the bank first. Zigzagging through the watery maze, they posted men at all the sharp angles in the ford, relieving the guides the 2nd Kentucky had left behind. Even so, three Company D boys got "a good ducking." All three bobbed to the surface unhurt and eventually made their way ashore, but Private William R. Julian suffered a severe leg injury when his horse stumbled and fell, pinning him against a rock. Some of Julian's comrades saw his predicament in time to rescue him, but fishing an injured man out of the water was no easy task. The passage of the 5th Iowa, 4th Tennessee, 9th Ohio, and 2nd Kentucky had made the east bank so wet and slippery the Hoosiers had to dismount and hold on to their horses' tails to negotiate the steep climb.

It was 2:00 or 3:00 A.M., July 17, before the last troopers scrambled ashore. A half-mile downstream at Stowe's Ferry, Lieutenant William T. Hays and Company H of the 5th Iowa worked feverishly for most of the night, shuttling across pack mules, ambulances, and artillery. When the last load was safely delivered, the Iowans presumably scuttled the ferry to keep the Rebels from using it.

The Tallapoosa was the severest test the raiders had yet encountered. "Ever after," wrote Colonel Hamilton, "we referred to the crossing of that river, in that night, with a shudder, for the thought of it was as unpleasant as that of any battle we were ever in." Yet despite the darkness and the difficulty of the ford, there was only one apparent fatality, a Negro boy riding with the 9th Ohio who drowned when the swift current swept away his mule.[19]

After reaching the east side of the river, Company D of the 8th Indiana was ordered to picket the eastern approaches to the ferry and moved downstream. Taking a position astride the main road just as day began to dawn, Privates Jerry Houtz and George Nock spied a house about 400 yards away. Hoping to talk the owner out of some bread or maybe even a few hot biscuits, they decided to pay a visit.

These two hungry Hoosiers were not the only ones drawn toward the house. During the night, vague rumors of Rousseau's approach had reached Captain John W. Browne, the county enrolling officer at Dadeville, nine miles east of Stowe's Ferry. A veteran of the 2nd Louisiana Infantry, hobbled by a gunshot wound suffered a year earlier at the battle of Chancellorsville, Browne hastily mustered a company of twenty old men and boys and set out to sink the ferry before the Yankees could cross the Tallapoosa.

Daylight found the captain and his stalwart band just short of the river. As a precaution, Browne sent Lieutenant Calder, Dr. Ridgway, and a Mr. Norris forward to reconnoiter; then he rode ahead of the rest of the company, looking for more volunteers. He overtook his three scouts in front of the house the two Yankee troopers had just entered.

Private Jesse E. Culbertson of the 8th Indiana was on the picket line, 400 yards to the west, when he spotted the little group of horsemen. He aimed his Spencer rifle and fired. His bullet struck Captain Browne squarely in the head, killing him instantly. Other Yankee pickets also opened fire, just as Privates Houtz and Nock dashed out of the house, leveling their guns at Lieutenant Calder and Dr. Ridgway. The two men threw up their hands, surrendering a revolver and a double-barreled shotgun. Their companion, Mr. Norris, somehow managed to escape, and fled with the rest of the frightened volunteers.[20]

Captain Browne's lifeless body was still lying in the road when Rousseau's advance guard, Company K of the 8th Indiana, passed through the picket lines about 8:00 A.M. Shortly afterward, Privates Culbertson, Houtz, Nock, and the rest of Company D remounted and hurried to overtake their regiment. They had ridden thirty-two miles the previous day, spent most of the night fording a treacherous river, and their haggard faces all told the same story. These men were tired; dead tired. Even Rousseau acknowledged, "the men were much exhausted," but he added, "being within a day's march of the railroad, I deemed it important to press forward."

It was amazing he did not have more stragglers than he did, but all of Rousseau's men had heard about the horrible conditions at the Rebel prison camp at Andersonville and they knew what would happen if they lagged behind. So they kept going, mile after weary mile. Funneling through a narrow defile known as Jackson's Gap, they rode south toward Montgomery for about four miles before turning back to the east. They met no opposition, and by 11:00 A.M. the advance guard was within a mile of Dadeville.

The town shimmered tranquilly in the Sunday morning calm. Everything was strangely quiet, especially since the remnants of Captain Browne's little company had surely spread the alarm by now. Fearing an ambush, the entire 8th Indiana charged into the west side of the courthouse square. Yelling and shouting like demons, they swept down the adjacent side streets, capturing four or five Rebel soldiers.

Many of the residents were on their way to church, but the Yankees quickly cordoned off the town, firing at anyone who did not halt promptly when challenged. Once the approaches had been secured, Rousseau passed the word to his regimental commanders to have the men dismount and rest. As had been the case at Ashville and Talladega, the Yankees generally respected private property, but the residents of Dadeville were understandably cool toward their guests. Sergeant Jackson of the 8th Indiana "exchanged a few smiles," but Rousseau acknowledged he "found damned few sympathizers, and they were damned timid."[21]

Of course, Rousseau's practice of confiscating horses, mules, and provisions was not calculated to win him many friends but to keep his column moving. "The day being extremely warm," explained Private Jack Wilson, "our horses began to give out in great numbers, hence every available animal was pressed for remounts, many being taken from buggies and carryalls, and vehicles of every description were left standing in the road, with the harness in front of them, the 'animiles' having disappeared. By far the greatest portion of the travelers thus brought to a stand, were ladies! some of whom took it as a good joke (not very easy to see though), others fumed and fretted, some 'sat like patience on a monument smiling in grief.' Others vented their indignation in no set phrases, and whose anger kept rising until they went off in an inarticulate, hysterical scream, like an African clown I once heard lecture on 'womans rights.'

"As for myself, my usual ill-starred fortune in the equine lottery gave me a double-action pump snorter which I managed to get along after a fashion until the charge at Dadesville [*sic*] took the starch completely out of him, and I was coagitating seriously to myself about stopping the next church-going vehicle, when luckily, enquiring of a negro where there was any horses to be found? he answered: 'plenty but half a mile off in the woods massa,' and by promising said nigger not to kill him, nor allow any one else to do so, got him to catch me a good horse. To which Jack and his fortunes were soon transferred and he went on his way rejoicing."

Others were not as fortunate. A remount detail of a corporal and eight men from Company K of the 9th Ohio was taken prisoner, bringing the total number of men captured from that ill-starred outfit during the last two days to eighteen.

After about an hour, Rousseau paroled his own prisoners and took his leave of Dadeville. Mindful of the orders issued in Ashville, officers tried to enforce discipline, even arresting Corporal J. P. Barrington of the 9th Ohio for straggling and leaving the ranks. But they could not be everywhere at once, and a few troopers lingered long enough to rob private homes of money and other valuables.[22]

These stragglers had to ride hard to catch up with the column as it plodded southeast at three miles an hour. By midafternoon, this steady pace had carried the raiders across Sandy Creek and past the crossroads village of De Soto. Here the column turned sharply to the southwest. This may have been a final effort on Rousseau's part to convince Confederate authorities he was indeed heading for Montgomery, but according to one source, Rousseau left the main road in order to bypass any opposition massing in front of him, and would have struck the Montgomery & West Point Railroad at Notasulga had he not received a report Clanton was leading a force from Montgomery to meet him. Whatever the reason, after passing through the little hamlet of Home, Rousseau's column suddenly veered back to the southeast and headed straight for Loachapoka.

Three miles short of the station, the advance guard captured Lieutenant Colonel Washington de Lafayette Craig of the 10th Texas Cavalry (dismounted) as he was enjoying the company of "a bevy of young ladies" at a house near the roadside. Taken completely by surprise, the colonel was much embarrassed. One of his companions, a tall, elegant-looking young woman, approached Rousseau with tears rolling down her cheeks and pleaded fervently for Craig's release. Rousseau received her with his characteristic courtesy and asked, "Are you the Colonel's wife, madam?"

"No, sir, I am his friend."

Rousseau smiled and said he presumed it amounted to the same thing. Assuring her the colonel would not be harmed, he directed one of his officers to take Craig's parole and leave him in the lady's custody.[23]

Continuing southward, Rousseau's leading regiment, the 8th Indiana, struck the Montgomery & West Point Railroad at Loachapoka at 6:00 P.M., capturing a few prisoners, seizing the mail, and cutting the telegraph wires. The rest of the Yankee column soon came shuffling up to the track, casting long shadows in the last slanting rays of the sun. Company by company, regiment by regiment, weary riders dismounted and squinted at a handful of weatherbeaten buildings, the station, and a scattering of houses. They had marched 240 miles, forded two raging rivers, fought a pitched battle, and endured endlessly long hours in the saddle to get to this seemingly insignificant little town with a name scarcely any of them could pronounce; but their mission was suddenly, abundantly clear. They were astride the major rail artery supplying the Confederate army in Atlanta, and every man knew the real work was about to begin.[24]

8
ROUSSEAU'S RAID
WORKING ON THE RAILROAD

JULY 17–JULY 18, 1864

And there was mounting in hot haste: the steed,
The mustering squadron, and the clattering car,
Went pouring forward with impetuous speed,
and swiftly forming in the ranks of war; . . .
While thronged the citizens with terror dumb,
Or whispering with white lips, — "The foe!
they come! they come!"

—Lord Byron, *Childe Harold's Pilgrimage*

It was about 8:00 P.M. before the last of Rousseau's regiments, the 5th Iowa, reached Loachapoka. Tired and hungry after the thirty-one-mile march from Stowe's Ferry, they dismounted and joined the other troops crowding around the railroad depot and a government warehouse bulging with supplies.

"Logopoca [*sic*] should have been defended to the last by the rebel soldiers," wrote Lieutenant Fanning of the 9th Ohio, "containing as it did the largest amount of quartermaster and commissary stores any of us ever saw gathered at any depot."[1]

Rousseau's adjutant, Captain Williams, estimated there were 2,000 pairs of harness, several hundred muskets, and just about anything else an army might require. But mostly there was food: flour, sugar, coffee, hardtack, corn, and oats.

Rousseau allowed his men to help themselves, but always careful of civilian property, he posted guards over private homes and stores. After a couple of hours to rest and feed, Company A of the 8th Indiana went to picket the roads north of town, while a 300-man detachment rode east along the railroad toward Auburn. Other patrols scouted west and south, looking for any sign of opposition, but Rousseau devoted most of his attention to the railroad. After a little experimenting, he found that twenty or thirty men using fence rails could easily pry up large sections of track. He directed Tom Harrison to organize the 1st Brigade into working parties and at 10:00 P.M. the destruction of the railroad began in earnest.

"The character of the superstructure of the road and the kind of timber used in its construction greatly facilitated the work," Rousseau explained. "The cross-ties were of pitch pine, and into these were sunken stringers of the same kind of wood, and a light bar of iron [called strap rail] spiked on the top through holes in a projection or flange. The wedges by which the string timbers were fastened into the cross-ties were readily driven out, and from 50 to 100 feet of the track raised from the ties at once by the use of fence rails as levers. The rails and timbers from one side of the road were placed upon those of the other, and fence rails and other combustible material piled on them, and fire applied. The dry pine burned so readily and produced such an

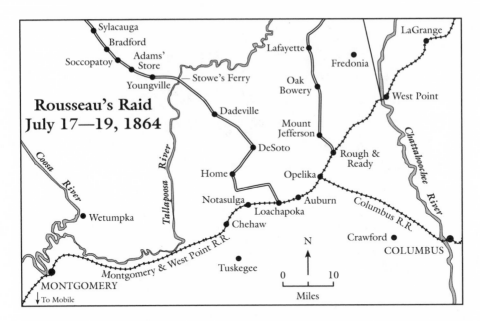

Rousseau's Raid
July 17—19, 1864

intense heat that the iron was warped and rendered worthless, and the ties burned off where the track rested on them, making the destruction complete."

Harrison's men soon had a string of bonfires burning brightly along the south side of the track. The flames hissed and crackled noisily, and the iron rails still spiked to the crossties writhed convulsively, buckling with "as loud an explosion as an extemporized 4th of July cannon."

Billowing clouds of thick black smoke boiled up into the night, and red-hot cinders, borne aloft by the intense heat, pelted down like fiery rain. What followed, said Jack Wilson, "came nearest to the stereotyped phrase of 'hell broke loose' of any thing I ever saw." A shower of sparks set the depot afire. Within minutes, the building was a "pyramid of flame," illuminating the whole town with a harsh red glare that made the fires along the railroad seem pale in comparison. The blaze quickly threatened to engulf a nearby hotel and "several fine buildings." Women and children shrieked and wailed. Officers yelled commands. Cavalrymen clambered to the rooftops with wet blankets and flailed furiously at the flames. Even Rousseau pitched in to help save the home of a widow, who expressed her surprise at the gallantry of these men she had previously regarded as "vandals."

Amid the smoke and confusion, horses left tied to the fences and hitching rails where Harrison's men had leaned their weapons grew increasingly restive. When some of the palings caught fire, the animals whinnied in terror and pulled fiercely at their reins. A few broke loose and galloped madly in all directions, threatening to start a general stampede. Frantic troopers chased after them, waving their arms and shouting, while others braved the searing heat to snatch up carbines and cartridge boxes and lead their frightened mounts to safety.

Rousseau's men eventually rounded up the strays and managed to confine the blaze

This lithograph shows Yankee infantrymen tearing up strap rail like that Rousseau's raiders encountered between Notasulga and Opelika. Strap rail was much easier to pry up and bend than T-rail, enabling Rousseau's men to obliterate more track in two days than the rest of Sherman's cavalry destroyed during the entire campaign. Reproduced from the Collections of the Library of Congress.

to the railroad buildings and a nearby blacksmith shop, undoubtedly saving much of Loachapoka from ruin. With the danger past, half the command went back to wrecking the railroad, while the other half slept beside their guns, fully expecting the bugles to summon them to arms before morning.

During the night, the large detachment Rousseau had sent eastward returned and reported a reconnaissance patrol probing the outskirts of Auburn had come under fire. No one was hit, but rather than press the issue, the patrol had fallen back.[2]

News of the approaching Yankee raid had reached Auburn earlier that day, when Major W. H. C. Price of the Nitre Bureau arrived on the noon train from Montgomery. Returning from an inspection tour, Price had met a Confederate courier ten miles east of Tuscaloosa on Thursday, July 14, who intimated he was carrying a dispatch warning a Yankee column had been sighted at Blountsville. Price heard little more about the raid until he reached the Alabama and Tennessee Rivers Railroad at Randolph, where he learned the Yankees had entered Talladega early Friday morning. Concerned for the safety of the government supplies in his care at Auburn, he had taken a northbound train, only to be turned back at the railroad trestle at Wilsonville. Resorting to a roundabout route through Selma, he finally got home, brimming with news about the raiders.

Price's warning took Auburn completely by surprise. "It was an unusually quiet and lovely Sunday," wrote Isabelle Shacklette. "There being few persons from the country in town, that I could hardly credit the news. But in the course of an hour, church alarm bells were commenced ringing, wagons were thundering through town, carriages, buggies, barouches, conveyances of all kinds containing women and children were rushing through the streets, excited people talking and crying on the corners, and the greatest confusion and noise possible, for the streets are very rocky and stoney. . . ."[3]

It was a familiar scene, one that had been repeated in almost every town along Rousseau's route, and Auburn was no better prepared than any of the others had been. Small groups of men, "some bareheaded, some coatless, all with hands in their pockets, with abstracted looks and vacant stares," gathered near the depot or along the railroad with seemingly no idea of what to do.

Captain Thomas H. Francis of the 4th Tennessee Infantry had assumed command of the post at Auburn the previous day. He had no provost guard, no organized force of any kind. Resolving to do what he could, he mustered a few convalescents from the Texas Hospital at the East Alabama Male College (later Auburn University) and a handful of local militia, some eighteen men and boys in all. He equipped them with shotguns and horses impressed from civilian barns and stables, and telegraphed Columbus, Georgia, requesting reinforcements. None came.

About 10:00 P.M., some of Francis's pickets traded shots with the Yankee patrol nosing around the edge of town. Presently, two horsemen, "one hatless, the other 'witless,'" came galloping down the main street, shouting that the Yankees were close behind, "as thick as the leaves of the forest." The two riders disappeared into the dark, leaving the men gathered around the depot alone with their thoughts. Most of them headed for home, but if they slept at all, noted one wag, it was "on lounges, with packed carpet bags for pillows, walking canes near by, dressed *cap-a-pie* for a woodland jaunt."

Late that night, a self-styled Scipio, described as "one of those noble spirits, 'who were born to command,'" rode into town at the head of five or six mounted militiamen. Halting in the street, he lavished loud praise on his troops for their dauntless courage in routing the foul invaders who had approached so boldly in the dark. Adding that he hoped they entertained "similar feelings" for him, he dismissed his followers for the night.

Over at the Nitre Bureau, Major Price was busy supervising the loading of wagons. Working diligently, he managed to remove his entire stock of nitre, all his records, and most of his supplies, except for a large quantity of lead and potash. Little or no attempt was made to save the quartermaster and commissary supplies stored in a warehouse near the railroad, but there were no more alarms during the night, and it began to look like a wholesale evacuation might not be necessary.

By daylight Auburn was rife with rumors the foe had fled, "awed by the formidable resistance he so unexpectedly encountered." The menfolk reassembled around the depot, and according to one observer, "As the report, that the enemy were retracing their steps gained credence as it spread from circle to circle, faces began to clear up, eyes to brighten and an occasional laugh, provoked by the previous night's incidents, would break into gentle ripples, the placid surfaces of the sombre feeling that pervades the scene, anon a belligerent feeling began to defuse [*sic*] itself through the crowd. Propositions for pursuit were suggested, and probable captures of the vandal foe hinted at. Finally some concern, as to the color of the State escutcheon would assume was expressed, should the enemy escape scot free. Then busy notes of preparations for pursuit could be heard, the clinking of blacksmith tools told of guns being repaired, rusted loads being drawn, broken tubes being filed, &c. Horses were 'inspected' and pronounced fit for service or condemned. Everything bespoke of an early departure."[4]

The Yankee column had indeed begun moving shortly after daylight, prodded by a gunshot that sent Corporal Ralph H. Jones and Private Uriah Oblinger of the 8th Indiana diving for cover at one of the picket posts north of Loachapoka. The bullet narrowly missed Jones, leaving its mark on the shoulder of his blue jacket. A few tense minutes passed, but when no Rebels appeared, Rousseau gave orders to mount up. Officers called in their pickets and relieved the men guarding private homes and businesses.

Private Jack Wilson and three troopers assigned to keep watch on a pharmacy and the shoe shop next door took a quick look inside before they left to make sure everything was all right. To their consternation, "nearly every scrap of leather" in the shoe shop had disappeared. All that remained in the pharmacy were "some jars containing various pulverized substances," and "a few bottles of various colored liquids, bitter as the waters of Marah." Wilson and his comrades had been so busy guarding the front door, they had forgotten about the back. Several other stores suffered similar fates, and Southern newspapers later excoriated the Yankees for breaking into the Masonic Hall and stealing the fraternal jewels and regalia.[5]

But most of the damage was done to the railroad. Working eastward from Loachapoka, by daylight Tom Harrison's men had torn up six miles of track. Well satisfied with the night's work, Rousseau recalled his section gangs at 5:00 A.M. Within an hour, the 5th Iowa was leading the column westward along a dirt road skirting the right-of-way.

Rousseau knew he had to work fast. Dividing his two brigades into five small detachments, he ordered Major Baird to proceed to Chehaw Station, thirteen miles southwest of Loachapoka, with Companies B, F, H, and M of the 5th Iowa and four companies of the 4th Tennessee. After burning the trestle over Uphaupee Creek, Baird's men were to work their way back toward Notasulga, tearing up the track as they went. The rest of Matt Patrick's 2nd Brigade, accompanied by the artillery, ambulances, and pack train, would strike the railroad somewhere west of Notasulga and work their way toward a junction with Baird. Jones's 8th Indiana would tear up the track in the immediate vicinity of Notasulga, leaving Elijah Watts's 2nd Kentucky to take care of the section between there and Loachapoka.[6]

Whether by accident or design, Rousseau had sent his best regiments toward Montgomery, the most likely source of any resistance. He was sitting astride his horse a half-mile west of Loachapoka, watching the long line of troopers file past, when he saw the 9th Ohio approaching at the head of the 1st Brigade. Calling Colonel Hamilton aside, he directed him to turn his regiment and the rest of the 4th Tennessee back to Loachapoka and tear up the track toward Atlanta. "Don't stop till you hear from me," Rousseau added. "If Clanton attacks you, fight him; if he is too much for you, fall back on me. But unless it becomes necessary, don't stop the work."

Hamilton thanked Rousseau for this vote of confidence and turned the head of his column eastward to do the general's bidding.[7]

By this time, news of the Yankee raid had spread far and wide. Late Thursday evening, July 14, the same Rebel courier Major Price had met on his way home galloped into Tuscaloosa, bringing Brigadier General Gideon J. Pillow a message Colonel Benjamin J. Lea had written at Elyton on July 13:

> On yesterday between 10 & 11 o'clock in the morning a Yankee force supposed to be about two thousand arrived at Blountsville, Ala. They were at Blountsville when my courier left at 4 o'clock P.M. Their number is altogether uncertain. I will probably get accurate information as to their number and destination by next courier. If they start this way I will immediately inform you. I have no force here to keep them in check.

Pillow promptly relayed this information to departmental headquarters at Tupelo, Mississippi. Without waiting for orders, he started his two cavalry brigades toward Montevallo to intercept the raiders.

As Pillow rode eastward, he received further reports of the Yankees' progress. Upon reaching Montevallo on July 16, his adjutant, Major John C. Burch, wrote to General Clanton:

> General Pillow directs me to say to you that he is informed by Major [Eugene F.] Falconnet and Colonel Lea, at Elyton, that the enemy's column divided at Ashville, over half going to Talladega, which you engaged; the other half coming down on the west side of [the] Coosa River, moving, as it was said, for this place. If we were to advance for the purpose of forming a junction with you that force might cut off your supplies and put both in a very awkward position by seizing this place. He has, therefore, determined not to advance until he can ascertain definitely whether the force on the west side of [the] Coosa is coming down. This information he will have in a day or two. The stock of this railroad is now ordered to run no farther than Coosa bridge, to which point it will be necessary for you to fall back temporarily to get forage and supplies. By that time he will advance his force, and the two united will be strong enough to take the field and advance to the former position at Oxford and Blue Mountain. He expects you to act promptly on this information, unless you are satisfied that no such column has come down on the west side of the river. Send by return courier whatever information you have of this column.

This wait-and-see attitude must have infuriated Clanton, but there is no record of his reply. When the Yankees failed to appear at Blue Mountain, he had hurried to Talladega to pick up their trail, and he had no intention of falling back to Wilsonville for "forage and supplies." If "bluebellies" could live off the country, so could he.[8]

The first vague rumors of Rousseau's approach had reached the city of Montgomery early on July 15 with the arrival of a day-old edition of the *Selma Mississippian*. According to a front-page article, a northbound passenger train on the Alabama and Tennessee Rivers Railroad had pulled into Blue Mountain at 10:00 P.M., July 13, to find the station buzzing over reports that 1,200 Yankee cavalrymen were at Ashville. Military authorities had sent the train back to Selma at 2:00 A.M., amid assertions the raiders had divided their force into three columns at Ashville and were heading for Talladega, Montevallo, and the Coosa River bridge at Wilsonville. The paper also reported General Clanton had captured a Yankee courier on Tuesday, July 12, supposedly carrying orders directing the Union commander at Decatur to send two cavalry columns to destroy the Alabama and Tennessee Rivers Railroad and lay waste to the countryside in conjunction with another mounted column moving south from Rome, Georgia. "We regard this intelligence as perfectly reliable," the *Mississippian* had concluded.[9]

This unsettling news and the failure of westbound trains from Atlanta to arrive the previous day (a result of Stoneman's Moore's Bridge raid) provided fresh grist for the rumor mills. Sidewalk strategists waxed loud and long about what the government should do, but after the initial scare, Montgomery "wrapped itself up with the cloak of incredulity and apathetic quiet," until the clatter of hoofbeats drummed along the city streets about noon on Saturday. A dust-covered rider brought dispatches; 1,500 Yankees were on their way to burn the statehouse and sack the city! Church bells rang and heralds sped through the streets, sounding the alarm. Crowds of concerned citizens gathered around the post office, anxious for the latest news, and the inevitable rumors began, always credited to some reliable but unidentified source. By sundown, the Yankee column had swelled from 1,500 to over 3,500, and many wide-eyed listeners hurried home to start packing, firmly convinced the city would soon be "wrapt in flames and half the community murdered in cold blood."[10]

Amid all the gossip and speculation, a delegation of some of Montgomery's most respected citizens called upon Major General Jones Mitchell Withers to inquire about the readiness of the city's defenses. A graying 1835 graduate of West Point, Withers commanded the Reserve Forces of Alabama, composed of men under eighteen and over forty-five years of age, but recent orders from Richmond had sent all his troops to meet a supposed Yankee threat to Mobile. He did not have a regiment under his command, he explained to his visitors; nor did he have the authority to call out, organize, or equip one. He would, however, render all the assistance he could and offered to command any troops the city raised for its defense. He would also telegraph Mobile, asking for the return of one of his borrowed battalions.

The citizens' committee earnestly requested him to do so, and that afternoon they circulated a handbill urging people of all classes and all ages to meet at the courthouse at 8:00 P.M. to "adopt measures for the defense of their homes and firesides." A large crowd gathered at the appointed hour and named Colonel James R. Powell to chair the proceedings. Calling the meeting to order, Powell briefly summarized the purpose of the assembly and the latest reports of the raiders' progress. When a citizen stood up and launched into an impassioned appeal for action, Powell reminded him that action, not speech-making, was why they were there. The haranguer called for General Withers. Several other voices joined in.

Responding to the clamor, Withers rose and looked out over an expectant audience. His speech, he announced as the room quieted, was going to be a short one. He needed a hundred men to volunteer immediately for cavalry service. He expected every Confederate officer in the city to report for duty at once and every man who could carry a musket to enroll by 10:00 P.M. in one of the volunteer companies that would assemble at points he would designate. He wanted obedience, he said in closing, not consultation.

One or two citizens took it upon themselves to offer a few suggestions, but as soon as they had their say, the meeting adjourned. Withers asked Captain Vincent M. Elmore, home on sick leave from the 1st Alabama Cavalry, to impress as many horses as he needed to organize two mounted companies and proceed that night to picket the nearby ferries over the Alabama and Tallapoosa rivers. At the same time, mustering officers appeared on darkened street corners to begin taking down the names of men answering the call to arms. They quickly enrolled two companies of volunteers and filled the ranks of two more that had previously been organized. By 11:00 P.M. the broad street in front of the city armory was crowded with men lining up to receive arms and ammunition. Shortly after midnight, orders came from Withers's headquarters directing the citizen soldiers to go home and wait until they heard the church bells ring. If no alarm sounded, they were to report to their companies at 7:00 A.M.

Anticipating the worst, government officials sent a recently arrived military payroll into the countryside for safekeeping. The Central Bank moved all its specie and bullion, much of it belonging to Atlanta banks, to the railroad depot under heavy guard. The precious cargo was loaded aboard a special train, and the locomotive kept up a full head of steam, ready to roll south at the first sign of trouble. Panicked civilians fled in droves, and scores of horse-drawn vehicles, groaning under the weight of household goods of every description, crowded the dark streets, all trying to get out of town before it was too late.

Sunday, July 17, dawned wet and overcast. Sleepless mustering officers added the last names to the long lists of volunteers. By 7:00 A.M., they had raised two companies of cavalry and five of infantry (one composed exclusively of old men), but this was nowhere near enough. The citizens who reported to their places of assembly that morning were detained while Withers sent out his provost guard with orders to collar every man who could carry a gun. Foreigners, city and state officials, congressmen, policemen, convalescent soldiers, men with medical deferments: there would be no exceptions. Most of the recalcitrants surrendered willingly enough, but a few were "highly indignant" and had to be forced into the ranks at the point of a bayonet. Dismissed until 11:00 A.M., the volunteers reassembled at the appointed time and waited in the hot sun for about an hour before receiving orders to report again at 5:00 P.M.[11]

By this time, news of the impending peril had spread to other anxious communities. After delivering "a most excellent discourse" in Greenville, a little railroad town about fifty miles to the south, the Reverend J. C. Davis of the Montgomery Methodist Church closed his Sunday sermon by saying, "And now my brethren, I have discharged one duty, but I have one other still to perform. Our enemy, the enemy of our country, is threatening the capital of our State. It is my duty and yours to go to its defense. I shall, and I want every man to go. All who are willing and ready to go will hold up their hands." Every man in the congregation raised his hand and followed the reverend out the door.[12]

By boat, by train, on horseback, and on foot, citizens and soldiers began converging on Montgomery from all points of the compass. Convinced the danger to Montevallo had passed, Gideon Pillow was moving his cavalry south toward Selma. At the same time, Lieutenant General Stephen D. Lee, commanding the Department of Alabama, Mississippi, and East Louisiana, ordered Lieutenant Colonel Marshall T. Polk and a trainload of 400 infantry eastward from Aberdeen, Mississippi. After repeated and urgent telegrams, Major General Dabney H. Maury, the Confederate commander at Mobile, was sending a battalion of Withers's reserves north from Pollard.

For the rest of the afternoon, disquieting reports continued trickling into Montgomery. The most accurate of them, already a day old by the time it arrived, put the

Yankee column at Sylacauga at 11:00 Friday night, moving south. More ominous news followed at 2:00 P.M., when a courier brought word the Yankees were just four miles above Wetumpka, only a six- or seven-hour ride from the capital. An attack seemed imminent until another rider reported the Yankees had left the Montgomery road twenty-six miles north of Wetumpka and headed east. The city breathed an almost audible sigh of relief, but military preparations continued.

Alabama Governor Thomas Hill Watts returned Sunday afternoon from commencement exercises at the University of Alabama at Tuscaloosa. Learning of the Yankee raid, he had canceled a fifteen-day furlough he had given the University Corps of Cadets and hurried back to the capital, directing all the cadets living around Montgomery to report for duty. Watts also issued his own call for volunteers and ordered the impressment of horses needed for artillery batteries. Despite his own military experience as colonel of the 17th Alabama Infantry, he seemed content to leave General Withers in command.[13]

It was probably just as well, because Montgomery was rapidly getting top-heavy with Rebel brass. General Braxton Bragg, President Davis's chief military advisor, had arrived unexpectedly on the train from Atlanta after his meeting with General Johnston. In his daily reports to Richmond, Bragg had stressed the vulnerability of Johnston's position and the need for his army to take some kind of offensive action. "Our railroad communication with Montgomery is now at the mercy of the enemy," he warned, "and a mere raid may destroy Montgomery, and we would not even know it had moved."

Leaving Atlanta late July 15 or early July 16 to meet with Stephen D. Lee in Mississippi, Bragg had passed through Loachapoka just five hours ahead of Rousseau. Despite his earlier presentiments, he apparently had no inkling of the Yankee raid until he reached Montgomery about 3:00 P.M.[14]

While he did not try to supplant Withers, an old friend and subordinate, he did try to coordinate the various detachments converging on the city. He sent a telegram to Selma urging Gideon Pillow to pursue the raiders "vigorously and rapidly in whatever direction they go."

Pillow wired back, acknowledging he had already received orders from Stephen Lee to dismount his cavalry at Selma and move them by boat and rail to Montgomery and West Point. "I will move my command by [the] first boat from this place on their arrival some time to-night," he advised. "Intelligence just received states that enemy has diverged from Wetumpka road toward Opelika."

Later that afternoon, Pillow sent Bragg a second telegram, suggesting the raid aimed to liberate 30,000 Yankee prisoners of war held at Andersonville. Anticipating the need for mounted operations if that happened, he asked if he should start his horses and wagons across country.

"Move your horses and train by direct road on the south side of [the] river," Bragg replied. "Indeed it would be as well for all your command to march by that route, as the city is now safe; move with all possible expedition."

But Pillow, a man of enormous ego, could never quite reconcile himself to a subordinate role. In a third telegram to Bragg, he asserted:

> Late New Orleans accounts that [Union General Edward R. S.] Canby has transportation for 30,000 troops. There is known to be but little force there. This transportation is intended to be thrown into the Chattahoochee River to bring out the

Andersonville prisoners. That is the object of Rousseau's movement. My judgment is that there is where your attention should be turned.

After this lecture to the nominal general-in-chief of the Confederate army, Pillow added that his wagon train was at Montevallo; his men and horses were at Plantersville, still twenty-two miles from Selma. He would leave Selma by train at 6:00 P.M. to meet them near the north bank of the Alabama River.

This exchange with Pillow was probably what led Bragg to wire Stephen Lee, "Nothing reliable from the raiders. They are reported as moving on this place and Opelika. The city will be defended but for want of cavalry no pursuit can be made."[15]

By this time, an exhausted Withers and his sleepless staff had mustered upwards of a thousand men, at least half of them volunteers. Fifty-four University of Alabama cadets had reported for duty and Companies A, B, D, E, and G of Major James L. Davidson's battalion of the 1st Alabama Reserves had arrived from Pollard. Each of Davidson's men carried forty rounds of buck and ball and an ancient but recently rifled musket capable of hurling this load (three buckshot and a one-ounce lead ball) perhaps a hundred yards. The rest of Withers's men, with the possible exception of his provost guard, were unarmed, and his officers worked frantically to equip them with whatever weapons they could find.

They succeeded well enough for the city volunteers to assemble at 5:00 Sunday evening in the square bounded by Adams, Alabama, Hull, and McDonough streets. In a show of force calculated to reassure even the most fainthearted residents, the troops paraded down Main Street, past Montgomery Hall and the Madison House hotel. An hour later, the dreaded news came. The telegraph had gone dead at Loachapoka. The Yankees were on the railroad.[16]

Rather than await the raiders' approach, Withers had already resolved to go after them. He put one of his staff officers, Major Bryan Morel Thomas, in command of Davidson's battalion, the provost guard, and the university cadets and ordered him to proceed eastward until he met the Yankees.

The twenty-eight-year-old Thomas had little experience leading troops. An 1858 graduate of West Point who had finished twenty-second in a class of twenty-five, he had spent most of the war on Withers's staff. In June 1864 he had briefly commanded a small regiment of Pillow's cavalry, and Withers had recently recommended him to President Davis as "capable and deserving" of promotion to brigadier general. Of course, Withers was understandably prejudiced. His oldest daughter was Thomas's fiancée.[17]

Now Withers was going to give his soon-to-be son-in-law a chance to earn that promotion. On the night of July 17, Montgomery's darkened streets echoed with the measured tread of marching feet as Thomas's troops tramped down to the depot to a waiting freight train. Some of the men climbed up into the cars and sat down against the walls, cradling their muskets beside them. Others scrambled for a seat on the roof. A few wrestled with two cannon Withers had conjured up from somewhere, along with the horses to pull them. Everything was hustle and bustle, confusion and noise, but once the troops were safely aboard, the engine gave a shrill whistle. The cars lurched violently, and the train pulled out of the station amid a chorus of good-byes and shouts of encouragement.

Any of these well-wishers who looked closely would not have been optimistic. Most of the troops crowded into the cars were mere boys, fifteen to seventeen years old, who had never been under fire. They were poorly armed, badly outnumbered, and commanded by an officer they had never seen. But they were full of high spirits and youthful bravado, and that would have to do.

The boys spent a restless night on the swaying cars. About forty miles east of Montgomery, their train stopped at Chehaw Station at 8:00 A.M., July 18, and it was probably here they met Major Edward S. Ready and an understrength battalion of young conscripts. Ready's five companies had left Camp Watts, two miles west of Notasulga, earlier that morning and they were probably the ones who told Major Thomas the Yankees were just six miles up the road.[18]

Fearing an ambush, Thomas ordered Lieutenant George F. Redwood's University of Alabama cadets to fan out on both sides of the track and advance as skirmishers. The rest of the command, about 450 strong with the addition of Ready's battalion, followed aboard the train, with riflemen riding in the tender to protect the fireman and the engineer from Yankee sharpshooters.

The locomotive kept pace with the cadets at first, but then slowed to a crawl as it approached Uphaupee Creek, snorting puffs of smoke and steam as it nosed across the trestle. Suddenly a shot rang out and a bullet thudded into the roof of one of the boxcars, right between Private Dave Scott's legs. Looking to the right, the startled Scott saw a Yankee soldier clearly silhouetted on the hill crowned by Beasley's gin house. Brakes squealed as the train lurched to a stop in front of a collection of wooden buildings known as Beasley's Station and Thomas's men began piling off the cars. Even Charley Marsh, "one of the cleverest conductors who ever demanded a ticket of a purseless traveler," grabbed a gun and took a place in the ranks.[19]

At Thomas's direction, Major Ready ordered his conscripts to "face out" and form ranks on the left side of the train. To his dismay, he soon discovered the train had stopped on an uphill grade, leaving the battalion insufficient room to maneuver. Trying to remedy the situation, he ordered his men to assemble on the more open ground around Beasley's Station.

Yankee troopers in the gin house on the south side of the track had a clear view of the station and started shooting as soon as Ready's raw recruits emerged from behind the train. The whole battalion recoiled before this baptism of fire, forcing Ready to realign his ranks to the left and rear of the whitewashed buildings at the station.

On the right side of the train, Major Davidson was busy deploying his battalion. Acting on orders from Thomas, he directed Captain Junius L. Walthall and Company E to form a skirmish line and move up the track and to the left, while Captain Brunot Yniestre and Company B moved to the right to drive the Yankees from the gin house. Captain William M. Donahoo and Company G would fill the gap between Walthall and Yniestre, leaving Companies A and D, commanded by Captains William C. Ward and James A. McCaa, in reserve.

These preparations were still under way when Lieutenant Redwood's cadets brought word the Yankees were massing north of the railroad, apparently intending to outflank the train from the left. There was no time to lose. Officers hurriedly dressed the ranks, and Thomas ordered his skirmishers forward. Walthall's men scarcely got beyond the locomotive when Yankee troopers, hiding among the willow trees in a bog near the track, stood up and aimed a volley into them at a range of less than twenty paces. Lieutenant T. R. Bethea fell dead, a bullet in his brain. His men quickly avenged his death, gunning down the Union soldier who had fired the fatal shot from behind a wrought-iron fence surrounding a small cemetery.

Major Ready moved his battalion toward the sound of the guns, only to get hopelessly entangled in the dense undergrowth north of the railroad. His two rightmost companies came under fire and were soon hotly engaged. Several of Ready's men fell, but the Yankees realized the tables had been turned and soon began retreating to avoid being outflanked themselves.

While this fighting raged on the left, Yniestre's company of Davidson's battalion, supported by Captain Donahoo, began moving up the slope toward Beasley's gin house. Anticipating a fight, the Yankees had torn down sections of a rail fence running perpendicular to the railroad and built "pens" for their sharpshooters,[20] but they abandoned these makeshift fortifications as Yniestre and Donahoo charged up the hill, fleeing across a large field behind the gin house to take cover in some woods about 400 yards to the rear.

Pursuing Confederates reaching the top of the hill saw a troop of bluecoated cavalry in the middle of the field, apparently trying to cover the retreat. Sidling to the right along a rail fence behind the gin house, Yniestre's men opened fire, but the range was too great for their antiquated guns and the shots fell short. Yankee horsemen coolly returned the fire, their bullets splintering the fence rails protecting Yniestre's men and kicking up dust around their feet.

In an effort to outflank these mounted Federals, Major Thomas ordered Captain Ward to move Company A "by the left flank obliquely to the left," under cover of the woods near the railroad. Ward led his company forward at a double-quick, clambered over the fence at the corner close by the track, and formed his line in a thick stand of timber. By the time his boys were in position, their quarry had already trotted off the field, moving diagonally toward the woods where the other Yankees had taken refuge. Ward set out after them and Davidson followed with the rest of the battalion until he received orders from Thomas to halt at right angles with the railroad and form a skirmish line near the eastern edge of the field.

Davidson obediently deployed Ward's company on the extreme right, next to a dirt road paralleling the railroad. Companies G and E took cover on Ward's left in a ravine overgrown with persimmon trees, while Captain McCaa's Company D straddled the railroad near a copse of willow trees on the extreme left, and Captain Yniestre's company remained in reserve near the gin house.

Back at Beasley's Station, some University of Alabama boys, under the command of cadet chief of artillery Andrew Johnson Smith, dragged their two cannon off the train, only to discover the bore of one gun was so fouled as to render it useless. Hitching up the other, the eager cadets hurried forward, hoping to enfilade the Yankee line with case shot from the dirt road skirting Captain Ward's right flank. As they approached the front lines, the artillery horses, recently impressed from Montgomery stables, grew increasingly restive at the unaccustomed rattle of musketry. Equally inexperienced cadet drivers tried to keep the fractious animals under control, only to send the gun careening into a ditch. The terrified horses struggled to their feet, kicked off the harness, and bolted to the rear, leaving the gun lying upside down. Unable to right it, the cadets had to content themselves with forming ranks alongside Major Ready's conscripts.

Thomas had brought Ready's five companies across the railroad to form a line of battle directly behind Davidson's skirmishers. However, this maneuver left the battalion standing totally exposed in the middle of an open field. Ready had been wounded eleven times during his service with the Army of Northern Virginia and had no desire to go courting number twelve. He tried to get Thomas to change his orders, but the major was nowhere to be found. Taking matters into his own hands, Ready ordered his boys to march by the right flank into some woods on the south side of the dirt road and take cover behind a fence. While he waited to hear from Thomas, he deployed Lieutenant Redwood's cadets on the right side of the road, Lieutenant J. H. Steinmats's Company A on the left, and sent them forward as skirmishers to link up with Davidson's right flank.

This extended Thomas's line from just south of the dirt road to just north of the railroad, a front of about a half-mile, but his troops were spread paper thin, a good five paces apart with nothing behind them. Hoping to compensate for his lack of numbers, Thomas had the engineer back the train up and then pull into Chehaw again, blowing his whistle and ringing the bell as if fresh troops were arriving from Montgomery. To enhance the illusion, he had his own men cheer as if they were welcoming reinforcements.[21]

The trick worked. Convinced he was badly outnumbered when actually the odds were about even, the 5th Iowa's Major Baird sent a courier galloping eastward to tell Rousseau his detachment had been attacked by two trainloads of Rebel infantry.

By this time, Lieutenant Colonel Patrick and the five other Iowa companies had already passed Notasulga and were just a mile or two behind Baird. Together with the 8th Indiana and the 2nd Kentucky, they had moved up from Loachapoka in a column of twos, each regiment dismounting at appropriate intervals along the track. Fastening their carbines and accoutrements to their saddles and handing the reins to the men in the left-hand file, troopers on the right lined up shoulder to shoulder alongside the railroad. Using fence rails as levers, they overturned and set fire to the track just about as fast as a man could walk. The horseholders kept pace, moving through the adjacent fields, watching for any sign of the enemy.

Rousseau spent the morning with the 2nd Kentucky as they worked their way west of Loachapoka, and by 10:00 or 11:00 A.M., the Kentuckians had obliterated three miles of track. Farther west, the 8th Indiana destroyed the rails as far as Notasulga before stopping to rest a little and feed their horses. Companies A, C, D, E, and L of the 5th Iowa had torn up the track for another two or three miles beyond Notasulga but were hampered because a short distance above the station the road was laid with T-rail, which proved much more difficult to pry up than the flimsy wooden stringers they had previously encountered. When they tried to convince a black man to tell them where the railroad kept its crowbars and sledge hammers, he refused to talk, despite being rather roughly handled, and the raiders had to rely on fence rails and other makeshift tools.

The Iowans could clearly hear the echo of gunfire as they worked, and about 10:00 A.M. they met Baird's courier, who stopped long enough to tell them the major's detachment had been battling 1,200 to 1,500 Rebel infantrymen from Montgomery for the last hour. The courier then hurried eastward until he found Rousseau and repeated his story. Rousseau immediately ordered the 1st Brigade's Tom Harrison to send six companies of the 8th Indiana to reinforce Baird.[22]

A Kentucky farm boy who, like Rousseau, had moved to Indiana, studied law, and won election to the state legislature, Harrison was "strong, vigorous, tenacious—not specially quick to move, but, once in motion, almost resistless in weight and power."[23] At his command, six 8th Indiana companies—A, D, E, G, H, and perhaps F—dropped what they were doing and grabbed their rifles and carbines. Climbing into the saddle, they formed ranks and set out at a swinging trot. Stray bullets soon began whining overhead. The Hoosiers dismounted, formed in line of battle, and advanced into a patch of scrub oaks and pines, "so thick," said Private Eli Heaton, "you couldn't have seen a Johnnie two rods ahead of you." Emerging just north of the railroad, they saw Thomas's Confederates drawn up in the field on the other side of the track.

Harrison quickly sent two companies across the railroad to bolster Baird's embattled left flank and directed Fielder Jones to deploy the four remaining companies north of the track, where two companies of the 5th Iowa were endeavoring to turn the Confederate left. The rest of Lieutenant Colonel Patrick's detachment also came up and apparently supported the center and right of Baird's line, or may have remained in reserve.

While waiting for these reinforcements, Baird seems to have withdrawn at least some of his troops a couple of hundred yards to the rear. As a result, the shooting had slackened considerably by the time the university cadets and Lieutenant Steinmats's conscripts aligned themselves on the right flank of the Rebel line. They had scarcely gotten into position when Major Thomas received a report the Yankees were a mile away, advancing in line of battle. Immediately he ordered the rest of Ready's battalion forward.

Ready had advanced about 200 yards when another message from Thomas directed him to deploy his conscripts across the front of Davidson's battalion in a skirmish line stretching from the railroad to the dirt road on the right, leaving Lieutenant Steinmats's company to anchor his flank. This would have been a difficult maneuver even under the best of circumstances, Ready later explained, and "required great exertion on the part of the officers to effectively accomplish it from the fact that the principal portion of the command were uneducated in military discipline."

Once everyone was in place Thomas directed Davidson to align his troops sixty paces behind Ready's skirmishers and ordered both battalions up the wooded slope east of the ravine. Ready's line reached the top of the hill in good order and had just crouched behind a rail fence when a volley ripped through their left and left center. Screams rose above the din as Yankee bullets found their mark, but Ready's recruits gamely returned the fire. The opposing lines stood only thirty or forty yards apart, and the woods crackled with the roar of musketry. Muzzle flashes stabbed through billowing clouds of smoke like lightning in a storm, and the air reeked with the stench of burnt powder and sweat.

For over an hour, neither side seemed willing to give an inch. Then, at 12:20 P.M., an Iowa soldier yelled, "Major Baird is killed!"

Hearing this, Baird, who was very much alive, jumped up where everyone could see him. "That is a lie," he yelled, "give it to them boys!"

Baird's men levered fresh cartridges into their Sharps breechloaders, just as Tom Harrison swung two companies of the 8th Indiana across the railroad against the Confederate left.

The two conscript companies on the left of Ready's line, commanded by Major A. S. Bibb, had borne themselves gallantly up to this point, but they had never faced anything like the withering fire of the 8th Indiana's Spencers. Both companies wavered, then broke and ran. Panic spread down the length of the line as Ready's whole battalion crumbled and fled, despite the best efforts of their officers to stop them.

Colonel Thomas Joshua Harrison of the 8th Indiana Cavalry
commanded Rousseau's 1st Brigade. A big, powerful Kentuckian, like Rousseau, he had studied law and served a term
in the Indiana legislature. He led what was generally regarded as one of the best regiments in the Union army.
Courtesy of James Barnett. Used by permission.

Davidson's battalion was lying down, sixty paces to the rear, listening to Yankee
bullets clipping the leaves off the persimmon trees overhead. They did not realize
what was happening until Ready's fugitives came charging through their ranks,
taking some of Davidson's men with them. At the same instant, a scything volley
shredded the front and left flank of Companies D and E. Captain McCaa went down,
shot through both thighs. Private William Hunt set aside his gun and knelt beside the
captain to see what he could do to help. He was giving McCaa a drink from his
canteen when he toppled with a bullet in his thigh. The rest of Company D ran for their
lives, leaving Hunt and McCaa where they fell. When some of Rousseau's men came
up shortly afterward, a big, bearded, redheaded trooper looked at Hunt's youthful
face. It was "a damned shame," he said, turning to his comrades, "to be shooting at a
bunch of boys."

Farther to the right, Captain Junius Walthall of Company E saw a Yankee creeping
toward him through the brush. Walthall raised his pistol and was about to fire when
another bunch of bluecoats took him by surprise, demanding his surrender. Bolting
toward the rear, the captain took cover behind a tree, only to have a bullet tear through
his boot. The blow spun him to the ground, next to Private Thomas T. Durrett, who
was bleeding to death with wounds in both legs. Walthall's own wound was not
serious, but knowing the Yankees would soon be upon him, he covered his hands and
boot with the dying boy's blood and clutched his leg as if it were broken. When his
pursuers caught up with him, they saw the crimson stain oozing between the

Confederate captain's fingers and all the classic signs of a crushed femoral artery. "Leave him alone, men," one of them said. "He is done for." Once the Yankees were out of sight, Walthall struggled to his feet and hobbled toward the rear.

With the rout of Companies D and E, the fighting swept down the ravine, engulfing Captain Donahoo and Company G. Hit from front, flank, and rear, Donahoo's men scattered. Only Captain Ward's Company A and the university cadets escaped the carnage relatively unscathed. They managed to hold their positions on the right, but the rest of Davidson's battalion, like Ready's, ran for their lives.

Major Thomas was trying to rally these fugitives and form a line near the gin house when a band of mounted militiamen from Tuskegee rode up and dismounted. Nattily attired in brown linen uniforms, they took cover behind the stout rail fence that had sheltered Captain Yniestre's men at the outset of the battle. Their arrival, together with Thomas's stubborn stand, convinced Rousseau he could not reach the trestle at Uphaupee Creek without diverting more troops from the work on the railroad. Reluctantly, he sent word for Harrison to withdraw and Yankee buglers soon began sounding "Recall."

Seeing what looked like a retreat, the Tuskegee militia whooped and hollered from behind the relative security of the rail fence, taunting the Yankees to come back and fight. But there would be no more fighting that day. The battle of Chehaw, or Beasley's Station, was over.

As the firing sputtered and died, Major Thomas ordered Ward's company of Davidson's battalion to fall back and cover the approaches to the Uphaupee trestle.[24] Other companies began the grim task of caring for the dead and dying who lay sprawled on the battlefield. Fully 19 percent of Thomas's boys were casualties. Five of Davidson's battalion had been killed, forty-three wounded, some mortally, and at least four were missing. Ready's battalion had seventeen wounded, including two University of Alabama cadets, and seventeen missing.

The Yankees also left behind some casualties. "One of these was found after the battle with his brains oozing out from a shot through the head," wrote Confederate Captain William Ward. "One of the boys attempted to remove a silver cup fastened to his belt, when he begged that it not be taken from him, as it was the gift of his mother. To this reply that it could do him no good, as he could only live a few minutes longer, he said: 'You don't think this little thing will kill a man.'" A few minutes later, the Yankee soldier was dead.[25]

Rousseau had become increasingly agitated as the echo of gunfire swelled in the distance and wounded men began trickling to the rear. Twirling the ends of his thick black mustache between his fingers, he muttered over and over again, "I shouldn't have got into this affair. I'm very much afraid this isn't judicious."

Noting Rousseau's anxiety, the ever-present Captain Elkin took matters into his own hands. Riding toward the sound of the guns, he struggled through the thickets until he overtook the 8th Indiana. Seeing the Rebels being driven back, he returned and told Rousseau what he had learned, adding, "There's no reason to be uneasy about Harrison, General."

"Uneasy about Harrison!" Rousseau exclaimed. "Tom Harrison can whip all the militia in Alabama. But what shall I do with my poor wounded boys? We are a thousand miles from home, and no way to carry them comfortably."

Fortunately, Rousseau's casualties were relatively light, but this did not become apparent until the troops engaged at Chehaw began returning to Notasulga later that afternoon. The 5th Iowa had borne the brunt of the battle. Privates D. D. Sage and James M. Harris had been killed. Private William Britt had been mortally wounded and left on the field, and a 4th Tennessee trooper had been captured.

Eight other Iowans and an 8th Indiana cavalryman suffered less serious wounds, and two Michigan artillerymen had suffered "contusions" when they fell off a fence. Chief Surgeon Luther D. Waterman and his colleagues ministered to them as best they could, but artilleryman David Gorman, Sergeant Gustav Krusch, and Privates Stephen Gleeson, Hypolett Graff, William S. Van Slyke, and Cerro P. Witcomb of the 5th Iowa were too badly hurt to continue. Reluctantly, Rousseau decided to leave them in the Confederate hospital at Camp Watts, two miles west of Notasulga.

Before leaving, he had some parting words for the young Confederates his men had captured at Chehaw. "Boys," he said, "go home and tell your parents that Rousseau does not war on women and children; and, mark you, do *you* see that they don't make war on wounded prisoners." The boys listened to the eloquent Kentuckian and upon being released, they did what they could for the wounded Yankees left at Notasulga.[26]

Rousseau also paroled approximately one hundred patients recuperating at the Confederate hospital, but he put the rest of Camp Watts to the torch. His troopers set fire to wooden barracks capable of housing two or three thousand men, sixty tents complete with poles and pins, and a large quantity of quartermaster and commissary supplies, including several thousand pounds of "fine chewing tobacco." They also burned the water tank at Notasulga and all the railroad buildings, including a warehouse containing 500 bales of cotton belonging to the Central Bank of Montgomery. When this work was done, the raiders mounted their horses about 4:00 P.M. and retraced their steps eastward along the charred ruins of the railroad.[27]

They found an old nemesis dogging their footsteps. True to his word, James Clanton had taken up the pursuit of the Yankees when they failed to appear at Blue Mountain. His column had passed through Talladega about dark on July 15, a good eight hours behind Rousseau. During the next two days, Clanton had steadily narrowed the gap, but along the whole route he did not see where the raiders had lost so much as a horseshoe. After trailing the Yankees for over a hundred miles, he finally caught up with the tail end of Rousseau's column late on July 17 and captured four prisoners. During the night, he scouted the perimeter of the Yankee encampment, and it was probably his men who fired on the 8th Indiana's pickets early on July 18. When the Yankees left Loachapoka shortly afterward and headed west toward Notasulga, Clanton had moved astride the railroad to follow. However, his plans went awry when Rousseau turned Colonel Hamilton's detachment back toward Loachapoka.

Seeing Clanton's Confederates blocking his path, Hamilton ordered his buglers to sound "Charge." Swinging into line of battle along the road leading from the Methodist church northward to Loachapoka Creek, his men thundered forward, their sabers gleaming in the sun. Clanton's cavalrymen, posted along the cemetery road, wilted before the two ranks could collide, and what followed was a horse race for the cover of some nearby woods. Clanton's men got there first, forcing Hamilton to halt and send in a line of dismounted skirmishers to root them out. The Rebels waited until the bluecoated troopers were within a hundred yards and opened fire, wounding a Yankee sergeant in the arm. Hamilton's men pressed forward and quickly cleared the woods.

Leaving a detachment of the 4th Tennessee to keep an eye on Clanton, Hamilton recalled his skirmishers and moved east of Loachapoka to the point where work on the railroad had ceased shortly before dawn. While half his command stood guard, the other half dismounted and handed their reins to the number fours. Officers quickly organized working parties, and the systematic destruction of the railroad began anew. Two men carrying axes they had found at Loachapoka led the way, driving out the wooden wedges holding the track in place. Troopers armed with handspikes and crowbars followed, prying up the north side of the track and heaving it south. Others piled up crossties, fence rails, and anything else that would burn, kindling huge bonfires in the wake of the work gangs. The number fours followed with the horses, while Hamilton's vedettes hovered about the front, flanks, and rear.

"The way led through a poor country thickly overgrown with bushes and scrub timber," Hamilton wrote, "through which it was difficult to handle cavalry or to watch their movements. Clanton was about us all day and occasionally tried to stop our work. Early in the day he made an attack from the front, which, however, we repulsed, and one of his men was left dead on the track."

At appropriate intervals, the vedettes changed places with the sweating section hands, and despite the heat, the work progressed rapidly. By 11:00 A.M., Hamilton's men had destroyed three miles of track. They were approaching the outskirts of Auburn when some slaves brought them a warning: Confederate officers were arming civilians and preparing to defend the town.

The dense undergrowth on either side of the railroad made an ambush seem likely. Rather than take any chances, Hamilton halted the work just short of Auburn and ordered his entire command to mount. His horsemen formed ranks and buglers sounded "Charge." "The rush through the thickets," Hamilton recounted, "could be better heard than seen."[28]

Isabelle Shacklette watched in horror from her room at the Railroad Hotel as the Yankees "dashed in shouting and firing at everyone in the streets and into the hospital, the wounded and sick running in every direction . . . and one who was just entering our gate was shot down before my eyes."[29]

Instead of putting up a fight, Captain Francis, the post commander, had ordered his troops to scatter and save themselves. Auburn's menfolk hardly needed any encouragement. One "substantial" citizen fled to a distant canebrake, where he climbed on a stump and sat there "froglike" for the next several hours, imagining every rustle among the leaves was a Yankee soldier. Another panic-stricken gentleman sprinted out of town, but not before equipping himself with three extra hats.

A hefty 225-pound commissary officer "larded the dusty road as he hurried along," accompanied by a member of the local medical examining board. Twelve miles out of town, the panting pair finally stopped at a cool spring to quench their thirst. They were still trying to catch their breath when a Negro warned them the Yankees were coming. Springing to his feet, the medical officer cleared an intervening bog with a single bound and disappeared into the woods. The portly commissary essayed the mire apprehensively. Not wanting to be left behind, he launched his ponderous bulk into the air. What followed could best be described as "a fierce struggle between gravitation and momentum." Gravity prevailed.

Elsewhere, a burly parson galloped up to the home of one of his parishioners. "Where is brother ——?" he demanded of the layman's wife. When told the man had already fled, the preacher rolled his eyes heavenward and exclaimed, "O! Lord what shall I do! What shall I do!"

"Go to the woods!" the woman shouted. "Go to the woods!"

While this seemed to be the consensus among Auburn's male population, most of the ladies stood their ground, determined to defend hearth and home. They watched the Yankees ride into town, and quite a few waved hastily prepared white flags from their windows.

Within a matter of minutes, Auburn was overrun with bluecoated cavalrymen. Hamilton put half his soldiers back to work on the railroad, while the rest stood guard or took possession of the depot and a nearby warehouse. After liberally supplying his men with Confederate stocks of food, clothing, tobacco, shoes, and underwear, Hamilton followed Rousseau's example at Talladega and invited civilians to come take whatever they wanted. This brought throngs of women and children, both black and white, running down to the warehouse, grabbing up everything in sight, including twenty-seven barrels of potash. One rather elegant lady, obviously unaccustomed to the first-come, first-served spirit of the affair, brought along her Negro manservant and proceeded to point out some hams she wanted him to take back to the house. "Haint got time, Missus, haint got time," the slave replied as he waded into the crowd, leaving the lady to fend for herself.

Hamilton watched as the beneficiaries of his generosity trotted home with all they could carry and then hurried back for more. "It was a God send to some of them who I think would welcome such a raid every week," he wrote.

However, Isabelle Shacklette remembered it as "a terrible time of carnage, thieving, and destruction." She watched apprehensively as a Union officer brazenly strode into the hotel where she was staying and ordered the hotelkeeper's wife, Martha Moore, to bake bread for sixty men or he would burn the place down over her head. Mrs. Moore told him he could have anything he wanted; one of the Negro cooks out in the kitchen would see that he was fed, but *she* was not baking bread for any Yankees. The officer stalked off to the kitchen, where he commanded Lucy, the cook, to bake bread for sixty men "damn quick," or "I'll skin you alive."

As Lucy and four other servant girls scurried to the pantry and began bringing out armloads of flour, meat, and eggs, more Yankees came crowding into the long dining hall adjacent to the kitchen. They had worked up a powerful appetite that morning, and they made their desires known in no uncertain terms. The hotel owner, James S. Moore, came over to where Lucy and her companions were working and told them they "might as well go to cooking for the soldiers, as they had asked for something to eat & would have it, & it would be better . . . to get the things & cook them up, rather than have the soldiers go in & hull everything about." The girls mixed and kneaded and rolled at a furious pace, and the hotel's huge sheet-iron stove, capable of cooking for fifty men, was soon turning out mountains of loaves, hoecakes, and biscuits.

Outside, Hamilton's horses fared as sumptuously as their riders. The first arrivals, comfortably quartered in Moore's barn, gorged on a crib full of corn and a loft full of forage. Latecomers crowded around feed troughs or ate off the ground as troopers brought them fodder hastily bundled with ropes, bridle reins, and harness leather, and corn scooped out of the crib in buckets, boxes, sacks, pans, and even saddle blankets.[30]

Down by the railroad, the townspeople were still picking through what was left of the government stores when a train whistle wailed mournfully in the distance. Everyone, soldier and civilian alike, stopped and listened. The Yankees exchanged questioning glances, a shadow of apprehension clouding their grimy faces. It was a troop train bringing Confederate reinforcements from Atlanta, someone said. Fearing the worst, Hamilton sent Captain Asbury P. Gatch and Company L of the 9th Ohio to investigate, then put the rest of his troopers to work barricading the streets. Frightened civilians asked if he meant to fight right there in the middle of town. It looked that way, Hamilton replied, but if any of the townspeople got hurt, it would be by their friends on that train, not by any of his men.

Two miles east of Auburn, Captain Gatch's company reined up behind a high railroad embankment and waited for the oncoming train. Soon a locomotive hove into sight, pulling a tender. Gatch let it pass, then he and his men swarmed over the track and pulled up a few rails. The engineer must have looked back and seen this or perhaps there were more troopers blocking the road up ahead. In any event, he threw the engine into reverse and opened the throttle wide, trying to back out of trouble. He backed into it instead, and the train derailed when it hit the gap in the track. Soon the engineer and the two railroad employees riding with him were looking down the barrels of Yankee carbines. When questioned by Captain Gatch, the trio said they had left Columbus, Georgia, around noon with orders to reconnoiter toward Auburn. There was no troop train following them.

Satisfied with the answers he got, Gatch sent a courier back to Auburn. His report persuaded Hamilton to abandon his barricades and resume work on the railroad. While one detachment set fire to a large tannery just east of town, others burned the depot and the warehouse, destroying what was left of the quartermaster and commissary supplies and a considerable quantity of lumber. The raiders even rolled 12,000 pounds of lead out of the Nitre Bureau and consigned it to the flames.

Nonetheless, residents admitted the Yankees were "very civil, and did not insult any one or disturb anything, with few exceptions. A few houses were burned immediately on the road, and mules and horses were taken wherever found. The negroes . . . seemed to enjoy their presence, but only a few left with them."[31]

Leaving Auburn wreathed in a pall of smoke, the raiders continued eastward, tearing up the railroad as they went. Late that afternoon, they found the locomotive and tender Captain Gatch and his men had waylaid. The engineer told Hamilton he had no sympathy for the Confederate cause. He was just a Northerner who happened to be working down South when the war began and was unable to get home. If the colonel would let him come along, he could be a guide.

Hamilton studied the man carefully and asked him where he was from.

"Massachusetts," the engineer replied.

"I concluded," Hamilton later wrote, "from the way he 'guessed' instead of 'reckoned' that he was telling the truth." He told the engineer to come along and ordered the other two men set free.

As for the locomotive and tender, some of Hamilton's men took sledge hammers they found on board and smashed the dials and instruments. Then they piled up crossties and fence rails in a futile effort to set the engine ablaze.[32]

While Hamilton's troopers worked their way eastward, leaving a string of bonfires in their wake, Rousseau and the rest of the command moved back from Notasulga under gray and lowering skies. Late that afternoon they plodded into Auburn, where a word of command halted the head of the column in front of the Railroad Hotel. Bone-tired, battle-weary troopers slid from their saddles and tied their horses to the fence palings on either side of the road in two parallel lines stretching westward as far as the eye could see. Picking up where Hamilton's men had left off, they took the last of James Moore's corn and fodder to feed to their hungry mounts.

Moore watched the seemingly endless stream of men crowding into his hotel, clamoring for something to eat. A New Yorker by birth and a cousin of Union General Alexander Stewart Webb, he felt entitled to at least some consideration and complained bitterly to Rousseau and some of his officers. The answer was always the same. The troops were in enemy territory. They were hungry and any food within their reach was fair game.

Rousseau settled into an upstairs room and had some "refreshments" sent up. After resting awhile, he came downstairs shortly before dark and ordered his troopers to mount up. A mad scramble followed.

"There was a great many men that ate," remembered Moore's exhausted cook, Lucy, "and a great many who couldn't get a chance to eat carried off the meat &c. raw. All the biscuit, bread, &c., not eaten there they carried off; every bit they could rake up." They rode off in a pelting rainstorm with sacks, pots, pans, and bundles of provisions dangling from their saddles, leaving Moore poorer by one horse, a whole lot of food and forage, and an untold number of knives, forks, and spoons.[33]

It was nearly midnight before Rousseau overtook Hamilton three miles east of Auburn. Ordered not to stop until he heard otherwise, Hamilton had followed his instructions literally. He was sitting on his horse, watching his men pry up rails in the dark when he heard someone asking for him. Presently a staff officer rode up, presented Rousseau's compliments and told Hamilton the general wanted to see him. Hamilton asked where Rousseau was. "Back there among the men," the aide replied.

Turning his horse in the direction indicated, Hamilton made his way to the rear. Rousseau saw him coming. "Hamilton," he called out, "are you going to Atlanta tonight?"

"I don't know," Hamilton answered, "my orders, as I understand them, were to keep at work till I heard from you, and whether that would take me in to Atlanta or not I was not certain."

"Well, sir," said Rousseau, "I want to thank you for your day's work. You have made this expedition a success. I saw a dead rebel or two by the road as I came. Did you have much trouble?"

He listened as Hamilton described his two brief encounters with the Rebels. "Well," he said, "I will take pleasure in giving you and your command proper credit in my report. I was not very successful on the other end. When I reached the railroad bridge I found it guarded by a company in a block [gin?] house, and as I had no artillery, I could not dislodge them. Call off your men and let them sleep till morning. I see a house with a porch yonder, let us lie down and take a nap."[34]

Hamilton recalled his section gangs, officers posted pickets for the night, and the raiders settled down along a desolate two-mile stretch of the right-of-way beginning a mile east of Auburn. There was no forage for the horses and no water, but most of the men who sprawled on the muddy ground that night in the glare of the blazing bonfires were simply too tired to care. In the past twenty-six hours, they had destroyed nineteen miles of railroad and telegraph lines and burned every water tank, railroad depot, and government warehouse between Auburn and Notasulga. Most fell asleep as soon as they lay down, but it was a troubled sleep, interrupted by splashes of rain and sporadic bursts of gunfire along the picket line. "Reports were current during the night that the West Point force was approaching . . . ," wrote Oscar Reese. Nothing was seen of them, but everyone knew the Rebels could not be far away.[35]

9

ROUSSEAU'S RAID
OPELIKA TO MARIETTA

JULY 19–JULY 22, 1864

Men will keep going on their nerve or their head,
But you cannot ride a horse when he's dead.

—Leonard Bacon, "Colorado Morton's Ride"

They were coming by companies and battalions, by regiments and brigades; volunteers and veterans, all converging on the West Point railroad to "welcome the raiders 'with bloody hands to hospitable graves.'" Gideon Pillow's dismounted cavalry reached Montgomery late on July 18. A trainload of infantry arrived from Pollard and promptly continued eastward for Chehaw. An urgent telegram from Major Thomas had already summoned Montgomery's volunteer battalion and one of hospital convalescents, but they reached Chehaw too late to see action at Beasley's Station. Leaving these newcomers to guard the trestle over Uphaupee Creek, Thomas led the remnants of Ready's and Davidson's battalions toward Auburn.

James Clanton was also moving east. After being swept aside by Hamilton's detachment early on July 18, he had taken his tiny brigade, less than 200 strong, down the wagon road toward Tuskegee, hoping to head off the Yankee column tearing up the railroad west of Loachapoka. Before he could get into position, he learned about Thomas's force and the fighting that had turned back the raiders at Beasley's Station. Reversing his line of march, Clanton retraced his steps toward Auburn to begin shadowing Rousseau's column again.[1]

Other Confederate troops were closing in from the east, drawn there, initially at least, by Stoneman's foray down the west bank of the Chattahoochee to Moore's Bridge. Rumors of Stoneman's approach had rapidly spread downriver, precipitating the usual panic. Citizens of West Point, the little railroad village straddling the state line between Alabama and Georgia, fled in droves. The mayor issued a call for all men and boys between the ages of sixteen and sixty to take up arms, and gangs of slaves, supervised by Major F. W. Capers, superintendent of the Georgia Military Institute, began digging fortifications around the vital railroad bridge spanning the Chattahoochee. Capers had about 160 GMI cadets with him, hardly enough to man the works, much less protect the bridge, and he apparently wired Atlanta, begging for reinforcements.[2]

All too aware of the importance of the bridge at West Point, Joe Johnston had responded by pulling Brigadier General R. W. Carswell's 1st Brigade out of the trenches west of Atlanta at 8:00 P.M., Saturday, July 16. Carswell's four units, the 1st, 2nd, and 5th Regiments and 1st Battalion of Georgia militia, marched down to the Atlanta & West Point depot, where a thirteen-car freight train waited to take them south. As it turned out, only five of the cars were empty, and these were soon filled to capacity. The rest of Carswell's 375 men were perched on top of the train when it

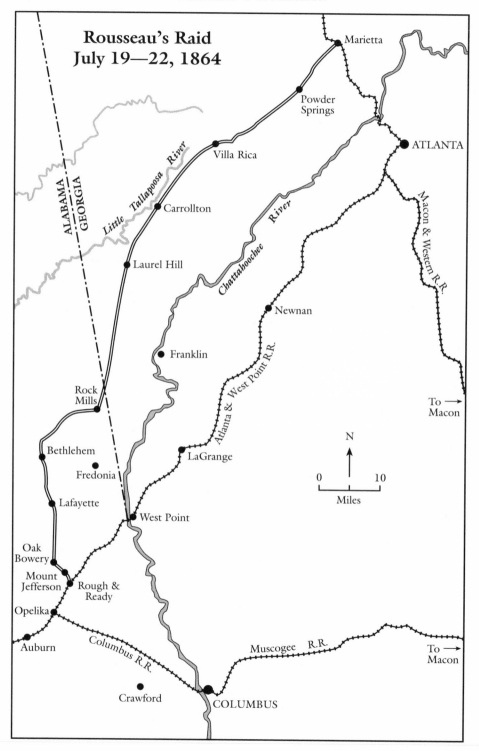

Rousseau's Raid
July 19—22, 1864

pulled out of Atlanta at 10:00 P.M. It was insufferably hot and stuffy inside the boxcars, and at every stop, more and more men climbed to the roof, seeking relief. Soon it was almost as crowded on top of the cars as it was inside, and two men fell off before the brigade reached West Point about 10:00 Sunday morning.

By that time, Stoneman's cavalry had already returned to Sherman's army and the danger had diminished considerably. "The citizens of the place say that no Yanks are in 30 miles of here," wrote A. T. Holliday of the 1st Georgia Militia. "I hope it is true."

Taking advantage of this unexpected but welcome respite, most of Carswell's men lounged around the train, trying to catch up on lost sleep. A few took note of the Sabbath. "We stopped within 20 steps of a Methodist church," wrote Vincent Montgomery of the 2nd Regiment, "where there was preaching at 11 o'clock and [at] three for the negroes and prayer meeting at five. I went every time."

Unaccustomed to army life, these citizen soldiers also did a lot of grumbling. "I have now one dollar in my pocket," A. T. Holliday complained in a letter to his wife, "and we have 2 days of rations cooked which was all we had and it may have to do us 5 or 6 days; we do not know. Some of the Brigade have nothing to eat at all. . . . We have a shabby set of officers and our Col. is a perfect fool. I believe if he was ordered to cross the Atlantic Ocean to-night he is just simpleton enough to try it."

Shortly after midnight, the authorities at West Point learned of a new threat, this time from the west. Yankee cavalry had cut the Montgomery railroad near Loachapoka, only thirty miles away. Carswell promptly marched his militia down to the railroad bridge and joined the GMI cadets throwing up earthworks on the east bank of the Chattahoochee. Scores of civilians who had earlier fled to the Alabama side of the river to get out of Stoneman's way now came crowding back into Georgia. "Such a stampede . . . you never heard of," wrote Cadet Seaborn Montgomery, Jr. "Every wagon, cart or pack horse that could be started was loaded with household chattels and started across the river."[3]

The panic soon spread thirty-five miles downstream to Columbus, Georgia, where Major George O. Dawson, the post commander, learned of the Yankee raid at "an early hour" on July 18. Fire bells and church bells rang to rouse the sleeping city, "all of which contributed," complained one observer, "in addition to calling out the male population, to greatly alarm the women, children, negroes, and non-combatants generally."

The city's 15,000 inhabitants had good reason to be alarmed, for Columbus was a tempting prize. With the possible exception of Selma, it was the greatest industrial center in the deep South. The Naval Iron Works turned out cannon, shot and shell, steam boilers, and iron plate. An ironclad ram, the *Muscogee,* was under construction near the steamboat wharf. Other government installations included an ammunition factory, a wagon works, the Confederate arsenal and armory, and two shoe factories employing over 500 men, most of them Negroes.

Private concerns, like L. Haiman & Brother, directly across Franklin Street from the arsenal, manufactured swords, pistols, bayonets, belts, buckles, saddles, harness, oilcloth, camp equipment, and assorted accoutrements. Greenwood & Gray's rifle factory stood nearby. On the east bank of the Chattahoochee, the Clapp Factory, the Coweta Factory, and two mills of the Eagle Manufacturing Company ran day and night, spinning sewing thread, yarn, rope, cotton goods and woolen cloth, while two large gristmills, Empire Mills and Palace Mills, ground corn and wheat for civilian and military consumption. There were also railroad shops, depots, a match factory, a paper mill, a brass foundry, a peanut oil mill, a nail factory, and warehouses of every description scattered throughout the city and the neighboring suburb of Girard, Alabama.[4]

But business came to an abrupt halt on July 18. All three Columbus newspapers, the *Times,* the *Daily Enquirer,* and the *Daily Sun,* suspended publication. Railroad officials began running rolling stock eastward to Fort Valley, and not a few residents took advantage of this opportunity to book passage to safer locales.

"The panic . . . revealed . . . who were true and who were not," noted the editor of the *Daily Sun,* "and tore the mask of blatant hypocrisy from some half dozen or more loud-mouthed gentlemen who had been industriously engaged in getting up town meetings and resolutions denunciatory of those who refused to participate in the *wind work* of defending the city."

But for every one of these sunshine patriots, there were a hundred stalwart men, and "soldiers sprung up like armed men from the fabled dragon's teeth," noted the *Columbus Times.* Even boys, some of them only ten years old, shouldered muskets taller than they were and took places in the ranks. Most of the white males employed in the various businesses and factories around town had previously been organized into home defense companies, and news of the Yankee raid now led to the formation of two new units composed entirely of arsenal workers. Other volunteer organizations, which had previously advertised in vain for recruits in the local papers, suddenly found their ranks filled to overflowing.[5]

Major Dawson, a twice-wounded veteran of the Virginia campaigns, worked tirelessly to organize, arm, and equip them. Convinced the raiders meant to destroy Columbus, he ordered slaves impressed to dig earthworks and sent scouts (including the ill-fated locomotive Rousseau's men derailed near Auburn) to determine the strength and location of the Yankee column. He also kept the telegraph wires humming, requesting reinforcements from Atlanta, Macon, Savannah, and as far away as Charleston.

"The enemy are reported within thirty miles of this city, advancing from the direction of Montgomery," he wired the post commander at Macon. "Their number is not known. If you can send me assistance, do so at once."

Dawson also wired Brigadier General John H. Winder at the infamous Rebel prison at Andersonville, advising him the Yankee force consisted of ten regiments of cavalry and two pieces of artillery.[6]

Both of these messages ultimately made their way to the Macon headquarters of Major General Howell Cobb, commanding the Georgia Reserves. Cobb forwarded Dawson's telegram to Andersonville in a letter to General Winder on July 18, and added:

> The only additional information I have is a telegram from Opelika saying that the Yankees were at Auburn tearing up the railroad track and they were expected to reach Opelika to-night. . . . I do not think there is much cause to apprehend an attack on Andersonville, still I thought it best to advize [*sic*] you of what was going on, that you may be prepared for any emergency.

With less than 2,500 poorly armed, poorly equipped troops to guard the 30,000 Union prisoners in his custody, Winder was understandably concerned over the whereabouts of the Yankee column. Ever since Johnston's army retreated across the Chattahoochee on July 9, he had grown increasingly fearful of just such a raid and had even proposed transferring some of his prisoners to a more secure spot near Silver Run, Alabama. Upon receipt of Cobb's letter and Major Dawson's accompanying telegram (probably on July 19), Winder immediately impressed all the Negroes and horses in the neighborhood and worked them round the clock, building earthworks commanding the approaches to the twenty-seven-acre stockade.[7]

There was also concern about the security of Camp Oglethorpe, a smaller prison accommodating approximately 1,500 Union officers on the south side of Macon. In one of his first acts after replacing Joe Johnston as commander of the Army of Tennessee, John Bell Hood wired Cobb on July 18 asking if he had enough men to defend both Columbus and Camp Oglethorpe.

"I am doing all I can to prepare for the defense of Columbus as well as for the safety of the prison at Andersonville. . . ," Cobb wrote to his wife, Mary. "It keeps me quite busy—telegraphing—writing & sending expresses, etc., etc., etc. I am not apprehensive of any serious results—but these thing[s] show that the enemy is being active, energetic, and will spare no pains to inflict all the injury he can upon us. . . ."

During the day, Cobb had received several replies to Major Dawson's requests for reinforcements. "Impossible to reinforce him from this point[,]" Brigadier General Henry R. Jackson telegraphed from Savannah; "troops too few & scattered[;] the design of the enemy may be on Andersonville." Major General Sam Jones sent a similar message from Charleston, urging Cobb, "if you can send him [Dawson] any reserves please do it without delay."

The only positive response came from Atlanta, where Hood wired Cobb:

> If Andersonville is seriously threatened & there is danger of release of [the] prisoners I will send reinforcements[,] if necessary a Brigade from this army to that point. Keep me advised that I may have notice in time. I can only detach if the danger is pressing. Brig. Genl. Armstrong with two guns and hundred [?] cavalry has started in the direction of Opelika to intercept the raiders.[8]

Armstrong's brigade had returned to the vicinity of Campbellton after turning back Stoneman's feeble foray at Moore's Bridge. About 6:00 P.M. on July 18, a courier delivered Hood's orders to hasten south again, this time to repel a Yankee column threatening the railroad bridge at West Point. While Armstrong called in his pickets, troopers fed their horses and hastily cooked what few rations were on hand. About an hour before sundown, buglers sounded "Boots and Saddles," and Armstrong's four regiments—Ballentine's, the 1st, 2nd, and 28th Mississippi—and a section of Captain Houston King's Missouri Battery started downriver. There was none of the chatter and joking usually incident to a march. Word of "the noble Johnston's" removal had come with Hood's orders and the troopers rode with a downcast air. "I will never forget the gloom of that march," wrote Lieutenant Colonel Frank Montgomery of the 1st Mississippi.[9]

Armstrong's Mississippians were not the only Confederate cavalrymen converging on the Georgia-Alabama border. A train carrying Colonel Duncan L. Clinch's 4th Georgia Cavalry from Fort Valley reached Columbus late on July 18, about the same time Major Dawson heard from the scouts he had sent out that morning. Anxious to learn more of the raiders' whereabouts, Dawson directed Clinch to proceed to

Opelika. A train was readied, but about an hour before it was to depart, a telegram arrived from Atlanta, directing Clinch to hold his regiment ready to move to the defense of Andersonville at a moment's notice.[10]

This left Dawson with few options. After consulting with his staff and veteran officers attached to various government installations, he decided the city could best be defended from the high ground on the Alabama side of the Chattahoochee. At 5:00 P.M., his troops began crossing the river.

"The citizen soldiery looked determined and performed well," reported an observer who watched them cross the bridges into the neighboring village of Girard; "the detailed men from the numerous government work-shops were joined by about a thousand convalescents from the various hospitals, and united this brigade presented a truly veteran appearance."

First across the river was the City Battalion, commanded by Columbus Mayor F. G. Wilkins. Organized by trades, the City Battalion consisted of Captain C. E. White's wainwrights, the Johnson Guards; Captain W. R. Kent's oilcloth makers; Captain F. S. Chapman's company of exempted men, the Georgia Defenders; Captain William H. Williams's Vigilant Fire Company; and Captain J. M. Russell's Typo Guards, temporarily attached to Captain Kent's company. Mayor Wilkins, a wounded veteran of the Army of Northern Virginia, led them out on the Crawford road for five miles before calling a halt at sundown. The men wearily unshouldered their muskets, expecting to make camp, but soon learned they had either missed a turn or gone too far. At any rate, they were not where they were supposed to be.

"We were told to retrace our steps," wrote one of the Typo Guards, "which manoeuver we executed with considerable celerity considering the jaded condition incident to a day of organization and the first march which many had ever undertaken."

After backtracking a mile or so in the midst of the same summer shower that was dousing Rousseau's men at Auburn, Wilkins called another halt and ordered the battalion to bivouac for the night. The clouds parted, revealing a full moon and a thousand twinkling stars overhead, but this was small comfort for tired, wet, hungry men with no food and scarcely a blanket among them. They lay down to sleep, but before they could get their eyes closed officers began bawling, "Fall in men!" Reforming their ranks, the tired troops tramped down the muddy road until they reached a line of hills only two miles west of Columbus. Here, about a quarter-mile beyond Godwin's old mill, Mayor Wilkins had them block the Crawford road with a barricade of fence rails which Captain Williams of the Vigilant Fire Company promptly dubbed "Fort Wilkins."

Leaving Captain Kent's oilcloth company and the Typo Guards to man the works, Wilkins deployed Chapman's Georgia Defenders in a cornfield on the left of the road, the Johnson Guards on the right, and Captain Williams's firemen as skirmishers. The men were in a bad humor, muttering about incompetent officers who marched them eight miles to get them two miles from where they had started, when Captain Williams stood up and called to them in a loud voice:

"*Fellow Soldiers!* The wisdom of our commander is apparent in giving our division the post of honor and danger. Time will illustrate the sagacity of the selection. Men, you are every one expected to fight on this line, even unto the death of the last one of you, if it takes all summer. This fortification shall never be given up as long as there remains an inch of ground to stand upon, or a drop of blood in your veins. The enemy may soon be upon you—perhaps in an hour—fight them till the last armed foe expires, or as long as there is a rail on this fort." The captain then "picked out a soft place in the road and lay down, amidst vociferous applause. . . ."

Major Samuel R. Jacques's 1st City Battalion of shoemakers and mill hands from the Eagle Manufacturing Company camped nearby. Other units included the Columbus Arsenal Battalion, composed of two companies organized only a few hours earlier; the Naval Iron Works Battalion; the venerable Independent Columbus Guards, composed exclusively of men over forty-five years old; Youngblood's Pistol Factory Company (which may have been part of Major Jacques's battalion); a generous leavening of convalescent soldiers from Columbus military hospitals; and a battery of four bronze Napoleon guns manned by the Dawson Artillery. Captain John S. Pemberton (who would later invent Coca-Cola) and his cavalry company, the Dawson Rangers, scouted the western approaches to the city, while Clinch's 4th Georgia Cavalry was up nearly all night carrying rations to the different commands.

It was a formidable force, an estimated 2,800 to 3,000 men and boys, who awaited the raiders' approach. Leaving Lieutenant Colonel Julius Adolph de Lagnel, the commander of the Columbus Arsenal, to take charge in the field, Dawson remained in Columbus to coordinate the defense. As a precaution he had the railroad bridge and two wagon bridges over the Chattahoochee dressed with "tar, pitch, turpentine and lumber."

A night of watchful waiting passed quietly. Early on July 19 members of the City Battalion awoke to hear the stentorian tones of the irrepressible Captain Williams booming over the bivouac:

"*Fellow Soldiers!* I am happy to find that each one of you has gallantly maintained his position during the night. Judging from the number of dead Yankees around us, I am satisfied that you are invincible. (Here he pointed to Chapman's division, who were lying prostrate in the sand of the adjacent cornfield.) A few more such fights and the victory will be ours. (Some one here called his attention to a number of mushmellows that some of the rascally boys had stolen during the night.)—Yes, says he, this is the strongest evidence that Providence is with us. See this pile of shells which the enemy had thrown among us, and yet, wonderful to contemplate, not a hair of your heads has been injured. A few more sacrifices and the day will be ours."

Not to be outdone, one of the Typo Guards, editor T. J. Jackson of the *Columbus Times,* tried to show off his own oratorical skill. "It is due him," noted the editor of the rival *Daily Columbus Enquirer,* "to say that for a new recruit he made the best 'old soldier' we ever saw, while the eloquence and oratory which he displayed on several occasions won for him the admiration and applause of all who listened to his harangues: and when his mess were in need of an axe, frying pan, or other implement of *warfare,* they sent him out to borrow it, and before he had made speeches at half of the bush arbors some one would bring forth the needed article and present it to him in a manner that made you feel that it was the lender who was being accommodated instead of the borrower."

Daylight brought no sign of the Yankees, and the Columbus volunteers soon found themselves with little to do besides drill and stand guard. "Lying up in the shade seemed to be the most agreeable pastime," wrote one citizen soldier, "and many of the boys got so lazy that they murmured at having to change spots to keep in the shade."[11]

"All quiet today," Major Dawson telegraphed Howell Cobb, "the latest from the enemy is they were four miles this side of Auburn last night."

But the calm did not last and that afternoon Dawson wired Cobb:

> The enemy were reported at noon today four miles this side of Opelika destroying rail road. Opelika has been burnt. Today I learn from reliable authority that the enemy is 4,000 strong with [twelve] pieces of artillery.[12]

Rousseau's men were only vaguely aware of the widespread consternation and confusion they were creating. Exhausted from their day-long labors, they had spent a restless night sprawled alongside the smoldering ruins of the railroad. There were, however, a few sleepless soldiers prowling the countryside. A group of about thirty-nine enlisted men from the 9th Ohio, including the brawling bugler, James Doran, was moving down a "dark and devious" road through the woods near Opelika when the night suddenly erupted with a fiery blast of musketry. Horses whinnied and reared. A bullet smashed into Doran's right ankle. Another shot felled his horse, pitching him face-first into the ground. His comrades fled, leaving Doran to be captured by some of Clanton's men.[13]

In nearby Auburn, Isabelle Shacklette spent the night hiding behind the door to her upstairs room at the Railroad Hotel. "I passed the night without once closing my eyes, in mortal terror . . . ," she wrote, "and as the door remained open all night, no one of the intruders thought of looking behind it. There I stood in terrible agony of fear, shaking and quaking the blessed night, praying as I never prayed before, for if one Yankee soldier entered that room to steal, 50 did I know, but as it was soon emptied of furniture and clothing the last ones lingered not long, but ran out to seek elsewhere for plunder. I could hear them shouting on the streets that the whole town would be burned down because it was near the house of William P. Yanc[e]y the great secessionist, his plantation being just a mile out of town. They burnt his dwelling house, but not the houses in town. . . . People were robbed of everything they possessed, and the awful carousing continued through the night. In the morning the alarm was sounded that the Confederates were coming in force to capture them. Then I looked out of the window and such a hurrying and scurrying to mount and haste away I never saw."[14]

Apparently unaware of the pillaging in Auburn, Rousseau roused his men at 4:00 A.M., July 19, and started eastward. Dividing the command into three or four detachments, he left Tom Harrison with the 2nd Kentucky and part of the 8th Indiana to continue destroying the railroad toward Opelika. The rest of the 8th Indiana probably guarded the flanks and rear of this force, while Rousseau's other regiments and the artillery moved southeast. Striking the Columbus Branch Railroad two miles below its junction with the Montgomery & West Point at Opelika, Hamilton's 9th Ohio began working their way northward, while Matt Patrick moved on to Opelika with the 5th Iowa and the 4th Tennessee to destroy the switching yards and depots and wreck the main line in the direction of West Point.

"The weather was excessively hot," noted Corporal Alexander Eckel of the 4th Tennessee, "and the men had to work by reliefs. . . . Everything was very dry and hot and the destruction was thorough."

By 10:00 A.M., Patrick's men had destroyed all the switches at Opelika, a turntable for rerouting cars, and the wye where the Columbus Branch Road connected with the Montgomery line. The 8th Indiana and the 2nd Kentucky wrecked the last two or three miles of track immediately west of the junction, and the 9th Ohio tore up a two-mile stretch of the branch line just south of town. Well satisfied, Rousseau reassembled his scattered detachments a mile north of Opelika near the only source of water, a branch of Sougahatchee Creek, and ordered each company to send a few troopers into town to bring back supplies from the tons of quartermaster and commissary stores Matt Patrick had found stockpiled at the junction.

"Opelika was a pretty country town apparently of some importance," noted Corporal Eckel. Besides the usual collection of stores and houses, there was an express office, a tool shop, two railroad depots, and three large government warehouses. The warehouses were filled to the rafters with 10,000 to 14,000 pounds of sugar, 12,000 pounds of flour, 10,000 to 20,000 pounds of bacon, and a large quantity of whisky, while the express office yielded thirty boxes of chewing tobacco.[15]

"This was a happy find," wrote Eckel, "as rations were getting scarce. The bacon was fine, and it was not long until the men were having some nice broils. To lovers of the weed, tobacco was particularly a welcome find, and many of the boys supplied themselves, besides carrying out with them considerable quantities, which they disposed of at good prices. This they were forbidden to do, but they succeeded in smuggling it through."

About 10:30 A.M., the troops settled down to breakfast, "a magnificent treat," declared Lieutenant Tom Fanning of the 9th Ohio, "as we regard one meal a day as a luxury beyond anything known to the sultans of Asia, leaving European kings and emperors aside." The 8th Indiana's John Jones agreed, and noted, "as the sun had already reached its zenith, we added the noonday meal and enjoyed a feast of the luxuries accumulated in our haversacks."

Rousseau and his staff dined at the Sledge House, near the railroad. Owner Nathaniel Sledge at first insisted he had nothing prepared, but acquiesced when asked if his Negroes would cook something. After enjoying a hearty meal, Rousseau and his officers paid the cooks fifty dollars for their trouble.

When his men had eaten their fill of Rebel rations, Rousseau issued his customary invitation for the people to come and take what was left. The familiar scenes already played in Auburn and Talladega were repeated as men, women, and children, black and white, young and old, flocked to the warehouses, grabbing up everything in sight.

These Yankees certainly did not act like Yankees, noted one Southerner. "They . . . respected private property, except sufficient for subsistence, and took such horses as needed. Indeed, they acted as if they were out on an electioneering tour, . . . supplied everybody with all the provisions they could carry off. . . . They stated they came with full expectation of being captured, and were willing to risk it in order to cut communications west. This accounts for their courtesy, as it is an anomaly in Yankee character."

Rousseau chatted amiably with several residents, telling them "he had been ordered to Opelika, and that he had gotten there, and he had expected to be captured." He told one lady he "knew many parties in that region, and it would have afforded him great pleasure to have met his old acquaintance General Pillow."

About noon, Matt Patrick and a detachment of the 4th Tennessee and the 5th Iowa shooed away the townspeople and set fire to the depots and storehouses. They also burned the express office, a tool shop, 450 bales of cotton, and six or seven freight cars loaded with hides, shovels, nails, and various other items.[16]

Once the flames had gotten a good start, both regiments moved to the east side of town and began tearing up the track in the direction of West Point. A closely spaced curtain of small trees and bushes veiled each side of the right-of-way, offering ideal cover for bushwhackers, and as a precaution, Lieutenant William Hays was ordered to take twenty men from Company H of the 5th Iowa and form a skirmish line to protect the work details. Moving to the right of the railroad, Hays and his men had waded through about 300 yards of heavy undergrowth when a shot rang out, instantly killing Private James Koontz. A frantic search failed to turn up any sign of whoever fired the fatal bullet and the rest of Patrick's brigade only had time to wreck a mile and a half of track before Rousseau sent word for them to rejoin the rest of the command. Recalling Hays's skirmishers, the brigade mounted and started back toward Opelika.[17]

Since prying up the first rail at Loachapoka at 10:00 P.M., Sunday, July 17, the raiders had destroyed twenty-six miles of railroad and telegraph lines, stretching from three miles west of Notasulga to a mile and a half east of Opelika. They had burned the depots, water tanks, and warehouses at Notasulga, Loachapoka, Auburn, and Opelika, the barracks at Camp Watts, a locomotive and tender, six or seven freight cars, and several million dollars' worth of Confederate supplies. In the words of one Rebel prisoner, they had put "a big hole in Johnston's haversack."[18]

Now it was time to head for home, and about 1:00 P.M. the 8th Indiana led the column northeast on a road paralleling the railroad. Flags fluttered gaily in the summer breeze and the men were in high spirits, laughing and singing while a regimental band played "I Wish I Was in Dixie."[19]

The Yankees had "a great many negroes with them," noted a Columbus lady visiting relatives near Opelika. "Only one or two houses escaped them in that neighborhood. They would go in and ransack the whole house, and took off a great many horses, buggies, and anything else that they wanted, such as corn, oats, frying pans, clothes, and all kinds of things."[20]

Five miles above Opelika, at Rough and Ready, the raiders left the railroad and turned north toward Lafayette. Passing through Mount Jefferson late that afternoon, they heard rumors a large force was gathering at West Point—as many as 2,000 infantry and 3,000 cavalry with artillery, according to one report.

That was not far from the truth. During the night, Frank Armstrong had hurried his Mississippians south, past the scene of their recent clash with Stoneman's cavalry at Moore's Bridge. Just before daylight, he called a brief halt, telling the men to leave their horses saddled. Within an hour, they were on the march again.

About 9:00 A.M., they passed the little river town of Franklin. Continuing down the east side of the Chattahoochee for another twenty miles, late that afternoon they reached the Atlanta & West Point Railroad at LaGrange. Only then did Armstrong allow his tired troopers to unsaddle and feed their weary mounts.

"Many soldiers have passed through here on the R.R.," noted Lieutenant William M. Worthington of the 1st Mississippi Cavalry, "but our Brig. is the first body of troops with guns in hand and artillery 'limbered up' that has ever come through the town. I tell you there was a great excitement among the 'small boys & niggers' and considerable 'flutteration' among the fair sex when we entered. We were very kindly treated. Buckets of cold water were at every door & at many houses biscuits, meat, buttermilk, they seemed to know the 'Cavalry peculiarity,' and fruit of all kinds were handed to us. The young ladies were out in full force, 'on dress parade.' There were many very pretty ones among them. They made many complimentary remarks about the 'gallant Mississippians.' Such shaking of handkerchiefs & waving of flags, I have not seen for a long time."

Worthington and his comrades rested for about an hour before bugles summoned them back into the saddle. Keeping up a steady pace, they reached West Point about midnight, having traveled eighty miles in thirty hours. There was no sign of any Yankees, and the railroad bridge was well guarded by General Carswell's brigade, Major Capers's cadets, the Troup County militia, and two artillery batteries. Satisfied these troops had the situation in hand, Armstrong ordered his exhausted Mississippians to unsaddle, feed their horses, and get some sleep.

It was not long, however, before some of them discovered a freight train parked on the siding next to their bivouac was packed full of provisions. The news acted like a magnet, and soon Armstrong's whole brigade was crowded around the cars. A light shining from a boxcar doorway revealed the stern silhouette of a commissary officer, but when asked to issue rations to the men, he adamantly refused. The contents of this train were bound for Virginia.

An angry murmur rippled through the crowd, and hungry cavalrymen would have undoubtedly taken matters into their own hands if the noise had not attracted Armstrong's attention. Galloping up on his horse, he demanded to know what was going on. Some of his troopers explained they were just trying to get something to eat, but this commissary seemed intent on feeding them chapter and verse of army regulations, right poor fare for fightin' men.

Sympathizing with their plight, Armstrong tried to explain how his Mississippians had ridden long and hard to come to West Point's defense, but the commissary shook his head. "You know I am entrusted with these supplies and cannot let them go except on proper authority," he said.

"Authority or no authority," shouted one trooper, "we are going to have enough of them to do us until morning, if we have to turn you, car and all, sunnyside batamus."

"Silence, boys," Armstrong commanded sternly, "you shall have them, and in a more legitimate manner." Gesturing to his brigade quartermaster, he said, "Sit down there at that table, draw up a requisition for a day's rations for the whole brigade, and I will write a statement for this man showing the emergency of the case."

Sensing it was useless, perhaps even unwise, to argue any further, the bean counter said, "General, while this is not at all regular, yet I will honor the requisition and issue the ration to your quartermaster, you bearing me blameless in the matter."

Turning to look upon the sea of anxious, upturned faces shining in the lamplight, Armstrong said, "Boys, go quietly back to your fires and send your regimental commissaries here, then each company can draw its own ration in due form." Soon the night air was fragrant with the tantalizing aroma of fresh, hot dough and fried bacon.[21]

At that moment, Rousseau's column was scarcely a dozen miles to the west. His advance guard had charged into Lafayette, Alabama, about 8:00 or 9:00 that night, half expecting to find Rebel cavalry waiting for them. Instead, everything was quiet, almost too quiet.

Seeing a light in a nearby church, Corporal Hezekiah Turner of the 8th Indiana swung down from his horse and led a squad of men to investigate. As the bluecoated troopers eased inside the door, the minister looked up from his sermon. A look of utter consternation crossed his face.

"I believe there's some 'federal' soldiers present," he stammered.

The entire congregation wheeled around and gaped at the dirty, heavily armed men standing behind the pews. There was a collective gasp, a few stifled screams, then a moment of expectant silence.

"Go on with your preaching," Turner said, "we only want the rebel soldiers that are here." As the startled congregation watched in disbelief, Turner's men trooped down the aisle, hauled perhaps a half-dozen Confederates out of their seats, and herded them outside.[22]

Rousseau may have intended to spend the night at Lafayette or some place nearby; at least that was the impression prevailing among the first arrivals. They had ridden eighteen miles since leaving Opelika, and they were tired and hungry. According to one account, "they entered nearly every store and dwelling house about the square, [and] took large quantities of bacon, corn, fodder, etc. They ransacked a number of private houses and took all the valuables they could find."[23]

The foraging was interrupted when some of Rousseau's scouts galloped into town to report a column of Rebel cavalry had crossed the Chattahoochee at Franklin and was rapidly bearing down on Lafayette. Rousseau immediately deployed his men in line of battle and ordered the pack train broken up, the extra ammunition distributed, and the packsaddles burned while he pondered his next move.

"For a time," wrote Captain Williams, "the prospect of a successful retreat looked rather gloomy. Gen. Rousseau, however, after carefully sifting the rumors, determined to move in the direction he had started, and fight the way through, if necessary."

About 10:30 P.M., orders passed down the line: fall back to the horses and prepare to mount. No bugles sounded "Boots and Saddles" for fear of advertising their whereabouts, and Rebel prisoners were hastily paroled, Lieutenant Fanning noted, "much to their gratification and that of their courtseying, hoop-skirted friends."

Guided by a full moon, Rousseau's column threaded through the dense forests north of Lafayette. Nerves worn raw with fatigue drew taut, waiting for the blinding flash, the crashing volley to erupt from the shadows. But the weary troopers plodded on unchallenged, twelve, thirteen miles and more, past a nondescript little community called Bethlehem, before Rousseau finally called a halt at 2:00 A.M.

Troopers in the rearmost units got perhaps an hour's rest before being summoned "To Horse" at 4:00 A.M., July 20. As usual, there was no time for breakfast. Rousseau paused only long enough to exchange his escort of Kentuckians for one composed of Companies E and G of the 9th Ohio, commanded by Lieutenants St. Clair J. Fechner and Tom Fanning, then set out at a torrid pace.[24]

However, Captain Ruger, the civilian McBurney, or some renegade guide Rousseau had picked up along the way steered the column down the road leading directly to West Point. Instead of outdistancing any would-be pursuers, the raiders were marching straight at them. Fortunately, someone recognized the mistake and rerouted the column before too much time was lost. "We moved on towards the Tallapoosa River till within 8 miles of it," wrote Sergeant Tom Jackson of the 8th Indiana, "then changed our course to the right and marched towards Carlton [Carrollton]."[25]

With scarcely a pause, Rousseau's men plodded on, stealing a few horses at a little country settlement called Bethel. They had ridden seventeen miles on empty stomachs before the welcome word "Halt" finally echoed down the column at Rock Mills about noon. Located on the banks of Wehadkee Creek, Rock Mills was the site of a small woolen factory, gristmill, sawmill, cotton gin, and general store, all owned and operated by Wilkins Stevens and his partner, Thomas Johnson. While hungry troopers methodically emptied the barns and smokehouses in the neighborhood, Rousseau and his staff sat down to dinner in Stevens's parlor. They were still eating when Stevens strode in and begged them to do something to keep their men from ransacking his house. A big officer, perhaps Rousseau himself, got up, accompanied Stevens to the foyer, and posted a guard at the doorway, but it was too late. Prowling troopers had already carried off most everything of value, including Stevens's watch, $300 in gold and silver coin, and even the covers off his bed. When Rousseau left Rock Mills after an hour or so, Stevens's handsome silver-mounted rockaway carriage was missing, too.[26]

Hoping to avoid another potentially fatal error in direction, Rousseau took one of Stevens's employees, a miller named Green R. Harper, along as a guide. Taking a northeasterly track, the column crossed the state line into Georgia about 2:00 P.M., stealing mules, horses, and provisions from the scattered farms along the way.[27]

"The route during the day was nearly parallel with the Chattahoochee, and with the railroad from West Point to Atlanta, and from ten to twenty miles distant from it," wrote Rousseau's adjutant, Captain Williams. "There are many roads running from the railroad and river across to that on which we were moving, and it was expected that the rebels would move across on one or more of these to intercept our retreat or harass our rear; but one after another of these intersecting roads was passed, and still no rebel force made its appearance."

Led by the 5th Iowa, the raiders covered another thirty-one miles before Rousseau finally called a halt at 9:00 P.M. and made camp in the woods. The Iowans and Tennesseans at the head of the column who had been first to reach the barns and smokehouses along the road prepared hearty suppers, but troopers riding farther to the rear apparently did not fare as well. "Did not get much to eat at this place," complained Sergeant Jackson of the 8th Indiana, but, Oscar Reese noted, "We . . . had the first good night's rest we have had on the trip."

At 5:00 the next morning, July 21, the raiders broke camp without breakfast and headed "almost due north" toward Carrollton. Following the directions of Green Harper, the miller pressed into service at Rock Mills, the column passed through six or seven miles of wilderness before reaching the Laurel Hill community about 9:00 A.M.

William L. Bell, his son, and two neighbors were threshing wheat when a soldier "with stripes on his sleeves" rode into the field where they were working and asked how far it was to Carrollton. About twelve miles, Bell replied. As the soldier wheeled and galloped away, Bell cast a quizzical glance at his companions. Then it dawned on him. That was a Yankee sergeant! Hurrying to his house, Bell found the yard and the road beyond crowded with bluecoated cavalrymen. The doors to his barns and corn-cribs stood ajar. The fence was down in several places, and his mouse-colored mule and bay mare were gone. A steady stream of soldiers filed from the smokehouse, laden with bacon and flour. Inside the barn, troopers were tying fodder into bundles and carrying out sheaves of oats. Another crowd was filling sacks at his corncrib, while a Federal captain sat on the piazza, giving directions. When Bell begged him to leave his family some provisions, the captain merely shrugged and said soldiers had to live too.

Rousseau kept the column moving so rapidly there was little chance for news of his approach to get ahead of him. Dr. James T. Thomason lived just a mile up the road from William Bell and was not aware of anything unusual until an officer called him out of the house. Seeing the road crowded with cavalry, Thomason asked whose command it was. Rousseau's, the officer replied, and pointed out the general, who spoke briefly with the doctor before riding on.

Thomason supported a family of twenty, and his children came swarming out of the house to stare at the seemingly endless parade of men and horses. Nothing escaped their bright eyes, and soon they began jumping up and down, shouting, "They have got Mr. Bell's mules."

Thomason saw it was true. As he watched, scores of Yankee troopers left the road and crowded around his house. "There were a good many soldiers . . . walking," he noted, "who said they had broke down their horses." One of them went into the stable and took the doctor's sorrel. Others bridled the family's mare and helped themselves to bacon, corn, oats, and wheat. They took Thomason's surgical and cupping instruments, his shirts, and several large feather pillows sunning in the yard, saying they needed them to make their wounded more comfortable. Mrs. Thomason indig-nantly asked a cavalryman wandering through her kitchen if he had any influence over the ruffians looting her home. He said no and explained he and his comrades had just come through some of the poorest county he had ever seen and were very hungry. "This must have been true," Mrs. Thomason conceded, "for they would stand around and eat raw bacon quite greedily."

The Yankees were three hours passing Thomason's house. About a mile beyond, the head of the column stopped at 10:00 A.M. to cook breakfast and feed their horses. Within an hour they were back in the saddle.[28]

"Our horses as well as the men are becoming very worn out," wrote Williamson Ward of the 8th Indiana. Five horses in Company H had collapsed in the past two days. Ignoring the vigorous prod of boot and spur, an exhausted animal would simply stop and sink to the ground with a guttural groan. Rolling to one side, nostrils flaring, glassy eyes staring, it would lie stoically while the trooper stripped off his saddle and bridle and moved on, leaving the poor beast to its fate. Time and again, the company books recorded the same grim epitaph: "fell down and could not be got up."[29]

About 2:00 P.M., Rousseau's advance guard, the 8th Indiana, charged into Carroll-ton. Only six days earlier, the townspeople had feted a battalion of Stoneman's cavalry with cakes and pies, but Rousseau did not linger long enough to sample their hospitality. His 1st Brigade marched straight through town without incident, but someone took a shot at Harlon Baird's Iowans as they brought up the rear. Baird's men returned the fire, reportedly killing a civilian. There were no Union casualties, and the raiders pressed on toward Villa Rica, except for Green Harper. Having fulfilled his promise to guide the Yankees as far as Carrollton, he started the long ride back to Rock Mills.[30]

Late that afternoon, Rousseau's column passed P. H. Hesterly's farm near Allen's Mill. Hesterly had received a visit from some of Stoneman's men on July 15 and been robbed of almost everything he had. Picking up the shattered pieces of his existence, he had spent July 19 cutting a four-acre field of oats and binding them into fifty dozen large bundles. The bundles were still curing in the sun when Rousseau's advance guard appeared on July 21. Troopers took every one of the oversize sheaves and tied them to their saddles. Others rounded up about a dozen of Hesterly's chickens, telling him they were "for the officers," and took his cooking utensils and seven or eight sacks of corn. "They seemed to be in rather a hurry," Hesterly noted stoically.[31]

About 8:00 P.M., the 8th Indiana dashed into Villa Rica, sixteen miles northeast of Carrollton, surprising fifteen or twenty Rebels. Most of them fled, but the Hoosiers managed to capture two or three. When questioned, the prisoners said they were scouts for Confederate General "Red" Jackson and indicated Yankee pickets from Stoneman's command were only sixteen miles up the road at Powder Springs. Contrary to his previous policy, Rousseau did not parole these latest prisoners but took them along for safekeeping. Three or four miles beyond Villa Rica, he left the main road at 9:00 P.M. to bivouac along Mud Creek.[32]

Daylight on July 22 found the weary raiders still in camp. "The General was very kind this morning," wrote John Jones of the 8th Indiana, "and gave us ample time for breakfast." It was perhaps as late as 6:00 A.M. before they were called "To Horse."

Taking the Marietta road, they came to a rickety wooden bridge over Sweetwater Creek about 11:00 A.M. As they crossed, troopers noticed a hand-shaped sign nailed to a large oak tree near the creek bank. The index finger pointed back toward Villa Rica, and scrawled in big, black, crooked letters were the words, "3 miles to hell."

"I thought perhaps the fellow who had nailed it up there was mistaken in the direction and the distance too," noted Private Eli Heaton.

Another hour's ride brought the column to Powder Springs. A mile east of town, at the bridge over Noyes' Creek, the raiders met a lieutenant and a platoon of men dressed in blue, the first friendly faces they had seen in twelve days. As each of Rousseau's regiments approached the bridge, these pickets, a detachment of Stoneman's 14th Illinois Cavalry, snapped to attention and held their guns in salute. "My eyes filled with tears as I returned it," wrote Colonel Hamilton of the 9th Ohio, ". . . I thought them the handsomest men I ever saw."

Cheer after cheer echoed from one end of the column to the other as jubilant troopers stood up in the stirrups and swung their hats in the air. They were home, safely inside the Union lines. The sense of relief was "better imagined than described," said Oscar Reese.

From Noyes' Creek the road led eastward, past the silent, scarred slopes of Kennesaw Mountain, past the abandoned breastworks, the shattered trees thrusting naked limbs toward the sky, and the long rows of freshly dug graves lining both sides of the road. Amid these desolate scenes, Rousseau called a halt about 1:00 P.M., five miles short of Marietta. Leaving his men to rest and feed their horses, he and his staff rode on, apparently accompanied by the two Ohio companies of his escort.

Upon reaching Marietta, Rousseau sought out the telegraph office on the public square and wired Sherman:

> I have torn up and destroyed nearly thirty 30 miles of the railroad between Montgomery and Opelika and three miles of it between Opelika & Columbus & two miles between West Point & Opelika also the Y & turn table & the depots filled with stores at Opelika & many depots of supplies at other points.
>
> My trip was entirely successfull [*sic*] in all respects. I destroyed 30 miles of R R in 36 hours. My command will be here in three hours. My whole loss does not exceed 12 killed & 30 wounded. I captured 400 fine mules & 300 horses.[33]

Rousseau could hear the distant roar of the great battle raging east of Atlanta. His men heard it, too, and speculated about what it meant as they ate their midday meal. After two hours' rest, they climbed back into the saddle one more time for the five-mile ride to Marietta.

The day had been clear and hot, but as they rode eastward, the clouds began to gather. It was raining steadily by the time Rousseau's rear guard, the 8th Indiana, plodded into the outskirts of Marietta at 8:00 P.M. and dismounted in the shadow of the Georgia Military Institute, now being used as a Union field hospital.

"We are nearly worn out with the constant travel and loss of sleep," noted Williamson Ward. "The boys look hollow eyed and care worn, the worst I have ever seen. The constant strain of excitement is enough to break the strongest ones among us."

The horses were in even worse shape, and before settling down for the night, each company drew forage for their hungry mounts. There were also several disciplinary matters to resolve. One trooper, caught earlier that day while trying to steal a chicken, had been strapped to his saddle and forced to ride all the way to Marietta slumped over the pommel with his head tied to the horse's neck. Another soldier, Corporal J. P. Barrington of the 9th Ohio, under arrest since July 17, was sent to the guardhouse for straggling and disobeying orders.

Barrington at least had a dry place to sleep. The rest of the command had left all their tents and blankets in Decatur and spent a miserable night in the rain. "We had a very poor night's rest, . . ." complained Lieutenant Tom Fanning.

July 23 dawned clear and unusually cool. "This morning finds us still in camp hardly knowing what to do as we are not ordered out," wrote Sergeant Tom Jackson, "but we contented ourselves and occupy our time in writing to Father, Mother, Brother, and Sister and perhaps a wife, if not a wife to a Lover or intended." And what a story they had to tell.

In twelve days, they had marched through the heart of Dixie, averaging thirty-four miles a day. They had destroyed $20,000,000 to $25,000,000 worth of Rebel property, including twenty-six miles of railroad and telegraph lines, eight or nine boxcars, a locomotive and tender, thirteen depots and warehouses, two gun factories, an iron works, a conscript camp, over 1,000 bales of cotton, several tons of tobacco, at least four wagons, and huge quantities of quartermaster, commissary, and ordnance supplies. In addition, they had brought in about 300 Negroes and roughly 300 horses and 400 mules, although estimates of captured stock ranged anywhere from 500 to 1,100.

They had fought pitched battles at Ten Islands and Chehaw, and skirmished at Sand Mountain, Stowe's Ferry, Loachapoka, and Auburn, killing at least twenty-five Confederates, wounding about a hundred, and capturing sixty-one, including two lieutenant colonels, a major, two captains, and two or three lieutenants. These prisoners had been paroled, along with another 243 Confederates captured at the military hospitals at Talladega and Notasulga.

The raiders' own losses were minimal: four killed, eight severely wounded and left behind, and thirty-five taken prisoner. Another fifteen had been hurt or wounded, but were able to return to the Union lines. These included two who had fallen from their horses, one with a slight contusion, another with a badly bruised leg, and a Kentuckian who had received a saber cut on his nose during a "personal altercation."[34]

Some of the totals were greatly exaggerated in the telling, but in a war marked by great cavalry raids, this had been the most daring, most successful expedition since Colonel Benjamin H. Grierson's sweep through Mississippi in the spring of 1863, and, unlike Grierson, Rousseau had succeeded in reinforcing a Federal army in the midst of an important campaign.

Justifiably proud of his men and all they had accomplished, Rousseau issued a congratulatory order:

HEADQUARTERS ROUSSEAU'S CAVALRY EXPEDITION,
Marietta, Ga., July 23, 1864.

The Major-General Commanding desires to express to the officers and men of his command his grateful appreciation of the arduous labors they have performed, and the energy and gallantry they have shown, in carrying out the important objects of the expedition. Having endured the fatigues and privations of forced marches; penetrated further into the enemy's rear than any similar expedition had done; forced the passage of rivers in the face of the foe, defeating him with heavy loss; effectually destroying over thirty miles of an important railroad, with all its appurtenances, several military manufacturing establishments, and immense quantities of supplies, and having throughout borne uncomplainingly and cheerfully the hardships incident to such service, and at all times shown a heroic readiness to meet the enemy, and an enthusiastic energy in accomplishing the work to be performed, the Major-General Commanding feels that he cannot too highly commend their fortitude, courage and patriotism. He regrets that duty, which calls him to service apart from the command, prevents him from expressing in person his thanks for their services, but wishes to assure officers and men that he will ever hold them in grateful remembrance.

By command of Major Gen. ROUSSEAU.
Thos. C. Williams, A.A.A.G.[35]

Rousseau had planned to return to Nashville to resume command of the District of Tennessee, but Sherman had other ideas. Upon receipt of the telegram announcing the raiders' arrival, he sent one of his aides, Captain Audenried, to George Thomas's headquarters at 2:00 A.M., July 23, with instructions for Thomas to have Rousseau relieve Stoneman's cavalry on the north side of the Chattahoochee and "let General Stoneman come to me with his whole force."

Enclosed with this message were orders to be forwarded to Rousseau "at once," in which Sherman acknowledged:

> Your dispatch is received, and you have done well. I hate to call on you so soon for more service, *but time is pressing* [author's italics]. I want you to move down right away to the railroad bridge and relieve General Stoneman, who is watching the Chattahoochee below Turner's Ferry. He will describe to you the country and what is needed. I want him relieved as soon as possible, that he may come over here. I hope to see you in a few days.

Thomas sent these orders to Marietta, but by the time they arrived Rousseau had already left Tom Harrison in command and started for the front at daylight. His first stop was Thomas's headquarters on the Marietta Road, a half mile behind the Union lines, where he learned of the orders to relieve Stoneman's troops. Knowing Harrison would do whatever was necessary, Rousseau continued to Sherman's headquarters, just north of Atlanta, at the intersection of the North Decatur and Durand's Mill roads.

He arrived sometime after 10:30 A.M. and received a warm welcome. Sherman was eager to hear all about the raid, and especially enjoyed the story about the unsuspecting planter below Talladega who had mistaken Rousseau and his men for Rebels.

"That's well done, Rousseau, well done," Sherman chuckled, "but I didn't expect to see you back."

"Why not?" Rousseau asked.

"I expected you to tear up the road," Sherman explained, "but I thought they would gobble you."

"You are a pretty fellow," Rousseau said in mock resentment, "to send me off on such a trip."

"You proposed it yourself," Sherman reminded him, "besides, I knew they wouldn't hurt you, and I thought you would pay for yourself."

Rousseau's visit was a short one. That evening he stopped at the headquarters of his old command, the 1st Division of the XIV Corps, and chatted amiably with friends and former subordinates for a few hours before returning to Marietta later that night.[36]

Early on July 24, Rousseau wired his adjutant, Major Polk, from Marietta:

> We arrived here day before yesterday, and have been eminently successful, and have executed the orders of Gen. Sherman to the letter. Our loss does not exceed twelve in killed and wounded. I start today for Nashville.

Rousseau would go on to other triumphs, but his role in the Atlanta campaign was finished. He and his staff, except for his civilian guide, McBurney, boarded a northbound train at Marietta at midnight, July 25, and arrived in Nashville on the night of July 26–27. There the rigors of the past three weeks began to tell. "Major-General Rousseau has not returned unscathed from his expedition to Opelika," a correspondent of the *Cincinnati Gazette* reported on August 1, "but on the contrary, is confined to his bed with a fever."[37]

But there would be no rest for the colonels, captains, and common horse soldiers he left behind.

10

GARRARD'S RAID

JULY 21–JULY 24, 1864

Nothing in his life
Became him like the leaving of it; he died
As one that had studied in his death
To throw away the dearest thing he owned
As 'twere a careless trifle.

—William Shakespeare, *Macbeth*

While delighted with Rousseau's success, Sherman was also anxious to hear from Kenner Garrard. Ordered to block the approach of any Rebel reinforcements from Virginia by destroying the railroad trestles over the Yellow and Alcovy rivers, forty miles east of Atlanta, Garrard's division had ridden out of Decatur on the evening of July 21. Heads bowed beneath a pelting rain that beat a steady tattoo on their hat brims, troopers of Eli Long's and Abe Miller's brigades had plodded past their old camps at Browning's Courthouse. Peering off to the right they could vaguely discern Stone Mountain's brooding silhouette. Somewhere off to the left were the ruins of McAfee's Bridge, where they had crossed the Chattahoochee only four days earlier.

As the leaden skies lowered into night, the column turned sharply to the southeast at Choice's store, occasionally rousing bewildered farmers out of bed to demand the keys to barns, stables, and smokehouses. No Rebels contested the march, and Eli Long's advance guard had put twenty-two miles behind them by the time they clattered across the Rockbridge over Yellow River shortly after midnight.[1]

Just beyond the river lay the "Promised Land," a sprawling 956-acre plantation belonging to Thomas Maguire. Calling a halt, Garrard bedded down under the sheltering boughs of some pines on the right side of the road, directing his men to keep their horses saddled and forbidding fires for fear of advertising their line of march to Wheeler's cavalry.

While Garrard slept, his men descended on the "Promised Land" like a plague out of Egypt, relieving Thomas Maguire of his watch and pocketbook, ransacking his house and barns, and taking everything that was not nailed down, including two bee gums. "They must have practiced roguery from their childhood," Maguire observed bitterly, ". . . so well they appear to know their art."[2]

The eastern sky was beginning to pale by the time Bob Minty's 1st Brigade reached Rockbridge. His men had made consecutive marches from New Cross Keys and Decatur, a total of thirty-two miles, to overtake the division. Dead tired, they stripped the saddles off their weary mounts and lay down to sleep. Within an hour heavy-handed sergeants were shaking them awake. Orders were to mount up, and in the hurry to break camp, Garrard's servant rolled up the general's rain-soaked bedding, tied it with a rope, and carelessly tossed it into the back of the headquarters wagon.

Leaving a small rear guard to burn Rockbridge, Garrard ordered his column

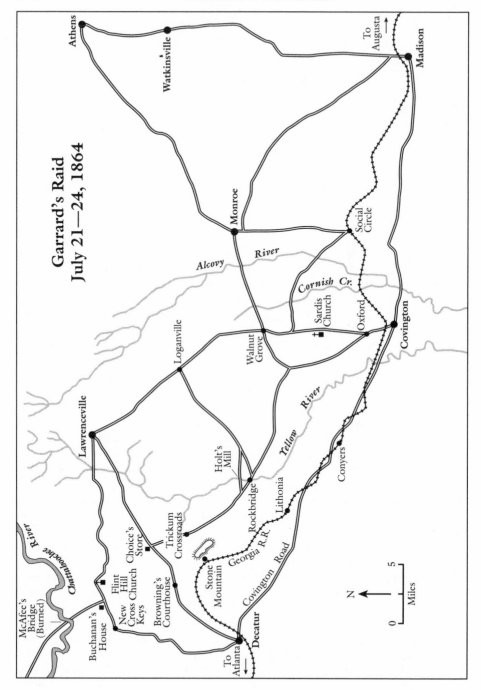

Garrard's Raid
July 21–24, 1864

forward at 5:00 A.M. The Georgia Railroad trestle over Yellow River lay only five or six miles to the right, and in the dawn's gray light he sent two companies of the 98th Illinois Mounted Infantry riding south to destroy it.[3]

Recrossing the Yellow River a few miles below Rockbridge, these two companies charged into Conyers about midmorning, just as a locomotive chugged up to the depot pulling a passenger coach and twelve freight cars. A hail of gunfire routed the engineer and conductor, and the raiders quickly made prisoners of sixteen Confederate soldiers and civilians before setting fire to the train and the depot and riding out of town.[4]

Following the railroad eastward, the Illinois troopers soon came to their main objective, the 555-foot trestle over Yellow River. A handful of old men and boys guarded the huge wooden span and a wagon bridge a few yards downstream, but ancient muzzle-loaders and shotguns were no match for forty or fifty veteran troopers armed with Spencers. The first exchange of gunfire killed a white-haired old man named Brown. The others simply ran away. Crossing to the east bank, the Yankees set fire to the wagon bridge and trestle, a large flour mill a short distance downstream, and the house of the miller, Albert P. Torrence.[5]

The rest of the division, 3,500 strong, traveled a parallel road a few miles farther north. Early that morning, some of Garrard's scouts, ranging far ahead of the column, surprised three Confederate troopers sleeping on the front porch of Mrs. Margaret Weaver's house. A gunfight began right in the front yard, and as Mrs. Weaver looked on, a young Kentuckian, John Davis, fell mortally wounded, almost at the feet of her eleven-year-old niece, Eudora. Another Rebel was shot and taken prisoner. The third grayjacket bolted out the back door and escaped into a nearby orchard with four other Confederates who had been sleeping in the barn.

The Yankees dragged Davis off the porch, searched him, and left him lying in the yard, bleeding from a bullet wound in his head. Mrs. Weaver had two of her Negro men carry him back to the porch and lay him on a mattress. While her children fanned the dying man's pallid brow with peacock feathers and peach branches, the Yankees searched the barn and rounded up Rebel horses. Mrs. Weaver took the precaution of locking her trunks and dresser drawers, just as her father, Thomas Maguire, had done the night before, but it did no good. The Yankees broke open the locks, ransacked her home, and emptied her smokehouse.[6]

"Our march had been through the finest and best country we had seen in the whole South," noted Sergeant Thomas Crofts of the 3rd Ohio. "Fine plantations, large mansions, everything indicating wealth and prosperity."

Garrard's men also encountered the wagons and buggies of several Atlanta families refugeeing eastward in hopes of getting themselves and a few precious belongings aboard a train bound for Madison, Augusta, or any place beyond Sherman's reach. Seeing the approaching Yankee horsemen, some drivers unhitched their teams and galloped off bareback, leaving their wives and children stranded by the roadside. Others, like Reverend Joshua Knowles, abandoned their vehicles and tried to flee on foot. When this failed, Knowles surrendered gracefully, but complained bitterly when he saw a trooper unhitching his buggy horse. The Yankees obligingly left him a stolen mule, and rumor had it the parson "got the best of the swap."[7]

"The men seemed to have no mercy on this class of people," observed Sergeant

Ben Magee of the 72nd Indiana, "and made free with horses, mules, and everything else that seemed to strike their fancy; and it was sometimes distressing to see their blank, vacant stare, as they would be left with their wagons in the road minus horses or mules, when they hadn't thought there was a Yankee nearer them than Decatur."

Bobbing in the midst of the bluecoated cavalcade was a bee gum troopers from Company G of the 7th Pennsylvania had stolen during the night. After slipping a forage bag over the hive, they had wrapped it in a rubber blanket or poncho and were taking turns balancing the cumbersome load on the pommels of their saddles. This worked well enough until the cover suddenly slipped off that morning, leaving a hapless trooper literally holding the bag. As the bees began buzzing around his head, he unceremoniously dumped the hive in the middle of the road, loosing a swarm of angry attackers. Horses reared and bucked wildly. Shouting, cursing troopers sawed on the reins with one hand and swatted furiously with the other. Before their fury was spent, the enraged insects had stung a horse to death and nearly stampeded the whole regiment.[8]

With troopers constantly leaving the ranks for one reason and another, some regiments began lagging far behind. Garrard called a halt about 11:00 A.M., and after closing up his column he sent Eli Long's 2nd Brigade eastward to burn the railroad trestle over the Alcovy River. The rest of the division followed Abe Miller's mounted infantry south toward Oxford.

A staid bastion of north Georgia Methodism, Oxford was built around the church-sponsored Emory College. Mathematics professor and deputy county clerk Gustavus John Orr was coming home for dinner that day when a horseman raced past his buggy shouting, "The Yankees are coming!" Reining up at his front gate, Orr hurled a carpetbag full of tax receipts over the fence. After raking up a few handfuls of leaves in a hurried effort to hide it, he ran into the house, blurted a brief explanation to his wife, who was in bed with a five-day-old daughter, and bolted out the back door.

While Professor Orr cowered in a weed-choked ditch in the garden, his thirteen-year-old son, Edgar, ran to the front gate just as the first bluecoats boldly rode down the street. He was standing beside his father's buggy when a Yankee officer commanded a passing trooper to "Take that horse." Drawing a knife, the soldier stepped toward the rig.

"Let me unharness it, Sir!" Edgar volunteered. "It won't take a minute."

"Cut that harness," the officer barked. Edgar watched helplessly as the trooper hacked the leather into little pieces and led the horse away.

"They came upon us with the suddenness of a whirlwind," wrote one astonished resident, "and were galloping through our streets ere we were aware of their approach."[9]

The clatter of hooves came just as Sergeant Walter A. Clark and other sick and wounded Confederates at Oxford's Hood Hospital were sitting down to dinner in the Emory College chapel. Crowding to the front door, they saw a big, redheaded Yankee astride a panting, sweat-lathered horse. Being of a philosophical turn of mind, Sergeant Clark sat back down to finish his dinner, but scores of previously bedridden patients housed in the college's main building and two literary society halls suddenly found the strength to limp, hobble, walk, and even run.

Yankee troopers quickly overtook the slower ones, but "in the main," noted one resident, "they treated the citizenship of Oxford, if not as well as they had a right to expect, certainly much better than they had feared. Their officers were invariably civil and polite; and Gen. Garrard, in his intercourse with us, I must say to his credit, showed himself the gentleman. Private property was generally respected, and yet there were few houses that were not robbed of articles of one kind or another by lawless soldiers as opportunity offered . . . there was not the first indignity offered to any of our ladies; nor do I know of an instance in which any gentleman was treated with rudeness or injury.

"Several were deprived of their watches, who did not take the precaution to hide them; but as they were surrendered upon demand, no personal violence was used. Our greatest loss was in mules and horses and negroes. . . . The Yankees offered many inducements, and tried every art to persuade many of our servants to go, but in vain. I confess that the fidelity of our negro population under this trying ordeal surpassed my most sanguine expectations."[10]

No one knew this better than Confederate Congressman Warren Akin. He was refugeeing at Oxford when his mulatto coachman, Bob Beavers, burst into the house yelling, "Run, Marst'r! The Fed'rals are comin'."

Akin fled to the woods, barely making his escape, but his pursuers inquired closely for him, offering Bob $500 in gold if he would show them where his master was hiding. When the faithful servant refused, they raised their bid to $1,000. "I had to tell a heap of lies," Bob later confessed, "but I said nothing about Marster."

Mrs. Akin watched fearfully as some of the raiders began ransacking her house. Then she saw Bob holding an ax behind his back. What are you doing, she asked? "Why, Miss Mary," he replied, gesturing toward a Yankee soldier, "if that man insults you, I will kill him." Mrs. Akin gently coaxed the ax out of his hands and put it out of sight.[11]

The ladies did their part, too. When Sergeant James Mount led a squad of the 72nd Indiana up to one stately residence, he was met by the icy stares of several calicoed Confederates. Dismounting, he announced he had orders to search the house.

"What for?" the ladies asked indignantly.

"For Rebel soldiers," Mount replied.

"Do you suppose we would harbor Rebel soldiers in our private parlors?"

"Rebel soldiers are not so unpopular in Georgia as to be deprived of the privacy of your parlors . . . when Union soldiers are in town," the sergeant answered.

"You must not enter our house."

"My orders are imperative," Mount said politely.

"There are no Rebels in our house."

"Ladies," Mount said firmly, "without further controversy, I shall soon settle the question." Stepping across the threshold, he mounted the stairs. At the top of the landing, he heard a door close. Flinging it open, he found two Rebel officers huddled inside and summarily ushered them downstairs, much to the dismay of their gallant defenders.[12]

The Yankees also visited the home of a noted Methodist clergyman. The minister was away, but his Northern-born wife received her callers courteously. "They'll never trouble me or mine," she confidently assured a neighbor. "I am just going to sit down and see the salvation of the Lord."

Garrard's men put her faith to the test, snatching up chickens and looting her smokehouse, but she managed to keep her composure until a trooper put a bridle on the family horse and led him off to "jine the cavalry." This was more than the poor lady could bear. Jumping to her feet, she denounced the Yankee army in general and these particular specimens in "plain and vigorous English."

Some of the raiders rode up to the back door of the Branham home, demanding something to eat, but the Negro cook tried to put them off, saying, "the white folks ain't et yet." When these ruffians threatened to burn the house down if they did not get fed, frail old Grandmother Branham came storming out and told them exactly what she thought of them.[13]

Another Oxford lady was sitting on her front porch when a Michigan soldier rode up to her front gate. "See what a fine Georgia 'hoss' I have," he gloated.

"Yes," she said contemptuously, "one you stole I suppose."

Taking umbrage at the woman's harsh tone, the trooper turned to her son. "Here, boy," he growled, "hold this 'hoss.'"

"I'd see you at the devil first," the lad shot back. Years later, he would recall this was his "first and last use of improper language in the presence of his Christian mother, and that for some reason she failed on that occasion to administer even a mild reproof."[14]

Anxious to get to the railroad, Garrard did not linger in Oxford. Leaving the 72nd Indiana's regimental surgeon, Dr. William Cole, and a few troopers behind to determine if any of the convalescent Confederates at Hood Hospital were fit to travel, he hurried the rest of Abe Miller's brigade down a road diverging to the right and ordered Bob Minty to send a battalion straight into Covington.

Minty assigned this task to Captain John C. Hathaway's 1st battalion (Companies A, D, G, and I) of the 4th Michigan. Hurrying forward, Hathaway's men passed a Rebel conscript camp housing thirty officers and two or three hundred recruits, "who all escaped," Minty's inspector general, Captain Heber S. Thompson, noted in disgust, "owing to the blundering of those worthless scouts of ours."

By this time, Covington had seen the pillars of smoke billowing from the burning bridges over Yellow River, and heard the Yankees had captured the westbound train at Conyers. This precipitated what one young lady called a veritable stampede of "wagons, buggies, cows, hogs, folk, women and children in terror, screaming and crying, calling for others."

News of the Yankees' approach reached Covington's two military hospitals, Hill and Lumpkin, just as Mrs. S. E. D. "Grandma" Smith was serving dinner. "If ever I saw what is called pell-mell," she wrote, "I saw it there and then. Everyone who could walk broke for the pine thicket . . . and before I was half done, there were not hands sufficient to carry the waiters to the rooms."

Nurse Allie Travis recounted how "one man, tall and lank, who was a member of the tribe known as 'hospital rats,' had long attracted attention by his woe-begone, dying-by-inches look and his slow, snail-like pace. The reported proximity of the Yankees infused new life into his veins, and he was soon seen rushing comet-like through the air, his long hair streaming in the wind; and as his reserve force was all brought into play he soon out-distanced all competitors. A lady who had come from Alabama to nurse her wounded husband was looking out at our front door when the racer flitted past, and, in spite of her distress, could not restrain a laugh, while she cried 'Look at Duncan! Look at Duncan!' But Duncan was gone."[15]

Presley Jones pulled back on his plow lines and watched the crowds of fleeing convalescents in disgust. A fifty-nine-year-old father of eight, he was too old to be a soldier, but not too old to fight. Leaving his plow, he went home to get his squirrel rifle, vowing to kill the first "damn Yankee" he saw. He was standing at the corner of Railroad and Usher streets when the first of Garrard's scouts, Private John Williams of the 17th Indiana Mounted Infantry and Private William Travellion of the 4th U.S. Cavalry, rode into town.

"[If] nobody will fight for my country, I will," Jones cried, leveling his gun at the first bluecoat.

"Don't shoot," the scout pleaded, but a rifle blast lifted him out of the saddle. Ducking around the corner, Jones hastily reloaded his gun and emerged on another street. His rifle cracked again, felling the second Yankee soldier. Before Jones could reload, the rest of Garrard's scouts were upon him. Clubbing his rifle, the old farmer stood his ground, glaring defiance until he went down in a hail of bullets.

As Jones lay dying, one of his daughters shouldered through the crowd of surrounding cavalrymen and knelt beside him, weeping bitterly.

"Boys don't she cry," said a Yankee trooper with a callous laugh. Another held out his hat, offering to "catch her tears." Still another assured her "if her father had had a thousand lives they would have taken them all." Then a third soldier shoved the muzzle of his pistol against Jones's graying temple and blew the old man's brains out.[16]

As the last echoes of the shot faded away, the Yankee scouts stalked the hushed, expectant streets. They wanted an eye for an eye, and they found George Hewitt Daniel.

A genteel and sophisticated English émigré, Daniel had established a small grocery business in Covington, acquired land, and become thoroughly Southern in his convictions. Twice married but now a widower, the forty-seven-year-old father of three young daughters had been serving as adjutant of the 8th Regiment of Georgia militia in the trenches north of Atlanta until sometime after July 3, when he came home on sick leave.

There are several versions of what happened in Covington on July 22, but the two earliest accounts insist Daniel had gone to the depot to see his youngest daughter off on the morning train to Conyers. When word arrived after her departure that the Yankees had captured the train, he became frantic with fatherly concern. The two stories differ slightly over just what happened next, but everyone agrees Daniel was "a very quiet, passionate man . . . acting on the impulse of the moment . . . a man of high prejudice . . . desirous to carry everything his own way."

According to Allie Travis, a nurse at one of the Covington hospitals, the distraught father vowed to rescue his daughter or die trying. He was at the depot, waiting for someone to bring him his horse, when some of Garrard's men rode up, saw he was wearing a cartridge box, and took him prisoner.

The other account, printed only two weeks after the event, maintained Daniel was still waiting for his horse when a friend advised him his daughter was safe. Greatly relieved, Daniel returned to his store but had scarcely gotten inside when Yankee troopers barged in and asked if he was a soldier. When Daniel admitted he was, his interrogators seemed skeptical. Two of them went outside. "Who is this man George Daniel?" they demanded of a passerby. The frightened civilian, perhaps thinking the Yankees would make prisoners of any Confederate soldiers they found in Covington, unwittingly sealed Daniel's fate by describing him as "a citizen and merchant."

"We'll have that man to shoot," declared one of the troopers.

Convening a mock trial, they summarily convicted Daniel as a bushwhacker. Since a neighbor had identified him as a civilian rather than a soldier, his captors refused to treat him as a prisoner of war. Instead, two of them led Daniel to a grove of oak trees on Colonel W. W. Clark's property and shot him dead. Daniel's three daughters did not learn of the tragedy until later that afternoon, when a neighbor heard a Yankee soldier say something about leaving "a dead Reb in the woods."[17]

Perhaps a half hour after this incident, Captain Hathaway's battalion of the 4th Michigan charged into town, overtaking some ward orderlies and attendants. When asked if they were with the hospitals, the frightened fugitives stammered, "Yes sir."

"Well, you damned fools, what are you running for? Stay inside your ward and you will not be troubled."

Spurred by reports of a Rebel wagon train parked somewhere on the outskirts of town, Hathaway's battalion galloped off in pursuit. Abe Miller's 3rd Brigade arrived a little later. They had struck the railroad two miles west of Covington, presumably meeting the two companies of the 98th Illinois Garrard had sent to Conyers that morning. Dismounting and laying their Spencers aside while Bob Minty's brigade formed a skirmish line to protect them, Miller's men began pulling down fences along the right-of-way and soon had dozens of fires blazing at the joints in the track. Utilizing the technique they had perfected at Stone Mountain on July 18, they steadily worked their way eastward until they reached the railroad depot on the north side of Covington at 2:00 P.M. They put the brick building, crammed with furniture belonging to refugee families, to the torch along with a nearby water tank and a large warehouse full of cotton and Confederate commissary supplies. "This made the largest single fire we ever saw," wrote Sergeant Ben Magee; "we are satisfied the blaze reached 100 feet high."[18]

While members of Magee's regiment set a string of flatcars ablaze, other detachments destroyed a cache of powder and ammunition, thirty stands of arms, fifty barrels of salt, and some brand new hospital tents. Sparing nothing of value, they even burned the old Bethlehem Baptist Church on the east side of Dried Indian Creek when they discovered it was full of cotton.

Troopers also set fire to several large, unfinished hospital buildings on Rogers Branch, and "a very large lot" of imported carpenters' tools used in their construction. The flames raged out of control and quickly spread, destroying a nearby workshop and smithy belonging to Lewis Freeland.[19]

Most of the stores ringing the town square had already closed for dinner before the first Yankees arrived, but a detail led by Lieutenant Colonel Biggs of the 123rd Illinois forced the doors open. While officers posted guards, teamsters backed six or seven big army wagons up to the buildings along with three or four more commandeered off the street and troopers began loading boxes, barrels, and sacks of tobacco, sugar, meat, flour, coffee, salt, soda, rice, corn, syrup, soap, candles, nails, cutlery, shoes, clothing, and yard goods. "Only such men as were ordered to go into the store went in," noted a harried shop clerk, "there was no grab & snatching about the taking. They pressed 2 or 3 Negroes into service & made them help load the goods as they were heavy."

One store owner, Charles L. Bowker, introduced himself to Biggs as a Massachusetts man and asked that his property be spared. Biggs politely refused, saying he had strict orders to take all the commissary supplies and tobacco he could find. When

Bowker asked for a receipt or some sort of voucher, Biggs put him off, saying he did not have time; he was expecting Wheeler's cavalry at any moment.

Occasionally, Biggs urged his men to hurry up, but even with his prodding it took them two and a half hours to empty Bowker's store. Apparently not one to hold a grudge, Bowker persuaded a refugee woman named Mrs. High to prepare dinner at J. W. Pace's house for four Yankee officers. How he managed this is something of a mystery, because Mrs. High had a reputation as "a *thoroughbred Rebel.*" She heaped abuse on her guests during the course of the meal and reportedly hung a small Confederate flag on the piazza until Bowker pulled it down and tore it to shreds.

The Yankees allowed Mrs. High her little act of defiance and even offered to pay for their meal. Such courtesies were not uncommon. Several officers advised citizens to hide their money, watches, silverware, and jewelry from prowling enlisted men. But except for Biggs's detachment, a few scouts, and Captain Hathaway's battalion, which returned after a fruitless search for Rebel wagons, most of the raiders seemed reluctant to venture too far from the railroad depot on the north side of town, where Garrard had made his headquarters.[20]

"Grandma" Smith had watched the first contingent of Yankee troopers race through the streets. Returning to her duties at Hill Hospital, she found the wards empty except for men too sick or too badly wounded to run away. "It was indeed a pitiful sight . . . ," she wrote, "to see them unable to help themselves, and . . . the first question, almost simultaneously asked by all, was, if I was going to leave them. I assured them that I had not thought of such a thing as to leave them—more especially as the ward master and the nurses had about all gone; and I would stay and see that they were cared for to the best of my ability, if all the others left, and not to let that trouble them in the least."

"Well," one of her patients said hopefully, "we are all right then, if you stay."

Assisted by a kindly black woman, Mrs. Smith began her rounds. In between fluffing pillows and checking bandages, her companion said she could not understand what made "all de fool niggers an' wimmin run for, no how; de Yanks didn't want dem." If she were "old miss," she would not allow such folk to "put dar foots back here, after leaving her and de poor helpless boys to take care ob demselves."

While the woman prattled on, Mrs. Smith left the ward for a few minutes to see how the surgeons were doing. To her horror and dismay, she found Drs. William H. Robertson and Benjamin R. Doyle surrounded by a Yankee captain and half a dozen heavily armed troopers.

"You have come and taken me prisoner while performing my duty as surgeon," Dr. Robertson defiantly told his captors. "The men whom you have disabled while contending for their just rights on the battle field, are under my care. You have gone contrary to military rules in molesting me. I shall, therefore, appeal to General Girard [sic] for redress. I could have made my escape, but before I would have forsaken these, my wounded comrades, I would suffer myself to be shot down here in this yard."

Noticing Mrs. Smith, Dr. Robertson said to the Yankee captain, "Let me introduce to you my chief matron. She is in hopes you will not suffer her to be molested. She wishes to be allowed to remain with these, her patients. She is the only one out of five ladies who were willing to run the risk of being captured for their sake; and I ask you to see she is respected."

The Yankee officer politely assured Mrs. Smith she would be treated with all due consideration. If anyone bothered her, she need only report the matter to General Garrard, who would deal with the culprits severely. "By the way, madam," he added, "two of our men [the scouts Williams and Travellion] have been wounded since coming in the place. If I send them here, will you have them taken care of?"

"Certainly, I will," she replied; "send them on, and they shall be taken care of."

Her main concern, of course, was her own sick and wounded boys, and she begged the Yankee captain to allow Dr. Robertson to continue his rounds. The captain promised to do everything in his power to secure the doctor's release but insisted on taking him to Garrard's headquarters first.

"I felt like my last friend was gone," wrote Mrs. Smith, "and I left alone, with no one to look to for protection and assistance. I suppose that out of at least fifty patients, not one was able to give the other a drink of water. Some were almost in a dying condition; and one died about midnight of the same day, with no one to watch over him but the humble writer and the hired young man, named Chris., of the Fifteenth Arkansas Regiment, who played off sick on the approach of the Federals, and saved himself from being captured."

Two wounded Yankees would have only added to her burdens, but both men died before they could be moved to the hospital. Officers left one of the bodies with storekeeper Charles Bowker. "I never heard what became of the other," wrote Mrs. Smith.[21]

She was still anxiously awaiting Dr. Robertson's return when several Yankee troopers burst into the ward, brandishing their weapons. "You're not going to molest us, are you?" a bedridden Confederate asked timorously.

"Oh no," replied one of the Yanks, "we will only parole you now, and when you are able to be moved, we will send you to prison."

"Well, you will not trouble grandma, will you?" the patient implored. "She stays with us."

"Well," said the trooper, "I suppose we will have to banish her to the North, or make her take the oath."

"Nary time will you do either," snapped Mrs. Smith. "One who ranks a little higher than you requested me to report to General Girard [sic] if one of you dared to molest me, and I will do so."[22]

Taken aback by this revelation, the Yankees soon retreated out into the yard. They also visited the Lumpkin Hospital before the day was over, and most were genuinely impressed with what they saw. "Judging from appearances," wrote Captain William W. Van Antwerp of the 4th Michigan, "I would say that these hospitals are as comfortable, in every respect as our own, as any place south of the Ohio River."

"The hospital was clean and nice as any you will see in the North," agreed Quartermaster Sergeant Othniel Gooding after seeing some of the patients. "Our boys went to the stores and got tobbaco, sugar, candies and wine & everthing else and gave to them. They thought we were a merry set of Yanks. I can't begin to tell you what we did not do, enough to say we acted bad enough."

Anticipating just such a visit, Covington's chief commissary officer, Major J. D. Maney, had previously urged the hospitals to draw ten days' rations for their staff and patients. "I was prompted to this," he later explained, "from the belief that, in the event of a raid, all the stores actually in the possession of the Hospitals would be respected by the Enemy, while I *knew,* that, if found in the Com'sy Department of the Post, they would all be destroyed as property of the Confederate states. The results proved the correctness of my opinion, for while the small remnant of Stores left in my Com'sy house were utterly destroyed by the Enemy . . . , they did not even touch or otherwise injure a single article in the possession of the Hospitals."

The only recorded loss came when five or six surgeons, overly anxious to appease their Yankee visitors, began dispensing medicinal whisky in a manner one trooper said "would have done credit to the leading artists behind a metropolitan bar."[23]

While the 1st and 3rd Brigades were wreaking heartbreak and havoc in and around Covington, Eli Long's 3rd and 4th Ohio moved east of town to capture the 250-foot covered railroad bridge over the Alcovy River. Unlike the bridges at Yellow River, the Alcovy span and the adjacent wagon bridge had been left completely defenseless. Long's advance guard crossed the wagon bridge and charged up the railroad embankment toward a parked train before any of the passengers knew what was happening. The engine had a full head of steam and just barely managed to escape, but only by leaving a string of baggage cars stranded on the west side of the river. Long allowed the terrified passengers to unload their possessions before ordering the trestle, wagon bridge, and cars burned. Then his men went to work on the railroad, destroying two and a half or three miles of track and the trestle over Cornish Creek before they reached the outskirts of Covington early that evening.[24]

Bob Minty later claimed he asked for permission to dismount his brigade, commandeer a train, and travel 120 miles east to destroy the great gunpowder mill at Augusta, but Garrard rejected the idea. Wheeler's cavalry was reportedly only five miles away and coming fast, and shortly before dark Garrard started all three of his brigades back to Oxford.[25]

He ordered Dr. Robertson and the other Confederate surgeons released, but his men made prisoners of several convalescents, including Lieutenant Colonel Joseph Hamilton of Phillips' Legion and some enlisted men who worked as hospital orderlies and attendants. "I thought it one of the most hateful and low down tricks I had ever seen," wrote "Grandma" Smith. "After assuring them that they should not be troubled, as they belonged to the hospital, and getting all of them who heard of it back in the yard and house, then to take advantage of them and easily secure them as prisoner."[26]

More prisoners were waiting at Oxford, where Dr. Cole of the 72nd Indiana had counted off some forty or fifty reasonably healthy Rebels and marched them outside at 3:00 P.M. to be turned over to the provost guard. However, one of Garrard's officers intervened and ordered the convalescents to wait in their wards until 5:00.

Among those contemplating their last few hours of freedom was Walter Clark, the imperturbable sergeant who had insisted on finishing his dinner. Returning to his cot in the college chapel, he tried to interest himself in Augusta Jane Evans's novel, *Macaria,* which he had borrowed from a Miss Harrison, but it was no use. "Visions of a Federal prison peered at me from every page," he wrote, "and I gave it up."

Remembering he had promised to have tea with the Harrisons that afternoon, Clark waited until he saw another patient saunter up the street without being challenged. Assuming a casual air, he stepped out the door and walked to the Harrisons' house, where he found Mr. Harrison hiding in the garden and Mrs. Harrison quavering with concern. Returning the borrowed book, Clark explained that due to circumstances beyond his control, he would not be joining them for tea. When Mrs. Harrison insisted he wait with them until the guards came for him, he took a seat on the piazza and watched apprehensively as a brigade of bluecoated cavalry rode past, followed by a crowd of contrabands. One of the Yankee troopers dismounted, came into the house, and took a ham out of the pantry. Others strolled across the yard, but no one said a word to the quiet young man on the piazza.

"I made no special effort to attract their attention," Clark admitted, ". . . but I was doing some pretty tall thinking. The idea had occurred to me, . . . that if I remained quietly where I was, I might be overlooked and decided to make the experiment. At 5 P.M. the squad of convalescents was re-formed and marched off under guard, passing within a short distance of where I sat. Possibly I felt that my place was properly among them, but I felt no disposition to halt them in order to secure it and my heart grew lighter as the line grew dim in the distance and finally vanished."[27]

As the rest of Garrard's column retired through Oxford, the rear brigade, Abe Miller's mounted infantry, set fire to a large warehouse and some smaller buildings bulging with several hundred bales of cotton. The resulting conflagration also engulfed the home of an elderly gentleman, William Irvine, and burned it to the ground.

"The cotton we burned was all in one pile and made the hottest fire we ever saw," wrote Sergeant Ben Magee; "as we urged our horses along the street past it, it was so hot as to scorch our clothes and singe the hair on our horses."

Miller's men also broke into another large warehouse containing an estimated 8,000 pairs of shoes and eighty to a hundred boxes of tobacco. "You ought to have seen our boys go for the tobacco . . . ," chuckled Magee. "Here it was, more than our whole division could carry off, and oh! what a chew the boys did take; and then you would have smiled to see them load themselves down with it; every pocket and haversack and saddle-bags, crammed to their utmost capacity, and yet some of them not satisfied, would, after mounting, have their comrades to hand them up 'another box.' Though there were shoes enough to supply the whole division, it was only after they found they could not possibly carry any more tobacco that they thought of taking the shoes; and then we saw men take a box of shoes before them and hand them out to the men after we began to move."

Loaded down with plunder, the raiders left Oxford strewing both sides of the road with tobacco, then shoes, then tobacco and shoes mixed together. Troopers also confiscated the mail and distributed it with equal abandon. Even Colonel Miller pocketed a letter from a young lady named "Annie" to her "Darling Sister."[28]

"Oh! this is a strange life!" Private John Lemmon of the 4th Michigan mused in his diary. "Creeping [sic] stealthily along all night & suddenly falling upon the foe at day-light or galloping right after them at other times & distributing shot and thrust right & left among the panic stricken foe. Of course it has its reverse, a dark side of regretfulness—even sorrow, but conscience is easily appeased by the reflection 'Who began it?' 'They that resort to the sword shall perish by the sword.'"

As the column plodded northward through the darkness, troopers occasionally cast an anxious glance toward the west. For several hours, they had clearly heard cannon booming in the direction of Atlanta. Obviously a great battle had been fought that afternoon, but they could only guess at its outcome. Sherman's armies might be marching triumphantly into the city. They also might be streaming across the

Chattahoochee in defeat. Uncertainty, fatigue, and the disturbing rumble of the guns had a decidedly sobering effect on the column. "We never knew our regiment to move so noiselessly as it did to-night," noted Ben Magee. "The men scarcely spoke at all, and when they did it was in subdued tones."

The huge fires burning in Oxford lit their way for a considerable distance and a bright yellow moon climbed in the sky a couple of hours after sundown, but somehow the column lost its way. "We either missed the road we wished to go, or else our officers anticipated we should be followed, or something was the matter," noted Ben Magee, "as we doubled on our track, and once in the night went square across a road we had traveled on an hour before. . . ."

Bob Minty's brigade was only six and a half miles north of Oxford when Garrard called a halt at Sardis Church at 10:00 P.M. The rear of the column arrived about midnight, and the provost guard, Company B of the 72nd Indiana, herded more than 200 prisoners into the church for safekeeping.

"Of course we were tired and hungry," noted Ben Magee, "and sadly needed our coffee, as that above every thing else was a panacea for all our ills; but we had to lie down without it, not even unsaddling our horses, and were soon sleeping the sleep of the innocent."

Garrard bedded down on the left side of the road at a shanty surrounded by a rail fence. He awoke the next morning to learn his prize prisoner, Lieutenant Colonel Hamilton, had escaped from the ambulance where he was confined during the night. Garrard angrily demanded an explanation, but all he got from the guard was lame excuses. "I always thought the guard was bought off on this occasion," asserted headquarters clerk Silas Stevens.[29]

Under the circumstances, however, there was little that could be done, and shortly before 6:00 A.M. Garrard started his column northward again. A few individuals in the 4th Michigan had risen early enough to breakfast on some potatoes they dug up along the roadside, but most troopers began this second day of the raid just like the first, on an empty stomach.

Two miles north of Sardis Church, the column passed through the little crossroads community of Walnut Grove. The rear guard paused long enough to burn three or four hundred bales of cotton, but the destruction was not just confined to Garrard's immediate line of march. Each brigade sent detachments ranging down the side roads to round up horses and mules and burn all the cotton they could find.

Second Lieutenant William L. Birney of the 17th Indiana led some of the division's freewheeling scouts across the Alcovy River and charged into Social Circle, eleven miles east of Covington, about midmorning. The scouts took several prisoners, captured the mail, and were "very insolent to the ladies" according to one resident, going into houses and plundering them of "such things as they fancied."

Birney ordered the town's only hotel burned, but after repeated entreaties, he allowed the owner, H. L. Spencer, enough time to get some of his furniture out into the street. Troopers also set fire to the railroad depot, the wood station, a water tank, several new Confederate wagons, and a store filled with commissary supplies. The flames reportedly destroyed five nearby houses, but there is conflicting evidence on this point. In any event, Birney's men left "the Circle" wreathed in smoke before they galloped out of town, swearing vengeance against the residents of nearby Madison for allegedly mistreating a Union general imprisoned there after the battle of Shiloh.[30]

These threats were apparently a ruse to throw any would-be pursuers off the trail. Instead of following the railroad east to Madison, Birney and his men rode ten miles north to Monroe, where they broke into the community's only general store, C. G. Nowell & Company, and carried off twenty-four reams of English writing paper and thirty boxes of tobacco, leaving the rest of the store's contents at the mercy of a rapacious crowd of women, children, and Negroes who followed them inside.

Some of Birney's men also stopped at the Broad Street home of Stephen Felker, a wealthy contractor and cabinetmaker who was rumored to keep large sums of money. Felker had fled, and a ransack search of his house yielded neither gold nor silver. Disappointed, a redheaded Irish trooper took Felker's overcoat before Birney's brigands rode out of town that hot July afternoon to rejoin Garrard.[31]

Garrard's column had marched leisurely northward from Sardis Church, unmolested except for a brief encounter that left Lieutenant Calvin S. Kimball of the 3rd Ohio a prisoner of war and one of his troopers, Private John Sullivan, dead from an accidental gunshot wound. Nine and a half miles north of Sardis Church, some of Bob Minty's troopers charged into Loganville, capturing a Rebel private and a lieutenant of engineers.[32]

Calling a noonday halt, Garrard lingered in Loganville long enough to burn another three or four hundred bales of cotton and scatter some Rebel rice. His troopers also emptied corncribs and hauled freshly shocked oats out of nearby fields, feeding their horses in the middle of the road while officers sat down to dinner in the homes of several reluctant Southerners. After an hour's rest, Garrard divided his command, sending Minty's 1st Brigade north toward Lawrenceville, while he led the 2nd and 3rd Brigades southwest on the Stone Mountain Road.

Anticipating their route, an intrepid civilian living near Loganville had already jumped into his buggy and sped northward to spread the alarm. Late that afternoon, a hastily assembled force of perhaps fifty Confederates confronted Minty's column near Tilford McConnell's farm, four miles southeast of Lawrenceville, only to scatter before a charge of the 4th U.S. Cavalry that chased them all the way back to town. When the dust settled, Minty's men had captured a captain, four sergeants, a corporal, and twelve privates representing fourteen different regiments, batteries, and battalions. They also arrested five civilians, all of whom were eventually released, except one man Minty held for the provost marshal.[33]

"Lawrenceville has been a really nice little place," noted Captain Heber S. Thompson. "In Covington, Oxford and indeed all the towns in Georgia, the conduct of our Division has been disgraceful—houses plundered, women insulted and every species of outrage committed."

"In Lawrenceville[,] on the contrary, when our Brigade was alone nothing of the kind occurred. The people, especially the ladies, and the town contained some really nice ones, were very much pleased with our orderly conduct."

A fire a few weeks earlier had destroyed the town's only major industry, a large cotton mill, leaving little else to tempt the raiders. "We found plenty of corn for our horses . . . ," noted a Michigan soldier, "but nothing else, as it had all been taken off before we got there."[34]

Marching his brigade out of Lawrenceville, Minty halted for the night about three miles out of town on the banks of Yellow River. While sentries stood watch on the picket lines and tired, hungry troopers huddled over flickering fires, dozens of runaway slaves peered from the dancing shadows.

"They were all intelligent looking people," observed a Michigan trooper. "What pleased me most was to see those who had been most against the freedom of the slave. The impulse to help the helpless was too much for Yanks, and spite of principles they divided their rations, and it seemed as though they could not do enough to make them comfortable. If a person wants to become fixed against slavery, he wants to go on a raid into slave lands. These same negroes tell us they had been made to believe that the Yanks killed all the niggers. But they preferred death by the Yanks than longer to live with their cruel masters, in slavery. Is not that enough of an argument against slavery, when the slave prefers to go where he has been made to believe he will meet certain death, to longer remain in bondage?"[35]

While most of Minty's brigade bivouacked on the banks of Yellow River, one outfit was missing. Company C of the 4th Michigan had spent the morning looking for horses and mules west of the main road to Loganville. Unaware the 1st Brigade had detoured north to Lawrenceville, they fell in with Garrard's column, crossing Yellow River late that afternoon at Holt's Mill, twelve miles southwest of Loganville. Presumably burning the bridge behind them, the raiders continued westward for three miles until they struck the familiar road from Choice's Store to Rockbridge. Turning to the right, the column rode on for another three miles before halting at 6:00 P.M. to camp on a branch of Stone Mountain Creek at Trickum Crossroads.[36]

Private Jacob Malott of the 72nd Indiana had just ridden to his post on the picket line when he noticed his bedroll was loose. Twisting in the saddle, he was tugging at the slack coat strap when the Spencer rifle hanging at his right side snagged on something. The hammer sprang forward, and the resulting blast put a bullet through Malott's right foot. The wound was not serious, but Garrard's troopers were inflicting as many casualties on themselves as the Rebels were.[37]

The men not assigned to picket duty dismounted stiffly and unsaddled their horses for the first time since leaving Decatur on July 21. Once the animals had been watered and fed, troopers looked to their own comfort, kindling cook fires and rummaging through haversacks. For some, supper was a few stale pieces of hardtack washed down with a cup of hot coffee, while liberal foragers such as Alva Griest of the 72nd Indiana dined on milk, eggs, ham, and butter.

Another Hoosier, Sergeant Ben Magee, made his first-ever attempt at brewing coffee that evening. After a few cautious sips, his messmates pronounced the results satisfactory and drained the pot before bedding down on the dead leaves carpeting the forest floor.

Sleep proved elusive for Garrard and his staff. "The headquarter[s] wagon was ordered up from the rear," recounted Silas Stevens, "and we went into camp . . . at a very pretty spot among the hills; pleasant groves, and streams of water on every side of the tenting place. The General ordered the fly of his tent pitched in a secluded retreat, away from the noise and view of the regular part of the camp, and directed his servant to bring his blankets, and make up his bed on the ground beneath the tent so he could sleep for he, as ourselves, of the headquarter[s] force, had had very little sleep or rest since the beginning of the raid."

These were the same wet blankets Garrard's servant had thrown into the back of a baggage wagon on the morning of July 22, where they had been fermenting ever since. Laying down, Garrard pulled the soured covers over him, but it was not long before he felt an odd, crawling sensation. Sitting bolt upright, he was horrified to discover a horde of freshly hatched maggots blindly groping over his body. "He awoke the entire headquarter[s] camp," wrote Silas Stevens, berating his staff in general and his servant in particular for not airing out his bedding.

Garrard's departure from Decatur had not gone unnoticed. About the same time he broke camp at Rockbridge on July 22, Rebel scouts were reporting the strength and direction of his column to Confederate cavalry chieftain Joe Wheeler. Wheeler was busy deploying his own troopers to attack the Federal wagon trains parked at Decatur and could only forward this information to Lieutenant General William J. Hardee, commanding the infantry on his left. Writing Hardee again shortly before noon, he advised, "Several more of my scouts have come in, all corroborating the report I sent you this morning that General Garrard had moved toward Covington with his division. Shall I pursue and break up Garrard, or shall I detach a force to follow him?"

Preoccupied with positioning his own troops to attack Sherman's unprotected left flank, Hardee replied, "I cannot spare you or any force to pursue Garrard now." While hopeful his impending assault would bring Garrard back, he suggested Wheeler report the facts to General Hood.

Wheeler was soon in the midst of the furious fight at Decatur and apparently did not advise Hood of Garrard's whereabouts until sometime later. Even then, it was 11:30 the next morning before he received orders authorizing him "to take what you think a sufficient force and pursue the raiding party you report as moving on the Covington road." Within ten minutes, Wheeler was in the saddle.

By that time, Hood was already spreading the alarm. At 10:00 A.M., he had wired Colonel George Washington Rains, the post commandant at Augusta:

> Night before last a body of [the] enemy's cavalry, estimated at about three brigades, was reported moving toward Covington and Augusta. Our cavalry is pursuing, but the information is sent you that you take measures for defense.

Rains took precautions to "prevent a surprise and give the vandals a warm reception," but Augusta's complacent civilian population seemed convinced the raiders were too far away to pose any real danger.[38]

It was a different story at Madison, sixty miles east of Atlanta, where news of the raid precipitated what one observer called "a regular Yankee panic." Confederate authorities hurriedly organized three companies of convalescents from the local military hospitals on July 22 and marched them out to take up positions astride the main approaches into Madison. Late the next day, all three companies were suddenly disbanded. Commissary officers threw open the doors to their warehouses and invited the public to help themselves. Military hospitals packed up and took the train for Augusta, a hundred miles to the east, while patients were loaded into wagons and sent to Eatonton, twenty miles to the south.

The wild rumors and speculation these sick and wounded Confederates brought with them soon had Eatonton in an uproar. When a courier brought word early on July 24 that the Yankees had allegedly burned Dennis' Factory, only seventeen miles north of town, whole families loaded everything they could carry into wagons, buggies, and carriages and fled. Some even boarded the southbound train on the Milledgeville and Eatonton Railroad and did not stop until they got to Savannah.

News of the raid reached the state capital at Milledgeville late Saturday, July 23. More reports arrived on Sunday, leading the post commander, Major W. K. DeGraffenried, to call the civilian population to arms. Georgia Governor Joseph E. Brown went a step further and ordered 1,000 militiamen rushed to the city's defense. He sent a similar request to Howell Cobb, commanding the Georgia Reserves at Macon, who immediately ordered Captain W. C. Humphrey's cavalry company to cook whatever rations they had and march to Milledgeville at once.[39]

Troops also mustered in Athens, twenty-five miles north of Madison. Situated between the upper forks of the Oconee River at the northern terminus of a short line connecting with the Georgia Railroad, Athens boasted a population of about 4,000, half of them slaves. It was also the home of Franklin College (which later became the University of Georgia), the Cook & Brother rifle works, a foundry, and a cotton mill.

Long considered a prime target for Yankee raids, the community had dug earthworks commanding all the main approaches. Workers at Ferdinand Cook's rifle factory had been organized into the 23rd Georgia Infantry Battalion, and at least three companies of home guards were also ready for duty. One of Cook's companies, equipped as cavalry, was mounted on horses recently confiscated from Dr. Richard D. Moore's volunteer battery, which was parked near the public square. Another artillery company, commanded by Captain Edward P. Lumpkin, was stationed just west of Athens on the Mitchell Bridge Road, while Lieutenant Colonel Andrew Young's 30th Georgia Cavalry Battalion bivouacked at the fairgrounds just south of town.

The call to arms came at 3:00 A.M. Saturday morning, July 23, when someone brought word that several thousand Yankee cavalrymen were at High Shoals, twelve miles south of town. Church bells rang and cannon boomed. Jumping out of bed, Cosmo Richardson ran bareheaded and barefooted to get an omnibus to take his mother and sister to the railroad depot. When he got back home he did not even give his sister time to fasten her dress but hurried her out the door *dishabille,* while Mary Franklin defied all modesty by dashing to the depot clutching her corsets and three pairs of stockings.

The Athens *Southern Watchman* later praised the way "our local companies and other military forces in the neighborhood, and every man in town, were at once under arms," but Julia Stanley noted, "Some of our men were so scared . . . that they ran off."

Editor John Christy of the *Southern Watchman* met a steady stream of refugees as he returned to Athens that morning. When he asked the reason for the exodus, he was told 30,000 or 40,000 Yankees had burned the cotton mill at High Shoals and would be in Athens by noon. Christy continued his journey, and the closer he got to Athens, the smaller the Yankee force became, "going from thirty or forty thousand down to twenty, fifteen, ten, six, four; and when within three miles of town, . . . it had dwindled down to nothing."

The military authorities eventually dismissed all the local companies, but not before agreeing on a signal to assemble in case of another alarm. A few more reports arrived that afternoon, crediting the Yankees with burning the factory at High Shoals and the county seat at Watkinsville, but most people went about their business as usual.

Many of the townsfolk were attending Sunday services the next morning when a man burst into several churches about 11:00 and warned the Yankees were coming. This was followed by three window-jarring blasts from Dr. Moore's battery, parked outside the town hall.

The worshippers dispersed "unceremoniously," according to the *Southern Watchman.* "There was very little apparent excitement," agreed the rival *Athens Southern*

Banner, "and the congregations retired from their respective churches with their usual order and decorum." However, Julia Pope Moss noted in the margin of her Bible, "Everyone left in a great state of excitement," and John A. Cobb asserted, "All the churches broke up in great confusion & there was great excitement for some time. . . ."

The Yankees were reportedly at a Mrs. Jackson's plantation, twelve miles out of town, but soon a message arrived from Lieutenant Colonel Young, explaining it was all a mistake. There were no Yankees. But a good rumor dies hard, and that afternoon brought reports Monroe had been captured by anywhere from 800 to 3,000 Yankees, depending on who told the story. Two gentlemen who volunteered to ride out and get to the truth of the matter returned after meeting a resident who advised them Monroe had been sacked by eighteen Yankee soldiers.[40]

Joe Wheeler probably heard equally exaggerated accounts as he hurried elements of Brigadier General John H. Kelly's division eastward through Lithonia and Conyers on the Covington Road. After a twenty-five-mile march, he reached the Yellow River about midnight on July 23–24, only to discover the Yankees had already burned the wagon bridge and the railroad trestle. Unaware that the raiders were bivouacked only a few miles upstream, Wheeler concluded any further pursuit was futile and ordered his men to make camp near the river.[41]

Garrard's tired troopers slept equally unaware and did not begin stirring until well after daylight on July 24. Knowing they would have little or no time for breakfast, Sergeant Ben Magee's mess had prudently filled their coffeepot the night before from a nearby stream. The first man up put the pot on the fire and added the ground beans. By the time the horses were saddled and fed, the dark, rich brew had come to a boil. Each man was nursing a steaming cup when someone mentioned the coffee tasted a little peculiar this morning. Magee and the others shrugged off the idea and had just swallowed the last drops when orders came to mount. A trooper turned the coffeepot upside down to empty it and out spilled the reason for the funny taste. Mixed in with the coffee grounds was a very large, very dead scorpion. "No serious results followed," noted Magee, "but you may well believe there was a deal of spitting done during the day."

Reversing the previous day's order of march, Eli Long's 2nd Brigade led the column northward at 6:00 A.M. Company B of the 72nd Indiana brought up the rear. Turning left at Choice's Store, the advance guard reached the outskirts of Decatur about noon, but instead of being greeted by their own pickets, they were met by Rebel horsemen. Uncertain of what lay ahead, Garrard ordered Abe Miller's brigade to dismount and advance on foot. Evidence of a fierce struggle lay on every side, and upon reaching the public square, Miller halted his line of battle and sent skirmishers ahead to reconnoiter.

Garrard dispatched a courier advising Sherman of his return, then sat down with Miller on the battle-scarred steps of the courthouse and dictated his report to an aide. In three days, his men had marched ninety miles, destroying three wagon bridges and the railroad trestle over the Yellow River, the wagon bridge and trestle over the Alcovy, and six miles of track between the two rivers. They had also burned a locomotive and train captured at Conyers, some flatcars at Covington, and a string of baggage cars near the Alcovy River, and citizens said a passenger train and a construction train, "both with engines," were cut off between Yellow River and the

The courthouse at Decatur, Georgia, was the scene of heavy fighting
between Confederate cavalry and the Chicago Board of Trade Battery
on July 22, 1864. Kenner Garrard sat on the front steps after returning
from his raid to Covington on July 24 and dictated his report to an aide.
The clock tower was added after the war. Courtesy of the DeKalb
Historical Society Archives. Used by permission.

break in the track at Stone Mountain. In addition, the division had burned 2,000 bales
of cotton, the depot and a considerable quantity of supplies at Covington, several
large tents, and thirty unfinished hospital buildings. Garrard noted the brigade he had
sent to Lawrenceville had not yet arrived, but the troops returning with him had
brought in 151 prisoners and 200 Negroes, who were being forwarded to the provost
marshal of the Army of the Tennessee. He calculated his own losses at just two killed
and commended "the zeal and promptness" of his whole command for making the
raid a success. "Since leaving Marietta," he concluded, "the division has been so
constantly in motion, it is now very much out of condition, and I would be pleased to
have a few days' quiet, to shoe horses and repair equipments."[42]

Early that afternoon, a courier delivered news of Garrard's return to Sherman's
headquarters at a big white house on the Peachtree Road, just north of Atlanta. "I am
rejoiced to hear that you are back safe and successful," Sherman replied at 2:00 P.M.
"General Rousseau has brought me 2,500 good cavalry, having been to Opelika and
destroyed thirty miles of road between West Point and Montgomery. I will give you
time to rest and then we must make quick work of Atlanta. I await your report with
impatience, and in the mean time tender you the assurance of my great consideration." He signed the dispatch, "Your friend, W. T. Sherman," a sure indication the
successful raid had put Garrard back in the redhead's good graces.[43]

Garrard spent the rest of the afternoon regrouping the scattered pieces of his
command. He found Lieutenant Griffin and the 1st and 3rd sections of the Board of

Trade Battery parked near Pea Vine Creek, two miles northwest of Decatur, with the division pack mules, led horses, and the sick and dismounted men. Eli Long's brigade joined them with the center section of the battery about 1:00 P.M., and Abe Miller's mounted infantry arrived that evening after spending the afternoon in Decatur waiting in line of battle. Bob Minty's brigade rode in at dark, after a twenty-seven-mile march via Flint Hill Church and New Cross Keys.[44]

Minty brought in another 100 contrabands, who were turned over to the pioneer corps of the 4th Division of the XV Corps, together with those who had come in with Miller and Long. Minty's men also added 21 prisoners to the 151 Garrard had sent to the provost marshal.[45]

That night, troopers who had been with Garrard gathered around the campfires, sipping coffee and listening as the men who had stayed behind described the fight at Decatur. "It was a very hard battle," concluded Alva Griest, "and the worst of it was (for us) that they captured our surplus baggage. I lost my overcoat, portfolia full of letters, papers and envelopes and stamps, one poncho and one blanket."

But the raiders brought back more than enough loot to offset their losses. There was cornmeal, sugar, paper, and personal items of every description, and the estimates of captured horses and mules ranged from 200 to 2,500. But mostly there was tobacco, and the news quickly spread to the nearby infantry camps. "It seemed like half of the army visited us," complained a tired Ben Magee. "Every hour of the night could be heard some one calling out: 'Is this Wilder's Brigade?' 'Give me a chew of tobacco.'"[46]

11

CONVERGING COLUMNS

JULY 24–JULY 31, 1864

The cautious seldom err.

—Confucius

Sherman had been willing to sacrifice a quarter of Garrard's command to cripple the Georgia Railroad. Garrard had returned with five casualties. His success, coupled with Rousseau's destruction of twenty-six miles of the Montgomery & West Point route, had completely severed Atlanta's direct rail connections to the east and west. "The question now," Sherman mused, "is, What next?"

The obvious answer lay to the south, where trains still hauled supplies and ammunition over the Macon & Western Railroad. This slender ribbon of rails was Atlanta's last tenuous link with the Confederacy. Cut it, and the city must fall.

"I would let Stoneman try it," Sherman confided in a dispatch he sent to George Thomas at 11:00 A.M., July 22, "but I hate to base any calculations on the cavalry. McCook might attempt it, but he is not strong enough, for I take it the main cavalry force of the enemy is now on that flank."

But that was before Rousseau reached Marietta and Garrard returned to Decatur. Within an hour of learning of Garrard's easy success, Sherman had made up his mind. "As soon as my cavalry rests," he declared, "I propose to swing the Army of the Tennessee round by the right rapidly and interpose between Atlanta and Macon, the only line open to the enemy."[1]

First, however, he had to bring the rest of his cavalry across the Chattahoochee. Since returning from their Moore's Bridge raid, George Stoneman's three brigades had been picketing the riverbank from Sweetwater Creek to Turner's Ferry. Upstream, Ed McCook's 1st Cavalry Division had moved their camps from Rottenwood Creek to Vining's Station on July 15 to begin patrolling from Pace's Ferry down to Turner's Ferry.

Except for sniping at Rebel pickets on the other side of the river and a fierce artillery duel McCook's 18th Indiana Battery had fought on July 17 to facilitate the XIV and XX Corps' crossing at Pace's Ferry, both divisions had lain more or less idle until July 22, when reports of empty Rebel trenches in front of Atlanta briefly convinced Sherman that Hood was retreating. Summoning his cavalry, he had George Thomas order McCook's division to cross the river on a newly completed trestle bridge at Pace's Ferry, to cover "the right flank of our army as it moves in pursuit." At the same time, Thomas directed Colonel George Buell's 58th Indiana Infantry to dismantle the pontoons they had laid at Pace's Ferry on July 17 and "move down to General Stoneman, to put the bridge across at the point selected by him."

McCook crossed the Chattahoochee at 10:00 A.M., July 22, and got as far as Peachtree Creek before he learned the Rebels were not retreating. Ordered to link up

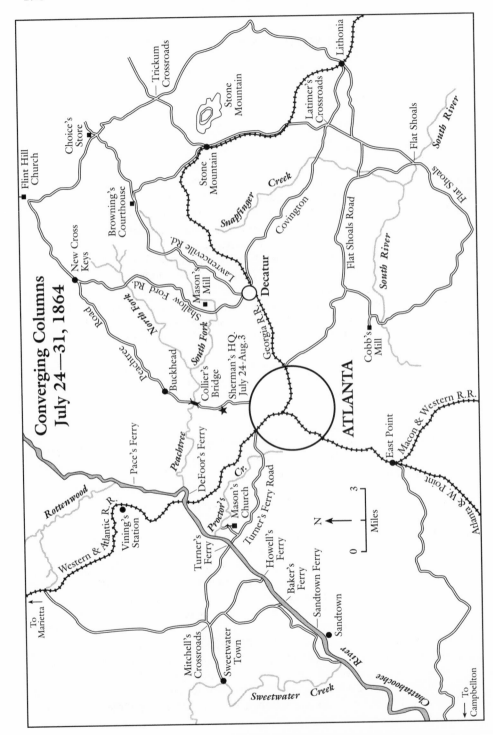

Converting Columns
July 24–31, 1864

with the XIV Corps and extend Thomas's right flank across the Western & Atlantic Railroad and the Marietta Road, he pushed on to Proctor's Creek, where dismounted Rebel cavalry, a burned bridge, and thick woods compelled him to halt for the night. Renewing his advance early on July 23, he reached Mason's Church without difficulty and sent four companies of the 8th Iowa Cavalry east on the Turner's Ferry Road to open communication with Thomas's infantry.[2]

The rest of McCook's men began building breastworks around Mason's Church. They had been reinforced on July 18 by the arrival of Colonel John T. Croxton's 4th Kentucky Mounted Infantry. Like other mounted infantry, Croxton's Kentuckians had seen considerable service as foot soldiers, but this was their first campaign on horseback. Nevertheless, this infusion of 550 well-mounted troopers armed with Spencer carbines and Ballard breech-loading rifles was a welcome one, swelling McCook's woefully understrength ranks to about 1,500 officers and men. He had assigned them to Colonel Joseph Dorr's 1st Brigade to replace the 2nd Michigan Cavalry, whose three-year enlistment had expired at the end of June. Croxton, by virtue of a senior commission, succeeded Dorr as the brigade commander.

Croxton's three regiments dug in on McCook's right flank at Mason's Church on July 23. Lieutenant Colonel William H. Torrey, who had recently resumed command of the 2nd Brigade, posted his three on the left, while the 18th Indiana Battery unlimbered between the two camps in the clearing around the church. Most of Croxton's men were still piling up dirt and fence rails at 4:00 P.M., but Torrey's troopers had finished their works, unsaddled their horses, and were starting to cook supper. A foraging detail from the 1st Wisconsin Cavalry was returning with their horses loaded down with cornstalks when about a hundred Rebel cavalrymen suddenly swooped down upon them. Digging in their spurs, the Wisconsin boys came racing up the Turner's Ferry Road, leaving a trail of green stalks in their wake. Croxton's troopers heard wild yells and the crackle of gunfire. "It increased and grew nearer," wrote Lieutenant Henry H. Belfield of the 8th Iowa. "The picket was evidently driven in, for the band of the 2d Brigade came streaming by—some mounted, some on foot, but all exerting themselves to the utmost to get to the rear. The rebels seemed to have struck the 2d brigade 'on eend' [sic], as they phrase it, for in a moment the road was filled with men, both black and white, ambulances, wagons, all hurrying to the rear. The battery took the alarm, and their caissons, not yet unlimbered, added to the throng. The firing still increased. The division sutler, the only representative of his numerous race who has favored us with his presence on this campaign, and whose stock in trade is carried in a buggy, early took alarm, and finding the progress of his Rosinante impeded by the vehicle, cut the traces and fled, leaving the buggy and contents to its fate."

Spurring into the midst of this maelstrom, the 8th Iowa's Joseph Dorr got out on the Turner's Ferry Road long enough to see what was happening and then raced back to camp, ordering his men to mount. As the Iowans snatched up saddles and bridles, Colonel Croxton, the newly named brigade commander, came galloping toward the sound of the guns yelling, "Save the battery!" McCook and his staff also sped past. As soon as the throng of fugitives were sufficiently out of the way, Lieutenant William B. Rippetoe's Indiana battery opened fire with canister and shell. Colonel Jim Brownlow appeared at the head of his 1st Tennessee. Dorr brought up the 8th

Iowa. While some troopers piled into the 1st Brigade's breastworks, others remained mounted, ready to charge the Rebels if the opportunity offered.

"This is the greatest scare I ever saw," wrote Lieutenant Belfield, "and but for the promptness of the battery in opening and the celerity with which the 1st Brigade showed themselves on the top of the hill in support, the rebels might have dashed into camp and done great harm. But the boys generally, of both brigades, showed great spirit, the running being done chiefly by camp followers, teamsters, negro servants &c. . . . The celerity with which the whole division (excepting, of course, the few cowards found in every division,) drew up in line of battle was surprising, and . . . some of the officers almost danced with delight at the prospect of getting at the rebels on ground of our own choosing."

McCook's 2nd Brigade captured two of the attackers, but a half dozen Yankee troopers were killed, wounded, or missing before the Rebels withdrew. "It was not deemed prudent to follow," noted Lieutenant Belfield, "as the timber completely masked the enemy; and the boldness of the attack seemed to augur the presense of a large force."[3]

About the same time McCook's men began digging in at Mason's Church on July 23, George Stoneman's division was dismounting on the other side of the Chattahoochee to cover the laying of Buell's pontoons at Sandtown Ferry. They came "straggling along on foot," wrote one of the pontoniers, "like so many colts going to water. The officers were without swords, but some of them instead carried revolvers in their hands. . . . They were far from presenting a bold appearance. They looked as if a Regiment of infantry on the other side could drive off the whole Division."

Work on the bridge had scarcely begun when orders from Thomas's headquarters, already over twelve hours old, countermanded the crossing. Apparently concerned for the safety of his pontoon train after McCook reported encountering heavy resistance at Proctor's Creek and the Turner's Ferry Road on July 22, Thomas directed Buell to move back upstream and lay his bridge "at Howell's Ferry near the railroad bridge." The pontoniers loaded their wagons and started toward Vining's Station at noon, followed by the 5th Indiana Cavalry. The rest of Stoneman's troopers remained at or near the riverbank until about dark when Horace Capron's brigade began backtracking from Mitchell's Crossroads to the bridge at Sweetwater Town. About 9:00 P.M., a courier brought Capron orders to turn east, toward Vining's Station.[4]

This abrupt about-face resulted from the orders Sherman's aide, Captain Audenried, had delivered to George Thomas in the wee hours of July 23, directing him to bring Stoneman's cavalry across the Chattahoochee. "I have just learned that General Rousseau has arrived at Marietta from Opelika and have ordered him to relieve you," Sherman explained in a separate note he enclosed for Stoneman. "Have all your men ready to start the moment General Rousseau comes. Turn over to him your instructions and the use of your pontoon train that he may cross over at Turner's [Ferry] the moment his horses are rested and General Thomas orders him."

Thomas forwarded this note to McCook, who was busy digging in at Mason's Church. McCook sent it across the Chattahoochee at Turner's Ferry sometime before 8:30 A.M. on July 23, but Rousseau's cavalry, still "sadly jaded" after the rigors of the raid to Opelika, did not even begin leaving Marietta until 9:00 that night. Now led by Tom Harrison, they had orders to move down the Atlanta Road and relieve Stoneman at the railroad bridge. The only problem was Stoneman's troopers were not at the railroad bridge. They were scattered from Vining's Station all the way down to Sweetwater Creek. Whether Harrison actually marched to the bridge before turning downstream is unclear, but his men and most of Stoneman's spent the night of July 23 groping along the dark roads north of the Chattahoochee.[5]

The welter of contradictory and conflicting orders also left bridge builder George Buell confused. Shortly before dark, he had halted his wagons near Vining's Station, where he met Captain William Kossak and the Army of the Tennessee's pontoon train. Both men had instructions to lay their pontoons "at Howell's Ferry near the railroad bridge," but Howell's Ferry was fully eight miles below the ruined trestle. After some discussion, they concluded their orders must be referring to DeFoor's Ferry, which was just above it. Rather than risk losing their way in the dark, they decided to camp where they were and march in the morning.

Buell started at 2:00 A.M., July 24, and reached the river shortly after daylight. Kossak was not far behind. Interpreting Thomas's orders literally, Buell's men put down two bridges and Kossak's crew had laid a third by the time Colonel James Biddle's 5th and 6th Indiana Cavalry arrived. The Hoosiers crossed the river about 9:00 A.M. and rode eastward until noon before halting near Buckhead to eat a late breakfast and feed their horses. Turning south on the Peachtree Road, then east through Decatur, they camped at 9:00 P.M., two miles north of town, near Mason's Mill on the South Fork of Peachtree Creek.

Horace Capron's brigade also reached DeFoor's Ferry that morning but did not begin crossing until sometime late that afternoon or early that evening. As daylight dwindled into dark, the long line of men and horses filed down the road toward Buckhead, past tumble-down cabins and lone chimneys standing watch over farms without fences and fields stripped of crops. Cannon rumbled in the distance and the night turned uncommonly cool. A sudden commotion in the front ranks brought the weary riders to a halt. The column had met a train of ambulances heading north with the grim harvest collected in front of Atlanta on July 22.

"It was the crossing of a creek having steep banks and a rough and stony bottom," wrote Captain James M. Wells of the 8th Michigan. "We were compelled to stand by the roadside while seventy-five ambulances with wounded men passed over. The condition of the ground shook the ambulances, rolling and wrenching the men so as to open afresh their wounds, and the prayers, groans, and curses caused by this rough handling were distressing to hear. For two long hours we sat there in the gloomy night, waiting for this procession to pass."[6]

While his division was all day crossing the bridges at DeFoor's Ferry, Stoneman apparently went over with Biddle's brigade early on July 24. His route led past Sherman's headquarters at the big white house on the Peachtree Road, where he stopped that afternoon, about the same time a courier brought the news of Garrard's return to Decatur. Sherman's fertile mind immediately seized upon a plan. Until now, his cavalry had always been in four different places, doing four different things. Now, he told Stoneman, it was time to bring all four divisions together at the same place, at the same time, to do the same thing: wreck the Macon railroad.

Just how long the two men conferred is uncertain, but that night Stoneman appeared at Garrard's bivouac near Decatur. "The night was cold and the wind blustering," recalled Garrard's clerk, Silas Stevens, "and the camp was not pleasantly located. . . . The General and Stoneman talked at a nearby camp fire the greater portion of the night."[7]

Stoneman told his old comrade-in-arms to prepare for another expedition. Tired and haggard after three days in the saddle, Garrard said he would "try to carry out all orders." But the next day, after assessing reports from his subordinates, he wrote to Sherman, "It will take three or four days to put my command in order. My wagons are not up, and I do not know where they are. I have also over 1,000 horses unshod. I can do all duty required of me on this flank, but, if possible, would like it to be so arranged as not to send me off again for some days."

Garrard also had reservations about the plan Stoneman had outlined. "I think it will amount to a fight with rebel cavalry," he asserted, "and [I am] very doubtful if much damage can be done."

He did, however, issue his Special Field Orders No. 4 on July 25, directing "that every effort be made to get the command in as good condition as possible without delay." Horses were to be shod and worn-out animals sent to the rear to rest and recover. Any judged unfit for further service would be abandoned. All Negroes, except one servant for each officer and two cooks for each company, would be sent to headquarters under guard and turned over to the provost marshal. Captured horses and mules were to be reported to the division quartermaster and branded "at once." "The column must not be encumbered and lengthened by a lot of worthless negroes and non combatants and broken down stock," Garrard warned.

The branding and shoeing had hardly begun when Garrard's troopers got orders at 2:00 P.M. to move. Major General John Logan, who had succeeded the late, lamented McPherson as commander of the Army of the Tennessee, was pulling John Sprague's battered infantry brigade out of the line and he wanted Garrard's cavalry to take their place. He instructed Garrard to leave the 1st Ohio at Roswell to help guard the bridge over the Chattahoochee and commandeered some of the cavalry's empty supply wagons to convey his crush of sick and wounded to Marietta.

After drawing rations and forage, Garrard's division climbed into the saddle at 5:00 P.M. and shuffled through Decatur, pausing briefly to allow some of Stoneman's cavalry (apparently Capron's brigade) to pass. Following the railroad westward, they relieved Sprague's pickets screening the left flank of the Army of the Tennessee. That night, some troopers bivouacked almost within rifleshot of Atlanta.[8]

In the midst of these maneuvers, Garrard received a note Stoneman had written from Sherman's headquarters on the Peachtree Road:

> General Sherman says that day after to-morrow will be soon enough, provided the enemy does not leave Atlanta before that time. In the mean time he wishes us to get our commands well in hand and to be ready to act vigorously in case we are called upon suddenly to push a retreating army. The general says that you can call in the regiment you now have at the [Roswell] Factory bridge, and that you can replace it with such portion of your command (under an officer), as you cannot make available in contemplated operations. . . . The success of your recent expedition warrants the general in expecting important results from the efforts of our forces combined.

This was more than the punctilious Garrard could swallow. Stoneman was giving orders as if he commanded all of Sherman's cavalry instead of a small division. Folding the message, Garrard wrote across the outside:

> Respectfully referred to General Sherman, through General Logan, to know under whose orders I am serving.
>
> I have been all day occupied in carrying out General Logan's orders and now this letter orders an entirely different disposition of my troops. Of course I do not recognize General Stoneman, but wish this matter settled in some way. I should not move for two or three days.

"I would like to give all the time you ask for rest, reshoeing, etc.," Sherman explained patiently in his reply,

> but am advised by General Grant that I must be prepared for a re-enforcement to the rebel army from Virginia, and want to prevent it. I am afraid I will have to call on you and also on General Rousseau's cavalry to start again the day after to-morrow, but I propose that yours and Rousseau's should be in the nature of support to General Stoneman and General McCook, who will be charged to make the circuit and break the Macon road well to the rear, say below McDonough.
>
> I wanted General Stoneman to consult and advise with you and bring me your opinion, but my plan is that all my army shall swing round by the right against East Point, whilst the cavalry right and left move by a circuit, and by detachments reach the railroad so as to cut off the last link of the enemy's communications. That done, I think we can pause for rest and all sorts of repairs. Every minute we delay will add to the magnitude of the undertaking, which I take it for granted the enemy must apprehend, and will be calling in his scattered cavalry to thwart and prevent it.[9]

Sherman had already asked George Thomas to send word to McCook to have his division and Tom Harrison's ready for "the big raid" by daylight on July 27. He also wanted to talk to McCook in person, if it was "convenient."

As a preliminary, Sherman had sent his chief engineer, Captain Orlando M. Poe, to lay a pontoon bridge at Turner's Ferry so McCook could communicate with Harrison. Poe left headquarters at daylight on July 25 and rode to DeFoor's Ferry, where he ordered Captain Kossak to take up his bridge and move it to Turner's Ferry.

Kossak dismantled his pontoons, and at 4:00 P.M. his wagons started down the south side of the river. An hour later, he penciled a note asking Poe to "send instructions," because, according to a lieutenant commanding McCook's pickets at the bridge over Proctor's Creek, the Rebels still held Turner's Ferry.

Poe hurried forward and found Kossak's pontoons waiting three-quarters of a mile north of Proctor's Creek. He talked with McCook, who confirmed his cavalry did not hold Turner's Ferry. His orders were to screen Thomas's right flank and the previous afternoon, July 24, he had abandoned the breastworks at Mason's Church and moved his division two miles closer to Atlanta. Unwilling to risk losing the pontoon train, Poe did not have much choice. After considerable effort, he got Kossak's big wagons turned around in the narrow road and started them back to DeFoor's Ferry. Then he hurried to Sherman's headquarters.

"I understood General Thomas to say yesterday that you had possession of Turner's Ferry road out for three miles from the river, . . . " Sherman wrote to McCook that night. "I wish that bridge laid down, and you to establish communication with

Colonel Harrison to-morrow. Captain Poe will see that the bridge is put down, and one of my inspectors will inspect Colonel Harrison's command to-morrow. Cover the bridge with all your cavalry."

Prodded by Sherman's message and a curt order from Thomas to "cover that ferry," McCook's division marched at 4:00 A.M., July 26, and quickly drove away the Rebel pickets on the Turner's Ferry Road. Poe and Kossak arrived shortly afterward with the pontoon train and had a bridge across the Chattahoochee by 2:00 P.M.[10]

By that time, Thomas had acquainted McCook with the outline of Sherman's "big raid," and the cavalryman had issued a circular directing his division to be ready to march at daylight on the 27th. Regimental and company officers were to make a thorough inspection of the entire command and see that each man carried five days' rations, 100 rounds of ammunition, two horseshoes, and "the requisite amount of nails." No wagons would accompany the column, and each regiment was responsible for furnishing four men with axes, two with spades, and two with picks. A second circular prescribed the order of march as 2nd Brigade, the battery, then the 1st Brigade followed by the regimental ambulances. All camp followers, led horses, and pack mules were to be left behind.

Leaving his officers to complete these preparations, McCook reported to the big white house on the Peachtree Road, where Sherman explained the raid in detail. His plans called for Thomas and Schofield to keep Hood busy on the north side of Atlanta while the Army of the Tennessee quit the trenches east of the city that night and marched westward to threaten the junction of the Montgomery and Macon railroads at East Point. As the infantry shifted from left to right, the entire cavalry corps, almost 10,000 strong, would move out at daylight on July 27. McCook would lead his own division and Harrison's around the west side of Atlanta, toward Fayetteville, at the same time Stoneman and Garrard circled to the east, toward McDonough. Allowing that Garrard's and Harrison's troopers were still fatigued from their recent forays, Sherman stressed they would be held in reserve. McCook and Stoneman were to rely on their own commands to reach the Macon & Western Railroad, rendezvousing south of Atlanta sometime on July 28. After destroying two to five miles of track and pulling down the telegraph wires, each division would return to its proper place on the flanks of the army, unless of course the break in Hood's communications compelled him to abandon Atlanta. In that case, Sherman expected his cavalry to obstruct the Rebel retreat with "all the energy in their power."

While Sherman felt he had "explained the movement perfectly," McCook had misgivings. The plan called for his column to march down the south side of the Chattahoochee, but the skirmishing to retake Turner's Ferry that morning had convinced him Rebel cavalry and infantry held a continuous line of works stretching from the west side of Atlanta all the way to the river. Any attempt to breach those defenses at the outset of the raid would be time-consuming, if not costly, and betray McCook's purpose before he had fairly begun.

It would be better, he suggested, for his command to cross the pontoons at Turner's Ferry, join Harrison, and move down the north bank of the river. This would enable him to outflank the Rebel defenses without firing a shot and use the Chattahoochee to screen his movements. Once safely downstream, his column could recross the river near Campbellton and march for Fayetteville over the more open country south of Atlanta. Sherman agreed to the proposal and McCook started back to his headquarters.[11]

Late afternoon found McCook's troopers lounging in the camps they had reoccupied at Mason's Church. Some were writing letters. Others tended smoky fires, cooking up the last of three days' rations they had drawn from the supply wagons the day before. The 18th Indiana Battery's six black Rodman rifles crouched in a semicircle on the same little rise they had occupied on July 23, and pickets from Company M of the 4th Indiana were loading their horses with forage bundled in a nearby field. The comforting clink of tin cups mingled with the low murmur of voices. Horses snorted, stamped their feet, and swished their tails at swarms of bloodthirsty black flies, while cicadas sang their scratchy songs in the surrounding woods.

If the scene seemed familiar, it was because history was about to repeat itself. A gunshot echoed in the distance. There were yells, more shots, the sudden drumming of hooves as the Indiana boys came galloping into camp, struggling to stay astride the bundles of forage hanging from their saddles. Close behind the Hoosiers came two companies of the 9th Texas Cavalry, led by Captain Ewell M. Wright and Lieutenant W. T. McClatchey, knifing through the 1st Brigade's picket line on the right, bowling over a portion of the 4th Kentucky Mounted Infantry, and chasing the fugitives across the clearing around Mason's Church. Pressing the reckless attack to within 200 yards of McCook's breastworks, the Texans soon had more prisoners than they could handle.

They were trying to herd their captives toward the rear when Lieutenant Rippetoe's battery loosed a hail of canister into their midst. Captured Kentuckians threw themselves to the ground in the indiscriminate storm of shot and refused to get up. The Texans angrily emptied their pistols into the backs of the prostrate prisoners, then spurred away, taking four Yankees with them and leaving one dead and three wounded. Rippetoe's gunners switched to shells as the Texans sped out of sight and quickly silenced an unseen Rebel battery firing from the woods, but the intermittent pop of carbines continued until dark.[12]

For the second time in three days, a handful of Rebel horsemen had nearly stampeded McCook's division at Mason's Church. Somewhere there was a lack of vigilance, a want of attention to detail, and this hinted at a larger problem in the Yankee cavalry's chain of command. With Sherman giving orders directly to Stoneman, Stoneman trying to give orders to Garrard, Thomas and Sherman both giving orders to McCook, and the Army of the Cumberland's chief of cavalry, General Elliott, not giving orders to anybody, there was a decided lack of coordination in the preparations for Sherman's "big raid."

Nowhere was this more apparent than on the north side of the Chattahoochee. After an all-night roundabout march from Marietta, Tom Harrison and the Rousseau raiders had reached Turner's Ferry at noon on July 24. While Harrison deployed a few companies to picket the riverbank as far down as Sweetwater Creek, the rest of his men had settled into an almost Spartan existence. They had left their tents and blankets at Decatur, Alabama. Stoneman's men and horses had already stripped the nearby farms and fields, and rations and forage soon ran out, forcing Harrison to send his pack mules back to Marietta for supplies on July 25. Company F of the 8th Indiana left on July 26 to escort a supply train into camp from Vining's Station, but apparently it was not until that afternoon, when completion of the pontoon bridge at Turner's Ferry opened communication with McCook, that Harrison learned he had less than twelve hours to provision his men for another raid.

"We start tomorrow on a raid to the rear of the Rebel Army," he wrote to his wife, "and if possible cut the Macon Road from Atlanta. . . . I am well. So is my Command. Generally we are very busy making preparations and I have little time [to] write. Give my love to all friends. I am in great haste."[13]

The cavalry camps on the left flank of the army were busy, too. Sunrise on July 26 found Garrard's 123rd Illinois Mounted Infantry bivouacked near the Georgia Railroad, about 300 yards behind the front lines. Most of the men not on picket duty were still rolled up in their blankets when Rebel shells overshooting the XVI Corps' breastworks suddenly began crashing into their midst. The rude awakening sent several troopers scurrying to the rear with their clothes tucked under their arms. Others clung defiantly to their blankets, declaring they were there first and it was going to take more than a shell to move them.

"I noticed one man sitting eating," wrote Private Jerome B. Quinn. "A shell fell within five feet of him and lay hissing. The balance of us around who were up fell flat on the ground, but the comrade who was eating looked at it, then put his hand over his can of oysters and remarked that he would _ _ if it should throw dirt in his food."

Early that morning, in obedience to instructions from Sherman, Garrard issued his Special Field Orders No. 5, directing all unserviceable horses be sent to Marietta by some safe road. Rations were to be issued and all pack mules and led horses started to the rear at 4:00 P.M. "The command will be held in readiness to move tomorrow morning at 4 o'clock towards Decatur in the following order," Garrard concluded. "First Brigade, Battery, Third Brigade, Second Brigade. No bugles will be sounded."

Blacksmiths' hammers echoed under an overcast sky. Troopers loaded greasy haversacks with rations, filled canteens and cartridge boxes, and cleaned their weapons. "*On the rampage again!*" Private John Lemmon of the 4th Michigan scrawled in his diary.

Corporal John Barnard of the 72nd Indiana was less enthusiastic. "We are going on a raid," he wrote to his wife, "so this will be thay last you will hear from me till we get back if I ever do . . . I don't feel like going on a raid as I am woren out & half sick all thay time."[14]

Members of the Chicago Board of Trade Battery spent the day refilling ammunition chests, inspecting harness, "fixing everything, sending away old horses and getting new ones in their place," noted John Nourse. The artillerymen also took up a collection of over $700 for their comrade, Tom McClelland, wounded in the fight at Decatur on July 22. Surgeons had amputated McClelland's left arm that day, above the elbow. When Private Charles Baldwin went to visit him in the hospital, McClelland complained his left hand hurt. He asked anxiously about what had become of his missing arm. Baldwin told him he had buried it beside a tree near the hospital. McClelland insisted something must be pressing on his hand and pleaded with Baldwin to find out what it was. Baldwin gently assured him he would. Soon he returned. Yes, he had dug the arm up. He had thrown away a dirt clod gouging the hand and carefully straightened out the fingers before burying it again. Soon McClelland was resting comfortably and Baldwin never told his friend that surgeons had simply pitched the severed arm out with a pile of other bloody limbs.

"Cannonading and skirmishing is constant," wrote Alva Griest of the 72nd Indiana. At least three times that afternoon squads of Rebel cavalry probed Garrard's picket line on the outskirts of Decatur. Each time, a few shots from alert vedettes drove them away.[15]

Stoneman's camps were also abuzz. "Flies everywhere . . . ," complained Lieutenant Nathan S. Boynton of the 8th Michigan Cavalry, "above, below, to the right, to the left, may be seen flies. I imagine myself in a beehive. We have a variety of flies, the 'hoss' fly, the green fly, the brown fly, the house fly, the blue tail fly, and the fly without a tail. The air is thick with them and they serve a good purpose when the sun shines for they form a complete shield—the sun's rays cannot penetrate. Sat down to dinner to day—had a sumptuous repast—sour belly and hard tack—coffee and hard tack. Flies determined to be guests—massed themselves for an attack on the sugar and hard tack—a furious assault commenced—was successful—hard tack went flying through the air with a fly grasping it and laughing in his sleeve—sugar disappeared—I became alarmed—food was scarce—called loudly for my darkey—darkey came puffing and blowing surrounded by flies . . . told him to brush away the flies—seized a huge tree and made one sweep through the atmosphere—four thousand fell dead and wounded upon the table—in the coffee—amongst the sour belly. I remonstrated against so much fresh meat—could not seperate it—shut my eyes and ate rapidly—finished the meal—took my pipe and smoked unconscious of the future."[16]

While his troopers drew clothing and rations on July 26, Stoneman addressed an eleventh-hour proposal to Sherman, asking permission to continue south after cutting the railroad below Atlanta and liberate the 30,000 Union prisoners being held at the infamous Rebel prisons at Macon and Andersonville. "I would like to try it," Stoneman averred, "and am willing to run any risks, and I can vouch for my little command. Now is the time to do it before the rebel army falls back and covers that country, and I have every inducement to try it. If we accomplish the desired object it will compensate for the loss as prisoners of us all, and I would feel compensated for almost any sacrifice."

This did not sound like the same man who had previously complained about the "utter incompetency" of his officers. Perhaps he had been encouraged by the recent acquisition of Horace Capron's brigade. Perhaps he had rekindled old ambitions or saw a chance to redeem himself. In any event, while Sherman foresaw "many difficulties" in Stoneman's proposed 150-mile dash to Andersonville, he admitted there was something "captivating" about the idea.

"You may after having fulfilled my present orders, send General Garrard back to the left flank of the army, and proceed with your command proper to accomplish both or either of the objects named," he wrote. The rest of the army would keep Hood busy, so Stoneman would have only cavalry to contend with, but Sherman cautioned him to cut the railroads and telegraph wires wherever he went, to keep the Rebels from following him. "If you can bring back to the army any or all of those prisoners of war," he added, "it will be an achievement that will entitle you and the men of your command to the love and admiration of the whole country."

As the day wore on, however, Sherman had second thoughts. In a telegram to General Halleck that night, he confided that liberating the prisoners at Andersonville "is probably more than he [Stoneman] can accomplish, but it is worthy of a determined effort."

Halleck was apparently the only man Sherman took into his confidence that night. Neither McCook nor Harrison nor Garrard had any inkling that Stoneman was about to attempt the most daring rescue of the war.

Sometime on July 26, Stoneman summoned his brigade and regimental command-ers to his headquarters. They were going to make an important raid on the rear of Hood's army, he announced. The division would move east and south of Atlanta in conjunction with Garrard and rendezvous with McCook's column at Lovejoy's Station on the Macon & Western Railroad. Together, the troops would wreck the railroad, cut Hood's supply line, and compel him to come out of the trenches ringing Atlanta.

After cutting the railroad, Stoneman explained, he had discretionary orders to march south, if he thought it expedient, to free 1,500 Union officers held at Macon and 30,000 enlisted men imprisoned at Andersonville. He suggested he would then strike for the Gulf coast of Florida and the Union garrison at Pensacola, but he offered no explanation about how he intended to feed and equip a huge army of sick and starving soldiers.

Perhaps there was a moment of stunned silence, a few raised eyebrows, or maybe a long whistle of surprise. One thing is certain. Not everyone liked what they heard. As the officers were returning to their respective commands, Colonel Thomas Butler of the 5th Indiana advised Colonel James Biddle to write his wife and tell her they were going on a raid and she might not hear from him for a long time because they were all probably going to spend the rest of the war in a Rebel prison pen.

What made him think that, Biddle asked?

Because, Butler replied solemnly, "I have no confidence in General Stoneman's ability to command a raiding party."[17]

While the cavalry completed last-minute preparations, Sherman turned his attention to the nagging question of who should succeed McPherson as commander of the Army of the Tennessee. John Logan seemed like the logical choice. The men adored him and he had performed admirably on the day McPherson fell. Sherman had as much as told him the command was his, but then George Thomas suggested one-armed Oliver Otis Howard would be a better choice.

Sherman countered that Logan's rough and tumble westerners might resent a Bible-thumping easterner like Howard, who did not drink, smoke, or swear. It might "dampen" their enthusiasm.

Thomas reiterated his opposition and insisted he could not get along with Logan. Bowing to the wishes of his senior subordinate, Sherman submitted Howard's nomination to the War Department. Confirmation came back shortly before 10:00 P.M., July 26, just as the Army of the Tennessee was leaving the trenches to play its part in Sherman's ambitious maneuver to cut the railroads south of Atlanta.

Early the next morning, Grenville Dodge found Logan sitting dejectedly on the front porch of Sherman's headquarters on the Peachtree Road. He had just come from a meeting with Sherman and there were tears in his eyes. Dodge spoke to him cordially, acknowledging his disappointment with the change in command, and his hope that everything would turn out "all right." Logan brightened, assuring him it would, but he was obviously and bitterly disappointed. Publicly, he accepted the news of Howard's promotion gracefully and resumed command of the XV Corps. Privately, he confided in a letter to his wife, Sherman was "an infernal *brute.*"

Major General "Fighting Joe" Hooker, commanding Thomas's XX Corps, made no secret of his feelings. He had led the Army of the Potomac at the battle of Chancellorsville, where Howard's failure to secure the right flank had resulted in a humiliating defeat. He saw Howard's promotion as "an *insult* to my rank and services" and immediately asked to be relieved. Sherman, who regarded Hooker as "envious, imperious, and [a] braggart," was only too happy to oblige.[18]

Howard assumed his new command as the Army of the Tennessee was crossing the

Peachtree Road near Sherman's headquarters. Sherman joined the one-armed general and they rode together until they came to some high ground near the right flank of Thomas's Army of the Cumberland. Pointing to a ridge running almost due south, Sherman said he wanted Howard to deploy there, adding that his lines should be long enough to reach the railroad junction at East Point before Hood could interfere.

Howard did not share his optimism, and asked permission for each of his divisions to go into line on Thomas's right before swinging into position. That way, each succeeding division would be able to protect the flank of the one preceding it.

"I don't think Hood will trouble you now," Sherman replied cheerfully, but he left Howard to deploy as he pleased and rode back to headquarters.

Howard got Dodge's XVI Corps into line before nightfall, and "at the first glimmer of light" on July 28 he put Blair's XVII and Logan's XV Corps in motion again. As they advanced, driving dismounted Rebel cavalry before them, the woods echoed with the rattle of musketry and the occasional roar of artillery. Sherman was following close behind when a cannonball whistled over his shoulder, killing the horse of the orderly behind him. Dismounting, he approached the front lines on foot and found Howard and Logan near Ezra Church, a little Methodist meetinghouse on the Lick Skillet Road. As they talked, a blast of Rebel canister rattled through the branches overhead.

"General Hood will attack me here," Howard asserted.

"I guess not," Sherman scoffed; "he will hardly try it again."

Events soon proved otherwise. About 11:30 A.M., Lieutenant General Stephen D. Lee, recently arrived from Mississippi to take command of Hood's old corps, sent two divisions charging across the Lick Skillet Road. Raising their fearsome Rebel yell, the butternut brigades swept across the sun-drenched fields, their faded battle flags flapping in the breeze. The irresistible rush fell on John Logan's XV Corps, driving back his right, pummeling his center. Accompanied by a single staff officer, Logan spurred into the midst of a retreating regiment. Swearing curses that carried over the battle's roar, beating skulkers with the flat of his sword, he seized the colors and led the men forward again.

Sherman had ridden back to the headquarters of Thomas's XIV Corps before the fighting began and was listening to the rising rattle of musketry when one of Howard's aides galloped up and reported Logan's men were under heavy attack. "Good," Sherman prattled happily, "that's fine, just what I wanted, just what I wanted, tell Howard to invite them to attack, it will save us trouble, save us trouble, they'll only beat their own brains out, beat their own brains out."

After an initial repulse, Lee sent a fresh brigade forward, the same South Carolinians who had broken the XV Corps' line at Atlanta on July 22. "Hold 'em! Hold 'em!" Logan growled. Sweating like demons under a blazing sun, his men fought furiously. All afternoon, their lips black and swollen from tearing open cartridges, they beat back one Rebel assault after another.

It was "perfect murder," wrote one appalled Union officer. Three thousand Confederate soldiers fell on that bloody afternoon, and when night finally drew its folds over the bodies heaped in front of Logan's breastworks, a Federal picket called across the lines, "Well, Johnny, how many of you are left?"

"Oh! about enough for another killing," came the sobering reply.[19]

Tactically, Ezra Church was the third bloody defeat Hood had suffered since taking command ten days earlier. The carnage had, however, stopped the Yankee infantry about two miles short of the coveted railroad. Sherman's bold flanking maneuver had failed. "It is time we heard something of our cavalry," he declared the next day.[20]

The Army of the Tennessee had already left the trenches on the east side of Atlanta when Stoneman's camps on the South Fork of Peachtree Creek began stirring at 2:00 A.M. on July 27. "Boots and Saddles" sounded an hour later, and the men marched without breakfast, 2,150 strong.

Orders sending to the rear every man and horse that could not go through "fire and water" had culled the 1st and 11th Kentucky of Colonel Silas Adams's brigade down to 550 officers and men. The 5th and 6th Indiana of Colonel James Biddle's brigade tallied about 700, and even Stoneman's largest brigade, Colonel Horace Capron's 14th Illinois, 8th Michigan, and McLaughlin's Ohio Squadron, could muster only 800 troopers. Fifty-four artillerymen shepherded a pair of 3-inch rifles from Captain Alexander Hardy's 24th Indiana Battery, while Lieutenant Washington W. Manning and thirty-two troopers from Company D of the 7th Ohio Cavalry escorted Stoneman and the seven members of his staff.[21]

About the same time Stoneman's command left Peachtree Creek, "Reveille" sounded in Garrard's camps west of Decatur. At 4:00 A.M., Bob Minty motioned his 1st Brigade forward without the sound of a bugle. The Board of Trade Battery, Eli Long's 2nd Brigade, and Abe Miller's 3rd Brigade followed, the last of Miller's regiments leaving camp about 6:00 A.M.[22]

As the two divisions converged on Decatur in the dark and drizzly dawn, a vedette from Company C of Garrard's 4th Michigan stood watch on the edge of town. Perhaps he was half asleep. Perhaps his challenge went unanswered. Throwing his Spencer to his shoulder, he loosed a shot at the sound of approaching horsemen. The rest of his detachment quickly formed into line, ready to give a good account of themselves.

The vedette had fired on the advance guard of Stoneman's command. No one was hurt, but this unexpected reception, the darkness, and the resulting confusion may have been what caused Stoneman to deploy his division in line of battle and wait while skirmishers scouted well to the right and right front. No Rebels were found, and about 8:00 A.M. Stoneman resumed his march, leaving Garrard to deal with any pursuit.

Lieutenant Joseph Hasty of the 6th Indiana and fifty picked men from each of Biddle's two regiments led Stoneman's column over the railroad embankment on the south side of town and down the Covington Road, a well-traveled route coursing over the low, rolling hills to the southeast. Dense woods, choked with undergrowth, lined both sides of the road, interrupted occasionally by a field or clearing around a weathered farmhouse.

The morning's march was uneventful. Crossing Snapfinger Creek, the column reached Latimer's Crossroads, eight miles southeast of Decatur, about 11:00 A.M. Here Stoneman dismounted and took a seat on the piazza of John N. Swift's house to wait for Garrard.[23]

Garrard had called in his pickets about 6:00 A.M. and followed Stoneman with 4,000 officers and men and six pieces of artillery. The troops were "in good spirits," wrote a soldier who watched them leave, "jubilant and confident of having a gallant and dashing ride before them."

"Gen. Garrard's division . . . is the best I ever saw," he added, "good men, splendidly armed and mounted and he is a good commander."[24]

Reaching Latimer's Crossroads about 1:00 P.M., Garrard joined Stoneman for dinner at the Swift house. Neither man left any record of their conversation, but Garrard understood he was to proceed to the South River, covering Stoneman's right flank, and wait there for further orders.

After relieving Swift of several mules and horses, Stoneman's column continued toward Lithonia, while Garrard's three brigades turned to the right toward South River. About 2:00 P.M., as Bob Minty's advance guard approached Flat Rock, or Flat Shoals as the locals called it, they surprised and burned six Rebel wagons and an ambulance, and captured three or four Confederate soldiers.[25]

Upon reaching South River, the column halted. As was customary when going into camp, the leading brigade stopped, allowing the others to pass. This reversed the next day's order of march, so that Minty's brigade became the rear guard and Eli Long's two Ohio regiments took the advance near the bridge at Flat Shoals. Troopers in both commands unsaddled their horses under threatening skies and began the familiar camp routine. By the time Abe Miller's 3rd Brigade dismounted, it was raining steadily. Miller kept his horses saddled until the rain stopped, shortly after dark. Then girths were loosened, and the men cooked their suppers over smoky little fires and pitched their tents. They were only nine miles from the Macon railroad.

Their departure had not gone unnoticed. Garrard's rearmost regiments had not even left Decatur when a Rebel scout advised Colonel William C. P. Breckinridge of the 9th Kentucky Cavalry that a large column of Yankee horsemen was moving down the Covington Road, carrying five days' rations. Breckinridge promptly relayed this information to Joe Wheeler.

Wheeler knew the Covington Road. He had followed it to the Yellow River in his fruitless effort to overtake Garrard on July 23. Returning to the right flank of the army late on July 24, his cavalry had relieved the Rebel infantry in the trenches east of Atlanta at 3:00 A.M., July 27, about the same time Stoneman was breaking camp. Pushing a skirmish line forward in the predawn darkness, Wheeler found that the Yankee infantry in his front had unexpectedly abandoned their entrenchments. He was contemplating what this meant when Breckinridge's report arrived.

Wheeler immediately ordered a regiment to follow the Yankee column and report its progress. He also sent a courier to alert Hood, but Hood's headquarters were five miles to the rear, at the L. Windsor Smith house on Atlanta's Whitehall Street, and communication was slow. At 7:00 A.M., Wheeler received two dispatches from Hood, dated 4:15 A.M. and "daylight," but neither acknowledged the departure of the Yankee cavalry. Instead, they stressed the importance of holding the trenches on the right because "indications are that the enemy will attack our left."

During the morning, Wheeler forwarded more reports from his scouts, but Hood remained unimpressed. Preoccupied with the infantry massing on his left, he may have regarded the Yankee cavalry on his right as merely a diversion. It was 11:00 A.M. before he authorized Wheeler to "detach what force you can spare to follow this raid and keep it in observation."

This was followed by a message Hood's chief of staff, Brigadier General Francis A. Shoup, sent at 1:30 P.M., directing Wheeler to "dispatch such force as you may deem sufficient to bring the raid you speak of to bay." Although still not convinced the Yankee column was "a heavy force," Hood had asked "Red" Jackson, commanding the cavalry on the left of the army, to send two of Brigadier General William Y. C. Humes's brigades to Wheeler's assistance, and he wanted Wheeler to keep an eye on the Macon railroad. "Come in this evening, if not too much engaged," Shoup concluded. "You must not go in person unless you think it important."

By this time, Wheeler was convinced the Yankees meant to cross the South River at Flat Shoals and cut the Macon railroad at Jonesboro or Lovejoy's Station. Upon receipt of Shoup's message, he sent Brigadier General Alfred Iverson hurrying down the Flat Shoals Road with his Alabama, Georgia, and Kentucky brigades. Ride hard, Wheeler ordered, parallel the Covington Road, overtake the Yankee column, and bring it to bay near South River.

Iverson's men welcomed the opportunity to get back in the saddle. "Being entrenched in the city was a tedious experience . . . ," complained a 3rd Alabama cavalryman. "No fresh buttermilk, no fresh pork, no hot cornbread or biscuits. . . . We entered into this chase like schoolboys in a game of baseball."

Hood, however, remained cautious, and at 5:00 P.M. he had Shoup instruct Wheeler:

> If you decide to go against the raiders please come to headquarters first. You can start Humes to Flat Rock to-night, as you suggest. The enemy seems about to attack our left. He is now pressing Humes back.

A half hour later, Hood conceded the raid toward Covington was "stronger than first reported," and at 5:40 P.M., Shoup advised Wheeler:

> You can send forward a part of [Brigadier General John H.] Kelly's command, and the general will send Humes to-night to Flat Rock. He thinks you will have artillery enough with Humes'. If it be not too much out of your way, ride by this way before you go.

Wheeler apparently declined this invitation, and at 9:00 P.M. Shoup finally sent him the message he had been waiting for:

> General Hood directs that you go yourself in pursuit of the enemy. Direct whoever you leave in command to report to General Hardee. Humes' division starts for Flat Rock to-night, and will there await your orders. General [Samuel Wragg] Ferguson's brigade will move to the right to-night.

Shoup repeated these instructions at 9:30 P.M., but Wheeler did not need any prompting. Leaving Ferguson's cavalry to hold the trenches east of Atlanta, he spurred his horse down the Flat Shoals Road, accompanied by his staff and escort.[26]

Wheeler had started the campaign with three divisions commanded by Major General William T. Martin, Brigadier General John H. Kelly, and Brigadier General William Y. C. Humes. On paper, this force had mustered 8,062 officers and men, but only 6,239 were mounted and ready for battle. Martin's whole division and all of Wheeler's artillery except a single section were in the rear recruiting their half-starved horses when the fighting began in May.

Most of these units had joined Wheeler north of the Etowah River, and the May 17 arrival of William H. Jackson's division had added three fresh brigades and three 4-gun batteries to the cavalry corps. Although Jackson's division was not properly a part of Wheeler's command and reported directly to army headquarters, by the last week of July, Wheeler could field 10,291 horsemen and thirty guns.

This gave him a small numerical edge over Sherman's cavalry, but the Federals, armed exclusively with rapid-firing breechloaders and repeaters, had an overwhelming advantage in firepower. Most of Wheeler's men relied on clumsy, single-shot Springfield, Enfield, and Mississippi rifles. Only about half of them had pistols, and a Confederate deserter asserted not more than three of Wheeler's regiments carried sabers.[27]

There were also deficiencies in the officer corps. Since the outset of the campaign, at least seven of Wheeler's regimental commanders and three of Jackson's had been killed, captured, or wounded. General Martin had taken twenty days' sick leave on July 2. Three-hundred-pound Brigadier General John S. Williams was also ill. Brigadier General John T. Morgan had been arrested for drunkenness in the face of the enemy, and "Red" Jackson had challenged an insubordinate brigadier, Samuel Wragg Ferguson, to a duel. Jackson had recanted, but the two men were so at odds that Ferguson's brigade had been assigned to Wheeler's corps about the time the army crossed the Chattahoochee.[28]

Since then, Wheeler had contested Thomas's advance toward Peachtree Creek on July 17, 18, and 19. His troopers had held the trenches on the east side of Atlanta against McPherson's infantry on July 20 and 21, driven the Yankees out of Decatur on July 22, and chased Garrard as far as Yellow River on the 23rd. Two of Jackson's brigades and two of Humes's screened the left flank of the army, picketing the Chattahoochee as far south as Campbellton. Martin's and Kelly's divisions, along with Williams's and Ferguson's brigades, had been watching the right until Hood sent orders at 10:00 A.M., July 26, summoning Wheeler and Kelly to his headquarters "without delay."

Outlining plans for a raid of his own, Hood had sent Kelly's division and Ferguson's brigade marching southwest early that afternoon with a day's rations. Halting near East Point about 11:00 P.M., troopers lay down in the road beside their mounts and slept until 3:00 A.M., when they were summoned back into the saddle. Shortly after daylight on July 27, they reached the Chattahoochee River at Campbellton. Engineers laid a pontoon bridge, but before Kelly and Ferguson could cross, a courier arrived with orders calling them back. Leaving Kelly's 3rd Confederate Cavalry to cover dismantling of the pontoons, the column mounted to the tune of "Boots and Saddles" and started back to East Point at 10:00 A.M.

Ferguson's brigade rode all afternoon to reoccupy the trenches on the east side of Atlanta vacated by the three brigades Wheeler sent with Alfred Iverson, while Kelly's division halted at 4:00 P.M. a few miles southeast of the city at Cobb's Mill on the Fayetteville Road. It was raining. The men were tired, the horses hungry, but there would be no rest that night. "Boots and Saddles" sounded again at 10:00 P.M. Companies and regiments trying to form ranks blundered into each other in the dark woods, but soon Kelly's division was riding southeast with orders to get ahead of the Yankee column heading for Flat Shoals.

The other arm of the Rebel pincer was already closing in from the north. At 9:00 P.M., the three brigades Wheeler had sent with Alfred Iverson had collided with Yankee pickets guarding the bridge that carried the Flat Shoals Road across Snapfinger Creek.[29]

Most of Garrard's men were just bedding down for the night when the canebrake crackle of rifles and carbines erupted to the west. The first few fitful shots quickly swelled to a roar, and by 10:00 P.M., Yankee sergeants were kicking at booted feet and blankets, bawling orders to saddle up. Troopers groped blindly for straps and buckles, swearing at skittish horses to hold still. Companies mounted, regiments formed, sending column after column hurrying toward the sound of the guns.

Minty's 4th Michigan halted just short of the picket lines, dismounted, and deployed across the Flat Shoals Road. The 1st section of the Board of Trade Battery unlimbered on a knoll just to the right of Company H, while the 7th Pennsylvania and 4th Regulars dismounted on the Michigan regiment's left and right. Long's and Miller's brigades came up too, forming a perimeter perhaps a half mile in diameter, and began fortifying the low hills commanding the approaches to South River.

"Our line was like a horse-shoe," explained Lieutenant Albert Potter of the 4th Michigan. Bob Minty's 1st Brigade and the 1st section of the Board of Trade Battery held the left shank. Abe Miller's 3rd Brigade and the 3rd section of the battery anchored the right, while Eli Long's 2nd Brigade and the 2nd section formed their line near the bridge over South River.

"I had to give up my blanket to put under the saddle and so could not lay down in the mud again," wrote artilleryman John Nourse. "I spent the rest of the night walking in the road and laying on the caisson limber. . . ."

Other troopers crouched behind hastily heaped piles of logs, rocks, and fence rails, waiting for daylight. Amid the occasional crack of carbines, the 1st Brigade band ventured as close to the firing line as they dared and launched into a stirring medley, including a rousing rendition of "Dixie" that brought cheers from the men on both sides.

Hard-riding Joe Wheeler arrived by midnight to take command of the situation. En route, a courier had overtaken him with orders from Shoup, dated 9:30 P.M., July 27, directing

> that in pursuing the enemy you take the smallest number of troops possible. Should the enemy's course prove such as not to require the greater part of your command, you will detach an officer to continue the pursuit and return with the balance, as he [Hood] needs you here with all the cavalry we can concentrate. He, however, leaves the general management in your hands, relying on your judgment, in which he has full confidence.[30]

Small arms fire alternately flared and sputtered as Wheeler jockeyed Alfred Iverson's three brigades into position to surround the bluecoated troopers who watched and waited in the darkness. As soon as it was light enough to see, he sent his skirmishers forward, driving the Yankee pickets across Snapfinger Creek. His scouts reported Garrard's division camped near Flat Shoals, but Stoneman's column had moved on, apparently intending to cross the South River and march through McDonough to strike the Macon railroad. Feeling Hood's orders constrained him from leading the pursuit himself, Wheeler directed Iverson to leave one regiment to confront Garrard while the rest of his division moved across the South River to "follow Stoneman rapidly and attack him wherever found."

Leaving Colonel Alfred A. Russell's 4th Alabama Cavalry to keep the Yankees busy, Iverson hurried toward McDonough with the Alabama, Georgia, and Kentucky brigades. This left Wheeler facing 4,000 Federals with a single regiment, but the Alabama boys kept up a bold front until two brigades of John Kelly's division, commanded by Colonels Robert Anderson and George G. Dibrell, began arriving about 8:00 A.M.

The all-night march from Cobb's Mill via Tucker's Cabin had left both of Kelly's brigades "completely outdone." Exhausted troopers had gone to sleep in the saddle and fallen off their horses. Others had been left behind when their mounts broke down, but Anderson's depleted ranks dismounted, deployed, and quickly drove some of the 7th Pennsylvania's pickets back across the shoals at South River. They were preparing to follow when Wheeler rode up and told Kelly to wait for his guns to soften up the Yankee defenses.[31]

"It is 8 o'clock and we can see the rebel lines are being constantly augmented by fresh troops from Atlanta," Sergeant Ben Magee of the 72nd Indiana noted apprehensively; "their skirmishers are still crawling up closer and closer; . . . the bullets are now whistling over our heads in chorus, and the bursting shells roar above us more frequently."

Fighting erupted on all sides. "The rebs first used artillery, opening with two 12-pd. brass howitzers on our rear," observed Private John Fleming of the Board of Trade Battery. "Our [2nd] section was ordered out, and got in position under a shower of bullets and in 3 minutes obliged the rebel pieces to make themselves scarce."

"Long shut them up as a big bull-dog would a little cur by one blow from his guns," Lieutenant Albert Potter added approvingly.

For the next hour Long's two guns, supported by the 3rd Ohio Cavalry, kept Anderson's Confederates pinned down behind fences and ditches on the south side of the river. During this interval, word leaked out that Garrard had orders to hold the crossing at Flat Shoals until noon at all costs, giving Stoneman a day's head start on the Rebel cavalry. The men were mulling this over when Garrard convened a council of his senior commanders.

Everyone knew they were in a tight place. A captured Confederate intimated Garrard was surrounded by seven brigades of Wheeler's cavalry. Rebel infantry might already be closing in from Atlanta, and every moment's delay only increased that possibility. Garrard asked for advice.

"Protect my flanks," Abe Miller said quietly, "and I will cut the length of my brigade."[32]

Returning to his brigade, Miller rode down the line, amiably chatting with his men like the frank, friendly country doctor he was. They were surrounded by a greatly superior force, he told them, but they were going to cut their way out because he knew what sort of stuff they were made of, and he was confident they could run over anything the Rebels put in front of them.

Miller was still getting his men into position when a Rebel officer approached Bob Minty's brigade about 10:00 A.M., carrying a white flag. A Federal officer met him and led him blindfolded to the old log house that was division headquarters. Aides shut the door behind him and quickly covered the windows with blankets to hide Garrard's dispositions. When the blindfold was removed, the emissary explained his mission. He had been sent by General Wheeler, he said, to demand Garrard's immediate and unconditional surrender and save the unnecessary effusion of blood.

Garrard dragged out the conversation as long as he could, making small talk, stalling for time, but soon the civilities came to an end. The Rebel officer repeated his demand. Garrard's gray eyes narrowed with contempt.

"My men do not know what surrender is and I will not teach them such a lesson," he said icily. "Tell your general that as soon as I get ready I will walk out of here."[33]

As the Rebel officer was led away, his blindfold kept him from seeing the 123rd

Illinois formed in a skirmish line across a large cornfield just below the log cabin where he met with Garrard. The rest of Miller's Lightning Brigade lined up behind them. The 1st section of the Board of Trade Battery unlimbered in close support, and Miller had his number fours bring the led horses right up behind the guns. Bob Minty's brigade left their works, a squad at a time, and quietly withdrew to the trees where their horses were tied. The 4th Regulars mounted, deploying two battalions of six companies each to cover Miller's flanks. The 4th Michigan and 7th Pennsylvania formed ranks behind Miller's led horses and drew sabers. Wagons, ambulances, and pack mules followed with the rest of the artillery, while Eli Long's 3rd and 4th Ohio brought up the rear.

As they waited for the order to advance, some of the boys in Company B of the 72nd Indiana were discussing their prospects of getting to the Macon railroad when they saw Lieutenant Byrns, the regimental adjutant, coming down the line. How far was it to the Macon River? a trooper guyed earnestly. How far to the Macon Road? inquired another. Corporal James Daugherty got a good laugh at the adjutant's expense when he asked how far it was to "Macon our escape."[34]

Not everyone was optimistic. "On an occurrence of this kind, and at such a time and in a fight like this, I am instructed to destroy the signal code and key I carry on my person," the signal officer attached to division headquarters told Garrard's clerk, Silas Stevens.

"He thereupon unfastened the relic[s] from around his neck and destroyed them at once," Stevens noted.

As the last preparations were being made, Lieutenant Colonel Jonathan Biggs surveyed the ranks of his 123rd Illinois. "Boys," he asked, "which is your choice—to cut the way out or be captured?"

"Cut our way out," his regiment roared back.[35]

A few moments later, the two ten-pounder Parrotts behind Miller's line boomed, sending a pair of shells hurtling up the Lithonia Road. Biggs's skirmishers leaped over their breastworks and broke into a run. A bugle blared and the rest of the brigade surged after them, a great blue phalanx sweeping across the broad fields with parade ground precision. The 4th Regulars threw down an intervening fence and quickly aligned themselves on either flank.

On they came, irresistible, grim, and silent except for the jostling of accoutrements. Fifty yards passed, a hundred and more before the first flicker of flame rippled down the Rebel skirmish line.

"We opened on them with our Spencers," wrote Ben Magee, "killed a few and captured others. They were taken so completely by surprise that many of them never even fired a single round, but skinned out for Atlanta as fast as their legs could carry them. We now raised a cheer and charged right into the main line along with their own skirmishers. Never was a surprise more complete. We are sure that not half of the main line ever fired a shot, and those who did were so badly scared that scarcely a shot took effect. The last mother's son of them ran away . . . we never saw men make better time. Had our cavalry been there mounted and ready to follow us we could have captured the whole force of rebels in front of us; but the cavalry were engaged in the rear, and by the time we had run 600 yards we were all given out, and were still 600 yards from the rebel lead [led] horses; the best we could do was for our battery to throw shells into them as they were mounting."

Some of the opposing skirmishers were posted near a house, and just as the shooting started, Sergeant Magee and his comrades saw a Rebel soldier jump up and down, slap at himself, and then throw himself on the ground, rolling over and over. At first they thought he was dodging bullets, but when they got a little closer, they saw he had knocked over a beehive. The Hoosiers gave him a wide berth, leaving him to be captured by the rear ranks.

In less than twenty minutes, it was over. Miller's winded troopers halted after a half mile and waited for the number fours to bring up their horses. Minty's brigade passed through their ranks and pressed on toward Latimer's Crossroads. The Rebels did not pursue, and shortly after noon Garrard halted the division on a three-mile stretch of road between Latimer's Crossroads and Lithonia. There, he waited.[36]

While surgeons attended the wounded, troopers relieved John Swift and his neighbors of livestock and provisions. Night came. Pickets kept their sleepless vigils, but no shots broke the stillness, no bugles sounded "To Arms."

"All was quiet last night and up to this hour 8 A.M.," Alva Griest noted on July 29.

"We seem to be taking things very coolly," observed Ben Magee. "We wonder why the rebels do not pay us their respects to-day, as we are only 10 miles from where they surrounded us yesterday."

Garrard wondered the same thing, and sent scouting parties in every direction, looking for some news of Stoneman. "Bub, where does this road go?" a Yankee sergeant asked as a roving squad of the 72nd Indiana passed a little boy sitting on a fence by the roadside.

"It don't go anywhere," the lad replied, "and never has went anywhere since I've been here."

"This is quite level country," observed artilleryman John Nourse, "—open—but poor soil—people take no care to make their plantations look neat—very hot day."

"Most devilish hot," agreed the 4th Michigan's Albert Potter, adding, "Our horses are doing well—lots of forage."

The afternoon trembled with the distant thunder of Sherman's guns. That evening, a slow drizzle brought some relief from the heat, and foragers returned with welcome supplies of corn, oats, meat, molasses, flour, eggs, preserves, potatoes, apples, and watermelons. "Had a good supper," Alva Griest noted in his diary before turning in for the night.

"Reveille" sounded at 4:00 A.M., July 30. There was no news from Stoneman. Seven wounded men lay suffering in the ambulances, and an eighth, Private Abraham Bishop of the 123rd Illinois, had died the day before.[37] Garrard made a decision. At 6:00 A.M. his division left Lithonia on the Lawrenceville Road, with Companies B and K of the 72nd Indiana bringing up the rear. The column kept this northeasterly course for about an hour, then turned northwest on the Rockbridge Road, leaving Stone Mountain's sugar-loaf silhouette towering to their left.

"Truly it is one of the 7 wonders of the world," marveled John Nourse. "A huge round stone . . . not a pile of stones—but one solid even stone—no gullies down the sides, but nice and rounding. The top is narrow, not sharp. It is twelve miles round the base, has but a few trees on the top, no foliage on the sides, not even grass—there is but one path up, which has been cut—and the stone is so very gray or white in the sun that a man going up the side can be seen from a distance of 10 miles with the aid of a very common field glass."

A brief morning shower soaked everyone as the column toiled through what Nourse described as "a flat, open, rough country," strewn with slabs of granite. About midday, the advance guard reached the intersection at Choice's Store, but instead of turning left at this familiar landmark and taking the direct road to Decatur, Garrard steered the division straight ahead. He had heard reports the Rebels had reoccupied Decatur and detoured north for another six miles until the division reached Flint Hill Church. There the column turned left on the Peachtree Road, passing Buchanan's and New Cross Keys before halting in the rain at 6:00 P.M. after a twenty-five-mile march.

Dark clouds still hung low overhead when Garrard's troopers broke camp and climbed into the saddle at 6:30 the next morning. Led by the 2nd battalion of Minty's 4th Michigan, the column plodded six miles south, past Buckhead and across Collier's Bridge. Just beyond the bridge, not far from Sherman's headquarters, the welcome orders to halt and dismount brought their four-day journey to an end. Swinging down from their saddles, sodden troopers sought shelter under the dripping pines that had witnessed the savage fighting at Peachtree Creek on July 20.

"The effluvia from the decaying horses, killed in the battle, was anything but pleasant," wrote Lieutenant William Doyle of the 17th Indiana, "and most of the Confederate dead, buried by their own man [sic] under [a] flag of truce, were partially exposed from the rains, they having been barely covered with earth. In many instances no trench was dug at all, when the body lay on a hillside. Then they dug earth from the upper side and threw upon it. In contrast to this general state of affairs was a graveyard of a Mississippi brigade into which they had gathered their fallen, burying the men of each regiment in a row, in separate graves, and marking the number of the regiment on a piece of board."[38]

A new grave was soon added to the mounds of earth dotting the rolling hills south of Peachtree Creek. Private John Boyd of the 72nd Indiana, accidentally shot in the left hip by another trooper during the breakout from Flat Shoals, died shortly after the column returned. "He was a noble boy," wrote Ben Magee, "a good soldier, and sadly missed by his comrades. Peace to his ashes."

The fight at Flat Shoals had cost Garrard two dead, two officers and four enlisted men wounded, and four captured. Three other troopers had been taken prisoner while foraging near Buckhead on July 30.[39]

Late that morning, Sherman learned of the column's return. "A cavalryman, just in, says General Garrard is coming in by the Peach Tree road," he telegraphed Generals Thomas and Howard; "had a small fight first day, none since. Says General Stoneman has gone on, so that branch of the raid seems to be doing well. I now want news of General McCook."[40]

12

McCOOK'S RAID
TURNER'S FERRY TO FLINT RIVER

JULY 27–JULY 29, 1864

No useless coffin enclosed his breast,
Not in sheet or in shroud we wound him;
But he lay like a warrior taking his rest
With his martial cloak around him.

—Charles Wolfe, "The Burial of Sir John Moore"

McCook's troopers woke to a drizzling rain when "Reveille" sounded at 2:00 A.M., July 27. Standing to horse, they waited while company officers inspected the ranks and dismissed the sick and the lame. Then they were ordered to turn over their blankets and excess baggage to the regimental quartermasters and prepare to march at once. "We consoled those who had to stay behind with the promise that we would bring them a plug of tobacco when we came back," wrote Sergeant John B. Vaughter of the 4th Kentucky Mounted Infantry.

Most of the men had already drawn three days' rations. This, together with what they already had in their haversacks, was supposed to last five days, but there were shortages. When Colonel Joseph Dorr asked his commissary officer if the 8th Iowa had been fully provisioned, he learned rations had run out before the noncommissioned staff could be supplied. They would have to live off the country, but no one anticipated any difficulty doing that.

"Boots and Saddles" sounded at 4:00 A.M. A few moments later the command "Right forward, fours right, march," echoed through the ranks and the column filed past Mason's Church to turn right on the Turner's Ferry Road. The 3rd section of the 18th Indiana Battery stayed behind, covering the rear, until most of the division had passed, before limbering up to follow.

Upon reaching Turner's Ferry, troopers dismounted and led their horses over the pontoon bridge. Once across, they halted and ate breakfast while Captain Kossak's pontoniers dismantled the bridge and ferried the last of McCook's pickets to the north side of the river.

Predawn inspections had reduced Colonel John T. Croxton's 1st Brigade—the 4th Kentucky, 8th Iowa, and 1st Tennessee—to 940 officers and men. The three small regiments of Lieutenant Colonel William H. Torrey's 2nd Brigade—the 2nd Indiana, 4th Indiana, and 1st Wisconsin—numbered at most 600. Together with 98 officers and men of Lieutenant William B. Rippetoe's 18th Indiana Battery, McCook brought no more than 1,638 officers and men across the Chattahoochee, and probably fewer than 1,300.[1]

To McCook's dismay, Tom Harrison's division was nowhere in sight. Company F of the 8th Indiana had been halfway back to Turner's Ferry, escorting the supply train they had met at Vining's Station, when they learned the rest of Harrison's command

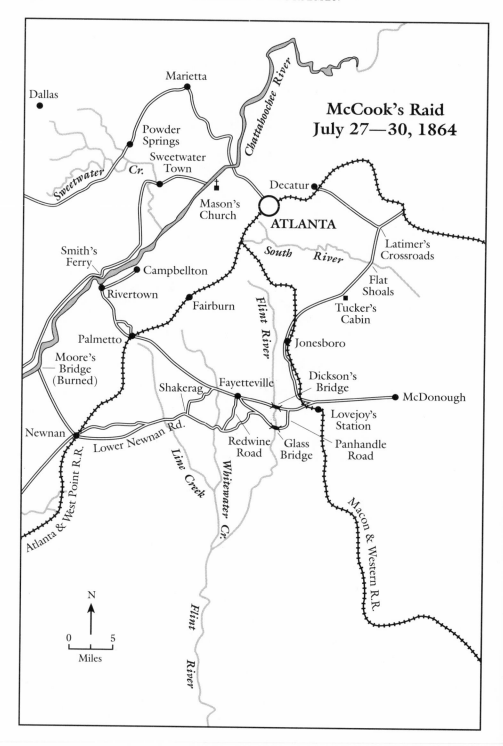

Dallas

Marietta

Powder
Springs

Sweetwater
Town

Sweetwater **Cr.**

Chattahoochee River

McCook's Raid
July 27—30, 1864

Decatur

Mason's
Church

ATLANTA

South *River*

Latimer's
Crossroads

Smith's
Ferry

Campbellton

Rivertown

Fairburn

Flint River

Flat
Shoals

Tucker's
Cabin

Jonesboro

Palmetto

Moore's
Bridge
(Burned)

Shakerag

Fayetteville

Dickson's
Bridge

McDonough

Newnan

Lower Newnan *Rd.*

Redwine
Road

Glass
Bridge

Lovejoy's
Station

Panhandle
Road

Atlanta & West Point R.R.

Lime Creek

Whitewater Cr.

Macon & Western R.R.

N

0   5
Miles

Flint River

was coming to meet them. The Hoosiers had halted by the roadside and waited. The 9th Ohio arrived after midnight, but owing to the darkness and what Fielder Jones angrily described as "the carelessness of some person unknown," the rest of Harrison's column got separated and Jones's 8th Indiana became hopelessly lost. With only an occasional flash of lightning to guide them, they had marched and countermarched until nearly daylight before reaching Vining's Station after an all-night odyssey of thirty-five miles.

While Harrison's men drew three days' rations, forage, and a few horseshoes, Sherman's brother-in-law, Major Charles Ewing, gave each regiment a cursory inspection. Sherman had calculated McCook and Harrison would have 3,500 troopers between them, but he had not counted on the effects of broken-down horses, debility, and diarrhea. Jones's powerful 8th Indiana had left Decatur, Alabama, on July 10 with 613 officers and men. Now it could count only 366 mounted and equipped for duty. Colonel William D. Hamilton's 9th Ohio had dwindled to 270. Major Owen Star's 2nd Kentucky, previously led by Lieutenant Colonel Elijah S. Watts, fielded only 205. The 5th Iowa, commanded by Major Harlon Baird in the absence of Lieutenant Colonel Matthewson T. Patrick, mustered 260, and Major Meshack Stephens's 4th Tennessee numbered no more than 300.[2]

Harrison started his 1,400 officers and men back to Turner's Ferry about 5:00 A.M. Their arrival bolstered McCook's strength to 2,700, perhaps even 3,000, and about 9:00 A.M. the combined commands headed northwest on the Old Alabama Road, past Mitchell's Crossroads, and across the familiar bridge at Sweetwater Town.

McCook's provost marshal, Captain Seneca P. Goulding, rode at the head of the column with Company C of the 4th Kentucky Mounted Infantry. John Croxton's 1st Brigade followed a few hundred yards behind; then came Rippetoe's six rifled guns, eleven regimental ambulances, the pack mules, and Captain Kossak's lumbering pontoon train. William Torrey's 2nd Brigade plodded behind the pontoons, while Tom Harrison's five regiments brought up the rear.

After crossing Sweetwater Creek, the column turned south at Salt Springs toward Campbellton, where McCook intended to recross the Chattahoochee. The advance guard, led by Lieutenant Granville C. West, scouted all the roads and paths leading to the river, and early that afternoon they discovered Rebel pickets guarding Gorman's Ferry. Moving another three miles downstream to the Campbellton Ferry, West concealed his company in some woods about 3:00 P.M. and led a squad ahead to reconnoiter. A short distance from the river, the road turned sharply to the left, in plain sight of the town on the opposite bank. As West and his men rounded the bend, Rebel pickets greeted them with a volley of musketry.

Quickly retreating out of range, West rejoined the men he had left in the woods, where a courier brought him orders to wait for further instructions. Realizing they might not get another opportunity, West told his men to cook a hasty supper.

They had not finished eating when McCook rode up at 4:00 P.M. and dismounted. At West's invitation, he accepted a knife, picked up a piece of hardtack, and fished a sizzling piece of pork out of a frying pan. West's servant handed him a cup of black coffee, which McCook nursed silently while the lieutenant made his report. "He was not at all communicative," West noted, "and seemed to me to be worried and, I thought, a little absent minded."[3]

Unlike Garrard and Stoneman, McCook was no hand-me-down horse soldier from the Army of the Potomac. He was a westerner, one of Ohio's fourteen famous

"Capable but unstable," Brigadier General Edward Moody McCook was a "pompous" frontier politician with no military training who commanded the 1st Cavalry Division. After the war, he was twice appointed governor of the Colorado Territory before charges of corruption hounded him out of office. Used by permission of the Massachusetts Commandery, Military Order of the Loyal Legion, and the U.S. Army Military History Institute.

"Fighting McCooks." Born in Steubenville on June 15, 1833, the eldest son of Dr. John and Catharine Julia Sheldon McCook, he had completed a public school education and gone to Minnesota at the age of sixteen to seek his fortune. Gold fever soon lured him to the sprawling Kansas Territory, where he became one of the first settlers of Pike's Peak. He studied law, hung out his shingle, and won election to the territorial legislature in 1860.

When the war began, McCook was in Washington, D.C., lobbying for creation of the Colorado territory. Together with several other western politicos, he joined Kansas Senator James H. Lane's Frontier Guards, a company of volunteers initially quartered in the East Room of the White House. This company soon disbanded, but by that time McCook had wrangled a job as an aide to General-in-Chief Winfield Scott. Disguised as a hobo, he had smuggled important dispatches through the howling mobs during bloody pro-Southern riots in Baltimore, a feat which earned him a second lieutenant's commission in the 1st U.S. Cavalry.

This unit was soon redesignated as the 4th U.S. Cavalry, but McCook did not share its subsequent history. Knowing that prospects for promotion were much brighter in volunteer regiments, he accepted a major's commission in the 2nd Indiana Cavalry. Within seven months, he was a colonel. He commanded a brigade at the battle of Perryville and a division at Chickamauga, where George Thomas cited him for "efficiency and gallantry."

Eager for promotion, in June 1863 McCook had written directly to the Secretary of

War, requesting permission to raise a brigade of black cavalrymen. "With a few regiments of picked, well-mounted, even though indifferently drilled, men," he asserted, "I am persuaded I could penetrate farther into the rebel country and . . . do much more toward upsetting the abnormal fabric of the rebellion than any white troops have as yet attempted or accomplished."

Nothing came of the idea, and it was April 1864 before he was promoted to brigadier general of volunteers. Receipt of his commission in mid-June only seemed to whet his appetite. "I am so tired of taking my share of this fight in little skirmishes and scouting parties," he complained, "that I would cheerfully risk the lives of and wind of the few anatomical steeds I have left for the purpose of getting my proportion of the glory, if there is any for the cavalry, of this campaign."

The youngest of Sherman's cavalry commanders, McCook was a bachelor, "unusually handsome, strong and vigorous," according to a contemporary, "and while not specially a student nor learned in the military art, he had had excellent experience and was always prompt and cheerful in such duties as fell to his lot."[4]

If he seemed worried as he listened to Lieutenant West that hot, muggy afternoon, he had reason to be. He had wasted five hours waiting for Harrison that morning. His column was strung out for miles on the road behind him, and Rebel pickets barred the way across the Chattahoochee.

McCook had intended to be in Fayetteville by nightfall, but there was no chance of that now. The best he could do was remain opposite Campbellton until the rest of the column caught up, then slip downstream under the cover of darkness in hopes of finding an unguarded ford or ferry. Until then, all he could do was wait.

John Croxton's brigade and the artillery arrived shortly before sundown and bivouacked in the woods three miles back from the river. Not wanting to betray his whereabouts, McCook would not allow them to build fires, so the men had to be content with cold hardtack and raw bacon.

Night fell, but there was still no sign of Kossak's pontoons. At 9:00 P.M., McCook wrote to Sherman's headquarters:

> I arrived opposite Campbellton at 4 p.m. The rebels have the whole river picketed in this vicinity, though not in sufficient force to have prevented my crossing. The pontoon train, however, at the hour I write, is not yet within six miles of me. Captain Kossak has found it impossible to pull it up with his mules. I will take some of my cavalry horses and pull it up. This delay will involve the probable necessity of crossing below here, as the attention of the enemy has, I think, been attracted to this point for some reason, as there have been none of them here recently until last night, when a brigade came down to picket their different ferries. I have endeavored to conceal my force, and think the rebels are not yet seriously alarmed. I expected to have reached Fayetteville to-night, and but for the disability on the part of the pontoon train would have done so. I now think I will be able to cross by day break at some point. Nothing has been found on this side of the river except small scouting parties of Texas cavalry. . . .[5]

Kossak's mules were in "miserable condition" when the march began and suffered severely trying to keep pace with the cavalry. A heavy rain that evening brought the struggling teams some relief from the heat, but the downpour also made the difficult roads only worse. Kossak fell farther and farther behind. It was 2:00 A.M. before his wagons finally trundled into camp, closely followed by Torrey and Tom Harrison.

McCook wanted to start downstream at once, but Kossak's mules were simply not up to the task. Eighteen of them had dropped dead in the harness during the twenty-six-mile march from Turner's Ferry. The rest were close to collapse. Kossak knew he had to lighten his loads, perhaps double up his teams. McCook agreed. He would take only enough pontoons for a small bridge, leaving Captain Lewis H. Bowlus's 2nd battalion of the 9th Ohio and the 3rd section of Rippetoe's battery to guard the excess equipment and distract the Rebel pickets at Campbellton.

McCook was eager to get started. Scouts had already found a little-used crossing six miles below Campbellton, and as the pontoniers began reshuffling their mules and wagons, John Croxton's brigade started downstream at 3:00 A.M. Sometimes in field, sometimes in forest, Croxton's three regiments snaked through the narrow bottomlands. At daylight, the advance guard surprised and captured a lone Rebel scout at Smith's Ferry, but the high ground on the other side of the river seemed undefended. Anxious to secure a bridgehead, McCook hurried one of Kossak's canvas pontoons forward and Croxton began ferrying his 4th Kentucky across the river, four men at a time.[6]

The rest of McCook's column started south with Kossak's pontoons at 4:00 A.M., July 28. The 4th and 8th Indiana drew fire as they passed Campbellton, and several horses were wounded before Captain Bowlus's stay-behind battalion of the 9th Ohio silenced the Rebel sharpshooters.[7] Even after reducing the size of the pontoon train, progress was ploddingly slow. It was nearly noon before Kossak covered the six miles to Smith's Ferry. By that time, Croxton had already shuttled across almost his entire brigade.

While the pontoniers assembled and launched their frame and canvas craft, McCook ordered his officers to winnow the ranks one more time before crossing the river. "All the horses & men in the cavalry that were not fit to stand the hardships were left to escort the Pontoon train back," noted artilleryman Henry Campbell. "The 1st Sec. was detailed to go with the expidition & all the best horses in the battery were given to it—all the mens clothing was left behind—their valises filled with rations, everything cleared off the caissons to make them as light as possible."

Within two hours, the pontoniers had finished, and at 2:00 P.M. Major Nathan Paine's 1st Wisconsin led Torrey's 2nd Brigade across the bridge and up the winding road to the top of the bluff overlooking the river. To save time, no one was allowed to dismount; the column thundered across "in a grand rush." Then the 1st Brigade's horses were led across to the troopers already waiting on the east bank. Lieutenant Martin J. Miller followed with the 1st section of the 18th Indiana Battery, and Harrison's division, led by the 8th Indiana, brought up the rear.

"The boys were all in high glee and full of hopes of the good results of the expedition," wrote Henry Campbell, who was among those left behind with Lieutenant Rippetoe and the 2nd section of the battery. McCook wanted them and the 1st and 3rd battalions of Hamilton's 9th Ohio to hold the bridge for twenty-four hours, to make the Rebels believe he intended to return that way. After that, Kossak was to load up his pontoons and move back upstream with Rippetoe and Hamilton.[8]

Already a day behind schedule, McCook was convinced Rebel scouts had surely reported his whereabouts by now. He needed a diversion, something to throw them off the scent for awhile. With this in mind, he ordered Major Paine to take his 1st Wisconsin up the east side of the Chattahoochee to Campbellton, while the rest of the command marched straight for the Atlanta & West Point Railroad at Palmetto. Upon reaching Campbellton, Paine was to turn east, cut the railroad at Fairburn, then strike south to rejoin McCook somewhere near Fayetteville. It was a difficult assignment, but if Paine had any misgivings he kept them to himself.

"If that order is in the limit of human possibility," McCook remarked as he watched the 1st Wisconsin ride away, "Paine will execute it."

"A noble officer" and "a thorough gentleman," "admired and loved by all who knew him," Paine had fallen from his horse at the battle of Varnell's Station, severely dislocating his elbow at the very outset of the campaign. The injured arm was still cradled in a sling as he led his little regiment northward under a slate-gray sky on July 28. His men were reputedly the best skirmishers in the division, but disease, wounds, and death had taken such a heavy toll that his twelve companies now maneuvered as two battalions instead of the usual three.

The 1st battalion's carbines began popping almost as soon as Paine's column started up the river. Pressing ahead, the advance guard chased an estimated 100 horsemen through Campbellton early that evening. As they turned east on the Fairburn Road, the Wisconsin troopers met increasingly stubborn resistance. Three or four times, they drew their sabers; each time the Rebels recoiled before them.

Two miles east of Campbellton, Paine called a halt to close ranks and rest his horses. Before climbing back into the saddle, he ordered the advance guard to dismount at the first sign of trouble and use their carbines. Soon afterward, only a half mile down the road, his troopers scattered some Confederate cavalry. When they tried to pursue, they found a whole brigade of Rebels manning a hastily constructed barricade flanked by an impassable swamp on one end and a high hill on the other. A flurry of gunshots brought Paine hurrying forward with Companies C and G. Putting himself at the head of the column, he drew his sword with his good arm and ordered the charge in a clear, ringing voice. A bugle blared, and Paine's horse leaped forward under the prod of the spur.

The impetuous charge drove the Rebel vedettes back to and over the barricade. Paine was in their midst, wielding his saber, when a dismounted Rebel trooper took aim and fired. His bullet struck the Yankee major squarely in the chest. Paine slid from his saddle. He was leaning weakly against his horse when Captain Charles F. Robinson rushed to his side.

"I'm shot," Paine gasped, "I'm shot dead." Turning to his men, he raised his saber. "Forward!" he yelled. Then he pitched into the dirt.

More shots rang out, emptying more saddles. The three remaining companies of the 1st battalion came up to confront a Rebel column moving to their right, but Paine's charge had lost all its momentum. The Wisconsin troopers eddied in confusion in the face of a withering fire, then wheeled and dashed devil-take-the-hindmost to the rear.

Paine's 2nd battalion had dismounted and was trying to deploy in the heavy underbrush on either side of the road when these fugitives stampeded through their ranks. Company M let them pass and then formed a line just in time to check the pursuing Rebels, but Major Paine, Lieutenant John W. Warren, and nine enlisted men from Companies C and G were killed, wounded, or missing.

The 1st battalion rallied in a nearby thicket, where Captain Lewis M. B. Smith, the senior surviving officer, hastily consulted with the other company commanders. No one had any idea what Paine's orders were. The men were "demoralized," their horses exhausted, and what looked like an entire Rebel brigade straddled the road to Fairburn. As bullets zipped through the branches overhead, Smith reluctantly ordered the regiment to fall back.

As he retreated through Campbellton, Smith sent Sergeant Milton Martin and a squad of men riding south to find McCook and tell him what had happened. The rest of the 1st Wisconsin reached Smith's Ferry at 10:00 P.M. Smith reported to Colonel Hamilton and then asked for two volunteers to overtake McCook, just in case Sergeant Martin's squad failed to get through. Sergeant Brazier Ellis and another man from Company H stepped forward. After drawing two fresh horses and listening to part of Smith's impassioned speech about how their names would be handed down to posterity, they mounted and sped into the night.[9]

News of the Yankee column had reached Confederate Brigadier General William Hicks Jackson several hours earlier. A big, burly man, familiarly known as "Red," Jackson commanded the Confederate cavalry screening Hood's left flank. A West Point graduate, class of 1856, he had a reputation for cool, calculated courage, and still carried a Yankee bullet in his side from a battle in 1861.[10]

He was sleeping in an abandoned house near the intersection of the Sandtown and East Point roads when his adjutant, Captain Edward T. Sykes, woke him early on July 28 with a message from Captain Addison Harvey, his chief of scouts. Harvey reported Yankee cavalry was crossing the Chattahoochee near Campbellton, but he had not yet determined how many or who was in command.

Forward the message to Hood's headquarters, Jackson directed; alert the brigade commanders. Then he went back to sleep.

Hood reacted to the news of Yankee cavalry on his left the same way he had responded to Stoneman's passage around his right. "The general directs me to inform you that he wishes the enemy resisted to the best of your power, and that he desires to hear what is passing on your line," Hood's chief of staff, Francis Shoup, wrote Jackson at 9:30 A.M.

Jackson was contesting Howard's advance toward Ezra Church when he received this message at 10:45 A.M. Responding to an earlier request from Hood, he had already relieved parts of four of Brigadier General William Y. C. Humes's regiments from the picket line and sent them riding eastward to assist Joe Wheeler. Their replacements, Frank Armstrong's brigade of much-traveled Mississippians, were hotly engaged and rapidly being pressed back toward the Lick Skillet Road. Suspecting the bluecoated cavalry moving down the west bank of the Chattahoochee might be acting in concert with Sherman's advancing infantry, Jackson asked for permission to pull his two remaining brigades off the west end of his picket line and start them for Campbellton.

"Draw out Ross and Harrison, as you suggest," Shoup replied at 11:20 A.M., "leaving only sufficient men to keep a good lookout and communications with our left."

"The General prefers you do not go yourself to Campbellton," Shoup added at 11:45; "but if you think it necessary for you to go, he desires that you will direct Gen. Armstrong to come to headquarters this evening."

Jackson, however, apparently renewed his request to lead the pursuit, and at 2:00 P.M. Shoup advised him that Hood "approves your proposition to go with the brigades to the left."

Couriers delivered this message at 2:30, but it was 4:00 P.M. before Brigadier General Lawrence Sullivan Ross got Jackson's orders to withdraw his Texas brigade from the Lick Skillet Road and fall back to Owl Rock Church. Upon reaching the church, Ross's men made camp, but just before dark a second note from Jackson, dated 7:00 P.M., again summoned them into the saddle. Marching south on the Campbellton Road, they overtook Colonel Thomas Harrison and part of his brigade near the scene of their recent encounter with the 1st Wisconsin.

Harrison's men had taken about a half dozen Yankee prisoners, including Major Paine, who lay on a blacksmith's bench, where a Rebel surgeon examined the small blue hole in his chest. Paine knew it was a fatal wound. No doubt his thoughts turned toward home, his wife, and the infant daughter he had never seen, but he accepted his fate with stoic dignity. He had never approved of the invasion of the South, he told some Confederate officers gathered around him, and he deplored the effects of the war.

"If that is the case why have you not left the army?" asked Captain J. W. Sneed, commanding Jackson's escort.

Paine raised himself up on his elbow, his brown eyes flashing. "You insult me Sir!" he exclaimed. "Can you believe me a *traitor*?"

Exhausted, the young major fell back on the bench and soon breathed his last. The next morning, Rebel cavalrymen stood respectfully at attention and officers doffed their hats as a gallant soldier was laid to rest.

From Paine and the other prisoners, Jackson learned he was facing McCook's division. "I move in an hour to Fairburn," he wrote to Hood at 9:00 P.M., "thence

With his arm cradled in a sling, Major Nathan Paine led his 1st Wisconsin Cavalry in a charge near Fairburn, Georgia, on July 28. Shot in the chest, he issued his last command: "Forward!" Used by permission of the State Historical Society of Wisconsin. Catalogue number WHi (X3) 33680.

below to intercept or strike them in the flank, and shall endeavor to protect the railroad." By that time, the night sky to the south had already turned a fiery red.[11]

After crossing the Chattahoochee, McCook had hurried east. Two miles beyond the river, the road from Smith's Ferry forked. Learning both roads led to Palmetto, McCook divided his command, sending the 4th and 2nd Indiana of William Torrey's brigade to the left while Brownlow's 1st Tennessee led the rest of the column to the right, past a crudely lettered sign nailed to a tree. Shaped like a hand, it pointed east and announced, "Five miles to Hell!"[12]

McCook's scouts easily shoved aside a few Rebels trying to dispute their advance, but sharpshooters soon began sniping at them from seemingly "every hill on the road." Within a mile, the scouts were calling for help. McCook passed the word not to stop for anything, and sent Brownlow's Tennesseans forward, quickly routing the Rebels. "The race after them was a lively one for the next five miles," wrote Sergeant John E. Farnsworth, one of the division scouts.

But it was McCook's northern column that got to Palmetto first, led by William Torrey, a rough-and-tumble lumberman from Green Bay, Wisconsin, with a reputation as a "very shrewd . . . [and] splendid officer."

"Whenever a difficult job of bridge building or repairing, or in fact any other forlorn hope, was to be executed . . . ," acknowledged one subordinate, "Torrey was the man to do it."

A rigid disciplinarian who did not hesitate to have his men bucked and gagged, or strung up by their thumbs, Torrey could be "a terror when he felt like it, and he most generally did feel like it," complained one trooper.[13]

Riding at the head of the 4th Indiana, he charged into Palmetto about 6:00 P.M., scattering a handful of rear-echelon Rebels. Ignoring the maledictions of "a few fearfully tempered women," his men quickly cut the telegraph wire and barricaded the main street before setting fire to three or four freight cars loaded with flour, cornmeal, bacon, salt, tobacco, and railroad supplies.

A half hour later, Jim Brownlow rode into town with his 1st Tennessee. He took a seat on Ezekial Jackson's porch while his men ransacked the post office and joined Torrey's troopers tearing up the railroad. The 8th Iowa and the 4th Kentucky arrived next. Halting at the foot of the steep railroad embankment running through the center of town, they counted off by fours and dismounted. While their horses stood in the road, contentedly munching on corn carried from nearby cribs, the number ones, twos, and threes joined the other regiments already lined up along the railroad. Together, they had torn up several hundred yards of track by the time the 8th Indiana arrived at the head of Harrison's division at 8:00 P.M.

"One set of men with hand spikes would turn over one length of rails, other sets back and forward would turn over other lengths as far ahead and back as the eye could reach," explained Private William Lightcap of the 5th Iowa. "The ties were then easily knocked off, piled up cross ways, the rails placed on top and the pile set on fire. The heat would soften the center of the rails so that the ends with their weight would bend to the ground and thus destroy them for further use. As soon as the pile was fired, that party would rush for their horses, mount and ride as fast as their horses could run until ahead of all at work, sometimes two miles distant. A constant stream of other squads would be riding still further ahead and so continue until the desired amount of track was torn up."

"It was a stirring sight," noted Sergeant Thomas A. Reed of the 4th Indiana, "to see the men moving rapidly about in the light of the burning buildings, and the railroad track writhing like a huge serpent as it turned over down the embankment."

McCook's men also burned three small trestles that carried the railroad over Palmetto's east-west streets. They pulled down two and a half miles of telegraph wire, torched a warehouse filled with government cotton, another full of baled corn shucks, and burned the depot, containing 1,000 bushels of corn, 300 sacks of flour, and several sides of bacon. The raiders also looted John Carleton's grocery store of bacon, flour, lard, salt, cornmeal, soda, shirting, and sundries, and apparently invited some of the townsfolk to take what was left.

Silhouetted by "a scene of fire, of ruin, and devastation," Torrey's 2nd Brigade mounted shortly before dark and rode out of town on the Fayetteville Road, leaving Croxton and Harrison to put the finishing touches to the conflagration. "I never in my life saw such flames of fire," wrote an awed Kentuckian; "it seemed that they would reach hundreds of yards high."

"The clouds overhead reflected the light and shone like red sunset," added Sergeant John B. Vaughter. "The fire became so hot that no one could pass along the street. It spread to adjacent buildings. The citizens were seen scampering in all directions. Even women—some of them in their night clothes, with white, scared faces—flitted from alley to street and from street to alley."

The fires were raging out of control when the first pelting drops of rain fell from the dark clouds overhead. As if a merciful God had heard the town's anguished prayer for help, a torrential downpour all but doused the bonfires blazing along two and a half miles of railroad, quite possibly saving Palmetto from total destruction.

Croxton's and Harrison's commands waited an hour before following Torrey at 9:00 P.M. Company C of the 4th Tennessee had salvaged some commissary whisky from the depot and rode out of town yelling and singing, leaving yards of gaily colored ribbon from John Carleton's store trampled in the mud behind them.[14]

About two miles southeast of Palmetto, McCook's bluecoated column trooped past a large plantation, where scores of slaves watched silently from the roadside. A wizened old Negro woman who had seen the pillar of fire spiraling into the night sky raised her gnarled hands to the heavens. "Bress de Lord!" she exclaimed, "de jubilee hab come!"

The rain stopped and the stars came out as Torrey's troopers led the procession past the piney hills southeast of Palmetto. They had gone about seven miles when Sergeant Martin's squad overtook them with news of the 1st Wisconsin's repulse east of Campbellton. McCook listened to the report glumly but kept his column moving.

Tired troopers were nodding in their saddles, struggling to stay awake, when Torrey suddenly called a halt shortly after midnight and ordered his two regiments to dismount and stand to horse. "I laid down by the side of the road with the bridlerein on my arm," recalled Sergeant Thomas Reed of the 4th Indiana, "and slept, as nearly as I could tell, about one hour, when orders came down the column in a low voice, to mount. Orders also came in a whisper, to secure our sabres so that they would make no noise, and not to fire a gun under any circumstances. . . ."

Torrey's advance guard had encountered a Rebel wagon train sitting beside the road. While his two regiments waited silently, his inspector general, Lieutenant Daniel S. Moulton, intrepidly rode from one end of the Confederate camp to the other.

Unchallenged, he returned and was leading Torrey's column past the rows of parked wagons when a sleepy teamster poked his head out of a pup tent and demanded, "What cavalry is that?"

"Wheeler's," came the reply.

A few moments later, a sleeping Rebel officer was awakened and told "that he must get up and put out some pickets as *the Yanks* were expected."

"Go away," the officer growled, in no mood for pranks at such an early hour. Then he lit a candle and saw a Yankee sergeant standing before him.

"Words can not picture their astonishment and abject terror when they gradually became conscious of the situation," the 4th Indiana's Major George H. Purdy wrote of the Rebel quartermasters and teamsters. "Some, dragged ruthlessly from their slumbers, were disposed to show fight at what they considered a very unhappy practical joke. Others were altogether incredulous, and nothing convinced them that they were really surprised until our men commenced destroying their trains."

Led by the 4th Indiana, Torrey's brigade moved swiftly and silently down the Fayetteville Road, capturing more wagons and teams, but what they saw upon reaching Smith's Crossroads made them blink their sleepless red eyes in disbelief. Six hundred canvas-covered wagons, parked tongue to tailboard and hub to hub, lined both sides of the road. Torrey's troopers swarmed over them, capturing bewildered teamsters, clerks, quartermasters, and commissaries without firing a shot.

"We marched slowly through the camp," explained Sergeant Reed, "the rear guard doing most of the work of killing mules, burning wagons and taking prisoners. It was strange to hear, in the darkness, as we occasionally did, a mule groan when a sabre was thrust into him, or to hear the gurgling sound, when a throat was cut."

Continuing eastward, Torrey's troopers splashed across Whitewater Creek at a half dozen fords. They were approaching the outskirts of Fayetteville when a Confederate officer dashed up to the head of the column, demanding to know what command it was.

"Fourth Georgia," came the weary reply.

"He rode away as though not still entirely assured," noted Sergeant Barnes Hutson of the 2nd Indiana, "but in the dark was unable to see the color of our uniforms."

Halting on the courthouse square, Torrey's troopers formed a line and waited while dismounted details began a door-to-door search, rousting Rebel officers out of their comfortable beds. "They came on us entirely unexpected," admitted a Confederate captain. "We was looking for a raid from the opposite direction [Stoneman] and was guarding against it—had moved our train some two miles from camp the evening before so as to get it, as we thought, in a safe place—when we moved it exactly on the road that the raid was coming."[15]

Colonel Andrew J. McBride of the 10th Georgia Infantry was sound asleep when twenty-year-old Mattie Tidwell burst into his room. Get up, she warned, the Yankees were coming.

"She got to me in time . . . to secret my watch in her—well she hid it," McBride confided modestly, but it was too late. Heavy boots sounded in the hallway. A bluecoated soldier barged into the room, followed by three carbine-carrying companions. Brandishing a revolver in one hand and a light in the other, he ordered the Rebel colonel out of bed.

"I objected, told them I was not able," recounted McBride, convalescing from a head wound he had recently suffered in Virginia. "At this they presented their guns so close to my head that I could almost feel the cold steel and told me that they would blow my brains out if I did not get up immediately. Just then Miss Mattie . . . fell upon her knees, begging them not to kill me. . . . In spite of all our pleading and protest two of them took hold of me, one by each arm, and pulled me out of bed, helped me to dress and carried me across the square to a small law office, where General McCook and his staff and a number of officers were assembled. Seeing that my head was bandaged and that I appeared to be weak, one of them gave me a chair. General McCook, his staff and most of the officers and troopers were a fine looking body of men. . . . I met Colonel [Major] Purdy, Colonel Lamson, Colonel Dorr, General [Colonel] Croxton and Colonel James Brownlow . . . and many others, all of whom treated me with soldierly courtesy, asking me a great many questions about the distance to Jonesboro, Lovejoy, etc., the whereabouts and number of our cavalry, all of which I answered so as to give as little information as possible."[16]

While Torrey's men rounded up prisoners, the rest of McCook's command was busy with captured wagons. Each vehicle bore the name of its division and brigade painted in large letters on both sides of the white canvas cover, and troopers quickly set fire to those loaded with forage and crackers. They were more meticulous with the ones containing officers' baggage, relieving them of fine liquor, cigars, and curious pieces of Masonic and Odd Fellows' regalia before applying the torch. They also broke open paymasters' safes and quartermasters' trunks, filling their pockets with thousands of dollars in Confederate "bluebacks."[17]

"It was in sheets, and by the bale," wrote Corporal Alexander Eckel of the 4th Tennessee. "If a man didn't have plenty of money, it was his own fault."

"For a long time thereafter the boys were flush with depreciated currency," agreed Private Samson L. Ward of the 8th Indiana, "and had no hesitation in offering to buy anything, from a slippery-elm pie to a farm."

"Every one along with the raid, (except those that were sleeping on their horses) were soon heavily laden with spoils taken from the captured wagons," added the 8th Indiana's Jack Wilson, "while the road was strewn with papers, shirts, drawers, rebel uniform coats, saddle bags, corn, forage, &c., razors and razor-straps, watches, and pocket-books, containing large amounts of Confederate currency, besides considerable sums of green-backs, were found stowed away in trunks, boxes, barrels and sacks, revolvers were also found in great numbers."

Corporal Eckel, left afoot when his horse gave out three miles after crossing the Chattahoochee, had spent the night perched on three cracker boxes strapped to the back of a pack mule. He and scores of others eagerly claimed fresh mounts from hundreds of what Lieutenant Granville West described as "the finest horses and mules I ever saw." Horse trading on a grand scale, artillerymen replaced the worn-out teams pulling their limbers and caissons with mules, and Jim Brownlow rode away on a handsome charger purportedly belonging to Confederate Brigadier General Mark P. Lowrey.[18]

The raiders mounted their prisoners on the best of the remaining stock and still had more animals than they could use. "Hundreds upon hundreds of mules were slaughtered—," acknowledged Major Purdy, "all, in fact, which were not in prime condition. They were run through the body, one after another, by our troopers, whose sabers, that night and early morning, dripped with more innocent blood than ever stained them before."

Laden with spoils, John Croxton's brigade rode into Fayetteville at daylight, capturing the mail and destroying 3,000 empty sacks and twenty boxes of tobacco. There was whisky, too. Torrey had already ordered the heads knocked out of seven barrels; Croxton's men found and destroyed at least four more before McCook ordered them back in the saddle at 5:00 A.M. to take the advance. Torrey's brigade followed at 7:00 A.M.

As the column began moving out, one of McCook's aides directed Andrew McBride to mount one of the captured mules. "I told him it would kill me," McBride protested. When the aide insisted, McBride appealed to McCook. After asking a few questions, McCook directed a surgeon to examine the wounded Rebel colonel.

"The surgeon took the bandage off my wound, felt my pulse and said that it would endanger my life to ride with the prisoners," McBride recalled. "General McCook gave me a parole and bade me goodbye. . . . As the last one passed out of sight over the hills . . . I felt better than I had since being wounded."

Others were not so fortunate. Colonels Andrew Ewing, Alexander W. Campbell, and Edward S. Worthington, Colonel McBride's host, Mial M. Tidwell, and 126 other Confederates captured at Fayetteville were mounted on mules and herded into the column. The Yankees put the 250-pound Tidwell, a retired lieutenant colonel of the 30th Georgia Infantry, on a small white mule outfitted with a saddle blanket and a rope halter. His remarks about his Sancho Panza–like appearance soon had captors and captives alike roaring with laughter.[19]

At the head of the column, Jim Brownlow's 1st Tennessee surprised and captured another 500 Confederate wagons parked east of Fayetteville on the McDonough Road. "It was my fortune to capture the Chief Quartermaster of Gen. [William W.] Loring's corps, Maj. [E. A.] Banks, with his chest of Government funds . . . ," wrote Captain Moses Wiley. "I stuffed my pockets full . . . so did some of the men. . . . When I would meet with an officer I was acquainted with, I would make him a present of a few thousand dollars by way of a joke. I think, however, most of the money was used for kindling fires."

"In this way," added Sergeant William Carter, "we were able to help many a distressed quartermaster to make settlement and 'balance accounts.'"

One surprised Rebel paymaster, confronted in his ambulance, surrendered his revolver to Sergeant Daniel C. Bishard of the 8th Iowa. Reaching into his pocket, he drew out a handsome gold watch and chain. "I will give you this and all the money in this ambulance," he said, "if you will let me go."

"We are not thieves," Bishard answered. "We don't want your watch and we already have you and the ambulance and the money." The paymaster laughed. He had not thought of it that way, he confessed, and climbed down to take his place with the other prisoners.

Leaving the wagons for the rear guard to burn, the 1st Tennessee pressed ahead.[20] A drove of Rebel officers, clerks, and teamsters fleeing across the Flint River tried to set fire to Dickson's Bridge, four miles east of Fayetteville, but Jim Brownlow boldly led a charge through the flames, scattering the defenders and putting out the blaze.

The rest of Croxton's brigade followed close behind, striking the Macon & Western Railroad a half mile north of Lovejoy's Station at 7:00 A.M. After cutting the telegraph wires and posting pickets, Croxton sent Major Russell Thornburgh's battalion of the 1st Tennessee and Major Richard Root's 2nd battalion of the 8th Iowa down to the station, where they destroyed the depot, water tank, and woodshed, $300,000 worth of cotton, two trains loaded with an estimated $100,000 to $120,000

McCook's surprise and capture of the Rebel wagon trains parked near Fayetteville, Georgia, as depicted in *Harper's Weekly*. Courtesy of the Hargrett Rare Book and Manuscript Library, University of Georgia Libraries. Used by permission.

worth of tobacco, large quantities of bacon, lard, salt, and ordnance, and almost a mile of track. Torrey's brigade arrived about 10:00 A.M. and joined in the work, but the rest of McCook's column was strung out all the way back to Fayetteville and beyond.

Two miles west of Fayetteville, seventy-five-year-old William Bennett, his daughter-in-law, Emily, and her children were just sitting down to breakfast when a squad of Yankees burst into their home. A slave named "Old Bull" claimed the Bennetts, who owned a large gristmill on Whitewater Creek, had lots of silver and jewelry, and these ruffians began ransacking the two-story house from top to bottom. They dumped the frightened family's breakfast on the floor, ripped open featherbeds, and poured syrup over them. One trooper tried to ride his horse up the stairs. Others put a rope around Bennett's neck and threatened to hang the old man unless he told them where the family valuables were hidden.

"I can not stand this any longer," Emily Bennett wailed. Hurrying to the front gate with her eleven-year-old daughter, Viney, in tow, she raised her hand over her head and made the Masonic sign of distress three times. A tall Yankee officer came across the road and saluted. "Madame," he asked, "what can I do for you?"

"My son and my husband are in Virginia fighting the war," Mrs. Bennett explained. "I am here with six daughters and a young son. I want my home cleared and protected."

The officer purposefully strode through the gate, past the trampled flowerbeds, and mounted the front porch. "Out of the house," he demanded.

The scavengers looked at him blankly.

"Out, or your life," he roared.

This sent bluecoats piling out the doors and windows. Once the house had emptied, the officer posted a guard at the gate and the Bennetts had no more trouble that day.[21]

Tom Harrison's division, bringing up the rear of McCook's column, did not reach

Fayetteville until well after daylight. They halted long enough to feed their horses and reverse their order of march; then, leaving the 8th Indiana to destroy the wagons and teams captured east of town, Harrison's other three regiments remounted and rode on after Torrey. Upon reaching the railroad about 11:00 A.M., details from the 4th Tennessee, 5th Iowa, and 2nd Kentucky joined the troopers prying up rails and ties. "This track being better than what is usually found in the Confederacy, it was harder to destroy . . . ," observed Private Oscar Reese.

By early afternoon, the raiders had torn up a mile and a half of the railroad at intervals extending for five miles.[22] Company A of the 8th Indiana, under the direction of Harrison's adjutant, Captain Edward Reeves, had chopped down the telegraph poles along the right-of-way and cut up and carried off four miles of wire.

As the rails came up and the wires went down, McCook and his staff nooned at Judge Stephen G. Dorsey's house on the McDonough Road, a mile east of the railroad. A day late reaching Lovejoy's, McCook had expected to find an impatient George Stoneman waiting for him, but there was no sign of the crusty old cavalryman. Puzzled, McCook sent several squads of the 8th Iowa riding toward McDonough to reconnoiter.

While Brownlow's 1st Tennessee fed their horses on corn hauled from Judge Dorsey's crib, troopers not assigned to work or picket details took advantage of the opportunity to eat or catch up on some much-needed sleep. Private Williamson Ward of the 8th Indiana traded his lame mount for a one-eyed Rebel mule, which promptly threw him against the root of a tree, badly bruising his back and shoulder, and Sergeant William Buchanan of the 4th Indiana donned a splendid Confederate officer's coat he had captured and paraded before the hoots and catcalls of his comrades.[23]

During this respite, Sergeant Brazier Ellis and his companion overtook the column after an all-night ride from Smith's Ferry, and delivered their message to Lieutenant Colonel Torrey about the same time McCook was casting anxious eyes to the north and east. The 8th Iowa detachments he had sent out had returned and reported cavalry coming toward the railroad. But it was not Stoneman. It was Joe Wheeler.

Stunned, McCook called a meeting of his senior officers and asked for their advice. William Torrey wanted to turn back, arguing that "to advance would be to lose what had been gained and probably sacrifice the command."[24] Croxton, Brownlow, and others urged McCook to press forward, passing around Hood's right in hopes of meeting Stoneman. McCook listened to their arguments. Then he made his decision.

At 2:00 P.M., Tom Harrison's 5th Iowa led the column back toward Fayetteville. However, McCook had no intention of retracing his steps to Smith's Ferry. Knowing Kossak had probably already dismantled the pontoons and the Rebels had undoubtedly discovered the trail of ruin and wreckage from Palmetto, he directed the advance guard to turn left on the Panhandle Road, a mile and a half west of the railroad, intending to march south of Fayetteville and cross the Chattahoochee at Moore's Bridge.

Torrey's brigade followed Harrison, but McCook lingered at Lovejoy vainly hoping to catch a glimpse of Stoneman's guidons fluttering against the sky. It was nearly 3:00 P.M. before he gave up and started westward, unaware that Stoneman had destroyed Moore's Bridge two weeks earlier.

"Red" Jackson was also belatedly on the move. After advising Hood he would

Familiarly known as "Red," Confederate Brigadier General William Hicks Jackson once cleaved a grizzly bear's skull with his saber while riding a horse that was blind in one eye. After the war, he acquired Belle Meade plantation, near Nashville, and became one of the most famous breeders of Thoroughbred racehorses in the South. Reproduced from the Collections of the Library of Congress.

march for Fairburn within an hour, he had dawdled, apparently waiting for his troopers to draw three days' rations. It was daylight before he finally ordered Harrison's and Ross's brigades forward.[25]

"It was now become generally circulated that we were in pursuit of a party of raiders who . . . were moving toward the railroad," noted Brigadier General Sul Ross, "and the utmost eagerness and enthusiasm prevailed among men and officers."

Leaving Campbellton to their right, Jackson's troopers marched through Fairburn and then followed the railroad until they came to the smoking ruins at Palmetto. Turning east on the Fayetteville Road, they halted at 9:45 A.M., munching apples plucked from trees along the roadside before moving on again at 10:30. By noon the consequences of Jackson's long delay in mounting the pursuit were painfully apparent. The charred ruins of burned-out wagons lined both sides of the road. Mule carcasses lay bloating in the sun. "The eagerness of all to overtake and chastise the insolent despoiler was increased two fold," wrote Sul Ross.

Captain William W. Mullendore's company of the 5th Tennessee Cavalry and some of Jackson's escort led the way east. "We had much fun at the residents' expense," wrote W. P. Witt, a sixteen-year-old private in Mullendore's company. "They seemed to think we were all there was of us, and we spoke as if we were going to thrash the Yankees at sight."

At one house, an old lady and two teen-aged girls came to the fence, offering water and a plate of pies to the passing troops. Witt got a drink of water and a piece of pie and was about to move on when the old lady threw up her hands and exclaimed, "Boys, for God's sake go back! They will kill every one of you."

"O[h] no," Witt replied with the brazen confidence of youth, "we will whip them if we can catch them."

"O[h] no you can't!" the lady said, shaking her head. "There are too many of them."

Early that afternoon, the Rebels reached Dickson's Bridge over the Flint River. "The Yankees had burned the floor of the bridge, but the sills were wet and would not burn," wrote Witt. "There was a fence handy, and we soon had a pile of rails fixed so we could lead our horses over.

"After this we started on, and just as I got to the top of the hill I saw three Yankees run across the road afoot into the bushes at the other end of a long lane. I rode back down the hill and reported the fact to Captain Mullendore."

"Red" Jackson rode up a moment later and spurred his big black horse to the top of the hill. Taking in the scene with a glance, he turned to Mullendore's little company and bellowed, "Charge them, boys!"[26]

The dismounted men Witt saw were apparently members of the 4th Indiana who had been detailed to steer John Croxton's brigade to the left on the Panhandle Road. The rest of McCook's column had long since made the turn, but Croxton's three regiments trailed far behind. His pickets had not even left Lovejoy's Station.

Croxton saw the Rebels almost as soon as they saw him. He sent an orderly galloping to find McCook and ordered Colonel Joseph Dorr forward with the 1st battalion of the 8th Iowa. Dorr trotted up on his gray horse and drew rein alongside Croxton. Charge those Rebels crowding the road up ahead, Croxton directed the erstwhile editor of the *Dubuque Herald*; hold them back until the 1st Tennessee and the rest of the 8th Iowa can get into line.

Dorr took his place in the first set of fours. Draw pistols, he ordered his Iowans, forward at a trot. The battalion spurred after him. Hoofbeats drummed on the hardpacked earth, sabers rattled in their scabbards as the column bore down on the oncoming Rebels, breaking into a relentless rush as Dorr ordered "Charge."

"Halt!" Captain Mullendore commanded his little company of Tennesseans. "Throw down the fence on both sides and get out of the lane!" Swerving aside, his men had just pulled down a few rails when they heard a bugle coming down the road behind them "as fast as a horse could bring it." Sul Ross and his bugler galloped past, closely followed by Ross's escort and Colonel Dudley W. Jones's 9th Texas Cavalry.

Crowding the McDonough Road in a compact column of fours, the Texans charged with a shout. Jackson and his escort joined them and generals and privates alike used their pistols in a wild melee. Dudley Jones, the beardless, twenty-two-year-old commander of the 9th Texas who carried a volume of Shakespeare in his saddlebags, killed a bluecoated cavalryman and was muzzle to muzzle with another when his pistol failed. Another Texan blasted the Yankee trooper just in time to save Jones's life.[27]

The hail of bullets cut down Dorr's first set of fours "like grass before a scythe." Dorr was shot through his right side. Two officers, Lieutenant James Horton and Lieutenant Joseph H. Cobb, were killed beside him. Sergeant Major William Christy was hit in the right side, left shoulder, left hand, and finger, and staggered to the rear, bleeding profusely. "A fiercer hand to hand fight never occurred," wrote Lieutenant

A former editor of the *Dubuque Herald,* Colonel Joseph B. Dorr commanded the 8th Iowa Cavalry. "Stocky and vigorous," he was shot through his side near Lovejoy's Station on July 29, but had the wound sewn shut and resolutely rode back into the fight. Courtesy of the State Historical Society of Iowa—Des Moines.

Henry Belfield of the 8th Iowa. "The red flag of the Texans, and our starry guidons almost touched."

The Iowans met the seemingly irresistible charge head on and drove the Texans back, but even as Jones's regiment recoiled, Ross's 6th Texas Cavalry dismounted and rushed into line. While they poured a flanking fire into the left of Dorr's column, a Rebel captain calmly sat on his horse in the middle of the road, firing a revolver with each hand until Jones's 9th Texas could rally, reform, and charge again.

Despite his wound, Joseph Dorr resolutely refused to leave the field. Seeing the dismounted Rebels raking his left, he ordered his eight remaining companies forward.

But Croxton had already turned the rest of the 8th Iowa aside with directions to deploy in a field to cover the mouth of the Panhandle Road. He also brought up Jim Brownlow's 1st Tennessee, intending to extend Dorr's right and keep the intersection open until his rearmost regiment, the 4th Kentucky Mounted Infantry, could get into position on the Panhandle Road to cover the brigade's retreat.

This left Dorr, with not even a hundred men, confronting Ross's whole brigade. Caught in a murderous crossfire, he withdrew before Dudley Jones's second charge and fell back 150 yards, to the small angle in the McDonough Road where his column had first collided with the Texans. Reinforced on the right and left by the timely arrival of Brownlow's 1st Tennessee and the rest of the 8th Iowa, Dorr ordered his battalion to dismount and draw their carbines.

Only then did he allow Hospital Steward Hiram T. Bird to hurry him back to the nearest house. Procuring a bucket of fresh water, "Little Medicine," as the men called him, washed and rewashed the hole in the colonel's side, then took a needle and thread and sewed both ends of the wound shut. When the last stitch was in place, Dorr pulled down his shirt and climbed back into the saddle to rejoin his regiment.

By this time, heavy firing had spread to both sides of the McDonough Road as Ross's 3rd and 27th Texas dismounted alongside the 6th and 9th Texas and Thomas Harrison's brigade deployed on the right. The pressure they brought to bear on the thin blue line soon forced Croxton to commit eight companies of the 4th Kentucky on the right flank of the 1st Tennessee. He was preparing to turn the Rebels' left flank when the orderly he had sent after McCook returned with disturbing news. The Rebels had crossed the Panhandle Road. Croxton's brigade was cut off.

At this crucial moment, Captain James I. Hudnall arrived from Lovejoy's Station with Companies I and K of the 4th Kentucky. Previously detailed for picket duty, these were two of four companies in that regiment armed with Spencer carbines. Croxton immediately ordered them to dismount, "move up the road, communicate with the column, and hold the road open." The rest of the brigade he directed to "move forward and drive the enemy from our front and be ready to withdraw promptly."

Advancing on foot, eight companies of the 4th Kentucky pushed the dismounted Rebel troopers out of the woods on the north side of the McDonough Road and across an adjacent field before halting to wait for further orders. While they bided time, the heaviest fighting shifted south, and soon became so severe Croxton pulled a Kentucky company from his extreme right to reinforce his threatened left.

"This movement separated me entirely from the rest of the command," explained Lieutenant Granville West of Company C, "for the topography of the ground was such that I could not see to my left. I was thus isolated from the regiment, and, without orders was at a loss to know what to do. The enemy in my front kept up a rapid fusil[l]ade of musketry from the woods in which he was stationed across an open field. But we were in that business, also, and held the foe at bay, for I had taken a position in a little ravine cut by the erosion of water in the side of the hill. . . . I scanned the faces of my men to see the effect of the firing in the rear, and was gratified that no sign of trepidation was visible. They were veterans, and had been in serious situations before. . . ."

While West waited anxiously for orders to fall back, Captain Hudnall's Spencers opened a gap in the Rebel ranks just as one of McCook's aides, Lieutenant Roswell S. Hill, brought part of Torrey's 2nd Brigade pounding back down the Panhandle Road. "As we were charging I noticed a good many gray suits in the road," wrote Sergeant L. M. Dickerson of the 4th Indiana, "which the boys had captured, and which they had . . . concluded they did not want when going into a fight."

The 4th Indiana dismounted. In the confusion Lieutenant Colonel Horace Lamson's horse fell on him. Major John Austin was shot in the arm and both men quit the field, leaving Major George Purdy in command. Assisted by a detachment of the 2nd Indiana, Purdy pushed a skirmish line into the woods west of the Panhandle Road.

The ensuing encounter was "not much," according to Lieutenant Stanley Hall, but it bought John Croxton enough time to mount up and move out. Leaving behind about twenty dead and wounded, he directed Companies D and H of the 4th Kentucky to cover the retreat, but Lieutenant Charles T. Swoope, commanding Company D, apparently misunderstood. Captain Henry P. Merrill of Company H refused to withdraw without unequivocal orders to do so. In the hurry to get away, both companies were left behind.[28]

William Torrey's 2nd and 4th Indiana skirmished for about an hour before they withdrew a short distance and barricaded the Panhandle Road with fence rails, fending off the pursuit until the Rebels threatened to turn their flank. Falling back, they built another barricade, and defended it until they were again forced to retreat.

Fight and fall back. Fight and fall back. The process was repeated over and over again that long, hot afternoon. "At times," said Sergeant Dickerson, "the perspiration would roll down our faces in such profusion that we could barely see to shoot."

The only casualty during this fighting retreat was Will Buchanan, the sergeant who had modeled a Rebel officer's coat only a few hours earlier. He was behind the skirmish line, holding horses for the dismounted men, when he collected his last souvenir, a Rebel bullet. A few of his comrades hastily buried him by the roadside and then rode on.

By this time, Major Harlon Baird's 5th Iowa had reached the Flint River at Glass Bridge, just as some Rebels were about to put a match to a liberal dose of kindling and turpentine. Baird's men drove them away and had already crossed the river, followed by the 4th Tennessee, when a courier brought word the rear guard had been attacked.

Both regiments dismounted and began pulling down fences to build breastworks on the west bank. Lieutenant Martin Miller wheeled up his section of artillery to sweep the eastern approaches, while Tom Harrison sent his rearmost regiment, the 8th Indiana, back to help Croxton.

The Hoosiers dismounted and formed their line of battle on both sides of the Panhandle Road. Screened by a swarm of skirmishers from Company D, they had advanced about a mile when they met Croxton's brigade riding toward the river. Facing about, the regiment remounted and resumed their place in the column.

The last of Torrey's troopers reached the Flint River just before sunset. Leaving a battalion of the 4th Indiana to burn Glass Bridge behind them, McCook ordered the column forward again at 6:00 P.M.

"Up to this time our raid had been a picnic . . . ," wrote Captain Moses Wiley of the 1st Tennessee. "But from this time on it was not so funny."[29]

13

McCOOK'S RAID
FLINT RIVER TO NEWNAN

JULY 29–JULY 30, 1864

Adversity reveals the genius of a general;
good fortune conceals it.

—Horace, *Satires,* ii

Joe Wheeler did not learn of the events unfolding south of Atlanta until July 29. After the fight at Flat Shoals, he had pursued the retreating Yankees toward Lithonia, capturing three abandoned wagons, some horses, and a few prisoners. The prisoners confirmed he was facing Garrard's division, which had been left at Flat Shoals to cover Stoneman's march toward Covington. Citizens and captured Confederates who had escaped from the Yankees corroborated this information, and scouts brought in some of Stoneman's stragglers, who intimated they had expected to meet another column south of Atlanta and make a dash for Macon.

Leaving Brigadier General John Kelly with Dibrell's Tennessee brigade to keep a watchful eye on Garrard, Wheeler had returned to Flat Shoals with the balance of his command, when a courier delivered two messages from Hood's headquarters early on July 29. One acknowledged the receipt of a couple of day-old dispatches and approved Wheeler's arrangements to guard the Macon railroad. The other, dated 6:20 P.M., July 28, advised:

> The enemy reported to be attempting a raid on our left, and crossing at Camp-bellton. If you can spare Humes, send him back. Use your discretion.

The news of this third Yankee column found Wheeler with very few troops to spare. He had already detailed one brigade to watch Garrard and sent three others after Stoneman. Humes and the 500 men he had brought with him were bivouacked on the McDonough Road, five miles west of Flat Shoals, where they had been waiting since midday, July 28, for orders to move east or south. The only other troops close at hand, Robert Anderson's brigade of John Kelly's division, were at South River, still weary from their hurried march from Campbellton and the previous day's fight at Flat Shoals. Directing Kelly to keep track of Garrard's division with Dibrell's brigade and start Anderson's men south as soon as possible, Wheeler sent word for Humes to march for Jonesboro and hurried to overtake him.[1]

Born on a 600-acre plantation near Augusta, Georgia, on September 10, 1836, Joseph Wheeler, Jr., was the son of a well-to-do Connecticut merchant who had married Julia Knox Hull, the daughter of William Hull, an American general remembered mainly for surrendering Detroit to the British in the War of 1812. Inheriting his father's frail physique and grandfather's love of adventure, Wheeler frequently mustered his playmates to build "forts" and fight "Indians." When his doting parents presented him with a small brass cannon, he resolved to fire it that

Fourth of July, but some mishap occurred, burning his hand very badly. Fearing his parents would confiscate his prized gun, he tried to keep the injury a secret, but during the night the pain became unbearable. A groan escaped his lips and only then did the family discover his hand required immediate attention.

"In swimming and skating he was the most expert of all his companions," wrote a relative. "*Fear* was a word he never could comprehend and he was always planning such daring feats that his family were kept in a most unpleasant anxiety."[2]

The youngest of four children, "Little Joe" was only five years old when his mother died. His father, bankrupted by a series of financial reverses, took the children to Derby, Connecticut, where they lived until the family returned to Augusta in 1845. When his father's efforts to recoup his fortunes failed, two maternal aunts took young Joseph into their Cheshire, Connecticut, home in 1849. After completing his schooling at Cheshire's Episcopal Academy, he moved to New York City, working as a clerk while he lived with an older sister and her husband.

In 1854 he successfully solicited a New York congressman for an appointment to West Point, where fellow cadets promptly dubbed him "Point" Wheeler, because he had "neither length, breadth, nor thickness." A voracious reader, he spent many hours in the library poring over books of military history, but he was a mediocre student and graduated nineteenth in the twenty-two-member class of 1859, finishing dead last in a course in cavalry tactics taught by William J. Hardee.

Assigned to the 1st U.S. Dragoons but transferred to the 1st U.S. Mounted Rifles in the spring of 1860, Wheeler got his first taste of combat when he reported to Hannibal, Missouri, as part of the escort for a wagon train bound for the New Mexico Territory. The third day out of Hannibal, a woman traveling with the train went into labor. Wheeler, along with a surgeon and a half-breed ambulance driver, was left behind to attend her. After an all-night vigil, a child was born and the next morning the ambulance continued serenely across the trackless prairie until a small band of marauding Indians spotted the lone wagon and gave chase. The driver lashed his team into a gallop, but army mules were no match for fleet-footed Indian ponies. Handing his reins to the surgeon, the driver sprang to the ground with a rifle, dropped to one knee and fired, tumbling the closest warrior into the dust. The others rushed him before he could reload, filling the air with arrows.

"That was my chance," Wheeler recalled many years later. "I charged the crowd knocking down a horse with a shot from my musket. Then I threw away my gun and went at them with my Colt pistol. The driver came in with his Colt and the Indians were on the run."

Upon overtaking the rest of the train, the surgeon told how the young lieutenant had pitched into the Indians. The incident earned Wheeler a new nickname, "Fightin' Joe," that would follow him the rest of his life.[3]

During his tour of duty in the New Mexico Territory, Wheeler watched the secession crisis unfold from afar. "Much as I love the Union," he wrote, "and much as I am attached to my profession. . . . If Georgia withdraws, and becomes a separate State, I cannot, with propriety and justice to my people, hesitate in resigning my commission."

Late in February 1861 he learned Georgia had seceded six weeks earlier. "Accept my commission in the Southern Army for me," he telegraphed his older brother. "I . . . have resigned."[4]

Mustered as a first lieutenant of artillery, Wheeler was ordered to Pensacola, Florida, where Confederate volunteers were trying, without much success, to train heavy guns on federally held Fort Pickens. Seeing an opportunity, Wheeler introduced himself to the commanding general, Braxton Bragg, and explained he had studied engineering at West Point. Bragg accepted his services, and within two weeks, the Confederate batteries were ready for action.

Wheeler was not one to rest on his laurels. Apparently at the urging of some Alabama politicians, he wrote to Leroy Pope Walker, the Confederate Secretary of War:

> Sir—I have the honor to ask for increased rank in the army.
> I have the honor to be, very respectfully,
>
> Your obt. Servant, JOS. WHEELER.[5]

The War Department appointed the brazen little lieutenant as colonel of the 19th Alabama Infantry and ordered him to Mobile. While other officers resided in the city's best hotel and idled away the hours drinking, gambling, and socializing, Wheeler remained in camp, turning raw recruits into soldiers. In their trial by fire at Shiloh, his men fought well. Wheeler had two horses shot from under him and was struck by a spent ball but remained at the head of his regiment, fighting on foot, "bearing the colors of his command."

Transferred to a cavalry brigade, late in the summer of 1862 Wheeler screened the army's advance into Kentucky. At the battle of Perryville, he confronted an entire Federal infantry corps with five small regiments. "No cavalry was ever more handsomely handled and no army better covered," Bragg assured him.

In the battle's aftermath, Bragg made Wheeler his chief of cavalry and directed him to protect the army's retreat southward. "Do not destroy anything. Do not abandon anything," Wheeler assured an anxious general. "Push on as rapidly as you can, and I will keep back the enemy."

During the next week, Wheeler fought on horseback, on foot, from sunrise to sunset. At night he studied the ground he would contest the next day and so delayed the pursuing Yankees that Bragg was able to cross the Cumberland Mountains without losing a wagon or gun.

Upon returning to Tennessee, Bragg traveled to Richmond to confer with President Davis. During their talks, he asked Davis to make the twenty-six-year-old Wheeler a brigadier general. When Davis demurred at promoting someone so young, Bragg asked, "Is not my chief of staff entitled to a brigadier's rank?" Davis allowed he was. "Then," said Bragg, "I nominate Joseph Wheeler."[6]

Wheeler quickly proved himself worthy of his new rank. On December 26, 1862, he notified Bragg the Union army had left its camps around Nashville and was advancing toward the Confederate position behind Stone's River, thirty miles to the southeast.

"How long can you hold them on the road?" Bragg asked.

"About four days, general," Wheeler replied.

Lieutenant General William Hardee shot his erstwhile student a critical glance. "They will run right over you," he declared.

Wheeler not only stymied the advance of 60,000 Yankee soldiers for four days; in

A note on a faded image of Confederate Major General Joseph Wheeler in the National Archives credits Sherman with suggesting, "In the event of war with a foreign country, Joe Wheeler is the man to command the cavalry of our army." In 1898, after serving nine terms in Congress, Wheeler donned a blue uniform to fight in the Spanish-American War. Reproduced from the Collections of the Library of Congress.

a raid reminiscent of Jeb Stuart's famous ride around McClellan, he led 1,100 troopers around the Union army not once but two and a half times, wreaking havoc on Yankee supply trains.

"Four hundred and fifty to five hundred wagons, 600 prisoners, hundreds of mules and horses captured, sums up our achievements . . . ," wrote one of Wheeler's officers. "We also had an immense deal of fun."[7]

A week later, Wheeler captured five transports and a Yankee gunboat on the Cumberland River, northwest of Nashville, leading one wag to suggest his troopers rode "iron-clad horses." Some of his men also swam the icy river and burned an enormous supply depot at Ashland, Tennessee, which, combined with the loss of hundreds of wagons at Stone's River, virtually immobilized the Army of the Cumberland for the next six months.

"We read often in the Richmond papers of the return of Stuart, with what would be considered out here as a mere handful of the spoils of war," noted one newspaper. "Stuart with all his dash, spirit and brilliancy, is not to be mentioned in the same breath with young Wheeler."[8]

In recognition of his exploits on the Cumberland River, President Davis nominated Wheeler to the rank of major general. The Confederate Congress honored him with a vote of thanks, but Wheeler was not without his detractors. In February 1863, after the bloody repulse of an ill-advised frontal assault on the fortified Federal garrison at Dover, Tennessee, an angry Nathan Bedford Forrest told Wheeler, "you can have my sword if you demand it; but . . . I will be in my coffin before I will fight again under your command." Other officers, such as John Hunt Morgan, Earl Van Dorn, and John Wharton regarded Wheeler as Bragg's pet. They resented taking orders from "that boy," and Forrest allegedly swore "that no man who wore number five boots could command him."[9]

At the height of his fame, the "War Child," as his men called him, stood five feet, five inches tall. Brown-eyed and bearded, he might have weighed 120 pounds with his spurs on. "In conversation, his gestures are frequent and rapid," wrote one admirer, "while his articulation is often so rapid as to become somewhat indistinct. His mind is not of the class that would be styled brilliant . . . or rapid in reaching its conclusions. Somewhat slow in its workings, it is only the more sure and reliable. . . . Cool, self-controlled, vigilant of every point . . . Wheeler, in battle, is an admirable study."[10]

By early 1864, he had fought over 600 battles and skirmishes. Five horses had been killed under him and several more wounded. He had suffered three slight wounds himself, but there is no evidence he ever took a leave of absence. In his spare moments, he authored *A Revised System of Cavalry Tactics for the Use of the Cavalry and Mounted Infantry, C.S.A.,* "the most complete and perfect work yet published" on the subject, according to the *Southern Literary Messenger,* which added: "Where sobriety, accomplished manners, and highly cultivated morals are admired . . . this Young General is a beautiful model, *sans reproche!*"[11]

Such fulsome praise paled in light of the acrimonious debate in the Confederate Senate over the merits of Wheeler's nomination to major general. "As a brigadier he was successful, sober, industrious, and methodical," acknowledged one critic. "He succeeded well in organizing, but when the field of his operations was enlarged the draft on his intellect, which is one of mediocrity, became too heavy. He has signally failed to give satisfaction. Moreover, his person is small, and in his manner there is nothing manly and commanding. He evidently handles men awkwardly in battle, for he has but few engaged at a time. In short, I consider that the interest of the service . . . demands that the Senate should refuse to confirm General Wheeler's nomination." Seeking to promote one of their own favorites, the Texas and Kentucky delegations blocked confirmation until January 1864 and only relented then after a direct appeal from Bragg's successor, Joseph E. Johnston.[12]

The promotion enhanced Wheeler's reputation, but not his popularity. He was a humorless martinet whose West Point ways left his high-spirited horse soldiers shaking their heads. "Our discipline is the most rigid that I have ever known volunteers to be subjected to," one of them complained in April 1864. "Some of it has good effect, some bad. The routine of camp and field duty is so great that we can scarcely find time to eat half rations."

"There was little overt hostility," noted one biographer, "but under the surface there was probably a feeling that perhaps Wheeler could not manage his men if orders and military etiquette failed him."[13]

After a fight at Noonday Creek on June 20, three captured Yankees were brought to him for questioning. Guards had relieved them of their carbines, but in the darkness had overlooked a revolver carried by Private Jim Davis of the 17th Indiana Mounted

Infantry. Upon being presented to Wheeler, Davis took dead aim at the Rebel general and pulled the trigger. The cap failed to explode, a guard grabbed Davis's wrist, and pistols clicked to full cock as staff officers drew their side arms.

"Don't shoot! Don't shoot!" Wheeler ordered. "Don't you know," he demanded of Davis, "that if you had shot me you would have been killed instantly?"

"Well," Davis replied, "I didn't know, General Wheeler, how I could do the cause more good than to dispose of you, and I thought it would be a big exchange, a general for a private."

Davis was led to the rear, where a Rebel officer gave him an appraising look and muttered, "It's a damn shame you didn't get him, is all I have to say."[14]

Southern newspapers had also taken Wheeler to task for failing to cut the railroad that was Sherman's sole source of supply. "We have a brave, gallant corps of Cavalry," wrote a correspondent for the *Atlanta Southern Confederacy,* "but there seems to be something lacking."

"It is hardly necessary for me to tell you that this all started by some members of General Forrest's staff who still think that his elevation can be facilitated by my detraction," Wheeler confided in a letter to Braxton Bragg. "They seem bent upon carrying out their ends but I am happy to state that their efforts have as yet had but little if any detrimental influences upon my command. I have begged General Johnston to allow me to go to the enemy's rear nearly every day for the last three months and he is anxious that it should be done but states that my presence is necessary upon the flanks, and here I am with one third rations of corn for horses, with my men building and defending rifle pits and the papers abusing me for not being in Sherman's rear.

"General Johnston tells me not to mind the papers and I try not to do so, but these things are disagreeable."[15]

Now he faced the most formidable challenge of his career. Three splendidly equipped columns of Yankee cavalry, almost 10,000 strong, were converging on the Macon Railroad. Against them, Wheeler could muster only 3,800 indifferently armed troopers. If he concentrated his strength against one Yankee column, the others were sure to wreak havoc with Hood's supply line. If he divided his command, he risked having each detachment defeated in detail. Outnumbered, outgunned, and hopelessly outdistanced, he spurred southward past Tucker's Cabin that afternoon to confront what he called "the most stupendous cavalry operation of the war."[16]

En route to Jonesboro, a courier brought him a message that had left Hood's headquarters at 4:30 A.M. Acknowledging a note from Wheeler and one "Red" Jackson had sent from Campbellton at 9:00 P.M., July 28, it advised:

> the force which crossed the river near that point was McCook's division of cavalry ... evidently making for the Macon and Western Railroad, moving via Fairburn. The commanding general directs that you send a force to co-operate with General Jackson, moving across to such a point as you may deem best calculated to intercept the enemy. Use your own discretion in selecting force, and in general instructions given them. It is intended that you should exercise your own judgment in detaching this force from your command. General Jackson says:
>
> > I move in an hour to Fairburn, thence below to intercept or strike them in flank, and shall endeavor to protect [the] railroad.
>
> He has two brigades—Harrison's and Ross'—and will probably require assistance.

This was followed by a telegram from Hood's chief of staff, Francis Shoup, who reported:

> A raid from the left has struck the Macon railroad below Jonesborough about six miles. Troops have gone from here by rail. Important to prevent damage as far as possible. . . . Take such steps as your judgment suggests. Force unknown.

The troops Hood had dispatched by rail, 700 hard-fighting Kentuckians from Brigadier General Joseph H. Lewis's brigade, reached Jonesboro about 3:30 P.M. Wheeler rode into town a half hour later with parts of four of Humes's regiments he had overtaken on his way south.

"The mothers and maidens were upon the roadside with water for the thirsty," noted Chaplain Robert F. Bunting of Humes's 8th Texas Cavalry. "What a wonderous change does the presence of the foe work upon the patriotism of some folks! Ten days ago they would have looked upon us as intruders, and Gadarene-like in their hearts, wished us to depart from their plantations."

While Wheeler's column continued south, the train carrying Lewis's infantry chugged on down to the break in the track, six miles below Jonesboro. There the foot soldiers met Dudley Jones's 9th Texas Cavalry, sent to assess the damage at Lovejoy's Station. The Texans soon doubled back toward the Flint River to pursue the retreating raiders. Wheeler was not far behind and reached the scene of the fighting on the McDonough Road shortly before dark. While pausing to allow Humes's men to feed their horses, he received another telegram from Shoup, reiterating the importance of protecting the Macon railroad. "General Hood desires your return as soon as you get through with those fellows in the rear," Shoup added. "He has most important service for you."

A staff officer Wheeler had sent to find "Red" Jackson now returned with a message in which Jackson proposed to get in front of the raiders while Wheeler pressed their rear. Wheeler immediately agreed and sent a note urging Jackson to move quickly to cut off the Yankee column while he pursued with Humes's men.

Learning the raiders had taken the road crossing the Flint River at Glass Bridge, Wheeler sent a staff officer to ascertain if the bridge was still standing and ordered scouts to scour the roads leading back to the railroad at Griffin. The officer soon returned and reported the bridge had been burned and all the Yankees appeared to be heading for Fayetteville. After an hour's rest, Wheeler resumed his march, crossing the Flint River at Dickson's Bridge.

Moving as rapidly as the jaded condition of his horses would allow, he was still east of Fayetteville when he received a second message from Jackson, who wrote at 10:00 P.M., "Two Miles and a Half from Fayetteville":

> The latest reports represent the enemy moving toward Fayetteville. I am quite certain they are moving back to cross the Chattahoochee. I have Harrison's brigade in their front at Fayetteville, and am moving now with Ross' brigade to that place. Should [the] enemy attempt to pass around the place I will gain their front or flank them about Newnan. If you can follow and push them in [the] rear, it would be well.

Wheeler reached Fayetteville about midnight, only to be told the Yankees had passed through town an hour ahead of him without meeting "any opposition whatever." That meant McCook was probably only three or four miles up the road, moving toward the Chattahoochee, just as Jackson had anticipated. Wheeler, however, could find no sign of Jackson or his men. Puzzled, he had his adjutant, Major William E. Wailes, write to Jackson:

> Major-General Wheeler directs me, in reply to your dispatch of 10 P.M., to say that he finds the enemy have moved on through the town of Fayetteville and on the Newnan road; that he will press on rapidly on this road in pursuit of them, and desires you, as you suggested, to gain their front on the upper Fayetteville and Newnan Road. He cannot hear of [Thomas] Harrison's brigade.

During this brief pause in Fayetteville, a courier overtook Wheeler with a message Hood had wired to Jonesboro at 6:30 P.M., acknowledging Wheeler's dispatch of 1:15 P.M., and belatedly advising him:

> Jackson engaged the raid from the West at 3 P.M. Enemy said to be 3,000 strong. Infantry sent; 3,000 militia at Macon; some directed to be sent to Griffin. Send information south when important to them.

Wheeler dispatched a brief report to Hood and the commanding officer at Griffin. Then, rousing Humes's weary horsemen, he spurred away at a gallop.

But the column of cavalry that had passed through Fayetteville at 11:00 P.M. was not McCook. It was "Red" Jackson. At 10:00 P.M., he was "Two Miles and a Half from Fayetteville" when he informed Wheeler, " I . . . am moving now with Ross' brigade to that place."

Ross's men had been on the march since daylight and seen some heavy fighting on the McDonough Road. It probably took them about an hour to cover the two and a half miles to Fayetteville, where a jittery population apparently mistook them for the returning raiders. The moon did not rise until after midnight on July 30, and even experienced soldiers had been known to mistake gray riders for blue ones in the dark.[17]

McCook's route was actually well south of Fayetteville that night. After crossing the Flint River at Glass Bridge, he had pulled John Croxton's 1st Brigade to the side of the road so William Torrey's two regiments could regain their place in the column. Once Torrey's troopers had passed, Croxton brought up the rear while Tom Harrison's division took the advance on a road leading north to Fayetteville.

Harrison's advance guard, the 5th Iowa, had gone about two miles when McCook called them back. Retracing their steps, they found the rest of the command waiting quietly. Ordered to about-face, the Iowans resumed the march. They had gone about two miles when McCook again countermanded his orders. The Iowans returned and found the rest of the column still had not moved.

McCook apparently had been stymied by reports a large Rebel force was between him and Fayetteville. He was pondering his options when a knowledgeable Negro volunteered to act as a guide. McCook eagerly accepted his offer, and around 6:00 P.M. the black man pointed the way west on a little-used byroad about two miles beyond Glass Bridge.

Lieutenant William Hays's Company H of the 5th Iowa led the way, with instructions "not to suffer the column to halt for a moment." Company E of the 5th Iowa was directed to wait for the rest of the command to pass and bring up the rear, while Captain David Waters and Companies B, D, L, and M were left behind with orders to move about three-quarters of a mile toward Fayetteville, barricade the road, and hold that position "at *all hazards* and against *any force*" for three hours.[18]

What followed was a nightmarish trek over a narrow, twisting road cut by countless streams and bogs. "The night was warm," noted Sergeant John B. Vaughter of the 4th Kentucky; "there was no wind, and a haze crept up, till the only stars visible were those near the zenith."

The stygian darkness soon compelled McCook to leave guides at every intersection, and their voices droned monotonously over the chorus of chirping crickets and croaking frogs: "to the right," "to the left," and occasionally "where the hell are you going?" As the night progressed, the strain of sixty sleepless hours began to tell. Tired troopers dozed in the saddle. Feeling the reins go slack, exhausted horses wandered off into the woods or simply halted in the middle of the road, unwilling to take another step. A few such sleeping riders brought whole regiments to a halt. Officers soon had to detail men to ride up and down the column, prodding nodding troopers awake.

"Our mules could scarcely be urged along by coaxing or beating when we crossed a stream," noted William Crouse of the 18th Indiana Battery, "but the orders were imperative 'not to stop for water or any other purpose.' If a horse or mule fell dead, the carriage was driven to the roadside and a fresh one put in harness, and the carriage must regain its place the best way it could."

At one point the battery lost its way and got tangled up in the woods. To the cannoneers' amazement, McCook rode back and ordered both guns disabled and abandoned; but this was one order Crouse and his comrades had no intention of obeying. "The strong affection a soldier has for his arms actuated us when we refused to leave them," he wrote, "and after a half hour's delay we succeeded in getting them through on the road again."

In the midst of this plodding procession, 72 captured Confederate officers and 350 enlisted men guarded by the 4th Indiana were doing everything in their power to hinder the march. They let their mules set their own pace and tried to misdirect the column at every crossroads. "Half the time it was so dark I could not see our prisoners," complained Sergeant John Y. Urick of the 4th Indiana, and many of the captured Confederates quietly slipped away.[19]

At the rear of the column, an angry John Croxton fumed and fretted as his brigade toiled in the wake of what he called that "everlasting train of pack mules." "No pack animals started with my brigade," he stormed, "because I understood distinctly from the general commanding the division that nobody was expected to go except soldiers to fight and officers to command them." He repeatedly sent staff officers to hurry up the recalcitrant mules and twice rode ahead himself. On one of these trips he met McCook's aide, Lieutenant Roswell Hill, who told him the 1st Brigade was lagging too far behind. McCook wanted him to close up. Croxton pointed an indignant finger at the mule train and waited by the roadside for his brigade to arrive.

By midnight, the Chattahoochee was still twenty-five miles away, and despite repeated orders to "keep well closed up," McCook's column was strung out for eight or nine miles on the roads south of Fayetteville. Realizing something had to be done, McCook sent Companies D and E of the 8th Indiana to the head of the column with their Spencer rifles to relieve Lieutenant Hays's advance guard. At the same time, he sent his adjutant, Captain Robert LeRoy, with orders for Colonel Croxton's rear guard to buy some time for the rest of the command.

Captain LeRoy found Croxton at a bridge over Whitewater Creek, the first sizable stream the column had encountered since crossing the Flint River. As troopers filed through the scrub oaks on five or six parallel ruts that sloped down to the bridge, LeRoy conveyed McCook's compliments to Croxton and ordered him to detail a company to hold the bridge until daylight, then burn it, and overtake the command. Croxton directed his boyhood school chum, Lieutenant Colonel Robert M. Kelly of the 4th Kentucky Mounted Infantry, to furnish the required company and rode on.

Kelly reined up at the west end of the bridge and beckoned to Lieutenant Granville West. Urging his horse to the side of the road, West listened as Kelly instructed him to halt his company and report to Captain LeRoy as soon as the rest of the brigade had passed. As Kelly disappeared into the darkness, West halted Company C and reported as ordered.

"Yes; well, the General directs that you remain here at this bridge till daylight and destroy it and then follow on after the command," LeRoy explained.

"Why, Captain," West protested, "it might be a difficult matter for the whole command to hold this position until daylight."

LeRoy shrugged off the objection and offered that West probably would not meet any resistance unless it came from "wandering guerrillas."

"To say that I was struck with amazement at such an order, at such a time, is using a very mild term," West later wrote. "The absurdity of the order provoked me, and had not the situation been so serious, its naivete would have been amusing." He knew the column had only eluded trouble by taking to the backroads. The enemy had undoubtedly picked up their trail by now, and begun the pursuit in earnest. "I was sure he would soon be upon us," West asserted, "and there was no time to lose."

He ordered his troopers to dismount and had the number fours lead the horses around a sharp bend in the road a quarter of a mile beyond the bridge. This left him with forty-five men. Sending Corporal Tom Bowlin to keep a sharp lookout from a hilltop a hundred yards east of the creek and posting a few others on the west bank, West put the rest of his troopers to work wrecking the bridge.

The bridge rested on three cribs or pens of logs, roughly six-by-sixteen feet and ten feet tall. These cribs sat about twenty feet apart, bridged by four round sleepers covered with a floor of split logs. After heaving these rough-hewn planks into the water, West's men pulled down ten or fifteen sections of a nearby fence, piled the rails on the sleepers, and kindled a fire in the road, within easy reach.

Captain LeRoy disapproved, and suggested if West tore up the bridge now instead of waiting until daylight it would hamper any stragglers trying to catch up with the column. "There was no time to consider this objection," West insisted, "for I was sure that there were none of our men behind who could get to that bridge that night."

The work continued undisturbed for about half an hour when Corporal Bowlin challenged, "Who comes there?"

"Who the hell are you?" a voice demanded.

"Who comes there?" Bowlin repeated firmly.

"Who are you?" came the insistent reply.

That was enough for West. Thrusting a burning brand into the rails piled on the bridge and ordering his men to take cover behind a fence in the timber bordering the creek, he yelled to Bowlin, "Tell him it is none of his damned business who you are."

Bowlin aimed an eloquent blast from his Ballard rifle in the direction of his unseen antagonist. A Rebel bullet answered, burying itself in one of the bridge timbers with a resounding thud, just as Bowlin came sprinting down the hill like a jackrabbit, followed by a hail of bullets that rattled the branches overhead. West's men answered with a ringing volley of their own.[20]

The woods fell silent as Lieutenant W. R. Friend of the 8th Texas Cavalry and the advance guard of Joe Wheeler's column recoiled into the darkness. After leaving Fayetteville, they had marched southwest, apparently on the Redwine Road. Whether by accident or by design, this had put them on the Lower Fayetteville and Newnan Road, squarely behind the fleeing Federals.

Dismounting, Friend and his men reloaded their guns. Joined by Wheeler's escort, they advanced again, aiming a second volley into the woods on the other side of the creek.

West's troopers returned the fire. Another ominous silence followed, broken only by the snap and crackle of burning rails and timbers as flames began to gnaw at the bridge. Then the shooting erupted again as Wheeler fed fifty troopers from Humes's 4th Tennessee Cavalry into the fight.

"The firing now became general on both sides and continuous," West observed. "I could readily tell when reinforcements would come up by the fire coming from different points where they would take up positions." The glare of the burning bridge soon illuminated the creek bank and Rebel bullets began splintering the rail fence where his men had taken cover. Deeming it "prudent to make a change," West directed his company to cease fire and fall back to where the road turned sharply to the left after crossing the bridge and then abruptly bent back to the right, cutting through a little ridge two or three rods beyond the creek.

As the Kentuckians slipped into the shadows, Wheeler's men continued to blaze away. When their fire drew no response, a Rebel officer ordered, "Onto the bridge and throw off that fire. Quick!"

About a hundred shadowy figures sprang forward. The first to reach the bridge heaved a burning rail over the side. Others crowded close behind.

"Then we let them have it," recounted Sergeant John Vaughter of the 4th Kentucky. "The range was about seventy-five yards. Some fell on the bridge, some went over its sides into the river, and some retreated. We cleared the bridge; nobody could stand our well-directed fire."

The night echoed with the resounding rattle of rifles and carbines. Muzzle flashes stabbed at the darkness. West had not suffered a single casualty and was beginning to believe he could hold his position until the bridge collapsed. Then he saw Rebels moving downstream toward a bend in the creek that would enable them to enfilade the entire length of his line.

"I considered that my little band had done all that mortal[s] could do in that situation," he declared, "and, to avoid the destructive sweep of the impending volley which would surely have annihilated my company, I ceased firing, quietly withdrew, mounted my horses, and started on up the road in the darkness I hardly knew where."[21]

While West's company was fighting to buy the column a couple of precious hours, the mincing pace of the mule train had once again slowed John Croxton's progress to a crawl. Two miles beyond Whitewater Creek, McCook's inspector general, Captain Joseph A. S. Mitchell, met the thoroughly vexed Kentuckian with orders to hurry up.

The two officers rode together for a few hundred yards in the darkness when the column came to a complete halt. Mitchell galloped ahead to determine the reason for the delay, and found an absolutely ludicrous scene. The entire mule train was standing in the middle of the road, sound asleep. Mitchell tried to get the exhausted animals moving again, but they defied his every effort. Finally the exasperated captain drew his saber and began jabbing the point into their tender flanks. Awaking with indignant snorts, the startled beasts bolted down the road at a mad gallop.

The 8th Iowa and 1st Tennessee spurred after them, but Croxton halted his rearmost regiment, Robert Kelly's 4th Kentucky, three miles beyond Whitewater Creek, where the Upper and Lower Newnan roads met at Shakerag. Ordered to form a line of battle and stave off the pursuit until daylight, Kelly directed Captain James Hudnall to dismount Companies A and I and barricade the road where it crossed the brow of a hill. His five remaining companies, B, E, F, G, and K, halted a few hundred yards to the rear and waited.

Shortly before daylight, Company C came galloping up the road, fresh from the fight at Whitewater Creek. Lieutenant West warned Kelly a large force of Rebel cavalry was close behind. Kelly calmly recounted Croxton's orders to stand fast until daylight and sent West and his winded troopers to the rear to dismount and wait for instructions.[22]

Three miles to the east, Joe Wheeler was laboring under the illusion he was at Line Creek. As soon as the Yankees retreated, he had his men extinguish the blaze on the bridge and begin replacing the flooring. An hour's hard work made the span passable.

"After crossing the bridge I pressed on rapidly . . . ," Wheeler recounted. He had not gone far when a courier brought him a message from "Red" Jackson. Dated "Three miles and a half from Fayetteville, July 30th—3 a.m.," it advised Wheeler:

> Since arrival of your courier I received notice from Colonel [Thomas] Harrison that he is opposite the enemy at Shakerag, three miles from here. The enemy has gone into camp there. I move at once with Ross' brigade. . . .[23]

Believing he had just passed Line Creek, three and a half miles west of Shakerag, Wheeler concluded if Jackson was still three miles east of Shakerag, he must still be at least two hours behind him and obviously mistaken about McCook's whereabouts. Sending a courier to hurry up Jackson, Wheeler pushed ahead, thoroughly convinced his was the only force within striking distance of the Yankees.

Private Clem Bassett and five other members of the 8th Texas were riding point at the head of Wheeler's column when they encountered a barricade of fence rails in the darkness. No one challenged them, and the Texans, thinking the obstruction had been abandoned, urged their horses around it. Just then, "a murderous volley" exploded "right in their faces," wounding Private Volney Catron in the leg.

Bassett and his companions had blundered into the 4th Kentucky's pickets, who quickly retreated into the darkness. The Texas troopers followed, trading occasional gunshots with them, and sent word to Wheeler that the Yankees were drawn up in line and ready for a fight.

"This is exactly what I wished," Wheeler later explained, "notwithstanding the disparity of our numbers, as I felt I would at least gain time and thus be enabled to join to my force that of [Robert] Anderson and Jackson."

Concerned the Yankees might withdraw if he did not attack immediately, Wheeler ordered Lieutenant Colonel Paul Anderson's 4th Tennessee Cavalry forward on foot. "Paul's People," as the Tennesseans styled themselves, promptly dismounted and pushed a line of skirmishers toward the barricade, only to meet a solid sheet of flame from Captain Hudnall's Spencers. Reforming their ranks, the Tennesseans tried again. Another rattling volley roared from the Yankee repeaters. Unable to make any headway in front, Wheeler sent General Humes and Colonel Henry M. Ashby spurring to the left and right with mounted elements of the 8th Texas, 1st Tennessee, and the 9th Tennessee Battalion.

Granville West was asleep, his reins wrapped around his arm, his head pillowed on a pile of leaves and small branches covered with his handkerchief, when he heard the sound of heavy firing. A moment later, an orderly dashed up and directed him to move his company to the extreme right flank at once. "The Colonel says drive those fellows back out of the woods," the orderly emphasized before he turned and galloped away.

West hurried Company C into line just in time to meet the charge of the 8th Texas. Working the balky breeches on their Ballard rifles as fast as they could, his troopers laid down a "galling" fire. "We held the ground," West noted, "but the firing was now continuous and incessant, . . . a blaze of musketry all along the line. . . ."

Sunrise found Kelly's entire regiment fighting on foot, except for Company G, which was guarding the horses. Officers on the left flank were pleading for reinforcements and Captain W. B. Riggs, commanding the two companies on the right, sent West an order to take part of his company and part of Company I to their support.

West left Sergeant John Vaughter and a few men to keep fighting on the right, telling him to do "the best he could." The sergeant warned him about something West already knew: the men were almost out of ammunition.

Undaunted, West and Company I's Lieutenant James McDermott hurried troopers across the Newnan Road and to the top of a little knoll, just in time to see a swarm of Rebels coming up the other side. "A bold, fierce and ferocious assault on this line checked them and drove them back in confusion," West recounted proudly, "and we held the ground."

The 4th Kentucky had weathered five separate assaults, but now the dawn's gray light revealed another line of Rebels coming through the woods at right angles to West's left flank. Facing his men to the left and rear, West tried desperately to form a new line paralleling the road. No sooner had he changed front than the 8th Texas renewed their assault on the regiment's right flank, cutting the road 200 yards behind the barricades, just as Joe Wheeler led a headlong charge that broke the center of Kelly's line. Out of ammunition, hit from front, flank, and rear, the 4th Kentucky collapsed like a house of cards.

"Get out of here, everybody!" yelled Lieutenant Charles T. Schable.

"I took him at his word," said Sergeant Henry M. Reed, "—I got; that is, I mounted my horse, put spurs to him, and rode to the rear as fast as I could go."

The rest of the regiment was trying to follow when Lieutenant Friend and Private Bassett of the 8th Texas fell in with a company of the 9th Tennessee Battalion and led them charging through the troopers guarding Kelly's horses. "There was only about 30 of us," Bassett recounted, ". . . the men were poorly armed, very few having pistols. We drove the Yankees back among the horse holders and fought our way through the lane. I killed five in eight shots as we went through. By that time the ones that were dismounted were whipped and driven back to their horses. They mounted and attempted to come out the lane where we were. I rallied a part of the company, my pistols were empty; waved my hat and told the men to forward. We bluffed them, us being at one end of the lane and the rest of the command coming up to the other. We captured most of them."

"Surrender you damned Yankee!" a Rebel officer roared at Granville West.

"Go to hell!" West shot back.

Raising his saber to point the way, West dug in his spurs. His horse bounded into a gallop and seventy or eighty bluejacketed troopers followed. "It was a reckless move," West admitted, "but the result was instantaneous. A convulsive tremor, a rush, a crash as of a thunderbolt, and in defiance of a chorus of demands to surrender, we were out, and away, and gone."

But Lieutenant Colonel Kelly and an estimated 150 to 200 officers and men were captured with all their horses and equipment. Forty or fifty others lay dead on the battlefield. In two short hours, McCook's biggest regiment had simply ceased to exist.

A quarter of a mile beyond Shakerag, the road bridged a deep gully. McCook's passing troopers had previously laid fence rails across the floor to reinforce the rickety span, but Henry Reed and the other fugitives "rushed over it as though it was the smoothest bridge in existence."[24]

Ahead of them, the rest of the 1st Brigade was going at a gallop behind the stampeded mule train. John Croxton had repeatedly sent his orderlies and two staff officers back to urge the 8th Iowa and 1st Tennessee to close up and the pounding of hooves drowned out the sounds of the struggle at Shakerag. The brigade had traveled seven miles at a furious pace when a messenger overtook Croxton with news the 4th Kentucky had been attacked. A moment later, a handful of survivors galloped up, exclaiming the regiment had been cut off and surrounded, and the Rebels were in hot pursuit. Even as they spoke, gunshots sounded sharply in the rear.

For Croxton, the question now became "not how to rescue the Fourth Kentucky, but rather how to save the remainder of my brigade from a similar catastrophe and protect the rear of the column." He ordered Jim Brownlow's 1st Tennessee to dismount, destroy the bridge over Line Creek, and cover the rear "from that point to Newnan, about ten miles," and sent an orderly, fourteen-year-old Johnny Mitch, to tell McCook what had happened.[25]

Troopers at the front of the struggling column had no idea what was going on behind them. They had marched more or less unmolested until about 3:00 A.M., when a Rebel sentry fired on McCook's advance guard, Company D of the 8th Indiana. The front ranks replied with a volley from their Spencers and charged with Company E into what proved to be the camp of Harvey's Scouts, capturing several wagons, mules, and horses. Leaving the wagons for the rear guard to destroy, the Hoosiers sent a few men to escort a handful of captured Rebels to the rear and resumed the march so quickly the rest of the column scarcely even slowed down.

In the confusion, some of the Rebel scouts had gotten away and an occasional gunshot sounded as the two companies pressed ahead. "I think their conduct . . . is worthy of all praise," Fielder Jones wrote of his men. "Fired on at almost every turn of the road, they charged repeatedly through the darkness without knowing or caring if their foe numbered 1 man or 1,000."[26]

Newnan, Georgia, circa 1885, looking west from the Lower Fayetteville Road. This is the same view McCook's advance guard had when they approached the town early on July 30. Note the railroad depot on the right at the bottom of the hill and the A.&W.P.R.R. boxcar waiting in front of it. Courtesy of Weyman C. Evans. Used by permission.

The occasional capture of a mule or a "Johnny" kept the Hoosiers alert, but it also thinned their ranks as troopers were detailed to usher prisoners to the rear. Company D had been reduced to only twenty-five men by the time McCook hurried the other eight companies of the 8th Indiana past the 5th Iowa to support them.

"Morning opens on us a tired lot of soldiers," a weary Tom Jackson noted in his diary. About 8:00 A.M. Companies D and E crested the hill overlooking the railroad depot at Newnan. The Chattahoochee lay just nine miles beyond the spires and rooftops of the sleepy little town. With any luck, they would be there by noon. Then they saw the train parked at the bottom of the hill. It was crowded with Confederate soldiers.[27]

News of the raid had reached Newnan on the evening of July 28 when scouts brought word a large force of Yankee cavalry was crossing the Chattahoochee. Already wearied by a series of false alarms following Stoneman's recent appearance at Moore's Bridge, no one had paid much attention to the report at first. Then a huge fireball had mushroomed into the night sky over Palmetto. "We knew what we had to expect," noted nurse Kate Cumming, "and got ready as usual; whisky and everything of any consequence, was sent off; the men who were able taking to the woods."

The next day, scouts reported the Yankees had moved eastward and the town relaxed its vigil. Convalescents returned to the wards, nurses continued their endless rounds, and about 10:00 that night a northbound train carrying Brigadier General Philip Dale Roddey and 550 dismounted cavalrymen pulled into the depot at the foot of Broad Street.

A one-time tailor, county sheriff, and Tennessee River steamboat captain, Roddey had enlisted as a private at the outbreak of the war and risen to command a division. His troops had seen action with Bedford Forrest at the battle of Tupelo on July 14 before orders summoned them to replace some of the heavy losses Hood had suffered at Peachtree Creek and Atlanta. Leaving Meridian, Mississippi, on July 24 and traveling by rail and river steamer to Montgomery, they had legged across the burnt section of track between Notasulga and Opelika to board a train for Atlanta. Even as they rode north, Braxton Bragg was sending telegrams from Montgomery, trying to call them back. The orders transferring them to Hood's army had been a mistake.

However, it was the break in the railroad at Palmetto, not Bragg, that had stopped their train at Newnan on July 29. Learning a Yankee raid was imminent, Roddey had posted his men on all the likely approaches into town. Early the next morning, one of the scouts sent out by the post commander, Colonel Thomas M. Griffin, reined up on the courthouse square and told a crowd of anxious listeners the nearest Yankees were miles away. Believing the danger had passed, Roddey ordered the train whistle sounded to recall his troops to the depot. The engineer pulled the cord hanging over his head just as Companies D and E of the 8th Indiana came charging down the hill.

"Yonder comes the Yanks now," a startled Rebel exclaimed over the wail of the locomotive.

Roddey's departure from the Tennessee Valley to reinforce Forrest had enabled Rousseau's raiders to plunder and pillage across northern Alabama almost at will. Now his timely arrival at Newnan put him squarely across the path of those same Yankees. When bluecoated troopers galloped to within thirty yards of where he stood on the platform, boldly demanding his surrender, Roddey replied he "did not come there to surrender" and ordered his escort to grab their guns.[28]

Outnumbered ten to one, the Hoosiers fired a few scattering shots into the troops crowded around the depot. Then, as one officer put it, "We charged out a damn sight faster than we charged in."

There were probably not a dozen loaded guns in Roddey's command. This enabled Company D to escape unscathed, but two troopers in Company E were severely wounded. Retreating to the top of the hill, Captains Josiah Stanley and John Boyer quickly formed a skirmish line and troopers began banging away at Rebels firing from the cover of railroad cars, the station platform, windows, cellar doors, and rooftops.

The "whistling of the cars" and the sudden crackle of gunfire brought up the rest of the 8th Indiana, the four advance companies of the 5th Iowa, and the 4th Tennessee. While these troopers dismounted and went into line alongside the advance guard, McCook waited for the rest of his straggling column.

When Johnny Mitch rode up he found McCook "encamped for dinner, as if nothing was going on." The little orderly reported the 4th Kentucky had been cut off and captured; the rear guard was being hard pressed. McCook's reply was to order Croxton to hold the pursuing Rebels in check. Beyond that, he seemed at a loss about what to do. Rebel cavalry was closing in from behind. What looked like a whole trainload of infantry blocked the road up ahead. To make matters worse, McCook's Negro guide now confessed he was unfamiliar with the country around Newnan.

The halt dragged on for at least an hour while McCook conferred with his officers. Rejecting a suggestion to ride right over the opposing Rebels, he left Tom Harrison and the men on the skirmish line to contend with the troop train and turned Major Owen Star's 2nd Kentucky aside with orders to find another way to the river. Two and a half miles south of Newnan, the Kentuckians discovered a road intersecting the Atlanta & West Point Railroad at Wright's Crossing. Pausing long enough to tear up five rails and cut the telegraph in three places, Star sent back word he had found a way to bypass the town and started toward the northwest.

William Torrey's little 2nd Brigade caught up with the head of the column about

10:00 A.M. "Soldiers were placed along the side of the pack train column with long switches with instructions to whip the negroes whenever caught asleep," explained Sergeant Barnes Hutson of the 2nd Indiana, "and in that way we kept the column moving until . . . we overtook the remainder of the force."

Reinforced by the five companies McCook had detached from the 5th Iowa the previous evening, Torrey's 2nd and 4th Indiana turned south with the ambulances, pack trains, prisoners, and artillery. Upon reaching the railroad, the 4th Indiana turned the prisoners over to a detachment of the 2nd Indiana and followed the 2nd Kentucky.[29]

By this time, Newnan was the scene of utter bedlam. People were running, shouting, jostling, crying. Rumor fed upon rumor. The Yankees were planting cannon on the hill above the depot. The Yankees had the town surrounded.

"The Yankees! The Yankees!"

The cry resounded through the narrow streets. People fled in droves, offering fantastic prices for rides on horses, buggies, carts, anything that would get them out of town. "The citizens stampeded; there was no time for deliberation," observed Fannie Beers, a nurse at Newnan's Buckner Hospital. "They could not move goods or chattels, only a few articles of clothing—no room for trunks and boxes."

Doctors and nurses crowded some of the most seriously injured patients behind the courthouse's stout brick walls. Many of the walking wounded, assistant surgeons, druggists, and orderlies hastily armed themselves and, together with some "impetuous boys," took their places in Roddey's ranks. Roddey was in their midst, riding back and forth in his shirtsleeves, ordering, exhorting, encouraging.

"A lady and myself tried to procure him a saddle, but were unsuccessful," recounted Kate Cumming; "the lady got him a blanket."

After about an hour, news came the raiders were wrecking the railroad south of town. Roddey loaded his cavalrymen aboard the train and backed down the track, but by the time he arrived the Yankees had moved on. Pausing briefly to survey the damage, Roddey remounted the cars and ordered the train back to Newnan.

Joe Wheeler got there first. After the fight at Shakerag, he had pressed after McCook's rear guard, which, according to Chaplain R. F. Bunting of the 8th Texas, "took advantage of every eminence and threw temporary breastworks of rails across the road."

By 9:00 A.M., the Yankees had succeeded in outdistancing Wheeler's exhausted troopers and it was nearly noon before he caught up with them again, capturing an officer and twenty-five enlisted men two miles east of Newnan. These prisoners volunteered that McCook had been repulsed by Rebel infantry and detoured to the south.[30]

As Wheeler hurried on, he was overtaken by Lieutenant Colonel Gustave Cook of Humes's division and seventy of the 8th Texas Cavalry. Sul Ross rode up with fragments of two of his regiments, the 3rd and the 27th Texas, each about a hundred strong. These reinforcements boosted Wheeler's ranks to 720 soldiers, but he was still outnumbered three to one and his men and horses were utterly exhausted. Some of them had traveled over fifty miles by the time they pounded into Newnan early that afternoon.[31]

"O[h], how joyfully we hailed them!" chronicled Kate Cumming, who watched the mottled columns come galloping in on two different roads.

"They . . . came to a halt in front of the hospital," recounted Fannie Beers, "but had not time to dismount, hungry and thirsty though they were. The regimental servants, however, came in search of water with dozens of canteens hung round them, rattling in such a manner as to show that they were empty. For the next half-hour, I believe, I had almost the strength of Samson. Rushing to the bakery, I loaded baskets with bread and handed them up to the soldier-boys to be passed along until emptied. I then poured all the milk I had into a large bucket, added a dipper, and, threading in and out among the horses, ladled out dipperfuls until it was all gone. I then distributed about four buckets of water in the same way. . . . Horses to the right of me, horses to the left of me, horses in front of me, snorted and pawed; but God gave me strength and courage: I was not afraid."

Before she could finish her ministrations, Wheeler had procured a guide and assigned him to Colonel Henry M. Ashby. Convinced the raiders had to enter the Corinth Road four miles southwest of town, he ordered Ashby to take his 1st Tennessee Regiment and 9th Tennessee Battalion through Newnan at a gallop to intercept them. After sending scouts and pickets to secure the other approaches into town, Wheeler was preparing to lead the rest of his little command down between the Corinth and Grantville roads to strike the Yankee column in flank when one of his brigade commanders suggested waiting for "Red" Jackson and Robert Anderson, who were still somewhere east of Newnan with six or seven hundred men.

"But we haven't a moment to lose," Wheeler snapped. "Form your men."[32]

14

McCOOK'S RAID
BATTLE AT BROWN'S MILL

July 30–July 31, 1864

Ten soldiers, wisely led,
Will beat a hundred without a head.

—D'Arcy Thompson, *Paraphrase of Euripides*

It was hot, and the noonday sun offered neither shade nor solace on July 30 as four companies of the 2nd Kentucky led McCook's shuffling column northwest on the Ricketyback Road. The regiment's motto was "Always Ready," but nothing in their three years of service had prepared them for the rigors of the past three days. Sullen, sleep-starved troopers slumped in the saddle as they approached the intersection with the Corinth Road. The withering blast of musketry delivered at point-blank range from the woods on their right and the high-pitched Rebel yell of Henry Ashby's Tennesseans took them completely by surprise.

Frightened horses reared and plunged. Officers bellowed commands, and men fell bleeding on the hardpacked earth. Neatly ordered ranks dissolved into a headlong stampede as troopers turned and bolted to the rear.

William Torrey's 2nd and 4th Indiana were toiling along, half a mile behind the advance guard, when the first shots rang out. Dismounting and sending the number fours to the rear, 123 Hoosiers formed a line across the road just as the runaway Kentuckians charged into their midst, receiving what Sergeant Thomas Reed called "the most terrible abuse from Col. Torrey I ever heard a body of men get."

Hastily reforming his partially broken ranks, Torrey sent the 4th Indiana forward with two companies of the 2nd Indiana, the five recently assigned companies of the 5th Iowa, and some of the 2nd Kentucky. The intermittent crack of carbines erupted almost immediately, mingling with the ringing reports of Rebel rifles.

"We . . . advanced in line of battle, dismounted, till we came to the public [Corinth] road," recounted Sergeant Reed. "We found no enemy, but plenty of tracks made as they were marching." Crossing the Corinth Road, troopers halted in a field and began pulling down the surrounding fence to build breastworks. While they waited for the number fours to bring up their horses, Torrey sent a series of aides and orderlies galloping down the Ricketyback Road to hurry up the rest of McCook's column. Five minutes passed. Ten. Fifteen. The number fours emerged from the woods. Men claimed their mounts and stood to horse. Still there was no sign of McCook.

Torrey became increasingly impatient. He could not keep the road open all day. Then, in the distance, he saw them approaching his flank. More Rebels! He had to find McCook. Escorted by an orderly and a few troopers, he spurred into the woods. Shots rang out. A moment later, Torrey's horse came back, the empty stirrups dangling at its sides.

A Wisconsin lumberman, Lieutenant Colonel William H. Torrey commanded McCook's 2nd Brigade. A tyrannical officer who could be "a terror when he felt like it," Torrey was mortally wounded at the outset of the Battle of Brown's Mill and died on August 2, "abusing the 2d Kentucky till the last." Courtesy of the Wisconsin Veterans Museum. Used by permission.

Command fell on the 4th Indiana's Major Purdy. Having received orders from McCook to rejoin the rest of the command, Purdy lined up his horsemen on the Corinth Road, facing Newnan. Sergeant Reed thought this was "the most curious formation" he had ever seen for going into a fight, much less attempting to cut through an opposing line, but before Purdy could act the woods in front of him erupted with the roar of renewed gunfire.

No commissioned officers were with the 4th Indiana's Companies G and H, so Reed and Corporal Sam Clark took command, exhorting their men, about twenty-five in all, to stand fast. As they watched, the Rebels advanced on foot through the dense undergrowth and halted about seventy-five yards away, "firing rapidly, overshooting us," Reed noted, "but cutting the twigs uncomfortably close to our heads."

The two Hoosier companies were still in the saddle, anxiously awaiting the order to charge, when Reed looked around and saw Purdy and the rest of the 2nd Brigade riding hell-bent for the rear. "We were in squads of tens, twenties, and thirties," said Sergeant John Urick, and it was every man for himself.

Not wanting to be left behind, Reed and his men spurred after them. Most of the fugitives rallied around a log house and some outbuildings on a knoll 300 yards north of the Corinth Road. Looking back, Reed saw the Rebels had not pursued, but had marched by their right flank into a field about five or six hundred yards from the house. "They stopped when fully out in the field," he observed, "front-faced,

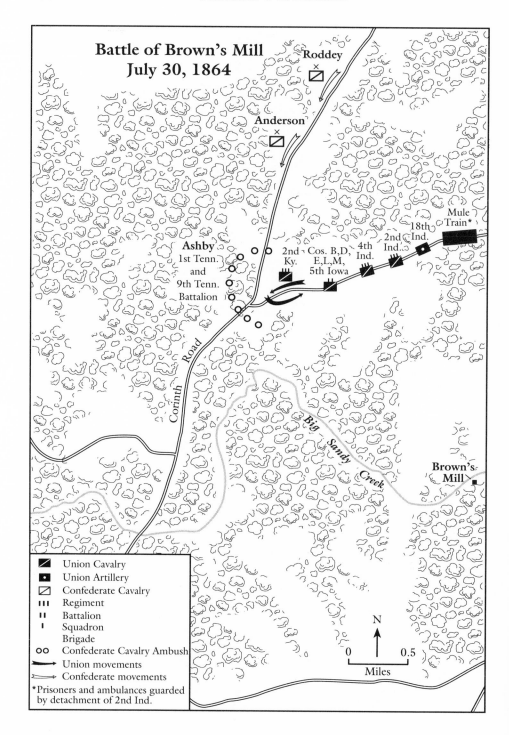

Battle of Brown's Mill
July 30, 1864

Roddey

Anderson

Ashby
1st Tenn.
and
9th Tenn.
Battalion

2nd
Ky.

Cos. B,D,
E,L,M,
5th Iowa

4th
Ind.

18th
Ind.

2nd
Ind.

Mule
Train*

Corinth Road

Big Sandy Creek

Brown's
Mill

Union Cavalry
Union Artillery
Confederate Cavalry
III   Regiment
II   Battalion
I   Squadron
      Brigade
oo   Confederate Cavalry Ambush
      Union movements
      Confederate movements
*Prisoners and ambulances guarded
 by detachment of 2nd Ind.

N

0   0.5
     Miles

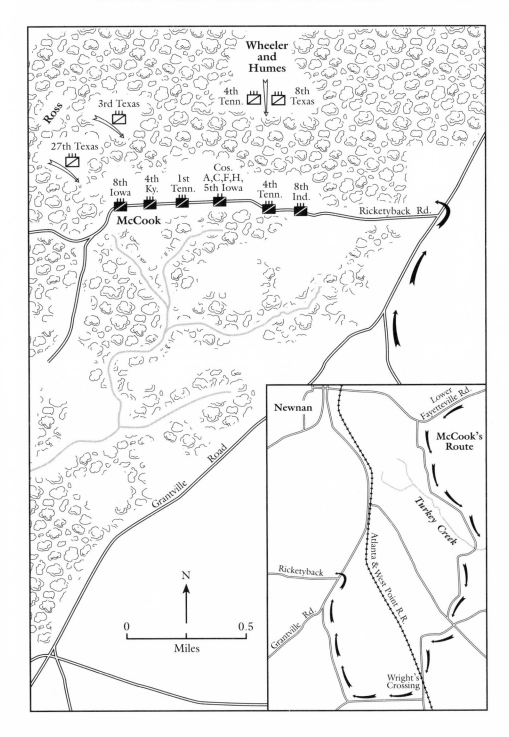

Wheeler and Humes

4th Tenn.   8th Texas

Ross

3rd Texas

27th Texas

8th Iowa   4th Ky.   1st Tenn.   Cos. A,C,F,H, 5th Iowa   4th Tenn.   8th Ind.

McCook

Ricketyback Rd.

Grantville Road

N

0   0.5
Miles

Newnan

Lower Fayetteville Rd.

McCook's Route

Turkey Creek

Ricketyback

Grantville Rd.

Atlanta & West Point R.R.

Wright's Crossing

grounded arms, and took a good look at the fleeing Yanks, but made no attempt to follow. There was not to exceed seventy-five of them, and they were dismounted men at that."

But without the iron-fisted Torrey to lead them, the 2nd Brigade simply fell apart. "Major Purdy was wild," Reed continued, "and he and some of the men were going pell-mell down the hill, vying with each other who should get out of danger first. I here saw a lieutenant who was a staff officer . . . that was the worst scared and worst looking live man I ever beheld. This stampede was all unnecessary and uncalled for; but the commanding officers had completely lost their heads and this was the result."

One hundred eighty men followed Purdy down the long slope and into a field of tasseling corn. Trampling the green stalks underfoot, they raced on until a gaping ditch yawned before them. Digging in their spurs, some of the officers tried to jump the ten-foot chasm, but their tired horses fell short and tumbled to the bottom.

"I saw several men dismount and take to the woods," Reed recounted. "Among them was the Adjutant of the 4th Indiana, who dismounted from a mule, and, when we assured him that there was no one pursuing us, he said that he would risk himself on foot rather than on that mule."

Bidding their dismounted comrades good-bye, Sergeant Reed, Corporal Clark, and several others who had kept their wits followed the ditch northward for a quarter of a mile until it narrowed. Crossing over, they soon came to a little creek, where the brigade adjutant, Lieutenant P. J. Williamson, had rallied about a hundred runaway troopers on the other side. Purdy's detachment soon joined them. After some discussion, Purdy assigned Captain Samuel Dickerson of the 4th Indiana to bring up the rear and struck out for the Chattahoochee with the sound of McCook's artillery booming in his ears.[1]

The sudden flurry of gunfire at the head of the column had sent McCook galloping to the rear, looking for his brigade commanders. The Rebels were in front and on the right flank, he told John Croxton. He wanted the 1st Brigade to cover a side road that seemed to lead back toward Newnan.

Croxton immediately ordered his three regiments to dismount and face right into line, the 8th Iowa on the left, the 1st Tennessee on the right, and a few survivors from the 4th Kentucky in the center. Tom Harrison received similar instructions. Dismounting and handing his reins to an orderly, he hurried his 4th Tennessee and the four remaining companies of the 5th Iowa into line on Croxton's right.

Moments later, a lone gunshot echoed through the woods, killing a horse at the head of Joe Wheeler's column. As the Rebel rider struggled to extricate himself, Wheeler's 4th Tennessee quickly dismounted and filed to the right, followed by the 8th Texas. A bugler sounded "Forward," and the thin gray line advanced.

"We were then within fifty yards of the enemy," recalled Private William H. Davis of the Confederate 4th Tennessee. "The underbrush was very dense and rendered our advance very difficult. We were within twenty-five yards of their line, and yet could not see them when they poured a volley into us."

Davis and his comrades had collided with their opposite number, the Federal 4th Tennessee, along with the 5th Iowa and Croxton's 1st Tennessee. Their answering volley drove the Yankee right flank back about a hundred yards, but Tom Harrison quickly rallied his two regiments and regained the lost ground by sheer weight of numbers.

His success allowed McCook to recall Croxton's brigade to face a new threat. The Rebels had cut off Torrey's brigade; Croxton must send a regiment to reopen the road at once. Croxton sent his adjutant, Captain William A. Sutherland, to deliver the order to Colonel Joseph Dorr. Sutherland found Dorr several hundred yards to the rear. Hampered by the painful wound in his side, he had not accompanied his regiment into the woods when it dismounted. Upon receiving Croxton's order, he asked Sutherland to give it to his second in command, Major Richard Root.

But Joe Wheeler was not so easily brushed aside. Seeing his attack on the Federal right flank begin to falter, he hurried to the front of his line and ordered a bugler to sound the charge.

"Follow me! My brave men!" he commanded.

A wild Rebel yell echoed up and down the line as the little general, conspicuous in his black plumed hat and crimson sash, led his Tennesseans and Texans back into the fight.

Wheeler's renewed assault coincided with the timely arrival of Sul Ross's 3rd and 27th Texas on his right. They were advancing through the woods from the west end of the Ricketyback Road when they encountered Yankee skirmishers. "Dismount! Left front into line," ordered Colonel Edward R. Hawkins of the 27th Texas.[2]

"As many of our men were behind, instead of detailing the usual number of horse-holders, we tied the horses, leaving two men of the company to watch them," recounted Lieutenant Samuel B. Barron of the 3rd Texas. "Almost immediately we were ordered into line, and before we could be properly formed were ordered to charge, through an undergrowth so dense that we could only see a few paces in any direction. As I was moving to my place in line I passed John Watkins, who was to remain with the horses, and on a sudden impulse I snatched his Sharpe's [sic] carbine and a half dozen cartridges. On we went in the charge, whooping and running, stooping and creeping, as best we could through the tangled brush. I had seen no enemy in our front, but supposed they must be in the brush or beyond it. Lieutenant Sam Terrell, of Company F, and myself had got in advance of the regiment, as it was impossible to maintain a line in the brush, Terrell only a few paces to my right. . . . Seeing him stop I did likewise, casting my eyes to the front, and there, less than twenty-five yards from me, stood a fine specimen of a Federal soldier, behind a black jack tree, some fifteen inches in diameter, with his seven-shooting Spencer rifle resting against the tree, coolly and deliberately taking aim at me. Only his face, right shoulder, and part of his right breast were exposed. I could see his eyes and his features plainly, and . . . quick as thought I threw up the carbine and fired at his face. He fired almost at the same instant and missed me. Of course I missed him, as I expected I would, but my shot had the desired effect of diverting his aim and it evidently saved my life.

"Directly in front of Terrell was another man, whom Terrell shot in the arm with his pistol. The Federals both turned around and were in the act of retreating when two or three of Terrell's men came up and in less time than it takes to tell it two dead bodies lay face downwards where, a moment before, two brave soldiers had stood. I walked up to the one who had confronted me, examined his guns, and found he had fired his last cartridge at me. Somehow I could not feel glad to see these two brave fellows killed. Their whole line had fallen back, demoralized by the racket we had made, while these two had bravely stood at their posts."[3]

Wheeler's sudden onslaught overlapped the Federal right, threatening to get between Tom Harrison's men and their horses. Unable to find the orderly who was supposed to bring him his mount, Harrison began a fighting retreat, but three "personal encounters" with pursuing Rebels soon separated him from his command. He was alone, afoot, and the heat and exertion were more than his forty-year-old legs could stand. The muscles in his right calf cramped, felling him just as surely as a gunshot wound. When he looked up, he was staring into the muzzles of Rebel rifles.[4]

The rest of Wheeler's troopers swept past the Yankee colonel, driving the 5th Iowa, the 4th Tennessee, and their led horses across the Ricketyback Road, through an intervening belt of timber and into a hundred-acre field. In forty furious minutes, Wheeler had captured 250 prisoners, including Tom Harrison and a badly wounded William Torrey. Joined by the 1st Tennessee and the 9th Tennessee Battalion, he was preparing to renew the assault when a courier brought word Ashby had successfully ambushed the head of the Yankee column just as it was entering the Corinth Road and the Federals were forming in line of battle. Convinced he had struck the right flank of this line, Wheeler directed Ashby to press the attack. He was reforming his own lines when he heard heavy firing to his right and rear.

It was Dorr's 8th Iowa. Shortly before 3:00 P.M., Major Root had formed the regiment in a compact column of fours and trotted past the pack train and prisoners. A half mile beyond, he encountered two of Ross's Texas regiments. Draw sabers, Root ordered. Bluecoated buglers sounded "Charge."

Tipped with steel, the Iowa column sped down the road, knifing through the right side of the Rebel line. Pausing long enough to rally part of the regiment behind an impenetrable thicket, Major John Isett then charged Ross's horseholders, nearly running down the 27th Texas's color-bearer. A group of Rebel officers standing in the road, gamely firing their revolvers as the Iowans raced past, were quickly overwhelmed. Lieutenant George M. Detwiler captured one of them, who was none other than Sul Ross himself.[5]

Detwiler was escorting his prisoner and another captured officer to the rear when Colonel Dorr caught up with the regiment. Advised the road was open, Dorr relayed this information to John Croxton. "Had the whole division then moved forward," Dorr insisted, "we should have been able to hold the road."

But before the rest of McCook's column could advance, Lieutenant Colonel Giles S. Boggess turned to his 3rd Texas. "Now, boys," he yelled, "you've got to fight your way back to your horses or take it afoot. About face! Charge!"

Turning on the 8th Iowa with a fury that "indicated a fondness for horseflesh that could have only been acquired by long and intimate association," the 3rd and 27th Texas quickly cut Dorr's column in half, taking Lieutenant Detwiler prisoner and recapturing Sul Ross. "The fighting occurred in thick woods, the underbrush concealing the combatants until within a few paces of each other," Ross later wrote. "Friends and foes were mixed up in the struggle, without regard to order or organization, and frequent hand-to-hand encounters were the consequence. Many instances of capture and recapture occurred . . . the victor one moment becoming a captive to his prisoner the next."

Wheeler was trying to decide what all this firing meant when Ross rode up and reported his brigade had advanced, leaving their horses where they first dismounted.

Convinced the Yankees were stampeding Ross's horses, Wheeler ordered his 4th Tennessee and 8th Texas to about-face and hurry toward the sound of the guns.

"Here," declared Lieutenant Samuel Barron of the 3rd Texas, "followed a battle which I could not describe if I would."

Three times Wheeler's men surrounded the embattled Iowans. Three times the Iowans cut their way out. Charge met countercharge. It was, said Private William Davis of Wheeler's 4th Tennessee, "a Kilkenny cat fight for nearly an hour."

Momentum in the thickets seesawed back and forth in dizzying succession. The 4th Tennessee's Lieutenant Colonel Paul Anderson, a former Texas Ranger who "affected all the vagaries of the cowboy costume," including "the white sombrero, leather-fringed breeches, and jangling spurs," was captured and recaptured three times in sixty minutes. "Boys," he drawled in his peculiar nasal tone after being rescued for the third time, "it looks like the Yankees were determined to have me, anyhow."

"The fighting all along the line was terrific . . . ," acknowledged the 8th Iowa's Major Root. "The enlisted men fought like tigers." Root himself had two horses shot from under him. One fall fractured his shoulder. His clothes were riddled with bullet holes. Surrounded by what he called "the enemy's infantry," he ordered his surviving officers to fight their way back to the column as best they could.[6]

Among the Iowa troopers left scattered through the woods was seventeen-year-old George K. Dolsen. Reining up alongside a riderless horse, he was untying a sack of hardtack from the saddle when he noticed two Rebels pointing their guns at him. "Git off that critter," one of them demanded. Dolsen moved as if to comply, then quickly drew his revolver and fired.

"Not yet gentlemen," he yelled as he spurred away. A bullet ploughed through his pistol arm and into his right side. A second shot went through his left leg and killed his horse. Left for dead, Dolsen lay bleeding for an hour before a squad of Rebels passed by. They ignored him, except to remark that if all dead Yankees went to heaven he would be joining the angels soon. Then a lone Johnny came along. He allowed Dolsen looked done for but carefully propped him up and left him a canteen of cool, clear water.

Late that afternoon, Dolsen noticed a wounded horse wandering nearby. Gathering his strength, he loosened his feedbag from his saddle and, clutching it beside him, slowly and painfully inched across the forest floor. After what seemed like an eternity, he dumped a small pile of corn in front of the horse's nose. While the horse ate hungrily, Dolsen grabbed one of the stirrups and hauled himself into the saddle. With his good arm, he reined toward the roar of McCook's artillery. The horse headed in the right direction and soon carried his wounded rider into the midst of Lieutenant Martin Miller's battery, where strong hands carefully eased Dolsen out of the saddle.[7]

Lieutenant Miller had unlimbered his two guns beside a log cabin on the crest of a little rise on the left of the Ricketyback Road.[8] "In our immediate front," he observed, "was an open field bounded by a thick woods, the edge of which our skirmishers occupied. The distance from the battery to the woods was about 150 yards, when suddenly a terrible fire of musketry from the enemy drove back and completely routed the skirmishers, some of whom threw away their guns as they passed the battery."

As these fugitives fled to the right and rear, Miller's sweating gunners hurled lethal loads of canister at the advancing Rebels. For the next half hour, they fought alone, firing as fast as they could ram the charges home. Rebel skirmishers were only eighty yards away when Lieutenant Roswell Hill of McCook's staff hurried twenty or twenty-five 2nd Indiana troopers into line on Miller's right.

The rest of the 2nd Indiana corralled prisoners, pack mules, and ambulances in a shallow depression behind the battery. The swale offered scant protection from the hail of bullets that seemed to fly from every point of the compass, and a wounded Yankee lying in one of the ambulances was hit a second time.

"The Federal commander of the guard was much confused and suggested no change of position . . . ," complained a captured Confederate. Only after earnest entreaties did he allow his prisoners to dismount and lie down.

By this time, John Croxton had reoriented the 4th Kentucky on the right side of the Ricketyback Road, in line with the battery. Joseph Dorr rallied what was left of the 8th Iowa on the right of the 4th Kentucky. Companies dismounted. Officers hurried skirmishers into line, who sprawled behind logs and trees. But even as the woods shook and the artillery roared, some exhausted troopers sighted down their carbines and promptly fell asleep.

McCook stood in the midst of the confusion, first on one foot, then on the other, anxiously rubbing his hands together as he turned around and around. "What shall we do? What shall we do?" he implored over the thunder of the guns. "What shall we do?"

John Croxton fixed him with a contemptuous glare. "Why _ _ them, fight them—fight them!" he roared.

But McCook had lost control of both himself and his men. "Take command and do the best you can," he ordered Croxton.

Croxton sent Captain James H. West and what was left of the 4th Kentucky to drive back a line of Rebel riflemen volleying at Miller's battery from the edge of the opposite woods. West could field only about a hundred men after the debacle at Shakerag, but they quickly scattered the Rebel skirmishers in their front and captured some horses. They also expended the last of their ammunition.

"This left us in a situation that is liable to produce a feeling of helplessness in a soldier," confided Lieutenant Granville West. When confronted by a "line of infantry," the Kentuckians had no choice but to abandon their captured horses and fall back.

Shortly afterward, Jim Brownlow's 1st Tennessee, previously sent to reconnoiter a right-hand road, rejoined the brigade and Croxton posted them behind the line to cover his left flank and rear. It was not long before the Rebels advanced a second time. Ordered to charge, the Tennesseans raised a yell and spurred to the attack, capturing several prisoners. Among them was a well-dressed officer wearing a black plumed hat, the left side pinned up with a silver buckle, who proved to be General Humes.

Pressing on, Brownlow's boys encountered a second Rebel line. "Here the firing was very heavy," recounted Sergeant William Carter, "and all that saved us was they fired too high."

Brownlow's regiment began retreating just as Joe Wheeler counterattacked with one or two mounted squadrons he had held in reserve. Seeing Humes being led to the rear, the Rebel Tennesseans charged recklessly into the midst of their retreating rivals, freeing their general and capturing his astonished guards. Overcome with emotion, Humes tearfully shook hands with each of his rescuers. "They had taken his hat, plume and silver buckle," noted Lieutenant William Gibbs Allen of the 5th Tennessee, "[and] had put an old planters hat on his head."

While McCook watched the 8th Iowa, 4th Kentucky, and 1st Tennessee being fed into the fight piecemeal, he held back Fielder Jones's powerful 8th Indiana with orders to "cover the rear and left flank of the column, and to guard those points at all hazards." Dismounting six of his ten companies, Jones held his ground with only a little intermittent skirmishing. Then he saw the Rebel battle lines "skirting the timber in a front of nearly two miles, completely enveloping the right, left, and rear of the column."[9]

What Jones saw was Joe Wheeler getting reinforcements. Shortly after Humes's rescue, Robert H. Anderson reported to Wheeler with 400 men. A tall, slender man with piercing black eyes, jet black hair, and flowing black beard who had only learned of his promotion to brigadier general the previous day, Anderson had left Flat Shoals about 2:00 P.M. on July 29. After an eighteen-mile march, he had halted his brigade just outside Jonesboro at 10:00 P.M. and rested for a couple of hours before climbing back into the saddle. After another halt at 3:00 A.M., he had resumed the march at daylight, pushing through Fayetteville, past broken-down horses and dismounted troopers straggling along on foot, and dead and wounded Yankees lying in the road at Shakerag. "On, on we went," Sergeant John Ash of the 5th Georgia Cavalry wrote in his diary, "galloping a part of the way and reached Newnan after noon."

Anderson did not even halt long enough for his panting horses to catch their breath. Hearing the distant roar of artillery, he led his brigade through the streets at a gallop, sending Company A of the 5th Georgia ahead to reconnoiter. Lieutenant Fredrick H. Blois, Sergeant Ash, another noncommissioned officer, and ten privates (all who had been able to keep up), pounded down the dusty road until they got within sight of the fighting, then hurried back to report to Anderson.

Anderson reached the field about the same time as Philip Roddey. Responding to an urgent summons from Wheeler, Roddey had marched from Newnan with perhaps a thousand dismounted cavalrymen, hospital convalescents, druggists, assistant surgeons, and anyone else who could shoulder a gun. Although "lame of ankle" after the previous day's twenty-mile trek across the burnt section of railroad between Notasulga and Opelika, Roddey limped down the Corinth Road like a common soldier, much to the delight of his men.

His arrival, combined with that of Anderson and straggling detachments from Ashby's, Harrison's, and Ross's brigades, gave Wheeler upwards of 1,800 men, about as many as McCook had left on the field. Wheeler immediately ordered the newcomers into line, deploying Roddey on his left and Anderson on the right.

"We were at once dismounted and formed in line," recounted John Ash of the 5th Georgia. "Just at this time some of our mounted men on our right were stampeded [apparently by Brownlow] . . . , but as soon as they saw us, they were reassured and turned upon the enemy, firing and dashing upon the foe. Our line of battle was marched forward in the woods, throwing out skirmishers. After awhile the enemy advanced on our left, so we were double quicked by the left flank and then moved forward by the left flank, coming up with the enemy in a few moments. . . ."

At the same time, Anderson ordered his mounted companies to charge. The 8th

Confederate was slow to respond, but Company G of the 5th Georgia "moved out instantly under a heavy fire." The "new issue," as Wheeler's veterans condescendingly called these recent arrivals from the Georgia coast, swept the Federals from the field, then dismounted and boldly advanced with the rest of the brigade, driving the Yankees from the cover of a fence at the edge of the woods. Anderson lavished praise on his old regiment, telling them they had "won their spurs." A moment later, he was wounded in the thigh.[10]

Anderson's sudden shift to the left may have been prompted by Harlon Baird's four companies of the 5th Iowa. Ordered to relieve Croxton's brigade and open the way to the Corinth Road, they charged down the wooded slope on the left of the battery and disappeared into the heavy undergrowth.

"It was quite difficult to keep our alignments and intervals," wrote Private George Healey. Becoming separated from his company, young Healey resolutely forged ahead until he heard a Confederate officer ordering his troops to "mount and count fours." Realizing he had somehow slipped between the Rebel skirmishers and their supports, Healey began backing away. He had not gone far when he encountered a solitary Confederate sitting on a log. Leveling his Spencer carbine, Healey hastily relieved the Rebel of his gun and tossed it into a nearby creek. He was about to march his prisoner to the rear when he heard footsteps. Ordering the Rebel to lie down, Healey took cover behind a tree. To his immense relief, he saw his comrade, Oscar "Oc" Martin approaching.

"The woods are full of them [Rebels]," the bareheaded Martin announced as he trotted up, pointing over his shoulder.

"Yes, and over here too," Healey said, gesturing behind him.

"Where did you get this fellow?" Martin asked, nodding toward Healey's prisoner.

"Right here," Healey answered.

"What have you in that bag?" Martin demanded of the Confederate.

"Chewing tobacco."

"For God's sake," Martin exclaimed, "give me some."

He and Healey both helped themselves to a "chaw" and were discussing their predicament when they heard voices. Ducking behind a tree, they saw four Confederate soldiers filing through the woods. Healey let them get within a hundred feet and then stepped into the open.

"Halt!" he commanded. "Drop those guns!" The startled Rebels were slow to comply. "Drop those guns!" Healey demanded menacingly. Three Spencer carbines fell to the ground. Healey ordered the four Rebels to take a few steps past the guns. Then he had them come forward one at a time, where Martin relieved them of three holstered revolvers.

Anxious to rejoin his regiment, he lined up his prisoners, leaving Martin to herd them behind him. Which way to go? Artillery and small arms fire seemed to echo in every direction and Healey admitted he was lost. "Your men were there," one of the Rebels volunteered.

That seemed like as good a direction as any, so Healey started forward, halting to pick up the three carbines left lying on the ground. Realizing he and Martin could not guard five Rebels and carry an armful of guns, he opened the butt of each Spencer and emptied the cartridges from the magazine, handing the weapons to the prisoners. A talkative Rebel explained they had captured the guns the day before (presumably from the 4th Kentucky) and asked, "How do you load them?"

After a brief explanation, Healey and Martin ordered their prisoners forward and soon reached the Federal lines. Pausing at a well, they shared a drink with their thirsty captives and then escorted them to McCook.

"Where did you get them?" McCook asked as he and his staff officers crowded around the five prisoners.

"On the skirmish line," the two Iowans replied.

Ordered to rejoin their company, Healey and Martin shared their captured tobacco with their comrades as they recounted their adventure. It was just one of countless little dramas played out on that bloody field, but this one would win Private Healey the Congressional Medal of Honor.[11]

Despite such heroics, Anderson's brigade advanced steadily on the right, while Roddey's men kept pace on the left. Attacking with "vigor and telling effect," they drove the Yankee skirmishers through clearings and thickets until they came to a large, bowl-shaped field divided by a formidable ravine.

McCook's men held the high ground on the other side and immediately opened with small arms and artillery. Roddey "advised strongly against attacking the position." Wheeler agreed. "To charge the position with fresh troops would have been hardly expedient," he later wrote, "but with men in our fatigued condition, it was out of the question."

Leaving Roddey, who reported his command too exhausted to travel any farther, to begin escorting prisoners and captured property back to Newnan, Wheeler ordered the rest of his command to mount up and move to the right to cut off McCook's line of retreat.

As the Rebel regiments withdrew to their horses, Reverend Edward Hudson of the 6th Texas noticed a wounded Confederate lying on the field. Dismounting, the chaplain and another trooper carried the helpless man to safety. When the two Samaritans went back for their horses, they found they had been left afoot. An erstwhile cavalryman himself, Hudson quickly caught a riderless mount and had started diagonally across a field when a Yankee volley slammed him to the ground. The horse was killed. Hudson was shot through the abdomen and would never walk again without the aid of crutches.[12]

McCook and his staff were riding through the woods when they found another wounded Rebel, Lieutenant T. J. Towles of the 3rd Texas, propped against a tree. McCook reined up his horse. "Major," he said, mistaking the cut of Towles's uniform, "you appear to be suffering."

Towles replied he feared he was mortally wounded and asked for a doctor. McCook shook his head. His surgeons already had more wounded than they could handle. "You have been a soldier long enough to know how these things are," he said, "and you must not think hard of me."

He then asked Towles how many Confederates were on the field. Towles refused to answer directly, except to say Wheeler, Jackson, and Roddey were all present. Visibly shaken, McCook turned to his officers and exclaimed, *"We must get out of this!"*[13]

About 5:00 P.M., McCook, his staff, and senior subordinates assembled on horseback behind the knoll where Lieutenant Miller's guns now stood silent. They were "completely surrounded," McCook announced, by "an overwhelming force." Wheeler and Jackson and Roddey were there with their cavalry, along with two brigades of infantry en route to Atlanta. McCook had already put every available man on the firing line, including his escort. Casualties were heavy. Torrey was missing. So was

Colonel James Patton Brownlow of the 1st Tennessee Cavalry was only twenty-one years old in the summer of 1864, but his exploits were already legendary. The youngest son of Tennessee's Union Governor "Parson" Brownlow, he told a wavering McCook at Brown's Mill, "You can all surrender and be damned." Used by permission of the Massachusetts Commandery, Military Order of the Loyal Legion, and the U.S. Army Military History Institute.

Tom Harrison. Lieutenant Miller reported the artillery had expended its last round of canister and almost all its shells. The rest of the command would soon be out of ammunition. McCook could see no alternative. They had to surrender.

"Gentlemen," Jim Brownlow said, "you can all surrender and be damned. I am going out with my regiment."

"What will you do?" McCook asked skeptically. "How can you help it?"

"Why, I can and will cut my way out," Brownlow insisted. "I would about as soon be killed in the attempt as to be captured and sent to Andersonville or Libby. They treat us Southern soldiers worse in those prisons than they do you Northern soldiers, and I am going to cut my way out if my men will follow me."

John Croxton agreed with Brownlow and asked McCook to let him take out his whole brigade. Fielder Jones spoke up, too, saying his 8th Indiana would "charge the gates of hell" before surrendering to Rebels.[14]

After some discussion McCook agreed to let them try to cut through the Rebel lines and find a road leading toward the Chattahoochee. He ordered Miller to disable his guns while John Croxton and Fielder Jones formed what was left of the command into two columns. Croxton's brigade would go first. Jones would follow, taking command of Tom Harrison's division. Ambulances, pack mules, and prisoners were to be abandoned, regimental surgeons left behind to take care of the wounded.

Told to get his troops "well in hand" and wait for instructions, Fielder Jones rode back to his command. He had left the 8th Indiana on the right of the prisoners, facing toward the rear, but during his absence some "unauthorized party" had ordered the regiment away. To make matters worse, troopers assigned to the pack train had unceremoniously turned loose their mules and led horses when directed to rejoin their companies and the resulting stampede nearly swept the Hoosiers off the field. Only after the "energetic co-operation" of his officers was Jones able to extricate the 8th Indiana, Major Baird's detachment of the 5th Iowa, and most of the 4th Tennessee from the mob.

Spying a neck of woods where the Rebels had not yet appeared, Jones sent Baird's Iowans south to reconnoiter. Baird soon returned and reported he had found "an obscure road," but was uncertain where it led. Trusting Providence to show the way, Jones ordered a bridge built across an obstructing ravine and lined up his brigade "as nice as though on dress-parade."

"The rebels are on three sides of us and all is now excitement and confusion," Private Williamson Ward of the 8th Indiana scrawled in his diary. "We are ready for the worst that can come, and will make some rebel bite the dust before we surrender."

A few moments later, Major Thomas Herring rode up to the head of Ward's company. Taking charge of the 8th Indiana after Jones assumed command of the brigade, Herring ordered Captain Josiah Stanley to "count off sixteen of your best men for advance guard."

My men are all the best men," Stanley asserted and ordered his first four sets of fours forward.[15]

While cavalrymen cast aside blankets, haversacks, a veritable "cloud-burst" of Confederate money, and anything else they thought would slow them down, Lieutenant Martin Miller sat on a mule he had mounted when his horse was shot out from under him and supervised the disabling of the artillery. His men spiked the vent of each gun, loaded both pieces to the muzzle with their last shells, cut up the harness, and chopped down the wheels. "The rebs will not use this gun on us," declared a grimy-faced cannoneer.[16]

John Croxton was busy, too. After advising the 8th Iowa and 4th Kentucky of the impending breakout, he rode south into a large field with Jim Brownlow and a few aides and orderlies. A precipitous ravine, coursed by a branch of Sandy Creek, cut across the south end of the clearing, but Brownlow soon pointed out a small wooden bridge (perhaps the one Jones had built) near Brown's Mill. Croxton sent Brownlow to bring up the 1st Tennessee and dispatched another rider to summon the rest of the brigade, while he waited with McCook, who had joined the little cluster of horsemen gathered near the mill.

Brownlow's regiment had just crossed the bridge when heavy firing erupted far behind them. Fearing Dorr's 8th Iowa was having trouble disengaging, Croxton halted the Tennesseans on the cleared crest of a high ridge just south of Sandy Creek and faced them to the rear. The firing soon ceased, and when Croxton saw the 4th Kentucky coming across the field, followed by what looked like the 8th Iowa, he parted company with McCook and ordered Brownlow to move out.

There were probably only 250 to 300 troopers in the column that filed through the woods, across the Corinth Road, and into a byroad leading toward the Chattahoochee. Directing Brownlow to keep moving, Croxton reined to the side of the road with three orderlies to wait for Dorr's 8th Iowa. He sent one orderly back to tell McCook the road to the river was clear and was still waiting anxiously for the 8th Iowa when the Rebel horsemen Wheeler had sent to cut off the raiders' escape suddenly appeared in the wake of Brownlow's retreating column. Croxton dashed back to the Corinth Road with his two orderlies to hurry up Dorr's Iowans, but the road was blocked. Rebels were everywhere, and Croxton and his two companions were suddenly very much alone.[17]

Joseph Dorr was still on the battlefield. Ignoring the wound in his side, he had risen from his ambulance to lead his regiment when Croxton informed him of the plan to cut through the Rebel lines. He was still waiting for orders when he received a report Croxton was missing and he was now in command of the 1st Brigade. Turning the 8th Iowa over to Major Isett, Dorr inquired after the 1st Tennessee and 4th Kentucky. Captain Sutherland, the brigade adjutant, soon reported neither regiment could be found.

This left Dorr with barely a hundred men. Some of them were wounded. Others had lost their weapons. Those who still had guns were almost out of ammunition. Dorr ordered them to move to the left, intending to follow the route Croxton had taken.

The head of his column was just entering the narrow woods that screened the big field to the south when McCook came galloping back and asked if Dorr could form his regiment on the crest of a little hill they had just passed to "check the enemy."

"I can," Dorr answered.

McCook ordered him to do so at once, adding, "This retreat must be protected."

As McCook hurried away, Dorr directed Major Isett to deploy the regiment. "This was in plain sight of the enemy," Dorr noted, "who were seen advancing."[18]

McCook continued to the rear, rounding up Miller's artillerymen and remnants of the 2nd and 4th Indiana. Among those who fell in behind him was Lieutenant Colonel Horace P. Lamson. Unable to exercise command of his regiment after his horse fell on him on July 29, Lamson had sat out the fight in an ambulance. Now he suddenly found the strength to climb into the saddle again.

"We then made a feint on one side of the Confederate front," recounted Sergeant Barnes Hutson of the 2nd Indiana, "charging as though we were attempting to go out and immediately wheeled and passed the Confederate soldiers who had been our prisoners, who waved at us and yelled, 'Get out boys, if you can.'"

Overtaking the 8th Indiana, McCook told Fielder Jones to give the order to advance. "Forward Gallop March!"

Company D of the 8th Indiana thundered down the narrow road four abreast, through the neck of woods, and into the sprawling field Croxton's brigade had crossed earlier. The rest of the 8th Indiana followed at a brisk trot, so suddenly and in such close order that half the regiment got through the Rebel lines before a shot was fired. "The enemy was in some places near enough to almost touch the horses," marveled Fielder Jones, and by the time his rear ranks reached the woods, the column was under a heavy fire. The fleeing Federals ran the gauntlet virtually unscathed, but a short distance beyond the woods, they came to the little bridge over Sandy Creek, slowing down as men and horses bunched up trying to get across this bottleneck.

"The enemy now became more bold," noted Corporal Alexander Eckel of the 4th Tennessee, "and rallied on a rise in the field and was firing into the rear of the column when a detachment of Co. C was ordered to charge on them and drive them back."[19]

Joseph Dorr watched as the tail end of McCook's column disappeared in the distance. "In this position we were obliged to remain," he recalled, "seeing the enemy moving towards our flank, until the fragments of regiments, the stragglers and skulkers, who filled the road upon which the column had moved, got out of our way. Every minute's delay I knew lessened our chances of escape, but there was no help for it, and the regiment, with a few exceptions, gallantly did their duty, calmly awaiting orders."

Dorr heard heavy firing to the south as McCook's column cut its way out, then silence. Realizing the Rebels were ignoring him and racing down the Corinth Road to intercept the retreat, he ordered his men back to their horses, intending to move cross-country and interpose his regiment between the pursuing Confederates and the flank of the fleeing column. The tangled woods quickly frustrated this attempt. Retracing his steps, Dorr then tried to follow McCook's route, but had gone only a short distance when part of the Federal 4th Tennessee came stampeding toward him, screaming they had been cut off. The forest road was so narrow Dorr and his men had to backtrack to let them pass. When they tried to move forward again, it was too late.

Sul Ross's brigade, reinforced by the arrival of the 6th and 9th Texas Cavalry, stood squarely between the retreating Iowans and the rear of McCook's column. There was no escape. At the urging of most of his officers, Dorr reluctantly agreed to surrender, but game to the last, he turned command of the regiment over to Major Isett and fled into the woods on foot with his adjutant, Lieutenant Henry Belfield.

At 5:30 P.M., Isett raised a white flag. Colonel Edward S. Worthington and Captain Thomas W. Brown, two of the Confederate officers McCook had captured at Fayetteville, accepted the surrender. A half hour passed. When no guards appeared, the Iowans began getting restless. Captain Brown finally had to summon some of Ross's Texans to make things official.[20]

The 8th Iowa's sacrifice enabled McCook and 1,200 officers and men to get across Sandy Creek. Skirting the high ground overlooking Brown's Mill, the fleeing horsemen soon came to a road about a mile south of the battlefield and turned to the right. Fielder Jones saw a Negro standing by the roadside and reined up. There was a question, a nod, and a few words of affirmation. Given a choice of guiding the Yankees to the Chattahoochee or a bullet in his brain, the black man quickly mounted a led horse and steered Jones's column into the Corinth Road.

Sergeant Edward Scott and "the best men" from Company D of the 8th Indiana led the way south. Ordered to ride through or over everything that got in their way, they had gone six and a half miles at what Private Jack Wilson called "a slapping rate" when they came to the bridge over New River. The flooring had been torn out, but Scott and his men dismounted, replaced the missing planks with fence rails, and the column hurried on, burning the bridge behind them.[21]

Joe Wheeler was about two and a half miles short of the bridge when darkness overtook him. By that time, it was clear the Yankees had fled in two directions. One column was moving southwest on the Corinth Road. The other was heading west, obviously intending to cross the Chattahoochee somewhere above Franklin.

Wheeler had anticipated that. Two hours earlier, he had sent Colonel George W. McKenzie's 5th Tennessee Cavalry and Colonel Amson W. Hobson's 3rd Arkansas Cavalry riding north to seize the nearest ford over the river. Now he ordered Robert Anderson's brigade, led by Colonel Edward Bird of the 5th Georgia after Anderson was wounded, to vigorously pursue the Federals fleeing down the Corinth Road.

Leaving "Red" Jackson, who had reported for duty just before sundown, to take charge of the prisoners and captured property, Wheeler and his staff started back to Newnan. It was getting late by the time they stopped and dismounted in front of Hugh Buchanan's white-pillared home on LaGrange Street. Buchanan was soldiering in Virginia. His frightened wife and children had spent much of the day cowering in the cellar, but they welcomed the little general, who politely asked permission to use their house as his headquarters. Shown to the study, Wheeler sat down behind a big plantation desk, spread his maps before him, and fell sound asleep.[22]

But there was no sleep for the frightened, hungry, demoralized fugitives riding hell-bent for the Chattahoochee that night. The first group to flee the battlefield, Major George Purdy and 310 officers and men from the 2nd and 4th Indiana, 5th Iowa, and 2nd Kentucky, enlisted the help of a Negro, who piloted them in "a zigzag direction through thick woods, miry swamps, and over rough hills" before striking a road leading directly to the Chattahoochee. About 9:00 that night, they reached Williams' (later Bowen's) Ferry, fifteen miles above Franklin. There was no ferryboat, but a bold trooper swam the muddy river and roused a resident on the west bank, telling him that 3,000 Rebels, on their way to burn a Yankee wagon train, were waiting to cross. The civilian obligingly showed his visitor three dugout canoes which were promptly pressed into service.

Purdy put the citizen under arrest to keep him from spreading the alarm, posted a strong rear guard, and ordered his troopers to strip their mounts. After each canoe was loaded with as many saddles as it could safely carry, two men paddled while a third held the reins of four horses who were forced to swim alongside. Purdy got his horses across first, then the mules, but it was maddeningly slow work.

All night long, the makeshift fleet shuttled back and forth. One horse drowned, but the rest of the command crossed with only a few mishaps, and at 6:00 A.M., July 31, Major Purdy, Sergeant Thomas Reed, and the last squad stepped safely ashore.[23]

The scene was repeated a few miles downstream, where Jim Brownlow's column, following "hasty directions" from several friendly Negroes, reached the Chattahoochee near Hollingsworth's Ferry at 1:00 A.M., July 31. Contrary to expectations, they found neither ford nor ferryboat and the precipitous banks made it virtually impossible to get their horses down to the water. Two frail canoes were the only boats at hand.

Utterly exhausted, many troopers lay down and went to sleep while they waited for their turn to cross. A few prodded their tired mounts over the bank, clinging to fistfuls of mane or tail as the animal swam for the far shore. But many of these men were east Tennessee mountaineers who could not swim. Doffing his hat, coat, boots, and breeches, Brownlow repeatedly braved the current to help men struggling in the water.

Despite his heroics, fewer than 150 troopers had gotten across when a flurry of gunshots erupted at daybreak. Hoofbeats pounded through the corn tasseling along the riverbank as Wheeler's 5th Tennessee and 3rd Arkansas regiments stampeded Brownlow's startled rear guard. In the wild, confused fight that followed, frightened Federals who had waited all night for their turn to cross the river leaped into the water and swam for their lives, only to flounder in a hail of lead. Others, too tired to fight, too demoralized to run, threw up their hands and surrendered.

"Col. Brownlow . . . escaped capture by our regiment by a hair's breadth," noted 5th Tennessee cavalryman William E. Sloane. Abandoning the fine horse he had

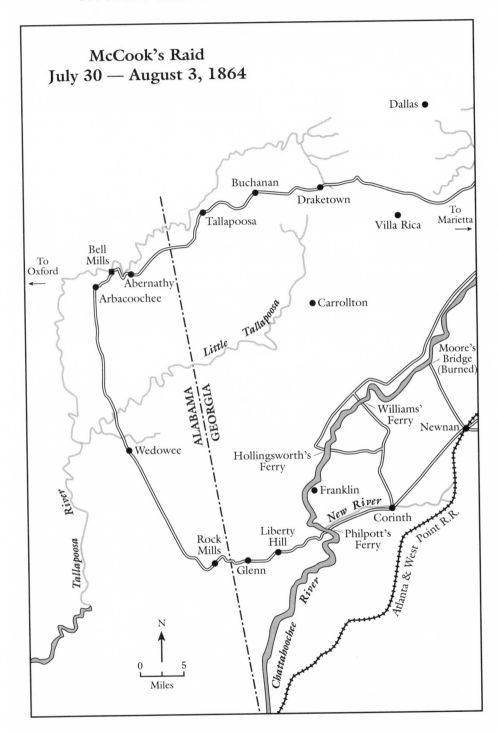

McCook's Raid
July 30 — August 3, 1864

captured at Fayetteville, Brownlow leaped from the bank and swam the river under a heavy fire. Barefoot, bareheaded, and not wearing much else in between, he purloined some civilian clothes as soon as he came ashore and began rounding up survivors.

Captain James West of the 4th Kentucky and about a hundred men stranded on the east bank were taken prisoner. "No sooner had we surrendered our arms than the work of robbing us began," recorded Private A. J. Tharp. "They took our pocket-knives from us, traded us hats that were worn out and full of holes for ours, exchanged their worn-out coats with us, and the next thing was to trade shoes with us, but some little trouble came up in the way of getting a fit. I soon saw that it did not amount to much, because if one man could not fit another could, so it was not long until we were dispossessed of all our clothes, pocket-knives, watches, gold pens, and everything of value."

Rebel troopers captured quite a few stragglers in the surrounding woods and swamps, and soon herded perhaps as many as 300 prisoners down the dusty road toward Newnan. "They rode," noted Sergeant John Vaughter of the 4th Kentucky. "We walked." Marching four abreast, surrounded by a cordon of guards, they had not gone far when one of the Rebel officers stopped at a farmhouse and asked for a drink of water. A nice-looking lady, accompanied by a Negro girl, brought a pitcher to the front gate and after listening to the officer give a glowing account of the fight at the river, she turned with a pleasant smile and asked, "Would any of you soldiers like a drink?"

"Madam," answered a captured cavalryman, "I would like a drink, please."

The woman's warm smile hardened into icy contempt. "You low-flung, thieving Yank," she sneered, "—would I give *you* a drink? Not unless it had strychnine in it. You ought to be hung, every one of you."[24]

The third and largest Yankee column, 1,200 horsemen who had fled down the Corinth Road with McCook, also reached the Chattahoochee in the waning hours of July 30. Crossing the hastily repaired bridge at New River and galloping through the crossroads village of Corinth, they turned right on the Franklin Road, overtaking Major Root and about a dozen 8th Iowa cavalrymen who had gotten separated from their regiment after charging through Ross's brigade. Two miles beyond Corinth, the fleeing Federals turned sharply to the southwest on the road that led to Philpott's Ferry, eight and a half miles below Franklin.

Sixty-six-year-old David Philpott had either heard the distant rumble of artillery that afternoon or somehow gotten word the Yankees were coming. By the time McCook's advance guard, Company D of the 8th Indiana, reached the river about 11:00 that night, the ferryboat was gone. Realizing something had to be done to buy the exhausted column some time, Fielder Jones sent Captains Francis M. Scott and Jacob Mitchell and Companies I and K of the 8th Indiana backtracking toward Corinth. Ordered to frustrate any pursuit, these Hoosiers rode hard and set fire to the only remaining bridge over New River, just as Rebel horsemen appeared on the other side.

In the meantime, the crowd of men left standing at Philpott's Ferry swelled with the arrival of each succeeding company. "The room between the river and the bluff was about sufficient for half our number," noted William Lightcap of the 5th Iowa, and the broad current coursed wide and deep under the black dome of a moonless sky.

Anyone trying to swim to the west bank risked drowning. Anyone lingering on the east bank faced a slow death in the Rebel prison at Andersonville. Weighing these grim prospects, some of the men began building rafts of fence rails tied together with link straps and bridle reins. Others, looking to more immediate needs, looted Philpott's smokehouse, emptied his corncrib, and butchered one of his sows. Still others simply slid from their saddles and slept soundly in the middle of the road.

Late that night, some of Philpott's slaves told the 8th Indiana's Captain Edward Reeves that the ferryboat had been poled about a third of a mile upstream and scuttled in the mouth of New River. Following an obliging Negro to the spot, troopers waded into the quiet, still water and began wrestling stone ballast out of the bottom of the sunken craft. The gunwales broke the surface and after some furious bailing, they were able to float the ferry back downstream at 4:00 A.M.

Company D of the 8th Indiana ferried across first, pulling the boat hand over hand on a chain of long metal rods stretched across the river by a windlass on the east bank. The rest of the regiment followed, loading the twenty-by-eight-foot flat with as many men and horses as it could carry.

"Tremendous efforts were put forth to get the command over, and various methods were resorted to," noted Corporal Alexander Eckel. "Every horse that could be carried over in the boat was put on it, while many forced their horses into the water and compelled them to swim over, beside the boat while they held their heads firmly by the bridle over the gunwale. But few of the horses were able to climb out of the water when they reached the shore, being so badly jaded before reaching the river, and struggling so desperately while crossing that they dropped down in the water and were drowned. Many forced their horses in the river and they swam across, but many of them were too exhausted to get up the bank and they too were drowned. A few men, when they got their horses to swimming, caught hold of their tails and by this means secured a crossing for themselves."

As the ferry plied back and forth, a ten-man squad from Company D of the 8th Indiana deployed to picket the road on the west side of the river. "Sunday morning, the last day of July, found us still busy crossing over men and horses," wrote Private Jack Wilson, "horses being driven into the river, either to sink, or swim, turn back to the same side, or get across, just as chance might determine, at the same time might be seen men crossing, by swiming, hanging to a log, or a rail; some on horses' backs, others clinging to the manes and tails of animals, all seeming determined to get the river between them and Johnny Reb."[25]

But Johnny Reb was tired, too. Shortly after leaving Brown's Mill, Edward Bird had halted Anderson's brigade long enough for the men to feed their horses. Five miles down the Corinth Road, he halted again and allowed his men to sleep until nearly daylight. Then he had to repair the damaged bridge over New River. As a result, it took Bird twelve hours to travel the same distance the Yankees had covered in five. It was after 8:00 A.M. before his troopers finally reached the heights overlooking Philpott's Ferry.

"I do not know which were in the worst plight, pursuers or pursued," admitted Sergeant John Ash of the 5th Georgia. He and his comrades had been marching and fighting almost constantly since July 26. Riding from Atlanta to Campbellton, Campbellton to Flat Shoals, and Flat Shoals to Newnan, they had put more miles behind them than any of Wheeler's other brigades. So many horses and riders had given out that when Bird ordered the column to dismount and deploy on foot, Ash's company could field only one officer and five men. From the hilltops ringing the landing, they aimed a plunging fire into the mass of men and horses struggling down below.[26]

Captain Josiah Stanley had just formed Company D of the 8th Indiana to take the advance when the first shots rang out. Every head snapped toward the sound. Powder-stained fingers probed nearly empty cartridge boxes and chambered a few precious rounds. A carbine cracked, then another and another, as Yankee troopers on both sides of the river began returning the Rebel fire. Scores of men still waiting to get across thronged around the landing, but the soldiers operating the ferry cravenly refused to return until troopers on the west bank compelled them at gunpoint.

"By that time there were no more than two or three boat loads of soldiers left on the east side of the river . . . ," recounted Sergeant Barnes Hutson of the 2nd Indiana. "When the boat approached the bank . . . the rush began, everyone wanted to be first on the boat. I was among the front ranks, and was pushed off into the river, but swam and climbed into the boat."

As the bullets whined overhead, Private William Lightcap of the 5th Iowa stripped the saddle and bridle off his horse and drove it into the river. Yelling encouragement, he clambered into the ferry, urging his mount to keep swimming. "I kept my eyes on him from the start," Lightcap recalled, "for fear that another might get him when he landed, for many were wading into the river nearly to their necks to get anybody's horse that was nearing the shore. About the time we pulled up along side of him, to my utter disgust and dismay, I saw him turn back and land at the starting point. I then lost sight of him forever."

As soon as the ferry nudged the west bank, there was a mad scramble to get ashore, get a horse, get out of range. The last troopers to disembark knocked a hole in the bottom of the ferry and sank it. This foiled any pursuit, but it also stranded the rear guard on the east side of the river.

Seeing they were being left behind, Lieutenant Pleasant C. Smith of the 4th Tennessee abandoned the rail breastworks his detachment had built at the foot of the hills and bolted through Philpott's cornfield. Ducking into a ravine that emptied into the river a short distance downstream, he and three or four of his men hastily fashioned and launched a raft out of fence rails. Lieutenant Stanley Hall of the 4th Indiana spurred his horse over the steep bank, clinging to the animal until he gained the opposite shore. Others abandoned their mounts and swam for their lives. Some of them drowned in the attempt.

Corporal David Sherry of the 8th Indiana was mortally wounded when a bullet broke his left thigh. Sergeant Tom Jackson recorded that a sergeant who had reached the supposed safety of the west bank was killed in the ranks of the 8th Indiana, but no one knew his name because "there were a no. who did not belong."[27]

At least three more of McCook's men were killed and three were wounded. About sixty troopers trapped on the east side of the river fought until they ran out of ammunition and surrendered. "They cheerfully sacrificed themselves to insure the safety of their comrades," McCook later wrote. "History contains no nobler example of devotion, or names more worthy to be handed down to posterity as heroes."[28]

Victorious Confederates also captured a hundred stand of arms, but it was the loss of an estimated 200 to 400 horses and mules that McCook's men felt most keenly.

"There were no more than half enough horses to mount us," William Lightcap lamented after reaching the west bank. "Some had other's horses, and many a hot discussion arose, not only between the owners and those who had possession, but between their respective captains."

Fielder Jones urged McCook to order all those who had horses to ride five miles, dismount, then let those who were afoot ride an equal distance, changing back and forth until foragers found enough horses and mules to mount the command. McCook refused to listen. "We will go with the mounted [men] and the rest will have to look out for themselves," he said.

Private Lightcap concluded, "McCook . . . was a little scared."[29]

Joe Wheeler, on the other hand, was furious. He reached Philpott's Ferry late that morning and immediately took Colonel Bird to task. "His instructions from me were to press on rapidly after the enemy and to report to me by courier . . . ," railed the little general who had nodded off over his maps. "It was full daylight before I heard from him at all, and then I learned that he had fallen asleep and allowed the demoralized mass to escape to the river."[30]

15

McCOOK'S RAID
THE CHATTAHOOCHEE RIVER TO MARIETTA

JULY 31–AUGUST 3, 1864

O for a horse with wings!

—William Shakespeare, *Cymbeline*

The first wounded men began trickling into Newnan about 4:00 P.M., July 30. Fannie Beers was at work in the wards of Buckner Hospital when a messenger handed her a note from chief surgeon William T. McAllister:

> Some of our men too badly wounded to be moved right away. Come out at once. Bring cordials and brandy,—soup, if you have it,—also fill the enclosed requisition at the drug-store. Lose no time.

Loading bandages, lint, and other supplies into a buggy, Mrs. Beers sped down the Corinth Road. She found Dr. McAllister at an improvised field hospital about three miles out of town.

"From the hospital-tent distressing groans and screams came forth," she later wrote. "The surgeons, both Confederate and Federal, were busy, with coats off, sleeves rolled up, shirt-fronts and hands bloody."

Supplied with a bottle of peach brandy and two canteens of water she slung over her shoulder, Mrs. Beers accompanied Dr. McAllister across a plowed field littered with guns, haversacks, accoutrements, and all the blood-red wreckage of war. "The plaintive cries and awful struggles of the horses first impressed me," she noted. "They were shot in every conceivable manner, showing shattered heads, broken and bleeding limbs, and protruding entrails. They would not yield quietly to death, but continually raised their heads or struggled half-way to their feet, uttering cries of pain, while their distorted eyes seemed to reveal their suffering and implore relief." A gunshot echoed close by, as a soldier put one of the suffering animals out of his misery.

"The dead lay around us on every side," she continued, "singly and in groups and *piles*; men and horses, in some cases, apparently inextricably mingled. Some lay as if peacefully sleeping; others, with open eyes, seemed to glare at any who bent above them. Two men lay as they had died, the 'Blue' and the 'Gray,' clasped in fierce embrace . . . one was shot in the head, the throat of the other was partly torn away. . . . In a corner of the field, supported by a pile of broken fence-rails, a soldier sat apparently beckoning us. On approaching him we discovered that he was quite dead, although he sat upright, with open eyes and extended arm."

By the time Mrs. Beers crossed the field, her shoes were smeared with blood. The hem of her dress was soaked with it. As she approached a shady spot where several wounded men lay, she was greeted with plaintive cries of "Water! Water!"

Mixing water and brandy in a small cup she drew from her pocket, she knelt beside a Yankee sergeant. A stream of blood trickled from his mouth when she tried to raise his head. Gently wiping it off, she pressed the cup to his lips, but he could not swallow. Reluctantly, she eased him down and moved on to the next man, who drank eagerly. A third soldier, unable to speak, beseeched her with doleful eyes. As she cradled his head against her arm, an ugly crimson stain spread across the sleeve of her dress.

"So we went on," she recounted wearily, "giving water, brandy, or soup; sometimes successful in reviving a patient, sometimes only able to whisper a few words of comfort to the dying. There were many more left, and Dr. McAllister never for a moment intermitted his efforts to save them. Later came more help, surgeons, and attendants with stretchers, etc. Soon all were moved who could bear it."

Accompanied by Dr. E. P. Wellford, Mrs. Beers started back to her buggy. As they walked past two overturned cannon lying near the road, they heard muffled cries coming from a log cabin. At first, no one appeared to be inside, but upon investigating, Dr. Wellford found a pair of legs dangling in the fireplace. Grasping the flailing limbs, the doctor pulled with all his might. The screams got louder.

"Stop your infernal noise," the doctor commanded, "and try to help yourself while I pull."

Assisted by several others who had heard the commotion, Wellford yanked and tugged until a black man emerged from the chimney; "not a negro," explained Mrs. Beers, "but a white man, whose blue eyes, glassy with terror, shone through the soot which had begrimed his face." He had climbed into the chimney to escape the battle's fury and the sight of him sent Mrs. Beers into gales of hysterical laughter. Then, overwhelmed by a flood of pent-up emotions, she began sobbing uncontrollably.[1]

Lieutenant George Griscom of Ross's 9th Texas estimated at least 150 dead Yankees lay sprawled on the battlefield and more than twice that many were wounded. Captain George Knox Miller of the 8th Confederate called it "the greatest slaughter I ever saw in front of a cavalry line. . . ." Despite these assertions, Federal losses probably numbered only about a hundred.[2]

Confederate casualties were surprisingly light. Ross's brigade reported five dead, eleven wounded. The hard-fighting 8th Texas had two killed and about ten wounded. Partial returns from the 4th Tennessee showed two dead and six wounded, while Anderson's brigade counted at least three killed and four or five wounded. The hospitals in Newnan admitted thirty-five severely wounded Confederates, twenty-seven belonging to Wheeler's cavalry and eight from Roddey's command. "Our hospital rats did good service," added Newnan's chief surgeon, Dr. B. W. Wible. "Cripples of all kinds mounted horses and aided in the fight. One was wounded."[3]

Private A. W. Sparks of the 9th Texas was among those searching the woods that evening for missing comrades. He had just laid a badly wounded man in the yard of a farmhouse when he discovered a Union officer had taken refuge inside. Sparks went in and ordered the man to give up his side arms. He refused. Wide-eyed with terror, the lady of the house darted from the room and up a flight of stairs, with the fugitive Federal in hot pursuit. Sparks bounded after them and found the Yankee at the top of the stairs, using the woman as a shield. Sparks ordered him to surrender by the count of ten or face the consequences. The Yankee held his hostage closer, vowing never to surrender his arms to the enemies of his country. The woman screamed. More Confederate soldiers crowded up the stairs. Sparks nervously began counting off the seconds. In one swift motion, the Yankee reached for his gunbelt, clasped it around the hysterical woman's waist, and was quickly ushered downstairs.[4]

Another Yankee officer lay in a pool of blood at the back door of John Carpenter's house near the Corinth Road, his head pillowed on his uniform coat. He wore a fine white linen shirt with a tucked front, and a diamond ring shone on his finger. A straggling Federal, possibly looking for a fat wallet, knelt beside him and was pulling the coat out from under his head when the officer roused, hurling furious invectives at the thief. The incident made a profound impression on twelve-year-old Tommy Carpenter, who later recalled he never heard such cussing in his life.[5]

The fighting had scarcely ended when Roddey's troops began escorting the first Federal prisoners back to Newnan. They had gone about two miles when they met a crowd of curious soldiers and civilians coming down the Corinth Road.

"You have the sons of bitches!" one man sneered contemptuously.

"That comes from the lips of a damned coward," roared the 8th Indiana's Tom Harrison. "None but slinks and cowards would talk like that to prisoners."

"I'll show you whether I'm a coward and a slink," the Rebel yelled, lunging at Harrison.

"Col. Harrison reached out as though he meant to take the Johnny in," observed Sergeant John Farnsworth of the 1st Wisconsin, "but at this juncture the guard interfered, and drove the little piece of impertinence away and we were marched silently to Newnan."

Jeering crowds of men and women gathered on the sidewalks to gawk at them. Guards halted the procession on Perry Street and herded the prisoners into a two-story cotton warehouse, midway between the courthouse and the depot.[6]

However, most of the captured Yankees spent the night of July 30–31 on the battlefield. "After our surrender," explained Hiram Bird of the 8th Iowa, "the officers had a grand hand-shake, for we had many Kentuckians and Tennesseeans in our brigade, and as the fight was over old acquaintances met as friends. We were then allowed to sleep till morning on the battlefield, which we did with a will, having been on the raid for three days and nights. Early in the morning the scalping process began, and those who had nothing were the most fortunate, for they did not suffer the humiliation that attended those who had valuables on their persons. My loss was a gold watch, a present from home. We all suffered alike, on the supposition that we had secured everything in our possession on the raid."

By daylight, Ross's Texans had corralled 587 prisoners, including the 8th Iowa's Colonel Dorr. He and Lieutenant Belfield had wandered through the woods all night, hoping to escape on foot, only to be challenged by Rebel pickets at every turn. Captured at daybreak, they were reunited with the rest of the 8th Iowa and chided for "not taking a night's sleep on the ground when it was offered."

Dorr surveyed the battlefield with a heavy heart. "Our dead . . . were robbed of all valuables," he wrote, "and in most cases entirely denuded of their clothes. I saw fifteen of my own regiment lying thus beside the road."

Iowa Sergeant John Huff was part of a detail assigned to bury these men. He alleged that several bodies, wounded in the arms, legs, or torso, also had powder burns on their faces where they had been shot at point-blank range.

Later that morning, guards started the prisoners toward Newnan. It was a six-mile march and throats were dry, lips parched, by the time they reached the warehouse on

Perry Street. Desperate for something to drink, Sergeant Daniel Bishard and several others broke ranks as the column passed a horse trough. Guards forced them back into line at gunpoint, just as a lone horseman galloped up.

"Stop those men and let them have all the water that they want," he demanded. "I have been a prisoner with them for two days and they let me have all the water I wanted."

Looking up as he cupped the brackish water to his lips, Sergeant Bishard recognized the Rebel paymaster he had captured at Fayetteville.[7]

The long, shuffling column of bluecoated captives gave Newnan ample reason for rejoicing, but even amid the cheers and jubilation, Kate Cumming heard "many complaints against General Wheeler."

"It seems that General Roddy [sic] had his men all ready to make a charge," she wrote, "and General Wheeler would not give the word of command. Many of the prisoners say, had the charge been made, all would have surrendered. . . ."

"Our forces were handled miserably . . . ," added Captain George Knox Miller of the 8th Confederate Cavalry. "If we had had a commanding officer with any brains not a one of them would have escaped."

"Oh! for a few more Forrests and Whartons to command our cavalry," lamented Chaplain Bunting of the 8th Texas.

Despite his detractors, Wheeler had won an impressive victory. In addition to over 500 prisoners, his men had captured two cannon, eleven ambulances, several hundred horses and mules, and enough saddles, bridles, blankets, halters, pistols, carbines, and accoutrements to outfit the whole Texas brigade in true regulation style. Other trophies included the regimental colors of the 2nd Indiana and the 8th Iowa and two Confederate flags (one belonging to the 2nd Arkansas Dismounted Cavalry) the raiders had looted from Rebel wagons at Fayetteville.

Company A of the 8th Confederate Cavalry also captured the colors of McCook's 4th Tennessee. "The same," Captain George Knox Miller noted smugly in a letter of his wife, "that on the 15th ult. waved over our homes in Talladega."[8]

Private John Will Dyer's share of the spoils was a big black mule he rode into town about midday.

"Glad to see you," hailed an elderly gent, "where did you get my mule?"

"Your mule?" Dyer asked skeptically. "Is this your mule?"

"Yes," came the reply. "That's Prince. Everybody in this country knows Prince. Why, I've owned Prince for twenty years."

Dyer demanded proof. In less than ten minutes, the old man had gathered twenty witnesses, each of whom affirmed, "Yes, that's Prince."

As Dyer surrendered the reins, the old man introduced himself as Mr. Griffith. He was the postmaster at Palmetto and the Yankees had stolen Prince when they passed through there three days earlier. Grateful for the return of his mule, he asked how much Dyer was going to charge him.

Dyer modestly claimed he was only doing his duty as a soldier, but the postmaster persisted. "If you won't take any pay," he said, "I am going to make you a nice present anyhow."

Reaching into his pocket, he drew out a fat leather wallet bulging with crisp new Confederate bills. Dyer watched in keen anticipation as he leafed through them in descending order, from five-hundred-dollar notes down to twenties. Repeating the procedure, he finally found what he was looking for and handed Dyer a fifty-cent shinplaster.[9]

By this time, Newnan was buzzing about a convalescent captain who had gone to the battlefield as a spectator on July 30 and volunteered to take a captured Yankee back to town. Instead of escorting his prisoner to Newnan, he had taken him into some woods and shot him, claiming vengeance for his mother and sister, who had been mistreated by Union soldiers.

"Such men ought not to be permitted to bring dishonor on a brave people, and deserve punishment," wrote Kate Cumming, and some of Wheeler's men vowed to hang the cowardly wretch if they caught him.[10]

For the most part, however, the captured raiders were well treated. The already crowded Confederate hospitals in Newnan admitted at least sixty-four wounded Federals, about half of them from the 8th Iowa. Among the latter was Captain Elliott Shurtz. A bullet had broken his left arm near the wrist; two of the fingers on his right hand had been amputated.

"He was a pitiful sight," noted Kate Cumming. "I told him I had more sympathy for him than I had for our own men." When he asked why, she said because "his conscience could not be at rest, like theirs."

Another nurse could scarcely conceal her enmity when she saw a captured Kentucky surgeon she knew. "His wife was one of my most intimate school friends," Laetitia Nutt recalled, "I know him very well, was at his wedding and went to school with his sister." Now she could not "entertain a thought or feeling that was not perfectly antagonistic."

As Fannie Beers made her rounds that morning, she recognized one of her favorite patients, Willie Hutson, a Mississippi boy she had nursed through a bout of typhoid fever. "Bright as a lark" the day before, "pleading to be sent back to the front," he had marched toward the sound of the guns at Brown's Mill. Now he lay with a Yankee bullet through his breast, so near death he did not recognize her. As Mrs. Beers hovered over him, she felt a hand on her shoulder. Turning, she saw the kindly face of Dr. Joshua Gore and a Yankee surgeon at his side.

"This is one of my old chums . . . ," Dr. Gore began.

"Oh, doctor!" Mrs. Beers cried. "I *cannot,*—look," she said gesturing toward the dying boy and then the entire ward. Hot tears streamed down her face as she hurried from the room and locked herself in her office. She did not want to meet any Yankees. She did not want to nurse them. They had killed her poor Willie.

Soon there was a knock at the door. Someone handed her a note, which read:

> I know how bitterly you feel, but pray for strength to cast out evil spirits from your heart. Forget that the suffering men, thrown upon our kindness and forbearance, are *Yankees.* Remember only that they are God's creatures and helpless prisoners. They need you. Think the matter over and do not disappoint me.
>
> Gore.

Drying her tears, Mrs. Beers strode resolutely toward the low brick building where the most seriously wounded Federals lay. On her way, she passed more than one hospital orderly carrying away a bloody arm or leg. Upon entering the dimly lit ward, she found her new patients "silent, repellent, and evidently expectant of insult and abuse." Suffering was etched on every face.

A Yankee surgeon sensed her antipathy. "Madam," he said, "one-half the attention you give to your own men will save life here."

Reluctantly, Mrs. Beers moved among the wounded prisoners, giving this one a sip of water and that one a few spoonfuls of soup. Contempt soon gave way to compassion, and she performed her duties diligently. Nothing, however, could mollify her disdain for the Yankee doctors.

"These Federal surgeons appeared to me to be very indifferent to the comfort of their patients and to avoid all unnecessary trouble," she noted scornfully. "They were tardy in beginning their work on the morning after the battle, and, when they were ready, coolly sent in *requisitions* for *chloroform,* which, having been . . . long since declared by their government 'contraband of war,' was almost unattainable, and used by our Confederate surgeons only in extreme cases."[11]

Hiram Bird, the 8th Iowa's hospital steward, learned a lesson about wartime shortages that evening when he asked a guard for a match to light a candle, the only illumination for a room nearly half a block long.

"We have not seen a match or pin since the war commenced," the guard replied, "as we depended on the North for these supplies."

When Bird asked what he was supposed to do, the guard took him to a back window and pointed to a banked fire in the yard, explaining that everyone in town depended on this fire to keep their stoves burning and their candles lit.

"I informed him that if he would go with me to a drug store I could fix this match business in a minute," Bird recounted. "So I used my knowledge gained in the Iowa Wesleyan College Chemistry Laboratory and had the druggist make a powder of chlorite of potash and sugar. When I touched this powder with a taper saturated with nitric acid I had a blaze." For months afterward, the druggist used Bird's formula to provide everyone in the county with "Yankee matches."[12]

McCook had left five surgeons and six assistant surgeons to treat his wounded. Seven of them were taken to Newnan with the prisoners, but surgeons Horace T. Persons of the 1st Wisconsin and John F. Taggart of the 4th Indiana and assistant surgeons Daniel H. Warren of the 8th Iowa and William V. Rutledge of the 2nd Indiana labored for three days at a makeshift field hospital, caring for men too badly wounded to be moved. Despite their best efforts, Lieutenant Colonel Torrey died on August 2, "abusing the 2d Kentucky till the last."[13]

Fannie Beers believed the Federal surgeons were "far rougher and less merciful" than their Confederate counterparts. "I do not believe they ever gave the poor shattered fellows the benefit of a doubt," she wrote. "It was easier to amputate than to attend a tedious, troublesome recovery. So, off went legs and arms by the wholesale."[14]

The continuing influx of prisoners put a severe strain on Newnan's limited resources. Hospital quartermasters dipped into their own supplies to furnish bareheaded, barefoot Yankees with hats and shoes. Kate Cumming even saw some of her patients give up their rations.

Early on August 1, Wheeler telegraphed Hood's headquarters:

> We have just completed the killing, capturing, and breaking up of the entire raiding party under General McCook—some nine hundred and fifty (950) prisoners—two pieces of Artillery, and twelve hundred horses and equipments captured.

Scouts and patrols brought in an additional 31 Yankees the next day. Another 122 arrived on August 3, bringing the total number of prisoners to 35 officers and about 1,250 enlisted men. The officers occupied two small rooms on the second floor of the warehouse on Perry Street.

"I made them as comfortable as I could, and fed them well," wrote Lieutenant Samuel Barron of the 3rd Texas, who commanded the guard detail. "I would turn the officers out every day into the front porch or vestibule of the warehouse, where they would get fresh air. They were quite a lively lot of fellows, except one old man, Colonel Harrison, I believe, of the Eighth Iowa [Indiana]. They appreciated my kindness and made me quite a number of small presents when the time came for them to leave."[15]

On the day orders came transferring them to the Confederate prison at Macon, the officers bid farewell to their men, which was not done, noted Lieutenant Henry Belfield, "without tears on both sides." Guards soon marched them down to the depot, and as the Yankee officers stood on the platform, waiting for the train, they regaled a crowd of curious onlookers with a medley of patriotic songs. "I remember particularly that 'Down with the traitor, up with the star,' was rendered with great unction," Belfield recalled. "The crowd surrounding us not only manifested no symptoms of anger, but applauded. Seeing that they were interested, and not having had our hunger satisfied for several days, we declined to continue our musical exercises until we were supplied with food. In this way we procured some cold victuals." A train soon arrived and carried them first to East Point, then to Macon, over the same tracks they had torn up at Palmetto and Lovejoy's Station only a few days earlier.[16]

By this time, Sherman was getting decidedly concerned about his cavalry. On July 29 and again on July 30, as part of "a vigorous demonstration" to "create a diversion" in favor of his raiding columns, he sent Colonel Israel Garrard's 7th Ohio nosing into Decatur.

Garrard's regiment was part of Stoneman's division. Arriving from Kentucky on July 27, too late to accompany the expedition, they had been assigned to cover the left flank of Schofield's XXIII Corps, picketing the roads to the east and north after the Army of the Tennessee moved to the west side of Atlanta. Their first foray into Decatur on July 29 yielded nothing of note, but on July 30 they brought back an interesting rumor: Yankee cavalry had cut the Macon railroad at Jonesboro.

"Order Colonel Garrard to feel into Decatur again in the morning," Sherman telegraphed Schofield late that evening, "and, without seeming anxious, to pick up further news of our cavalry."

Early the next morning, Garrard reoccupied Decatur for the third time in three days. He talked with a Mrs. Smith, who confided a Rebel scout had told her there had been "a fight of no great importance" with a force left at Flat Shoals and the rest of Stoneman's column had gone on to Jonesboro, destroyed ten miles of railroad, and moved down to Macon, tearing up the track as they went.

This information reached Sherman after a returning cavalryman told him Kenner Garrard's division was coming in on the Peachtree Road, and that Stoneman had gone on toward Macon. Fearing McCook "may be disappointed" if Stoneman failed to join him at Lovejoy's Station, Sherman ordered Schofield to send Israel Garrard's regiment to Vining's Station and down the west bank of the Chattahoochee to find the pontoon bridge McCook had left near Campbellton and to watch for his return, making the "utmost endeavors" to help him get back across the river.

After an all-night march, Garrard reached Vining's Station early on August 1, only to discover Captain Kossak's pontoon train had arrived the previous evening, escorted by the 9th Ohio, the 1st Wisconsin, and four guns from the 18th Indiana Battery. "Under these circumstances," Garrard advised Schofield at 9:00 A.M., "I have deemed it proper to report the facts and await your orders to move the pontoon train down the river to the vicinity of Campbellton."

Sherman had already learned of Kossak's return and McCook's apparent intention to ride completely around Atlanta. During the night, he had canceled the orders sending Israel Garrard down the Chattahoochee, and was eagerly awaiting further news. The first reports filtering into his headquarters on August 1 were encouraging. McCook had supposedly burned 300 wagonloads of Rebel clothing and broken up twelve miles of the Macon railroad. This was followed by a message that some of McCook's men had reached Marietta.[17]

Major Purdy was the first to arrive. After crossing the Chattahoochee at Williams' Ferry, he had secured a civilian guide and headed north. The overcast skies soon cleared and the sun beat down unmercifully. Several men were left afoot when their exhausted horses collapsed, but except for an hour's halt at noon, Purdy kept moving.

"The men and animals were completely played out . . . ," recounted Sergeant Reed of the 4th Indiana. "After dark it was impossible for the men to keep their places in the column. The horses would reel and stagger along the road, with the men asleep on them: and no wonder, for neither man nor beast had had as much as one good meal in five days and nights, and all the time were either fighting or marching rapidly."

Purdy had covered forty-five miles by the time he called a halt two miles short of the bridge at Sweetwater Town at 11:00 P.M. After a good night's rest, he rode into Marietta at noon on August 1 with 283 officers and men and went into camp on the north edge of town.[18]

Shortly afterward, a barefoot and bedraggled Jim Brownlow led nineteen equally haggard-looking horsemen into town. McCook had put the West Point and Macon railroads out of action for at least fifteen days, he told Colonel John G. Parkhurst, the Army of the Cumberland's provost marshal, and burned 500 Rebel wagons, including Hood's and Hardee's headquarters baggage. When Stoneman failed to keep the appointed rendezvous at Lovejoy's Station, McCook had doubled back, only to be overtaken near Newnan by Kelly's and Humes's divisions of Rebel cavalry and a division of Rebel infantry. In the fight that followed, Tom Harrison had been killed; McCook and the rest of the command had probably been captured.

Parkhurst immediately telegraphed this startling news to George Thomas's headquarters and started for the front at 12:30 P.M. with Brownlow in tow.

Thomas was in his shirtsleeves, sitting on a camp stool in front of his tent in the shade of a brush arbor, when Brownlow rode up that evening on "an ill favored horse, with an old bridle, and a blanket for a saddle." Dismounting, he raised a salute to the shabby straw hat he was wearing and repeated his story to the general.

Thomas listened quietly. Then he asked what became of McCook and the rest of the men.

"I don't know where in the devil they are," Brownlow replied.

Thomas gave the barefoot colonel a pair of boots and relayed his story to Sherman's headquarters.

"I can hardly believe it . . . ," a stunned Sherman wired General Halleck at 8:00 P.M., "[McCook] had 3,000 picked cavalry. . . ."

During the night, Thomas reported nearly 500 of McCook's men had reached Marietta, but that still left 2,500 cavalrymen unaccounted for. "I am quite unwell . . . ," Sherman telegraphed Thomas the next morning.[19]

While Sherman waited and worried, the hatless, coatless, half-famished remnants of McCook's command limped away from Philpott's Ferry on July 31, gnawing on roasting ears plucked from Philpott's cornfield. Many of the men had lost their weapons or thrown them away. Two or three hundred were on foot.[20]

Company D of the 8th Indiana led the way west, passing through Liberty Hill at 11:00 A.M. They would be the first to find trouble if it was waiting for them, but they also got first crack at "bread and biscuit, apple cobblers, with various other dainties" at the farms and plantations along the way. "At some places," noted Jack Wilson, "they gave us eatables very willingly, and seemed very glad to get us away on any terms."

The raiders also searched barns, corrals, and pastures for horses and mules, but riding stock was scarce in this sparsely settled part of Georgia. At the Garrett farm, just west of Liberty Hill, troopers discovered several mules, and the fact that one of them had not been broken to ride did nothing to dissuade one footsore Federal. "I'll ride him if the hair stays on him," he declared as he climbed aboard.

Unaccustomed to the weight of a rider on his back, the mule dashed down the road with a snort, bucking and kicking wildly. It soon came trotting home, alone.[21]

"Some of the men, in their desperation to keep up with the column, yoked cattle to carts, buggies and carriages—any kind of a vehicle that would carry men," recorded Alexander Eckel. "Some were mounted on oxen, and even cows, and the cavalcade presented many grotesque scenes, and, even desperate as the situation was, there was much merriment at the expense of the riders as the boys trudged along trying to keep up with the column."

The morning overcast soon burned off and the dismounted men, many of whom were barefooted, suffered terribly as they tried to keep pace with the column. Thirsty troopers flocked around every roadside well they passed and upon reaching a little creek that flowed across the road about five miles beyond the river, many of the men lay down in it, clothes and all. A summer shower brought some relief from the stifling heat, but even this was a mixed blessing. The thick, red Georgia clay clung to boots and shoes, "sticking closer than a brother," said Corporal Eckel.

The sun was at its zenith when one of the dismounted men staggered and collapsed with a mournful cry. Some of his comrades gingerly picked him up and carried him into J. C. Gamble's yard, just west of a little settlement called Glenn. Gamble offered what assistance he could, but the stricken trooper never regained consciousness and soon died.[22]

Private William Lightcap was also on the verge of collapse by the time the column crossed the Alabama state line that afternoon. He was about to seek refuge in the woods when Corporal Thomas Allen rode up alongside. "He insisted on me riding his horse a few miles," Lightcap recalled, "and by staying by him and changing often, he thought the horse would take us both through." Lightcap gladly accepted the offer and climbed into the saddle. Cresting the top of a long hill, he looked back and saw his friend limping up the road, obviously and painfully lame. Lightcap immediately dismounted and despite Allen's entreaties, refused to ride any farther. "I saw that it was useless to try to keep up," he confessed, "so seeing a squad of seven fall out to the left, I went with them."

Scores of men, surrendering to fatigue, had dropped out of the ranks by the time the weary column straggled into Rock Mills, Alabama, that afternoon. Troopers who had been with Rousseau remembered stopping here on July 20, and McCook halted, too.

Scouts had brought him a captured dispatch, indicating Robert Anderson's brigade had already crossed the Chattahoochee at Philpott's Ferry. Realizing the plodding pace of his dismounted detail only slowed him down, McCook called in his rear guard and sent an orderly galloping back down the road, ordering the men still on foot to scatter and make their way north toward Atlanta while the rest of the command continued westward to draw off the pursuit.

Leaving these unfortunates to their fate, the column moved on, "as fast," noted Williamson Ward, "as our jaded horses could travel." Afternoon wore into evening, evening slipped into night. Horses staggered and fell, unable to take another step. Troopers rode double or grimly trudged along on foot, but except for a few brief halts to press fresh horses or mules or to ask some sullen farmer to point the way to Rome, Georgia, the killing pace continued.

At 9:00 Sunday evening, Company D of the 8th Indiana approached the outskirts of Wedowee, Alabama, eighteen miles northwest of Rock Mills. The dark streets were deserted as they rode into town, but as the Hoosiers dismounted in the public square, they could plainly hear the loud voice of an impassioned preacher. "I say unto the white man, to the black man, and to the red man of the forest. . . ," they heard him exclaim as they gathered in the pools of yellow light spilling from the church windows and peered inside. Just then Corporal Hez Turner stepped through the front door with his Spencer cradled in his arms. A hush fell over the congregation. "A Yankee! A Yankee!" whispered some black brethren sitting in the back pews. Turner, just as he had done in LaFayette a few days earlier, bid the sermon to continue but the startled minister was suddenly at a loss for words and the entire congregation stampeded for the door.[23]

Wedowee was the first town of any size the raiders had encountered since leaving Newnan. It was also a hotbed of Union sentiment, but troopers made few distinctions between friend and foe as they searched barns and storehouses, dumping sacks of wheat, ears of corn, and shocks of oats into the streets to feed their mules and horses. "They were very hungry," sixty-three-year-old Joseph Benton noted of some officers who lingered at his house to eat dinner, "and told me that this was the first place they had come to where they had found any friends."

The stay in Wedowee was a short one. After the horses and mules had been fed, the raiders moved on, led by Richard Wadkins, an elderly Negro McCook enlisted as a guide. A few officers stayed behind and spent the night with former Alabama state senator Robert S. Heflin, a Union sympathizer, but McCook and most of his men bedded down between Wedowee Creek and the south bank of the Little Tallapoosa River.

Early the next morning, McCook summoned Heflin and his next-door neighbor, Robert S. M. Hunter, to his bivouac, a mile and a half north of town. As they rode into camp, Captain Edward Reeves of the 8th Indiana confiscated their mounts, saying he regretted taking property from Union men, but his soldiers needed horses. Hunter did not complain much, but Heflin, who had come home the night before to an empty barn and ransacked storerooms, protested that the raiders had taken everything the Rebels had not confiscated from him. McCook apologized and had an aide give Heflin a receipt for his livestock and provisions. For the next two hours he questioned both men about "the state of affairs generally" and asked directions to Marietta before parting company with them about 8:00 or 9:00 A.M.

The head of McCook's column had started northward some three or four hours earlier, "taking our leisure and feeding as often as the country would admit," noted Sergeant Tom Jackson. August 1 was election day in Randolph County, and after crossing the Little Tallapoosa, the advance guard encountered several voters on their way to the polls, whom they summarily set afoot.

At 10:00 A.M., the column stopped at Solomon E. Jordan's farm on Piney Woods Creek, twelve miles north of Wedowee. While troopers fed their horses and mules on oats and barley from Jordan's barn, McCook and his staff lunched on cornbread, biscuits, and bacon prepared in the family kitchen. In an effort to make conversation, some of the officers asked nineteen-year-old Nancy Ann Jordan what her brothers' names were.

William, John C., Henry Clay, and Daniel Webster Jordan, she replied.

"Your father must have been a Whig," one of the Federals chuckled.

The hordes of ravenous soldiers alarmed Mrs. Jordan and she begged McCook to leave her family something to eat. He asked her how her husband stood on the war. Her husband was a Union man, she declared. He had gone to Wedowee that morning to cast a vote for Robert Heflin.

Taking a little book from his pocket, McCook jotted down Jordan's name and assured her everything would be all right. That night the family sat down to a supper of freshly dug Irish potatoes and ate with their fingers because the Yankees had stolen all their knives and forks.[24]

As the raiders continued northward that afternoon, the well-stocked farms and plantations gave way to low, rolling hills covered with scrub oaks. About the time the column was approaching the little community of Arbacoochee, scouts brought McCook a Rebel courier and a captured dispatch from a Lieutenant J. A. Vaughan, "Commanding Scouts." Writing from "W. B. Wood's Farm-House, Fourteen miles southeast of Wedowee," on July 31, Vaughan reported McCook's raiders had been driven across the Chattahoochee River at Philpott's Ferry and were inquiring about the way to Rome, Georgia, and Oxford, Alabama. Many of them were unarmed and on foot and Vaughan believed they could be captured. They had abandoned their artillery and ambulances in the fight at Brown's Mill, and all their wounded. Two brigade commanders, Colonel Harrison and Lieutenant Colonel Torrey, had been captured, and Torrey severely wounded. "I have got twelve men with me from the Eighth Confederate Cavalry Regiment, and a few from Harrison's Texas brigade, making twenty-four men . . . ," Vaughan concluded. "We have captured 8 of the enemy."

The 8th Indiana rejoiced at the news Colonel Harrison was still alive, but McCook was concerned. The captured message was addressed to Rousseau's old nemesis, General James H. Clanton, at Oxford, Alabama. Oxford was only twenty miles to the west, and McCook had been marching in that direction, intending to burn the iron works there.[25]

Clanton's presence required an abrupt change in plans. Turning sharply to the northeast at Arbacoochee, the Yankee column crossed the Big Tallapoosa River at Bell Mills in the waning hours of the afternoon. Company A of the 8th Indiana hurried ahead and secured a second bridge, four miles upstream, where McCook called a halt for the night.

Resuming the march at daylight on August 2, the raiders passed through Abernathy,

Records in the National Archives credit McCook's raiders with capturing this red and white flag with the motto "Our Country Our Rights" on July 29, 1864, at or near Fayetteville, Georgia. However, a diary kept by Private Uriah Oblinger of the 8th Indiana Cavalry strongly suggests that it was actually taken at Tallapoosa, Georgia, on August 2, 1864. Used by permission of the Museum of the Confederacy, Richmond, Virginia. Photography by Katherine Wetzel.

a mile and a half beyond the Big Tallapoosa, picking up two Rebel deserters. The advance guard crossed the Georgia state line at 7:00 A.M. and charged into Tallapoosa late that morning, capturing a Rebel flag.[26]

Tallapoosa, or "Possum Snout," as some of the residents still called it, boasted a school, a few houses, and a surprisingly well-stocked store owned by Norvell M. Robinson. Troopers looted the store and took Robinson prisoner when they discovered he was also a Rebel enrolling officer. Toiling eastward under a cloudless sky, they passed through Buchanan at 3:00 P.M. and Draketown a couple of hours later. At 8:30, the column halted on the banks of the Tallapoosa, thirteen miles southwest of Dallas.[27]

That night McCook wrote a preliminary report to Sherman, detailing his accomplishments: cutting the West Point railroad; destroying two and a half miles of the Macon road and five miles of telegraph wire; burning two trains, about 100 bales of cotton, and over 500 wagons; killing about 800 mules, and capturing over 400 prisoners before being "completely surrounded" near Newnan by Jackson's, Wheeler's, and Roddey's cavalry and two brigades of infantry. "My loss very heavy," he concluded. "No co-operation from Stoneman. Will be in Marietta to-morrow."[28]

Sending a courier to deliver this gross misrepresentation of the truth to Sherman's headquarters, McCook marched at dawn. At 9:00 A.M., his column halted somewhere near Dallas to eat a late breakfast and feed their jaded stock. An hour later, the men were back in the saddle, plodding eastward on the road to Powder Springs. As they approached the headwaters of Sweetwater Creek, Private Eli Heaton noticed the signboard he had seen on the return from Rousseau's raid and the words "3 miles to hell" scrawled in big, black letters. This time, he could only nod in agreement.

Crossing the rickety wooden bridge over the creek, the weary troopers rode on in silence, their shoulders stooped with fatigue. That afternoon, as they crossed the Kolb's Farm battlefield south of Kennesaw Mountain, the sunny skies clouded over. The wind began to rise. Lightning flashed overhead and thunder rumbled angrily as a fast-moving storm swept down on the column. McCook's cavalrymen bowed their heads under the lash of the pelting rain that churned the road into mud. Wet and weary, their 250-mile ordeal finally came to a close at 5:30 P.M., when the column halted just west of Marietta at the Georgia Military Academy, on the same ground where Rousseau's raid had ended twelve days earlier.

"It was a sorry-looking body of men that returned to Marietta," noted Sergeant Thomas Reed of the 4th Indiana as he watched the mud-spattered column file past his bivouac. "Six days and nights without sleep, and next to nothing to eat; marching rapidly, and fighting almost constantly for two days, was enough to make men look seedy."

Some troopers who had been with Rousseau had not had a full night's rest since they left Nashville on July 8. Worn beyond all endurance, they dismounted. They ungirthed their saddles and they wondered. Where was Stoneman?[29]

16

STONEMAN'S RAID
LATIMER'S CROSSROADS TO CLINTON AND THE OCONEE RIVER

JULY 27–JULY 30, 1864

No reliance can be placed on the conduct of troops in action
with the enemy, who have been accustomed to plunder.

—Wellington

After parting with Garrard at Latimer's Crossroads on July 27, Stoneman's division had ridden east. Stone Mountain's bald dome loomed stark and gray against the bright summer sky on their left, and farms and plantations of "astonishing abundance" lay on either side. The jangling column marched slowly, plundering horses, mules, bacon, and corn, before halting early that evening on the Georgia Railroad at Lithonia. After a hasty supper, the raiders moved on, crossing and recrossing the track on the meandering road that led to Conyers.

Garrard's troopers had burned the railroad and wagon bridges directly east of Conyers on July 22, so crossing the Yellow River posed a problem, one Stoneman apparently solved by detouring three miles downstream to Brown's Bridge.[1] The head of his straggling column got to the east bank by midnight and halted two miles southwest of Covington, but the rear ranks took all night to close up. Some troopers barely got an hour's sleep before they climbed back in the saddle at dawn.

Covington awoke unaware of the raiders' approach. "Grandma" Smith was preparing to serve breakfast to her patients in Hill Hospital when the ward master called out, "The Yankees are in town again."

"Oh, surely you are mistaken," exclaimed Mrs. Smith.

"No, I am not," the ward master insisted. "Just look up the street, yonder, and you will see them yourself."

Mrs. Smith went to the door just as Stoneman's advance guard swept past. There was no panic, no hysteria. There was no time. The chief surgeon, Dr. H. L. Nichol, immediately surrendered both Confederate hospitals, and Dr. William H. Robertson instructed Mrs. Smith to see that none of her patients tried to escape. A moment later four or five drunken Yankee troopers galloped up to the hospital door.

"Oh, you damned Rebels," one of them called, "come out of there and march on the square, where General Stoneman is. We will show you how to fight against the Union."

"Go with them, boys," Mrs. Smith urged two of her patients, "like gentlemen and soldiers; they won't keep you long."

She went back to serving breakfast, but before she could finish, three or four Federals rode up to the kitchen window. "Hand us out them biscuit there," they demanded, "and that chicken; we are hungry."

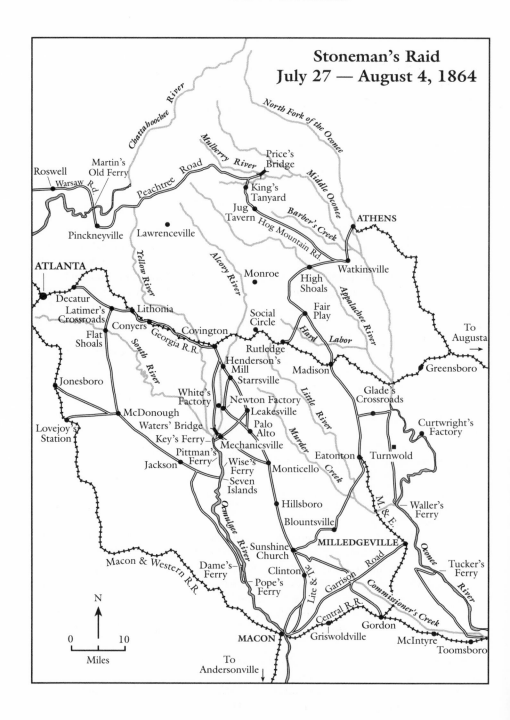

**Stoneman's Raid
July 27 — August 4, 1864**

Mrs. Smith bid the cook to give them what they wanted, and the Yankees sat on their horses, wolfing down everything offered to them. When they had devoured all the cook had prepared, they began swearing.

"Gentlemen," Mrs. Smith interrupted, "I hope you will not so far forget the dignity of gentlemen, and that your mothers were women, as to impose on a lone woman because she is in your power."

A tipsy trooper turned unsteadily in his saddle and spat. "Oh, no, madam," he said, "we will not forget our mother; she was a nice and mighty good woman."

Mrs. Smith thought these new Yanks were "not as civil" as Garrard's men had been, but, for the most part, they were more disorderly than dangerous.[2]

"Covington is quite a nice place," noted Lieutenant Richard E. Huffman of the 1st Kentucky. The ladies were better dressed than any he had previously seen in Georgia, and two who came out to talk to him were "very polite." He gave them a copy of the *Louisville Journal,* which they seemed pleased to get.

Huffman's regiment was the first to reach Covington that morning, and troopers had gone straight to the nearest bar. They found enough whisky and brandy to get noisily drunk and began boasting to anyone who would listen that they were on their way to Macon and intended to liberate the Union prisoners at Andersonville. In the midst of these revels, Stoneman rode into town. Bellowing curses, he charged about in a dyspeptic rage, much to the amusement of Lieutenant Huffman, who "could not help laughing at the General's imprecations, and the noise of the men."

Stoneman was still in a foul mood when he dismounted in the town square. As guards presented the two captured convalescents from Hill Hospital, a courier galloped up with a message. Stoneman read the slip of paper, then turned to his prisoners. "You can go to hell, for all I care," he growled, "I have no use for you now."

Elsewhere on the square, a staff officer approached Charles Bowker, one of the storekeepers Garrard's men had cleaned out on July 22. Confiding that some citizens had pointed him out as a Union man, the officer asked Bowker about the dispositions of Wheeler's cavalry, the best road to Macon, and the size of the garrison there. Bowker asserted Stoneman did not have enough men to force his way into Macon, but he told the aide what he knew and shook his hand, bidding him Godspeed.

The vanguard of Stoneman's column began filing out of Covington about 8:00 A.M., their saddles piled high with "every article they could possibly steal."

"Howdy, Johnnie Reb," passing troopers called to the bandaged and crippled patients gathered in front of Hill Hospital. "How are you? Our boys gave you a wounded furlough; and they shot your leg off—ah, ha. Well, all right. We are the Yanks that can whip you. Go home, and stay there."

A troop of runaway slaves, mounted on stolen horses and mules, followed in their wake. Waving good-bye to friends and acquaintances, they loudly proclaimed their intention to go with the Yanks to fight "de white trash."

As "Grandma" Smith watched this raucous procession parade past, a bareheaded trooper dashed up. "I want this hat," he said, snatching it off the head of one of her patients.

"You have the power now, and can use it," the crippled Confederate said quietly as the bullying bluecoat rode away, "but perhaps it will not always be so."[3]

Leaving on the Monticello Road, Stoneman diverted Silas Adams's Kentucky brigade down the west side of the Alcovy River with orders to scout toward

Mechanicsville and "watch movements of the enemy" before rejoining the command at Monticello at dark. His other two brigades crossed the Alcovy at Henderson's Mill. "The people are all taken by surprise when the Yanks ride along . . . ," noted Surgeon Andrew Weir of the 6th Indiana, "they had no warning of our approach."

Three miles southeast of Covington, Stoneman stopped long enough at Starrsville to order Horace Capron to send a detachment back to burn Henderson's flour mill and the bridge over the Alcovy once the rear guard had passed, as well as a nearby cotton mill called Newton Factory. While the rest of the column, led by Lieutenant Joseph Hasty and fifty handpicked Hoosiers from the 5th and 6th Indiana, continued to Leaksville and Palo Alto, foraging details scattered in every direction. "You may talk about [John Hunt] Morgan pressing horses," declared the 1st Kentucky's Lieutenant Huffman. "He knew nothing about it. Stoneman can steal horses where Morgan can find none."

"They robbed every house on the road of its provisions," lamented one lady, "sometimes taking every piece of meat, blankets and wearing apparel, silver and arms of every description. They would take silk dresses and put them under their saddles, and many other things for which they had no use."

Troopers also preyed upon the wagons of several refugee families fleeing south to escape the fighting around Atlanta. "Got all the preserves that we could eat," wrote Sergeant Oliver Haskell of Hasty's detachment. "Captured considerable stock."

Except for a couple of frightened Rebels who abandoned their horses and fled on foot at the raiders' approach, the ride south was unopposed. At dark, Stoneman halted his column on the outskirts of Monticello, expecting to meet Adams. Troopers dismounted. Fires began to flicker along the roadside and the smell of wood smoke mingled with the aromatic scent of coffee. But as the dark hours slipped past and there was still no sign of Adams, Stoneman became increasingly impatient. Along about midnight he sent half of Hasty's detachment back toward Mechanicsville to look for him.[4]

Crossing the Alcovy had put Stoneman on the east side of the Ocmulgee River. At first glance, this seemed to preclude keeping his prescribed rendezvous with McCook at Lovejoy's Station, and Sherman would later charge Stoneman had "not obeyed his orders." Historians have repeated and amplified this accusation, using words like "blundering" and "glory-hunting" to vilify Stoneman for deliberately deserting McCook and striking straight for the prison camps at Macon and Andersonville.[5]

Militarily, however, Stoneman's roundabout route made sense. He commanded the smallest of the three cavalry columns converging on the Macon railroad. He knew he would be pursued, and probably outnumbered. By leaving Garrard to keep Joe Wheeler busy at Flat Shoals and crossing both the Yellow River and the Alcovy before turning south, Stoneman could use the Ocmulgee to shield his right flank and rear, just as McCook used the Chattahoochee to screen his march to Campbellton and Smith's Ferry.

At some point, however, he had to cross the Ocmulgee and, since he had no pontoon train, he had to rely on the existing bridges. Stoneman claimed that before leaving Atlanta he had received repeated assurances there were three bridges spanning the Ocmulgee north of Macon. He intended to cross the one at Seven Islands, ten miles southwest of Monticello, where a hard day's ride on a good road would carry him to Lovejoy's Station via Jackson and McDonough.

Everything depended on moving quickly, but it was midnight before Silas Adams and his Kentuckians halted about four miles from Monticello, apparently in the rear of Horace Capron's brigade. As Stoneman had ordered, Adams had moved down the west bank of the Alcovy, destroying a cotton mill called White's Factory. After crossing the Alcovy near its mouth and burning Waters' Bridge behind him, he had taken the road south to Mechanicsville, sending scouting detachments far down the east side of the Ocmulgee. These scouts brought Stoneman some disquieting news. There was no bridge at Seven Islands. There was no bridge anywhere along this stretch of the Ocmulgee.

There were three widely separated ferries—Key's, Pittman's, and Wise's—but Stoneman rejected the idea of using them. Ferrying 2,200 men across the Ocmulgee would be time-consuming at best and expose his little division to attack. As he saw it, there were only two alternatives. He could turn back, or he could keep going south toward Macon; but there was no hope of meeting McCook at Lovejoy's Station.

Reluctantly, Stoneman elected to move south. He could play havoc with the railroad linking Macon with Augusta and Savannah, and perhaps release 1,500 Union officers held prisoner at Macon's Camp Oglethorpe. But as Stoneman waited for his scattered detachments to regroup, his chief of staff, Lieutenant Colonel Robert W. Smith, noted the general seemed "much disheartened and filled with gloomy forebodings."[6]

At 4:00 A.M., Capron's adjutant, Captain Samuel Wells, returned with eighty-eight men from McLaughlin's Ohio Squadron and reported burning Henderson's Mill and the nearby bridge over the Alcovy, as well as Newton Factory and the bridge connecting it with White's Factory.[7] Lieutenant Hasty's Hoosiers also returned just as the rest of the column was preparing to march. "Didn't have time to get any breakfast," Sergeant Haskell groused after a night of looking for wayward Kentuckians.

As his serried ranks shuffled past the courthouse at Monticello, Stoneman once again divided the command into two columns, sending Silas Adams's brigade to the right to scout the country immediately east of the Ocmulgee River, while he marched straight ahead with Biddle's and Capron's brigades and the artillery. They would reunite that evening at Clinton.

Six miles below Monticello, some of Stoneman's men stopped at Carden Goolsby's plantation and ordered him, in language more forceful than polite, to mount an old mule they had and show them where he kept his stock. "I'll be damned if I do," the feisty old planter shot back. "I have never ridden a mule in my life and I'll not ride one for any damned Yankee."

An officer persuaded him it was in his best interest to cooperate. As he escorted Goolsby out the front gate, he enjoined his men to stay out of the house. Before they were out of sight, Goolsby heard furniture being tossed about, glass shattering, and wood splintering. "Damned rascals," the officer muttered.

"We had but little rations with us . . . ," wrote the 1st Kentucky's Richard Huffman, "yet we did not suffer." Apples, peaches, and watermelons were just turning ripe, and every farm and plantation seemed to have a keg or two of peach brandy. Shoving, jostling troopers eagerly filled cups and canteens, and some of them were decidedly drunk by the time the column clattered into Hillsboro late that morning.[8]

Seventy-year-old John McKissack had often vowed he would kill the first Yankee who tried to steal anything he owned. Fearing he would make good on his threat, Mrs. McKissack persuaded him to leave the house. He went out the back just as some of Stoneman's men came barging in the front, but as he stepped over the threshold, he grabbed a shotgun he kept hanging above the door. Several troopers ran after him, demanding his surrender. McKissack slowed and then renewed his stride. Halt, a soldier demanded angrily. McKissack turned. Seeing a gun aimed at him, he emptied a load of buckshot into the chest of his closest pursuer. Before the echoes of the blast died away, the enraged Yankees were upon him. Tearing the shotgun from his hands, they hoisted him on a horse, telling his terrified wife and mother-in-law to bid him farewell "forever." Heaping curses on the two helpless women, they smashed every dish in the house, and vowed to burn it to the ground.[9]

"If I had my way with the damned rebel I would hang him from his own door post," asserted a Yankee captain quaffing buttermilk as he sat on a piano stool in Mrs. Tabitha Reese's parlor with Stoneman and several other officers. Stoneman's presence spared Mrs. Reese, her widowed daughter, and granddaughter the intrusions of enlisted men, but pillaging outside the house went unchecked. When it came time to leave, the Yankee captain rose from his stool. "What would we think," he asked, pausing to admire his reflection in the mirror hanging over the mantel, "if we could see ourselves as others see us?"[10]

With the condemned Mr. McKissack and perhaps a half dozen captured Rebels in tow, the wanton raiders rode on, past Round Oak and Sunshine Church. They took horses. They took mules. They robbed everyone and respected none. When widowed, sixty-six-year-old Sarah Allen pleaded with an officer to stop the men who were ransacking her home, he merely shrugged and said he could not control them.

At noon, Stoneman halted Horace Capron's brigade eight miles below Hillsboro and gave orders diverting Major Francis Davidson and five companies of the 14th Illinois to strike the Central Railroad at its junction with the Milledgeville and Eatonton branch at Gordon, eighteen miles to the southeast. After destroying "all public property that he could find on either railroad," and doing "all the damage he could," Davidson was to "bring his command out safely." Just how he was supposed to accomplish that was a point Stoneman apparently left to the major's discretion.

As Davidson's little detachment disappeared in the distance, the rest of the Yankee column shuffled southward in the shimmering heat. Early that afternoon, Lieutenant Hasty's advance guard charged into Clinton, scattering a handful of Rebels.

Clinton was "a most beautiful little town" noted Sergeant Oliver Haskell. An imposing brick courthouse dominated the town square, and shaded streets bearing names like Washington, Madison, and Jackson bounded the pillared homes of some of Jones County's wealthiest citizens. Stoneman stopped at Dr. James F. Barron's big white house on the southeast corner of the square and asked him about crossing the Ocmulgee at Macon. The doctor assured him there was no bridge at Macon. It had been swept away by a June freshet.[11]

Uncertainty tugged at Stoneman's elbow. If what the doctor said was true and there was no bridge at Macon, then there was no chance of rescuing the prisoners at Camp Oglethorpe. Left to mull over his options while he waited for Silas Adams to arrive, Stoneman gave orders for the men to dismount and unsaddle their horses.

Clinton never forgot what happened next. "The boys went after everything that they wanted," recorded Oliver Haskell, "especially whisky."

Troopers lined up outside Mrs. Elizabeth Lowther's house and forced her and Colonel William DeForrest Holly to serve up the contents of the wine cellar. They barged into homes, broke open trunks, and rifled drawers. They robbed gray-haired old men of money and watches at gunpoint, snatched rings off ladies' fingers, and plucked pins and broaches from their bosoms. According to one account, some of them even ravished slave women in front of their mistresses. "Sham guards were sometimes posted around houses," a Macon newspaper later reported, "but the guard and the officer commanding it would straightaway fall to work and sack the premises."

Richard W. Bonner was not at home when ax-wielding troopers pushed past his two small sons. Smashing open bureaus and splintering his desk, they pocketed money, notes, titles, and deeds. They carried off silverware, cutlery, bed covers, Bonner's hat, shoes, all his clothes, and his only picture of his dead wife. "My servants begged them not to take that as well as everything else," Bonner recounted bitterly, "but they plundered on even to the underwear and dresses my wife left at her death. . . ."[12]

The first vague rumors of Stoneman's approach had reached Macon on July 27, when Major General Howell Cobb received a telegram from Hood's headquarters advising, "A Small raid moving towards Covington[,] our cavalry in pursuit."

Another tersely worded wire, sent at 7:20 P.M., warned Cobb, "The destination of the raiding party is still unknown[,] prepare for it."

This was followed by a third telegram, reiterating, "The raid toward Covington is stronger than at first reported. Destination still unknown. We have a heavy force in pursuit."[13]

Cobb was skeptical the Yankees would venture this far south, but he forwarded copies of the telegrams to Georgia's adjutant general, Major General Henry C. Wayne, who was in Macon mustering the state militia at Camp Rescue, a shady grove near Macon's Rose Hill Cemetery. He also sent scouts up both sides of the Ocmulgee and posted additional pickets on the outskirts of the city, "to be prepared for any emergency."[14]

The personification of Southern aristocracy, Cobb, a former Speaker of the House of Representatives, governor of Georgia, and secretary of the treasury, commanded the state Reserves, five regiments of boys, aged seventeen and eighteen, and able-bodied men between forty-five and fifty. His troops had originally been assigned to guard the Yankee prisoners held at Andersonville and Macon, but the pressing need for manpower after the recent bloodletting at Peachtree Creek and Atlanta had compelled Hood to order them to the front on July 26.

Cobb believed this order was "attended with serious danger to the country," and news of an approaching raid only confirmed his misgivings. Hood apparently agreed and at 5:10 P.M., July 28, a telegram from his headquarters directed Cobb to let the Reserves remain at Andersonville for the present. "Raiders reported across South River[,] one column moving towards McDonough," it added.[15]

As the evening sun cast its lengthening shadows down the dusty streets, machinists at the Macon Armory shut down the production line that made Spiller & Burr revolvers and the lathes that turned rifle stocks for Rebel arsenals in North Carolina and Virginia. At Macon's own arsenal and laboratory, quitting time suspended work on percussion caps, medicines, and a wide variety of ordnance. Foundrymen banked the fires at Findlay's Iron Works, and mechanics, artisans, and smiths streamed home from Schofield Brothers' Foundry, Gustin's Factory, W. J. McElroy, and half a dozen private concerns that produced all the assorted accoutrements of war.

Among those leaving work that evening was the man who ran the ferry that had replaced the washed-out city bridge. Cobb had encountered considerable difficulty trying to get his scouts and pickets across the Ocmulgee the previous evening, and tonight he could not find the ferryman at all. When a direct appeal to Macon Mayor Stephen Collins failed to elicit a response, Cobb simply gave up and left the eastern approaches to the city unguarded.[16]

He was more concerned about the enemy within, 1,500 Union officers confined behind the twelve-foot-high board fence enclosing Camp Oglethorpe, a three-acre stockade at the southwest corner of the city. "The prison at Macon is not secure . . . ," Brigadier General John H. Winder, commanding the garrison at Andersonville, had recently warned the War Department. "It is within a few hundred yards of three important railroad depots and very large workshops, which escaped prisoners might and probably would burn." He had urged the inmates be moved to Charleston, South Carolina.

The War Department concurred, and after calling the roll at Camp Oglethorpe on the morning of July 27, a Rebel lieutenant announced 600 prisoners were to be ready to leave for Charleston at 5:00 P.M. "It was a busy time till that hour," noted one inmate. "Clothes were washed, pones baked, haversacks made ready and filled for *emergencies.*"

No one anticipated conditions would be any better at Charleston, but the long train ride promised a welcome change of scenery and perhaps a chance to escape. At 5:00 P.M., 600 faded and frayed-edged Yankee officers eagerly stepped through the inner gate when the Rebel lieutenant called their names. Some sort of delay ensued while they waited between the deadline and the stockade, and shortly after dark the remaining prisoners created enough disturbance to distract the guards. When the Rebel lieutenant counted heads at the front gate at 11:00 P.M., he found fifty more than he needed. These were quickly winnowed out. Then a hundred-man detachment of Cobb's 5th Georgia Reserves escorted those to be transferred to the Central Railroad depot, where they boarded a train that left for Charleston at 4:00 A.M., July 28.

Another 600 prisoners left Macon at 4:00 the next morning, but for the rest of the city, business began as usual. Long a marketplace for the cotton plantations of central Georgia, Macon was the terminus of four railroads. Trains regularly arrived and departed for Atlanta, Augusta, Columbus, Savannah, and the state capital at Milledgeville.[17]

Among those waiting at the depot on July 29 was Howell Cobb. He scanned the sea of arriving passengers, looking for a familiar face. Disappointed, he returned to his headquarters. "I have been at the depot for two successive mornings with the hope of meeting you . . . ," he wrote to his wife, Mary Ann. "Whilst I do not doubt your presence [at their home in Athens, Georgia] is very agreeable to Howell [their son], I beg to inform you that there is *another Howell* that is even more anxious to see you & to whom your presence would be *even more agreeable.* Think of *him* in your arrangements."

There had been "some excitement" about a Yankee cavalry raid for the last two days, Cobb added. He, however, had "no serious apprehension."[18]

Neither did Dr. William Felton. He and his wife, Rebecca, had refugeed from north Georgia's war-torn Cherokee County in May and rented an "unfinished, cheap dwelling" on the Clinton Road, about four miles northeast of Macon. It had no well, no ceilings, and not a pane of glass in any of the windows, but for the time being it was home.

Mrs. Felton sent her Negro maid to Macon on July 29 to pick up the mail. She was entertaining some neighbors that afternoon when the slave woman came rushing into the house like a cyclone, so winded she could only pant and stutter about meeting a Confederate soldier riding a half-dead horse dripping with foam. "I met a soldier on the bridge when I was comin' out," she finally blurted, "an' he said the Yankees wus comin'—a perfect army—comin' to Macon. He sont word to hide your money and send your horses to the canebrake. They will shore be here tonight."

Mrs. Felton and her guests could not help but laugh. There were no Yankees closer than Atlanta, they assured the frightened servant. The soldier was April fooling her. "If I had that man here," Mrs. Felton said angrily, "I'd bless him out for treating you so shabbily."[19]

But Mrs. Felton's maid had not been deceived. The lone rider she had encountered at the railroad bridge over the Ocmulgee may have been Captain Samuel S. Dunlap. The enrolling officer for Jones County, Dunlap had traded shots with some of Stoneman's men just south of Clinton and came pounding into Macon at noon to spread the alarm.[20]

Cobb's first reaction was to take this important news to Henry Wayne. The adjutant general was not in his office. Bowing before the exigencies of the moment, Cobb wrote directly to Georgia Governor Joseph E. Brown:

> I have just received positive information that the enemy have taken Monticello and are marching on Clinton. I am preparing to send a cavalry force to meet them. I called to see Genl. Wayne but there was no one in his office and supposing you would desire to take steps for the protection of Milledgeville as well as this place I send you the information and am prepared to cooperate with you in any course you may adopt for the protecting of the two points.

Ever jealous of his prerogatives, Brown had taken the train to Macon after receiving the order calling his militia to the front. He had, no doubt, been privy to the telegrams Cobb had shared with General Wayne on July 27, and upon receipt of Cobb's note, he replied:

> I will be at my office in the Club room at half past 3 o'clock and will be glad to see you and cooperate with you for the defense of this place and Milledgeville against the raid. I will detain the troops who are armed and send part of them to Milledgeville.[21]

Brown and Cobb had quarreled politically and loathed each other personally, but with a Yankee raid bearing down on the state capital, the boorish, rawboned governor and the wealthy, rotund general were willing to set their differences aside. Neither left any record of their meeting, but it was probably brief. At 3:30 P.M., orders from Brown reached Camp Rescue, directing 1,000 men to start for the capital at once. Two militia regiments and a section of artillery duly reported to the Central Railroad depot at 5:00 P.M., where General Wayne began loading them on a train for the thirty-eight-mile trip to Milledgeville.

Cobb, in the meantime, hastily organized a cavalry company under Major W. S. Wallace and ferried them across the Ocmulgee at 5:00 P.M. with orders to scout toward Clinton. Two miles beyond Macon, Wallace divided his little command, sending four men to scout to the left on the River Road while the rest of the company continued toward Clinton.

"It is of vital importance that the ferry near the rail road bridge should be kept ready to pass couriers and cavalry at all times day & night," Cobb wrote to Macon Mayor Stephen Collins. Recounting the "great trouble and difficulty" he had experienced getting his scouts and pickets across the river the past two evenings, he reiterated it was "of utmost importance that ferrymen should be kept at the ferry all the time and especially at night." "You may rest assured," he concluded, "that the safety of your city is involved in the question."[22]

The rest of Macon was already rallying to the call to arms. Colonel James H. Burton, superintendent of the Macon Armory, got his orders at 4:45 P.M. and immediately assembled his workers in the armory yard. After roll was called, he gave Captain W. L. Reid written orders to march the company to Hodgkins's armory, where each man drew a .69 caliber smoothbore musket, a set of infantry accoutrements, and forty rounds of ammunition. Once equipped, Captain Reid and the Armory Guards reported to Lieutenant Colonel John W. Mallet, superintendent of the Macon Laboratory.

Mallet's battalion, 350 strong with the addition of Reid's men, consisted of two companies from the Macon Arsenal and Captain Samuel Kirkpatrick's Wright Guards. Together with 1,500 of Governor Brown's militia and all of Cobb's 5th Georgia Reserves that were not escorting prisoners to Charleston, they crossed the railroad bridge over the Ocmulgee at 8:00 P.M.

Cobb divided this force into two wings, commanded by Colonel John B. Cumming of the 5th Georgia Reserves and Colonel George Washington Lee of the state militia. Cumming marched his regiment, now led by Lieutenant Colonel Christopher D. Findlay, out on the Clinton Road with Mallet's battalion and a couple of guns commanded by Cobb's chief of artillery, Major Edward Taliaferro. Halting about a mile beyond the Ocmulgee, his column made camp in an old field, while Colonel Lee moved four regiments of his militia down the Garrison Road and bivouacked a few hundred yards beyond Cobb's East Macon command post.

On the west side of the Ocmulgee, Macon's recently appointed post commander, Colonel George C. Gibbs, assembled the City Battalion at the Vineville Academy. Composed of "old men, preachers, exempts, rheumatics, &c., &c.," Gibbs's battalion deployed to watch the northern approaches to the city.

At 7:00 P.M., the train carrying General Wayne's militia to Milledgeville pulled out of the depot. A second train followed about three hours later, loaded with another regiment of militia Cobb had ordered to Griswoldville, nine miles east of Macon, ostensibly to protect the Griswold & Gunnison factory, the South's largest producer of revolvers. Wary of an ambush, Wayne proceeded cautiously. But the track was clear and, after safely passing Griswoldville, his train sped on to Gordon, eighteen miles east of Macon.[23]

His arrival did not go unnoticed. After parting company with Stoneman, Major Francis Davidson and Companies A, D, F, G, and H of the 14th Illinois Cavalry had taken a southeasterly course past Dr. Palacia Stewart's place and Pine Ridge Church.

Crossing the headwaters of Commissioners Creek above Salem Church, they had captured a couple of well-to-do farmers, Taylor Pitts and Bill Wood, and compelled them to act as guides. Mounted on a pair of mules, Pitts and Wood led the Yankees back across Commissioners Creek at Flat Shoals. About an hour before sundown, they came to Thomas W. Choate's plantation on the Garrison Road.

Davidson's men swiftly relieved Squire Choate of all his riding stock and forced him to accompany them at gunpoint. The "fat old gentleman" bounced all over the back of a hard-trotting mule as the Yankee column hurried south toward Gordon.

The painful ride was uneventful until Bill Wood suddenly bolted from his captors. A flurry of pistol shots flared in the darkness, but Wood was off, away, and gone before anyone could stop him. The Yankees let him go. "They moved rapidly, but cautiously," Thomas Choate later related; "not a word spoken nor an accoutrement rattled."

About 9:00 P.M., they reached Walden's shanty, a mile west of Gordon, just as a trainload of Wayne's militia came puffing and wheezing into the depot. Realizing he was badly outnumbered, Davidson hurriedly secreted his men on the north side of the track and waited.

The tracks and sidings at Gordon were crowded that night. Besides General Wayne's train and an eastbound passenger train from Macon that arrived shortly afterward, there was a westbound passenger train from Eatonton and Milledgeville. There were also several engines and cars belonging to the Western & Atlantic Railroad, sent south after Sherman put that route out of business. Davidson and his officers counted eleven trains in all: eleven engines, forty passenger cars, eighty boxcars, and twenty flatcars.[24]

After a twenty-minute stop to take on firewood and water, the train crowded with militia chugged off toward Milledgeville. The passenger train soon followed. About 10:30 P.M., Sergeant Joseph B. Agnew and five raiders scurried from the shadows to cut the telegraph wires. Leaving a sizable picket on the outskirts of town to watch for the approach of any more troop trains, Davidson and the rest of his men dashed into Gordon.

They surprised H. K. Walker, the railroad agent and telegrapher, and robbed his office of an estimated ten or eleven thousand dollars in Confederate money. In quick succession, they set fire to the depot, a substantial brick building filled with bacon, cornmeal, flour, and refugee furniture; two adjacent storehouses; and the passenger shed. They rekindled the blaze in the passenger shed three times before it caught but spared a nearby diner and the Wayside Home for traveling soldiers, declaring it was not their purpose to destroy private property.

While some of Davidson's men put the railroad buildings to the torch, others surrounded the Milledgeville train and herded off the frightened passengers. Mrs. Jefferson Lamar watched angrily as troopers looted her trunk of several pieces of jewelry and silver plate. The Yankees also confiscated the mail pouch and then set fire to the cars and 500 Enfield rifles bound for Macon.

Several refugee families who had temporarily set up housekeeping in Western & Atlantic boxcars did not fare any better. It seemed for every Yankee willing to help frightened mothers and wailing children unload a few precious belongings, there was another intent on rifling their baggage. Soon the cars were engulfed in flames that hissed and crackled as troopers with axes methodically moved up and down the sidings, smashing the controls of parked locomotives. Other details destroyed fifty to a hundred yards of track on the Central line and the Milledgeville branch, and burned the turntable. Taylor Pitts, the captured farmer, apparently managed to slip away in the confusion, but when the Yankees rode out of Gordon about a half hour after midnight, they took H. K. Walker and Squire Choate with them.

That was when the citizens of Gordon, men and women, black and white, sprang into action. Dousing the fire in the passenger shed, they saved four carloads of bacon, some engines, and six or seven flatcars loaded with machinery belonging to the Western & Atlantic Railroad. Despite these efforts, at least seven engines were damaged and perhaps as many as twelve passenger cars and forty boxcars were destroyed.[25]

The lurid flames lit up the night sky like a beacon as Davidson and his men filed past Solomon's gristmill. Following a road running roughly parallel and about a half mile north of the Central Railroad, they spent another long night in the saddle. 125 men, a hundred miles behind enemy lines, depending on the directions of two surly civilian guides. If they were too bold and hurried down the track, they were liable to run into a trainload of trouble. If they were too cautious, trouble was sure to come looking for them. Either way, they would end up just as dead, and so they plodded on.[26]

Dawn was tinting the edge of the horizon by the time they charged into McIntyre, eight and a half miles east of Gordon. Gunfire sputtered as the advance guard traded shots with about twenty Confederate soldiers, who quickly surrendered. During the next hour, the raiders burned the depot full of tax-in-kind bacon, the water tank, and the side track and confiscated the mail. Before leaving McIntyre at 6:00 A.M., Davidson paroled his prisoners, including his reluctant guides, Choate and Walker, but not before a trooper relieved Walker of his expensive gold watch.

Just east of McIntyre, the advance guard fired at a farmer who refused to halt and surrender his mule. Hammering his heels into the animal's flanks, the frightened farmer escaped with a bullet wound but did not stop his frenzied flight until he literally rode the poor mule to death.

Continuing eastward, Davidson's men set fire to two railroad trestles between the 157 and 158 mileposts. About 9:00 A.M., they dashed into Toomsboro, seven miles beyond McIntyre, burned the depot, and set fire to the siding.[27] Swamps barred the way east of Toomsboro, and after torching Deas and Jackson's gristmill and sawmill on the edge of town and the 300-foot wagon bridge over Commissioners Creek, Davidson quit the railroad at 10:00 A.M. in favor of a road diverging to the north. Four miles beyond Toomsboro, this road intersected the railroad again at Beech Hill, where the raiders burned three sections of track between the 152 and 153 mileposts and set fire to a thousand cords of well-seasoned wood stacked along the right-of-way, which was consumed "much quicker," a Yankee officer noted, "than it would have been, had it been used as our erring Southern brethren proposed it should be when it was corded up."

While the rest of the command halted and built barricades, Davidson sent Lieutenant Lewis W. Boren and Companies G and A to burn the railroad bridge over the Oconee River. Footing down a trestle spanning a mile and a half of swamp, Boren and his men reached the Oconee about noon. Sergeant Agnew and ten or twelve troopers hurried across and liberally sprinkled the Savannah end of the bridge with some sort of flammable liquid. A fire was lit and the pine timbers blazed furiously. Fifteen minutes later the 700-foot span slid off its pilings and fell into the river. In that instant, Atlanta became an isolated city. All its rail connections, east, south, and west, had been severed by Sherman's horsemen.[28]

17

STONEMAN'S RAID
CLINTON TO WALNUT CREEK

JULY 29–JULY 30, 1864

Raw in the fields, the rude militia swarms, . . .

—John Dryden, *Cyman and Iphigenia*

Leaving a pall of smoke billowing behind them, Davidson's little detachment headed northwest on the narrow road that hugged the crest of the high ground bordering the backwater swamps on the banks of the Oconee. About 9:00 that evening, just six miles short of the state capital at Milledgeville, the column abruptly turned to the right and struck the river at Tucker's Ferry, twenty-two miles above the railroad bridge.[1]

It was dark. Rain was coming down in sheets and the thunder rolled. Peering across the river as lightning flickered overhead, Davidson and his men dimly saw the low silhouette of a ferryboat lying against the distant shore. Lieutenant John S. Anderson, commanding Company H, volunteered to go get it.

Shucking off his boots, the lieutenant waded into the black water. Arms stroking rhythmically against the pull of the current, he swam to the other side, boarded the ferry, and steered it back to the west bank, where Davidson began the slow and difficult task of shuttling men and swimming mules and horses across the rainswept river.

Exhausted troopers sprawled in the wet grass while they waited for their turn to cross. Some slept so soundly their comrades had to carry them aboard. By 2:00 A.M., July 31, Davidson had all of his men safely across, but citizens later reported fifty horses and mules drowned.

The raiders also lost a two-mule wagon carrying the mail, jewelry, and silverware they had stolen at Gordon. The soldier driving it had stopped near Tucker's plantation to raid a watermelon patch when one of Tucker's slaves jumped into the seat. Laying the lash to the team, he drove the wagon to Milledgeville and delivered its contents to the military authorities.

Georgia's capital was already on the alert. A telegram, announcing the approach of Yankee raiders, had arrived from Macon the afternoon of July 29, and the city had immediately mobilized its defenses; 120 old men and boys organized into three companies: the Milledgeville Guards, the Armory Guards, and the Factory Guards, all under the command of Major McMahon.[2]

Across the river from Milledgeville, on the east bank of the Oconee, Lucy Barrow Cobb had spent most of the day in bed, sandwiched between hot bricks and alternating sips of tansy tea with doses of Jacob's cordial. July 29 was her first wedding anniversary, and she was feeling ill and a little sad at being separated from her husband, John, who was attending family business in Macon while she stayed with her Uncle William McKinley's family.

About 6:00 p.m., she dragged her "trembling limbs" to the portico and sat down on the front steps to enjoy the sunset as she wrote to her "Johnny darling." She had composed only a few lines when some little boys came "tearing 'round the circle like mad."

"They must have important news," Lucy mused. They did. Six thousand Yankees were at Monticello! Scouts reported they had split into two groups and one of them was heading for Milledgeville. "Startling news if true—," Lucy wrote, as the rest of the family gathered on the front steps.

"Lay aside your writing Lucy, & join us," urged cousin Mary McKinley as they anxiously awaited Uncle William's return from the city. As darkness came and the night air grew cool, the family retreated inside. Then they heard Uncle William galloping up the driveway.

"*Uncle William galloping* was in itself alarming," Lucy noted, joining the crowd that rushed "en masse" to the front door.

"Be quick girls," Uncle William announced gravely as he alighted from his panting horse. "Hear what I have to say. . . . The Yankees are in ten miles of Milledgeville. We are certainly informed of that. They may not come before morning—may not come at all if Genl. Wayne with his thousand men get here in time. They are expected at ten o'clock. Compose yourselves, but be prepared for the worst!"

He then described the piteous scene he had witnessed at the governor's mansion. Mrs. Brown, "in the greatest distress, pale & terror stricken flying hither & thither . . . fearing that the house would be burned over her head before morning." In the space of an hour, she had received three telegrams from the governor, telling her to take the children and flee to Scottsboro, a little village four miles south of Milledgeville. But besides her own large family, Mrs. Brown had an elderly mother-in-law, sick with fever, and a sister-in-law with a newborn baby. She could not abandon them. Hearing of her plight, Uncle William had put aside past political differences and gallantly offered the governor's family refuge in his home.

His own family listened silently until he had finished. Then they burst into a spontaneous round of applause, declaring themselves ready and willing to welcome the Browns. "But one dissenting voice was raised . . . ," noted Lucy, that of Uncle William's stepdaughter, Gracie, "who spoke for herself & her cowardly cousin Mrs. Moore. *They* thought the presence of Gov. Brown's family would endanger the house—& loudly expressed their discontent. . . ."

Lucy countered by arguing, "Christian-like behavior, such as forgetfulness of *self* would bring upon us the blessing of Heaven, would insure for us the special care & protection of Providence." The rest of the family agreed and began preparing to receive their guests while Uncle William hurried back to Milledgeville. "Of course no rest was taken by any of us . . . ," Lucy wrote, "everything we had valuable was bundled up & concealed about our person's. My two precious pictures I hid in my bosom—& I must confess . . . sharp, shooting pains warn me that 'tis not advisable to let them remain there. Everything else that I value I have put in a bag, which I shall fasten to my hoop at the first signal of alarm—hoping that my person will be held inviolate."

The first of several carriages from the governor's mansion soon appeared, and before morning three generations of Browns had arrived "bag and baggage," filling the hallway with sugar, coffee, syrup, and other scarcities six-year-old Guy McKinley declared they "took from the government."

"Gracie is more badly frightened than any of us . . . ," noted Lucy. "Her wrath explodes whenever she catches sight of a Brown or a piece of Brown property—& you can't turn around without having some little deformed face peering at you from behind a corner. I never saw such an afflicted family."

It was 1:00 A.M., July 30, before the train carrying General Wayne's militia finally arrived from Macon. The heavily laden engine had been unable to pull the long grade between Scottsboro and Midway, but instead of unloading his troops and marching the last three or four miles into Milledgeville, Wayne had spent two hours waiting for the engine to get up enough steam to finish the trip. Upon reaching the depot, he was met by Stith P. Myrick, whom he had telegraphed before leaving Macon, asking him to recruit some citizens to act as scouts. Myrick had a few volunteers ready and Wayne immediately sent them riding north, south, and west to look for the approaching Yankees. The two regiments he had brought from Macon relieved the home guards picketing the roads leading into the city, and an anxious Lucy Cobb found their presence very reassuring, "'milish' though they be."[3]

Her father-in-law Howell Cobb's troops were busy, too. Major Wallace's company, reduced to forty-eight men after dispatching four riders up the River Road, had probed seven miles beyond Macon in the fading twilight on July 29 when they learned a column of Yankee cavalry was approaching the road fork at Coxe's. Wallace sent a civilian volunteer, Dr. Robert Collins, to take a detachment forward and secret someone by the roadside to count the raiders as they passed. Collins promised to perform the task personally.

The Yankees had left Clinton late that afternoon, when Stoneman, advised of the approach of Silas Adams's Kentuckians, had started Lieutenant Hasty's self-styled "Hatchet Brigade" down the Lite-n-Tie Road. James Biddle's and Horace Capron's brigades had followed with the artillery, but Stoneman diverted Adams's men and the pack train to the right on the direct road to Macon. "We had not gone far before dark came," recounted the 1st Kentucky's Richard Huffman. "It was so dark and cloudy that we could scarcely see anything."

About 10:00 P.M., a Kentucky trooper came hurrying back through the gloom on foot. He had been riding with the advance guard, he told Adams, when he was captured by some Rebels, but managed to escape. Concerned, Adams sent a few men forward to reinforce his front ranks. Moments later, a flurry of gunshots crackled in the darkness.

The explosive encounter sent Dr. Collins diving for cover. His cohorts hastily fired their guns and fled. Racing down the road until they met the rest of their company, the doctor's detachment halted, blanched and breathless, while Major Wallace doubled their numbers and hurried them back to face the Yankees again.

At the same time, Silas Adams sent Lieutenant Huffman spurring up to investigate. Overtaking the head of the column, Huffman found a 1st Kentucky trooper dead and another critically wounded. Chastened and more cautious now, the advance guard moved forward again.

They had not gone far when a second volley shattered the stillness, inflicting more casualties. The Kentuckians loosed a few shots in reply and again Wallace's rattled recruits beat a hasty retreat. Recklessly, the Kentuckians raced after them. Wallace let them get within thirty yards of his position. Open fire, he ordered. A withering blast leaped from the roadside, followed by yells, groans, and the clatter of hooves. Seeing the Yankees "in confusion & retreating hastily," Wallace ordered his men to charge. Nothing happened, a result Wallace attributed to "the men never having been under fire before & their horses being badly frightened."

One of Wallace's men had been killed in the exchange. Another was mortally wounded, presumably the same one who later told his Kentucky captors they were facing a company of forty-seven men. However, when Wallace withdrew a short distance to regroup his little command, he could count only fourteen men and only six of these were still armed. The rest of his company had scattered, including a lieutenant who, in Wallace's estimation, "did not behave with that gallantry that becomes an officer." Wallace later claimed he and his six stalwart companions defended every hilltop on the Clinton Road, but Adams's Kentuckians reported they were "not interrupted any more that night."

Hearing the firing to his right, George Stoneman dispatched his acting commissary officer, Lieutenant W. C. Root of the 1st Kentucky, to find out what all the shooting was about. Root hurried away with a few troopers but soon returned and reported he had encountered Rebels on a road bisecting the angle between the Clinton and Lite-n-Tie roads. Stoneman reinforced Root's escort and gruffly told the young lieutenant to "go through or die."

"This was about two o'clock in the morning," recounted one of the raiders. "The darkness, thickets, and creeks made it anything but pleasant."

With Stoneman's parting words prodding him on, Root reached the Clinton Road, but in the darkness he blundered into Major Anderson T. Keen's battalion of Adams's 1st Kentucky. A shot rang out. Carbines began blazing. Root tried to shout above the din, asking his opponents to identify themselves. Someone apparently recognized the lieutenant's voice, Root's men captured a bluecoated Kentuckian, and both sides realized their mistake before anyone was hurt. Late that night, Adams called a halt about five miles short of Macon.[4]

"It was a night of sweltering heat, as frequently happens at that time of the year," recalled Rebecca Latimer Felton, who had retired early that evening. "We tossed about, fanned the children and slept 'cat naps' until just before day when I went to sleep soundly. . . ."

Her husband was restless, however. He got dressed and had gone out on the front steps for some fresh air when a Negro boy burst through the back door screaming, "Dar, Marse William, dar's dey comin', shore nuff."

Hearing the commotion, Mrs. Felton hastily pulled a wrapper on over her nightgown and stepped into her slippers. As she hurried to the front door, she heard her husband talking with a Yankee cavalryman, who demanded to know "the quickest route to Macon."

"By the time I could peep through the half opened shutter," she later wrote, "the woods in front of the dwelling were literally working with blue coats mounted on horses . . . [they] had turned our cows and sheep out of the big enclosure nearby and had loosened saddles and fed horses, while less than a hundred yards distant we were trying to sleep with everything in the house accessible to anybody . . . who chose to come in at the open windows. . . ."

The Yankees were back in the saddle before dawn. Silas Adams had received orders, perhaps from Lieutenant Root, to "strike the river at some point above Macon, sound it for fords or examine for ferries or some other means of crossing, and feel the enemy as he advanced down the river and drive him in if found." Mrs. Felton watched as the jangling column clattered past and was convinced "Macon would have a hard time of it."[5]

Over on the Lite-n-Tie Road, Stoneman had briefly halted Biddle's and Capron's brigades a little after dark, about five miles south of Clinton. "We didn't get to sleep any . . . ," complained a weary Oliver Haskell, "they kept send[ing] orders to us all night, to build fires then to put them out then to make a detail to go some where with some officer then go on picket. . . ."

"We marched and stopped, marched and stopped . . . ," agreed Colonel Tom Butler of the 5th Indiana. It was nearly daylight before orders halted the head of the column at Mrs. Morton's farmhouse, nine miles from Macon.

The men scarcely had time to close their eyes before officers roused the weary column at 4:00 A.M. on July 30. Girths were tightened, carbines slung, and James Biddle's 5th and 6th Indiana soon began crowding down the Garrison Road. Horace Capron's brigade followed as far as Joseph Stiles's place, seven miles east of Macon, where Stoneman directed them to leave a strong picket. The rest of the brigade he sent south on the Griswoldville Road with orders to wreck the Central Railroad before rejoining the division in front of Macon.

Giving Griswoldville and its defending militia a wide berth, Capron divided his brigade into detachments, striking the railroad at intervals from three to six and a half miles east of Macon. Despite the destruction at Gordon during the night, officials had neglected to stop traffic on this part of the line, and about a mile and a half west of Griswoldville, Capron's son, Albert, and a detachment of the 14th Illinois captured a train loaded with quartermaster and commissary stores. Troopers allowed the engineer and some Negroes on board to remove their private possessions; then they uncoupled the engine and set the cars on fire. As the smoke and flames billowed into the sky, the younger Capron backed the engine up to the inferno and gave it a push. "Blazing and snapping in a frightful manner," the cars hurtled down the grade toward Griswoldville. Railroadmen and the militia sent to guard the pistol factory saw the conflagration coming and stopped the train by throwing ties across the track before it did any damage.

Lieutenant Capron was not through, however. Draining the engine's boiler, leaving only enough water to get up a head of steam, he stoked the firebox full of dry pine, then compelled a Negro boy to climb into the cab and pull the throttle open before leaping to safety. The lieutenant may have intended to send the engine hurtling into Macon, but there was an obstacle in the way. About three miles east of the city, another Yankee detachment had stopped a train full of refugees, loaded to its "utmost capacity," noted the elder Capron, "with costly furniture, printing presses, and type, private carriages and horses; in fact, every conceivable form of moveable property." The runaway locomotive the lieutenant had set in motion ploughed into the back of this train at fifty miles an hour, slicing the rear car in half and smashing halfway through the next one. Both cars had been uncoupled from the train, but the tremendous crash derailed three more passenger cars, loaded with screaming women and children. Miraculously, no one was hurt.

In the meantime, Capron's other detachments bent to the task of uprooting railroad. "Our first halt was at a point where the track ran along the steep bank of a millpond on which was located a large flouring mill," said Captain James Wells of the 8th Michigan. "The various devices in vogue by the army for destroying rails were now resorted to. First, about 200 yards of track were taken up and turned over bodily down the embankment into the pond—ties, rails and all. Meantime[,] fires were built on the track in other places, so that the expansion of the rails doubled them into the form of an elbow. Still others, taking up rails, placed them side by side with the ends resting on ties or some other object elevated a few feet above the ground, and fires were built on top of the rails in the center. As the heat increased they settled, forming a bend till the ground was reached, rendering them worthless for the time being. Often a half dozen men would pick up a rail already heated in the middle (the ends remaining cool) and wind it around the nearest tree or telegraph pole. After completing this work, just as we started away I looked back and saw with regret the flouring mill in flames. Even after the most diligent inquiry among the men I was never able to find out who set the mill on fire."

While this work was going on, pickets posted on Capron's left flank heard an approaching locomotive. Taking cover by the right-of-way as an engine and three or four cars sped past, they waited until the train stopped for the break in the track, then rushed out and captured the engineer, his crew, and a handful of Confederate soldiers they promptly paroled. Three cars were loaded with horses and mules, but no one bothered to let them out. They "burned with the train" noted a Michigan trooper.

Working their way westward, Capron's men destroyed about a mile of track, three locomotives, twenty-two boxcars, three passenger coaches, and some stock cars. They burned Owen W. Massey's machine shop and sawmill five miles east of Macon, a tannery and 2,000 hides, and plundered the farms of James Dukes, Thomas Wimberly, J. A. Tharp, Henry Champion, and a Mr. McCall before joining James Biddle's brigade in front of Macon late that morning.[6]

Biddle's two regiments had closed to within three miles of the city before gunfire crackled at the head of the column. Lieutenant Hasty's advance guard quickly put the Rebel pickets to flight and advanced steadily until about 6:00 A.M., when a few musket shots and a torn-up bridge over Walnut Creek brought them up short, a mile and a half east of Macon.

Hasty's men dismounted to fight on foot. A horse thudded to the ground, killed by a Rebel bullet. As number fours hurried the others out of range, Sergeant Oliver Haskell and a few troopers charged across the stringers of the ruined bridge. Keeping up "a constant fire," they got half a mile beyond Walnut Creek before they saw the long lines of Rebel infantry massed in the morning sun. Beating a prudent retreat, Haskell reported to Lieutenant Hasty, who directed him to take charge of the number fours and led horses while the rest of the advance guard hurried into the fight.

A lively skirmish was pop-pop-popping by the time James Biddle rode up with the 5th and 6th Indiana. After "fooling around for an hour or so," apparently waiting for the artillery to arrive, he ordered both regiments to dismount. As number fours led the horses to the rear, Major Orlando J. Smith's battalion of the 6th Indiana marched south to burn the railroad trestle over Walnut Creek. The rest of the brigade—barely enough to make "a respectable skirmish line," noted Colonel Tom Butler—crossed the creek to confront the Rebel infantry.

As Biddle's skirmishers moved forward, drivers urged the teams pulling Captain Hardy's limbers and caissons across the hastily repaired bridge and up the slopes of Dunlap's Hill, just south of the Garrison Road. The battery unlimbered next to Captain Samuel Dunlap's house, the same Dunlap who had fired at the raiders the previous day. The captain was not at home, but his wife was, and she watched fearfully as the Yankees began tearing down the stable and outbuildings and throwing up breastworks across her yard. One of Stoneman's staff officers assured the frightened lady she would not be harmed. Gesturing toward Macon, he asked how many men were defending the city and who commanded them. Then he boasted how General Stoneman had come to rescue the poor prisoners held there and would soon set them free.

Stoneman repaired to Dunlap's Hill after breakfasting at a Mrs. Loyd's. He spoke briefly with Mrs. Dunlap, who told him the prisoners at Camp Oglethorpe had been removed. Scarcely able to conceal his disappointment, Stoneman confided their release was one of the "principal objects" of his expedition.[7]

Just how much influence this conversation had on subsequent events is uncertain, but Camp Oglethorpe was not empty. At least 300 prisoners were still waiting to be sent to Charleston. Guards had marched them to the depot at 11:00 P.M. on July 29 and herded them into the cars. Doors slid closed, locks clicked shut, but the train did not move.

"Nothing is so irksome and annoying as to be lying still on a railroad train," complained one prisoner, "especially when one is along with sixty or seventy companions, squeezed into a stock car without seats, and with scarcely room to stand, as was the case with us."

Hours ticked by; daylight began seeping through the cracks in the cars, and the stale air grew hot and fetid. When some of the prisoners loudly inquired about the reason for the delay, guards told them Yankee cavalry was threatening the railroad east of Macon. This only made the inmates more eager to be off, and they listened anxiously for the shrill of the locomotive's whistle.

About 7:00 A.M., they heard the first rumble, distant but distinct, like a blast from Gabriel's trumpet. It was the sound of salvation, the roar of redemption. It was the thunder of Stoneman's artillery.

The car doors slid open. Get out, the guards commanded gruffly. Blinking at the bright sunshine, the prisoners climbed down and were hurried back to Camp Oglethorpe as the sounds of battle swelled in the distance.[8]

A steady stream of couriers had kept Howell Cobb advised of the Yankees' progress during the night and now that the wolf was at the door, Governor Brown issued a proclamation:

TO THE CITIZENS OF MACON.
HEAD QUARTERS.
Macon. July 30, 1864.

The enemy is now in sight of your houses. We lack force. I appeal to every man, Citizen or Refugee, who has a gun of any kind, or can get one, to report at the Court House with the least possible delay, that you may be thrown into Companies and aid in the defense of the city. A prompt response is expected from every patriot.

JOSEPH E. BROWN,

Report to Col. Cary W. Styles who will forward an organization as rapidly as possible.[9]

As heralds broadsided the governor's call to arms through the streets, Dr. Samuel H. Stout, medical director of the Army of Tennessee, ordered surgeons at the Macon hospitals to send "every man able to bear a musket, officer and soldier, . . . to the ordnance officer in charge of the gun factory adjoining this office to aid in repelling the raid now being made on Macon.

"They will report all who shirk from this duty," Stout added, "that charges may be preferred against them."

The edict had the desired effect. A Macon newspaper reported seeing "a number of officers and soldiers who were wounded in the late battles, . . . some of them with wounded arms in bandages, others with wounded heads. One man was hobbling along with a crutch under one arm and a gun on the other; numbers of them were pulling themselves along, using their muskets for walking sticks, all determined and anxious to go to the field." One crippled Confederate asserted that those unable to walk were *taken out to the fight in vehicles!*"

Even the guards at Camp Oglethorpe were pressed into service. Only twenty-five men and Captain Edward S. Lathrop's battery of four light guns were left behind, with orders to open fire on the prisoners if they tried to escape.[10]

Among those hurrying through the busy streets that morning was Joseph E. Johnston, the recently relieved commander of the Army of Tennessee. After leaving Atlanta on a southbound freight on the evening of July 19, he and his wife had arrived in Macon about noon the next day. Met by an invitation from Howell Cobb, offering them the hospitality of his home on Walnut Street, the Johnstons had gratefully accepted. They had stayed with Cobb until July 26, then moved to Vineville, a northern suburb of the city, to share a house with Johnston's former chief of staff, Brigadier General William W. Mackall.

When the alarm sounded on July 30, Johnston mounted his bay mare and rapidly rode into Macon to tender his services. Cobb immediately offered him command of the men mustering to defend the city, but Johnston politely declined and volunteered instead to serve as Cobb's advisor. "I take pleasure in acknowledging my great obligation to him," Cobb later wrote. "He showed himself not only to be the General but the gentleman that I had always believed him to be."[11]

Against the advice of several of his own officers, Cobb had already decided to give battle with his back to the Ocmulgee. It was a risky move. If his reserves and raw militia gave way, they would be hopelessly trapped against an unfordable river, with no place to run. Perhaps Cobb reasoned this would make them fight better.

Early that morning, he had ordered his field commander, Colonel Lee, to shift Colonel W. J. Armstrong's militia regiment to the left to extend Colonel Cumming's flank across the Clinton Road. He directed Lee's two remaining regiments to form their line astride the Garrison Road where it crested the second hill beyond East Macon.

Lee's militia began moving into position at 5:00 A.M.; Colonel Tarpley L. Holt's regiment on the left side of the road, Colonel Charles Jenkins Harris's regiment on the right. "Captain," an aged militiaman called to his company commander as Holt's regiment formed its line in a cornfield, "what must an old man do who can't run? I have rheumatism so bad."

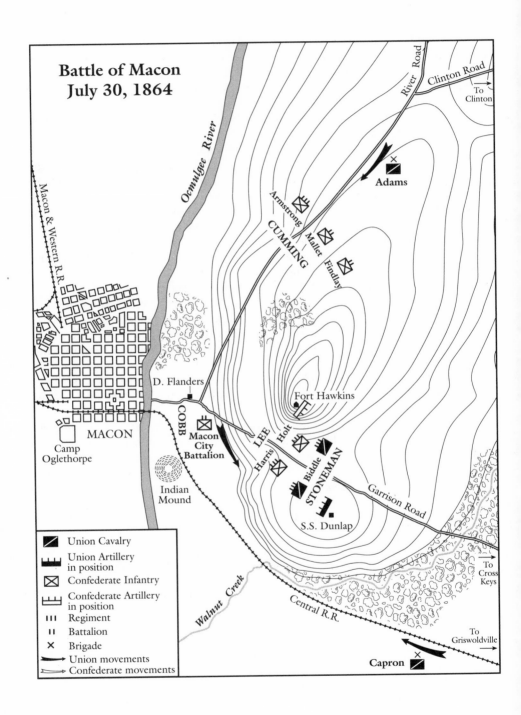

Battle of Macon
July 30, 1864

Ocmulgee River

River Road

Clinton Road

To Clinton

Macon & Western R.R.

Adams

Armstrong

Mallet

CUMMING

Findlay

D. Flanders

COBB

Fort Hawkins

Macon City Battalion

LEE

Holt

MACON

Camp Oglethorpe

Harris

Biddle

STONEMAN

Indian Mound

S.S. Dunlap

Garrison Road

To Cross Keys

Walnut Creek

Central R.R.

To Griswoldville

Capron

Legend

- Union Cavalry
- Union Artillery in position
- Confederate Infantry
- Confederate Artillery in position
- ııı Regiment
- ıı Battalion
- × Brigade
- → Union movements
- ⇒ Confederate movements

That was just the sort of man they needed, the officer replied, one who would not run away.

Captain Brooks's company of Harris's regiment had moved forward to form a skirmish line across the Garrison Road when they encountered Lieutenant Hasty's "Hatchet Brigade" at Walnut Creek. Pressed by "superior numbers," the militiamen began falling back.

The first blue wave of Yankee skirmishers began advancing about 7:00 A.M., and soon both of Lee's regiments were hotly engaged. Then one of the Yankee guns on Dunlap's Hill suddenly opened fire. The militiamen cowered. Some of them started for the rear. Lee, accompanied by his aides, Captains John C. Hendrix, W. H. Paxton, and William Gibbs McAdoo, spurred into their midst. Rally! Rally! Stand fast, Captain Hendrix implored just as his horse was shot out from under him. Captain Paxton dismounted and was urging the men forward when he was shot through the leg. Several other officers, sent by Cobb, galloped up to steady the wavering ranks. "All confusion disappeared," Lee later wrote, "and the men were again advanced into line . . . ," where they began building breastworks of earth and rails.[12]

Macon's City Battalion was still at Vineville, guarding the northern approaches into town, when the first rattle of musketry sounded on the other side of the Ocmulgee. At 7:00 A.M., Colonel Gibbs received orders advising him the Yankees were within a mile and a half of the city. A "cultivated, urbane, and humane" old officer who had commanded the Rebel prisons at Richmond and Danville, Virginia, and Salisbury, North Carolina, before coming to Camp Oglethorpe, Gibbs assembled his battalion: two companies of "aged gentlemen," Captain J. W. Armstrong's appropriately named Silver Greys and Captain B. F. Ross's Home Guards; Lieutenant Nichols's Fire Guards; Major M. R. Rodgers's Factory Company; and a company of convalescents led by Lieutenant Charles M. Wiley. Gibbs gave them a short, patriotic speech, then ordered them "forward."[13]

As the battalion trooped down Georgia Avenue and into Mulberry Street, the venerable Silver Greys and Home Guards were met by crowds of boys carrying baskets their mothers had filled with "hot coffee, sandwiches, fried chicken, hard-boiled eggs, biscuits, etc.," for fathers, grandfathers, and uncles. "The hungry men kept us engaged until the center of town was reached," recounted fourteen-year-old Arthur Boardman, "when the lads scurried home to return the empty baskets and get their shot-guns, to aid in repelling the enemy. The thoughtful mothers had carefully put away and locked up the shot-guns and ammunition and the lads feared to make too apparent [a] search for them lest they be forbidden to leave the premises. So they stole away and soon were seen following close in the rear of the columns. . . ."[14]

As Gibbs's battalion approached the railroad bridge over the Ocmulgee, the disquieting roar of battle was punctuated by jarring blasts of artillery. Firing from Dunlap's Hill, Yankee gunners hurled an estimated fifteen shells into Macon itself. Six shots were aimed at the old magazine; two or three fell near the Ocmulgee Hospital. Others struck near the riverbank or exploded in the air.[15]

Stoneman's battery had apparently done little or nothing to improve the quality of its ammunition since the Moore's Bridge raid two weeks earlier. A Hotchkiss shell ploughed into the sand sidewalk in front of Judge Asa G. Holt's four-columned home on Mulberry Street, ricocheted upward, and gouged a chunk out of the second column from the left, smashing through the top of a window sash and shattering the glass before landing with a thud in the front hallway, where Mrs. Holt had been sitting only fifteen minutes earlier. It did not explode.[16]

"Mein Gott in Himmel!" Abraham Dessau of the Silver Greys muttered over and over again as the shells screamed overhead. One explosion startled John L. Jones so badly he lost his footing as he emerged from the east end of the railroad bridge and tumbled down the steep embankment. "Fortunately, no bones were broken," recorded young Arthur Boardman, "but he was so bruised and shaken by the fall that it was deemed advisable to send him home, and there was no lack of volunteers to carry him there."

Just beyond the river, Gibbs halted the battalion at the foot of Sixth Street and ordered the men to load their muskets. Leaving the Silver Greys to guard the railroad bridge, he led the Home Guards, the Fire Guards, the Factory Company, and convalescents up the hill toward the sound of the guns. "As we passed the river . . . ," noted one citizen soldier, "the women, children, and negroes from East Macon came pell-mell down the streets in the wildest confusion—couriers were passing at full speed to and fro, as though we were really to have a battle."

Looking to their left as they crested the top of the hill, Gibbs's men saw Governor Brown, General Johnston, and several other officers gathered under the shade of a chinaberry tree in front of David Flanders's house. The gray-bearded, corpulent Cobb sat in their midst in an oversized armchair, flanked by a small table set with a palm-leaf fan and a tall glass of "something iced." The City Battalion recognized him with a cheer.[17]

At 9:00 A.M., about the same time Gibbs's men marched into East Macon, Orlando Smith's battalion of the 6th Indiana was setting fire to the 200-foot railroad trestle over Walnut Creek. The plume of thick, black smoke quickly attracted the attention of Lieutenant Charles A. McClung, who, at Cobb's direction, had wheeled a twelve-pounder Napoleon into position in front of Fort Hawkins, a weathered old blockhouse dating back to the War of 1812. With the help of an officer posted in the upper story, McClung immediately opened a well-directed fire.[18]

"Our battery could get no position from which it could operate effectively against that of the enemy in Fort Hawkins," complained one of Stoneman's staff officers, and Rebel shells rained down on Dunlap's Hill. One hurtled through Captain Dunlap's house, forcing Mrs. Dunlap and her children to flee for their lives. Others burst in a watermelon field, showering some of Biddle's horseholders with shell fragments and melon rinds.

But Major Smith was "not the man to be driven off until his work was well done," noted a Yankee trooper. He cut the telegraph wire with his own hands. Then, reinforced by the arrival of some of Capron's men, he led his battalion up the Central Railroad toward Macon.[19]

Seeing this effort to turn his flank, Lee sent a courier galloping to Cobb with an urgent request for reinforcements. Gibbs's battalion arrived soon afterward, and Lee hurried them across George W. Adams's cornfield under "a very heavy fire" with orders to hold the right "at all hazards."

Springing over a rail fence, the Home Guards and Fire Guards formed their ranks just behind the cornfield. The Factory Company deployed a little farther to the right as skirmishers, while the convalescents passed down the rear of Gibbs's line to anchor the extreme right in an orchard.

Fort Hawkins, near Macon, Georgia, as it appeared circa 1876. Built in 1806 as a defense against hostile Indians, the old blockhouse helped turn back George Stoneman's assault on the city. A full-scale replica, reconstructed by the Daughters of the American Revolution, now stands on the site. Used by permission of the Middle Georgia Archives, Washington Memorial Library, Macon, Georgia.

"We went into line of battle in a swamp; deployed as skirmishers and were all well posted behind trees," recounted Campbell Tracy, a wounded veteran who hobbled to the field on crutches with the Home Guards. "I was well flanked: the venerable Dr. [David] Wills, pastor [of the] First Presbyterian Church, was on my right; and . . . the Reverend J. E. Evans, Mulberry Street Methodist Church, was on my left, a veteran soldier having been thus *wisely* placed, all along the line between the citizens!"

They had scarcely gotten into position when some of Lee's militia came racing toward them in full retreat. Then the first bluejacketed Federals came into view. "Fire," an officer ordered, and the City Battalion's front blazed with the crash of three hundred muskets.

"His [Stoneman's] first advance was repulsed," continued Campbell Tracy, "but he soon got a battery in position, and opened on us with that. A second charge on our line was driven back and everything was going on as lively as in old Virginia when on their third advance a Yank got a side shot at me as I leaned against my tree to shoot. His bullet went between my lip and the bark, the shock knocking me off my crutches. As I fell, the blood flowed freely, my lip having been cut by pieces of the bark.

"Old Parsons Wills and Evans quit firing, and ran to my assistance. I told them I was not much hurt; to help me up, and go back and keep firing or the enemy would break through the line! But wishing to help me—(*thinking I needed surgical aid*) and *knowing they needed to get off the firing line!*—they insisted on picking me up, *nolens volens.* They had me hoisted up as high as their shoulders with me just *a kickin' and a cussin'!*"

"Campbell," Reverend Evans admonished, "ain't you afraid to take the name of the Lord in vain, right here in the presence of death, hell, and destruction?"

Just then a shell burst nearby. "They let me drop and *broke for the rear,*" Tracy noted disparagingly. "I called to them for God's sake to come back, or the Yanks would break through the line. I *swore some more* and they came back and helped me to my tree."

"I tell you, boys," Tracy said hotly as his two companions lifted him to his feet, "you like to have broke my wounded leg over! Don't you try that stunt again!"

Another Methodist minister who took his place on the skirmish line was Reverend Jacob R. Danforth. His black broadcloth suit and silk top hat made him a conspicuous target, and it was not long before a Yankee bullet sent his headgear spinning. Danforth knelt down and picked it up, ruefully inspecting the damage as he knocked the dust off with a brush of his sleeve. "No gentleman would be guilty of such bad manners," he remarked, putting the ruined chapeau back on his head.

The Reverends Ebenezer W. Warren and F. M. Haygood of the First Baptist Church of Christ; Samuel Boykin, editor of the *Christian Index*; and John W. Burke of the Methodist Book Depository also saw action with the City Battalion. Reverend Warren had shouldered a musket, even though he had been too ill to fulfill his ministerial duties. He and the rest of the clergy gave a good account of themselves, and the City Battalion stood fast. "We are giving them hell!" shouted a wounded man who was brought back to Macon.[20]

The work waxed hotter as the sun climbed higher. One of the militiamen collapsed from the heat and died. Eager young boys, mindless of the danger, scurried up and down the lines, ladling out cartridges and cool water. Everything was noise and confusion. The militia lacked experienced officers, and according to one observer, "their maneuverings were bungled and their firing done at random—most of which being a waste of ammunition. . . . [O]ur men frequently fired into each other, and . . . our loss in killed and wounded is chiefly owing to these mistakes."

On the left of Cobb's line, along the Clinton Road, Lieutenant Colonel John W. Mallet had roused his battalion of ordnance workers before dawn and spent two hours building breastworks. Mallet held a degree from the University of Dublin and a doctorate from the University of Gottingen, but he was a chemist, not an engineer. He had sited his works "in so exposed a position," noted one of the Wright Guards, "that had the enemy engaged us, he could have poured a withering cross fire upon the entire line from a wooded elevation in front."

Work was interrupted about 9:00 A.M., when couriers galloped up and reported the Yankees were only a half mile away, coming down the Clinton Road. Mallet immediately sent a squad of pickets forward, but they soon came back, loading and firing as they retired before swarms of Yankee skirmishers. "Minie balls were soon flying about us," observed one of Mallet's men, "filling the air with their mournful whistlings. . . ."

The fighting alternately flared and sputtered, but the "withering cross fire" that would have swept the rude Rebel works never materialized. For some reason, the Yankees did not press the attack on the Clinton Road, and shortly before noon, in response to repeated requests from Lee, Cobb ordered Colonel Cumming to send

Mallet's battalion and part of the 5th Georgia Reserves to reinforce the threatened right. As Mallet's battalion marched through East Macon, the Wright Guards were detached to round up stragglers. The rest of the column, led by Lieutenant Colonel Gustavus A. Henry, Jr., hurried toward the railroad.

An aide to General Hood, Henry had little or no experience handling troops, but what he lacked in expertise, he made up for with enthusiasm. He had a horse shot out from under him as he deployed Major Charles E. McGregor's battalion of the 5th Georgia Reserves on the extreme right of Lee's line, and for the next two hours, his "daring and chivalric bearing" steadied the artisans, foundrymen, and arsenal workers, who beat back every attempt of Stoneman's veterans to advance up the railroad.

In the face of such stubborn opposition, the fighting shifted north of the Garrison Road again, where Yankee skirmishers began probing a gap between the left and right wings of the Rebel line. This brought another urgent request from Lee, asking Cobb to shift Colonel Cumming's command to the right to connect with his left. Cumming speedily complied and with the help of the artillery at Fort Hawkins easily checked the assault.[21]

On the Clinton Road, Silas Adams's brigade made only halfhearted efforts to advance. The 1st Kentucky's Lieutenant Huffman found time to feast on watermelons, and Rebecca Latimer Felton complained her house was overrun with Yankee troopers who "chased and shot chickens," stripped her peach trees, and were "continually going and coming."

"Canteens were filled with brandy instead of water," she wrote. "Along about 4 p.m. the drinking ones got to fussing among themselves—shots begun to be exchanged. I huddled in a back room with my two little boys, one five and the other ten years old. I had sense enough left to put as many partition walls as possible between us and the shooting crowd in the front yard. I backed up against a chimney. . . . Finally, a trooper who had occupied a chair on the rude piazza in the rear, sought me out. One of the little boys went toward him with a weary little smile and took his hand. The sight of the child and my tearful helplessness got the better of him. He stood in the door, going out in the hall, and with his gun in his hand he motioned the wild, half drunk men who made continual rushes through the hall to go on."

Mrs. Felton's husband was sitting on the front-yard fence when a Yankee officer perched beside him suddenly stood up and asked, "How's that?"

"Coming this way. Is it not?" ventured Dr. Felton, cocking an ear toward the pounding of approaching hooves. A moment later the road was filled with horsemen streaming back toward Clinton. The firing around Macon grew faint and distant and finally ceased altogether.

Mrs. Felton and her family heaved a collective sigh of relief. But in Camp Oglethorpe, shoulders sagged in despair and strong men's eyes welled with tears. "All was quiet as the still morning air which it had first broken," a prisoner noted as the last shot echoed in the distance, "and with it *died all hope*."[22]

Believing the prison was empty, Stoneman decided he had done all that could be done, and at 3:00 P.M. he ordered his brigade commanders to withdraw. Eight hours of skirmishing had cost his most heavily engaged regiments, the 5th and 6th Indiana, one man killed and five or six wounded. He still had a potent striking force and fully intended to "press on to Andersonville," sixty miles to the southwest.[23]

Summoning the Kentucky brigade from the Clinton Road, he ordered Silas Adams to take the pack train down the east bank of the Ocmulgee and hold a ford seven or eight miles below Macon until the rest of the command arrived. Adams had gone about two miles in that direction when one of Stoneman's scouts reported a column of Rebel cavalry, 1,000 to 1,500 strong, coming into Macon. Fearing this force might get to the ford before he could, Stoneman countermanded his orders and called Adams back.

While awaiting Adams's return, Stoneman convened a council of some of his senior officers at the Cross Keys Hotel. They could not get into Macon, he announced; the wagon bridge was washed out. A sizable force of Rebel cavalry was moving to block the road to Andersonville. There was nothing else they could do. It was time to head back toward Atlanta.

"There is the railroad bridge . . . ," suggested Tom Butler, "give me the order and the 5th Cavalry will take it."

Stoneman eyed him sourly. "Colonel Butler," he said gravely, "I want you to understand that I am in command here and when I want you to go I will order it."[24]

Repeating his instructions to withdraw, he left his officers casting questioning glances among themselves. They talked in low tones, anxious to know how Stoneman intended to get back to Sherman's lines. "We reasoned that the main force of the enemy would certainly be on the same road that we came down on," explained Tom Butler, "and to go back [on] that road would be disastrous in the extreme."

After some discussion, Butler's fellow officers delegated him to speak to Stoneman, discern his plan "if possible," and acquaint him with their suggestions, which they felt "were entitled to his consideration."

The six-foot, black-bearded Butler approached Stoneman and asked how he intended to get back to Atlanta. Stoneman curtly replied he had not decided yet.

"I then asked the privilege of making a suggestion," Butler recounted, "which was granted. The suggestion was that he should return on the Milledgeville road [Griswoldville road], leaving the Macon [Garrison] road, on which we had marched down, to our left, and by so doing, with rapid marching that night, we could put our pursuers in our rear; then destroying a bridge or two across some of those narrow, deep streams, would insure us of safe passage to Sherman's lines."[25]

Stoneman allowed the idea had merit and told his chief of staff, Robert Smith, he intended to strike eastward for Milledgeville "as soon as practicable." Anticipating a long night in the saddle, he ordered Horace Capron to form a line on the first elevated ground near the road forks at Cross Keys and rest his men and horses for one hour.

Capron's brigade arrived at the intersection and found Stoneman "in a white heat." The wife of a Confederate general had come to him complaining a soldier had stolen a tin box full of money and jewelry from her. Stoneman had the man arrested and was threatening to have him tied to a gun carriage and shot when Captain James Wells of the 8th Michigan intervened.

The money and jewelry could all be returned, Wells hastily explained. His men had "taken it thoughtlessly, as they would pick up a coin or a purse on a public highway," and he related how a slave woman had told one of his pickets where the box was buried. The soldier had followed her to the spot, dug the box up, and, being a generous sort, had shared watches, rings, bracelets, gold coins, and "trinkets galore" with his comrades.

Canvassing his company, Wells restored most of the money and jewelry to its rightful owner, but Stoneman's mood had not improved. Scouts had brought him word the force he had dispatched toward Gordon the day before had drawn the Rebel pursuit toward Milledgeville.

Compelled to rethink his route, Stoneman reasoned if the Rebels were converging on Milledgeville, this would leave only a small force to block the road back to Covington. He would have to ride all night, but if he could retrace his steps as far as Hillsboro by daylight, he would then have his choice of three roads to travel. Abandoning any designs he had on Milledgeville, he started Capron's brigade toward Clinton at 5:00 P.M.[26]

James Biddle's brigade brought up the rear, burning the wagon bridge over Walnut Creek behind them. Seeing the retreat, Rebel artilleryman Charles McClung limbered up the Napoleon gun he commanded at Fort Hawkins and followed the Yankees as far as the ruined bridge, hurling a few shells to hurry them on their way. According to some captured Confederates who escaped in the ensuing confusion, these parting shots killed two Yankees and wounded others before the rear ranks got out of range.

Early that evening, Biddle's brigade reached the intersection of the Garrison and Griswoldville roads at Cross Keys. There they met a soldier Stoneman had left behind with orders for Biddle to rest his horses for an hour, then close up on Capron as quickly as possible.

While the Hoosiers halted under a dark and suddenly threatening sky, a mounted company of Macon volunteers, led by Lieutenant J. D. Bostwick, splashed across Walnut Creek and followed at a respectful distance. When John Cleghorn, a bookkeeper for the Macon firm of Ross & Seymour, asked for permission to press ahead, Bostwick tried hard to dissuade him, but the plucky Scot refused to listen. Slipping through the cornfields, he soon found the Yankees halted on the right of the Garrison Road. Lying down behind a fence, the bookkeeper coolly began counting horses. When he had finished, he took down a section of rails, resolving to bring back proof he had actually been in the Yankee camp. Pulling off his silk neckerchief and tying it around the neck of a grazing horse, he lead the animal through the gap just as a sentry sounded the alarm. A buzz of bullets whizzed past, but Cleghorn escaped and soon advised his astounded lieutenant there were 800 Yankees camped just a quarter-mile up the road.

The two Indiana regiments Cleghorn had counted sat hunched in their saddles for about an hour, "during which," declared one of the raiders, "the hardest rain fell I ever saw." Then they headed north on the familiar road back to Clinton, and everyone, from colonels down to the lowliest enlisted man, knew what it meant.

"I guess," Sergeant Erastus Holmes mused in his diary, "we are to fight Wheeler tomorrow."[27]

18

STONEMAN'S RAID
CROSS KEYS TO SUNSHINE CHURCH

JULY 30–JULY 31, 1864

Fatigue makes cowards of us all.

—George S. Patton, Jr.,
War as I Knew It

Lightning arced across the slate-gray sky as Company F of the 8th Michigan Cavalry led Stoneman's straggling column northward on the Lite-n-Tie Road. Thunder rumbled somewhere in the fading twilight and a wet breeze stirred through fields of green corn on both sides of the road. The weary, rain-soaked troopers rode in slack-reined silence as their horses and mules shuffled past the darkened doors of the farmhouses and plantations they had looted only a few hours earlier.

About a mile and a half below Clinton, a Negro man approached the head of the column. The town was full of Rebs, he said, maybe fifty of them. Officers gave a few hurried commands. Troopers drew their revolvers and quickly divided into small squads, sweeping into Clinton from several directions. Pistol shots mixed with the drumming of hooves as Rebel scouts raced out of town at a gallop, occasionally turning in their saddles to snap a shot at their pursuers as they sped north and west.[1]

Stoneman's advance guard took perhaps twenty prisoners in this brief skirmish and released thirty-three of their own stragglers who had been captured and confined in the Jones County jail. Someone set the two-story stone building ablaze and the lurid flames cast long shadows as the Yankee troopers filed past. The red glare slowly receded in the distance as they rode northward, and by 9:00 P.M. the head of the column was three miles beyond Clinton. That was when the first gunshots sounded in the darkness.[2]

Capron's advance guard had collided with a column of oncoming Confederates. Two days earlier, Joe Wheeler had sent Brigadier General Alfred Holt Iverson's command toward McDonough to protect the Macon railroad. Leaving the 4th Alabama Cavalry at Flat Shoals with Wheeler, Iverson had hurried south with the 1st, 2nd, 3rd, and 4th Georgia regiments of his own brigade, commanded by Colonel Charles C. Crews; the 1st, 3rd, 7th, 12th, and 51st Alabama of Brigadier General William Wirt Allen's brigade; the 1st, 2nd, and 9th Kentucky of Colonel John Russell Butler's brigade; a pair of three-inch rifled guns from Huggins's Battery, commanded by Lieutenant Nat Baxter; and two six-pounders belonging to Captain Benjamin F. White's Battery.

Early on July 28, Iverson had halted his column, about 1,400 strong, on the McDonough Road, a mile and a half from Hollingsworth's Mill. He intended to move through McDonough to Jonesboro as soon as his men fed their horses, but a courier overtook him with instructions to wait for further orders. Scouts had discovered the Yankees were marching toward Monticello, not McDonough, but it was not until 11:00 P.M., July 29, that Iverson received Wheeler's dispatch to follow Stoneman rapidly and "attack him wherever found."[3]

Iverson advised Wheeler his march would be in the general direction of Milledgeville. On the morning of July 30, he turned Allen's and Crews's brigades eastward, crossing the Yellow and Alcovy rivers, while Russ Butler's Kentucky brigade apparently continued south, through McDonough and Jackson, to block any attempt by Stoneman to cross the Ocmulgee and join the other raiding column threatening the railroad between Atlanta and Macon.

"The difficulty now," one of Iverson's staff officers pointed out, "was to ascertain whether the Yankees would go to Milledgeville, to Macon, or having twenty-four hours start, would attempt the passage of the Ocmulgee from the East, and strike at Macon and the Macon and Western Railroad, on the West bank, and thence to Andersonville. In this latter case, if General Iverson . . . committed himself to the direct pursuit of Stoneman, he would find the ferries burned, and the enemy in a situation to inflict with impunity whatever damage they pleased. All this necessary information had to be obtained, and General Iverson accordingly filled the country before him with a cloud of scouts, moving at the same time in such a manner as to be closing on Stoneman, and . . . not to be thrown off the track in case he attempted a ruse."

Iverson's scouts picked up Stoneman's trail somewhere below Covington and followed it south, through Monticello. "We knew that Gov. Brown had militia forces in Macon and that they and the citizens ought to prevent the enemy from crossing the river," explained Iverson's aide, ". . . if they did not, it would be impossible for us, by marching ever so hard, to save the city, or catch them afterwards, while, if they were repulsed from Macon and attempted to escape toward Eatonton, we could have the short cut across their line of retreat."

While Allen's and Crews's brigades moved southward through Monticello, Russ Butler's Kentuckians apparently crossed the Ocmulgee at Pope's and Dame's ferries, fourteen and sixteen miles above Macon. In fact, Butler's three regiments were almost certainly the mysterious column of Rebel cavalry one of Stoneman's scouts reported moving down the west side of the Ocmulgee that afternoon. By nightfall, all three of Iverson's brigades were fast converging on Hillsboro.[4]

Iverson was a native of nearby Clinton, but despite oft-repeated claims to the contrary, he was not intimately familiar with the surrounding countryside. The son of Alfred and Sarah Caroline Holt Iverson, he was barely a year old when his mother died. Soon afterward, his father had quit Clinton for good and moved the family to Columbus, Georgia.[5]

The elder Iverson became a U.S. congressman and senator, and apparently had no qualms about using his influence on his son's behalf. After briefly attending the Alabama Military and Scientific Institute at Tuskegee, eighteen-year-old Alfred became a second lieutenant in a Georgia battalion his father helped raise and equip for the Mexican War. The unit reached Mexico too late to see any action, and young Iverson spent eight of his eleven months in the army on sick leave.[6]

After a failed attempt at reading law and a stint as a railroad contractor, in 1855 he received a first lieutenant's commission in the newly created 1st U.S. Cavalry. The

There are no known images of Confederate Brigadier General Alfred Holt Iverson in uniform. This is how he appeared in 1858. The spoiled son of a Georgia senator, he spent most of his prewar career in the old 1st U.S. Cavalry on leave of absence and came to the Army of Tennessee trying to restore a ruined reputation. Courtesy of Gary Kross. Used by permission.

regiment was posted to the turbulent Kansas frontier, but Iverson soon returned to Georgia, married his second cousin, and spent almost two years on a recruiting detail in Carlisle, Pennsylvania. When finally ordered to rejoin his regiment in May 1858, he spent more time on furlough than he did in the field.

Resigning his commission in March 1861, he was elected colonel of the 20th North Carolina Infantry. He suffered a severe wound during the Seven Days battles around Richmond and served creditably in the Confederate invasion of Maryland. Upon the recommendation of both "Stonewall" Jackson and Robert E. Lee, he was promoted to brigadier general, but camp gossip hinted he owed his promotion to his father's political influence. A widower now, with two small children, Iverson wrote to "Stonewall" Jackson in February 1863, threatening to resign unless he got a leave of absence. Jackson replied he would rather accept Iverson's resignation than give him a furlough.

Iverson reluctantly stayed with the army and stood his trial by fire as a brigade commander at the battle of Chancellorsville. During the second day's savage fighting in the tangled woods, he walked away from his hard-pressed brigade to "procure re-enforcements." After summoning help, he did not rejoin his troops because "I received a contusion in the groin from a spent ball, which made walking very painful. . . ."

Any questions Chancellorsville raised about Iverson's fitness for command were answered on the first day at the battle of Gettysburg, when he committed a serious tactical blunder and then remained far to the rear while his brigade was butchered. Quietly relieved of command, Iverson was sent to Georgia at the request of Howell Cobb to command the cavalry of the State Guard. When the Guard's enlistment expired in February 1864, he was transferred to the Army of Tennessee and assigned to Major General William T. Martin's division of Wheeler's cavalry. Martin took sick leave on July 2, and Iverson assumed command as the senior brigadier. His courage was questionable, his abilities suspect, but fate was going to give him a second chance, almost within sight of the town where he was born.[7]

The skirmishing that started three miles above Clinton that night rapidly moved north. Ordered to ride over anything that got in their way, Stoneman's advance guard shoved Iverson's men back half a mile. The Rebels met reinforcements and more shots rang out in the darkness. As resistance stiffened, Horace Capron sent a squadron of the 8th Michigan forward. Two companies, D and I, deployed in line of battle. "We . . . made a charge and run them two miles," wrote Sergeant John Kesler, "and followed them all night, when we could not get another man to rally." Finally, Captain Muir A. McDonald led Company I in a headlong charge that drove the Rebels out of three successive barricades.

"Tigers," exclaimed Stoneman's inspector general, Major Myles Keogh. These Michigan boys fought like tigers.

"The route took us through wooded country," noted Captain James Wells, "and about midnight, after turning an angle in the road, from an elevated position a few yards ahead, there came a succession of volleys that brought our command to a halt, and at the first round two or three men and horses were wounded. This rapid fire compelled us to dismount and lead out into the timber for shelter, there to await orders from the commanding General."

Capron advised Stoneman it was "still too dark for us to form an estimate of the force opposing us or the nature of their defences," and received instructions to halt and build barricades. Troopers pulled down fences and crouched behind piles of rails as the surrounding woods echoed with the incessant, ringing reports of rifles and carbines.

Stoneman, in the meantime, waited for the rest of his column to close up. Adams's brigade had passed through Clinton shortly after dark, while the jail was still ablaze. Biddle's brigade followed about 11:00 P.M.

"The march that night . . . was very tedious," wrote the 5th Indiana's Tom Butler, "and sometimes I imagined the whole command was asleep. Indeed many did sleep upon their horses, which was not to be wondered at, as that was the third day and night without sleep and with very little food."

Well after midnight, Biddle's exhausted troopers halted about three miles beyond Clinton and lay down in the road to try to get some rest. "An order came about every 2 minutes for the rear guard to do something," complained Sergeant Oliver Haskell, ". . . couldn't sleep."

At 3:30 A.M., Stoneman ordered Capron to push a skirmish line up both sides of the Hillsboro Road. Captain James Wells formed Company F of the 8th Michigan on the right flank, but it was so dark the only way he could keep his alignment in the tangled woods was to pass orders from left to right in a low voice. He had not gone far when someone demanded, "Who comes there?"

"The Eighth," Wells replied.

"Eighth what?"

"Eighth Michigan," Wells retorted. "What regiment is that?"

"First Alabama."

"Fire and advance," Wells yelled.

The dark woods rang with the roar of the answering volley. Wells plunged forward, stepping past a dead Rebel who lay sprawled with a bullet hole in his head, the same man who had challenged him a moment earlier.

The fighting in the predawn darkness was close and brutal. A muzzle blast blossomed a few feet in front of Sergeant Homer Manvel. A bullet whistled past. Then a dark form hurtled at him, pinning his arms to his sides, calling to unseen companions for help. Manvel shoved the muzzle of his Colt revolver against the man's ribs and pulled the trigger. There was a jarring blast and Manvel felt the man's suddenly lifeless grip slip away.

Loading and firing, the Michigan men waded through briars and honeysuckle and scrambled across gullies, driving the Rebels before them. The slanting rays of the morning sun were just spilling through the trees when they pushed past Sunshine Church, "an unpretending little house of God," on the left side of the road. But there would be no services this Sunday. Just beyond the chinked log chapel, on either side of John J. Barfield's house, Brigadier General William Wirt Allen's Alabama brigade waited behind a rail barricade blocking the Hillsboro Road.[8]

A Princeton graduate, Allen had begun his military career as a lieutenant in the cavalry company captained by James H. Clanton and later succeeded him as colonel of the 1st Alabama. He was shot in the shoulder while leading a charge at the battle of Perryville. At Stone's River, a disabling wound had cost him part of his right hand. A tall, stout man, "cool amid danger, and faithful and tireless in the discharge of his duty," he had hurried ahead with his brigade at dusk the previous evening with orders to delay the approaching Yankees. All night long, his men had been fighting and falling back, fighting and falling back. Now, as they watched the oncoming enemy fill their gunsights, they eared back the hammers on their rifles and carbines once again.[9]

A half mile behind them, Alfred Iverson was furiously fortifying a gentle rise straddling the Hillsboro Road. He had arrived at daylight with his Georgia and Kentucky brigades, and as soon as they had piled up enough fence rails to cover their front, he ordered his hard-pressed Alabamians to fall back. Bluecoated skirmishers swarming over Allen's abandoned barricade quickly came within range and Iverson's Georgia and Kentucky cavalrymen opened fire. The blast staggered the Yankees and a salvo from Captain Benjamin White's twin six-pounders sent them scrambling for cover in a thin strip of woods.

While Horace Capron peered through the intervening foliage, trying to get a good look at Iverson's position, his exhausted Michigan troopers slumped to the ground. "It was impossible to keep the men awake . . . on the skirmish line," Captain James Wells noted with alarm. "As soon as a partial cover was reached, a stump, a rock, or a bush, they fell asleep, oblivious to all danger."

The roar of the guns brought Stoneman hurrying to the front. What he saw and heard convinced him the Rebel line formed a rough semicircle or an inverted "V," completely overlapping both of his flanks. He immediately ordered the rest of Capron's and Adams's brigades to dismount, deploying Capron's 8th Michigan and Adams's 1st and 11th Kentucky on the left of the Hillsboro Road; the 14th Illinois and McLaughlin's Ohio Squadron on the right. Captain Hardy unlimbered one of his

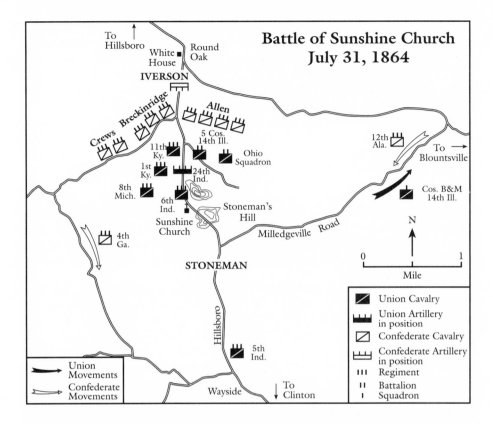

Battle of Sunshine Church
July 31, 1864

3-inch rifles just outside the churchyard, while the other waited in reserve. His gunners quickly found the range and put a shell right through the floor sills of Iverson's headquarters at Joseph White's house, just north of Round Oak. Once again, their aim was better than their ammunition and the shell failed to explode.

While Hardy dueled with the Rebel battery at the head of the column, officers at the rear were trying to shoo away perhaps as many as 5,000 Negroes who had followed them from Macon. "You could see them . . . their eyes shining in a most wonderful manner . . . ," noted Lieutenant Richard Huffman, "black cotton-field, genuine negroes . . . huddled together with the led stock. . . . When the shells commenced flying and bursting, you never saw such running as there was of negroes and mules."

By the time the guns fell silent about 8:00 A.M., preparations on both sides were complete. Iverson had sent Major Augustus R. Stewart's 4th Georgia Cavalry sweeping around the right to attack Stoneman's rear and moved Allen's Alabama brigade to his left to keep the Yankees from escaping on the Milledgeville Road.

Stoneman, however, made no pretense of maneuver and simply ordered Adams's and Capron's brigades to drive straight ahead. When Capron protested his 8th Michigan had not come up, leaving him with only seven companies of the 14th Illinois and two companies of McLaughlin's Ohio Squadron, Stoneman peremptorily ordered him to attack and drive the Rebels off the Hillsboro Road.

"Gen. Stoneman seemed infatuated with the idea that he could cut his way through and return by the same route," recorded a Michigan officer, "although he had sufficient evidence that a large force was in his front, and that the force in Macon would follow up in his rear. Almost every officer and man in his command felt certain that remaining in that position and attempting to fight our way through would prove a failure. Even General Stoneman's staff officers begged him to avoid the enemy's main force, and move around to the right. . . ."

Stoneman, however, was adamant and went out on the skirmish line, urging his men forward. "Gen. Stoneman appeared almost mad," noted Lieutenant Huffman, and Capron later speculated there were other reasons, "physical perhaps," which compelled Stoneman to insist on taking the most direct route back to Atlanta. In other words, four days in the saddle may have been all his hemorrhoids could stand.

Whatever the reason, Stoneman massed his troops on the west side of the Hillsboro Road. Screened by the woods, his skirmishers advanced to within 220 yards of the Rebel line before taking cover in a deep gully. After resting a few minutes, the 8th Michigan and 1st and 11th Kentucky scrambled over the top and rushed up the slope. Captain Watson B. Smith, commanding Company K of the 8th Michigan, was among the first to clamber over the rail fence crowning the top of the hill. Other companies followed close behind.

"It occurred to me that there might be some Johnnies there," recounted Sergeant Charles A. Wing of the 8th Michigan. "I jumped back a few paces, intending to fire through the fence and stir them up if there were any there, and then fall on the ground behind the brush to learn the result."

He raised his Spencer just as a Rebel bullet struck the muzzle of the gun and coursed down the right side of the barrel, splitting the stock, gouging his left hand, tearing the end off his right thumb, and searing the right side of his face. The impact knocked him down, but Wing scrambled to his feet and angrily fired a shot across the fence before showing the Rebels his heels.

"Halt! Halt! you damn Yankee," a half-dozen voices demanded angrily, but Wing never looked back. Two bullets ripped through his coat. Two more holed his trousers below the knee. Lieutenant Colonel Elisha Mix, commanding the 8th Michigan, saw Wing come bounding past and the bloody stain spreading over his hands. Where are you hit? he asked.

"By thunder," Wing railed, "my gun-stock is split in two."

The rest of the 8th Michigan had managed to get across the fence in a few places when Colonel Charles Crews's 1st and 3rd Georgia suddenly rose up fifteen or twenty yards beyond and aimed a withering volley at the advancing Federals. Stoneman's two Kentucky regiments balked in the face of this fire, refusing to advance. Silas Adams rushed to the front. Bareheaded, sword in hand, he implored his Kentuckians to push on, but to no avail. Many of his men were due to be mustered out in two weeks, and neither Adams nor his appeals to state pride could get them moving again. "We gave back some distance," confessed Lieutenant Richard Huffman of the 1st Kentucky, "and it was with great difficulty that we could get the men to halt and form."

"This staggered the whole line," added Captain James Wells, and the fierce Rebel counterattack swung the 8th Michigan's left flank a quarter of the way around before the regiment finally broke and fled in disarray. Finding themselves surrounded, Captain Muir McDonald and six Michigan troopers took cover in a log house and put up a furious defense for the next hour. When their Spencers began running out of ammunition, they bolted out the door. Two troopers were shot down, but McDonald and the others escaped unscathed.

In the meantime, Captain Wells's company fell back with the rest of the regiment and soon came to the ravine that had sheltered them only a few minutes earlier. Wells jumped in, calling for his men to follow. They piled in after him, but as Wells led them along the bottom, the ravine gullied deeper and deeper until it abruptly came to a dead end. The sheer walls rose eight feet on either side, the bottom mired ankle deep in ooze, and Rebel bullets whined overhead. They were trapped.

Desperate troopers leaped vainly at the lip of the gully, snatching at limbs and roots that dangled just out of reach. Each time they missed, they sank a little deeper in the mire. As Wells grabbed at an overhanging bush, a tall, powerful corporal named Jeff Mills seized him by the hips and hoisted him up. Wells got a handhold and hauled himself out. Rolling over, he reached back into the ditch, grabbed the corporal's outstretched hand and pulled him up. Mills, in turn, plucked another comrade out until, one after another, the whole company had escaped.

That was when Wells heard a plaintive voice in the bottom of the ditch. Turning around, his gaze met the anxious, upturned eyes of his cousin, Corporal William S. Wells. They had been raised together and now the corporal stood mired up to his knees. "Cap," he implored, "you're not going to leave me here, are you?"

Bullets clipped the branches overhead and the woods echoed with the wild yells of approaching Rebels as Wells sprawled on his stomach at the edge of the ditch, extending his arm as far as he could reach. His fingers grazed the corporal's outstretched hand and gripped it hard. Gritting his teeth, trying not to be pulled in himself, Wells hauled his cousin out and together they fled to the rear.[10]

The sudden collapse of the Kentucky brigade caught Captain Hardy's battery unprepared. Gunners were frantically trying to limber up their pieces when Major Myles Keogh galloped up astride his horse, Tom.

A dapper young Irishman, Keogh had served with distinction in the eastern theatre before accepting a place on Stoneman's staff and accompanying him west. "He was as handsome a young man as I ever saw . . . ," recalled an Ohio cavalryman. "He rode a horse like a Centaur. He had a fresh Irish complexion like the pink side of a ripe peach—more like the complexion of a 16-year-old girl than of a cavalry soldier. His uniform was spotless, and fitted him like the skin of a sausage, and if there had been any more of the man or any less of the uniform it would have been a misfit." This was "altogether too much style" to suit some of Stoneman's jaded veterans. They had initially refused to share their canteens with Keogh and made snide remarks, like "I wonder if his mother cuts his hair?" and "What laundry do you think he uses?" The snubbing ended the first time they saw him in battle.

Displaying the same cool, conspicuous courage that would distinguish him twelve years later on the banks of the Little Big Horn, Keogh rallied a handful of troopers and charged the advancing Rebels. Hopelessly outnumbered, his men soon turned and fled. Keogh and a few officers pressed ahead. Bullets emptied several saddles, horses tumbled in midstride, but Keogh's charge checked the Southern skirmishers just long enough for Captain Hardy to haul his guns away.[11]

On the east side of the Hillsboro Road, Horace Capron had previously sent Captain William R. Sanford and Companies B and M of the 14th Illinois to screen his right flank and rear. As the rest of the regiment dismounted, Capron reined up behind a log cabin and ordered Lieutenant Colonel David Jenkins to deploy his five remaining companies and McLaughlin's Ohio Squadron along the lane fronting the house and "form his line connecting his left with the right of the 11th Kentucky."

Three minutes later, Capron received a report of Rebels advancing on his right and rear. The two mounted companies he had sent with Captain Sanford had emerged from the woods and halted about a mile to the east with the Milledgeville Road to their left and front when some of Allen's Alabama brigade suddenly bore down on them, loosing a shower of bullets at long range. Sanford ordered his squadron to hold their fire and sent a trooper racing back to report to Capron. The rest of his men stoically endured several volleys before some of them got impatient and drew their carbines. They were banging away at the distant riders when one of Capron's couriers galloped up with orders for Sanford to charge. Forming by platoons, Sanford's men drew their sabers and spurred ahead with a lusty cheer.

The Rebel horsemen wheeled and fled before this sudden onslaught, racing down the Milledgeville Road for about half a mile before abruptly turning to the left on a country lane. The pursuing Yankees followed close behind, with loud calls to "Surrender!"

As Private Isaac M. Dennis of the 14th Illinois spurred past the gate at the mouth of the lane, he saw some dismounted Rebels taking cover behind the trees to his right. He called to Captain Thomas S. Lupton, commanding Company M, to suggest leaving a few men behind to deal with them.

"Onward, and catch those in front," Lupton yelled. "We will attend to those when we return."

"Our horses were fleeter than those of the enemy," Dennis noted, "and soon after entering the lane the advance of our crowd were among the foe, cutting and slashing. Rebs were knocked and yanked from their saddles and told to remain there till we returned. I noticed several as I flew by who had been wounded unto death, two who had arms half-severed from saber cuts, and one officer who had received a terrible slash in the cheek."

Leaving this wreckage writhing in their wake, Sanford's men stormed up the lane for about a mile, until they came to several slave cabins clustered around a cotton gin. Rebel riflemen firing from the cover of these buildings greeted them with a ringing volley.

"In a few seconds all our men were huddled together at the end of the lane," Private Dennis continued, "giving an excellent chance to the rebs to take 'pot shots.' They did not miss the opportunity. Bullets came in showers. Huddled together as we were we peppered away with our revolvers and made the Johnnies dodge, you bet."

The dazed Federals milled about until someone yelled, "Why don't you dismount and lower the fence?"

"We will when the order is given," came the reply.

Someone bellowed a command and troopers sprang from the saddle, pulling down the rails on the right of the lane. The rest of the squadron bounded through the gap to rally and reform in an adjoining field. They scarcely had time to realign their ranks before they heard the wailing defiant fury of the Rebel yell. Confederate cavalry came swarming over the top of a little rise in front of them, yelling and shooting. Sanford's men replied with their carbines, then began falling back, paralleling the lane.

What started as a retreat quickly became a rout. Frantic officers tried to rally the men when they reached a strip of woods, but the wild-eyed fugitives rode right past them until they came to a double staked-and-ridered fence, fifteen rails high. It was every man for himself as troopers tried to urge their mounts over the top.

"Rein back, and give me a show," commanded Private Daniel York, roweling his mount forward. The big horse crashed into the top of the fence, pulling down several rails as it fell back on its haunches. York tumbled out of the saddle with a mournful cry, shot in the back.

Isaac Dennis spurred his mare at the same spot and jumped over cleanly. Looking to his right, he saw Rebel horsemen thundering down the lane. Urging the mare for all her speed, Dennis raced down the outside of the bordering fence. As he drew abreast of a half dozen Rebel riders, a gray-clad officer pointed a revolver across the fence. "Surrender! Surrender!" he demanded.

"Go to hell!" Dennis yelled.

A gunshot exploded so close to his head he could smell the sulfur. Dennis turned in his saddle and raised his revolver. "Take that!" he snarled, aiming two shots at the Rebel's face. Both missed.

"By this time," Dennis recounted, "the lane was full of Yanks and rebs, everybody yelling 'Surrender!' shooting, cutting, and slashing. We would not stop, and coming to the gate we found that those devils whom I had seen in the timber as we charged past had come out, shut and barricaded the gateway.

"Now was a wild scene for a few minutes. Such yelling and wild shooting I never before had heard nor seen. Men were knocked from their saddles. We were so mixed up that one was afraid to shoot for fear of hitting a friend."

In the midst of this hilt-to-hilt melee, the fence got knocked down. Seeing his chance, Dennis spurred through the opening. A bullet struck his mare; she fell to her knees, almost pitching him over her head. Dennis hauled back on the reins, trying to get her to her feet, just as four fresh companies of the 14th Illinois came charging to the rescue.[12]

Seeing Sanford's squadron being driven back in confusion, Capron had personally ordered Major David Quigg's 2nd battalion of the 14th Illinois into the saddle. As Quigg and his men prepared to charge, Private John C. Hall of the 14th Illinois rode up to Capron with a message from Stoneman. Placing his hand on the pommel of the colonel's saddle, Hall leaned forward to make himself heard, just as a bullet, obviously meant for Capron, struck his outstretched left arm and chest.[13]

Perhaps in response to the orders the severely wounded Hall brought, Capron directed his adjutant, Captain Samuel Wells, to deploy McLaughlin's Ohio Squadron on foot. As Wells rode away, Quigg's battalion dashed down the Milledgeville Road.

Captain Sanford saw them coming. Wheeling his shattered squadron about at a dead run, he turned savagely on his attackers. Lieutenant Henry H. Mayo of Company B led the way, spurring into the midst of the Rebel horsemen. Emptying both his revolvers, Mayo drew his saber, cutting and slashing at all who dared oppose him. A bullet struck him in the chest, under his upraised right arm. As he thudded to the ground, retreating Rebels fired three or four shots at him, but the trampling hooves soon thundered past. Dragging himself into some nearby bushes, Mayo lay down to die.[14]

Capron was watching the Rebels being routed on his right when a courier rode up and reported Lieutenant Colonel Jenkins "couldn't find the line" on his left and wanted a staff officer to come and "give him directions." With a snort of disgust, Capron hastily recalled Captain Wells and told him to go find Jenkins; place him under arrest if it seemed necessary, but put someone in command who would link up with the 11th Kentucky.

Leaving the Ohio Squadron to fend for themselves, Wells hurried up the lane to the log house where Capron had given Jenkins his orders half an hour earlier. He found Jenkins standing in front of the house and some of his men forted up inside. Others crouched behind the rail fence bordering the lane. Pointing to the left, Wells directed Jenkins to form his line on the right of the 11th Kentucky immediately.

The forty-year-old Jenkins was a cantankerous sort. The son of orthodox Ohio Quakers, he had upset his parents by announcing his intention to attend West Point. Compelled to settle for a law career instead, he had a practicing attorney's penchant for prerogatives. Capron had already irritated him by ordering Quigg's battalion away without consulting him. This left Jenkins with less than a hundred men, but he promptly moved them in the direction Wells indicated, only to discover he had been sent on a fool's errand. The 11th Kentucky and all the troops west of the Hillsboro Road had "skedaddled."[15]

The Kentuckians had bolted for the rear just as Stoneman summoned the 6th Indiana to their support. Ordered forward at a gallop, the Hoosiers were forming their ranks under a heavy fire when Colonel Biddle and Lieutenant Colonel Court Matson saw the Rebels driving back the broken blue ranks.

"Dismount, and go into them," Biddle shouted as the Kentuckians streamed past.

The 6th Indiana answered with a yell and slid from their saddles, scarcely leaving anyone to hold their horses.

"The boys rushed forward at [a] double-quick, pouring a well-aimed volley into the enemy's ranks, which made them waver and halt for a short time, but the advantage thus gained at a bloody sacrifice, was not long to be held," lamented an Indiana officer. "Our line was too weak, being only one rank; the enemy's a double line, two ranks each. The fight was desperate, almost hand to hand, each party knowing the importance of the position. Our men were ordered to fall back to their horses, which had been taken a short distance to the rear. This they did in good order, leaving many of their comrades dead and wounded on the field. . . ."

Among those who fell was Captain Elijah W. Peck of Company H. Under arrest when preparations for the raid began, he had begged for permission to accompany his men. He was serving in the ranks as a common soldier when he was shot through the neck and killed instantly.

Firing also erupted behind the Hoosiers, where Biddle's rear guard, the 5th Indiana, brushed aside a feeble probe by Iverson's 4th Georgia. "The attack . . . was of short duration," noted Colonel Tom Butler, "after which the rear seemed to be abandoned by the enemy entirely."[16]

But it was not long before Silas Adams's panic-stricken Kentucky brigade came crowding back in confusion. Butler quickly formed a battalion of the 5th Indiana across the Hillsboro Road. Shoot any man who tries to get past, he ordered, but this proved unnecessary. The Kentuckians rallied, and as they marched back into line a courier brought Butler orders to report to Stoneman.

On his way up the road, Butler met Myles Keogh and other members of Stoneman's staff. Things were going badly, they explained. They urged him to persuade the general to back away from this fight, slide around to the right, and move east on the Milledgeville Road.

Stoneman was "very much excited, walking to and fro and swinging his arms violently," when Butler rode up, saluted, and reported his regiment was ready for duty.

"I am glad that you are here," Stoneman replied warmly. "I want a regiment that I can depend upon, and if I had a dozen regiments like the 5th Indiana Cavalry I could whip all the cavalry in the Confederacy. Why, that brigade [Adams's] broke before there were two hundred shots fired, and I couldn't rally twenty-five men around me."

Butler asked what he planned to do.

"I intend to fight it out right here," Stoneman declared.

Butler reminded him "a raiding party should never make a standing fight; that every minute we were there we grew weaker, both man and horse, and that every round of ammunition that was fired weakened our strength."

Stoneman would not listen. After exhausting all his arguments, Butler finally proposed if Stoneman would lead the column down the Milledgeville Road, the 5th Indiana and the picked men in Lieutenant Hasty's detachment would take care of the rear.

"No sir," Stoneman said adamantly, "we will fight it out right here."[17]

He directed Colonel Biddle to move the 6th Indiana back to a crossroads to cover the rear and protect the ambulances and pack trains. Butler was to bring up his regiment to support the artillery.

By this time an uneasy calm had settled over the battlefield. Tired troopers, unable to keep their eyes open any longer, dozed fitfully with the butts of their carbines pressed against their cheeks. Others, too weary or too anxious to sleep, stared numbly into the distance. Behind the lines, horses snorted and stamped their feet. Flies buzzed and an occasional gunshot sounded, like the one that knocked Lieutenant Huffman's horse out from under him. Dismounting, Huffman quickly pulled off his saddle as his steed slowly sank to the ground, rolling its great glassy eyes. "Poor old gray!" he mused, "he seemed to know what was the matter."

During this lull in the fighting, Captain Delany R. Carr's company of the 1st Kentucky was on picket when a young woman came up and asked for permission to pass through the lines. She lived with her mother, she said, pointing to a nearby house, but when Carr went to investigate, the old lady denied the woman was her daughter. Suspicious, Carr came back and examined the applicant more closely. "She" proved to be nineteen-year-old Joe Funderburk, a furloughed Confederate soldier disguised in one of his mother's dresses. Carr promptly arrested him as a spy and sent him to Stoneman, who compelled Funderburk to keep on the dress.

Just what Stoneman hoped to gain by idling the morning away defied explanation. "Here we are in a most beautiful predicament," Sergeant Erastus Holmes of the 5th Indiana complained in his diary. "Old Wheeler or somebody else of large size, right square in front & rumors coming to us that the very devil is to pay on both fronts and in the rear. . . . We are now lying in the sun in an open field. Instead of cutting out, we lay like some easy set of gents whose fortunes are made. Maybe like Micawber, we are waiting for something to turn up."

As the sun climbed higher, the 1st Kentucky's Lieutenant Huffman noted the men "began to lose confidence in their commanding officers." Perhaps Stoneman, after seeing the Kentuckians so easily routed that morning, began losing confidence in his men.

It was 12:30 P.M. before he finally ordered Adams and Capron to strengthen their lines in preparation for renewing the advance. Capron had previously pulled back from his original position to realign with the rest of the division, leaving Captain William A. Lord and Companies C and E of the 14th Illinois to picket the Milledgeville Road. But while Capron was putting every available man, including his provost guard, into line, Silas Adams received orders to keep one of his two regiments in reserve.[18]

Preparations were also under way at Confederate headquarters. Iverson had already moved both his batteries to support his right flank; now he ordered Russ Butler's Kentucky brigade forward to help hold the ground Crews's Georgians had gained. As the Kentuckians deployed between Crews's left flank and the west side of the Hillsboro Road, Iverson directed William Wirt Allen to leave two of his Alabama regiments to picket the road to Milledgeville. The rest of Allen's brigade came trotting through the woods and fields to extend Iverson's line east of the Hillsboro Road.

"We had now driven the enemy back into the pine thickets, from whence they could not see our movements, nor could we see theirs," explained one of Iverson's aides, "but we knew from the minies that they were there. Their lines were extended over two miles, while ours was concentrated in length not over one fourth of a mile, directly in front of their centre. Two [of Allen's] mounted regiments, a mile or more to our left, and one [the 4th Georgia] in the rear, connected with us by a few skirmishers, deceived Gen. Stoneman as to the extent of the line opposed to him. Our artillery was so placed as to enfilade his left flank."

Once all three brigades were in position, Iverson convened his commanding officers. Crews's skirmishers were to make a convincing demonstration in front of the Yankee left, he explained, while White's and Baxter's batteries pummeled that flank with all four of their guns. He wanted Butler's Kentuckians to stand fast while three of Allen's Alabama regiments advanced in two lines, two ranks deep, against the right center of the Yankee line, breaking it "at all hazards." Once the line was breached, Allen was to pivot on his left flank and begin rolling up the Yankee right. At the same time, the left wing of Butler's brigade would pour into the gap Allen had opened, wheel to the right, and enfilade the Yankee left.

About 1:00 P.M. the battle renewed with the sudden roar of artillery. Allen waited long enough for the distant crackle of musketry to announce Crews's skirmishers were at work and ordered his brigade forward.

"How beautifully and steadily they march," exclaimed several officers as they watched Allen's right regiment, the 51st Alabama Mounted Infantry, disappear into the pines.[19]

Capron had just ordered the 14th Illinois and McLaughlin's Ohio Squadron forward when the fierce howl of a Rebel yell and a terrific blast of musketry stopped his thin blue line in its tracks. Capron's men stood fast for a few moments, loading and firing. A few troopers crumpled in agony. A few others fled in panic. Suddenly, dismounted Rebel cavalrymen seemed to be everywhere, yelling and cheering, engulfing the right, the left, driving everything before them.

Capron watched horrified as his men bolted for the rear. "The rush of the enemy toward the spot where the horses were held was more than they could stand," he acknowledged. "The distance was about equal, as before my line broke, the enemy had gained their flank. . . . A foot race and a rough and tumble fight for the possession of the horses ensued."[20]

Capron had previously put half his number fours on the firing line, leaving each of the remaining horseholders to contend with eight fractious mounts. They were struggling to control their recently captured horses and mules when Lieutenant William Rowcliff of the 14th Illinois dashed up and told them to get ready to ride. A moment later a blue wave of panic-striken soldiers crashed through the underbrush.

"Here, Ben, take your horse, quick," Private Isaac Dennis of the 14th Illinois yelled when he saw his friend, Sergeant Benjamin Kaufman.

"No, Dennis; I won't go," Kaufman said flatly. "I will not violate the rules of war."

"Rules of war?" Dennis asked incredulously. "We know no rules of war to-day. This is hell we're in, and he who surrenders goes to Andersonville and starvation."

Climbing into the saddle, Dennis again held out Kaufman's reins. Kaufman shook his head. "No, no," he said with tears streaming down his cheeks; "I can't go. I will trust to fate. Good-bye."

As Dennis spurred away, other troopers struggled to get a foot in their stirrups. Shouts and oaths mingled with the roar of artillery and rattle of musketry as wild-eyed horses and mules, unaccustomed to the frightful racket, reared and plunged. Ears laid back and nostrils flared, some broke away and bolted through the woods. Frantic troopers chased after them, their cumbersome sabers banging against their booted calves.

"So closely did the enemy press my command," Capron recounted, "many of the men were unable to mount their horses, the enemy capturing and mounting the horses repeatedly charged my rear as I continued to retreat."

Staff officers sent to communicate with Stoneman failed to return. In desperation, Capron sent his son, Albert, galloping to the right to recall Captain Lord's two companies. It was too late. Seeing Capron's brigade being rapidly swept off the field, Captain Lord had already formed his squadron and was leading them eastward through the woods bordering the Milledgeville Road. He had gone about a mile when he encountered a rail barricade manned by some of Allen's Alabamians. Rifles, pistols, and carbines blazed defiance, but Lord rode right over the defenders. Just beyond the barricade his men collided with Iverson's mounted reserve, and a wild, running fight whirled down the Milledgeville Road.

Capron saw the "confused and continuous line of horsemen" fast disappearing in the distance and with it his only hope of rallying his command. "The sight was mortifying, and to some extent paralyzing," he admitted, "and for an instant I thought of surrender." Then his eyes fell upon the face of his youngest son, an eighteen-year-old private. The thought of condemning him to Andersonville steeled his resolve. Calling for the boy to keep him in sight, Capron gathered up about a hundred fugitives and dug in his spurs.

The headlong retreat sped eastward across fallow fields overgrown with bushes and saplings and rutted with gullies. Briars and branches snagged uniforms and tore cruelly at exposed arms, legs, and faces, but the panic-stricken Federals rode down everything in their path, cutting a swath close to thirty feet wide.

"It was almost as clear of bushes, weeds, and everything of that kind as a regular public road," marveled a pursuing Confederate. "Even the ground rails of fences were torn from their places, and one could scarcely tell that there had ever been a fence there except by the fences on either side of the newly made road."

In a pine thicket about two miles east of the Hillsboro Road, the head of the fleeing column suddenly confronted a yawning chasm, eight feet deep and twelve or fifteen feet wide. The front rank reined up on the rim of the gully, only to be pushed over the edge by those who piled in from behind. Men and horses tumbled in headfirst until the ditch was bridged with a bloody, writhing mass of torn flesh, trampled under the pounding hooves of the mindless mob.[21]

Back on the battlefield, Confederate Colonel Russ Butler's 1st, 2nd, and 9th Kentucky stormed into the gap Allen's brigade had opened. Pivoting to their right, they flanked and quickly routed Silas Adams's 1st and 11th Kentucky. The bluecoated Kentuckians fled shamelessly across an old field and vaulted over a rail fence where Tom Butler's 5th Indiana lay waiting.

"There they come boys," Stoneman yelled as the howling Rebel ranks emerged from the woods, "go for them."

Loosing a volley from their .50 caliber Smith carbines, the Hoosiers clambered over the fence and charged across the field into the opposite woods. "Here we formed a line and had some very hot practice with our carbines & pistols," noted Sergeant Erastus Holmes, "falling back when the occasion required."

In the course of one such retreat, Holmes's company came to a deep ravine, the banks cut up by several smaller gullies angling in from either side. Any semblance of order and alignment disappeared as the men bunched up, looking for the best place to cross. Seeing the confusion, Captain Russell P. Finney let fly with a few choice words Sergeant Holmes described as "more expressive than polite."

Scrambling across the ravine, troopers about-faced and promptly reformed their ranks. "Beg your pardon gentlemen," Finney smiled with an apologetic tip of his hat, "I did not see the ditch before."

A short distance to the rear, Stoneman, Major Keogh, and Colonel Butler sat on their horses, twenty feet behind the brow of a small hill. Companies D and K of the 5th Indiana crouched behind the rail fence at the crest, anxiously watching the steady approach of a double rank of Rebel skirmishers. The ground heaved under the jarring impact of exploding shells that flung fence rails around like matchsticks. Several troopers were killed before Lieutenant William W. Angel, commanding Company D, turned angrily to Stoneman and demanded, "Are you going to let us stay here and have all our men slaughtered?"

"Hold on a few minutes, until Capt. Hardy's Battery comes up," Stoneman ordered gruffly.

Hardy's two black guns soon came bounding through the cut Lieutenant Angel and his men were defending. Skirting the hill, the battery hastily unlimbered in full view of the Rebel skirmishers and raked them with an enfilading fire that drove them back into the woods.

Stoneman was intently observing all this when a cannon shot struck just behind his leg. Slipping out of the stirrups, he hastily dismounted as his horse sank to the ground. "My poor Beauregard is killed," he groaned, with tears welling up in his eyes.

Wearily climbing on the back of a worn-out cavalry horse someone had abandoned, Stoneman dolefully surveyed the scene. Shells exploded all around. Men were falling and dying. A third of his command had run away. Another third cowered uselessly in the rear. "5th Indiana," he called, "you have done your duty, mount your horses and fall back."[22]

As the Hoosiers hastily mounted and sped away under the prod of the Rebel barrage, a solid shot struck in the midst of Company D, tearing through the breast of the mule Private John Smaltz was riding. Smaltz hit the ground with a sickening thud. When he regained his senses, he saw a gaping wound where his knee had been, his left leg hanging by a single shred of skin. The rest of the company had already swept past, but then Smaltz saw Lieutenant Angel bringing up the rear. Don't leave me, he begged. Angel stopped, flagged down one of Captain Hardy's caissons and tried to help Smaltz climb on top of one of the limber chests. The shattered leg flopped and dangled awkwardly. It was of no further use, Smaltz said stoically. Opening one of the blades on his pocketknife, he calmly reached down and cut it off.

Big, burly Fred Warner, the company blacksmith, saw what was happening. Dismounting, he hoisted Smaltz into his saddle and ushered him across the battlefield toward the large yellow hospital flag hanging outside Sunshine Church.

Inside the little log building, the rude floor ran red with the blood of wounded Federals. Shirtsleeved surgeons were doing what little they could to alleviate the suffering and comfort the dying when Smaltz was led into the churchyard, still clutching his severed leg.

Leaving Smaltz in the care of the surgeons, Warner rejoined his company on an abrupt hill, a hundred yards east of the Hillsboro Road. Stoneman was already there, determined to continue the fight.

"Never did a man display more daring heroism than Gen. Stoneman," declared a Kentucky officer. "He was everywhere along the line cheering the men, calling upon them to hold on to the last. . . . He grasped the muddy wheels of the guns, getting them into position, aimed them himself, showing he could execute as well as command."[23]

The 5th Indiana took up positions on either side of the guns. The 8th Michigan was skirmishing somewhere to the left. The 6th Indiana still covered the rear. Silas Adams's brigade had reached their horses by this time, but it was only with difficulty that Major Anderson T. Keen of the 1st Kentucky succeeded in rallying enough men to form a skirmish line. The rest of Adams's men took refuge at the bottom of a ravine, while solid shot and shell rained down with unnerving accuracy.

Captain William P. Pierce had just formed Company A of the 11th Kentucky and was talking with Captain Frank Wolford, commanding Company A of the 1st Kentucky, when a shellburst sent a hot piece of iron slicing into Lieutenant James Humphrey's left knee. As the fair-haired Humphrey hauled his shattered limb over the pommel of his saddle, Captain Wolford and several others dismounted to assist him. At that instant, there was another searing blast. When the smoke cleared, Wolford lay in a pool of blood, his head nearly torn off by a piece of shell.[24]

Captain Pierce hurried his company out of range. They could not stay here, he exclaimed upon meeting Colonel Adams. They had to cut their way through the Rebel lines. Adams had come to the same conclusion. He had just heard Stoneman was going to surrender.

Surrender! The word went through the brigade like an electric shock. "I have seen excitement in our regiment," noted the 1st Kentucky's Richard Huffman, "but when our men . . . learned that they were about to be made prisoners, the excitement was uncontrollable."

Adams went directly to Stoneman. The 1st Kentucky's enlistment was about to

Colonel Silas Adams refused to surrender at Sunshine Church and successfully led his Kentucky brigade off the battlefield. He is pictured here
as a member of the Kentucky House of Representatives in 1891. Courtesy
of the Kentucky Historical Society. Used by permission.

expire, he declared; it was unfair to condemn them to captivity at Andersonville.
Many of the 11th Kentucky were ex-Confederates. If they were captured, the Rebels
would shoot them as deserters.

Stoneman argued it was impossible to move the whole division without being
discovered. The Rebels were sure to pursue, and when they did, they would have
fresher horses and the inside track to Atlanta. His own men did not have enough
ammunition left to resist them, and Stoneman gloomily predicted if they tried to run
for it, half of them would lose their horses or get separated from the command. While
troopers captured by organized bodies of Confederate cavalry could expect to be
treated as prisoners of war, stragglers would be at the mercy of bushwhackers or small
squads unrestrained "by an officer of rank." They would be shot down like dogs,
Stoneman warned; any man left afoot would have little or no chance of escape, and
he was not going to be responsible for that. He told Adams to take a flag of truce and
surrender the division.

"General," the "stalwart, square-built, kindly-faced Kentuckian" implored, "do
you order me to do it?"

"What else do you propose to do, Colonel Adams?" Stoneman asked.

"To cut my way out," the young commander answered confidently, "and where *I* go
my brigade will follow."

"Well," said Stoneman with an air of resignation, "if you think you can go out
without too great a sacrifice of your men, go, Colonel. I will remain, and may God
bless you."

As Stoneman's staff looked on, the two men tearfully shook hands.

"Go, Colonel," Stoneman said solemnly, "and all who wish to go with you. I will engage the enemy's attention in our front with Colonel Biddle's brigade; will fire the last musket, will use the last charge of ammunition."[25]

As Adams rode off to rejoin his two regiments, he met Stoneman's chief of staff, Bob Smith, who had been sent to rally a wavering skirmish line. Stoneman was about to surrender, Adams announced, but he was going to cut his way out and the general had given his permission to anyone else who wanted to try. Smith followed the Kentucky colonel to the ravine where his brigade lay waiting. Mount up, Adams ordered in a clear, ringing voice. Artillery roared, rifles and carbines crackled as his troopers swung into the saddle. Squads and platoons, companies and battalions quickly took their place in the lengthening column, and with all the skill of a seasoned fox hunter, Adams boldly led them south, then east and north.

"We went through woodlands, across open fields, leaped fences and ditches, and performed many wonderful equestrian feats," marveled Private John C. Weddle of the 1st Kentucky. No obstacle was too formidable. In the midst of the column rode calicoed Joe Funderburk, his mother's dress hiked up over his thighs. Briars and branches tore the garment to shreds, ripping off everything but the collar and the clothes he wore underneath.

"I know not how Col. Adams found the way," confessed Lieutenant Huffman; "but he led us over hills and deep ditches—not a sign of a path being there—and took us out between the Rebel pickets without being seen, and without firing a gun. It was one of the most wonderful feats he ever accomplished."[26]

Stoneman, in the meantime, was making good on his promise. Hardy's battery hurled shells and canister in every direction until the last round of ammunition had been fired. Hardy then took out a couple of files, intending to spike the guns, but to his consternation, Stoneman forbade him. Hardy broke down in tears.

Tom Butler then pleaded for permission for the 5th Indiana to save itself. "General Stoneman," he said, "if you will get on your horse and let me withdraw my command from the front line and follow me; I will take the ambulances with the wounded and the balance of the command out of this place, and back to our lines."

"I am going to fight it out here," Stoneman said coldly.

"Fight out[,] hell[,] without ammunition!" Butler exploded.

"I said to him that I would rather sacrifice the regiment in an effort to escape than to have them made prisoners and die in those prison pens," Butler recounted, "and that our friends at home would honor me for it. His reply was, 'that they would condemn me for it.'"

Butler angrily rejoined his regiment, but other officers apparently tried to convince Stoneman there was no point in fighting any longer. They had given Capron and Adams the head start they needed. The men were almost out of ammunition and there was no hope of escape. If they surrendered now, the Rebels would treat them as prisoners of war. Keep fighting and the men would be needlessly slaughtered.

Stoneman saw he had no choice. After a fruitless search among his officers for a handkerchief white enough to be recognized as a flag of truce, he tore the tail off his shirt and handed it to Major Duvall English of his staff. Surrender the division, he ordered, but try to keep the Rebels talking as long as possible. That would give Capron and Adams more time to get away.

Tall, black-haired Colonel Thomas H. Butler commanded the 5th
Indiana Cavalry of Biddle's brigade. He begged Stoneman not to
surrender at Sunshine Church and initially refused to let the officer
carrying the white flag pass through his lines. Reproduced from the
Collections of the Library of Congress.

Accompanied by Lieutenant Rufus Somersby of the 11th Kentucky, English rode
to the front line. When Tom Butler saw the white flag approaching, he was incredulous. He confronted English and refused to let him pass. Hastily polling some of his
officers, he asked if they thought it was time to surrender.

"Not by a damned sight," came the reply.

Butler accompanied Major English back to see Stoneman and again pleaded for
permission to let the 5th Indiana save itself.

Stoneman told him to "be a man and surrender."

Enraged, Butler called him "a liar and a coward."

"Col. Butler," Stoneman said icily, "I want you to understand that I am in
command."

Returning to his regiment, Butler called some of his officers together. "Has it come
to this?" he wailed, grasping some of them by the hand as tears streamed down his dirt
stained face. "We must obey orders."

Reluctantly, he detailed Lieutenant Angel to accompany Major English and
Lieutenant Somersby. "Boys," he said as he watched the scrap of flag pass through his
line, "we are gone."[27]

News of the impending surrender quickly spread to the ranks of the 8th Michigan,
where it was greeted with curses and cries of "Officers we will follow you out!"
"Captain lead us out!" "By God, we won't surrender!"

The 8th Michigan's senior officer, Elisha Mix, and twenty troopers who had gotten separated from the regiment early that afternoon had already fled with Capron's 14th Illinois, leaving Major Buck in command. Hastily conferring with his officers, Buck elected to follow Adams's brigade.

Lieutenant Colonel Court Matson of the 6th Indiana had no intention of surrendering, either. He rode up to Lieutenant Hasty's "Hatchet Brigade," which had been guarding the rear all day, and announced anyone who wanted to escape should follow him.

The rest of the 6th Indiana was waiting for orders when Major Orlando Smith rode down the line. "Boys," he said, "all of you that don't want to go to prison, follow me." About 300 officers and men fell in behind him and trotted into the woods east of the Hillsboro Road.[28]

In the meantime, Stoneman's three emissaries approached the advancing Rebel skirmish line. Just north of Sunshine Church, near Frank Hascall's house, they were met by Captain Jeff Rogers of the Confederate 1st Kentucky and Captain J. F. Smith of the 9th Kentucky. Major English announced he had come to ask for terms of surrender. An awkward wait ensued while this information was relayed to Russ Butler, who immediately sent a rider racing to find General Iverson.

Unlike Wheeler, who commanded from the front ranks, Iverson was about a mile to the rear, trying to recall Allen's brigade, which had long since been outdistanced by Capron's fleeing Federals. He instructed Allen to gather up his horses, fall back to Hillsboro, and hurry east to cut off the Yankee retreat toward Milledgeville. He also sent a message directing Major Stewart's 4th Georgia to renew the attack on the Yankee rear and was dictating similar orders for the rest of Crews's brigade when Butler's courier rode up and reported a flag of truce approaching on the right. Iverson hastily finished his note to Crews, adding if the Yankees wished to surrender, they must do so unconditionally. Otherwise, he was to attack at once.[29]

Major English and his companions were still waiting patiently when Russ Butler galloped up with his staff and reined to a halt, demanding to know what they wanted. English said they wanted to surrender.

"Who is the flag from?" Butler asked.

"From Maj. Gen. Stoneman," came the reply.

"Is Maj. Gen. Stoneman there in person?"

"Yes."

"What are your terms?"

"Under the cartel," English answered.

"I accept of the terms," Butler said.

A second Rebel officer rode up with about fifteen or twenty men. He posed the same questions Colonel Butler had already asked and seemed surprised to learn a Yankee general wanted to surrender.

Then Colonel Crews rode up with his staff, asking what the flag meant. Advised that Stoneman proposed to surrender, he too accepted the terms and suggested English send someone back to arrange for the Yankee division to march to a nearby hill and lay down their arms.

"That made me smile," Lieutenant Angel later wrote; "in fact, I laughed out [loud]. He asked me what tickled me. We had only part of one regiment to surrender. One of the staff asked me how many batteries we had. I told him we had but two pieces of the 24th Ind. Battery. He said he didn't ask me for a lie. Another said if that was all the guns we had that they had done some mighty good work in killing lots of their men."

While the officers talked, some of Butler's men edged closer. Several of them recognized English and Somersby and bombarded the two Kentuckians with questions about friends, home, and family. Finally, Butler intervened, telling the three Federal officers he would go with them to accept Stoneman's surrender.

As they started for the rear, Colonel Crews dashed up and told Butler to stay with his command. He was the ranking officer and he would accept the surrender. A few hot words were exchanged before Butler backed down. Crews directed him to send the 1st Kentucky to guard the prisoners and ordered his own 3rd Georgia to take charge of captured property. Then, accompanied by a few officers, he set out for the Federal lines with English, Somersby, and Angel.[30]

Stoneman's men were drawn up in line, awaiting the results of the parley, when Major Stewart's 4th Georgia charged their left and rear. Stewart had not received the orders countermanding his attack and for a few anxious moments it seemed like the fighting was about to start all over again. Then the Georgians saw the flutter of white flags. "Dismount, you Yankey sons of bitches," they demanded.

"We did," recounted Private John Sammons of the 5th Indiana; "but it was not our own will to do so. We were ordered to take our . . . [weapons] off and lay them in front of us. One squad took our arms and another, our horses, and a third took us."

The Rebels also released several soldiers and civilians Stoneman had taken prisoner, including John McKissack, the old man who had shotgunned a Yankee trooper at Hillsboro on July 29.

By the time Crews arrived, it was all over. Stoneman was waiting on horseback, just east of the Hillsboro Road, on the steep hill that would afterwards bear his name. Four hundred and forty downcast Federals stood nearby, their arms stacked before them.

Crews saluted as he rode up and announced he had come to receive the surrender. Stoneman said he preferred to surrender to the officer in command. The Rebel colonel politely, but very firmly, refused. Reluctantly, Stoneman handed over his sword. Then the tired old dragoon sat down on a log and cried.[31]

19

STONEMAN'S RAID
SUNSHINE CHURCH TO MARIETTA

JULY 31–AUGUST 4, 1864

A horse is a vain thing for safety.

Psalms 33:17

"Why did you not surrender when Stoneman did?"

The angry words rang in Private Perry Quick's ears as he lay near Sunshine Church, bleeding from a wound in his leg. A split second later, a vicious blow from a Rebel rifle butt knocked the Michigan trooper senseless.

Such brutality was rare, however. Most of Iverson's men honored the spirit, if not the letter, of the terms of surrender as they swarmed around the captured Yankees. "Took our private horses & most everything they could get . . . ," conceded Dr. Andrew Weir of the 6th Indiana, "[but] they treated us very kindly."[1]

As the swaggering Southern soldiers herded their sullen prisoners into the road, Stoneman's adjutant, Captain William Perkins, recognized an old schoolmate, Colonel Russ Butler, among the Confederates and presented him with a pair of pistols. "Thank you sir," Butler acknowledged politely. "I hope I will do good service with them the next fight I get into." At the same time, Captain Hardy and officers of the 24th Indiana Battery gave Confederate Captain Benjamin White a fine field glass in grudging admiration of his skill as an artilleryman.[2]

"Three cheers for Colonel Crews!" someone yelled as his Georgians prepared to march the captured Yankees to the rear. As the last hoarse "hooray" rose from raspy Rebel throats, the downcast blue column began shuffling across the battlefield.

Crews had already separated the Yankee officers from their men and sent a message to Iverson confirming Stoneman's surrender and promising to deliver him to headquarters in half an hour. Iverson and his staff were waiting when guards halted the captured officers in front of Joseph White's house, a mile and a half north of Sunshine Church. The Yankees dismounted, marched into the yard, and lined up in front of the house, where Iverson greeted Stoneman cordially.

As the Rebel general passed down the line shaking hands with the other officers, he was surprised to see Colonel Tom Butler of the 5th Indiana still wearing his side arms. The colonel seemed "well fixed," Iverson observed, nodding toward the weapons; if Butler had "no further objections," he would take charge of them.[3]

After supplying his guests with supper, Iverson offered them complete freedom within the grounds of White's plantation if they promised not to escape. Stoneman accepted the offer and bedded down under some trees in front of the house with Colonels Biddle and Butler, Majors Keogh and English, Captains Perkins and Hardy, and the other officers.

The rest of the yard was filled with Rebel wounded. Iverson estimated his casualties at "less than eighty," and the sighs, moans, and murmurs of their private agonies mingled with the soft patter of a passing shower.

Most of the enlisted men captured with Stoneman spent the night corralled in a hog pen on a low piece of ground near White's house. "The cobs were rough," conceded Sergeant Erastus Holmes, "but we were tired, after a four days['] ride, interspersed with three hard fights, the last one lasting eight hours, and the whole day without food, we were soon in dreamless sleep."[4]

Yet night brought no relief for the hundreds of Yankee horsemen fleeing from Sunshine Church. The darkness hung before their eyes like a veil, masking all dangers, magnifying all terrors, as they groped blindly through the countryside. There was no moon, no maps, no familiar landmarks. The mustering of Joe Brown's militia and the impressment of slaves to dig fortifications around Atlanta had left very few men, white or black, on the farms and plantations, and in their absence it was slave women who answered officers' anxious questions and padded barefoot alongside the blue columns, eagerly pointing out fords, obscure paths, and little-used roads.

"At a rugged crossing in a deep forest where all were compelled to dismount and lead," recounted Captain James Wells, "two young colored women with red turbaned handkerchiefs around their heads and carrying torches (our guides for a long distance) stood on the banks of the stream and lighted the command across. The varying and uncertain glare of the burning pine knots cast weird shadows into the waters below, and over men and horses as they plunged down the banks; while the forest, lighted up but a few yards overhead and beyond, soon shaded off into impenetrable darkness. There was just enough light to reveal the desperate earnestness depicted on the faces of these slave girls (with flashing eyes darker than the night itself) who had entered upon this task that might prove death or torture to them."

Most of the raiders had scarcely had four hours' sleep in the past four days, but fear of capture pushed them on all night long with hardly a pause. Horses and mules, lamed by the loss of a shoe or prodded past the point of exhaustion, staggered and collapsed. Troopers, desperate to lighten their loads, jettisoned sabers, blankets, and ponchos. Many of those with empty cartridge boxes threw their carbines away or smashed the stock against a tree trunk, hurling the pieces into the brush.[5]

After emerging from the woods, Silas Adams's brigade followed the Milledgeville Road as far as Blountsville before turning north toward Eatonton. "We marched leisurely," recounted Lieutenant Richard Huffman, "and learned that Col. Capron's command was on ahead of us, and running their horses to kill. We . . . learned this from the number of dead horses found on the road."

Shortly after midnight, the Kentuckians rode wearily into Eatonton, "a sleepy little town" with "a court-house and town square, a tavern, several wide streets, many fine trees, and a number of old colonial homes."

"This is said to be one of the finest parts of Georgia," noted Lieutenant Huffman, "but we had no time to stop and see." The Kentuckians lingered long enough to sack a couple of stores and plunder the tithe collector's house and then hurried north on the Madison Road.

About an hour later, Major Buck's 8th Michigan and Lieutenant Colonel Court Matson's 6th Indiana rode into town. Most of the column continued on after Adams, but Major Orlando Smith and two companies of the 6th Indiana stayed behind to burn quartermaster and commissary supplies. The Hoosiers barely had time to set fire to the railroad depot, containing an estimated 800 to 1,000 Enfield rifles, before they heard the huffing and puffing of an approaching locomotive.[6]

The train carried Major McMahon and 130 Hancock and Baldwin County militia-men General Wayne had dispatched from Milledgeville early that morning. Seeing smoke clouding the sky over Eatonton, McMahon stopped the train just south of town and sent a few scouts ahead to reconnoiter. The rest of his old men and boys climbed down from the cars and cautiously moved up the track. As they approached the ruined depot, McMahon saw some of the raiders and demanded their surrender. A few doffed their hats as if to comply, but some of McMahon's anxious militia misunderstood the gesture and opened fire, perhaps wounding one man. The Hoosiers answered with a few scattering shots, then mounted their horses and raced out of town.[7]

Five miles north of Eatonton, Silas Adams had called a brief halt shortly before daylight to rest his jaded command. It was here, perhaps, that Joe Funderburk, faced with the prospect of being hanged as a "female" spy, managed to slip away from the column and fled into the woods. His captors did not bother to look for him and were soon on the march again.

Adams's grueling pace outdistanced not only the pursuit but also the news of the fighting at Sunshine Church. About 9:00 that hot Monday morning, J. R. Kendrick and several men were lounging in front of a store on the public square in Madison, twenty-two miles north of Eatonton, debating the merits of a rumor that Yankee cavalry had been seen in the county. A farmer rode up and after listening to the course of the conversation for a few moments, offered to "eat all the Union soldiers within ten miles of Madison."

At that instant, a gray-clad rider galloped around the corner, closely followed by a bluecoated horseman firing his pistol. "Yankees!" cried the startled group of onlook-ers, springing to their feet.

"Don't run!" Kendrick yelled, but most of his friends were already in full stride. Shots rang out as a flood of Federals poured into the square and spurred down the narrow streets, firing at any man who ran away. Women screamed, but despite the bedlam, Kendrick boldly stood his ground. Approaching an officer, he asked for permission to return to his home on the outskirts of town. The officer told him he would have to wait until the colonel arrived.

Five or ten minutes later, Silas Adams rode into Madison. His troopers had already arrested several civilians, but when Kendrick renewed his request, Adams promptly assigned an officer to escort him through the mob of soldiers crowding the street. Noticing the covetous glances cast at his gold watch chain, Kendrick hastily buttoned his coat. He reached his front gate safely, where two or three soldiers approached him and politely asked for something to eat. Kendrick provided them with what he could spare and answered their anxious questions about how far it was to Atlanta.

"They were good looking and rather gentlemanly fellows," conceded one resident, "and conducted themselves very well for Yankees."

That meant they stole every horse and mule they could find. Colonel William M. Browne, the state superintendent of the Confederate Conscription Bureau, was left sitting behind the empty shafts of his buggy as he waited to catch the morning train. The raiders also ransacked his baggage, but "with the exception of the theft of a few gold watches," noted J. R. Kendrick, "I do not remember that our citizens had much to complain of."

They would have burned the depot if railroad agent James Porter had not persuaded them the flames would likely spread to some nearby homes. Hauling several boxes of government clothing and canvas shoes out into the street instead, they encouraged a gaping crowd of Negroes to help themselves. After setting fire to what was left and riding about town, "receiving the hospitalities of some of the citizens," the Kentuckians took their leave.

Major Buck's 8th Michigan rode into Madison shortly afterward but soon hurried on after Adams. Court Matson and the 6th Indiana arrived about 2:00 P.M. and picked up where the Kentuckians had left off, breaking into stores, filling their pockets with smoking tobacco, and urging slaves to take whatever was left. What they could not carry away, they piled in the street and burned. By the time Matson's men left town an hour later, they had purportedly destroyed 50,000 pounds of bacon, 500 bags of Rio coffee, and several bales of cotton. They had also emptied two or three barrels of liquor.

As the tail end of the Yankee column filed northward across the Georgia railroad, two drunken stragglers stayed behind. They rode around the square, yelling and cursing and generally making themselves obnoxious until James P. Smith, a refugee from Pontotoc County, Mississippi, emerged from a knot of citizens watching silently from the courthouse steps. It was a shame, Smith said, for a whole town to let itself be cowed by a pair of drunken desperados. Drawing a pistol, he confronted the ruffians on Main Street and demanded their surrender. The two Yankees slowly dismounted, keeping their horses between them and Smith. Eyewitnesses disagreed about what happened next. Some said Smith fired first; others blamed the bluecoats, but the end result was the same. One or two shots struck home, and Smith crumpled in the street, clutching a mortal wound in his bowels. The two Yankees remounted and rode out of town, swearing they would soon return with reinforcements and put Madison to the torch.[8]

By this time, the 6th Indiana had already crossed Hard Labor Creek on the Monroe Road, following in the wake of the 1st and 11th Kentucky and the 8th Michigan. "I never experienced such a hard time in my life," declared Sergeant Oliver Haskell, "in the saddle from sunrise till night, from night till morning, no time for sleeping, no time for eating, the boys sleep on their horses as they move along on the road, half of them are without hats, have lost them while asleep."

They all wore the pinched, haggard faces of hunted men. "About one half only of them were armed," noted a citizen who saw them pass, "the rest having thrown away their guns in their flight, and all of them seemed very much demoralized and alarmed with the idea of a pursuit."

Adams's brigade had ridden fifty-six miles in twenty-one hours by the time they reached George F. Ponder's place early that afternoon. Ponder raised fine horses on his 3,500 acres and ran a store at a crossroads called Fair Play. Troopers compelled some of his slaves to halter and bridle eight horses and broodmares and sixteen fat mules. Then they emptied his crib, barn, and smokehouse. Adams arrived in time to post a guard around Ponder's white-pillared home but turned a deaf ear to the planter's pleas to spare his livestock and provisions. His dismounted men must be mounted, Adams said simply, and the hungry had to be fed.

The Kentuckians had just begun broiling bacon and feeding their horses and mules on piles of Ponder's corn, oats, and fodder when Major Buck's 8th Michigan caught up with them. Court Matson's 6th Indiana arrived later that afternoon. About the same time, another column was seen approaching from the southwest. It was Horace Capron's brigade.[9]

Capron's men had been the first to bolt from the battlefield at Sunshine Church. Pursuing Rebels had chased them up the Milledgeville Road for seven or eight miles, killing and wounding several troopers before Capron overhauled Captain Lord's two companies, turned on his attackers and beat them back. He had halted to rest his blown horses when Lieutenant Colonel Mix of the 8th Michigan rode up and reported Stoneman had surrendered.

"Stoneman surrendered?" Capron asked incredulously. "Never while I have a horse under me will I surrender."

He immediately began reorganizing the rabble that had been his brigade, putting those who still had pistols and carbines at the front and rear of the column. The best mounted, best equipped troopers he assigned to the rear guard, reasoning they had the best chance to catch up if they had to stop and fend off the Rebels.

The arrival of several small squads and detachments had swelled his ranks to about 300 men by the time Capron resumed the march. Captain Lord led the way north on the Eatonton Road, but Lieutenant Colonel Mix, commanding the rear guard, was left afoot when his horse gave out. "The last was seen of him," noted a Michigan sergeant, "he was leaping a fence to keep from falling into the enemy's hands. . . ."

Negroes warned that Confederate forces were massing at Eatonton, and after fording Murder Creek, Capron bore off to the left near the present-day crossroads community of Note. Leaving Eatonton well to the right, he and his men marched all night. About 9:00 the next morning they met Major Francis Davidson and the five companies of the 14th Illinois Stoneman had sent to wreck the Central Railroad.

Davidson's detachment had moved up the east side of the Oconee River after crossing at Tucker's Ferry, passing within two and a half miles of Milledgeville at daylight on July 31, probably within sight of the McKinley house where Governor Brown's family had taken refuge. Davidson, however, had no intention of testing the capital's defenses. Pressing a Mr. Briscol of Hancock County into service as a guide, he kept to the backroads until he reached Waller's Ferry, at the mouth of Little River, eight miles above Milledgeville. By noon he had safely shuttled his men and a herd of about seventy-five captured mules to the west side of the Oconee.

Dismissing Briscol and several attendant Negroes, Davidson headed north on the Sparta and Macon Road. His troopers had put another fifteen miles behind them by the time they reached Pop-Castle plantation at 5:00 P.M.

"They . . . had captured . . . Stephen B. Marshall, Esq., at his plantation, on the Oconee, and Jesse T. Batchelor, Esq., at the plantation of Mrs. [Caroline] Beall," noted Joseph Addison Turner, a country editor and publisher. "They were reported to have other prisoners with them.

"At the house of Wm. Little . . . , our nearest neighbor, they behaved very well, taking only something to eat, and one or two other needed articles. At the house of Mrs. [Martha A.] Johnson, they also behaved well, requiring only something to eat, and one horse, leaving one in the place of the one they took. Their comparatively good conduct was continued at the house of Mrs. [B. F.] Hubert, where they took four hams, and two horses. Their courtesy and respect for the ladies generally prevailed, wherever we heard from them."[10]

At James C. Denham's tannery, the raiders outfitted themselves with boots and shoes from one of the most extensive footwear factories in the South. Davidson then ordered the place burned, but relented upon learning it was privately owned and a fire would imperil a nearby church and dwellings.

Turning west at Glade's Crossroads, the little column struck the Eatonton and Madison Road well ahead of the first fugitives from Sunshine Church. Davidson followed this road northward for another five miles before turning west again on the Seven Islands Road. Several troopers, unable to keep up the grueling pace, fell asleep in their saddles and were soon left far behind. The others hung on grimly until Davidson finally called a halt at 2:00 A.M., August 1, and allowed them three hours' sleep. Back in the saddle at daylight, they stopped again three miles down the road to eat breakfast and feed their horses. They were haggard and tired when they met Capron's column at a fork in the road that morning, but they still had full cartridge boxes. Capron immediately sent them to relieve his rear guard.

Davidson had been heading northwest, intending to cross the Georgia Railroad west of Social Circle. Capron agreed to follow that route, but sometime that morning, the column abruptly changed direction and marched rapidly to the northeast. "We moved forward without rest," Capron recorded, "riding through corn-fields, where the men pulled an ear for themselves and a few for their horses, never halting during this entire day." Late that afternoon, they crossed the Georgia Railroad at Rutledge Station without even pausing to burn the depot. Seven miles beyond Rutledge, they met Silas Adams, William Buck, and Court Matson at Fair Play.[11]

Capron, by virtue of his senior commission, immediately asserted his right to command. Adams objected his own rank was sufficient to take care of his brigade, and some sharp words ensued before he agreed to obey Capron's orders. There was also an intense discussion about which direction to take. Adams had been moving northwest, intending to reenter the Union lines via Monroe and Lawrenceville. Capron had been heading northeast, aiming for Athens. Apparently on the strength of a report placing Rebel cavalry near Monroe, the whole column began moving toward Athens shortly after dark.

Every step took them farther away from Atlanta, but the weary raiders doggedly plodded on, putting another twelve miles behind them by the time they halted at High Shoals about midnight. The little village straddled both sides of the Appalachee River, surrounding a cotton mill that hugged the south bank. Troopers lingered long enough to destroy some cloth and thread, but they moved on across the Appalachee without setting fire to the mill. They preyed heavily, however, on the farms north of the river. Families like the Gobers, the Thompsons, the Middletons, the Turnells, and the Murrays were robbed of "the last peck of grain, the last bundle of oats, the last pound of meat, and all the horses and mules."[12]

As the Yankees passed Dickens' Crossroads, they were confronted by fifty-nine-year-old Jacob Klutts. Klutts had lost a son in the war and legend has it he came out of his house and roundly cursed the raiders as every species of rogue and scoundrel. He and a neighbor, Charley Burger, were promptly taken prisoner.

Capron relied on captured civilians to show him the roads, but a squad of scouts, led by a lean, sinewy Kentuckian named Ransom S. Wilshire, ranged far ahead of the column. Early that morning, about four miles beyond High Shoals, Wilshire and his men surprised and captured six Rebel pickets. Before sending his prisoners to the rear, Wilshire got permission from Colonel Adams to relieve them of their uniforms.

Thus disguised, he and his men—Sergeant Milford A. Purdy, Corporals John Rhodes and Nicholas M. Waymen, and Privates John A. Lawhorn, John P. Logan, and John J. Elliott of the 1st Kentucky—approached the picket reserve post about two miles up the road. "Rally on Lieutenant Quirk," Wilshire commanded as he galloped up. The Yankees were coming!

Lieutenant P. E. Bush of the 30th Georgia Cavalry Battalion obediently ordered his men into line. Seeing the newcomers drawing their pistols and forming right behind him, he turned to Wilshire. "You are a man after my own heart," he said, giving the Kentuckian a friendly slap on the back.

Wilshire leveled his pistol on the lieutenant and coldly demanded his surrender. Bush and his seventeen men meekly threw down their guns.

Wilshire's ruse enabled Adams's brigade to charge into Watkinsville virtually unannounced. "The Yankees came very near getting right in town before we believed it," an astonished Louisa Booth Ashford wrote to her son. "Such a scampering out of the way our men had, some on horseback and some on foot in different directions, till there was not one left on the street to welcome (?) the Yankees but your pa and Mr. John Harris; they did not attempt to go at all, but talked to them very cleverly, as the Yankees did to us."

Mrs. Ashford, her husband, William, and their children watched from the front porch as the troopers rode down the main street. "I asked them a great many questions," she continued, "and they answered me very politely. We had a plate full of biscuit left from breakfast I intended for supper that night, but when they came in and asked for bread, I gave them all to them; and when the dinner I had prepared was done I gave it to them, and all the buttermilk I had. I was not troubled cooking for them as some of our neighbors were."

A few Yankees came to the back of the house and ransacked Mr. Ashford's tailor shop. They did not bother anything in the house, Mrs. Ashford noted, but "at a few places in town they searched everything in the dwellings, and took nearly all the corn and meat they could find, and many other things they needed, such as clothing, hats, boots, shoes, etc. They took all the watches they could find everywhere; made Mr. John Harris take his out of his pocket and give it to them, also Mrs. Wilson, Mrs. Lee, and some others. They went into the post-office, all the shoe shops, both of the clerk's offices, took out all they wanted themselves, gave away other things to the negroes, then broke, tore up, and destroyed everything else. . . ."

Ignoring a considerable quantity of cotton stored in the old Methodist and Baptist churches and Dickens' Grocery on the courthouse square, the raiders soon moved on toward Athens. Riding in the midst of the column with the other prisoners, Jacob Klutts waved good-bye to friends and acquaintances and laughingly told Louisa Booth Ashford he did not know what the Yankees intended to do with him.

Just north of Watkinsville, Horace Capron called a halt. While his men fed their exhausted mules and horses, he consulted with Silas Adams about which direction to take. One road branched off to the west, toward a reportedly passable ford across the middle fork of the Oconee River, two and a half miles above Athens. The other crossed the Oconee just south of the city. Adams argued in favor of pushing straight into Athens, destroying the Confederate armory there, and putting the Oconee between them and any would-be pursuers. Capron reluctantly agreed.

"His instructions, distinctly given and understood," Capron later insisted, "were that if he found the crossing could or could not be made without a detention, he should report the facts to me by a courier at once. In case we could not pass the bridge he was ordered to meet me at the ford with his command, sending a guide to pilot me to that point."[13]

Athens, however, would not be caught napping. Mrs. Howell Cobb and the other members of the Soldiers' Aid Society were in the town hall, tearing up skirting for use as bandages, when one of the ladies looked out the window about 10:00 A.M. and noticed a commotion in the street. "Something must be happening," she exclaimed, "there goes Mrs. Cobb's carriage again loaded up."

A moment later, the Cobbs' servant, Israel, appeared at the door and announced "Mas Howell" wanted "to see Mistress." Putting down her work, Mrs. Cobb went outside, where she met her son, Howell, Jr. The Yankees were at Watkinsville, he blurted, 800 of them. There was no mistake about it this time; they were marching for Athens. A scout had just brought the news to Colonel William J. Magill, the post commander.

Mrs. Cobb, Mrs. Mary Clancy, and Julia Pope Moss climbed into the rockaway and Howell urged the team through the crowded streets. "Great activity ensued among masculine and feminine," noted Mrs. Cobb, "but little consternation or fright—everybody solemn & resolute. The military quietly went to work, no alarm guns, no alarm bells. Such a contrast to Saturday & Sunday [July 23–24] when no Yankees were in a hundred miles—here they were at the breastworks and the people were calm."

Major Ferdinand Cook's battalion of armory workers shouldered their muskets. So did three companies of home guards commanded by Captains James White, Richard S. Taylor, and John Billups. Several hundred strong, these artisans and mechanics, mill hands and merchants, judges and lawyers, doctors and college professors, newspapermen, bankers, old men, and boys marched down Lumpkin Street like the minutemen of an earlier generation, vowing that if the Yankees entered Athens it would be "over the dead bodies of the last one of us."

Early that afternoon the column reached the Pioneer Paper Mill on the Watkinsville Road, three and a half miles south of town, and filed into the previously prepared trenches overlooking the bridge just below the confluence of McNutt's and Barber's creeks. While Captain Taylor's company crossed the bridge and deployed as skirmishers on the south bank, Captain Ed Lumpkin sited his battery in three gun emplacements, tiered on the slope behind them. They were ready and waiting when an estimated eighty bluecoated troopers appeared on the hill across the creek.

Gripping their muskets a little tighter, the home guards held their fire, hoping to coax the Yankees closer to the breastworks. Several anxious moments passed. Then Captain Lumpkin, a veteran artilleryman who had served in the Army of Northern Virginia, gave the command. His bronze-throated 12-pounders boomed in quick succession, scattering the clustered riders in every direction.[14]

The Yankees had no artillery of their own, and with his brigade's enlistments about to expire, Adams was not inclined to push matters. Despairing of crossing the creek, he withdrew his Kentuckians and detoured westward along the present-day Daniels Bridge, Virgil Langford, and Mars Hill roads, sending a courier and a guide to report to Capron.

The news that infantry and artillery blocked the road to Athens found Capron still waiting in the woods north of Watkinsville. Eager to reunite with Adams, he ordered his troopers back into the saddle and was soon plodding westward. He had gone six miles before he discovered his civilian guide had deliberately led the column astray.[15]

After six hours of delay and repeated efforts to communicate with Adams, Capron finally abandoned the idea of fording the Oconee. Learning a "heavy body of infantry and cavalry" was approaching on his right, he struck off to the northwest on the Hog Mountain Road about 4:00 P.M.[16]

"Both men and animals had about reached the limit of endurance," noted Captain James Wells of the 8th Michigan, "and it was found to be impossible, except by the most strenuous effort, to keep either awake. With both hands locked over the horns of their saddles, the men would fall asleep, when their horses, taking advantage of the situation, turned out by the roadside and stopped. In this manner the command was often strung out a distance of two or three miles."

At 9:00 P.M., Capron finally called an hour's halt at Jug Tavern to rest and feed. This scarcely gave troopers in the rear ranks time to catch up, and when a bugle sounded "To Horse" at 10:00 P.M., officers had to prod some of the men awake with the points of their sabers.

Capron compelled Wiley Bush, a furloughed Confederate his men had captured at Jug Tavern, to show the way northwest, toward the Peachtree Road. He wanted to put the Mulberry River behind him before halting again, but as his troopers blindly groped through the gloom of a moonless night, it quickly became apparent they just could not go any farther. "We had to keep a guard on each side of the column . . . to keep the men from riding into the woods while sleeping on their horses," recorded Lieutenant Isaac M. Brown of the 6th Indiana, "and the horses were as sleepy as the men."

Despite these precautions, troopers tumbled out of their saddles and sprawled senseless in the road until the rear guard shook them awake. Uncertain of how far it was to the Mulberry River, at 1:00 A.M., shortly after crossing the Lawrenceville and Jefferson Road, Capron wearily called a halt at King's Tanyard on Rocky Creek.

Dismounting, he instructed the head of the column to move on far enough for the rear to close up on the tanyard. He reckoned they had come fifty-six miles (actually it was closer to thirty-six) in the last twenty-four hours, more than enough to outdistance even the most dogged pursuit. He would let the men get a couple of hours' sleep, but, as a precaution, he put part of the 8th Michigan at the head of the column with the last few rounds in their Spencers and sent his adjutant, Captain Samuel Wells, to have Major Davidson's battalion of the 14th Illinois barricade the road a mile to the rear, post vedettes, and keep a sharp lookout.

Capron later insisted he directed the rest of his men to dismount and lie down "without removing the saddles." Private Isaac Dennis of the 14th Illinois said he heard his captain give orders to "dismount: make no noise; don't unsaddle; throw the bridle-rein over the horse's head, and lie down with arm through the bridle-rein."

But Lieutenant Isaac Brown and Sergeant Oliver Haskell of the 6th Indiana both insisted they were told to unsaddle. "It was said to be an order from Colonel Capron," recounted an 8th Michigan cavalryman, and most of the men unbuckled their girths, slid the saddles off the matted, sweat-stained backs of their mounts, and collapsed in the middle of the road.[17]

"The night was very warm," noted Captain James Wells, "and from long continuance in the saddle many of the men had swollen feet, and for greater comfort removed their boots, while others took off their coats and used them for pillows."

Capron shunted about 300 Negroes—old men, women, and children mounted on mules, donkeys, and broken-down horses—into the fields on the left side of the road, between the rear guard and the main column. He had retired to the front porch of a nearby house with his son and an orderly when Court Matson of the 6th Indiana confronted him. It could not be that far to the Mulberry River, Matson argued. They should keep going, get across the river and destroy the bridge behind them before stopping for the night. Capron assured him they were perfectly safe and curled up on his blanket.[18]

By this time, Capron's Confederate guide, Wiley Bush, had either escaped or been released. He was on his way back to Jug Tavern when he met a small group of horsemen. They were Rebels.

Alfred Iverson had started William Wirt Allen's Alabama brigade after the fleeing Federals before dark on July 31. Allen was supposed to get ahead of them before they got to Eatonton but had taken the wrong road, allowing the fugitives to escape. As he approached Madison early on August 1, a courier overtook him with a report that 700 Yankees had crossed the Oconee River at Curtwright's Factory, a cotton mill at Long Shoals. Hastily backtracking his brigade, Allen camped a few miles south of Madison while his scouts scoured the roads west of the Oconee.[19]

Iverson also sent Russ Butler's Confederate Kentuckians to join the chase, and they pounded northward all day and all night, reaching Madison early on August 2, several hours behind the raiders. Realizing his fatigued force could never catch up unless he did something drastic, Butler assembled his brigade, now reduced to fewer than 500, and had his inspector general select the fittest horses and men. Later that morning, ninety-eight carefully culled Kentuckians spurred out of Madison, led by Captains J. F. Smith and Jeff Rogers, the same officers who had received Stoneman's flag of truce.[20]

They were soon overtaken by William Campbell Preston Breckinridge, the able and energetic colonel of the 9th Kentucky Cavalry. Assuming command, the twenty-seven-year-old Breckinridge relentlessly rode northward, through Fair Play, High Shoals, and Watkinsville. Horses broke down. Men collapsed with fatigue. About eighty-five riders were left by the time Captain Smith's advance guard encountered Wiley Bush on the road to Jug Tavern.

Learning Bush had just come from the Yankee camp, the Kentuckians asked him to lead them to it. He refused. The Yanks would shoot him, he protested. Besides, he was home on furlough and "not due to fight." He did volunteer how to get there, and Captain Smith and his men, armed with these directions, warily rode ahead.

Night was just beginning to gray into dawn when two of Smith's scouts, Timothy L. Jones and Clark Johnson, discerned a couple of Yankee vedettes in the darkness and quietly took them prisoner. Dismounting, both scouts cautiously continued up the road on foot. They had not gone far when they discovered the picket reserve post, manned by ten troopers from Company D of the 14th Illinois. No one challenged their approach. The exhausted Yankees were all asleep until Jones and Johnson prodded them awake at gunpoint. Colonel Breckinridge then quietly brought up the rest of his little command and eased his men into the woods on both sides of Capron's slumbering column.[21]

Private Isaac Dennis of the 14th Illinois had let down a section of fence by the roadside, unsaddled his captured mare, looped the reins over a tree limb, and been asleep for about an hour and a half when he felt someone shake him awake. "Who is it?" he asked groggily.

"Captain Lupton," a voice whispered. "Get up quick and saddle your horse, we are surrounded by the enemy." Dennis stirred slowly. "For God's sake," Lupton hissed, grabbing him by the shoulder and yanking him to his feet, "be quick and mount. I have not closed my eyes to-night. An old darky found me and gave me the alarm. He is now passing along the line. I have my company all mounted and in line. It is just a scratch that I found you in here. Quick! Quick! Mount and fall into line!"

Dennis was buckling his saddle girth when a pistol shot stabbed at the darkness, immediately followed by "unearthly yells and screams," as Breckinridge's left wing came charging through the sleeping Negroes.

"Get up quick, Cap, for God's sake," cried Sergeant Miles Horn, shaking Captain James Wells like a rag doll, "they are right onto us."

Horace Capron awoke with a start, just in time to see the shadowy figures of frightened Negroes, galloping horses, and braying mules and donkeys stampeding into the midst of his sleeping troopers. Bareheaded, he bounded off the porch, calling for his young son to follow. Discovering his orderly had unsaddled his horse, he mounted bareback, shouting for his men to stay together and stand fast.

At the rear of the column, Lieutenant Albert Capron and seventy-five 14th Illinois cavalrymen stationed at a fork in the road mounted at the first alarm and fought desperately for a few moments, but the Rebels swarmed past them, yelling and shooting. Jolted from a sound sleep, McLaughlin's Ohio Squadron sprang to their feet, threw saddles on their horses' backs, and frantically spurred down the road into the throng of dazed troopers and terrified Negroes. Some soldiers bolted aimlessly into the woods. Others lay quiet and still, shot dead in their sleep.

"Rally men! Rally! and charge them!" Court Matson bellowed at the 6th Indiana. Major Orlando Smith managed to extract thirty or forty mounted Hoosiers from the mob and got them into line on the right side of the road. They showed "no evidence of a panic or disposition for retreat," noted a Confederate cavalryman, ". . . the situation was critical in the extreme."

Breckinridge hesitated. Casualties and details to guard his burgeoning catch of prisoners had already whittled down his little force to perhaps only forty men. Pressing the attack now might mean losing all he had won.

At that instant, Sergeant Phil Pointer of the 1st Kentucky Cavalry spurred up beside him. Charge them again, Pointer yelled, standing up in his stirrups, charge them again and victory was certain.

Charge! Breckinridge ordered and his handful of horsemen hurled themselves at the waiting Hoosiers.

Pistols crackled in the gray dawn. Major Smith of the 6th Indiana took a bullet in his left thigh. His men fled.

Horace Capron had dismounted, grabbed a saddle, and was in the act of throwing it across his horse's withers when a dozen Rebel riders raced past, pistols blazing, and knocked him sprawling. Scrambling to his feet, Capron sprang upon his horse's back and started toward the road, where he could see about 150 of his men trying to form a line. Another surge of yelling, cursing, shooting riders cut him off. Caught up in the confused crush of men and horses, Capron announced it was "every man for himself."

"You are right, Colonel," agreed Isaac Dennis, "and I guess I will get out of this in a hurry." Digging in his spurs, he sped down the road until a voice ordered him to "Halt!"

"Where are you going?" demanded an officer.

"I am going to get away from that rebel yell while I have a chance," Dennis replied as he reined up.

"No you don't," the officer snapped. "If you attempt to pass I will shoot you. Ride in there, and form a line with my men."

"All right," Dennis said, but as soon as the officer turned his back, he put the spurs to his horse again.

At the head of the column, Major Buck was on foot, desperately trying to rally the 8th Michigan. None of his men had more than three or four cartridges left, and despite orders, pleas, and threats from their officers, they began scrambling over the stake-and-rider fences on either side of the road. Others savagely spurred their horses up the Hog Moutain Road. Just after crossing a shallow ford on the Little Mulberry River, the road forked, and in the pale first light of dawn, panicked troopers sped past the left turn that led toward Atlanta. Bearing to the right, toward Jefferson, they struck Price's Bridge over the Mulberry River at a dead run. The old span shuddered under the weight of hurrying hooves and then snapped like a twig, spilling horses and riders into the muddy water, sixteen feet below. A few men drowned. Others, trying to swim across, were mired in the low, marshy bank when Captains J. F. Smith, S. O. Peyton, Lieutenant J. C. Pickett, and a handful of Confederate Kentuckians rode up and opened fire. "The slaughter was fearful," declared a Michigan soldier.[22]

Major Buck and Captain Muir McDonald had managed to get a few troopers into line on the right side of the road when McDonald noticed some others milling around on the left. Spurring over, he dismounted and was trying to get them to fall in when a rider dashed out of the darkness demanding to know who was "the son of a bitch" giving orders to his men. "What regiment do you belong to, sir?" he asked McDonald, drawing his revolver.

"The 8th Michigan, sir," McDonald answered.

The rider's pistol roared, sending a bullet whizzing past McDonald's head. Dismounting, he cocked his gun again. McDonald immediately surrendered and asked his assailant if he intended to shoot his prisoners.

"I'll show you," the Rebel answered as he pulled the trigger. The cap failed to explode. Angrily, he pulled McDonald to the side of the road. "Surrender, do you," he sneered, "you Yankee son of a bitch! We don't give quarter; we intend to shoot every damned one of you!" Opening the flap of a small pouch on the front of his belt, he fumbled for a percussion cap. "I'll show you how to surrender!" he snarled as he reprimed his revolver. "What the hell made you run away after Stoneman had surrendered you?"

McDonald slid a hand into his pocket and pulled out a small pistol. He pressed it within an inch of his opponent's head and pulled the trigger. Hearing the sharp report, two more Rebels dashed up. They were about to avenge their comrade when a pair of Yankee bullets struck them down.[23]

It was Silas Adams's brigade. His 1st and 11th Kentucky had halted and unsaddled along Rocky Creek at midnight, a scant three miles east of Capron's bivouac. Awaking early on August 3, they had mounted and resumed their westward march along the Mulberry Road. The advance guard had gone about two and a half miles when Private Terrance O'Brien of the 14th Illinois came galloping out of the woods shouting, "Capron has been attacked and cut all to pieces."

Spurring ahead, the Kentuckians soon reached the intersection of the Mulberry and Hog Mountain roads. A blueclad body lay sprawled amid a welter of hoofprints, and it only took a moment to discern which direction the stampede had gone. Turning to the right, Adams ordered his front ranks forward at a gallop.

The column raced northward, splashing across the Little Mulberry River. "As we charged down the road," noted Lieutenant Richard Huffman, "we came across several Union soldiers lying dead. . . . The road was strewn with the guns, pistols, blankets, etc., of Capron's men."[24]

They had gone about a mile when they collided with Rebel cavalrymen escorting a bunch of prisoners back from Price's Bridge. Adams's men pounded into their midst with shouts and pistol shots. Confederate Colonel Breckinridge, just remounting after his horse was wounded, was swallowed up in the wild melee and quickly captured. Clad in a jeans hunting shirt, he went unrecognized and soon slipped away. Captain Smith also escaped after a hand-to-hand encounter with two Yankee horsemen, but Captain Peyton and Lieutenant Pickett were taken prisoner.

Peyton assured the Federals they would not get much farther. They were up against Kentucky boys. His captors volunteered they were Kentucky boys themselves. Adams's brigade, Peyton asked? Adams's brigade, came the reply. "Then our squadron is gone up," Peyton said gloomily.

Realizing fate had pitted them against their home state rivals, some of Breckinridge's men shouted, "Where is the 1st Kentucky Federal cavalry?"

"Here we are," answered the bluecoated Kentuckians, rushing in to duel with sabers and pistols. "We are the 11th," roared the 11th Kentucky as they galloped up to join the fray.

The two regiments went through the Rebels like a dose of salts. "When we went charging after them they were so confused that they did not know what to do," noted Lieutenant Huffman. "Many of them made no attempt to escape, while others went as fast as their horses would carry them."[25]

Adams, however, had no intention of pressing the pursuit. Besides nearly exhausting what little ammunition his men had left, the charge had uncovered a road leading directly to the Chattahoochee. Detailing Captain Delany Carr and some of the 1st Kentucky to push the retreating Rebels a little farther up the road toward Price's Bridge, Adams paused long enough to gather up his wounded and what few of Capron's men he could find. Then he turned his column squarely to the left on the Hog Mountain Road. "You never saw brighter faces than ours when we learned that we were in advance of our foes," confessed a relieved Lieutenant Huffman.

Prodded by reports another Rebel brigade was angling toward their left to cut them off from the Chattahoochee, the Kentuckians crossed Hog Mountain without incident that morning and filed into the Peachtree Road. This route would have taken them back to Decatur via Flint Hill Church and New Cross Keys, but as they solemnly shuffled westward, citizens assured them Sherman had been driven across the Chattahoochee. "If this was true," noted Stoneman's aide, Lieutenant Colonel Bob Smith, "our situation was still more perilous." Faced with this uncertainty, Adams decided to take no chances. Abandoning the Peachtree Road at Pinckneyville, he detoured due north. About an hour before sundown his advance guard struck the

Chattahoochee at a ford a couple of miles above the ruins of McAfee's Bridge, probably at or near Martin's Old Ferry. The ford was rough, the current swift, but by 9:00 P.M. everyone had crossed safely. About two miles beyond the river, the Kentuckians halted and camped in a cornfield near Newtown Crossroads. Since sunrise, they had ridden nearly forty miles. Utterly exhausted, they lay down and slept so soundly that two captured Confederates, Captain Peyton and Lieutenant Pickett, were able to escape during the night.

Early on August 4, Adams and his men mounted their horses and leisurely continued westward on the Warsaw Road through Roswell. About 11:00 A.M., they began straggling into Marietta.[26]

"Colonel Adams, commanding [a] brigade of Stoneman's cavalry, is here with the First and Eleventh Kentucky Cavalry, about 900 [sic] strong," the post commander wired Sherman that afternoon. "He thinks that the balance of the command are prisoners, including General Stoneman. He cut the railroad south of Macon. The command was overwhelmed by the rebels between Monticello and Clinton."

"Tell Colonel Adams to make a minute report of the facts," Sherman replied from his new headquarters on the west side of Atlanta, "and let me draw conclusions."[27]

20

BACK FROM OBLIVION

JULY 30–AUGUST 12, 1864

The woods are lovely, dark and deep,
But I have promises to keep,
And miles to go before I sleep,
And miles to go before I sleep.

—Robert Frost,
"Stopping by Woods on a Snowy Evening"

It was dark when Sergeant Charles Wing awoke and saw the Rebel soldiers standing around Sunshine Church. Shot in both hands when a bullet split his gunstock, the Michigan trooper had fallen asleep after a busy surgeon had hurriedly bound his wounds. Confused and bloody, he got up from the ground where he lay and walked to a nearby house where Dr. Charles G. Robinson of the 8th Michigan Cavalry was laboring over dozens of other casualties. What did it mean? Wing asked, gesturing toward the Rebel guards outside.

"Stoneman has surrendered," the doctor snapped. "Where have you been?"

"Out there on the ground, asleep," Wing replied.

"Well," Robinson exclaimed, "if you could sleep there you could sleep in Bedlam, for the hardest of the fighting has been there, and that ground has been taken and retaken by both parties."

Wing pondered this for a moment and then asked if there was anything dishonorable about trying to escape after being surrendered by a superior officer. Robertson said he could not answer that; the sergeant would have to decide for himself. "Well, Doctor," Wing said, "I haven't surrendered yet, and I am going to get out of this."

Enlisting the help of an old black man, he soon slipped past the guards and spent the rest of the night aimlessly stumbling around the dark woods. Fearing his guide had deliberately misled him, he finally sent the old man home and hid in a cornfield. Shortly after daylight on August 1, a half dozen Rebel cavalrymen flushed out the hapless sergeant and escorted him back to Sunshine Church.[1]

Guards were already prodding the other prisoners into line when Tom Butler came down to say good-bye to his men. "Boys," he said solemnly, "I did all I could to keep you from being captured yesterday, but to no avail. You, my brave boys, have taken an oath to support the Constitution of the U.S.: never take an oath to fight under their flag. If you have to die, die like men."

Together with Major Mell Soper, he tearfully moved down the ranks, shaking hands with the men who had faithfully stood by him to the last. "There was not a dry eye in all that line that unfortunate morning," recorded Private John Sammons.[2]

Butler soon rejoined the other officers in front of Joseph White's house to begin the march to Macon. The night before, a young Rebel soldier had promised him he could ride his own mount if Butler would give him the big black horse and persuade Iverson to let him keep it. Butler made the request and the little Rebel kept his word. The black was saddled and ready when the captured officers were ordered to mount up at 9:00 A.M.[3]

Escorted by Iverson and his staff, they rode to the field hospital at Sunshine Church where Stoneman's medical director, Dr. Hawkins Brown of the 1st Kentucky, and regimental surgeons and assistant surgeons from the 5th and 6th Indiana, 14th Illinois, and 8th Michigan had labored far into the night, assisted by "a very pleasant" Rebel physician from the Confederate 1st Kentucky Cavalry. Leaving Dr. John Wilkins of the 14th Illinois to care for the wounded Federals, Dr. Brown and his associates joined the cavalcade of captured officers and started down the much-traveled road to Macon.

Iverson was a convivial companion, and even Stoneman conceded the Confederate general had handled his troops handsomely. As the two men rode side by side, Stoneman confided he had come down the east bank of the Ocmulgee expecting to find a bridge at Seven Islands, cross over, and strike the Macon & Western Railroad. When this proved impossible, he had continued south, aiming for the Central Road, rather than expose his division to attack while trying to ferry across the Ocmulgee.

About midday, the procession passed through Clinton. Iverson had returned to his hometown, a conquering hero, and perhaps he paused a moment on the courthouse square, accepting the accolades of old family friends.

Stoneman sat quietly on his horse until he recognized Dr. James Barron standing on his porch with his seven-year-old son. "Doctor," the captured general called, "what you told me was true. The bridge was gone."

For the rest of the afternoon, the blue and gray officers rode along companionably in the stifling August heat. Iverson had previously sent a message to Macon, announcing Stoneman's capture and asking Howell Cobb to provide rations for 1,400 men, including the prisoners. Cobb and his staff met the column two or three miles east of the city at 5:00 P.M. and escorted it to the Ocmulgee River, where the city ferry began shuttling across the men and horses. As the procession started up Fifth Street, a large crowd of all ages, sexes, and colors gathered on the sidewalks, eager to catch a glimpse of "Stoneman and his thieves."

The lone expression of sympathy came from Lieutenant Colonel Richard M. Cuyler, commander of the Macon Arsenal. Running into the street, he heartily shook both of Stoneman's hands, proffering his pocketbook and his services "at any time, and under all circumstances."

The rest of the crowd hooted and jeered. "Some of the ladies shook their fists at us," noted Dr. Andrew Weir, "& call[ed] us all kinds of names such as real ladies ought to be ashamed to repeat."

"Ha! Ha!" jeered a heavyset woman sitting in a buggy as a dejected, haggard-looking Stoneman rode past. "I bet you don't feel as big as you did Saturday morning when your men came into my house."

Ignoring the insults and epithets hurled at him, Stoneman rode silently down the dusty street until the stout prison stockade at Camp Oglethorpe loomed before him. Ordered to dismount, he and his officers strode into the sandy backyard of the provost marshal's office, a small frame house that stood on pilings two or three feet above the ground. Summoned inside, Stoneman was searched and stripped of all his valuables.

A native of Philadelphia, Colonel James Biddle (seen here as a
captain) commanded Stoneman's Indiana brigade and was captured
at Sunshine Church. After the war, he served as a cavalry officer on
the frontier for almost thirty years and retired as a brigadier general.
Courtesy of Roger D. Hunt. Used by permission.

He came out carrying a small stool. Setting it by the side of the house, he sat down,
buried his bronzed face in his hands, and wept bitterly.

Then another officer was called in. Those left standing in the yard were puzzled by
these proceedings until they caught a glimpse of what was going on through a crack
in the wall. Tom Butler had sixty-five dollars in his wallet, but never one to give up
easily, he hastily chewed a fifty into a small wad and secreted it in his pocket before
being called inside.

"What a beautiful belt," Captain Edward Lathrop, the Rebel provost marshal
exclaimed, admiring the silver eagle on Butler's buckle. Hoping the belt might be the
key to keeping the rest of his cash, Butler gave it to him. Lathrop thanked him and in
the same breath demanded his wallet.

Colonel James Biddle had better luck. Escorted by Colonel Crews, he arrived
somewhat belatedly and strolled into the yard with a pair of saddlebags slung over his
arm. Noticing some of his officers standing on the other side of the fence, he asked
what was happening.

"We have been searched," one of them answered, "to see what money or papers we
might have."

"Have you been searched?" Biddle asked.

When the officer acknowledged he had, Biddle quietly tossed him the saddlebags
with instructions to hold on to them. When he was searched a few moments later, he

meekly surrendered a handful of greenbacks and a few official papers. Outside the office, he reclaimed the saddlebags, which contained a thousand dollars in Confederate money his adjutant, Lieutenant G. A. Brown, had captured from a Rebel tax collector. In the dark days to come, Biddle's bundle would buy food for Stoneman and his staff.

That night, in a brief note which the Rebels promised to send through the lines, Stoneman wrote his wife, Mary:

> I am somewhat unwell but safe love. My horse shot. My command was driven off the field except the artillery and [a] portion of one brigade which I held together to cover the rest of the force. This & myself were forced to surrender after having used up our ammunition. Rest assured I did all I could to perform my duty to my men, myself and my government.[4]

The men he had surrendered would have scoffed at that notion as they trudged south, two abreast, flanked by a file of Rebel horsemen on either side. As they passed the scenes of some of the heaviest fighting at Sunshine Church, 5th Indiana troopers noticed a dead comrade lying beside the road, "his breast bone lifted up and the flies swarming over him." Their pleas to stop long enough to bury him were in vain.

The guards riding alongside the column belonged to Crews's Georgia brigade. They seemed like "verry onerable men," noted one Hoosier, although some of them were "insulting."

"We were pretty well worn out and discouraged," admitted Private John Sammons. "We had but little to say to each other. The rebels were in high glee and taunted us in many ways, but we dare not say one word back."

The road south led past many of the same farms and plantations the raiders had plundered on their way to Macon, and distraught owners rushed out to meet the column, loudly demanding the return of stolen horses and mules. At first, Rebel troopers handed over the reins with no questions asked, but as the morning wore on and the supply of captured stock began to dwindle, the country folk began laying claim to animals Crews's men had raised themselves. "This," reported one observer, "rather 'opened their eyes.' They were thereafter not so accommodating. . . ."

The Yankee prisoners paid little attention to these transactions. Unaccustomed to walking, they suffered terribly in the heat and dust. Plaintive cries for water rose at every stream they passed, but the Rebels refused to let anyone break ranks until the column briefly paused by a branch at noon. Some of the guards climbed over the fence into an adjacent cornfield and began tossing roasting ears into the road, where hungry prisoners scrambled for them "like so many hogs."

The march continued until nightfall halted the column at a bridge over a little stream about eight miles from Macon on the Clinton Road. Fires were built, and captor and captive alike dined on a supper of green corn roasted in the shuck. "We went to bed very early that night with very heavy hearts," recounted Private Sammons, "not much talking. . . ."[5]

They awoke on August 2 to an overcast, unsettled dawn. Storm clouds were brewing, and as the gray skies darkened Crews's tattered Georgians ordered the finely outfitted Federals to hand over their oil cloths and extra clothing. When prisoners protested that the terms of surrender protected their personal belongings, Crews's men simply laughed. "Oh!" they said, "that's no difference, they will strip you at the prison anyhow, and we need your traps worse than the guards, so will take them now."

The raiders reluctantly gave up their baggage and after another meal of green corn and creek water, marched on to Macon. As they trudged past a farmhouse, a white woman standing by the front gate drawled disdainfully, "That is the way I like to see you all come."

"Old Billy Sherman will be along in a few days," a prisoner shouted back.

On the outskirts of Macon, some of Joe Brown's militia relieved Crews's cavalry and escorted the raiders into the city about 10:00 A.M. Angry crowds greeted them with taunts and curses, but the captured Yankees "appeared in good spirits," reported the *Macon Telegraph,* "and . . . are a very good looking body of men. . . ."

Their stay at Camp Oglethorpe was a short one. Guards quickly herded 442 of them aboard a train waiting at the depot, cramming them into the cars as thick as they could stand. With a shrill whistle, the engine started south, and for the next several hours the closely packed captives sweated, swayed, and suffered. About 4:00 P.M. the cars lurched to a stop. The doors slid open. Squinting their eyes against the sun's shimmering glare, the troopers climbed down from the cars and got their first look at Camp Sumter, the palisaded Rebel prison otherwise known as Andersonville.

The Rebels had made special arrangements for their arrival. The train had stopped before it got to the depot and extra guards were waiting. "You were going to release the prisoners here," one of them jeered; "we'll show you Andersonville."

Herded into line, the woebegone raiders shuffled across the sandy plain for about a half mile before the prison commandant, Captain Henry Wirz, halted them two or three hundred yards from the stockade. He lined them up, four ranks deep, while guards surrounded them with muskets and shotguns already at half cock.

"After looking at us for a few minutes he commenced one of the most unique performances I was ever permitted to witness," recounted Sergeant Erastus Holmes. "He raved up and down the line like a wild beast, swearing and abusing us in the vilest language and billingsgate I ever heard. He fairly foamed at the mouth, and the sweat poured off of him at a rate wonderful to see. . . . After he was fairly tired out, he gave this order: 'Strip them! Strip them every one! Take everything away! They are all raiders and they are all thieves.'"[6]

A Rebel sergeant repeated the order. Reluctantly, the prisoners disrobed and stood naked in the sweltering heat as Wirz's guards moved through the ranks, turning pockets inside out, fingering waistbands and suspicious seams, crushing coat collars, and inspecting hatbands, relieving them of watches, money, and jewelry, hats, boots, and shoes, pocketknives, postage stamps, pictures, Masonic pins, and anything else they wanted. The process was repeated the next day, August 3, when the first contingent of McCook's men arrived.[7]

Back in Macon, Alfred Iverson and his men accepted the plaudits of a grateful city. The Southwestern Railroad Company contributed $500, the Macon & Western Railroad made a matching donation, and a Jones County resident collected $1,000, all of which was presented to Iverson for the benefit of his command. A detail of ten men went out and spent a sizable portion of these funds on watermelons. "Such a water melon feast and such a war with melon rinds I never witnessed before or since," recalled Private J. A. Wynn of the 1st Georgia Cavalry.

The city also laid plans for a "complimentary entertainment" to be held at 5:00 P.M., August 4, in the grove behind the Wesleyan Female College. Macon Mayor Stephen Collins appointed a Committee of Arrangements and called upon citizens to show "their appreciation of the services of these heroic defenders of our fields and firesides" by contributing "provisions, coffee, milk, and other supplies." In the midst of these preparations, word came that Iverson had received orders to move his troops back to Atlanta without delay.

The gala event was canceled and, in its place, a thanksgiving service was held at 5:00 P.M., August 5, at the Baptist church. "It was larger than I expected," wrote Howell Cobb, "being about two thirds the size of the ordinary Sunday congregation. . . . The services were conducted by Dr. Wills, the Presbyterian minister. His remarks were personally offensive to me and all other officers charged with the defense of the city . . . & I shall not give him another opportunity of repeating the offense as I shall attend no more of the meetings unless I know that he will not be there."[8]

One of the sore points in Macon was the disposition of captured horses and mules. Cobb had issued orders on August 2 and again on August 4 specifying that any citizens able to identify their animals among the captured stock could reclaim them. Those who had acquired broken-down mounts with Yankee brands to replace those the raiders had stolen could keep them, and officers were authorized to provide captured animals to poor families that had lost their only horse or mule.

These orders, however, applied only to the troops under Cobb's immediate command. When Dr. J. F. Barrow found his buggy horse under one of Iverson's cavalrymen and tried to reclaim it, the trooper told him it would cost him $3,000 in cash. "Several of my neighbors, as well as myself, visited Macon to recover some portion of our mules, but you can hardly judge of our astonishment when we saw them offered for sale in the streets of your hospitable city . . . ," a Jasper County citizen complained. "The best efforts of us poor country folks, . . . to obtain any redress, were fruitless. The soldiers laughed at us for claiming legitimate spoil, had they not fought for it? We said—in an under tone—'not much'; this pleased them worst of all; they cursed and said, 'we wouldn't have thought so if we had been there.'"[9]

While Iverson's Georgians were wearing out their welcome in Macon, his Kentuckians marched Lieutenant Colonel Matson, Major Buck, Major Davidson, 206 other bluecoated captives, 17 Negroes, and 210 horses and mules into Athens about 3:00 P.M., August 3. Tired and hungry after the long hours in the saddle and the wild, confused fight at King's Tanyard, the Confederate cavaliers deposited their prisoners behind the wrought-iron fence surrounding the Franklin College campus and called upon one of the local defense companies, the venerable Mitchell Thunderbolts, to guard them.

When the Thunderbolts' commander, Captain John Billups, tried to muster his men, Dr. Henry Hull sent word that guard duty was "contrary to his habit of life and he didn't expect to reverse it." Others insisted their only obligation was to protect Athens from attack. A few, however, expressed their willingness to serve, if only for "the privilege of pointing their guns at the yankees and making them behave themselves." One of the volunteers was Dr. Edward R. Ware. With his rifle primed and ready, he sat on the fence surrounding the campus for hours at a time, compelling the prisoners to lie on the ground and remain perfectly still.

This was Athens' first glimpse of Yankee soldiers, and crowds of curious citizens, under the pretext of going to prayer meeting, gathered outside the fence, gawking at them. "The prisoners presented a sorry spectacle," reported the *Athens Southern Watchman*. "Ragged, some of them bare-headed, some bare-footed, and all very dirty, we have never seen an equal number of men looking so badly. The great mass of them appeared to be the 'rag, tag and bobtail' of the communities from whence they came. We recognized 'the rich Irish brogue and sweet German accent' among them. It is true that, now and then, a respectable looking man was to be seen among the officers and men. The great mass of them, however, looked like 'hard cases.'"

"The Yankees were impudent," Mrs. Howell Cobb observed indignantly. "One told Sukey Daugherty he had seen many girls a great sight prettier than she—he saw one yesterday—she was a *yellow girl*."

Athens set aside the next day, August 4, to honor Colonel Breckinridge and his brave men. Preceded by the blare of a marching band, the Kentucky brigade paraded down Broad Street at 3:00 P.M. A citizens' committee met them at the center of town and conducted them to the college chapel, where they were greeted by the enthusiastic applause of hoopskirted ladies who waved handkerchiefs and showered them with bouquets.

When the ovation ended, heads bowed in prayer as a minister gave fervent thanks for the city's deliverance from the foul hands of the invader. Then, in "a perfect little gem of a speech," Dr. Andrew A. Lipscomb, the college chancellor, extended the heartfelt hospitality of the Classic City to Kentucky's gallant sons. Captain Given Campbell of the 2nd Kentucky rose and responded "in a brief and eloquent manner." Then citizens and soldiers alike turned their attention to six tables, extending the entire length of the chapel, piled high with "all the substantials and delicacies of the season."

"Our soldiers were a motley looking set compared with those well-dressed people," conceded Major J. P. Austin of the 9th Kentucky. "We had not seen our wagon-train for a month, and were as dirty as pigs."

For the rest of the afternoon, jangling spurs mixed with "the clicking of knives and forks" and "the merry converse of belted knights and fair dames" as Athens feted its heroes. When everyone had eaten, there were loud calls for Colonel Breckinridge. Mounting the rostrum, dressed in a worn jeans hunting shirt which contrasted sharply with the gold braid of some of his resplendent subordinates, he made a "manly and touching speech" which provided a fitting end to the festivities.

The surfeit of food left on the tables was sent to the captured Yankees lounging under the oak trees in front of the chapel. "The prisoners 'curse and damn' old Stoneman at a furious rate," reported the *Athens Southern Watchman;* "nor do they spare Sherman—alleging that every man of common sense must have known that a raid upon Macon, Milledgeville, &c., would inevitably fail."[10]

During the next two days, Breckinridge's men brought several more stragglers into town. On Saturday morning, August 6, guards marched 271 Yankees down Broad Street, across the bridge over the Oconee River, and up the slopes of Carr's Hill. There the prisoners boarded a train that carried them to Augusta, where they bivouacked on the banks of the Savannah River. From Augusta, a train took them south to Millen, then west to the burned bridge at the Oconee River. Ferried across, they boarded another train that traveled to Macon over the already repaired track they had wrecked only nine days earlier. "The train on the Central Railroad yesterday was crowded beyond precedent," the *Macon Daily Confederate* reported on August 9. "Besides three hundred Yankee prisoners [from Athens], a large number of passengers were on board. . . . About the most unpleasant predicament a person can be placed in now is a railroad train."

Between August 3 and August 14, soldiers and stalwart civilians rounded up 431 of Stoneman's raiders and brought them to Athens to be sent to the prisons at Macon and Andersonville. Among them was a tired, hungry, Irish trooper "fresh from the Emerald Isle." He was sitting on the stairs to the provost marshal's office on Broad Street when a pompous Athenian came up, cursed him, and kicked him. Sixteen-year-old Augustus Longstreet Hull watched in disgust. "Boy as I was," he later recalled, "I boiled over with indignation and I felt like apologizing to the prisoner for the whole state of Georgia. . . ."[11]

To the frightened, footsore Federals desperately trying to get back to Sherman's lines, it seemed like the whole state of Georgia was hunting them. When Mrs. M. A. Robey spotted two stragglers skulking about her farm near Eatonton, she sent her Negro man, Anderson, after them. Taking a double-barreled shotgun, the slave dutifully mounted his mule and called to his dogs. The hounds quickly picked up the scent and tracked the two fugitives into the swamps along Murder Creek. Brought to bay, the Yankees tried to fight off the dogs until a shotgun blast made them think better of it. Anderson then marched his captives to Eatonton, where a cheering crowd greeted him with cries of "Make way for *Captain* Robey." When some citizens got up a reward and presented him with several hundred dollars, Anderson modestly proclaimed his readiness to fight to the last "in *suspense* of his country."

These two prisoners, together with twenty-six others already in custody in Eatonton and another dozen held in Milledgeville, were soon sent to Macon. For the next two weeks, captured Yankees were brought in almost daily, despite the most determined efforts to escape. One of the raiders, claiming to belong to a Confederate cavalry command, boarded the train at Madison on the evening of August 15. His partially blue uniform and "broad Puritan dialect" aroused the suspicion of other passengers, and a provost guard took him into custody before the train got to Greensboro.

Macon watched this daily influx of captured Federals with undisguised delight. The overwhelming victories at Brown's Mill, Philpott's Ferry, Sunshine Church, and King's Tanyard breathed new hope into Southern hearts and renewed confidence in the prowess of Confederate arms.[12]

But the raids also left the city seething with rage. The Yankees had deliberately hurled shells into homes and hospitals. They had looted and pillaged shamelessly. The *Southern Confederacy,* reminding its readers of the treatment Confederate General John Hunt Morgan had received a year earlier when he was captured during an ill-fated raid through Indiana and Ohio, demanded "a cell and a shaved head for Stoneman." Other Macon papers took up the cry. "Now is the chance, now is the time for retaliation," declared the *Daily Intelligencer.* "The indignities that were offered to General John H. Morgan can be ballanced [*sic*] by an indignity to General Stoneman."

Confederate authorities seemed content to treat Stoneman as a prisoner of war and, to the dismay of some, nothing was done. But on August 10, the *Intelligencer* fanned the flames of public outrage to new heights when it reported Stoneman had entered the home of a "highly respectable" citizen of Jones County, who had fled to avoid capture, and compelled the man's wife, "an accomplished lady," to cook breakfast for him and his staff. After gorging himself at her table, the "*Federal General* proceeded . . . to draw his sword and cut to pieces several of the lady's dresses that were hanging against the wall of one of the chambers, and having thus vented his diabolical malice, he next exhibited his licentious and beastly nature, by making dishonorable propositions to the lady of the house herself." Crediting the story to a gentleman of "unimpeachable" veracity, the *Intelligencer* demanded not just "a cell and a shaved head" for the Yankee fiend, but "the rope and the scaffold" as well.

Stoneman emphatically denied the allegations and immediately sent *Intelligencer* editor J. H. Steele a note requesting "the honor of an interview to day upon a subject of importance to myself."

Steele received the general's note about sundown and applied early the next morning at the post commandant's office for permission to visit him. Upon arriving at Camp Oglethorpe, Steele found Stoneman and his officers had been removed to Charleston.

Some Southern newspapers reprinted the *Intelligencer*'s allegations. Others rejected the story as "not fit to be related in a public journal." Only the *Savannah Republican,* on the principle that "the Devil should have his due," averred that Confederate officers who knew Stoneman represented him as "a soldier of the old school, and above a dishonorable act."

"If what the journals say of Stoneman be true," the *Columbus Daily Sun* concluded, "he should have been tried, condemned, and executed by the Civil Code of the State in which his crimes were perpetuated. If false and designed only to inflame the passions of a people . . . those journals are unworthy of the people whom they claim to represent, and cannot be looked to as exponents of the habits, sentiments and feelings of the Southern people."[13]

No one demonstrated the "sentiments and feelings" of the Southern people better than the ladies of Jones and Jasper counties. Day after day, Dr. Palacia Stewart loaded her buggy with medicines and supplies and drove to Sunshine Church to nurse the sick and wounded soldiers on both sides. Mrs. Frank Haskell took some of the hated Yankees into her home, where her sister, Mrs. Jesse Hunt, visited them daily, bringing food, changing bandages, and writing letters. When the time came to move the less seriously wounded prisoners to the general hospital at Macon, the Yankee surgeon, Dr. John Wilkins, and eight of his patients presented Mrs. Hunt with a heartfelt letter of thanks, extolling "her many acts of kindness and sympathy," and enjoining any Union troops who passed through the neighborhood to "refrain from injuring her property in every respect."

Nine of the most seriously wounded men remained at Sunshine Church with Dr. Wilkins. Three others, Lieutenants Daniel Murphy and James Humphrey and Sergeant Thomas J. Jenkins of the 1st Kentucky, were taken to Joseph White's house. Murphy had been shot in the spine. Humphrey and Jenkins were amputees, each having lost his left leg, but Humphrey's wound festered, compelling a Confederate surgeon, Dr. John L. Ancrum, to perform a second operation about two weeks later.

"I visited the hospital frequently," wrote Hillsboro's Louise Caroline Cornwell, "as it was near my mother's residence and some of our wounded was also there. I never went through curiosity, but to carry them something for their comfort. Once in a while . . . this man Humphrey asked me to write a letter for him, he felt that he would die. He was engaged to be married to a Miss Buchanan, Casey City, Ky., and he had her likeness[,] a small daguerrotype, which he wished me to take and return to her. . . . I took it and gave the required promise, wrote the letter for him and sent it off. He died there. I cut a lock of hair from his head and kept it with the likeness awaiting an opportunity to send it to her."

Mrs. Cornwell also saw a Yankee trooper lifted onto a table so doctors could amputate his shattered hip. "I can see his face now," she later wrote, "as he raised himself on his elbow and looked around at the face of each one present to see if he could find one to sympathize with him in this, his hour of deepest trial; though suffering greatly not a groan escaped his lips as he fell back and resigned himself to his fate."

Upon examining the wound, the attending surgeon decided an operation was useless and had the young soldier carried back to his bed. About a week later, Mrs. Cornwell brought him some wine. He sat up long enough to drink it and then said feebly, "You never come only to bring something. I always feel so sorry when I see you."

Mrs. Cornwell asked why, but the trooper made no reply. Half an hour later, he died. Some ladies who lived two or three miles from Hillsboro later identified him as the Yankee who had broken open a trunk in their home and robbed them of about three hundred dollars in gold.[14]

Five of the twelve raiders left at Sunshine Church died of their wounds. Slaves hauled their bodies away in carts and buried them on Frank Haskell's farm. The lonely, unmarked graves of about twenty-five more of Stoneman's men dotted the woods and fields between Clinton and Hillsboro. At least nine troopers who escaped the surrender at Sunshine Church were cut down in the carnage at King's Tanyard, and countless others perished trying to reach the safety of Sherman's lines.[15]

For the next month, the survivors straggled back, alone, in pairs, sometimes in small squads, bearded, hatless, haggard, half-starved men dressed in faded, mud-stained clothes that hung from their stooped shoulders in rags. They had been hunted by bloodhounds and shot at by home guards. Fear and hunger had been their constant companions.

Many of the dismounted men McCook callously cast adrift at Rock Mills, Alabama, on July 31 had been with Rousseau's column and at least had the advantage of being familiar with the road to Atlanta. There was a certain amount of ambivalence toward the war in that part of the country and some families who had suffered heavily at the hands of Rousseau's raiders only a few days before shared what little food they had with groups of fugitives and gave them directions. After a couple of days of hiding in the woods and dodging Rebel patrols, Captain Erastus G. McNeely of the 5th Iowa and six hungry, exhausted troopers reached P. H. Hesterly's house at Allen's Mill near Carrollton. Some of Stoneman's men had visited Hesterly on July 16, robbed him of mules, chickens, and provisions, and thoroughly looted his house. Rousseau's column had followed on July 21 and taken most of what was left, but when these hunted men appeared on his doorstep, asking for help, Hesterly fed them, hid them from the home guards, and hired a man to guide them to the Union lines. "If any of our troops pass this man[']s house at any time Protect him for he is a good union man[,] he fed and helped some of Gen McCook[']s command that were dismounted," Privates William Moyer, T. J. Channer, Henry H. Bellows, William Martin, and Chief Bugler Joseph Hensman of the 5th Iowa and Private James McKeehan of the 4th Tennessee gratefully attested in a note they signed and left with him.

Slaves befriended one of Stoneman's men, Sergeant John V. Munger of the 14th Illinois, and guided him to Covington. Dressed in a stolen Rebel uniform, he followed the Georgia Railroad westward and walked into Kenner Garrard's lines near Buckhead on August 8 without even being challenged.

A week later, some of Garrard's soldiers picketing the railroad between Atlanta and Decatur saw a barefooted scarecrow of a man staggering toward them, dressed in a ragged pair of drawers and a flannel blouse matted with blood. It was Lieutenant Herbert Mayo of the 14th Illinois. Shot while leading a charge at Sunshine Church, he had crawled into the bushes to die. Passing Rebels had robbed him of his boots, money, and clothing, but when he came to he dragged himself to his feet and unsteadily started north. Traveling at night, wading swamps and rivers, he never met a soul. His wound bled profusely and one day, while he was bathing in a stream, his probing finger chanced upon a hole between his shoulder blades. The Rebel bullet had gone all the way through.

Then there were three 2nd Indiana cavalrymen who became separated from McCook's column and rode completely around Atlanta, crossing the Chattahoochee forty miles above the Western & Atlantic Railroad bridge, hiding by day and stealing south at night until they reached Marietta. Even more remarkable was the odyssey of Lieutenant John S. Welch and Sergeant George W. Norris of the 14th Illinois. Left afoot during the fight at King's Tanyard, they wandered through the wilderness for twenty-two days before reaching the Union lines, at Knoxville, Tennessee.[16]

White-haired Horace Capron's ordeal also began at King's Tanyard. Calling for his young son, Osmond, and a few troopers to stay with him, he had plunged his barebacked mount into the dense thickets bordering the road. Emerging in a field where several riderless horses were wandering around, both he and his son stopped long enough to procure a couple of saddles. They scarcely had time to pull the cinches tight before the Rebels burst from the woods behind them, yelling and shooting.

Father and son mounted and raced for the trees on the other side of the field. Joined by Lieutenant Almeron E. Calkins of the 8th Michigan, they outdistanced their pursuers, and after briefly resting their winded horses, they cautiously set out on a road leading toward the Chattahoochee. They had gone two or three miles when they heard hoofbeats. Looking back, they saw about ten gray riders coming at a gallop. These were some of Silas Adams's scouts, still dressed in captured uniforms, but to Capron and his companions, they looked like real Rebels. With a prod of their spurs, the three bluecoated cavalrymen quit the road, leaped fences, and bounded over ditches, sweeping down bushes and brambles at breakneck speed. Racing through the thickets, along the shaded edges of the cornfields crowding the south bank of the Mulberry River, they came to a deeply washed streambed. Capron swerved in and led the way down the muddy ditch, ducking under an overhanging archway of limbs and branches as he plunged his horse into the dark, deep waters of the Mulberry. Wet, winded, and weary, all three men gained the other side just in time to hear hoofbeats fading in the distance. They were safe, for the moment at least, and reined their horses into the shade of a nearby thicket to rest.

A month shy of sixty, Capron was undoubtedly the oldest cavalry officer in Sherman's army. A hale and hearty campaigner despite his years, he had already seen the war claim the life of his namesake son. He had left a second son, Albert, on the field at King's Tanyard and was grimly determined not to lose another.

In the shade of the thicket, Capron and his companions took stock of their arsenal. His was the only pistol they had, and it contained a single suspect cartridge, dampened by the plunge into the river. That and one poncho were their only encumbrances when they ventured forth once again.

Capron figured if they kept to the woods and rode northwest they would eventually reach the Chattahoochee. They could steal a boat, float downstream, and hopefully reenter the Union lines near the Roswell bridge. Avoiding the main roads, they gave cabins and houses a wide berth. When compelled to cross a road, they first looked carefully in both directions and always tried to cover their horses' tracks. Night came, but they kept going, only to blunder into a tangled swamp. Hopelessly lost, they waited anxiously for daylight.

They were picking their way through the woods the next afternoon when they encountered a lean, rough-cut Georgian, commonly known as a Cracker. Unarmed and obviously fearful, he claimed to be a Union man who was hiding out to keep from being conscripted into the Rebel army. After a lengthy discussion, he convinced the Yankee colonel and his companions to leave their horses with his mother and sister, who lived nearby, and promised to guide them through the trackless wilds on foot, traveling at night to avoid surprise. Once they were safely inside the Union lines, he wanted a hundred dollars for his trouble and a horse to take him home.

Capron was wary, but he needed a guide, and he knew getting through on horseback would be virtually impossible. To provide some relief for his already swollen feet, he cut the toes off his jackboots, which were still full of river water. Then, as darkness set in, he bid an affectionate farewell to his faithful steed, seized the guide by the coattail, and told him to lead on, while his son and Lieutenant Calkins brought up the rear. Single file, they groped through an unbroken wilderness, stumbling, falling, bloodying their hands, wearing blisters on their feet. By 2:00 A.M., they could go no farther and sprawled exhausted on a wooded knoll.

When they awoke the next morning, their guide was gone, no doubt chuckling about how he had slickered the Yanks out of three good horses. There was not a moment to lose, Capron declared. They had to get moving before their friend brought back the home guards.

For the next two days, they lived on blackberries and a biscuit begged from a passing Negro. Twice they hugged the ground while armed bands of men, women, and children passed close by, beating the bushes for Yankee soldiers. Once, three fierce-looking guerrillas topped a hill just as the trio were about to dart across a country road. Throwing themselves under a bridge over a narrow streambed, the fugitives held their breath as hoofbeats sounded on the timbers overhead.

Late in the afternoon on August 6, a sliver of silver glimmered through the trees. It was the Chattahoochee. As Capron and company cautiously approached the south bank, they met a Negro. He was timid and fearful at first, but they persuaded him to follow them back into the woods so they could talk. When they told him they needed a boat, he shook his head. Rebel soldiers had the whole river picketed, he said; every ferryboat had either been sunk or hauled out of reach.

Surely there must be something, Capron persisted. Well, the slave admitted, there was a dugout chained on the other side of the river. The Rebels used it to ferry their pickets back and forth. Prodded by Capron, the promise of Osmond's silver watch, and some Confederate notes Lieutenant Calkins had, he finally agreed to get it for them as soon as it was dark.

The little group then moved to the top of a bluff to reconnoiter while there was still enough light to see. They had just taken cover in some tall grass when about a hundred Rebel soldiers approached the north bank with forty or fifty bluecoated prisoners. A muted peal of thunder muttered somewhere in the distance as the little dugout cast off.

Twelve or fifteen feet long and only fifteen inches wide, it was barely big enough to carry three or four men. Capron watched, picking his fingernails with his pearl-handled pocketknife, as it shuttled back and forth. It was nearly 9:00 P.M. before the last load came ashore.

Just as Capron was about to emerge from his hiding place, more Rebels suddenly appeared with a second group of prisoners. They were about to commence crossing when a white hot flash of lightning seared overhead. A terrific thunderclap shook the black heavens and trees thrashed violently under the lash of wind and rain.

Capron's Negro guide wailed in dismay and "trembled from head to foot like an aspen leaf." The colonel kept a firm grip on him and tugged at him to come on; they had to take advantage of the storm. The black man balked. Capron pleaded. The slave shook his head. It was going to take more than a silver watch and a few paper dollars to get him moving. He wanted the colonel's pearl-handled pocketknife. Capron surrendered it, grabbed the slave by the shirt and dashed down to the river, holding hands with his companions to keep from getting separated in the darkness.

The thunder crashed again. "Massa Colonel," the Negro pleaded when they reached the riverbank, "I'se can't go in dar in dis lightener."

It took half an hour and all Capron's powers of persuasion to coax him into the water. The colonel, his son, and the lieutenant waited, nerves strained to the breaking point, half dreading, half expecting the sharp report of a Rebel rifle to punctuate the darkness as they crouched on the riverbank. Finally they heard the beat of the slave's brawny black arms and saw his head bobbing in the rain-spattered waves, the dugout's chain clenched tightly in his teeth. Instantly, all three men sprang into the water and pulled the boat ashore. Capron took a seat in the stern. His son sat in the bow and Lieutenant Calkins, the heaviest of the three, settled in the center. Using a piece of plank for a paddle, Capron pushed off and aimed the boat downstream.

The frail craft caught the current and quickly gathered speed. Mindful of the perils they had left behind, the crew could not repress an exultant shout that was quickly swallowed up in the storm. Lightning flashed overhead, illuminating the night at glaring intervals, and the riverbank began speeding past at an alarming rate. They were going too fast. Then they caught a flickering glimpse of white water and heard a fearful roar.

Rapids! Neither Capron nor his son could swim, and they clung fiercely to the gunwales as the little dugout pitched and heaved wildly. Water poured in over the sides, threatening to swamp them. They were bucked and buffeted and bumped; then, just as suddenly as it had started, it was over. The dugout was wallowing gently on smooth water.

"Father," young Osmond called anxiously, "are you in?"

Capron was in, but the boat was awash. Bail, he commanded, and they worked furiously, using their hats for buckets. About a mile downstream, they heard the approaching roar of a second set of rapids. Capron had no stomach for another such encounter and paddled for shore. Grabbing an overhanging branch, he and his comrades hauled the dugout out of the water and clambered up the bank. Parting the screen of dripping boughs and brambles, they hid in a large cornfield and unrolled their tattered poncho among the puddles. As the rain drummed on their huddled bodies, they fell into an exhausted sleep.

They awoke wet, cold, and miserable on August 7. Lieutenant Calkins was for

Colonel Horace Capron was a nationally renowned expert on scientific farming and animal husbandry. At age fifty-nine, he was undoubtedly the oldest cavalry officer in Sherman's army, but seemed to have no trouble keeping up with the brigade he led during Stoneman's raid. Reproduced from the Collections of the Library of Congress.

surrendering to the first picket they met. Osmond sat on a log, stiff, sore footed, and despondent, begging his father to leave them and go on by himself. The old man sat down beside his son, put his arms around him, and spoke a father's words of reassurance.

He convinced both his companions to get back in the dugout. The sun came out and they shot the rapids without difficulty, then hugged the bank, using the leafy green canopy hanging out over the water to conceal their movements. There were occasional breaks in the foliage where roads came down to fords or ferries, but the Rebel pickets guarding the crossings were watching the roads, not the river, and the dugout slipped past unseen.

Twice during the day, Capron ran the boat ashore and then set it adrift over some rough-looking rapids. Lieutenant Calkins, the only swimmer in the group, waited at the foot of the shoals and retrieved it when it reached still water.

They passed a few black fishermen in canoes that afternoon, but the Negroes always seemed to lower their eyes or look the other way. "Masters, look out," one of them called softly as he paddled past; "pickets just ahead; killing your people just as fast as they can catch them."

The sun was slipping behind the trees when Capron thought he recognized some familiar terrain. Smoke was wafting into the evening sky, and as they rounded a bend in the river, they saw the south end of the bridge General Dodge had thrown across the

Chattahoochee at Roswell with such amazing speed three weeks earlier. They laughed, they cheered, they clapped, rocking the dugout dangerously. An instant later, their elation turned to horror. The bridge was on fire.

Capron could think of only one explanation. Paddling to the north bank, he sprang ashore and some civilians soon confirmed his worst fears: Sherman's army had been driven back across the Chattahoochee. Determined to overtake the rear guard, the three cavalrymen set out as fast as they could run.

"A more forlorn looking trio were seldom seen," Capron noted. "My two companions hatless and shoeless, all were in tatters, clothes torn to shreds by rushing through bushes and brambles, skin lacerated, hair and beards long and matted with Georgia clay and mud."

Night fell, and with it gloom and despair. There was no army, no escape, no hope. Then a voice challenged from the darkness. "Halt! Who goes there?"

Friends, Capron answered hopefully. A sentry stepped from the shadows and eyed him suspiciously. It was one of Capron's own men, part of a detail Sherman had ordered Silas Adams to send from Marietta on August 4 to picket the roads around Roswell. The bedraggled fugitives collapsed at his feet, overcome with emotion and fatigue. Hard-bitten troopers tenderly draped them in blankets, brought them hot coffee and hardtack, and assured them the army was not retreating. Sherman was merely shifting the focus of his operations to the west side of Atlanta and had burned the bridge at Roswell to shorten his lines.[17]

The odyssey of Sherman's oldest cavalryman was rivaled by the exploits of one of the youngest. Fourteen-year-old Johnny Mitch was one of two orderlies who had been cut off with Colonel John Thomas Croxton when McCook fled the Brown's Mill battlefield on July 30. Everywhere he and his companions looked, they saw Rebel cavalrymen. There was only one way out and, together with four other soldiers, they ducked into the woods. Riding hard, they soon struck the road again. Surely they had gotten ahead of the Rebels, someone suggested, but Johnny was not so sure.

Determined to find out, he shouldered a Confederate guidon one of the men had captured and pressed ahead. The army did not make sack coats and trousers small enough to fit him, and he wore a weathered outfit Croxton had bought for him that could pass just as easily for gray as for blue. Putting on a bold front, he approached some women standing near a large white house on the left side of the road.

Glorious news, he shouted as he spurred his weary mount into the yard. General Wheeler had completely routed the Yankees and driven them into the woods. Some of them had escaped down the road, but the "Independent Scouts," were trying to overtake them. Had the ladies seen any Yankees?

Oh yes, replied an elderly matron, the Yankees had come flying down the road with Wheeler's men right behind them. Johnny thanked her for this information, then added he and his comrades had been so busy chasing Yankees they had not had time to eat. They were very hungry.

"Run, girls," the woman commanded, "get some pies." The young ladies soon returned and handed the little scout a pie cut into five pieces just as his six companions rode up. Johnny gobbled up the first piece and handed the rest to Colonel Croxton to pass around to the others. He had just finished a hasty report of what he had learned when a column of Confederate cavalry come pounding down the road.

"Quick," Croxton cried, "to the woods."

The seven bluecoated riders bounded over a low fence and soon disappeared from sight. No one followed, and with Johnny leading the way, they threaded through the thick woods until it was too dark to see.

Coming to a clear place that looked like a road, Johnny urged his mount forward. The horse shied. Johnny dug in his spurs and the horse responded with a mighty leap, landing squarely in the middle of what proved to be a bog. Shouting a warning to the others, Johnny slid from his saddle and immediately sank to his knees. He pulled and tugged on the reins, but the frightened, floundering horse only sank deeper. Realizing his efforts were in vain, Johnny pulled himself free and joined Croxton and the others. He had lost his horse, he announced.

Croxton suggested they all might stand a better chance on foot than on horseback. Dismounting, he ungirthed his saddle and gave his faithful gray a friendly pat before unbuckling the bridle and turning it loose. When the others had done the same, Croxton called them together. He was too sick to go on, he said. They should leave him and try to escape.

Four of the men edged away to discuss the idea. Johnny soon joined them and was shocked to learn they had decided to abandon the colonel. He argued with them, tried to talk them out of it. When this failed, he walked back to where Croxton was lying on his saddle blanket.

Where are the others? Croxton asked. Up the hill a little, Johnny said. Croxton sent him to fetch them, but Johnny soon came back, alone. Croxton asked him where the boys were. When Johnny did not answer, he repeated the question. Johnny made no reply.

"Yes!" Croxton said softly. "I see, they are gone."

Croxton's other orderly, Private Ben Schultz of the 1st Tennessee, lounged nearby. "Johnny," he said, "come on; I have waited on purpose for you. Let's go."

Johnny turned on him angrily. No, he insisted, they must stay the colonel. Why should they? Ben argued. Croxton had already said he was too sick to go any farther. If they stayed with him, they were sure to be captured or maybe shot.

Croxton heard every heated word and urged Johnny to go with his friend. The little private indignantly turned on the colonel and asked what made him think he would abandon him under any circumstances. Croxton stood up and gently put an arm around the boy's shoulders. "Johnny," he said, "you shall stay with me." He told Ben to go on and catch up with the others, but Ben sheepishly decided to stay. They should get some sleep then, Croxton said. He stretched out on his saddle blanket with Johnny by his side.

They were an unlikely pair, the tall, dark-haired Kentuckian and the little Ohio farm boy. Croxton was a Yale graduate. Johnny had run away from home when he was only twelve years old and tried to enlist in Company C of the 3rd Ohio Cavalry. When this failed, he crossed the Ohio River, went to Louisville, lied about his age, and got himself mustered into Company K of the 4th Kentucky Infantry. The blocky little recruit soon attracted Croxton's attention, and he made Johnny his orderly.

At the battle of Chickamauga, Croxton was shot through the leg. Propping himself up, he continued yelling orders and encouragement to his hard-pressed command until he was carried fainting from the field. Johnny stayed behind. Picking up a musket from a fallen comrade, he manfully took his place on the firing line. A Rebel bullet bloodied his left hand. Another hit him in the head. A third struck him squarely in the mouth, shattering his hard pallet and lodging next to his spine. For four days, he lay on the battlefield more dead than alive. Captured and exchanged, he soon rejoined his regiment, although his speech was slightly impaired and he still had a bullet lodged in his neck.

The rigors of the last four days had apparently aggravated Croxton's old wound, and perhaps this was why he had told the others to leave him behind. He awoke on July 31 feeling much better. Agreeing they must try to get to the Chattahoochee, he and Ben and Johnny resolutely trudged westward until they came to a crossroads at the edge of the forest. Broad fields stretched before them, but a distant hill, overgrown with vines and saplings, looked like a good place to hide. Scurrying across the open, they took cover in the leafy shade, hungrily devouring handfuls of half-ripe blackberries.

About 2:00 P.M., a young Negro wandered past. Croxton called out to him, identifying himself and his companions as Union soldiers. They were desperately hungry and begged him to bring them something to eat. The slave promised to do what he could, but it would be dangerous. If the white folks caught him, they would make him suffer.

For the rest of the afternoon, Croxton, Ben, and Johnny eagerly awaited his return. Toward sundown, they began to get impatient. They could see a house about a half mile away, and thinking the slave might have gone there, Johnny convinced Croxton to let him reconnoiter. With his captured guidon in one hand and his Spencer carbine in the other, he darted into a nearby cornfield, pausing long enough to shuck and greedily gnaw on a few ears that were barely in blisters. Weeds choked the rows, screening him from view as he crept to the edge of the field. Sprawling in an overgrown ditch, he watched the house for about an hour before venturing out to tell a woman their cavalry had won a great victory. The "Independent Scouts" were so busy rounding up Yankee stragglers they scarcely had time to eat or sleep, he added. His captain had sent him to see if she would prepare a meal for him and two of his men. He would gladly pay for her trouble.

While the woman began slicing ham and making biscuits, Johnny waited outside. Just as the biscuits were about to go in the oven, he saw six mounted Confederates coming down the road. The question was, would they stop? The inviting aromas wafting from the kitchen left no doubt in Johnny's mind, and as the Rebels dismounted at the front gate, he scurried out the back, telling his hostess he was going to fetch his captain. He sped through a watermelon patch, pausing briefly in the overgrown ditch to make sure he was not being followed, then disappeared behind the tasseled curtain of corn.

In "a bad mood over losing a magnificent dinner," he rejoined his crestfallen comrades and related what had happened. To his dismay, they insisted on raiding the watermelon patch. Johnny offered a half dozen arguments against it, but the majority prevailed, and as soon as it got dark, he led them through the cornfield, over the ditch, and to the melons.

Most of them were nowhere near ripe and Johnny broke open three or four before he found one fit to eat. Reaching up, he tugged on Croxton's coat and the colonel knelt beside him. As they dug their fingers into the juicy red fruit, Ben wandered between them and the house, thumping melons.

"Halt!" a voice demanded. "Who comes there?"

"A friend," Ben answered, trying to sound confident.

"Then advance and give an account of yourself."

"Who are you?" Ben asked.

"Who are you?" the voice insisted, and then added hotly, "I'll shoot! By God, I'll shoot!" A gunshot exploded in the darkness. Then six or eight more. Ben went down like he had been poleaxed. Johnny threw his carbine to his shoulder and was just about to return the fire when Croxton grabbed his arm. "It can do no good to fight," Croxton hissed. "Our object is to get away. Ben is dead. We can accomplish nothing staying here."

Hiding by day, groping through field and forest at night, they made their way westward on swollen, blistered feet that seemed to become more painful with every step they took. It rained "almost incessantly." Hunger gnawed at their bellies, and sleep brought neither rest nor relief from fear and fatigue. They had been on the run about six days when a white-haired old Negro wandered past the tangled underbrush where they were hiding one morning. Croxton called to him and begged him to bring them something to eat. The old man promised to do his best and about 4:00 P.M., he returned with a jug of buttermilk and a corn pone that looked as big as a baby grindstone. Leading the half-starved wanderers to a cabin in the middle of a cornfield, he answered their anxious questions as they wolfed down mouthfuls of cornbread. It was not far to the Chattahoochee, he said. No, he was too old and feeble to get them across, but he had friends who might. If they would wait in the cabin he would try to find someone. He would signal them with a whistle, like this, when he returned.

It was getting dark before Johnny and the colonel finally heard the long-awaited signal. They answered and a moment later the old man appeared. He had another slave with him, who would pilot them to the Chattahoochee. Closing his eyes, the old Negro bowed his head and in a deep voice asked God's blessing on Mr. Lincoln's soldiers and their guide.

With their bellies full of cornbread and buttermilk, Johnny and Croxton had a hard time keeping up with the younger Negro as he jogged down a well-worn path. They soon reached the river and were overjoyed to find a boat tied at the water's edge. Clambering aboard, they cast off and paddled swiftly to the west bank. Croxton gratefully gave their guide five dollars and after listening to some directions about which road to travel and which houses to avoid, he and Johnny headed north.

They found nothing to eat but a little green corn and the last of the summer's blackberries. When these became scarce, they gnawed the bark off twigs. Croxton damned McCook bitterly and grew increasingly despondent. It was all Johnny could do to keep him from approaching houses to beg for food and shelter. Once, they lost their way in the woods and wasted a whole night traveling in the wrong direction before realizing their mistake. Another night, they came to a signpost at a crossroads. Croxton hoisted his little orderly up on his shoulders to see what it said, but it was too dark to read. At the colonel's suggestion, Johnny carefully ran his hand over the weather-beaten board, tracing the letters with a dirty finger. To his relief, the sign confirmed they were heading in the right direction.

At daylight on Sunday, August 7, they stopped on a ridge studded with tall pines. While Croxton slumped in the shade, Johnny shinnied up a tree to survey the route they would travel when it got dark. As he clung to the branches, he spotted a fine, big house in the distance and watched as several people came and went. That afternoon, he heard the melodic notes of a piano and a young woman singing in a clear, sweet voice. She started with some well-remembered tunes, and her guests joined in, adding their voices to the martial strains of war songs from both North and South. Johnny listened, spellbound, as she concluded with the sad, haunting words of "Home, Sweet Home":

> I gaze on the moon as I tread the drear wild,
> And feel that my mother now thinks of her child,
> As she looks on that moon from our own cottage door
> Thro' the woodbine, whose fragrance shall cheer me no more.
> Home, home, sweet, sweet home!
> There's no place like home. . . .

Johnny waited until all the visitors had departed before climbing down from his perch. Croxton sat with his back against a tree. He had heard the singing, too. He did not raise his eyes when Johnny approached. He did not say a word. He just sat there, an absolute picture of despair.

It was a long time before Johnny finally broke the silence. The road up ahead looked good, he said, but they would have to wade another swamp to get to it. That evening, they got an early start and slogged through two or three miles of standing water before reaching dry ground.

Late that night, they approached a large plantation house surrounded by slave cabins. What looked like the overseer's quarters sat off to one side, and at Croxton's insistence they quietly mounted the porch, hoping to get something to eat. Johnny knocked softly on the door. There was no answer. He knocked again, a little harder. There was still no answer. He was about to knock a third time when a clock began to strike. The hair stood up on the back of his neck and a chill shivered down his spine as the chimes sounded: one, two, three, four, five, six, seven, eight, nine, ten, eleven, twelve. Johnny felt something rap on his carbine. Hastily backing away from the door, he asked if the colonel had thrown a pebble at him. No, Croxton said, grabbing him by the arm and hurrying back to the road.

When they were a safe distance away, Croxton confessed he had never experienced anything like the sheer terror he felt when that clock began counting out the hour. Johnny admitted it scared him, too, and wondered what had struck his carbine. Then he noticed the gun's hammer swinging loosely back and forth. When they stopped to hide the next morning, he backed the screws out of the lockplate and found the mainspring had broken cleanly in half.

The gun was useless, but instead of throwing it away, Johnny selected a rock, hoping he could hit the hammer hard enough to fire it if that became necessary. Croxton, however, was ready to give up. He was sick and tired and kept talking about surrendering. Johnny begged and pleaded with him to keep going. It could not be that much farther to the Union lines, he argued, just a few more days and they would be safe. When Croxton would not listen, Johnny threatened to leave him and reminded him of his wife and children. If he ever wanted to see them again, they had to keep going.

Croxton's expression changed as some hidden reserve of strength welled up inside him. Not waiting for sundown, he and Johnny set out early that evening and walked all night. Rain was drumming down steadily when they came to a cotton gin just before dawn. They slipped through the surrounding fence only to find a whole company of Confederate cavalry sleeping under the shed. Horses were tied along the fence, and motioning silently to one another, Johnny and the colonel each eased up to a likely looking mount. Johnny was about to untie the reins when he noticed a Rebel soldier sitting on the fence under the shed awning, barely an arm's length away. "Hello, boys," the sentry said sleepily, "where are you going?"

Bounding through the fence, across the road, and over another fence, Johnny and the colonel crouched in the corner of a field, their hearts pounding wildly as the Rebels swarmed out of the shed and vaulted into their saddles. The stubbled field offered no cover at all and as soon as the road was clear they sprinted toward the dim outline of some woods.

The trees were too far apart to fully conceal them, but Croxton could go no farther. Still clinging to the saddle blanket he had carried from the first day, he asked Johnny to make a shelter for him in a thick stand of pines. Fashioning some pegs to hold down the corners, Johnny propped up the middle of the blanket with a stick. Croxton crawled inside, pulling off his boots, despite Johnny's remonstrances, and pillowed them under his head. He invited Johnny to join him, but the boy refused and crouched sullenly under one end of the blanket, saying someone had to keep watch.

Croxton had been asleep about two hours when a gunshot echoed nearby. "Hello, boys," a woman called, "are you going down in the hollow?" Then Johnny saw the muzzles of several rifles cresting a little rise. Jerking the blanket down with one hand, grabbing Croxton's leg with the other, he sprang behind a huge pine tree. Croxton followed close behind. Flattening themselves against the trunk, they inched around its circumference, keeping it between them and the passing soldiers. "Well, Johnny," Croxton breathed when the Rebels were out of sight, "that certainly was a close call. But for your watchfulness they certainly would have caught us."

Much refreshed by his nap, Croxton resolved to press on, and late that morning they came to a road at the edge of the woods. Desperate for something to eat, they decided to take a chance and approached a log cabin. Luck smiled on them. A kindly Union man and his wife provided them with a hearty meal and a room where they could rest for the day, promising to warn them if any Rebel soldiers came along. Croxton undressed and crawled into bed, but Johnny was too wary to relax. Noticing a pond across the road, he excused himself and took a good bath. Returning to Croxton's room, he crawled under the bed, dug some of the chinking from between the logs so he could see, and spent the rest of the afternoon watching the road.

Croxton awoke early that evening. After eating a light supper, he and Johnny bid their friends farewell and set out with a lunch the woman had packed for them. It was only thirty-five miles to Sweetwater Creek, the man said; they should make it without any trouble.

Just before dark they came to a footlog spanning a large creek. Croxton essayed out first, but halfway across, the log began to sag and wobble. Flailing his arms frantically as he tried to keep his balance, Croxton fell in. This struck Johnny as uproariously funny and he cackled heartily. Croxton did not see the humor in it and said so.

For the rest of the night, they kept up a steady pace, but Johnny was wearing out. Each time they stopped, he fell asleep and Croxton had to shake him vigorously to wake him up. Several times, the sound of approaching horsemen compelled them to step off the road and hide.

August 12 dawned hot and humid, but they kept going, determined to reach their

A Yale graduate and an ardent opponent of slavery, Colonel John Thomas Croxton led McCook's 1st Brigade. Cut off from his command at the Battle of Brown's Mill, he and a young orderly wandered through the wilderness for almost two weeks before reaching the Union lines. In 1873 Croxton became the United States ambassador to Bolivia. Author's collection.

goal. Coming to a crossroads, they saw a big house on their right and a log cabin about 200 yards behind it. As Johnny approached the cabin to ask for directions a beautiful young woman came out. "For God's sake," she hissed, throwing up her arms, "go away quick. Only last evening a man was killed right there." She pointed to a dark stain on the ground and then to the big house. "There is a whole company of Confederate soldiers right there," she said. "For God's sake, go on."

The two weary travelers detoured unseen around the Rebel pickets. Regaining the road, Johnny trotted ahead and had not gone far when he met a Union soldier. The startled Yank aimed his gun. Game to the last, Johnny raised his useless carbine just as Croxton came up and disarmed the soldier with a sharp reprimand.

A few minutes later, their long ordeal ended at a Yankee picket post at the foot of a hill where the Stars and Stripes waved a hearty welcome overhead. There Croxton learned that on July 30, the same day as the battle at Brown's Mill, he had been promoted to brigadier general.

Fate had one more surprise in store for him. Several days later, another straggler reported for duty. It was Ben Schultz, the orderly Croxton had left for dead in the watermelon patch. Hit in his left shoulder, right side, and left thigh when the bullets started flying, he had managed to crawl away before the Rebels came out to look for him. Some Negroes found him, hid him in a swamp until he was well enough to travel, then smuggled him north, sometimes by wagon, sometimes on foot, until he reached the Union lines.[18]

Capron, Croxton, and every cavalryman who came back told a mounting tale of disaster. When company clerks prepared the muster rolls for July and August, 1,230 of the 3,000 officers and men who had started south with McCook were listed as dead, wounded, or missing.[19] Stoneman's losses were even worse. No fewer than 1,329 of the 2,144 cavalrymen in his column had been killed, captured, or wounded.[20]

Even more sobering was the realization these sacrifices had been in vain. The prison pens at Macon and Andersonville were more crowded than ever, and trains loaded with supplies for the Rebel army were rolling into Atlanta before McCook's and Stoneman's men even got back to Marietta. Sherman listened to the shrill whistles of locomotives steaming up from the south but said surprisingly little about the failure of his "big raid." He accepted and even commended McCook's self-serving report of the expedition, including McCook's ridiculous assertion that his whole loss "will not exceed 500." "His management," Sherman concluded, "was all that could be expected throughout."

He did not seem particularly surprised to learn Stoneman had failed to join forces with McCook at Lovejoy's Station. "I think Stoneman has gone to Macon, east of Yellow River, and that is well," he wrote after Garrard returned from Flat Shoals and reported Stoneman had gone toward Covington; "a desperate move," he conceded, "but may succeed for its desperation." Far from being angry, he seemed hopeful. "I think Stoneman has a chance of rescuing those prisoners," he wrote. "It was a bold and rash adventure, but I sanctioned it and hoped for its success from its very rashness."[21]

Coming from a practical man and a master of logistics, such optimism seems incredibly naive. Little, if any, thought had been given to the problem of arming and feeding 30,000 sick and starving men once they were released, or getting them to the Florida coast. While there was probably some vague notion of giving them carte blanche to prey on the surrounding countryside, there did not seem to be any plan beyond that. Sherman had hastily endorsed a commendable but otherwise ill-conceived effort and simply seemed to be hoping for the best.

Writing to his wife on August 2, he confided Stoneman was "attempting to reach our prisoners confined at Andersonville." This letter and another he wrote on August 9, admitting his cavalry had suffered heavy losses "attempting to rescue the prisoners at Macon," would eventually lead to speculation Sherman might have given Stoneman secret orders to forgo the rendezvous with McCook and march directly south.[22]

Such a scenario seems highly unlikely, for three reasons. First, Stoneman had sound military motives for moving down the east side of the Ocmulgee. Second, while he was not particularly popular with his staff and senior subordinates, they agreed the failure to meet McCook at Lovejoy's Station was the result of faulty intelligence about the bridges over the Ocmulgee and not a willful act of abandonment. Finally, far from hinting at some secret plan, Sherman repeatedly asserted Stoneman "had not obeyed his orders." But instead of condemning the cavalryman for errors in judgment, he laid the blame for the disaster squarely at the feet of Kenner Garrard.[23]

21

TROOPERS IN THE TRENCHES

AUGUST 1–AUGUST 17, 1864

We have met the enemy and he is us.

—Pogo

"I must have a bolder commander for General Garrard's cavalry . . . ," Sherman wired George Thomas after receiving Garrard's report on July 31. His 3,500 troopers had sat idly at Flat Shoals and Latimer's Crossroads, doing little or nothing to keep the Rebel cavalry from going after McCook and Stoneman, then returned to Buckhead with "trifling" losses.

Thomas tried to defend his former student. "I do not know of a better cavalry commander in my army than Garrard," he replied that night. "He is an excellent administrative officer, and I have no doubt you will find on inquiry that his orders from Stoneman were indefinite. . . . I think if you will bear with Garrard you will find in a short time he will be the best cavalry commander you have."

"I think I appreciate General Garrard's good qualities," Sherman conceded, "but he is so cautious that if forced to make a bold move . . . I doubt if he would attempt it."

In deference to Thomas, he did not press the issue, and on August 1 he ordered Garrard's cavalry to relieve Schofield's XXIII Corps in the trenches northeast of Atlanta. From there, Garrard was to patrol the roads around Decatur, picket toward Roswell, and "be prepared to sally out as cavalry from his trenches, in case of necessity."[1]

These orders reached Garrard's headquarters tent on the south bank of Peachtree Creek about the same time the 2nd Division's supply trains arrived from Marietta, escorted by the long-absent 1st Ohio. Garrard had summoned the wagons the day before, to "bring forward rations and forage . . . and also a good supply of horse-shoes." The sight of their faded canvas covers, still sodden from a soaking morning shower, was a welcome one, and Garrard's three brigades, bivouacked on both sides of Peachtree Creek after their recent foray to Flat Shoals, spent the rest of the afternoon refilling haversacks and cartridge boxes. Quartermasters had supplied each man with a day's rations and one hundred rounds of ammunition by the time buglers sounded "The General" at 5:00 P.M.

The brassy summons to prepare to march sent the 17th and 72nd Indiana and the 98th and 123rd Illinois of Abe Miller's Lightning Brigade bustling to break camp on the south side of the creek. As Sherman's artillery thundered in the distance, they hauled in clothes hung out to dry, rolled up blankets, and saddled horses. Evening's gray twilight was fading into the black shadows of a near moonless night when the bristling blue column formed in the Peachtree Road and started south, followed by the Board of Trade Battery's six breech-banded Parrotts.

Miller's brigade had gone about four miles when officers abruptly turned the column into a large field and called a halt at 9:00 P.M. Soon afterward, Garrard rode up with the 7th Pennsylvania, 4th Regulars, and 4th Michigan of Bob Minty's 1st Brigade and ordered the men to dismount. Swinging down from their saddles and shouldering a rattling assortment of rifles, carbines, haversacks, and canteens, both brigades formed ranks. Leaving the artillery and the number fours to guard the horses, they started down the rough and rutted road to the southeast.

"The mud was very deep & tenacious," complained Private John Lemmon, trudging at the rear of the column with Minty's 4th Michigan. "As we floundered along the great and unusual exercise caused curses loud & deep to rend the midnight air for the boys['] feet were blistered. We soon began to pass in the dark what seemed to be intrenchments—deep ditches & high banks (with slippery sides). . . ."

Swearing, mud-spattered troopers slogged through the muck in their heavy high-topped boots for three miles before orders halted them at midnight behind the trenches Schofield's XXIII Corps had vacated earlier that evening. Minty's rear guard, the 4th Michigan, did not arrive until 3:00 A.M., "and a more tired lot of fellows you never saw," noted Lieutenant Albert Potter.

Both brigades posted a regiment on the picket lines. The rest of the men tumbled into the muddy red ditches or sprawled by the roadside "like cobs thrown from a basket" and were soon fast asleep.

They awoke the next morning to the rattling fusillade of rifles and carbines. "We are soldiering now with a vengeance," wrote Minty's adjutant, Captain Robert Burns. "Our horses are five miles in the rear, and we . . . are doing infantry duty in the dirt. I am sitting on the ground writing on my knee, surrounded by the debris of an exceedingly dirty infantry camp. If we ever get clean again it will require an immense amount of washing. . . . Can get no clothes, hats, or boots. We are ragged, black, and uncombed. Have not received a cent of pay since Dec. 31st. To crown all, there is a little insect in the woods here, called 'chickor' or 'jigger' which now almost torments us out of our senses. It is so small that it is almost imperceptible. It pierces the skin and makes a terrible itching. My body is covered with the marks of the remorseless little monster. I can do nothing but groan and scratch as the chickor is too small to be found and taken off. We all suffer terribly from him. We are also troubled with wood-ticks, scorpions, and all sorts of accursed bugs. The other night a snake ran across my body when [I was] asleep, scaring Capt. [Heber S.] Thompson, who was lying near me, almost out of his seven (?) senses."

Unlike Rebel troopers, who had spent much of the campaign fighting on foot, this was the Yankee cavalry's first experience in the trenches. "A ditch, about two and half feet deep and four feet wide was dug out," observed Lieutenant William Doyle of the 17th Indiana, "the earth being thrown to the front, forming the breastwork. This breastwork would be but about three feet high from the outside, but about five feet from the inside, standing in the ditch. Then on top of the breastwork a 'head log' was laid parallel to the work, supported on cross pieces. The guns were fired under this head log, which served as a protection."

About a hundred yards beyond the trenches were the rifle pits. These shallow, hastily dug holes, big enough for two to four men, extended all the way down to the unfinished red-brick walls of the Troup Hurt house on the Georgia Railroad, covering the approaches to the main line.

Bob Minty's brigade manned an angle in the works in front of the Howard house, where Sherman had watched the battle of Atlanta on July 22. The city's spires and rooftops were plainly visible a mile and a half away, and troopers passed the time picking out homes and occupations for themselves, anticipating the day they would march down the bowered streets in triumph.

Just beyond the Howard house, the works angled back to the northeast, so that part of Minty's men faced the Georgia Railroad. On their left, Abe Miller's brigade held the trenches paralleling the Decatur Road. It was a gamble, sending two brigades, not even 2,000 strong, to take the place of 11,000 infantry, but Sherman was betting their seven-shot Spencers made them more than equal to the task.[2]

The foot soldiers they replaced spent August 2 toiling along the roads north and west of Atlanta. Led by Colonel Israel Garrard's 7th Ohio Cavalry, Schofield's XXIII Corps moved behind Thomas's Army of the Cumberland, across the Lick Skillet Road and down to Utoy Creek, deploying on the right flank of Howard's Army of the Tennessee. Major General John M. Palmer's XIV Corps, over 18,000 strong, followed the next day.

These two corps had done little fighting during the desperate, bloody battles of July 20, 22, and 28. Together, they almost outnumbered Hood's whole army and Sherman decided it was time to put them to work. He spent August 3 personally reconnoitering the right flank and gave Schofield orders to push his XXIII Corps and Palmer's XIV Corps across the Sandtown Road to cut the Atlanta & West Point Railroad near East Point.

The next morning, Sherman sent instructions for Palmer to "report to and receive orders from General Schofield."

"I am General Schofield's senior," Palmer replied curtly. "We may co-operate but I respectfully decline to report to or take orders from him."

In another note, he advised Schofield, "You are my junior. . . . I will not obey either General Sherman's orders or yours, as they violate my self-respect."

While Schofield fumed and Palmer pouted, five divisions of Yankee infantry spent the day vainly waiting for the word to attack. That night an exasperated Sherman patiently explained that while Palmer's and Schofield's commissions as major generals both bore the same date, Schofield was senior because his promotion to brigadier general predated Palmer's. More important, Sherman added, Schofield led an army, Palmer only a corps, and Sherman sent him emphatic orders to report to Schofield and cut that railroad, even if "it costs half your command."

Palmer petulantly asked to be relieved. Sherman ordered him to obey Schofield, who was planning to use two of Palmer's three divisions and two of his own to attack on August 5. Palmer did as he was told, but he did it so slowly it was nearly dark by the time his troops got into position.

"I would prefer to move a rock than to move that corps," Sherman stormed.

Palmer withdrew his request to be relieved, but that night Sherman angrily summoned him to headquarters and practically ordered him to resign. Despairing of getting any cooperation out of the XIV Corps, Schofield ordered his own troops forward early on August 6.

But two days of petty bickering had given Hood ample time to strengthen the Confederate defenses along the Sandtown Road. When the long lines of Yankee infantry began advancing about 10:00 A.M., his riflemen were ready. Two futile assaults in a driving rain cost Schofield over 300 casualties. Confederate losses numbered only fifteen or twenty.[3]

For the first time in the campaign, Sherman seemed uncertain about what to do next. His cavalry had failed. His infantry was stretched thin along twelve miles of trenches curving in a great arc from near the Howard house on the east side of Atlanta to Utoy Post Office on the west. "I am too impatient for a siege," he wrote on August 7, but that same day he ordered a battery of 4½-inch guns sent down from Chattanooga.[4]

While he waited for this artillery to arrive, the two opposing armies glared at each other from their muddy trenches, each waiting for the other to make the first move. On the east side of Atlanta, some of Bob Minty's skirmishers were posted within 200 yards of the Rebel works and gunfire crackled from dawn till dark and sometimes far into the night.

Each of Minty's regiments took turns in the rifle pits, once every three days. At the end of a twenty-four-hour shift, another regiment would come out to relieve them. This generally occurred just before daybreak, but on moonlit nights heavy skirmishing sometimes kept the relief waiting in the trenches. Daylight brought scorching heat or soaking rain, empty canteens and growling bellies. Finally, some tired, hungry soldier would shout, "Stop the darned firing and let the relief come on." The shooting would cease. Fresh troops would scurry into the red ditches. The old occupants would clamber out. Then the firing would begin again.

For men not on duty in the rifle pits, life quickly settled into a monotonous routine. "Nothing to do," noted the 4th Michigan's John McLain, "but cook, eat, sleep and keep a sharp lookout."

Some of Garrard's men took advantage of the opportunity to visit friends and relatives serving with the neighboring IV Corps. Others, like Alva Griest of the 72nd Indiana, explored the nearby July 22nd battlefield. "It is an awful sight," he wrote. "Thousands lie comparatively unburied. I saw one . . . poor fellow [who] had been standing behind a tree in the act of loading, when the fatal ball reached his heart and he still stood leaning against the tree with his hand extended holding the rammer and the other holding the gun-barrel. Such scenes make me shudder even yet." But they did not keep him from palming "a watch and two Mexican dollars" he found in a dead man's pockets.

When sunset brought the day to a close, the men not assigned to the rifle pits sought the crude comforts of camp. "I am sitting in a kind of arbor made of the branches of oaks (we have no tents or shelters), writing on a table made of cracker boxes which we fixed up this afternoon," Captain Robert Burns noted at 8:00 P.M. on August 4. "In one corner of our arbor are lying Capt. [Heber S.] Thompson and Lieutenant [Samuel C.] Dixon on their ponchos, smoking, laughing, and talking, being 'jolly under creditable circumstances.' Col. Minty is looking over and comparing a monthly return I have just made out, and at the same time telling me he is father of a new boy. Our darkeys are outside singing and humming 'nigger' songs, and a little farther off is another crowd of them, dancing their liveliest to a sort of chant they have. A few rods from us the band of an infantry brigade is playing infantry waltzes and other airs, which strangely mingles with the bray of mules. A steady rattle of musketry is kept up by the skirmishers about a half mile or less from us; every few minutes comes in the great 'boom' of the cannon followed in a few seconds by the report of the bursting of the shell. Most of the firing is done by our men, as the enemy has very little ammunition to waste. Sometimes the firing gets so sharp that we stop to listen, thinking that an attack has been made. At other times we pay no attention to it. Crickets and tree-toads also keep up their perpetual chatter. This is our usual evening entertainment 'before Atlanta.'"

Tedium in the trenches was rivaled only by the boredom behind the lines, where members of the Board of Trade Battery had been left with the number fours and led horses. "There are two cattle pens that are too near for the good health of either men or horses," wrote Private John Nourse, and on the morning of August 3 the battery moved back a thousand yards to "a beautiful camp" in the woods west of the Peachtree Road. The artillerymen repacked limber chests, oiled harness, and wrote letters, but there was little or nothing to do until noon on August 6, when Lieutenant Griffin and the 1st section were ordered to the front. The two guns rattled down the road and went into battery between Minty's 1st Brigade and the left flank of the IV Corps, next to the 88th Illinois Infantry.[5]

While most of Garrard's division wallowed in the trenches, Eli Long's 2nd Brigade remained at Buckhead, where the return of the 1st Ohio with the division wagon trains on August 1 had reunited his three regiments for the first time since crossing the Chattahoochee. Eager to get a look at Atlanta, some of his men had nailed steps to the trunk of a big oak tree shading their bivouac and built an observation platform in its branches. On a clear day, they could see for miles, but that first week of August soon turned disagreeably dark and dreary. Troopers on foraging details, patrolling the labyrinth of muddy roads between Decatur and Roswell, or manning lonely outposts had almost daily encounters with bushwhackers and roving bands of Rebel cavalry. Between August 1 and August 16, Long's brigade would suffer at least eight casualties, more than the rest of Garrard's entire division.[6]

For troopers in the trenches, the novelty of foot soldiering was rapidly wearing thin. It rained every day. At times, the stench of rotting flesh from the nearby battlefield was almost unbearable. "Everything seems covered with mud," Alva Griest complained in his diary. "We sleep in mud, eat in mud, walk in mud. . . ."

Foraging details wandered as far as ten and twelve miles from camp searching ravaged fields and orchards for apples, sweet corn, and peaches. Orders on August 10 cut their already meager rations in half. "Pork interdicted by special order," John Lemmon noted in disgust, "—on account of scurvy in the Inf[antry]."[7]

Like it or not, Sherman found himself doing the very thing he had hoped to avoid, laying siege to Atlanta. Sieges took time, and that was a luxury he could not afford. Time was already whittling away his army faster than Rebel shells and bullets. Every day saw the departure of veteran regiments whose enlistments had expired, "diminishing my fighting force by its best material," he complained.[8]

In the midst of these uncertainties, a southbound train belching black soot and cinders rolled into Resaca, Georgia, at 9:00 P.M., July 21. As the rattling cars squealed to a stop, a small man in a tightly tailored blue uniform appeared in one of the doorways, supported by a pair of crutches. A set of dundrearies, a shade darker than his sandy red hair, framed his oval face, softening the effects of a prominent nose perched over a lantern jaw. Pursing his thin lips, he gingerly eased himself down the steps, flashing a row of perfect white teeth at the officers and men who rushed to greet him. The news spread through the camps like wildfire. "Kill Cavalry" was back.

Brigadier General Hugh Judson Kilpatrick propped himself on his crutches, basking in the moment as men of the 92nd Illinois Mounted Infantry eagerly crowded around the station platform. "Boys," he said, "you have been disgraced; you have been disgraced. Here you are guarding railroads. This would not have been, had I been here. You are brave, noble men, and shall not be treated in this manner. I promise you that within three days you shall be at the front winning glory for yourselves." The men answered with wild cheers that made the blue hills ring.[9]

Like Elliott, Garrard, and Stoneman, Kilpatrick was another cast-off cavalier from the Army of the Potomac. Born near Deckertown, New Jersey, on January 14, 1836, he had always aspired to be a soldier. As a boy he pored over books recounting the lives of great captains like Alexander, Hannibal, Caesar, and Napoleon. He also took a precocious interest in politics and won an appointment to West Point by tirelessly campaigning for an incumbent congressman.[10]

Kilpatrick was a good student and the only man in his class who did not receive a single demerit during his plebe year. Moving steadily up the chain of command, he became a cadet lance corporal in 1857, corporal in 1858, sergeant in 1859, and lieutenant in 1860. "His ambition was simply boundless," recalled an upperclassman, "and from his intimates he did not disguise his faith that . . . he would become governor of New Jersey, and ultimately president of the United States."

On one occasion, Kilpatrick put another cadet on report for some infraction of the rules. The other boy was much larger and warned him of dire consequences. Ignoring the threats, Kilpatrick did his duty, then accepted the bully's challenge. A slender five feet, seven inches tall, he dodged and darted and jabbed and clung to his opponent for forty-five grueling minutes, ultimately battering him into submission.

Kilpatrick was a frequent actor in cadet plays and a rousing orator. As war clouds gathered in the fall of 1860, he spoke unabashedly for the Union, and his unflinching "I'll lick you out of your boots" brand of patriotism led to several confrontations with Southern cadets.

His class was still two months short of graduation when North and South went to war. He and his classmates successfully petitioned to be commissioned at once, and at commencement exercises Kilpatrick delivered the valedictory address before an audience of friends, relatives, and distinguished guests, including his fiancée, Alice Shailer of New York City. "Kill is going to the field, and may not return," a fellow cadet remarked afterward. "Better get married now." The impulsive Kilpatrick married Alice in the cadet chapel that afternoon.[11]

Finishing seventeenth in a class of forty-five and commissioned a brevet second lieutenant in the 1st U.S. Artillery, Kilpatrick quickly realized the shortest path to promotion lay in the ranks of the volunteers. Three days after his wedding, he enrolled as a captain in the 5th New York Infantry. A month later, at Big Bethel, Virginia, he was struck in his right leg by a piece of grapeshot and immediately lionized as the first regular army officer wounded in the first battle of the war.

After a brief convalescence, Kilpatrick quit the infantry to become lieutenant colonel of the 2nd New York Cavalry. He quickly proved himself an able and aggressive commander, but in October 1862 he was arrested when one of his officers, the regimental sutler, and a Virginia farmer accused him of selling captured horses, mules, and tobacco for personal gain. Kilpatrick adamantly denied the allegations but languished in Washington's Old Capitol Prison for three months before the Secretary of War ordered the charges dropped.

Promoted to colonel during his incarceration, Kilpatrick rejoined his regiment and was one of the few officers to enhance his reputation during George Stoneman's abortive Richmond raid. His personal flag, adorned with his wife's name, fluttered at the front of the brigade he bravely led into the biggest cavalry battle of the war at Brandy Station, Virginia. Scarcely two years after leaving West Point, he became a brigadier general.

"Kill Cavalry," as his men called him, had always been an aggressive officer, but as a division commander, his hilt-to-hilt, hell-for-leather style had its limits. On the third day of the battle of Gettysburg, he goaded one of his subordinates, Brigadier General Elon J. Farnsworth, into a senseless charge that cost Farnsworth his life. Spurring after the Confederate columns that retreated from that bloody battlefield, he made shamelessly inflated claims about the number of prisoners, guns, and battle flags his division captured.

He was unquestionably brave, but when truth interfered with ambition, he ran over it roughshod. He swore furiously and had a reputation as a rake. "Kilpatrick is the most vain, conceited, egotistical little popinjay I ever saw," asserted one officer. "He is a very ungraceful rider, looking more like a monkey than a man on horseback."

Kilpatrick's aide, Captain Lewellyn G. Estes, also noticed he "usually rode stooping and bent over the saddle." When asked about it, Kilpatrick said "his kidneys troubled him and caused him a pain in the back." He spoke of passing too much urine on some occasions, too little at others. Often the pain became so severe he could not ride a horse and had to lie down in an ambulance, relying on Estes to convey his orders.[12]

The third day at Gettysburg marked the beginning of a long, slow decline in Kilpatrick's personal and professional fortunes. His wife died in November 1863. Less than two months later he received news of the death of his infant son. With only his ambition left to interest him, Kilpatrick hatched a plan to liberate thousands of captured Union soldiers imprisoned at Richmond and used his political connections to float the idea in Washington. President Lincoln endorsed the scheme, and on the evening of February 28 Kilpatrick started south with 3,500 men, vowing he would not come back alive unless he succeeded. Two days later, his skirmishers approached the defenses a mile north of the Confederate capital, held by only a handful of Rebel militia. Kilpatrick stood on the threshold of greatness, and wilted. When he did not hear from a small detachment sent to strike the west side of the city, he ordered a retreat, leaving his dead and wounded behind. This time, there was nothing he could say or do to hide the ugly face of failure.

Relieved of command, he was ordered to Chattanooga and reassigned to the newly created 3rd Cavalry Division of the Army of the Cumberland. "Gentlemen," he announced quietly upon his arrival, "I am General Kilpatrick, and have been ordered to take command of this division."

Three weeks later, on May 13, at the very outset of the Georgia campaign, his skirmishers encountered a force of Rebel infantry and cavalry a mile and a half west of Resaca. Riding to the front, Kilpatrick ordered a charge. Moments later, a Rebel bullet plowed through his horse's neck, striking Kilpatrick on the inner side of his left thigh and passing through his hip. He tumbled out of the saddle, bleeding "like a stuck pig."

"Shot in the —," the ashen general moaned, "by —. That will be a — — pretty story to go back to New Jersey."[13]

Sherman once described Brigadier General Hugh Judson Kilpatrick as "a hell of a damned fool." A vain, reckless lothario, Kilpatrick was still recovering from a painful wound when he reassumed command of the 3rd Cavalry Division on July 22. After the war he wrote a bad play and served as America's ambassador to Chile. Reproduced from the Collections of the Library of Congress.

Kilpatrick spent the next two months convalescing at Buttermilk Falls, New York, a mile south of West Point. He was well enough by June 22 to attend graduation exercises at Rutgers College and accept an honorary A.M. degree, but his wound remained troublesome and he feared Atlanta would fall before he could recover. In mid-July, newspapers reported the city's capture seemed imminent. Ignoring his doctor's advice and the admonition of friends, Kilpatrick quit his sickbed, took his crutches, crossed the Hudson River, and boarded the first southbound train.[14]

Upon reaching Resaca on July 21, he discovered three of his regiments, the 8th Indiana, 2nd Kentucky, and 5th Iowa, were already at the front, where they had seen hard service with Rousseau and McCook. The rest of his troopers were scattered up and down the Western & Atlantic Railroad, protecting Sherman's supply line. The 3rd Indiana, 10th Ohio, and the 10th Wisconsin Battery were at Cartersville. The 3rd Kentucky, 5th Kentucky, and the 92nd Illinois Mounted Infantry were at Resaca.[15]

Arriving at division headquarters at Cartersville on July 23, Kilpatrick reassumed command from Colonel William W. Lowe of the 5th Iowa. "I find the Division in good condition[,] much improved during my absence," he wired the Army of the Cumberland's chief of cavalry, General Elliott. "Col. Lowe deserves great credit."

In this same telegram, Kilpatrick asked permission to move the 3rd Kentucky, 5th Kentucky, and 92nd Illinois from Resaca down to Calhoun. "The RR can be guarded as well from that point as Resaca," he argued, and it would put all three regiments nearer "good grazing & oats." More important, it would get them closer to the fighting at Atlanta.

Orders came on July 24 authorizing the 3rd Kentucky and the 92nd Illinois to move south to Calhoun as Kilpatrick had requested, but the 5th Kentucky was sent north to Dalton. Kilpatrick did not give up. "It may be unmilitary," he wired Elliott on July 25,

> but I am forced to request that if consistent with the opinions my superiors have formed of this Division and its commander, we be ordered to the front. I can march with over 2,000 men in good condition, with my command now at the front the Division will be large. We have been in rear of the army nearly two months, all this country is quiet. May we not come to the front, and share with the army of the Cumberland its Dangers and its Glories?[16]

It was a brazen request, but it also made sense. Kilpatrick's division was larger than McCook's, better mounted, and better equipped, and on July 27 George Thomas summoned the 10th Ohio, a detachment of the 2nd Kentucky, and a section of the 10th Wisconsin Battery to the front. As soon as they arrived, McCook's understrength command would fall back to Cartersville and relieve the rest of Kilpatrick's scattered regiments.

Kilpatrick's timing could not have been better. The same day he received these orders, McCook started on the raid that all but destroyed his division. Suddenly Sherman needed all the cavalry he could get.

"You had better order General Kilpatrick to march at once down by Marietta to our right flank," he wired George Thomas after receiving barefooted Jim Brownlow's report on August 1, ". . . for the enemy will surely cross over to that flank."

Thomas relayed these instructions to General Elliott, who immediately wired Kilpatrick to "proceed with your division to [the] Chattahoochee River, taking the Sandtown Road."

"Your dispatch has been received," Kilpatrick replied cheerfully from Cartersville that night. "I have ordered in my people and will march at the earliest possible moment."[17]

It was still dark when the bugles began blaring in the cavalry camps near Calhoun on August 2. The orders to march had come "very unexpectedly" and captains cursed and sergeants swore as Colonel Eli H. Murray's 3rd Kentucky and 92nd Illinois scrambled to get their horses saddled and form ranks. At 5:00 A.M., the long blue column started down the straight red road hugging the right shoulder of the Western & Atlantic Railroad. They followed the track down the broad green valley, past the wooded hills, through Adairsville and Kingston for thirty-five wearying miles. Late that evening, they joined Kilpatrick at Cartersville.

Perhaps delayed by waiting for the 5th Kentucky to arrive from Dalton, it was 9:00 the next morning before Kilpatrick, still unable to sit a horse, wheeled out of Cartersville in a handsome carriage his men had fixed up for him. While Company A of Lieutenant Colonel Thomas W. Sanderson's 10th Ohio Cavalry rode ahead to lead the advance, the rest of the regiment fell in behind Kilpatrick, followed by six companies of Lieutenant Colonel Robert Klein's 3rd Indiana Cavalry, a detachment of the 2nd Kentucky, Captain Yates V. Beebe's four-gun 10th Wisconsin Battery, and a ponderous train of wagons and ambulances. Eli Murray's 3rd Brigade brought up the rear.

Two miles south of Cartersville, the column crossed the recently rebuilt wagon bridge over the Etowah River and followed the Western & Atlantic Railroad through the mountain pass at Allatoona. Somewhere along the route, Kilpatrick received a telegram from General Elliott, warning, "I have reports that 500 to 1,000 rebels crossed the Chattahoochee at Campbellton last night and moved in the direction of Burnt Hickory. Look out for them on the railroad."

"Your telegram received," Kilpatrick answered from Allatoona. "I will look out for the enemy reported to have crossed the river."[18]

Sending patrols to scout to the west and south or perhaps the mountainous nature of an otherwise good road slowed Kilpatrick's progress to a snail's pace. His column had traveled only sixteen miles when the advance halted at 6:00 P.M. on August 3 to bivouac in the woods along Allatoona Creek. Eli Murray's rear guard, following in the lumbering wake of the wagon train, did not arrive until 9:00 P.M.

"Reveille" sounded at 2:00 A.M. Reversing the previous day's order of march, Murray's brigade left camp at daylight, but once again progress was painfully slow. It was 10:00 A.M. before Kilpatrick's rear guard, the 10th Ohio, even got out of camp.

"The scenes of this day were much the same as those of the day before," noted Sergeant Warren McCain of the 3rd Indiana as the column plodded south on the Sandtown Road, "and we marched over many a hard contested battlefield, and saw the graves of hundreds of our fallen soldiers."

Late that afternoon elements of the 92nd Illinois reached the Chattahoochee River opposite Sandtown and made camp after a march of eighteen miles. The rest of the division bivouacked behind them at places like Mitchell's Crossroads and Sweetwater Bridge.

Kilpatrick made his headquarters on the Sandtown Road, near the river, and waited to hear from patrols probing to the west. He had already established a courier line to communicate with the telegraph office at Vining's Station and that afternoon he advised General Elliott, "I hear nothing of any force of the enemy. I shall have reports this evening from Burnt Hickory and vicinity. I shall move at daylight."[19]

But the order Kilpatrick was waiting for, the order to cross the Chattahoochee, did not come, and his division remained on the north side of the river. Kilpatrick was disappointed, but he used August 5 to remedy some glaring deficiencies he had noticed during the march south. The "large amount of officers' stores and baggage" encumbering the column must be sent to the rear "at once," he announced. He also noted it had come to his attention that ambulances were being used to haul personal effects and supplies. Henceforth, anything found in an ambulance that did not belong there would be thrown out.[20]

In the absence of orders to cross the Chattahoochee, Kilpatrick began withdrawing his regiments from the riverbank about noon on August 5. The 92nd Illinois halted after only two miles. The 3rd Indiana continued for another four, the 10th Ohio for seven, but Kilpatrick did not like what he saw. The next day, he laid down the law to the whole division:

> It has been found that the efficiency of this command is greatly impaired by the neglect of company, squadron and regimental commanders to observe the primary rules of cavalry tactics. Detachments, companies, and even squadrons have become separated from their command. This, together with the extreme length of the column on the march renders it necessary to adopt some measures to obviate this evil.

Regiments forming under all circumstances should be told off into fours and squadrons formed into platoons and divisions. This organization should be preserved intact and when in motion on the march should always move by fours.

The distance between companies and squadrons should be regulated with regard to the number of men composing them. Companies of 40 or 50 men and squadrons of eighty or a hundred men must not observe the distance prescribed by Cav. Tactics for a squadron of one hundred and sixty four men. The distance observed by squadrons now on the march is deemed more than sufficient for the distance between regiments such as compose this command.

By observing these rules and existing orders in regard to straggling we can never be surprised but are ever ready for any and every emergency.[21]

This edict coincided with a reshuffling of the division's command structure. Kilpatrick had left Cartersville with five regiments: the 3rd Indiana and 10th Ohio of Lieutenant Colonel Robert Klein's 2nd Brigade and the 3rd Kentucky, 5th Kentucky, and the 92nd Illinois of Colonel Eli Murray's 3rd Brigade. Three others—the 8th Indiana, 2nd Kentucky, and 5th Iowa—were camped at Marietta, recuperating from the Rousseau and McCook raids, and Kilpatrick had already taken steps to retrieve them.

At 10:30 A.M., August 6, Fielder Jones's 8th Indiana, outfitted in brand new uniforms they had drawn the day before, left their bivouac at the Georgia Military Institute. Apparently accompanied by the 2nd Kentucky and 5th Iowa, they moved down the Powder Springs Road to Sweetwater Bridge. By virtue of seniority, Jones immediately assumed command of Kilpatrick's 2nd Brigade, consisting of the 8th Indiana, 2nd Kentucky, and 10th Ohio. This displaced Lieutenant Colonel Klein, but Kilpatrick assigned him to a newly formed 1st Brigade, composed of the 3rd Indiana and the 5th Iowa.[22]

Sherman's decision to keep Kilpatrick on the north side of the Chattahoochee left only 400 cavalrymen guarding Schofield's right flank on Utoy Creek. Schofield regarded this force as "entirely inadequate," but unless Kilpatrick crossed the river, there was simply no other cavalry available. The transfer of the 8th Indiana, 5th Iowa, and 2nd Kentucky to Kilpatrick's command and the 4th Tennessee's impending departure for Decatur, Alabama, had reduced McCook's 1st Cavalry Division to only 536 mounted officers and men.[23] Stoneman's division could muster only 424, and more than half of them belonged to Silas Adams's Kentucky brigade, whose three-year enlistment was about to expire. Desperate for more horse soldiers, Sherman had already telegraphed his commanders in Tennessee and Kentucky to "send me all the cavalry that can possibly be spared." On August 7 he authorized Schofield to dismount Adams's brigade, which was waiting at Marietta to be mustered out, and turn their horses over to other regiments.

Schofield soon discovered the Kentuckians, unlike most Union cavalrymen, rode their own mounts. It would take his quartermasters a week to appraise, purchase, and brand that much stock. In the meantime, the only other horse soldiers within reach were a battalion of the 9th Illinois Mounted Infantry belonging to the XVI Corps and Colonel George S. Acker's 9th Michigan Cavalry, which had ridden into Marietta on July 31, escorting Israel Garrard's wagon train from Kentucky. Schofield asked for them all.[24]

He was awaiting their arrival when he received a warning at 11:15 A.M., August 8, that Rebel infantry and cavalry were probing his right flank. "I presume the design is to cross Utoy Creek and strike our trains," he wired Sherman at 1:50 P.M. "I will try to prevent it, but may not be able."

At 6:00 P.M., he advised Sherman Rebel cavalry was "all along Utoy Creek beyond our right, but has made no attempt to cross."

Sherman seemed unconcerned. "If [Israel] Garrard watches well the passes of Utoy Creek," he replied at 9:20 P.M., "I have no fear for that flank."

Shortly after 10:00 P.M., a second telegram from Schofield warned Rebel cavalry had attempted to cross the bridge near the mouth of Utoy Creek and a nearby ford at dark, but had been repulsed. This coincided with a report several hundred horsemen had been seen making camp on the south side of Utoy Creek, two miles from its mouth.

"I will order Kilpatrick's cavalry down on the other bank of the Chattahoochee to feign a crossing at Sandtown," Sherman reassured the anxious Schofield. This would get the Rebels' attention and make them think twice before sending any sizable force across Utoy Creek.

Unsure of Kilpatrick's dispositions, Sherman telegraphed George Thomas, asking, "Where is General Kilpatrick's cavalry at this time?"

"General Kilpatrick's headquarters are at the junction of the Powder Springs and Sandtown roads," Thomas replied. "He covers Sweet Water and patrols to Dallas."

A few minutes later, the telegraph key at Thomas's bivouac chattered to life with another message from Sherman:

> The enemy's cavalry manifests activity on our right, threatening to cross Utoy Creek to General Schofield's rear. He has little or no cavalry. I want him to-morrow to develop well the enemy's flank, which I believe is along the south fork of Utoy Creek, covering East Point. To enable him to do this I want a general cannonading to-morrow, the 4½-inch guns included, if they come in time; and I want you to order General Garrard to send a brigade out to and beyond Decatur on your left, and let General Kilpatrick move down to Sandtown and feign as though intending to cross over. Send orders for him tonight, that the effect may be felt as early in the day as possible. I cannot move General Schofield with any activity as long as that cavalry hovers on his right and rear. We are now as much extended as possible, and must test the strength of our flanks and line.

Thomas relayed these instructions to General Elliott's headquarters, and at 11:30 P.M. orders were sent advising Kilpatrick:

> The enemy's cavalry on the south side of the Chattahoochee threatens General Schofield's right flank on or near the Sandtown and Atlanta road. The general commanding directs that you make a demonstration opposite to and below Sand–town as if you intended to cross the river. Make the greatest show of force by countermarching [your] command. Let this be done at an early hour but without harassing your animals more than is necessary.[25]

Kilpatrick had two brigades in the saddle by 8:00 A.M., August 9. Led by the 92nd Illinois, Eli Murray's 3rd Brigade and a section of the 10th Wisconsin Battery moved down the Sandtown Road to the Chattahoochee. While Murray's skirmishers fanned out along the riverbank, trading shots with Rebel pickets, the artillery unlimbered on a hill overlooking the Sandtown Ferry and added their deep-throated thunder to the din. Desultory firing continued until dark, when Murray withdrew and made camp about a mile from the river.

To further the illusion a crossing was imminent, Fielder Jones's 2nd Brigade left Sweetwater Bridge that morning with three days' rations and the remaining section of the 10th Wisconsin Battery. Striking the Chattahoochee opposite Campbellton, Jones's men began banging away while the Wisconsin battery's 3-inch rifles lobbed shells across the river. They kept up this charade until just before dark, when Jones had his men build campfires in the woods to make it look like a large force had moved down to the river. The brigade then quietly moved upstream, crossed the mouth of Sweetwater Creek, and camped near Alexander's Mill before returning to Sweetwater Bridge on August 10.[26]

On the opposite end of the far-flung Federal line, Kenner Garrard got orders from Thomas's headquarters sometime after midnight on August 9, directing him to send out a brigade "at as early an hour as possible," "to and beyond Decatur," to "make a demonstration against the enemy," in conjunction with Kilpatrick's show of force near Campbellton. "The enemy's cavalry manifested unusual activity on our right yesterday, threatening to cross Utoy Creek," the orders explained. "This movement of the cavalry is ordered to occupy the attention of the enemy's and prevent him in any way embarrassing the movements of General Schofield to-day while he endeavors to find the rebel left flank."

Garrard sent these instructions to Eli Long, and early on August 9 the 2nd Brigade and the 3rd section of the Board of Trade Battery marched from Buckhead to Decatur. Patrols pounded up and down the puddled roads, capturing a few pickets, but most of Long's men spent a wet, dreary day on the courthouse square, waiting for something to happen. Unable to bait the Rebel cavalry into battle, they started back to Buckhead at sundown. Lathered artillery horses strained in their harness, heads down, nostrils flaring, as they hauled the heavy guns across the muddy miles, and two of them died of exhaustion before the column returned to camp at 8:30 P.M.[27]

While Thomas's cavalrymen were making these showy demonstrations at Sandtown, Campbellton, and Decatur, Israel Garrard's 7th Ohio spent August 9 guarding the fords and bridges over Utoy Creek. Late the previous day, Garrard had been reinforced by the arrival of Colonel George S. Acker's 9th Michigan Cavalry and seven companies of Captain Samuel T. Hughes's 9th Illinois Infantry (mounted on mules), but even three regiments were hard pressed to do all the picketing and scouting on the right flank.

"If you have a good cavalry brigadier," Sherman offered Schofield on August 9, "I will give you Colonel Hamilton's regiment, Ninth Ohio, with a full regiment and nearly 500 horses to make a brigade of cavalry, but I must have a real head, one that will give it personal attention."

"I have no good cavalry commander," Schofield wired back. "Colonel Adams is probably the best I have. Can you not assign one from some other department?"

"I have no cavalry commander at all," Sherman answered gruffly. "All the cavalry of the old Army of the Tennessee is back in Mississippi, and General Thomas' cavalry is not well commanded. Colonel Adams told me his time was out, and he is going back to Kentucky. . . . Colonel Capron is back; how is he?"

Schofield confessed he did not know Capron personally, but dismissed him as "not of much account," and disparaged Israel Garrard as "wanting in dash." "I cannot do better for the present," he concluded, "than to put Colonel Garrard in command, unless Colonel Hamilton is better. I know nothing of him."

Sherman agreed to leave the choice of a brigade commander to Schofield. He sent a telegram to Vining's Station assigning Hamilton to the Army of the Ohio and directed him to bring his regiment across the river to report to Schofield.[28]

As the rain pelted down that afternoon and Sherman waited for news from Sandtown and Decatur, the heavens roared, the air shook, and the earth trembled. It was not thunder, it was artillery. Sherman had ordered George Thomas to begin "a general cannonading" in conjunction with the cavalry movements, and the Army of the Cumberland's artillery responded with a will. From the time the first cannon roared about 10:00 A.M. until the guns finally fell silent between 3:00 and 4:00 P.M., Thomas's batteries hurled 3,157 rounds of solid shot and shell into Atlanta.

"All the fires of hell, and all the thunders of the universe seemed to be blazing and roaring over Atlanta," wrote a dazed civilian, but this was only the beginning. In the midst of the fierce bombardment, a train rolled across the recently rebuilt railroad bridge over the Chattahoochee River. Lashed aboard the flatcars were three 4½-inch siege rifles Sherman had ordered from Chattanooga.

A detachment from Captain Arnold Sutermeister's 11th Indiana Battery hauled the heavy guns from the railroad to a site George Thomas had personally selected on the left flank of the XX Corps, about a mile and a half east of the Marietta Road, and positioned them in embrasures cut into the works of the 149th New York Infantry. A thousand Schenkl shells arrived the next morning, and at 4:00 P.M., August 10, in the midst of a heavy rainstorm, all three guns opened fire. Four of Sutermeister's 20-pounder Parrotts, posted 500 yards east of the Marietta Road, added their weight to the barrage, and both batteries worked nonstop for the next forty-eight hours, lobbing shells into Atlanta at a rate of one every five minutes.[29]

"I want the 4½-inch and 20-pounder guns to hammer away," Sherman wired Thomas, "and I will think of the next move."

Schofield had suggested detaching his corps and one other and sending them to make a lodgement on the West Point railroad near East Point, but Sherman rejected the idea. "I . . . despair of making a quick move," he replied. "It takes two days to do what ought to be done in one."

"I cannot extend more without making my lines too weak," he confided in a telegram to General Grant at 8:00 P.M. "I may have to leave a corps at the railroad bridge, well intrenched, and cut loose with the balance and make a desolating circle around Atlanta."

He had already discussed that possibility with Generals Thomas and Howard, but moving all three of his armies around the west side of Atlanta was a step he was clearly reluctant to take. "My own experience is the enemy can build parapets faster than we can march . . . ," he complained. "In a single night we would find ourselves confronted with parapets which we would fear to attack in the morning."

Before he could contemplate any sort of move around the west side of Atlanta, he had to know more about the lay of the land south of Utoy Creek, and shortly before 11:00 P.M. on August 10 he ordered Schofield to have Israel Garrard rebuild the bridge over the mouth of Utoy Creek and "feel across to the south bank."[30]

Repairing the bridge apparently took some time. It was 3:00 P.M., August 11, before Garrard led part of his 7th Ohio, three companies of the newly arrived 9th Michigan,

A Harvard Law School graduate, Israel Ludlow Garrard abandoned his practice before the war to enjoy the solitude of a Minnesota hunting lodge. Unlike his brother, Kenner, he had no military training, but he certainly dressed the part when he became colonel of the 7th Ohio Cavalry. Courtesy of the Western Reserve Historical Society, Cleveland, Ohio. Used by permission.

and a battalion of the 9th Illinois Mounted Infantry across the creek toward Sandtown. His column, about 450 strong, quickly routed some vedettes on the south side of the creek, pushed on another mile and a half, and drove the Rebel pickets out of Sandtown. They then followed the Sandtown Road eastward for two and a half miles before turning south at Dry Pond, "a one-horse settlement with no pond, but two or three houses & a blacksmith shop." As they approached Owl Rock Church, Garrard saw telltale piles of horse dung, withered corn fronds, and scores of smoldering campfires. An old man named McWilliams who lived near the church said three brigades of Frank Armstrong's cavalry had left there for Campbellton early on August 10, "on a raid," but about 200 of them had returned that morning, heading toward East Point.

Garrard retraced his steps to the Sandtown Road to follow them. The abandoned picket posts he found at every crossroads as he continued eastward convinced him the Rebel cavalry had quit this part of the country. Upon reaching one of his own outposts behind Schofield's lines near Utoy Post Office, he sent most of his troopers back to camp and led the others on a brief scout to the right of the infantry. He returned that evening without finding any Rebels and advised Schofield, "I do not think it practicable to picket the line of road traveled to-day, and think that the line of Utoy

Creek is the best one for the protection of the flank from the right of our line to the river. There are no natural advantages on the line of the Sandtown Road."

That night, Garrard received orders from Schofield officially giving him command of "all the cavalry of the Army of the Ohio serving with the troops in the field." He was to move his brigade forward the next morning, clearing the Rebel cavalry from the right flank of the XXIII Corps, and picket all the roads leading back to the Chattahoochee.

With his neatly barbered beard and mustache and prominent Gallic nose, Garrard cut a dapper, if not altogether handsome, figure. A graduate of the Harvard law school who had abandoned his profession for the unfettered life of a sportsman, he suddenly found himself and his younger brother, Kenner, in command of all of Sherman's cavalry south of the Chattahoochee River. In obedience to Schofield's orders, early on August 12 he sent a small force across the bridge at the mouth of Utoy Creek to scout down to Sandtown again. Another detachment, two companies of the 9th Michigan led by Major William C. Stevens, crossed Utoy Creek at Donohue's Mill with orders to go to the intersection of the Campbellton and Sandtown roads at Dry Pond. About a mile north of the settlement, Stevens's men encountered some Rebel cavalry. After skirmishing for half an hour and driving them back to the crossroads, Stevens found the Rebels getting "*too* thick" and withdrew.

The rest of the 9th Michigan went with Israel Garrard as part of a reconnaissance in force Sherman had ordered Schofield to push toward the West Point railroad. After screening the advance of an infantry division down a crossroad connecting the Sandtown and Campbellton roads, Garrard's troopers turned west, toward Dry Pond. Within half a mile, they began skirmishing with dismounted Confederate cavalry and were unable to make any further progress until Schofield's infantry came up. Pressing ahead again, they encountered some of Sul Ross's vedettes at Mrs. Patterson's about 3:00 P.M. Company C of the 9th Michigan charged, only to meet a countercharge by the 9th Texas. Pistols popped, horses tumbled in headlong heaps of harness and hooves, and two Michigan men were captured when their mounts were shot out from under them. The sharp skirmishing convinced Garrard "the country over which I scouted yesterday had been reoccupied." He fell back on his infantry support and at dark Schofield recalled the entire expedition.[31]

Sherman had spent the day with Schofield, hoping to prod him forward. "He thinks all the Confederate Army with the Reserves are on his flank," Sherman complained, "& seems over cautious about a small gap in his lines." When it became apparent the railroad would not be reached, he returned to his headquarters that evening and issued orders summoning his army commanders to a meeting at 10:00 the next morning.[32]

The conference lasted nearly all day. Thomas, Howard, and Schofield were present with their staffs, along with several corps and division commanders, and Sherman's chief engineer, Captain Poe. Anyone who came with expectations of being asked for advice was disappointed. Sherman had already decided what he wanted to do and merely convened his subordinates to work out the details. That evening, in a cipher to General Halleck in Washington, he announced, "I have ordered army commanders to prepare for the following plan: Leave one corps strongly entrenched at the Chattahoochee bridge in charge of our surplus wagon trains and artillery; with 60,000 men, reduced to fighting trim, to make a circuit of devastation around the town, with a radius of fifteen or twenty miles."[33]

While Sherman and his generals bent over Captain Poe's maps, Companies E, F, G, and H of Eli Long's 4th Ohio rode out of Buckhead early on August 13 to investigate a disturbing report that Rebel infantry was moving toward Decatur. The Ohio cavalrymen jangled into town and probed down the McDonough Road for two or three miles, hunted the roads to the north and east for five or six miles, then returned to Buckhead that evening without seeing any sign of a Rebel column.

The rest of Kenner Garrard's 2nd Cavalry Division spent August 13 lounging in their bivouacs or crouched behind breastworks. At Buckhead, 3rd Ohio troopers turned in their single-shot Sharps and Burnside breechloaders for Spencer repeaters. Out in the trenches, Minty's 4th Regulars relieved the 4th Michigan in the rifle pits at 10:00 A.M., and many of the men took advantage of the first clear skies in a week to dry their sodden blankets.

Quiet reigned along the lines until about 8:00 P.M., when several of Thomas's batteries began lobbing shells into Atlanta. Flames erupted near the courthouse, sending a plume of thick black smoke floating off to the northwest on the evening breeze. Some of Bob Minty's men had climbed on top of the breastworks to get a better look at the blaze when a Rebel fort opposite the Howard house suddenly loosed a thunderous salvo at 9:00 P.M.

Hood's gunners had the range perfectly. Cracker boxes, camp kettles, and brush arbors were blown sky high and then came raining down again. Troopers standing on the breastworks hurled themselves into the trenches. Others who had been lolling around camp in various states of disarray sprinted for the ditches in what was ever afterward remembered as the "shirt-tail dress parade."

Major William H. Jennings, commanding the 7th Pennsylvania, and three of his officers were sitting around a makeshift table when a 64-pound shell hurtled through their lean-to, smashed the table into kindling, struck the log breastwork behind Captain Charles C. McCormick, and exploded a foot from his head. The searing blast flung Private Robert Bridgens, sitting on the rampart almost directly above the hut, into the air like a rag doll, fearfully mangling his leg.[34]

The 7th Pennsylvania's regimental surgeon, Dr. John L. Sherk, rushed to the aid of the stricken officers. Major Jennings and two of his companions stirred feebly, dazed but unhurt. Captain McCormick lay unscathed, but seemingly lifeless. Detecting a feeble pulse, Dr. Sherk labored over him for almost an hour before he revived. By the time he turned his attention to Robert Bridgens, it was too late. The private had lost too much blood and died in a field hospital that night when doctors tried to amputate his leg.

Among those diving for cover as the shells screamed overhead was Bob Minty's Negro cook, George. George frequently boasted about his bravery and his eagerness to enlist so he could put down the rebellion, but he had always managed to stay out of harm's way until a Rebel shell ploughed into the cookhouse where he was sleeping. For the next three hours, Minty's men hugged the ground in a passionate embrace as shells boomed and burst and blasted all around them. There was no sign of George until the next morning, when Minty's adjutant, Captain Robert Burns, saw him coming back into camp. "George," he asked, "where were you last night when the rebels were shelling us? We wanted you to clean up things a little, after they quit."

"Well," George replied, "de fac is Cap'n, when dey t'row'd de big sell into de cook-house, I tought I's not wanted hea'h, an' jumped inter dat 'gofer hole,' wid a lot of you all, den I went to de bres' works an' fit 'til I got to *de bottom of my brave,* an' dat wah a deal shallerer dan I tought; so I jest let out, an' did'n't stop till I had run about a mile an' haf." He paused a moment and then added gravely, "It wah a tempestuous night, wah'n't it, Cap'n!"[35]

The 2nd Division's tenure in the trenches abruptly ended at 4:00 P.M., August 14, when Abe Miller's brigade and the 1st section of the Board of Trade Battery were ordered back to the Peachtree Road. The cannoneers harnessed up their teams, then unhitched when their move was countermanded, but Miller's men were soon footing for the rear, "very well satisfied to be out of the ditches."

Advised of their approach, the number fours quickly saddled the horses that had been left in their care and led them out to meet the column. The animals had been on half rations of grain and had not had a blade of forage since August 1, but two weeks of rest appeared to have done them good. The men mounted and moved back to their old camps on the south side of Peachtree Creek, where they drew five days' rations, 100 rounds of ammunition, and orders to be ready to march for Dalton at 4:00 A.M.[36]

This sudden about-face resulted from a telegram Sherman had received from Resaca. Joe Wheeler and 3,000 Rebel cavalry had captured a herd of 1,000 army beeves at Adairsville, crossed the Oostenaula, and were demanding the surrender of the Union garrison at Dalton.

The news did not come as a complete surprise. Three days earlier, on August 11, Sherman had received a copy of a report Kenner Garrard had sent to General Elliott, describing how stragglers returning from Stoneman's raid had seen a huge force of Rebel cavalry concentrating near Covington. An officer of the 14th Illinois (probably Lieutenant Mayo), brought to Garrard's headquarters with a bullet wound in his shoulder, asserted he had never seen so many horsemen in one place and they seemed to be preparing for a big raid into Tennessee or Kentucky.

"I don't see as we can at this time prevent them from going," Sherman had confided to George Thomas after reading the report, "but [we] must study to be ready for the effect."

He was reasonably certain Wheeler could not do any lasting harm. Blockhouses guarded all the major bridges. Infantry, cavalry, and artillery garrisoned strategic depots, and well-rehearsed section gangs stood ready to repair any damage done to the railroad he depended on for supplies. Instead of seeing the raid as a threat, Sherman saw it as an opportunity.

"I would not be surprised if Wheeler is up at Dalton," he wired George Thomas that evening. "If so, now is the time for General Elliott to collect all his cavalry and make a break round the enemy by either flank."

Thomas disagreed. "I think it better to pursue Wheeler with our cavalry than to attempt another raid with it on the enemy's communications . . . ," he counseled; "but Elliott will be over to see you."

Sherman, however, was insistent. "We should either act offensively with our cavalry or so place it that it catch Wheeler on his return," he asserted. "Let General Elliott give orders that those cattle must be recovered at all hazards, and we will await further news as to the force Wheeler carried off with him; but Generals Garrard's and Kilpatrick's cavalry could operate in the absence of Wheeler from Decatur without risk."

"Your dispatch received and shown to Elliott," Thomas answered. "He will be over

Brigadier General Washington Lafayette Elliott commanded the Cavalry Corps of the Army of the Cumberland. "An old cavalryman of high character," Elliott was an excellent administrator, but rarely ventured very far from his tent. "He once in a great while sent us an order," noted Judson Kilpatrick, "but I never saw him on the field." Reproduced from the Collections of the Library of Congress.

to see you. But do you think it prudent to risk any more cavalry on their communications until our [cavalry] force is materially increased?"

Sherman seemed to relent after meeting with Elliott that night. "Inasmuch as we propose to throw our army on the enemy's communications I will not risk our cavalry," he wired Thomas, "but will get General Elliott to have General Kilpatrick make a bold reconnaissance toward Fairburn and engage any cavalry he meets to test its strength; General Schofield's cavalry to go with him."

Shortly before 8:45 P.M., he telegraphed Schofield, "There is no doubt Wheeler is up about Dalton with a large cavalry force. I want our cavalry now to feel the enemy's flanks strong, and will order General Kilpatrick to cross at Sandtown and make a bold push for Fairburn, and General Garrard in like manner to feel well round the enemy's right flank. Let your cavalry go down in the morning to Sandtown and report for the expedition to General Kilpatrick."

By 11:00 P.M., Sherman had directed Thomas to pull the rest of Kenner Garrard's cavalry out of the trenches and revoked the orders sending Abe Miller's mounted infantry after Wheeler. Thomas passed these instructions to Elliott, who ordered Garrard to march early the next morning with his entire force to determine how much of Wheeler's cavalry was left around Decatur. "Give him a hard fight if the opportunity offers, . . ." Elliott urged. "If the opportunity offers to reach the Macon [rail]road without too much risk, don't fail to avail yourself of it."

Garrard immediately went to Elliott's headquarters and stayed until after midnight, airing his usual litany of complaints. Minty's brigade was still in the trenches. There would not be any forage for the horses until noon. As for the whereabouts of the Rebel cavalry, he already knew that. There was at least a brigade, perhaps a division, behind breastworks extending the right flank of Hood's line, and he had tried repeatedly to lure them out. Long's whole brigade and two pieces of artillery had gone to Decatur for that purpose on August 9. A battalion of the 4th Ohio had been there just yesterday, but the Rebel horsemen still clung to their trenches. If Sherman needed proof, a brigade could do the job just as well as a division. If he wanted to draw the remaining Rebel cavalry into battle, why not send a column to Covington, where Wheeler had reportedly left his convalescent horses? If his object was to cut the Macon railroad, Garrard knew enough about the roads on this side of Atlanta to get there quickly, but uncovering that flank while his division marched south would endanger the wagon trains parked in Sherman's rear.

Elliott promised to convey these concerns to headquarters. "Have presented your statement to General Thomas," he advised Garrard early on August 15; "he says he cannot give you more definite orders—to use your discretion. I say, if the enemy won't come out and fight you can't make him, but can drive him to his works. If, in connection with your reconnaissance, you think you cannot strike the railroad, I would not attempt it. Such is my understanding of General Sherman's orders."[37]

Garrard had his 2nd and 3rd Brigades saddled and ready to march early on August 15, but it was daylight before infantry from Thomas's IV Corps relieved Bob Minty's brigade in front of the Howard house. Number fours brought the trench-bound troopers their horses and "a more pleased set of men you never saw," noted Michigan cavalryman George Chase.

At 6:00 A.M. Minty's faded, mud-stained column started back to the horse camp on the Peachtree Road with the 1st section of the Board of Trade Battery. The rest of the division dawdled: sipping coffee, writing hasty letters home, dozing fitfully. Garrard may have been waiting to make sure Minty got out of the trenches, but he had also received two urgent messages from General Elliott warning that 500 Rebel cavalry were reportedly threatening Vining's Station. "Send a cavalry force there immediately," Elliott commanded, "without regard to other orders."

Garrard dispatched one of Minty's regiments, the 7th Pennsylvania, to Vining's Station and ordered the 4th Michigan and 4th Regulars to relieve Eli Long's pickets guarding the roads back to Roswell. It was 8:00 or 9:00 A.M. before Abe Miller's brigade, led by the 72nd Indiana, and the 3rd section of the Board of Trade Battery started for Decatur. Eli Long followed with the 2nd Brigade at noon, as soon as his pickets returned from the outposts they had turned over to Minty's men.

By that time, Abe Miller's scouts had dashed into Decatur, capturing two or three Rebel soldiers. Eight roads—to Atlanta, Fayetteville, McDonough, Flat Shoals, Covington, Stone Mountain, Lawrenceville, and Roswell—converged on the courthouse square and Garrard soon sent regiments trotting down six of them.

The 72nd Indiana headed out on the Atlanta Road. They had gone about a mile and a half when the advance guard encountered a Rebel outpost. Company C dismounted and quickly drove the opposing pickets away, capturing two of them. Pressing ahead for another mile, they found what Sherman was looking for, Rebel cavalry—lots of it. Outnumbered, with no reinforcements within reach, the regiment about-faced and began a fighting retreat. As gunfire crackled at the rear of the column, where Company D tried to discourage the pursuit, the leaden skies lowered and a cold rain began to fall. Gray riders raced up a parallel road, trying to head off the Yankee regiment, but the Hoosiers got there first, dismounted, and hastily formed behind a rail fence running along the crest of a prominent ridge a half mile below Decatur. A broad field stretched before them, sloping away to the south for almost a mile, and through the heavy downpour they could see Rebel cavalrymen preparing to fight on foot.

Soon a long gray line of skirmishers came forward, but they seemed wary of approaching the long-barreled Spencers aimed at them. They were only halfway across the field when they began firing and their shots fell short by fifty to a hundred yards.

The Hoosiers hooted at the "no account" Rebel rifles. "Come closer," they yelled. "Come and get a piece of corn bread."

The Rebels raised their defiant yell and started up the rain-slick slope only to meet a withering volley that sent them diving for cover.

"Get up out of the mud," the Indiana troopers taunted. "Get up out of the mud."

The Rebels rose up and rushed forward again. A few more shots from behind the rail fence quickly pinned them to the ground.

About this time the 72nd's officers realized the railroad between Atlanta and Decatur ran through a deep cut in the woods on their right. Company G and part of Company D hurried into position on that flank just in time to meet a Confederate column coming through the defile. Both sides opened fire. A bluecoated soldier fell, severely wounded in the chest. Others took cover in the woods on either side of the cut and easily held the attackers at bay.

"Just as the firing began on our right the rebels made another attempt to advance on our front," noted Sergeant Ben Magee, "and although it was still raining as hard as it could pour we could see them so plainly and our men opened on them with such deliberation that they scarcely got a dozen rods till they were all flat on their bellies again. They then tried shooting at us from their positions on the ground. A few shots went over our heads, and a few struck the fence in front of us, but most of them dropped short of their mark; no rebel dare stick up his head for a second but he was glad to get it down again."

For the rest of the afternoon, the Hoosiers kept their opponents hugging the ground. They laughed at them, taunted them, jeered them. As darkness fell, the regiment slowly retired to Decatur, mounted their horses, and joined the rest of Garrard's rain-soaked column as it started back to Buckhead.

The other patrols Garrard had sent out had ventured southwest to Cobb's Mill, southeast toward Covington and Flat Shoals, and west toward Stone Mountain. Except for the 72nd Indiana's fight on the Atlanta Road and a smaller skirmish on the McDonough Road, there was no opposition, and the 2nd and 3rd brigades reached Buckhead about midnight.[38]

Sherman was waiting impatiently for them. Early on August 16 he inquired of both Elliott and Thomas, "Have you anything from Generals Garrard and Kilpatrick?"

Elliott reported the 7th Pennsylvania had returned from Vining's Station without seeing any Rebels, but there was still no news from Garrard. Sherman then asked Major General David Stanley, whose IV Corps had relieved the cavalrymen in the trenches, "Have you heard anything from General Garrard since he started out?"

Stanley replied he had not heard anything, but he sent a messenger to Garrard's headquarters on the Peachtree Road and soon reported, "General Garrard came back last night. He had some fighting with the rebels. He found them in force, about seven regiments. They fell back behind breastworks. Some rebel cavalry passed our flank about [New] Cross Keys yesterday. They killed one man on picket. I presume General Garrard has already reported."

This only honed Sherman's impatience to a fine edge. "General Stanley reports General Garrard as back," he telegraphed Thomas. "Has he reported? General Stanley says some cavalry passed to our rear at Cross Keys and killed a picket. Does General Garrard manifest enough activity? Get his report and let me have the substance."

Thomas did not immediately reply, but Sherman was in no mood to wait. He was poised on the brink of a difficult and potentially dangerous maneuver, Confederate cavalry was raiding his supply line, and in the last two weeks he had had his fill of intractable, insubordinate, and insipid officers.

"General Garrard will not attempt anything if there be a show of resistance," he wired Thomas. "If you consent, and can give command of that cavalry to Colonel Long, I will put General Garrard on my staff and send him to Nashville to supervise the equipment and armament of our cavalry."

Once again, Thomas sprang to the defense of his former student. "Garrard returned last night about 12 o'clock," he replied at 10:00 A.M. "His report is being copied to be sent to you. I think you will find it satisfactory. . . . Garrard's services on the Augusta road [during the raid to Covington] show how thoroughly he performs his work when he undertakes what he has to do. By not rashly pushing on the main road, regardless of the forces opposed to him, he has preserved to us his fine division, with which I believe he will yet do good service."

Soon afterward, Sherman received a copy of Garrard's report to General Elliott. In it Garrard advised, "with some degree of certainty," that Ferguson's brigade and two regiments just up from Savannah were the only cavalry on the Rebel right flank. All the signs indicated Wheeler had taken his whole effective force to raid in Sherman's rear, but Garrard had not ventured near the Macon railroad because "I did not deem it advisable to attempt it."

The report made Sherman more determined than ever to find someone else to command the 2nd Cavalry Division. "General Garrard . . . went seven miles; saw some horsemen and came back," he sneered. He had not even tried to reach the Macon railroad. In Sherman's eyes, that was unforgivable.

"I am willing to admit that General Garrard's excessive prudence saves his cavalry to us," he telegraphed George Thomas after reading the report, "but though saved, it is as useless as so many sticks. Saving himself, he sacrifices others operating in conjoint expeditions. I am so thoroughly convinced that if he can see a horseman in the distance with a spy-glass he will turn back, that I cannot again depend on his making an effort, though he knows a commander depends on him. If we cannot use that cavalry now, at this moment, when can we? Wheeler is out of the way, and when shall we use cavalry, if not now? If we wait till Wheeler returns, of course an opportunity is lost, which never is repeated in war."

Thomas noted several colonels in Garrard's division were senior to Eli Long and the only way to get around that was to have him promoted.

"Do I understand if Long can be promoted you will approve him as the division commander?" Sherman asked that afternoon. "I don't want to act in this matter without your full and cordial consent, as this cavalry is properly in your command, and it is for you to regulate it." But he added, "I want that road broken bad, and I believe now is the time."

When Thomas replied he was "perfectly willing" to make the change, Sherman telegraphed Washington, asking the War Department to promote Eli Long to brigadier general. Then he waited to hear from Kilpatrick.[39]

After returning from the feinted river crossings at Sandtown and Campbellton on August 9, Kilpatrick had reestablished his headquarters at the intersection of the Powder Springs and Sandtown roads, probably in the front yard of Andrew J. Cheney's house. Since then, he had subjected his command to almost daily reviews and inspections.[40]

As sunset dimmed the evening sky on August 14, he and his staff sat around on rough benches, laughing, smoking, telling funny stories. As usual, Kilpatrick was the center of attention. He was regaling his listeners when Lieutenant Theodore F. Northrop rode up and dismounted. Northrop called him aside and delivered orders from General Elliott:

> You will make a bold reconnaissance in the direction of Fairburn to [the West Point] railroad if you can reach it. It is reported that Wheeler with 6,000 cavalry and artillery has gone north. If true, you will have only Jackson's cavalry to contend with. If the opportunity offers try to break him up. General Schofield's small force of cavalry will be ordered to co-operate with you. It is on the south side of Utoy Creek, and will report to you at Sandtown to-morrow.

Kilpatrick read the message, then slowly walked over to a low fence. These were the orders he had been waiting for, and he paused for a few seconds, looking at the moon. Then he spun on his heel and quickly strode back toward his officers, summoning his adjutant, Captain Estes. The division would march at 3:00 A.M., he announced. He talked quietly with Estes for about five minutes, then sat back down and resumed his story.

Within half an hour, Estes had dispatched orders for the division to be ready to move "at a moments notice." Brigade commanders were to make certain their men carried one day's forage, three days' rations, and sufficient ammunition. "*Only effective horses*" would accompany the column, and pioneers must be equipped with axes, picks, and shovels.[41]

"Reveille" sounded in the 3rd Division's bivouacs at 1:00 A.M. on August 15. Bleary-eyed, half-buttoned troopers scuffled to the picket ropes in the dark, hastily groomed and fed their horses, then gathered around flickering fires, squatting in the shallow circles of light to fry bacon and hardtack and boil coffee.

In the midst of these preparations a circular came from Kilpatrick:

> Soldiers
>   The long wished for opportunity to strike the foe has at last arrived. In obedience to orders I am about to attempt the accomplishment of a most important object. Let each soldier remember, that he is to follow me into danger, that his good name and mine depends on his own individual conduct. Let us be determined, cool and brave and success shall be ours.[42]

Fielder Jones's 2nd Brigade finished breakfast, saddled their horses, and began moving south from the bridge at Sweetwater Town at 3:00 A.M. Clattering down the

Sandtown Road, they joined Robert Klein's 1st Brigade at Mitchell's Crossroads, then halted briefly at 4:00 A.M. while Eli Murray's 3rd Brigade and the artillery filed into the road ahead of them.

A pale moon set on their right and a red sun rose on their left as Murray's 92nd Illinois led the way to the Chattahoochee. Half a mile from the river, the regiment halted, dismounted, and formed in line of battle while Captain Beebe's 10th Wisconsin Battery unlimbered on a hill behind them. Someone barked an order and Murray's skirmishers started across the dewy fields. A thunderous report erupted behind them as the Wisconsin battery went into action, but the shells fell short, bursting in front of and behind the thin blue line with a fiery roar, ploughing up the ground and pelting the men with dirt. A little cussing from Kilpatrick quickly compelled Beebe's careless cannoneers to take better aim, and the 92nd reached the riverbank without loss. As they began banging away with their Spencers, a shell whistled overhead and exploded in Sandtown, scattering surprised Rebel pickets "like frightened deer."

A few moments later, some of Colonel George Buell's 58th Indiana pontoniers appeared with one of their canvas boats and began ferrying the 92nd Illinois across the river. The rest of Buell's men "went to work with a will," as wagons laden with balks and chesses rolled down to the water's edge. By 10:00 A.M., they had spanned the muddy river and Kilpatrick had all eight of his regiments across by noon.[43]

Leaving a portion of his command to fortify the bridgehead at Sandtown, Kilpatrick sent the rest of his column south. Shortly after 1:00 P.M. they met Israel Garrard's brigade at Owl Rock Church.

Garrard had received orders from Schofield during the night to "move close to Sandtown early to-morrow with your command, aid General Kilpatrick in crossing the river, and report to him for duty. . . ." Leaving his camp near Mrs. Kennedy's on the south side of Utoy Creek, Garrard had marched early on August 15 with close to a thousand men from the 7th Ohio, 9th Michigan, 9th Illinois Mounted Infantry, and the recently transferred 9th Ohio. Unlike Kilpatrick's troopers, who were carrying picks, axes, shovels, and three days' rations, his men came totally unprepared. "We did not expect to be gone more than five or six hours," complained Major William C. Stevens of the 9th Michigan, "so did not take any rations with us but when we got, as we supposed, to our destination . . . and then learned for the first [time] that we were to go ten or twelve miles farther, you may be sure the intelligence . . . was not very agreeable."

Assuming Garrard's men were more familiar with the country on this side of the river, Kilpatrick put them out front. As the 9th Michigan led the way south toward Campbellton and then southeast on the Fayetteville Road, a gust of wind unfurled the flags and guidons that had been hanging limply from their staffs. Dark clouds curtained the glaring sun and thunder rumbled overhead as the same downpour that would drench Kenner Garrard's troopers later that afternoon at Decatur soaked the Yankee soldiers filing across the bridge over Camp Creek and past Bethel Church. About a mile and a half beyond the church, the road forked. Kilpatrick sent Israel Garrard's four regiments to the left on the Fairburn Road to block the approach of any Rebel cavalry. The rest of the column turned to the right, toward the railroad.

Garrard's 9th Michigan had not gone a mile when they collided with two regiments of Sul Ross's Texans at Wolf Creek. The Yankee troopers held their ground in the face of heavy small arms and artillery fire, but Ross quickly recognized this was only a diversion to distract his attention. Leaving two companies to contend with Garrard, he ordered his whole brigade south toward Fairburn at 5:20 P.M.[44]

He was too late. Kilpatrick's division had already struck the West Point railroad about halfway between Fairburn and Red Oak, cut the telegraph wire, and begun working their way south, tearing up track as they went. Just before sunset, about 200 troopers from Robert Klein's 1st Brigade galloped into Fairburn, chased the telegraph operator out of town, set fire to the depot, water tank, and woodshed, and tore up about three-quarters of a mile of track.

As smoke and flames billowed into the evening sky, the 92nd Illinois's band played "sweet music" on their silver instruments. Companies and regiments sprawled along the right-of-way, drying wet clothes and cooking supper. Corporal Cass Bell of the 8th Indiana was sitting beside a fire when a big black snake came coursing out of the gloom. Confused and frightened by the heat and smoke, it slithered up the first dark hole it could find, the leg of Bell's trousers. Bell bounded to his feet, yelling and wriggling like a wild man. "He flew around lively," chuckled Williamson Ward, "but the snake did no harm other than frightening him."

Shortly before dark, Kilpatrick ordered his column to mount up and retrace their route along the railroad. The smoke from the burning buildings was also Garrard's signal to withdraw and the two commands fell back about four miles before halting for the night at Camp Creek.

"Thus far my reconnaissance has been a success," Kilpatrick wrote to General Elliott from the north side of the creek at 9:00 P.M.:

> I crossed the river at 11:00 a.m., and passed out at once for Fairburn. I forced the enemy back into his camp near the railroad, five miles above the station. Destroyed the station, public buildings, telegraph and railroad for about three miles. Jackson's division of cavalry has thus far refused to give me battle. I rather expect an attempt will be made in the morning to prevent my return. This will give me the opportunity I seek to destroy Jackson and his command, provided his cavalry alone meets me.[45]

Eager to pick a fight with "Red" Jackson, Kilpatrick started his column back toward Sandtown at 6:00 A.M. on August 16. His rear guard, the 92nd Illinois, had spent the night in a dry camp at Bethel Church, and upon reaching the bridge over Camp Creek, they stopped to water their thirsty horses. Corporal Edward O. Trask and a squad were keeping watch from the crest of a hill just south of the creek when a sizable force of Rebel cavalry came charging up the road. Seemingly outnumbered ten to one, the corporal's men hesitated, trying to decide whether to run or fight. "We must stand," Trask yelled; "we belong to the Ninety-Second; we can whip them." The answering crackle of his squad's Spencers compelled the Rebels to do an abrupt about-face, and the rest of the regiment calmly finished watering their horses before moving on to catch up with the division.

As the Yankee column slowly retired toward the Chattahoochee, scouts reported Jackson's cavalry was camped several miles to the east, at Mt. Gilead Church. Upon reaching Owl Rock Church, instead of continuing toward Sandtown or the camps on Utoy Creek as Israel Garrard's hungry troopers hoped, Kilpatrick turned to the right and sent them eastward on the Campbellton Road, past Dry Pond. About noon, they reached the crossroads at Mrs. Patterson's, the scene of their skirmish with the 9th Texas Cavalry during Schofield's reconnaissance on August 12. While Garrard's men formed a line of battle astride the Campbellton Road, facing Atlanta, Kilpatrick turned the head of his column south toward Mt. Gilead. Scouts ranging far ahead soon returned and reported finding only fifty or a hundred Rebels at the church. The rest of Jackson's division was gone.

Leaving Garrard's command to cover his withdrawal, Kilpatrick reversed his order of march and retired to Sandtown. Eli Murray's 3rd Brigade arrived about 3:00 P.M. and trooped across the pontoon bridge to make camp on the north side of the Chattahoochee. The 1st and 2nd Brigades halted on the south side and began building breastworks and posting a screen of pickets stretching in a broad arc through Dry Pond and Owl Rock Church, while Company D of the 8th Indiana moved to establish a courier line linking Sandtown with General Elliott's headquarters.[46]

Kilpatrick was pleased with his success. He had reached the West Point railroad, torn up what he claimed was three miles of track, and returned to Sandtown without losing a man. "I scouted the entire country between Camp Creek and the railroad to within one mile and a half of East Point . . . ," he wrote to General Elliott at 4:00 P.M. "The enemy seemed to make but little or no effort to prevent me from reaching the railroad at any point below East Point Station. I infer from this that the road is to be abandoned. The enemy's cavalry has certainly all been withdrawn from this portion of his line save two brigades, of Jackson's division, which force is not at all formidable. You will see by the accompanying sketch that if I am able to maintain the line of pickets indicated, the enemy's lines will be very much contracted and both [the West Point and Macon] railroads exposed to raids from this point."[47]

Sherman was still waiting to hear from Kenner Garrard's scout toward Decatur when Elliott sent him a copy of the initial report Kilpatrick had written at Camp Creek. "The news from Kilpatrick is first rate," the exultant redhead replied. "He acts in earnest. I believe General Kilpatrick, with his own and General [Kenner] Garrard's cavalry, could go straight for Rough and Ready, and break the Macon road all to pieces."

That night, in a telegram to George Thomas, Sherman asked, "What say you to letting General Kilpatrick have two of General Garrard's brigades and then strike across to the Macon road and tear it up good? He has scouted the country now and knows it, and can act with confidence and due caution. . . . I like the plan better than to send General Garrard up to Cartersville, for the enemy will simply run off, but General Kilpatrick, with two good brigades, can reach across to the Macon road about Rough and Ready, and tear up about six or eight miles by to-morrow night or next day."

Thomas had no objections. "If you think a cavalry raid can destroy the Macon road sufficiently to force Hood to retreat," he replied, "I think now would be a good time to send against it."

Perhaps anticipating Thomas's answer, Sherman wired Schofield shortly before 10:00 P.M., August 16, asking him to communicate with Kilpatrick and get "a definite report of his operations."

Schofield had already dispatched a courier to Sandtown when a second telegram arrived twenty minutes later. "Ascertain from General Kilpatrick if he does not think with two of General Garrard's brigades in addition to his own he could break the Macon road effectually," Sherman instructed. "I do not think General Garrard will try."

Schofield sent a second messenger speeding through the night. Early the next morning he received a copy of Kilpatrick's second report to General Elliott. "I am satisfied," Kilpatrick wrote in an accompanying note, "that, with two of General Garrard's brigades and my own division, I can break the Macon road effectually at any point the major general commanding may be pleased to indicate. Such an opportunity to strike the enemy a terrible blow has never been offered."

Schofield dispatched a rider to deliver the report to Sherman. A short time later, Sherman had a message for Kilpatrick telegraphed to Schofield's headquarters. "Put your command in good shape for rest and security," he ordered; "and come up to see me."[48]

22

KILPATRICK'S RAID
SANDTOWN TO STEVENS' CROSSROADS

AUGUST 17–AUGUST 19, 1864

Booted and spurred and mounted,
Away at the bugle call; . . .
To conquer, or fighting fall.

—Clifford McKinney Taylor,
"A Ride with Stuart"

Sherman's decision to summon Kilpatrick came less than twelve hours after he had issued Special Field Orders Number 57, the ambitious plan which would put 60,000 infantry in motion around the west side of Atlanta. The march was scheduled to begin at dark on August 18, but by 10:40 A.M. on August 17, Sherman was contemplating giving his cavalry one last crack at the Macon railroad.

"I do not want to move this vast army and its paraphernalia round Atlanta unless forced to do so," he confided in a telegram to George Thomas, "and it seems the enemy has offered us the very opportunity we seek. We know positively that Wheeler is above Dalton, and that he must have taken the very flower of his cavalry. He has, and may do us harm, but that we cannot help. I do not think he can carry any point of our road that he can maintain, and his own necessities will force him back soon with jaded and worn-out horses. Now, ours can be quickly moved to Sandtown at a walk, and according to General Kilpatrick can reach Red Oak or any point below the enemy's infantry and break up many miles of that railroad."

Sherman believed one of Kenner Garrard's powerful brigades could easily "amuse" whatever Rebel cavalry remained east of Atlanta, enabling Kilpatrick's division and the rest of Garrard's troopers to make a sudden dash from Sandtown and tear up enough railroad south of the city to "disturb Hood seriously." "The risk will be comparatively small . . . ," he assured Thomas. "I am perfectly alive to the fact that the loss of our cavalry would be most serious, but I do think such an opportunity if neglected will never again appear."

Thomas conceded this was "as good a time as could be taken to make another raid on the Macon railroad," but he insisted Kilpatrick must take "the most practicable route and avoid the enemy's infantry as much as possible."

Sherman vowed to give Kilpatrick strict orders so that he "would not be rash," and shortly before noon, he directed Thomas to notify Kenner Garrard to have a brigade ready to make a demonstration toward Decatur. Garrard's other two brigades, led by Eli Long if possible, were to prepare to march by moonlight across the trestle bridge at Pace's Ferry and down the north side of the Chattahoochee to join Kilpatrick's command at Sandtown. "They will not move," Sherman instructed, "till I see Kilpatrick in person and have a clear understanding."[1]

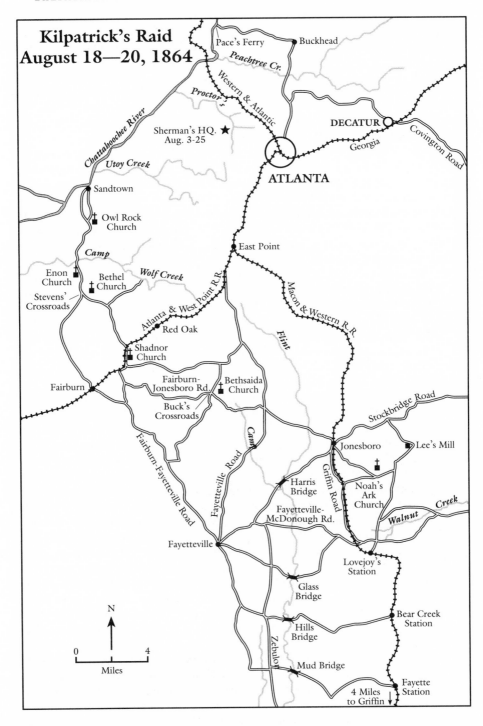

**Kilpatrick's Raid
August 18—20, 1864**

Pace's Ferry   Buckhead

Peachtree Cr.

Western & Atlantic

Proctor's

Chattahoochee River

DECATUR

Sherman's HQ. ★
Aug. 3-25

Georgia   Covington Road

Utoy Creek

ATLANTA

Sandtown

Owl Rock
Church

East Point

Camp

Enon
Church   Bethel
Church   Wolf Creek

Stevens'
Crossroads

Macon & Western R.R.

Atlanta & West Point R.R.

Red Oak

Flint

Shadnor
Church

Fairburn-
Jonesboro Rd.   Bethsaida
Church

Stockbridge Road

Fairburn   Buck's
Crossroads

Camp   Jonesboro   Lee's Mill

Fairburn-Fayetteville Road   Fayetteville Road   Griffin Road   Noah's
Ark
Church   Creek

Harris
Bridge   Walnut

Fayetteville-
McDonough Rd.

N

Fayetteville

0   4
Miles   Lovejoy's
Station

Glass
Bridge

Bear Creek
Station

Hills
Bridge

Zebulon

Mud Bridge

4 Miles
to Griffin   Fayette
Station

Kilpatrick arrived that afternoon at the collection of tent flies, camp stools, and cracker boxes that served as Sherman's headquarters. After a hearty handshake and some small talk, the two men got down to business. Sherman wanted Kilpatrick to take his own division and two of Garrard's brigades and move out tomorrow night, as soon as it got dark. Upon reaching the West Point railroad, somewhere between Red Oak and Fairburn, a detail should stop, if there was time, and tear up a small portion of track, "without using fire," to prevent Rebel infantry from coming down on the cars and blocking their return. The main column would continue eastward, strike the Macon railroad near Jonesboro, and "tear it up thoroughly."

This was not a raid, Sherman emphasized, "but a deliberate attack for the purpose of so disabling the road that the enemy will be unable to supply his army in Atlanta." Kilpatrick could not tear up too much track or twist too much iron. Sherman expected him to work, not to fight. He would have Schofield move as far to the right as prudence would allow on August 19 to prevent the Rebels from sending infantry after the column. The rest of the army would keep Hood so busy he would not be able to interfere. Whip any cavalry that got in the way, Sherman added, but steer clear of Rebel infantry and artillery.

Once the railroad was cut, Kilpatrick was to return to his post on the right flank of the army, sending Garrard's borrowed brigades back to the left. If they did their work well, Hood would have to abandon his trenches, Atlanta would fall, and Sherman would smash the retreating Rebel army on the open ground south of the city.

Kilpatrick listened attentively and assured Sherman he could destroy enough track to put the Macon railroad out of commission for two weeks. That was the kind of talk Sherman wanted to hear and he telegraphed George Thomas to start two of Kenner Garrard's brigades for Sandtown.[2]

After returning from their recent reconnaissance to Decatur, Garrard's troopers had settled into their old camps along Peachtree Creek. Men who had spent the past two weeks crouching in the muddy ditches in front of Atlanta thronged to the creekbank, bathing and washing clothes. An occasional breeze stirring among the pines brought some relief from the midday heat but reeked of death and decay. Mounds of raw, red earth marked the graves of hundreds of brave men, silent monuments to the fierce fighting that had raged through the nearby fields and thickets on July 20. Captain Robert Burns counted ten bullet holes, all within six feet of the ground, in the tree where his tent fly was tied, twenty-three in another, forty-seven in another, and sixty-one in another. "I hope we shall not have to stay here long," he wrote, "as the stench is sometimes almost intolerable. Dead horses and mules still lie about entirely too near. The whole of this country is one great Golgotha."

Early on August 17, Garrard had advised his brigade commanders that marching orders were "liable to be received any moment," and instructed them to have horses shod and everything prepared for "active operations." "We have no orders in regard to moving yet," Private Alva Griest noted in his diary, "although rumors are plentiful. Some say we go to Tennessee to scout for Gruillas and horse thieves, but I doubt it."

Shortly before 1:00 P.M., Garrard received a warning from Thomas's headquarters: Rebel infantry was massing on the army's left flank. Cautioned to "keep a strict lookout" and "resist any ordinary attack made on your lines," Garrard apparently ordered his whole division to "saddle up immediately" and directed Bob Minty to send a regiment to strengthen the picket line. Buglers sounded "The General," followed at once by "Boots and Saddles." Flinging saddles on their horses' backs, buckling girths and bridles, Minty's men had just climbed into the stirrups when "Recall" echoed through the camps. It was a false alarm. There were no Rebels. The men dismounted, unsaddled, and spent the rest of the afternoon "lying around loose."

Those not out on the picket lines or on patrol were dozing in the shade when Garrard got orders from General Elliott's headquarters to have "the effective force of two brigades, under command of Colonel Long, ready to move to-night by moonlight, via Pace's Ferry and Sandtown bridge, to Sandtown."

Later that afternoon, after meeting with Kilpatrick, Sherman elaborated on these instructions in a telegram directing George Thomas to have Garrard send two brigades of cavalry and a battery of artillery to Sandtown. "The horses should be well fed," Sherman added, "and could take some wagons of shelled corn as far as Sandtown, when the wagons may return. Men provided with full ammunition and five days' bread, sugar, coffee, and plenty of salt. . . . Instruct Garrard to be sure to send the pioneers along with the cavalry, provided with the tools to break up [the] railroad. Kilpatrick ranks Garrard, and the latter may go along if you prefer."[3]

Thomas had General Elliott's headquarters forward Garrard a copy of these instructions, along with a postscript suggesting the column could save six or eight miles by moving down the south side of the Chattahoochee instead of crossing the bridge at Pace's Ferry.

Garrard, however, had no intention of serving under Kilpatrick. Upon receipt of Sherman's message, he promptly issued his Special Field Orders Number 6, directing the 1st and 2nd Brigades and two sections of the Board of Trade Battery to report to Sandtown "by the nearest and best possible routes." Bob Minty, the senior colonel, would command. The men would draw five days' rations, to be carried on pack mules, and "an ample supply of ammunition." "The command will move to-night as soon as the rations are issued," Garrard ordered.

Shortly before 6:00 P.M., he summoned Minty to his headquarters. "Your force will consist of your own and Long's Brigades," he explained, "and four guns from the battery. You will march as soon as it is dark, pass round the rear of our army and report to General Kilpatrick at Sandtown as early as possible tomorrow morning."[4]

In the meantime, pickets had to be relieved, rations issued, ammunition distributed, horses inspected, mules packed, and wagons sent to the rear. Orders were issued to march at 10:00 P.M., "without bugle calls," but due to delays in procuring rations, it was 1:00 A.M., August 18, before the column got started.

Major Frank W. Mix's 4th Michigan, 19 officers and 231 men, led the way, followed by 11 officers and 262 men belonging to Captain James B. McIntyre's 4th Regulars. Then came Major William H. Jennings's 7th Pennsylvania, 16 officers and 313 men. Together with 8 staff officers and 65 enlisted men attached to Minty's headquarters, the 1st Brigade fielded 54 officers and 871 men.

Eli Long's 2nd Brigade brought up the rear. His three regiments—Colonel Beroth B. Eggleston's 1st Ohio, 16 officers and 330 men; Colonel Charles B. Seidel's 3rd Ohio, 27 officers and 450 men; and Lieutenant Colonel Oliver P. Robie's 4th Ohio, 24 officers and 455 men—together with Long's headquarters detachment of 8 officers and 73 men totaled 75 officers and 1,308 men.

Lieutenants George Robinson and Henry Bennett and 88 artillerymen accompanied the column with the number 1, 3, 4, and 5 guns from the Chicago Board of Trade

A former ensign in the British army, Colonel Robert Horatio George Minty was the combative commander of the 1st Brigade of Garrard's 2nd Cavalry Division. Although he was repeatedly recommended for promotion, an unmerited court martial and the apparent enmity of Major General Henry Halleck kept him from becoming a brigadier. Used by permission of the Massachusetts Commandery, Military Order of the Loyal Legion, and the U.S. Army Military History Institute.

Battery. Teams of eight horses pulled each of the 10-pounder Parrotts, while six-horse hitches towed the limbers packed with shell and canister. On orders from Garrard, the caissons were left behind.

They rode southwest, a long, clattering column of 2,398 men and four guns. Bathed in the soft silver light of a full moon, they filed across the Western & Atlantic Railroad, past Sherman's headquarters, and down the south side of the Chatta-hoochee.[5]

Near the head of the column rode "natty, fair-haired, and debonair" Robert Horatio George Minty. Born in Westport, County Mayo, Ireland, on December 4, 1831, Minty had spent much of his youth in the British West Indies, where his father was a highly respected captain in the 1st West India Regiment of Foot, a black regiment commanded by white officers. When the elder Minty died of a tropical fever in 1848, arrangements were made for his seventeen-year-old son to join the regiment as an ensign. After serving in Jamaica, Honduras, and Sierra Leone, Minty sold his commission in 1853 and emigrated to the United States.[6]

Settling in Detroit, he got a job with the railroad. When his adopted country went to war, he helped organize the 2nd Michigan Cavalry and briefly served with the rank of major. A fellow officer remembered him as "a very genial gentleman, who endeared himself to the men by his unassuming yet soldierly manners. He lived in his tent in camp and could call his men by name, and was ever ready to impart any instructions or listen to any communications they might make."

Trained officers were in great demand, and a week after mustering in, Minty was named lieutenant colonel of the 3rd Michigan Cavalry. He led this regiment in thirty-six battles and skirmishes before resigning in July 1862 to accept the colonelcy of the 4th Michigan Cavalry. The following December, he succeeded Ed McCook in command of the brigade that would be associated with his name for the rest of the war.

Generally regarded as one of the best cavalrymen in the army, Minty taught his troopers to sharpen their sabers and to use them. He repeatedly won praise for his "able, undaunted spirit and ability," and was three times recommended for promotion to brigadier general. But on October 7, 1863, in a sharp encounter with Joe Wheeler's cavalry at Farmington, Tennessee, his brigade was unaccountably late. The division commander, Brigadier General George Crook, angrily arrested him for insubordination.

"There is no foundation for the charges," Minty asserted, but he languished in arrest for almost four months, "cast aside like a piece of useless furniture," he complained, before a court martial convened in February 1864 to try him on charges of "disobedience of orders" and "conduct subversive of good order and military discipline." General Crook took the stand and testified that on the day in question he had given Minty orders to be ready to march at daylight. When asked if he had specified what road and which direction Minty's brigade was supposed to take, Crook confessed he could not remember, and as the trial progressed, it became increasingly apparent his orders had been vague. The court acquitted Minty of all charges and restored him to duty.[7]

A temperate man who neither drank nor swore, Minty loved music and was extolled by one of his contemporaries as "an educated soldier of great intelligence and enterprise . . . a dandy cavalryman . . . an excellent disciplinarian, and as good a leader as Murat himself." But the most flattering compliment came from a Confederate cavalryman who wrote, "Col. Minty is one of the most gallant and dashing officers in the Federal army, and those who 'scare him up' may count on having to fight."[8]

After an all-night march from Buckhead, Minty halted his column at 6:00 A.M., August 18, on the banks of Utoy Creek. Leaving instructions for his men to unsaddle, water, feed, and groom their horses, he and his adjutant, Captain Burns, rode on to Sandtown with a couple of orderlies.

Sandtown was not much to look at, only a public house and a few log cabins, most of which had been torn down to build breastworks. When Minty arrived, Kilpatrick was still in bed, but he dressed hurriedly, greeted his visitor cordially, and sent for his brigade commanders.

"Gentlemen," he announced after everyone had assembled in his tent, "our organization will be two divisions: Colonel Minty commands the Second, Colonel Murray will command the Third. I command the corps. We will march at 6 o'clock this evening. Murray's division in the advance; we will move in light marching order; all impedimenta, including ambulances, will be left in camp."

Kilpatrick calculated they would reach the West Point railroad at Red Oak by daylight. The horses would still be fresh and if they rode hard they should get to Jonesboro sometime between noon and 2:00 P.M. "At Jonesboro," he explained, "Murray's Division will at once set to work to destroy the railroad; Minty's division will form line of battle facing Atlanta and take position to protect the working party from any force advancing from that point. As soon as the Third Division has destroyed its own length of the railroad it will move south and repeat the operation. Col. Minty will follow the Third Division and continue to protect it by showing a bold front toward Atlanta, the only point from which we may expect opposition. These movements will be repeated indefinitely until further orders. Gentlemen, let me have an expression of your opinions. Colonel Minty, what do you say?"

"General," Minty replied, "I like your plan in every particular but one."

"What is that, sir?" Kilpatrick demanded.

"Leaving our ambulances in camp," Minty said. "I do not like the idea of having to abandon my wounded men to the mercy of the enemy; and I have always found, and I have no doubt, General, that your experience is the same, that our men will fight with better heart when they know that if wounded they will be taken home with their comrades and not left in the hands of the enemy. Allow me to take my ambulances, and I pledge myself that you will not find them an incumbrance. If they are, I will destroy them."

Kilpatrick thought a moment. "Well, Colonel Minty," he said, "you can take your ambulances; but if they impede our movements or delay us in the slightest degree you must burn them. Colonel Murray, you will leave your ambulances in camp."[9]

Sherman expected the expedition to swing back to the west after wrecking the track at Jonesboro and "make another big tear up" on the West Point road before returning to Sandtown. But after meeting with Minty, Kilpatrick sent a message to General Elliott at 10:00 A.M., inquiring about the roads and rivers east of Jonesboro and the disposition of the rest of Kenner Garrard's division.

"Our cavalry on our left is on [the] Augusta railroad, near and east of Atlanta," replied Elliott's adjutant. "Decatur is occupied alternately by scouts from both armies. Should you find it necessary to return by our left, the route by Flat Rock [Flat Shoals], Latimar's [Latimer's], and Decatur would probably be best. You will have many officers of Garrard's division, who can give you more information about South River and its branches than I am able to get for you. The entire cavalry force on the left cannot be detached, but orders will be given to make a demonstration this evening and early to-morrow morning to engage the attention of the enemy's cavalry on our left and draw him in that direction."

Sherman had already urged George Thomas "to instruct Kenner Garrard minutely" in that regard. "He will obey orders," Sherman admonished, "but if left to himself does not persevere long enough."

But while Garrard needed prodding, Kilpatrick had to be kept on a tight rein. "Now, of all times, is the time for our cavalry to do its work well," Sherman telegraphed John Schofield at 11:30 A.M. on August 18. At his behest, Schofield wrote to Kilpatrick that afternoon, reminding him his task was not to pick a fight with Rebel cavalry but to

break as much of the Macon road as you possibly can, and, as you swing back, to rest on the West Point road somewhere below Fairburn, and make another big break there. If you find you are master of the situation on that road, take time enough and destroy as long a line of track as possible. Do the work thoroughly by heating and twisting the rails, and burning ties, &c. In places where you have not time to work, you can still do great damage by prying up the track (rails and ties together), propping it up on the surface of the ground, piling in large quantities of dry fence rails and burning them. There is good reason to hope that you may be able to accomplish what the whole army would otherwise have to do, at great risk, by a long and difficult flank movement. Early to-morrow I will move with a corps of infantry toward the railroad near East Point, and engage the enemy so as to prevent his sending infantry to oppose you. General Sherman directs me to assure you that he will have the same done all along the line, especially on our extreme left, and he will see that Garrard occupies the attention of the enemy's cavalry about Decatur and Stone Mountain. The most abundant success to you.[10]

In the meantime, Kilpatrick had ordered his troopers to draw one hundred rounds of ammunition, one day's forage, three days' rations of hardtack, a six-day supply of sugar and coffee, and to be ready to march at 6:00 P.M. Similar preparations consumed the long, hot afternoon at Utoy Creek, where Minty's men packed an additional sixty cartridges into their saddlebags to go with what they already had in their cartridge boxes. Artillerymen with the Board of Trade Battery scrubbed down their horses, inspected harness, and distributed what little forage they had for their teams. Here and there, troopers dozed in whatever shade they could find. "The weather was very hot," complained Lieutenant Will Curry of the 1st Ohio, "the flies and insects were swarming and the surroundings were anything but inviting for a good day's rest."

Afternoon's sharp shadows were melding into evening's softer shades when Minty's men got orders at 5:00 P.M. to feed and water their horses, eat supper, and be ready to saddle in an hour. At Sandtown, hoofbeats sounded woodenly on the floor of the pontoon bridge as Eli Murray's 3rd Brigade, now commanded by Lieutenant Colonel Robert H. King, began filing across the Chattahoochee to join the rest of Kilpatrick's column.[11] South of the river, Company D of the 8th Indiana was relieved from courier duty and ordered to report to their regiment immediately.

At 6:00 P.M., Minty's headquarters bugler sounded "Boots and Saddles." The brassy notes echoed and reechoed as brigade and regimental buglers took up the call, only to be drowned out by the groans of hundreds of weary troopers who had vainly hoped to avoid another sleepless night in the saddle.

"The expression of many a man as he braced his knee against his horse's ribs and drew tight his saddle girth was certainly more expressive than elegant," noted Lieutenant George Robinson, "and when all was ready and waiting the call to mount, occasionally a man, to give more forcible expression to his disappointment and disgust, would go back and set fire to the little bunch of straw or sunburned grass that he had gathered for a bed for the purpose of making his night's rest more comfortable and enjoyable."[12]

Colonel Charles Seidel watched solemnly as his 3rd Ohio led their horses into a large field on the right side of the road and lined up by battalions. When they were all in position, he took out a circular every regimental commander had received that afternoon. The closely scrawled sheet of paper trembled slightly in his hand as he brought it closer to a lighted candle he was holding. Then, in a loud voice, he read:

Soldiers!
You have been selected from the Cavalry Divisions of the Army of the Cumberland. You have been well organized, equipped and rendered formidable at great expense to accomplish an object vital to the success of our cause. I am about to lead you, not on a raid, but in a deliberate and well combined attack upon the enemy's communications in order that he may be unable to supply his army in Atlanta. Two expeditions have already failed. We are the last cavalry troops of the army. Let each

soldier remember this and resolve to accomplish the great object for which so much is risked or die trying.

(Signed) J. Kilpatrick
Brig Genl
Comdg. Expedition[13]

There was a moment of silence when Seidel finished. Then he directed the pack train to fall out and anyone with a lame horse to go to the rear. Similar commands sounded in the 1st and 4th Ohio and about a hundred troopers led their limping, sore-backed steeds away. The rest of the brigade was ordered to mount. Sabers rattled and stirrup leathers creaked as the men swung lightly into their saddles.

"Right, forward, fours right!"

The 3rd Ohio answered with wild cheers as they turned and led Eli Long's 2nd Brigade into the road.[14]

By this time, the head of Kilpatrick's column was already in motion. The 92nd Illinois had left Sandtown at 7:00 P.M., followed by the 3rd Kentucky and 5th Kentucky of Robert King's 3rd Brigade and four 3-inch rifled guns belonging to Captain Yates Beebe's 10th Wisconsin Battery. The 10th Ohio, 8th Indiana, and 2nd Kentucky of Fielder Jones's 2nd Brigade were next in line, followed by the 3rd Indiana and 5th Iowa of Robert Klein's 1st Brigade. Then came the troopers from the 2nd Division: Eli Long's 2nd Brigade, led by the 3rd Ohio, the Board of Trade Battery's four Parrott guns, six ambulances, and Minty's 1st Brigade. From head to tail, the serpentine column stretched for two and a half miles and it was nearly 9:00 P.M. before Minty's rearmost regiments, the 4th Regulars, 7th Pennsylvania, and 4th Michigan, even got started.

They came down the road at a swinging trot, 4,500 men and eight pieces of artillery. Seven of the fourteen regiments carried Spencer rifles or carbines slung from their shoulders. It was more men, more firepower, and more formidable than any mounted column Sherman had ever assembled.[15]

Half an hour after dark, a bright yellow moon rose overhead. Crickets and tree frogs began chirruping noisily, and startled birds flitted from their roosts along the roadside as the grim troopers swept past. At darkened farmhouses, yard dogs bounded out of the shadows, barking and yapping and then retreating before the endless rush of men and horses.

Captain Matthew Van Buskirk and Companies D, E, and K of the 92nd Illinois were riding at the head of the column when Kilpatrick overtook them. "Boys," he said, "is this the advance guard?"

"Yes, sir."

"All right," Kilpatrick said, "I am with you; we'll have some fun tonight. When the rebel pickets challenge you let me respond."

About five miles south of Sandtown, a detachment of the 6th Texas Cavalry, led by Captain James S. Porter, guarded the bridge over Camp Creek. "An ignorant old goose," according to one of his men, Porter had left only six pickets at the bridge and neglected to pull up the flooring. His reserves were about 300 yards to the rear, where the road passed through a cut eight or ten feet deep, bordered on both sides by a high fence and dense thickets of blackjack trees. When some of his men suggested cutting down a few of these trees to block the road, Porter scoffed at the idea. "I know how to manage the Yanks," he said.

At 9:00 P.M. Porter's pickets heard hoofbeats approaching. "Halt there!" a sentry demanded.

"Friends without the countersign," a voice answered.

The padding of hooves on the dirt road came closer. Again the sentry hurled his challenge. Then he bolted out of the way. The other pickets barely had time to fire a few scattering shots before Kilpatrick's advance guard came pounding over the bridge.

"They came at full speed right up the road four deep and paid no attention to us," recounted Private Newton A. Keen of the 6th Texas, "but dashed through our lines and on down the road they went." Keen and his comrades hastily mounted and piled down the sides of the cut, whooping and yelling. The dust and the darkness made it impossible to tell friend from foe, and only a few shots were fired as Yanks and Rebs raced along almost side by side.

Half a mile beyond the cut, someone had chopped down a post oak tree, leaving two feet of the trunk jutting into the road. "Logs are good things to throw horses down in case we beat a hasty retreat," Private Keen had remarked on the way to guard the bridge that morning. Now, as luck would have it, his little black mule hit this obstacle at full stride and tumbled head over heels. Keen landed flat on his back on the north side of the road, but quickly scrambled to his feet and disappeared into the bushes.

The Yankee horsemen swept past him, "yelling with all their might." About a mile beyond Camp Creek they saw the fires of the 6th Texas's bivouac flickering in the distance.

"Attention—trot—march! Charge!" a voice bellowed.

With wild shouts, Kilpatrick's advance guard descended upon the sleepy Texans, scattering them in every direction.

Newton Keen heard the gunshots echoing up ahead as he groped through the tangled woods. He had gone about two miles on a course paralleling the road when he came to a small field. Looking to his right, he saw a crowd of Yankee horsemen milling around on the other side of the road. Keen edged to his left, feeling his way around the wooded fringe of the field. He had taken only a score of steps when he encountered six or seven shadowy figures.

"Who's this?" one of them asked.

"Johnny," Keen replied.

"Give up your gun, Johnny," demanded a Yankee trooper.

Keen surrendered his rifle and two of his captors led him away. A few minutes later, he was face to face with Judson Kilpatrick. The general asked him where he was born.

"The State of Indiana, Harrison County," Keen answered.

What regiment did he belong to? Who commanded his brigade? How many regiments in the brigade? How old was he? How long had he been in the army? Where were his parents born? Where did they live? Was his father a Mason? For half an hour, Kilpatrick plied his prisoner with questions.

"I told him . . . everything just as I knew it," Keen recounted. "I knew it would add nothing either one way or the other, and did not propose to misrepresent anything."

Finally, Kilpatrick got to the point. None of his officers were familiar with the roads south of Atlanta. He needed a guide, and he offered Keen a good horse and $300 if he would take the job. Keen replied he had taken an oath to fight for the

Confederacy; folks would not respect him if he broke his word. Kilpatrick offered to send him out West where no one knew him, or back home to Indiana. Keen refused. Kilpatrick reminded him he could also send him to a prison camp. Keen said he would rather be a prisoner than break his word. Kilpatrick argued, but to no avail. Finally, he summoned a guard and had Keen marched to the rear.

By this time, the head of the Yankee column had reached Stevens' Crossroads, two and a half miles beyond Camp Creek. The advance guard had captured four or five Texans, killed one, and wounded others at a cost of only one horse and one injured trooper among themselves. The march was right on schedule, and at 11:00 P.M. Kilpatrick sent a courier back to Sandtown with a short message assuring Sherman the column would reach the Macon railroad by 12:30 the next afternoon.[16]

During the halt at Stevens' Crossroads, Kilpatrick ordered Fielder Jones's 2nd Brigade forward to relieve his winded 3rd Brigade and take the advance. He also summoned Robert Klein. He needed a diversion, and he wanted Klein's 1st Brigade to turn south, cut the West Point railroad at Fairburn, and then continue southeast to the Macon road. The rest of the column would cross the track below East Point, strike the Macon road near Jonesboro, and follow it south to meet Klein near Griffin.

Klein turned his brigade of 13 officers and 292 men south at Stevens' Crossroads and disappeared into the night. Following a zigzag course over seven miles of country roads, they reached the West Point railroad at Fairburn at 1:30 A.M., August 19, cut the telegraph, and captured the mail. Troopers overturned a few sections of track and set them ablaze, silhouetting the charred ruins of the depot and the water tank they had burned three days earlier. At 2:00 A.M., they climbed back into the saddle.

Heading southeast on the Fairburn and Fayetteville Road, Klein's little column moved on in the moonlight. Dawn came, and at 9:00 A.M. they surprised an estimated eighteen to twenty Rebel forage wagons just outside Fayetteville, capturing seven teamsters. "We got several good horses and mules out of the train," noted Sergeant Warren McCain, "and these proved to be the best part of the booty, for some of our horses had already begun to fail."

After burning the wagons, Klein paused in Fayetteville long enough to capture the mail before continuing southeast on the Griffin Road. Turning to the left near Mount Zion Church, he crossed the Flint River, probably at Mud Bridge, intending to cut the Macon railroad near Fayette Station. But somewhere along the way a guide he had pressed into service made a mistake. Instead of Fayette Station, Klein's column struck the railroad four miles farther north, at Bear Creek Station, at 11:00 A.M.

Troopers promptly cut the telegraph wire and began tearing up track. Noticing a freight train parked about a half mile north of the station, Privates Samuel N. Hamilton and James Jeffries of the 3rd Indiana galloped up to the engine and leveled their carbines at the engineer, fireman, and conductor, demanding their surrender. Sergeant Warren McCain and the rest of a ten-man detachment followed close behind. After taking charge of the trainmen and six or eight Negroes, they pried open the doors to the boxcars with a crowbar and found them loaded with whisky, meal, wheat, lard, and railroad car wheels. Some of them were filling their canteens with whisky when Klein rode up and ordered the train burned. The men obediently poured liquor on the wheat and set it on fire. Private David Babb climbed aboard the engine, fired the boiler until it was red hot, pulled the throttle wide open, and with a yank on

A former Prussian soldier, Lieutenant Colonel Robert Klein commanded the 1st Brigade of Kilpatrick's division. An exacting drillmaster, he was "especially versed in the sword exercise," recalled a trooper, "and knew more about this weapon than we ever cared to learn." Reproduced from *History of the Third Indiana Cavalry* by W. N. Pickerill (Indianapolis, 1906).

the whistle cord, sent the train caterwauling toward Bear Creek Station. With a screech of twisting metal and the hiss of escaping steam, the engine hit the break in the track and tumbled down an embankment.

Engineer James Knight watched the smoke spiraling up from the jumbled wreckage of his train. The crash distracted his captors, and seeing his chance, he bolted for the woods. Ten or twelve shots rang out behind him, but he escaped, leaving his conductor to answer the questions the Yankee colonel asked in a heavy German accent.

Klein was anxious for news of Kilpatrick, but it soon became apparent the conductor knew nothing about another Yankee column. After lingering long enough to tear up about 300 yards of track and burn the trestle over Bear Creek, the raiders headed north, toward Lovejoy's Station, pulling down the telegraph wire and pausing at intervals to tear up a few rails. Two miles south of Lovejoy, they saw a train approaching. It was crowded with Confederate soldiers.[17]

News of the Yankee raid had reached John Bell Hood's headquarters on the night of August 18. Realizing the absence of Wheeler's cavalry had left the railroads south of Atlanta extremely vulnerable, he had ordered Major General Edward C. Walthall to move his infantry division out of the trenches fronting the Marietta Road at 3:00 A.M., holding his troops in readiness to march "to any point where support might be needed." He also pulled Frank Armstrong's cavalry brigade off the picket lines west of Atlanta with orders to start for Jonesboro as soon as it was light. Similar instructions sent to the east side of the city put Samuel Wragg Ferguson's troopers in motion toward Rough and Ready.

More reports of the raiders' progress came in during the dark hours before dawn, and early on August 19 Hood ordered Walthall to send one of his brigades to help "Red" Jackson defend the Macon railroad. At 10:00 A.M., Brigadier General Daniel Harris Reynolds's brigade—the 1st Arkansas Mounted Rifles (dismounted), 2nd Arkansas Mounted Rifles (dismounted), 4th Arkansas Infantry, 9th Arkansas Infantry, and 25th Arkansas Infantry—climbed aboard the cars, reinforced by the 48th Tennessee.

The trip south was a slow one, a welcome respite from weeks of fire and fury. Reynolds had lost almost half his men in the headlong assaults at Ezra Church on July 28. Captains commanded four of his five regiments. Attrition had also caused the recent consolidation of two other units, both of whom laid claim to the proud name of 48th Tennessee. Altogether, Reynolds had about 300 lean, battle-tested veterans.

His train chugged into Jonesboro at 1:00 P.M., just about the same time Armstrong's and Ferguson's cavalry rode into town. "Red" Jackson met the train at the depot and told Reynolds to continue south to Lovejoy's Station and then toward Griffin if the Yankees seemed to be headed in that direction. Armstrong and Ferguson would follow on the wagon road paralleling the track.

Reynolds reached Lovejoy and saw a black, ugly smear of smoke against the southern sky. Learning the Yankees had cut the railroad at Bear Creek Station, he commandeered another locomotive, put some of his men aboard two flatcars piled high with crossties, and sent them ahead to reconnoiter. The rest of the brigade followed cautiously.

About two miles below Lovejoy, one of Jackson's scouts flagged down Reynolds's train and reported a thousand Yankee cavalrymen had crossed the railroad not ten minutes before, heading west. Wary of being ambushed in the thick woods, Reynolds had the engineer move the train into a clearing 400 yards down the line.

The rear cars had just passed a dirt road when a flurry of shots rang out. Two of Reynolds's men fell wounded. The others piled off the cars as the train jolted to a stop. After some initial confusion, they formed ranks and sent out a skirmish line.

Yankee troopers, hidden in the brush, had allowed Reynolds's scout train to pass unmolested. Seeing the second one "packed full of Johnnies," they opened fire. Klein was deploying for a more concerted attack when a brigade of Rebel cavalry suddenly appeared on his flank. "Boys," he shouted, "get out of this."[18]

Turning to the left, his troopers beat what Sergeant Warren McCain called "a hasty, though orderly retreat," and captured several prisoners. From them, Klein learned he was facing Reynolds's Rebel infantry and Armstrong's and Ferguson's cavalry. Outnumbered, unable to hear anything from Kilpatrick, he had to decide between turning south toward Griffin and almost certain capture, or trying to get back across the Flint River.

"Under the circumstances," Klein concluded, "I deemed it prudent to get out of there." Abandoning the railroad at 4:30 P.M., he headed west toward Fayetteville, intending to return on the same road he had traveled that morning. He reached the Flint River, probably at Hill's Bridge, about three miles north of Mud Bridge, only to find the floor had been pulled up. Replacing the missing planks with some rails from a nearby fence, his men quickly crossed over and burned the bridge behind them.

Turning north, the head of the column was two miles short of Fayetteville when gunshots suddenly sounded in the distance. Some of Frank Armstrong's Mississippians, crossing the Flint River at a ford on the road from Fayetteville to Lovejoy's Station, had overtaken the rear guard.[19] Klein urged his men to keep moving, but the disquieting crackle of rifles and carbines swelled sharply behind them. As the advance guard approached Fayetteville, more Rebels appeared in the road up ahead. They were surrounded, an outnumbered little brigade on tired horses, and thoughts of what had happened to McCook and Stoneman flashed through more than one trooper's head.

There was not a moment to lose. Draw sabers, Klein commanded. The sunset shimmered on cold steel and spurs roweled deep as the Yankee column charged straight through the Rebels blocking the road, causing them to "skedaddle" in what Private James Thompson of the 3rd Indiana called "the most approved Confederate style."

Dashing through Fayetteville, the fleeing Federals sped toward the northwest. Armstrong's weary Mississippians, who had ridden nearly forty-five miles since daylight, did not pursue, and the raiders reached Fairburn well after dark without further incident. Crossing the blackened scar that marked where the railroad had been, they marched on until midnight before Klein finally called a halt at Stevens' Crossroads. Three of his men were missing. Two others were wounded. The rest were utterly exhausted and sprawled in the road beside their horses.

Arising early on August 20, Klein's little command crossed Camp Creek and rode into Sandtown about 8:00 A.M., reporting to Lieutenant Colonel Matt Patrick of the 5th Iowa, who had been left in charge of the 3rd Division's dismounted men. They brought seventeen prisoners and forty captured mules with them, but more important, they had decoyed two Rebel cavalry brigades and a trainload of infantry away from Kilpatrick.

"I feel certain that General Kilpatrick is doing good work," Sherman wired George Thomas after reading Klein's report on August 21; "still it is time for us to hear from him direct."[20]

23

KILPATRICK'S RAID
STEVENS' CROSSROADS TO LEE'S MILL

AUGUST 19–AUGUST 20, 1864

An army of asses led by a lion is vastly superior to
an army of lions led by an ass.

—George Washington

After halting briefly at Stevens' Crossroads and sending Klein's brigade south, Kilpatrick had continued east. Fielder Jones's 2nd Brigade, 900 strong, led the way, and about a mile beyond the crossroads his 10th Ohio collided with pickets from the 6th Texas. Ohio troopers charged, driving the Texans back a half mile. The advance pressed ahead, unhindered, until half an hour after midnight, when Colonel Dudley W. Jones's 9th Texas came dashing out of the darkness in a column of fours. Pistols blazing, the Texans struck like the crack of a whip. The Ohio regiment recoiled, dismounted, and hurriedly deployed skirmishers. Fielder Jones sent the 8th Indiana galloping up to reinforce them, and for the next hour, a fierce, noisy fight raged at point-blank range. "It was very dark," complained Williamson Ward, "and we could only see the flash of their guns."

Dudley Jones was injured when his horse fell on him, and his outnumbered Texans slowly began retreating down a road leading northward to Wolf Creek. Confused accounts of the fighting soon reached Brigadier General Lawrence Sullivan Ross's headquarters just north of the creek, at Sewell's house.[1]

A tall, soft-spoken Texan sporting a thick black mustache and a short goatee, the twenty-five-year-old Ross sweated with a "hot fever" and shook with chills almost every three days. He was probably suffering from tertiary malaria but resolutely stayed in the field. On the night of August 18, his 400 Texans were all that stood between 4,000 Yankee cavalrymen and the vital railroads south of Atlanta.[2]

"The enemy is advancing on [the] Sandtown and Fairburn road in force," he wrote to "Red" Jackson at 1:30 A.M. "Scouts from their flanks and rear report at least a brigade of cavalry, followed closely by infantry. My pickets are now fighting them between Bethel and Enon Church."

Ross soon discovered his outnumbered Texans were rapidly retiring eastward and at 2:00 A.M., he advised Jackson:

> I am convinced the enemy I have been fighting is Kilpatrick's division on a raid. It has passed our flank and gone on in the direction of Fairburn. Scouts from their rear now report the column two miles and a half long and all cavalry. I have sent the Third Texas across to get in their front, and will move on after with the rest of my command at once. We had a severe skirmish with the enemy's advance and have lost several men.[3]

The fight for possession of the Sandtown and Fairburn Road also cost Fielder Jones's brigade at least a half dozen casualties before the Texans withdrew. Leaving

In his youth, Confederate Brigadier General Lawrence Sullivan Ross once rode 700 miles on a mule to attend Florence Wesleyan University. He spent his college vacations fighting Comanches. A wiry, soft-spoken man, he later became governor of Texas and president of Texas A&M. Used by permission of the Texas Collection, Baylor University, Waco, Texas.

the 10th Ohio to hold the road open, the 8th Indiana fell back, mounted their horses, and waited while the 92nd Illinois and Robert King's 3rd Brigade led the rest of the column past.[4]

Bob Minty's two brigades followed King. Unlike Kilpatrick's men, this was their second night in the saddle and it showed. "Discussions on the general conduct of the war and upon the probable object of our present movement ended early that evening," noted Lieutenant George Robinson of the Board of Trade Battery, "and for several hours afterward you might have ridden up and down the column (of the battery at least) and not found a half-dozen men, aside from the drivers of the wheel teams, but what were soundly asleep, and up and down the column of the second division, as far as we could hear, the clicking of the sabre-scabbards against the stirrup, the jingle of the flying ends of the traces of the artillery harness, the dull rattle of the wheels of the gun carriages and limbers, and the low pattering of the horses' hoofs on the hard dirt road, were the only sounds to break the otherwise almost breathless silence. A human voice was seldom heard along this part of the column, except when semi-occasionally, a man would, by the miss-step or sudden lurch of his horse, become half aroused, when you would hear him yawn and utter the self-addressed expression: 'My God, how sleepy I am.'"

Gunfire occasionally echoed somewhere up ahead, compelling whole companies to dismount and scout the woods on both sides of the road. "The entire night," Bob Minty noted impatiently, "was passed in that most tiresome of all experiences to an active soldier—halt, dismount, wait, mount, advance a few hundred yards, halt, dismount, wait, and so on."[5]

Despite these frequent halts, Lieutenant William W. Webb of the 4th Regulars complained companies at the rear of the column were kept at a trot for much of the night, "and often would have to close up at a gallop, as no falling back or intervals between the different regiments or brigades were allowed."

About 3:00 A.M., Kilpatrick's advance guard, the 92nd Illinois, reached the Atlanta & West Point Railroad three miles north of Fairburn. While most of the men dismounted to cut the telegraph wire and begin tearing up track, one of the raiders playfully pulled out a letter he had taken from a dead Rebel and read to his comrades, "The Yankees are encamped not far from here. We are liable to have a fight at any moment. I may never see you again. I commend you, my dear wife, and our little ones, to heaven's protection." The page was stained with blood and the Yankee trooper's eyes clouded with tears before he could finish.[6]

In the meantime, work details had lined up along one side of the railroad. Standing "as thick as they could stand," the men laid hold of the near rail and ties and heaved the track on its side. Then they began prying off crossties and wrenching the rails loose. Heaping the ties into piles, they had several fires blazing up and down the track when bugles sounded "To Horse."

"This is not the road we are after," Kilpatrick shouted as he rode up; "we want the one that runs southward from Atlanta."[7]

A large part of Robert King's 3rd Brigade had congregated about a quarter mile east of the railroad. Kilpatrick waited impatiently for them to get moving again and sent orders summoning Bob Minty to the front. Daylight was spilling over the horizon, veiled with silvered patches of fog that hugged the hills and hollows, when he saw the bearded Minty and his staff approaching.

"Here are men coming who will not be delayed by trifles," Kilpatrick said crossly to Eli Murray. "Colonel Minty," he ordered, "you will take the advance; push forward to Jonesboro as rapidly as possible; let nothing delay you; we should be there now."[8]

As he spoke, King's 3rd Brigade was already moving down the east side of the railroad. Led by the 92nd Illinois, they rode about two miles before turning left at Fremont's Corners on the Fairburn and Jonesboro Road. Eli Long's 2nd Brigade followed, and as his column crossed the railroad, Long halted his rear guard, the 1st Ohio, with orders to dismount and tear up more track.

The command echoed down the length of the regiment and the number one, two, and three troopers in each rank swung down from their saddles. The number threes handed their reins to the number fours, who remained mounted. The number twos tied their reins to number threes' bits, and number ones tied theirs to number twos' reins. Then the dismounted men lined up alongside the track and went to work.

They had wrecked about a half mile of rails and ties by the time the Board of Trade Battery rolled up to the crossing. "I shall never forget how the road looked when we came up to it," recalled a drowsy Private John Nourse, ". . . the fire was in a 'cut' and the banks of red clay, it looked in the gray of morning like a very fiery furnace."

One section of the battery had crossed the track when a 12-pounder shell hurtled overhead, crashed through the trees on their right, and ploughed into the ground. A second shell struck even closer. Jolted awake, John Nourse urged the tired team pulling his gun over the crossing at a trot, just as a third shell burst directly in front of him, sending searing slivers of hot metal slicing in every direction.

Kilpatrick was at least a mile away, sitting on the fence in front of a log house, questioning a woman about roads, when he heard the distant report of the cannon's roar. "That means fight," he said, turning to Major Albert Woodcock of the 92nd Illinois. "Move your men rapidly to the rear and assist in the engagement."[9]

By this time, the rear of the straggling Yankee column was in shambles. The 1st Ohio had just uprighted another 150-yard section of track when the first shell struck. They promptly let go. Eli Long came galloping back, yelling orders for the regiment to mount up. Springing into the saddle, they swung into line alongside the 4th Ohio just as the Board of Trade Battery came rattling down the road and unlimbered on a little knoll to their right.

Captain James McIntyre's 4th Regulars followed the battery, dodging a few Rebel shells as they crossed the railroad. The next regiment, the 7th Pennsylvania, was halfway across when the woods on their left erupted with gunfire.

It was Ross's 3rd Texas, supported by Lieutenant George B. Young and a 12-pound howitzer from the Columbus Light Artillery. Moving eastward from Wolf Creek on whatever roads they could find, they had paralleled Kilpatrick's column so closely, noted Lieutenant Sam Barron, "that we could distinctly hear the clatter of their horses' hoofs, the rumbling of their artillery, and the familiar rattle of sabers and canteens." Upon reaching the West Point railroad, Lieutenant Young had sited his gun on a commanding ridge, while the Texans dismounted and crept through the woods under the cover of the heavy morning mist. Closing to within 200 yards of the Sandtown and Fairburn Road, they opened fire.[10]

The volley caught Companies G and M of the 7th Pennsylvania squarely in the left flank. Wounded horses screamed and stampeded through the ranks, throwing the column into confusion. Bugler Orin F. Wilson doubled over in agony with a bullet in his belly, but somehow stayed in the saddle as his regiment ran the gauntlet.

The 7th Pennsylvania's commanding officer, Major William Jennings, reined up about 300 yards past the railroad and ordered Company E to dismount. While they about-faced to deploy as skirmishers, Jennings formed his 1st and 2nd battalions into line behind them to hold the road open for the 3rd battalion. But the 3rd battalion was nowhere in sight. The Rebel volley had cut the Yankee column cleanly in two.

Minty's ambulance train, pack mules, and led horses were following just behind the 7th Pennsylvania when the shooting started. "They of course skedaddled," acknowledged Captain Robert Burns, "each nigger and ambulance driver bolted for the woods. Several shells exploded among the colored brethren and they thought the kingdom had come."

Major Frank Mix, commanding the 4th Michigan, heard the noisy crackle of gunfire punctuated by point-blank blasts of artillery and saw the ambulance drivers frantically laying the lash to their teams. He followed with his regiment, but instead of crossing the railroad, the ambulances suddenly veered to the right and careened down a narrow bridle path. Mix spurred after them.

On the other side of the track, Eli Long had just started the 1st and 4th Ohio across a gullied field when Kilpatrick came dashing down the line with his staff and directed him to move forward at a gallop. "For a moment each of the staff officers and orderlies seemed possessed of a devil bent on making him break his neck," noted Private Lucien Wulsin as he watched them hurry over the ruts and washes to deliver the urgent command. The blue ranks surged ahead and Kilpatrick led the way, effortlessly leaping his spotted horse over an intervening ditch. A few troopers who tried to follow his example ingloriously thudded to the ground when their horses failed to make the jump, but within five minutes the two Ohio regiments had reached the edge of the woods, a half mile away, and dismounted to fight on foot.

The resulting Union line resembled a large, disjointed "V" with wings on either side of the railroad. As the two wings began to converge, the 10th Wisconsin Battery unlimbered and, together with at least one section of the Chicago Board of Trade Battery, started shelling the woods above the railroad crossing. "All the while," observed Captain John P. Rea of the 1st Ohio, "the enemy were firing in a more or less desultory way upon the entire command; scattered parties stealing up under cover[,] firing and running away."

Fielder Jones and his 2nd Brigade were still on the west side of the track, bringing up the rear of the column. Hearing the shooting, Jones immediately sent Captain Horace S. Foote ahead with Companies A and B of the 8th Indiana to reconnoiter, but a Rebel volley raked them before they could reach the railroad. Both companies hastily dismounted and formed a skirmish line in the woods north of the Sandtown and Fairburn Road. As their Spencers spat out a rapid fusillade, the rest of the regiment came up on foot and went into line with orders to pivot to the right and take the Rebels in flank. The Hoosiers advanced 500 yards and had been fighting for about a half hour when Jones realized the regiment on his right, Frank Mix's 4th Michigan, had disappeared.

Mix had found the stampeded ambulances bunched up at the end of the bridle path. While they were being turned around, he had Captain L. Briggs Eldridge's 3rd battalion dismount and deploy on the left side of the path, facing the Sandtown and Fairburn Road. About the same time, Major James F. Andress came up with the missing 3rd battalion of the 7th Pennsylvania. As the senior officer present, Mix assumed command and put the Pennsylvanians into line on Eldridge's right. Bullets began clipping the branches overhead as Ross's Texans pushed across the main road. Mix ordered both battalions to advance as skirmishers and drive them back.

Captain Eldridge's battalion forged through the woods "in fine style," suffering several casualties, but Major Andress seemed more concerned about rejoining his regiment than retaking the road. Without bothering to tell Mix, he led his men across the railroad, exposing the Michigan battalion's right flank. When Mix learned this, he immediately directed Captain John C. Hathaway's 1st battalion of the 4th Michigan to dismount and move up to support Eldridge. Before Hathaway could get into position, Captain Eldridge sent word he had reached the road.

Mix ordered his regiment to mount and sent his adjutant, Lieutenant Julian G. Dickerson, to have the ambulances fall in between the 1st and 2nd battalions. The lieutenant soon returned. Some of the ambulances had been wrecked, he reported, and no one was around to take charge of the others. Mix decided there was no time to wait. Forward by fours, he ordered, at a gallop!

As the blue ranks roweled forward, Sergeant Reuben A. Ray of Company M hurriedly unhitched the team from an overturned ambulance and urged them ahead of his horse. Up the path and over the brow of a hill, the Michigan regiment then turned to the right and spurred across the railroad.

This left Fielder Jones in a dilemma. Realizing his command had been cut off from the main column, he had two choices: charge through the Rebel lines or go back to Sandtown. Jones resolved to press ahead. He hastily recalled the 8th Indiana with orders to mount up and hurry after the 4th Michigan. Just as his front fours emerged from the woods and turned into the road, they came under a heavy fire. Captain Justice G. Crowell immediately wheeled Company C into line to cover the left flank while the 8th Indiana, 2nd Kentucky, and 10th Ohio galloped past.

By this time, Major Jennings and the 7th Pennsylvania had received orders to close up on the head of the column. As they fell back to Fremont's Corners, two miles south of the railroad crossing, Major Andress's wayward battalion rejoined them. The Pennsylvania boys had halted to build barricades when Frank Mix's 4th Michigan came pounding down the road and wheeled into line beside them. While both regiments piled up fence rails, Mix sent Lieutenant Jacob Bedtelyon and Company K of the 4th Michigan galloping back to the crossing to find the missing pack mules and ambulances.

"If there is any fun in such a place," noted John Nourse of the Board of Trade Battery, "we had it now. The ambulances came up two abreast, horses on the run. Two of the ambulance drivers thought to dodge some of the shot and shell by leaving the road and taking to the brush. They got through: that is the horses and the running gear did; the tops and all the contents of the wagons were left in the brush. And now come the pack mules. Sometimes two files; sometimes as many as four files; and occasionally one file: and every mule on the jump and braying in terror; camp kettles and pans rattling, drivers cracking their whips and swearing at the top of their voices: occasionally a rebel shell bursts near the road and the bullets keep [up] a continuous zip, zip."[11]

Lieutenant Bedtelyon brought back three of Minty's ambulances, but panic-striken drivers had wrecked three others, with heartrending results. When Orin Wilson, the fair-haired bugler shot in the stomach during the first flare of fighting, asked his comrades to take him off his horse and put him on a litter, the ambulance sergeant refused to receive him. He had orders to accept only those who were likely to recover, the sergeant said, and this man "will die inside of a few hours."

"Then will you leave me to die in the hands of the enemy?" Wilson implored. Three of his comrades carried him into Shadnor Church, a little white building by the roadside, and gently laid him on a plain wooden bench near the door. "Please," Wilson begged as his friends turned to leave, "write to my mother, and tell her all about it."[12]

As the firing fitfully sputtered to a close, Minty ordered Eli Long's 2nd Brigade back into the saddle and withdrew his artillery. His 1st Brigade followed, led by the 2nd battalion of the 7th Pennsylvania, while Major Jennings and his other two battalions brought up the rear.

Robert King's 3rd Brigade waited until the entire command had passed before falling in behind Fielder Jones's 10th Ohio. Wary of another ambush, King deployed the 92nd Illinois as flankers on the left side of his column, where they marched single file, four or five rods apart, stumbling over logs, scrambling over ditches, and toiling through the dense underbrush.

Having delayed the raiders for the better part of two hours, Sul Ross also withdrew. "I am again moving on the flank of the enemy on [the] Fairburn and Jonesborough road," the tall, wiry Texan advised "Red" Jackson at 9:00 A.M. He accurately reported the Yankee column had divided, the greatest number going east, toward Jonesboro, while a smaller force (Klein's) was heading for Fayetteville. "Some companies of my command have only a few rounds left," he added. "Cannot you hurry forward to me a wagon lightly loaded with ammunition?"[13]

His quarry was rapidly moving away, trying to make up for lost time. Jangling past Robert King's brigade at a trot, Eli Long's Ohio boys took their place at the head of the column as Kilpatrick had previously ordered. The advance guard had gone about a half mile when some of Sul Ross's Texans suddenly opened fire from behind a barricade of felled trees and fence rails. The tangled woods on either side of the road were too thick for horsemen to maneuver, and when Minty came up he ordered Long to send his leading regiment forward on foot. Dismounting and handing their reins to the number fours, the 3rd Ohio formed a line and advanced at a double-quick. There was a crackling flurry of gunfire as they shouldered the Texans aside, then the regiment remounted and moved forward another half mile. Cresting a hill and looking across an intervening swale, they saw an even more imposing barricade crowning the next ridge. This time the Texans had artillery in place and thunderous blasts shook the woods as a couple of shells hurtled overhead.

Once again the 3rd Ohio dismounted and went into line. One section of the Board of Trade Battery hastily unlimbered in the road behind them, the other in a field a few yards to the left. As they roared in reply to the Rebels, Minty directed Long to have his number fours lead the horses off the road while the 4th and 1st Ohio, remaining mounted, quickly moved up on either side of the 3rd Ohio. The outnumbered Texans retreated before this show of force, only to pitch into the Yankees again at Bucks Crossroads.

"Delay . . . was their great object," asserted Captain John Rea of the 1st Ohio. "On one occasion from a wood perhaps two hundred yards from the narrow sunken road on which we were marching, and right opposite my squadron there was a volley fired direct into our flank, it luckily passed over our heads, wounding, as I remember, one horse. I immediately had the fence thrown down and clambering up the abrupt road side, made for the wood at a gallop only to find that the Rebs had gone."

After two or three such encounters, Minty finally ordered Long to have the 3rd Ohio dismount and press ahead on foot while the number fours followed close behind with the led horses. "The advance would often be briskly engaged with the enemy," noted Lieutenant William Webb of the 4th Regulars, "but owing to the length of the column, those in the rear would know nothing of it—only conjecture, by the halts and hitches, that there was trouble at the front; then, the obstruction being overcome, we would see the files in front light out at a trot or gallop to close up, following in the movement by all, on to the rear, until close order was again resumed."

The 3rd Ohio had driven the Texans from four good positions by the time Long's brigade halted at noon, just beyond Camp Creek, to rest near Martha H. McLeroy's house. Wiping the sweat from their brows, hot, thirsty troopers took long pulls on their canteens and dug into their haversacks for something to eat. They were sprawled in the shade, gnawing on pieces of raw bacon and hardtack, when Ross's ubiquitous Texans charged again.

Seeing his advance guard being driven back before the reserves could mount, Long ordered his whole brigade forward on foot. Part of the 1st Ohio deployed on the right side of the road, where they passed through a watermelon patch. "It was amusing to see the boys grab for the melons; regardless of the balls that were knocking up the dust on all sides," chuckled Lieutenant Will Curry. "As it was very hot and the men were almost famished after the long run, the melons were very refreshing after the rebel rear guard was routed."[14]

A mile beyond Camp Creek, Minty left his own rear guard, Major Jennings's 1st and 3rd battalions of the 7th Pennsylvania, to picket the intersection of the Jonesboro and Fayetteville roads and keep the crossroads open until the entire command had passed. At the head of the column, Eli Long sent the 4th Ohio to relieve the 3rd Ohio, deploying Companies G and H in a strong skirmish line covering the front and both flanks. Advancing on foot, these two companies steadily drove the Rebels back. "Occasionally the firing of the skirmishers became quite lively," noted Private Lucien Wulsin of the 4th Ohio; "the rebel bullets in return mowed and sang over the column at a lively rate. Sometimes the rebels would raise a yell, to which our skirmishers would respond with voice and carbine, then we in the column would take it up, being encouraged thereto by Colonel Minty, who with some of Kilpatrick's staff, was directly in our rear and would say whenever we yelled: 'That's right, boys; keep it up. Show them you're coming.'"

Companies E and M of the 4th Ohio had moved forward to relieve Companies G and H by the time Minty's skirmish line crested the top of a low, wooded ridge at 2:00 P.M. Looking to the east, they could see the church spires at Jonesboro poking above the pines, a mile and a half away. Before them, the road descended into a cornfield and across the Flint River, a deep, narrow, high-banked stream, where the Rebels were hard at work, tearing the floor out of the bridge.

"Charge, charge. Let's charge," the Ohio troopers urged their officers. As Lieutenant Colonel Oliver Robie swung the rest of his regiment into line, Private Peter Diebold fell with a Rebel bullet through his leg. Forward, Robie ordered. Clambering over a rail fence, his men dashed across the cornfield and down to the river's edge, yelling at the top of their lungs. The Rebels answered with a rattling volley and scampered across the ruined bridge. Ross's artillery boomed from the east bank to cover the retreat, the bursting shells showering Bob Minty and some officers watching from the top of the ridge with dirt and tree bark and creating a commotion among the led horses.

The 4th Ohio dived for cover behind a fence on the right side of the road. As they began trading shots with Rebel sharpshooters crouched in rifle pits honeycombing the opposite bank, the 3rd Ohio came legging across the cornfield and tumbled into a ravine on the left.

On the ridge behind them, Lieutenant Robinson unlimbered the leading section of the Board of Trade Battery in the road and opened fire. While these two guns swept the approaches to the bridge, Minty ordered the rest of his command to dismount. Leaving the 2nd battalion of the 7th Pennsylvania to guard the horses, he hurried the 1st Ohio, 4th Regulars, and 4th Michigan through the woods on either side of the road. As they lined up to support the 3rd and 4th Ohio, Lieutenant Henry Bennett's section of the Board of Trade Battery wheeled into position on some high ground to the left of the road and began hurling shells across the river. "The very first shot struck a rebel artilleryman," noted Captain Robert Burns, "burst in him, and blew him to atoms."[15]

For the next fifteen minutes there raged what Ohio Captain John Rea called "as pretty a little artillery duel as I ever witnessed." Bennett's section soon forced the Rebel gunners to withdraw, enabling Lieutenant Robinson to move the two guns he had unlimbered in the road and redeploy on Bennett's left. Kilpatrick also ordered Captain Beebe's 10th Wisconsin Battery into line and with a noise like a thunderclap, all eight guns let loose.

Firing by volleys over the heads of Minty's skirmishers, the two batteries pounded the Rebel rifle pits. After four salvoes, the guns fell silent. As the last rolling echoes faded away, the 3rd and 4th Ohio sprang to their feet with a ringing cheer and rushed to the riverbank. After pausing long enough to aim two or three volleys, they sprinted for the bridge, closely followed by a second line composed of the 1st Ohio and 4th Regulars.

Company L of the 4th Ohio got to the span first and nimbly negotiated the bare stringers. Some 3rd Ohio troopers were clambering across when Kilpatrick rode up, shouting orders for them to retrieve the flooring planks still floating in the water. The Ohio boys ignored him and hurried after their comrades.

"Damn you go on," Kilpatrick yelled, "the 3d Ohio had rather fight than to build bridges, anyway."[16]

One red-faced cavalryman collapsed with sunstroke. The others raced on, panting and puffing, for about three-quarters of a mile before their officers ordered a halt. "We were completely tired out," confessed a winded trooper. "We had marched five miles on foot and charged three times, with the heat 112 degrees in the shade."[17]

While Companies K, L, and M of the 4th Ohio deployed as skirmishers on the left-hand side of the road, twenty other companies formed a line in the woods on the right and waited for the rest of the column to come up. Kilpatrick personally supervised repairs to the bridge and once enough planks and rails had been relaid, he ordered Minty to bring up the balance of his command and drive the Rebels out of Jonesboro. The 4th Michigan, 4th Regulars, and the 1st Ohio began crossing on foot and, at the suggestion of Lieutenant Robinson, gunners wheeled a section of the Board of Trade Battery across by hand.

Fanning out on either side of the road, Captain William Van Antwerp's 2nd battalion of the 4th Michigan relieved the exhausted Ohio troopers on the skirmish line. The rest of the regiment deployed in close support, and the 4th Regulars and 1st Ohio assembled a second line a few paces to the rear. While the 3rd and 4th Ohio reformed in the road to follow the front ranks in a dismounted column of fours, Lieutenant Robinson's sweating artillerymen dragged their two guns right up on the skirmish line. At 4:30 P.M., Minty ordered them forward.[18]

Resistance was light. The Rebel artillery had disappeared and within half an hour Minty's skirmishers were approaching the outskirts of Jonesboro. Sweeping across the town common, they saw Sul Ross's Texans manning a hastily constructed barricade of cotton bales and fence rails extending northeast to southwest, from the iron water tank near the Macon railroad, across the front of the depot and past several nearby warehouses. A sheet of flame blazed near the water tank. Private Oliver Warner of the 4th Michigan staggered and fell dead. His comrades answered with a hail of lead from their Spencers and Lieutenant Robinson's men wheeled one of their 10-pounder Parrotts into position. The big gun boomed, putting a shell through the bottom half of the water tank. Water gushed from the gaping hole, flushing out the nearby defenders.

Robinson then turned his attention to some Rebels firing from the freight depot and ordered one of his gun crews to load a shell with a short fuse. An instant later the cannon recoiled with a roar. The shell struck the building just below the eaves and exploded inside. A vented cupola in the center of the roof leaped ten or fifteen feet into the air and hung there for a moment before crashing back down and tumbling to the ground. Robinson's gunners put two more shells into the building, one of which struck an iron safe, filling the air with a blizzard of railway tickets marked "Jonesboro to Atlanta" and "Jonesboro to Macon."

Five minutes later, Minty's skirmishers were standing on the Macon railroad. Captain Van Antwerp was the first to set foot on the track and he immediately put his battalion to work tearing up the rails. Then he noticed some Rebel officers racing back and forth, rallying Ross's Texans on some higher ground a quarter mile south of the depot.

Minty's thin blue ranks hastily reformed and surged forward to meet them. Keeping pace with the skirmishers, Lieutenant Robinson's artillerymen dragged their two guns past the depot, halting to hurl a few shells down the length of the main street paralleling the west side of the railroad. At the same time, Lieutenant Bennett's section dashed up, unlimbered a short distance to the right and rear, and opened an oblique fire on Ross's left.

The center of the Rebel line soon broke under the weight of this barrage and fled in disorder. Turning to Minty, who was standing nearby, Lieutenant Robinson said he could put his section on the rise the Rebels had just abandoned if the skirmish line would support him.

"Go ahead," Minty replied, "the [F]ourth Michigan will be with you in a moment."[19]

Robinson ordered his limbers up from the rear. At the command to fix prolonges, his cannoneers uncoiled the tow ropes attached to each gun, secured them to the limbers, and then clung to the limber chests and trail pieces as Robinson led them down the street at a rattling gallop. Wheeling into battery on the crest of the disputed ground, the section opened fire on the retreating Rebels.

A single shell killed Captain A. R. Wells of the 9th Texas Cavalry, a citizen named William Christian, and two horses. Taking refuge in some buildings on Robinson's right, Texas troopers began firing at the Yankee gunners from windows and doorways.

Shell them, Minty ordered Robinson. A blast from one of his big black guns chased the Texans away from a white frame house, except for a seemingly unconcerned fellow, who calmly sat on the porch with his chair tilted back and his legs crossed. When several more shots failed to dislodge him, Robinson dismounted, vowing to make him move. Ordering a shell loaded, he personally aimed the sights and yanked the lanyard. The gun recoiled with a roar and the shell struck home, bursting with a puff of white smoke. When the smoke cleared, the "Johnny" was nowhere in sight.

On the right side of the line, Captain John Rea of the 1st Ohio watched as Lieutenant Bennett put two shells into a frame house sheltering some Rebel sharp-shooters. "I was within ten feet of him and had misgivings at the time," Rea later wrote. "I thought of women and children but I afterwards concluded that he was right, war is cruelty."[20]

The mayor of Jonesboro and several frightened civilians soon appeared in the main street, waving a white flag. The Yankee gunners ceased fire and not long afterward Kilpatrick rode up to the skirmish line.

"General," Minty reported with a salute, "in obedience to your orders, I have taken possession of Jonesboro."

"You have done nobly," Kilpatrick replied, grasping him by the hand and pumping it firmly. The bridge across the Flint River had been repaired, he added; the number fours were bringing across the led horses. In the meantime, there was work to be done and he directed Minty to post his pickets and begin tearing up the railroad.[21]

Any attack would most likely come from Atlanta, and Minty deployed a heavy skirmish line facing northward. The 4th Ohio settled in next to the freight depot, covering the northeast section of town. While detachments from other regiments picketed the roads radiating to the east, west, and south, Minty sent Captain James McIntyre's 4th U.S. Cavalry to burn the depot and begin destroying the railroad. Setting their Spencers aside, the Regulars lined up along the track and laid hold of the rail.

"Now, then, men," an officer commanded, "altogether! Heave ho!" A long section of track slowly rose upright and then turned bottom up. There were wild, exultant cheers, then soldiers with crowbars and sledge hammers began prying the ties loose, piling them up, and laying the rails on top. Bonfires began to blaze and crackle. A plume of smoke spiraled from the hole in the depot roof where the cupola had been. Flames appeared, rapidly engulfing the whole building, as well as a large stone warehouse filled with cotton and three railroad cars loaded with leather and furniture.

As the Regulars bent to their work, Kilpatrick sat astride his dappled Arabian, Spot, and watched, surrounded by his staff. "Damn the Southern Confederacy," he yelled, standing in his stirrups and swinging his hat over his head; "I can ride right through it!"

Lieutenant Joseph Hedges of the 4th Cavalry was more circumspect. "We may sing a different tune to-morrow," he said.

"What's that, my man?" Kilpatrick asked.

"I was merely remarking," Hedges replied, "that when infantry begins to come down from Atlanta we will not have it all our own way."

"Oh," Kilpatrick said blithely, "we will not fight their infantry—we will run away from it; but we can lick hell out of their cavalry. Don't you see?"[22]

As the dusky twilight faded into dark, lurid tongues of flame leaped into the sky above Jonesboro. Troopers not assigned to wrecking the railroad moved down the main street, looting and torching the courthouse, the jail, the provost marshal's office, and two tax-in-kind warehouses.

"A brisk wind sprung up," recounted a Union officer, "and very soon the flames spread to stores and other buildings, and over two-thirds of the town was burned to the ground, together with considerable public property and effects of the citizens."[23]

The fires destroyed a smithy, D. H. Rea's harness shop, and L. C. Hutcheson's blacksmith shop. The vacant residence of Captain William B. Elliott and the home of Mrs. Elijah Rountree Hanes also went up in flames.

"We set fire . . . to *one house*," admitted John Nourse, "because the owner cut the well rope and dropped both bucket and rope down the well. He ought to have been shot."[24]

Other thirsty troopers broke into James H. Morrow's grocery and helped themselves to an ample supply of whisky. Then they knocked the heads off the barrels and dumped the remaining liquor into the street. Vandals twice set the building ablaze; each time better men put the flames out.

"My smokehouse was broken open and robbed of every piece of meat I had," complained Guy L. Warren, an agent for the Macon & Western Railroad. "My horse was stolen from the stable, and, as they entered my house, a Major rode up and ordered them out, thus saving it from pillage."[25]

Mattie Johnson Hanes was not so fortunate. Thieving Yankees brutally ransacked her house, stole all her bacon, meal, syrup, and sugar, broke open her trunks, and shredded her clothes and dresses. A 4th Michigan trooper also snatched the silken battle flag her sister, Mary Frances Johnson, had presented to the Benjamin Infantry, Company E of the 10th Georgia Regiment, at the outset of the war. Mattie's husband, Lieutenant Joshua J. Hanes, had brought it home from Virginia the previous summer for safekeeping. A variation of the first Confederate colors, with three broad horizontal bars of red, white, and red and a circle of eight 5-pointed stars centered in a rectangular blue canton, the flag bore a scrolled legend painted in gold letters, enjoining its defenders to "Strike for Your Altars and Your Firesides."[26]

Kilpatrick's men also looted the hotel, James B. Key's house, and several others, breaking up crockery and taking all the knives and forks and provisions they could find. While this "contemptible plundering of ladies' trunks and wardrobes" outraged civilians, one of them acknowledged that, overall, the Yankees' conduct was "not so reprehensible as on several other occasions that have fallen under my observation."[27]

Thomas Byrne was cowering in the back of his store when an unruly crowd of cavalrymen began pounding on the front door about 7:00 P.M., loudly demanding to be let in. Before Byrne could get the door unlocked, it splintered under the heavy blows of an ax. A mob of Yankees and Negroes swarmed in, taking everything in sight, including thirty-three 100-pound boxes of chewing tobacco they found stacked under the counter. Byrne watched helplessly until a squad arrested him and marched the old Irishman to Kilpatrick's headquarters for questioning.[28]

Kilpatrick had already interrogated several other civilians, and by 6:00 P.M. he knew a Yankee column had cut the Macon railroad at Bear Creek Station that morning. This was obviously Klein's little brigade, but no one seemed to know where it had gone. These same civilians also intimated Frank Armstrong's Mississippi cavalry had passed through Jonesboro at 1:00 P.M., heading south. This was a force to be reckoned with if it came back, and when Fielder Jones rode into town at dark, Eli Murray met him with orders to move his brigade past Minty's work gangs and wait for instructions. Continuing down the main street, Jones halted his three regiments just south of Jonesboro and began building barricades.

The 92nd Illinois arrived next, scratched up and worn out after a long day of wading through briars and thickets, shielding the left flank of Robert King's brigade. Halting in the cornfield on the west side of the Flint River, they fed their horses while King sent Captain John M. Schermerhorn with Companies A, G, H, and I and a detachment of the 3rd Kentucky to examine Harris' Bridge, about three miles downstream. After trading shots with a few Rebels, Schermerhorn returned and reported both the bridge and an adjacent ford were impassable.

The rest of the 92nd Illinois led King's column into Jonesboro at 8:00 P.M. "The torch had been applied to the depot, and all public buildings," noted one of the mounted infantrymen, "and very soon the little town was a sea of fire, and the heavens lurid with the flames of the burning buildings. No time to wait—no time to eat—no time to rest—the whole command fell to work."[29]

Leaving King's brigade to continue tearing up track, Minty's 4th Regulars and 4th Michigan mounted and moved into a field on the north side of town. Joined by the 7th

Pennsylvania, which had been left to picket the intersection of the Jonesboro and Fayetteville roads until the rest of the column passed, they unsaddled and fed their horses in the glare of the burning buildings and then began putting up barricades along the crest of a ridge running at right angles to the railroad.

Eli Long's Ohio regiments also went into camp, on the east side of the track. The air reeked with smoke and whisky, and the 92nd Illinois band formed in the firelight and began playing "Yankee Doodle," "Hail Columbia," "The Star Spangled Banner," and "Come Johnny Fill Up the Bowl."

"The effect of this upon us can better be imagined than described—," recounted a weary Lucien Wulsin of the 4th Ohio, "it was meat, drink and rest; all fatigue was forgotten. Some of the boys jumped up, threw their hats in the air and danced like wild men, while the cheers of the other regiments in town were responded to till we were all hoarse with shouting. It would have been a splendid scene for an artist—the black sky for a background, the huge fires, the mounted band playing and the groups of men mounted and dismounted, in front, forming such a scene as is rarely seen."

While his comrades marveled at the awesome spectacle, Private Christopher Slaven of the 3rd Ohio seemed restless, withdrawn, ill at ease. Sergeant John Anderson told him to lie down and get some sleep.

"I can't," Slaven said; "we are in a much tighter place than our officers think; some of us will never get out of this place alive, and I am one of them."[30]

Minty's troopers were still building barricades when Kilpatrick sent word at 10:00 P.M. that the 3rd Division had destroyed about two miles of track and was preparing to move farther south. He wanted Minty's men to fall back along the railroad and take up a new position to cover them.

Fielder Jones had already received orders to move his 2nd Brigade ahead of the work details to clear the front and flanks. Wearily climbing back into the saddle, Tom Sanderson's 10th Ohio led Jones's column down the Griffin Road. They had gone about a quarter mile when a crashing volley blazed from the dark woods.

After his brief encounter with Klein's cavalry that afternoon, Confederate General Dan Reynolds had put his men back on the cars and moved down to the break in the track at Bear Creek Station. "Red" Jackson overtook him there with orders to hurry back to Jonesboro and help Sul Ross's hard-pressed Texans. Setting the train in reverse, Reynolds arrived about three miles south of Jonesboro at dark and saw the huge fireball illuminating the night sky. He proceeded cautiously for another mile and a half before ordering his brigade off the cars and sending Captain A. F. Aydolett and three companies of the 48th Tennessee Infantry forward as skirmishers. Aydolett halted some 600 yards south of town, while Reynolds formed his main line another 200 yards to the rear, the right flank resting on the railroad, the left stretching across the Griffin Road. His Arkansas regiments had just started relieving Captain Aydolett's skirmishers when the 10th Ohio came trooping down the road. Men who had soldiered at Shiloh, Stone's River, Chickamauga, Peachtree Creek, and Ezra Church leveled their Enfield rifles at the shadowy figures silhouetted against the blazing sky and opened fire.[31]

The withering blast felled men and horses, stopping the 10th Ohio in its tracks. Hearing the firing, Fielder Jones hurried the 2nd Kentucky and then the 8th Indiana forward at a gallop. Reaching the head of the stalled column, he ordered both regiments to dismount and build barricades on the left, while the 10th Ohio remained on horseback in the road to their right.

Robert King's 3rd Kentucky soon came up and dismounted on Jones's left. The 92nd Illinois, having stripped off their short woolen jackets for hot work on the railroad, came double-quicking out of the dark in their shirtsleeves and lay down behind Jones's line, while the 5th Kentucky moved to support his right.

At the same time, Bob Minty's 4th Michigan, 4th Regulars, and 7th Pennsylvania abandoned their unfinished barricades on the north side of town and moved about a mile down the railroad to guard Jones's left flank. Eli Long's Ohio brigade followed, extending Minty's line westward across the railroad.

"It was a wild night and a most graphic scene," recounted Lieutenant Will Curry. "The sky was lighted up with burning timbers, buildings and cotton bales; the continuous bang of carbines, the galloping of staff officers and orderlies up and down the streets carrying orders or dispatches, the terrified citizens peering out their windows, the constant marching of troops changing position . . . all made up a weird scene never to be forgotten. . . ."[32]

By 11:00 P.M., Kilpatrick had his entire force in line of battle. The full moon slid behind a thick bank of clouds. Lightning flickered overhead. Thunder rumbled and rain was pouring down when the 8th Indiana and 2nd Kentucky quietly got up and warily approached the unseen Rebel barricades, 250 yards away. They had gone about a hundred yards when the opposing skirmishers opened fire. Both regiments cheered lustily and charged, riddling the night with rapid volleys from their Spencers. Rushing blindly through the rain and darkness, they closed to within forty yards of the Rebel works, only to falter in the face of a heavy fire.

"We were now catching it from the front, also upon both flanks," noted the 8th Indiana's commanding officer, Major Thomas Herring. "The order was given to lie down."[33]

As the Hoosiers hugged the muddy ground, Kilpatrick brought the 92nd Illinois band right up behind his lines, among the guns of the Board of Trade Battery, and ordered them to play. Mounted on milk-white horses, the musicians raised their German silver instruments to their lips and launched into a rousing rendition of "Yankee Doodle," followed by "The Star Spangled Banner" and "Dixie."

"The effect was almost magical," declared Captain William Van Antwerp. "Cheer after cheer arose along the entire line."

"It was," added Captain Albert Potter, "as much as to say, come and take us if you *can*, but you *can't.*"

But the band and its white horses also made excellent targets, and Rebel bullets soon began droning past, sounding sour notes. Cannoneers caught in the line of fire became "quite indignant," according to John Nourse, "and used their ramrods to drive the band out of the battery."[34]

In the meantime, the 8th Indiana and 2nd Kentucky continued blazing away at the muzzle blasts of Rebel rifles, but with seemingly little effect. Corporal Ben Pontious of the 8th Indiana was killed and several others were wounded. After an hour, both regiments had nearly exhausted their ammunition. Ordered to fall back, they retired about fifty feet behind the barricade they had previously built and began refilling their cartridge boxes.

Major Albert Woodcock's 92nd Illinois moved forward to relieve them, stumbling over a dead cavalryman sprawled in the darkness. Ordered to lie down, the Illinois infantrymen watched as a sheet of flame erupted in front of them. They answered with a rattling reply from their Spencers, and both sides kept up a furious fusillade.

"I do not see how men can live any length of time under such fire," Lieutenant George R. Skinner, a brigade staff officer, remarked when he brought orders for Major Woodcock to withdraw.[35]

Woodcock's regiment quietly retired behind the fence rails the cavalry had piled up and waited as an uneasy calm settled over the battlefield. Some of the men were so weary they could scarcely keep their eyes open, and officers were kept busy, moving up and down the line, prodding them awake.

There were occasional bursts of firing. The gunshot that killed Illinois Private Alycrah W. Latham sounded so close his comrades at first thought he had accidentally shot himself. Then they discovered his Spencer was still loaded.[36]

As the rain continued to beat down, Kilpatrick convened a meeting of his officers on the veranda of a house in Jonesboro. He faced a dilemma. Wet ties would not burn. Cold rails would not bend. Rebel infantry blocked the road to the south and Sul Ross and Frank Armstrong were undoubtedly lurking close by.

Someone suggested if Kilpatrick simply abandoned the railroad and moved east to regain Sherman's lines, Rebel cavalry was sure to follow. On the other hand, if he flanked the force in front of him, he might be able to strike the railroad somewhere farther south, beyond the reach of the Rebel infantry. He could tear up more track, fight off any Rebel cavalry that tried to interfere, and then fall back.

The wail of locomotives could be plainly heard to the north. Fearing an attack from Atlanta, Kilpatrick decided to move south. He ordered Bob Minty to start his 1st Brigade and Lieutenant Robinson's section of the Board of Trade Battery east on the Stockbridge Road. Eli Murray would follow with both brigades of the 3rd Division, leaving Minty with Long's 2nd Brigade and Lieutenant Bennett's section of artillery to hold the Rebel infantry in check. The plan was quickly agreed upon, but nearly every officer in Minty's command took "quiet exception" to the idea of placing one of his brigades at the head of Kilpatrick's column and the other in the rear. They realized if there was any fighting to be done, they would have to do most of it.

Some of Minty's pickets and vedettes had scarcely gotten into position when the order came to fall back on the number fours. After a half hour's delay, the 4th Regulars mounted and began retiring down the rubble-strewn streets at 2:00 A.M. The 7th Pennsylvania followed, then the 4th Michigan. "The rain had now nearly ceased," Lieutenant Robinson noted as his two guns joined the column leaving on the Stockbridge Road, "the night was, however, very dark, the roads muddy and the low places full of water, but the march was kept up as rapidly as the conditions would admit. . . ."

Robert King's 3rd and 5th Kentucky moved out next. His other regiment, the 92nd Illinois, got orders about 3:00 A.M. to hold their position for another fifteen minutes. Then they crawled away from the barricades on their hands and knees until they were safely out of range. Lieutenant George Skinner was on his horse, waiting for the last two or three companies to mount, when a drunken trooper rode past, vowing to whip the entire Southern Confederacy. Skinner told him to get back to his unit, but the soldier said he was not going to take orders from any staff officer. He was going to fight, he brayed loudly, and he would just as soon start with the lieutenant. Hearing the commotion, Rebel riflemen sent a swarm of bullets whizzing overhead. Quiet down, Skinner warned, but in the ensuing exchange, the trooper swayed drunkenly in the saddle and fell. Skinner left him lying senseless in the mud and rode on.[37]

Fielder Jones's brigade soon followed the 92nd Illinois off the field, leaving Bob Minty to confront the Confederate infantry with Eli Long's three Ohio regiments and Lieutenant Bennett's two guns. Long's men were erecting a barricade on the south side of Jonesboro when officers double-quicked them back to the center of town to build another. They pulled down fences and outbuildings and had barely finished this second line when they were ordered back to complete the first one. The nearest supply of fence rails was some distance away and troopers made repeated trips, back and forth, before Minty finally gave the order to mount up at 4:00 A.M.

"Never did rails feel so heavy," complained Lucien Wulsin of the 4th Ohio. "We had now been out thirty-six hours without a halt, about twenty hours of which our regiment had been dismounted, marching, fighting and working. When, upon starting back toward our horses the order was given to double-quick some of us learned the meaning of 'giving out.' Fortunately our horses had been sent to meet us."

While waiting for Long's brigade to mount, Minty's adjutant, Captain Robert Burns, lay down on the rain-soaked ground. Like most of the men, he had been awake and in the saddle for the better part of seventy-two hours. Exhausted, he soon fell fast asleep. When he awoke, the first pink blush of dawn was beginning to color the eastern sky and the rear guard was quietly riding away. Scrambling to his feet, Burns mounted his horse and hurried after them.

The pursuit was not far behind. During the night, "Red" Jackson had positioned his largest brigade, Samuel Wragg Ferguson's, a mile and a half or two miles east of Jonesboro and Sul Ross's tired Texans to the west. His cavalry had the town surrounded, he assured Dan Reynolds. If the Yankees attempted to leave, his troopers would open fire. That would be the signal for Reynolds's infantry to advance.

All night long, Reynolds waited for the sound of the guns. A "reliable citizen" who lived near the Stockbridge Road subsequently reported some of Ferguson's men had come to his house and made his family put out the lights and keep quiet while the Yankees marched past "without interruption."

"If Gen. Ferguson had stationed his men along the ridge on which he was and thrown up temporary breastworks of rails, of which there were plenty, and made any fight at all," railroad agent Guy Warren concluded after hearing this story, "the enemy could not have passed him, and Gen. Jackson would have pressed them in the rear, and the whole force would have been captured there between two hills, for there was no path for them to get out at unless they cut roads through the thick woods."[38]

By all accounts (including his own), Sam Ferguson was the spoiled scion of a wealthy Charleston family. At West Point, he had amassed a huge number of demerits and a suspension had compelled him to repeat his second year before he finally graduated in 1857.

"Red" Jackson was an old classmate, but they had been at odds since May, when Jackson charged Ferguson's brigade had acted "disgracefully" at the battle of New Hope Church. Ferguson demanded an official investigation and sent Jackson a letter, calling him a liar. Jackson challenged him to a duel. He later conveyed his apologies and the matter was "honorably adjusted," but the truce did not last. By the time the army crossed the Chattahoochee, the bickering had become so bad Joe Johnston felt compelled to transfer Ferguson's brigade to Joe Wheeler's corps, despite Wheeler's strenuous objections. When Jackson ordered Ferguson to leave behind the battery attached to his brigade, Ferguson had disobeyed. Jackson had filed charges against him, charges which were still pending when Wheeler rode northward to cut Sherman's supply line, leaving a disgruntled Ferguson once again under Jackson's command.

"General Ferguson was insubordinate as a cadet, insubordinate as a lieutenant in the U.S. Army, and insubordinate as a brigadier under General Jackson," Joe Wheeler later wrote. Perhaps that was why 4,000 Yankee cavalrymen could march out of Jonesboro right under his nose.[39]

Dan Reynolds's infantry cautiously moved into town with Sul Ross's cavalry at daylight on August 20 and captured four or five stragglers, but it quickly became apparent the rest of the raiders were gone. Convinced Kilpatrick was trying to get back to the Union lines, Jackson sent Ross's Texans down the Stockbridge Road and dispatched orders for Ferguson to move his brigade up the railroad toward Rough and Ready in case the Yankees headed in that direction. He also directed Reynolds to march his infantry to the north side of Jonesboro to wait for a train to take them back to Atlanta.[40]

By that time, the head of Kilpatrick's column had already reached the little crossroads called Pittsburg, three and a half miles east of Jonesboro. Turning south, they were approaching Lee's Mill on Line Creek when the advance guard surprised a small Rebel wagon train that had fled Jonesboro the previous evening. Bluecoated troopers quickly made prisoners of sleepy teamsters and the captain in command, then continued up the road. As they approached Samuel Lee's house, they saw a uniformed figure standing in the road.

"Surrender, surrender, and hold up your arms," they demanded. The man slowly raised his hands and, with as much dignity as possible, identified himself as Major L. P. Thomas of the 42nd Georgia Infantry.

Thomas had come from Atlanta on a three-day pass to visit his wife, Jennie, and their two small children, who had fled their home in Lawrenceville for the supposed safety of her grandfather Lee's farm. As troopers took Thomas into custody, he asked one of them for permission to step to the rear of the house and say good-bye to his family. The guard shook his head sternly.

"You cannot refuse me this request," Thomas pleaded. "You can't make me believe that you would treat a prisoner that way. Only allow me to kiss my wife and little ones good-bye. Oh, no, you can't refuse to do that. You are too brave a soldier to do a thing of that kind."

The guard dropped his gaze to the ground, but said nothing. Thomas turned and let himself into the yard through a side gate, secretly palming a small Confederate bill and an old silver watch his father had given him. With his guard following close behind, he calmly walked to the back of the house, where he met his wife and tenderly kissed her good-bye, discreetly pressing the treasured heirloom and the almost worthless scrap of paper into her hand, which she hid in the billowing folds of her dress.

Under the watchful eyes of his guard, Thomas strode through the big front gate and into the road to join the other prisoners. "Major," the captain of the captured wagon train greeted him, "ain't we in a hell of a fix?"

Thomas agreed they were and asked if there was a horse he could ride. Told to help himself, he untied a likely looking mount and led it by the halter down the line of captured wagons. "Boys, loan me a bridle," he said loudly, looking first in one wagon and then another. After repeating this request several times, he turned back toward the house. The front gate stood slightly ajar, and just as Thomas got even with it, he bolted through the opening, leaving the horse between him and his startled guard. Past the house, over the back fence and across the fields beyond, his headlong flight carried him into a copse of woods. Crouching breathlessly behind a rail fence, he looked back and heard gunshots, the screams of his children, and the squealing of pigs. There were oaths and shouts as the Yankees ransacked the house and out-buildings, and threats to burn the place down.

He was so close to the road, he could hear two Yankee troopers quarreling over a pocketknife. A section of artillery came rattling up the hill and there was the murmur of voices and the muted clatter of sabers and scabbards as Minty's brigade dismounted to feed their horses. King's and Jones's brigades halted on another hilltop about a mile behind them. Both hills had been cleared, with only a few trees in the valley between them, and little fires soon flickered to life as troopers began boiling their morning coffee to wash down a few mouthfuls of hardtack.[41]

Eli Long's Ohio brigade caught up with the column about 6:00 A.M., turning from the Stockbridge Road and halting in a wooded valley on the south side of a small stream. "When the boys found that we were again moving [away] from our lines there was some tall swearing done," noted Private Lucien Wulsin, "and remarks made that 'Kill-Horse' was bound to get into a muss before going back."

Long posted his rear guard, a battalion of the 1st Ohio, on the north side of the stream. While they dismounted and began building barricades, Bob Minty and Captain Burns rode ahead to rejoin the 1st Brigade and get something to eat.

Kilpatrick breakfasted at Lee's Mill that morning and promised gray-haired old Samuel Lee he would not burn it. His men, however, took Lee's mules and emptied his smokehouse before bugles sounded the advance again at 8:00 A.M.[42]

Major Benjamin S. Dartt's 2nd battalion of the 7th Pennsylvania led the way, turning sharply to the right on the road to Noah's Ark Church. Two miles behind them, Eli Long's men were still feeding horses and cooling coffee when the crackle of gunshots shattered the morning stillness. There were shouts and oaths. A stray bullet spilled Captain John Rea's cup of coffee into the fire and Yankee bugles urgently began blaring "To Horse."

"Here's my last drink!" announced Chris Slaven of the 3rd Ohio, lifting up his cup. "Good-by, boys."[43]

Other troopers, whose coffee was still too hot to drink, mounted with steaming cups in their hands. Eli Long hurried them to some high ground overlooking the stream and then spurred toward the sound of the guns.

Sul Ross's redoubtable 3rd Texas had pitched into Long's rear guard, quickly overlapping the outnumbered Ohio battalion on both flanks. The Yankee officer in command fled in "a most disgraceful manner,"[44] but Captains John Rea, William H. Woodlief, Lieutenants James W. Kirkendall, Joseph A. O. Yeoman, and Will Curry gamely kept their companies in line until Long brought up the rest of the regiment and drove the Texans back.

As the embattled rear guard began to withdraw, about twenty troopers from Companies F and G of the 3rd Ohio dismounted at the corner of a small field to help cover the retreat. When Ross's men came dashing out of the woods, both companies opened fire. The Texans answered and Chris Slaven was killed instantly, just as he had predicted. Two or three other Ohio troopers fell wounded.[45]

As the fighting alternately flared and sputtered, Kilpatrick looked on from a hill near Lee's Mill. After watching for a few moments, he remarked, "Long can easily attend to them fellows."[46]

Sending orders for Long to hold the Rebels in check and close up on the rest of the column as quickly as possible, he and his staff rode on, but Minty's aide, Captain Burns, lingered a moment, looking across the valley. "It was a beautiful sight," he noted. "The rebels could be perceived moving towards our men, and were driven back whenever seen by them. It was the best chance of seeing the *whole* of a skirmish I ever had. I remained as long as I could, and then galloped after our column."

Keeping two regiments on the skirmish line while the other fell back to a new position, Long methodically withdrew his brigade for half a mile. A Texas detachment charging down a right-hand road briefly threatened to get between him and the main column, but the 4th Ohio quickly repulsed them and the retreat continued with what one officer called "as little confusion and as much precision as if on review."[47]

Falling back on Fielder Jones's brigade, Long received Kilpatrick's order to catch up with the rest of Minty's command at the head of the column. Leaving Jones to contend with Ross's hard-charging Texans, he led his troopers trotting past the 3rd Division.

As the fighting rolled toward Lee's Mill, L. P. Thomas, the runaway Rebel major, abandoned his hiding place and shinnied up the grapevine-tangled branches of a nearby oak tree. Perched on a limb, he hugged the trunk, watching the events unfolding beneath him. "I was just about as comfortable as a man riding a rail," he confessed. "Soon the skirmishing opened up[;] shelling was done by a light battery placed in the road by our cavalry, and the limbs of the trees, as the balls would strike them near me, were disturbed considerably. Underneath my tree rode one of the raiders, and nearby their line of skirmishers was placed by a fence; and they kept a continual skirmish fire on us."

Seeing a company of Confederate cavalry in the distance, Thomas cautiously climbed down and hit the ground running as Yankee bullets clipped the branches all around him. He reached Ross's lines unhurt but angry. Concerned for the safety of his family, he implored the Texans to attack. "I was certain we could capture all [the raiders] on that side of the creek," he assured them. "They refused however, and had me to report to General Ross in person; and here I joined the cavalry for one day."[48]

At 8:30 A.M., the weariless Ross wrote to "Red" Jackson:

> We came upon the enemy halted to feed and have driven his rear guard from two lines of rail works. He is now formed, a brigade strong, on the hill at the far side of an open field some three quarters of a mile in my front, and has artillery in position and at work. We are on the road leading toward McDonough, and from the direction the enemy has chosen I infer his raid will be continued on farther down the country.

In a second note, written at 10:00 A.M. from Mrs. Carnes's gin house, halfway between the Stockbridge Road and Lee's Mill, he advised:

> The enemy's whole force has been formed near Lee's Mill, . . . and is now just commencing to withdraw. The direction they are moving will lead them into the

Jonesborough and McDonough road, about half a mile from Lee's Mill, but whether they will continue straight across that road to Lovejoy's Station, or will go on through McDonough, is yet undecided. Their force is large. I have had a plain view of at least 4,000 formed in line. The road they are moving on intersects the Jonesborough and McDonough road at Noah's Ark Church.[49]

Ross's first report made it clear the Yankees were heading south, not east, and at 10:00 A.M. Jackson ordered Dan Reynolds's brigade to hurry down to Lovejoy's Station. While the foot soldiers' route stepped past the smoldering ruins of the railroad to board the train that had brought them from Atlanta, Jackson hurried ahead on the Griffin Road. Just south of Jonesboro, he and his escort passed some Yankees killed in the fighting during the night. "A gray soldier had one crotched against a small tree," noted a Rebel trooper, "endeavoring to pull off his boots."[50]

24

KILPATRICK'S RAID
LEE'S MILL TO BUCKHEAD

AUGUST 20–AUGUST 22, 1864

So they've got us surrounded,
the poor bastards!

—An American GI
at Bastogne, 1944

Late that morning a Yankee cavalryman stopped at Rachel Abercromby's house. Is this Dorsey's plantation? he asked. No, she said, the Dorsey place was a little farther down the road. The soldier hurried on, followed by the advance guard of Kilpatrick's column.

Judge Stephen G. Dorsey had already had one visit from the Yankees. On July 29, Ed McCook and Jim Brownlow had taken dinner at his house, along with a hundred bushels of corn. While professing to be a Union sympathizer, Dorsey feared arrest and fled at Kilpatrick's approach, leaving behind his wife, Lucinda, and three children sick with the measles.

Soon afterward, a horde of rapacious raiders descended on his yard. Crowding around the smokehouse, they began filling canteens and buckets with syrup and pulling out sides of bacon packed in some big barrels. They hauled sacks of wheat and shelled corn out of the gin house and poured several hundred bushels on the ground for their hungry horses. They ransacked his house and began scooping a hogshead full of flour into pillow cases. They took crockery and tinware, clothing and bed linens, and even the India rubber cover off the piano in the parlor. When Mrs. Dorsey protested her husband was a Union man, who had nothing to do with the war, and "narry son in it," a bluecoated officer assured her "the innocent had to suffer as well as the guilty."[1]

Just beyond Judge Dorsey's house, the road from Lee's Mill crossed the Fayetteville-McDonough Road. When the first Yankees approached the intersection at 11:00 A.M., about a dozen of "Red" Jackson's scouts who had been hovering just out of rifle range all morning suddenly opened fire. The sharp crack of carbines brought Bob Minty and his staff galloping to the front. Reining up their mud-spattered horses at the crossroads, they found Captain Dartt's battalion fighting on foot. The firing soon ceased, but as Dartt's men remounted to continue south, Minty heard a new sound, the labored approach of a locomotive. Eager to capture it, he diverted Frank Mix's 4th Michigan to the right on the Fayetteville-McDonough Road with orders to cut the Macon railroad. He also detached Lieutenant William Webb's 3rd battalion of the 4th Regulars to watch the roads to the left and sent a staff officer to ask Kilpatrick to hurry Long's brigade forward.

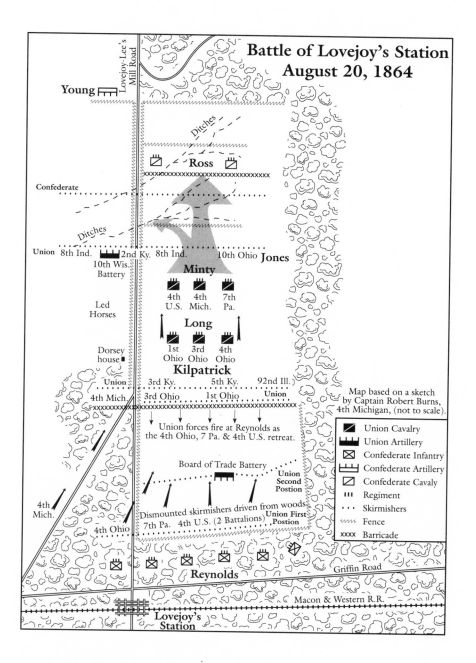

Battle of Lovejoy's Station
August 20, 1864

Young

Loveyjoy-Lee's Mill Road

Ditches

Ross

Confederate

Ditches

Union 8th Ind. 2nd Ky. 8th Ind. 10th Ohio Jones

10th Wis. Battery

Minty

Led Horses

4th U.S. 4th Mich. 7th Pa.

Long

Dorsey house

1st Ohio 3rd Ohio 4th Ohio

Kilpatrick

Union 3rd Ky. 5th Ky. 92nd Ill.

4th Mich. 3rd Ohio 1st Ohio Union

Union forces fire at Reynolds as the 4th Ohio, 7 Pa. & 4th U.S. retreat.

Board of Trade Battery

Union Second Postion

4th Mich.

Dismounted skirmishers driven from woods
7th Pa. 4th U.S. (2 Battalions)

Union First Postion

4th Ohio

Map based on a sketch by Captain Robert Burns, 4th Michigan, (not to scale).

Union Cavalry
Union Artillery
Confederate Infantry
Confederate Artillery
Confederate Cavaly
III Regiment
••• Skirmishers
wwww Fence
xxxx Barricade

Reynolds

Griffin Road

Macon & Western R.R.

Lovejoy's Station

As Minty's aide raced away, Frank Mix ordered Captain Briggs Eldridge's 3rd battalion of the 4th Michigan to dismount and deploy as skirmishers. Forming an extended line on either side of the Fayetteville-McDonough Road, Eldridge's troopers pushed through the woods and fields for about three-quarters of a mile and reached the Macon railroad without meeting any opposition. Mix brought Captain Van Antwerp's 2nd battalion forward to reinforce them and sent a courier riding down the Griffin Road to advise Minty he had reached the railroad. The rest of his regiment went to work wrecking the same track McCook's men had razed only three weeks earlier.

While Mix moved toward the railroad, Minty was following close behind Captain Dartt's battalion. The Pennsylvanians had gone about 300 yards when a squad of mounted Rebels suddenly crested the next rise in the road. Charge them, Minty ordered. Captain Joseph G. Vale and the men of Company M drew their sabers and spurred ahead. The Rebel horsemen wheeled and fled. Vale's men pressed after them, leaving Dartt's dismounted skirmishers far behind. They were within fifteen or twenty rods of the depot at Lovejoy's Station when Vale slowed the company to a trot.[2]

That was as close as they got. The train carrying Dan Reynolds's infantry from Jonesboro had rolled into Lovejoy about 11:00 A.M. "Red" Jackson rode up soon afterward and reported the Yankees were just down the road, coming fast. He directed Reynolds to deploy his brigade on the east side of the track at once.

Nelson Rainey, a nineteen-year-old private in Jackson's escort, Company A of the 7th Tennessee Cavalry, had just taken his post at the corner of the depot when he saw his brother, Joe, leap from the cars with the 48th Tennessee Infantry.

"Nelse, come on go into the fight with me!" Joe called cheerfully as his regiment formed ranks in front of the depot.

Turning to General Jackson, Nelson said, "I ask leave to go into the fight with my brother who stands there!"

"Are you on duty sir?" Jackson asked sternly.

"Yes sir," the private answered.

"Keep your station sir!"

To make the thin gray line longer and at least look stronger, Reynolds deployed his infantry in a single rank. He had 300 rifles waiting when Captain Vale's bluecoated company of the 7th Pennsylvania came trotting toward the depot.[3]

"I had been with the advance urging them forward," recounted Minty's adjutant, Captain Burns, "as it was extremely necessary to reach the Rail Road as soon as possible, and rode back to have more men sent to reinforce the advance guard when a *devil* of a fusil[l]ade took place."

The hail of lead ripped through Vale's ranks just as Frank Mix's courier brought Bob Minty word the 4th Michigan had reached the railroad. Minty bellowed a command. The rest of Captain Dartt's battalion dismounted and rushed into line about 600 yards from the depot with shouts of "Forward to the railroad!"

Minty brought up the rest of the 7th Pennsylvania to help clear the woods, but the command Lieutenant George Robinson of the Board of Trade Battery heard pass down the column was "Fours, left about." Thinking some retrograde movement was planned, he faced his section of artillery to the rear, a difficult task in the confines of a narrow road bordered on both sides by a split-rail fence. His men had to unlimber both guns and turn them around by hand. By the time they completed this maneuver, the cavalry had faced to the front again and was slowly moving forward.

At the head of the column, the rest of the 7th Pennsylvania soon dismounted and went into line alongside Captain Dartt's men. When gunfire continued to echo in the woods on the right, Minty dispatched Captain Burns to hurry up two of Eli Long's regiments and ordered the 1st and 2nd battalions of the 4th Regulars forward at a gallop. He sent a mounted squadron of the Regulars to anchor the left and directed Captain McIntyre to take the rest of the regiment into the woods to extend the line to the right.

"Prepare to fight on foot," McIntyre ordered.

The Regulars slid from their saddles, but before they could tie their horses, Reynolds's infantry came charging through the woods. On the right of the Rebel line, Lieutenant Colonel Henry Evans had deployed three companies of the 48th Tennessee as flankers, instructing Captain E. C. Cantrell to maintain contact with the right of the regiment while advancing his own right as rapidly as possible. Approaching Minty's line at an oblique angle, these three companies triggered a rolling volley that raked the 7th Pennsylvania and 4th Regulars from left to right at a range of less than 150 yards.

The murderous blast unhorsed Minty. An orderly quickly brought him a fresh mount and he climbed into the saddle, appalled at what he saw. "It appeared for a moment," he confessed, "as if the two regiments had been annihilated. . . ."

"The first volley of the enemy killed *four brave men* out of Captain Schaeffer's company," lamented Corporal Frank Dornblaser of the 7th Pennsylvania. "Sergeant [Samuel] Foster, whose manly form was seen in front of many a sabre-charge, and whose stentorian shout was heard a moment before, fell dead on his face; David McDonald, a gallant soldier, dropped like one shot in the heart; Emery Else, a Christian young man, whose voice was frequently heard in our prayer-circle, was shot dead with his face to the foe; George Caldwell, the singer of the Company, whose cheerful songs and ringing laughter were heard round many a campfire, was mortally wounded, the ball passing from cheek to cheek, and severing the tongue far back in the mouth."

Dornblaser himself was struck in his instep, the bullet piercing his sock and searing the skin around his left ankle before lodging in the heel of his boot. His friend, Sergeant Bill Hays, urged him to go to the rear to find an ambulance, but Dornblaser, flexing his foot and finding no broken bones, said there was no need. Go on, Hays insisted as the firing waxed hotter, "All of us will have to go after a little."

Looking around, Dornblaser saw Hays was the only man still standing on that part of the line. Reluctantly, he started toward the rear. He had only gone a few yards when the chilling shrill of the Rebel yell echoed through the woods.

Minty's men fired rapidly, emptying the last rounds from the seven-shot magazines of their Spencers. Before they could reload, howling Rebels were on them with fixed bayonets. Dornblaser ran, hurt foot and all, and soon came to the fence surrounding a large cornfield on the left of the Lovejoy Road where the number fours were waiting with the led horses. His company commander, Captain Israel B. Schaeffer, was sitting where his skirmishers had pulled down the rails a few moments earlier. "Where are Hays, and Foster, and the rest of the boys?" Schaeffer asked.

"They are killed or captured," Dornblaser said simply.

Some of the panicked Pennsylvanians fled through the woods and up the Griffin Road. They rushed past the 4th Michigan's startled pickets, shouting their regiment had been butchered by a brigade—a division—two divisions of Rebel infantry. Frank Mix immediately suspended work on the railroad, where his 1st battalion had uprooted two lengths of track and had several bonfires blazing. Recalling his pickets, he formed his regiment for battle and waited for orders as the sound of sharp firing welled up from the south.[4]

Lieutenant George Robinson was also waiting for orders when he saw Eli Long's Ohio brigade coming up the road from Lee's Mill at a trot. Realizing it was useless to leave his two guns limbered toward the rear, he spurred to the front, where he saw Minty's skirmishers streaming out of the woods in wild disorder.

"The situation looked somewhat serious," Robinson noted, "and I was a little apprehensive of a stampede, unless a rallying point could be fixed, and I hurried back to the battery, determined to get it into position at the first opening, believing that if I could demonstrate to the division that I was prepared and ready to help them, they would rally to our support and make the best fight possible."

The only open ground in sight was the big cornfield, about 400 yards long and half as wide, on the south side of the road. Robinson turned his guns through a gap in the fence just about the same time Lieutenant Henry Bennett's section rolled up. Trampling cornstalks underfoot, the battery quickly went into action in the center of the furrowed field, sending a salvo of shells hurtling over the heads of Minty's skirmishers. The hard-pressed troopers answered with a cheer.

Eli Long, in the meantime, rode ahead to report to Minty. After a hurried conversation, he galloped back to where he had left his brigade waiting in the road and ordered the leading battalion of the 4th Ohio to dismount. Company B promptly let down a section of fence on their left and filed into the cornfield, but on the right of the regiment there was confusion as officers gave conflicting orders to left wheel, dismount, and then mount. Finally, Long personally ordered Captain James Thomson's squadron, Companies E and L, forward on foot to stop the Rebel advance.

"The firing in front was now very rapid, and the yells of the rebels almost appalling," asserted Private Lucien Wulsin; "stragglers began to appear, and we were in danger of breaking, when a number of men from each company near the head of the column dismounted and rushed forward with cheers into the woods to the right of the road."

They had gone about a hundred yards when they came to a large fallen tree. Taking cover behind this admirable breastwork, they were trying to form a line when a mob of Minty's men burst from the woods, running "pell mell, every man for himself, and devil for the hindmost."

It was no use, a bluecoated captain yelled as he sprinted past; better get moving or they would all be captured. The Ohio troopers shook their heads. Climbing on top of the log and waving their hats, they yelled, they cursed, they threatened, pleading for Minty's men to stop "for God's sake."

Some of them did stop. Rallying on the left of Long's line, just as Lieutenants John M. Hedrick and Jacob Rief brought up portions of Companies C and K of the 4th Ohio, the cavalrymen poured a furious fire into the oncoming Confederates.

The gray ranks hesitated. "Charge them," a bluecoated soldier yelled. The raiders rushed forward and paid dearly for their enthusiasm. An orange sheet of flame blazed down the length of the Rebel line. Corporal John Aberdeen of the 4th Ohio fell, shot through the hips. When he tried to crawl away, he was shot again and mortally wounded. Lieutenant Rief was hit. So was Lieutenant Hedrick.

The blue line staggered. Captain Jim Thomson's squadron of the 4th Ohio was cut off. Thomson was captured. The men began falling back, firing their carbines as they went, before pausing to rally on either side of the Board of Trade Battery.

The 4th Regulars were reforming their ranks to the right and rear of the guns when someone noticed Captain McIntyre was missing. Word quickly passed down the line and instantly, noted artilleryman John Nourse, "every man seemed to have the fury of a demon." With carbines blazing, they rushed into the woods and soon brought their captain back in triumph.[5]

Their retreat gave the Board of Trade Battery a clear field of fire, and gunners began ramming double loads of canister down the maws of their guns just as the fluttering Rebel battle flags emerged from the woods at the west end of the field. There was a crashing volley of musketry, the wild rush of an infantry charge, and the high-pitched howl of the Rebel yell. The battery answered with lethal blasts of canister that scythed through the cornfield cutting down everything in its path.

Switching from canister to shell as the riddled Rebel ranks retired into the woods, the Board of Trade boys worked furiously. Again and again their four rifles roared. The furrowed ground, soaked from the previous night's rain, yielded with each blast, sinking the spoked wheels of the gun carriages halfway up to the axle. Gunners had to drag their pieces out of the mud to resight and reload, but the crew of Lieutenant Bennett's number one gun were so intent on firing they failed to notice when its heavy wooden trail lodged against a tree stump. The recoil from the next shot snapped the trail cleanly in two at the elevating screw, leaving the Parrott hanging by the trunnions, its muzzle pointing uselessly toward the sky.

Robinson sent the disabled gun's limber to the rear. "We had now slacked our firing," he noted, "but still continued shelling the woods in our front, although at longer intervals, when suddenly the rebels came out of the woods and in position under the fence along the road to my right and let us have it. . . ."[6]

Robinson immediately changed front to face the road. Pulling his right piece back, bringing the left one forward, his gunners opened with canister again. Rails and splinters flew in every direction as the riddling hail of little round balls struck home, but no sooner was the right flank cleared than the battery came under fire from the woods on its left. Robinson had the left gun swung around, and soon the battery was firing in three different directions.

"It fought magnificently," applauded Minty's adjutant, Captain Burns. "It was a glorious sight to see it sweep those woods with . . . canister, sending many a howling rebel to eternity."

But Robinson's limber chests were nearly empty. In fifteen minutes, his four guns had each fired seventy rounds of shell and canister. One piece had been disabled, six or seven horses shot. Private Thomas Wygant had been killed. Five other artillerymen were wounded, and the withering cross fire from the road and the woods had driven back the dismounted cavalrymen on both flanks. Robinson ordered the battery to fall back.[7]

Leaving their disabled gun behind, the artillerymen withdrew about a hundred yards to where Eli Long and the 1st Ohio were waiting near the east end of the cornfield. These troopers had been the length of a regiment behind the 4th Ohio when Long ordered the column to dismount, and this had given them enough time to throw together a fairly substantial barricade of logs and fence rails. Cautioned to hold their fire, they hunkered behind their hastily built breastworks as the flood of dismounted men, led horses, and artillery bounded past. Then the Rebel infantry appeared.

"My God!" exclaimed a crouching 1st Ohio cavalryman when he saw the long gray line coming through the head-high rows of corn, "Captain, look at that thousand legged worm."

A moment later, the 1st Ohio loosed a blazing volley at a range of only 100 feet. The Rebels pressed closer. Yankee officers emptied their revolvers into them, but the Rebels kept coming through the corn.

"I had my men take the ammunition from their boxes and place it on the ground right under their chins, to enable more rapid firing . . . ," recounted Captain John Rea. "There was not over 200 men in the regiment, but as often as the enemy advanced for the next ten minutes or half hour, I couldn't have told which, when it was over, we drove them back with terrible slaughter."

Taking cover with two troopers behind a rotten old stump, Rea picked up a Sharps carbine someone had dropped and blazed away until a Rebel bullet half-blinded him with a shower of dirt. Blinking the grit out of his eyes, he looked up and saw Eli Long standing close by. Rea pointed proudly to his carbine. Long flashed a smile and sauntered on down the firing line, quietly puffing on his pipe.

By this time, the 3rd Ohio had dismounted and deployed on the 1st Ohio's right, extending Long's line from the Lovejoy–Lee's Mill Road to the Fayetteville-McDonough Road. Eli Murray arrived shortly afterward with Robert King's 3rd Brigade and sent the 92nd Illinois to hold the left, while the 3rd and 5th Kentucky formed behind Minty and Long. Fielder Jones's 2nd Brigade came up next, led by the 8th Indiana.

These reinforcements quickly overlapped Dan Reynolds's outnumbered Rebel infantry by several hundred yards on both flanks. Running low on ammunition and reluctant to reveal just how small his force really was, he halted his six regiments 300 yards beyond the Griffin Road and quietly retired to the tree line at the west end of the cornfield, with casualties of ten killed, thirty-seven wounded, and one missing.[8]

But as the Rebel infantry withdrew, Yankee troopers heard the disquieting rattle of musketry in the rear. They listened as the echoes swelled sharper and more insistent in the shimmering heat. It was unexpected. It was unnerving. It was hard-riding Sul Ross and his tenacious Texans, storming down the road from Lee's Mill.

While two of Ross's regiments dismounted to advance on foot, one of Fielder Jones's staff officers, Captain Samuel Lyon, took command of a squadron of the 10th Ohio that hastily barricaded the road. Loading and firing, these troopers held up the Texans long enough for Jones to get his brigade into line in a field on the right of the road and face to the rear. Sending Captain Jacob Mitchell and Company K of the 8th Indiana to screen his left flank, Jones hurried his three regiments back to the crest of a commanding ridge. Captain Beebe reported with his 10th Wisconsin Battery. As the artillerymen unlimbered their guns in a patch of sorghum cane, Jones directed Major Charles A. Gordon to dismount five companies of the 8th Indiana and the little 2nd Kentucky, mustering only eighty-three men, to support them.

A tall, handsome Kentuckian, Colonel Eli Huston Murray (seen here as a brigadier general) was only twenty-one years old when he took command of Kilpatrick's 3rd Brigade. Despite his youth, he was "always cool, self-possessed, . . . and equal to every emergency." In 1880 he became governor of the Utah Territory. Reproduced from the Collections of the Library of Congress.

Cannoneers and cavalrymen began pulling down some nearby slave cabins. While they barricaded Beebe's guns behind planks and fence rails, Jones deployed the four remaining companies of the 8th Indiana on the battery's left and ordered the 10th Ohio into line on the right. An anxious Eli Murray also sent a staff officer galloping off to find Kilpatrick.

Kilpatrick soon dashed up on his spotted horse. "Hold your fire . . . until you can see the whites of their eyes," he bellowed; "don't shoot until you hear the order." Captain Beebe's men double-shotted their guns with canister. Cavalrymen squinted down the sights of their carbines.

"Fire!"

A deafening blast boomed from Beebe's battery. The rattle of carbines rose to a steady roar. Ross's Texans answered with small arms and artillery. Bullets began smacking into the side of Judge Dorsey's house. Put the children flat on the floor, a Yankee officer commanded a terrified Lucinda Dorsey.[9]

"A fierce battle seemed now to be going on in every direction, but which was the front or main point of the attack I could not for the life of me tell . . . ," noted Lieutenant William Webb when he rode up with the 3rd battalion of the 4th Regulars, left to picket the roads to the east until the rear guard had passed. "Artillery and musketry were pouring their deadly missiles into our front, rear and both flanks. I could find for the moment no one to report to, and was uncertain and somewhat bewildered as to what I should do with my handful of men. Finally, I recognized the led horses of the Fourth Cavalry in the distance, and hastening to join them, discovered that the balance of the regiment were fighting on foot somewhere, but where, no one could tell me."

About this time one of Kilpatrick's aides dashed up and directed Webb to take his battalion to some high ground on the left and build a barricade. "Which way shall I face it?" Webb asked.

"Suit yourself," the aide shouted as he galloped away.

Webb hurried to the position indicated and ordered his battalion to dismount. Leaving the number fours and led horses sheltered in a shallow depression, he and his men began piling up some half-rotten rails that lay nearby. "Although I had been given *carte blanche* in the matter of facing the wretched affair," Webb recounted, "I soon found that unless I constructed a pen and got inside of it with my men, I might as well save myself the trouble of building at all; and there were not enough rails for such a purpose. We therefore lay as low as possible in the grass, and popped at the enemy with our seven-shooters in whatever direction he showed himself, and were popped at in return from all sides."[10]

In the midst of this mayhem, Captain Burns rode up to Bob Minty and reported Kilpatrick wanted to see him at once. Confederate General Pat Cleburne's infantry division was closing in on the right, he added. Ferguson's, Ross's, and Armstrong's cavalry were pressing the left and rear, and Minty had already seen "what is in front of us."

Minty sent Burns riding toward the railroad to bring the 4th Michigan back to the intersection of the Lee's Mill and McDonough roads before they got cut off from the main column. Then he galloped to the rear to report to Kilpatrick. He found the general waiting near Judge Dorsey's house.

"Colonel Minty," Kilpatrick said excitedly, "we are surrounded. You know what is in our front; Jackson with 5,000 cavalry is in rear of our left, and Pat Cleburne with 10,000 infantry is closing on our right; our only salvation is to cut our way out. We will form here, facing our present rear; you will form line on the right of the road, Colonel Murray will form on the left; you will charge simultaneously."

Minty studied the ground Kilpatrick had indicated, an old field, cut up by several deep gullies and two small fences.

"General," he said, "I will form in any way you direct; but, if it was left to me, I would never charge in line over this ground; when we strike the enemy, if we ever do so, it will be a thin, wavering blow that will amount to nothing."

"How, then, would you charge?" Kilpatrick asked.

"In column, sir," Minty replied. "Our momentum would be like that of a railroad where we strike, something has to break."

Kilpatrick pondered this for a moment and then said, "Form in any way you please."[11]

Minty was returning to his command when he met Lieutenant Robinson. The artilleryman reported one of his guns had been disabled and was still out in the cornfield. He asked Minty to give him enough men to help bring it back.

Minty crept into the field, close enough to make sure the gun was still there, then backtracked to his lines and called for twenty volunteers. The 4th Michigan, just returned from the railroad, was building a barricade on the right of the 3rd Ohio, and when Captain Burns repeated the appeal, Lieutenant Alfred B. Purinton and every man of Company I, except the horseholders, stepped forward. Minty, however, had already rounded up Captain Charles L. Greeno and a handful of 7th Pennsylvania cavalrymen. With these troopers, and some from the 3rd Ohio, he started across the cornfield again with Lieutenant Robinson and a few artillerymen. The Rebel infantry waiting at the edge of the woods had virtually ceased firing by this time and, crouching low, Minty and his men reached the disabled gun without mishap. Attaching a couple of horse halters to one end of a fence rail, they slipped the halters over the Parrott's upturned muzzle and levered it down to a horizontal position. Prodded by a few bullets Rebel sharpshooters aimed at them, they worked quickly and dragged the gun safely inside the Union lines.

Lieutenant Robinson immediately had the cannon dismounted and the broken carriage chopped to pieces. His men tried to suspend the breech-banded barrel underneath its limber, but when prolonges proved too weak to bear the weight, they wrestled the 890-pound Parrott into the back of one of the battery wagons. They buried their dead comrade, Private Wygant, in a shallow grave between the corn rows and were loading their wounded into ambulances when orders came to send a section back to the hill where Captain Beebe's battery was dueling with the Rebel artillery.

Robinson assigned this task to Lieutenant Bennett. As two guns started toward the rear, Minty passed the word to Major Mix, Major Jennings, and Captain McIntyre to have their regiments mount up and form ranks on the south side of the Lovejoy–Lee's Mill Road, facing the rear. They were going to cut their way through the Rebel cavalry, and he sent Captain Burns to tell Eli Long to line up his 2nd Brigade close behind the 1st, "in columns with regimental front, and sweep up what we break through."[12]

Leaving a thin line of skirmishers to cover their retreat, both of Minty's brigades began falling back. There was no hurrying, no confusion. The 1st Ohio retired from the sheltering split rail barricades in perfect order when officers told them to mount their horses. Captain John Rea, bringing up the rear of Company I, had gone perhaps twenty yards when he stopped behind a tree to see if the Rebels were following. Hearing a noise about twenty feet to his left, he turned just in time to see a trooper crumple beside a tree, a bullet through his brain. At that instant, about ten feet to Rea's left, a fair-haired young soldier who had also turned to look fell with a wound in his back. Thinking he recognized the boy, Rea rushed to his side. As he knelt beside the lifeless body, a Rebel bullet parted his shoulder-length hair. Terrified at the prospect of being wounded and captured, Rea ran to rejoin his company. While they mounted their horses, he hastily called the roll. Seventeen-year-old Alonzo Conover failed to answer.[13]

As the last of Minty's skirmishers withdrew, Kilpatrick had Eli Murray realign King's 3rd and 5th Kentucky to confront the quiescent Confederate infantry. At the other end of the field, facing the opposite direction, Fielder Jones's brigade, Captain Beebe's battery, and Lieutenant Bennett's two guns blazed away at Ross's cavalry.

The led horses for the entire command had been corralled behind King's Kentuckians, and Captain Burns watched as troopers from Minty's 4th Regulars, 4th Michigan, and 7th Pennsylvania mounted and began lining up behind the brow of the hill Fielder Jones's brigade was defending. All three of Minty's regiments were just getting into position when Kilpatrick rode up about 2:00 P.M.

"Captain," the general asked, turning to Burns, "can your men charge through and break those rebels in front of us?"

"Yes, sir," Burns replied confidently, "they can."

"What would be the best formation, do you think?" Kilpatrick queried. "In line or in column?"

"In columns of four, I think," Burns said, "each regiment to form a column and then the rebels' attention would be distracted."

"We will have them so," Kilpatrick resolved. "How do they generally charge—with sabre or firing?"

"With sabre, sir."

"Good!" Kilpatrick snapped. "Go tell Colonel Minty to have them charge in that way and drive the damn rebels to hell."

At that point, Bob Minty rode up.

"Colonel Minty," Kilpatrick beckoned, "have you determined upon the best way to make this charge?"

"I have," Minty replied, "in column of fours; the regiments of my brigade side by side."

"That is, I think, the proper way," Kilpatrick concurred. "You will break them . . . Long will follow with his brigade . . . and clean them out."

Minty summoned Frank Mix and told him to form his 4th Michigan in a column of fours, leaving room for the 4th Regulars on his left and the 7th Pennsylvania on his right. He gave similar instructions to Captain McIntyre and Major Jennings and sent an aide, Captain Heber Thompson, to remind Eli Long to keep his 2nd Brigade close behind the 1st.[14]

As the men formed for the charge, some of them recalled the words of a famous poem they had read in their youth. Rebels to the right of them, Rebels to the left of them, Rebels in front of them. They were surrounded, and grim visions flashed through their minds as they tightened their saddle girths, reloaded revolvers, checked their spurs, and nervously readjusted saber belts. "The men threw away all extra . . . trap of all kinds," noted artilleryman John Nourse, "horseshoes, blankets, haversacks, ammunition, carbines, camp utensils and clothing."

Officers sent troopers who had no sabers to the rear ranks of their companies. Negro cooks and servants, brandishing long hickory switches, prodded pack mules into line behind their regiments. Take good care of the mule carrying the officers' rations, Lieutenant Will Curry warned "Brick" and Henry, serving with Company K of the 1st Ohio, or "two darkies would dangle from the nearest tree."

Getting the different regiments into position took time. Occasionally there was a jarring blast as a Rebel shell burst overhead. Horses snorted and stamped their feet impatiently in the sweltering heat. Men shifted uneasily in their saddles. Private George Cassel was waiting in the rear ranks of the 4th Regulars when a stray bullet struck him in the chest. He slumped across the neck of his horse and died before his comrades could take him down.

"There is a certain feeling which I cannot tell you of," noted Captain Albert Potter of the 4th Michigan, "—when a man stands waiting the word, which perhaps will send him to Eternity. . . ."

As Minty's men lined up, Lieutenant Robinson and the rest of the Board of Trade Battery reunited with Lieutenant Bennett's two guns. Limbers, ambulances, and wagons crowded into the Lovejoy Road to the left and rear of Eli Long's brigade.

Lieutenant William Webb's battalion of Regulars were still on foot when someone called their attention to the columns forming in the cornfield. "Although ordered to remain where I was until relieved," Webb confessed, "there was not enough of the Roman soldier of romance about me to remain where I knew I could do nothing, especially when I could see that we should shortly be left alone. . . ." He yelled for his men to mount up.[15]

Before Webb's troopers could rejoin their regiment, Bob Minty rode over to the Lovejoy Road to report to Kilpatrick. Eli Murray came up about the same time.

"General," Murray said, "my men cannot charge over this ground."

"Why not, sir?" Kilpatrick demanded.

"They cannot do it, General," Murray repeated.

Kilpatrick turned to Minty. "Colonel Minty," he said, "are you ready?"

"All ready, sir."

"Then charge when you please."[16]

Spurring back to his command, Minty halted his sorrel mare in front of Company C of the 4th Michigan. Captain Burns and Captain Thompson reined up on his left as he fixed his gaze on the grim-faced men who had ridden with him at Stone's River, Shelbyville, Chickamauga, and a hundred other battles.

"Attention!" he commanded in a clear, ringing voice. "Draw sabers!"

There was the sharp, metallic rasp of cold steel being drawn from the scabbard.

Minty's bugler bounded to the top of the hill where Fielder Jones's brigade and the artillery were keeping Sul Ross's Texans at bay. Silhouetted against the summer sky, he lifted the bugle to his lips and sounded "Forward."

"Forward—trot," Minty ordered, "regulate by the center column! March!"

Red, white, and blue guidons unfurled overhead as all three regiments started up the slope, the 4th Regulars on the left, the 4th Michigan in the center, the 7th Pennsylvania on the right. Lieutenant Webb's battalion came racing up from the flank just in time to fall in behind the Regulars. As the first riders reached the crest, Jones's skirmishers threw down the fence in front of them.

"Gallop! March!" Minty roared, swinging his saber over his head. "Charge!"

"Charge!" the bugles echoed. A wild cheer rose in the throats of a thousand troopers as three compact columns of fours surged up and over the crest. Boot to boot, stirrup to stirrup, they spurred hell-for-leather, here-we-come down the gullied slope, their upraised sabers flashing in the sun. About a dozen men Minty had detailed from each column to race ahead on foot pulled down sections of the rail fence at the bottom of the hill and the horsemen hurtled through the gaps.[17]

"The rapid gait through this field brought the stout corn-stalks against our legs with such force, and seemed to cause the horses so much distress," noted Lieutenant Webb, "that by common consent," after passing this first fence, "the Fourth Cavalry obliqued to the left and struck the dirt road, down which we went at break-neck speed."

In front of them, a lone Rebel howitzer roared from a stand of walnut trees on a hill on the left side of the road. A shell burst overhead. Then another. Then the Rebel gunners switched to canister. As the Regulars raced on, a frightful hail of round balls shivered a mulberry tree next to the fence on their right. Yelling and shouting, they dug their spurs in deep. An instant later they were galloping past the belching gun, so close they could feel its hot breath on their faces.[18]

Sul Ross's caissons, led horses, and ambulances crowded the narrow road behind the gun and the Yankee regiment slammed into them at a dead run. The impact was terrific. The white horse Captain McIntyre was riding collided with an artillery limber, hurling him headlong into the fence. Catch that horse, he yelled. An orderly retrieved the runaway and the captain quickly remounted. A Tennessee-born Texan who had finished five places behind John Bell Hood at West Point, McIntyre counted many friends and acquaintances in Ross's ranks. Brandishing his saber, he charged into the wild melee as men and horses, limbers and ambulances, hemmed in by high fences on both sides of the road, piled together in "inextricable confusion." Some of Ross's horseholders, including L. P. Thomas, the Rebel major who had narrowly escaped capture that morning at Lee's Mill, "fled for dear life." Others, trying to dodge the flailing hooves of their frightened mounts, threw up their hands to surrender, only to be cut down by the Regulars' slashing blades. "The sabres were plied with vigor all the time we were detained in this road," noted Lieutenant Webb, "and many fierce hand-to-hand encounters took place."

A withering blast ripped through the struggling mass, felling friend and foe alike. In their haste, the Regulars had left Ross's howitzer sitting beside the road, untouched. As the Yankee troopers swept past, the Rebel gunners swung the piece around and hurled a double load of canister into their backs. Then they faced to the front again, bringing the gun to bear on the rest of Minty's brigade.

The 4th Michigan and 7th Pennsylvania struck the Rebel line perhaps half a minute behind the Regulars, boring straight across a field at least a half-mile wide, obstructed by three fences, one hastily built barricade, and half a dozen gullies, two to six feet deep and five to twelve feet wide. No sooner had the charging columns cleared one obstacle than they had to leap another. "Our horses went kiting over the fences," recounted Captain Robert Burns; "some of them they knocked down. Of course a good many of our men were dismounted."

The others spurred on. The muddy ground trembled under the urgent fury of pounding hooves. The smoky air shook with each fiery blast of case shot and canister. Horses screamed in agony, men shouted, and the clanging of camp kettles strapped on the backs of panicked pack mules, said one officer, "beat any noise I ever heard."

The charge caught Sul Ross in the act of withdrawing the two Texas regiments he had previously sent forward to fight on foot. His skirmishers fled before the Yankee onslaught without attempting to make a stand, while his main line crouched behind the hastily built barricade about halfway across the field, watching as the oncoming blue columns rapidly closed to within 300 yards. A few unforgiving seconds passed. The distance dwindled to 200 yards. Ross's men waited. The range shrank to 100 yards.

"No order was heard; not a word was spoken," noted Lieutenant Sam Barron of the 3rd Texas; "every officer and every man took in the whole situation at a glance: no one asked or gave advice: no one waited for orders. The line was maintained intact for a few seconds, the men emptying their pieces at the heads of the columns. This created a momentary flutter without checking their speed, and on they came in fine style."

Before they could reload, the Yankee horsemen were upon them. The Texans threw down their guns and ran, but it was too late.

"Our men were mounted and on the gallop and . . . cut them down right and left," exulted Captain Burns. "I was just about to strike two, when they threw up their hands and surrendered. I passed them by, leaving someone in the rear to take care of them.

A third who did not surrender quick enough, I struck full on the top of the head, felt my sabre sink in, saw him fall, and dashed on."

Private Sam Waters, riding in the front ranks of the 7th Pennsylvania, stood up in his stirrups as he overtook a mounted Confederate and raised his saber. The Rebel rider threw his arm up to ward off the blow. The Yankee blade flashed, cutting off his hand at the wrist. Another blow nearly severed the man's head from his body.

"They surrender[ed] by dozens," noted the 4th Michigan's Albert Potter, "—but many of them were cut down without mercy, for my part I could not strike them after they had given up and but very few did hit them in our regiment, but the Regulars— slashed right and left, and many a poor devil's brains lay scattered on the ground— from there it was nothing but a Panic, they just ran like dogs."

Lieutenant Sam Barron was among the last of Ross's men to reach the deep ditch fronting the fence on the far side of the field. He leaped across, cleared the fence, and had gone ten or fifteen steps when he heard hoofbeats drumming behind him.

"Surrender, sir!" a voice demanded.

Barron looked back and saw a stalwart bluecoat towering in the stirrups, his gleaming saber poised to strike. Barron hesitated.

"That's all I ask of you, sir," the Yankee implored in a stern but gentler tone.

Barron dropped the rifle he was carrying.

"All right," the soldier said, spurring on to overtake his comrades.

At that instant, a Rebel shell burst directly over Barron's head, showering his would-be captors with shrapnel. Taking advantage of the momentary confusion, Barron grabbed his left hip, as if he had been struck, and staggered into the open space between the charging columns. Falling on his right side to conceal the pistol he wore, he played possum as the Yankee horsemen thundered past.

In the forefront of the charge, Bob Minty sabered a Texan across the head just before his mare was hit by a rifle bullet and fell into the ditch at the far end of the field. Frank Mix reined up long enough to ask if he were hurt. Minty asserted he was all right, hauled the mare to her feet, and hurried on to keep pace with the front ranks.

"Upon reaching the woods, we could not go so fast," explained Captain Burns, "and could not keep in column." The troops became scattered, chasing dismounted and demoralized Texans in every direction.

In the confusion, Frank Mix became separated from his command. Off to the left, Ross's howitzer roared again.

"Boys," Mix yelled over the din, "let's take that gun out with us."

Minty's aide, Captain Heber Thompson, along with Captain Van Antwerp and about a dozen others, turned down a narrow lane to follow him. A blast of canister ripped through the underbrush on their right. Most of the shot missed, but a single ball struck Mix in his left hand, forcing him to drop his reins. Before he could sheath the saber in his other hand and regain control, his horse veered into the path of a runaway mule. The jarring collision hurled Mix to the ground.

While some of the men stopped to help him back into the saddle, Captain Thompson and a few 4th Michigan troopers forged ahead. Emerging from the woods into a field, they met Lieutenant Ed Fitzgerald of the 4th Regulars and spurred toward the troublesome gun. A dismounted Rebel took aim from about fifty yards away and fired. His bullet struck Thompson's mare squarely in the chest. She reared straight up and fell over backwards, dead before she hit the ground. Thompson swiftly extricated himself but had taken only a few steps when he encountered a dozen of Ross's men, who immediately took him prisoner.

As Thompson's captors hurried him away, Bob Minty had the "Rally" sounded. The bugle's urgent blare halted the 7th Pennsylvania in the woods at the end of the field, and Minty ordered Major Jennings to move to the left until he reached the main road. Threading through the thickets, encountering a few Rebel stragglers along the way, the Pennsylvanians reached the road just as Eli Long's 2nd Brigade emerged on their left.[19]

Minty had intended for Long to follow him in line of regiments. Long, however, had formed his three regiments in columns of fours, just like the 1st Brigade, and that was how they charged, sailing over fences, leaping ditches, and yelling like demons.[20]

"Owing to the irregular nature of the ground," explained Long's adjutant, Captain William E. Crane, "after leaving the corn-field, no regular alignment was possible, and it soon became a charge of squadrons, companies, squads, and single riders."

The lone Rebel howitzer roared defiantly at their approach, but the thunderous stampede kept coming. Twice, Sul Ross sent messages urging Lieutenant George Young to leave the gun and save his men.

"Not while I have a shot left!" Young replied.

Finally, Ross gathered about thirty men and led them to the top of the knoll. "Well, Young," he said, "if you are determined to stay with your gun, we will stay with you."

"Our men stood manfully and fought like madmen . . . ," declared a Rebel gunner. Ramming home canister and case shot, they fired in three or four different directions, cutting down men and horses in midstride.

"Take the guns!" yelled Captain William H. Scott, spurring ahead of the 1st Ohio. A blast of canister spun the young Irishman out of the saddle. Dazed and covered with blood, he sprawled at the foot of a tree, his shattered right arm hanging limply at his side.[21]

Company I of the 1st Ohio was crossing the gully in front of the Rebel barricade when a piece of canister struck a large man in the first set of fours. His frightened horse dashed past Captain John Rea, who turned and saw the hole in the trooper's neck. "The blood had not begun to flow and the light shone plainly through it," Rea recounted. "He held on to his horse's mane—was the first to reach the barricade when he slid to the earth already dead."

Company K of the 1st Ohio was going at a gallop when their Negro cook, "Brick," streaked past them, flailing his mule furiously. His eyes "bulged out as large as two saucers," and the pack mule with the officers' rations he was supposed to be leading was nowhere in sight.

In the ranks of the 3rd Ohio, a trooper was hurled ten feet in the air when a shell struck his mount and exploded. In Company C, a horse fell dead, pinning its rider to the ground. "Help!" the trooper pleaded as his company galloped past, "for the love of God, help, or I am a prisoner."

Fearing for their own lives, his comrades raced on, leaving him to his fate. Company D followed close behind. Seeing the struggling soldier and hearing his plaintive cries for help, Private Edward W. Amsden dismounted and pulled him free. As the rest of the regiment sped out of sight, Amsden remounted and spurred after them, crouching low over his horse's neck as he passed within fifty yards of the booming howitzer.

Ahead of him, the 4th Ohio had already reached the thick woods on the far side of the field and filed to the left. Emerging behind the Rebel artillery, they found the main road crowded with galloping horsemen, waving their sabers and cheering. Some of Ross's Texans who had recovered from their fright were firing from the dense undergrowth, picking off riders in what Private Lucien Wulsin called "regular bushwhacking style." Turning to the right, the 4th Ohio moved down the road for about 300 yards before halting to reform their ranks.

Orderly Sergeant Garner Stimsen of the 3rd Ohio and two of his companions who had gotten separated from their regiment also reached the main road, where they met Bob Minty and two of his aides.

"Orderly," Minty beckoned, "where do you belong?"

"To the Second Brigade, Second Division," Stimsen replied.

"Where is the rest of your command?" Minty asked.

"This is all I know anything about," Stimsen answered. "Where is the First Brigade?"

Minty flashed a grin. "This is all of the First Brigade that I know anything about," he said, nodding toward his aides.[22]

By this time, the 4th Regulars had hacked their way through Ross's led horses and limbers. While Sergeant John C. Rose led the way with his saber and "almost cut a road for the rear," Private Thomas Douglas followed with Captain McIntyre, taking prisoners left and right. Emerging from the melee, he rode up to Bob Minty, herding several captured Rebels ahead of him. "Here, Colonel, are fifteen Johnnies," he said with a salute, "the trophies of Captain McIntyre and Private Douglas, 4th Regulars."[23]

Other troopers swarmed over Rebel wagons and ambulances. Dismounting and taking hatchets from their saddlebags, they chopped down the wheels, unhitched the mules, and looted anything of value. Private Isaac Sollers of the 4th Cavalry took Sul Ross's dress cap, trimmed in gold lace. Another Regular rode away with the battle flag of the 3rd Texas Cavalry.[24]

Lieutenant Robinson's Board of Trade Battery followed in the Regulars' wake, lashing their lathered teams down the road at a gallop. As they pulled off to one side to pass a couple of Rebel caissons, Robinson stopped and detailed a few men with axes to dismount the Negro drivers, cut down the wheels, and shoot the horses. They had scarcely finished this work when an officer rode up, yelling, "For God's sake, Robinson, hurry along out of here, the rebs have reformed and are close upon us!"

Behind him, the 3rd Division was preparing to run the gauntlet. Eli Murray had instructed Fielder Jones to wait until Minty's columns were "well out" before sending his 2nd Brigade forward. As the last of Minty's men swept past, Jones gave orders to "withdraw quickly, mount and follow." His men ran back through the sorghum cane, retrieved their horses, and in less than three minutes the 8th Indiana was formed in column, followed by the 2nd Kentucky and 10th Ohio. Murray joined Jones on the right side of the road at the front rank of the 8th Indiana and sent word for Robert King's 3rd Brigade to begin withdrawing, too.

"Never did men obey an order with more alacrity or determination," King noted as his Kentuckians sprinted for their horses.

The Wisconsin battery did not waste any time either. Captain Beebe had kept his teams right behind the barricades and when Jones ordered him to fall in behind the

2nd Brigade, his men limbered up so quickly they got into the road ahead of Jones's column instead of behind it. They were plying whip and spur when Kilpatrick's adjutant, Captain Lewellyn Estes, raced up alongside yelling, "Halt that battery!"[25]

Then Kilpatrick sped past on his spotted horse, surrounded by his staff and escort. A Rebel shell ripped through his personal flag, adorned with the names of the battles he had fought, hurling the color-bearer to the ground. Leaving the road, Kilpatrick and about thirty horsemen veered to the left, spurring straight toward the smoking mouth of the gun. A high stake-and-rider fence barred the way. Some of the men dismounted and began tearing it apart.

"Boys, there's time enough to give them one more shot," yelled a Rebel cannoneer.[26]

The powder-grimed gunners apparently could not depress the muzzle far enough to reach the bluecoated troopers furiously pulling down fence rails at the foot of the knoll and a blast of canister ripped into the ranks of the oncoming 8th Indiana, felling men and horses. Having fired their last round, the Rebel artillerymen fled, just as the Yankees opened a hole in the fence wide enough for two or three horsemen. Private William Bailey, a dark-skinned little orderly Minty had sent with a message for Kilpatrick, spurred through the gap. "Come on boys!" he yelled as he galloped toward the gun, firing his revolver.

Bailey allegedly shot down one of the defenders. Kilpatrick urged his spotted horse over the fence in what one trooper called "beautiful style" and followed the little orderly with his staff and escort, brandishing his saber and yelling at the top of his voice.[27]

Immediately behind them came Companies D and E of the 8th Indiana. These were the men who had marched 800 miles in the past forty days, ridden half the length of Alabama with Rousseau, and been to hell and back with McCook. Led by Captain Josiah Stanley and the brigade inspector, Captain Samuel Lyon, they swarmed over the abandoned gun. Captain Lyon's horse went down, struck by a bullet. A Rebel who had already surrendered suddenly fired at Private Eli Boring, cutting the boy's cartridge box sling and grazing his hip. Another Hoosier shot the Rebel dead and the brigade raced on, leaving three men to take possession of the prized howitzer.

At the rear of Jones's column, nineteen-year-old Hector Looker of the 10th Ohio tumbled from his saddle, shot through the head. Private James Looker dismounted and rushed to his side. As he knelt over his dead boy's body, a Rebel bullet struck him down.

The 5th and 3rd Kentucky of King's brigade swept past the fallen father and son, then wheeled around to cover the retreat of the ambulances, ammunition wagons, and artillery. Someone brought back the Board of Trade Battery's spare limber, and troopers hurriedly hitched up the captured Rebel howitzer and hauled it away.

Last to leave the field was Major Albert Woodcock's 92nd Illinois. They had not gotten into the fight, explained Sergeant Ed Cort, "but we were dissmounted and double quicked arround untill we were about rundown." Ordered to mount, they fell in behind Beebe's Wisconsin battery and spurred down the road. Just as they reached the foot of the little knoll, some of Ross's men opened fire from the woods on their left at point-blank range.

Instantly, the left wing of the regiment wheeled into line. Leveling their Spencers, they pumped a withering hail of lead into the woods. The Rebels answered with a second volley, wounding Lieutenant William B. Mayer in the knee and slightly injuring a few other troopers before they ran away. "[T]hey were not 20 yds from us when we wheeled and fired on them," said Sergeant Cort. "One ball passed through the bundle on the front of my saddle within three inches of me."[28]

The 4th Ohio had just reformed their ranks when this rattle of small arms erupted behind them. Ordered to save the threatened artillery and ambulances, they turned around but had not gone far when someone cried, "Make way for the artillery." As the column moved aside, the Board of Trade Battery trundled past towing the Rebel howitzer that had inflicted so many casualties. "Bully for you, boys," the Ohio troopers cheered.

Then came the ambulances, loaded down with wounded, and the regiment watched somberly as the grim cargoes rolled past. Many of their comrades were still lying on the battlefield, but Kilpatrick could not stop to collect them. He had to keep moving, and he was not going to make the same mistake McCook and Stoneman had made. Instead of trying to retrace his route back to Sandtown, he turned the head of his column east, toward McDonough, leaving Bob Minty's two brigades to bring up the rear.

The entire command was badly disorganized. Troopers who had lost their mounts were chasing runaway Rebel horses and mules. Men were looking for their officers. Officers were looking for their regiments. It took Frank Mix almost an hour before he found his 4th Michigan lined up about a mile down the road with the rest of Minty's brigade. A surgeon dressed his wounded left hand and gave him "a good drink of whisky." Kilpatrick stopped and spoke to him briefly, and Mix advised him the rear guard was likely to be "hard pressed."

Bob Minty apparently agreed and had his provost marshal, Lieutenant Samuel C. Dixon of the 7th Pennsylvania, transfer forty-nine captured Confederates to the custody of Kilpatrick's division. He also sent Lieutenant John H. Simpson with orders for Eli Long's Ohio brigade to dismount and hold the Rebels at bay while the rest of the column moved off toward McDonough.[29]

"The motion of forming and moving out was slow . . . ," Long noted disapprovingly. An 1855 graduate of the Kentucky Military Institute who had served in the old 1st U.S. Cavalry with Alfred Iverson and James B. McIntyre, Long was "a perfect soldier in appearance and dress," and much beloved by his men. "He was serious, deliberate, methodical, 'still as the breeze, but dreadful as the storm'. . . ," wrote a fellow officer. "As modest and noiseless as a woman but as intrepid as one of Cromwell's 'Ironsides,' he was . . . serene under all conditions, . . . without a trace of the fanfaronade and fondness for dress and display which are supposed to be the characteristics of the cavalryman. Looking out constantly for the comfort of his men and horses, he needed no supervision and but few orders. He was always in his right place and always ready for such service as might come his way."[30]

Knowing the Rebels would soon be after them, he waited impatiently for Kilpatrick's confused column to get started. When the restless eddies of men and horses finally began filing off to the east, he halted his rearmost regiment, the 3rd Ohio, only recently armed with Spencers, and ordered a battalion to hold the crest of a small ridge until the tail end of the column was out of sight. Companies B and D dismounted along with two others, sending their horses with the rest of the regiment. Taking cover behind a couple of log cabins and some apple trees, they waited.[31]

They did not have to wait long. Half an hour after the Yankees rode over Ross's Texans, Frank Armstrong's Mississippi brigade arrived on the field. Decoyed away from Kilpatrick's column by Robert Klein's feint toward Bear Creek Station the previous day, they had spent the night near Fayetteville before being ordered back to Jonesboro early on August 20. They had gone eight or ten miles in that direction when a courier met them with news the Yankees were moving toward Griffin. Hurrying south, Armstrong's men heard the first faint rumble of artillery about 1:00 P.M. and reached the battlefield about an hour later.

"I was amazed at the sight that presented itself to my view," wrote Lieutenant Sydney Champion of the 28th Mississippi Cavalry. The ground was covered with guns, pistols, sabers, sacks of corn, oats, coffee, cooking utensils, cups, pans, buckets, cartridge boxes, ammunition, blankets, overcoats, and saddlebags. Horses, some trailing skewed saddles behind them, stood in suffering silence or struggled violently, crazed with pain and fear. Others sprawled glassy-eyed and still, the flies already swarming over torn bodies and protruding entrails. Nearby lay their riders, some in ashen-faced agony, others to rise no more.[32]

As Armstrong's brigade followed the trampled wake of the retreating raiders, Ross's men flocked to the side of the road, many of them bleeding from saber cuts. "Go ahead boys," the Texans yelled, "they are not over a mile ahead and too badly scared and hurt to fight you very hard."[33]

Colonel Robert Pinson's 1st Mississippi Cavalry pressed ahead. Followed by part of Ballentine's Regiment and a section of King's Battery, they soon overtook the Yankee rear guard. "By the left flank into line; then charge," Pinson ordered.[34]

The Ohio battalion Eli Long had left behind fired a volley and then ran to rejoin their regiment, pausing occasionally to snap a shot at Pinson's pursuing skirmishers. Racing across a cornfield, they soon came to the banks of Walnut Creek, a small stream much swollen from the previous night's rain. "Thinking it was shallow," recounted Sergeant Garner Stimsen, "we stepped in and down we went, head first, but managed to get across. We . . . did not stop to pull off our boots to empty the water out, but held up our feet so that it would run out, and then hastened to our horses and mounted."

Eli Long sat on horseback, watching grimly as his skirmishers came splashing across the creek. In front of him, Colonel Charles Seidel's 3rd Ohio was lined up on both sides of the road, crouching behind a rail fence on a little rise at the edge of the woods. Behind him, Private Henry Prince raced away with orders for the number fours to form the led horses in a compact column facing the rear. Soon the Rebels appeared on the far side of the creek. Hold your fire, Long ordered. Wait until they try to cross, then "fire rapidly and with precision."

The 1st Mississippi burst out of the corn rows and rushed to the creekbank. "Talk about thirst!" recalled Lieutenant Colonel Frank Montgomery. "I felt it that day as I never did before or since; and coming to a small, sluggish stream, over which the entire federal command had crossed, and the water of which was almost thick enough to cut with a knife, those of us crossing in the road stooped and scooping the stuff up in our hands, I thought it the sweetest morsel I ever tasted."

Most of the men waded into the waist-deep water, but some members of Company A, 1st Mississippi, tried to keep their feet dry by filing over a hewn footlog bridging the narrow stream. Sergeant Bob Perkins had just started across when he was shot through the throat and fell dying into the water. The next man in line, Corporal Alphonse Hearn, was hit in the shoulder. He tumbled off the log and would have drowned if Private G. N. Smith had not jumped in after him. "None of the rest of the

Colonel Eli Long commanded the 2nd Brigade of Garrard's division. An 1855 graduate of the Kentucky Military Institute, he was a quiet, pipe-smoking officer, "brave as a lion, gentle as a woman," and always in the thick of a fight. By the war's end he was sporting a full beard. Reproduced from *The Story of the Fourth Regiment Ohio Veteran Volunteer Cavalry: From the Organization of the Regiment, August, 1861, to Its 50th Anniversary, August, 1911.* Based on the book of 1890 by Lucien Wulsin (Cincinnati, Ohio, 1912).

boys attempted to cross the creek on that log," Private W. C. Smith noted solemnly, "but preferred wading even if they did get a little wet."

Rifles held high, they plunged into the water and mounted the opposite bank, where they were met by what Private Smith called "a perfect fusil[l]ade of rifle shots." "Seeking all the protection the dead trees, stumps and the nature of the ground afforded," he related, "we continued to slowly advance. . . ."

Eli Long watched the approaching Rebel skirmishers. "The enemy presented a formidable front, extending well to my right," he noted, "and poured in heavy volleys of musketry, while his artillery opened with excellent precision upon the other regiments in column in the road."

The remaining gun of Lieutenant Bennett's section roared in reply. His shells hurtled over the heads of the 3rd Ohio to burst in the gray ranks, but it was not enough.

"The rebs came running on, yelling like mad demons . . . ," recounted Sergeant Garner Stimsen. "They had to cross a corn field in full view of us; but on they came, their lines well closed and deep. We poured volley after volley into them from our seven shooting guns, but it never wavered their lines in the least."

Eli Long's horse was shot in the head. Colonel Seidel's mount was hit, too. A moment later, Rebels appeared in the woods on the 3rd Ohio's right.

"We are surrounded," Seidel exclaimed.

Raising his hand, he motioned frantically for the regiment to fall back. This was done in what Long described as "a disorderly manner," but before he could intervene, he was shot twice, in his right thigh and forearm.

"The 3d Ohio was here under the most terrible fire that they ever experienced," declared Sergeant Stimsen. "When we were falling back the man on my right was instantly killed, the man on my left was shot through both arms. . . ." Directly in front of him, Lieutenant George Garfield fell from his horse, badly wounded. Private John Grabach asked for and quickly got permission to stay with him. The rest of the regiment hurried past the 4th Ohio, which had dismounted on the north side of the road to cover their retreat.[35]

As Eli Long was led off the field, "pale and bleeding," he turned command of the brigade over to his senior colonel, Beroth Eggleston of the 1st Ohio. A pettifogging lawyer, farmer, and father of five from Chillicothe, Ohio, Eggleston sent word to Bob Minty that Rebel infantry was trying to turn his flanks. Soon a courier galloped up with orders directing him to fall back.

Minty had halted the 1st Brigade a few hundred yards to the rear. Learning Captain McIntyre's Regulars were completely out of carbine ammunition, he sent them ahead with Kilpatrick's column and ordered his two remaining regiments to dismount. The 4th Michigan, led by Captain Briggs Eldridge after Major Mix's wound proved troublesome, took cover behind a rail fence on the left side of the road. The 7th Pennsylvania deployed on the right.[36]

The 1st, 3rd, and 4th Ohio retired through this line in good order, one regiment at a time, using bugle calls to signal the commands. Minty watched approvingly and directed Eggleston to have his men double-quick to the rear, mount their horses, and cross an intervening swamp to support the Board of Trade Battery on the next piece of high ground.

Eggleston's own 1st Ohio got there first. They had just swung into line when Eli Long rode past, supported by an orderly on either side. He smiled wanly and bowed and the men answered with cheers. "He rode forward passing within four feet of me," recounted Captain John Rea, "and I would not have known he was hurt had not his orderly whispered it to me with the remark, 'He wants it kept from the men.'"

About this time, the Board of Trade Battery's three guns galloped up under whip and spur and wheeled through the gateposts of the Foster house on the north side of the road. As the artillery unlimbered in the yard, some women and small children watched anxiously from the front porch.[37]

Suddenly, heavy firing sounded on the other side of the swamp, where Rebel skirmishers were crowding Minty's 4th Michigan and 7th Pennsylvania. "[T]he reception with which they were met a few moments before prevented them from attacking us with the same impetuosity with which they had rushed on to Colonel Long's command," noted Captain William Van Antwerp of the 4th Michigan, but for the next half hour, Minty's rear guard crouched behind hastily built rail breastworks, levering round after round into their Spencers. It was, asserted Frank Mix, "the hardest fighting that we had seen during the raid."

The Rebels brought up a section of King's Battery, which opened fire with what Minty called "great precision." At least one Rebel shell struck the roof of the Foster house. Terrified mothers hurried their children inside and huddled in the brick fireplace, wailing and crying as stray bullets splintered the wooden walls.

Out in the yard, the Board of Trade Battery was firing as fast as the gunners could load. They had just rammed a shell with a two-and-a-half-second fuse down the mouth of the number five gun when there was a terrific explosion. In the blink of an eye, the big cast-iron cannon simply disappeared. The fiery blast shattered all the spokes on both wheels above the hubs and knocked the entire gun crew to the ground. Miraculously, no one was seriously hurt, but when the smoke cleared all that remained of the big Parrott was a small piece of the reinforcing band around the breech.

Moments later, a shell became wedged halfway down the bore of a second gun. Unable to ram the round home or worm it out, Lieutenant Robinson ordered the piece limbered up and sent to the rear along with the wreckage of the number five gun carriage. Leaving Lieutenant Bennett in charge of the remaining gun and what little ammunition was left, he rode across the swamp to ask Minty to have Beebe's battery sent back to relieve him.[38]

Unable to find Minty, Robinson returned and soon received orders to withdraw. Once his battery and the Ohio brigade were safely out of the way, the 4th Michigan and 7th Pennsylvania fell back after repelling three separate assaults.

By now it was nearly 6:00 P.M. Long and Minty had held off the pursuing Rebels for an hour and forty minutes, giving Kilpatrick enough time to get his 3rd Division moving toward McDonough. As the rear guard wearily climbed into their saddles to follow, dark clouds rolled in from the west. Thunder rumbled across the slate-gray sky and rain slanted down in torrents. "I had lost both hat and rubber overcoat in the brush," grumbled Robert Burns, "and in just five seconds was soaked, saturated, even my boots were so filled that the water ran out of the tops."[39]

When the rain began, the head of Kilpatrick's column was already five or six miles down the road. Led by Captain Egbert Q. E. Becker, Companies B, C, and I of the 92nd Illinois charged into McDonough about 5:00 P.M.

Residents had heard the racket west of town that afternoon, and some disabled veterans had immediately recognized it as the rattle of small arms and the roar of artillery. Two or three citizens had ridden out to investigate, and it was not long before the crowd gathered around the courthouse saw them coming back at a gallop, flailing their foam-flecked mounts and yelling the Yankees were coming.

Men sprinted for the woods. Women snatched up their children and hurried home. There they watched as more men and horses than they had ever seen came crowding down the deserted street; stubble-faced, fierce-looking men who looted the commissary store and ransacked the two-story brick courthouse, scattering the county ordinary's records across the floor in a layer six inches deep.

At some point that evening, the raiders learned a group of men had slipped out of town, apparently intending to burn the bridges ahead of them. Captain Matthew Van Buskirk received orders to take a hundred 92nd Illinois mounted infantrymen and a similar sized detachment from the 3rd Kentucky, hurry to Peachstone Shoals and seize the bridge over South River, eight miles to the northeast. Shortly before dark, Van Buskirk rode out of McDonough with an advance guard of fifty men.

They had gone about a mile on the Covington Road when they overtook the squad of would-be bridge burners. "We run them off the track," recorded Sergeant Ed Cort, "and got a head [sic]." Riding hard in the driving rain, Van Buskirk and his men reached the South River at 9:00 P.M. and captured the bridge over the dam at Persall's Mill without difficulty. The rest of the detachment, led by Captain John P. Cummings of the 3rd Kentucky, arrived about five hours later. "We had had no sleep for 60 hours," recounted a weary Illinois soldier, "so we dismounted, wrapped the halter-straps to our wrists, felt our way to a fence and selected three rails, leaned them

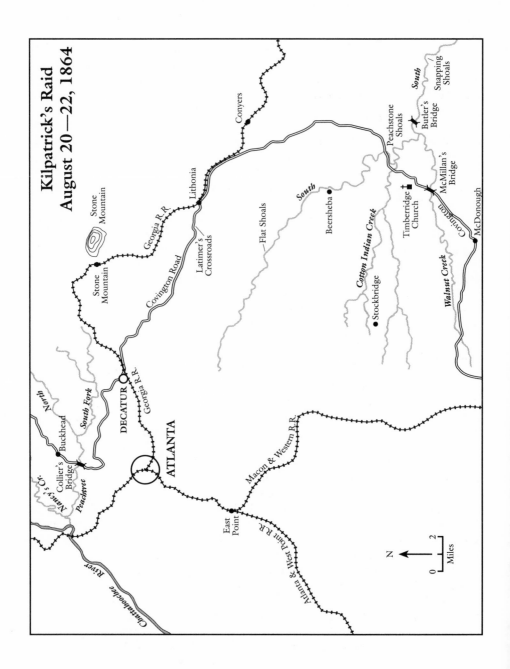

Kilpatrick's Raid
August 20–22, 1864

against the fence at an angle of 45 degrees, lay ourselves upon them, covered ourselves with our rubber ponchos, and were soon lost in sleep."[40]

The rest of the 92nd Illinois followed only as far as McMullen's Bridge over Walnut Creek, four miles northeast of McDonough, before halting at 8:00 P.M. "You will go in there to the left and await further orders," directed an orderly who splashed up alongside the regiment. Moving into what proved to be a plowed field, nearly knee deep in mud, some of the men dismounted and tried to sleep while leaning against their horses. Others, past the point of caring, lay down in the flooded furrows.[41]

The balance of Kilpatrick's plodding column was strung out for miles. The two brigades in front had not slept for two nights. The two in the rear had not slept in three. As darkness descended from the stormy skies on the night of August 20, the Rebels abandoned their pursuit and from that point on, noted Captain John Rea, "it was a column of sleeping horsemen. . . ."[42]

"None but soldiers . . . know what it is to be thoroughly tired . . . ," mused Lieutenant William Webb. "The spectacle of a body of 5,000 [4,000] men marching along through torrents of rain, and four-fifths of that number sound asleep, some sitting bolt upright, others with their arms crossed on the necks of their horses as a support to their heads, must have been a novel sight to any one who could have gazed at us as we passed; but there were no spectators. . . ."

Lightning flashed. The thunder rolled. Wrapped in rubber ponchos if they still had them, soaked to the skin if they did not, troopers swayed in their saddles under the lash of the driving rain, silently cursing the man they called "Kill Cavalry." Many had lost their hats in the charge at Lovejoy's Station. Others, awaking to find their hats had fallen off while they slept, reached out in the darkness, and if a dozing neighbor still had his, immediately appropriated it. "Of those who had hats next morning," chuckled Captain John Rea, "very few had their own."

"[I]t was utterly impossible to march in any kind of order or to keep out an advance guard," added Lieutenant Will Curry of the 1st Ohio, "as men and officers would go to sleep. In some instances the horses would halt along the road in fence corners and the riders would either unconsciously dismount or fall off and sleep until dragged out by the rear guard and compelled to mount and move on with the column."

"I fell asleep on my horse for two hours," admitted Captain Burns, "during which time we had a terrible storm of rain which drenched me more, if possible, than I was. I knew nothing of it until I awoke and then found myself in a strange crowd."

Two or three sleeping riders were enough to stop whole regiments. Thinking there was some obstacle up ahead, the ranks behind them would halt, the men invariably began to nod, and would soon be asleep, too. The 4th Ohio halted about 9:00 P.M. and stood in the pelting rain for nearly an hour because the rear of the 3rd Ohio had gone to sleep. "Upon their awakening we started on such a ride as 'Tam O'Shanter's' must have been on the stormy night when the devils chased him," recounted Private Lucien Wulsin. "It was dark as pitch, raining, thundering and lightning as it only does in the South, while we were going at a hard gallop. . . . Almost every moment some poor fellow would come down into a mud-hole, receiving as encouragement the curses of those following for getting in their way. This continued about an hour, when we rejoined the column."

The 1st Ohio floundered through the darkness until about midnight, when the column halted and orders summoned them forward. "Who guided us and why we moved at all I have never quite understood," noted Captain Rea.

Upon overtaking Minty's front ranks, Rea was placed in command of the advance battalion. He detailed two of his sergeants to keep the men awake, but it was an impossible task. At one point during that wet and miserable night, Rea rode back along the plodding procession and found his reserve squadron standing stock-still beside a fence. The commanding captain was sound asleep. "He was a good Methodist," recounted Rea, "I a Presbyterian, [and] there was a religious war for a moment. I am afraid . . . I swore mildly at him."

The rain had stopped by the time Rea's four companies plodded across McMullen's Bridge at 2:00 A.M. Moving on past Kilpatrick's slumbering soldiers, they halted on a flat, flooded piece of ground. "We dismounted," Rea recalled, "just what else we did I do not remember, but I threw myself on the ground in the water and was wrapped in sleep in a second."

He had scarcely closed his eyes when the regimental sergeant major shook him awake. Orders, the sergeant major explained; Rea's company was to mount up at once and report for picket duty.

Rea started to protest but soon realized there was no point in arguing with the sergeant major. Convinced the orders probably resulted from the recent change in command of the 1st Ohio, he got up and went to regimental headquarters. There must be some mistake, he told Lieutenant Colonel Thomas J. Patten, who had succeeded Beroth Eggleston after Eli Long was wounded. His men had been on picket the night before and had just been relieved as the advance guard. They could scarcely keep their eyes open.

Patten sleepily waved him away, saying he had no time to listen to complaints. Everyone was exhausted and the orders would not be changed.

Rea angrily stalked off to brigade headquarters, a few yards away, and repeated his story to Colonel Eggleston. The colonel said he would select another company and told him to go get some sleep.

As Rea returned to his soggy billet, Minty's rear guard, the 4th Michigan, crossed Walnut Creek. Leaving a detachment to burn the bridge behind them, at least part of the regiment apparently continued up the Covington Road for another two and a half miles before halting near two old churches, Timberridge Presbyterian and Little Sharon Primitive Baptist. Cold, wet, and miserable, Yankee troopers pulled down both buildings and used them for firewood.[43]

They also ransacked the James Jefferson Turner house, almost directly across the road from the Timberridge Church. It was probably here that a Michigan trooper found a handsome silk flag with eleven white stars surrounding a gold rendering of the Georgia state seal on a blue square in the upper staff corner. A blue ribbon, scrolled across three horizontal bars of red, white, and red, bore the words, "Presented by the Ladies of Henry" painted in gold letters on one side, and "Victory or Death," and "Zachry Rangers" on the other. Turner's son-in-law, Charles T. Zachry, had raised the company at the outset of the war. Mustered into service as Company H of the 27th Georgia Infantry, the Rangers were sent to Virginia, where Zachry rose to the rank of colonel. At some point, apparently after acquiring title to the two-story house on the Covington Road from Turner's widow in December 1863, Zachry had sent the flag home for safekeeping, and this was how Kilpatrick's men captured a second set of colors belonging to an infantry company serving in the Army of Northern Virginia.[44]

Despite these depredations and others, most of the raiders managed to get some much-needed rest. "Four hours sleep helps a man amazingly . . . ," marveled Captain Albert Potter when he awoke on August 21 as a new day dawned behind the gray overcast.

"Oh! but what a [sorry] looking crowd we were!" confessed Lieutenant George W. Clark of the 4th Michigan. Everything and everybody was caked with mud. Downcast and dispirited, the weary, rain-soaked riders hauled their stiff, aching bodies into wet saddles and shambled into line on horses half dead with fatigue.[45]

Plodding up the Covington Road for perhaps a half mile, at 6:00 A.M. the head of the column came to the banks of Cotton Indian Creek. Ordinarily a quiet country stream about twenty-five-feet wide and two-and-a-half-feet deep, the recent rains had swelled it to a raging torrent, three times its normal size. There was no bridge and troopers who had braved a hundred battles quailed at the sight. "It was the most formidable torrent I have ever met . . . ," declared Captain John Rea. "The current rushed down between high, steep banks, that made the channel appear like a great trough through the earth, with a swiftness that appalled us all. . . ."[46]

Realizing anyone attempting to swim straight across was sure to be swept past the flooded roadbed on the other side, troopers moved twelve or fifteen rods upstream before roweling their snorting, wide-eyed mounts over the bank. By keeping their horses' heads pointed upstream and swimming against the current, the advance guard reached the east bank without mishap.

Kilpatrick was among the first to cross. Those who followed saw him standing waist-deep in the roiling, brown water, ready with a rope and a helping hand for anyone who needed it.

"Take your saber to that horse," he yelled to a trooper with a reluctant mount. "Let go the bridle reins and let the horses guide themselves," he ordered another.

Cursing one moment, encouraging the next, he was hauling floundering horses out of the water by their bridles when Eli Murray rode up to the edge of the west bank.

"General," Murray called over the rush of the muddy torrent, "the enemy are pressing my command in the rear."

"Then what in hell are you doing here?" Kilpatrick shot back.

The contrite Kentuckian hurried away.[47]

Getting 4,000 men and horses across the eighty-foot freshet was agonizingly slow work. One by one, they plunged down the slippery bank and neck-deep into the swirling water. In the rear ranks of Company K of the 1st Ohio, Private Francis M. Jones watched from the back of a small mule he was riding after losing his horse in the charge at Lovejoy's Station. When his turn came, he prodded his mount into the flood. Halfway across, the mule panicked. Broadsided by the relentless current, it rolled over and Jones went under, weighed down by his carbine and accoutrements. He did not come up. There was a moment of stunned silence as his comrades watched helplessly from the shore. Then the next man spurred over the bank.[48]

They could not wait for the rushing waters to recede. "If we had been attacked by a large force before we had succeeded in crossing, a great number of us would have been captured," asserted Captain Burns. "We were almost wholly out of ammunition, and many an anxious glance was cast to the rear."

The artillery crossed after Minty's cavalry, one gun at a time. Cannoneers and postilions clutching all the powder bags they could carry drove their teams in at the ford and headed upstream for several yards before turning toward the east bank. "This task of swimming eight horses all harnessed together, attached to a heavy gun and carriage which was sunk far below the surface was as dangerous as facing a Rebel charge," declared John Nourse. "As every man was weighted with ammunition a slight tangling of the harness meant sure drowning." But by the time the wheel horses had to swim, the leaders had already gained the opposite shore and the guns crossed safely.

"The most difficult and trying work," averred Bob Minty, "was getting our poor wounded comrades across. . . ." Some were strapped to their saddles and led across, but the most seriously injured had to be carried over in the ambulances. Kilpatrick's headquarters ambulance made the first attempt and was immediately swept downstream, mules, driver, and all.[49] A few men with axes were subsequently dispatched to the east bank, where they felled a big tree into the muddy torrent. The ring of axes also sounded on the west bank, where a second tree soon crashed into the creek. Lieutenant Robinson then sent some of his artillerymen across this tangled bridge of trunks and branches with a picket rope. Tying one end to the wagon tongue and looping the other around a big rock on the east bank, they towed the ambulances and teams across with the help of a few cavalrymen, who swam their horses on the upstream side to break the force of the current.

This worked well enough until one of the ambulances suddenly tipped over, spilling three wounded men into the water. Calling to some troopers on the east bank for help, Kilpatrick plunged in after them. Struggling in water up to his armpits, he and the ambulance driver pulled Lieutenant William Mayer of the 92nd Illinois ashore.

Bystanders rescued the other two men, and once the wounded were safely across troopers began driving the pack mules into the water. Burdened with top-heavy loads of camp kettles, rations, and equipment, the poor beasts never had a chance. "As soon as they reached the swift current they would roll over and down the stream they went," noted John Nourse: "generally all we could see was four legs sticking up out of the water kicking vigorously." Very few reached the east bank.

The scene must have reminded members of the 8th Indiana and the 2nd Kentucky of the perils they had faced at Ten Islands and the Tallapoosa River during Rousseau's raid. By the time it was their turn to cross, the only vehicles remaining on the west bank were two or three ammunition wagons belonging to the Board of Trade and 10th Wisconsin batteries. When Kilpatrick ordered these destroyed, Lieutenant Robinson reminded him one of them carried the gun that had been dismounted at Lovejoy's Station. If the general would give him the privilege of attempting it, he felt sure he could tow the wagon across with his picket ropes.

"Damn the gun!" Kilpatrick roared. "Destroy the wagon."[50]

Retorting he would "dam the river by throwing the damned gun into it," Robinson led a few men back to the west bank, spiked the prized Parrott and pitched it into four feet of water. Then they cut down the wagons and set them ablaze. "I . . . have frequently, though mentally, damned Kilpatrick from then till now . . . ," Robinson later wrote.

It was late that morning before the last trooper crossed Cotton Indian Creek. Private Jones and at least fifty mules and horses had drowned and there was not a dry stitch of clothing in the command, but at least, noted a mounted infantryman, the water had "washed away the mud."[51]

Kilpatrick's advance guard had already pressed ahead, and a mile beyond Cotton Indian Creek they came to Peachstone Shoals on the South River. Skirting the face of the rocky bluff rising along the river's edge, they filed down to the bridge Captain Van Buskirk's detachment had captured during the night at Persall's Mill. Just as they started across, the mill burst into flames. "It was pretty hot passing it," acknowledged Sergeant Garner Stimsen of the 3rd Ohio, "but our clothes needed drying. . . ."

Once everyone was across, Kilpatrick's rear guard, Company D of the 8th Indiana, burned the bridge behind them. Shortly after midday the column halted to rest and feed. "I don't remember of dark, strong, army camp-kettle coffee ever tasting better or having a more exhilarating effect than at this particular time," noted a weary Lieutenant Robinson.

During this halt, Kilpatrick sent several small detachments ranging up and down the east bank of the South River. These patrols burned the bridges at Beersheba, Landum's, and Snapping Shoals, effectively forestalling any Rebel pursuit. After resting a couple of hours, the raiders continued northward. "A few bushwhackers fired into us," reported Sergeant Ed Cort of the 92nd Illinois, "but we were not troubled much."

About 3:00 P.M., the advance guard encountered several carriages and buggies loaded with families returning from church. Troopers immediately shucked the horses out of the shafts and led them away, leaving old men, women, and children stranded in the middle of the road. As the Yankee column filed past the frightened worshipers, an Illinois soldier noticed an attractive young lady of about eighteen dressed in her Sunday best. "Sissy," he called wolfishly, "are you in favor of *our* Union?"

She shook her dark curls emphatically, her black eyes flashing angrily.[52]

For the rest of that overcast afternoon, the blue column wearily plodded past farms and plantations, looting provisions and riding stock.[53] "This is a good country," observed Corporal John McLain of the 4th Michigan, "and there is a good crop of corn growing."

"A detail has been in the rear all day," he added, "shooting horses that could go no further." The 10th Wisconsin Battery alone abandoned six exhausted animals before the column finally halted along the Georgia Railroad at Lithonia about 7:00 P.M. Haggard and hollow-eyed, the men stripped the saddles off the backs of their worn-out mounts for the first time since leaving Sandtown. In some cases, noted one trooper, "our blankets brought off hair and all."[54]

They were reasonably certain they had outdistanced the Rebel cavalry and infantry they had fought at Lovejoy, but their safety was by no means ensured. Tired as they were, the possibility a force might have been sent from Atlanta to intercept them compelled the 92nd Illinois to stand watch east of the railroad, while detachments from other regiments picketed the other points of the compass.

No fires were allowed. Rations were scarce. "John Shoemaker and I got a sack of peanuts at Jonesborough, a commercial sack, about 3 bushels, emptied part out, and that is all we have eaten since . . . ," John McLain complained to his diary.

During the night, the rain poured down again. A few troopers found shelter in the railroad depot, but everyone else had to sleep out in the open. Lieutenant Ebenezer Stetson and Private William Cash of the 10th Wisconsin curled up in a cornfield. They awoke the next morning to find a layer of mud had washed up around them, leaving a high-water mark that stretched from head to heel.

Wet and weary, the mud-caked cavaliers began stirring early on August 22. "The men [are] much worn out," noted Captain John Paisley of the 10th Ohio. A few managed to coax flickering fires to life and boil coffee, but most had nothing to eat before Bob Minty's brigade led the column west on the Covington Road at 6:00 A.M.

The skies had cleared. The sun shone brightly, and Stone Mountain's familiar shape rose up on the right as Minty's men led the way past Latimer's Crossroads and other landmarks they remembered seeing three weeks earlier during their part in Stoneman's raid. "Moved fast all day, losing many horses and picking up all we could find," recorded the 10th Ohio's Captain Paisley. "Many of our men who were dismounted had to foot it and keep up or be taken prisoners. They chose the former and pressed along, many of them about half asleep and if we dismounted [for more] than a moment had to go round and waken them up before [we] could start. . . ."

About noon, the column halted on the outskirts of Decatur while Kilpatrick hurried the 4th Ohio forward to meet a small Rebel force that sallied out to challenge his approach. Taking advantage of this delay, the 92nd Illinois fed their horses in a nearby cornfield, pulled down the cedar fence rails, built bonfires, stripped off their wet clothes, and hung them up to dry. Some of the Illinois boys had stolen the fraternal regalia from the burning Masonic Hall in Jonesboro. While waiting for their clothes to dry, they donned the little Masonic aprons embroidered with gold and silver bullion and marched around in a circle, "in commemoration," they said, "of old father Adam, who was partial to that kind of dress."

After a halt of about two hours, the column moved on through Decatur. "The town is in a dilapidated condition and nearly deserted of Inhabitants," the 8th Indiana's Williamson Ward noted as the rear guard ambled past the empty houses. Continuing westward, across the scarred battlefield of July 22, late that afternoon the raiders began filing past the trenches held by David Stanley's IV Corps. Curious foot soldiers flocked to the roadside, asking whose cavalry they were.

"Kilpatrick's," came the reply.

The infantrymen greeted them with wild cheers. "We heard you were all captured," someone yelled.

The tired troopers assured them the rumors of their demise had been greatly exaggerated, but they were mightily hungry and asked, "Do you have any hard bread you could give me?"

Some soldiers from the 74th Illinois dug into their haversacks and handed passing horsemen pieces of hardtack and sowbelly, which Private William Cash of the 10th Wisconsin Battery noted was eaten "ravenously raw as we moved along."[55]

As the column turned northward on the Peachtree Road, Kilpatrick stopped briefly at the big white house that now served as General Stanley's headquarters. After telegraphing news of his return, he lingered long enough to regale Stanley and his staff with a brief account of the raid before riding on to report to General Thomas.[56]

In the meantime, Bob Minty's brigade plodded north and reached their old camps on Peachtree Creek at sundown. The Ohio brigade crossed Collier's Bridge and continued to their old bivouac at Buckhead, where they greeted the news of Eli Long's promotion to brigadier general with hearty cheers before breaking ranks and rushing to secure their billets and water their horses.

The 3rd Division arrived shortly afterward and halted at Peachtree Creek. There the 92nd Illinois received an enthusiastic welcome from their former comrades-in-arms, the mounted infantrymen of Abe Miller's Lightning Brigade. "They had got word that we were coming, and were hungry and weary," recounted Corporal Charles Holbrook; "and, noble men that they were, when we came up they greeted us with three hearty cheers, and what was better, kettlesful of hot coffee, fried pork, and hardtack."[57]

As troopers lifted their stiff, aching limbs out of the saddle, equally weary regimental surgeons, assisted by colleagues from Miller's Lightning Brigade, turned their attention to the wounded. Far into the night, they labored over men like Captain William Scott of Eli Long's staff, who had been struck down when he charged the Rebel howitzer at Lovejoy's Station and now lay in an ambulance with a shattered right shoulder. When doctors told "Scotty" they would have to amputate his arm, he steadfastly refused, even though he knew it meant he would die.[58]

Casualty lists left no doubt who had done most of the fighting. Bob Minty's 1st Brigade counted 106 killed, wounded, or missing. Losses totaled 94 in Eli Long's brigade, and 7 in the Board of Trade Battery.

In contrast, Fielder Jones's 2nd Brigade of Kilpatrick's division had 49 dead, wounded, and missing. The 10th Wisconsin Battery had 6 casualties, while Robert King's entire 3rd Brigade could count only 15. Many of the missing troopers were wounded men who had been left behind because there were not enough ambulances to carry them.[59]

"I wish to see General Kilpatrick soon as possible," Sherman wired George Thomas shortly before 6:00 P.M. when he learned of the cavalry's return. In a second telegram at 6:30 P.M., he asked Thomas to send him "in general terms" the results of Kilpatrick's raid. "If General Kilpatrick be tired," he added, "let him rest with you. . . ."

"General Kilpatrick is about to start for your headquarters," Thomas wired at 7:30 P.M. Recounting the gist of his conversation with the cavalryman, he reported Kilpatrick claimed to have torn up four miles of railroad between Rough and Ready and Jonesboro, another ten miles at intervals, and destroyed two trains, including the one Klein had wrecked at Bear Creek Station. He had fought off Jackson's cavalry and a whole division of infantry, and "virtually captured" Ross's entire Texas brigade, but was able to bring away only about seventy prisoners. He also brought back three Rebel battle flags and a captured cannon and had taken three other guns, destroying two of them and nine caissons. He asserted his own losses totaled ninety-seven killed and missing, including four officers, and he had brought back all his wounded.

A little later that evening, a tired but enthusiastic Kilpatrick arrived at Sherman's headquarters on the west side of Atlanta. Elaborating on the exaggerated tale he had already told Thomas, he spoke of his accomplishments in glowing terms and assured Sherman his men had destroyed enough track between Jonesboro and Bear Creek Station to disable the Macon railroad for ten days.

Far off in the distance, trumpeting over the treetops and lingering on the night air, came the high shrill notes that made his words a lie. It was the defiant wail of a Rebel locomotive chugging into Atlanta from the south.[60]

EPILOGUE

An army weak in cavalry
rarely achieves great success.

—Napoleon

The trains kept rolling into Atlanta and by 9:15 A.M., August 23, Sherman knew Kilpatrick had failed. "I became more than ever convinced," he later wrote, "that cavalry could not or would not work hard enough to disable a railroad properly, and therefore resolved at once to proceed to the execution of my original plan."[1]

Resurrecting the intricate flanking maneuver that would send his armies swinging around the west side of Atlanta, Sherman corralled his surplus wagons and baggage on the north bank of the Chattahoochee. On the night of August 25, George Thomas's XX Corps quietly abandoned the trenches north of Atlanta and retired to the south side of the river to fortify three small enclaves embracing the railroad trestle, the wagon bridge at Pace's Ferry, and a pontoon bridge at Turner's Ferry. Thomas's IV Corps followed as far as the Marietta Road and then turned south to join the XIV Corps on the far right flank of Sherman's line. The next night, the XV, XVI, and XVII Corps of Oliver Otis Howard's Army of the Tennessee quit the trenches west of Atlanta and slogged through heavy rain and muddy roads to deploy on the right of the IV Corps.[2]

To the pale, war-weary Atlantans who cautiously crept out of the cellars and bombproofs where they had huddled for the last month, the empty trenches could only mean one thing. Sherman had quit, given up, gone home. John Bell Hood wanted to believe that. He had received glowing (and grossly inflated) reports of Joe Wheeler's success on the Western & Atlantic Railroad, and scouts and deserters assured him the Yankee army was hungry, cut off from supplies. Hood remained cautious, however, and while Atlanta basked in the unaccustomed quiet, he sent "Red" Jackson's cavalry to locate Sherman's bluecoated columns and alerted his infantry to be ready to move "at a moment's notice."

By the afternoon of August 27, Jackson's troopers were sparring with Yankee skirmishers just west of the Atlanta & West Point Railroad. Realizing Sherman was not retreating, Hood dispatched two infantry brigades to Jonesboro and three more to Rough and Ready to protect the Macon railroad. The rest of his army sat in the trenches, waiting.[3]

The Yankees easily pushed aside Jackson's cavalry and by nightfall, August 28, Thomas and Howard were astride the West Point railroad between Red Oak and Fairburn. But instead of pressing ahead, Sherman, whose fixation with railroads bordered on obsession, directed both armies to halt and devote the next day to tearing up track. "Let the destruction be so thorough that not a rail or tie can be used again," he ordered.

While Schofield's XXIII Corps confronted the Confederate trenches at East Point, the IV, XIV, XV, XVI, and XVII Corps spent the next thirty-six hours wrecking twelve and a half miles of railroad between Red Oak and Fairburn. "The track was heaved up in sections the length of a regiment," Sherman noted approvingly, "then separated rail by rail; bonfires were made of the ties and of fence rails on which the rails were heated, carried to trees or telegraph poles, wrapped around and left to cool."[4]

Satisfied with the scope of the destruction, early on August 30 he sent all three of his armies advancing eastward on a broad front. Uncertain of where the next blow would fall, Hood countered by shifting his three corps west and south of Atlanta, extending his left toward Rough and Ready.

Late that evening, Sherman's southernmost column, spearheaded by Judson Kilpatrick's 3rd Cavalry Division, crossed the Flint River near Jonesboro. John Logan's XV Corps dug in on the high ground just west of the Macon railroad, where the rest of Howard's Army of the Tennessee joined them the next morning.

Realizing the threat this posed to his supply line, Hood sent General William J. Hardee to drive the Yankees into the Flint River "at all hazards." Arriving at Jonesboro with his own corps and Stephen D. Lee's, Hardee attacked at 3:00 P.M. on August 31. Some of his infantry pressed to within pistol shot of Howard's lines before heavy volleys forced them to hug the ground. Other units were slow to advance and the assault quickly degenerated into a futile series of rushes at the blazing Yankee breastworks. Forty-five minutes of fierce fighting cost Hardee no less than 1,900 casualties. Howard's losses numbered only about 200.

Fearing a counterattack, Hardee withdrew to begin digging in around Jonesboro. During the night, orders from Hood directed him to send back Lee's corps. "There are indications," Hood advised, "that the enemy may make an attempt on Atlanta to-morrow."[5]

Sherman, however, was trying to concentrate all three of his armies in front of Jonesboro and thoroughly wreck the Macon railroad. He ordered Schofield's XXIII Corps and Thomas's IV and XIV Corps to push south from Rough and Ready, tearing up the track as they went. While he anxiously awaited their approach, Howard's XV, XVI, and XVII Corps inched forward early on September 1, pinning down the three divisions Hood had left with Hardee.

Late that morning, the XIV Corps arrived, commanded by Jefferson C. Davis, a combative, thirty-six-year-old Kentuckian with an unlikely name and an unsavory reputation. Aggrieved over a supposed insult, Davis had murdered another Union general in a Louisville hotel lobby in September 1862 and had never been brought to trial. Sherman believed he was just the sort of fellow who could put some fire into Thomas's sluggish XIV Corps, and had promoted him to replace the recalcitrant John Palmer.

Davis found Hardee's Confederates manning a fishhook-shaped line of works paralleling the west side of the Macon railroad, the right flank bending back across the track about a mile north of Jonesboro. Under the cover of a fierce artillery barrage, Davis deployed two divisions in front of the angle at the railroad. At 4:00 P.M., his front ranks stepped forward. Dense undergrowth, mires, and gullies hampered the advance, and while one of Davis's divisions halted at the edge of an old cornfield to realign its ranks, the other resolutely pressed ahead.

Hardee's grim veterans were stretched paper thin, standing six feet apart in some places, but they went to work manfully, biting the ends off paper cartridges, ramming the loads down the muzzles of their long-barreled Enfields, and fumbling with the musket caps that made them fire. Artillerymen cursed and sweated, swabbed and loaded, filling the air with torrents of canister and case shot.

The disjointed Federal assault stacked up in the face of a withering fire, faltered and fell back. Davis brought up reinforcements, and at 4:45 P.M., the XIV Corps lunged forward.

"There was no chance for flinching here," declared Major James A. Connolly. "Generals, Colonels, Majors, Captains and privates, all had to go forward together over that open field, facing and drawing nearer to death at every step we took, our horses crazy, frantic with the howling of shells, the rattling of canister and the whistling of bullets, ourselves delirious with the wild excitement of the moment, and thinking only of getting over those breast works. . . ."[6]

Rebel gunners redoubled their efforts. Men jolted convulsively and pitched to the ground, but the living pressed on; with wild shouts and yells, they poured over the Rebel works at the angle "like a drove of Texas beeves." Then it was gun butt and bayonet, bullets at point-blank range.

Seeing the breakthrough, Sherman sent "Old Slow Trot" Thomas to hurry the IV Corps down the east side of the Macon railroad to cut the Rebel line of retreat. It was, Sherman noted, "the only time during the campaign I can recall seeing General Thomas urge his horse into a gallop."[7]

Before the IV Corps could get into position, a Confederate counterattack stemmed the initial onslaught and darkness soon drew the fighting to a close. Losses were heavy on both sides, Davis's XIV Corps suffering 1,200 casualties, while Hardee lost 1,000 men just as prisoners.

At 11:00 P.M., Hardee quietly began pulling his three divisions out of the trenches. Defeated, dispirited, encumbered with Hood's supply and ordnance wagons, the long columns somehow slipped through the noose Sherman was trying to close around them and headed south for Lovejoy's Station.[8]

Behind them, a series of thunderous explosions shook the night. A sleepless Sherman cocked his ear toward Atlanta and wondered what it meant.

The jarring blasts also rattled the XX Corps' headquarters near the railroad bridge over the Chattahoochee River. Major General Henry Warner Slocum, recently arrived to take the departed Joe Hooker's place, ordered each of his three divisions to send patrols toward Atlanta to reconnoiter.

Shortly after daylight on September 2, Colonel John Coburn left Turner's Ferry with a detachment of 900 infantrymen. Deploying a heavy skirmish line on both sides of the road and screened by Lieutenant Lewis W. Boren and about forty troopers from Companies E and G of the 14th Illinois Cavalry, Coburn marched eastward for five miles before halting behind the breastworks his men had abandoned a week earlier.

Accompanied by two cavalrymen, Captain Henry M. Scott of the 70th Ohio Infantry and three other officers rode ahead to reconnoiter. From a hilltop behind their old lines, they saw a pall of smoke hanging over Atlanta. Directly in front of them, the once bristling Rebel forts and trenches stood silent and still. Sending a courier to take this information back to Colonel Coburn, Scott and his companions continued toward the city. As they entered the empty Rebel breastworks, they saw a line of graycoated cavalry forming across the road ahead of them. Shots rang out, and the handful of Yankee horsemen beat a hasty retreat.

Falling back on Coburn's skirmishers, Captain Scott made a brief report and then led Lieutenant Boren's cavalry to the left. Boren's troopers outflanked the opposing Rebels and soon reached the Marietta Road. As they approached the abandoned earthworks, they saw a group of riders coming toward them, carrying a flag of truce. Captain Scott rode ahead and met a stately gentleman on a white horse who identified himself as James M. Calhoun, the mayor of Atlanta.

Calhoun asked if Scott was the officer in command.

"No," the Yankee captain replied.

With as much dignity as he could muster, the mayor reiterated his request to speak with the commanding officer. Hood had abandoned Atlanta during the night, blown up twenty-eight freight carloads of ammunition left standing in a rail yard, and marched south to rejoin Lee and Hardee. Calhoun had come to surrender the city.

Scott sent a courier galloping back to Turner's Ferry with this news and escorted Colonel Coburn forward to meet the mayor's delegation. Then he hurried on to overtake Lieutenant Boren's cavalry, who became the first Union soldiers to enter the conquered city.[9]

About 4:00 that afternoon, one of Kenner Garrard's staff officers, Captain Lewis M. Hosea, caught up with Sherman and George Thomas a mile and a half north of Lovejoy's Station and told them the glorious news. Hood had abandoned Atlanta.

"They both gave extravagant vent to the joy of the announcement," Hosea recalled. "After a rapid cross-questioning, and assurance that I had personally seen the inside of the works, they let loose and actually danced and flung up their hats, and embraced each other, while I bore the brunt of hand-shaking that made my arms sore."[10]

"Atlanta is ours, and fairly won," Sherman telegraphed Washington on September 3. Hood's retreating columns were at his mercy, but in his long-awaited hour of triumph, Sherman let them go.

"Atlanta . . . ," he confided in a letter to his friend Henry Halleck, "was the prize I fought for."[11]

He seemed to have forgotten Grant's original instructions, back in April, to move against the Rebel army and "break it up." His whole focus after crossing the Chattahoochee had shifted from destroying the opposing army to capturing Atlanta. He had talked confidently of taking the city within a week and counted heavily on his cavalry to cut the railroads that kept the defenders supplied with beef, bacon, and cornmeal, bullets, gunpowder, and shells. Instead, it had taken six weeks to force the city's surrender, and when Sherman did not win the quick victory he wanted, he accused his horsemen of not working hard enough.[12]

This was not true. Lovell Rousseau had obliterated twenty-six miles of railroad and telegraph during the forty-four hours he spent astride the Montgomery & West Point route, and the effects of his raid were keenly felt in Atlanta. By August 1, a Rebel artillery officer was complaining, "Because the Atlanta and Montgomery Railroad has been cut, depriving us, at least temporarily of our source of supplies, the artillery horses are becoming materially reduced from lack of their usual number of pounds of corn. We are now foraging from the fields of green corn." The interruption of grain supplies from Alabama and Mississippi and the need to range far afield for forage may have also been what sent a sizable portion of Hood's wagon train all the way down to Fayetteville, where McCook captured it on July 29.[13]

Kenner Garrard's destruction of the trestles over the Yellow and Alcovy rivers on

July 22 also had important results. His raid, when combined with Sherman's presence on the east side of Atlanta, denied the Rebel defenders direct access to reinforcements and munitions from Virginia and the Carolinas and put the Georgia Railroad out of commission for the rest of the war.[14]

In less than two weeks, at a cost of less than a hundred casualties, Rousseau and Garrard effectively crippled two of the three railroads supplying the Confederate army in Atlanta. No wonder Sherman was optimistic when he sent McCook and Stoneman to cut the tracks south of the city on July 27. "I estimated this joint cavalry could whip all of Wheeler's cavalry, and otherwise accomplish its task," he later wrote, "and I think so still."[15]

Instead, both columns met with disaster and the trains kept coming into Atlanta. Kilpatrick did not do much better when Sherman sent him out three weeks later in a last desperate effort to cut the Macon railroad. So the question arises, how could Rousseau and Garrard be so successful and suffer so few casualties while McCook, Stoneman, and Kilpatrick accomplished little or nothing at such a tremendous cost?

The first explanations were both simple and self-serving. By August 4, a rumor was circulating in Sherman's army that McCook's command had captured "a large quantity of 'John Barleycorn'. . . got on a tight—and while in that condition were surrounded . . . and captured."

That same day, a story appeared in the *Nashville Dispatch,* attributing McCook's misfortune "to the liquor captured with the Rebel [wagon] train" at Fayetteville. Newspapers throughout the North repeated the allegation, leading the editor of the *Milwaukee Sentinel* to charge, "The officers in command must have been criminally negligent of their duty to have allowed their men to indulge in the use of liquor to the extent hinted at by the dispatches."

The denial from the 1st Cavalry Division was swift and unequivocal. "The story is a lie from beginning to end . . . ," McCook's adjutant, Captain Robert LeRoy, asserted in a letter to the *Philadelphia Press.*

"On the night of the 28th of July, a wagon train . . . was captured," a 5th Iowa trooper elaborated in the *Dubuque Daily Times,* "and I believe about six barrels of whisky, at least about half a pint to a man, providing it was equally divided and none wasted. Now the fight [at Brown's Mill] happened on the 30th, . . . did the men get drunk and stay drunk for *two days and two nights,* or did they put it in their canteens and carry it these *two days* for *this* occasion when marching in this hot weather over dusty roads when canteens had to be used to carry water?"

"I *know* that the barrels were *immediately* destroyed," added Lieutenant Henry Belfield of the 8th Iowa; "I did not see a man drunk, and I had an opportunity of seeing most of the command. . . . I *do* know that men fell from their horses from want of sleep and exhaustion."

"I was on said raid," a 1st Wisconsin trooper told the *Milwaukee Sentinel,* ". . . and what I *saw I know.* . . . though there had been a quantity of poor liquor captured and destroyed, and some canteens were filled, I can safely say I did not see a single private soldier in the least intoxicated. . . . I did notice several *officers* slightly intoxicated, though by no means drunk."

McCook did not respond to these allegations of drunkenness directly, but he did point an accusing finger at George Stoneman. He contended, with some justification, that Stoneman's failure to join him at Lovejoy's Station had pitted him against impossible odds at Brown's Mill. "I was surrounded by an overwhelming force," he declared; "Roddey, Wheeler, and Jackson were all there with cavalry, and a large infantry force besides."[16]

Indeed, if there is a common thread in Federal accounts of the fighting at Brown's Mill, Sunshine Church, and Lovejoy's Station, it is this stubborn insistence McCook, Stoneman, and Kilpatrick were all surrounded by swarms of Confederate cavalry and infantry. Since Sherman's raiding columns were under orders to avoid pitched battles with opposing infantry, some officers seem to have seized upon this as a convenient excuse to explain their lack of success.[17]

However, Confederate records make it clear there was no infantry at Brown's Mill or at Sunshine Church. Instead of being surrounded, McCook and Stoneman initially outnumbered the Rebels opposing them. While Kilpatrick could truthfully claim he encountered Confederate foot soldiers at Jonesboro on the night of August 19 and at Lovejoy's Station on August 20, he grossly overestimated their strength.

He was not alone. Even a reliable observer like Captain Robert Burns believed the Rebels had "a brigade of Infantry on our front and partly to our left [at Lovejoy's Station]; a division moving to hit us on the right, and . . . three Brigades of Cavalry in our rear."

"They had surrounded us with 20,000 picked men," Sergeant Garner B. Stimsen of the 3rd Ohio asserted in a letter to the *Norwalk Reflector.*

As the years went by, this story gained credence. Citing a wartime letter a Confederate eyewitness had allegedly sent to the *Atlanta Appeal,* Captain Joseph Vale of the 7th Pennsylvania insisted the brigade of Rebel infantry Kilpatrick encountered at Lovejoy's Station was quickly reinforced by Ross's and Ferguson's cavalry, Pat Cleburne's infantry, twelve pieces of artillery, Major General William T. Martin's cavalry division, and a brigade of Georgia militia. "It thus appears," Vale wrote in 1886, "that the rebels had on the ground, now surrounding Kilpatrick, five brigades of infantry, eighteen pieces of artillery, and six brigades of cavalry, in all a force of twelve thousand men of all arms."

This was patently incorrect, but Bob Minty quoted Vale's figures as gospel in his 1890 account of the raid. So did Lieutenant Will Curry in 1898 and artilleryman John Nourse in 1900. Vale's assertions also found their way into the regimental histories of the 1st Ohio, 3rd Ohio, and 7th Pennsylvania Cavalry, published in 1899, 1910, and 1906. Minty even went a step further and cited the captured colors of the Benjamin Infantry and Zachry's Rangers (which were actually taken from houses his men had plundered) as proof his brigade had been attacked by Georgia militia.[18]

Vale, however, was vague about the date the *Appeal* article appeared, except to say it was sometime in September 1864. Files of the *Appeal* for that month apparently have not survived the ravages of time, but editors in that era were very good about "borrowing" interesting copy from other newspapers. The article Vale quoted does not appear in the surviving issues of any other Georgia newspaper. Even if it did, other sources make it abundantly clear Pat Cleburne's infantry never left Atlanta. Will Martin's cavalry was unquestionably with Joe Wheeler in Tennessee. Sam Ferguson's brigade did not participate in the fight at Lovejoy's Station, and the nearest brigade of Georgia militia was twenty miles away.

Inflating the size of the opposition might make an obviously embarrassing defeat more palatable, but why would so many otherwise reliable Yankee eyewitnesses insist they saw Rebel infantry when there were none? Fatigue may have been a factor. When the hour of crisis came at Brown's Mill, Sunshine Church, and Lovejoy's Station, most of these men had not slept in three or four days. This could have led them to misinterpret some of the things they saw. Also, much of the fighting took place in dense woods and, at a distance, there was not too much to distinguish a dismounted Rebel cavalryman from a Rebel foot soldier. They wore the same hats, clothes, and accoutrements and carried the same long-barreled Springfield and Enfield rifles.

Federal troopers, on the other hand, were equipped with sabers, revolvers, and short-barreled carbines, "effective weapons in a cavalry charge," noted Lieutenant Washington L. Sanford of the 14th Illinois Cavalry, "but inferior in fighting dismounted."

In other words, a Confederate soldier armed with a muzzle-loading rifle could open fire from ranges at which a Yankee trooper could not effectively reply. Did this make a difference? Confederate General Dan Reynolds thought it did. "My Enfield rifles were much more effective in the small timber than their short cavalry guns," he noted in his report of his encounter with Kilpatrick's raiders.[19]

Still, 4,000 Yankee cavalrymen should have been more than a match for the 300 Rebel infantry they initially encountered at Lovejoy's Station. The same holds true for all of Sherman's raiding columns. They were better armed, better mounted, and better equipped than their opponents, and they usually had a numerical advantage. If they were tired by the time they got to Brown's Mill, Sunshine Church, or Lovejoy's Station, so were the Rebels who pursued them. If they fought believing they were badly outnumbered, Joe Wheeler, Alfred Iverson, "Red" Jackson, and Sul Ross all went into action knowing the odds were against them.

Sometimes the difference between victory and defeat simply boils down to those subtle qualities called leadership. There are men like Lovell Rousseau, who inspired confidence and enthusiasm wherever he went. This and a natural instinct for soldiering more than made up for whatever shortcomings he had as a general. He was conspicuously brave, a self-made man who inspired other men to follow him, and he led them on one of the most successful cavalry raids of the war.

Kenner Garrard had a completely different style. Genteel, reserved, always concerned about the welfare of his horses and men, he lacked the callousness that combat requires of a good commander. His soldiers revered him because they knew he would not risk their lives unnecessarily, but his failure to keep Wheeler and Iverson busy at Flat Shoals contributed mightily to the fate that befell troopers with McCook and Stoneman. He was cautious when he should have been bold, and some of his own officers lamented his "want of generalship." However, Garrard was blessed with three extraordinarily gifted brigade commanders in Bob Minty, Eli Long, and Abe Miller, who made his cavalry division the best in Sherman's army.[20]

George Stoneman had none of these advantages. A gruff, by-the-book old soldier whose flaws were probably aggravated by a chronic case of hemorrhoids, he blamed his defeat at Sunshine Church principally on "the bad conduct of the Kentucky brigade." Yet his whole division lacked cohesion and discipline, qualities a good commander would have instilled. "I know Stoneman like a book," declared a Union general while the army was anxiously awaiting news of his raid. "He will go to the proper spot like a cannon-ball, but when he gets there, like a shell, he'll burst."[21]

Ed McCook also performed well enough as long as things went smoothly, but when

Stoneman failed to meet him at Lovejoy's Station, he had to contend with limitations of his own. He had orders to retrace his steps to the Chattahoochee after breaching the Macon railroad and he blindly obeyed them, even though hindsight suggests he should have continued around the east side of Atlanta. Unexpected events seemed to unnerve him and his subsequent conduct raised serious questions about his fitness for command. Twice during the fighting at Brown's Mill, McCook essentially surrendered his duties to subordinates, first to John Croxton, then to Fielder Jones, and the image of him turning around and around, asking "What shall we do? What shall we do?" could hardly have been inspiring.

Aside from Rousseau, Judson Kilpatrick was the only one of Sherman's cavalry commanders who consistently projected the charisma and elan that makes tired men win desperate battles. He was also an arrogant, conceited, prevaricating braggart, but as a veteran sergeant of the 92nd Illinois explained, "He is the *Prince of Raiders.* I would sooner go under him on a raid than any other man that I know of."[22]

But Kilpatrick, like all of Sherman's cavalry generals except for Rousseau and McCook, was a castoff from the Army of the Potomac, and this underscores an important point. The Union cavalry in the Atlanta campaign simply lacked competent, aggressive leaders. Instead of promoting capable subordinate officers from within the ranks, the politics of command saddled Sherman's horsemen with outsiders who had already been tried elsewhere and found wanting. One can only wonder what would have happened at Brown's Mill or Sunshine Church if Bob Minty or Eli Long had been in command.

The burden of leadership also weighs heavily on the shoulders of William Tecumseh Sherman. He was, after all, the officer who ordered the raids and expected them to bring Atlanta to its knees. Rousseau's and Garrard's expeditions admittedly gave him reasons to believe this could be done. What he failed to realize was Rousseau owed much of his spectacular success to the flimsy strap rail construction of the Montgomery & West Point route and the absence of Bedford Forrest and Philip Roddey, who had been ordered to Mississippi to confront a powerful Federal column from Memphis. Kenner Garrard was able to cripple the Georgia Railroad for the same reasons. There were simply no sizable forces of Confederate cavalry around to keep him from destroying the vulnerable trestles over the Yellow and Alcovy rivers.

But the tactical situation that fostered these two successful raids changed dramatically on July 22, when the bloody battle of Atlanta forced Hood's army into the heavily fortified inner ring of the city's defenses. Prior to this, Confederate cavalrymen had spent most of the campaign fighting on foot alongside the outnumbered Rebel infantry, trying to keep the thin gray lines from being overlapped. After July 22, the contracted Southern lines no longer had vulnerable flanks the cavalry had to protect. This freed Joe Wheeler, for the first time in the campaign, to lead his ill-equipped, undersized regiments after Sherman's raiding columns, and his relentless pursuit of McCook and Stoneman in the sweltering heat of July was nothing short of brilliant.

To his credit, Sherman quickly realized the futility of trying to race Wheeler to the railroads south of Atlanta and did not mount another raid for almost three weeks. Only after learning Wheeler had ridden himself right out of the campaign on an ill-starred expedition of his own did he risk sending out his cavalry again. Eschewing the converging columns and complicated rendezvous that had ruined his previous plans, he doubled the size of Kilpatrick's command, gave him explicit orders, and sent him to succeed where McCook and Stoneman had failed. However, Sherman allowed the rest of his army to remain relatively idle and did not pin Atlanta's defenders in their trenches. When the Rebels realized the threat to the railroads, they were able to use their interior lines of communication to rush reinforcements to Jonesboro and Lovejoy's Station, keeping Kilpatrick from doing any serious harm.

Despite these tactical difficulties and the lack of effective leadership, despite sweltering heat, choking dust, raging rivers, and daunting distances, Sherman's horsemen completely severed Atlanta's vital railroads on July 29–30 and again on August 19–20. What they failed to reckon with was the South's surprising ability to repair the damage. Piles of ties were still burning when a train carrying telegraphers and linemen reached the break Rousseau's men had made in the Columbus Branch road on July 20. A concerted effort mended the wires between Columbus and Opelika in a day or two, while crews from Montgomery completed repairs between Notasulga and Opelika by the night of July 23. The new telegraph poles were hastily planted and a violent thunderstorm blew many of them down that same night, but communication was quickly restored.

Meeting in Montgomery on July 20, the board of directors of the Montgomery & West Point Railroad sent a party eastward to determine the full extent of the damage to the road. The news was not encouraging, and on July 23 Braxton Bragg urged Richmond to complete construction of forty miles of track from Columbus to Montgomery, via Union Springs. Most of the route had already been graded and he estimated the remaining work could be done in three or four months, "giving us a uniform gauge all the way to Richmond."

On July 26, Major General Jeremy F. Gilmer, chief of the Confederate Engineer Bureau, sent Lieutenant Colonel Minor Meriwether to Montgomery to study the feasibility of this proposal. At the same time, he ordered Captain L. P. Grant and Major George Whitfield "to assist in pressing forward the work on the West Point Road."[23]

Mail and passenger service between Montgomery and Atlanta resumed on July 29, with the establishment of a stage line bridging the burnt miles of track. As a temporary measure, Captain S. M. Lanier, chief quartermaster of the Alabama Reserves, advertised on July 24 for 200 wagons, teams, and drivers to haul army supplies across the twenty-mile gap between Notasulga and Opelika. "The planters of Alabama have never yet flagged in the hour of trial," he wrote, "and it is therefore confidently believed they will promptly respond to this appeal."

By August 3, the flow of supplies from Montgomery to Atlanta had returned to 50 percent of normal and repairs to the railroad were progressing steadily. Rejecting Bragg's proposed completion of the route from Union Springs to Montgomery, Lieutenant Colonel Meriwether confiscated railroad iron from less important lines, while other officers impressed slave laborers from the surrounding counties and imported carpenters and workmen from as far away as Meridian, Mississippi. Major Whitfield, only recently recovered from a broken leg, arrived on August 4 to personally oversee the work, assisted by Major John M. Hottel of the Engineer Bureau. Under their supervision, section hands hammered home the last spike on August 26, forty days after Rousseau's raiders uprooted the first rail at Loachapoka.[24]

Track laid with T-rail was more difficult to destroy; consequently, Sherman's raids against the railroads immediately south of Atlanta did comparatively little damage. Ed McCook's men tore up several hundred yards of the Atlanta & West Point road at Palmetto on July 28, and parts of a mile-and-a-half stretch of the Macon & Western route at Lovejoy's Station on July 29. Section gangs had the Macon road running again by July 31, and traffic over the West Point route resumed perhaps as early as August 2 and certainly no later than August 6.[25]

George Stoneman's troopers wrecked about a mile of the Central of Georgia road at intervals between Griswoldville and Macon on July 30 and burned the trestles over Walnut Creek and the Oconee River. By August 7, Rebel work crews had the cars running from Macon to the west bank of the Oconee. Building a Howe truss bridge over the river to replace the burned trestle took until August 20, but in the interim, the railroad ferried across freight and passengers with minimal delays.[26]

Judson Kilpatrick's expedition, despite his extravagant claims, only succeeded in destroying a small section of the West Point railroad above Fairburn on August 19 and maybe a mile and a half of the Macon railroad at Jonesboro before heavy rain and Rebel infantry brought the work to a halt. Once again, the damage was quickly undone and trains were running between Macon and Atlanta before Kilpatrick got back to Buckhead.[27]

This is not to imply that the man on horseback was some sort of medieval anachronism who had outlived his usefulness on the battlefield. On the contrary, mounted troops were unsurpassed at scouting, picketing, protecting the flanks of an army, and screening its movements from the enemy. Their presence could be, and often was, decisive. Confederate cavalryman Earl Van Dorn frustrated Grant's first campaign against Vicksburg when his horse soldiers destroyed the Union supply depot at Holly Springs, Mississippi, in December 1862. The following April, Colonel Benjamin H. Grierson's raid through the heart of Mississippi diverted Confederate attention while Grant maneuvered his army into position for the assault that ultimately forced Vicksburg's surrender. In the eastern theater of the war, Jeb Stuart's celebrated "ride around McClellan" in June 1862 exposed a weakness in the Federal commander's dispositions that enabled Robert E. Lee to drive the Union army away from Richmond during the Seven Days battles. Eleven months later, Lee won his greatest victory when Stuart's horsemen reported the Federal right flank was "in the air" at Chancellorsville. On the other hand, Stuart's absence during Lee's subsequent invasion of Pennsylvania is often cited as a primary factor in the Confederate defeat at Gettysburg.

Unlike Lee, Sherman had never served with the cavalry. He had no affinity for horse soldiers, no grasp of their capabilities, and no patience with their limitations. He never understood that cavalry, to be successful, generally had to work in close conjunction with the rest of the army. Instead of sending his troopers to strike the West Point and Macon railroads a little closer to Atlanta and boldly following them with heavy columns of infantry, he was constantly sending his horsemen far behind the Rebel lines, beyond any hope of support or assistance. Once they reached their objective, even after a protracted march, there was no time to rest. They had to get to work. While every fourth trooper held horses, other sizable detachments deployed as pickets and vedettes, reducing the number of men a commander could line up beside the track by almost half. Even if the work of burning ties and bending rails progressed smoothly, the raiders could not linger for more than a day or two. Confederate cavalry was too vigilant, telegraphic communications were too good, and nearby Southern cities and towns such as Montgomery, Columbus, Macon, Milledgeville, and Athens were too well defended for two or three thousand Yankee horsemen to roam at will for very long. Safety depended upon mobility, and once they moved on to avoid the approach of opposing infantry or cavalry, there was nothing to prevent the Rebels from beginning repairs on the railroads.

But Sherman, blinded by Rousseau's dazzling success, followed so closely by Garrard's, kept waiting for his cavalry to make a substantial break in Atlanta's supply lines *before* committing his infantry to a sustained offensive. When this failed, he seemed to be at a loss for what to do next. Wary of Hood, reluctant to take risks, he seemed haunted by the old fears of failure. His armies wallowed in the trenches for almost a month before he finally decided he had no other options and sent his foot soldiers to cut the railroads south of Atlanta. This forced the city's surrender, but by waiting for his cavalry to win a quick victory, Sherman undoubtedly prolonged the campaign.

As the war progressed, Sherman grew into a gifted and farseeing strategist, but he remained an indifferent tactician. He allowed a dangerous gap to open in his lines just prior to the battle of Peachtree Creek on July 20. He left a vulnerable flank uncovered on July 22, with nearly disastrous results, and negated his superiority in numbers by rarely bringing all three of his armies into action at the same time.

The cavalry raids he mounted against Atlanta's railroads during the summer of 1864 made casualties of more than 3,000 of his horsemen, almost one in every three. By the last week of August, their ranks were so sadly depleted that probably no more than 5,000 troopers accompanied the infantry columns that swept around the south side of the city.[28] When two days of bloody fighting at Jonesboro subsequently left these forces squarely between the beaten wings of the Rebel army, fate presented Sherman's horsemen with a golden opportunity, what could have been their finest hour.

But Sherman had neither the inspiration nor the inclination to seize it. He wanted Atlanta. The city's subsequent surrender had tremendous strategic, political, and personal implications, but tactically it was a hollow victory. No bold squadrons went slashing at the flanks and rear of the weary Rebel column that shuffled southward on the night of September 1. No triumphant troopers returned herding crowds of dispirited prisoners before them. Hood's army would escape, regroup, and strike northward into Tennessee, where Union generals would be seriously hampered by the shortage of cavalry. It would be the spring of 1865, when Major General James H. Wilson led an army of 13,000 mounted men in a massive raid across Alabama and Georgia, before Sherman's cavalry corps fully recovered from the losses at Brown's Mill, Sunshine Church, King's Tanyard, and Lovejoy's Station and took the field in sufficient numbers to play a significant role in the war's final campaign.

But in the warm September days following the fall of Atlanta, Sherman withdrew his armies from Lovejoy's Station and Jonesboro to occupy the abandoned Rebel defenses. Content with his victory and determined to make the conquered city a secure garrison, he expelled what was left of the civilian population. Then, turning to more humanitarian concerns, he accepted Hood's offer to exchange 2,000 prisoners of war. About 1,100 enlisted men, including many of Sherman's captured cavalrymen, were brought up from Andersonville to be repatriated at Rough and Ready on

September 19 and 22. Nine hundred eighty-two were exchanged, but 137 others, to their unspeakable horror, were sent back to Andersonville because Sherman refused to swap for anyone who did not belong to his army.

On September 27, another train deposited about 150 captured Union officers at Griffin. Among them were such familiar names as Major General George Stoneman, Major Myles Keogh, Colonel Joseph Dorr, Colonel Tom Harrison, and Colonel James Biddle, all recent inmates of the Confederate military prison at Charleston, South Carolina. Upon learning of the pending exchange of Stoneman and his staff, Biddle had added his name to a list of the general's aides as "chief commissary." The ruse worked well until he climbed off the cars at Griffin and met General Alfred Iverson and Colonel Charles Crews, the Confederate officers who had captured him at Sunshine Church.

"Why, Biddle," Iverson exclaimed after renewing old acquaintances, "you are a brigade commander and not a chief commissary."

"We are both cavalrymen and have been hammering at each other for a long time," Biddle begged; "can't you help me out?"

Iverson explained Sherman and Hood had agreed to exchange prisoners according to the cartel of 1862. A colonel was the equivalent of fifteen privates and the Federals simply had not sent down enough men to swap for him. Biddle pleaded so fervently, however, that Iverson finally agreed to give him a temporary parole and a pass to get through the lines to Sherman's headquarters to see if something could be arranged. "If there are not enough men to exchange for you," Iverson warned, "you will give no information whatever but will return here and give yourself up."

The next morning, Biddle started for Atlanta on foot. He reached the lines of the XVII Corps that evening and was promptly escorted to Sherman's headquarters, a handsome residence at the corner of Mitchell and Washington streets. "Biddle, I am awfully sorry," Sherman said after hearing his story; "I have exchanged every man prisoner I have."

On September 30, Biddle glumly climbed into a luxuriously appointed caboose with three officers Sherman had appointed to handle the exchange. The ride to Rough and Ready was a short one, and as the train braked to a halt, the officer in charge said, "Colonel Biddle, remain here; I will let you know when you are wanted."

"You understand," Biddle said solemnly, "my word is pledged to go back unless everything is all right."

After what seemed like an eternity, the officer returned with Stoneman and his staff and assurances that everything was "all right." The Rebel emissaries handling the exchange were fine fellows, he explained. "We all took a drink and looked at the rolls to compare them. Then we all talked over things and compared them again. Then we all talked over things and let the clerks, who also had had drinks, figure out the rolls to see how they compared." Then they all had a few more drinks. "Biddle," the officer confided as the train began backing toward Atlanta, "to tell the truth, I believe you were exchanged for a keg of whiskey."[29]

NOTES

ABBREVIATIONS

ACS	Augusta (Ga.) *Daily Chronicle & Sentinel*	MDA	*Montgomery Daily Advertiser*
		MDC	*Macon (Ga.) Daily Confederate*
ADA	*Atlanta Daily Appeal*	MDM	Military Division of the Mississippi
ADC	Augusta (Ga.) *Daily Constitutionalist*	MDS	*Milwaukee Daily Sentinel*
ADI	*Atlanta Daily Intelligencer*	MDT	Macon (Ga.) *Daily Telegraph*
AJ	Allegan (Mich.) *Journal*	MJPGA	*The Miners' Journal and Pottsville* (Pa.) *General Advertiser*
AP	Albany (Ga.) *Patriot*		
ASB	Athens (Ga.) *Southern Banner*	MM	*Montgomery Daily Mail*
ASC	*Atlanta Southern Confederacy*	MSR	Milledgeville (Ga.) *Southern Recorder*
ASW	Athens (Ga.) *Southern Watchman*	MWA	*Montgomery Weekly Advertiser*
AT	*American Tribune*	ND	*Nashville Dispatch*
BAH	Birmingham (Ala.) *Age-Herald*	NR	Norwalk (Ohio) *Reflector*
BDH	Burlington (Iowa) *Daily Hawk-Eye*	NT	*National Tribune*
BDW	Bellefonte (Pa.) *Democratic Watchman*	NYH	*New York Herald*
BKWRV	Brownlow's Knoxville (Tenn.) *Whig and Rebel Ventilator*	NYT	*New York Times*
		NYTB	*New York Tribune*
CCMDM	Cavalry Corps Military Division of the Mississippi	OR	*Official Records of the Union and Confederate Armies*
CDC	*Cincinnati Daily Commercial*	OSJ	Ohio (Columbus) *State Journal*
CDS	Columbus (Ga.) *Daily Sun*	PC	*Pittsburgh Commercial*
CE	*Cincinnati Enquirer*	PCD	Portage County (Ravenna, Ohio) *Democrat*
CI	Christian (Macon, Ga.) *Index*		
CMH	*Confederate Military History, Extended Edition*	PDT	Peoria (Ill.) *Daily Transcript*
		PHP	Port Huron (Mich.) *Press*
CPR	Clinton (Pa.) *Republican*	PI	*Philadelphia Inquirer*
CR	Columbus (Ind.) *Republican*	PRB	Putnam (Ind.) *Republican Banner*
CT	Columbus (Ga.) *Times*	RG	Record Group
DAB	*Dictionary of American Biography*	RIU	Rock Island (Ill.) *Union*
DAT	*Detroit Advertiser and Tribune*	RWC	Ripon (Wis.) *Commonwealth*
DCE	Daily Columbus (Ga.) *Enquirer*	SCR	Sandusky (Ohio) *Daily Commercial Register*
DDT	*Dubuque Daily Times*		
DFP	*Detroit Free Press*	SHSP	*Southern Historical Society Papers*
DMT	District of Middle Tennessee	SMR	Selma (Ala.) *Morning Reporter*
DN	District of Nashville	SOG	Scioto (Ohio) *Gazette*
DSH	Daily Steubenville (Ohio) *Herald*	SR	Savannah (Ga.) *Republican*
DTB	Daily Toledo (Ohio) *Blade*	SWW	Semi-Weekly (Milwaukee) *Wisconsin*
DZC	Daily Zanesville (Ohio) *Courier*	TC	The (Turnwold, Ga.) *Countryman*
ECN	Early County (Blakely, Ga.) *News*	UDC	United Daughters of the Confederacy
EDJ	Evansville (Ind.) *Daily Journal*	TWA	The (Wellsboro, Pa.) *Agitator*
HDT	Houston (Tex.) *Daily Telegraph*	WBB	West Branch (Williamsport, Pa.) *Bulletin*
HT	Howard (Kokomo, Ind.) *Tribune*		
IDJ	*Indianapolis Daily Journal*	WC	Wolverine (Flint, Mich.) *Citizen*
JDG	Janesville (Wis.) *Daily Gazette*	WES	Washington (D.C.) *Evening Star*
KDGC	Keokuk (Iowa) *Daily Gate City*	WF	Waukesha (Wis.) *Freeman*
LDJ	Louisville (Ky.) *Daily Journal*	WSJ	Wisconsin (Madison) *State Journal*
LP	Lebanon (Ind.) *Patriot*		
MAR	*Mobile Advertiser and Register*		
MCU	Milledgeville (Ga.) *Confederate Union*		

Full details on works cited may be found in the bibliography following the notes.

INTRODUCTION

1. U.S. War Department, *The War of the Rebellion* (hereafter cited as *OR*), series I, vol. 38, pt. 1, p. 69; pt. 3, pp. 280, 286, 293, 309, 318, 324, 341, 348, 350, 352, 357; pt. 5, p. 30 (all citations are series I unless otherwise indicated); Temple, *The First Hundred Years*, pp. 321–24; William H. Records Diary, 3 July 1864; Magee, *History of the 72d Indiana Volunteer Infantry*, pp. 326–28; Sherman, *Memoirs*, 2:65.

2. Williams, "The Military Leadership of North and South," p. 43.

3. Rusling, *Men and Things I Saw in Civil War Days*, pp. 106–7 (hereafter cited as *Civil War Days*). Sherman's biographer Lloyd Lewis noted, "Always there would be a dispute among his closest friends and relatives about the color of his eyes, some saying that they were dark blue, others black, others hazel, others brown—but all agreed that they were sharp and piercing." See Lewis, *Sherman: Fighting Prophet*, pp. 48–49 (hereafter cited as *Fighting Prophet*).

4. Lewis, *Fighting Prophet*, pp. 197, 274; *CDC*, 28 June 1864, p. 1; Richardson, *The Secret Service*, p. 249; Gray and Ropes, *War Letters*, p. 427; Rusling, *Civil War Days*, pp. 107, 113 (Sherman's "gamey" qualities); Shanks, "Recollections of Sherman," pp. 641–46; *NT*, 11 August 1892, p. 2 (Sherman's rapid speech like the long roll); Shanks, *Personal Recollections of Distinguished Generals*, pp. 23–26, 37–38, 53–54, 56–57 (hereafter cited as *Distinguished Generals*); Villard, *Memoirs*, 1:210–11; Bradford, *Union Portraits*, pp. 134, 156–57, 161; *NT*, 26 April 1923, p. 6; Nichols, *The Story of the Great March*, p. 121; Hitchcock, *Marching with Sherman*, pp. 112–13.

5. Shanks, *Distinguished Generals*, pp. 38–39; Sherman, *Memoirs*, 1:218–19; Villard, *Memoirs*, 1:209, 272; Shanks, "Recollections of Sherman," p. 643. The best account of Sherman's stormy relations with the press is Marszalek, *Sherman's Other War*.

6. Shanks, *Distinguished Generals*, pp. 17–18.

7. Unless otherwise noted, the details of Sherman's life before the Atlanta campaign are drawn from Sherman, *Memoirs*; Shanks, "Recollections of Sherman," pp. 640–46; Shanks, *Distinguished Generals*, pp. 17–57; Reid, *Ohio in the War*, 1:417–93; Cullum, *Biographical Register of the Officers and Graduates of the U.S. Military Academy*, 2:27–29; McCrory, "Early Life and Personal Reminiscences of General William T. Sherman"; Smalley, "General Sherman"; Fleming, "William Tecumseh Sherman as College President"; Fleming, *General William T. Sherman as College President*; Lewis, *Fighting Prophet*; Clarke, *William Tecumseh Sherman: Gold Rush Banker*; Merrill, *Sherman*; Castel, "The Life of a Rising Son, Part I: The Failure"; Castel, "The Life of a Rising Son, Part II: The Subordinate"; Marszalek, *Sherman*.

8. U.S. Military Academy, *Official Register of the Officers and Cadets of the U.S. Military Academy*, 1837:4, 22, 1838:11, 22, 1839:8, 22, 1840:6, 19.

9. Howe, ed., *Home Letters of General Sherman*, p. 24.

10. Sherman to John Sherman, 5 November 1857, William T. Sherman Papers.

11. Sherman to Thomas Ewing, 2 April 1858, Ewing Papers.

12. Sherman to "Dearest Ellen," 15 April 1859, Sherman Family Papers.

13. Sherman, *Memoirs*, 1:183–84; Fleming, "William Tecumseh Sherman," p. 54.

14. Thorndike, ed., *Sherman Letters*, pp. 110–12, 122–23; Lewis, *Fighting Prophet*, pp. 161–62.

15. Howe, ed., *Home Letters of General Sherman*, pp. 199–200, 203–10, 212.

16. *OR*, 52, pt. 1, p. 198 (Halleck's assessment of Sherman's physical and mental state); *CDC*, 11 December 1861, p. 1; Villard, *Memoirs*, 1:212–13; Marszalek, *Sherman's Other War*, pp. 64–74; *OR*, 38, pt. 5, p. 791.

17. Howe, ed., *Home Letters of General Sherman,* pp. 220–25; Thorndike, ed., *Sherman Letters,* pp. 141, 143–46; John T. Taylor, "Reminiscences," pp. 128–33.

18. Marszalek, *Sherman's Other War,* pp. 76–83, 119–21, 123–26; Wilson, *Under the Old Flag,* 1:235.

19. Merrill, *Sherman,* pp. 223–24; Howe, ed., *Home Letters of General Sherman,* pp. 247–48, 250–54, 256–58; Thorndike, ed., *Sherman Letters,* pp. 197, 201–3, 205–6; Grant, *Personal Memoirs,* 1:542.

20. Howe, ed., *Home Letters of General Sherman,* p. 270; *OR,* 30, pt. 4, p. 73; Sherman to "Dearest Ellen," 6 October 1863, Sherman Family Papers.

21. *OR,* 30, pt. 4, pp. 470, 475–76; *OR,* 31, pt. 2, pp. 568–71; pt. 1, pp. 712, 713; Howe, ed., *Home Letters of General Sherman,* pp. 279–80.

22. *OR,* 31, pt. 2, p. 340.

23. Sherman's command initially included the Army of the Cumberland, the Army of the Tennessee, the Army of the Ohio, and the Army of Arkansas. The Army of Arkansas soon proved too distant for Sherman to exercise direct control, and on May 8, 1864, it was transferred to Major General E. R. S. Canby's Military Division of West Mississippi. See Sherman, *Memoirs,* 2:14; *OR,* 34, pt. 3, p. 505.

24. For insights into Sherman's fear of failure, see Williams, *McClellan, Sherman and Grant,* pp. 50–52; Walters, *Merchant of Terror,* pp. 16, 33, 37; Marszalek, *Sherman,* pp. 15–16.

25. Grant, *Personal Memoirs,* 2:118–20; Sherman, *Memoirs,* 2:5; Society of the Army of the Tennessee, *22nd Meeting,* p. 316; *OR,* 32, pt. 3, pp. 245–46, 312–14.

26. Sherman, *Memoirs,* 2:9–12 (Sherman's reasons for curtailing shipments of forage); Shanks, "Recollections of Sherman," p. 641; Shanks, *Distinguished Generals,* pp. 20–22; *OR,* 32, pt. 3, pp. 174, 220, 223, 240–41, 279–80, 311, 330, 420, 434, 466, 469, 490; *OR,* series III, vol. 4, pp. 962–65; series III vol. 5. p. 985; Lewis, *Fighting Prophet,* p. 352; *OR,* 38, pt. 4, pp. 25, 33–34; Dana, *Recollections,* pp. 165–67; *OR,* 52, pt. 1, p. 622; Rusling, *Civil War Days,* p. 111.

27. Sherman, *Memoirs,* 2:15; *OR,* 38, pt. 1, pp. 62–63, 89–115; DuBose, *General Joseph Wheeler,* p. 282.

28. *OR,* 38, pt. 1, pp. 59, 63; *OR,* 32, pt. 1, p. 19; pt. 3, p. 466; Howe, ed., *Home Letters of General Sherman,* p. 292; Van Horne, *History of the Army of the Cumberland,* 2:24–25; Boynton, *Sherman's Historical Raid,* pp. 96–103; Liddell Hart, *Sherman,* pp. 239–40; Burne, *Lee, Grant and Sherman,* pp. 75–81; *OR,* 38, pt. 4, p. 40.

29. *OR,* 38, pt. 1, pp. 63–64; pt. 4, pp. 105–6, 125–26; DuBose, *General Joseph Wheeler,* p. 283 (Sherman's reaction to the news McPherson had seized Snake Creek Gap); Cox, "Snake Creek Gap, and Atlanta," p. 341.

30. *OR,* 38, pt. 4, pp. 138–39, 158, 160–63; pt. 3, pp. 614–15; Connelly, *Autumn of Glory,* pp. 326–42; Hitchcock, *Marching with Sherman,* p. 113; Conyngham, *Sherman's March,* pp. 48–49.

31. *OR,* 38, pt. 1, pp. 64–65; pt. 3, p. 615; Shanks, *Distinguished Generals,* p. 24. See also McMurry, "Resaca"; Secrist, "Resaca"; McMurry, "The Atlanta Campaign." The engineer officer Sherman addressed, Colonel William W. Wright, later reported, "reconstruction commenced while the old bridge was still burning, and was somewhat delayed because the iron rods were so hot that the men could not handle them to remove the wreck." The work was completed in sixty hours. See *OR,* series III, vol. 4, p. 957; *OR,* 38, pt. 4, p. 248; *CDC,* 31 May 1864, p. 1.

32. Sherman, *Memoirs,* 2:42; Howard, *Autobiography,* 1:535, 539; *OR,* 38, pt. 1, p. 65; pt. 4, p. 299. For the controversial events leading to Johnston's retreat from Cassville, see Johnston, *Narrative,* pp. 319–24; *OR,* 38, pt. 3, pp. 615–16; Hood, *Advance and Retreat,* pp. 98–116; Polk, *Leonidas Polk,* 2:355–57, 376–82; Connelly, *Autumn of Glory,* pp. 343–54; McMurry, "Cassville"; McMurry, *John Bell Hood,* pp. 107–9; Castel, *Decision in the West,* pp. 198–206.

33. Sherman, *Memoirs,* 2:52–54; Johnston, *Narrative,* p. 337; *OR,* 38, pt. 1, pp. 65–67, 223,

243; pt. 3, pp. 616–17; Howard, *Autobiography,* 1:563; *NT,* 21 May 1903, p. 3; Polk, *Leonidas Polk,* 2:372–74; *ADC,* 17 June 1864, p. 1; *MDT,* 30 June 1864, p. 1. See also McMurry, "'The Hell Hole'"; Davis, "The Death of Bishop Polk."

34. *OR,* 38, pt. 4, p. 507.

35. James, "McCook's Brigade at the Assault upon Kenesaw Mountain"; Watkins, *"Co. Aytch,"* pp. 156–57; *OR,* 38, pt. 1, pp. 67–69; pt. 5, p. 91; Howe, ed., *Home Letters of General Sherman,* p. 299. See also McMurry, "Kennesaw Mountain"; Kelly, "The Atlanta Campaign."

36. *OR,* 38, pt. 1, p. 69; pt. 5, pp. 14, 30–31, 36–37.

37. Gates, ed., *The Rough Side of War,* p. 234; *OR,* 38, pt. 1, p. 892; *NT,* 24 January 1895, p. 1; Howard, "The Battles about Atlanta," pp. 385–86; Howard, *Autobiography,* 1:596.

38. *OR,* 38, pt. 1, p. 69; pt. 5, pp. 46–47, 50–51; McKinney, *Education in Violence,* pp. 11, 209, 331; Johnston, *Narrative,* p. 346; Shoup, "Dalton Campaign"; Sherman, *Memoirs,* 2:66–67; Connolly, *Three Years in the Army of the Cumberland,* p. 234.

39. "Generals in the Saddle," pp. 169–70; Sherman, *Memoirs,* 2:67; *NT,* 10 September 1925, p. 6; *OR,* 38, pt. 5, p. 61.

40. Garrett, *Atlanta and Environs,* 1:567–69; Howe, ed., *Home Letters of General Sherman,* pp. 299–300.

1. CROSSING THE CHATTAHOOCHEE, JULY 3–JULY 10, 1864

1. Quoted in Henderson, *The Science of War,* pp. 56–57.

2. *OR,* 38, pt. 5, p. 14; Black, *Railroads of the Confederacy,* pp. 9–10, map; *ADC,* 21 July 1864, p. 3; Avary and Bowie, *The West Point Route,* p. 11; Garrett, *Atlanta and Environs,* 1:482–84.

3. *OR,* 32, pt. 3, p. 313.

4. The best overview of the training, organization, and exploits of Yankee horse soldiers in the western armies is found in Stephen Z. Starr's excellent study, *The Union Cavalry in the Civil War,* vol. 3: *The War in the West 1861–1865.* For the condition of Sherman's mounted regiments at the outset of the Atlanta campaign and his mistrust of cavalry, see Curry, comp., *Four Years in the Saddle,* p. 164; *OR,* 38, pt. 4, p. 120.

5. *OR,* 38, pt. 1, pp. 101–2, 114–15; U.S. War Department, *U.S. Department of War, Adjutant General's Office, General Orders, 1863,* 1: General Orders Number 110, pp. 1–2; Gist, "The Ages of the Soldiers in the Civil War." This estimate of the effective strength of Sherman's cavalry at the outset of the campaign does not include independent companies serving as generals' escorts or three small regiments, the 1st Alabama Cavalry, the 5th Ohio Cavalry, and the 9th Illinois Mounted Infantry, attached to McPherson's Army of the Tennessee. The bulk of McPherson's cavalry corps had been left near Memphis to defend western Tennessee against the feared Confederate raider, Major General Nathan Bedford Forrest.

6. Warner, *Generals in Blue,* pp. 141–42, 481–82; Wilson, *Under the Old Flag,* 2:20; *OR,* 38, pt. 1, pp. 101, 114; pt. 4, p. 224.

7. *OR,* 38, pt. 2, pp. 746–47, 766, 803–4, 857–58; George Knox Miller to "My darling Wife," 1 July 1864, George Knox Miller Papers; William M. Worthington to "My Dear Father," 26 June 1864, Worthington Family Papers.

8. *OR,* 38, pt. 4, pp. 268, 287, 336, 387 (McCook's complaints about serving alongside the infantry and horses dying of starvation), 399, 627–28; pt. 2, pp. 766, 832; Dornblaser, *Sabre Strokes,* p. 160; *OR,* 38, pt. 1, p. 116.

9. *OR,* 38, pt. 4, pp. 507; pt. 2, pp. 747, 858.

10. *MDT,* 7 July 1864, p. 2; *MAR,* 25 June 1864, p. 2; *ACS,* 14 July 1864, p. 2.

11. *OR,* 38, pt. 5, pp. 11–12, 20, 25, 48–49; Sherman to "General Garrard," 4 July 1864, Letter Book G, Sherman Papers, Records of the Adjutant General's Office, RG 94.

12. *OR,* 38, pt. 4, pp. 125, 187, 197–98, 367, 450, 507, 555.

13. Some authors insist Garrard was born in September 1828, citing the *Official Register of the U.S. Military Academy,* 1848:14, which notes Garrard signed a letter upon entering the Academy on July 1, 1847, giving his age as eighteen years and ten months. However, in researching *Generals in Blue,* Ezra J. Warner discovered "that the 'letter' above-mentioned was invariably signed upon the putative cadet's arrival at the Academy, and not on July 1st, which was the beginning of the school year. In those days many cadets arrived in May and June. There are records of some who arrived even earlier, in order to 'tutor' for the entrance exams." Warner also pointed out Garrard had a younger brother, Lewis, born in May 1829, and noted it was unlikely they were born only seven or eight months apart. See Warner to Reference Librarian, Cincinnati Public Library, 28 July 1960, Ethel L. Hutchins to Warner, 2 August 1960, and James Barnett to Warner, 23 December 1967, Ezra J. Warner Papers; Biographical File; Barnett, "Forty for the Union: Civil War Generals Buried in Spring Grove Cemetery," p. 101.

14. Des Cognets, *Governor Garrard, of Kentucky,* pp. 29–33; Reid, *Ohio in the War,* 1:852; Association of the Graduates of the United States Military Academy, *10th Annual Reunion,* pp. 94–99; Price, comp., *Across the Continent with the Fifth Cavalry,* pp. 345–47; Cullum, *Biographical Register,* 2:441–42; *DAB,* 1928 ed., s.v. "Kenner Garrard," by Charles Dudley Rhodes; Warner, *Generals in Blue,* pp. 167–68; Bethany College, "Matriculation List 1841–1881"; *Official Register of the U.S. Military Academy,* 1848:14, 19, 1849:11, 17, 1850:11, 19, 1851:9, 19; McKinney, *Education in Violence,* pp. 51–54; Roland and Robbins, eds., "The Diary of Eliza (Mrs. Albert Sidney) Johnston" pp. 470–71, 488; Stanley, *Personal Memoirs,* pp. 29, 31; *OR,* 1, pp. 553, 555.

15. Garrard, ed., *Nolan's System,* introduction.

16. Cassius M. Clay to Lincoln, 19 August 1862, Abraham Lincoln Papers; Basler, ed., *The Collected Works of Abraham Lincoln,* 5:390; *OR,* series II, vol. 4, p. 439; Brainard, comp., *Campaigns of the One Hundred and Forty-Sixth Regiment New York State Volunteers,* pp. 6, 7, 25–45, 48, 65–87, 104–26, 132, 135, 147; *OR,* 21, pt. 1, pp. 429–30; *OR,* 25, pt. 1, pp. 541–44; *OR,* 27, pt. 1, pp. 97, 635, 651–52; *OR,* 51, pt. 1, p. 1131; *OR,* series III, vol. 4, pp. 2, 47; Wilson, *Under the Old Flag,* 1:327 (Garrard's conversation with Stanton); *OR,* 32, pt. 2, p. 263; *OR,* 52, pt. 1, pp. 513–14, 516; *NT,* 4 October 1900, p. 3 (Garrard and Private Walker); Price, comp., *5th Cavalry,* p. 349.

17. The *Macon Daily Telegraph,* 6 July 1864, p. 1, and 9 July 1864, p. 2, put Garrard's losses on July 3 at "about thirty killed and fifty wounded, together with fifty Spencer rifles and about thirty horses." Garrard's casualties actually numbered one killed, two wounded, and two missing (one of whom returned the next morning) on July 3, and three wounded, one of them mortally, on July 4. See *OR,* 38, pt. 2, pp. 804, 813, 837–38, 842; pt. 5, p. 48; Crofts, comp., *History of the Service of the Third Ohio Veteran Volunteer Cavalry,* p. 152; *DTB,* 18 July 1864, p. 2; *SCR,* 20 July 1864, p. 2; Magee, *72nd Indiana,* pp. 328–31; Records Diary, 3–4 July 1864; Ambrose Remley to "Father and Mother, Sister and Brothers," 2 July 1864, Ambrose Remley Papers; Morning Reports, 3–4 July 1864, Company A, 72nd Indiana Mounted Infantry, RG 94; "List of Casualties in the 2d Brigade 2d Division Cavalry U.S.A.," pp. 64–65, vol. 57/140, Cavalry Corps Military Division of the Mississippi (hereafter cited as CCMDM), Records of U.S. Army Continental Commands, 1821–1920, RG 393; Compiled Service Records, RG 94.

18. Unless otherwise noted, the movements of Garrard's division on July 5 are based on the following sources: *OR,* 38, pt. 2, p. 813; pt. 5, p. 60; Stanley Lathrop to "Dear Father and Folks at Home," 9 July 1864 (description of camp routine), Stanley Lathrop Papers; Vale, *Minty and the Cavalry,* pp. 265, 321; John G. Lemmon Diary, 4 July 1864; John C. McLain Diary, 5 July 1864; Henry Albert Potter Diary, 5 July 1864; Henry Albert Potter to "Dear Father," 10 July 1864, Henry Albert Potter Papers; *DFP,* 19 July 1864, p. 1; Regimental Return, July 1864, 4th Michigan Cavalry, reel 83, M-594, Compiled Records Showing Service of Military Units in Volunteer Union Organizations, RG 94; *MJPGA,* 20 August 1864, p. 1; Sipes, *The Seventh*

Pennsylvania Veteran Volunteer Cavalry, p. 114; Tri-Monthly Report, 10 July 1864, 1st Ohio Cavalry Papers, RG 94; Regimental Return, July 1864, 1st Ohio Cavalry, reel 140, M-594, RG 94; George Kryder to "Dear Beloved Wife," 15 July 1864, George Kryder Papers; Crofts, comp., *3rd Ohio,* pp. 152–53; William H. Kemper Diary, 5 July 1864; Regimental Return, July 1864, 17th Indiana Mounted Infantry, reel 38, M-594, RG 94; Doyle, *History of the Seventeenth Indiana,* p. 20; *AT,* 2 December 1897, p. 6; Alva C. Griest Diary, 5 July 1864; Remley to "Father and Mother, Sister and Brothers," 2 July 1864; Records Diary, 4–5 July 1864; Magee, *72nd Indiana,* pp. 331–32; John C. Fleming to "Dear Father," 12 July 1864, John C. Fleming Papers; A. W. Lester Diary, 5 July 1864; John A. Nourse Diary, 4–5 July 1864.

19. Compiled Service Records, RG 94; Ohio Roster Commission, *Official Roster of the Soldiers of the State of Ohio in the War of the Rebellion,* 11:127; Nourse Diary, 4–5 July 1864.

20. Compiled Service Records, RG 94; Pension Records, Records of the Veterans Administration, RG 15; Carded Medical Records, RG 94; *PC,* 28 July 1864, p. 1; *PI,* 1 August 1864, p. 2.

21. Candler and Evans, eds., *Georgia: Comprising Sketches of Counties, Towns, Events, and Persons,* 3:93–94; *ADI,* 8 July 1864, p. 1.

22. Power, "Bulloch Hall, I Love You," p. 25; *KDGC,* 23 July 1864, p. 4; Griffin, "Cobb County: The Roswell Manufacturing Company 1838," pp. [1–2]; *AT,* 2 December 1897, p. 6 (Yankee lieutenant's quote); Garrett, *Atlanta and Environs,* 1:153–54; White, *Statistics of the State of Georgia,* p. 189; White, *Historical Collections of Georgia,* p. 402; Scruggs, ed., *Georgia Historical Markers,* pp. 205, 237; Temple, *The First Hundred Years,* pp. 111–12; Fleming to "My Dear Father," 12 July 1864; Nourse Diary, 7 July 1864; Coleman, *A Short History of the Roswell Manufacturing Company,* pp. 3, 5; *SWW,* 30 July 1864, p. 4; Theophile Roche vs. the U.S., Case Number 466, French and American Claims Commission, Records of the Department of State, RG 76; *OR,* 38, pt. 5, p. 68; Pratt, "Captain Thomas E. King"; A. S. Atkinson and Others, Executor of Charles J. McDonald vs. A. V. Brumby, Case Number 9,821.

23. *ADI,* 6 July 1864, p. 1. Writing in the *American Tribune,* 2 December 1897, p. 6, Lieutenant William E. Doyle of the 17th Indiana Mounted Infantry said, "One of the younger Rosses [i.e., Kings] held a commission as major in the Confederate army and was in command of a battalion formed out of the employes [*sic*] of the factories, which, with two brass guns, was stationed in an earthwork on the road. How it came that he was not ordered to retreat I can't tell, but while the 7th Pennsylvania Cavalry was chasing the retreating Confederate cavalry down the main street of Rosswell [*sic*] and over the Chattahoochie [*sic*] he still remained at his post until some of his stragglers informed him that the Yanks were in his rear, and he had just time to escape with his guns, but the 17th Indiana got some prisoners." Doyle's account seems suspect for several reasons. First, the Major Ross he mentions could only have been James Roswell King, who testified on two occasions he left Roswell *before* the Yankees arrived. Second, the 7th Pennsylvania's route led them right past the lone earthwork guarding Roswell's main approaches. It is inconceivable that King, if he had been there, would not have seen them. Third, and perhaps most important, Captain Will Clark, the actual commander of the Roswell Battalion, told the *Atlanta Daily Intelligencer* his troops evacuated Roswell at 8:00 A.M., July 5, three hours before the Yankees appeared. While the 17th Indiana did take some prisoners during the march to Roswell, Doyle was apparently mistaken about their identity. This author has been unable to find a list of prisoners captured by the 17th Indiana, but such a document compiled by Garrard's 1st Brigade, which included the 7th Pennsylvania, does not include any members of the Roswell Battalion. See Roche vs. the U.S., Case Number 466, RG 76; A. S. Atkinson and Others, Executor of Charles J. McDonald vs. A. V. Brumby, Case Number 9,821; *ADI,* 8 July 1864, p. 1; "Rebel Prisoners of War," vol. 50/108, CCMDM, RG 393.

24. Roche vs. the U.S., Case Number 466, RG 76; *NT,* 31 May 1894, p. 1. In his article for

the *National Tribune,* Minty said a delegation of "French and British gentlemen" visited his headquarters on July 5. Several other sources, such as Vale, *Minty and the Cavalry,* p. 321; Magee, *72nd Indiana,* p. 337; *NYTB,* 25 July 1864, p. 1; and *ACS,* 8 July 1864, p. 3, also asserted both French and British flags were flying over some of the mills in Roswell. However, all these accounts were either written long after the war, or by persons who were not actually in Roswell on July 5. Garrard was in as good a position to know the facts as anyone, and in *OR,* 38, pt. 5, p. 68, he said his troops found a French flag flying over the woolen mill. He made no mention of any British flags. Other reliable accounts, such as Silas C. Stevens to E. B. Stevens, 7 January 1905, Silas C. Stevens Papers; Crofts, comp., *3rd Ohio,* p. 153; *DFP,* 22 July 1864, p. 3; *SCR,* 22 July 1864, p. 2; *CDC,* 22 July 1864, p. 1; and the *NYTB,* 21 July 1864, p. 1, do not mention any British flags either. One of the owners of the Ivy Mill, James Roswell King, also disputed the presence of any British flags. Testifying in 1869, he said, "I never knew or heard of any English flag being raised over the Roswell Mills. I understood a Frenchman in my employ raised a French flag over the Ivy Woolen Mill." See A. S. Atkinson and Others vs. A. V. Brumby and William J. Russell, Case Number 9,821.

25. *NT,* 31 May 1894, p. 1; *OR,* 38, pt. 5, pp. 48–49, 60; Sherman, *Memoirs,* 2:31–32; Sherman to "General Garrard," 4 July 1864, Letter Book G, Sherman Papers, RG 94; Roche vs. the U.S., Case Number 466, RG 76. There is conflicting evidence regarding Roche's residence in Roswell. Testifying in Roche vs. the U.S., John N. Brown said Roche was boarding with Brown's father. However, in this same case, James Roswell King asserted Roche was living in the home of Thomas Edward King "as a guest & not as a boarder." Another witness, T. D. Adams, the manager of the company store, stated Roche had been "staying around" the King home "for the purpose of protection." This would account for the French flag flying over Bulloch Hall when the Federals arrived on July 5.

26. *SCR,* 22 July 1864, p. 2; Roche vs. the U.S., Case Number 466, RG 76.

27. Silas C. Stevens to E. B. Stevens, 7 January 1905; Vale, *Minty and the Cavalry,* pp. 321–22; *NT,* 31 May 1894, p. 1; *DFP,* 22 July 1864, p. 3; Griffin, "The Roswell Manufacturing Company," p. [2]; *AT,* 2 December 1897, p. 6; Roche vs. the U.S., Case Number 466, RG 76; *SCR,* 22 July 1864, p. 2; Crofts, comp., *3rd Ohio,* p. 153; Magee, *72nd Indiana,* p. 332; Doyle, *17th Indiana,* p. 20; Nourse Diary, 7 July 1864; *MJPGA,* 20 August 1864, p. 1; Regimental Return, July 1864, 17th Indiana Mounted Infantry, reel 38 M-594, RG 94; *OR,* 38, pt. 5, p. 68; U.S. War Department, *The Official Military Atlas of the Civil War* (hereafter cited as *OR,* Atlas), plate LXIII, no. 5; Sherman Map #103. In all probability, the decision to burn the mills was Sherman's. Roche testified, "an order was received, as your memorialist [Roche] is informed and believes[,] by the Commanding officers of the Federal forces in Roswell from Gen. Sherman, commanding him to burn the factories." Several other sources, such as Crofts, comp., *3rd Ohio,* p. 153; Sipes, *7th Pennsylvania,* p. 114; Lester Diary, 6 July 1864; Fleming to "My Dear Father," 12 July 1864; and Silas C. Stevens to E. B. Stevens, 7 January 1905, also credit Sherman with issuing the order to burn the mills. While this author has been unable to locate a written copy of any such order, it could have been verbal, delivered by Sherman's aide, Major McCoy, on July 4. As previously noted, Garrard may have been acknowledging such instructions when he wrote to Sherman on July 5, promising to "destroy all buildings." On the other hand, he may have made this decision on his own. Sherman seemed to hint at that in *OR,* 38, pt. 5, p. 76, when he wrote Garrard on July 7, "Their [the mills] utter destruction is right and meets my entire approval." However, it seems more likely Sherman was merely trying to reassure Garrard, who may have been concerned about Roche's persistent claims of neutrality. In any event, Sherman assumed full responsibility for the incident in a July 7 telegram to Washington, stating the mills were burned "by my order." He repeated this assertion in another telegram on July 9. See *OR,* 38, pt. 5, pp. 73, 91–92.

28. *OR,* 38, pt. 5, p. 68; Morning Reports, 6 July 1864, Company B, 7th Pennsylvania Cavalry, RG 94; Compiled Service Records, RG 94.

29. *OR,* 38, pt. 5, p. 69.

30. Lathrop to "Dear Father and Folks at Home," 9 July 1864; Stanley A. Hall Diary, 1–6 July 1864; Henry Campbell Diary, 1–6 July 1864; James Henry Harris Diary, 1–6 July 1864; William M. Winkler Diary, 1–6 July 1864; Record of Events, July–August 1864, Company G, 4th Indiana Cavalry, reel 34, M-594, RG 94; Regimental Return, July 1864, 1st Wisconsin Cavalry, reel 197, M-594, RG 94; Record of Events, July–August 1864, Company L, 1st Wisconsin Cavalry, reel 197, M-594, RG 94; Love, *Wisconsin in the War,* p. 720; Scruggs, ed., *Georgia Historical Markers,* p. 149; *OR,* 38, pt. 2, pp. 759–60, 767, 782, 789, 791; pt. 4, p. 643; pt. 5, pp. 21, 22–24, 33, 44, 53, 60–61, 67; McCook to David F. How, 6 July 1864, p. 162, vol. 24/48, CCMDM, RG 393.

31. Hunt and Brown, *Brevet Brigadier Generals in Blue,* p. 86; Powell, comp., *List of Officers of the Army of the United States from 1779 to 1900,* p. 217; Tennessee Adjutant General, *Report of the Adjutant General of the State of Tennessee,* p. 303; Carter, *History of the First Regiment of Tennessee Volunteer Cavalry,* pp. 38, 69–70, 141, 169–70, 269; *MDT,* 11 July 1864, p. 2; *OR,* 38, pt. 5, p. 75.

32. *OR,* 38, pt. 5, pp. 75, 77–78; pt. 2, p. 515; Schofield to Sherman, 7 July 1864, p. 73, vol. 19/28, Military Division of the Mississippi (hereafter cited as MDM), RG 393; McMurry, ed., "More on 'Raw Courage,'" p. 37 (Brownlow quote); Hall Diary, 7 July 1864; Harris Diary, 7 July 1864; Lathrop to "Dear Father and Folks at Home," 9 July 1864.

33. Nourse Diary, 5–6 July 1864; Magee, *72nd Indiana,* p. 332; *OR,* 38, pt. 2, p. 813; pt. 5, pp. 69, 75–76, 869–70; Audenried to Sherman, 7 July 1864, p. 70, vol. 19/28, MDM, RG 393.

34. Sherman, *Memoirs,* 2:68–69; *OR,* 38, pt. 5, pp. 50, 55–59, 76–77, 80.

35. Roche vs. the U.S., Case Number 466, RG 76; Audenried to Sherman, 7 July 1864, p. 70, vol. 19/28, MDM, RG 393.

36. "Circular, Hd. Qurs. 2d Brig. 2d Divin. Cav., Near Roswell Ga., July 8th 1864," p. 45, vol. 40/79, CCMDM, RG 393; Tri-Monthly Reports, 10 July and 31 July 1864, 1st Ohio Cavalry Papers, RG 94; Tri-Monthly Report, 10 July 1864, 3rd Ohio Cavalry Papers, RG 94; Tri-Monthly Report, 10 July 1864, 4th Ohio Cavalry Papers, RG 94; Long to Robert P. Kennedy, 1 July 1864, p. 39, vol. 40/79, CCMDM, RG 393; Eggleston to E. S. Wood, 8 July 1864, 1st Ohio Cavalry Papers, RG 94; *OR,* 38, pt. 1, pp. 89, 101, 115–16; "Weekly Report of 4th Mich. Cavy. for the Week Ending Monday, July 11th, 1864," 4th Michigan Cavalry Papers, RG 94; "Weekly Report of Effective Force Present from the Week Ending Monday [July] 11th 1864 for the 7th Penn. Vol. Cavy.," 7th Pennsylvania Cavalry Papers, RG 94; Regimental Return, July 1864, 4th U.S. Cavalry, reel 41, Returns from Regular Army Cavalry Regiments 1833–1916, M-744, RG 94; "Report of Men Present in the 17th Ind. Mtd. Inftry. from a Muster Held July 8th 1864," 17th Indiana Mounted Infantry Papers, RG 94; "Semi Weekly Return of the Effective Force of the 72nd Rgt. Ind. Vols. for July 7th 1864," 72nd Indiana Mounted Infantry Papers, RG 94; "Effective Force 98th Ills. Vols. July 7th 1864," 98th Illinois Mounted Infantry Papers, RG 94; Tri-Monthly Report, 13 July 1864, 123rd Illinois Mounted Infantry Papers, RG 94; Magee, *72nd Indiana,* p. 333. While there is no concrete evidence of an inspection in Minty's 1st Brigade on July 8, it seems unlikely Garrard would order an accounting of the 2nd and 3rd Brigades and not the 1st.

37. Hunt and Brown, *Brevet Brigadier Generals in Blue,* p. 414; Steiner, *Physician-Generals in the Civil War,* pp. 81–82; Magee, *72nd Indiana,* pp. 34–36, 108–9, 119–22, 313, 333; Sunderland, *Lightning at Hoover's Gap,* pp. 17–19, 24–26, 28–29, 154; Marcot, *Spencer Repeating Firearms,* pp. 28, 51; *AT,* September 24, 1903, p. 1; 28; *AT,* 2 October 1897, p. 2; *IDJ,* 19 July 1864, p. 1; Wilson, *Under the Old Flag,* 2:172.

38. Roche vs. the U.S., Case Number 466, RG 76; *DFP,* 22 July 1864, p. 3; *CDC,* 19 July 1864, p. 1; Dornblaser, *Sabre Strokes,* p. 167; "List of Casualties in the 2d Brigade, 2d Division Cavalry," pp. 66–67, vol. 57/140, CCMDM, RG 393. The exact number of mill hands is uncertain. In *OR,* 38, pt. 5, p. 68, Garrard, said 400 women worked in the mill he visited. A correspondent for the *New York Tribune,* 21 July 1864, p. 1, said each of Roswell's three mills employed 300 women and girls. General Thomas, in *OR,* 38, pt. 5, p. 104, reported "400 or

500" Roswell factory hands reached Marietta on July 10, while a correspondent who saw them after their arrival advised the *Cincinnati Daily Commercial,* 20 July 1864, p. 1, they numbered about 700. Garrard's men gave estimates of anywhere from 500 to 1,100, including 200 small boys, in *OSJ,* 26 July 1864, p. 2; Records Diary, 8 July 1864; Kemper Diary, 9 July 1864; Nourse Diary, 7 July 1864; Fleming to "My Dear Father," 12 July 1864; *DTB,* 27 July 1864, p. 2; *SCR,* 22 July 1864, p. 2. Even the highest of these figures seems within reason. Sherwood's *Gazetteer of Georgia,* p. 52, said Roswell had a population of 1,000 in 1860. Garrard, in *OR,* Atlas, plate LXIII, no. 5 (Sherman Map #103), estimated there were about 4,000 inhabitants in 1864. Hauling even a fraction of that number to Marietta must have taxed his wagon train severely. "General Order No. 10, Head Quarters Chief of Cavalry, D. C., Chattanooga, Tenn., April 15, 1864," in Order Books, Companies A to K except D, 92nd Illinois Mounted Infantry, RG 94, allotted each cavalry division in the Army of the Cumberland fifty supply wagons; twenty-five ordnance wagons; one wagon for every regimental, brigade, and division headquarters; one for every twelve company officers; one for every ten staff officers not attached to any headquarters; one for every eighty enlisted men; and two ambulances for every brigade and division. This might have given Garrard as many as 160 wagons and ambulances, minus the inevitable number of losses, breakdowns, and detachments. Long after the war, Major General Grenville M. Dodge of the XVI Corps incorrectly asserted in his *Personal Recollections,* p. 150, that Garrard moved the mill hands to Marietta "by detailing a regiment of cavalry, each member of which took one of the operatives on his horse. . . ."

39. Unless otherwise noted, the movements of Garrard's cavalry and artillery on July 8 and 9 are based on the following sources: *OR,* 38, pt. 2, pp. 813, 838, 842, 848, 850–51; Vale, *Minty and the Cavalry,* p. 323; *NT,* 31 May 1894, pp. 1–2; Othniel Gooding to "(the Boys are all looking and guessing)," 10 July 1864, Othniel Gooding Papers; Lemmon Diary, 9 July 1864; McLain Diary, 8–9 July 1864; Potter to "Dear Father," 10 July 1864; Potter Diary, 8–9 July 1864; *DAT,* 28 July 1864, p. 4; *DFP,* 22 July 1864, p. 3; *WC,* 23 July 1864, p. 2; *WC,* 6 August 1864, p. 2; Regimental Return, July 1864, 4th Michigan Cavalry, reel 83, M-594, RG 94; *MJPGA,* 20 August 1864, p. 1; Larson, *Sergeant Larson,* p. 265; "Circular, Hd. Qurs. 2d Brig. 2d Divin. Cav. Roswell, Ga., July 8th 1864," pp. 39–40, vol. 40/79, CCMDM, RG 393; Magee, *72nd Indiana,* pp. 333–37; Griest Diary, 8–9 July 1864; Records Diary, 8–9 July 1864; John Barnard to "Dear Wife," 11 July 1864, John M. Barnard Letters; *IDJ,* 19 July 1864, p. 1; *NT,* 22 May 1884, p. 7; *AT,* 24 January 1901, p. 2; *NT,* 13 March 1919, p. 2 (Eugenius B. Dunwoody's account); Doyle, *17th Indiana,* p. 20; Kemper Diary, 8–9 July 1864; *AT,* 2 December 1897, p. 6; *AT,* 4 October 1900, p. 1; *NT,* 18 October 1900, p. 3; *NT,* 3 April 1919, p. 3; Fleming to "My Dear Father," 12 July 1864; Lester Diary, 8–9 July 1864; Nourse Diary, 8–9 July 1864.

40. "Circular, Hd. Qurs. 2d Brig. 2d Divin. Cav. Roswell, Ga., July 8th 1864," pp. 39–40, vol. 40/79, CCMDM, RG 393.

41. *OR,* 38, pt. 5, pp. 91. In Letter Book G, Sherman Papers, RG 94, this dispatch is simply marked "courier." For evidence it was delivered by Major McCoy, see *NT,* 19 December 1889, p. 3.

42. Magee, *72nd Indiana,* pp. 334–35.

43. Corporal John Barnard of the 72nd Indiana added, "The rebs tried to get a position with artillery on the other side but our artillery men caught them at it and let the Shells in to them so thick they had to get out." None of the other eyewitnesses made any mention of a Rebel battery.

44. Vale, *Minty and the Cavalry,* p. 323.

45. According to Indiana Adjutant General, *Report of the Adjutant General of the State of Indiana,* 4:365, Private James M. Case of the 17th Indiana Mounted Infantry died of wounds received at the front on July 9, 1864. However, Compiled Service Records in RG 94 make it clear Case died on July 19 of wounds received at Noonday Creek on June 20.

46. Potter to "Dear Father," 10 July 1864. Estimates of the number of Rebel prisoners taken at Shallow Ford vary from a ridiculously high 200 in Sipes, *7th Pennsylvania*, p. 114, and Vale, *Minty and the Cavalry*, p. 323, to a more modest forty or fifty in *NT*, 31 May 1894, pp. 1–2, and Larson, *Sergeant Larson 4th Cav.*, p. 265. However, contemporary accounts agree only a handful of Rebels were captured. In a letter to "Dear Father," 10 July 1864, Lieutenant Albert Potter of the 4th Michigan Cavalry said there were only thirty Rebel pickets guarding the ford, and three or four were taken prisoner. Another member of the 4th Michigan, probably Captain William W. Van Antwerp, noted only two in a letter to the *Detroit Free Press,* 22 July 1864. A list in "Rebel Prisoners of War," vol. 50/108, CCMDM, RG 393, shows Garrard's 1st Brigade, to which the 4th Michigan belonged, captured four Rebels on July 9, all of them members of the 53rd Alabama Mounted Infantry. This author has been unable to locate a similar list for Garrard's 3rd Brigade, but Sergeant Ben Magee, *72nd Indiana*, p. 336, said his regiment captured three or four Rebels, while his comrade, Corporal William Records, noted in his diary, "Five prisoners were taken." Another Hoosier, Private Alva Griest, put the number at seven.

47. *OR,* 38, pt. 5, pp. 99–100.

48. *OR,* 38, pt. 5, p. 76; pt. 2, pp. 515–16, 683–85, 703–735 passim, 838; *NYTB,* 21 July 1864, p. 1; *CDC,* 19 July 1864, p. 1. Garrard also may have brought a few mounted companies of Eli Long's 2nd Brigade across Shallow Ford to picket the roads to the south. See Crofts, comp., *3rd Ohio*, p. 153.

49. *OR,* 38, pt. 5, pp. 96, 99–100; pt. 1, pp. 296–371 passim, 896; *CDC,* 20 July 1864, p. 1. In his 10:00 A.M. dispatch, Sherman had told Garrard to expect reinforcements on the "river road." However, Newton's men apparently took the Roswell Road because the "river road" was still impassable due to the destruction of the bridge near the mouth of Sope Creek and the presence of Schofield's XXIII Corps. Moreover, Newton had orders to "march by such roads as not to be seen by the enemy." This would preclude use of the "river road." See *OR,* 38, pt. 5, pp. 93, 100; pt. 2, pp. 683–84.

50. *NT,* 18 October 1900, p. 3.

51. *WC,* 23 July 1864, p. 2.

52. *OR,* 38, pt. 2, pp. 838, 843, 848; James Thomson Diary, 9 July 1864; White, *Statistics of Georgia*, p. 297; "List of Prisoners of War Captured by 2d Brigade 2d Division Cavalry U.S.A.," pp. 4–5, vol. 57/140, CCMDM, RG 393; "List of Casualties in 2d Brigade 2d Division Cavalry," pp. 66–67, vol. 57/140, CCMDM, RG 393. Reid noted in *Ohio in the War,* 2:769, "At McAfee Bridge (or Shakerack), on the 9th of July, four companies of the Third [Ohio] Cavalry, under command of Captain E. M. Colver, engaged a superior force of Rebel Texan cavalry, killing a Lieutenant and seven men, and capturing a large number of prisoners and horses." While Garrard may have sent a battalion of the 3rd Ohio up the river on July 9, it seems odd a skirmish of this size is not mentioned in the *Official Records,* Crofts's *3rd Ohio,* the regimental papers, or any surviving letters or diaries. The 3rd Ohio had been left in Roswell as a mounted reserve, and all of Wheeler's Texas regiments were operating on the opposite end of the Confederate line. It seems likely this skirmish, if it ever took place, occurred not in July, but in June, somewhere near McAfee's Crossroads, north of Marietta.

53. *OR,* 38, pt. 5, p. 100.

54. *OR,* 38, pt. 2, pp. 760–61; pt. 5, pp. 95–96; McMurry, ed., "More on 'Raw Courage,'" p. 37; *CDC,* 19 July 1864, p. 1; Carter, *1st Tennessee*, p. 170; John H. Ash Diary, 10 July 1864. While sources differ about the exact number of men Brownlow took with him and whether he crossed the river in a canoe or on a raft made of two logs, this author has accepted Brownlow's version of the story, which appeared in the *Knoxville Tri-Weekly Whig and Rebel Ventilator,* 29 July 1864, p. 1, quoted by McMurry in "More on 'Raw Courage.'"

55. *OR,* 38, pt. 2, p. 761; "Raw Courage," p. 46. McCook credited Brownlow with capturing three privates and a noncommissioned officer. However, Major General Oliver Otis Howard,

who was closer to the scene, put the number at three, as did Sergeant John Ash of the 5th Georgia Cavalry, who even gave their names. See *OR,* 38, pt. 5, pp. 95–96; Ash Diary, 10 July 1864.

56. *MDS,* 26 July 1864, p. 1; *Harper's Weekly,* 13 August 1864, p. 525.

2. "AN ASS OF EMINENT GIFTS"

1. Rousseau to William D. Whipple, 16 June 1864, pp. 184–85, Letters Sent, November 1863–January 1866, District of Middle Tennessee (hereafter cited as Letters Sent, DMT), RG 393.

2. *OR,* 38, pt. 4, pp. 530–31, 582, 624–25, 638, 648.

3. *OR,* 38, pt. 5, pp. 16–17, 19, 41.

4. Unless otherwise noted, the details of Rousseau's life are drawn from *DAB,* 1928 ed., s.v. "Lovell Harrison Rousseau," by E. Merton Coulter; Warner, *Generals in Blue,* pp. 412–13; Rousseau to Charles Lanman, 23 October 1865, Charles Lanman Papers; *The National Cyclopaedia of American Biography,* 1904 ed., s.v. "Richard Hilaire Rousseau"; *Appletons' Annual Cyclopaedia and Register of Important Events,* 1869 ed., s.v. "Lovell H. Rousseau"; Fitch, *Annals of the Army of the Cumberland,* p. 87; Shanks, *Distinguished Generals,* pp. 199–241; Shanks, "Recollections of General Rousseau," pp. 763–68.

5. U.S. Congress, Senate, *Reports and Subreports of the Battle of Buena Vista,* 1:180, 194; *AT,* 30 October, 1891, p. 1. Colonel Jefferson Davis of the 1st Mississippi Rifles was also at Buena Vista and may have been referring to Rousseau when he noted in his report: "In every approbatory sense of these remarks, I wish to be included a party of Colonel Bowles' Indiana Regiment, which served with us during the greater part of the day, under the immediate command of an officer of that regiment, whose gallantry attracted my particular attention, but whose name I regret is unknown to me."

6. Speed, Kelly, and Pirtle, *Union Regiments of Kentucky,* pp. 320–21.

7. *OR,* 10, pt. 1, pp. 105, 120, 251–52, 296, 304–5; *OR,* 16, pt. 2, p. 127; pt. 1, pp. 1026–27, 1038–58, 1155–56; *OR,* 20, pt. 1, pp. 193, 373, 376, 377–406; Shanks, "Recollections of General Rousseau," p. 766; Shanks, *Distinguished Generals,* p. 231.

8. Scribner, *How Soldiers Were Made,* pp. 276–77; *NT,* March 1879, p. 19; *NT,* 31 October 1907, p. 6.

9. *OR,* 23, pt. 2, pp. 598–600; Basler, ed., *Collected Works of Lincoln,* 6:352, 394; *OR,* 30, pt. 1, p. 211; pt. 3, pp. 62, 947; *OR,* 31, pt. 1, pp. 69, 669.

10. *OR,* 31, pt. 1, p. 847; pt. 2, p. 54; pt. 3, p. 109; Beatty, *The Citizen Soldier,* p. 354.

11. *OR,* 30, pt. 1, p. 305; *OR,* 38, pt. 2, p. 904.

12. *NT,* 7 February 1895, p. 3; Iowa Adjutant General, *Roster and Record of Iowa Soldiers,* 4:845–55; Iowa Adjutant General, *Report of the Adjutant General and Acting Quartermaster General of the State of Iowa,* pp. 977–98; Records of Ordnance and Ordnance Stores, vol. 7, 5th Iowa Cavalry, Records of the Chief of Ordnance, RG 156; Regimental Return, July 1864, 5th Iowa Cavalry, reel 51, M-594, RG 94; B. H. Polk to "Comd'g Officer 5th Iowa Cavalry," 12 June 1864, p. 183, Letters Sent, DMT, RG 393; Rousseau to Starkweather, 4 July 1864 (telegram), 5th Iowa Cavalry Papers, RG 94; Special Orders Number 39, Starkweather to Baird, 4 July 1864, 5th Iowa Cavalry Papers, RG 94; Morning Reports, 7 July 1864, Companies A and C, 5th Iowa Cavalry, RG 94.

13. Reid, *Ohio in the War,* 2:809–11; Ohio Roster Commission, *Official Roster,* 11:459; Goodloe, *Some Rebel Relics from the Seat of the War,* pp. 222–23; Hamilton, *Recollections of a Cavalryman,* pp. 1, 5; General Orders Number 58 and 59, 18 June 1864, and General Orders, 27 June 1864, Order Books, Companies A-K, 9th Ohio Cavalry, RG 94; Fanning, *The Hairbreadth Escapes and Humerous [sic] Adventures of a Volunteer,* p. 106; Rousseau to

Starkweather, 5 July 1864, p. 145, Telegrams Sent, November 1863-January 1866, District of Nashville (hereafter cited as Telegrams Sent, DN), RG 393; Morning Reports, 1–9 July 1864, Companies C, E, G, H, and M, 9th Ohio Cavalry, RG 94.

14. *OR,* 38, pt. 5, p. 71.

15. Magill to "Com'dg Officer 8th Ind. Cav.," 29 June 1864, p. 197, Letters Sent, DMT, RG 393; *OR,* 38, pt. 2, p. 878; Owen Star to William D. Whipple, 2 September 1864, Regimental Letter and Endorsement Book, 2nd Kentucky Cavalry, RG 94; Polk to G. M. L. Johnson, 6 July 1864, p. 146, Telegrams Sent, DN, RG 393; Thomas J. Jordan to Washington L. Elliott, 10 July 1864, General Orders Issued, November 1863–January 1866 (hereafter cited as General Orders), DMT, RG 393; Rowell, *Yankee Cavalrymen: Through the Civil War with the Ninth Pennsylvania Cavalry,* p. 183.

16. Aurelius M. Willoughby Diary, 8 July 1864; Williamson D. Ward Diary, 6 July 1864; Thomas Jackson Diary, 7 July 1864; Morning Reports, 6–7 July 1864, Company D, 8th Indiana Cavalry, RG 94; *NT,* 2 May 1901, p. 5; Heaton, "The Rousseau Raid," p. 11; Hamilton, *Recollections,* pp. 130–31.

17. *OR,* 39, pt. 2, p. 169; *OR,* 38, pt. 5, p. 81; Rousseau to Dodge, 7 July 1864, p. 148, Telegrams Sent, DN, RG 393.

18. *OR,* 38, pt. 5, p. 82.

19. Carmony, ed., "Jacob W. Bartmess Civil War Letters," pp. 163–64; Willoughby Diary, 8 July 1864; Ward Diary, 6–8 July 1864; Uriah W. Oblinger Diary, 7–8 July 1864; Orders, Company L, 7 July 1864, Order Books, Companies B, C, F, G, K, and L, 8th Indiana Cavalry, RG 94; Indiana Adjutant General, *Report,* 2:390–91; *NT,* 2 May 1901, p. 5; Jackson Diary, 8 July 1864; Heaton, "The Rousseau Raid," p. 11; Morning Reports, 6–8 July 1864, Companies D and H, 8th Indiana Cavalry, RG 94; Regimental Return, July 1864, 8th Indiana Cavalry, reel 35, M-594, RG 94.

20. Iowa Adjutant General, *Report,* pp. 998–99; Regimental Return, July 1864, 5th Iowa Cavalry, reel 51, M-594, RG 94; *DDT,* 14 July 1864, p. 1; Josiah Conzett, "Memoirs," pp. 71–72, Josiah Conzett Papers.

21. Owen Star to William D. Whipple, 2 September 1864, Regimental Letter and Endorsement Book, 2nd Kentucky Cavalry, RG 94; *NT,* 16 January 1896, p. 3; *OR,* 20, pt. 1, p. 379; Speed, Kelly, and Pirtle, *Union Regiments of Kentucky,* pp. 120–23; Kentucky Adjutant General, *Report of the Adjutant General of the State of Kentucky,* 1:63; Muster Roll, July–August 1864, Company L, 2nd Kentucky Cavalry, RG 94; Rousseau and Magill to Eifort, 4 July 1864, p. 144, Telegrams Sent, DN, RG 393; Rousseau and Polk to Eifort, 5 July 1864, Polk to Watts, 8 July 1864, pp. 200, 202–3, Letters Sent, DMT, RG 393; Regimental Returns, June, July, and August, 1864, 2nd Kentucky Cavalry, RG 94; Record of Ordnance and Ordnance Stores, vol. 7, 2nd Kentucky Cavalry, RG 156; "Weekly Report of the Effective Force of the 8th Indiana Cavalry, Monday Morning, June 27, 1864," 8th Indiana Cavalry Papers, RG 94; Orders, Company L, 7 July 1864, Order Books, Companies B, C, F, G, K, and L, 8th Indiana Cavalry, RG 94; Owen Star to William D. Whipple, 2 September 1864, Regimental Letter and Endorsement Book, 2nd Kentucky Cavalry, RG 94. Rousseau and his staff may have traveled south with the 2nd Kentucky, but the records do not offer any concrete evidence to that effect.

22. *NYH,* 23 July 1864, p. 1; Polk to Robert S. Granger, 8 July 1864, p. 148, Telegrams Sent, DN, RG 393. Shanks did not betray this trust. It was July 23, 1864, before his story appeared on the front page of the *New York Herald.* Even so, he was criticized in some circles for his "premature disclosure" of the raid. See *IDJ,* 25 July 1864, p. 2.

23. *OR,* 38, pt. 2, p. 905; *LDJ,* 30 July 1864, p. 1; *CDC,* 1 August 1864, p. 1; *NYH,* 23 July 1864, p. 1.

24. *OR,* 38, pt. 2, p. 909; McBurney Family Bible; James C. McBurney, Typewritten Memoir, James C. McBurney Papers; "A Brief biography of James Carol [*sic*] McBurney,"

McBurney Papers; U.S. Department of the Interior, Census Office, Twelfth Census of the United States, 1900: Population, Georgia, Bibb County, Enumeration District 28, Sheet 19; Agnes L. Dickson to Mrs. Willard B. McBurney, 15 October 1940 and 21 January 1963, McBurney Family Papers; Garrett, *Atlanta and Environs*, 3:537; *Jersey City Evening News*, 1 April 1905, p. 1; *Jersey Journal*, 8 July 1960, p. 8; Superior Court, Hudson County, New Jersey, Deeds and Mortgages, vol. 71, pp. 413–15, reel 4521a; James C. Freeman, Case Number 2,783, Records of the Southern Claims Commission, RG 233; James C. McBurney File, Collector of Customs Applications, General Records of the Department of the Treasury, RG 56; Simon et al., eds., *The Papers of Ulysses S. Grant*, 8:373, 413 (McBurney's activities during the Vicksburg campaign); Superior Court, Bibb County, Georgia, Deeds and Mortgages, vol. R–17, 1863–1866, pp. 286–87, reel 181–21; James C. McBurney File, Confederate Papers Relating to Citizens or Business Firms, M-346, War Department Collection of Confederate Records, RG 109; *OR*, 38, pt. 4, pp. 624–25; Special Order No. 159, 8 July 1864, p. 136, vol. 10, Orders, District of Nashville, RG 393.

25. *OR*, 38, pt. 2, pp. 904–5; *LDJ*, 30 July 1864, p. 1; *NYH*, 23 July 1864, p. 1; Orders, Company E, 10 July 1864, Order Books, Companies A–M, except F, 5th Iowa Cavalry, RG 94; Iowa Adjutant General, *Report*, p. 999; Fanning, *Hairbreadth Escapes*, p. 106; Morning Reports, 9 July 1864, Companies C, E, G, H, K, and M, 9th Ohio Cavalry, RG 94; Eckel, *History of the Fourth Tennessee Cavalry*, p. 50.

26. Jackson Diary, 9 July 1864; Ward Diary, 9 July 1864; Oblinger Diary, 9 July 1864; Morning Reports, 9 July 1864, Companies D and H, 8th Indiana Cavalry, RG 94; Heaton, "The Rousseau Raid," p. 11; Washington L. Elliott to William D. Whipple, 19 July 1864, with enclosure (J. E. Jacobs to Elliott, 18 July 1864), General Orders, DMT, RG 393; *OR*, 38, pt. 2, p. 878; Special Orders No. 27, 9 July 1864, Regimental Descriptive, Letter, Order, Guard Report, and Pass Book, 8th Indiana Cavalry, RG 94; *NT*, 2 May 1901, p. 5; *HT*, 25 August 1864, p. 1; *LDJ*, 30 July 1864, p. 1.

27. Owen Star to William D. Whipple, 28 September 1864, Regimental Letter and Endorsement Book, 2nd Kentucky Cavalry, RG 94; Washington L. Elliott to William D. Whipple, 19 July 1864, with enclosures (Thomas J. Jordan to Elliott, 10 July 1864; Robert S. Granger to J. L. Donaldson, 12 July 1864; J. E. Jacobs to Elliott, 18 July 1864), General Orders, DMT, RG 393; *DDT*, 1 August 1864, p. 1; Iowa Adjutant General, *Report*, p. 999.

28. Special Orders, 9 July 1864, Order Books, Companies A–K, 9th Ohio Cavalry, RG 94; Fanning, *Hairbreadth Escapes*, p. 106; Morning Reports, 8–10 July 1864, Companies C, E, G, H, K, and M, 9th Ohio Cavalry, RG 94; Eckel, *4th Tennessee*, p. 50; Regimental Return, July 1864, 4th Tennessee Cavalry, RG 94; Muster Roll, July–August 1864, Company M, 4th Tennessee Cavalry, RG 94.

29. *OR*, 38, pt. 2, pp. 904–5; *NYH*, 23 July 1864, p. 1; *LDJ*, 30 July 1864, p. 1; Hamilton, *Recollections*, p. 131; Circular, 9 July 1864, Regimental Descriptive, Letter, Order, Guard Report, and Pass Book, 8th Indiana Cavalry, RG 94; Morning Reports, 9 July 1864, Battery E, 1st Michigan Light Artillery, RG 94; *CDC*, 1 August 1864, p. 1.

30. *LDJ*, 30 July 1864, p. 1; *NT*, 2 May 1901, p. 5; Oblinger Diary, 9 July 1864; George W. Healey to "My Dear Mother," 9 July 1864, George W. Healey Papers; Jackson Diary, 9–10 July 1864; Ward Diary, 10 July 1864; *NYH*, 23 July 1864, p. 1; Cooke, *Cavalry Tactics*, p. 18; Steffen, *The Horse Soldier 1776–1943*, 2:59–62; U.S. War Department, *The Ordnance Manual for the Use of the Officers of the United States Army*, pp. 155–58; Heaton, "The Rousseau Raid," p. 12; *OR*, 38, pt. 2, pp. 878, 905.

31. Tennessee Adjutant General, *Report*, pp. 354, 388.

32. This telegram, found on p. 73, vol. 19/28, MDM, RG 393, is dated 8 July instead of 10 July 1864. It was not included in the *OR*'s, but did appear in U.S. Congress, Joint Committee on the Conduct of the War, *Supplemental Report*, 1:113, also dated 8 July 1864. However, Rousseau was still in Nashville on July 8, and had already telegraphed Sherman he would not leave Decatur until July 9. Any message he sent on July 8 should have reached Sherman's

headquarters at Vining's Station that same day or the next, but Sherman did not acknowledge receipt of this wire until July 11, when he advised George Thomas in *OR,* 38, pt. 5, p. 114, "General Rousseau telegraphs from Decatur *on the 8th* [author's italics] that he started that day and would be on the Montgomery and Opelika road in eight or nine days." This same telegram also appears on p. 77, Letter Book G, Sherman Papers, RG 94. However, another version of Sherman's July 11 communique appeared in the Joint Committee on the Conduct of the War's *Supplemental Report,* 1:121, twenty-five years before the publication of the *OR'*s. It stated: "General Dodge reports the enemy's cavalry alone above Peach Tree Creek, at Buckhead. He says he has an Atlanta paper of *the 10th;* . . . General Rousseau telegraphs from Decatur that he started *that day* [author's italics] and would be on the Montgomery and Opelika road in eight (8) or nine (9) days." Apparently, someone later inserted the words "on the 8th" in a misguided attempt to clarify the meaning of "that day." Rousseau undoubtedly sent his message on July 10.

33. Harrison to "Dear Wife," 11 [*sic*] July 1864, Thomas Joshua Harrison Papers.

34. Granger to J. L. Donaldson, 12 July 1864, General Orders, DMT, RG 393; Jackson Diary, 10 July 1864; Ward Diary, 9–10 July 1864; Oblinger Diary, 10 July 1864; Morning Reports, 6, 9–10 July 1864, Companies D and H, 8th Indiana Cavalry, RG 94; Regimental Return, July 1864, 8th Indiana Cavalry, reel 35, M-594, RG 94; Morning Reports, 10 July 1864, Company A, 5th Iowa Cavalry, RG 94; Morning Reports, 10 July 1864, Companies G, H, and K, 9th Ohio Cavalry, RG 94; *NYH,* 23 July 1864, p. 1; *LDJ,* 30 July 1864, p. 1; *DDT,* 1 August 1864, p. 1; *HT,* 25 August 1864, p. 1; *NYT,* 31 July 1864, p. 6; *NT,* 2 May 1901, p. 5; *OR,* 38, pt. 2, p. 905; Iowa Adjutant General, *Report,* p. 999; Eckel, *4th Tennessee,* p. 50; Fanning, *Hairbreadth Escapes,* p. 106; U.S. War Department, *Ordnance Manual,* pp. 155–59, 167–68, 224, 233; Record of Ordnance and Ordnance Stores, vol. 7, 8th Indiana, 5th Iowa, 2nd Kentucky, 9th Ohio, and 4th Tennessee Cavalry, RG 156; Reedstrom, *Bugles, Banners and War Bonnets,* pp. 227, 245; *CDC,* 1 August 1864, p. 1; Healey to "My Dear Mother," 9 July 1864. The supply of rations apparently varied from regiment to regiment. Lieutenant Thomas W. Fanning of the 9th Ohio Cavalry said he received only a twelve-day supply of coffee and sugar and four of hardtack and sowbelly. Several men make no mention of receiving salt, but this could have been carried on the pack mules.

35. *LDJ,* 30 July 1864, p. 1; *HT,* 25 August 1864, p. 1; Iowa Adjutant General, *Report,* p. 999; Heaton, "The Rousseau Raid," p. 12; *NT,* 2 May 1901, p. 5; Healey to "My Dear Mother," 9 July 1864.

3. TO MOORE'S BRIDGE AND BACK, JULY 1–JULY 18, 1864

1. *OR,* 38, pt. 5, pp. 80, 86, 90–91; pt. 3, pp. 38, 382; Dodge, *Personal Recollections,* p. 149; *NT,* 12 June 1902, p. 3.

2. *LDJ,* 14 September 1864, p. 1; Morrison, ed., "Getting through West Point," p. 315; Association of the Graduates of the United States Military Academy, *26th Annual Reunion,* p. 27. Unless otherwise noted, the details of Stoneman's life are drawn from *DAB,* 1928 ed., s.v. "George Stoneman," by Oliver L. Spaulding, Jr.; Warner, *Generals in Blue,* p. 481; *MAR,* 18 August 1864, p. 1; Bancroft, *The Works of Hubert Howe Bancroft,* vol. 24: *History of California,* p. 432; *Official Register of the U.S. Military Academy,* 1843:12, 17, 1844:10, 17, 1845:9, 17, 1846:7, 18; Cullum, *Biographical Register,* 2:280–81; Price, comp., *5th Cavalry,* pp. 86–87, 315–19.

3. Clendenen, *Blood on the Border,* pp. 39–40; Ford, *Rip Ford's Texas,* pp. 290–95; U.S. Congress, House, *Troubles on Texas Frontier,* pp. 80–82.

4. Ford, *Rip Ford's Texas,* pp. 320–21; *NYT,* 12 April 1861, p. 8; *NYT,* 13 April 1861, p. 8; *NYTB,* 12 April 1861, pp. 3, 5; *NYTB,* 13 April 1861, p. 5; *WES,* 11 May 1861, p. 2; Grimsley, ed., "'We Prepare to Receive the Enemy Where We Stand,'" pp. 18–24; Thiele, "The

Evolution of Cavalry in the American Civil War; 1861–1863" (Ph.D. diss.), pp. 265–66, 269–71; Averell, *Ten Years in the Saddle,* p. 356; *OR,* 51, pt. 1, pp. 698, 700; Averell, "With the Cavalry on the Peninsula," p. 430; *OR,* 51, pt. 1, pp. 709, 713.

5. Averell, *Ten Years in the Saddle,* pp. 365–66; *OR,* 51, pt. 1, pp. 754, 830, 946; *OR,* 25, pt. 2, pp. 51, 59, 71–72, 212, 543 (Hooker accuses Stoneman of destroying half his cavalry); pt. 1, pp. 1060 (Stoneman's bursting shell speech), 1066–67 (Hooker's orders to Stoneman); Bigelow, *The Campaign of Chancellorsville,* p. 458 (Stoneman's hemorrhoids); *NT,* 14 June 1888, p. 1 (Stoneman "too much of an old Regular"). Long after the war, Hooker complained the army's seniority system had forced him to appoint "a wooden man" to command his cavalry. See Owens, *Sword and Pen,* p. 146.

6. *NT,* 7 June 1888, p. 1; *NT,* 14 June 1888, p. 1; *OR,* 25, pt. 2, p. 513; *OR,* series III, vol. 3, p. 581; *OR,* 52, pt. 1, pp. 509–10; Wilson, *Under the Old Flag,* 1:327; Cox, *Military Reminiscences,* 2:137–39; *OR,* 32, pt. 2, pp. 166, 229–30, 251, 363; pt. 3, p. 312; Tarrant, *The Wild Riders of the First Kentucky Cavalry,* pp. 314–20, 324, 328–29; *OR,* 38, pt. 4, pp. 267–68.

7. *OR,* 38, pt. 1, pp. 114, 116; pt. 2, p. 683; pt. 4, pp. 649–50; pt. 5, pp. 10, 23–24, 36–79 passim, 174. Stoneman did not assign numbers to his brigades as was done in the rest of Sherman's cavalry but referred to them by the names of their commanding officers. See R. W. Smith to Horace Capron, 18 July 1864, Horace Capron Papers.

8. *OR,* 38, pt. 5, pp. 68, 91, 99.

9. White, *Statistics of Georgia,* p. 144; White, *Historical Collections of Georgia,* p. 293; A. S. Atkinson and Others vs. A. V. Brumby and William J. Russell, Case Number 9,821; *NYTB,* 21 July 1864, p. 1; Russell, "Georgia Towns Moved in War," p. 6; Sanford, *History of Fourteenth Illinois Cavalry,* p. 177; Martin West Diary, 10 July 1864; *NT,* 16 January 1902, p. 3; *OR,* 38, pt. 5, pp. 21, 76–77, 104; Upson, *With Sherman to the Sea,* p. 119. The *New York Tribune*'s account confused the destruction of the Sweetwater Factory with the mills at Roswell, asserting, "Five cotton factories at Rossville [*sic*] . . . were destroyed on the 12th [*sic*] by order of Gen. Sherman," and credited Major Tompkins with burning the mills at both places. Apparently the *Tribune*'s correspondent got his information second- or thirdhand and failed to distinguish between events at Roswell and Sweetwater Town. Monroe M. King asserted in *Destruction of New Manchester, Georgia,* p. 4, that Major Tompkins ordered a battery of twelve-pounder guns to "breach the great 300-foot long wooden dam across the creek above the mill," only to have one of the cannon swept away in the ensuing flood. Relic hunters have reportedly located a bronze Napoleon gun in the creek below the mill, but it seems to be set in concrete or stone, as if it were part of some sort of monument. Stoneman's artillery consisted of four wrought-iron Rodman rifles, all of which were still in service after July 9. The identity of the mill destroyed by Captain Benjamin Crandle's detachment of the 14th Illinois is uncertain, but it may have been Perkerson's Mill on Olley's Creek. It was burned by an unidentified group of Federals who "detached the mill stones and rolled them into the creek bed before they fired the mill." See *Marietta Daily Journal,* 8 March 1974, p. 1D.

10. Samuel D. Reniker Diary, 9 July 1864; Andrew N. Weir Diary, 9 July 1864; West Diary, 9 July 1864; Oliver C. Haskell Diary, 9 July 1864; Compiled Service Records, RG 94; Pension Records, RG 15; Tarrant, *1st Kentucky,* p. 348; Morning Reports, 8–9 July 1864, Company B, 5th Indiana Cavalry, RG 94; Record of Events, July–August 1864, Company D, 5th Indiana Cavalry, reel 34, M-594, RG 94; *OR,* 38, pt. 1, pp. 70, 155, 896–97; pt. 3, p. 617; pt. 5, pp. 70, 102–4, 107, 109, 114, 872–73.

11. *OR,* 38, pt. 5, pp. 107, 109; Levi Nickel Diary, 10 July 1864; Weir Diary, 10 July 1864; Haskell Diary, 10 July 1864; West Diary, 10 July 1864; Sanford, *14th Illinois,* p. 177; R. W. Smith to Capron, 10 July 1864, Capron Papers.

12. This author has been unable to find any specific evidence Hardy's battery accompanied Adams and Capron, but it seems unlikely the limbers and caissons would have forded

Sweetwater Creek with Butler's brigade after the heavy rains of July 10. None of Butler's troopers mention the presence of any artillery.

13. Citing a diary he kept, in *NT,* 16 January 1902, p. 3, assistant surgeon Samuel D. Tobey of the 8th Michigan Cavalry credited Adams's men with capturing two Rebel lieutenants and twenty privates. Stoneman, writing two days after the event in *OR,* 38, pt. 2, p. 913, put the number at only one lieutenant and sixteen or seventeen men. The wounded officer was probably Lieutenant William N. (or N. B.) Webster of the 1st Tennessee Cavalry. See Lindsley, ed., *The Military Annals of Tennessee,* pp. 611, 890. There are indications in *CDS,* 16 July 1864, p. 2, he either escaped or was released to seek medical attention at the nearby Confederate hospitals in Newnan.

14. The ferryboat Stoneman's men used probably came from Reese's Ferry, about a mile below Moore's Bridge.

15. The narrative describing Stoneman's foray down the west bank of the Chattahoochee is drawn from *OR,* 38, pt. 2, pp. 912–13; pt. 5, pp. 107, 130, 133, 135, 145, 878; West Diary, 11 July 1864; Sanford, *14th Illinois,* pp. 173, 177–78; *DAT,* 14 July 1864, p. 4; *DAT,* 8 August 1864, p. 4; *DFP,* 10 August 1864, p. 3; *PHP,* 17 August 1864, p. 1; *NT,* 16 January 1902, p. 3 (Dr. Tobey's account of the bombardment of Campbellton); Record of Events, July–August 1864, Companies E and K, 8th Michigan Cavalry, reel 84, M-594, RG 94; Hinman, *The Story of the Sherman Brigade,* pp. 886–88; Morning Reports, 11 July 1864, Company K, 5th Indiana Cavalry, RG 94; Record of Events, July–August 1864, Company H, 5th Indiana Cavalry, reel 34, M-594, RG 94; Haskell Diary, 11–12 July 1864; Weir Diary, 11–12 July 1864; Morning Reports, 11 July 1864, Company I, 6th Indiana Cavalry, RG 94; Tarrant, *1st Kentucky,* pp. 348–49; *CDS,* 15 July 1864, p. 1; George J. Haynes vs. the U.S., Congressional Jurisdiction Case File Number 3,698, Records of the United States Court of Claims, RG 123; Leroy Brown, Case Number 11,391, RG 233 (Stoneman's camp at Dog Creek); John M. Strickland, Case Number 14,607, RG 233; *NYTB,* 25 July 1864, p. 1 (Adams's attack on Moore's Bridge); *CDS,* 16 July 1864, p. 2; Horace King, Claim Number 19,661, RG 233; William Chasteen vs. the U.S., Case Number 3,346, RG 123.

16. Scruggs, ed., *Georgia Historical Markers,* p. 156; Cumming, *Kate: The Journal of a Confederate Nurse,* pp. 210–11; *OR,* 38, pt. 5, p. 878; Combined Reports of Bragg, Buckner, Foard, and Gamble Hospitals, 30 June, 7 July, 31 July, 1864, Samuel H. Stout Papers; *CDS,* 16 July 1864, p. 2.

17. Sydney S. Champion to "My Precious Wife," 14 July 1864, Sydney S. Champion Papers; Harry St. John Dixon Diary, 16 and 24 July 1864; Dixon, "Recollections of a Rebel Private," p. 147; Weir Diary, 12–13 July 1864; Haskell Diary, 12–13 July 1864; *OR,* 38, pt. 2, pp. 912–13; pt. 3, p. 618; pt. 5, pp. 133, 135, 145, 880; J. A. Bigger Diary, 15 July 1864; Record of Events, July–August 1864, Captain Farris's Battery (Clark Artillery, King's Battery), Light Artillery, reel 34, M-861; Compiled Records Showing Service of Military Units in Confederate Organizations, RG 109; Record of Events, July–August 1864, Company G, 2nd Mississippi Cavalry, reel 27, M-861, RG 109; Muster Roll, July–August 1864, Company H, Ballentine's Regiment, 2nd Mississippi Partisan Rangers, RG 109; Powell, comp., *List of Officers,* p. 165; Hickman, "Confederate Generals of Tennessee," p. 171; Wright, *Arkansas in the War,* p. 56; Evans, ed., *Confederate Military History,* vol. 10: *Tennessee,* by James D. Porter, pp. 288–91; *DAB,* 1928 ed., s.v. "Frank C. Armstrong," by Walter S. Grant; Foreman, "The Armstrongs of Indian Territory, Part III: General Frank Crawford Armstrong," pp. 56–58, 63–65; Warner, *Generals in Gray,* pp. 12–13; *OR,* 2, p. 393.

18. *NT,* 16 January 1902, p. 3; *OR,* 38, pt. 2, p. 913; pt. 4, p. 656; pt. 5, pp. 145, 880; Bigger Diary, 15 July 1864; Record of Events, July–August 1864, Captain Farris's Battery (Clark Artillery, King's Battery), reel 34, M-861, RG 109; Smith, *The Private in Gray,* p. 99; Sanford, *14th Illinois,* p. 178; Compiled Service Records, RG 94. Stoneman said the Rebels had four guns at Moore's Bridge. Confederate sources mention only two. J. A. Bigger of the 2nd Mississippi Cavalry credited the 7th Tennessee Cavalry with charging the Yankee rifle pits,

but the only part of the 7th Tennessee participating in the Atlanta campaign was Company A, which served as General Jackson's escort. Since Jackson did not accompany Armstrong to Moore's Bridge, it seems unlikely he would have sent his escort. The only other numbered regiment with Armstrong, besides Bigger's, was the 1st Mississippi Cavalry.

19. *OR,* 38, pt. 5, p. 880.

20. *OR,* 38, pt. 2, p. 913; pt. 5, p. 145; Tarrant, *1st Kentucky,* p. 349; Sanford, *14th Illinois,* p. 178; *PHP,* 17 August 1864, p. 1. After the war, two of Armstrong's men, Montgomery, in *Reminiscences of a Mississippian in Peace and War,* p. 182, and Deupree, in "The Noxubee Squadron of the First Mississippi Cavalry," p. 100, claimed Confederate troops burned Moore's Bridge. However, the wording of these two accounts is so similar it seems likely Deupree borrowed heavily from Montgomery's earlier work. All the other reliable sources agree Moore's Bridge was burned by Union troops.

21. John M. Strickland, Case Number 14,607, RG 233; Blanton F. Thornton, Southern Claims Commission Case File Number 9,297, Records of the General Accounting Office, RG 217; Simeon Bridges, Case Number 9,299, RG 217; Allen D. Sims, Case Number 9,298, RG 217; *OR,* 38, pt. 2, p. 913; pt. 5, p. 145; Sanford, *14th Illinois,* pp. 178–79; George J. Haynes vs. the U.S., Case Number 3,698, RG 123; Leroy Brown, Case Number 11,391, RG 233.

22. *DFP,* 10 August 1864, p. 3; Record of Events, July–August 1864, Companies C, E, F, and K, 8th Michigan Cavalry, reel 84, M-594, RG 94; William F. Brown, Case Number 3,016, RG 233; *PHP,* 17 August 1864, p. 1 (Michigan trooper's quotation); *NT,* 16 January 1902, p. 3. Samuel D. Tobey, the assistant surgeon accompanying Buck's column, noted there were only sixty men in the detachment. However, Miss Susan W. Brown, eleven or twelve years old in the summer of 1864, testified in 1871 that she saw 150 Yankees ride into Carrollton.

23. *NT,* 16 January 1902, p. 3; Sanford, *14th Illinois,* p. 179; P. H. Hesterly, Case Number 6,560, RG 217; William H. Austin vs. the U.S., Case Number 3,439, RG 123; Mary A. Cartwright vs. the U.S., Case Number 7,195, RG 123; William Chasteen vs. the U.S., Case Number 3,346, RG 123; John H. Giles vs. the U.S., Case Number 7,418, RG 123; James M. Green vs. the U.S., Case Number 601, RG 123; George J. Haynes vs. the U.S., Case Number 3,698, RG 123; Annie Hilderbrand vs. the U.S., Case Number 4,717, RG 123; Thomas Millis vs. the U.S., Case Number 4,204, RG 123; Aquilla Reeves vs. the U.S., Case Number 3,507, RG 123; Drucilla Winn vs. the U.S., Case Number 6,946, RG 123; Leroy Brown, Case Number 11,391, RG 233; Wilson Cartwright, Case Number 10,967, RG 233; Sanford, *14th Illinois,* p. 179; *OR,* 38, pt. 2, p. 913; pt. 5, pp. 145–46; Tarrant, *1st Kentucky,* p. 349.

24. *OR,* 38, pt. 5, pp. 117–18, 127–28, 134–35, 139–40, 144–46. This dispatch is also found in Letter Book G, Sherman Papers, RG 94, and in Telegrams Sent in the Field, April to November 1864, vol. 16/23, MDM, RG 393, indicating it may have been telegraphed to Marietta to be forwarded to Stoneman by courier. Signal corpsmen may also have stretched a telegraph wire linking Sherman's headquarters at Vining's Station with Blair's bivouac, but there is no mention of this in the *Official Records.*

25. *OR,* 38, pt. 5, p. 147.

26. Nickel Diary, 16 July 1864; *OR,* 38, pt. 3, pp. 553, 571, 573, 579; pt. 5, pp. 147–48; Thomas B. Mackall Diary, 16 July 1864, Joseph E. Johnston Papers. Lieutenant George Griscom of the 9th Texas Cavalry noted the skirmishing around Howell's Ferry abruptly ceased about 6:00 A.M., July 16, and for the next twelve hours Rebel pickets ventured freely into the open spaces along the riverbank without coming under fire. See Kerr, ed., *Fighting with Ross' Texas Cavalry Brigade, C.S.A., The Diary of George L. Griscom,* p. 158.

27. Tarrant, *1st Kentucky,* p. 349; Sanford, *14th Illinois,* pp. 179–80; Haskell Diary, 16 July 1864; Weir Diary 17 July 1864; Morning Reports, 16–17 July 1864, Companies B and K, 5th Indiana Cavalry, RG 94; Record of Events, July–August 1864, Companies D and H, 5th Indiana Cavalry, reel 34, M-594, RG 94; Morning Reports, 17 July 1864, 6th Indiana Cavalry, RG 94; *OR,* 38, pt. 5, pp. 174, 192; Stoneman to Capron, 17 July 1864, Capron Papers; Hinman, *The Sherman Brigade,* p. 888; "Proceedings of a Court Martial which convened at

Nashville, Tenn. in the case of Lieut. Col. D. P. Jenkins, 14th Ills. Vol. Cav." (hereafter cited as Jenkins), Case Number 00694, Records of the Judge Advocate General's Office, RG 153; Beall, *In Barrack and Field,* pp. 402–3 (Major Buck's campsite on July 15); William F. Brown, Case Number 3,016, RG 233; *NT,* 16 January 1902, p. 3; *DFP,* 10 August 1864, p. 3.

28. *DFP,* 10 August 1864, p. 3; *DAT,* 8 August 1864, p. 4; John J. Applegate to "Dear Wife," 18 July 1864, John Sickles Collection; *OR,* 38, pt. 2, p. 913; pt. 5, pp. 145–46, 192; Tarrant, *1st Kentucky,* p. 414; Kentucky Adjutant General, *Report,* 1:12–13, 38–39, 274–75, 308–9, 312–13, 342–43; Indiana Adjutant General, *Report,* 6:158, 467; Compiled Service Records, RG 94; Pension Records, RG 15. In his July 15 report, written at Dog Creek, Stoneman told Sherman he had sent forty prisoners to the rear. However, in a letter dated 1 November 1864, Lieutenant John M. Baird reported the 8th Michigan alone had captured seventy-four prisoners on the Moore's Bridge raid. See Baird to Adjutant General, State of Michigan, 1 November 1864, Records of the Michigan Military Establishment, RG 59–14.

29. Finney, "The 5th Ind. Cavalry in the War and in Civil Life," p. 21; Whitenack, "Reminiscences of Army Life," pp. 36–37; Whitenack, "Reminiscences of the Civil War: Andersonville," pp. 129–30; Compiled Service Records, RG 94; "History of Company F, 5th Indiana Cavalry," Regimental Correspondence of the 90th Regiment; Indiana Adjutant General, *Report,* 3:105; Quartermaster General's Office, *Roll of Honor,* 23:71. A citation in Loomis's compiled service record reads, "Died of wounds received on the morning of the 17th of July. On evening of the same day wounded again by guard of Federal soldiers."

30. Hinman, *The Sherman Brigade,* p. 888; Sanford, *14th Illinois,* pp. 178–79.

4. TO THE GATES OF ATLANTA, JULY 10–JULY 20, 1864

1. *OR,* 38, pt. 5, p. 123.

2. George Knox Miller to "My Darling Wife," 12 July 1864; Gibbons, *The Recollections of an Old Confederate Soldier,* p. 6; *CDS,* 17 July 1864, p. 2; Payne, *History of the Thirty-fourth Regiment of Illinois Volunteer Infantry,* p. 179; *CDC,* 20 July 1864, p. 1.

3. *OR,* 38, pt. 5, pp. 101, 111–12; pt. 2, p. 838; Morning Reports, 10 July 1864, Company G, 4th Ohio Cavalry, RG 94; Record of Events, July–August 1864, Muster Roll, Company E, 4th U.S. Cavalry, RG 94; McLain Diary, 8 and 10 July 1864; Lemmon Diary, 10 July 1864; Regimental Return, July 1864, 4th Michigan Cavalry, reel 83, M-594, RG 94; Potter to "Dear Father," 10 July 1864; Gooding to "(the Boys are all looking and guessing)," 10 July 1864; *WC,* 23 July 1864, p. 2; *DFP,* 22 July 1864, p. 3; *MJPGA,* 20 August 1864, p. 1; Lester Diary, 10 July 1864; Nourse Diary, 9–10 July 1864.

4. Records Diary, 10 July 1864; Magee, *72nd Indiana,* pp. 337–38; Temple, *The First Hundred Years,* p. 335; *OR,* 38, pt. 5, p. 109; Lemmon Diary, 10 July 1864.

5. Griest Diary, 10 July 1864; Records Diary, 10 July 1864; Kemper Diary, 10 July 1864; Magee, *72nd Indiana,* p. 338; Doyle, *17th Indiana,* p. 20; Jeremiah Mosteller, Case Number 3,600, RG 233; Lester Diary, 10 July 1864; Nourse Diary, 10 and 12 July 1864; Fleming to "My Dear Father," 12 July 1864; Durand, *Calvin Durand–Sarah Gould Downs Durand, A Memorial,* pp. 63–65; Crofts, comp., *3rd Ohio,* p. 153; "List of Prisoners of War Captured by 2d Brigade 2d Division Cavalry," pp. 4–5, vol. 57/140, CCMDM, RG 393; "List of Casualties in 2d Brigade 2d Division Cavalry," pp. 66–67, vol. 57/140, CCMDM, RG 393; Compiled Service Records, RG 94; Pension Records, RG 15; Ohio Roster Commission, *Official Roster,* 11:33, 153, 156–57, 186, 228; *OR,* 38, pt. 2, p. 838; pt. 5, pp. 111–12, 119.

6. Records Diary, 11 July 1864; Magee, *72nd Indiana,* p. 339; Brown, *The Signal Corps,* p. 530.

7. Regimental Return, July 1864, 4th Michigan Cavalry, reel 83, M-594, RG 94; *MJPGA,* 20 August 1864, p. 1; Lemmon Diary, 11 July 1864; McLain Diary, 11 July 1864; Crofts, comp., *3rd Ohio,* p. 152; Morning Reports, 11 July 1864, Company G, 4th Ohio Cavalry, RG

94; Lester Diary, 11 July 1864; Nourse Diary, 11 July 1864; Fleming to "My Dear Father," 12 July 1864; *OR*, 38, pt. 2, p. 838; pt. 3, p. 121; pt. 5, p. 119.

8. *OR*, 38, pt. 5, pp. 114–15; pt. 1, pp. 155–500 passim, 897–98.

9. James Ball, Case Number 6,443, RG 233; Grenville M. Dodge Diary, 11–13 July 1864; Grenville M. Dodge, "Personal Biography of Major General Grenville Mellon Dodge," 1:232, Grenville M. Dodge Papers; *OR*, 38, pt. 3, pp. 38–383 passim; pt. 5, pp. 109, 117–19, 130–32, 134, 136, 139.

10. Lester Diary, 14 July 1864; Nourse Diary, 14 July 1864; Magee, *72nd Indiana*, p. 340; Doyle, *17th Indiana*, p. 20; Griest Diary, 14 July 1864; Records Diary, 14 July 1864; Kemper Diary, 14 July 1864; Regimental Return, July 1864, 17th Indiana Mounted Infantry, reel 38, M-594, RG 94; William H. Scott, Case Number 2,949, RG 233; Larson, *Sergeant Larson*, pp. 259–65; Regimental Return, July 1864, 4th Michigan Cavalry, reel 83, M-594, RG 94; McLain Diary, 14 July 1864; *MJPGA*, 20 August 1864, p. 1.

11. *OR*, 38, pt. 5, pp. 139–40, 142–43.

12. In a 14 July 1864 letter to Sherman, found on p. 90, vol. 19/28, MDM, RG 393, McPherson said the regiment sent to Cumming numbered "700 strong." A Tri-Monthly Report, 10 July 1864, 3rd Ohio Cavalry Papers, RG 94, confirms the 3rd Ohio numbered 724 officers and men, but the four companies of the regiment's 3rd battalion had been sent to escort Garrard's wagon train to Marietta on July 13 and had not yet returned. This would have reduced Seidel's strength by a third. Seidel could conceivably have borrowed a battalion from another regiment in the 2nd Brigade, but the records of the 1st and 4th Ohio make no mention of this. Most likely, McPherson's estimate of Seidel's strength was simply too high. Private George Kryder said most of the troopers who were out foraging when Seidel left for Cumming had already ridden thirty-five or forty miles by the time they got back to camp and were too tired to follow.

13. *OR*, 38, pt. 2, p. 846; *SCR*, 28 July 1864, p. 2; *DTB*, 27 July 1864, p. 2; Crofts, comp., *3rd Ohio*, p. 153; Kryder to "Dear Beloved Wife," 15 July 1864; John T. Brown, administrator of the estate of Almon G. Hutchins, Case Number 4,955, RG 233; White, *Statistics of Georgia*, p. 253; Frank H. Nichols vs. the U.S., Case Number 744, RG 123; John G. Lott, Case Number 4,960, RG 217. Crofts said Seidel "had a little skirmishing and captured a number of prisoners." Seidel did not mention any fighting in his report in *OR*, 38, pt. 2, p. 846, and Private George Kryder, in a letter to his wife, said troopers returning from the raid told him "they did not even see any Rebs." The skirmish Crofts referred to may have involved troopers Seidel left at Lebanon Church. According to Kryder, foragers from the 3rd Ohio clashed with some Rebel scouts on July 14 and "killed two and took two prisoner." However, the "List of Prisoners of War Captured by 2d Brigade 2d Division Cavalry," pp. 4–5, vol. 57/140, CCMDM, RG 393, does not show any Confederate prisoners taken by the 3rd Ohio on July 14 or 15.

14. Wilson, *Under the Old Flag*, 2:224; Illinois Adjutant General, *Report of the Adjutant General of the State of Illinois*, 6:419; Griest Diary, 15 July 1864; Records Diary, 15 July 1864; "Semi-Weekly Report of Effective Forces [of] the 123rd Ills. Vols., 14 July 1864," 123rd Illinois Mounted Infantry Papers, RG 94; "Semi-Weekly Return of the Effective Force of the 72nd Ind. Vols. for July 14th 1864," 72nd Indiana Mounted Infantry Papers, RG 94; "Weekly Report of Effective Force Present from the Week Ending Monday [July] 11th, 1864 for the 7th Penn. Vol. Cavy.," 7th Pennsylvania Cavalry Papers, RG 94; Magee, *72nd Indiana*, pp. 340–41; *ACS*, 19 July 1864, p. 2; Records of Ordnance and Ordnance Stores, vol. 7, 123rd Illinois Mounted Infantry, 72nd Indiana Mounted Infantry, 7th Pennsylvania Cavalry, RG 156; *MJPGA*, 20 August 1864, p. 1; Dornblaser, *Sabre Strokes*, p. 168. The oats may have belonged to Alexander Baker, a farmer who lived in Gwinnett County on the main road between Atlanta and Cumming. He testified that a large force of Union cavalry, including an Illinois regiment, "went into the field & took the oats, they were cut & shocked. They carried them off on their horses. There were about 500 hundred dozen of the oats." See Alexander Baker, Case Number 12,696, RG 217.

15. Long to William D. Whipple, 14 July 1864, Eggleston to E. S. Wood, 8 July 1864, Robert P. Kennedy to Long, 15 July 1864, 1st Ohio Papers, RG 94; Tri-Monthly Report, 31 July 1864, 1st Ohio Cavalry Papers, RG 94; Curry, comp., *Four Years in the Saddle,* p. 21; Reid, *Ohio in the War,* 2:747. Earlier reports of "disgraceful and wanton pillaging and destruction of property" had led Garrard to issue standing orders for officers to accompany all foraging parties to "prevent pillaging and destruction" and in all cases to leave "a limited but sufficient supply of corn and bacon . . . for the support of the women and children. . . ." See General Order No. 16, 14 June 1864, Regimental and Descriptive Order Book, 72nd Indiana Mounted Infantry, RG 94.

16. McLain Diary, 16 July 1864; Potter Diary, 16 July 1864; Lester Diary, 16 July 1864; Nourse Diary, 16 July 1864; Pension Records, RG 15; L. B. Eldridge to John Robertson, 28 August 1864, RG 59–14; Lemmon Diary, 15 [16] July 1864.

17. *OR,* 38, pt. 5, pp. 147, 156–57.

18. Robert P. Kennedy to Eggleston, 16 July 1864, 1st Ohio Cavalry Papers, RG 94; "Circular, Hd. Qrs. 2d Brig. 2d Divn. Cav., Near Roswell, Ga., 16 July 1864," 1st Ohio Cavalry Papers, RG 94; "Circular, Hd. Qrs. 2d Brig. 2d Divn. Cav., Near Roswell, Ga., 16 July 1864," p. 44, vol. 40/79, CCMDM, RG 393; *OR,* 38, pt. 2, pp. 843, 845, 846; pt. 5, p. 155; Tri-Monthly Report, 20 July 1864, 1st Ohio Cavalry Papers, RG 94; Kryder to "Dear Beloved Wife," 18 July 1864; Crofts, comp., *3rd Ohio,* p. 153; Tri-Monthly Report, 20 July 1864, 3rd Ohio Cavalry Papers, RG 94; James Thomson Diary, 16 July 1864; Morning Reports, 16 July 1864, Company G, 4th Ohio Cavalry, RG 94; Tri-Monthly Report, 21 July 1864, 4th Ohio Cavalry Papers, RG 94; Griest Diary, 16 July 1864; Records Diary, 16 July 1864.

19. *OR,* 38, pt. 5, pp. 152–53; pt. 1, passim; pt. 2, pp. 16–487 passim; pt. 5, pp. 155–56, 159, 161; Stormont, comp., *History of the Fifty-Eighth Regiment of Indiana Volunteer Infantry,* pp. 341–42; Rosenberger, ed., "Ohiowa Soldier," p. 138; *CDC,* 2 July 1864, p. 1.

20. Unless otherwise noted, the narrative describing the movements of Garrard's division from July 17 to July 20 is based on *OR,* 38, pt. 2, pp. 808, 813 (Garrard's report), 842, 848; pt. 3, pp. 121–22; pt. 5, p. 221; *OR,* 52, pt. 1, p. 569; Vale, *Minty and the Cavalry,* p. 325; *NT,* 31 May 1894, p. 2; Heber S. Thompson Diary, 18 July 1864; Regimental Return, July 1864, 4th Michigan Cavalry, reel 83, M-594, RG 94; Gooding to "Dear Lucy," 26 July 1864; Lemmon Diary, 17–20 July 1864; McLain Diary, 18–20 July 1864; Potter Diary, 17–20 July 1864; Potter to "Dear Father," 1 August 1864; *DFP,* 6 August 1864, p. 1; *WC,* 6 August 1864, p. 2; *WC,* 13 August 1864, p. 2; *WC,* 20 August 1864, p. 2; *MJPGA,* 20 August 1864, p. 1; Record of Events, Muster Rolls, July–August 1864, Companies E and G, 4th U.S. Cavalry, RG 94; Regimental Return, July 1864, 4th U.S. Cavalry, reel 41, M-744, RG 94; Larson, *Sergeant Larson,* p. 266; Crofts, comp., *3rd Ohio,* p. 154; James Thomson Diary, 19–20 July 1864; Morning Reports, 20 July 1864, Company G, 4th Ohio Cavalry, RG 94; Griest Diary, 17–20 July 1864; Records Diary, 17–20 July 1864; Barnard to "Dear Mag," 22 July 1864; Magee, *72nd Indiana,* pp. 341–44; Kemper Diary, 17–20 July 1864; Doyle, *17th Indiana,* pp. 20–21; *AT,* 16 December 1897, p. 6; "Effective Force 98th Ill. Vols. July 21st/64," 98th Illinois Mounted Infantry Papers, RG 94; Illinois Adjutant General, *Report,* 5:516, 6:419; *NT,* 18 October 1900, p. 3; Lester Diary, 17–20 July 1864; Nourse Diary, 17–20 July 1864; Abram D. Binion, Case Number 3,561, RG 217; George W. Cash, Case Number 7,399, RG 217; Thomas M. Bryson, Case Number 15,604, RG 233.

21. *OR,* 38, pt. 5, p. 165. Garrard added his headquarters were near the house of a "Mr. Chester." A search of census records and an interview with noted Atlanta historian Franklin Garrett has failed to locate any Chester families living in the vicinity. Several families named Chestnut did live in this area, and Garrard's headquarters was probably located near the Chestnut house shown on Map N221–34, Civil War Map File, Records of the Office of the Chief of Engineers, RG 77.

22. Orlando M. Poe Diary, 16–17 July 1864; *OR,* Atlas, plate LVI, no. 4; *OR,* 38, pt. 1, pp. 211, 260, 898, 900; pt. 3, p. 68; pt. 5, pp. 152, 158–60, 162, 166, 168.

23. A cavalry battalion usually consisted of four companies, but Company D of the 7th Pennsylvania's 1st battalion was on detached duty, serving as Garrard's escort. See *MJPGA,* 9 July 1864, p. 1; Regimental Return, August 1864, 7th Pennsylvania Cavalry, reel 165, M-594, RG 94.

24. Newspaper accounts differed over the exact hour Garrard's division reached the Georgia Railroad, putting the time at 11:00 A.M. or 2:00 P.M. See *ADC,* 20 July 1864, p. 1; *NYTB,* 28 July 1864, p. 1.

25. Garrard's apprehension about large bodies of Confederate troops near the railroad apparently stemmed from reports he received from the Army of the Tennessee. A Confederate deserter who surrendered to Logan's XV Corps on July 17 indicated Brigadier General John H. Kelly's cavalry division, 4,000 strong, was facing Logan on the north side of Peachtree Creek, while Major General William B. Bates's infantry division was waiting on the south side. Grenville Dodge forwarded a similar report to McPherson early on July 18. Both Logan and McPherson were in close contact with Garrard's headquarters and either of them could have shared this information with him. See *OR,* 38, pt. 5, p. 166; Dodge, "Personal Biography," 1:237.

26. The 17th Indiana may have adopted a slightly different technique. Adjutant William E. Doyle, writing in the *American Tribune,* 16 December 1897, p. 6, said, "Poles were cut for levers, and the track turned over in sections thirty to one hundred feet in length, on which fence rails were piled and set on fire."

27. The narrative describing the activities of Lightburn's infantry on July 18 is based on *OR,* 38, pt. 3, pp. 19–20, 38, 101, 188, 210, 228, 235, 237, 240, 245, 253, 260; pt. 5, pp. 176–77; *OR,* 52, pt. 1, p. 569.

28. *OR,* 38, pt. 2, p. 808. The destruction of the wood station is mentioned in William H. Histel[?] to "Dear Mr. Stephens," 20 July 1864, Alexander H. Stephens Papers, and *ACS,* 20 July 1864, p. 1. In the sources previously cited, Garrard's officers and men estimated the amount of track destroyed at anywhere from one to seven miles. McPherson reported in *OR,* 38, pt. 3, pp. 19–20, and pt. 5, p. 176, his infantry and Garrard's cavalry "thoroughly destroyed over three miles of track." Estimates by Lightburn's regimental commanders ranged from one to five miles, but Captain Gordon Lofland, assistant adjutant general for the 2nd Division, XV Corps, probably came closest to the truth in *OR,* 38, pt. 3, p. 188, when he noted Lightburn's brigade "destroyed one mile and a half of the road." Confederate accounts in *ACS,* 20 July 1864, p. 3; *ADC,* 20 July 1864, p. 3; *MDT,* 21 July 1864, p. 1; *ACS,* 22 July 1864, p. 3; and *DFP,* 28 July 1864, p. 3, admitted the loss of a half mile to three miles of track.

29. *OR,* 38, pt. 3, pp. 19–20; pt. 5, pp. 170, 175–76, 179–81.

30. *OR,* Atlas, plate LX, no. 1; "Special Field Orders No. 1, Head Qrs. 2nd Cavalry Division D.C., Cochran's House, July 19th 1864," p. 219, vol. 35/74, CCMDM, RG 393.

31. *NT,* 30 May 1895, p. 3. The evidence seems to indicate Garrard had Long's men build fires at the ends of the rails, rather than overturn the track and burn the crossties as Sherman would have preferred.

32. *ACS,* 23 July 1864, p. 3. In a letter to the *Detroit Free Press,* 6 August 1864, p. 1, Captain William W. Van Antwerp of the 4th Michigan Cavalry said a train of cars carrying "Quartermaster's stores for the rebel army at Atlanta" arrived from Augusta on the night of July 18–19. Unable to proceed to Atlanta because of the break in the track, the train unloaded its cargo at Stone Mountain. Southern sources neither confirm nor deny this story. An article in the *ACS,* 20 July 1864, p. 1, reported the freight train which left Augusta for Atlanta on the morning of July 18 "went within sight of the raiders, before it turned back." The *ADC* of 20 July 1864, p. 1, said a train which left Augusta on Monday, July 18, "proceeded to Conyers fifteen miles this side of Stone Mountain, but learning of the presence of the Yankees returned." Even the evening passenger train to Augusta was "about two miles below Decatur" before the engineer learned the Yankees had torn up the track at Stone Mountain. See *DFP,* 28 July 1864, p. 3. Since there was no telegraph along this stretch of the Georgia Railroad, it was

impossible to warn westbound trains of the break in the track until they were within a few miles of Stone Mountain. See *OR,* 38, pt. 3, p. 20; pt. 5, p. 176.

33. Magee, *72nd Indiana,* pp. 342–43. Magee said the 2nd Cavalry Division took several prisoners at Stone Mountain, but in a report submitted that same night, Garrard declared, "We captured no prisoners. . . ." Confederate General Joseph Wheeler admitted the loss of thirteen men, but he also estimated Federal casualties at seventy, a ridiculously high figure. There is a small cemetery in Stone Mountain containing the bodies of approximately 150 unknown Confederate soldiers, but most of them died from wounds or disease in makeshift military hospitals in the vicinity. See Evans, ed., *CMH,* vol 8: *Alabama,* by Joseph Wheeler, p. 368; Scruggs, ed., *Georgia Historical Markers,* p. 170.

34. Garrard's assertion he engaged two Rebel brigades at Stone Mountain is somewhat suspect. None of the other members of his command mention such a large force, and Private Alva Griest of the 72nd Indiana, writing in his diary on July 19, said there were only 300 or 400 Rebels at Stone Mountain. The only corroboration comes from Joseph Wheeler, in *Alabama,* vol. 8 of *CMH,* p. 368, who stated all three brigades of Brigadier General John H. Kelly's division saw action at Stone Mountain on July 19. Stephen A. Jordan's diary for 19 July 1864 leaves no doubt Dibrell's Tennessee brigade was present, while Sergeant John Ash of the 5th Georgia Cavalry noted in his diary that Colonel Robert H. Anderson's brigade

> marched down the R.R. and along the track and once we were so near our men skirmishing with the Yanks that the enemy's balls passed over our heads. Halt. Halt and dismount was the order several times but we did not go out on foot till about the 3rd time we were dismounted. Having seen the R.R. burning we marched in that direction and dismounting, scoured the woods and saw here about 2 miles of the R.R. were burnt. Gen. Kelly finding the Yankees were in too great a force for us retreated with us safely from the R.R. into the country going toward Stone Mountain and Covington on Ga. R.R. We halted by a school house or church and were just about sending out to press provisions when the enemy pressed us so hard we had to get up and get.

In the "Eighth Confederate Cavalry," George Knox Miller Papers, another member of Anderson's brigade, Captain George Knox Miller, makes no mention of doing any fighting at Stone Mountain on July 19. This author has been unable to locate any records for Colonel Moses W. Hannon's brigade of Kelly's division, but it seems likely Garrard only confronted Dibrell's brigade at Stone Mountain, although Anderson's was close by.

35. McLain Diary, 19 July 1864; Regimental Return, July 1864, 4th Michigan Cavalry, reel 83, M-594, RG 94; Compiled Service Records, RG 94; Michigan Adjutant General, *Record of Service of Michigan Volunteers,* vol. 34: *Fourth Michigan Cavalry,* p. 16; Muster Roll, July–August 1864, Company K, 4th U.S. Cavalry, RG 94; Pension Records, RG 15; Sherman, *Memoirs,* 2:72.

36. *OR,* 39, pt. 2, pp. 695–96, 712; *MDT,* 15 July 1864, p. 1; *ADC,* 16 July 1864, p. 1; Mackall Diary, 13 July 1864; Scruggs, ed., *Georgia Historical Markers,* p. 227; Garrett, *Atlanta and Environs,* 1:100; Johnston, *Narrative,* p. 364; *OR,* 38, pt. 5, p. 878 (Bragg's telegrams to Davis). Some historians have made much of a seemingly cryptic telegram Davis sent to Atlanta on July 14 advising Bragg, "The selection of a place must depend upon military considerations so mainly that I can only say that if C. is thus indicated adopt advice and execute as proposed." They assert "C" must have referred to a list of options Bragg received before he left Richmond, probably giving him the authority to relieve Johnston and replace him with Hardee. However, a careful reading of the *Official Records* reveals this telegram was actually part of a protracted exchange about moving Union prisoners from Andersonville to either Cahaba or Silver Run, Alabama. "C" was simply an abbreviation for Cahaba. See *OR,* 52, pt. 2, p. 704; *OR,* series III, vol. 7, pp. 441–44, 445–46, 448, 458, 463, 467, 469, 473, 476; *OR,* 38, pt. 5, p. 877.

37. Mackall Diary, 14 July 1864; *MDT,* 18 July 1864, p. 1; *OR,* 38, pt. 5, pp. 879–81; *OR,* 39, pt. 2, p. 714. For a thorough and thoughtful look at the relations between Bragg, Johnston, and officers of the Army of Tennessee, see Connelly, *Autumn of Glory,* passim, and McMurry, *John Bell Hood,* pp. 95–97, 109–10, 114–15.

38. *OR,* 38, pt. 5, pp. 882–83, 885, 888, 889; Kurtz, "At the Dexter Niles House," pp. 6, 20; Johnston, *Narrative,* pp. 348–50; *Advance and Retreat,* pp. 126–27; Hay, "The Davis-Hood-Johnston Controversy of 1864," p. 66n.39 (quoting Johnston); *OR,* 52, pt. 2, pp. 708–9; Hood, *Advance and Retreat,* pp. 127–28; Mackall Diary, 17–19 July 1864.

39. Schofield, *Forty-Six Years in the Army,* pp. 231–32; Society of the Army of the Cumberland, *Fourth Re-Union,* p. 154. In his *Memoirs,* 2:72, Sherman said, "one of General Thomas's staff officers brought me a citizen, one of our spies, who had just come out of Atlanta, and had brought a newspaper of the same day, or the day before, containing Johnston's order relinquishing the command of the Confederate forces in Atlanta, and Hood's order assuming the command." Challenging Sherman's recollection of this incident, Schofield insisted he was the one who brought Sherman the Atlanta newspaper. Two factors strongly suggest Schofield was correct. First, Sherman was traveling with Schofield's column on July 19; and second, a careful reading of *OR,* 38, pt. 5, pp. 183–84, clearly shows it was Sherman who informed Thomas of the change in the Confederate high command.

40. *Official Register of the U.S. Military Academy,* 1853:4, 7–8; Cullum, *Biographical Register,* 2:515, 524, 567; Schofield, *Forty-Six Years in the Army,* p. 138; Hood, *Advance and Retreat,* pp. 7, 59, 64, 182; O'Connor, *Hood: Cavalier General,* pp. 18–22, 26–28, 151–52, 155, 165–67, 169; McMurry, *John Bell Hood,* pp. 15, 75–77, 83–84; Steiner, *Medical-Military Portraits of Union and Confederate Generals,* pp. 220–21; Warner, *Generals in Gray,* pp. 142–43; *DAB,* 1928 ed., s.v. "John Bell Hood," by Douglas Southall Freeman.

41. Sherman, *Memoirs,* 2:72; Perkins, *Trails, Rails and War: The Life of General G. M. Dodge,* p. 149; Dodge, "Personal Biography," 1:238; Dodge, *Personal Recollections,* p. 152; *NT,* 12 June 1902, p. 3.

42. *OR,* 38, pt. 5, pp. 193–94.

43. "Special Field Orders No. 2, Head Qrs. 2nd Cavalry Division, Near Decatur, Ga., July 20th 1864," p. 219, vol. 35/74, CCMDM, RG 393. McPherson did issue a written order, dated July 20, 1864, directing Garrard to burn McAfee's Bridge, but this same order, found in *OR,* 38, pt. 5, p. 210, also named Brigadier General Giles A. Smith to succeed wounded Brigadier General Walter Q. Gresham as commander of the 4th Division of the XVII Corps. Gresham was shot in the left leg on the evening of July 20, while Garrard issued orders to burn McAfee's Bridge sometime before noon. Obviously, he had received authorization to do this several hours before the receipt of McPherson's written instructions.

44. Gay, *Life in Dixie during the War,* pp. 127–28.

45. *OR,* 38, pt. 3, pp. 630–31, 698–99, 871–942 passim; pt. 5, pp. 195–96; pt. 1, pp. 71–557 passim, 904–5; pt. 2, pp. 16, 25, 33–487 passim; Hood, *Advance and Retreat,* pp. 165–72; Connelly, *Autumn of Glory,* pp. 439–44; Newton, "Battle of Peachtree Creek," pp. 395–405; Stone, "The Atlanta Campaign," p. 442; McKinney, *Education in Violence,* p. 349; Merrill, *The Seventieth Indiana Volunteer Infantry,* pp. 152–53.

46. *OR,* 38, pt. 1, pp. 71, 156, 291; pt. 2, pp. 34, 141, 329; 538–57 passim; pt. 3, pp. 733, 748–49, 751, 756, 877–942 passim; pt. 5, pp. 197, 211; Stone, "The Atlanta Campaign," pp. 441–42, 449; Merrill, *70th Indiana,* p. 144.

5. A COSTLY MISTAKE, JULY 21–JULY 22, 1864

1. *OR,* 38, pt. 5, p. 208; McAllister, *Ellen Ewing: Wife of General Sherman,* pp. 284–85.
2. *OR,* 38, pt. 5, pp. 149–50; *OR,* 39, pt. 3, p. 135; Wilson, *Under the Old Flag,* 2:17.
3. *OR,* 38, pt. 5, pp. 139–40, 209, 221.

4. *OR,* 38, pt. 3, pp. 39, 384, 486, 506, 512, 519, 524; pt. 5, p. 220; Illinois Adjutant General, *Report,* 5:516; Thomas M. Sanders, Case Number 6,476, RG 233. Kitchell did not submit a report on the burning of McAfee's Bridge, but in "Student Historian Researches McAfee-Holcombe Bridge," p. 2, Mrs. C. C. Garrard related how her aunt, Miss Ida Benson, often told a story she had heard from her grandparents, who lived near the bridge. She said, "the Yanks emptied a feather bed, scattered the feathers in the road between the [McAfee] house and the store . . . , rode their horses through the feathers, galloped over the bridge toward Roswell and burned the bridge." Kitchell's orders were to rejoin the division via "the most direct road from Cross Keys," and if this story is true, it would seem to indicate his regiment recrossed the Chattahoochee at Roswell before heading south to Decatur.

5. *WC,* 20 August 1864, p. 2; Lester Diary, 21 July 1864; Nourse Diary, 21 July 1864; Heber S. Thompson Diary, 21 July 1864; Regimental Return, July 1864, 4th Michigan Cavalry, reel 83, M-594, RG 94; McLain Diary, 21 July 1864; Potter Diary, 21 July 1864; Magee, *72nd Indiana,* p. 345. Private Andrew J. Ward of the 4th Michigan said Minty's brigade left camp at 9:00 A.M. Private John Nourse of the Chicago Board of Trade Battery recorded the hour as 10:00 A.M., while another artilleryman, Private A. W. Lester, noted the battery left New Cross Keys at noon. Captain Heber S. Thompson, a member of Minty's staff, wrote in his diary that the march began at 11:00 A.M., as did Lieutenant Henry Albert Potter of the 4th Michigan. The regimental return agreed, but Corporal John C. McLain of the 4th Michigan recorded the brigade received orders to march "after dinner." It may be that different detachments of Minty's brigade, picketing roads at all four points of the compass, all marched at slightly different times.

6. "Special Field Orders No. 3, Head Qrs. 2nd Cavalry Division D.C., Decatur, Ga., July 21st 1864," p. 220, vol. 35/74, CCMDM, RG 393; *DTB,* 8 August 1864, p. 2; Crofts, comp., *3rd Ohio,* p. 157; James Thomson Diary, 21 July 1864; Lester Diary, 21 July 1864; Nourse Diary, 21 July 1864; Fleming to "My Dear Parents," 25 July 1864; Magee, *72nd Indiana,* p. 345; Griest Diary, 21 July 1864; Hosea, "Some Side Lights on the War for the Union," p. 41; Regimental Return, July 1864, 4th Michigan Cavalry, reel 83, M-594, RG 94; McLain Diary, 21 July 1864; Potter Diary, 21 July 1864; Heber S. Thompson Diary, 21 July 1864; Gooding to "Dear Lucy," 26 July 1864; *WC,* 13 August 1864, p. 2; *WC,* 20 August 1864, p. 2; *WC,* 6 August 1864, p. 2.

7. Union sources used in describing the battle of Decatur on July 22, 1864, are *WC,* 20 August 1864, p. 2; Fleming to "My Dear Parents," 25 July 1864; Lester Diary, 22 July 1864; Nourse Diary, 21–22 July 1864; *OR,* 52, pt. 1, pp. 108–9 (Lieutenant Trumball D. Griffin's quote); Silas C. Stevens to E. B. Stevens, 8 February 1905; Chicago Board of Trade Battery Memorial Association, *Historical Sketch of the Chicago Board of Trade Battery,* pp. 28, 69, 72–75, 77–78; Illinois Adjutant General, *Report,* 8:728, 736; Barnard to "Dear Mag," 23 July 1864; Records Diary, 22 July 1864; Magee, *72nd Indiana,* p. 352; Compiled Service Records, RG 94; *OR,* 38, pt. 3, pp. 371, 373–74, 453, 478, 506–7, 509–12, 513, 516–17, 519, 521, 524, 536–37; pt. 5, pp. 289, 300; *CDC,* 30 July 1864, p. 1; *CDC,* 2 August 1864, p. 1; *Portland Oregonian,* 26 December 1893, p. 2 (quoting Major John W. Fouts); "List of Casualties in 2d Brigade 2d Division Cavalry," pp. 66–67, vol. 57/140, CCMDM, RG 393; Ohio Roster Commission, *Official Roster,* 11:173–74, 187, 189, 209, 222, 228; *NT,* 9 July 1885, p. 3; *NT,* 13 August 1885, p. 3; U.S. Congress, Senate, Committee on Veterans' Affairs, *Medal of Honor Recipients,* p. 232. Confederate sources *OR,* 38, pt. 3, p. 953, Dodson, ed., *Campaigns of Wheeler and His Cavalry,* p. 211; Evans, ed., *CMH,* vol. 8: *Alabama,* p. 368. Wheeler's claims in the *Official Records* of capturing "225 prisoners, a large number of small arms, 1 12-pounder gun, 1 forage, 1 caisson, and 6 wagons and teams, together with the captain of the battery and most of his men," are greatly exaggerated. In *OR,* 38, pt. 1, p. 74, Sherman noted the loss of only three wagons and added the teamsters got away with their mules.

8. *OR,* 38, pt. 1, pp. 72–73; pt. 2, pp. 516, 572; pt. 3, pp. 22–23, 82, 88, 102, 122, 369–546 passim, 631, 699; pt. 5, pp. 222–31, 899–900; Sherman, *Memoirs,* 2:74–77, 532–33, 540–41;

Society of the Army of the Tennessee, *23rd Meeting,* pp. 497–98; Hood, *Advance and Retreat,* pp. 129–35, 173–82, 188–89; Buck, *Cleburne and His Command,* pp. 235–41; Roy, "General Hardee and the Military Operations Around Atlanta," pp. 354–68; Brown, ed., *One of Cleburne's Command: The Civil War Reminiscences and Diary of Capt. Samuel T. Foster,* pp. 110–12; Dodge, "The Battle of Atlanta," pp. 490–96; Dodge, "Personal Biography," 1:240–42, 245; Compton, "The Second Division of the 16th Army Corps, in the Atlanta Campaign," pp. 251–53; Chamberlin, "Recollections of the Battle of Atlanta," pp. 455–58; Strong, "The Death of General James B. McPherson."

9. *OR,* 38, pt. 1, p. 73; Sherman, *Memoirs,* 2:76–77. The so-called Howard house actually belonged to Augustus F. Hurt, but the Hurt family had fled sometime earlier, leaving behind their furniture and many personal possessions. When Sherman's army arrived, Thomas C. Howard, who operated a distillery in the nearby Clear Creek valley, had taken up residence there. Consequently, all Federal dispatches refer to this dwelling as the Howard house. See Kurtz, "Civil War Days in Georgia, No. 6: The Augustus F. Hurt House," p. 6.

10. Society of the Army of the Tennessee, *23rd Meeting,* p. 498; *NT,* 25 August 1892, p. 4; Society of the Army of the Tennessee, *14th Meeting,* p. 114; David C. Bradley, "Recollections of the Autumn and Winter of 1864," p. 3, David C. Bradley Papers.

11. *OR,* 38, pt. 1, pp. 73–74; pt. 3, pp. 25–26, 103, 139, 165, 179–819 passim; Munson, "Battle of Atlanta," pp. 420–26; Tuthill, "An Artilleryman's Recollections of the Battle of Atlanta," pp. 445–46; Society of the Army of the Tennessee, *16th Meeting,* pp. 486–87; Manigault, *A Carolinian Goes to War,* pp. 226–28, 260–62, 290–93; Sherman, *Memoirs,* 2:77–78; Strong, "The Death of General McPherson," p. 530; Schofield, *Forty-Six Years in the Army,* p. 146; Davis, "With Sherman in His Army Home," p. 202.

12. Sherman, *Memoirs,* 2:80–81, 536, 543–44; Society of the Army of the Tennessee, *23rd Meeting,* pp. 499–500; *OR,* 38, pt. 1, p. 74; pt. 2, p. 517; pt. 3, pp. 25–26, 59, 103, 116–464 passim, 778–80, 787–88, 819; Schofield, *Forty-Six Years in the Army,* pp. 147–48; Howard, *Autobiography,* 2:13–14; Howard, "The Battles about Atlanta," p. 395; *NT,* 28 February 1895, p. 1.

13. *OR,* 38, pt. 1, p. 75; pt. 3, pp. 21, 28, 48, 547, 565, 582–83, 588, 594–95, 602, 606, 732; Livermore, *Numbers & Losses,* p. 123; Castel, *Decision in the West,* p. 412; Sherman, *Memoirs,* 2:82, 544; Society of the Army of the Tennessee, *23rd Meeting,* p. 500.

14. *OR,* Atlas, plate LXXXVIII, no. 1; *OR,* 38, pt. 5, p. 235; Rousseau to Sherman, telegram, 22 July 1864, Sherman Papers.

6. ROUSSEAU'S RAID: DECATUR TO EASTABOGA, JULY 10–JULY 15, 1864

1. The 9th Ohio Cavalry's Lieutenant Fanning, in *Hairbreadth Escapes,* p. 107, identified Rousseau's escort as Companies E and K of the 2nd Kentucky. However, Company K had previously been incorporated into Company I. See Kentucky Adjutant General, *Report,* 1:60; Regimental Return, July 1864, 2nd Kentucky Cavalry, RG 94.

2. Unless otherwise noted, the narrative describing Rousseau's march from Decatur to Eastaboga is based on the following sources. Union: *OR,* 38, pt. 2, pp. 905–6 (Rousseau's report); *CDC,* 1 August 1864, p. 1; *LDJ,* 30 July 1864, p. 1 (Captain Thomas C. Williams's account); *LDJ,* 30 August 1864, p. 2; Jackson Diary, 11–14 July 1864; Oblinger Diary, 11–14 July 1864; Ward Diary, 11–14 July 1864; *HT,* 25 August 1864, p. 1 (Private Jack Wilson's account); Heaton, "The Rousseau Raid," pp. 13–15; *NT,* 16 October 1884, p. 3; *NT,* 2 May 1901, p. 5 (Private John N. Jones's account and Rousseau's encounter with the Rebel prisoner); Morning Reports, 11–14 July 1864, Companies D and H, 8th Indiana Cavalry, RG 94; Regimental Return, July 1864, 8th Indiana Cavalry, reel 35, M-594, RG 94; Iowa Adjutant General, *Report,* pp. 999–1000; *NYT,* 31 July 1864, p. 6 (Private Oscar Reese's first account); *DDT,* 1 August 1864, p. 1 (Private Oscar Reese's second account); *NT,* 28 August 1884, p. 3; Morning Reports, 11–14 July 1864, Company C, 5th Iowa Cavalry, RG 94; Fanning,

Hairbreadth Escapes, pp. 107–9; Hamilton, *Recollections,* pp. 131–33; *NT,* 6 April 1905, p. 3 (Private James W. Swan's account); Morning Reports, 12 July 1864, Company H, 9th Ohio Cavalry, RG 94; Eckel, *4th Tennessee,* pp. 50–52, 56–57; Eckel, "The Rousseau and McCook Raids," pp. 4–5; Record of Events, July–August 1864, Companies B, C, and I, 4th Tennessee Cavalry, reel 188, M-594, RG 94. Confederate: *SMR,* 26 July 1864, p. 1 (Rousseau at Ashville); Ezekiel J. Halbrooks, Case Number 19,237 (Return of Rousseau's wagon train to Decatur), RG 233.

3. Lieutenant Fanning claimed Rousseau's pickets captured thirty-three Rebel scouts, "who had come from Mumfordsville, Alabama, through the darkness, expecting to achieve great things in the bushwhacking line. . . ." This seems highly unlikely. There is no Mumfordsville in the vicinity of Somerville, and neither Rousseau nor anyone else in his command mentioned a capture of this size. Much of *Hairbreadth Escapes and Humerous Adventures* is sheer fantasy, but there is just enough truth in what Fanning says to make his book an important source.

4. Just which regiment these musicians belonged to is uncertain. At one time, both the 5th Iowa and the 8th Indiana had regimental bands, but these were apparently broken up in 1862 and it seems unlikely any of the regiments Rousseau brought from Nashville would have burdened themselves with musical instruments. In all probability, the music came from Hamilton's 9th Ohio, which had a regimental band as late as May 22, 1864. See Iowa Adjutant General, *Roster and Record,* 4:867–68; Indiana Adjutant General, *Report,* 5:222, 8:168–71; Fanning, *Hairbreadth Escapes,* p. 95.

5. The identity of these two Rebel scouts will probably never be known, but Mrs. Henry J. Livingston noted in an undated manuscript in Livingston's 8th Alabama Cavalry Papers:

> In a skirmish near Greensport, trying to cut off Rousseau's raid, one of the 8th Alabama boys, Luther Rice, had a breakneck ride equal to that of Putnam of Revolutionary fame. Rice and a comrade had been ordered to guard a certain pass in a "mountain gorge" and before they were aware of it, the Yankees had surrounded them. There was no way to escape except up the perpendicular sides of the mountain. It seemed death in either case. Rice was determined not to be captured, so putting spurs to his horse and lying flat on the back of his steed to escape the bullets flying all around, he had a run for his life up the rugged cliffs where a goat could scarcely climb, he made the perilous ascent. He finally reached the top of the mountain as his horse fell almost dead from exhaustion. Rice's companion was never seen again and it is more than probable that his bleaching bones now lie entombed in that mountain gorge. . . .

While Mrs. Livingston said this incident took place near Greensport, her description of the "mountain gorge" and "rugged cliffs" does not fit the terrain in that vicinity. A more likely spot lies five miles southeast of Somerville, where the road to Blue Springs threads through a narrow mountain pass before crossing Six Mile Creek. If the incident did indeed take place here, it would mean Rice and his comrade were acting as scouts, far in advance of the 8th Alabama's camp at Blue Mountain. This is not beyond the realm of possibility, because Confederate scouts had detected Rousseau's column by the time it reached Blountsville on July 12. See *MAR,* 27 July 1864, p. 1.

6. *OR,* Atlas, plate CXVII and CXVIII, no. 1; John W. Nesmith, Case Number 12,986, RG 217; Uriah W. Nesmith, Case Number 12,987, RG 217. Plate CXVII shows Rousseau passing through Mt. Alvis, Alabama, but his route was much farther east, as shown on the map drawn by Rousseau's topographical engineer, Captain Edward Ruger, on plate CXVIII.

7. Unaccustomed to long hours in the saddle, Rousseau either acquired this carriage after he reached Decatur or took it from the plantation where he spent the night of July 10. See *MM,* 29 July 1864, p. 2.

8. The raiders disagreed about how many prisoners Elkin's men captured. In a letter to the

Nashville Union (quoted by the *New York Times,* 31 July 1864, p. 6), Oscar Reese of the 5th Iowa said there were seven. Private John N. Jones of the 8th Indiana, writing for the *National Tribune,* 2 May 1901, p. 5, noted "two or three furloughed Johnnies, [and] three or four citizens." Lieutenant Fanning of the 9th Ohio counted seven soldiers and a Rebel chaplain in *Hairbreadth Escapes,* p. 107. Private Reese added the raiders also burned forty stands of arms and 150 bales of cotton, but it seems unusual for that much material to be stored in a remote mountain village like Summit. None of the other sources mention such a conflagration, and Reese probably confused events at Summit with those four days later at Talladega.

9. Writing in the *Louisville Daily Journal,* Rousseau's adjutant, Captain Thomas C. Williams, said this ambush at Sand Mountain was the first armed opposition the column had encountered since leaving Decatur. However, if Williams was traveling with Rousseau on the first day of the march, two hours behind the head of the column, he may not have heard about the shots fired at the advance guard just beyond Flint River on July 10.

10. Thomas Nation, Case Number 11,189, RG 217.

11. William L. Trask Journal, p. 192; *BKWRV,* 17 August 1864, p. 1. In *4th Tennessee,* pp. 50, 56, Corporal Eckel said one of the inmates joined Rousseau's column, but none of the other sources mention this.

12. James Brown, Case Number 9,844, RG 233.

13. Eckel, *4th Tennessee,* p. 57.

14. *NT,* 6 April 1905, p. 3. Private Oscar Reese, writing for the *Dubuque Daily Times,* reported the artillery was lowered down the side of Sand Mountain on July 11, but he was probably mistaken. The descent from Blount Mountain is much steeper than Sand Mountain and Reese had a tendency to confuse days and events. In an article for the *Louisville Daily Journal,* 30 July 1864, p. 1, Rousseau's adjutant, Captain Williams, described the descent through Aughtry's Gap as "remarkably steep and rugged."

15. Hurd, ed., *A Treasury of Great American Quotations,* p. 40.

16. *LDJ,* 30 July 1864, p. 1.

17. Ibid.; "Headquarters Cavalry Forces, in the Field, July 13th., 1864," serial Z, vol. 37, William T. Walthall Papers.

18. *MAR,* 21 July 1864, p. 1; *CDC,* 1 August 1864, p. 1. See also Harper, "Rousseau's Alabama Raid" (Master's thesis), p. 22.

19. Iowa Adjutant General, *Roster and Record,* 4:845–55, 887; Stuart, *Iowa Colonels and Regiments,* p. 628; U.S. War Department, *Revised United States Army Regulations of 1861. With an Appendix Containing the Changes and Laws Affecting Army Regulations and Articles of War to June 25, 1863,* p. 361, 545; Compiled Service Records, RG 94; Pension Records, RG 15; "List of Casualties in Cavalry Division under Command of Maj. Gen. L. H. Rousseau from July 10th to July 23rd (hereafter cited as "List of Casualties")," RG 94. Immediately after the war, the United States government made a concerted effort to locate the bodies of Union soldiers who had died in the service of their country. Special details scoured the South, looking for graves. Whenever they found a Union soldier's body, the remains were disinterred for reburial at one of the national cemeteries. The following citation, regarding the national cemetery at Marietta, Georgia, is found in Quartermaster General's Office, *Roll of Honor,* 23:236:

No.	Name	Sec.	Grave	Original Place of Interment
9932	Unknown	K	P	Greenport [*sic*], Alabama

This is undoubtedly Captain Curl, but despite an overwhelming array of evidence, the Veterans Administration steadfastly refuses to acknowledge this is his final resting place. The captain lies beneath a weathered stone, his only epitaph the word "Unknown."

20. *MAR,* 21 July 1864, p. 1.

21. J. W. Dubose, "Eighth Alabama Cavalry," p. 24, manuscript in Livingston's 8th Alabama Cavalry Papers; Irons, "River Ferries in Alabama before 1861," pp. 28–29. In

Recollections of a Cavalryman, p. 132, Colonel Hamilton credited Captain A. P. Gatch and thirty men from Company L of the 9th Ohio with crossing the Coosa at Green's Ferry on the night of July 13–14. There is no further evidence to support his statement. Writing fifty years after the actual event, Hamilton may have simply confused the names Gatch and Graham.

22. *DCE,* 24 July 1864, p. 2; *NYT,* 29 July 1864, p. 2; *OR,* 32, pt. 3, p. 751; *OR,* 38, pt. 3, p. 975, *CT,* 23 July 1864, p. 1.

23. Garrett, *Reminiscences of Public Men in Alabama,* pp. 625, 632–33, 638, 644; Brewer, *Alabama: Her History, Resources, War Record, and Public Men,* pp. 466–67; Evans, ed., *CMH,* vol. 8: *Alabama,* pp. 398–99; Owen, *History of Alabama and Dictionary of Alabama Biography,* 3:327; Warner, *Generals in Gray,* p. 50; Drake, ed., *The Annals of the Army of Tennessee,* p. 334 (Clanton "a perfect demon"); Going, "A Shooting Affray in Knoxville with Interstate Repercussions: The Killing of James H. Clanton by David M. Nelson, 1871," pp. 40, 46; *OR,* 10, pt. 2, p. 299 ("gallant to rashness"); *OR,* 25, pt. 2, pp. 740–41; Jones, "A Roster of General Officers," pp. A32–A33; *OR,* 26, pt. 2, pp. 511, 548–57; *OR,* 52, pt. 2, pp. 48–49, 601, 679; *OR,* 39, pt. 2, pp. 601, 691–92.

24. *MAR,* 3 August 1864, p. 1; *DCE,* 24 July 1864, p. 2; *CT,* 23 July 1864, p. 1; *NYT,* 29 July 1864, p. 2; *SMR,* 26 July 1864, p. 1; *OR,* 38, pt. 3, p. 975.

25. An estimated forty to seventy of Daniels's men were on foot when the column left Greensport, but they soon remedied this by taking mules and horses from the farms along their route. By dint of some hard marching, they reached the Tennessee River at Guntersville about 11:00 that night and began ferrying across the half-mile width of the river, swimming their horses alongside two old canoes they found near the steamboat landing. By 7:00 A.M., everyone had crossed safely, including the wounded Captain Wilcox. Their sudden appearance threw the entire Department of Northern Alabama into a panic. Brigadier General Robert S. Granger wired General Thomas that 2,800 Rebel cavalrymen had crossed the Tennessee, and the Union garrisons at Claysville, Whitesburg, Huntsville, Stevenson, and Bridgeport shouldered arms and spent the next day or two in the trenches, awaiting an attack. See Carswell Battles, Case Number 3,351, RG 233; *OR,* 38, pt. 5, pp. 148, 154; Robert H. Milroy and Burr H. Polk to Horatio P. Van Cleve, 15 July 1864, p. 153, Polk to Granger, 15 July 1864, p. 154, Milroy and Polk to Wladimir Krzyzanowski, 15 July 1864, p. 154, Milroy to James B. Steedman, 16 July 1864, p. 155, Telegrams Sent DN, RG 393; Hamilton, *Recollections,* pp. 276–77; Lyon, comp., *Reminiscences of the Civil War Compiled from the War Correspondence of Colonel William P. Lyon,* pp. 152–53; Chadick, "Civil War Days in Huntsville, A Diary of Mrs. W. D. Chadick," p. 259; *NYH,* 24 July 1864, p. 5; *PCD,* 24 August 1864, p. 1.

26. Heaton, "The Rousseau Raid," p. 14.

27. Confederate accounts of the fighting at Whisenant's Mill and Ten Islands are drawn from *SMR,* 26 July 1864, p. 1; *DCE,* 24 July 1864, p. 2; *MAR,* 21 July 1864, p. 1; *CT,* 23 July 1864, p. 1; *CDS,* 29 July 1864, p. 1; Coleman, "Master and His Faithful Slave," p. 410; *MAR,* 19 July 1864, p. 1; *MAR,* 3 August 1864, p. 1. Captain Abercrombie and Clanton's wife, Parthenia, were cousins. See Cherry, "The History of Opelika and her Agricultural Tributary Territory, Embracing More Particularly Lee and Russell Counties," pp. 245–47.

28. "List of Casualties," RG 94; *LDJ,* 30 August 1864, p. 2; Compiled Service Records, RG 94; Pension Records, RG 15. Privates Ward and Wilson of the 8th Indiana reported a third man was slightly wounded, but they were not with Graham's battalion and medical records do not corroborate their story.

29. *NT,* 16 October 1884, p. 3. Other Union sources put Confederate casualties at Whisenant's Mill at anywhere from fifteen to twenty-two killed and forty wounded. See *OR,* 38, pt. 2, p. 906; *LDJ,* 30 July 1864, p. 1; Regimental Return, July 1864, 8th Indiana Cavalry, reel 35, M-594, RG 94; Ward Diary, 14 July 1864; Oblinger Diary, 14 July 1864; *HT,* 25 August 1864, p. 1; Fanning, *Hairbreadth Escapes,* p. 108; *CDC,* 1 August 1864, p. 1; *NT,* 16 October 1884, p. 3. The editors of the *Ashville Vidette* said Confederate losses were "about 8 killed, the same number wounded and five captured." See *SMR,* 26 July 1864, p. 1.

30. *NT,* 2 May 1901, p. 5.

31. Compiled Service Records, RG 94; Pension Records, RG 15; Hunt and Brown, *Brevet Brigadier Generals in Blue,* p. 318; Grayson, *"The Spirit of 1861." History of the Sixth Indiana Regiment,* pp. 3–4, 10–14, 37–42; Indiana Adjutant General, *Report,* 2:381; *OR,* 20, pt. 1, pp. 308, 313–15; *NT,* 22 July 1926, p. 6; *OR,* 23, pt. 1, pp. 137–38.

32. *NT,* 2 May 1901, p. 5. Companies A and B of the 2nd Kentucky were probably the recipients of the Spencer rifles and carbines that regiment had drawn from Companies L and M of the 8th Indiana before leaving Nashville on July 8.

33. Sources do not agree on the extent of Confederate losses at Ten Islands. Lieutenant William T. Hays of the 5th Iowa, writing in Iowa Adjutant General, *Report,* p. 1000, said the 8th Alabama left behind ten dead and many wounded. The *Selma Morning Reporter,* 26 July 1864, p. 1, put Livingston's casualties at only three or four. The *Mobile Advertiser and Register,* 3 August 1864, p. 1, and the *Jacksonville Republican* quoted by *Montgomery Daily Mail,* 27 July 1864, p. 2, reported the combined total of Confederate casualties at Whisenant's Mill and Ten Islands numbered thirty to thirty-five killed and wounded. Clanton admitted the loss of thirty-five men in the *Daily Columbus Enquirer,* 24 July 1864, p. 2. As for prisoners, Rousseau reported in *OR,* 38, pt. 2, p. 906, "as nearly as could be ascertained," his men captured eight prisoners at Ten Islands. Private Oscar Reese of the 5th Iowa, writing for the *Nashville Union* (quoted by the *New York Times*) and the *Dubuque Daily Times,* put the number at twelve, while correspondent W. F. G. Shanks's account in the *New York Herald,* 28 July 1864, p. 1, said two officers and twenty privates were captured. The 8th Indiana's Fielder Jones noted in *OR,* 38, pt. 2, p. 878, the raiders took "1 lieutenant-colonel, 1 major, 3 lieutenants, and 20 men" on July 14. Subtracting the lieutenant colonel, major, lieutenant, and at least three privates Graham's battalion captured in the skirmish near Green's Ferry, this would mean Rousseau took two lieutenants and approximately seventeen privates at Ten Islands. These figures are corroborated to some extent by Lieutenant Hays, who tallied fifteen Rebel prisoners at Ten Islands in Iowa Adjutant General, *Report,* p. 1000. For a ridiculously high estimate of Clanton's losses, see Fanning, *Hairbreadth Escapes,* pp. 108–9.

34. *MAR,* 3 August 1864, p. 1; *MAR,* 21 July 1864, p. 1; *CDS,* 29 July 1864, p. 1. Although Rousseau made no specific reference in his official report about the size of the Confederate force he encountered at the Coosa River, other sources—such as Ward Diary, 14 July 1864; Jackson Diary, 14 July 1864; *HT,* 25 August 1864, p. 1; *NYT,* 31 July 1864, p. 6; Record of Events, July–August 1864, Company G, 4th Tennessee Cavalry, reel 188, M-594, RG 94; Iowa Adjutant General, *Report,* p. 1000—credited Clanton with anywhere from 500 to 700 men. Actually, Clanton's brigade numbered only about 200. See *DCE,* 24 July 1864, p. 2; *CT,* 23 July 1864, p. 1; *MAR,* 3 August 1864, p. 1. For evidence Rousseau did not parole Clanton's officers until the next day, see Washington T. Lary and Eliphalet A. McWhorter, 6th Alabama Cavalry, Compiled Service Records, RG 109; *Memorial Record of Alabama,* 1:1016.

35. Agee, "Highway Markers in Alabama," p. 73. Estimates by Rousseau's men about the quantity of cotton destroyed on the afternoon of July 14 varied from "1900 bales" and "two cotton gins," to a "cotton factory." The *Jacksonville Republican,* quoted by *Mobile Advertiser and Register,* 26 July 1864, p. 1, reported the Yankees burned some cotton gins in Calhoun County and about one hundred bales of cotton "near Middleton," which is about three and a half miles east of the Jackson Trace. This author has been unable to locate any cotton mills in that vicinity.

36. *MAR,* 2 August 1864, p. 1. Private Reese of the 5th Iowa was the only source to mention the capture of a Rebel paymaster. In his letter to the *Nashville Union* (quoted by *New York Times,* 31 July 1864, p. 6), he said the paymaster was carrying $160,000 in "rebel shinplasters of almost every description, including some State money." In a concurrent article for the *Dubuque Daily Times,* he put the amount at $170,000, but this may have been a typesetting error. In both accounts, he said the paymaster was captured on July 12 at "a little place called Shakerag." If Reese was correct about the date, this would put Shakerag somewhere south of

Sand Mountain and west of the Coosa River. This author has been unable to locate any place called Shakerag in that vicinity, and it seems unlikely a Rebel paymaster would have any reason to venture so far into the wilderness. Even if he did, he probably would have been captured by Rousseau's advance guard. But the 5th Iowa rode in the rear with Harrison's 1st Brigade on July 12. They did not take their turn at the head of the column until July 14. This would put Shakerag somewhere east of the Coosa River. According to Krakow, *Georgia Place-Names*, p. 207, the name "Shakerag" was often given to "various early railroad stops, referring to the waving of a signal flag." Utley and Hemperley, eds., *Placenames of Georgia: Essays of John H. Goff*, p. 398, offered another definition. They said the expression apparently applied to "communities that prided themselves on being rough and tough; and any stranger who did not have business in such localities was liable to be chased away shaking his rag, i.e., with his shirttail flying." Since there were no railroads on raiders' line of march between July 12 and July 14, this latter definition seems more appropriate. The only other clue, found in Morning Reports, 14 July 1864, Company H, 8th Indiana Cavalry, RG 94, says the raiders bivouacked at Shakerag on the night of July 14–15. Rousseau's adjutant, Captain Williams, writing in the *Louisville Daily Journal,* 30 July 1864, p. 1, made it clear the raiders spent that night at Eastaboga, so it seems likely Shakerag was a slang term for Eastaboga.

7. ROUSSEAU'S RAID: EASTABOGA TO LOACHAPOKA, JULY 15–JULY 17, 1864

1. *OR,* 38, pt. 3, pp. 975, 977; Katz, "The Mysterious Prisoner, Assassination Suspect J. G. Ryan," p. 41; Jemison, *Historic Tales of Talladega,* pp. 140, 142–43; Vandiver, "Pioneer Talladega," pp. 134, 166–67, and appendix; Stewart, ed., "The Journal of James Mallory," p. 226; Barclay, "Reminiscences of Rousseau's Raid," pp. 208–9; *CDS,* 29 July 1864, p. 2 (flight of Congressman Chilton); *MAR,* 3 August 1864, p. 1; *MAR,* 4 August 1864, p. 2; *MAR,* 19 August 1864, p. 1; *DCE,* 2 August 1864, p. 2; Anna T. Walthall to William T. Walthall, 16 July 1864, and "Letters Written," 13–14 July 1864, serial Z, vol. 83, Walthall Papers. A correspondent of the *Selma Reporter,* quoted by *Mobile Advertiser and Tribune,* 26 July 1864, p. 1, castigated Major Walthall for abandoning Talladega and derelicting his duty. On August 3, Walthall petitioned Lieutenant General Stephen D. Lee, commanding the Department of Alabama, Mississippi, and East Louisiana, for a formal hearing before a court of inquiry. His request was denied. See Walthall to Stephen D. Lee, 3 August 1864, serial Z, vol. 83.

2. *MAR,* 2 August 1864, p. 1; *OR,* 38, pt. 3, p. 976; *NYT,* 29 July 1864, p. 2; Stewart, ed., "Journal of James Mallory," p. 226; Vandiver "Pioneer Talladega," p. 94. Unless otherwise noted, the narrative describing the movements of Rousseau's column from July 15 to July 17 is based on *OR,* Atlas, plate CXVIII, no. 1; *OR,* 38, pt. 2, pp. 906–7 (Rousseau's report); pt. 3, pp. 976–77; *LDJ,* 30 July 1864, p. 1 (Captain Thomas C. Williams's account); *CDC,* 1 August 1864, p. 1; Jackson Diary, 15–17 July 1864; Oblinger Diary, 15–17 July 1864; Ward Diary, 15–17 July 1864; *HT,* 25 August 1864, p. 1 (Jack Wilson's account); Heaton, "The Rousseau Raid," p. 15; *NT,* 2 May 1901, p. 5 (John Jones's account); Morning Reports, 15–17 July 1864, Companies D and H, 8th Indiana Cavalry, RG 94; Regimental Return, July 1864, 8th Indiana Cavalry, reel 35, M-594, RG 94; Iowa Adjutant General, *Report,* pp. 1000–1001; Morning Reports, 15–16 July 1864, Company C, 5th Iowa Cavalry, RG 94; *NYT,* 31 July 1864, p. 6 (Oscar Reese's first account); *DDT,* 1 August 1864, p. 1 (Oscar Reese's second account); *DZC,* 20 August 1864, p. 2 (Colonel William D. Hamilton's account); Fanning, *Hairbreadth Escapes,* pp. 109–10; Morning Reports, 15–17 July 1864, Companies H and M, 9th Ohio Cavalry, RG 94; Eckel, *4th Tennessee,* pp. 52–53.

3. Vandiver "Pioneer Talladega," pp. 127–28, 176–79, and appendix; Docket Numbers 347–50, 558, 687–91, 701, U.S. District Court, Montgomery, Alabama, Records of the District Courts of the United States, RG 21; Donald, "Alabama Confederate Hospitals (Part

II)," p. 65. For a grossly exaggerated estimate of the number of patients in Wayside Hospital, see Fanning, *Hairbreadth Escapes,* p. 109.

4. *OR,* pt. 3, p. 976; *MAR,* 2 August 1864, p. 1; *DCE,* 2 August 1864, p. 2; Barclay, "Reminiscences of Rousseau's Raid," p. 208.

5. These are Rousseau's figures. According to the *Alabama Reporter,* 27 July 1864, quoted by *Montgomery Daily Advertiser,* 8 August 1864, p. 2, the depot contained 1,200 to 1,500 pounds of loose cotton, twenty bushels of wheat, and one and a half bushels of rye and some empty sacks, while the commissary warehouse held about 8,000 pounds of bacon, 200 sacks of flour, forty bags of meal, nine and a half hogsheads of sugar, one or two tierces of rice, 100 pounds of candles, 1,800 sacks, and several barrels of soap. Major Walthall submitted a detailed account from the post commissary officer with his report of 21 July 1864, but it has been lost.

6. *OR,* 38, pt. 3, p. 976; Barclay, "Reminiscences of Rousseau's Raid," p. 209; Vandiver "Pioneer Talladega," p. 176 and appendix; Docket Numbers 350, 688, 690, 701, U.S. District Court, Montgomery, Alabama, RG 21; *DCE,* 2 August 1864, p. 2; *MAR,* 19 July 1864, p. 1; *MAR,* 21 July 1864, p. 1; *MAR,* 26 July 1864, p. 1; *MAR,* 2 August 1864, p. 2.

7. "List of Casualties," RG 94; Compiled Service Records, RG 94; Pension Records, RG 15; *MAR,* 2 August 1864, p. 1.

8. Nitre, or saltpeter, is one of three main ingredients in the manufacture of gunpowder. Natural supplies of this important commodity were scarce, so the South tried to produce it artificially by dumping decaying animal and vegetable matter in a shallow pit and periodically dousing it with urine or some other suitable liquid. After eighteen months, the soil at the bottom of the pit was dug up, placed in vats, and mixed with water to leach out the valuable nitre. A government Nitre Bureau was responsible for collecting the raw ingredients, and Captain Jonathan Harrolson (Harrelson, Haralson), in charge of the nitre works at Selma, even placed an advertisement in local newspapers asking ladies to save the contents of their chamber pots. This inspired one Thomas B. Wetmore (?) to write:

> John Harrolson! John Harrolson! You are a wretched creature,
> You've added to this bloody war a new and awful feature.
> You'd have us think while every man is bound to be a fighter,
> That ladies, bless the dears, should save their pee for nitre.
>
> . . . .
>
> John Harrolson! John Harrolson! Do pray invent a neater;
> And somewhat more modest mode of making your saltpetre;
> But 'tis an awful idea John, gunpowdery and cranky,
> That when a lady lifts her skirts she's killing off a Yankee!

See Wiley and Milhollen, *Embattled Confederates,* p. 108; Albaugh and Simmons, *Confederate Arms,* p. 227; Lowry, *The Story the Soldiers Wouldn't Tell,* pp. 51–52.

9. *MAR,* 2 August 1864, p. 1; Vandiver, "Pioneer Talladega," p. 178 and appendix; Docket Numbers 691 and 348, U.S. District Court, Montgomery, Alabama, RG 21; *OR,* 38, pt. 3, pp. 976–77; Fuller and Steuart, *Firearms of the Confederacy,* pp. 157–58; Albaugh and Simmons, *Confederate Arms,* p. 266; *MAR,* 21 July 1864, p. 1; *MDA,* 8 August 1864, p. 2. Rousseau's adjutant, Captain Williams, said the raiders destroyed several cases of Mississippi rifles. Major Walthall and the *Alabama Reporter,* 27 July 1864, quoted by *Montgomery Daily Advertiser,* 8 August 1864, p. 2, admitted only one.

10. Jemison, *Tales of Talladega,* pp. 141–43; Vandiver, "Pioneer Talladega," p. 167; *DCE,* 2 August 1864, p. 2; Compiled Service Records, RG 94; *MAR,* 2 August 1864, p. 1; Fanning, *Hairbreadth Escapes,* pp. 109, 119.

11. Stewart, ed., "Journal of James Mallory," p. 226; Harris, *Dead Towns of Alabama,* p. 92; Lee, "Old Homes of Talladega County," pp. 90–93; Jemison, *Tales of Talladega,* p. 142;

Vandiver, "Pioneer Talladega," p. 167. The *Selma Reporter,* 18 July 1864, quoted by *Mobile Advertiser and Register,* 21 July 1864, p. 1, incorrectly reported the raiders burned Mrs. Hardie's house, "in retaliation for the killing of one or two of their men by her young son as they were passing."

12. Stewart, ed., "Journal of James Mallory," p. 226.

13. Lee, "Old Homes of Talladega County," pp. 84–88; Stewart, ed., "Journal of James Mallory," p. 226; Jemison, *Tales of Talladega,* p. 142; Vandiver, "Pioneer Talladega," pp. 167–68; *DCE,* 2 August 1864, p. 2; *MAR,* 20 July 1864, p. 1; *MAR,* 2 August 1864, p. 1.

14. Brewer, "History of Coosa County," pp. 94–95; *MAR,* 3 August 1864, p. 1. Williamson Ward and John Jones of the 8th Indiana noted the Bradford mill was burned, but the *Mobile Advertiser and Register*'s correspondent, one of Clanton's men, asserted it was spared.

15. Brewer, "History of Coosa County," p. 100; Sherman, *Memoirs,* 2:69–70. Previous accounts of Rousseau's raid all place this incident just "below" Talladega. However, there had been a steady exodus of refugees along the roads south of Talladega for several hours before Rousseau arrived on July 15, 1864, and it is inconceivable a planter living anywhere in that vicinity would not have heard of his approach. On the other hand, Soccopatoy is directly south or "below" Talladega, and Rousseau's sudden appearance there on July 16 took residents completely by surprise. This would explain the planter's misconceived hospitality.

16. "List of Casualties," RG 94; Compiled Service Records, RG 94; Pension Records, RG 15; Morning Reports, 16 July 1864, Company K, 9th Ohio Cavalry, RG 94; Company Descriptive Book, Company K, 9th Ohio Cavalry, RG 94; Ohio Roster Commission, *Official Roster,* 11:488–90, 491–93, 498. The *Mobile Advertiser and Register,* 21 July 1864, p. 1, quoting the *Montgomery Daily Advertiser,* reported, "six Yankee scouts; belonging to the 9th Ohio, mistook Clanton's lines for their own and were captured, together with twelve horses." Two of the 9th Ohio troopers may have been captured the night before at Sylacauga. See *NYT,* 7 August 1864, p. 8.

17. Hamilton, *Recollections,* pp. 133–34; McKeever, *He Rode with Sherman from Atlanta to the Sea,* pp. 14–15.

18. McKeever, *He Rode with Sherman,* pp. 14–15; *AT,* 18 July 1895, p. 6; *NT,* 24 December 1925, p. 3.

19. Hamilton, *Recollections,* p. 134; Morning Reports, 16 July 1864, Company K, 9th Ohio Cavalry, RG 94. Fanning, in *Hairbreadth Escapes,* p. 110, said the Tallapoosa claimed three men and seven horses, but there is no evidence in any of the other records to support this statement.

20. *NYH,* 28 July 1864, p. 1; *CV* 6:533; *CDS,* 6 August 1864, p. 2; Compiled Service Records, RG 109. The citizens who buried Browne's body were unable to learn anything about him except his last name. Hoping the grave could be properly marked, M. J. Bulger of Jackson's Gap, Ala., advertised in *Confederate Veteran* 6:533, for more information. His query apparently went unanswered, and in 1909 Benjamin Walker of Alexander City, Ala., posed the question again in *Confederate Veteran* 17:302 on behalf of the Sidney Lanier Chapter of the United Daughters of the Confederacy. Again there was apparently no response. To the best of the author's knowledge, this is the first time the mysterious Captain Browne has been positively identified.

21. *CDS,* 6 August 1864, p. 2.

22. Morning Reports, 17 July 1864, Companies G and K, 9th Ohio Cavalry, RG 94; Company Descriptive Book, Company K, 9th Ohio Cavalry, RG 94; Pension Records, RG 15; Compiled Service Records, RG 94; Ohio Roster Commission, *Official Roster,* 11:491–493; Hamilton, *Recollections,* p. 133; Moses, "Prison Life During the Civil War," p. 22; *CDS,* 6 August 1864, p. 2. Private Oscar Reese, writing for the *Dubuque Daily Times,* said the raiders "captured supplies and burned them," while the *Cincinnati Daily Commercial* reported, "two supply depots were destroyed, and they were full of wheat, whisky, bacon, and powder." None

of the other sources, Federal or Confederate, mention any burning at Dadeville. Reese and the *Daily Commercial*'s correspondent may have simply confused Dadeville with the tax-in-kind warehouses at Youngville.

23. *LDJ,* 30 July 1864, p. 1

24. Fretwell, "Rousseau's Alabama Raid," p. 537.

8. ROUSSEAU'S RAID: WORKING ON THE RAILROAD, JULY 17–JULY 18, 1864

1. *DDT,* 1 August 1864, p. 1; Iowa Adjutant General, *Report,* p. 1001; Morning Reports, 17 July 1864, Company C, 5th Iowa Cavalry, RG 94; Fanning, *Hairbreadth Escapes,* p. 110. The government warehouse Fanning referred to was probably the Carlisle building, a red stucco structure still standing in Loachapoka as late as 1968. See Nunn, *Yesterdays in Loachapoka,* pp. 56, 83.

2. *LDJ,* 30 July 1864, p. 1 (Captain Williams's account); *DDT,* 1 August 1864, p. 1; *NYT,* 31 July 1864, p. 6; Iowa Adjutant General, *Report,* p. 1001; *HT,* 25 August 1864, p. 1 (Jack Wilson's account); *NT,* 2 May 1901, p. 5; Eckel, *4th Tennessee,* p. 53; *OR,* 38, pt. 2, p. 907 (Rousseau's report); *MM,* 26 July 1864, p. 1; *MAR,* 27 July 1864, p. 1; *MDA,* 15 August 1864, p. 1; *MWA,* 17 August 1864, p. 3.

3. *MAR,* 27 July 1864, p. 1; Isabelle Wood Johnston Shacklette Narrative. Shacklette said she was later told the racket of wagons and carriages racing down Auburn's rocky streets convinced Rousseau's scouts the Rebels were bringing up artillery.

4. *OR,* 38, pt. 3, p. 973; Donald, "Alabama Confederate Hospitals," p. 67; *MAR,* 27 July 1864, p. 1; *MDA,* 15 August 1864, p. 1; *MWA,* 17 August 1864, p. 3.

5. Oblinger Diary, 18 July 1864; *NT,* 2 May 1901, p. 5; *HT,* 25 August 1864, pp. 1, 4; *MM,* 26 July 1864, p. 1. The Masonic jewels were returned after the war. See Nunn, *Yesterdays in Loachapoka,* p. 85.

6. Jackson Diary, 17 July 1864; Fanning, *Hairbreadth Escapes,* p. 110; *LDJ,* 30 July 1864, p. 1; *OR,* 38, pt. 2, pp. 907–8; *DDT,* 1 August 1864, p. 1; *NYT,* 31 July 1864, p. 6; Iowa Adjutant General, *Report,* p. 1001; Ward Diary, 18 July 1864; *HT,* 25 August 1864, p. 4. Rousseau's adjutant, Captain Williams, said four companies of the 4th Tennessee accompanied Major Baird's detachment. Private Oscar Reese of the 5th Iowa said three or four, while Lieutenant William T. Hays, also of the 5th Iowa, said there were only two. A close examination of Regimental Return, July 1864, 4th Tennessee Cavalry, reel 188, M-594, RG 94, and Record of Events, July–August 1864, Companies A-L, 4th Tennessee Cavalry, reel 188, M-594, RG 94, does little to resolve these discrepancies, except to make it clear Company D of the 4th Tennessee was part of Baird's force.

7. Hamilton, *Recollections,* p. 135. According to Captain Williams's account in the *Louisville Daily Journal,* 30 July 1864, p. 1, four companies of the 4th Tennessee went with Major Baird's detachment, while "part" of the regiment accompanied Colonel Hamilton. Record of Events, July–August 1864, Companies A-L, 4th Tennessee Cavalry, reel 188, M-594, RG 94, gives the impression Rousseau sent at least three Tennessee companies, B, C, and I, with Hamilton, but reports from the other companies are inconclusive.

8. *MAR,* 27 July 1864, p. 1; Benjamin J. Lea to Gideon J. Pillow, 13 July 1864, Gideon J. Pillow Papers, RG 109; *OR,* 39, pt. 2, p. 714; *OR,* 52, pt. 2, p. 708; *OR,* 38, pt. 3, p. 978 (Burch to Clanton); *DCE,* 24 July 1864, p. 2; *CT,* 23 July 1864, p. 1; *MAR,* 3 August 1864, p. 1.

9. *MDA,* 15 July 1864, p. 1; *MM,* 16 July 1864, p. 1. Clanton did not mention capturing any couriers in his account of the raid in the *Daily Columbus Enquirer,* 24 July 1864, p. 2. This incident, together with a story in the *Selma Dispatch,* 15 July 1864, quoted by *Montgomery Daily Mail,* 17 July 1864, p. 2, about two Yankee spies arrested in Jacksonville, Alabama,

while carrying plans for the raid to Sherman's headquarters appears to be the product of one of the fanciful rumors current at the time.

10. *MDA,* 15 July 1864, p. 2; *MM,* 14 July 1864, p. 2; *MAR,* 20 July 1864, pp. 1, 2; *NYT,* 7 August 1864, p. 8; *MM,* 17 July 1864, p. 2.

11. *MAR,* 3 August 1864, p. 1; Cullum, *Biographical Register,* 1:620; *OR,* 52, pt. 2, pp. 664, 682, 708; *OR,* 39, pt. 2, pp. 695, 709, 712; *NYT,* 7 August 1864, p. 8; *MM,* 17 July 1864, p. 2; *MM,* 24 July 1864, p. 2; *MDA,* 24 July 1864, p. 2; *MAR,* 20 July 1864, p. 2; *MAR,* 3 August 1864, p. 1.

12. *MM,* 20 July 1864, p. 1; *MAR,* 21 July 1864, p. 1.

13. *OR,* 38, pt. 5, pp. 883–84; *OR,* 52, pt. 2, p. 708; *MDA,* 24 July 1864, p. 2; *ACS,* 19 July 1864, p. 2; *MM,* 24 July 1864, p. 2; *CDS,* 29 July 1864, p. 1; *MAR,* 21 July 1864, p. 1; *MAR,* 20 July 1864, p. 2; *MAR,* 3 August 1864, p. 1; John, "Alabama Corps of Cadets," p. 12; Sewell, "Rousseau's Raid through Northern-Eastern Alabama, July 10–22, 1864, Which Culminated in the Battle of Chehaw or Beasley's Farm" (Master's thesis), pp. 14–15; Brewer, *Alabama,* p. 460; Garrett, *Reminiscences,* p. 723; Evans, ed., *CMH,* vol. 8: *Alabama,* pp. 836–37.

14. *OR,* 39, pt. 2, p. 713; *CDS,* 3 August 1864, p. 2.

15. *OR,* 38, pt. 5, pp. 884, 887; *OR,* 52, pt. 2, p. 708; Braxton Bragg to Stephen D. Lee, telegram, 17 July 1864, Stephen D. Lee Papers. Bragg apparently made no effort to alert Joe Johnston about this threat to his supply line. The only report Johnston received that Sunday indicated 1,200 Yankee cavalrymen had passed through Blountsville on July 12, and even this outdated piece of information did not come from Bragg. See Mackall Diary, 17 July 1864.

16. *CDS,* 29 July 1864, p. 1; *BAH,* 10 August 1902, p. 12; John, "Alabama Corps of Cadets," p. 12; Sewell, "Rousseau's Raid," p. 14; Record of Events, May–October 1864, Companies A, B, D, E, and G, 62nd Alabama Infantry, reel 5, M-861, RG 109; *NYT,* 7 August 1864, p. 8; *MM,* 24 July 1864, p. 2; *MAR,* 21 July 1864, p. 1; *MAR,* 3 August 1864, p. 1.

17. Northen, ed., *Men of Mark in Georgia,* 3:27–30; Evans, ed., *CMH,* vol. 7: *Georgia,* by Joseph T. Derry, pp. 443–44; Cullum, *Biographical Register,* 2:711; "The Last Roll: Gen. B. M. Thomas," pp. 424–25; Powell, comp., *List of Officers,* p. 626; Estes, comp., *List of Officers, Regiments and Battalions in the Confederate States Army,* p. 123; *OR,* 10, pt. 1, pp. 535–36; *OR,* 20, pt. 1, p. 758; *OR,* 32, pt. 3, p. 594; *OR,* 38, pt. 4, p. 760; Jones M. Withers to Jefferson Davis, 15 July 1864, Papers of General and Staff Officers, RG 109. The records do not substantiate a claim in "The Last Roll," *Confederate Veteran* p. 424, that Thomas served as an instructor at West Point after his graduation. Given his low standing in the class of 1858, such an assignment seems unlikely.

18. A correspondent, apparently one of General Withers's staff, said in the *Mobile Advertiser and Register,* 3 August 1864, p. 1, that the conscript battalion was one of the units Withers had summoned to Montgomery and it left Sunday evening on the train carrying Davidson's battalion and the university cadets. However, in a handwritten endorsement on Major Edward S. Ready's report, 26 July 1864 (hereafter cited as Ready's Report), filed with Muster Rolls, Ready's Battalion, RG 109, Major Thomas said he picked up Ready's command "as we moved up the road towards Opelika from Montg'y."

19. In "Rousseau's Raid through Northern-Eastern Alabama," p. 16, Sewell quotes a Captain Scott, who said the Yankee sharpshooter was killed in an exchange of gunfire with the Rebel troops riding atop the cars.

20. According to an eyewitness account in the *Montgomery Daily Mail,* 21 July 1864, p. 2, Baird's men forced some Negroes to build these crude breastworks.

21. *MM,* 24 July 1864, p. 2; *MAR,* 3 August 1864, p. 1; *BAH,* 10 August 1902, p. 12; "The Last Roll: J. I. Cannon," p. 130; Ready's Report, RG 109; *MM,* 21 July 1864, p. 2; Major James L. Davidson's report, 23 July 1864 (hereafter cited as Davidson's Report), filed with Muster Rolls, 62nd Alabama Infantry, RG 109; *CDS,* 29 July 1864, pp. 1 (describing Conductor Charley Marsh), 2; Evans, ed., *CMH,* vol. 8: *Alabama,* p. 802; *CDS,* 29 July 1864, p. 2; Sewell,

"Rousseau's Raid," p. 16. Federal estimates of Confederate troop strength at Beasley's Station ranged from 1,200 to 1,500, but Thomas actually had only about 450 men. See *OR*, 38, pt. 2, p. 908; *LDJ*, 30 July 1864, p. 1; *NYT*, 31 July 1864, p. 6; *DDT*, 1 August 1864, p. 1; *CDC*, 1 August 1864, p. 1; Iowa Adjutant General, *Report*, p. 1001; Handwritten endorsement by Bryan M. Thomas on Ready's Report, RG 109.

22. *DDT*, 1 August 1864, p. 1; *NYT*, 31 July 1864, p. 6; *HT*, 25 August 1864, p. 4; *OR*, 38, pt. 2, p. 908 (quote by Rousseau); Jackson Diary, 18 July 1864; Ward Diary, 18 July 1864; *NT*, 2 May 1901, p. 5; *CDS*, 29 July 1864, pp. 1, 2; *LDJ*, 30 July 1864, p. 1.

23. Hunt and Brown, *Brevet Brigadier Generals in Blue*, p. 265; Blanchard, ed., *Counties of Howard and Tipton, Indiana*, pp. 58, 80, 180; Grayson, *6th Indiana*, pp. 10–15; Indiana Adjutant General, *Report*, 2:381, 390; Society of the Army of the Cumberland, *5th Re-Union*, pp. 191–94.

24. Privates Oscar Reese of the 5th Iowa and J. N. Jones of the 8th Indiana asserted the raiders burned the railroad bridge over Uphaupee Creek. Southern newspapers made it clear the trestle was saved. See *NYT*, 31 July 1864, p. 6; *NT*, 2 May 1901, p. 5; *MDA*, 24 July 1864, p. 2; *CDS*, 29 July 1864, p. 1; *DCE*, 30 July 1864, p. 1.

25. Union sources: *LDJ*, 30 July 1864, p. 1; *NT*, 2 May 1901, p. 5; *HT*, 25 August 1864, p. 4; Ward Diary, 18 July 1864; Jackson Diary, 18 July 1864; Oblinger Diary, 18 July 1864; Morning Reports, 18 July 1864, Companies D and H, 8th Indiana Cavalry, RG 94; Heaton, "The Rousseau Raid," pp. 15–16; *DDT*, 1 August 1864, p. 1 (quoting Major Baird); Iowa Adjutant General, *Report*, p. 1001; *OR*, 38, pt. 2, p. 908. Confederate sources: *BAH*, 10 August 1902, p. 12 (Captain William C. Ward's account and "He is done for" quote); Ready's Report, RG 109; Davidson's Report, RG 109; *MAR*, 21 July 1864, p. 1; *MAR*, 3 August 1864, p. 1; *MDA*, 24 July 1864, p. 2; *CDS*, 24 July 1864, p. 2; "Register, Gen'l. Hospital, Notasulga, Alabama, July 22, 1864," Stout Papers.

26. Shanks, "Recollections of General Rousseau," p. 767; Shanks, *Distinguished Generals*, pp. 234–36; Compiled Service Records, RG 94; Pension Records, RG 15; Morning Reports, 18–19 July 1864, Company M, 5th Iowa Cavalry, RG 94; Iowa Adjutant General, *Report*, p. 1001; Iowa Adjutant General, *Roster and Record*, 4:884, 914, 927, 934, 987, 1000, 1010; Eckel, *4th Tennessee*, p. 53; Record of Events, July–August 1864, Company D, 4th Tennessee Cavalry, reel 188, M-594, RG 94; *DAT*, 27 August 1864, p. 4; "Battery 'E' History &c 1864," RG 59–14; "List of Casualties," RG 94; Ward Diary, 18 July 1864; *LDJ*, 30 July 1864, p. 1; *CDC*, 1 August 1864, p. 1; *DDT*, 1 August 1864, p. 1; Donald, "Alabama Confederate Hospitals," p. 26; *MM*, 21 July 1864, p. 2; *CDS*, 29 July 1864, p. 1; "Register, Gen'l. Hospital, Notasulga, Alabama, July 22, 1864," Stout Papers. Both Sage and Harris may have been alive when Rousseau's troops withdrew. According to a letter in the *Montgomery Daily Mail*, 21 July 1864, p. 2, a Union soldier, "too badly wounded to be moved," was left at Beasley's, "shot through the breast and mouth." See also Captain Ward's account of the dying Yankee soldier in the *Birmingham Age-Herald*, 10 August 1902, p. 12. The Confederates moved Private Britt to the hospital at Camp Watts, where the raiders had left six other wounded Iowans. He died there on July 25, 1864. After the war, the United States government removed the bodies of Sage, Harris, and Britt for reburial. The following citation for the national cemetery at Marietta, Georgia, is found in the Quartermaster General's *Roll of Honor*, 23:235:

No.	Name	Sec.	Grave	Original Place of Interment
9926	Unknown	L	666	Near Beasley's Water-tank, Ga. [Ala.]
9927	Unknown	L	712	Near Beasley's Water-tank, Ga. [Ala.]
9930	Unknown	L	171	Camp Watts, n'r Tuskeegee, Ala.

The current burial register at Marietta even gives July 1864, as the date of death for the soldier buried in grave 666. Yet like Captain Curl, Privates Sage, Harris, and Britt lie buried among the unknowns.

27. *OR*, 38, pt. 2, p. 908; *LDJ*, 30 July 1864, p. 1; *CDS*, 29 July 1864, p. 1; Ward Diary, 18

July 1864; Morning Reports, 18 July 1864, Company C, 5th Iowa Cavalry, RG 94; Iowa Adjutant General, *Report,* p. 1001; Eckel, *4th Tennessee,* p. 54. Oscar Reese of the 5th Iowa wrote two accounts of the raid on or about July 23, 1864. In *Dubuque Daily Times,* 1 August 1864, p. 1, he said the raiders burned 2,000 pounds of tobacco at Notasulga. In the *Nashville Union,* 27 July 1864, quoted by *New York Times,* 31 July 1864, p. 6, he said it was 150,000 pounds. Obviously, the story just got better with the telling.

28. Anna Walthall to William T. Walthall, 16 July 1864; *MAR,* 3 August 1864, p. 1; *DCE,* 24 July 1864, p. 2; Compiled Service Records, RG 94; Pension Records, RG 15; Nunn, *Yesterdays in Loachapoka,* p. 83; Record of Events, July–August 1864, Companies A-G, and I, 4th Tennessee Cavalry, reel 188, M-594, RG 94; Fanning, *Hairbreadth Escapes,* pp. 110–11; James S. Moore, Case Number 20,751, RG 233; Hamilton, *Recollections,* pp. 135–37.

29. Either there were very few patients in the Texas Hospital or they all fled at Hamilton's approach. None of the reliable eyewitness accounts mention the capture or parole of any convalescents at Auburn.

30. Shacklette Narrative; *OR,* 38, pt. 3, p. 973; *MDA,* 15 August 1864, p. 1; *MWA,* 17 August 1864, p. 3; *MAR,* 27 July 1864, p. 1; Hamilton, *Recollections,* p. 137 (quoting slave); *DZC,* 20 August 1864, p. 2 (Colonel Hamilton's quotation); James S. Moore, Case Number 20,751, RG 233.

31. Shacklette Narrative; Hamilton, *Recollections,* pp. 137–38; *OR,* 38, pt. 2, p. 908; *LDJ,* 30 July 1864, p. 1; *CDS,* 29 July 1864, p. 1; *MAR,* 27 July 1864, p. 1. The *Daily Columbus Enquirer,* 24 July 1864, p. 1, erroneously reported the Yankees had burned Auburn's Railroad Hotel, owned by James S. Moore. For proof the hotel escaped the flames, see James S. Moore, Case Number 20,751, RG 233.

32. Hamilton, *Recollections,* p. 138; *MAR,* 26 July 1864, p. 1; *CDS,* 29 July 1864, p. 1. Some sources (such as the *Columbus Daily Sun,* 29 July 1864, p. 1; *Daily Columbus Enquirer,* 24 July 1864, p. 1; *Mobile Advertiser and Register,* 26 July 1864, p. 1; Fanning, *Hairbreadth Escapes,* p. 111; and the *National Tribune,* 2 May 1901, p. 5) indicate the Rebel train was captured and burned on Tuesday, July 19. However, the vast preponderance of evidence, both Union and Confederate, clearly shows this incident took place on Monday, July 18. See *OR,* 38, pt. 2, p. 907; *LDJ,* 30 July 1864, p. 1; *CDC,* 1 August 1864, p. 1; *MDT,* 21 July 1864, p. 2; *ACS,* 22 July 1864, p. 3; *DDT,* 1 August 1864, p. 1; Morning Reports, 18 July 1864, Company H, 9th Ohio Cavalry, RG 94; Ward Diary, 18 July 1864.

33. *NT,* 2 May 1901, p. 5; James S. Moore, Case Number 20,751, RG 233.

34. Hamilton, *Recollections,* pp. 138–39. Hamilton's recollection that Rousseau said he "had no artillery" is puzzling, since Rousseau certainly had the remaining gun of Lieutenant Wightman's section with him. The lack of roads and the tangled woods west of Notasulga may have kept him from getting it into position.

35. *OR,* 38, pt. 2, p. 908; *LDJ,* 30 July 1864, p. 1; *CDC,* 1 August 1864, p. 1; Jackson Diary, 18 July 1864; Ward Diary, 18 July 1864; Oblinger Diary, 18 July 1864; Morning Reports, 18 July 1864, Companies D and H, 8th Indiana Cavalry, RG 94; Heaton, "The Rousseau Raid," p. 16; *NT,* 2 May 1901, p. 5; Morning Reports, 18 July 1864, Company C, 5th Iowa Cavalry, RG 94; Iowa Adjutant General, *Report,* p. 1001; *DDT,* 1 August 1864, p. 1; *NYT,* 31 July 1864, p. 6.

9. ROUSSEAU'S RAID: OPELIKA TO MARIETTA, JULY 19–JULY 22, 1864

1. *MDA,* 22 July 1864, p. 2; *MM,* 20 July 1864, p. 1; Record of Events, July–August 1864, Company D, 12th Mississippi Cavalry, reel 27, M-861, RG 109; Record of Events, November–December 1864, Company F, 12th Mississippi Cavalry, reel 27, M-861, RG 109; *CDS,* 29 July 1864, p. 1; *MAR,* 3 August 1864, p. 1; *DCE,* 24 July 1864, p. 2.

2. *MM,* 21 July 1864, p. 2; Vincent Montgomery to "My Dear Companion," 18 July 1864,

Vincent Montgomery Papers; Holland, "Georgia Military Institute," pp. 244–45; Bonner, *Milledgeville*, p. 181. On behalf of General Joseph E. Johnston, Georgia Governor Joseph E. Brown had written Alabama Governor Thomas H. Watts on July 4, 1864, asking him to "send a sufficient State force to guard the Chattahoochee Bridge at West Point." Watts provided ten companies of Alabama Reserves, but these had recently been transferred to Mobile. See Joseph E. Brown to "His Excellency Governor Watts," 4 July 1864, Governor's Letter Book, 1860–1865; *OR,* 39, pt. 2, p. 710; *OR,* 52, pt. 2, pp. 692–93.

3. Evans, ed., *CMH,* vol. 7: *Georgia,* p. 142; *MDT,* 5 August 1864, p. 2; A. T. Holliday to "My Dear Wife," 17 July 1864, A. T. Holliday Papers; Vincent Montgomery to "My Dear Companion," 18 July 1864; Seaborn Montgomery, Jr., to "My Dear Mother," 21 July 1864, Seaborn Montgomery, Jr. Papers.

4. *ACS,* 22 July 1864, p. 3; Albaugh and Simmons, *Confederate Arms,* pp. 211, 217, 224–27; Standard, *Columbus, Georgia, in the Confederacy,* pp. 27–33, 35, 37–44; Telfair, *A History of Columbus, Georgia,* pp. 29, 117–19, 201–2; Etta Worsley, *Columbus on the Chattahoochee,* p. 285; Martin, comp., *Columbus,* p. 166.

5. *ACS,* 22 July 1864, p. 3; *ADC,* 26 July 1864, p. 1; *ACS,* 20 July 1864, p. 3; *MDT,* 19 July 1864, p. 2; *MM,* 28 July 1864, p. 2; *CDS,* 24 July 1864, p. 1 (quoted); *CT,* 23 July 1864, p. 2; (quoted); *DCE,* 24 July 1864, p. 1; *DCE,* 17 July 1864, p. 2; *CDS,* 14 July 1864, p. 2; *CDS,* 15 July 1864, p. 1; Smith, comp., "Organizational Summary of Military Organizations from Georgia in the Confederate States of America," pp. 56, 187, 194; *CDS,* 13–17 July 1864, p. 2; *CDS,* 14–17 July 1864, pp. 1, 2.

6. Henderson, comp., *Roster of the Confederate Soldiers of Georgia,* 1:980; Compiled Service Records, RG 109; *CT,* 6 August 1864, p. 2; *ACS,* 22 July 1864, p. 3; *ACS,* 24 July 1864, p. 3; *MDT,* 19 July 1864, p. 2 (Dawson's telegram to Macon); *ACS,* 20 July 1864, p. 3; Howell Cobb to John H. Winder, 18 July 1864, Howell Cobb Letter Book, Cobb-Erwin-Lamar Papers; *OR,* series II, vol. 7, p. 476; Cobb to "My Dear Wife," 18 July 1864, Howell Cobb Papers.

7. Cobb to John H. Winder, 18 July 1864, Cobb Letter Book; *OR,* series II, vol. 7, pp. 446, 463, 469, 480, 483.

8. Hood to Cobb, telegram, 18 July 1864, Cobb to "My Dear Wife," 18 July 1864, Henry R. Jackson to Cobb, telegram, 18 July 1864, Sam Jones to Cobb, telegram, 18 July 1864 (received 19 July 1864), Hood to Cobb, telegram, 18 July 1864, Cobb Papers.

9. Champion to "My Precious Wife," 16 July 1864; Dixon Diary, 24 July 1864; Dixon, "Recollections of a Rebel Private," p. 147; Smith, *Private in Gray,* p. 96; Bigger Diary, 18 July 1864; Record of Events, July–August 1864, Company G, 2nd Mississippi Cavalry, reel 27, M-861, RG 109; Record of Events, July–August 1864, Companies B, D, G, and I, 28th Mississippi Cavalry, reel 28, M-861, RG 109; Record of Events, July–August 1864, Captain Farris's Battery (Clark Artillery, King's Battery), reel 34, M-861, RG 109; Deupree, "Noxubee Squadron," p. 101; Montgomery, *Reminiscences,* p. 182.

10. *CT,* 6 August 1864, p. 2. According to the *Daily Columbus Enquirer,* 24 July 1864, p. 1, Clinch's cavalry reached Columbus on Tuesday, July 19, but the best evidence points to Monday, July 18. That was the date the author of "Letter from Columbus," *Augusta Daily Chronicle & Sentinel,* 22 July 1864, p. 3, noted the arrival of a mounted command in the city. Another letter, in the *Macon Daily Telegraph,* 21 July 1864, p. 2, concurred, and strongly implied Clinch himself was the author.

11. *CT,* 6 August 1864, p. 2; *ACS,* 22 July 1864, p. 3 (veteran appearance of the citizen soldiers); *CDS,* 9 July 1864, p. 2 (Johnson Guards); *CDS,* 15 July 1864, p. 1 (Johnson Guards); *CDS,* 14 July 1864, p. 2 (Georgia Defenders); *DCE,* 12 August 1864, p. 2 (Kent's Company); Coulter, *"A People Courageous," A History of Phenix City, Alabama,* pp. 157–58; *MDT,* 20 July 1864, p. 2; Smith, comp., "Military Organizations from Georgia," pp. 61, 187–88, 194; First City Battalion (Columbus) Infantry, reel 14, M-861, RG 109; Martin, comp., *Columbus,* pp. 160, 167–68; Worsley, *Columbus on the Chattahoochee,* p. 285; *CT,* 4 August 1864, p. 2 (Youngblood's Company); *CDS,* 13 August 1864, p. 1 (Youngblood's Company); *CDS,* 5

August 1864, p. 2 (Dawson Artillery); *CDS,* 28 July 1864, p. 2 (Dawson Rangers); *MDT,* 21 July 1864, p. 2 (Clinch's Cavalry); *CT,* 26 July 1864, p. 2 (Major Dawson); *CDS,* 3 August 1864, p. 2 (dressing the Columbus bridges with combustibles); *CT,* 25 July 1864, p. 2 (quoting one of the Typo Guards and Captain Wilkins); *DCE,* 24 July 1864, pp. 1–2 (troops lying in the shade).

12. Dawson to Cobb, two telegrams, 19 July 1864, Cobb Papers. The word "twelve" does not appear on Cobb's copy of this second telegram, but it is present in a transcript printed in the *Macon Daily Telegraph,* 21 July 1864, p. 2.

13. Compiled Service Records, RG 94; Pension Records, RG 15; Ohio Roster Commission, *Official Roster,* 11:476–77. In his *Recollections,* p. 133, Colonel Hamilton said Doran's bugle "fell into the hands of General Clanton. The General's widow returned it to me years afterward and I still have it." Hamilton added Doran had "found whiskey, got drunk and went to sleep and was captured," but there is no mention of this in the sworn statements in Doran's pension file. Doran may have been the central character in a story entitled "Must Have the Boots," in the *Columbus Daily Sun,* 26 August 1864, p. 2:

> A Yankee, rather badly wounded in the leg, told at Opelika, that, when the Confederate who captured him, wanted to pull off the fine boots he was wearing, Yank begged that he wouldn't do it. "Mighty sorry," replied Confed, "shoes are ragged and must have the boots." "Let me cut them off," pleaded Yank. "Can't stand cut boots when good ones are around," asserts Southern rights. "Pulling 'em off will kill me," entreats Yank. "Mighty sorry," repeats ragged shoes, "but you can't live more than 12 hours, and if I can't get the boots, somebody else will, and then I won't have any, so fork over." Result—a Yankee passed through Columbus Tuesday night with holy shoes.

14. Shacklette Narrative.

15. *ACS,* 23 July 1864, p. 3; *DCE,* 24 July 1864, p. 1; *CT,* 23 July 1864, p. 2. Unless otherwise noted, the narrative describing the movements of Rousseau's column from July 19–July 22 are based on *OR,* Atlas, plate CXVIII, no. 1; *OR,* 38, pt. 2, pp. 908–9 (Rousseau's report); *LDJ,* 30 July 1864, p. 1 (Captain Williams's account); *CDC,* 1 August 1864, p. 1; *NYH,* 23 July 1864, p. 1 (map); *NYH,* 28 July 1864, p. 1; Jackson Diary, 19–22 July 1864; Oblinger Diary, 19–22 July 1864; Ward Diary, 19–22 July 1864; Heaton, "The Rousseau Raid," pp. 16–17; *NT,* 2 May 1901, p. 5 (Private John N. Jones's account); Morning Reports, 19–22 July 1864, Companies D and H, 8th Indiana Cavalry, RG 94; Regimental Return, July 1864, 8th Indiana Cavalry, reel 35, M-594, RG 94; Hamilton, *Recollections,* p. 140; Fanning, *Hairbreadth Escapes,* pp. 111–12; Morning Reports, 22 July 1864, Company G, 19–21 July 1864, Company H, 9th Ohio Cavalry, RG 94; Iowa Adjutant General, *Report,* pp. 1001–2; *NYT,* 31 July 1864, p. 6 (Private Oscar Reese's first account); *DDT,* 1 August 1864, p. 1 (Private Oscar Reese's second account); Morning Reports, 19–22 July 1864, Company C, 5th Iowa Cavalry, RG 94; Eckel, *4th Tennessee,* pp. 54–55; William King Diary, 23 July 1864.

16. *CT,* 23 July 1864, p. 2 (quoting a Southerner on the raiders' conduct); *CDS,* 29 July 1864, pp. 1, 2 (quoting Rousseau); *ACS,* 23 July 1864, p. 3; *DCE,* 24 July 1864, p. 1.

17. "List of Casualties," RG 94; Compiled Service Records, RG 94; Pension Records, RG 15; Iowa Adjutant General, *Roster and Record,* 4:935. The identity of Koontz's killer may never be known for certain, but in an article entitled "The Raid," 24 July 1864, p. 1, the *Daily Columbus Enquirer* reported that "Mr. _____ of Opelika, killed three of the raiders by bushwhacking them." Similarly, a correspondent for the *Columbus Daily Sun* who made a trip from Montgomery to Opelika shortly after the raid noted, "We could hear of but one house (that of a Mr. Holtzclaw) which was burned, and, it is said, this was destroyed because the owner had abandoned it and bushwhacked their men." See *Columbus Daily Sun,* 29 July 1864, p. 1. Koontz was apparently left where he fell. The *Roll of Honor* makes no mention of any disinterments near Opelika.

18. *CDS,* 29 July 1864, p. 1; *DDT,* 1 August 1864, p. 1. Rousseau and his officers claimed they destroyed "over 30 miles" of the railroad in *OR,* 38, p. 2, pp. 878, 908; Regimental Return, July 1864, 8th Indiana Cavalry, reel 35, M-594, RG 94; Regimental Return, July 1864, 9th Ohio Cavalry, reel 141, M-594, RG 94; Regimental Return, July 1864, 4th Tennessee Cavalry, reel 188, M-594, RG 94. Other Union accounts estimated the distance at thirty to forty miles. Confederate sources reported the loss of about twenty-five miles of track, and this seems to be a more accurate estimate. According to Paul Carine of the Louisville & Nashville Railroad, it is 19.27 miles by rail from Opelika to Notasulga. Adding this figure to the three miles of track the raiders tore up west of Notasulga, the mile and a half east of Opelika, and the two miles on the Columbus Branch road, gives a total of 25.77 miles. See *MAR,* 23 July 1864, pp. 1, 2; *MAR,* 27 July 1864, p. 1; *MAR,* 3 August 1864, p. 1; *MDT,* 26 July 1864, p. 2; *CDS,* 29 July 1864, p. 1; George Whitfield to B. F. Jones, 9 September 1864, George Whitfield, Confederate Engineer Bureau, Compiled Service Records, RG 109.

19. Jack Wilson (*HT,* 25 August 1864, p. 4); Alexander Eckel, *4th Tennessee,* p. 55; and Oscar Reese (*NYT,* 31 July 1864, p. 6), cite 3:00, 4:00, and 5:00 P.M. as the hour of departure, but they may be referring to the time Rousseau's column left the railroad at Rough and Ready and turned north toward Lafayette.

20. *ACS,* 30 July 1864, p. 1. This unidentified woman counted twenty-three flags and two banners as a brigade of Yankee cavalry and a "fine large silver-mounted carriage" passed her Aunt B.'s house on the Lafayette Road. The flags were undoubtedly company guidons and the banners were regimental colors. Most likely, this was Patrick's 2nd Brigade, composed of eleven companies of the 4th Tennessee, nine companies of the 5th Iowa, and a section of Battery E, 1st Michigan Artillery. Rousseau traveled by carriage whenever possible, escorted by two companies of the 2nd Kentucky, each of which presumably had a guidon. These two companies, together with Patrick's twenty companies, and the artillery would have made a total of twenty-three guidons and two regimental colors. The woman made no reference to any other troops, which suggests Harrison's 1st Brigade left Opelika by a slightly different route. This same woman said the Yankees had three pieces of artillery, "two of their own and one they had captured from us." A letter in the *Atlanta Daily Appeal,* quoted by *Macon Daily Telegraph,* 23 July 1864, p. 2, also credited the raiders with three guns. Rousseau left Decatur with two Parrott rifles but abandoned one of them before reaching Talladega. There were three Rebel 6-pounders at Talladega, but in *OR,* 38, pt. 3, p. 976, Major Walthall reported these were destroyed before the Yankees arrived. Neither Rousseau nor any of his men mentioned capturing any artillery, so just what this obviously observant lady saw remains a mystery.

21. Bigger Diary, 18–19 July 1864; Champion to "My Precious Wife," 20 July 1864; Worthington to "Dear Sis," 25 July 1864; Record of Events, July–August 1864, Company G, 2nd Mississippi Cavalry, reel 27, M-861, RG 109; Record of Events, July–August 1864, Companies B, D, G, and I, 28th Mississippi Cavalry, reel 28, M-861, RG 109; Record of Events, July–August 1864, Captain Farris's Battery (Clark Artillery, King's Battery), reel 34, M-861, RG 109; Seaborn Montgomery, Jr. to "My Dear Mother," 21 July 1864; Smith, *Private in Gray,* pp. 96–98.

22. Ward Diary, 19 July 1864. Ward did not specify how many prisoners Corporal Turner took from the church, but Fanning, in *Hairbreadth Escapes,* p. 112, said, "We captured six officers who were secreted in houses here. . . ."

23. *CDS,* 9 August 1864, p. 2.

24. According to Rousseau's adjutant, Captain Williams, "Reveille was sounded at three o'clock and the march resumed." Similarly, Private Oscar Reese of the 5th Iowa reported, "At 5 o'clock A.M. the bugle sounded again, and the wearied men were once more on the road." However, Private John Jones of the 8th Indiana said, "We slept two hours, when we were aroused and ordered 'To horse' without the bugle call." Perhaps the bugles blew for the 2nd Brigade, but not the 1st.

25. The *Chambers Tribune,* quoted by *Columbus Daily Sun,* 9 August 1864, p. 2, reported "the notorious Bob Smith of Randolph" and "a number of other Southern renegades," guided

the raiders through eastern Alabama. This was the same R. T. Smith whose services Rousseau had requested in a coded telegram on July 7, but Rousseau made no mention of Smith in his official report and Smith apparently did not reach Decatur in time to accompany the column. See R. T. Smith to Ulysses S. Grant, 5 March 1869, R. T. Smith File, Collectors of Customs Applications, RG 56. Just how far the column traveled on this West Point road before someone realized the mistake is unclear. The only clue comes from Lieutenant Fanning's not always reliable memoirs. He wrote in *Hairbreadth Escapes,* p. 112, "Shortly after starting our brave General Rousseau heard the enemy was massing his forces at Fredonia, and there we went to engage him, but found no enemy at all." Fredonia is some seven miles southeast of Rousseau's bivouac of July 19–20 and it seems unlikely he would have gone so far out of his way looking for trouble.

26. One eyewitness asserted he heard Rousseau say he and his staff thought they were at the home of Stevens's partner, Thomas Johnson, an avowed secessionist. This might account for the thorough ransacking of Stevens's house.

27. Henry Stoker, Case Number 13,108, RG 233; James L. Vineyard, Sr., Case Number 6,522, RG 233; Mrs. H. H. Stevens, executrix of Wilkins Stevens, vs. the U.S., Case Number 8,605, RG 123; Edmund G. Arnett, Case Number 15,819, RG 233; Harriet M. Lewis, Case Number 15,820, RG 217; John J. Hendricks, Case Number 16,822, RG 233; Alexander Mooty, Case Number 4,546, RG 233.

28. William L. Bell, Case Number 11,791, RG 233; James R. Thomason, Case Number 10,792, RG 233; Ward Diary, 21 July 1864.

29. Morning Reports, 19–21 July 1864, Company H, 8th Indiana Cavalry, RG 94.

30. James L. Vineyard, Sr., Case Number 6,522, RG 233. J. S. Miller of Carroll County offered a clue to the identity of the civilian casualty. Testifying before the Fulton County Superior Court on April 1, 1869, in the case of A. S. Atkinson and Others, Executors of Charles J. McDonald vs. A. V. Brumby and William J. Russell, Case Number 9,821, Miller said he was employed in the summer of 1864 by his father-in-law, William Amis, who owned a large cotton mill at Bowenville (present-day Banning), eight miles southeast of Carrollton. According to Miller, Yankee troops first visited the mill on July 21, 1864. "Mr. Amis . . . did not remain at the Factory," he said, "but was shot while refugeing [*sic*] with his family on the day U.S. troops were at his factory." This fits together very nicely with the story of a civilian being shot by Rousseau's rear guard, but William Amis survived the war, and none of his descendants have any recollection of his being wounded. While Rousseau could have sent a detachment to Bowenville on July 21, Stoneman's cavalry camped in that vicinity on the night of July 13–14, and Major Buck's battalion of the 8th Michigan marched past the mill on their way to Carrollton on July 14. If Amis were shot on the day the Yankees *first* came to Bowenville, it would have been on July 14 or 15, not July 21.

31. P. H. Hesterly, Case Number 6,560, RG 217.

32. In the *New York Times,* 31 July 1864, p. 6, and the *Dubuque Daily Times,* 1 August 1864, p. 1, Oscar Reese said Rousseau's rear guard was fired on as it entered Villa Rica, but he may have confused Villa Rica with the shooting incident at Carrollton six hours earlier. On the other hand, there is absolutely no truth in Alexander Eckel's assertion in "The Rousseau and McCook Raid," p. 7, that on the night of July 21

> As . . . the advance guard was emerging from the woods . . . a little distance ahead they discovered troops passing on a road that crossed theirs, going south. Word was sent to Gen. Rousseau, the command was halted, and all parties ordered to keep quiet. . . . On investigation it was ascertained Wheeler was going south, hunting for Gen. Rousseau. After Wheeler had passed on at a safe distance the command "forward" was given, and they moved off at a brisk pace. The march was continued until well toward daybreak, when a halt was made and the men and horses given a short and much-needed rest.

Eckel told a slightly different version of this tale in *4th Tennessee,* pp. 55–56, making his own regiment the advance guard and crediting them with discovering Pillow's cavalry was crossing their front. However, the 4th Tennessee was not at the head of Rousseau's column on July 21, but far to the rear, and Wheeler's cavalry was hotly engaged on the east side of Atlanta. As for other Confederate columns in the vicinity, Pillow had moved to Talladega via Opelika, Clanton had given up the chase after Rousseau passed Lafayette, and Armstrong was retracing his steps to LaGrange after riding to Lafayette on July 20. Eckel's recollection that Rousseau's column marched "until well along toward daybreak" is also incorrect. The raiders bivouacked well before midnight on July 21–22. See Record of Events, July–August 1864, Company D, 12th Mississippi Cavalry, reel 27, M-861, RG 109; Record of Events, November–December 1864, Company F, 12th Mississippi Cavalry, reel 27, M-861, RG 109; *DCE,* 24 July 1864, pp. 1, 2; *MAR,* 3 August 1864, p. 1; Champion to "My Precious Wife," 20 July 1864; Bigger Diary, 20–21 July 1864; Record of Events, July–August 1864, Companies D and G, 28th Mississippi Cavalry, reel 28, M-861, RG 109.

33. Rousseau to Sherman, telegram, 22 July 1864, Sherman Papers.

34. Morning Reports, 10–22 July 1864, Company C, 5th Iowa Cavalry, RG 94; Harrison to Mrs. L. E. Harrison, 25 July 1864; *DDT,* 1 August 1864, p. 1; *LDJ,* 30 July 1864, p. 1; *NYH,* 28 July 1864, p. 1; Iowa Adjutant General, *Report,* p. 1002; Rousseau to Sherman, telegram, 22 July 1864, Sherman Papers; *OR,* 38, pt. 2, pp. 878, 909; *NYT,* 31 July 1864, p. 6; *CDC,* 1 August 1864, p. 1; *CDC,* 2 August 1864, p. 1; *NYT,* 28 July 1864, p. 1; *NYH,* 28 July 1864, p. 1; "List of Casualties," RG 94; "Register, Gen'l. Hospital, Notasulga, Alabama, July 22 1864," Stout Papers; Reid, *Ohio in the War,* 2:812; Fanning, *Hairbreadth Escapes,* pp. 111–12; *DTB,* 29 July 1864, p. 2; *HT,* 18 August 1864, p. 1; Morning Reports, 16 July 1864, Company G, 8th Indiana Cavalry, RG 94; Morning Reports, 16, 17, and 19 July 1864, Company K, 9th Ohio Cavalry, RG 94; Company Descriptive Book, Company K, 9th Ohio Cavalry, RG 94; Compiled Service Records, RG 94; Pension Records, RG 15; Muster Rolls, 8th Indiana, 5th Iowa, 2nd Kentucky, 9th Ohio, 4th Tennessee Cavalry, Battery E, 1st Michigan Light Artillery, RG 94; Ohio Roster Commission, *Official Roster,* 11:476–77, 488, 490–93, 495; Tennessee Adjutant General, *Report,* pp. 396, 406; *DCE,* 24 July 1864, p. 2; Ward Diary, 12, 14, and 16 July 1864; Jackson Diary, 14 July 1864; Oblinger Diary, 14 July 1864; *HT,* 25 August 1864, p. 1; *DAT,* 27 August 1864, p. 4; Eckel, *4th Tennessee Cavalry,* p. 52. For spurious claims crediting Rousseau with destroying over thirty miles of railroad, burning 800 wagons, killing 800 Rebels, capturing 2,000 more, etc., etc., etc., see *NYT,* 31 July 1864, p. 6; *DDT,* 1 August 1864, p. 1; *OSJ,* 29 July 1864, p. 3; *CDC,* 2 August 1864, p. 1; *NYT,* 28 July 1864, p. 1; *NYH,* 28 July 1864, p. 1; Anderson, *Fighting by Southern Federals,* pp. 216–17; Van Horne, *History of the Army of the Cumberland,* 2:118.

35. *NYT,* 14 August 1864, p. 2; *DFP,* 11 August 1864, p. 3.

36. *OR,* 38, pt. 5, pp. 234–37; Sherman, *Memoirs,* 2:69–70; Shanks, *Distinguished Generals,* p. 236; *NYT,* 1 August 1864, p. 2. D. P. Conyngham, the *New York Herald*'s correspondent with Sherman's army, did not mention Rousseau's visit to the XIV Corps. Instead, his dispatch to the *Herald,* 2 August 1864, p. 5, said Rousseau spent some time with Major General Oliver O. Howard's IV Corps. Howard, however, makes no mention of such a visit in his official reports or in his lengthy memoirs, nor does his adjutant, Lieutenant Colonel Joseph S. Fullerton, who kept a detailed daily diary of events at Howard's headquarters. A newcomer to the Army of the Cumberland, Howard had not previously served with Rousseau, and it seems unlikely Rousseau would have had any reason to visit him.

37. *NYT,* 26 July 1864, p. 1; *WES,* 27 July 1864, p. 1; *NYT,* 1 August 1864, p. 2; *NYT,* 28 July 1864, p. 1; *JDG,* 10 August 1864, p. 1. Rousseau was not the only one feeling the effects of the march. Captains Ruger and Elkin of his staff also complained of poor health and requested sick leave shortly after returning to Nashville. See Compiled Service Records, RG 94. Rousseau's guide, James McBurney, remained at the front as a volunteer aide to his cousin, Brigadier General Mortimer D. Leggett of the XVII Corps. See McBurney, Memoir, McBurney Papers; Leggett to L. M. Dayton, 22 August 1864, Sherman Papers; Leggett to "Friend Kaufmann," 6 June 1865, McBurney File, RG 56.

10. GARRARD'S RAID, JULY 21–JULY 24, 1864

1. Allen J. Veal vs. the U.S., Case Number 6,842, RG 123. Unless otherwise noted, the narrative describing Garrard's raid is based on *OR,* 38, pt. 2, pp. 809 (Garrard's report), 842–43, 846; *CDC,* 11 August 1864, p. 1; *NYTB,* 13 August 1864, p. 1; Hosea, "Side Lights on the War," p. 41; Vale, *Minty and the Cavalry,* p. 326; Heber S. Thompson Diary, 21–25 July 1864; Lemmon Diary, 21–24 July 1864; McLain Diary, 21–24 July 1864; Potter Diary, 21–24 July 1864; Gooding to "Dear Lucy," 26 July 1864; *DFP,* 6 August 1864, p. 1 (Captain William W. Van Antwerp's account); *WC,* 13 August 1864, p. 2; *WC,* 20 August 1864, p. 2; Regimental Return, July 1864, 4th Michigan Cavalry, reel 83, M-594, RG 94; *BDW,* 2 September 1864, p. 2; *MJPGA,* 20 August 1864, p. 1; *CPR,* 7 September 1864, p. 1; Record of Events, Muster Roll, July–August 1864, Companies E, H, and M, 4th U.S. Cavalry, RG 94; Kryder to "Dear Beloved Wife," 2 August 1864; *DTB,* 8 August 1864, p. 2; Crofts, comp., *3rd Ohio,* pp. 157–58; James Thomson Diary, 21–24 July 1864; Morning Reports, 22–23 July 1864, Company G, 4th Ohio Cavalry, RG 94; Griest Diary, 21–24 July 1864; Records Diary, 21, 24 July 1864; *NT,* 8 October 1891, p. 3; Magee, *72nd Indiana,* pp. 345–51; Kemper Diary, 21–24 July 1864; Doyle, *17th Indiana,* p. 21; *AT,* 16 December 1897, p. 6; *NT,* 18 October 1900, p. 3; Illinois Adjutant General, *Report,* 5:516; Silas C. Stevens to E. B. Stevens, 7 January and 8 February 1905; Nourse Diary, 24 July 1864; Fleming to "My Dear Parents," 25 July 1864; Thomas M. Bryson, Case Number 15,604, RG 233 (Garrard's route on July 24); Bartlett M. Jenkins, Case Number 7,572, RG 217 (Minty's route on July 24).

2. Flanigan, *History of Gwinnett County Georgia,* 2:189, 196–97; Thomas Maguire Diary, 21 July 1864. In "A list of the property stolen by the Yankees from Thomas Maguire which he herewith submits to the Honorable the Inferior Court of Gwinnett County and prays to be exempt from taxes for the year 1864," cited in Flanigan, 2:196–97, Maguire estimated his losses at $35,481.00.

3. Garrard's rear guard did not wait to make sure the fire did its work. "After they were gone I sent some hands to put it out," Thomas Maguire noted in his diary on July 22. "Plank nearly all burned and sleepers badly injured, but folks can cross on foot. Bad feelings against the Yankees. I hope they will never come back again." Four months later, the entire left wing of Sherman's army passed right through Maguire's front yard on the March to the Sea.

4. *ACS,* 24 July 1864, p. 1; *ADC,* 24 July 1864, p. 1; *ADC,* 26 July 1864, p. 1; *ACS,* 27 July 1864, p. 3; Jordan Diary, 23 July 1864. According to passengers interviewed by the *Augusta Daily Chronicle & Sentinel* and the *Augusta Daily Constitutionalist,* the raiders captured and burned a passenger train and a freight train at Conyers. Garrard, however, in *OR,* 38, pt. 2, p. 809, reported the destruction of only one train, adding that civilians told him the raid had left a passenger train and a construction train stranded between Stone Mountain and Yellow River. Captain Hosea of Garrard's staff, Sergeant Ben Magee of the 72nd Indiana, and Stephen Jordan, a Confederate cavalryman on picket duty near Lithonia, all noted the destruction of one train at Conyers, but Magee also mentioned a freight train had been stranded west of Yellow River. The number of prisoners taken at Conyers is also subject to dispute. Sergeant Magee said there was a colonel, a captain, and fifteen privates, but he was not on the scene. None of the other sources mention a captured colonel, and Magee may simply have confused this incident with a Rebel colonel taken prisoner at Covington later in the day. The most reliable information seems to come from the Illinois Adjutant General, *Report,* 5:516, which credits the 98th Illinois with taking sixteen Confederate prisoners at Conyers.

5. *ADC,* 24 July 1864, p. 1; *ACS,* 24 July 1864, p. 1; Record of Ordnance and Ordnance Stores, vol. 7, 98th Illinois Mounted Infantry, RG 156; Lovett, "Airy Mount—In Sherman's Track," p. 194.

6. Stephenson, "Refugeeing in War Time," pp. 136–37.

7. *ACS,* 2 August 1864, p. 1.

8. This incident, first related by Captain Joseph G. Vale in *Minty and the Cavalry,* pp. 323–24, and later quoted by Colonel William Sipes in *7th Pennsylvania,* pp. 114–15, supposedly

took place about July 10, while the 2nd Division was on a scouting expedition "up the river." However, Vale was uncertain about the exact date, and evidence from other sources strongly suggests the hives were actually stolen on the night of July 21–22. In a letter to the *Wolverine Citizen,* 13 August 1864, p. 2, a 4th Michigan trooper noted the 1st Brigade had plundered a farmer's beehives during the night, and Thomas Maguire, in his "List of the property stolen by the Yankees," noted the loss of "2 bee gums & contents."

9. Orr, "Life of Edgar Harold Orr as Revealed in Family Letters," pp. 35–36; Orr, "Gustavus John Orr: Georgia Educator," pp. 90–92; *ADC,* 2 August 1864, p. 3.

10. Putnam Weaver to Jenny Weaver, 26 May 1864, Putnam Weaver Letters; Clark, *Under the Stars and Bars,* p. 144; *ADC,* 2 August 1864, p. 3.

11. Prather, "When Sherman Marched through Georgia," p. 339; Akin, "Refugees of 1863," p. 115; Akin, "Faithful Slave, 'Col. Robert,'" p. 470.

12. Magee, *72nd Indiana,* pp. 347–48.

13. Clark, *Under the Stars and Bars,* pp. 144–46; White, "Emory in the Civil War," p. 14; Jarrell, *Oxford Echoes,* p. 89. According to oral tradition in the Branham family, the Yankees probably would have burned the house down if it were not for the presence of a Miss Johnson of Watertown, New York, who was boarding with the Branhams while she taught at the nearby Palmer Institute.

14. Clark, *Under the Stars and Bars,* p. 151.

15. *Covington News,* 21 October 1927, p. 7; *ADI,* 4 August 1864, p. 1; Williford, *The Glory of Covington,* p. 148; Smith, *The Soldier's Friend,* pp. 120–21; Travis, "Heroism at Home," p. 390.

16. *ACS,* 29 July 1864, p. 3; *MSR,* 3 August 1864, p. 2; Clark, *Under the Stars and Bars,* p. 149; Kathleen Middlebrooks Heard, "Reminiscence: Newton County Goes to War," in "UDC Bound Typescripts" (hereafter cited as UDC), 11:69; L. L. Cody, "Reminiscence by L. L. Cody," UDC 11:138–39; *Covington News,* 21 October 1927, p. 7; Williford, *Glory of Covington,* p. 153; Morning Reports, 22 July 1864, Company K, 17th Indiana Mounted Infantry, RG 94; Compiled Service Records, RG 94; Indiana Adjutant General, *Report,* 4:368, 8:449; Muster Roll, July–August 1864, Company G, 4th U.S. Cavalry, RG 94; Regimental Return, July 1864, 4th U.S. Cavalry, reel 41, M-744, RG 94; *ADC,* 2 August 1864, p. 3; Travis, "Heroism at Home," pp. 390–91. A slightly different version of this story, apparently based on oral tradition, in the *Covington News,* 21 October 1927, p. 7, says bystanders carried Jones to Richard King's house, where he died on the front porch. Another account, found in Clark, *Under the Stars and Bars,* p. 149, claims the Yankees shot Jones to death and then beat his brains out with their rifle butts, but Clark was not in Covington on July 22. Mrs. Travis was.

17. Alexander and Bogle, "George Hewitt Daniel," pp. 21–24, 32, 37, 43–47; Bogle, "George Hewitt Daniel Part II," pp. 31–32; *ADI,* 4 August 1864, p. 2; Travis, "Heroism at Home," p. 391; Charles L. Bowker vs. the U.S., Case Number 8,798, RG 123; *ACS,* 29 July 1864, p. 1; *ADC,* 2 August 1864, p. 3.

18. *Covington News,* 21 October 1927, p. 7; Smith, *The Soldier's Friend,* pp. 121–22; *ACS,* 24 July 1864, p. 1; *MSR,* 3 August 1864, p. 2; *ADC,* 2 August 1864, p. 3; *ACS,* 29 July 1864, p. 3; *CDS,* 9 August 1864, p. 2. Sergeant Magee also mentioned the destruction of "a very large mill containing 8,000 bushels of corn and a large quantity of flour," but he may have been referring to the gristmill on Yellow River the detachment from the 98th Illinois had burned earlier in the day. Captain William W. Van Antwerp of the 4th Michigan seemed to hint at this in a letter appearing in the *Detroit Free Press,* 6 August 1864, p. 1, when he said the raiders destroyed 2,000 bushels of corn "in and about the town." However, Private John Nourse of the Board of Trade Battery noted in his diary that troopers returning from the raid on 24 July 1864 told him the large warehouse Garrard's men burned in Covington was full of sacked grain. Nourse did not accompany the expedition, but he also mentioned the destruction of a rifle factory. This author has been unable to find any evidence of such a facility in Covington; nor

is there any apparent basis in fact for assertions in the *Wolverine Citizen,* 13 August 1864, p. 2, and the *National Tribune,* 18 October 1900, p. 3, crediting Garrard's men with destroying a wagon train and a railroad tunnel and spiking several cannon.

19. *CDS,* 9 August 1864, p. 2; *MSR,* 3 August 1864, p. 2; *Covington News,* 21 October 1927, p. 7; Williford, *Glory of Covington,* p. 6. Garrard said this unfinished hospital consisted of over thirty buildings capable of housing 10,000 patients. If so, it would have been the largest hospital in the South, but Captain Van Antwerp of the 4th Michigan, who was actually on the scene, counted only five buildings. The *Covington News,* 21 October 1927, p. 3, said this workshop belonged to Pringle Hyer, but according to the 1860 census, there was no one by that name living in Covington. There was an E. P. Hyer, but he was only fifteen years old. Lewis Freeland, on the other hand, is listed as a buggy maker with real and personal property valued at $6,200. See U.S. Department of the Interior, Census Office, Eighth Census of the United States, Free Inhabitants, Newton County, Georgia, 1860, pp. 427, 430.

20. Charles L. Bowker vs. the U.S., Case Number 8,798, RG 123; Simeon N. Stallings vs. the U.S., Case Number 9,252, RG 123; *MSR,* 3 August 1864, p. 2.

21. Later that evening, Charles L. Bowker buried the dead scout in a corner of the Covington cemetery, not far from where Presley Jones would be laid to rest. Three or four years later, the army disinterred the body entrusted to Bowker's care and moved it to the National Cemetery at Marietta, where it was apparently reburied with the unknowns. The location of the remains of the second scout is uncertain, but he was probably reinterred at Marietta. See Charles L. Bowker vs. the U.S., Case Number 8,798, RG 123; Quartermaster General's Office, *Statement of the Disposition of Some of the Bodies of Deceased Union Soldiers and Prisoners of War,* 2:25.

22. Smith, *The Soldier's Friend,* pp. 120–24.

23. Major J. D. Maney to Major J. F. Cummings, 18 September 1864, Stout Papers; *CDC,* 11 August 1864, p. 1.

24. *ACS,* 24 July 1864, p. 1; *ACS,* 27 July 1864, p. 3.

25. *NT,* 31 May 1894, p. 2; Charles L. Bowker vs. the U.S., Case Number 8,798, RG 123. In a deposition filed before the Court of Claims, Bowker testified:

> about 5 o'clock in the afternoon while Col. Bibb's [Biggs'] command was in town, a messenger from Wheeler's Cavalry came into Covington with information Wheeler was within five miles of Covington with 1500 cavalry. The fact was made known to me. I immediately went to one [of] Col. Bibb's Lieuts. & informed him of what I had heard; he immediately in turn informed Col. Bibb in *my presence.* Col. Bibb on the strength of this information at *once ordered* his command to get ready to leave—and when Col. Bibb's cavalry was leaving the north part of the city— Wheeler's cavalry was coming into the south part of it & camped in town that night. All of this I was *eyewitness* to.

While a messenger or scout may have indeed reported the approach of Wheeler's command, the latter portion of Bowker's testimony will not stand close scrutiny. Wheeler had spent most of the afternoon of July 22 trying to drive the Board of Trade Battery off the square in Decatur and was nowhere near Covington.

26. "List of Prisoners of War Captured by 2d Brigade 2d Division Cavalry," pp. 6–7, vol. 57/140, CCMDM, RG 393; *MSR,* 3 August 1864, p. 2; Smith, *The Soldier's Friend,* pp. 126–27. This author has been unable to substantiate a claim in the *Augusta Daily Constitutionalist,* 26 July 1864, p. 1, alleging "the Yankees murdered two or three negroes at Covington for refusing to leave with them."

27. *ADC,* 2 August 1864, p. 3; Clark, *Under the Stars and Bars,* pp. 146–47.

28. *ADC,* 2 August 1864, p. 3; *MSR,* 3 August 1864, p. 2; Clark, *Under the Stars and Bars,* p. 144; *Lebanon* (Ind.) *Patriot,* 6 August 1864, p. 2. It seems appropriate at this point to lay a myth to rest. According to Walter Clark in *Under the Stars and Bars,* pp. 150–51, among the

letters Garrard's men confiscated in Oxford on July 22 was one written by a young South Carolina refugee named Zora Fair. In it, she described to Georgia Governor Joseph E. Brown how she had disguised herself as a Negro, and sneaked into the Federal camps around Atlanta to learn Sherman's plans and troop dispositions. Supposedly, when Garrard's men discovered the contents of the letter they sent a squad back to Oxford to arrest its young author, but Miss Fair escaped by hiding in the attic of Mr. Rivers's house, while her father took refuge in a well. Other authors have repeated this story as gospel, and while it does have a certain amount of truth to it, it *did not* take place on July 22. The incident actually occurred in November 1864, during Sherman's march to the sea, and had absolutely nothing to do with Garrard's cavalry. See Hitchcock, *Marching with Sherman,* pp. 72–73.

29. Robert A. Guinn, "History of the Important Movements and Incidents of the Newton Rifles," UDC 10:12; "List of Prisoners Captured by 2d Brigade 2d Division Cavalry," pp. 4–7, vol. 57/140; CCMDM, RG 393; "Rebel Prisoners of War," vol. 50/108, CCMDM, RG 393. Silas Stevens identified the prisoner as a brigadier general, but the records in RG 393 make it clear he was a lieutenant colonel.

30. William R. Simpson, Case Number 7,712, RG 217; Elijah Palmer, Case Number 7,707, RG 217; Stephenson, "Refugeeing in War Time," p. 137; Maguire Diary, 21 and 24 July 1864; *ASW,* 27 July 1864, p. 2; *ACS,* 29 July 1864, p. 3; *ASB,* 27 July 1864, p. 3; Sams, *Wayfarers in Walton,* pp. 181, 638; *DCE,* 29 July 1864, p. 1; *ACS,* 27 July 1864, p. 3; *ACS,* 26 July 1864, p. 1; *ADC,* 26 July 1864, p. 1; *OR,* 38, pt. 1, p. 175; pt. 5, p. 250; Burge, *A Woman's Wartime Journal,* p. 7. A letter quoted by the *Daily Columbus Enquirer* claimed the Yankees carried off several small boys when they left town, but except for an almost identically worded account in the *Augusta Daily Chronicle & Sentinel,* 29 July 1864, p. 3, none of the other Southern sources mention any such outrage.

31. Sams, *Wayfarers in Walton,* p. 190; *ASW,* 27 July 1864, p. 2; *ASB,* 27 July 1864, p. 3. *Wayfarers in Walton* erroneously identifies Birney's troopers as part of Stoneman's command.

32. "List of Casualties in 2d Brigade 2d Division Cavalry," pp. 66–67, vol. 57/140, CCMDM, RG 393; Compiled Service Records, RG 94; Ohio Roster Commission, *Official Roster,* 11:149, 152; Crofts, comp., *3rd Ohio,* pp. 269, 272; *OR,* 38, pt. 1, p. 75; "Rebel Prisoners of War," vol. 50/108, CCMDM, RG 393.

33. Isaiah C. Brand, Case Number 7,392, RG 217; Edwin Johnson, Case Number 17,387, RG 217; Elisha Martin, Case Number 7,702, RG 233; James W. Hill vs. the U.S., Case Number 8,547, RG 123; Tilford McConnell vs. the U.S., Case Number 7,901, RG 123; "Rebel Prisoners of War," vol. 50/108, CCMDM, RG 393.

34. *WC,* 13 August 1864, p. 2.

35. Ibid.

36. Guinn, "History of the Newton Rifles," UDC 10:12; John Rannals, Case Number 7,436, RG 217; George W. Minor, Case Number 7,424, RG 233; Jackson H. Kimbrell, Case Number 7,698, RG 233. In *OR,* 38, pt. 2, p. 809, Garrard credited his men with burning three wagon bridges over Yellow River. The records specifically mention only two: one at Rockbridge, the other on the main road between Conyers and Covington. The third may have been the bridge at Holt's Mill.

37. Compiled Service Records, RG 94; Pension Records, RG 15.

38. *OR,* 38, pt. 5, pp. 900–901, 905–6; pt. 3, p. 953; Dodson, ed., *Wheeler and His Cavalry,* pp. 211–12; Ash Diary, 23 July 1864; Jordan Diary, 23 July 1864; *ADC,* 24 July 1864, p. 3.

39. J. W. Ward to "My Dear Father," 26 July 1864, Confederate States of America Records; *ACS,* 29 July 1864, p. 3; *SR,* 24 July 1864, p. 2; *ADC,* 27 July 1864, p. 1; *MCU,* 26 July 1864, p. 3; R. J. Hallett to W. C. Humphreys, 24 July 1864, Cobb Letter Book.

40. Stegeman, *These Men She Gave,* pp. 1–4, 79, 107–10, 113–15; Coleman, *Confederate Athens,* pp. 1–12, 95–116, 164, 169, 215; Record of Events, July 1864, Captain Richard D. Moore's Battery, reel 13, M-861, RG 109; Record of Events, July 1864, Captain Richard S. Taylor's Company, reel 19, M-861, RG 109; Record of Events, June 1864, Captain James

White's Company, reel 19, M-861, RG 109; *ASB,* 27 July 1864, p. 3; *ASW,* 27 July 1864, p. 2; Julia Pope Stanley to Marcellus Stanley, 1 August 1864, Marcellus Stanley Papers; John A. Cobb to "My Dear Wife," 28 July 1864, Cobb Papers.

41. *OR,* 38, pt. 3, p. 953; Ash Diary, 23 July 1864.

42. Garrard erred when he said he had only two casualties. Privates John Williams, William Travellion, and John Sullivan had been killed, Lieutenant Calvin S. Kimball captured, and Private Jacob Malott wounded. See *DTB,* 8 August 1864, p. 2; Hosea, "Side Lights on the War," p. 41. As for the number of Negro contrabands his column brought back, other sources gave estimates of anywhere from 93 to 800. See *NYTB,* 4 August 1864, p. 2; *CDC,* 2 August 1864, p. 1; *DTB,* 8 August 1864, p. 2; *WC,* 20 August 1864, p. 2; Nourse Diary, 24 July 1864; *WC,* 13 August 1864, p. 2. Garrard's report in *OR,* 38, pt. 2, p. 809, differs slightly from the one quoted in *NYTB,* 13 August 1864, p. 1.

43. *OR,* Atlas, plate LXXXVIII, no. 1; *OR,* 38, pt. 5, pp. 243, 245. Sherman received Garrard's written report within the hour. See *OR,* 38, pt. 5, p. 240.

44. Minty, in the *National Tribune,* 31 May 1894, p. 2, and Vale, in *Minty and the Cavalry,* p. 326, said the 1st Brigade did not reach Decatur until midnight, but letters and diaries from Minty's men make it clear they arrived about dark.

45. *OR,* 38, pt. 5, p. 250; *CDC,* 2 August 1864, p. 1; "Rebel Prisoners of War," vol. 50/108, CCMDM, RG 393.

46. Potter to "Dear Father," 1 August 1864; *MDS,* 12 August 1864, p. 1; *CDC,* 2 August 1864, p. 1; *CDC,* 18 August 1864, p. 2; *NYTB,* 4 August 1864, p. 2.

11. CONVERGING COLUMNS, JULY 24–JULY 31, 1864

1. *OR,* 38, pt. 5, pp. 209, 223, 238, 240.

2. Tarrant, *1st Kentucky,* p. 349; Sanford, *14th Illinois,* p. 180; Hinman, *The Sherman Brigade,* p. 888; Record of Events, July–August 1864, Companies E and K, 8th Michigan Cavalry, reel 84, M-594, RG 94; Record of Events, July–August 1864, Companies E and H, 5th Indiana Cavalry, reel 34, M-594, RG 94; Morning Reports, 21 July 1864, Company B, 5th Indiana Cavalry, RG 94; Weir Diary, 19–21 July 1864; Haskell Diary, 18–21 July 1864; Bird, *Memories,* p. 20; *BDH,* 28 July 1864, p. 2; *DDT,* 30 July 1864, p. 1; *DDT,* 4 August 1864, p. 1; Carter, *1st Tennessee,* p. 174; Hall Diary, 15–22 July 1864; Harris Diary, 15–22 July 1864; Winkler Diary, 16–22 July 1864; *EDJ,* 15 August 1864, p. 1; Record of Events, July–August 1864, Companies G, L, and M, 4th Indiana Cavalry, reel 34, M-594, RG 94; Regimental Return, July 1864, 1st Wisconsin Cavalry, reel 197, M-594, RG 94; Record of Events, July–August 1864, Companies G and L, 1st Wisconsin Cavalry, reel 197, M-594, RG 94; Lathrop to "Dear Father and Folks at Home," 20 July 1864, 1 August 1864; Nathan Paine to "My Dear Father," 19 July 1864, Edward L. Paine Family Papers; Swint, ed., "With the First Wisconsin Cavalry 1862–1865 (II): The Letters of Peter J. Williamson," pp. 439–40; Quiner, *The Military History of Wisconsin,* p. 893; Wisconsin Adjutant General, *Annual Report of the Adjutant General of the State of Wisconsin for the Year Ending December 30, 1865,* p. 426; Campbell Diary, 15–22 July 1864; William O. Crouse, "History of the Eighteenth Indiana Battery," pp. 16–17, William O. Crouse Papers; Rowell, *Yankee Artillerymen: Through the Civil War with Eli Lilly's Indiana Battery,* pp. 210–13; *OR,* 38, pt. 2, pp. 488, 761, 767, 782, 789, 791, 801; pt. 5, pp. 137, 145, 154, 160–62, 173–74, 191–92, 196, 206–7, 217–18, 222, 224, 228–29, 901–2.

3. Campbell Diary, 19, 23 July 1864; Speed, Kelly, and Pirtle, *Union Regiments of Kentucky,* pp. 302–10; Muster Rolls, July–August 1864, Companies A-K, 4th Kentucky Mounted Infantry, RG 94; Record of Ordnance and Ordnance Stores, vol. 7, 4th Kentucky Mounted Infantry, RG 156; Lathrop to "Dear Father and Folks at Home," 1 August 1864; Crouse, "18th Indiana Battery," p. 17; *DDT,* 4 August 1864, p. 1 (Lieutenant Henry H. Belfield's account); Winkler Diary, 23 July 1864; Carter, *1st Tennessee,* p. 174; Record of

Events, July–August 1864, Company G, 1st Wisconsin Cavalry, reel 197, M-594, RG 94; Compiled Service Records, RG 94; *OR,* 38, pt. 1, p. 101; pt. 2, pp. 777–78, 782, 793, 795–96; pt. 5, pp. 242, 257–58.

4. Horace Capron, "A Brief Record of the Military Services of General Horace Capron and the 14th Regiment of Illinois Cavalry Volunteers," p. 89a, Horace Capron Papers (microfilm); Tarrant, *1st Kentucky,* p. 349; Record of Events, July–August 1864, Companies D and H, 5th Indiana Cavalry, reel 34, M-594, RG 94; Morning Reports, 22 July 1864, Company 1, 6th Indiana Cavalry, RG 94; Haskell Diary, 22–23 July 1864; Weir Diary, 22–23 July 1864; Stormont, comp., *58th Indiana Infantry,* p. 346; *OR,* 38, pt. 5, pp. 224, 239; Stoneman to Capron, 23 July 1864, Capron Papers; Sanford, *14th Illinois,* pp. 180–81; Hinman, *The Sherman Brigade,* p. 888.

5. Sherman to "Major-General Thomas," 23 July 1864, Sherman to "General Stoneman," 23 July 1864, Letter Book G, Sherman Papers, RG 94; *OR,* 38, pt. 5, pp. 235–37; pt. 2, pp. 875, 878; pt. 5, pp. 235–36; Regimental Return, July 1864, 8th Indiana Cavalry, reel 35, M-594, RG 94; Morning Reports, 23–24 July 1864, Companies D and H, 8th Indiana Cavalry, RG 94; Jackson Diary, 24 July 1864; Oblinger Diary, 23–24 July 1864; Ward Diary, 23–24 July 1864; *HT,* 18 August 1864, p. 1; Regimental Return, July 1864, 5th Iowa Cavalry, reel 51, M-594, RG 94; Morning Reports, 23–24 July 1864, Company C, 5th Iowa Cavalry, RG 94; Iowa Adjutant General, *Report,* p. 1002; *DDT,* 12 August 1864, p. 1; *NT,* 6 June 1889, p. 3; Regimental Return, July 1864, 9th Ohio Cavalry, reel 141, M-594, RG 94; Morning Reports, 23–24 July 1864, Companies C, G, H, and K, 9th Ohio Cavalry, RG 94; Fanning, *Hairbreadth Escapes,* p. 113; *NT,* 10 October 1889, p. 5.

6. Stormont, comp., *58th Indiana Infantry,* p. 347; *OR,* 38, pt. 3, p. 68; pt. 5, p. 242; Morning Reports, 24–25 July 1864, Company I, 6th Indiana Cavalry, RG 94; Haskell Diary, 24 July 1864; Weir Diary, 24 July 1864; Record of Events, July–August 1864, Field and Staff, Companies A, C, D, E, and H, 5th Indiana Cavalry, reel 34, M-594, RG 94; Sanford, *14th Illinois,* p. 184; Record of Events, July–August 1864, Companies G, H, I, and M, 14th Illinois Cavalry, reel 13, M-594, RG 94; Regimental Return, July 1864, 8th Michigan Cavalry, reel 84, M-594, RG 94; Record of Events, July–August 1864, Field and Staff, Companies C, E, H, and K, 8th Michigan Cavalry, reel 84, M-594, RG 94; *NT,* 16 January 1902, p. 3; *PHP,* 17 August 1864, p. 1; Hinman, *The Sherman Brigade,* p. 888; Wells, *"With Touch of Elbow,"* pp. 202–3. There are no recorded temperatures for Atlanta on the night of July 24–25, 1864, but soldiers on both sides mentioned it was unseasonably cold. "I came near freezing after I lay down," wrote Lieutenant Chesley A. Mosman of the 59th Illinois Infantry. "Night very cold," agreed Lieutenant George L. Griscom of the 9th Texas Cavalry, "one blanket failing to keep a man comfortable." See Gates, ed., *The Rough Side of War,* p. 248; Kerr, ed., *Ross' Texas Cavalry,* p. 159.

7. *OR,* 38, pt. 5, p. 250; Silas C. Stevens to E. B. Stevens, 8 February 1905.

8. *OR,* 38, pt. 5, pp. 250–52; "Special Field Orders No. 4, Head Qrs. 2nd Cavalry Division D.C., Decatur, Ga., July 25th 1864," p. 221, vol. 35/74, CCMDM, RG 393; Lemmon Diary, 25 July 1864; McLain Diary, 25 July 1864; Potter Diary, 25 July 1864; *MJPGA,* 20 August 1864, p. 1; Regimental Return, July 1864, 4th Michigan Cavalry, reel 83, M-594, RG 94; James Thomson Diary, 25 July 1864; Morning Reports, 25 July 1864, Company G, 4th Ohio Cavalry, RG 94; Griest Diary, 25 July 1864; Records Diary, 25 July 1864; Kemper Diary, 25 July 1864; Barnard to "Dear Mag," 26 July 1864; Magee, *72nd Indiana,* p. 351; Lester Diary, 25 July 1864; Nourse Diary, 25 July 1864; Sanford, *14th Illinois,* p. 184. In a postwar reminiscence found in the *National Tribune,* 18 October 1900, p. 3, Private Jerome B. Quinn of the 123rd Illinois recalled that about 3:00 P.M. on July 25 his regiment "moved to the extreme right [left] to protect the wagon-bridge that crossed the Chattahoochee close to McAfee, but we found nothing to cause excitement and in the evening were ordered back . . . and . . . arrived at the left of the army about 4 o'clock in the morning." While there may be some truth to Quinn's story, it is highly unlikely the 123rd Illinois made the thirty-six-mile trip from Decatur to Roswell and back in only thirteen hours.

9. *OR,* 38, pt. 5, pp. 251–52.

10. *OR,* 38, pt. 5, pp. 248–50; pt. 3, pp. 68–69; pt. 2, p. 767; Poe Diary, 25–26 July 1864; Orlando M. Poe to "Dear Wife," 25 July 1864, Kossak to Poe, 25 July 1864, Orlando M. Poe Papers; *EDJ,* 15 August 1864, p. 1; Lathrop to "Dear Father and Folks at Home," 1 August 1864; Hall Diary, 24–26 July 1864; Harris Diary, 24–26 July 1864; Winkler Diary, 26 July 1864; Record of Events, July–August 1864, Company G, 4th Indiana Cavalry, reel 34, M-594, RG 94; Campbell Diary, 26 July 1864.

11. "Circular, In the Field Ga., July 25th 1864," p. 42, vol. 24/49, CCMDM, RG 393; "Circular, In the Field Ga., July 25th 1864," p. 43, vol. 24/49, CCMDM, RG 393; *OR,* 38, pt. 1, pp. 75, 116; pt. 5, pp. 255–56, 261.

12. Hall Diary, 26 July 1864; Record of Events, July–August 1864, Company G, 4th Indiana Cavalry, reel 34, M-594, RG 94; *EDJ,* 15 August 1864, p. 1; *NT,* 31 October 1895, p. 3; Lathrop to "Dear Father and Folks at Home," 1 August 1864; *NT,* 25 September 1890, p. 2; Campbell Diary, 26 July 1864; *OR,* 38, pt. 2, pt. 2, p. 767; pt. 5, pp. 911–12; Kerr, ed., *Ross' Texas Cavalry,* pp. 159–60; Compiled Service Records, RG 94; Company Returns, July, August 1864, Companies F, H, and I, 4th Kentucky Mounted Infantry, RG 94; Kentucky Adjutant General, *Report,* 1:656–57, 666–67, 670–71, 674–75.

13. *OR,* 38, pt. 2, p. 878; Regimental Return, July 1864, 8th Indiana Cavalry, reel 35, M-594, RG 94; Morning Reports, 24–26 July 1864, Companies D and H, 8th Indiana Cavalry, RG 94; Jackson Diary, 24–26 July 1864; Oblinger Diary, 24–26 July 1864; Ward Diary, 24–26 July 1864; *HT,* 18 August 1864, p. 1; Regimental Return, July 1864, 5th Iowa Cavalry, reel 51, M-594, RG 94; Morning Reports, 24, 26 July 1864, Company C, 5th Iowa Cavalry, RG 94; Iowa Adjutant General, *Report,* p. 1002; *DDT,* 12 August 1864, p. 1; Healy to "My dear Mother, sisters and brother," 24 July 1864; Lightcap, *The Horrors of Southern Prisons during the War of the Rebellion,* p. 9; Regimental Return, July 1864, 9th Ohio Cavalry, reel 141, M-594, RG 94; Morning Reports, 24–26 July 1864, Companies C, G, H, and K, 9th Ohio Cavalry, RG 94; *DTB,* 2 August 1864, p. 2; Fanning, *Hairbreadth Escapes,* p. 113; Harrison to "Mrs. Harrison," 26 July 1864.

14. *NT,* 18 October 1900, p. 3 (Private Jerome B. Quinn's account); Lester Diary, 26 July 1864; Records Diary, 26 July 1864; "Special Field Orders No. 5, Head Qrs. 2nd Cavalry Division, Near Decatur, Ga., July 26/64," p. 222, vol. 35/74, CCMDM, RG 393; McLain Diary, 26 July 1864; Potter Diary, 26 July 1864; James Vernor to "Dear Mother," 23 August 1864, Vernor Family Correspondence and Papers; Magee, *72nd Indiana,* p. 352; Nourse Diary, 26 July 1864; Lemmon Diary, 26 July 1864; Barnard to "Dear Mag," 26 July 1864.

15. Nourse Diary, 26 July 1864; Silas C. Stevens to E. B. Stevens, 8 February 1905; Griest Diary, 26 July 1864; Potter Diary, 26 July 1864; James Thomson Diary, 26 July 1864.

16. *PHP,* 17 August 1864, p. 1.

17. Haskell Diary, 26 July 1864; *OR,* 38, pt. 1, pp. 75–76; pt. 5, pp. 260–61, 264–65; Butler, "The Stoneman Raid and Why It Was a Failure," pp. 9–10.

18. Dawson, *Life and Services of Gen. John A. Logan,* pp. 71, 514, 517–18; Dodge, "Personal Biography," 1:257–58; *OR,* 38, pt. 5, pp. 240–41, 252–53, 260, 261, 266, 272–73; John A. Logan to "My dear wife," 6 August 1864, John A. Logan Papers; Joseph Hooker to "Mj Gen Logan," 27 July 1864, Logan Papers; Howe, ed., *Home Letters of General Sherman,* p. 303.

19. Howard, *Autobiography,* 2:17–19; Howard, "Battles about Atlanta," p. 396 (quoting Sherman, July 27); Sherman, *Memoirs,* 2:88–89; Garrett, *Atlanta and Environs,* 1:623; Society of the Army of the Tennessee, *26th Meeting,* p. 137 (quoting Sherman, July 28); *AT,* 8 November 1894, p. 1; Connolly, *Three Years in the Army of the Cumberland,* pp. 247–48 (quoting Sherman's reaction to the news Howard was under attack); Manigault, *A Carolinian Goes to War,* pp. 230–36, 263–65; Lewis, *Fighting Prophet,* p. 399 (quoting Logan); *OR,* 38, pt. 3, pp. 40–360 passim, 762–943 passim; pt. 1, p. 78; pt. 5, p. 289; Cox, *Atlanta,* p. 168.

20. *OR,* 38, pt. 5, p. 293.

21. *OR,* 38, pt. 2, pp. 915, 919, 925; Tarrant, *1st Kentucky,* p. 359; Morning Reports, 26 [27] July 1864, Company K, 5th Indiana Cavalry, RG 94; Record of Events, July–August 1864,

Field and Staff, Companies A, C, D, E, F, H, and L, 5th Indiana Cavalry, reel 34, M-594, RG 94; Morning Reports, 27 July 1864, Company I, 6th Indiana Cavalry, RG 94; Haskell Diary, 27 July 1864; Weir Diary, 27 July 1864; Sanford, *14th Illinois*, p. 185; *NT,* 12 September 1895, p. 3; Morning Reports, 27 July 1864, Company G, 14th Illinois Cavalry, RG 94; Record of Events, July-August 1864, Field and Staff, Companies B-M, 14th Illinois Cavalry, reel 13, M-594, RG 94; Regimental Return, July 1864, 14th Illinois Cavalry, reel 13, M-594, RG 94; Wells, *Touch of Elbow,* p. 205; *DFP,* 10 August 1864, p. 3; *DAT,* 12 August 1864, p. 1; Record of Events, July–August 1864, Field and Staff, Companies C, E, F, H, and K, 8th Michigan Cavalry, reel 84, M-594, RG 94; Regimental Return, July 1864, 8th Michigan Cavalry, reel 84, M-594, RG 94; Hinman, *The Sherman Brigade,* p. 890. In *OR,* 38, pt. 2, p. 915, Stoneman's inspector general, Lieutenant Colonel Robert W. Smith, estimated the column's strength at "about 2,104 officers and men," but his calculations did not include Stoneman's escort. Captain R. C. Rankin, writing in *History of the Seventh Ohio Volunteer Cavalry,* pp. 17–18, asserted Stoneman's column had been reinforced by the July 24 arrival of the 7th Ohio Cavalry, but Lieutenant Colonel George G. Miner, the commanding officer, lost his way while returning from Stoneman's headquarters on the night of July 26–27 and did not rejoin his regiment until it was too late to overtake the expedition. Rankin repeated this charge in the *National Tribune,* 16 November 1893, p. 1, adding that Miner was placed under arrest, but his story withers under close scrutiny. Miner's commanding officer, Colonel Israel Garrard, reported in *OR,* 38, pt. 2, p. 923, "the advance regiment of my brigade, marching from the outfitting camp in Kentucky, reached our lines near Atlanta on the 27th of July, too late to move with the expedition under Major-General Stoneman." A member of Garrard's staff corroborated this in a letter to the *Ohio State Journal,* 11 August 1864, p. 2, when he noted, "We (Colonel G. and myself) arrived here on the night of the 26th inst. The command did not reach the front till the day after."

22. Unless otherwise noted, the narrative describing Garrard's division from July 27 to July 31 is based on the following sources: *OR,* 38, pt. 2, pp. 804, 813, 843, 846, 848, 854; Hosea, "Side Lights on the War," p. 41; Vale, *Minty and the Cavalry,* pp. 326–28; *NT,* 31 May 1894, p. 2; Heber S. Thompson Diary, 27–31 July 1864; Lemmon Diary, 27–31 July, 1 August 1864; McLain Diary, 27–31 July 1864; Potter Diary, 27–31 July 1864; Potter to "Dear Father," 1 August 1864; Vernor to "Dear Mother," 23 August 1864; Regimental Return, July 1864, 4th Michigan Cavalry, reel 83, M-594, RG 94; Robertson, comp., *Michigan in the War,* p. 666; Lanman, *The Red Book of Michigan,* p. 279; *MJPGA,* 20 August 1864, p. 3; Sipes, *7th Pennsylvania,* p. 116; Record of Events, July–August 1864, Muster Roll, Company E, 4th U.S. Cavalry, RG 94; Larson, *Sergeant Larson,* pp. 267–68; *MDS,* 12 August 1864, p. 1; *SCR,* 20 August 1864, p. 2; Crofts, comp., *3rd Ohio,* pp. 158–59; James Thomson Diary, 27–31 July 1864; Morning Reports, 27–31 July 1864, Company G, 4th Ohio Cavalry, RG 94; Reid, *Ohio in the War,* 2:774; Griest Diary, 27–31 July 1864; Barnard to "My Dear Wife," 1 August 1864; Remley to "Dear Parents, Brothers and Sister," 1 August 1864; *NT,* 8 October 1891, p. 3; Magee, *72nd Indiana,* pp. 352–57; Kemper Diary, 27–31 July 1864; *EDJ,* 16 August 1864, p. 1; Doyle, *17th Indiana,* p. 21; *NT,* 30 May 1895, p. 3; *AT,* 16 December 1897, p. 6; *NT,* 18 October 1900, p. 3; Lester Diary, 27–31 July 1864; Nourse Diary, 27–31 July 1864; Fleming to "My Dear Parents," 3 August 1864; Silas C. Stevens to E. B. Stevens, 8 February 1905.

23. *AT,* 14 April 1898, p. 6; McLain Diary, 27 July 1864; Sanford, *14th Illinois,* p. 185; Weir Diary, 27 July 1864; *IDJ,* 16 August 1864, p. 2; *OR,* 38, pt. 2, p. 915; Haskell Diary, 27 July 1864; Hitchcock, *Marching with Sherman,* p. 60; John N. Swift vs. the U.S., Case Number 11,371, RG 123.

24. *OR,* 38, pt. 3, p. 957; pt. 5, pp. 257–58, 316; *OSJ,* 11 August 1864, p. 2.

25. John N. Swift vs. the U.S., Case Number 11,371, RG 123; *OR,* 38, pt. 5, pp. 308, 310, 314; Weir Diary, 27 July 1864; Sanford, *14th Illinois,* p. 185; *OR,* 39, pt. 1, p. 663; "Rebel Prisoners of War," vol. 50/108, CCMDM, RG 393.

26. *ASB,* 10 August 1864, p. 2; Dodson, ed., *Wheeler and His Cavalry,* pp. 217–19; Garrett, *Atlanta and Environs,* 1:625; *ADI,* 21 August 1864, p. 2; Mims, comp., *War History of the Prattville Dragoons,* p. 13; *OR,* 38, pt. 3, p. 953; pt. 5, pp. 267–68, 348, 910, 913–14, 916.

27. *OR,* 38, pt. 3, pp. 614–15, 642, 646, 676, 680, 943–44, 957; pt. 2, p. 915; pt. 5, pp. 257–58, 316, 319; pt. 4, pp. 782, 791; *OR,* 39, pt. 2, p. 610; Hood, *Advance and Retreat,* pp. 74–75; Photocopy of Numerical Returns of Wheeler's Cavalry Corps, January 1864–April 20, 1865, Author's Collection; "Statements Made by Prisoners of War, Scouts, CSA Deserters, May-August 1864," p. 18, vol. 178/249, DMT, RG 393.

28. Evans, ed., *CMH,* vol. 7: *Georgia,* p. 478; vol. 8: *Alabama,* pp. 255, 275, 289; Brewer, *Alabama,* p. 678; Lindsley, ed., *Military Annals of Tennessee,* p. 684; Robinson, *Civil War Diary of Capt. William J. Robinson,* p. 43; *ADA,* 22 May 1864, p. 1; *ADA,* 24 May 1864, p. 1; *ADA,* 28 May 1864, p. 1; *ADA,* 2 June 1864, p. 1; *SR,* 3 August 1864, p. 2; "Special Field Orders No. 35, Head Quarters Army Tenn., In the Field July 2, 1864," William T. Martin Papers; Dyer, *Reminiscences; or Four Years in the Confederate Army,* p. 193; *ASB,* 10 August 1864, p. 2; John T. Morgan to Joseph Wheeler, 28 August 1871, William T. Martin to John T. Morgan, 31 August 1871, copies with covering letter in Joseph Wheeler Papers; John T. Morgan to Isaac W. Avery, 8 June 1864, 20 July 1864, 20 July 1864, 3 August 1864, Isaac W. Avery Letters and Papers; "Answers to Interrogatories in the Case of John T. Morgan Brig. Genl. for Drunkeness July 28, 1864," Avery Letters and Papers; Cash and Howorth, eds., *My Dear Nellie: The Civil War Letters of William L. Nugent to Eleanor Smith Nugent,* pp. 190–91, 204–6, 209–10, 217; *OR,* 38, pt. 2, pp. 806, 828; pt. 5, pp. 877, 893; *OR,* 47, pt. 2, pp. 1004, 1012–13, 1027–28. Casualties among regimental commanders included Lt. Col. William E. DeMoss, 9th Tennessee Cavalry, captured May 13; Colonel Richard Gordon Earle, 2nd Alabama Cavalry, killed May 18; Colonel Isaac W. Avery, 4th Georgia Cavalry, wounded May 25; Lt. Col. J. L. Harris, 2nd Mississippi Cavalry, mortally wounded May 28; Colonel John T. Ballentine, Ballentine's Regiment, wounded May 1864; Colonel James C. Malone, Jr., 7th Alabama Cavalry, wounded June 20; Colonel P. H. Rice, 3rd Confederate Cavalry, wounded in Georgia; Colonel Robert Thompson, 3rd Georgia Cavalry, wounded July 3; Lt. Col. James Strickland, 1st Georgia Cavalry, mortally wounded July 21; Colonel John R. Hart, 6th Georgia Cavalry, wounded July 21.

29. *OR,* 38, pt. 3, pp. 951–53; pt. 5, pp. 885–86, 889–90, 892–902, 905, 910–11, 914; Ash Diary, 26–27 July 1864; Jordan Diary, 26–28 July 1864; Cash and Howorth, eds., *My Dear Nellie,* p. 189; Dodson, ed., *Wheeler and His Cavalry,* pp. 219–20; *ASB,* 10 August 1864, p. 2; *ADI,* 21 August 1864, p. 2.

30. *Synopsis of the Military Career of Gen. Joseph Wheeler,* p. 43, Dodson, ed., *Wheeler and His Cavalry,* pp. 220–21; *OR,* 38, pt. 3, p. 953; pt. 5, pp. 914–15. In what appears to be a rough draft of Dodson's book, Wheeler asserted in "Reports Made by Myself of [the] Battles of Murfreesboro and Perryville and also July and August 1864," Wheeler Papers, that he received Shoup's message late in the morning or early in the afternoon of July 28, after it had been "following me for thirty miles." This seems strange, because it was barely sixteen miles from Hood's headquarters to Flat Shoals. A copy of this message, in the Wheeler Papers, which apparently served as the source for the text in the *Official Records,* offers no clues as to when Wheeler received it, but in a little pamphlet entitled *Synopsis of the Military Career of Gen. Joseph Wheeler,* p. 43, a staff officer said Wheeler received Shoup's message "while en route" to Flat Shoals. This seems to be correct, since the orders Wheeler gave dispatching Alfred Iverson toward McDonough coincided exactly with Shoup's instructions.

31. Wheeler, "Reports"; Dodson, ed., *Wheeler and His Cavalry,* p. 220; *ADI,* 21 August 1864, p. 2; *OR,* 38, pt. 3, p. 953 (Wheeler's orders to Iverson); Iverson to Major E. S. Burford, 28 July 1864, Alfred Iverson, Jr., Papers; Ash Diary, 28 July, 1864; Jordan Diary, 28 July 1864.

32. *MDS,* 12 August 1864, p. 1. In a postwar account in the *National Tribune,* 18 October 1900, p. 3, Private Jerome B. Quinn credited a similar statement to Lieutenant Colonel Jonathan Biggs of the 123rd Illinois Mounted Infantry.

33. *CPR,* 7 September 1864, p. 1; Larson, *Sergeant Larson,* pp. 267–68.

34. Magee, *72nd Indiana,* pp. 355–56.

35. *NT,* 18 October 1900, p. 3.

36. John N. Swift vs. the U.S., Case Number 11,371, RG 123; Marvin H. Wesley vs. the

U.S., Case Number 5,174, RG 123; John A. Powell, Case Number 3,768, RG 233; Abner Turner, Case Number 9,167, RG 233.

37. "List of Casualties in the 2d Brigade 2d Division Cavalry," pp. 66–67, vol. 57/140, CCMDM, RG 393; Hospital Register, Cavalry Corps Army of the Cumberland, May 10–November 30, 1864, Register 730, p. 18, RG 94; Compiled Service Records, RG 94; Illinois Adjutant General, *Report,* 6:408; Quartermaster General's Office, *Roll of Honor,* 23:20.

38. *AT,* 16 December 1897, p. 6.

39. Compiled Service Records, RG 94; Quartermaster General's Office, *Roll of Honor,* 23:60; Hospital Register, Cavalry Corps Army of the Cumberland, May 10–November 30, 1864, Register 730, p. 18, RG 94; Morning Reports, 28 July 1864, Company L, 4th Ohio Cavalry, RG 94; "List of Casualties in the 2d Brigade 2d Division Cavalry," pp. 66–67, vol. 57/140, CCMDM, RG 393; Pension Records, RG 15; Indiana Adjutant General, *Report,* 6:163; 8:612; Illinois Adjutant General, *Report,* 6:408; Ohio Roster Commission, *Official Roster,* 11:197, 200, 229; Bates, *History of Pennsylvania Volunteers,* 2:1161, 1163; Sipes, *7th Pennsylvania,* p. 116.

40. *OR,* 38, pt. 5, p. 310.

12. McCOOK'S RAID: TURNER'S FERRY TO FLINT RIVER, JULY 27–JULY 29, 1864

1. Fanning, *Hairbreadth Escapes,* p. 113; Hall Diary, 25–27 July 1864; Harris Diary, 27 July 1864; Winkler Diary, 27 July 1864; *EDJ,* 15 August 1864, p. 1; *AT,* 26 January 1893, p. 2; *AT,* 14 April 1898, p. 6; Lathrop to "Dear Father and Folks at Home," 1 August 1864; *JDG,* 18 August 1864, p. 2; *NT,* 25 April 1889, p. 4; Monlux, *To My Comrades of Company "I" Eighth Iowa Cavalry,* p. 40; Vaughter, *Prison Life in Dixie,* p. 14; Campbell Diary, 27 July 1864; *OR,* 38, pt. 2, pp. 769, 774, 776, 782, 789, 791; pt. 3, p. 69; pt. 1, pp. 101, 116; pt. 5, pp. 257–58; Tri-Monthly Report, 20 July 1864, 2nd Indiana Cavalry Papers, RG 94; Tri-Monthly Report, 20 July 1864, 4th Indiana Cavalry Papers, RG 94; "Report of Effective Force 4th Indiana Cavalry July 17th 1864, 4th Indiana Cavalry Papers, RG 94; Paine to "Dear Father," 19 July 1864; "Weekly Report of Effective Force of the 18th Indiana Battery," 2 August 1864, 18th Indiana Battery Papers, RG 94.

2. Jackson Diary, 26–27 July 1864; Fanning, *Hairbreadth Escapes,* p. 113; Morning Reports, 26 July 1864, Company C, 5th Iowa Cavalry, RG 94; Ward Diary, 27 July 1864; *HT,* 18 August 1864, p. 1; *NT,* 24 May 1894, p. 3; Oblinger Diary, 26–27 July 1864; Morning Reports, 27 July 1864, Company D, 8th Indiana Cavalry, RG 94; Regimental Return, July 1864, 9th Ohio Cavalry, reel 141, M-594, RG 94; Morning Reports, 27 July 1864, Companies C and G, 9th Ohio Cavalry, RG 94; Iowa Adjutant General, *Report,* p. 1002; Hamilton, *Recollections,* pp. 140–41; Sherman to "Dearest Ellen," 26 July 1864, Sherman Family Papers; *OR,* 38, pt. 5, p. 260; pt. 2, pp. 875, 878; *DZC,* 20 August 1864, p. 2; *DDT,* 12 August 1864, p. 1; Eckel, *4th Tennessee,* p. 59; Eckel, "The Rousseau and Mc-Cook Raids," p. 8. Lieutenant William T. Hays, writing in Iowa Adjutant General, *Report,* p. 1002, stated that on the night of July 26, the 5th Iowa Cavalry "marched up the river some six miles, crossed on a pontoon, and proceeded to Gen. McCook's head-quarters near Burnt Church, where they received orders to proceed to Vining's station to draw three days' rations for another raid." None of the other accounts or surviving documents mention such a side trip across the Chattahoochee and this author believes Hays's intinerary is simply incorrect.

3. *NT,* 24 May 1894, p. 3; Campbell Diary, 27 July 1864; *NYH,* 11 August 1864, p. 1; *OR,* 38, pt. 2, pp. 769, 774–75, 782, 875; pt. 3, pp. 69, 965; pt. 5, pp. 261, 274; *AT,* 14 April 1898, p. 4; West, "McCook's Raid in the Rear of Atlanta and Hood's Army," p. 547.

4. Warner, *Generals in Blue,* p. 297; *DAB,* 1928 ed., s.v. "Edward Moody McCook," by Charles Dudley Rhodes; Gower, "Kansas Territory and the Pike's Peak Gold Rush," p. 311;

Edwards, "A Pedigreed Smith and Wesson," p. 142; Leech, *Reveille in Washington,* pp. 58–59; "The Soldiers of Kansas: The Frontier Guard at the White House, Washington, 1861," pp. 418–21; Dary, "Lincoln's Frontier Guard," pp. 12–14; Suppiger, "'In Defense of Washington,'" pp. 38–45; Powell, comp., *List of Officers,* pp. 463–64; Indiana Adjutant General, *Report,* 2:400–401; *OR,* 10, pt. 1, 354; *OR,* 16, pt. 1, pp. 1028, 1030; pt. 2, p. 596; *OR,* 23, pt. 2, pp. 580, 588; *OR,* 30, pt. 1, pp. 46, 894–97; *OR,* 32, pt. 2, p. 276; *OR,* series III, vol. 3, pp. 249–50 (McCook to Stanton); U.S. War Department, *U.S. Department of War, Adjutant General's Office, General Orders, 1864,* 3:General Orders Number 256, p. 58; Basler, ed., *Collected Works of Lincoln,* 7:311n; *OR,* 38, pt. 4, pp. 456–57, 470, 575 (quoting McCook); Wilson, *Under the Old Flag,* 2:168.

5. West, "McCook's Raid," p. 548; Campbell Diary, 27 July 1864; Monlux, *To My Comrades,* p. 40; Vaughter, *Prison Life,* p. 14; *NT,* 25 April 1889, p. 4; *NT,* 24 May 1894, p. 3; Lathrop to "Dear Father and Folks at Home," 1 August 1864; *OR,* 38, pt. 2, p. 769; pt. 5, p. 274. One reason for the increased Confederate presence at Campbellton may have been Kelly's and Ferguson's intention, described in chap. 11, to lay their own pontoon bridge there earlier on July 27.

6. In *OR,* 38, pt. 2, p. 769, Croxton said his men captured "a Rebel scout" on the west bank of the river at Smith's Ferry. However, Sergeant John Vaughter, apparently a member of the advance guard, wrote in *Prison Life in Dixie,* p. 15:

> Two [Confederate] companies were stationed at this point, and they had a picket-post on our side of the river; four men and an officer were on guard, but thinking the Yanks were far away they had set their guns against a tree, built a little fire to smoke off the mosquitoes, and were quietly snoozing when our scouts crept up, moved the guns from the tree, and then, with their own guns cocked and ready, waked up the pickets and told them to keep very quiet, as we wished to cross the river without disturbing any one.

Vaughter also remembered two pontoons were used to ferry the 4th Kentucky across the river, while Croxton emphasized there was only one. An account by correspondent David P. Conyngham in the *New York Herald,* 11 August 1864, p. 1, said the regiment crossed in "skiffs and rafts."

7. According to the *Atlanta Journal,* 9 November 1901, 2nd section, p. 2, the Confederate pickets at Campbellton were a battalion of Georgia militia commanded by Major William A. Turner.

8. *OR,* 38, pt. 3, p. 69; pt. 2, pp. 769, 774–76, 782, 786, 789–90, 791, 802, 875; pt. 5, pp. 274, 309, 324; *NT,* 5 August 1926, p. 5; Hall Diary, 27–28 July 1864; Harris Diary, 28 July 1864; Winkler Diary, 28 July 1864; *CDC,* 9 August 1864, p. 1; *EDJ,* 15 August 1864, p. 1; *NT,* 31 October 1895, p. 3; *AT,* 14 April 1898, p. 6; Lathrop to "Dear Father and Folks at Home," 1 August 1864; *JDG,* 18 August 1864, p. 2; *WF,* 23 August 1864, p. 1; Iowa Adjutant General, *Roster and Record,* 4:1513; Daniel C. Bishard, "A [*sic*] Abstract of My Life," p. [5], Daniel C. Bishard Papers; Monlux, *To My Comrades,* p. 40; Vaughter, *Prison Life,* pp. 14–15; West, "McCook's Raid," p. 548; *NT,* 16 January 1890, p. 3; *AT,* 26 January 1893, p. 2; Campbell Diary, 27 [28] July 1864; Crouse, "18th Indiana Battery," p. 17; Oblinger Diary, 27–28 July 1864; Ward Diary, 28 July 1864; *NT,* 24 May 1894, p. 3; Morning Reports, 28 July 1864, Company D, 8th Indiana Cavalry, RG 94; Lightcap, *Southern Prisons,* p. 9; Iowa Adjutant General, *Report,* pp. 1002–3; *DZC,* 20 August 1864, p. 2; Hamilton, *Recollections,* p. 141; Fanning, *Hairbreadth Escapes,* p. 115; Morning Reports, 28 July 1864, Companies H and K, 9th Ohio Cavalry, RG 94; Regimental Return, August 1864, 9th Ohio Cavalry, reel 141, M-594, RG 94; *NT,* 10 October 1889, p. 5; Eckel, *4th Tennessee,* p. 59; Eckel, "The Rousseau and McCook Raids," p. 8.

9. *OR,* 38, pt. 2, pp. 782–83, 786, 791–92; pt. 5, p. 309; Record of Events, July–August 1864, Companies G, I, and L, 1st Wisconsin Cavalry, reel 197, M-594, RG 94; Regimental

Return, July 1864, 1st Wisconsin Cavalry, reel 197, M-594, RG 94; *JDG,* 18 August 1864, p. 2; Quiner, *Military History of Wisconsin,* pp. 891–93; Love, *Wisconsin in the War,* pp. 738–41 (quoting McCook), 880; Wisconsin Adjutant General, *Report,* p. 426; Wisconsin Adjutant General, *Roster of Wisconsin Volunteers, War of the Rebellion,* 1:1, 25; *RWC,* 3 June 1864, p. 1; Lathrop to "Dear Father and Folks at Home," 1 August 1864; *EDJ,* 15 August 1864, p. 1; *WF,* 23 August 1864, p. 1; *WSJ,* 13 August 1864, p. 1; *WSJ,* 2 September 1864, p. 2; *WSJ,* 21 September 1864, p. 2; *NT,* 1 June 1899, p. 3.

10. Sparks, *The War between the States, as I Saw It,* p. 75; Evans, ed., *CMH,* vol. 10: *Tennessee,* p. 316; *DAB,* 1928 ed., s.v., "William Hicks Jackson," by Samuel C. Williams; Warner, *Generals in Gray,* pp. 152–53; Cullum, *Biographical Register,* 2:666–67; Maury, *Recollections of a Virginian,* p. 124; "Gen. William H. Jackson," p. 176.

11. Sykes, "Error in the Harris-Adair Article," p. 454; *OR,* 38, pt. 3, pp. 767, 963; pt. 5, pp. 309, 914, 922–23, 927 (Shoup-Jackson correspondence); William E. Sloane Diary, 28 July 1864; Bigger Diary, 28 July 1864; Dixon Diary, 29 July 1864; Dixon, "Recollections of a Rebel Private," p. 148; Kerr, ed., *Ross' Texas Cavalry,* p. 160; Barron, "Wheeler's Cavalry in Georgia Campaign," p. 70; William Gibbs Allen, "War Reminiscence," The Confederate Collection; Witt, "After M'Cook's Raid Below Atlanta," p. 115; Quiner, *Military History of Wisconsin,* p. 893; Love, *Wisconsin in the War,* pp. 740–41; I. N. Rainey, "Experiences of I. N. Rainey in the Confederate Army," p. 72 (quoting Paine), Civil War Collection; *WSJ,* 2 September 1864, p. 2; Fanning, *Hairbreadth Escapes,* p. 115.

12. Unless otherwise noted, the narrative describing the eastward march of McCook's column on July 28 and 29 is based on the following sources: *OR,* 38, pt. 2, pp. 761–63, 769–70, 774–76, 782–83, 785–86, 790, 875, 878; *NYH,* 11 August 1864, p. 1; *NYT,* 31 August 1864, p. 5; *NT,* 5 August 1926, p. 5 (Sergeant Barnes Hutson's account); Hall Diary, 28–29 July 1864; Harris Diary, 28–29 July 1864; Winkler Diary, 28–29 July 1864; *CDC,* 9 August 1864, p. 1 (Major George H. Purdy's account); *EDJ,* 15 August 1864, p. 1; *NT,* 31 October 1895, p. 3 (Sergeant L. M. Dickerson's account); *AT,* 14 April 1898, p. 6 (Sergeant Thomas A. Reed's account); Record of Events, July–August 1864, Companies G, L, and M, 4th Indiana Cavalry, reel 34, M-594, RG 94; *WF,* 23 August 1864, p. 1; *WSJ,* 2 September 1864, p. 2; *NT,* 25 September 1890, p. 2 (Sergeant John Farnsworth's account); *DDT,* 21 October 1864, p. 2; *NT,* 31 May 1883, p. 7; *NT,* 25 April 1889, p. 4; *NT,* 2 April 1891, p. 4; Belfield, "My Sixty Days in Hades," p. 449; Bishard, "Abstract of My Life," pp. [5–6]; Monlux, *To My Comrades,* p. 41; Iowa Adjutant General, *Roster and Record,* 4:1513–14; Vaughter, *Prison Life,* pp. 17–20 (quoting Negro woman); *NT,* 16 January 1890, p. 3; *AT,* 26 January 1893, p. 2 (Private A. J. Tharp's account); West, "McCook's Raid," pp. 548–50; *NT,* 26 May 1892, p. 1 (Captain Moses Wiley's account); *NT,* 2 September 1909, p. 7; Carter, *1st Tennessee,* pp. 177–79; Crouse, "18th Indiana Battery," pp. 17–18; Jackson Diary, 27 [28]–28 [29] July 1864; Oblinger Diary, 28–29 July 1864; Ward Diary, 28–29 July 1864; *HT,* 18 August 1864, p. 1; *NT,* 6 June 1889, p. 3 (Private Samson L. Ward's account); *NT,* 24 May 1894, p. 3; Morning Reports, 28–29 July 1864, Company D, 8th Indiana Cavalry, RG 94; *DDT,* 12 August 1864, p. 1 (Private Oscar Reese's account); Lightcap, *Southern Prisons,* pp. 10–11 ("Five Miles to Hell"); Morning Reports, 28–29 July 1864, Company C, 5th Iowa Cavalry, RG 94; Iowa Adjutant General, *Report,* p. 1003; Eckel, *4th Tennessee,* pp. 59–60; Eckel, "The Rousseau and McCook Raids," pp. 8–9; *NT,* 26 December 1889, p. 3; Record of Events, July–August 1864, Companies B, C, G, I, and K, 4th Tennessee Cavalry, reel 188, M-594, RG 94; Regimental Return, August 1864, 4th Tennessee Cavalry, reel 188, M-594, RG 94.

13. Wisconsin Adjutant General, *Roster,* 1:1; Lathrop to "Dear Father and Folks at Home," 22 May 1864; *NT,* 1 June 1899, p. 3; *NT,* 19 April 1900, p. 3; J. George Moore, "Biography of Our Grandfather—James George Moore," pp. 31–32, 63–64, James George Moore Papers.

14. *MDT,* 4 August 1864, p. 1; *Atlanta Journal,* 9 November 1901, 2nd section, p. 2; Arthur Hutcheson, administrator of John Carleton, vs. the U.S., Case Number 8,067, RG 123.

15. *AT,* 14 April 1898, p. 6 (quoting sleepy teamster); *WF,* 23 August 1864, p. 1 (quoting the grumpy Rebel officer); Dupree, *The War-Time Letters of Captain T. C. Dupree,* p. [20].

16. Andrew J. McBride to "Dear Fannie," 4 August 1864, Andrew J. McBride Papers; *Atlanta Journal,* 16 February 1901, 2nd section, p. 6.

17. Wilson, *Reminiscences of Thomas B. Wilson,* p. 30; *CDC,* 6 August 1864, pp. 1, 2.

18. Brownlow said the horse belonged to General Lowrey; however, Lieutenant William Berryhill of the 43rd Mississippi Infantry noted the raiders "captured Gen. [William W.] Loring's fine horse." See *BKWRV,* 10 August 1864, p. 2; Jones and Martin, eds., *The Gentle Rebel: The Civil War Letters of 1st Lt. William Harvey Berryhill,* p. 64.

19. *ACS,* 6 August 1864, p. 1; *CT,* 8 August 1864, p. 1; Sykes, "Error in the Harris-Adair Article," p. 454; Evans, ed., *CMH,* vol. 10: *Tennessee,* p. 386; *Atlanta Journal,* 24 August 1901, 2nd section, p. 2; *Atlanta Journal,* 16 February 1901, 2nd section, p. 6 (Andrew J. McBride's account). Oral tradition in Fayetteville credits Tidwell with hanging a large Confederate flag out of his window just as McCook's men were about to set fire to the courthouse. Promptly arrested, he so distracted his captors they forgot about burning the building. Just how much truth there is to this story is hard to say, but the *Official Records* credit McCook's 1st Cavalry Division with capturing a flag on July 29 bearing the inscription "Our Country Our Rights," and Fayetteville today boasts the oldest courthouse in the state of Georgia. See *OR,* 38, pt. 1, p. 172; Fayette County Historical Society, *The History of Fayette County,* pp. 42–43, 386.

20. On July 27, Braxton Bragg had complained to President Davis that Hood's army was encumbered with "more than 1,000 wagons and 5,000 mules in excess of the number allowed by General Johnston's orders." McCook apparently solved that problem in a single morning, reporting his men burned 1,160 Confederate wagons and destroyed or disabled 2,000 mules. Confederate newspapers gave a much more conservative estimate, putting the total number of destroyed wagons at only fifty to a hundred. See *OR,* 52, pt. 2, pp. 712–14; *OR,* 38, pt. 2, p. 762; *ACS,* 2 August 1864, p. 3; *CDS,* 31 July 1864, p. 2; *CDE,* 31 July 1864, p. 2; *CT,* 11 August 1864, p. 1; *ECN,* 3 August 1864, p. 2; *MDT,* 2 August 1864, p. 2; *SR,* 30 July 1864, p. 2.

21. Mrs. W. B. Stewart, "Some Reminiscences as Told by Mrs. W. B. Stewart to Mrs. A. J. Woodruff and Mrs. A. L. Wade," UDC 9:96–97; Fayette County Historical Society, *Fayette County,* p. 389.

22. These are Southern figures, cited in *ACS,* 2 August 1864, p. 3. McCook calculated he destroyed two and a half miles of track at Lovejoy. Most other Union accounts put the amount at two to six miles. See *OR,* 38, pt. 2, pp. 761–62; Regimental Return, July 1864; 8th Indiana Cavalry, reel 35, M-594, RG 94; Ward Diary, 29 July 1864; Winkler Diary, 29 July 1864; *CDC,* 9 August 1864, p. 1; *EDJ,* 15 August 1864, p. 1; *NYH,* 11 August 1864, p. 1.

23. Stephen G. Dorsey vs. the U.S., Case Number 119, RG 123. Carter, in *1st Tennessee,* p. 179, and Eckel, in *4th Tennessee,* p. 60, said at times the raiders had to quit work on the railroad and take up arms to repel Rebel skirmishers. None of the other sources mention any fighting during the halt at Lovejoy's Station. Similarly, Sergeant George K. Dolsen of the 8th Iowa, writing in the *National Tribune,* 31 May 1883, p. 7, claimed to have heard "the guns of Stoneman's men pounding away," but neither Stoneman's nor Garrard's artillery was in action on July 29.

24. *NT,* 1 June 1899, p. 3; *WSJ,* 2 September 1864, p. 2 (quoting Torrey). "His [McCook's] long delay at Lovejoy was not understood," Sergeant Henry M. Reed wrote in the *National Tribune,* 16 January 1890, p. 3. "It appeared suicidal. We knew nothing of the intended junction with Stoneman at that point. Some declared that McCook had imbibed too freely of the applejack we had secured in the wagon train, and that he was too drunk to realize his condition." Reed, however, wrote with the benefit of hindsight. Contemporary accounts give the unmistakable impression McCook's troopers welcomed a few hours' rest at Lovejoy's Station.

25. Postwar accounts by several veterans (including Barron, "Wheeler's Cavalry in Georgia," p. 70; Love, "Sharing Credit with General Wheeler," p. 343; Witt, "After M'Cook's Raid," p. 115; and Keen, *Living & Fighting with the Texas 6th Cavalry,* p. 64) claimed Jackson started after McCook about 9:00 P.M., July 28, and "marched all night." All the eyewitness wartime accounts indicate Jackson's column did not march until daylight, July 29.

26. Kerr, ed., *Ross' Texas Cavalry,* pp. 160–61; George Scott Milam Diary, 29 July 1864, McKinney Family Papers; *OR,* 38, pt. 3, p. 963 (Sul Ross quotation); Witt, "After M'Cook's Raid," p. 115.

27. In *OR,* 38, pt. 3, pp. 963–64, Ross asserted Jones's regiment had neither sabers nor revolvers, but Lieutenant George L. Griscom's diary contradicts the general and clearly states the 9th Texas charged "in a column of fours with pistols." See Kerr, ed., *Ross' Texas Cavalry,* p. 161.

28. Realizing he had been cut off, Lieutenant Swoope moved his company about two miles to the left, taking refuge on the crest of a wooded hill. After an anxious night of waiting, daylight revealed a heavy line of Rebel infantry advancing toward the Kentuckians. "What do you think of the situation, lieutenant?" asked Private James M. Burke. "If we had a hundred round[s] of ammunition," Swoope replied, "we would go out of this or take a few of the Johnnies with us to the happy hunting ground. As it is boys, I'm afraid there is nothing to do but to surrender." Swoope and thirty-four of his men surrendered to Brigadier General Joseph H. Lewis's Kentucky brigade, which had been sent down by train from Atlanta. Private Burke found many old acquaintances in Lewis's 4th Kentucky Infantry. "They treated me kindly," he wrote, "sharing their scanty rations with me, and doing all in their power for my comfort." Lieutenant Swoope, on the other hand, complained, "My hat was taken from my head by Lieut. Wickliff of the 9th Ky. Rebel Infty. The men of my company were robbed of their hats[,] overcoats[,] blankets[,] canteens[,] haversacks[,] money & pocketbooks. We were taken to Jonesboro & confined in a large brick building with nothing to eat for two days except what the men could buy with money they had sold their boots for." Captain Henry P. Merrill and Company H of the 4th Kentucky Mounted Infantry suffered a similar fate. After hiding their horses in some thick woods, they were apparently trying to make their way to the Federal lines on foot when they were confronted by some of Harvey's Scouts near Lovejoy's Station on July 31. Before the Kentuckians could offer any resistance, Lieutenant George Harvey boldly rode up to Captain Merrill and told him he was surrounded; if he did not surrender at once, his men could expect no quarter. Merrill meekly handed over his saber and ordered his men to stack arms, only to discover, to his utter mortification, Harvey had only seven men. After forcing one of the Yankees to show him where they had left their horses, Harvey marched back to the railroad and turned his prisoners over to General Lewis, having captured fifty-two Federals, fifty-two horses, forty-two Spencer rifles, and several pistols. To add insult to injury, Captain Merrill was robbed of his hat, watch, and money while talking with General Lewis. See *NT,* 24 June 1882, p. 8; Charles T. Swoope, Company D, 4th Kentucky Mounted Infantry, Compiled Service Records, RG 94; Morning Reports, 31 July 1864, Company H, 4th Kentucky Mounted Infantry, RG 94; Monthly Returns, July and August 1864, Company H, 4th Kentucky Mounted Infantry, RG 94; *MDT,* 2 October 1864, p. 2; Wiley Nash, "Harvey's Scouts," J. F. H. Claiborne Papers.

29. Union sources for the fighting on the Panhandle Road: *AT,* 14 April 1898, p. 6; *NT,* 16 January 1890, p. 3; *OR,* 38, pt. 2, pp. 763, 770 (Croxton's report), 774–76, 778–79, 783, 786, 790, 875, 878; Stuart, *Iowa Colonels and Regiments,* p. 639; Iowa Adjutant General, *Roster and Record,* 4:1514, 1523, 1541, 1544, 1573; Compiled Service Records, RG 94; *DDT,* 21 October 1864, p. 2 (Lieutenant Henry Belfield's account); *BDH,* 1 October 1864, p. 2; Belfield, "Sixty Days in Hades," p. 452; *NT,* 2 April 1891, p. 4; Bird, *Memories,* p. 22; *NT,* 25 April 1889, p. 4; *NT,* 27 September 1928, p. 5; Mead, *The Eighth Iowa Cavalry in the Civil War,* p. 13; Record of Ordnance and Ordnance Stores, vol. 7, 4th Kentucky Mounted Infantry, RG 156; West, "McCook's Raid," pp. 551–52; Harris Diary, 29 July 1864; Hall Diary, 29 July 1864; Winkler Diary, 29 July 1864; *EDJ,* 15 August 1864, p. 1; *NT,* 31 October 1895, p. 3

(Sergeant L. M. Dickerson's account); Vaughter, *Prison Life,* p. 20; *NT,* 24 June 1882, p. 8; Carter, *1st Tennessee,* pp. 179–80; Indiana Adjutant General, *Report,* 6:263, 8:624; Iowa Adjutant General, *Report,* p. 1003; *DDT,* 12 August 1864, p. 1; *DDT,* 15 August 1864, p. 4; Jackson Diary, 28 [29] July 1864; *HT,* 18 August 1864, p. 1; *NT,* 26 May 1892, p. 2 (Captain Moses Wiley's account). Confederate sources: *OR,* 38, pt. 3, pp. 963–64; Witt, "After M'Cook's Raid," p. 115; Rose, *Ross' Texas Brigade,* p. 149; Kerr, ed., *Ross' Texas Cavalry,* p. 161; Sparks, *War between the States,* pp. 66–68.

13. McCOOK'S RAID: FLINT RIVER TO NEWNAN, JULY 29–JULY 30, 1864

1. Wheeler, "Reports"; Dodson, ed., *Wheeler and His Cavalry,* pp. 220–23; *ADI,* 21 August 1864, p. 2; *OR,* 38, pt. 3, pp. 953–54; pt. 5, pp. 921–22; *CDS,* 9 August 1864, p. 2; Ash Diary, 26–29 July 1864; Miller to "My Darling Wife," 1 August 1864.

2. Joseph Wheeler Scrapbook, pp. 1–2. Unless otherwise noted, the details of Wheeler's life are drawn from the Wheeler Scrapbook, pp. 1–90; "Major Gen. Joseph Wheeler, Jr.," pp. 222–32; "Sketch of Major-General Joseph Wheeler," pp. 5–9; DeLeon, *Joseph Wheeler, the Man, the Statesman, the Soldier,* pp. 21–26, 51–54, 96–98, 102–7; Dodson, ed., *Wheeler and His Cavalry,* pp. 1–216; DuBose, *General Joseph Wheeler,* pp. 49–219; Dyer, *"Fightin' Joe" Wheeler,* pp. 4–155; Jones, "Roster of General Officers," pp. A18–A19, A72–A73; *DAB,* 1928 ed., s.v. "Joseph Wheeler," by Thomas Jeffries Betts; Warner, *Generals in Gray,* pp. 332–33.

3. Official Register of the U.S. Military Academy, 1855:13, 17, 1856:12, 17, 1857:10, 1858:8, 1859:7, 16; Cullum, *Biographical Register,* 2:730; Dyer, *"Fightin' Joe" Wheeler,* p. 17 (quoting Wheeler).

4. DuBose, *General Joseph Wheeler,* p. 52; Wheeler Scrapbook, p. 1.

5. Wheeler Scrapbook, pp. 3–4. See also DuBose, *General Joseph Wheeler,* p. 54; *OR,* 52, pt. 2, p. 169.

6. *OR,* 4, p. 416; *OR,* 10, pt. 1, pp. 468, 524, 534–35, 550, 552, 555, 558–60; *OR,* 17, pt. 1, p. 650; *OR,* 16, pt. 1, pp. 893–900; pt. 2, pp. 932 (quoting Bragg), 939–40; Dodson, ed., *Wheeler and His Cavalry,* pp. 27–28 (quoting Wheeler); Wheeler Scrapbook, p. 31.

7. DuBose, *General Joseph Wheeler,* pp. 120, 143; *OR,* 20, pt. 1, pp. 663–64, 667, 958–60.

8. *OR,* 20, pt. 1, pp. 961, 980–84; Dodson, ed., *Wheeler and His Cavalry,* p. 72.

9. *OR,* 23, pt. 1, pp. 39–41; Wyeth, *Life of Lieutenant-General Nathan Bedford Forrest,* p. 151 (quoting Forrest); Duke, *Morgan's Cavalry,* pp. 248–49; *OR,* 32, pt. 3, pp. 643–44; "Sketch of Lieutenant-General Joseph Wheeler," p. 242 (quoting Forrest).

10. *CDS,* 29 May 1864, p. 1; DeLeon, *Joseph Wheeler,* pp. 120, 131; Wheeler Scrapbook, p. 54. DuBose, p. 56, described Wheeler as "but five feet two inches in height and . . . not quite one hundred pounds."

11. *OR,* 32, pt. 2, p. 759; "Major Gen. Joseph Wheeler, Jr.," p. 232.

12. *OR,* 52, pt. 2, pp. 606, 611; Connelly, *Autumn of Glory,* p. 316.

13. DuBose, *General Joseph Wheeler,* p. 56; Dyer, *"Fightin' Joe" Wheeler,* pp. 4, 154–55.

14. *NT,* 26 January 1893, p. 4; *AT,* 2 December 1897, p. 6. Lieutenant William E. Doyle, author of the article in the *American Tribune,* identified Wheeler's detractor as "Colonel Jack Brown" of the 4th Georgia Cavalry. No officer by that name commanded the 4th Georgia or any of the other regiments of Wheeler's Georgia brigade.

15. *MSR,* 5 July 1864, p. 2; Wheeler to Bragg, 1 July 1864, Braxton Bragg Papers.

16. *OR,* 38, pt. 3, p. 957.

17. Dodson, ed., *Wheeler and His Cavalry,* pp. 222–24; Thompson, *History of the Orphan Brigade,* p. 264; Kirwan, ed., *Johnny Green of the Orphan Brigade,* p. 151; *HDT,* 19 October 1864, p. 1 (Robert F. Bunting quotation); Kerr, ed., *Ross' Texas Cavalry,* p. 161; Wheeler, "Reports"; *OR,* 38, pt. 3, pp. 688, 954; pt. 5, pp. 927–29 (Confederate correspondence).

18. The large force of Rebels McCook was trying to avoid by moving south of Fayetteville was probably Jackson's division retracing its steps westward on the McDonough Road.

19. *OR,* 38, pt. 2, pp. 761–62, 770–71, 875; Carter, *1st Tennessee,* p. 180; *NT,* 2 September 1909, p. 7; Iowa Adjutant General, *Report,* p. 1003; *CDC,* 9 August 1864, p. 2; *DDT,* 12 August 1864, p. 1 (McCook's orders to the 5th Iowa); *HT,* 18 August 1864, p. 1; Iowa Adjutant General, *Roster and Record,* 4:1514; Belfield, "Sixty Days in Hades," p. 452; Vaughter, *Prison Life,* p. 23; Eckel, "The Rousseau and McCook Raids," p. 9; Eckel, *4th Tennessee,* pp. 60–61; *NT,* 2 April 1891, p. 4; Crouse, "18th Indiana Battery," pp. 19–20; *Atlanta Journal,* 24 August 1901, 2nd section, p. 2; *Memorial Record of Alabama,* 1:425; *EDJ,* 15 August 1864, p. 1 (Sergeant John Y. Urick's account).

20. *OR,* 38, pt. 2, pp. 770–71, 773 (quoting Croxton), 779, 875–76, 878; Carter, *1st Tennessee,* p. 180; Crouse, "18th Indiana Battery," p. 20; Ward Diary, 30 July 1864; *HT,* 18 August 1864, p. 1; Morning Reports, 29 July 1864, Company D, 8th Indiana Cavalry, RG 94; Vaughter, *Prison Life,* pp. 23–25; Miller, "John Thomas Croxton," p. 283; West, "McCook's Raid," pp. 553–55. West wrote in 1898: "Two sentinels were sent back on the road a hundred yards or so. . . ." However, Sergeant John Vaughter, writing in 1880, remembered West sent back only one man, "Tom B—— . . . to go to the top of the hill in the barrens and stand picket." This author has accepted Vaughter's account, since it was written closer to the actual event. Close scrutiny of West's memoir appears to corroborate Vaughter, since West repeatedly refers to "the sentinel" instead of "the sentinels." As for the identity of the sentinel, Vaughter referred to him only as "Tom B——." A search of Kentucky Adjutant General, *Report,* 1:628–683, and Muster Roll, July–August 1864, Company C, 4th Kentucky Mounted Infantry, RG 94, reveals the only Tom B's in Company C of the 4th Kentucky were Corporal Tom Bowlin and Private Thomas Baird. Private Baird is listed on the Regimental Return, July 1864, 4th Kentucky Mounted Infantry, RG 94, as "absent sick at Marietta since July 18, 1864."

21. [Clem Bassett] to "Dear General," [1867?], Wheeler Papers; *ADC,* 10 August 1864, p. 3; Dodson, ed., *Wheeler and His Cavalry,* p. 239; Guild, *A Brief Narrative of the Fourth Tennessee Cavalry Regiment,* p. 69; Vaughter, *Prison Life,* pp. 25–27; West, "McCook's Raid," pp. 555–57. West was not the only one who was uncertain of his whereabouts that night. When Joe Wheeler wrote his account of this skirmish in October 1864, he stated, "I pressed on rapidly [after leaving Fayetteville] and overtook his [McCook's] rear at Line Creek. The enemy had destroyed the bridge and were holding the opposite side with troops in strong barricades." See *OR,* 38, pt. 3, p. 954. Most histories of the Atlanta campaign have accepted this statement at face value. However, none of the Federal officers who were present even mention Line Creek. They all insist the rear guard was first attacked at "White Water" or "White River." See *OR,* 38, pt. 2, pp. 771, 779; *NYH,* 11 August 1864, p. 1. The key to this conflicting evidence lies in the distances from Fayetteville to Line Creek and Fayetteville to Whitewater Creek. Wheeler had reached Fayetteville about 12:00 A.M. on the night of July 29–30, pausing long enough to receive a message from Hood and write dispatches to Hood, Jackson, and the post commander at Griffin. All this correspondence must have taken a considerable amount of time, and it is not unreasonable to assume it was perhaps 12:30 A.M. before Wheeler left Fayetteville. He said his column pushed on rapidly and soon overtook the Yankee rear guard. Lieutenant West said he was attacked about 2:00 A.M., and his account of the fight at Whitewater Creek parallels Wheeler's description of the encounter at Line Creek so closely there can be no doubt the two men are referring to the same incident. But Line Creek is twelve miles west of Fayetteville. For the fight to have taken place there, Wheeler would have had to march twelve miles in roughly an hour and a half. While this is not impossible, it is extremely unlikely Wheeler's jaded troopers, who had been moving at a fairly consistent pace of about three miles an hour, could have put on such a phenomenal burst of speed in the middle of the night in unfamiliar territory. Whitewater Creek, on the other hand, is about three and a half miles southwest of Fayetteville via the Redwine Road, well within the range of an hour and a half march by 400 weary Rebel cavalrymen. A fairly accurate account of the raid

in the *New York Herald,* 11 August 1864, p. 1, said McCook's column crossed Whitewater Creek "near Glen Grove [present day Starr's Mill]." However, Glen Grove is ten miles southwest of Fayetteville, much too far south to fit into the previously described timetable of events.

22. *OR,* 38, pt. 2, pp. 771, 779; West, "McCook's Raid," pp. 557–58.

23. Wheeler, "Reports"; Dodson, ed., *Wheeler and His Cavalry,* p. 225; *OR,* 38, pt. 3, p. 954. A slightly abbreviated version of this dispatch appears in *OR,* 38, pt. 5, p. 932. In all three of these accounts, Wheeler asserted he encountered Yankee barricades every few hundred yards after crossing the bridge over Whitewater Creek. This appears to be an exaggeration of events that occurred later that night. None of the Federal eyewitnesses mention barricading the road anywhere between Whitewater Creek and Shakerag.

24. Confederate sources: *OR,* 38, pt. 3, p. 955; Wheeler, "Reports"; Dodson, ed., *Wheeler and His Cavalry,* pp. 225, 239; [Clem Bassett] to "Dear General," Wheeler Papers; John W. Hill to Miss M. S. Hill, 7 August 1864, John W. Hill Papers; *ADC,* 10 August 1864, p. 3; *HDT,* 19 October 1864, p. 1; Davis, "Cavalry Service under Gen. Wheeler," p. 353. Union sources: *OR,* 38, pt. 2, pp. 773, 775, 779; West, "McCook's Raid," pp. 558–61, 562; *NT,* 16 January 1890, p. 3 (Sergeant Henry M. Reed's account).

25. *OR,* 38, pt. 2, pp. 771, 773; *NT,* 21 January 1915, p. 5; *NT,* 15 July 1926, p. 5; Carter, *1st Tennessee,* p. 180; *NT,* 2 September 1909, p. 2.

26. Jackson Diary, 29 [30] July 1864; Ward Diary, 30 July 1864; *HT,* 18 August 1864, p. 1; Record of Events, Regimental Return, July 1864, 8th Indiana Cavalry, reel 35, M-594, RG 94; Crouse, "18th Indiana Battery," pp. 19–20; Carter, *1st Tennessee,* p. 180; Nash, "Harvey's Scouts"; *OR,* 38, pt. 2, pp. 763, 787, 876. The exact number of wagons the 8th Indiana captured is uncertain. Major George Purdy of the 4th Indiana, who was in a position to know, said the rear guard destroyed eight C.S. wagons. Sergeant John Farnsworth, a division scout, said the raiders burned twenty-five to thirty captured wagons, while Private Crouse of the 18th Indiana Battery said fifty wagons were "cut down" rather than burned for fear of advertising the column's position. McCook reported the wagons were burned. See *OR,* 38, pt. 2, pp. 763, 787; *NT,* 25 September 1890, p. 1; Crouse, "18th Indiana Battery," pp. 19–20.

27. *HT,* 18 August 1864, p. 1; Jackson Diary, 29 [30] July 1864; Ward Diary, 30 July 1864; *NT,* 6 June 1889, p. 3; *NT,* 31 May 1894, p. 3. Private Ward, riding at the head of the column, noted the advance guard reached Newnan "a little after sun up." Lieutenant Colonel Fielder Jones, in *OR,* 38, pt. 2, p. 876, said it was early in the morning. Others were more precise. Private Oscar Reese of the 5th Iowa, Private Crouse of the 18th Indiana Battery, Lieutenant Stanley A. Hall of the 4th Indiana, Colonel Jim Brownlow of the 1st Tennessee, and nurse Fannie Beers all agreed it was 8:00 A.M. See *DDT,* 12 August 1864, p. 1; Crouse, "18th Indiana Battery," p. 20; Hall Diary, 30 July 1864; *OR,* 38, pt. 2, p. 774; Beers, *Memories,* p. 142. Others, such as Major Purdy of the 4th Indiana, Sergeant Jackson of the 8th Indiana, and Sergeant Carter of the 1st Tennessee, said McCook's column did not reach Newnan until 10:00 A.M. See *OR,* 38, pt. 2, p. 787; *CDC,* 9 August 1864, p. 1; Jackson Diary, 29 [30] July 1864; Carter, *1st Tennessee,* p. 180. This author believes the hour of 8:00 A.M. is correct, 10:00 A.M. referring to the time the rear ranks caught up with the advance. Most eyewitnesses agreed there was only one train parked at the depot that morning, but Major Purdy, Lieutenant Colonel Jones, and Sergeant John Farnsworth, a division scout, reported (in *OR,* 38, pt. 2, pp. 787, 876; *CDC,* 9 August 1864, p. 1, and *NT,* 25 September 1890, p. 1) that there were two. This author has chosen to rely on the testimony of those who were closest to the scene.

28. Beers, *Memories,* pp. 138–39; Cumming, *Confederate Nurse,* pp. 214–15; Nutt, *Courageous Journey: The Civil War Journal of Laetitia Lafon Ashmore Nutt,* p. 85; Brewer, *Alabama,* p. 310; Evans, *CMH,* vol. 8: *Alabama,* pp. 439–40; *DAB,* 1928 ed., s.v. "Philip Dale Roddey," by Donovan Yeuell; Warner, *Generals in Gray,* p. 262; James E. Saunders to Thomas Jordan, 13 February 1867, Leroy Moncure Nutt Papers; *OR,* 39, pt. 1, pp. 322–24; pt. 2, p. 724; Hancock, *Hancock's Diary: or, A History of the Second Tennessee Confederate Cavalry,* p. 439; Roddey to Braxton Bragg, 28 July 1864, Philip D. Roddey Papers; Wheeler, "Reports";

Dodson, ed., *Wheeler and His Cavalry,* p. 229; *OR,* 38, pt. 5, p. 926; *ADI,* 4 August 1864, p. 2; Benjamin F. McPherson, "I Must Tell," p. 41, Private Collection; Davis, ed., *Diary of a Confederate Soldier: John S. Jackman of the Orphan Brigade,* p. 144; *MDT,* 4 August 1864, p. 1; *MDA,* 11 August 1864, p. 1 (quoting Roddey).

29. *HT,* 18 August 1864, p. 1; Morning Reports, 30 July 1864, Company D, 8th Indiana Cavalry, RG 94; Jackson Diary, 29 [30] July 1864; Ward Diary, 30 July 1864; *NT,* 6 June 1889, p. 3; *NT,* 5 April 1900, p. 7; *NT,* 31 May 1894, p. 3 (quoting Yankee officer); McPherson, "I Must Tell," p. 41; *DDT,* 12 August 1864, p. 1; Iowa Adjutant General, *Report,* p. 1004; *NT,* 21 January 1915, p. 5 (Johnny Mitch's account); Crouse, "18th Indiana Battery," p. 20; *NT,* 25 September 1890, p. 1; *NYH,* 11 August 1864, p. 1; *MDA,* 11 August 1864, p. 1; Martha Camp to Lizzie Reynolds, 14 August 1864, Camp Family Papers; *NT,* 5 August 1926, p. 5 (Sergeant Barnes Hutson's account); Hall Diary, 30 July 1864; Winkler Diary, 30 July 1864; *EDJ,* 15 August 1864, p. 1; *AT,* 14 April 1898, p. 6; *OR,* 38, pt. 2, pp. 762, 763, 771, 783, 787, 876.

30. In postwar accounts, Wheeler increased the number of prisoners from one officer and twenty-five men to forty men. See Wheeler, "Reports"; Dodson, ed., *Wheeler and His Cavalry,* p. 226.

31. Wheeler repeatedly asserted his troops had "travelled about seventy miles" by the time they reached Newnan. The route he took from Flat Shoals to Newnan is actually about fifty-five miles.

32. Beers, *Memories,* pp. 139–41, 148–49; Cumming, *Confederate Nurse,* p. 215; B. W. Wible to Samuel H. Stout, 3 August 1864, Stout Papers; Dyer, *Reminiscences,* p. 238; McPherson, "I Must Tell," p. 41; *MDA,* 11 August 1864, p. 1; Wheeler, "Reports"; Dodson, ed., *Wheeler and His Cavalry,* p. 226; *OR,* 38, pt. 2, p. 955; *HDT,* 19 October 1864, p. 1; Guthrey, "Wheeler's Cavalry around Atlanta," p. 267.

14. McCOOK'S RAID: BATTLE AT BROWN'S MILL, JULY 30–JULY 31, 1864

1. *OR,* 38, pt. 2, pp. 783–84, 787; *CDC,* 9 August 1864, p. 1; Scaife, *The Campaign for Atlanta,* p. 83, plate XVIII; Speed, Kelly, and Pirtle, *Union Regiments of Kentucky,* p. 125; Lindsley, ed., *Military Annals of Tennessee,* pp. 890–91; Harris Diary, 30 July 1864; Winkler Diary, 30 July 1864; *DDT,* 12 August 1864, p. 1; *EDJ,* 15 August 1864, p. 1 (Sergeant John Urick's account); *WSJ,* 2 September 1864, p. 2; *NT,* 31 October 1895, p. 3; *NT,* 1 June 1899, p. 3; *AT,* 14 April 1898, p. 6 (Sergeant Thomas Reed's account); *AT,* 21 April 1898, p. 6 (Reed's account cont'd.).

2. Union sources: *OR,* 38, pt. 2, pp. 771–72, 776; pt. 5, p. 396; Iowa Adjutant General, *Report,* p. 1027; West, "McCook's Raid," p. 563; Carter, *1st Tennessee,* p. 181; Eckel, "The Rousseau and McCook Raids," p. 10; Eckel, *4th Tennessee,* p. 61. Confederate sources: Davis, "Cavalry Expeditions in Georgia," p. 261; Hill to Miss M. S. Hill, 7 August 1864; *ADC,* 10 August 1864, p. 3; *HDT,* 19 October 1864, p. 1; Wheeler, "Reports"; Dodson, ed., *Wheeler and His Cavalry,* p. 227; *OR,* 38, pt. 3, pp. 955, 964; John Witherspoon DuBose, "History of the 1st Alabama Cavalry, CSA," p. 105 (quoting Wheeler), 1st Alabama Cavalry Papers; Perkerson, *White Columns in Georgia,* p. 313; Johnson, *Texans Who Wore the Gray,* p. 365. I. E. Kellie, the color-bearer of the 27th Texas, recalled this order was given by Colonel John W. Whitfield. However, Whitfield had retired from active service in October 1863. See Kerr, ed., *Ross' Texas Cavalry,* pp. 102, 116(n); Warner, *Generals in Gray,* pp. 334, 398(n).

3. Barron, *Lone Star Defenders,* pp. 200–202.

4. Eckel, "The Rousseau and McCook Raids," p. 10; Eckel, *4th Tennessee,* p. 61; *OR,* 38, pt. 5, p. 396.

5. In his report to the Iowa Adjutant General, Colonel Dorr credited Lieutenant Detwiler with capturing General William Y. C. Humes. Dorr's adjutant, Lieutenant Henry Belfield, made the same assertion in the *Dubuque Daily Times,* 21 October 1864, p. 2, and in a postwar

account, "My Sixty Days in Hades," p. 453. All the other reliable contemporary accounts, including Major Root's report in *OR*, 38, pt. 2, p. 777, indicate Lieutenant Detwiler captured Sul Ross.

6. Confederate sources: Hill to Miss M. S. Hill, 7 August 1864; *ADC*, 10 August 1864, p. 3; *ADC*, 13 August 1864, p. 2; *HDT*, 19 October 1864, p. 1; Otey, "Story of Our Great War," p. 109 (quoting Lieutenant Colonel Anderson); Davis, "Cavalry Expeditions in Georgia," p. 261; Guild, *4th Tennessee*, p. 70; Barron, "Wheeler's Cavalry in Georgia Campaign," p. 70; Barron, *Lone Star Defenders*, pp. 200, 202; Giles, *Terry's Texas Rangers*, p. 84; Johnson, *Texans Who Wore the Gray*, pp. 365–66; Beall, *In Barrack and Field*, p. 408 (quoting Lieutenant Colonel Boggess); Wheeler, "Reports"; Dodson, ed., *Wheeler and His Cavalry*, pp. 227–28, 240; *OR*, 38, pt. 3, pp. 955, 964 (Ross quotation). Union sources: *OR*, 38, pt. 2, pp. 762, 763, 772, 776–77 (Major Root quotation); *NYH*, 11 August 1864, p. 1; *BDH*, 15 August 1864, p. 3; *DDT*, 21 October 1864, p. 2; Iowa Adjutant General, *Report*, pp. 1027–28 (Dorr quotation); *NT*, 31 May 1883, p. 7; *NT*, 2 April 1891, p. 4.

7. *NT*, 31 May 1883, p. 7.

8. McCook's troopers variously referred to the building on the crest of this hill as "an old log house" or "an old church." Sergeant Josiah Conzett, who did not accompany the column but who lost a brother on the raid, said the artillery unlimbered behind the log house of a retired Presbyterian minister named Cook. See Conzett, "Memoirs," p. 74.

9. *NT*, 31 May 1883, p. 7; *NT*, 16 January 1890, p. 3; *AT*, 26 January 1893, p. 2; Scaife, *Campaign for Atlanta*, p. 99, plate XVIII; Dr. W. Kerry Elliott, Newnan, Georgia, telephone interview with the author; *OR*, 38, pt. 2, pp. 772, 783, 802–3 (Lieutenant Miller quotation), 876; *NT*, 25 April 1889, p. 4; *NT*, 5 April 1900, p. 7; *NT*, 5 August 1926, p. 5; Evans, ed., *CMH*, vol. 10: *Tennessee*, p. 386 (quoting captured Confederate); Iowa Adjutant General, *Report*, p. 1028; *DDT*, 12 August 1864, p. 1; *NYT*, 31 August 1864, p. 5; *NT*, 21 January 1915, p. 5 and *NT*, 15 July 1926, p. 5 (quoting exchange between McCook and Croxton); West, "McCook's Raid," p. 563; Miller to "My Darling Wife," 1 August 1864; Wheeler, "Reports"; Dodson, ed., *Wheeler and His Cavalry*, p. 228; Carter, *1st Tennessee*, pp. 181–82; Allen, "War Reminiscence"; *HT*, 18 August 1864, p. 1.

10. Wheeler, "Reports"; Dodson, ed., *Wheeler and His Cavalry*, pp. 228–29; *OR*, 38, pt. 3, pp. 955–56; Miller to "My Darling Wife," 12 July 1864 and 1 August 1864; Ash Diary, 29–30 July 1864; *ADI*, 4 August 1864, p. 2; *ADC*, 13 August 1864, p. 2; Dyer, *Reminiscences*, p. 239; B. W. Wible to Samuel H. Stout, 3 August 1864, Stout Papers; Beers, *Memories*, p. 141; *MDA*, 11 August 1864, p. 1; *SR*, 18 August 1864, p. 1; *ADA*, 25 June 1864, p. 2; William Augustus Fleming, "Records and Reminiscences of the Liberty Independent Troop," *Civil War Times Illustrated Collection* (quoting Anderson).

11. *OR*, 38, pt. 2, p. 772; Conzett, "Memoirs," p. 74; George W. Healey to Col. D. B. Henderson, 24 November 1898, Record & Pension Office File 535308, RG 94; U.S. Congress, Senate Committee on Veterans' Affairs, *Medal of Honor Recipients*, p. 116.

12. *MM*, 11 August 1864, p. 1; *ADC*, 13 August 1864, p. 2; Dodson, ed., *Wheeler and His Cavalry*, p. 229; *OR*, 38, pt. 3, p. 956; Wheeler, "Reports"; Ash Diary, 30 July 1864; *MDA*, 11 August 1864, p. 1; Davis, "Cavalry Expeditions in Georgia," p. 261; Rose, *Ross' Texas Brigade*, pp. 120–21; Sparks, *War between the States*, pp. 285–86; Fowler, "Army Chaplains in Battle," p. 205. On pages 125 and 267–68 of *The War between the States*, Texas trooper A. W. Sparks said the 9th Texas's chaplain, T. A. Ish, was killed at Newnan while kneeling beside a wounded comrade. Ish, however, had resigned in August 1862. See Kerr, ed., *Ross' Texas Cavalry*, p. 211.

13. Rose, *Ross' Texas Brigade*, pp. 112–13; Sparks, *War between the States*, p. 242.

14. Iowa Adjutant General, *Report*, p. 1028; Belfield, "Sixty Days in Hades," p. 453; *NT*, 25 April 1889, p. 4; Eckel, *4th Tennessee*, p. 62; Ward Diary, 30 July 1864; *OR*, 38, pt. 2, pp. 762, 763, 772, 774–75, 803, 876; *HT*, 11 August 1864, p. 2; Eckel, "The Rousseau and McCook Raids," p. 10; *NT*, 26 December 1889, p. 3; *NT*, 3 November 1927, p. 3 (quoting Brownlow);

NT, 5 July 1900, p. 3; *NT,* 2 September 1909, p. 7; Carter, *1st Tennessee,* p. 182 (all quoting exchange between Brownlow and McCook); Jackson Diary, 29 [30] July 1864; *NT,* 31 May 1894, p. 3 (quoting Jones); *NT,* 5 April 1900, p. 7. Private J. N. Jones of the 8th Indiana, writing in the *National Tribune,* 5 April 1900, p. 7, said Colonel Brownlow had left the field before this meeting took place and Fielder Jones was the only officer who opposed surrender. This assertion was quickly challenged by Sergeant William Carter of the 1st Tennessee. See *NT,* 5 July 1900, p. 3.

15. *OR,* 38, pt. 2, pp. 762, 763, 772, 774–75, 803, 876; *NT,* 5 April 1900, p. 7; Jackson Diary, 29 [30] July 1864; Ward Diary, 30–31 July 1864.

16. Oblinger Diary, 30 July 1864; *HT,* 18 August 1864, p. 1; *DDT,* 21 October 1864, p. 2; *AT,* 26 January 1893, p. 2; DuBose, *General Joseph Wheeler,* p. 379; Iowa Adjutant General, *Report,* p. 1004; *NT,* 2 April 1891, p. 4; *NT,* 31 May 1894, p. 3; *NT,* 5 August 1926, p. 5; *OR,* 38, pt. 2, pp. 802–3; Campbell Diary, 5 August 1864; Crouse, "18th Indiana Battery," p. 21; *NT,* 14 October 1897, p. 2. Writing in the *American Tribune,* 26 January 1893, p. 2, Private A. J. Tharp of the 4th Kentucky Mounted Infantry said the preparations also included "killing the extra mules and horses we had captured." None of the other eyewitnesses mentioned such wholesale slaughter.

17. *OR,* 38, pt. 2, p. 772; Carter, *1st Tennessee,* pp. 182–83; *NT,* 21 January 1915, p. 5; *NT,* 15 July 1926, p. 5; *DDT,* 12 August 1864, p. 1. Brownlow, in *OR,* 38, pt. 2, p. 774, said there were 600 men in the column he led off the battlefield. This figure seems entirely too large. Croxton's whole brigade numbered only 940 officers and men when the raid began. The 4th Kentucky had suffered an estimated 300 casualties in the previous day's fighting on the Panhandle Road and at Shakerag. The 8th Iowa, 316 strong on July 27, had taken heavy losses in the charge Major Root led against Ross's brigade and did not accompany Brownlow when he slipped through the Rebel lines.

18. *OR,* 38, pt. 2, p. 772; Iowa Adjutant General, *Report,* p. 1028 (quoting Dorr); *DDT,* 21 October 1864, p. 2; Belfield, "Sixty Days in Hades," p. 453; Monlux, *To My Comrades,* p. 41. The question arises, why did Dorr fail to follow the rest of the 1st Brigade when Croxton specifically sent "an officer" to bring up both the 8th Iowa and the 4th Kentucky? The answer may lie with Croxton's young orderly, Private Johnny Mitch, who later wrote:

> The 1st Tenn. [*sic*] had been acting as rear guard and . . . Croxton . . . sent me back to have Brownlow [*sic*] fall back with his regiment and join forces for a final dash. I started back, but made slow progress, as there is a limit to the endurance of a good horse, and mine scarcely answered to the prod of the spur.
>
> I had gone some distance when I met Maj. [Captain] Hudnall [of the 4th Kentucky] and asked him to change horses with me, so I could carry out my order, but he told me that his horse could not be urged out of a walk, and, besides, that the 1st Tenn. [*sic*] had been completely scattered and advised me to go no further, as I would run into the enemy, which I soon saw was correct.

Mitch obviously confused Dorr's 8th Iowa with Brownlow's 1st Tennessee. Brownlow's regiment was the advance guard, not the rear guard, and was already across Sandy Creek when Croxton summoned the rest of his brigade. Otherwise, Mitch's account is perfectly plausible and exonerates Dorr, who failed to withdraw because he never got the order to do so. See *OR,* 38, pt. 2, p. 772; *NT,* 21 January 1915, p. 5; *NT,* 15 July 1926, p. 5.

19. *OR,* 38, pt. 2, pp. 790, 876–77; Crouse, "18th Indiana Battery," p. 21; Campbell Diary, 5 August 1864; *EDJ,* 15 August 1864, p. 1; *NT,* 31 October 1895, p. 3; *NT,* 5 August 1926, p. 5 (Sergeant Barnes Hutson's account); Ward Diary, 31 July 1864; Jackson Diary, 29 [30] July 1864; Morning Reports, 30 July 1864, Company D, 8th Indiana Cavalry, RG 94; *HT,* 18 August 1864, p. 1; *NT,* 6 June 1889, p. 3; *NT,* 31 May 1894, p. 3; *NT,* 5 April 1900, p. 7; Lightcap, *Southern Prisons,* p. 12; Eckel, "The Rousseau and McCook Raids," p. 10; Eckel, *4th Tennessee,* p. 62.

20. Iowa Adjutant General, *Report,* p. 1028; Belfield, "Sixty Days in Hades," pp. 453–54; *DDT,* 21 October 1864, p. 2; *OR,* 38, pt. 3, p. 965; Kerr, ed., *Ross' Texas Cavalry,* pp. 161–62; *ADC,* 13 August 1864, p. 2; Evans, ed., *CMH,* vol. 10: *Tennessee,* p. 386. Hiram Bird recounted that at one of the first postwar reunions of the 8th Iowa, a comrade confided a secret a dying trooper had shared with him during their captivity at Andersonville. This trooper had captured $8,000 in gold from a Rebel paymaster's wagon at Fayetteville. When the 8th Iowa surrendered the next day at Brown's Mill, he had buried his treasure on the battlefield. The comrade to whom he bequeathed this secret returned to Newnan shortly after the war. Posing as a Southerner, he spent two weeks with the family whose plantation encompassed the battlefield. After several unsuccessful attempts, he finally succeeded in slipping away one night to begin his search, only to be overtaken by his host. "You are nothing but a Yankee, and are here for no good," the planter accused, "and the sooner you get out the better it will be for you." The Iowan promptly took this advice and apparently did nothing more about the gold until he told the story to Bird. Bird decided to make the treasure a Masonic secret and wrote the Masonic Lodge in Newnan, offering to share it. Realizing any extensive digging on the old battlefield was bound to arouse suspicion, the master of the lodge, Dr. Bowman, took the planter into his confidence. The planter told him an interesting tale. One night just after the war, he had heard a commotion in his corral. Thinking someone was stealing his stock, he grabbed his gun, summoned his Negroes, and hurried outside. He was confronted by four soldiers and, in an exchange of gunfire, one of the soldiers was killed. Upon investigating, the planter found his visitors had dug a big hole in the corral. After several unsuccessful searches, Dr. Bowman and the planter concluded the four soldiers must have seen the gold buried in 1864 and returned to retrieve it. Interestingly, the 8th Iowa was part of a great cavalry raid that swept through Alabama and Georgia during the last weeks of the war and revisited the battlefield at Brown's Mill on April 27, 1865. See Bird, *Memories,* pp. 47, 49–50; *OR,* 49, pt. 1, p. 423.

21. *OR,* 38, pt. 2, pp. 762, 877, 879; Lightcap, *Southern Prisons,* p. 12; *NT,* 5 April 1900, p. 7; *NT,* 6 June 1889, p. 3; *HT,* 18 August 1864, p. 1; Ward Diary, 31 July 1864.

22. Wheeler, "Reports"; Dodson, ed., *Wheeler and His Cavalry,* pp. 228–29, 240; *ADC,* 10 August 1864, p. 3; Sloane Diary, 30–31 July 1864; Ash Diary, 30 July 1864; *OR,* 38, pt. 3, p. 956; Perkerson, *White Columns in Georgia,* pp. 312–13.

23. *OR,* 38, pt. 2, pp. 784, 787; Purdy to Washington L. Elliott, 1 August 1864, p. 200, vol. 20/28,39, CCMDM, RG 393; Harris Diary, 30 July 1864; Winkler Diary, 30 July 1864; *CDC,* 9 August 1864, p. 1; *EDJ,* 15 August 1864, p. 1; *NT,* 31 October 1895, p. 3; *AT,* 21 April 1898, p. 6.

24. Sworn statement of Major Henry G. Flagg, 1st Tennessee Cavalry, 14 September 1876, found in Benjamin F. Housley, Pension Records, RG 15; Hamilton, *Recollections,* p. 142; *OR,* 38, pt. 2, pp. 774–75, 780; pt. 3, p. 956; Carter, *1st Tennessee,* pp. 183–84; *NT,* 5 July 1900, p. 3; *NT,* 2 September 1909, p. 7; *NT,* 16 January 1890, p. 3; Wheeler, "Reports"; Dodson, ed., *Wheeler and His Cavalry,* p. 240; *ADC,* 10 August 1864, p. 3; Collier, *The War Child's Children: The Story of the Third Regiment, Arkansas Cavalry,* p. 105; Sloane Diary, 31 July 1864; Miller to "My Darling Wife," 1 August 1864; Isaac Fulkerson to his Sister, 10 August 1864, Isaac Fulkerson Letters; *BKWRV,* 10 August 1864, p. 2; *NT,* 5 July 1883, p. 3; *AT,* 2 February 1893, p. 2 (Private A. J. Tharpe's account); Vaughter, *Prison Life,* pp. 29–34. Federal muster rolls and casualty lists made little or no distinction between men killed, wounded, or captured at Shakerag, Newnan, and the Chattahoochee, so it is difficult to determine the extent of Brownlow's losses on July 31. Arkansas historian Calvin L. Collier said 85 of Brownlow's men were killed and 350 captured, but he gave no sources for these figures. Wheeler, in *OR,* 38, pt. 3, p. 956, said the 3rd Arkansas and 5th Tennessee took between 200 and 300 prisoners. Private William E. Sloane of the 5th Tennessee Cavalry noted in his diary, "We captured about 100 men." This was also the figure given by another cavalryman writing in the *Augusta Daily Constitutionalist,* 10 August 1864, p. 3. In *OR,* 38, pt. 2, p. 774, Brownlow admitted losing 450

men, but this figure is greater than the number of men who actually followed him off the battlefield and cannot be considered accurate. In a second report in *OR*, 38, pt. 2, p. 775, Brownlow also asserted he was attacked from both sides of the river. None of the other Union and Confederate accounts bear witness to this.

25. *OR*, 38, pt. 2, pp. 762–63, 777, 876–77, 879; Ward Diary, 31 July 1864; *NT*, 6 June 1889, p. 3; Crouse, "18th Indiana Battery," p. 21; Iowa Adjutant General, *Report*, p. 1004; Lightcap, *Southern Prisons*, p. 12; *NT*, 22 July 1909, p. 7; *NT*, 5 August 1926, p. 5; John Philpot, Franklin, Ga., interview with author; *NT*, 31 May 1894, p. 3; Iowa Adjutant General, *Report*, p. 1004; Eckel, "The Rousseau and McCook Raids," p. 11; Eckel, *4th Tennessee*, p. 63; *HT*, 18 August 1864, p. 1.

26. Ash Diary, 30–31 July 1864. Private Jack Wilson, writing in the *Howard Tribune*, 18 August 1864, p. 1, said the Rebels appeared on the east side of the river "about 9 A.M." B. H. King's assertion in "The Stoneman and McCook Raid," p. 262, that the pursuing Confederates reached Philpott's Ferry "seven hours" after leaving the Brown's Mill battlefield is incorrect.

27. *HT*, 18 August 1864, p. 1; *NT*, 5 August 1926, p. 5 (Sergeant Barnes Hutson's account); Lightcap, *Southern Prisons*, p. 13; *NT*, 31 May 1894, p. 3; *NT*, 5 April 1900, p. 7; *NT*, 22 July 1909, p. 7; Eckel, "The Rousseau and McCook Raids," p. 11; Eckel, *4th Tennessee*, p. 63; Hall Diary, 31 July 1864; *NT*, 28 August 1884, p. 3; Tennessee Adjutant General, *Report*, p. 410; Indiana Adjutant General, *Report*, 5:226, 8:168, 528; Morning Reports, 31 July 1864, Company B, 8th Indiana Cavalry, RG 94; Compiled Service Records, RG 94; Jackson Diary, 30 [31] July 1864. Sergeant Brazier Ellis of the 1st Wisconsin may have been referring to the same incident when he wrote in the *National Tribune*, 1 June 1899, p. 3, "While lying a mile or more back from the river, resting, feeling we were quite safe, as the enemy could be kept from crossing the river very easily, a stray minie came singing leisurely along, striking Jack Parson[s], of our regiment, and killing him instantly."

28. Quartermaster General's Office, *Roll of Honor*, 23:80, 234; *HT*, 18 August 1864, p. 1; Wheeler, "Reports"; *OR*, 38, pt. 2, pp. 763, 879. McCook said these troopers belonged to the 2nd and 8th Indiana, but most of them appear to have been members of the 4th Tennessee and 5th Iowa. See *DDT*, 12 August 1864, p. 1; *NT*, 26 December 1889, p. 3; Eckel, "The Rousseau and McCook Raids," p. 11; Eckel, *4th Tennessee*, p. 63.

29. *OR*, 38, pt. 2, p. 877; pt. 3, p. 976; Wheeler, "Reports"; Ash Diary, 31 July 1864; Lightcap, *Southern Prisons*, pp. 13–14. Lightcap's memory obviously failed him when he said this discussion was between McCook and Colonel Brownlow. Brownlow was not at Philpott's Ferry. For all intents and purposes, McCook had turned his command over to Fielder Jones, who most likely was the officer Lightcap overheard. See also *NT*, 31 May 1894, p. 3.

30. Wheeler, "Reports"; *OR*, 38, pt. 3, p. 956.

15. McCOOK'S RAID: THE CHATTAHOOCHEE RIVER TO MARIETTA, JULY 31–AUGUST 3, 1864

1. Cumming, *Confederate Nurse*, p. 216; Beers, *Memories*, pp. 152–55.

2. Kerr, ed., *Ross' Texas Cavalry*, p. 162; Miller to "My Darling Wife," 1 August 1864. Lists of wounded Yankee prisoners hospitalized in Newnan after the battle contain a total of sixty-five names, and some of these men, such as Colonel Joseph Dorr and Sergeant Major William Christy of the 8th Iowa, clearly incurred their injuries in the skirmishes prior to Brown's Mill. At least six of these men died of their wounds. After the war, burial details removed thirty to thirty-four bodies from Newnan and vicinity to the National Cemetery at Marietta. See "Register of Federal troops in Hospital Newnan, Ga.," Horace T. Persons Papers; "Register of Patients at Buckner Hospital Newnan Ga.," August 2, 3, 4, 5, 7, 11, and 12, 1864, Stout Papers; Quartermaster General's Office, *Roll of Honor*, 23:78, 86, 92, 95, 99,

196, 231; Quartermaster General's Office, *Disposition of Some of the Bodies of Deceased Union Soldiers and Prisoners of War,* 3:10.

3. *OR,* 38, pt. 3, p. 965; Hill to Miss M. S. Hill, 7 August 1864; *HDT,* 19 October 1864, p. 1; Giles, *Terry's Texas Rangers,* pp. 84–85; Guild, *4th Tennessee,* pp. 70, 156, 157, 158, 163; "Register of Patients at Buckner Hospital Newnan Ga.," August 12, 1864, "Register of Patients Foard Hospital Newnan Ga.," July 31, August 9, 1864, Stout Papers; Ash Diary, 30 July 1864; Miller to "My Darling Wife," 1 August 1864; B. W. Wible to Samuel H. Stout, 3 August 1864, Stout Papers. A letter in the *Augusta Daily Constitutionalist,* 13 August 1864, p. 2, said Roddey's command suffered about thirty casualties, but this figure seems high in light of the patient registers in the Stout Papers.

4. Sparks, *War between the States,* p. 103.

5. "The Battle of Brown's Mill," UDC 12:31. Carpenter offered no clues to the identity of this wounded Yankee officer, but his description sounds a lot like Lieutenant Colonel Torrey of the 1st Wisconsin.

6. *OR,* 38, pt. 3, p. 956; Wheeler, "Reports"; Dodson, ed., *Wheeler and His Cavalry,* p. 229; *MDA,* 11 August 1864, p. 1; *NT,* 25 September 1890, p. 1 (Sergeant John Farnsworth's account); Bird, *Memories,* p. 23; *NT,* 27 September 1928, p. 5; Belfield, "Sixty Days in Hades," p. 454; Barron, "Wheeler's Cavalry in Georgia Campaign," p. 70; Barron, *Lone Star Defenders,* p. 203; *Newnan Times-Herald,* 23 February 1978, p. 1.

7. *NT,* 8 August 1889, p. 3 (Hiram T. Bird's account); *OR,* 38, pt. 3, p. 965; Belfield, "Sixty Days in Hades," pp. 453–54; Iowa Adjutant General, *Report,* p. 1029 (quoting Dorr); *DDT,* 21 October 1864, p. 2; Bishard, "Abstract of My Life," p. [6].

8. Cumming, *Confederate Nurse,* p. 217; *HDT,* 19 October 1864, p. 1; *OR,* 38, pt. 3, p. 965; Kerr, ed., *Ross' Texas Cavalry,* p. 162; Miller to "My Darling Wife," 1 August 1864.

9. Dyer, *Reminiscences,* pp. 239–40.

10. Cumming, *Confederate Nurse,* p. 216. The exact circumstances surrounding this incident may never be known, but Simon Miltmore Dufur recounted in *Over the Dead Line; or, Tracked by Blood Hounds,* pp. 117–22, that among the prisoners arriving at Andersonville during "the latter part of July or the forepart of August [1864]" was a young man whose face was "literally cut to pieces." When questioned, the man said he had been taken prisoner in a skirmish and marched to a farmhouse about three miles away. After an hour, the Rebel soldier who captured him was relieved by another who took the Yankee's revolver and mounted a horse, herding the captive ahead of him. They had gone about a mile when the trooper heard a sharp report, accompanied by a searing pain in his body and "prickly sensation" in his legs. Realizing he had been shot, he ducked behind a large pine tree just as a second bullet whistled past his head. Dodging from tree to tree, he managed to foil the Rebel's aim until all six shots had been fired. He fell to the ground, begging for mercy. The Rebel dismounted. "Now you damned Yankee dog," he snarled as he drew his saber, "escape from me if you can." With a single blow, he laid open the trooper's forehead. He cut and thrust again and again, then pulled off the trooper's boots and left him for dead. A little girl found the wounded man, and returned with her mother, who dragged the trooper to her home with the help of a Negro servant. An elderly physician treated the Yankee's wounds until a squad of Rebel cavalry discovered him and sent him to Andersonville.

11. B. W. Wible to Samuel H. Stout, 3 August 1864, Stout Papers; "Register of Patients at Buckner Hospital Newnan Ga.," August 2, 3, 4, 5, 7, 11, and 12, 1864, Stout Papers; Iowa Adjutant General, *Report,* p. 1029; Iowa Adjutant General, *Roster and Record,* 4:1623; Compiled Service Records, RG 94; "Register of Federal troops in Hospital Newnan, Ga.," Persons Papers; Cumming, *Confederate Nurse,* p. 219; Nutt, *Courageous Journey,* p. 85; Beers, *Memories,* pp. 156–59.

12. Bird, *Memories,* p. 23; *NT,* 27 September 1928, p. 5.

13. "Register of Patients at Buckner Hospital Newnan Ga. August 3rd 1864," "Register of Patients at Buckner Hospital Newnan Ga. August 11th 1864," Stout Papers; *PI,* 13 September 1864, p. 2; Beers, *Memories,* p. 159; Persons to "My Dear Wife," 13 August 1864; Compiled

Service Records, RG 94; Wisconsin Adjutant General, *Roster,* 1:1; Quartermaster General's Office, *Roll of Honor,* 23:196; *AT,* 14 April 1898, p. 6. The "Register of Patients at Buckner Hospital Newnan Ga. August 3rd 1864," said Torrey died on August 3. However, his attending physician, Dr. Horace T. Persons, wrote in a letter to "My Dear Wife," 3 August 1864, "Col. Torry [*sic*] . . . died yesterday."

14. Beers, *Memories,* p. 158. A "Register of Federal troops in Hospital Newnan, Ga.," kept by Dr. Persons shows only four, perhaps five, amputations among fifty-nine patients. The mortality rate among these fifty-nine patients was over ten percent.

15. Cumming, *Confederate Nurse,* pp. 218–19; *OR,* 38, pt. 5, p. 939; pt. 3, p. 689; Hood, *Advance and Retreat,* p. 196 (quoting Wheeler's telegram); B. W. Wible to Samuel H. Stout, 3 August 1864, Stout Papers; Barron, "Wheeler's Cavalry in Georgia Campaign," p. 70; Barron, *Lone Star Defenders,* pp. 203–4.

16. Belfield, "Sixty Days in Hades," pp. 454–55; Vaughter, *Prison Life,* p. 35; *AT,* 2 February 1893, p. 2; Monlux, *To My Comrades,* p. 42. These captured officers must have left Newnan on or about August 2, since they reached the Confederate prison at Macon on August 3. Colonel Dorr, still suffering from his wound, did not arrive until August 8. See Smith, ed., "The Civil War Diary of Colonel John Henry Smith," pp. 152–53.

17. *OSJ,* 11 August 1864, p. 2; *OR,* 38, pt. 2, p. 923; pt. 5, pp. 293–96, 303–4, 308–10, 311–13, 323–24.

18. *OR,* 38, pt. 2, pp. 784, 787, 790; Harris Diary, 31 July 1864; Winkler Diary, 31 July 1864; *CDC,* 9 August 1864, p. 1; *EDJ,* 15 August 1864, p. 1; *NT,* 31 October 1895, p. 3; *AT,* 21 April 1898, p. 6 (Sergeant Thomas Reed's account). Purdy's column included Major Owen Star and approximately ninety-five officers and men of the 2nd Kentucky. See *OR,* 38, pt. 5, p. 337; Purdy to Washington L. Elliott, 1 August 1864, p. 200, vol. 20/28, 39, CCMDM, RG 393. In this letter to General Elliott, Purdy asserted he had marched eighty-five miles since leaving Williams' Ferry, taking "bye-paths in order to avoid discovery." He told essentially the same story to the *Cincinnati Daily Commercial,* 9 August 1864, p. 1, and in his official report, in *OR,* 38, pt. 2, p. 787. Sergeant John Urick of the 4th Indiana repeated this claim in a letter to the *Evansville Daily Journal,* 15 August 1864, p. 1, but the actual distance from Williams' Ferry and the bridge at Sweet-water Town is only forty-five to fifty miles, the figure cited in both the Harris and Winkler diaries.

19. Purdy to Washington L. Elliott, 1 August 1864, p. 200, vol. 20/28, 39, CCMDM, RG 393; Eben P. Sturges Diary, 1 August 1864; Hamilton, *Recollections,* pp. 142–43 (quoting Brownlow); *OR,* 38, pt. 2, p. 774; pt. 5, pp. 320–321, 323, 330.

20. Unless otherwise noted, the narrative describing the movements of McCook's column from July 31 to August 3 are based on *OR,* 38, pt. 2, pp. 761, 764, 877; pt. 3, p. 973; Hall Diary, 31 July–3 August 1864; Jackson Diary, 30 [31] July–3 August 1864; Oblinger Diary, 31 July–3 August 1864; Ward Diary, 31 July–3 August 1864; *HT,* 18 August 1864, p. 1 (Private Jack Wilson's account); Morning Reports, 31 July–3 August 1864, Company D, 8th Indiana Cavalry, RG 94; Regimental Return, August 1864, 8th Indiana Cavalry, reel 35, M-594, RG 94; Lightcap, *Southern Prisons,* p. 14; Iowa Adjutant General, *Report,* p. 1004; Eckel, "The Rousseau and McCook Raids," p. 11; Eckel, *4th Tennessee,* pp. 63–64; *NT,* 26 December 1889, p. 3; *NT,* 5 August 1926, p. 5.

21. James O. Wilson, Sr., Glenn, Ga., interview with the author.

22. Smith, "The Faded Coat of Blue," p. 15; Smith, "The Battle of Brown's Mill," p. 28. Gamble buried the unknown soldier in the Adamson cemetery, a mile and a half west of Glenn. In 1928, the grave was covered with two concrete slabs laboriously inscribed with a poem by N. R. "Bud" Adamson:

This dying man
His friends had fled

Left to his foes
Not a word he said

Away from home
Away from friends
And all that heart holds dear
A federal soldier buried here
No earthly friends was near

Five other verses, each followed by the chorus, recount how the soldier's body, which showed "not a mark of harm," was buried in a coffin of planks taken from a nearby barn the Yankees had robbed of "wheat and corn," the planks "loosely laid" because there were no nails.

23. *HT,* 18 August 1864, p. 1 (quoting impassioned preacher).

24. Joseph Benton, Case Number 723, RG 217; William Jordan, Case Number 12,098, RG 233; J. M. K. Guinn, administrator of Abraham Gordon, Case Number 12,096, RG 233; Alfred McBurnett, Case Number 12,920, RG 217; Berry Bolt, Case Number 6,481, RG 233; Lucinda West, Case Number 13,966, RG 217; Robert S. Heflin, Case Number 14, RG 217; Robert S. M. Hunter, Case Number 11,758, RG 217; John W. Martin, Case Number 2,072, RG 233; Sarah E. Satterwhite, Case Number 2,075, RG 233; Solomon E. Jordan, Case Number 7,609, RG 233.

25. Franklin S. Knott, Case Number 2,067, RG 233; *HT,* 11 August 1864, p. 2; *OR,* 38, pt. 3, pp. 972–73; Address on back of dispatch from J. A. Vaughan to James H. Clanton, 31 July 1864, RG 109.

26. This flag may be the one described in *OR,* 38, pt. 1, p. 172, bearing the inscription "Our Country Our Rights."

27. Norvell M. Robinson, Case Number 4,409, RG 233; David Stephens vs. the U.S., Case Number 4,149, RG 123.

28. *OR,* 38, pt. 2, pp. 761–62.

29. Heaton, "Rousseau's Raid," p. 16; King Diary, 3 August 1864; David Wiltsee Diary, 3 August 1864; *AT,* 21 October 1898, p. 6 (Sergeant Thomas Reed's account).

16. STONEMAN'S RAID: LATIMER'S CROSSROADS TO CLINTON AND THE OCONEE RIVER, JULY 27–JULY 30, 1864

1. The evidence that might clarify exactly where Stoneman crossed the Yellow River is fragmentary at best. In a letter to the *Detroit Advertiser and Tribune,* 12 August 1864, p. 1, an 8th Michigan cavalryman reported the column left the railroad and took a southeasterly direction, crossing "the Yellow River Bridge at a place called Mount Sterling." He did not specify whether this was a plantation or a small village and the name has since been obscured in the mists of time. Garrard had burned the railroad and wagon bridges immediately east of Conyers on July 22, and Major Henry Hitchcock, traveling this same route with Sherman's XIV Corps in November 1864, noted they had not been rebuilt. However, another bridge, "three miles below," was said to be still standing. Most likely, this was Brown's Bridge, which may be the site of Stoneman's crossing. See Hitchcock, *Marching with Sherman,* pp. 65, 68.

2. According to the Kentucky Adjutant General, *Report of the Adjutant General of the State of Kentucky: Confederate Kentucky Volunteers,* 1:318–19; and Thompson, *The Orphan Brigade,* p. 789, Private D. C. Prather of the 6th Kentucky Infantry was sick in the hospital at Covington when he was "taken prisoner by Stoneman's Raiders and probably killed, as he was never heard from." Stoneman, however, appears to have paroled the patients he captured at Covington. It seems more likely Prather was one of the convalescent Confederates Garrard rounded up on July 22.

3. William Sheppard vs. the U.S., Case Number 11,970, RG 123; Drury Mauldin, Case Number 7,157, RG 233; William J. Smith, Case Number 6,465, RG 233; John A. Powell, Case

Number 3,768, RG 233; *OR,* 38, pt. 2, pp. 915, 925–26; Tarrant, *1st Kentucky,* p. 360 (Lieutenant Richard Huffman's account); Erastus Holmes Diary, 27 July 1864; *CR,* 22 July 1875, p. 1; Haskell Diary, 27 July 1864; Weir Diary, 27–28 July 1864; Sanford, *14th Illinois,* pp. 184–86; *NT,* 12 September 1895, p. 3; Morning Reports, 27 July 1864, Company G, 14th Illinois Cavalry, RG 94; Horace Capron, "Stoneman's Raid to the South of Atlanta," p. 676; Albert Banfield Capron, "Stoneman Raid to Macon, Georgia, in 1864," p. 712; *ACS,* 31 July 1864, pp. 2, 3; *ADC,* 31 July 1864, p. 1; Burge, *A Woman's Wartime Journal,* p. 9; Smith, *The Soldier's Friend,* pp. 129–30, 131 (quoting Stoneman), 132–35; Charles L. Bowker vs. the U.S., Case Number 8,798, RG 123. Albert Capron plagiarized his father's earlier account of Stoneman's Raid almost word for word and will not be cited again except in instances where his article differs from his father's. The elder Capron's account was serialized in the *National Tribune* (23 November 1882, pp. 1–2; 30 November 1882, p. 1; 7 December 1882, p. 1; and 14 December 1882, p. 1) and also appears as a letter to Brigadier General R. C. Drum in the Horace Capron File, reel 8, Generals' Reports of Service, M-1098 (hereafter cited as M-1098), RG 94.

4. *ADC,* 31 July 1864, p. 1; *ACS,* 31 July 1864, pp. 2, 3; *AP,* 4 August 1864, p. 1; Burge, *A Woman's Wartime Journal,* p. 9; *OR,* 38, pt. 2, pp. 919, 926; *CDC,* 12 August 1864, p. 2; *LDJ,* 14 September 1864, p. 1; Tarrant, *1st Kentucky,* pp. 360, 369 (Lieutenant Huffman's account); Haskell Diary, 28 July 1864; Holmes Diary, 28 July 1864; Weir Diary, 28 July 1864; Sanford, *14th Illinois,* pp. 188–89; Capron, "Stoneman's Raid," p. 676.

5. Sherman, *Memoirs,* 2:98; Starr, *The Union Cavalry in the Civil War,* 3:468; Carter, *The Siege of Atlanta,* pp. 260–61, 264; McDonough and Jones, *War So Terrible,* p. 253; Bailey, *Battles for Atlanta,* p. 138; Bragg, "The Union General Lost in Georgia," p. 18; Castel, *Decision in the West,* p. 442.

6. *OR,* 38, pt. 2, pp. 919–20; Holmes Diary, 28 July 1864; Tarrant, *1st Kentucky,* p. 360; *ACS,* 5 August 1864, p. 3; John Webb, "Memoirs, 1861–1870," p. 111, John Webb Papers; Newton County Historical Society, comp., *History of Newton County,* p. 226; Henry C. Wayne to "Hon. Justices of Inferior Court, of Jasper County, Monticello, Geo.," 17 August 1864, Georgia Adjutant General's Letter Book 1861–1864, 25:387; *LDJ,* 14 September 1864, p. 1; "Map of the 9th District, Butts County [Ga.]," Map N221–22, RG 77; Vicinity of Newnan to Ocmulgee River in the Vicinity of Jackson, Showing Topography, etc., Sept. 7, 1864, Map N221–22, RG 77; *NT,* 5 September 1895, p. 3; *CDC,* 23 August 1864, p. 2.

7. Captain Wells apparently had to wait several hours for Stoneman's rear guard to cross the Alcovy. According to the *Augusta Daily Constitutionalist,* 31 July 1864, p. 1, Henderson's Mill was not burned until some time after 1:00 P.M. As for Newton Factory, the Newton County Historical Society's *History of Newton County,* p. 220, asserts it was not burned during the war, but this is contradicted by Colonel Capron's report in *OR,* 38, pt. 2, p. 926, and another reference to the destruction of the mill by C. C. Anderson in *A Preliminary Report on a Part of the Water-Powers of Georgia,* p. 45.

8. *OR,* 38, pt. 2, pp. 915, 920, 926; Capron, "Stoneman's Raid," p. 676; Webb, "Memoirs," p. 111; Haskell Diary, 28 July 1864; William Goolsby vs. the U.S., Case Number 5,702, RG 123; Sanford, *14th Illinois,* p. 186; Tarrant, *1st Kentucky,* pp. 360, 368 (Lieutenant Huffman's account); *LDJ,* 14 September 1864, p. 1; Mrs. Harvie Jordan, "Jasper County in War Times," UDC 13:168–69; Carden Goolsby vs. the U.S., Case Number 9,680, RG 123; Harwell and Racine, eds., *The Fiery Trail: A Union Officer's Account of Sherman's Last Campaigns,* p. 56.

9. *ACS,* 5 August 1864, p. 3; Louise Caroline Reese Cornwell, "A Paper Written and Read by Mrs. Louise Caroline Reese Cornwell before a Woman's Meeting in Hillsboro, Ga., in the Late Sixties," UDC 5:249–50. There is a typescript of Mrs. Cornwell's account, entitled "Stoneman's and Sherman's Visit to Jasper City," in the Iverson-Branham Family Papers. When compared with the UDC version, several curious omissions are evident and it will not be cited. Mrs. Cornwell said the man McKissack wounded was taken with the column. However, according to the Jasper County Historical Foundation, Inc., comp., *History of*

Jasper County, Georgia, p. 32, "A Federal soldier died in the McKissack House. He was given a respectful burial in the Baptist churchyard but nothing more is known of him or his family." A slightly muddled postwar reminiscence by H. C. Wells of the 8th Michigan Cavalry in *American Tribune,* 31 July 1891, p. 5, also asserted, "another of our boys met his death [on July 29] by being bushwhacked by a citizen with a load of buck-shot." The Quartermaster General's Office, *Disposition of Some of the Bodies of Deceased Union Soldiers and Prisoners of War,* contains no references to removing the bodies of any Union soldiers from Hillsboro churchyards after the war.

10. Cornwell, "A Paper by Louise Cornwell," UDC 5:250, 253. Mrs. Cornwell had a very good memory for names, and she identified this preening Federal as "Captain Buel, one of Gen. Stoneman['s] staff officers." There was, however, no one named Buel on Stoneman's staff and it seems likely Mrs. Cornwell confused names or dates with a visit she received from Major General Oliver Otis Howard during the March to the Sea. Howard's chief of ordnance was Captain David H. Buel. A thoroughly garbled account of events in Hillsboro, confusing Stoneman's raid with Sherman's March to the Sea, is found in McKenzie, "When Sherman Marched through Georgia," UDC 13:356–60.

11. Macon's City Bridge collapsed when the center pier gave way shortly before midnight on Sunday, June 19, 1864. See *DCE,* 23 June 1864, p. 1; *MDA,* 27 June 1864, p. 1.

12. Cornwell, "A Paper by Louise Cornwell," UDC 5:249; *MDT,* 2 August 1864, p. 2; Sarah Allen, Case Number 17,287, RG 233; *OR,* 38, pt. 2, pp. 915, 920, 926; Capron, "Stoneman's Raid," p. 676; *WBB,* 24 September 1864, p. 1; Morning Reports, 29 July 1864, Company G, 14th Illinois Cavalry, RG 94; Sanford, *14th Illinois,* pp. 189, 204; *NT,* 12 September 1895, p. 3; *NT,* 26 September 1895, p. 3; *DAT,* 12 August 1864, p. 1; Haskell Diary, 29 July 1864; Holmes Diary, 29 July 1864; *CR,* 22 July 1875, p. 1; Butler, "The Stoneman Raid," p. 10; Williams, *History of Jones County,* pp. 19, 146, 148, 162, 195–228, 231, 233–35, 237–39, 249; Butler, *Historical Record of Macon and Central Georgia,* p. 265; Cobb to "My Dear Wife," 3 August 1864, Cobb Papers; *DCE,* 5 August 1864, p. 1; *MDT,* 4 August 1864, p. 2. According to the *Macon Daily Confederate,* 3 August 1864, quoted by *Daily Columbus Enquirer,* 5 August 1864, p. 1, the "chief sufferers" in Jones County were "Mrs. Elizabeth Lowther, jewels, negroes, plate, brandies, wines, etc., $40,000. Col. Wm. DeForrest Holly, jewels and clothing, $20,000. Lee Clower, $40,000. Green Clower, $40,000. Maj. Ben Barron, 63 negroes, mules, horses, clothing, etc., $150,000. Drs. Browning and Barron lost everything on their plantations. Hon. Judge Robert V. Hardeman lost $30,000 in property. James H. Blunt and Daniel Blunt, had their plantations ravaged."

13. Shoup to Cobb, 3 telegrams, 27 July 1864, Cobb Papers. See also *OR,* 38, pt. 5, p. 917. At 5:30 P.M., Hood's headquarters also wired the post commanders at Macon and Columbus, instructing them to find Braxton Bragg, travelling by train between the two cities, and deliver a telegram advising him, "There is a raid moving toward Covington. Considerable force. Ten pieces of artillery. Wheeler in pursuit. Destination unknown. Please give such attention as you can." This telegram would have been sent to Colonel George C. Gibbs in Macon, and it is doubtful if Cobb ever saw it. See *OR* 38, pt. 5, p. 913.

14. Cobb to "My Dear Wife, 29 July 1864, Cobb Papers; *CDS,* 31 July 1864, p. 2; Cobb to Henry C. Wayne, 27 July 1864, Cobb Letter Book.

15. Evans, ed., *CMH,* vol. 7: *Georgia,* pp. 401–2; *DAB,* 1928 ed., s.v. "Howell Cobb," by R. P. Brooks; Warner, *Generals in Gray,* p. 55; *OR,* series II, vol. 7, p. 92; Hood to Joseph E. Brown, 26 July 1864, Brown to Cobb, 26 July 1864, Cobb to Brown, 26 July 1864, Governor's Letter Book, p. 671; F. A. Shoup to Cobb, telegram, 26 July 1864, Brown to Cobb, telegram, 26 July 1864, Shoup to Cobb, telegram, 28 July 1864, Cobb Papers; Cobb to Jno. H. Winder, telegram, 26 July 1864, Cobb Letter Book; *OR,* 38, pt. 5, p. 924.

16. Albaugh and Simmons, *Confederate Arms,* pp. 219, 229–30, 234, 239, 241, 243, 260, 263, 274, 276; Butler, *Historical Record of Macon,* pp. 257–58; Daniel and Gunter, *Confederate Cannon Foundries,* pp. 70–73; "Map of Macon and Vicinity compiled from Information

by Capt. E. Ruger under the Direction of Lt. Col. J. G. Wharton, Top. Engineer, Hd. Quartrs., Department of the Cumberland," Map N76–3, RG 77; Cobb to Stephen Collins, 29 July 1864, Cobb Letter Book.

17. *OR,* series II, vol. 7, pp. 463, 472; Cooper, *In and Out of Rebel Prisons,* p. 105; Isham, Davidson, and Furness, *Prisoners of War and Military Prisons,* pp. 54, 60; Abbott, *Prison Life in the South,* pp. 84–85; Drake, *Fast and Loose in Dixie,* p. 54; Ferguson, *Life-Struggles in Rebel Prisons,* p. 113; Newsome, *Experience in the War of the Great Rebellion,* p. 99; Glazier, *The Capture, the prison pen, and the escape,* pp. 129–30; R. J. Hallett to Col. J. B. Cumming, 27 July 1864, Cobb Letter Book. With the exception of Hadley, *Seven Months a Prisoner,* p. 78, all the Federal accounts agree two groups of 600 prisoners left Macon on July 28 and 29. Hadley put the number at 500. Isham said the selection process was left to the senior captured officer.

18. Cobb to "My Dear Wife," 29 July 1864, Cobb Papers.

19. *Atlanta Journal,* 12 February 1902, p. 6; Felton, "Mrs. Felton's War Memories," p. 5. Rebecca Latimer Felton was born at Latimer's Crossroads, where Garrard and Stoneman had stopped briefly before going their separate ways on July 27. In 1922, at age eighty-seven, she was appointed to fill the unexpired term of Georgia Senator Tom Watson, becoming the first woman member of the United States Senate. She served for one day.

20. *AP,* 4 August 1864, p. 1; *DCE,* 5 August 1864, p. 1; *MM,* 5 August 1864, p. 2; *MDT,* 30 July 1864, p. 2; *ACS,* 6 August 1864, p. 2; Butler, *Historical Record of Macon,* p. 263. Dunlap, a member of Phillips' Legion, had suffered a debilitating wound at Gettysburg. See Young, Gholson, and Hargrove, *History of Macon,* p. 256.

21. Cobb to Brown, 29 July 1864, Cobb Letter Book; Brown to Cobb, 29 July 1864, Cobb Papers.

22. *OR,* series IV, vol. 3, pp. 344–49, 381–86, 417–22, 431–39, 442–44, 455–57; *ACS,* 6 August 1864, p. 2; *CDS,* 4 August 1864, p. 1; *MSR,* 3 August 1864, p. 2; *ADI,* 3 August 1864, p. 1; *ADI,* 4 August 1864, p. 2; *ADI,* 6 August 1864, p. 2; Henry C. Wayne to Joseph E. Brown, 4 August 1864 (hereafter cited as Wayne's Report), Georgia Adjutant General's Letter Book, 25:218–19; *AP,* 4 August 1864, p. 1; *AP,* 11 August 1864, p. 2; W. S. Wallace to Lamar Cobb, 5 August 1864 (hereafter cited as Wallace's Report), Cobb Papers; Cobb to Stephen Collins, 29 July 1864, Cobb Letter Book.

23. James H. Burton to Captain W. L. Reid, 29 July 1864, Burton to Josiah Gorgas, 2 August 1864, Burton to Gorgas, 8 August 1864, Chapter IV, vols. 20, 29, and 31, pp. 517–18, 524, Records of the Arsenal at Macon, Georgia, RG 109; *ADI,* 4 August 1864, pp. 1, 2; *AP,* 11 August 1864, p. 2; *ADI,* 9 August 1864, p. 2; *CI,* 12 August 1864, p. 2; Butler, *Historical Record of Macon,* pp. 263–64; Wayne's Report, Georgia Adjutant General's Letter Book, 25:218–19; *CDS,* 31 July 1864, p. 2; *CDS,* 4 August 1864, p. 1; *ADI,* 3 August 1864, p. 1; Mary Callaway Jones, "Confederate Reminiscences: Mr. Robert H. Kingman," UDC 2:210; G. W. Lee to Howell Cobb, 4 August 1864 (hereafter cited as Lee's Report), Cobb Papers; Fuller and Steuart, *Firearms of the Confederacy,* pp. 284–87; Albaugh and Simmons, *Confederate Arms,* pp. 11, 225–26; *ADI,* 6 August 1864, p. 2. Butler, in *Historical Record of Macon,* pp. 263–64, said Macon was reinforced on the evening of July 29 by the timely arrival of "a battalion of six hundred Tennesseans, under command of Major John W. Nisbet," who were on their way from Andersonville to Atlanta. This statement has been repeated over and over again in books, magazines, and newspaper accounts of Stoneman's raid. However, a close check of the records reveals Major John W. Nisbet commanded the 26th Georgia Infantry Battalion. His three companies, which would have numbered nowhere near 600 men, had apparently been detailed from the Army of Tennessee sometime between May 16 and June 30, 1864, to escort Yankee prisoners to Andersonville. While Cobb did issue orders on July 29 directing the officer commanding Nisbet's battalion to stop at the depot and "report for instructions," none of his officers nor any of the accounts in the Macon newspapers mention the arrival of this unit. Nor do they mention the mysterious Captain Peschke, whom Butler credited with commanding a

three-gun battery on the Clinton Road. This author can find no evidence that such a battery even existed or that Cobb ever had more than two field pieces at his disposal. See Estes, comp., *List of Field Officers, Regiments and Battalions in the Confederate Army,* p. 94; Nisbet, *Four Years on the Firing Line,* pp. xiv, 138, 188, 255–56; Special Orders Number 61, Special Orders 1864–1865, Cobb-Erwin-Lamar Papers; *OR,* 38, pt. 3, p. 639; Mallet, "Work of the Ordnance Bureau," p. 17; *ADI,* 3 August 1864, p. 1; *CDS,* 4 August 1864, p. 1; *AP,* 4 August 1864, p. 1.

24. Other sources give other numbers. A correspondent of the *West Branch Bulletin,* 24 September 1864, p. 1, who was apparently a member of the 14th Illinois, said there were "a large number of engines," "about 40 passenger cars and 200 freight cars, 80 of the latter loaded with commissary and quartermaster's stores." Stoneman's provost marshal, Major Haviland Tompkins, reported in *OR,* 38, pt. 2, p. 920, that Davidson told him the railroad agent at Gordon (H. K. Walker) said there were 275 flat and box cars, 9 engines, and 150 passenger and express cars in the yard. William McNabb, an employee of the Western & Atlantic Railroad, told Union interrogators in *OR,* 38, pt. 5, p. 496, there were "4 trains, 4 engines, and about 50 cars" on the siding at Gordon. The *Macon Daily Telegraph,* 2 August 1864, p. 2, put the number at 150 to 200 cars and engines. All of the engines apparently belonged to the Western & Atlantic and Milledgeville & Eatonton Railroads. See Central Railroad and Banking Company of Georgia, *Reports of the Presidents and Superintendents,* pp. 274–75.

25. *OR,* 38, pt. 2, pp. 926, 929; *NYH,* 13 August 1864, p. 1; *WBB,* 24 September 1864, p. 1; Record of Events, July–August 1864, Company G, 14th Illinois Cavalry, reel 13, M-594, RG 94; *NT,* 26 September 1895, p. 3; Sanford, *14th Illinois,* pp. 189, 204; *DAT,* 22 August 1864, p. 1; Williams, *Jones County,* pp. 148, 162; *ADC,* 6 August 1864, p. 3; *ADI,* 3 August 1864, p. 2 (quoting Squire Choate); *CT,* 8 August 1864, p. 2; *MDT,* 2 August 1864, p. 2; Wayne's Report, Georgia Adjutant General's Letter Book, 25:218; *ACS,* 31 July 1864, p. 3; *ASB,* 3 August 1864, p. 3; *SR,* 1 August 1864, p. 1; *TC,* 16 August 1864, p. 442; *ACS,* 5 August 1864, p. 1; *ACS,* 6 August 1864, p. 3; *MSR,* 3 August 1864, p. 2; *ACS,* 2 August 1864, p. 1. The *Columbus Times* (quoting the *Macon Daily Confederate*), 8 August 1864, p. 2, reported, "One Yankee got left behind by helping women at the cars save their property, and Sunday morning [July 31] gave himself up as a prisoner."

26. Horace Capron, in *OR,* 38, pt. 2, p. 929, and his adjutant, Captain Samuel Wells, in the *Detroit Advertiser and Tribune,* 22 August 1864, p. 1, asserted Davidson followed the railroad to Emmett, sixteen miles east of Gordon and then moved another eight miles down the track to Toomsboro. This itinerary also appears in Sanford, *14th Illinois,* p. 204, but the actual facts are these: the events Capron and Wells described at Emmett actually took place at McIntyre. The railroad had closed the station at Emmett in 1856 and moved it a mile and a half west to Toomsboro, which is about sixteen miles east of Gordon, not twenty-four. See Davidson, *History of Wilkinson County,* pp. 221–22.

27. The *West Branch Bulletin*'s correspondent said that upon reaching Toomsboro, Davidson's detachment "met a train coming up with a guard to find out our force, but on seeing us they skedaddled to the cars, and we only took a dozen prisoners, a small amount of ammunition and some guns, which we destroyed." Major Haviland Tompkins went even further, in *OR,* 38, pt. 2, p. 921, claiming Davidson "caught 4 trains between Gordon and Buffalo Creek; destroyed them entire." No other sources, Union or Confederate, mention the destruction of any trains east of Gordon, and Tompkins's assertion that Davidson burned the trestle over Buffalo Creek, just east of the Oconee River, is incorrect.

28. *CT,* 8 August 1864, p. 2; *MDT,* 2 August 1864, p. 2; *SR,* 1 August 1864, p. 2; *WBB,* 24 September 1864, p. 1; Sanford, *14th Illinois,* p. 204; *NT,* 26 September 1895, p. 3; *OR,* 38, pt. 2, p. 929; *ADI,* 3 August 1864, p. 2; *ACS,* 5 August 1864, p. 1; Davidson, *Wilkinson County,* p. 258; *DAT,* 22 August 1864, p. 1 (quoting unidentified Union officer). Lieutenant Washington L. Sanford asserted in *14th Illinois,* pp. 204–5, and again in the *National Tribune,* 26 September 1895, p. 3, that Boren and his men attacked and routed a bridge guard of 150 men and two pieces of artillery. However, Sanford was not a member of Davidson's detachment,

and Major Haviland Tompkins reported Davidson "met no resistance." Several Southern newspapers reported a force of 150 men stationed at the bridge had been withdrawn the day *before* the raiders arrived. See *OR,* 38, pt. 2, p. 921; *MDT,* 2 August 1864, p. 2; *ACS,* 2 August 1864, p. 1; *SR,* 1 August 1864, p. 1; *SR,* 4 August 1864, p. 2.

17. STONEMAN'S RAID: CLINTON TO WALNUT CREEK, JULY 29–JULY 30, 1864

1. In *14th Illinois,* p. 205, Lieutenant Sanford claimed, "Lieutenant Boren and party now fell back to the main command, which moved back, and just as they entered the main road they discovered a large rebel force that had just passed down to guard the bridge (but now to mourn over its ashes). Our party struck in between the main force and its rear guard, and charging down on the latter, drove them in utter confusion, never stopping to gather up the arms and hats that strewed the road. They drove them several miles, capturing some, whom they paroled; and at the first favorable diverging road they dashed off in a direction to baffle pursuit if it were attempted." He repeated this story in *National Tribune,* 26 September 1895, p. 3, but there is nothing in the official reports or contemporary accounts to give it credence. According to the *Macon Daily Confederate,* quoted by *Columbus Times,* 8 August 1864, p. 2, after the Yankees left Toomsboro, they were followed by "eight or ten citizens to the Oconee bridge, . . . but no attack was made. . . ." Several other Southern newspapers criticized the army's failure to defend the bridge, further discrediting Sanford's story.

2. *OR,* 38, pt. 2, p. 929; *DAT,* 22 August 1864, p. 1; *WBB,* 24 September 1864, p. 1; Sanford, *14th Illinois,* pp. 204–5; *NT,* 26 September 1895, p. 3; *MDT,* 2 August 1864, p. 2; *ACS,* 31 July 1864, p. 1; *ACS,* 2 August 1864, pp. 1, 3; *SR,* 1 August 1864, p. 1; *CT,* 8 August 1864, p. 2; *MSR,* 3 August 1864, p. 2; Wayne's Report, Georgia Adjutant General's Letter Book, 25:222; *OR,* 44, p. 531; *ADI,* 3 August 1864, p. 2; *ACS,* 6 August 1864, p. 3; *MCU,* 9 August 1864, p. 3.

3. Montgomery, *Johnny Cobb: Confederate Aristocrat,* p. 66; Lucy Cobb to "Johnny darling," 29, 30 July, 1 August 1864, Cobb Papers; Wayne's Report, Georgia Adjutant General's Letter Book, 25:218–19; *MCU,* 9 August 1864, p. 3.

4. *MDT,* 30 July 1864, p. 2; *AP,* 4 August 1864, p. 1; Wallace's Report, Cobb Papers; Morning Reports, 29 July 1864, Company G, 14th Illinois Cavalry, RG 94; Haskell Diary, 29 July 1864; *OR,* 38, pt. 2, pp. 915, 920, 926; *LDJ* 14 September 1864, p. 1 (quoting Stoneman and unidentified raider); *NT,* 18 October 1888, p. 3; Tarrant, *1st Kentucky,* pp. 360–61; Compiled Service Records, RG 94; Kentucky Adjutant General, *Report,* 1:34–35, 42–43. Sources do not identify the detachment that accompanied Lieutenant Root on his cross-country jaunt, but Sanford, *14th Illinois,* p. 189, offered a tantalizing clue when he wrote: "A picket, under command of Lieutenant Wm. M. Moore, of Company 'L,' 14th Illinois Cavalry . . . had an exciting little adventure in being mistaken for rebels and were attacked by a detachment of our own forces. No great injury was suffered on either side, the mistake being soon discovered."

5. Felton, "War Memories," p. 5; *Atlanta Journal,* 12 February 1902, p. 6; *OR,* 38, pt. 2, p. 915 (Stoneman's orders to Adams).

6. Haskell Diary, 29–30 July 1864; Butler, "The Stoneman Raid," p. 10; *AT,* 31 July 1891, p. 5; Holmes Diary, 29 July 1864; *OR,* 38, pt. 2, pp. 915–16, 920, 926; Capron, "Stoneman's Raid," p. 677; Sanford, *14th Illinois,* pp. 189–90; *DAT,* 12 August 1864, p. 1; *DFP,* 16 August 1864, p. 1 (quote by Michigan trooper); *NT,* 16 January 1902, p. 3; Wells, *Touch of Elbow,* pp. 208–9; *NYH,* 13 August 1864, p. 1; "Map of the 6th District of Jones Co. [Ga.]," Map N221–23, RG 77; *ADI,* 5 August 1864, p. 3; *ACS,* 2 August 1864, p. 3; *ACS,* 6 August 1864, p. 3; *AP,* 11 August 1864, p. 2; *MDT,* 2 August 1864, p. 2; *ADI,* 3 August 1864, p. 2; *CT,* 4 August 1864, p. 1. The *Macon Daily Telegraph,* 2 August 1864, p. 2, and *Augusta Chronicle & Sentinel,* 2

August 1864, p. 3, credited Stoneman's raiders with burning twenty-seven cars at Griswoldville, and some of the Northern accounts cited above said the stock cars were loaded with horses and hogs. There is, however, no truth in a report by the *Columbus Daily Sun,* 2 August 1864, p. 1, that the Yankees burned the pistol factory at Griswoldville. It was not destroyed until November 1864, during Sherman's March to the Sea. See *OR,* 44, pp. 363, 508.

7. Holmes Diary, 30 July 1864; Haskell Diary, 30 July 1864; *ADI,* 3 August 1864, p. 1; Lee's Report, Cobb Papers; Sammons, *Personal Recollections of the Civil War,* p. 28; *IDJ,* 16 August 1864, p. 2; Butler, "The Stoneman Raid," p. 10; Butler, *Historical Record of Macon,* p. 264; *MDT,* 2 August 1864, p. 1; *CDS,* 3 August 1864, p. 1; *NYH,* 13 August 1864, p. 1. There is a strong possibility Stoneman sent one of Captain Hardy's two guns with Adams's Kentucky brigade. Colonel G. W. Lee reported the Yankees brought one piece of artillery into action on the Garrison Road, while Johnny Cobb, apparently serving on his father's staff in an unofficial capacity on July 30, noted Stoneman had a gun that fired into Macon from the Clinton Road. See Lee's Report, Cobb Papers; Cobb, "Civil War Incidents in Macon," p. 282.

8. Glazier, *Capture, Prison Pen, and Escape,* p. 131; Isham, *Prisoners of War,* p. 60; Calef, "Prison-Life in the Confederacy," p. 142; Smith, ed., "Diary of Colonel John Henry Smith," p. 152; Williams, "Captain Williams' Escape," p. 184; Prutsman, *A Soldier's Experience in Southern Prisons,* p. 35; Roach, *The Prisoner of War,* pp. 133–34 (prisoner's quotation); *ADI,* 3 August 1864, p. 1; Lee's Report, Cobb Papers.

9. "To the Citizens of Macon," 30 July 1864, Crandall Number 1574–1.

10. S. H. Stout to "The surgeon in charge of Hospitals in and near Macon," 30 July 1864, Stout Papers; *ACS,* 6 August 1864, p. 2; Nisbet, *Four Years on the Firing Line,* p. 245; Lathrop, "Gossipy Letter From Georgia," p. 520.

11. Johnston, *Narrative,* p. 369; Mackall Diary, 19 July 1864; Patterson, "Places of Historic Interest in Macon," p. 252; Mackall, *A Son's Recollections of His Father,* p. 221; John W. DuBose, "51st Ala. Cavalry, CSA," p. 107, 51st Alabama Cavalry Papers; Dubose, *General Joseph Wheeler,* p. 380; *ECN,* 3 August 1864, p. 3; Cobb to "My Dear Wife," 20 July, 26 July, and 3 August 1864, Cobb Papers.

12. *ADI,* 9 August 1864, p. 2; *ADI,* 3 August 1864, p. 1; Williams, *Jones County,* p. 146 (quoting aged militiaman); Lee's Report, Cobb Papers.

13. *AP,* 11 August 1864, p. 2; Jones, comp., "The Treatment of Prisoners during the War Between the States," p. 189; *OR,* 39, pt. 2, pp. 625, 709; *OR,* series II, vol. 3, pp. 533, 753, 770, 855, 861–62; *OR,* series II, vol. 4, pp. 779, 832–33, 838; *OR,* series II, vol. 7, pp. 372–73, 418–19, 463; Arthur E. Boardman to Mrs. Frank F. Jones, 28 April 1928, Arthur E. Boardman Papers; *ADI,* 9 August 1864, p. 2; *MDT,* 11 August 1864, p. 2; Butler, *Historical Record of Macon,* p. 264. Butler said Charles M. Wiley, commander of the convalescent company, was a lieutenant colonel. Wiley is not listed in Estes, comp., *List of Field Officers, Regiments and Battalions in the Confederate States Army,* and according to Henderson, comp., *Roster of the Confederate Soldiers of Georgia,* 4:726–27, 6:783, he was actually a lieutenant.

14. Boardman to Jones, 28 April 1928. Boardman added Captain Armstrong was not at the head of the Silver Greys when they marched through Macon. Captain A. G. Butts seemed to be in command; Armstrong may have joined the company later that morning.

15. The *Columbus Daily Sun,* 3 August 1864, p. 1, quoting the *Macon Daily Telegraph* and the *Atlanta* [Macon] *Daily Intelligencer,* said none of the six shells aimed at the magazine exploded. The *Macon Daily Confederate,* on the other hand, quoted by *The Countryman,* 23 August 1864, p. 449, reported five of the six shells burst and the sixth, which fell five steps short of the magazine, was on display at the *Confederate* office. The *Daily Columbus Enquirer,* 2 August 1864, p. 2, added to the confusion when it reported only two shells fell on Macon and one of them exploded, killing a Negro man. None of the Macon newspapers repeated this story, and the *Macon Daily Telegraph,* 2 August 1864, p. 1, specifically stated "no non-combatant was injured" in the bombardment. See also Mary Ann Lamar Cobb to "My Dear Mother," 31 July 1864, Cobb Papers; *ACS,* 6 August 1864, pp. 2, 3; *DCE,* 2 August 1864,

p. 1; *CDS,* 2 August 1864, p. 1; *CT,* 2 August 1864, p. 2; *ECN,* 3 August 1864, p. 3; *MDT,* 2 August 1864, p. 1; *SR,* 2 August 1864, p. 2.

16. Butler, *Historical Record of Macon,* p. 264; *OR,* 38, pt. 2, pp. 913, 916; Burton to Gorgas, 2 August 1864, Chapter IV, vols. 20, 29, and 31, p. 517, Records of the Arsenal at Macon, Georgia, RG 109; Mary Ann Lamar Cobb to "My Dear Mother," 31 July 1864, Cobb Papers; *AP,* 4 August 1864, pp. 1, 2; *DCE,* 2 August 1864, p. 1; *CDS,* 3 August 1864, p. 1; Young, Gholson, and Hargrove, *History of Macon,* p. 259; Cobb, "Civil War Incidents in Macon," p. 282. It is interesting to note that Colonel James H. Burton, commander of the Macon Armory, said Macon was bombarded by Hotchkiss shells, the type commonly fired from 3-inch ordnance rifled cannon like those Stoneman used. The projectile preserved by the United Daughters of the Confederacy at the Holt House is a 12-pounder solid shot that could only have been fired from a smoothbore gun.

17. Other high-ranking officers who were on the field, but not necessarily with Cobb's coterie, included Brigadier Generals William W. Mackall and Daniel Ruggles, and Colonel W. H. Wright. See *AP,* 4 August 1864, p. 1; *ADI,* 4 August 1864, p. 1.

18. Boardman to Jones, 28 April 1928 (description of Cobb); Butler, *Historical Record of Macon,* p. 264; *ADI,* 9 August 1864, p. 2; Smedes, *Memorials of a Southern Planter,* p. 206; *AP,* 11 August 1864, p. 2 (quoting citizen soldier); *CDS,* 3 August 1864, p. 1; *ADI,* 3 August 1864, p. 1; *ADI,* 4 August 1864, p. 1; Cobb to "My Dear Wife," 3 August 1864, Cobb Papers; *CI,* 12 August 1864, p. 2; *MDT,* 2 August 1864, p. 1; *IDJ,* 16 August 1864, p. 2; *MDT,* 4 August 1864, p. 2; *CDS,* 4 August 1864, p. 1; Lee's Report, Cobb Papers. McClung was a second lieutenant in Ramsey's Tennessee Battery. See Tennessee Civil War Centennial Commission, *Tennesseans in the Civil War,* 2:270.

19. *OR,* 38, pt. 2, pp. 916, 926; *MDT,* 2 August 1864, p. 1; Sammons, *Recollections,* pp. 28–29; *IDJ,* 16 August 1864, p. 2 (quoting Hoosier trooper). Lieutenant Colonel Smith's report in the *Official Records* and Confederate casualty lists published in the Macon newspapers belie Thomas Dabney, Jr.'s "recollection" in Smedes, *Memorials of a Southern Planter,* p. 206, that "none of the Silver Grays were touched until Major Taliaferro placed two cannon on our side of the river. . . . Volunteers to man the guns were called for. In an instant father and many other old gentlemen were busy loading the two twenty-pounders . . . and a perfect storm of shot and shell burst upon our devoted heads. In a few minutes our guns were silenced, but not until several of the Silver Grays lay dead beside the little brazen guns which brought us nothing but death."

20. Lee's Report, Cobb Papers; Butler, *Historical Record of Macon,* p. 265; *ADI,* 9 August 1864, p. 2; Nisbet, *Four Years on the Firing Line,* pp. 245–46; Boardman to Jones, 26 April 1928 (quoting Reverend Danforth); *CI,* 12 August 1864, p. 2; *MDT,* 17 August 1864, p. 2; Cobb to "My Dear Wife," 7 August 1864, Cobb Papers; *AP,* 4 August 1864, p. 2; *ECN,* 3 August 1864, p. 3. Reverend Warren's illness may have been a chronic throat condition that made public speaking difficult. See Batts, *History of the First Baptist Church of Christ at Macon,* p. 46. The *Christian Index* reported bullets grazed Dr. Wills's eyebrow and Reverend Burke's neck. The *Albany Patriot* added Reverend Warren was shot in the left arm and Reverend Burke was wounded in the cheek, but retracted the story in another column and announced both ministers came through the fight "unscathed."

21. Boardman to Jones, 26 April 1928; Smith, "The Georgia Militia about Atlanta," p. 331; *AP,* 4 August 1864, p. 2 (mistakes of the militia); Hoole, "John W. Mallet and the Confederate Ordnance Laboratories," pp. 33–34; *ADI,* 4 August 1864, p. 1 (quote by one of Mallet's men); *ADI,* 4 August 1864, p. 1; *MDT,* 11 August 1864, p. 2; Evans, ed., *CMH,* vol. 7: *Georgia,* p. 820; *OR,* 3, p. 329; *OR,* 7, pp. 284, 296–97; *OR,* 20, pt. 1, p. 915; *OR,* 38, pt. 3, p. 70; pt. 5, p. 988; *OR,* 52, pt. 2, p. 529; Lee's Report, Cobb Papers. Butler's *Historical Record of Macon,* p. 264, asserted:

Cumming ordered Peschke's battery to reserve their fire until the Federals were within two or three hundred yards of their front. They were then coming down the

Milledgeville [Garrison] road. The battery opened with a well directed fire, when Nisbet's battalion was ordered to charge. The militia and Findlay's command were held in reserve to follow the battalion if necessary. On the charge being made, and the fire of Peschke's battery kept up, the enemy retreated towards Cross Keys."

Cumming, however, was not in command on the Garrison Road. Lee was, and his report makes no references whatsoever to "Peschke's battery" or Nisbet's battalion. This author has been unable to confirm the existence of Peschke's battery, and there is absolutely no mention of Nisbet's 26th Georgia Battalion (which Butler mistakenly identified as a Tennessee outfit) in the detailed newspaper accounts of the fighting. Nisbet was the son of one of Macon's most prominent attorneys, and it seems highly unlikely his hometown papers would not have acknowledged him. A casualty list in the *Macon Daily Telegraph,* 2 August 1864, p. 1, includes a Lieutenant William Goldsmith, of the *27th* Georgia Battalion. At first glance, this might appear to be a typographical error, but Goldsmith was indeed a member of the 27th Georgia. This unit, also known as the Augusta Arsenal Battalion, had been guarding prisoners at Camp Oglethorpe until it was transferred to the Georgia coast sometime in June or July. For some reason, Goldsmith remained in Macon and marched into battle with Company B of the City Battalion on July 30. According to the *Augusta Chronicle & Sentinel,* 5 August 1864, p. 3, "After the fight near Macon he was proceeding to the field to ascertain the number of Yankees killed. Putting his gun on the opposite side of the fence, he rested his hand on the muzzle to assist him in springing over. As he did so the gun went off, the charge passing through his hand and into one eye, coming out of the back of his head. He died instantly." See *OR,* series IV, vol. 3, p. 474; *OR,* 35, pt. 2, pp. 598–99, 610–11; *MDT,* 8 August 1864, p. 2; *CI,* 12 August 1864, p. 3.

    22. Sanford, *14th Illinois,* p. 191; Tarrant, *1st Kentucky,* pp. 368–69; *Atlanta Journal,* 12 February 1902, p. 6; Felton, "War Memories," p. 24; Roach, *The Prisoner of War,* p. 135.

    23. *CDS,* 3 August 1864, p. 1; *OR,* 38, pt. 2, pp. 916, 926; Capron, "Stoneman's Raid," pp. 677–78; Haskell Diary, 30 July 1864; Weir Diary, 29 [30] July 1864; *IDJ,* 16 August 1864, p. 2; *LDJ,* 14 September 1864, p. 1. The paucity of detailed medical records makes it difficult to determine the full extent of Stoneman's losses in front of Macon. Stoneman's chief surgeon, Dr. Hawkins Brown, quoted by the *Macon Daily Confederate* in the *Montgomery Daily Mail,* 7 August 1864, p. 2, said he "did not *know* of but one man killed and five wounded." Stoneman himself allegedly told a citizen he had seventeen killed and twenty-seven wounded. The *Columbus Times,* 2 August 1864, p. 2, reported the Yankees buried seven of their dead at Cross Keys, a half mile east of Walnut Creek. Other Confederate estimates of Stoneman's casualties generally ranged from fifteen to twenty-nine killed and an unknown number wounded. See *AP,* 4 August 1864, p. 2; *MSR,* 3 August 1864, p. 2; *DCE,* 2 August 1864, p. 1; *SR,* 2 August 1864, p. 2; Mary Ann Lamar Cobb to "My Dear Mother," 31 July 1864, Cobb Papers.

    24. Tarrant, *1st Kentucky,* pp. 361–62; *LDJ,* 14 September 1864, p. 1; Sanford, *14th Illinois,* p. 190; *OR,* 38, pt. 2, p. 916; Angel, "To Secretary 5th Ind. Cav. Assn.," p. 28. "Why there was no attempt made to cross the bridge no one will ever know," Lieutenant Isaac M. Brown of the 6th Indiana wrote in the *Columbus Republican,* 22 July 1875, p. 1, "unless it was because Stoneman was too drunk to appreciate the situation. . . ." This, he added, was "the common opinion of all I talked with on the subject at that time and afterwards." Brown's accusation is questionable at best. He did not actually see Stoneman drunk, and Stoneman had a history of severe digestive problems which probably precluded the use of alcohol. When Major Thomas W. Osborne, chief of artillery of the Army of the Tennessee and a contemporary of Stoneman's in the Army of the Potomac, heard a similar story during the March to the Sea in November 1864, he asserted "the General never drinks intoxicating liquors of any kind." See Harwell and Racine, eds., *The Fiery Trail,* p. 56.

    25. L. J. Bruner, "A Seven Day's Ride In Rebeldom," p. 9; Butler, "The Stoneman Raid," p. 10.

    26. Butler, "The Stoneman Raid," p. 10; *OR,* 38, pt. 2, pp. 916, 920, 926; Capron,

"Stoneman's Raid," p. 678; Wells, *Touch of Elbow*, pp. 209–10. Stoneman's awareness of Rebel troops at Milledgeville lends credence to the idea he may have sent a sizable scouting detachment in that direction sometime after leaving Clinton. According to the *Milledgeville Southern Recorder*, 3 August 1864, p. 2, at daylight on July 30 eighty Yankee cavalrymen approached within two miles of the city on the Garrison Road and then withdrew "after looking at the military force near the depot." A correspondent for the *Atlanta* [Macon] *Daily Intelligencer*, 3 August 1864, p. 2, claimed two of these Yanks, dressed in jeans, slipped into the city on foot and actually conversed with the militiamen bivouacked around the depot while the rest of the detachment waited at Fishing Creek. A "respected" Milledgeville resident, Captain William Rice, whom the Yankees held prisoner from 6:00 A.M. until 10:00 A.M., told the *Southern Recorder* the officer in command was named Wheeler. The only officer by that name in Stoneman's whole division was Captain George H. Wheeler, who commanded Company H of the 11th Kentucky Cavalry.

27. *IDJ*, 16 August 1864, p. 2; Sammons, *Recollections*, p. 29; *CR*, 22 July 1875, p. 1; Haskell Diary, 30 July 1864; Butler, "The Stoneman Raid," p. 10; *MDT*, 4 August 1864, p. 2; *CDS*, 4 August 1864, p. 1; *AP*, 11 August 1864, p. 2; *ACS*, 6 August 1864, p. 1; Holmes Diary, 30 July 1864.

18. STONEMAN'S RAID: CROSS KEYS TO SUNSHINE CHURCH, JULY 30–JULY 31, 1864

1. These Rebel scouts were probably part of a detachment commanded by Captain S. O. Peyton of the 9th Kentucky Cavalry and Captain S. Jeff Rogers of the 1st Kentucky Cavalry. See *ASB*, 10 August 1864, p. 2.

2. Wells, *Touch of Elbow*, p. 211; Williams, *Jones County*, pp. 20, 242, 250; *OR*, 38, pt. 2, pp. 916, 926; Capron, "Stoneman's Raid," pp. 678–79; Sanford, *14th Illinois*, p. 192; *NT*, 12 September 1895, p. 3; *NT*, 30 August 1883, p. 7; Tarrant, *1st Kentucky*, p. 363; *CR*, 22 July 1875, p. 1; *DAT*, 18 August 1864, p. 1.

3. The *Daily Columbus Enquirer*, 5 August 1864, p. 1, quoting the *Macon Daily Confederate*, 3 August 1864, said Iverson's column numbered only 900 men, but all the other reliable accounts put the number at 1,300 to 1,400. See Dodson, ed., *Wheeler and His Cavalry*, pp. 222, 233; Ray, "Career of Gen. Iverson during Days of Sixties," p. 4; R. R. Gaines, "Reminiscences of the 3rd Alabama Cavalry," p. 14, 3rd Alabama Cavalry Papers; Young, *Confederate Wizards of the Saddle*, p. 582; Alfred Iverson, Jr., to Alfred Iverson, Sr., quoted by *The Countryman*, 23 August 1864, p. 458.

4. Wheeler, "Reports"; Dodson, ed., *Wheeler and His Cavalry*, pp. 220–22; *ADI*, 21 August 1864, p. 2 (quotes by Iverson's aide); Iverson to Major E. S. Burford, 28 July 1864, Alfred Iverson, Jr., Papers; *DCE*, 5 August 1864, p. 1; Recollection in J. A. Wynn Papers; Mims, *The Prattville Dragoons*, p. 9; Brewer, *Alabama*, pp. 679, 682, 688; Evans, ed., *CMH*, vol. 8: *Alabama*, pp. 257, 261, 279; *Memorial Record of Alabama*, 1:132; John W. DuBose, "Twelfth Alabama Cavalry 1863–1865," p. 5, 12th Alabama Cavalry Papers; Kentucky Adjutant General, *Report, Confederate Volunteers*, 1:538–39, 2:5, 236; Record of Events, July–December 1864, Companies A-G, 1st Kentucky Cavalry, reel 20, M-861, RG 109; Record of Events, July–December 1864, Companies B, C, D, and G, 2nd (Woodward's) Kentucky Cavalry, reel 20, M-861, RG 109; Lindsley, ed., *Military Annals of Tennessee*, p. 803; "B. F. White," pp. 561–62; Williams, *Jones County*, pp. 115–16; *OR*, 38, pt. 2, pp. 916, 920; pt. 3, p. 953. Except for a brief postwar reminiscence by Private B. C. Ward of the 1st Kentucky Cavalry, quoted by Mrs. Williams in *Jones County*, none of the Confederate sources make any mention of Iverson dividing his command and sending Butler's brigade down the west bank of the Ocmulgee. However, one of Iverson's aides hinted Ward's account might be correct when he noted in a lengthy letter to the *Atlanta* [Macon] *Daily Intelligencer*, 21 August

1864, p. 2, "General Iverson had committed himself to the direct pursuit . . . moving at the same time in such a manner as to be closing on Stoneman, and at the same time not to be thrown off the track, in case he should attempt a ruse."

5. The claim that Iverson was "very familiar with the country and people" around Clinton originated in Wheeler, "Reports," and was repeated in *Wheeler and His Cavalry,* pp. 221–22. However, in a letter to the *Macon Telegraph,* 20 November 1929, p. 4, Iverson's nephew, Alfred Iverson Branham, asserted his uncle "never visited Clinton after he left the town as a child."

6. Iverson's obituary in the *Atlanta Georgian,* 31 March 1911, p. 1, credited him with being the colonel of his regiment and "serving thru the Mexican campaign from Buena Vista to the City of Mexico, with signal honors." His compiled service records make it clear this is not true.

7. Evans, ed., *CMH,* vol. 7: *Georgia,* pp. 424–25; Northen, *Men of Mark in Georgia,* 2:339–40, 3:435–36; Warner, *Generals in Gray,* pp. 147–48; *Atlanta Georgian,* 31 March 1911, p. 1; Jones, comp., "Holt Genealogy," pp. 69–71, 73–74, 88; Williams, *Jones County,* p. 568; Compiled Service Records, RG 94; Pension Records, RG 15; "Pension Application," Iverson-Branham Papers; Flanigan, *Gwinnett County,* 2:499; Alfred Iverson, Jr., to Henry C. Wayne, 26 February and 5 March 1861, Alfred Iverson, Jr., Letters; *DCE,* 1 August 1861, p. 2; *OR,* 11, pt. 2, pp. 554, 625–26, 642, 644; *OR,* 19, pt. 1, pp. 939–940, 1020, 1024, 1029, 1040–45; pt. 2, pp. 684, 699; Jones, "Roster of General Officers," pp. A48–49; Clark, ed., *Histories of the Several Regiments and Battalions from North Carolina,* 1:633–37; 2:111–15, 119, 239–40; Tucker, *High Tide at Gettysburg,* pp. 62, 127–33; Freeman, *Lee's Lieutenants,* 2:499; 3:83–86, 201; Patterson, "The Death of Iverson's Brigade," pp. 13–18; Kross, "That One Error Fills Him with Faults," pp. 48–52; *OR,* 25, pt. 1, pp. 983–94; *OR,* 27, pt. 2, pp. 342, 444–45, 451, 552–55, 562, 578–81; pt. 3, pp. 993, 1016, 1025, 1059–60; *OR,* 29, pt. 1, pp. 399; pt. 2, pp. 771, 775; *OR,* 51, pt. 2, pp. 772, 844; *OR,* 32, pt. 2, p. 818; "Special Field Orders No. 35, Head Quarters Army Tenn., In the Field July 2, 1864," Martin Papers; *OR,* 38, pt. 3, p. 951.

8. *OR,* 38, pt. 2, pp. 916, 926–27; Capron, "Stoneman's Raid," pp. 679–80; Sanford, *14th Illinois,* p. 192; *DAT,* 18 August 1864, p. 1 (Sergeant John Kesler's account); *DAT,* 22 August 1864, p. 1 (quoting Major Myles Keogh); *DAT,* 12 August 1864, p. 1; *DFP,* 16 August 1864, p. 1; *RIU,* 17 August 1864, p. 2; *IDJ,* 16 August 1864, p. 2; Tarrant, *1st Kentucky,* p. 363; *CR,* 22 July 1875, p. 1; Butler, "The Stoneman Raid," p. 10; Haskell Diary, 30 July 1864; *DAT,* 2 September 1864, p. 4; Wells, *Touch of Elbow,* pp. 211–12; *DCE,* 5 August 1864, p. 1; *AP,* 4 August 1864, p. 1; *ADI,* 21 August 1864, p. 2. According to Williams, *Jones County,* pp. 272, 336, there is no record of Sunshine Church's denomination.

9. Jones, "The Late Maj. Gen. William Wirt Allen," p. 324; Evans, ed., *CMH,* vol. 8: *Alabama,* pp. 385–86; Wheeler Scrapbook, pp. 15, 33; *OR,* 16, pt. 1, p. 899; *OR,* 20, pt. 1, pp. 957–60; Jones, "Roster of General Officers," pp. A26–27, A76; Brewer, *Alabama,* p. 469.

10. *ADI,* 21 August 1864, p. 2; *DCE,* 5 August 1864, p. 1; *AP,* 4 August 1864, p. 1; Williams, *Jones County,* pp. 272–73; *OR,* 38, pt. 2, pp. 916, 927; Capron, "Stoneman's Raid," pp. 679–80; *DAT,* 12 August 1864, p. 1; *DAT,* 2 September 1864, p. 4; *DFP,* 16 August 1864, p. 1 (quote by Michigan officer); *IDJ,* 16 August 1864, p. 2; Sanford, *14th Illinois,* p. 194; *LDJ,* 14 September 1864, p. 1; Tarrant, *1st Kentucky,* pp. 363, 369 (Lieutenant Richard Huffman's account); Jenkins, Case Number 00694, RG 153; *DAT,* 22 August 1864, p. 1; *NT,* 19 September 1895, p. 3 (Sergeant Charles A. Wing's account); Wells, *Touch of Elbow,* pp. 63–64, 212–15. Wells remembered his cousin and Jeff Mills as sergeants; however, the Muster Roll, July–August 1864, Company F, 8th Michigan Cavalry, RG 94, lists them both as corporals.

11. Convis, *The Honor of Arms: A Biography of Myles W. Keogh,* pp. 3–34, 40, 42; *OR,* 12, pt. 1, p. 697; *OR,* 27, pt. 1, pp. 921, 930; Pohanka, "Myles Keogh from the Vatican to the Little Big Horn," pp. 15–19; *NT,* 13 October 1898, pp. 1–2 (quote by Ohio cavalryman); George H. Thomas to Edwin M. Stanton, 22 June 1865, Myles Keogh File, reel 102, Letters Received by

the Commission Branch of the Adjutant General's Office, 1863–1870, M-1064 (hereafter cited as M-1064), RG 94; *CDC,* 12 August 1864, p. 3; *NYH,* 13 August 1864, p. 1; *ADI,* 21 August 1864, p. 2. Keogh's horse, Tom, was killed under him during the battle of Sunshine Church, but it is not clear whether it was during this charge or sometime later in the day. See Convis, *The Honor of Arms,* p. 44; Pohanka, "Myles Keogh," p. 20.

12. *OR,* 38, pt. 2, p. 927; Capron, "Stoneman's Raid," p. 681; Jenkins, Case Number 00694, RG 153; *NT,* 8 February 1900, p. 3. Private Dennis's antagonists probably belonged to the 12th Alabama Cavalry of Allen's brigade. See Brewer, *Alabama,* p. 688; Evans, ed., *CMH,* vol. 8: *Alabama,* p. 279; *Memorial Record of Alabama,* 1:132.

13. After the war, Hall told a bizarre story in the *National Tribune,* 14 August 1884, p. 3, claiming that "Private John Smouse, of the 2d Ind. Cav." [Private John Smaltz, 5th Indiana Cavalry], who died from the effects of an amputation at Sunshine Church, was buried under a headboard bearing Hall's name, company, and regiment. His story was repeated by King and Derby, comps., *Camp-Fire Sketches and Battlefield Echoes of the Rebellion,* pp. 33–35. However, when Sherman's troops passed through Hillsboro in November 1864, a Federal surgeon reported Private John Smaltz, Company D, 5th Indiana Cavalry, was one of several of Stoneman's men whose bodies local residents had buried near Sunshine Church. John C. Hall's name did not appear on the list. Smaltz was later reinterred in the national cemetery at Andersonville, Georgia. See *OR,* 44, p. 80; Quartermaster General's Office, *Roll of Honor,* 17:497.

14. *OR,* 38, pt. 2, p. 927; Capron, "Stoneman's Raid," pp. 680–81; Jenkins, Case Number 00694, RG 153; Williams, *Jones County,* p. 115; *WBB,* 24 September 1864, p. 1; *NT,* 1 February 1883, p. 1. In "Stoneman's Raid," p. 681, Capron claimed he led Quigg's battalion "in person." This is not borne out by the testimony in Jenkins, RG 153.

15. Jenkins, Case Number 00694, RG 153; Sanford, *14th Illinois,* p. 306; Jenkins to James Grant Wilson, 3 October 1862, David P. Jenkins Letter. Major Henry C. Connelly recalled, "David P. Jenkins . . . was a pet of Governor [Richard] Yates. As an officer he was never a success in the regiment." See Connelly, "Recollections," p. 459.

16. *IDJ,* 16 August 1864, p. 2 (quote by Colonel Biddle and an Indiana officer); Compiled Service Records, RG 94; Morning Reports, 31 July 1864, Company H, 6th Indiana Cavalry, RG 94; Indiana Adjutant General, *Report,* 2:656, 8:609; *CR,* 22 July 1875, p. 1; Haskell Diary, 31 July 1864; Butler, "The Stoneman Raid," p. 11. Francis Green, a paroled Confederate who lived between Round Oak and Five Points, apparently led at least part of the 4th Georgia into position to attack Stoneman's rear guard. Hearing the firing that morning, he had ridden over to the Hillsboro Road, where he met a captain and twenty-five Confederate cavalrymen near Round Oak. Asked if he could show them a way to reach the rear of the Yankee column, Green replied he knew every pig path and led them past Ben Green's, the old Butts place, and Luke Mercer's before reentering the Hillsboro Road at Wayside. Yelling and shooting, the Rebels charged several Yankees clustered around Jonathan Holmes's well and sent them running up the road toward Sunshine Church. See Williams, *Jones County,* p. 117.

17. Butler, "The Stoneman Raid," p. 11.

18. *OR,* 38, pt. 2, pp. 914, 927; *IDJ,* 16 August 1864, p. 2; Butler, "The Stoneman Raid," p. 11; *PRB,* 18 August 1864, p. 2; *NT,* 12 September 1895, p. 3; Tarrant, *1st Kentucky,* p. 364 (Lieutenant Richard Huffman's account); *NT,* 12 May 1904, p. 3; Dodson, "Stampede of Federal Cavalry," p. 124; Henderson, comp., *Roster of the Confederate Soldiers of Georgia,* 4:884; Holmes Diary, 31 August [July] 1864; *LDJ,* 14 September 1864, p. 1; Jenkins, Case Number 00694, RG 153.

19. *AP,* 4 August 1864, p. 1; D. S. Bethune to John W. DuBose, 26 September 1906, 51st Alabama Cavalry Papers; *ADI,* 21 August 1864, p. 2.

20. In his postwar account, Capron juggled the facts, trying to place the blame for his brigade's collapse on the failure of Adams's Kentuckians to hold their ground. This is patently incorrect. Capron's troopers were the first to feel the brunt of the Confederate attack, and even

Stoneman asserted, "Capron's brigade gave way at once and was followed by Adams' (Kentucky) brigade. . . ." See *OR,* 38, pt. 2, pp. 914, 917.

21. *OR,* 38, pt. 2, p. 927; Capron, "Stoneman's Raid," pp. 681–83; *NT,* 9 November 1899, p. 3 (Private Isaac Dennis's account); Capron, "Stoneman Raid to Macon," pp. 716–17; Sanford, *14th Illinois,* pp. 198–99; *NT,* 19 September 1895, p. 3; Dodson, "Stampede of Federal Cavalry," p. 124.

22. *ADI,* 21 August 1864, p. 2; *OR,* 38, pt. 2, p. 914; *LDJ,* 14 September 1864, p. 1; Tarrant, *1st Kentucky,* p. 364; *NT,* 29 November 1888, p. 4 (quoting Stoneman); Record of Ordnance and Ordnance Stores, vol. 7, 5th Indiana Cavalry, RG 156; Holmes Diary, 31 August [July] 1864; Angel, "To Secretary 5th Ind. Cav. Assn.," pp. 28–29; *NT,* 3 April 1902, p. 2 (Stoneman's lament for his horse). Lieutenant Angel said Beauregard was a gift Pierre G. T. Beauregard had presented to Stoneman before the war. Given that Pierre Beauregard and Stoneman never served together, it seems more likely the horse was simply named for the Confederate general.

23. *NT,* 3 April 1902, p. 2; *NT,* 6 March 1902, p. 3; Holmes Diary, 31 August [July] 1864; *NT,* 6 February 1902, p. 3; *OR,* 38, pt. 2, p. 914; *LDJ,* 14 September 1864, p. 1.

24. Lieutenant Huffman reported Captain Wolford was killed after he had dismounted. However, in a postwar reminiscence in *National Tribune,* 16 November 1899, p. 7, Private John P. Logan of Company A, 1st Kentucky, said Wolford "wheeled round to the left of the company and asked for Dr. Brown. The next shot from the battery struck him in the head, severing it from his body. I saw him standing in his stirrups without a head." The *Macon Daily Confederate,* 3 August 1864, quoted by *Daily Columbus Enquirer,* 5 August 1864, p. 1, reported a rumor accusing Wolford of capturing Lieutenant William D. Burton of the 51st Alabama Cavalry and then shooting him through the head. However, Miller, *Wheeler's Favorites: A Regimental History of the 51st Alabama Cavalry Regiment,* p. 46, noted Burton was killed "leading a charge."

25. *OR,* 38, pt. 2, pp. 914, 917, 920; *DFP,* 16 August 1864, p. 1; *DAT,* 12 August 1864, p. 1; *IDJ,* 16 August 1864, p. 2; Tarrant, *1st Kentucky,* pp. 364–65 (Lieutenant Huffman's account), 371, 372, 396; *CE,* 23 September 1864, p. 1; *NT,* 16 November 1899, p. 7; Williams, *Jones County,* p. 115; Cornwell, "A Paper by Louise Cornwell," UDC 5:251; Kentucky Adjutant General, *Report,* 1:2–3; Compiled Service Records, RG 94; *CDC,* 23 August 1864, p. 2; Kendrick, "A Non-Combatant's War Reminiscences," p. 459; *LDJ,* 14 September 1864, p. 1. For a slightly different version of the exchange between Stoneman and Adams, see Tarrant, *1st Kentucky,* p. 365, and Quisenberry, "The First Kentucky Cavalry, U.S.A.," p. 17.

26. *OR,* 38, pt. 2, p. 917; *RIU,* 17 August 1864, p. 2; *NT,* 18 October 1888, p. 3; *NT,* 12 May 1904, p. 3 (Private John C. Weddle quotation); Dodson, "Stampede of Federal Cavalry," p. 124; Tarrant, *1st Kentucky,* pp. 365, 375.

27. *OR,* 38, pt. 2, pp. 914, 917; *ADI,* 21 August 1864, p. 2; Fifth Indiana Cavalry Association, *17th Annual Reunion,* p. 36; *NT,* 3 April 1902, p. 2; Finney, "A Digest History of the Fifth Indiana Cavalry during the War of the Rebellion," p. 46 (quoting initial exchange between Stoneman and Butler); Butler, "The Stoneman Raid," pp. 11–12; *AP,* 4 August 1864, p. 1; *DFP,* 16 August 1864, p. 1 (Butler calls Stoneman a liar and a coward); Angel, "To Secretary 5th Ind. Cav. Assn.," p. 29 (quoting Stoneman's assertion he was in command and exchanges between Butler and his officers); Sammons, *Recollections,* p. 30.

28. *DAT,* 2 September 1864, p. 4; *DFP,* 16 August 1864, p. 1; Haskell Diary, 31 July 1864; *NT,* 1 January 1914, p. 7; *NT,* 8 February 1923, p. 2. In a letter appearing in the *Columbus Republican,* 22 July 1875, p. 1, Lieutenant Isaac M. Brown of the 6th Indiana said, "Orders were given to see that every gun was loaded and a fresh cap on, and we moved up the hill in full view of rebels who stood in line all around us at . . . order arms. Field glasses were brought to bear upon us in the front and rear, yet no commands were given until we had orders to charge, when the line in front came up with their guns and fired just as we did. We scattered the line and the rebels run [sic] like scared sheep. We lost several men in this charge but the

rebels lost many more." However, Sergeant Winfield S. Matson of Company C painted a very different picture of the 6th Indiana's escape. Writing to the *Putnam Republican Banner,* 18 August 1864, p. 2, he reported, "We flanked Wheeler [Iverson] and got out with very little fighting." Sergeant Matson was Lieutenant Colonel Court Matson's younger brother.

29. *AP,* 4 August 1864, p. 1; *ASB,* 10 August 1864, p. 2; *NT,* 3 April 1902, p. 2; Hargis, *Thrilling Experiences of a First Georgia Cavalryman in the Civil War,* p. 22; *ADI,* 21 August 1864, p. 2. After the war, R. T. Logan and O. P. Hargis of the 1st Georgia Cavalry both asserted Iverson was in the rear because he was "ill" and "not on duty." See Robert Logan, "Membership Record," UDC 13:319; Hargis, *1st Georgia,* p. 22.

30. *ASB,* 10 August 1864, p. 2; *NT,* 3 April 1902, p. 2. In a postwar recollection, J. A. Wynn of the 1st Georgia Cavalry said about forty minutes elapsed between the appearance of the Federal flag of truce and agreement on the terms of surrender. See J. A. Wynn Papers.

31. *ADI,* 21 August 1864, p. 2; Butler, "The Stoneman Raid," p. 12; Sammons, *Recollections,* p. 30; *MSR,* 3 August 1864, p. 2; Cornwell, "A Paper by Louise Cornwell," UDC 5:251; *NT,* 3 April 1902, p. 2; Williams, *Jones County,* p. 151; Holmes Diary, 31 August [July] 1864; Hargis, *1st Georgia,* p. 22; *ECN,* 10 August 1864, p. 1; *DCE,* 5 August 1864, p. 1. The number of captured Federals is taken from the Holmes Diary. Eyewitness Confederate accounts in the *Athens Southern Banner,* 10 August 1864, p. 2, and *Macon Daily Confederate,* 3 August 1864, quoted by *Daily Columbus Enquirer,* 5 August 1864, p. 1, put the number at 525 and 600, but these figures probably include prisoners captured after the formal surrender.

19. STONEMAN'S RAID: SUNSHINE CHURCH TO MARIETTA, JULY 31–AUGUST 4, 1864

1. *NT,* 30 August 1883, p. 7; Weir Diary, 30 [31] July 1864. On page 147 of *History of Jones County,* Mrs. Williams noted, "A Negro belonging to Sam Griswold, named Minor, ran away and joined Sherman's forces and acted as a guide for him in Jones County. He made himself very obnoxious by leading the Yankees in their depredations on Jones County people and when . . . Stoneman surrendered, Minor was captured and swung to a limb of a nearby tree." None of the eyewitness accounts cited in these chapters make any mention of seeing a black man hanged. The incident may have been part of the March to the Sea instead of Stoneman's raid.

2. Hargis, *1st Georgia,* pp. 22–23; "B. F. White," pp. 561–62.

3. Hargis, *1st Georgia,* p. 23; *ADI,* 21 August 1864, p. 2; Fifth Indiana Cavalry Association, *2nd and 3rd Re-Unions,* p. 14. An anonymous handwritten account in the Iverson-Branham Family Papers entitled "A horse, some horses and two Captured Knights" asserts Stoneman and Iverson became "pleasantly acquainted" while serving together at Fort Riley, Kansas, and goes on to quote Stoneman as saying "that if he had to be captured, he could not think of anyone he would rather have had for his captors than the command of 'Gen. Alfred Iverson.'" Iverson allegedly replied "that if fates were such that Alfred Iverson were ever captured he hoped it would be by 'General George Stoneman.'" Stoneman, however, never served at Fort Riley and it is doubtful he ever met Iverson prior to the battle of Sunshine Church. He was much chagrined by his surrender, and while he did exchange greetings with the Rebel general, it seems highly unlikely he expressed any pleasure about the circumstances of his capture.

4. Fifth Indiana Cavalry Association, *2nd and 3rd Re-Unions,* p. 14; *ADI,* 21 August 1864, p. 2; Alfred Iverson, Jr., to Alfred Iverson, Sr., quoted by *TC,* 23 August 1864, p. 458; Charles W. Homsher, "A Few Notes While in Andersonville Prison, Ga.," p. 1, *Civil War Times Illustrated* Collection; Hargis, *1st Georgia,* p. 23; Sammons, *Recollections,* p. 31; Holmes, "Andersonville and How We Got There," p. 3.

5. Wells, *Touch of Elbow,* pp. 216–17.

6. *MDT,* 4 August 1864, p. 2; *TC,* 2 August 1864, p. 419; *OR,* 38, pt. 2, pp. 917, 929; *NT,* 12 May 1904, p. 3; Harris, *The Life and Letters of Joel Chandler Harris,* pp. 2–3 (description

of Eatonton); Tarrant, *1st Kentucky,* p. 366 (Lieutenant Huffman's account); *MDT,* 5 August 1864, p. 2; *DAT,* 12 August 1864, p. 1; *DAT,* 22 August 1864, p. 1; *DFP,* 16 August 1864, p. 1; *IDJ,* 16 August 1864, p. 2; Haskell Diary, 1 August 1864; *TC,* 9 August 1864, p. 427; *ACS,* 11 August 1864, p. 1. The correspondents of the *Detroit Free Press* and the *Detroit Advertiser and Tribune,* neither of whom accompanied the raid, both credited the 8th Michigan with burning the depot at Eatonton, as did Colonel Capron in his official report. The author believes the 6th Indiana's eyewitness account in the *Indianapolis Daily Journal* is more likely correct.

7. Wayne's Report, Georgia Adjutant General's Letter Book, 25:220; *MSR,* 3 August 1864, p. 2; *MCU,* 9 August 1864, p. 3; *ADC,* 6 August 1864, p. 3; *MDA,* 8 August 1864, p. 1. General Wayne complained that "owing to a want of court [concerted?] action, due to irregular troops without discipline, my orders were not carried out and the party escaped." *The Countryman,* 2 August 1864, p. 419, added that "a blunder on the part of an officer caused a delay which resulted in the burning of the depot at Eatonton."

8. *OR,* 38, pt. 2, p. 917; Dodson, "Stampede of Federal Cavalry," p. 124; *MDT,* 8 August 1864, p. 2; Kendrick, "War Reminiscences," pp. 458–59; *ACS,* 6 August 1864, p. 1; *CDC,* 23 August 1864, p. 2; *DFP,* 16 August 1864, p. 1; Record of Events, July–August 1864, Companies E and K, 8th Michigan Cavalry, reel 84, M-594, RG 94; Haskell Diary, 1 August 1864; *IDJ,* 16 August 1864, p. 2; *ADC,* 4 August 1864, p. 1; Mrs. Kirby-Smith Anderson, "Sherman's March to the Sea," UDC 12:102. The *Daily Constitutionalist* said the Yankees also wounded a Dr. Oglesby. The other eyewitness accounts do not mention a second casualty, but census records show a Dr. Hugh I. Ogilby was living in Madison in 1860. There are also conflicting accounts about what happened to Smith. Mrs. Kirby-Smith Anderson, apparently citing oral tradition in Madison, said he dragged himself down Main Street to Dr. Abram Saffold's office and died by the front steps. A similar account, written long after the war, is found in the Thomas Preston Gibbs Papers, but Louise McHenry Hicky asserted in *Rambles through Morgan County,* pp. 13–14, 52, that Smith managed to get to his sister's home, the Stokes-McHenry house, a block off Main Street, and died in the hallway. There may be a bit of truth in both versions of the story, since a contemporary account in the *Macon Daily Telegraph* reported Smith died the day after he was shot. As for the men who shot him, some of Russ Butler's Kentucky cavalrymen surprised and captured three Yankee stragglers and a runaway Negro they found sleeping twelve miles from Madison on August 2. Two of the prisoners were identified as the men who shot Mr. Smith. The *Macon Daily Telegraph,* 8 August 1864, p. 2, said they were sent to Augusta, but Captain T. J. Williams, an escaped Federal prisoner from Camp Oglethorpe, heard reports as he made his way back to Union lines that three of Stoneman's men and a Negro, captured near Madison, were "murdered in cold blood." See Williams, "Captain Williams' Escape," p. 186.

9. Haskell Diary, 1 August 1864; *MDT,* 8 August 1864, p. 2 (quoting a citizen); George F. Ponder vs. the U.S., Case Number 4,470, RG 123; Record of Events, July–August 1864, Companies E and K, 8th Michigan Cavalry, reel 84, M-594, RG 94; *DAT,* 12 August 1864, p. 1; *IDJ,* 16 August 1864, p. 2; *NT,* 12 May 1904, p. 3; *OR,* 38, pt. 2, pp. 917, 928; Capron, "Stoneman's Raid," p. 685; Sanford, *14th Illinois,* p. 201. Federal accounts paint a very confusing picture of just when and where the 8th Michigan and 6th Indiana overtook Adams's brigade. The *Detroit Advertiser and Tribune*'s correspondent, who, as previously mentioned, was not with the expedition, said the 8th Michigan "joined the two Kentucky regiments before we reached Eatonton." He retracted this statement in the 22 August 1864 issue, p. 1, but did not offer any further details. In his official report, Lieutenant Colonel Bob Smith said, "Adams' brigade was joined about noon by a detachment of the Eighth Michigan, under command of Major Buck, and the Sixth Indiana, under command of Lieutenant Colonel Matson, came through Madison about 2 p.m., and here destroyed a large amount of commissary and quartermaster stores." This ambiguously structured sentence can be read two ways. Either the 8th Michigan and the 6th Indiana both overtook Adams about noon and they all marched through Madison at 2:00 P.M., or the 8th Michigan caught up with Adams about noon

(after he had already passed Madison) and then the 6th Indiana rode into Madison at 2:00 P.M. This second interpretation is probably correct. All the Confederate eyewitness accounts agree Adams's brigade reached Madison about 9:00 A.M. and the company records cited in RG 94 specifically stated the 8th Michigan joined Adams *after* passing through Madison. As for the 6th Indiana, Sergeant Haskell noted in his diary the regiment caught up with Colonel Adams's brigade that evening, somewhere beyond Madison. The *Indianapolis Daily Journal*'s correspondent added the rendezvous took place "about fourteen miles" from Monroe. Fair Play is about eleven miles from Monroe.

10. Turner published his remarkable newspaper at his home, Turnwold Plantation, just southeast of Glade's Crossroads. His typesetter was young Joel Chandler Harris, who later became famous as the author of the Uncle Remus stories.

11. *OR*, 38, pt. 2, pp. 920–21, 927–30; Capron, "Stoneman's Raid," pp. 683–85; Sanford, *14th Illinois*, pp. 200, 205–6; *NT*, 19 September 1895, p. 3; Capron, "Stoneman Raid to Macon," p. 716 (quoting Horace Capron's reaction to Stoneman's surrender); *DAT*, 2 September 1864, p. 4; *AJ*, 5 September 1864, p. 2 (quote by Michigan sergeant); *WBB*, 24 September 1864, p. 1; *NT*, 26 September 1895, p. 3; Wayne's Report, Georgia Adjutant General's Letter Book, 25:220; *ADC*, 6 August 1864, p. 3; *OR*, 44, pp. 270, 271, 283, 291; *TC*, 2 August 1864, p. 419 (quote by Joseph Addison Turner); *TC*, 9 August 1864, p. 427. Just where Capron's column changed direction is uncertain. Sanford, in *14th Illinois*, pp. 200–201, and *National Tribune*, 19 September 1895, p. 3, said the column "marched rapidly through Columbus and Rutledge Station," but this author has been unable to find any record of a village or settlement called Columbus in Morgan or Jasper counties.

12. A story in the Athens Historical Society, *Newsletter*, May 1969, p. 2, alleges the Yankees gathered up a herd of mules at James C. Branch's plantation, south of Watkinsville, and began shooting them. When Branch made the Masonic sign of distress, an officer stopped the slaughter, saying, "This man has contributed enough." While the story undoubtedly has some basis in fact, it is hard to believe the raiders would waste what little ammunition they had to kill mules they desperately needed.

13. *OR*, 38, pt. 2, pp. 917, 928; *ADC*, 4 August 1864, p. 3; *ADC*, 6 August 1864, p. 1; *NT*, 19 September 1895, p. 3; *NT*, 21 May 1889, p. 3; *LDJ*, 14 September 1864, p. 1; *IDJ*, 16 August 1864, p. 2; *DAT*, 12 August 1864, p. 1; "High Shoals," p. 1; *ASW*, 10 August 1864, p. 2; Collier, "Yankees Raid Watkinsville," p. 18; Ashford, *Mother's Letters*, pp. 11–12; Tarrant, *1st Kentucky*, pp. 366, 369–70, Athens Daily Banner, 3 August 1922, pp. 1–2; Clarke County, Georgia, Inferior Court, Minutes of 9 August 1864, quoted in Athens Historical Society, *Newsletter*, p. 2; Haskell Diary, 2 August 1864; Sanford, *14th Illinois*, pp. 201–2; Capron, "Stoneman's Raid," pp. 679, 685–86.

14. *ASB*, 3 August 1864, p. 3; Mary Ann Cobb to "My Dear Husband," 3 August and 5 August 1864, Cobb Papers; Mary Ann Cobb to Colonel William M. Browne, 4 August 1864, William M. Browne Papers; *ASB*, 10 August 1864, p. 2; *ASW*, 10 August 1864, p. 2; *ADC*, 5 August 1864, p. 3; *Athens Daily Banner*, 3 August 1922, pp. 1–2; Stegeman, *These Men She Gave*, pp. 24, 107–8, 119–20. In her letters, Mrs. Cobb said Lumpkin's battery fired three shots. This seems credible, since there were three gun emplacements, but according to Record of Events, February 1864, reel 13, M-861, RG 109, Lumpkin's was a four-gun battery. While one gun might have been left to guard the Mitchell Bridge on the west side of town, the uppermost of the gun emplacements at the paper mill appears large enough to have held two guns. The *Athens Southern Banner* reported the battery fired four shells at the raiders, the first round allegedly killing a Yankee lieutenant and wounding four enlisted men. Federal accounts do not mention any casualties, and fifty-eight years later one of the home guards, G. L. Carson, Sr., told the *Athens Daily Banner*, "No one was killed in this skirmish. . . ." James W. Camak asserted in *Confederate Veteran* 23:310 that Athens's famous double-barreled cannon saw action at the paper mill, but he offered no evidence to support this claim. Later historians conjectured it was "very unlikely" the four-pounder gun was part of Lumpkin's battery and records in the National Archives leave no doubt Lumpkin's artillery consisted of four bronze

12-pounder howitzers. See Drewry, "The Double-Barrelled Cannon of Athens, Georgia," p. 446; Records Relating to Ordnance Stores, Powder Factory, 1862–1865, p. 358, Records of Ordnance Establishments at Augusta, Georgia, RG 109.

15. Capron offered no clues to the identity of his guide, but it was almost certainly one of the Clarke County civilians his men had taken prisoner: Jacob Klutts, Charley Burger, George Jarrell, David M. McClesky, Uriah Poss, and a Mr. Allen. Charley Burger was released fifteen miles above Watkinsville. McClesky, Poss, and Allen were also turned loose, but as of August 10, 1864, George Jarrell's whereabouts were unknown and Jacob Klutts never returned. One or both of them may have been shot or hanged for misdirecting Capron's column. See *ASB,* 10 August 1864, p. 2; *ASW,* 10 August 1864, p. 2; Ashford, *Mother's Letters,* p. 12; Collier, "Yankees Raid Watkinsville," pp. 7, 18; "High Shoals," p. 1.

16. After the war, Capron accused Adams of deliberately deserting him. "I can find no words of condemnation sufficiently strong in which to express my abhorrence of this cruel and uncalled-for desertion of my worn-out command," he wrote. However, contemporary accounts of the raid found no fault with Adams's conduct, and Capron in his official report placed the blame squarely on his guide for "leading me six miles away from the route agreed upon." The "heavy force" of infantry and cavalry Capron thought was threatening his right was probably an improvised mounted company consisting of thirty 16th Georgia cavalrymen and an equal number of civilians. Led by Major Ferdinand Cook, they left Athens on the Mitchell Bridge Road at sunset on August 2 but did not meet any Yankees. See Mary Ann Cobb to "My Dear Husband," 3 August and 5 August 1864, Cobb Papers; Mary Ann Cobb to Colonel William M. Browne, 4 August 1864, Browne Papers.

17. Lieutenant Colonel Robert W. Smith noted, "It is said . . . that instead of his giving orders to unsaddle, that he [Capron] had expressly forbidden it. Here statements seem to vary." See *OR,* 38, pt. 2, p. 918.

18. *OR,* 38, pt. 2, pp. 917–18, 928; Tarrant, *1st Kentucky,* pp. 366–67; Capron, "Stoneman's Raid," pp. 685–88; *IDJ,* 16 August 1864, p. 2; *NT,* 19 September 1895, p. 3; Wells, *Touch of Elbow,* p. 218; Haskell Diary, 2 August 1864; R. P. Williams, "A True Story of the Battle of King's Tan Yard," UDC 9:284; *CR,* 22 July 1875, p. 1 (Lieutenant Isaac M. Brown's account); *DAT,* 12 August 1864, p. 1; Sanford, *14th Illinois,* p. 202; *NT,* 24 January 1889, p. 3; *NT,* 9 September 1897, p. 2 (Private Isaac Dennis's account); *DAT,* 18 August 1864, p. 1; *DFP,* 16 August 1864, p. 1 (quote by 8th Michigan soldier); *PRB,* 18 August 1864, p. 2.

19. The march of Davidson's detachment up the west bank of the Oconee was responsible for the exaggerated reports of a Yankee column threatening Curtwright's Factory.

20. J. R. Kendrick said Butler's brigade reached Madison a little after midnight. Another eyewitness, Mr. T. Johnson, superintendent of the Southwestern Telegraph Company, told the *Macon Daily Telegraph,* 8 August 1864, p. 2, it was 7:00 A.M. Unnamed sources cited in the *Augusta Daily Constitutionalist,* 4 August 1864, pp. 1 and 3, gave times of 1:00 A.M. and 4:00 A.M. *Confederate Wizards of the Saddle,* p. 597, credited Lieutenant Robert L. Bowles of the 9th Kentucky Cavalry with command of the men picked to continue the pursuit, but this is obviously incorrect.

21. *ADI,* 21 August 1864, p. 2; *ADC,* 4 August 1864, pp. 1, 3; *ADC,* 6 August 1864, p. 1; *TC,* 9 August 1864, p. 427; *ASB,* 10 August 1864, p. 2; Kendrick, "War Reminiscences," p. 459; *MDT,* 8 August 1864, p. 2; Young, *Wizards of the Saddle,* pp. 596–97; Evans, ed., *CMH,* vol. 11: *Kentucky,* by J. Stoddard Johnston, pp. 287–88, 658; Mary Ann Cobb to Colonel William M. Browne, 4 August 1864, Browne Papers; Overley, "'Williams's Kentucky Brigade,' C.S.A.," pp. 460–61; Thompson, *The Orphan Brigade,* p. 960; Wheeler, "Reports"; Williams, "King's Tan Yard," UDC 9:284; Sanford, *14th Illinois,* p. 202; Capron, "Stoneman's Raid," p. 688; *DFP,* 16 August 1864, p. 1; *OR,* 38, pt. 2, p. 928; *CDC,* 15 August 1864, p. 1.

22. The *Athens Southern Banner,* 10 August 1864, p. 2, said seven Yankees drowned when the bridge collapsed.

23. *NT,* 9 September 1897, p. 2 (Private Isaac Dennis's account); Wells, *Touch of Elbow,* pp.

219–20; Capron, "Stoneman's Raid," pp. 688–89; *OR*, 38, pt. 2, pp. 928–29; *CDC*, 15 August 1864, p. 1; Capron, "Stoneman's Raid to Macon," p. 720; G. R. Pope to "Mrs. Col. Capron," 22 April 1865, Capron Papers; Sanford, *14th Illinois*, pp. 202–3; Haskell Diary, 3 August 1864; *PRB*, 18 August 1864, p. 2; *CR*, 22 July 1875, p. 1; *IDJ*, 16 August 1864, p. 2 (quoting Lieutenant Colonel Court Matson); Thompson, *The Orphan Brigade*, pp. 960–61 (quoting Confederate cavalryman); *NT*, 24 January 1889, p. 3; Wheeler, "Reports"; *ASW*, 10 August 1864, p. 2; *ASB*, 10 August 1864, p. 2; *DAT*, 12 August 1864, p. 1 (quoting Michigan trooper); *DFP*, 16 August 1864, p. 1 (quoting Captain Muir McDonald). Captain McDonald believed he had killed a Rebel officer, but Southern sources insist the only Confederate fatality at King's Tanyard was Private Martin Van Buren Parkhurst of the 9th Kentucky Cavalry. "We were intercepted by a Brigade that come in on another Road, capturing 2 and Killing Van instantly," wrote his kinsman, Captain J. F. Smith. "He had just went into the most gallant charge of the war and come out safe, but was killed I think by a person after he surrendered." See *ASW*, 10 August 1864, p. 2; Thompson, *The Orphan Brigade*, p. 944; Kentucky Adjutant General, *Report, Confederate Volunteers*, 2:28–29; J. F. Smith to "Dear Cousin," 15 August 1864, Christine Parkhurst Carruth Papers.

24. Huffman added "at one place there were six dead Rebels," but this appears to be an exaggeration.

25. The *Detroit Free Press* correspondent said the bridge over the Mulberry River collapsed at this point, *after* Adams's brigade had struck Breckinridge's column. However, Confederate eyewitnesses said they had already driven the Yankees into the river and were on their way back when Adams attacked. See *ASB*, 10 August 1864, p. 2; J. F. Smith to "Dear Cousin," 15 August 1864, Carruth Papers.

26. *NT*, 16 November 1899, p. 7; *DFP*, 16 August 1864, p. 1; *DAT*, 12 August 1864, p. 1; *RIU*, 17 August 1864, p. 2; *LDJ*, 14 September 1864, p. 1; *NT*, 21 March 1889, p. 3; *NT*, 12 May 1904, p. 3; Tarrant, *1st Kentucky*, pp. 367–68, 370 (Lieutenant Huffman's account and quoting Captain Peyton); *ASB*, 10 August 1864, p. 2; J. F. Smith to "Dear Cousin," 15 August 1864, Carruth Papers; *OR*, 38, pt. 2, p. 918 (quoting Lieutenant Colonel Smith); King Diary, 5 August 1864; *CE*, 23 September 1864, p. 1; Hitt, *Charged with Treason*, p. 106; Map N221–34, RG 77.

27. *OR*, 38, pt. 5, p. 363. The post commander at Marietta, Colonel Samuel Ross, greatly overestimated the strength of Adams's two regiments. Lieutenant Colonel Bob Smith, who was with the column, reported in *OR*, 38, pt. 2, p. 918, that Adams returned with about 490 men.

20. BACK FROM OBLIVION, JULY 30–AUGUST 12, 1864

1. *NT*, 19 September 1895, p. 3.

2. Sammons, *Recollections*, p. 31.

3. The fate of Stoneman's horse, or horses, is a bit of a mystery. After his favorite, Beauregard, was shot out from under him, he had mounted what he called a "worn down one." Sixty-five years later, in a letter to the *Macon Telegraph*, 20 November 1929, p. 4, Iverson's nephew recalled that at the time of his capture, "General Stoneman rode a magnificent black horse. He . . . asked General Iverson to take good care of his horse; not to let it go along with the other horses of his command. General Iverson sent the horse to my father's home on the Houston road, and there it stayed until General [James H.] Wilson captured Macon, and it was then delivered to an officer of Wilson's army." An anonymous account in the Iverson-Branham Family Papers, "A horse, some horses and two Captured Knights," pp. 6–7, surmised that on "a hard, fast raid such as the one planned to take Macon & Andersonville," Stoneman might have had more than one mount and added, "One of the captured General's horses was assigned to Adjutant [Richard F.] Lawton who kept it until after the war. . . . General Iverson's nephew,

Alfred Iverson Branham . . . recalls that tho' a small boy, he was present on the arrival of General Stoneman at the officers' camp in Macon. He remembered that General Stoneman was mounted on a 'beautiful black charger.' He was under the impression that General Stoneman asked his uncle, General Iverson, to keep his horse until after the war, that General Iverson agreed and that the horse was kept at 'Dunlop's farm' on Houston road and returned to General Stoneman at the close of the war." There is a chance, however, the "magnificent black horse" Iverson's nephew remembered was actually the one ridden by the 5th Indiana's Colonel Butler. In *A Source Book on the Early History of Cuthbert and Randolph County, Georgia,* p. 289, Annette McDonald Suarez asserted Stoneman was riding "a very beautiful sorrel horse, with black mane and tail" when he was captured. Colonel Crews's aide, James J. McDonald, claimed this horse and a matching mount from the captured Yankee stock and sent both animals to his home in Cuthbert. Stoneman did file a claim for one "Horse and Equipage lost . . . by capture in [the] Battle of Sunshine Church, Ga. July 30 [31] 1864," but this, presumably, was the horse shot out from under him shortly before he surrendered. See Horse Claim Awards, vol. 9, p. 71, Office of the Third Auditor, RG 217.

4. Fifth Indiana Cavalry Association, *2nd and 3rd Re-Unions,* p. 15 (Colonel Tom Butler's account); "Report of Disposition of Prisoners in Jones County Georgia," Samuel H. Stout Papers, Emory; *PI,* 13 September 1864, p. 2; *NT,* 16 January 1902, p. 3; Weir Diary, 30 [31] July, 31 July [1 August], 1–2 August 1864; *CT,* 4 August 1864, p. 1; *ADI,* 21 August 1864, p. 2; Williams, *Jones County,* pp. 115, 250 (quoting Stoneman); *OR,* 38, pt. 5, p. 937; *MDT,* 2 August 1864, p. 2; *Macon Telegraph,* 20 November 1929, p. 4; *CT,* 5 August 1864, p. 2; *AP,* 11 August 1864, p. 2 (Cuyler's expression of sympathy); *MDT,* 10 August 1864, p. 1 (quoting heavyset woman); Wells, *Touch of Elbow,* p. 227; Lathrop, "Gossipy Letter from Georgia," p. 520; Biddle, *Reminiscences of a Soldier's Wife,* pp. 247–49; Howell Cobb to F. A. Shoup, telegram, 1 August 1864, Sherman Papers. Stoneman's message apparently did not reach its destination until over a month later. See W. T. Sherman to Mrs. General Stoneman, 8 September 1864, Sherman Papers.

5. The prisoners and their guards probably bivouacked on Sand Creek in Jones County.

6. Most of Stoneman's men identified the Rebel captain as Henry Wirz, the prison commandant, but Private Perry Quick said it was Captain Winder. He did not specify whether he meant Captain W. S. Winder, the prison adjutant, or Captain Richard B. Winder, the post quartermaster. Captain Richard Winder later claimed he was on duty in Macon at this time. Captain Wirz swore he was absent on sick leave, but records prove he was at Andersonville on August 1, 1864, the day before Stoneman's men arrived. See *OR,* series II, vol. 8, pp. 731, 774; *OR,* series II, vol. 7, pp. 521–22; Page and Haley, *The True Story of Andersonville Prison,* p. 146.

7. Logan, "Membership Record," UDC 13:319; Recollection in Wynn Papers; Hargis, *1st Georgia,* p. 23; Holmes, "Andersonville," pp. 3–4 (quoting tattered Georgia cavalryman); Homsher, "Notes in Andersonville," pp. 1–2 (quotation by Hoosier soldier and exchange with woman at farmhouse); Sammons, *Recollections,* p. 32; *MSR,* 23 August 1864, p. 2 (citizens claiming troopers' horses); *Atlanta Journal,* 12 February 1902, p. 6; Felton, "War Memories," p. 24; *NT,* 30 August 1883, p. 7; Smith, ed., "Diary of Colonel John Henry Smith," p. 152; *ADI,* 3 August 1864, p. 2; *CT,* 5 August 1864, p. 2; *MDT,* 3 August 1864, p. 2; Whitenack, "Reminiscences," p. 131; Holmes Diary, 7 August 1864; Letteer[?], "Andersonville: Diary of a Prisoner," p. 5; Forbes, *Diary of a Soldier, and Prisoner of War in the Rebel Prisons,* p. 35; Kelley, *What I Saw and Suffered in Rebel Prisons,* pp. 60–61; Urban, *Battle Field and Prison Pen,* pp. 333–34; Spencer, *A Narrative of Andersonville,* pp. 72–74; *NT,* 6 December 1883, p. 7 (quoting guard at Andersonville); *AT,* 2 February 1893, p. 2; *NT,* 18 January 1883, p. 3; *NT,* 25 September 1890, p. 2; *NT,* 5 August 1897, p. 7; Vaughter, *Prison Life,* pp. 35, 40–44; *MDT,* 4 August 1864, p. 2; *OR,* series II, vol. 7, p. 565.

8. *MDT,* 4 August 1864, p. 2; Recollection in Wynn Papers; *ADI,* 4 August 1864, p. 1; *ADI,* 5 August 1864, p. 3; Cobb to "My Dear Wife," 5 August and 7 August 1864, Cobb Papers.

9. R. J. Hallett to Captain Tufts, 2 August 1864, Cobb to Captain S. S. Dunlap, 4 August 1864, Cobb Letter Book; *MSR,* 23 August 1864, p. 2; *MDT,* 11 August 1864, p. 2; *MDT,* 9 August 1864, p. 2.

10. *ASB,* 10 August 1864, p. 2; Thomas Crawford to "Mrs. Cobb," [3 August 1864?], Cobb Papers; Mary Ann Cobb to Colonel William M. Browne, 4 August 1864, Browne Papers; Hull, *Annals of Athens, Georgia,* pp. 263–64, 269, 273–74; *ASW,* 10 August 1864, p. 2; Mary Ann Cobb to "My Dear Husband," 5 August 1864, Cobb Papers; *ASW,* 10 August 1864, p. 2; *ASB,* 10 August 1864, p. 2; Austin, *The Blue and the Gray,* pp. 132–36; Mitchell, *Georgia Land and People,* p. 341; *ASW,* 17 August 1864, p. 2. Major Austin's recollections of the reception differed from the contemporary accounts in the Athens newspapers. Writing in 1899, he said that after the welcoming speech, it became incumbent upon the Kentuckians to make a reply. After an embarrassing silence, a ragged young private, James C. C. Black, was pushed forward. "The comments we overheard were by no means flattering," Austin recalled:

> Several elegantly dressed ladies occupied the seat just in front of the writer, who, overhearing some of their comments on the ludicrous appearance of our soldier-boy, remarked to them that, if they would withhold their criticisms for a moment, they might find themselves mistaken. To make the matter worse, our soldier wore a gray jacket which fell far short of concealing two very large abrasions in the seat of his pants, caused by long contact with the saddle. His attempt on the stage to stretch his jacket in order to hide this defect, brought forth a shout from all parts of the house. He was indeed an object of pity rather than of mirth. His hair was in a tangled mass, and his shirt had not felt the cleansing effect of water for months. With all these visible defects, the young man braced himself for the conflict, and . . . addressed himself to the "chair" with an ease and grace of manner which showed he was no novice in the part he was called upon to perform. As he warmed up to his subject, everyone seemed to lose sight of his outward appearance. His lofty and sublime thoughts, clothed in classically chosen language . . . completely captivated his hearers. . . . there was scarcely a dry eye left in the house. He held the crowd spellbound for an hour. When he descended the rostrum the ladies gathered about him, anxious to grasp the hand of the soldier-orator and congratulate him on his magnificent effort.

All this makes for a marvelous story, except that Private Black, who later became Congressman Black, kept a diary. On the day of the banquet, he was at a camp meeting ground near Covington, thirty-five miles southwest of Athens. See James Conquest Cross Black Diary, 4 August 1864.

11. *ASW,* 10 August 1864, p. 2; *ACS,* 7 August 1864, p. 3; *CR,* 22 July 1875, p. 1; *AT,* 31 July 1891, p. 5; Wells, *Touch of Elbow,* pp. 226–27; *MDC,* 9 August 1864, p. 1; *ASW,* 17 August 1864, p. 2; *ASB,* 10 August 1864, p. 2; Hull, *Annals of Athens,* p. 264. Some Jackson County residents banded together and brought in twenty-seven Yankee prisoners. These citizens may have belonged to a company of home guards led by Dr. Ange De Lapriere. Mitchell, in *Georgia Land and People,* p. 340, said Dr. De Lapriere's company fought at the battle of King's Tanyard, but none of the contemporary accounts mention the presence of any home guards. It seems more likely Dr. De Lapriere's men would have mustered after the predawn fighting to help round up Yankee stragglers.

12. *MSR,* 9 August 1864, p. 2; *MSR,* 3 August 1864, p. 2; *ACS,* 16 August 1864, p. 3; *ADI,* 3 August 1864, p. 2; *SR,* 2 August 1864, p. 2; *ACS,* 13 August 1864, p. 2.

13. *ADI,* 4 August 1864, p. 2; *ADI,* 11 August 1864, p. 2; *CT,* 12 August 1864, p. 1; *ADI,* 20 August 1864, p. 2 (quoting *Savannah Republican*); *CDS,* 20 August 1864, p. 1.

14. Hinman, *The Sherman Brigade,* pp. 894–95; Williams, *Jones County,* pp. 151–52, 429; Receipt, "Sunshine Church Jones County Ga Aug 14th/64," signed by Francis B. Haskell, Wilbur Kurtz Papers; "Report of Disposition of Prisoners in Jones County Georgia," Stout

Papers, Emory; Cornwell, "A Paper by Louise Cornwell," UDC 5:251–53. Mrs. Cornwell remembered this repentant raider as an Illinois soldier, but the only Illinois trooper with a wounded hip on the "Report of Disposition of Prisoners in Jones County" is Private Denny Donlouie of the 14th Illinois. He survived the war. Sergeant Andrew J. Catron also suffered a hip wound, but according to Tarrant, *1st Kentucky*, p. 371, and the *Roll of Honor*, 17:499, he died on July 31, not a week later, as Mrs. Cornwell recalled. The soldier she remembered may well have been Sergeant Thomas J. Jenkins of the 1st Kentucky, who had been taken to Joseph White's house with Lieutenants Humphrey and Murphy. Doctors had amputated his left leg and he died some time afterward. See Quartermaster General's Office, *Roll of Honor*, 17:499. Of the three Yankees Mrs. Cornwell nursed at Joseph White's house, only Lieutenant Murphy recovered from his wounds. After the war, he returned to Hillsboro and begged the young widow on bended knee to be his wife. She refused. See McKenzie, "When Sherman Marched through Georgia," UDC 13:358–59.

15. Cornwell, "A Paper by Louise Cornwell," UDC 5:252; Indiana Adjutant General, *Report*, 6:463, 8:662; Kentucky Adjutant General, *Report*, 1:2–3, 4–5, 20–21, 42–43; Tarrant, *1st Kentucky*, pp. 371, 396, 401, 429, 464; Compiled Service Records, RG 94; Quartermaster General's Office, *Roll of Honor*, 17:497–500; Quartermaster General's Office, *Disposition of Some of the Bodies of Deceased Union Soldiers and Prisoners of War*, 2:25–26; *OR*, 44, p. 80; Williams, "King's Tan Yard," UDC 9:285. An account in the *Athens Southern Banner*, 10 August 1864, p. 2, estimated Yankee casualties at King's Tanyard at about eighteen killed, forty wounded, and seven drowned.

16. Willoughby Diary, 3 September 1864; Harriet M. Lewis, Case Number 15,820, RG 217; Alexander Mooty, Case Number 4,546, RG 233; William L. Bell, Case Number 11,791, RG 233; James R. Thomason, Case Number 10,792, RG 233; P. H. Hesterly, Case Number 6,560, RG 217; "Statements Made by Prisoners of War, Scouts, CSA Deserters, May–August 1864," p. 25, vol. 178/249, DMT, RG 393; *WBB*, 24 September 1864, p. 1; *NT*, 1 February 1883, p. 1; Campbell Diary, 12 August 1864; Sanford, *14th Illinois*, pp. 212–23, 320.

17. *NT*, 16 November 1899, p. 7; Starr, "General Horace Capron," pp. 260, 274; *DAB*, 1928 ed., s.v. "Horace Capron," by Claribel Ruth Barnett; Sanford, *14th Illinois*, pp. 150, 305, 315; Capron, "Stoneman's Raid," pp. 689–705; *CDC*, 15 August 1864, p. 1; *OR*, 38, pt. 2, p. 929; pt. 5, pp. 363, 406, 439. In his report, Capron says he reached Marietta on the morning of August 7. A telegram in *OR*, 38, pt. 5, p. 439, makes it clear he arrived on August 8.

18. *AT*, 23 May 1901, p. 2; Crofts, comp., *3rd Ohio*, p. 17; Compiled Service Records, RG 94; Warner, *Generals in Blue*, p. 104; Society of the Army of the Cumberland, *8th Reunion*, pp. 171–73; Speed, Kelly, and Pirtle, *Union Regiments of Kentucky*, p. 72; Miller, "John Thomas Croxton," pp. 281–83; *OR*, 30, pt. 1, pp. 82, 404, 405, 423; *OR*, 31, pt. 3, p. 202; *NT*, 5 November 1925, p. 5; *Favorite Songs of the People*, p. 72; *NT*, 21 January 1915, p. 5; *NT*, 28 January 1915, p. 5, *NT*, 15 July 1926, p. 5; *OR*, 38, pt. 2, pp. 772–73; pt. 5, pp. 289, 300.

19. Regimental Returns and Muster Rolls, 8th Iowa Cavalry, 4th Kentucky Mounted Infantry, 1st Tennessee Cavalry, 2nd Indiana Cavalry, 4th Indiana Cavalry, 1st Wisconsin Cavalry, 18th Indiana Battery, 8th Indiana Cavalry, 2nd Kentucky Cavalry, 9th Ohio Cavalry, 5th Iowa Cavalry, 4th Tennessee Cavalry, RG 94; Muster Roll, May–August 1864, Company H, 2nd Kentucky Cavalry, Kentucky Adjutant General's Records; Campbell Diary, 5 August 1864; "Register of Patients at Buckner Hospital Newnan Ga. August 3rd 1864," "Register of Patients at Buckner Hospital Newnan Ga. August 11th 1864," Stout Papers; "Register of Federal troops in Hospital Newnan, Ga.," Persons Papers; Kentucky Adjutant General, *Report*, 1:46–62, 428–39, 628–683; Tennessee Adjutant General, *Report*, pp. 303–28, 389–415; Iowa Adjutant General, *Roster and Record*, 4:863–1013, 1523–1639; Indiana Adjutant General, *Report*, 2:381–90, 400–411, 3:12–19, 431, 5:222–50, 273–302, 6:245–67, 7:754–57, 8:174–79, 368, 525–29, 624–26, 737–38; Wisconsin Adjutant General, *Roster*, 1:1–49; Ohio Roster Commission, *Official Roster*, 11:461–501, 788–92; *OR*, 38, pt. 2, pp. 785, 788, 790, 791, 802.

20. *OR,* 38, pt. 2, p. 925; Muster Roll, July–August 1864, Company D, 7th Ohio Cavalry, RG 94; *CDC* 16 August 1864, p. 1; Regimental Returns and Muster Rolls, 5th Indiana Cavalry, 6th Indiana Cavalry, 14th Illinois Cavalry, 8th Michigan Cavalry, McLaughlin's Ohio Squadron, 1st Kentucky Cavalry, 11th Kentucky Cavalry, 24th Indiana Battery, RG 94; "Report of Casualties of Officers and Men of Co. D 7th Ohio Cav. During the late raid with Genl. Stoneman," "Report of Casualties in the 5th Regt. Ind. Vol. Cav. During the Late Raid with General Stoneman," "Report of the Casualties in the 6th Regiment Ind. Vol. Cavalry during the late Raid with Genl. Stoneman," "Report of the Casualties in the 6th Regiment Ind. Vol. Cavry. during the late Raid with Genl. Stoneman," "Report of Casualties in the 14th Regt. Ills. Vol. Cav. during the late Raid with Genl. Stoneman," "Report of Casualties in the 8th Regt. Mich. V. Cavy. during the late Raid with General Stoneman," "Report of Casualties of the 8th Regt. Mich. Vol. Cavalry during the late Raid with Major Genl. Stoneman from July 27th 1864 to Aug. 20th 1864," "Report of Casualties during the Stoneman raid in the McLaughlin Squadron and 24" Ind. Battery," Lists and Reports Received by the Cavalry January 1864– July 1864, RG 393; "Report of Casualties of the 8th Regt. Mich. Vol. Cavalry during the late Raid with General Stoneman from July 27th 1864 to Aug. 20th 1864," RG 59-14-A; "Report of Disposition of Prisoners in Jones County Georgia," Stout Papers, Emory; Ohio Roster Commission, *Official Roster,* 11:711–19; Indiana Adjutant General, *Report,* 2:652–63, 3:102–8, 444–45, 6:138–61, 455–80, 7:772–75, 8:282–84, 302–4, 371, 608–12, 659–62, 740; Illinois Adjutant General, *Report,* 8:453–85; Michigan Adjutant General, vol. 38: *Eighth Michigan Cavalry,* pp. 5–173; Kentucky Adjutant General, *Report,* 1:2–45, 270–351.

21. *CT,* 3 August 1864, p. 2; *ACS,* 2 August 1864, p. 3; *ADC,* 2 August 1864, p. 3; *CDS,* 2 August 1864, p. 2; *CDS,* 3 August 1864, p. 2; *MDT,* 4 August 1864, p. 2; *OR,* 38, pt. 5, pp. 310, 312, 340, 410; pt. 2, pp. 763–64.

22. Castel, *Decision in the West,* p. 569; Sherman to "Dearest Ellen," 2 August and 9 August 1864, Sherman Family Papers.

23. *CDC,* 23 August 1864, p. 2; Capron, "Stoneman's Raid," pp. 675–76; *OR,* 38, pt. 1, p. 76; pt. 5, p. 340; *OR,* series II, vol. 7, p. 857; Sherman, *Memoirs,* 2:98.

21. TROOPERS IN THE TRENCHES, AUGUST 1–AUGUST 17, 1864

1. *OR,* 38, pt. 5, pp. 248, 309–11, 314, 327–28.

2. *OR,* 38, pt. 1, pp. 211, 912, 916; pt. 2, pp. 813, 845; Silas C. Stevens to E. B. Stevens, 8 February 1905; General Orders No. 19, 1 August 1864, 1st Ohio Cavalry Papers, RG 94; Tri-Monthly Report, 10 August 1864, 1st Ohio Cavalry Papers, RG 94; Kenner Garrard to "Capt:," 31 July 1864, 1st Ohio Cavalry Papers, RG 94; Records Diary, 1 August 1864; William Allen Pepper Diary, 1 August 1864; Hosea, "Side Lights on the War," p. 41; Lemmon Diary, 1–2 August 1864; McLain Diary, 1–2 August 1864; Potter Diary, 31 July, 1–2 August 1864; Robert Burns to "My Dear Davidson," 2 August 1864, Robert Burns Papers; Regimental Return, August 1864, 4th Michigan Cavalry, reel 83, M-594, RG 94; *DFP,* 17 August 1864, p. 4; *MJPGA,* 20 August 1864, p. 3; Sipes, *7th Pennsylvania,* p. 115; Vale, *Minty and the Cavalry,* pp. 328–29; Doyle, *17th Indiana,* pp. 21–22; *AT,* 16 December 1897, p. 6 (quote by Lieutenant Doyle); Kemper Diary, 1–2 August 1864; Magee, *72nd Indiana,* pp. 357–59; Remley to "Dear Parents Brothers and Sister," 1 August 1864; Barnard to "My Dear Wife," 7 August 1864; Griest Diary, 2 August 1864; Nourse Diary, 1 August 1864; Lester Diary, 1 August 1864; "Weekly Report of Effective Force of 4th Regt. Mich. Vol. Cavalry for the week ending July 31 1864," 4th Michigan Cavalry Papers, RG 94; "Weekly Report of Effective Force of 7th Penna. Vol. Cavalry Monday August 1st 1864," 7th Pennsylvania Cavalry Papers, RG 94; Regimental Return, July 1864, 4th U.S. Cavalry, reel 41, M-744, RG 94; "Semi Weekly Report Effective Force 98th Ill. Vols. August 1 1864," 98th Illinois Mounted Infantry Papers, RG 94; "Weekly Report of Effective Forces of the 123d Regt. Ills. Vols. Aug 1st 1864,"

123rd Illinois Mounted Infantry Papers, RG 94; Tri-Monthly Report, 31 July 1864, 17th Indiana Mounted Infantry Papers, RG 94; "Semi Weekly report of Effective force of the 72nd Regt Ind. Vols. Aug 1st 1864," 72nd Indiana Mounted Infantry Papers, RG 94; Sherman, *Memoirs,* 2:135.

3. *OR,* 38, pt. 2, pp. 517–727 passim, 923; pt. 1, pp. 78–79, 133–34, 160–61, 525, 635, 744; pt. 5, pp. 316, 319, 333–35, 341–42, 348–49, 354–58 (Palmer quotation), 362, 364–66, 369–71 (Sherman quotation), 378–85, 390, 397–400, 424; pt. 3, p. 690; Sherman, *Memoirs,* 2:135; Bigger Diary, 6 August 1864; Champion to "My Precious Wife," 7 August 1864; Dixon Diary, 7 August 1864; Castel, "Union Fizzle at Atlanta: The Battle of Utoy Creek," pp. 26–32; Kelly, "Back in the Saddle," pp. 31–32.

4. *OR,* 38, pt. 5, pp. 408–9, 412.

5. Vale, *Minty and the Cavalry,* p. 328; *CPR,* 7 September 1864, p. 1; Lemmon Diary, 3, 5 August 1864; *AT,* 16 December 1897, p. 6; McLain Diary, 2 August 1864; Griest Diary, 4 August 1864; Burns to "My Dear Davidson," 4 August 1864; Nourse Diary, 2–6 August 1864; Lester Diary, 2–6 August 1864; John A. Nourse to "Dear Sister," 10 August 1864, John A. Nourse Letters. On pp. 330–31 of *Minty and the Cavalry,* Captain Robert Vale of the 7th Pennsylvania claimed Minty's 1st Brigade suffered ten casualties on August 7, while covering the left and rear of an assault by the IV Corps that captured nearly two miles of Rebel rifle pits. He also took credit for commanding the skirmish line that checked a Rebel charge which drove the Yankee infantry out of their rifle pits near the railroad on August 9. Minty repeated these stories in the *National Tribune,* 31 May 1894, p. 2, but the casualties his brigade supposedly sustained do not appear in the muster rolls, and for a very good reason. Nothing happened on the dates these incidents allegedly occurred. "Very quiet along the line," John McLain wrote in his diary on August 7. "No trouble," added Albert Potter. Nor do eyewitnesses mention any Rebel assault on August 9. Three divisions of Thomas's IV Corps did attack and capture the Rebel rifle pits in their front late on August 3 and made demonstrations on August 5 and 6, but all the reliable evidence indicates Minty's brigade did not participate.

6. *OR,* 38, pt. 2, pp. 838, 843, 845, 848; pt. 5, p. 420; Morning Reports, 1–8 August 1864, Company G, 4th Ohio Cavalry, RG 94; Brown, *Battle-Fields Revisited,* pp. 63–64; Long to T. J. Patten, 7 August 1864, p. 46, vol. 40/79, CCMDM, RG 393; Tri-Monthly Report, 10 August 1864, 1st Ohio Cavalry Papers, RG 94; *NT,* 29 September 1898, p. 9; Compiled Service Records, RG 94; Pension Records, RG 15; "List of Casualties in 2d Brigade 2d Division Cavalry," pp. 68–69, vol. 57/140, CCMDM, RG 393; Ohio Roster Commission, *Official Roster,* 11:127, 128, 215.

7. Magee, *72nd Indiana,* p. 365; Lester Diary, 10 August 1864; Records Diary, 8–10 August 1864; Griest Diary, 7–8, 10 August 1864; Lemmon Diary, 7, 10 August 1864. Strangely, at this time infantrymen in the neighboring IV and XX Corps were writing, "We are faring better in the eating line now than any time on the campaign." See Sylvester, ed., "'Gone for a Soldier': The Civil War Letters of Charles Harding Cox," p. 214; Snetsinger, ed., *Kiss Clara for Me: The Story of Joseph Whitney and his Family,* p. 143; Holzhueter, ed., "William Wallace's Civil War Letters: The Atlanta Campaign," p. 104.

8. Howe, ed., *Home Letters of General Sherman,* pp. 305, 307–8.

9. Tomlinson, ed., *"Dear Friends," The Civil War Letters and Diary of Charles Edwin Cort* (hereafter cited as *Sergeant Cort*), p. 150; Ninety-Second Illinois Reunion Association, *Ninety-Second Illinois Volunteers* (hereafter cited as *92nd Illinois*), p. 144; Association of the Graduates of the United States Military Academy, *13th Annual Reunion,* p. 45; Ninety-Second Illinois Reunion Association, *9th Triennial Re-Union,* p. 12.

10. Except where noted, Kilpatrick's biography is based on Judson Kilpatrick File, reel 345, M-1064, RG 94; Judson Kilpatrick File, reel 2, M-1098, RG 94; Moore, *Kilpatrick and Our Cavalry,* pp. 25–165; Brockett, "Brevet Major-General Hugh Judson Kilpatrick," pp. 419–28; Throckmorton, "Major-General Kilpatrick," pp. 590–600; Association of the Graduates of the United States Military Academy, *13th Annual Reunion,* pp. 45–48; Small, *Camp-*

Fire Talk on the Life and Military Services of Maj. Gen. Judson Kilpatrick, pp. 3–13; Cullum, *Biographical Register,* 2:784–89; *DAB,* s.v. "Hugh Judson Kilpatrick," by Charles Dudley Rhodes; Warner, *Generals in Blue,* p. 266; Longacre, "Judson Kilpatrick," pp. 25–30; King, "General Judson Kilpatrick," pp. 35–41; Pierce, "General Hugh Judson Kilpatrick in the American Civil War: A New Appraisal" (Ph.D. diss.), pp. 10–243 passim.

11. *Official Register of the U.S. Military Academy,* 1857:13, 1861:9; Sergent, *They Lie Forgotten,* pp. 82, 102, 150; Wilson, *Under the Old Flag,* 1:370–71 (quote by upperclassman); Moore, *Kilpatrick and Our Cavalry,* p. 34 (quoting classmate).

12. Connolly, *Three Years in the Army of the Cumberland,* p. 348; Pension Records, RG 15.

13. *OR,* 32, pt. 3, pp. 375, 465, 498, 557; Small, *Kilpatrick,* pp. 13 (Kilpatrick's arrival at 3rd Division headquarters), 19; *OR,* 38, pt. 2, pp. 858, 862, 886, 889, 895, 896, 903; pt. 3, pp. 91, 125, 225; Atkins, "With Sherman's Cavalry," p. 625; Pension Records, RG 15; Ninety-Second Illinois, *9th Re-Union,* p. 12; *Kennesaw Gazette,* 15 July 1887, p. 6. In an untitled article in *Confederate Veteran* 10:161, Polk Prince, a Kentucky cavalryman serving with John S. Williams's brigade, recounted:

> I was on our picket line and a party of five or six of the enemy rode up in the woods near where I was sitting on my horse. They did not see me until I fired on them with my spencer rifle. Then they hastily retired. I saw that I had shot one of them in the leg—my horse having moved his head just as I fired, my shot went lower than intended. Soon after this a youngster in citizen's dress, and mounted on a small horse, came riding up near me, and I "called" him in. He was badly scared, of course, but claimed to be a reporter for the Cincinnati Gazette. On questioning him he told me of the party I had fired on, and that Gen. Kilpatrick was wounded in the leg. This was in front of Resaca. . . . The man I shot was riding a white or gray horse.

14. *ASC,* 9 June 1864, p. 1; *ND,* 2 July 1864, p. 2; *DAT,* 8 July 1864, p. 4; Moore, *Kilpatrick and Our Cavalry,* p. 166.

15. Unless otherwise noted, the narrative describing the movements of Kilpatrick's division from July 21–August 6 are based on the following sources: *OR,* 38, pt. 1, p. 102; pt. 2, pp. 858, 887, 889, 898, 903; pt. 5, p. 299; Moore, *Kilpatrick and Our Cavalry,* p. 167; Brockett, "Hugh Judson Kilpatrick," p. 429; Throckmorton, "Kilpatrick," pp. 600–601; Small, *Kilpatrick,* p. 19; McCain, *A Soldier's Diary; or The History of Company "L," Third Indiana Cavalry,* p. 32; James S. Thompson Diary, 3–5 August 1864; Regimental Return, July 1864, 3rd Indiana Cavalry, reel 34, M-594, RG 94; Tri-Monthly Report, 31 July 1864, 3rd Indiana Cavalry Papers, RG 94; John Paisley Diary, 3–5 August 1864; Record of Events, May–August, July–August 1864, Companies A-L, 10th Ohio Cavalry, reel 141, M-594, RG 94; Tri-Monthly Report, 31 July 1864, 10th Ohio Cavalry Papers, RG 94; Semi-Monthly Inspection Report of the Batteries of the 3rd Cavalry Division, 15 July 1864, 10th Wisconsin Battery Papers, RG 94; Battery Return, August 1864, 10th Wisconsin Battery Papers, RG 94; William Henry Brown Diary, 21, 24–25 July, 2–5 August 1864; William Henry Brown Notebook, 25 July, 1, 3–5 [August] 1864, *Civil War Times Illustrated* Collection; James Munro Forbes to "Dear Sister," 26 July 1864, James Munro Forbes Papers; Tomlinson, ed., *Sergeant Cort,* pp. 150–51; Morning Reports, 2–5 August 1864, Companies A, B, and I, 92nd Illinois Mounted Infantry, RG 94; Record of Events, July–August 1864, Companies E and K, 92nd Illinois Mounted Infantry, reel 28, M-594, RG 94; *92nd Illinois,* p. 144; Tri-Monthly Report, 31 July 1864, 5th Kentucky Cavalry Papers, RG 94.

16. Kilpatrick to Elliott, 23 July 1864, p. 180, Kilpatrick to Elliott, 24 July 1864, p. 181, Kilpatrick to Elliott, 25 July 1864, p. 184, vol. 20/28, 39, CCMDM, RG 393.

17. *OR,* 38, pt. 5, pp. 258, 276, 321–22, 323; Kilpatrick to Elliott, 1 August 1864, p. 200, vol. 20/28, 39, CCMDM, RG 393.

18. Stormont, comp., *58th Indiana Infantry,* p. 321; *OR,* 38, pt. 5, p. 346; Kilpatrick to Elliott, 3 August 1864, p. 203, vol. 20/28, 39, CCMDM, RG 393.

19. Kilpatrick to Elliott, 4 August 1864, Kilpatrick to David F. How, 4 August 1864, p. 204, vol. 20/28, 39, CCMDM, RG 393.

20. "Circular, Head Quarters 3rd Cav. Div. D. C. In the field Ga. Aug. 5th 1864," 3rd Indiana Cavalry Papers, RG 94; "Circular, Head Quarters 3rd Cav. Div. Dep't Cumb'd. In the Field Ga. August 5th 1864," 8th Indiana Cavalry Papers, RG 94. See also Regimental Descriptive, Letter, Order, Guard Report, and Pass Book, 8th Indiana Cavalry Papers, RG 94.

21. "Genl Orders, Head Quarters 3d Div. Cavalry Dept Cumb. In the field Ga. August 6th 1864," Regimental Descriptive, Letter, Order, Guard Report, and Pass Book, 8th Indiana Cavalry Papers, RG 94.

22. *OR,* 38, pt. 1, p. 102; pt. 2, p. 879; Robert Klein to Lorenzo Thomas, 1 August 1864, 3rd Indiana Cavalry Papers, RG 94; Oblinger Diary, 5–6 August 1864; Ward Diary, 6 August 1864; Morning Reports, 5–6 August 1864, Company D, 8th Indiana Cavalry, RG 94; Regimental Return, August 1864, 8th Indiana Cavalry, reel 35, M-594, RG 94; Regimental Return, August 1864, 5th Iowa Cavalry, reel 51, M-594, RG 94; "General Orders No. 4, Head Quarters 2nd Brig 3rd Div Cavalry near Sweet Water Bridge Ga. August 6th 1864," p. 13, vol. 59/154, 155, 158, 159, 160, 160A, 161A, RG 393; James S. Thompson Diary, 8–10 August 1864.

23. The 4th Tennessee was ordered to turn all their horses and equipment over to Kilpatrick's division before leaving for Alabama.

24. *OR,* 38, pt. 5, pp. 320–21, 329, 340, 396, 414–15, 428, 432–33, 442, 635; pt. 3, p. 453; *OR,* 39, pt. 2, p. 219; *OR,* 52, pt. 1, p. 572; Tarrant, *1st Kentucky,* pp. 381–82; Regimental Return, July 1864, 9th Michigan Cavalry, reel 84, M-594, RG 94; Record of Events, July–August 1864, Companies A, B, D, F, H, I, and M, 9th Michigan Cavalry, reel 84, M-594, RG 94; Morning Reports, 31 July 1864, Company B, 9th Michigan Cavalry, RG 94; *DFP,* 12 August 1864, p. 4; William C. Stevens to "My Dear Father," 13 July 1864, William C. Stevens Papers.

25. *OR,* 38, pt. 5, pp. 418, 419, 421–24, 429–30.

26. *OR,* 38, pt. 2, p. 898; Morning Reports, 9 August 1864, Companies A and B, 92nd Illinois Mounted Infantry, RG 94; Brown Diary, 9 August 1864; Brown Notebook, 9 [August] 1864; Paisley Diary, 9–10 August 1864; Oblinger Diary, 9–10 August 1864; Ward Diary, 9–10 August 1864; Regimental Return, August 1864, 8th Indiana Cavalry, reel 35, M-594, RG 94; Morning Reports, 9–10 August 1864, Company D, 8th Indiana Cavalry, RG 94.

27. *OR,* 38, pt. 5, p. 439; pt. 2, p. 843; Morning Reports, 9 August 1864, Company G, 4th Ohio Cavalry, RG 94; Tri-Monthly Report, 10 August 1864, 1st Ohio Cavalry Papers, RG 94; Crofts, comp., *3rd Ohio,* p. 159; Nourse Diary, 9–10 August 1864.

28. Regimental Return, August 1864, 9th Michigan Cavalry, reel 84, M-594, RG 94; Record of Events, July–August 1864, Companies A, B, D, F, H, I, and M, 9th Michigan Cavalry, reel 84, M-594, RG 94; Morning Reports, 8 August 1864, Company B, 9th Michigan Cavalry, RG 94; William C. Stevens to "My Dear Bro & Sister," 12 August 1864; *NT,* 28 July 1904, p. 6; *AT,* 24 September 1903, p. 1; *NT,* 8 November 1923, p. 3; *OR,* 38, pt. 5, pp. 428, 442–43; Sherman to William D. Hamilton, 9 August 1864 (telegram), p. 288, vol. 16/23, MDM, RG 393.

29. *OR,* 38, pt. 1, pp. 79, 121, 134, 917; pt. 2, pp. 143, 303, 489–90; pt. 3, pp. 60, 387, 411; pt. 5, pp. 412, 418, 419, 431, 434–436, 447–50, 452–58, 465, 471–73; *OR,* 52, pt. 1, p. 698; Sturges Diary, 9–13 August 1864; Hoehling, *Last Train from Atlanta,* p. 279 (quoting civilian); Otto, *History of the 11th Indiana Battery,* p. 79; Poe Diary, 10–11 August 1864. A fourth gun arrived on the same train carrying the ammunition and went into action on the left of the XVI Corps on August 11. The relentless pounding continued until about 9:00 P.M., August 12, when two of Sutermeister's 20-pounder Parrotts burst, blowing the ends off the muzzles. His two remaining 20-pounders ceased firing, but the big 4½-inchers kept up a slow, deliberate barrage until August 19, when the vent holes in two of the guns in front of the XX Corps became so enlarged they were unsafe to shoot. The remaining gun and the one on the

left of the XVI Corps continued firing until they were replaced on August 23 by four new 4½-inch guns.

30. *OR,* 38, pt. 5, pp. 447–48, 450–53.

31. William C. Stevens to "My Dear Bro & Sister," 12 August 1864; Regimental Return, August 1864, 9th Michigan Cavalry, reel 84, M-594, RG 94; Record of Events, July–August 1864, Companies A, D, and I, 9th Michigan Cavalry, reel 84, M-594, RG 94; Scruggs, ed., *Georgia Historical Markers,* p. 247; Densmore, "The Garrard Family in Frontenac," pp. 31–36; Upham and Dunlap, comps., *Collections of the Minnesota Historical Society,* vol. 14: *Minnesota Biographies 1655–1912,* 14:247; Reid, *Ohio in the War,* 1:804, 943; 2:796–802; Hunt and Brown, *Brevet Brigadier Generals in Blue,* p. 225; William C. Stevens to "My Dear Mother," 13 August 1864, and to "My Dear Father," 18 August 1864; Kerr, ed., *Ross' Texas Cavalry,* pp. 163–64; Compiled Service Records, RG 94; Michigan Adjutant General, vol. 39: *Ninth Michigan Cavalry,* pp. 32, 78; *OR,* 38, pt. 2, pp. 921–22; pt. 5, pp. 460–65, 467–68, 470, 478–80.

32. Sherman to "Dear Thomas," 12 August 1864, William Tecumseh Sherman Papers; *OR,* 38, pt. 5, pp. 472, 473, 478, 481.

33. Sturges Diary, 13 August 1864; Poe Diary, 13 August 1864; *OR,* 38, pt. 5, p. 482. This telegram appears in the *Official Records* dated "August 13, 1864—8 a.m.," two hours *before* Sherman consulted with his army commanders. However, there are two other versions of this dispatch and they tell a different story. One is in U.S. Congress, Joint Committee on the Conduct of the War, *Supplemental Report,* 1:167, with the date "August 13, 1864—8 p.m.," not "8 a.m." A handwritten version, dated 7:30 p.m., is found on page 229, vol. 20, Telegrams Received by Major General Henry W. Halleck, July 30 1864 to September 16, 1864, Records of the Office of the Secretary of War, RG 107, and again on pp. 9021–22 of the Henry W. Halleck Papers, RG 94. Sherman usually waited until the end of the day before telegraphing Washington, and it seems clear he advised the War Department of his plans *after* conferring with Thomas, Howard, and Schofield, not before.

34. Vale identified the officers seated with Major Jennings as Captains Charles C. McCormick, Percy White, and "either Captain [William C.] Garrett or Lieutenant Edward P. Inhoff." McCormick, an acting assistant inspector general on W. L. Elliott's staff, was apparently visiting his old regiment. Writing in his diary sometime after the actual event, Private John Nourse mistakenly identified the dead soldier as a member of the 98th Illinois Mounted Infantry.

35. *OR,* 38, pt. 1, pp. 918–19; pt. 5, pp. 483–85; Morning Reports, 13 August 1864, Company G, 4th Ohio Cavalry, RG 94; Crofts, comp., *3rd Ohio,* p. 159; McLain Diary, 13 August 1864; Potter Diary, 13 August 1864; Griest Diary, 13 August 1864; *ADI,* 16 August 1864, p. 2; Nourse Diary, 13–14 August 1864; Lester Diary, 13 August 1864; Magee, *72nd Indiana,* p. 364; Sipes, *7th Pennsylvania,* pp. 116–17 and Roster p. 57; Dornblaser, *Sabre Strokes,* p. 171; Compiled Service Records, RG 94; Bates, *Pennsylvania Volunteers,* 2:1138; Vale, *Minty and the Cavalry,* pp. 329–32. Vale, who was not particularly keen at remembering dates, said this incident took place on August 3, but none of the other eyewitnesses mention any shelling that day. "All quiet in our front except constant picket firing," wrote John McLain. "All quiet in front of us," agreed John Lemmon. "No disturbance," added Albert Potter. The events Vale dated August 3 obviously took place on August 13. See McLain, Potter, and Lemmon Diaries, 3 and 13 August 1864.

36. Lester Diary, 14 August 1864; Nourse Diary, 14 August 1864; *OR,* 38, pt. 2, pp. 813, 833; Sipes, *7th Pennsylvania,* p. 117; Griest Diary, 14 August 1864; Records Diary, 14 August 1864; Barnard to "Well Mag," 15 August 1864; Doyle, *17th Indiana,* p. 22; Magee, *72nd Indiana,* pp. 366–67. Recounting a visit to Garrard's division on August 14, Colonel Albert G. Brackett, acting inspector general of cavalry for the Department of the Cumberland, noted in the *National Tribune,* 26 January 1888, p. 1, "that for two weeks previously his men had been . . . dismounted and serving as infantry in the trenches. The horses were left in the woods in

the rear, where there was no grazing, in charge of soldiers detailed for that purpose. On the whole the animals looked hearty, though they were thin, and appeared to have been as well cared for as circumstances would admit."

37. Sherman to "Dear Thomas," 12 August 1864, William Tecumseh Sherman Papers; *OR,* 38, pt. 1, p. 79; pt. 3, pp. 951, 957, 961; pt. 5, pp. 459, 489–91, 494, 497, 509.

38. Record of Events, July–August 1864, Field and Staff, 7th Pennsylvania Cavalry, reel 165, M-594, RG 94; Regimental Return, August 1864, 7th Pennsylvania Cavalry, reel 165, M-594, RG 94; George Chase to "Dear Mother," 19 August 1864, George Chase Papers; McLain Diary, 15 August 1864; Potter Diary, 15 August 1864; Record of Events, July–August 1864, Muster Roll, Company E, 4th U.S. Cavalry, RG 94; Vale, *Minty and the Cavalry,* p. 333; Morning Reports, 15 August 1864, Company G, 4th Ohio Cavalry, RG 94; Crofts, comp., *3rd Ohio,* p. 159; Griest Diary, 15 August 1864; Robinson, "With Kilpatrick around Atlanta," p. 573; Nourse Diary, 15 August 1864; Lester Diary, 15 August 1864; Barnard to "Well Mag," 15 August 1864; Remley to "Dear Parents Brothers and Sisters," 17 August 1864; Records Diary, 15 August 1864; Magee, *72nd Indiana,* pp. 367–68; Compiled Service Records, RG 94; *ACS,* 18 August 1864, p. 1; *MDT,* 19 August 1864, p. 2; *ACS,* 20 August 1864, p. 2; *OR,* 38, pt. 1, p. 919; pt. 2, pp. 809–10, 833; pt. 5, pp. 509–10, 526, 964. In *OR,* 38, pt. 1, p. 919, Lieutenant Colonel Joseph S. Fullerton of the IV Corps noted Garrard returned at 8:00 P.M. Garrard, however, reported he did not get back until midnight and the other sources agree with him. Fullerton may have seen the 4th U.S. Cavalry returning from a scout toward Decatur. See Record of Events, July–August 1864, Muster Roll, Company E, 4th U.S. Cavalry, RG 94.

39. *OR,* 38, pt. 2, pp. 809–10; pt. 5, pp. 521, 525–30, 532.

40. *OR,* 38, pt. 5, p. 419; "Circular, Head Quarters 2nd Brig 3rd Div Cavalry D.C. Sweet Water Bridge Ga. August 10th 1864," 8th Indiana Cavalry Papers, RG 94; "Circular, Head Qrs. 3d. Brig. 3d Cav. D. In the Field Ga. Aug 11/64," 92nd Illinois Mounted Infantry Papers, RG 94; "Circular, Head Qrs. 3rd Brig 3rd Cav Div In the field Ga. Aug 11/64," p. 42, vol. 59/ 154, 155, 158, 159, 160, 160A, 161A, CCMDM, RG 393; Robert Klein to Captain Alfred Gaddis, 13 August 1864, 3rd Indiana Cavalry Papers, RG 94; "Circular, Head Quarters 3rd Division Cavalry Department of the Cumberland In the Field Ga. August 13th 1864," 8th Indiana Cavalry Papers, RG 94; "Circular, Head Qur. 3d Brig 3d Cav Div In the field Ga. Aug 13/64," p. 43, vol. 59/154, 155, 158, 159, 160, 160A, 161A, CCMDM, RG 393; "Circular, Head Quarters 1st Brig" 3d Cav' Divis D.C. Aug" 14" 1864," 3rd Indiana Cavalry Papers, RG 94; Morning Reports, 12 August 1864, Company A, 92nd Illinois Mounted Infantry, RG 94; Brown Diary, 12, 14 August 1864; Paisley Diary, 11, 13–14 August, 1864; Morning Reports, 13–14 August 1864, Company D, 8th Indiana Cavalry, RG 94; Oblinger Diary, 11, 13–14 August 1864; Ward Diary, 11, 13–14 August 1864.

41. *AT,* 4 April 1901, p. 1; *OR,* 38, pt. 5, p. 493; "Circular, Head Quarters 3rd Cavalry Div D.C. In the Field Ga. August 14" 1864," 8th Indiana Cavalry Papers, RG 94. See also Regimental Descriptive, Letter, Order, Guard Report, and Pass Book, 8th Indiana Cavalry, RG 94.

42. Brown Diary, 15 August 1864; Brown Notebook, 15 [August] 1864; *92nd Illinois,* p. 146; "Circular, Head Quarters 3rd Cavalry Division D.C. In the Field Ga. Aug. 15th 1864," 8th Indiana Cavalry Papers, RG 94. See also Regimental Descriptive, Letter, Order, Guard Report, and Pass Book, 8th Indiana Cavalry, RG 94.

43. In his report in *OR,* 38, pt. 2, p. 858, Kilpatrick said he crossed to the south bank of the Chattahoochee, fortified, and remained in camp until 5:00 P.M. Other sources and a message Kilpatrick sent at 9:00 P.M., August 15, in *OR,* 38, pt. 5, p. 530, make it clear there was no such delay. Unless otherwise noted, the narrative describing Kilpatrick's foray from Sandtown to Fairburn on August 15–16 is based on the following sources. Union: *OR,* 38, pt. 2, pp. 858, 887, 889, 898, 922–24; pt. 5, pp. 451, 460, 466, 468–69, 499–500, 512, 530–31, 534–36; pt. 3, p. 453; McCain, *A Soldier's Diary,* p. 33; Regimental Return, August 1864, 3rd Indiana Cavalry, reel 34, M-594, RG 94; Regimental Return, August 1864, 5th Iowa Cavalry, reel 51,

M-594, RG 94; Oblinger Diary, 15–16 August 1864; Ward Diary, 15–16 August 1864; Morning Reports, 15–16 August 1864, Company D, 8th Indiana Cavalry, RG 94; Regimental Return, August 1864, 8th Indiana Cavalry, reel 35, M-594, RG 94; Paisley Diary, 15–16 August 1864; Record of Events, May–August 1864, Companies C, E-H, July–August 1864, Companies A, B, K, and L, 10th Ohio Cavalry, reel 141, M-594, RG 94; Brown Diary, 15–16 August 1864; Brown Notebook, 15–16 [August] 1864; Tomlinson, ed., *Sergeant Cort,* pp. 153–54; *92nd Illinois,* pp. 146–48; Morning Reports, 15–16 August 1864, Companies A, B, and I, 92nd Illinois Mounted Infantry, RG 94; Stormont, comp., *58th Indiana Infantry,* pp. 362–63; Sherman to William D. Hamilton, 9 August 1864 (telegram), p. 288, vol. 16/23, MDM, RG 393; William C. Stevens to "My Dear Father," 18 August 1864; *OSJ,* 29 August 1864, p. 2; *DFP,* 31 August 1864, p. 3; Record of Events, July–August 1864, Companies A, D, and I, 9th Michigan Cavalry, reel 84, M-594, RG 94; Regimental Return, August 1864, 9th Michigan Cavalry, reel 84, M-594, RG 94. Confederate: *OR,* 38, pt. 5, p. 968; Ross to "Gen. [William H. Jackson]", 16 [15] August 1864, George Moorman Papers, RG 109; Kerr, ed., *Ross' Texas Cavalry,* p. 164; *ACS,* 18 August 1864, p. 1; *MDT,* 19 August 1864, p. 2; *ACS,* 20 August 1864, p. 2; *ADI,* 19 August 1864, p. 2.

44. Ross's reports on the progress of Kilpatrick's column, found in *OR,* 38, pt. 5, p. 968, and in his Letter Book in the Lawrence Sullivan Ross Papers, are erroneously dated August 16 instead of August 15.

45. *OR,* 38, pt. 5, p. 530.

46. Garrard's four regiments remained in line of battle on the Campbellton Road until sundown, exchanging occasional shots with Rebel pickets, then retired to the Sandtown Road. As soon as they left, some of Sul Ross's Texans drove in a detachment of the 9th Illinois Mounted Infantry Garrard had posted at Patterson's Crossroads, wounding one man and capturing two others. See *OR,* 38, pt. 2, p. 922; pt. 3, p. 453; pt. 5, p. 536; Kerr, ed., *Ross' Texas Cavalry,* p. 164.

47. *OR,* 38, pt. 5, p. 531; *OR,* Atlas, plate XC, no. 2. Kilpatrick exaggerated the damage his men had done to the Atlanta & West Point Railroad. According to George Scott Milam of the 6th Texas Cavalry, the Yankees pulled up only about a half dozen rails. The track was repaired by August 16. See Milam Diary, 15 August 1864; *ACS,* 18 August 1864, p. 1.

48. *OR,* 38, pt. 5, pp. 524–25, 530, 532–33, 536, 556; U.S. Congress, Joint Committee on the Conduct of the War, *Supplemental Report,* 1:173; Sherman to "Genl Kilpatrick, Sandtown; via Gen Schofield," 17 August 1864 (telegram), p. 341, vol. 16/23, MDM, RG 393.

22. KILPATRICK'S RAID: SANDTOWN TO STEVENS' CROSSROADS, AUGUST 17– AUGUST 19, 1864

1. *OR,* 38, pt. 1, pp. 79, 168, 920; pt. 5, pp. 546, 548–49, 551, 555.

2. Rusling, *Civil War Days,* p. 113; *OR,* 38, pt. 5, pp. 549–50, 551, 555–57, 582, 583–84; pt. 1, p. 79.

3. Burns to "My Dear Davidson," 17 August 1864; "Special Field Orders No. 6, Head Qrs. 2nd Cavalry Division, Near Atlanta, Aug 17th 1864," 1st Ohio Cavalry Papers, RG 94; "Special Field Orders No. 6, Head Qrs. 2nd Cavalry Division, Near Atlanta, Aug 17th 1864," pp. 222–23, vol. 35/74, CCMDM, RG 393; Griest Diary, 16–17 August 1864; Records Diary, 17 August 1864; McLain Diary, 17 August 1864; Potter Diary, 17 August 1864; Magee, *72nd Indiana,* pp. 368–69; *OR,* 38, pt. 1, p. 920; pt. 5, pp. 548, 549–50, 553–55.

4. "Special Field Orders No. 6, Head Qrs. 2nd Cavalry Division, Near Atlanta, Aug 17th 1864," pp. 222–23, vol. 35/74, CCMDM, RG 393; Nourse Diary, 17 August 1864; Rough draft of an article appearing in the *National Tribune,* 22 January 1903, p. 6, found in the Robert H. G. Minty Papers.

5. The movements of Minty's and Long's brigades on August 17–18 are based on the following sources: "Circular, Hd. Qurs. 2d Brig. 2d Div. Cav., Buck Head, Ga., Aug 17th 64," 1st Ohio Cavalry Papers, RG 94; *OR,* 38, pt. 2, pp. 813, 824, 828–29, 833, 835, 839, 843, 845, 846, 848, 852, 854; Hosea, "Side Lights on the War," p. 41; Burns to "My Dear Davidson," 28 August 1864; Heber S. Thompson Diary, 17–18 August 1864; *CDC,* 31 August 1864, p. 1; *NT,* 10 July 1890, p. 1; *NT,* 22 January 1903, p. 6; Vale, *Minty and the Cavalry,* pp. 337–38; McLain Diary, 17–18 August 1864; Potter Diary, 17–18 August 1864; Potter to "Dear Father," 24 August 1864; *DFP,* 6 September 1864, p. 4; *DAT,* 8 September 1864, p. 4; *AJ,* 26 September 1864, p. 2; *NT,* 9 October 1924, p. 3; Regimental Return, August 1864, 4th Michigan Cavalry, reel 83, M-594, RG 94; *MJPGA,* 10 September 1864, p. 1; *MJPGA,* 17 September 1864, p. 1; Webb, "Kilpatrick's Great Raid," p. 729; Record of Events, Muster Roll, July–August 1864, Companies E and G, 4th U.S. Cavalry, RG 94; Regimental Return, August 1864, 4th U.S. Cavalry, reel 41, M-744, RG 94; *SOG,* 13 September 1864, p. 4; Crane, "Bugle Blasts," p. 244; Curry, "Raid of the Union Cavalry, Commanded by General Judson Kilpatrick, Around the Confederate Army in Atlanta, August, 1864," pp. 603–4; Curry, comp., *Four Years in the Saddle,* pp. 174–75; Rea, "Kilpatrick's Raid around Atlanta," p. 647; Crofts, comp., *3rd Ohio,* pp. 159–60; *DTB,* 6 September 1864, p. 2; *NR,* 13 September 1864, p. 3; James Thomson Diary, 17–18 August 1864; Wulsin, *The Story of the Fourth Regiment Ohio Veteran Volunteer Cavalry,* pp. 53–54; Morning Reports, 17 August 1864, Company L, 4th Ohio Cavalry, RG 94; Nourse Diary, 17–18 August 1864; Lester Diary, 17–19 August 1864; Fleming to "My Dear Parents," 13 September 1864; John A. Nourse, Untitled typescript account of Kilpatrick's raid (hereafter cited as Nourse, "Kilpatrick's Raid"), pp. 1–2, in Minty Papers; Robinson, "With Kilpatrick," pp. 574–76; Chicago Board of Trade Battery, *Historical Sketch,* p. 29. Robert Minty wrote two very similar accounts of Kilpatrick's raid in the 10 July 1890 and 22 January 1903 issues of the *National Tribune.* The 1890 article will be cited only when it adds information to the more detailed one published in 1903. Similarly, William L. Curry's description of Kilpatrick's raid in *Four Years in the Saddle,* pp. 174–87, is almost identical to his other account, "Raid of the Union Cavalry, Commanded by General Judson Kilpatrick," in *The Atlanta Papers,* pp. 597–622. It will not be cited again unless it elaborates on Curry's narrative in *The Atlanta Papers.* Another valuable source, Captain Robert Burns's letter of 28 August 1864, was reprinted almost verbatim in Vale, *Minty and the Cavalry,* pp. 357–65; Sipes, *7th Pennsylvania,* pp. 123–34; and Barron, *Lone Star Defenders,* pp. 216–27. Private Lucien Wulsin's equally informative account of the raid in the *4th Ohio,* pp. 53–61, also appears in *Roster of Surviving Members of the Fourth Regiment Ohio Volunteer Cavalry 1861–1865 with a Brief Historical Sketch of the Regiment,* pp. 20–32.

6. Wilson, *Under the Old Flag,* 2:171; Lanman, *Red Book of Michigan,* p. 468; *DAB,* 1928 ed., s.v. "Robert Horatio George Minty," by Charles Dudley Rhodes; Hunt and Brown, *Brevet Brigadier Generals in Blue,* p. 417; Robert Minty to Colonel Henry Capadose, 9 August 1847, Edward Rowley Hill to Lord Fitz Roy Somerset, 7 October and 20 November 1848, T. Bunbury[?] to Lord Fitz Roy Somerset, 25 November 1848, Commander in Chief, Memoranda Papers, 1793–1870, War Office Series (hereafter cited as WO) 31/956, XC14259; *A List of the Officers of the Army and of the Corps of Royal Marines on Full, Retired, and Half-Pay; with an Index* (hereafter cited as *Army List). 1848–9,* p. 312; *Army List, 1849–50,* pp. 320–21, 535; *Army List, 1850–51,* p. 321; *Army List, 1851–52,* p. 321; *Army List, 1852–53,* p. 337; Muster Roll, January–March 1849, 1st West India Regiment of Foot, General Muster Books and Pay Lists, 1732–1878, WO 12/11274, XC3310; Muster Roll, January–March 1851, 1st West India Regiment of Foot, WO 12/11280, XC3397; Muster Rolls, January–March 1852, January–March 1853, 1st West India Regiment of Foot, WO 12/11285, XC14954.

7. Lonn, *Foreigners in the Union Army and Navy,* pp. 228–29; Michigan Adjutant General, vol. 34: *Fourth Michigan Cavalry,* pp. 1, 102; Thatcher, *A Hundred Battles in the West,* p. 24 (quoting fellow officer) and roster; *NT,* 19 January 1888, p. 3; Vale, *Minty and the Cavalry,* pp. 108, 110, 148–49, 174–86, 224–40, 243–47, 508; Robertson, comp., *Michigan in the War,* p.

889; *OR,* 20, pt. 1, pp. 202, 620, 621; *OR,* 30, pt. 2, pp. 668–70, 686–87; pt. 4, pp. 185–86 (Minty to the commanding general), 291; *OR,* 31, pt. 1, p. 844 (Minty quoted); Minty to John Robertson, 13 January 1864, RG 59–14; "Proceedings of a General Court Martial convened at Nashville, Tenn., February 2nd 1864. In Case of Col. R. H. G. Minty 4th Mich. Vol. Cav'y, Com'd'g 1st Brigade 2nd Division Cavalry," Case Number NN1210, RG 153; *NT,* 7 September 1893, p. 3.

8. *NT,* 19 January 1888, p. 3; *NT,* 2 October 1913, p. 7; Wilson, *Under the Old Flag,* 2:171–72; *ADA,* 25 June 1864, p. 2.

9. "Map of 1st Distrt., Campbell Co., Georgia, South of the Cherokee Boundy. Line. Compiled under direction of Capt. W. E. Merrill, Chief Topl. Engr., D.C. by Sergt. Finegan from the notes of a captured Rebel Engineer & State Map," Map Z 10, RG 77; Oblinger Diary, 15–16 August 1864; Stormont, comp., *58th Indiana Infantry,* pp. 363–64; *OR,* 38, pt. 5, p. 574; *NT,* 22 January 1903, p. 6. For a slightly different version of this conversation, see *NT,* 10 July 1890, p. 1.

10. *OR,* 38, pt. 5, pp. 573, 579, 582, 583–84.

11. Construction of a trestle bridge had begun at Sandtown on August 16 and was apparently still in progress. See *OR,* 38, pt. 1, p. 135.

12. Paisley Diary, 17 [18] August 1864; Oblinger Diary, 18 August 1864; *HT,* 15 September 1864, p. 1; Brown Diary, 18 August 1864; Tomlinson, ed., *Sergeant Cort,* p. 154; *92nd Illinois,* p. 148; Crofts, comp., *3rd Ohio,* p. 160; Nourse Diary, 18 August 1864; Rea, "Kilpatrick's Raid," p. 647; Curry, comp., *Four Years in the Saddle,* p. 174; *OR,* 38, pt. 2, pp. 863, 889–90, 893; Morning Reports, 18 August 1864, Company B, 92nd Illinois Mounted Infantry, RG 94; Morning Reports, 18 August 1864, Company D, 8th Indiana Cavalry, RG 94; Ward Diary, 18 August 1864; Robinson, "With Kilpatrick," p. 575.

13. *DTB,* 6 September 1864, p. 2; *NR,* 13 September 1864, p. 3; *MJPGA,* 17 September 1864, p. 1. Copies of this circular, with a few minor variations in wording and punctuation, are found in the 3rd Indiana Cavalry Papers, RG 94, and the 4th Michigan Cavalry Papers, RG 94. A copy also appears in an article written by Eli Long's adjutant, William E. Crane, entitled "Bugle Blasts," p. 244.

14. Curry, "Raid around Atlanta," p. 606; Rea, "Kilpatrick's Raid," p. 647; *OR,* 38, pt. 2, p. 839; *DTB,* 6 September 1864, p. 2; Wulsin, *4th Ohio,* p. 53; Crofts, comp., *3rd Ohio,* p. 160. According to Lieutenant George Robinson of the Board of Trade Battery, bugles sounded "To Horse," and quickly followed with "Mount." Then the headquarters bugler sounded "Forward." However, Eli Long's adjutant, Captain Crane, asserted, "The expedition was designed to be a secret one, and there were no bugle blasts to awaken the echoes of the still night. . . ." See Robinson, "With Kilpatrick," p. 576; Crane, "Bugle Blasts," p. 244.

15. Tomlinson, ed., *Sergeant Cort,* p. 154; Brown Diary, 18 August 1864; Brown Notebook, 18 [August] 1864; Morning Reports, 18 August 1864, Companies A, B, and I, 92nd Illinois Mounted Infantry, RG 94; Ninety-Second Illinois Reunion Association, *5th Triennial Reunion,* p. 16; *92nd Illinois,* p. 148; *NT,* 17 July 1924, p. 7; Battery Return, August 1864, 10th Wisconsin Battery, RG 94; Paisley Diary, 18 August 1864; Morning Reports, 18 August 1864, Companies E and G, 10th Ohio Cavalry, RG 94; Record of Events, May–August, July–August 1864, Companies A–L, 10th Ohio Cavalry, reel 141, M-594, RG 94; Oblinger Diary, 18 August 1864; Ward Diary, 18–19 August 1864; *HT,* 15 September 1864, p. 1; Fielder Jones's report, p. 245, vol. 20/28, 39, CCMDM, RG 393; Unsigned report, dated "Head Quarters 8th Ind. Cavalry, Sandtown, Georgia, August 25th 1864," (probably by Major Thomas Herring and hereafter cited as Herring's Report), 8th Indiana Cavalry Papers, RG 94; Morning Reports, 18 August 1864, Company D, 8th Indiana Cavalry, RG 94; Regimental Return, August 1864, 8th Indiana Cavalry, reel 35, M-594, RG 94; James S. Thompson Diary, 18 August 1864; McCain, *A Soldier's Diary,* p. 34; Regimental Return, August 1864, 3rd Indiana Cavalry, reel 34, M-594, RG 94; Regimental Return, August 1864, 5th Iowa Cavalry, reel 51, M-594, RG 94; Iowa Adjutant General, *Report,* p. 1005; *OR,* 38, pt. 2, pp. 858, 863, 879, 887, 893, 896, 903; pt. 5,

p. 978; *LDJ,* 15 September 1864, p. 1; *NYTB,* 5 September 1864, p. 1. Sources citing the order and time of departure of Minty's and Long's brigades are found in note 5. In a letter to "My Dear Davidson," 28 August 1864, Minty's adjutant, Captain Robert Burns, estimated the strength of Kilpatrick's column at about 4,800 men. The *Cincinnati Daily Commercial,* 31 August 1864, p. 1, and Minty's postwar account of the raid in the *National Tribune,* 22 January 1903, p. 6, put the number a little higher, at about 5,000. However, reliable figures in *OR,* 38, pt. 2, pp. 824, 839, 858, 868, 879; *Louisville Daily Journal,* 15 September 1864, p. 1; *New York Tribune,* 5 September 1864, p. 1, indicate the actual number was closer to 4,500. For information on the seven regiments armed with Spencer rifles and carbines, see Record of Ordnance and Ordnance Stores, vol. 7, 92nd Illinois Mounted Infantry, 8th Indiana Cavalry, 2nd Kentucky Cavalry, 4th Michigan Cavalry, 3rd Ohio Cavalry, 7th Pennsylvania Cavalry, 4th U.S. Cavalry, RG 156; Orders, Company L, 7 July 1864, Order Books, Companies B, C, F, G, K, and L, 8th Indiana Cavalry, RG 94; Crofts, comp., *3rd Ohio,* p. 159.

16. Robinson, "With Kilpatrick," p. 576; *NT,* 1 March 1894, p. 3 (quoting Kilpatrick); *DCE,* 27 August 1864, p. 2; *LDJ,* 15 September 1864, p. 1; *NYTB,* 5 September 1864, p. 1; Ninety-Second Illinois, *5th Reunion,* p. 16; Keen, *6th Texas,* pp. 68–76; Brown Notebook, 18 [August] 1864; James Dawson to "Dear family and friends in General," 24 August 1864, James Dawson Papers; *92nd Illinois,* p. 148; *OR,* 38, pt. 2, pp. 858, 863, 896–97; pt. 5, pp. 601, 603.

17. *OR,* 38, pt. 2, pp. 855–56, 862–63, 868–69, 879; pt. 5, pp. 580, 595, 615; Ninety-Second Illinois, *5th Reunion,* p. 16; *HT,* 15 September 1864, p. 1; *NYTB,* 5 September 1864, p. 1; Regimental Return, August 1864, 3rd Indiana Cavalry, reel 34, M-594, RG 94; Iowa Adjutant General, *Report,* p. 1005; *NT,* 1 January 1885, p. 3; James S. Thompson Diary, 18–19 August 1864; McCain, *A Soldier's Diary,* pp. 35–36; Pickerill, *History of the Third Indiana Cavalry,* p. 118; *MDT,* 20 August 1864, p. 1; *CT,* 23 August 1864, p. 1; *ADI,* 20 August 1864, p. 1; *ADI,* 23 August 1864, pp. 1, 2; *CDS,* 24 August 1864, p. 1; Vicinity of Newnan to Ocmulgee River in the Vicinity of Jackson, Showing Topography, etc., Sept. 7, 1864, Map N221–2, RG 77; *ACS,* 27 August 1864, p. 3; *DCE,* 27 August 1864, p. 2; Daniel H. Reynolds's Report, dated "Hd. Qrs. Reynolds' Brigade, Walthall's Div. Army Tenn. Atlanta August 25, 1864" (hereafter cited as Reynolds's Report), Daniel H. Reynolds Papers; Watkins, "The 'Fighting' Forty-Eighth Tennessee Regiment," pp. 250–51. In *OR,* 38, pt. 2, pp. 862, 868–69, Klein said the train captured at Bear Creek Station consisted of an engine and nine cars, but Private James S. Thompson of the 3rd Indiana noted eighteen cars in his diary entry for 19 August 1864. The *Atlanta* [Macon] *Daily Intelligencer,* 20 August 1864, p. 1, said there was an engine and sixteen cars. A correspondent for the *Columbus Times,* 23 August 1864, p. 1, agreed, but the *Griffin Rebel,* 20 August 1864, quoted by *Atlanta* [Macon] *Daily Intelligencer,* 23 August 1864, p. 2, said the train consisted of eleven platform cars and four boxcars. A reporter writing from Jonesboro in the *Augusta Chronicle & Sentinel,* 25 August 1864, p. 2, cited these same numbers, and the *Griffin Rebel,* 22 August 1864, quoted by *Atlanta* [Macon] *Daily Intelligencer,* 23 August 1864, p. 1, added two of the boxcars escaped destruction.

18. *OR,* 38, pt. 5, pp. 975–77; pt. 3, pp. 928, 940; pt. 2, pp. 868–69; Champion to "My Precious Wife," 22 August 1864; Bigger Diary, 19 August 1864; Dixon Diary, 27 August 1864; Dixon, "Recollections of a Rebel Private," p. 218; Smith, *Private in Gray,* p. 117; Deupree, "Noxubee Squadron," p. 103; Montgomery, *Reminiscences,* p. 195; Record of Events, July–August 1864, Company G, 2nd Mississippi Cavalry, reel 27, M-861, RG 109; Record of Events, July–August 1864, Companies B and D, 28th Mississippi Cavalry, reel 28, M-861, RG 109; Record of Events, July–August 1864, Captain Farris's Battery (Clark Artillery, King's Battery), reel 34, M-861, RG 109; Reynolds's Report, Reynolds Papers; Henry G. Evans, Report dated "Hd. Qrs. 48th Ten. Regts. Cons., In the Field, Aug 28th 1864" (hereafter cited as Evans's Report), Reynolds Papers; Dacus, *Reminiscences of Company "H," First Arkansas Mounted Rifles,* p. [14]; Leeper, *Rebels Valiant: The Second Arkansas Mounted Rifles (Dismounted),* p. 245; Lavender, *The War Memoirs of Captain John W.*

Lavender, C.S.A., p. 99; Lindsley, ed., *Military Annals of Tennessee*, p. 548; Record of Events, July–August 1864, Companies A-K, 1st Arkansas Mounted Rifles, reel 6, M-861, RG 109; Record of Events, July–August 1864, Companies A, B, D-G, 2nd Arkansas Mounted Rifles, reel 6, M-861, RG 109; Record of Events, July–August 1864, Companies F-I, 4th Arkansas Infantry, reel 7, M-861, RG 109; Record of Events, July–August 1864, Company E, 9th Arkansas Infantry, reel 7, M-861, RG 109; Record of Events, July–August 1864, Field and Staff, Companies A, B, D, G, I, and K, 25th Arkansas Infantry, reel 8, M-861, RG 109; Milton Walls to "My dear Pa and Ma," 19 August 1864, Albert Milton Walls Papers; Watkins, "Forty-Eighth Tennessee," p. 250; *MDT,* 23 August 1864, p. 2; *CT,* 29 August 1864, p. 2; *DCE,* 27 August 1864, p. 2; *NT,* 1 January 1885, p. 3.

19. Klein did not identify this ford except to say it was on the road "from Lovejoy's to Fayetteville." While he might have been referring to the Cut Bank Ford, about two miles below Hill's Bridge, it seems more likely he was describing the ford above the ruins of Glass Bridge, two miles above Hill's Bridge. The 9th Texas Cavalry had used this ford to cross the Flint River on July 30 during their pursuit of McCook's raid, and it would have given Armstrong's men the inside track to Fayetteville. See *OR,* 38, pt. 2, pp. 869, 894; Vicinity of Newnan to Ocmulgee River in the Vicinity of Jackson, Showing Topography, etc., Sept. 7, 1864, Map N221–2, RG 77; Kerr, ed., *Ross' Texas Cavalry,* p. 161.

20. McCain, *A Soldier's Diary,* p. 36; Regimental Return, August 1864, 3rd Indiana Cavalry, reel 34, M-594, RG 94; James S. Thompson Diary, 19 August 1864; Dixon Diary, 27 August 1864; Dixon, "Recollections of a Rebel Private," p. 218; Champion to "My Precious Wife," 22 August 1864; Compiled Service Records, RG 94; Indiana Adjutant General, *Report,* 5:404–5; Iowa Adjutant General, *Report,* p. 1005; Iowa Adjutant General, *Roster and Record,* 4:885, 944; *LDJ,* 15 September 1864, p. 1; *OR,* 38, pt. 2, pp. 856, 868–69; pt. 5, pp. 615, 622.

23. KILPATRICK'S RAID: STEVENS' CROSSROADS TO LEE'S MILL, AUGUST 19–AUGUST 20, 1864

1. *OR,* 38, pt. 2, pp. 858, 863, 879; pt. 5, p. 978; Paisley Diary, 18 August 1864; Record of Events, May–August, July–August 1864, Companies C, H, I, and L, 10th Ohio Cavalry, reel 141, M-594, RG 94; Morning Reports, 18 August 1864, Company E, 10th Ohio Cavalry, RG 94; Jones's Report, p. 245, vol. 20/28, 39, CCMDM, RG 393; Regimental Return, August 1864, 8th Indiana Cavalry, reel 35, M-594, RG 94; Kerr, ed., *Ross' Texas Cavalry,* p. 165; Herring's Report, 8th Indiana Cavalry Papers, RG 94; *HT,* 15 September 1864, p. 1; Oblinger Diary, 19 August 1864; Ward Diary, 19 August 1864.

2. Benner, *Sul Ross: Soldier, Statesman, Educator,* pp. 15, 81, 91; Ross to "Dear Lizzie," 26 April 1864, Ross Family Papers. See also Shelton, "Personal Letters Written by Lawrence Sullivan Ross" (Master's thesis), pp. 165–66.

3. *OR,* 38, pt. 5, p. 978.

4. Unless otherwise noted, the movements of Kilpatrick's column described in this chapter are based on the following sources. Union: *OR,* 38, pt. 2, pp. 813–14, 824–25, 829–30, 833–34, 835, 839–40, 843, 845, 846, 852, 858, 862, 863, 879–80, 887, 893, 897, 903; *CDC,* 31 August 1864, p. 1; *NYTB,* 5 September 1864, p. 1; *LDJ,* 15 September 1864, p. 1; *LDJ,* 23 September 1864, p. 1; Burns to "My Dear Davidson," 28 August 1864; Heber S. Thompson Diary, 19–20 August 1864; Vale, *Minty and the Cavalry,* pp. 338–42; *NT,* 10 July 1890, p. 1; *NT,* 22 January 1903, p. 6; McLain Diary 19 August 1864; Potter Diary, 19–20 August 1864; Potter to "Dear Father," 24 August 1864; *DFP,* 6 September 1864, p. 4; *DAT,* 8 September 1864, p. 4; *AJ,* 26 September 1864, p. 2; Regimental Return, August 1864, 4th Michigan Cavalry, reel 83, M-594, RG 94; *MJPGA,* 10 September 1864, p. 3; *MJPGA,* 17 September 1864, p. 1; *MJPGA,* 1 October 1864, p. 2; *TWA,* 5 October 1864, p. 4; Dornblaser, *Saber Strokes,* pp. 174–76; Dornblaser, *My Life-Story for Young and Old,* pp. 62–63; Webb,

"Kilpatrick's Great Raid," pp. 729–32; *SOG,* 13 September 1864, p. 4; Crane, "Bugle Blasts," pp. 245–46; Curry, "Raid around Atlanta," pp. 606–12; Curry, comp., *Four Years in the Saddle,* pp. 175–79; Rea, "Kilpatrick's Raid," pp. 648–51; *DTB,* 6 September 1864, p. 2; *NR,* 13 September 1864, p. 3; *NT,* 15 May 1902, p. 3; Crofts, comp., *3rd Ohio,* pp. 161–62; Morning Reports, 19 August 1864, Companies G and L, 4th Ohio Cavalry, RG 94; Wulsin, *4th Ohio,* pp. 54–57; Lester Diary, 19–20 August 1864; Nourse Diary, [19]–20 August 1864; Nourse, "Kilpatrick's Raid," pp. 2–3; Nourse to Minty, 3 February 1903, Minty Papers; Robinson, "With Kilpatrick," pp. 576–84; Chicago Board of Trade Battery, *Historical Sketch,* pp. 66–67; Jones's Report, pp. 245–46, vol. 20/28, 39, CCMDM, RG 393; Herring's Report, 8th Indiana Cavalry Papers, RG 94; Oblinger Diary, 19–20 August 1864; Ward Diary, 19–20 August 1864; *HT,* 15 September 1864, p. 1; Morning Reports, 19 August 1864, Company D, 8th Indiana Cavalry, RG 94; Regimental Return, August 1864, 8th Indiana Cavalry, reel 35, M-594, RG 94; Paisley Diary, 19 August 1864; Morning Reports, 19–20 August 1864, Companies E and G, 10th Ohio Cavalry, RG 94; Record of Events, May–August, July–August 1864, Companies B, C, E, F, G, and L, 10th Ohio Cavalry, reel 141, M-594, RG 94; "List of Casualties in the 10th Ohio Cavy. During the Expedition Starting from Sandtown, Ga. Aug. 18th 1864," 10th Ohio Cavalry Papers, RG 94; Brown Diary, 19–20 August 1864; Brown Notebook, 19-[20] [August] 1864; Dawson to "Dear family and friends in General," 24 August 1864; Tomlinson, ed., *Sergeant Cort,* p. 154; Ninety-Second Illinois, *5th Reunion,* p. 16; *NT,* 1 March 1894, p. 3; *NT,* 10 April 1902, p. 3; *NT,* 15 December 1910, p. 7; *92nd Illinois,* pp. 149–51; Morning Reports, 18–20 August 1864, Companies A, B, and I, 92nd Illinois, RG 94; *NT,* 17 July 1924, p. 7; Battery Return, August 1864, 10th Wisconsin Battery, RG 94. Confederate sources: *OR,* 38, pt. 3, p. 691; Record of Events, July–August 1864, Croft's Battery, reel 13, M-861, RG 109; Kerr, ed., *Ross' Texas Cavalry,* pp. 165–66; Barron, *Lone Star Defenders,* pp. 206–7; *ADI,* 23 August 1864, p. 1; *CT,* 23 August 1864, p. 1; *DCE,* 23 August 1864, pp. 1, 2; *MDT,* 23 August 1864, p. 2; *ACS,* 25 August 1864, p. 2; *DCE,* 27 August 1864, p. 2; *CT,* 29 August 1864, p. 2.

5. *NT,* 22 January 1903, p. 6.

6. *92nd Illinois,* p. 149.

7. Ibid.

8. *NT,* 22 January 1903, p. 6, and rough draft of this article in Minty Papers. Minty's rough draft of the article in the *National Tribune* said Colonel Murray was with Kilpatrick, but this observation was deleted from the final text.

9. *92nd Illinois,* p. 149.

10. A 7th Pennsylvania trooper, writing to *The Miners' Journal and Pottsville General Advertiser,* 10 September 1864, p. 3, said the Rebels opened on the Yankee column with four guns. Another correspondent, Lieutenant George W. Fish of the 4th Michigan, told the *Detroit Advertiser and Tribune,* 8 September 1864, p. 4, there were only two. Colonel Minty agreed with Lieutenant Clark in his account of the raid in the *National Tribune,* 22 January 1903, p. 6, but the Confederate accounts cited in note 4 insist Ross had only one gun, a 12-pounder howitzer.

11. Nourse, "Kilpatrick's Raid," p. 2. Other sources identified the ambulance drivers as Return "Turn" T. Anderson of the 4th Michigan and Wilson H. Smith of the 7th Pennsylvania. See McLain Diary, 19 August 1864; Vale, *Minty and the Cavalry,* p. 339.

12. Dornblaser, *Saber Strokes,* pp. 175–76; Dornblaser, *My Life-Story,* pp. 62–63; Compiled Service Records, RG 94; Sipes, *7th Pennsylvania,* roster p. 81; Bates, *Pennsylvania Volunteers,* 2:1144.

13. *OR,* 38, pt. 5, pp. 600, 978.

14. Curry, comp., *Four Years in the Saddle,* pp. 176–77.

15. In his report in *OR,* 38, pt. 2, p. 852, Lieutenant Robinson said this shot dismounted one of the Rebel guns and killed a Confederate cannoneer. Private John Nourse of the Board of Trade Battery elaborated on the story in "Kilpatrick's Raid," p. 3, and asserted one shot was "fired to get the range," and the second shot "struck a Rebel gun in the trunnion, knocked that

gun out of service, and killed two cannoneers." Another eyewitness, in a letter appearing in the *New York Tribune,* 5 September 1864, p. 1, said the Rebel battery consisted of two guns. Private Lucien Wulsin agreed in *4th Ohio,* p. 55, but Confederate newspaper accounts all insist Ross had only one gun, a 12-pounder howitzer, which was positioned in front of Dr. John Baber's house. Lieutenant Colonel William Forbes II, in his carefully researched history of Croft's Battery, identified Corporal A. F. Knight as the Rebel artilleryman killed by the shell. See *DCE,* 27 August 1864, p. 2; *CT,* 26 August 1864, p. 2; *CT,* 29 August 1864, p. 2; Forbes, "The Old Bronze Gentleman of Lovejoy's Station," p. 29.

16. *NR,* 13 September 1864, p. 3.

17. Ibid.

18. Lieutenant William Curry remembered the 1st Ohio as being on the right of the 4th Regulars in *Four Years in the Saddle,* p. 177. In a November 1902 letter to artilleryman John Nourse, reprinted in the Chicago Board of Trade Battery's, *Historical Sketch,* p. 66, Minty drew a diagram of the formation, showing the 1st Ohio on the Regulars' left.

19. Robinson, "With Kilpatrick," p. 582.

20. In his reminiscences of the raid, Lieutenant William Curry said Rebel sharpshooters kept up a brisk fire from a brick church until a section of the Board of Trade Battery hurled several shells into the sanctuary, "making the bricks and mortar fly." Jonesboro had only two or three churches, and only one of them, the Jonesboro Baptist Church, was on the south side of town. It was made of wood. None of the other eyewitnesses mention a church being shelled, an incident that Southern newspapers would undoubtedly have cited as further evidence of Yankee depravity. A brick house belonging to Dr. Francis T. Gayden did stand opposite the Baptist Church. See Curry, comp., *Four Years in the Saddle,* p. 177; Curry, "Raid around Atlanta," p. 609; Moore, *A History of Clayton County, Georgia,* pp. 7, 9, 10, 81.

21. *NT,* 22 January 1903, p. 6. Writing in 1886, Lieutenant George Robinson recounted in "With Kilpatrick," p. 582, that after his guns had ceased firing, he noticed a telegraph office just to his right. Stepping inside, he heard the chatter of the telegrapher's key. "The message then on the wire was interpreted by a Yankee soldier who claimed to have been a telegraph operator," Robinson recalled, "and was said to be advices that Cleburne's division of infantry and Martin's brigade of cavalry were en-route to re-enforce Ross and Ferguson. Acting on this, Kilpatrick sent a force well up the road toward Atlanta, to tear up the road. . . ." Bob Minty apparently borrowed this story and repeated it in his accounts of the raid in the *National Tribune,* 10 July 1890, p. 1, and 22 January 1903, p. 6. So did Lieutenant William Curry, in *Four Years in the Saddle,* pp. 177–78, and "Raid around Atlanta," p. 610, in 1898; Private John Nourse, in "Kilpatrick's Raid," p. 4, in 1899; and Sergeant Tom Crofts, in *3rd Ohio,* p. 161, in 1910. However, the receipt of a telegram warning of the approach of Rebel infantry and cavalry appears nowhere else in the literature of Kilpatrick's raid, and perhaps with good reason. Kilpatrick does not mention receiving any such information in his report in the *Official Records,* or sending forces to tear up the railroad north of Jonesboro. Confederate correspondence in *OR,* 38, pt. 5, pp. 976, 979, and pt. 3, p. 958, also makes it clear Hood had no intention of sending Cleburne's infantry after the raiders, and Martin's division (see Lawson, *Wheeler's Last Raid,* pp. 140, 145–47, 150–51) was in Tennessee on August 19 with the rest of Wheeler's cavalry. If Kilpatrick learned anything from the telegraph office, it might have been news that Klein's brigade had broken the railroad at Bear Creek Station, and Reynolds's infantry brigade, supported by Armstrong's and Ferguson's cavalry, had passed through Jonesboro, heading south. See *LDJ,* 15 September 1864, p. 1.

22. Webb, "Kilpatrick's Great Raid," pp. 731–32.

23. *CDC,* 31 August 1864, p. 1. The *Atlanta* [Macon] *Southern Confederacy*'s correspondent, quoted by *Columbus Times,* 29 August 1864, p. 2, identified the tax-in-kind warehouses as belonging to a Mr. Kaigler. This name does not appear in Moore's extensive *History of Clayton County,* but Moore does note Jesse Coogler was one of a handful of merchants living in Jonesboro in 1860.

24. Nourse Diary, [19] August 1864. Nourse may have been referring to William Parker, an elderly farmer. According to the *Atlanta* [Macon] *Southern Confederacy,* quoted by *Columbus Times,* 29 August 1864, p. 2, Yankee troopers fired into Parker's house and robbed him of his watch, $800 in Confederate money, and all his clothes, bacon, and cornmeal. The *Atlanta* [Macon] *Daily Intelligencer,* 23 August 1864, p. 1, reported the raiders burned a total of five residences, while the *Columbus Times,* 23 August 1864, p. 1, put the number at ten or twelve "unoccupied tenements." However, correspondents writing from Jonesboro to the *Griffin Rebel,* quoted by *Daily Columbus Enquirer,* 27 August 1864, p. 2, and the *Atlanta* [Macon] *Southern Confederacy,* quoted by *Columbus Times,* 29 August 1864, p. 2, agreed that only two private dwellings were burned. A letter to the *Augusta Chronicle & Sentinel,* 25 August 1864, p. 2, noted the burned houses were unoccupied. The *Macon Daily Telegraph,* 23 August 1864, p. 2, also accused the Yankees of burning the residence of a Mrs. Johnson. Presumably, this was Mrs. James F. (Martha) Johnson, but the *Southern Confederacy*'s correspondent, railroad agent Guy L. Warren, made no mention of her in his inventory of outrages committed in Jonesboro and according to Moore's *Clayton County,* pp. 25, 313, the Johnson home was still standing on Main Street, just north of the business district, in 1983.

25. *CT,* 29 August 1864, p. 2.

26. Ibid.; *OR,* 38, pt. 1, p. 172; pt. 2, pp. 826, 859; *NYTB,* 5 September 1864, p. 1; Madaus and Needham, *The Battle Flags of the Confederate Army of Tennessee,* pp. 120, 126n.40; Travis Hutchins, Curator of Exhibits, Georgia State Museum of Science and Industry, Atlanta, Ga., telephone interview with the author. Earlier in 1864, Mary Frances Johnson had married Colonel Andrew J. McBride, whose encounter with McCook's raiders is described in chapter 12.

27. *ACS,* 25 August 1864, p. 2.

28. Thomas Byrne vs. the U.S., Case Number 8,005, RG 123.

29. *92nd Illinois,* p. 150.

30. *NT,* 1 September 1904, p. 3.

31. Reynolds's Report, Evans's Report, Reynolds Papers.

32. Curry, "Raid around Atlanta," pp. 610–11.

33. Reynolds's Report, Evans's Report, Reynolds Papers; Herring's Report, 8th Indiana Cavalry Papers, RG 94.

34. *NT,* 24 November 1887, p. 3; *92nd Illinois,* p. 145; *DFP,* 6 September 1864, p. 4 (quote by Captain Van Antwerp); Potter to "Dear Father," 24 August 1864; Nourse to Minty, 3 February 1903, Minty Papers. Potter had been promoted from first lieutenant to captain on August 5. See Potter to "Dear Father," 5 August 1864, and Potter to "Dear Sister," 5 August 1864.

35. Clifton, *Libby and Andersonville Prisons,* p. [2]; "List of Casualties in 2d Brig 3d Div Cavalry during the late Cavalry Expedition—Brig Genl Kilpatrick" (hereafter cited as "List of Casualties 2d Brig 3d Div,"), RG 94; *92nd Illinois,* pp. 150–51.

36. "Report of Casualties of the 3rd Cav Brig 3rd Cav Div D.C. during the recent Cav Expedition from Aug 18th to Aug 24th 1864" (hereafter cited as "Report of Casualties 3rd Brig 3rd Div,"), RG 94; Illinois Adjutant General, *Report,* 5:356.

37. Ninety-Second Illinois Reunion Association, *7th Tri-ennial Re-Union,* p. 13.

38. *DCE,* 27 August 1864, p. 2; Reynolds's Report, Reynolds Papers; Barron, *Lone Star Defenders,* pp. 206–7; *CT,* 29 August 1864, p. 2.

39. Samuel Wragg Ferguson, "Memoirs of S. W. Ferguson," chapter 1, pp. 11, 15, 17, 20–25, chapter 2, pp. 1–14, unpublished typescript in Heyward-Ferguson Papers; Freeman, *R. E. Lee: A Biography,* 1:332–33; Special Orders No. 6, 16 January 1854, vol. 13, Orders Received 1838–1866, Records of the Adjutant General, Records of the United States Military Academy, RG 404; *Official Register of the U.S.Military Academy,* 1853:13, 1854:12, 19, 1855:10, 18, 1856:9, 19, 1857:7; Cullum, *Biographical Register,* 2:688; Evans, ed., *CMH,* vol. 6: *South Carolina,* by Ellison Capers, p. 394; Association of the Graduates of the United States Military

Academy, *48th Annual Report,* pp. 99–100; Cash and Howorth, eds., *My Dear Nellie,* pp. 206, 209–10; *OR,* 38, pt. 5, pp. 877, 944; "Charges & Specifications vs. Brig. Genl. Samuel W. Ferguson P.A.C.S.," William Hicks Jackson Papers; *OR,* 47, pt. 2, pp. 1004, 1012, 1027.

40. Reynolds's Report, Reynolds Papers; Kerr, ed., *Ross' Texas Cavalry,* p. 165; *DCE,* 27 August 1864, p. 2.

41. L. P. Thomas, "A Thrilling Narrative of War Times," UDC 9:134–138.

42. William C. Lee, Administrator of Samuel Lee, vs. the U.S., Case Number 5,766, RG 123; Thomas, "A Thrilling Narrative," UDC 9:134.

43. *NT,* 1 September 1904, p. 3.

44. Curry, comp., *Four Years in the Saddle,* p. 179.

45. *NT,* 1 September 1904, p. 3; Ohio Roster Commission, *Official Roster,* 11:152; "List of Casualties in 2d Brigade 2d Division Cavalry," pp. 68–69, vol. 57/140, CCMDM, RG 393.

46. Vale, *Minty and the Cavalry,* p. 342.

47. Rea, "Kilpatrick's Raid," p. 651.

48. Thomas, "A Thrilling Narrative," UDC 9:138–39.

49. *OR,* 38, pt. 2, p. 981.

50. Reynolds's Report, Evans's Report, Reynolds Papers; Rainey, "Experiences," p. 67.

24. KILPATRICK'S RAID: LEE'S MILL TO BUCKHEAD, AUGUST 20–AUGUST 22, 1864

1. Stephen G. Dorsey vs. the U.S., Case Number 119, RG 123. Judge Dorsey owned forty-one slaves in 1861, making him the largest slaveholder in Clayton County. His neighbor, Philip Fitzgerald, the great-grandfather of author Margaret Mitchell and the model for Gerald O'Hara in *Gone with the Wind,* owned thirty-five. See Moore, *Clayton County,* pp. 16–17, 22, 241–46.

2. *LDJ,* 15 September 1864, p. 1; Rea, "Kilpatrick's Raid," p. 651; *TWA,* 5 October 1864, p. 4; *MJPGA,* 17 September 1864, p. 1; Vale, *Minty and the Cavalry,* pp. 343–44; Burns to "My Dear Davidson," 28 August 1864; Heber S. Thompson Diary, 20 August 1864; McLain Diary, 20 August 1864; *CDC,* 31 August 1864, p. 1; *NYTB,* 5 September 1864, p. 1; *NT,* 21 May 1891, p. 3; *NT,* 10 July 1890, p. 1; *NT,* 22 January 1903, p. 6; *OR,* 38, pt. 2, pp. 814, 825, 830, 834; Regimental Return, August 1864, 4th Michigan Cavalry, reel 83, M-594, RG 94; Potter Diary, 20 August 1864; *DFP,* 6 September 1864, p. 4; *DAT,* 8 September 1864, p. 4; Webb, "Kilpatrick's Great Raid," p. 732.

3. Reynolds's Report, Reynolds Papers; Lindsley, ed., *Military Annals of Tennessee,* p. 548; Watkins, "Forty-Eighth Tennessee," p. 251; Rainey, "Experiences," pp. 67–68.

4. Burns to "My Dear Davidson," 28 August 1864; *OR,* 38, pt. 2, pp. 814, 825, 830, 834, 835; *CDC,* 31 August 1864, p. 1; Heber S. Thompson Diary, 20 August 1864; Vale, *Minty and the Cavalry,* p. 344; *NYTB,* 5 September 1864, p. 1; *MJPGA,* 10 September 1864, p. 3; *MJPGA,* 17 September 1864, p. 1; Robinson, "With Kilpatrick," pp. 584–85; Evans's Report, Reynolds's Report, Reynolds Papers; Watkins, "Forty-Eighth Tennessee," p. 251; *NT,* 22 January 1903, p. 6 (quote by Minty); Dornblaser, *Sabre Strokes,* pp. 177–79; Dornblaser, *My Life-Story,* pp. 63–64; Regimental Return, August 1864, 4th Michigan Cavalry, reel 83, M-594, RG 94; *DFP,* 6 September 1864, p. 4; *DAT,* 8 September 1864, p. 4; Potter Diary, 20 August 1864; Potter to "Dear Father," 24 August 1864.

5. Robinson, "With Kilpatrick," pp. 585–86; Nourse Diary, 20 August 1864; *OR,* 38, pt. 2, pp. 814, 825, 840; *NT,* 22 January 1903, p. 6; Crane, "Bugle Blasts," p. 246; James Thomson Diary, 20 August 1864; Wulsin, *4th Ohio,* pp. 57–58; Nourse, "Kilpatrick's Raid," pp. 4–5.

6. Private Nelson Rainey of the 7th Tennessee Cavalry was probably describing this bombardment when he recalled seeing "Red" Jackson standing near a fence just as a shell burst directly overhead. "I saw my General's big head *sink* down into his shoulders," he wrote.

"I thought it strange that that big brave man should shrink from anything. But 'twas enough to make anybody shrink. I did so myself." See Rainey, "Experiences," p. 71.

7. Nourse Diary, 20 August 1864; Nourse, "Kilpatrick's Raid," pp. 4–5; Nourse to Minty, 3 February 1903, Minty Papers; Fleming to "My Dear Parents," 13 September 1864; *OR,* 38, pt. 2, pp. 825, 852–53; *NT,* 10 April 1890, p. 4; *NT,* 22 May 1890, p. 3; Robinson, "With Kilpatrick," pp. 586–87; Vale, *Minty and the Cavalry,* p. 345; Burns to "My Dear Davidson," 28 August 1864; Lester Diary, 20 August 1864; Chicago Board of Trade Battery, *Historical Sketch,* pp. 29, 46, 61, 71, 72, 74, 76, 80; Compiled Service Records, RG 94; Illinois Adjutant General, *Report,* 8:729, 731, 736.

8. Robinson, "With Kilpatrick," p. 587; Nourse Diary, 20 August 1864; Nourse, "Kilpatrick's Raid," p. 5; Wulsin, *4th Ohio,* p. 58; Crane, "Bugle Blasts," p. 246; Curry, "Raid around Atlanta," p. 612; Rea, "Kilpatrick's Raid," pp. 652–653; Crofts, comp., *3rd Ohio,* p. 162; *NR,* 13 September 1864, p. 3; Burns to "My Dear Davidson," 28 August 1864; *OR,* 38, pt. 2, pp. 814, 825, 840, 843, 852, 859, 863–64, 880, 893, 903; Brown Diary, 20 August 1864; Brown Notebook, [20] [August] 1864; *92nd Illinois,* p. 152; Ninety-Second Illinois, *5th Reunion,* p. 16; *NT,* 1 March 1894, p. 3; Herring's Report, 8th Indiana Cavalry Papers, RG 94; *HT,* 15 September 1864, p. 1; Ward Diary, 20 August 1864; Reynolds's Report, Evans's Report, Reynolds Papers; *DCE,* 27 August 1864, p. 2; "List of Casualties in Reynolds' Arks Brigade at Lovejoy Station, Geo: August 20th 1864," Reynolds Papers.

9. Potter to "Dear Father," 24 August 1864; *OR,* 38, pt. pp. 859, 880; *NYH,* 16 September 1864, p. 1; Paisley Diary, 20 August 1864; Morning Reports, 20 August 1864, Company E, 10th Ohio Cavalry, RG 94; Jones's Report, pp. 246–47, vol. 20/28, 39, CCMDM, RG 393; Herring's Report, 8th Indiana Cavalry Papers, RG 94; *HT,* 15 September 1864, p. 1; Ward Diary, 20 August 1864; *LDJ,* 15 September 1864, p. 1; *NT,* 17 July 1924, p. 7 (quoting Kilpatrick); Stephen G. Dorsey vs. the U.S., Case Number 119, RG 123.

10. Webb, "Kilpatrick's Great Raid," p. 732.

11. *OR,* 38, pt. 2, p. 830; Regimental Return, August 1864, 4th Michigan Cavalry, reel 83, M-594, RG 94; Burns to "My Dear Davidson," 28 August 1864; *NT,* 21 May 1891, p. 3; *NT,* 26 February 1891, p. 3; *NT,* 22 January 1903, p. 6 (Minty's account).

12. *NT,* 22 January 1903, p. 6; *NT,* 23 April 1903, p. 3; Burns to "My Dear Davidson," 28 August 1864; *OR,* 38, pt. 2, pp. 814, 825, 831, 852, 834, 835, 840, 843; Regimental Return, August 1864, 4th Michigan Cavalry, reel 83, M-594, RG 94; McLain Diary, 20 August 1864; *AJ,* 26 September 1864, p. 2; Potter to "Dear Father," 24 August 1864; Crofts, comp., *3rd Ohio,* p. 162; Ripley, *Artillery and Ammunition of the Civil War,* p. 370; Chicago Board of Trade Battery, *Historical Sketch,* p. 66; Fleming to "My Dear Parents," 13 September 1864; Nourse Diary, 20 August 1864; Nourse, "Kilpatrick's Raid," p. 5; *NT,* 10 April 1890, p. 4; *NT,* 22 May 1890, p. 3; Robinson, "With Kilpatrick," pp. 587–88; *NT,* 4 July 1895, p. 3.

13. *OR,* 38, pt. 2, p. 834; Crane, "Bugle Blasts," p. 247; Curry, "Raid around Atlanta," p. 613; Rea, "Kilpatrick's Raid," pp. 653–54; Compiled Service Records, RG 94; Ohio Roster Commission, *Official Roster,* 11:36.

14. *OR,* 38, pt. 2, pp. 814, 825, 831, 834, 835, 864, 880, 893–94, 903; Robinson, "With Kilpatrick," p. 588; Regimental Return, August 1864, 4th Michigan Cavalry, reel 83, M-594, RG 94; Burns to "My Dear Davidson," 28 August 1864 (exchange between Burns and Kilpatrick); *NT,* 3 December 1891, p. 4 (quoting Kilpatrick and Minty); *NT,* 21 May 1891, p. 3; Heber S. Thompson Diary, 20 August 1864.

15. *CDC,* 31 August 1864, p. 1; *MJPGA,* 10 September 1864, p. 1; *WC,* 24 September 1864, p. 2; *DAT,* 8 September 1864, p. 4; Robinson, "With Kilpatrick," pp. 588, 590; Curry, "Raid around Atlanta," pp. 614–15; Dornblaser, *Sabre Strokes,* p. 181; Nourse, "Kilpatrick's Raid," p. 5; Nourse Diary 20 August 1864; McLain Diary, 20 August 1864; Curry, comp., *Four Years in the Saddle,* p. 308; *OR,* 38, pt. 2, p. 859; *LDJ,* 15 September 1864, p. 1; Rea, "Kilpatrick's Raid," p. 655; *NYTB,* 5 September 1864, p. 1; *SOG,* 13 September 1864, p. 4; *MJPGA,* 17 September 1864, p. 1; Crofts, comp., *3rd Ohio,* p. 163; *NT,* 21 May 1891, p. 3; *NT,* 15

December 1892, p. 4; Potter to "Dear Father," 24 August 1864; Webb, "Kilpatrick's Great Raid," p. 732. During this lull, Captain Potter noted "a flag of truce from the Infantry in our rear . . . fluttering towards us." In postwar reminiscences, Corporal Frank Dornblaser of the 7th Pennsylvania, Lieutenant William Webb of the 4th Regulars, and Lieutenant P. R. Walker and Private F. A. Free of the 92nd Illinois Mounted Infantry also recalled the approach of a white flag, but according to William W. Watkins, a 5th Iowa private assigned to 3rd Division headquarters, Kilpatrick refused to receive it, saying he had "no time to swap jack-knives." While this story may be true, there is no evidence to support it in any of the contemporary accounts, and neither Kilpatrick, nor Minty, nor any of their brigade and regimental commanders made any mention of a flag of truce in their official reports. Nor did Confederate General Dan Reynolds, the man who would have sent it. See Potter Diary, 20 August 1864; Potter to "Dear Father," 24 August 1864; Dornblaser, *Sabre Strokes,* p. 179; Webb, "Kilpatrick's Great Raid," p. 732; *NT,* 15 December 1910, p. 7; Ninety-Second Illinois, *5th Reunion,* p. 16; *NT,* 4 December 1884, p. 3; *NT,* 23 April 1891, p. 3.

16. *NT,* 22 January 1903, p. 6.

17. In *Minty and the Cavalry,* p. 347, Vale asserted Companies B and M of the 7th Pennsylvania Cavalry deployed as skirmishers, covering the entire front of the brigade, and threw down the first fence. An anonymous account in the *Louisville Daily Journal,* 15 September 1864, p. 1, and Kilpatrick, in *OR,* 38, pt. 2, p. 859, credited pioneers advancing ahead of the charging columns. Minty corrected Kilpatrick in *NT,* 22 January 1903, p. 6, and insisted, "I sent from the head of each of my three columns about a dozen men, to charge as foragers and make the necessary gaps in the fences."

18. Major Thomas Herring of the 8th Indiana saw only one Rebel gun on the field. Colonel Minty and his adjutant, Captain Burns, put the number at seven, and the estimates of other Federal officers and men ranged from two to Captain Joseph Vale's ridiculously high figure of eighteen. The best Confederate evidence indicates Ross had one 12-pounder howitzer at his disposal. See *DCE,* 27 August 1864, p. 2; Record of Events, July–August 1864, Croft's Battery, reel 13, M-861, RG 109; *OR,* 52, pt. 2, p. 725.

19. The charge of Minty's brigade is based on the following sources. Union: *OR,* 38, pt. 2, pp. 814, 825–26, 831, 834, 835, 859; Burns to "My Dear Davidson," 28 August 1864; Heber S. Thompson Diary, 20 August 1864; *CDC,* 31 August 1864, p. 1 (quoting Minty); *NYTB,* 5 September 1864, p. 1; *LDJ,* 15 September 1864, p. 1; Vale, *Minty and the Cavalry,* p. 347; *NT,* 26 February 1891, p. 3; *NT,* 31 May 1894, p. 2; *NT,* 22 January 1903, p. 6; McLain Diary, 20 August 1864; Potter Diary, 20 August 1864; Potter to "Dear Father," 24 August 1864; *DFP,* 6 September 1864, p. 4; *DAT,* 8 September 1864, p. 4; *WC,* 24 September 1864, p. 2; *AJ,* 26 September 1864, p. 2; *NT,* 4 December 1884, p. 3; *NT,* 21 May 1891, p. 3 (Major Frank Mix quotation); *NT,* 14 January 1892, p. 4; Regimental Return, August 1864, 4th Michigan Cavalry, reel 83, M-594, RG 94; *MJPGA,* 10 September 1864, p. 3; *MJPGA,* 17 September 1864, p. 1; *NT,* 3 December 1891, p. 4; Dornblaser, *Sabre Strokes,* pp. 181–82; Webb, "Kilpatrick's Great Raid," pp. 732–33; *NT,* 23 April 1891, p. 3; *NT,* 15 December 1892, p. 4; Cullum, *Biographical Register,* 2:569–70; Robinson, "With Kilpatrick," pp. 588–89; Nourse Diary, 20 August 1864; Nourse, "Kilpatrick's Raid," p. 5; Crane, "Bugle Blasts," p. 247. Confederate: Record of Events, July–August 1864, Croft's Battery, reel 13, M-861, RG 109; *CT,* 26 August 1864, p. 2; *DCE,* 27 August 1864, p. 2; *NYH,* 16 September 1864, p. 1; *NT,* 30 October 1913, p. 8 (location of Croft's Batery); Thomas, "A Thrilling Narrative," UDC 9:139; Barron, *Lone Star Defenders,* pp. 208–11, 223–24; *Atlanta Journal,* 10 August 1901, 2nd section, p. 2.

20. After noting Minty's orders for Long's brigade to follow in column of regiments, W. S. Scott, in "Kilpatrick's Raid around Atlanta," p. 268, concluded, "There seems to have been either considerable confusion or disobedience at this point, for Long, in the charge, followed the leading brigade in columns of fours. . . ." To this, the usually reticent Long replied, "I have no recollection of said orders being received by me, and, of course, of any disobedience on my

part or that of my command, and therefore deny the statement 'in toto.' . . . If there was any confusion or disobedience on the part of the Second Brigade or its commander, it is somewhat singular that something should not have been done or said about it, at or about the time it occurred, and that it should be discovered and commented upon only some twenty-six years afterward." See Eli Long, "Letter from General Long," p. 429.

21. In postwar accounts of the raid, Curry, comp., *Four Years in the Saddle,* p. 281, and Rea, "Kilpatrick's Raid," p. 657, both said Captain Scott got to his feet, waving his saber in his left hand, and followed the column for two miles before overtaking an ambulance. However, Captain Crane, writing in the *Cincinnati Daily Commercial,* 31 August 1864, p. 1, said Scott "lay on the ground some time before being brought off," and Private Lucien Wulsin, *4th Ohio,* p. 59, recalled seeing him "shot through the arm and covered with blood, lying up against a tree."

22. The charge of Eli Long's brigade is based on the following sources. Union: *OR,* 38, pt. 2, pp. 814, 825, 834, 840, 843; Burns to "My Dear Davidson," 28 August 1864; *NT,* 31 May 1894, p. 2; *NT,* 26 July 1894, p. 3; *NT,* 4 July 1895, p. 3; *NT,* 22 January 1903, p. 6; *CDC,* 31 August 1864, p. 1; Crane, "Bugle Blasts," pp. 247–49; Curry, comp., *Four Years in the Saddle,* pp. 181, 211, 281, 308, 314 (quoting Captain William H. Scott); Curry, "Raid around Atlanta," pp. 614–16; Rea, "Kilpatrick's Raid," pp. 655–57, 662–63; *DTB,* 6 September 1864, p. 2; *NR,* 13 September 1864, p. 3; *NR,* 20 September 1864, p. 1 (quoting fallen 3rd Ohio trooper); Crofts, comp., *3rd Ohio,* p. 163; Wulsin, *4th Ohio,* p. 59; *NT,* 15 October 1891, p. 3 (Sergeant Garner Stimsen's account). Confederate: *DCE,* 27 August 1864, p. 2 (quoting Sul Ross and Lieutenant George Young); *Atlanta Journal,* 10 August 1901, 2nd section, p. 2 (quote by Rebel gunner); Record of Events, July–August 1864, Croft's Battery, reel 13, M-861, RG 109.

23. *OR,* 38, pt. 2, pp. 826, 836; *CDC,* 31 August 1864, p. 1. The *Cincinnati Daily Commercial*'s correspondent said Douglas's prisoners included a captain and a lieutenant, but Minty, in his report, credited Douglas with capturing four commissioned officers.

24. *OR,* 38, pt. 1, p. 172; pt. 2, pp. 826, 859; Dornblaser, *Sabre Strokes,* p. 182; *NT,* 15 December 1892, p. 4; *CDC,* 31 August 1864, p. 1; *NYTB,* 5 September 1864, p. 1; *LDJ,* 15 September 1864, p. 1; Potter to "Dear Father," 24 August 1864; Vale, *Minty and the Cavalry,* p. 350; Barron, *Lone Star Defenders,* p. 227; Madaus and Needham, *Battle Flags,* pp. 75–76. Lieutenant Barron noted the 3rd Texas's colors were not unfurled on this expedition and must have been taken from an ambulance.

25. Robinson, "With Kilpatrick," p. 590; Herring's Report, 8th Indiana Cavalry Papers, RG 94; *HT,* 15 September 1864, p. 1; Paisley Diary, 20 August 1864; *OR,* 38, pt. 2, pp. 864, 880, 887, 894 (quote by Lieutenant Colonel Robert H. King); *NT,* 17 July 1894, p. 7 (quoting Captain Estes).

26. The *Savannah Republican,* quoted by *Charleston Daily Courier,* 27 August 1864, p. 1, reported a Yankee prisoner told his Confederate captors Kilpatrick had a narrow brush with death when a bullet cut off a lock of hair just above his forehead.

27. *AJ,* 26 September 1864, p. 2; *DFP,* 6 September 1864, p. 4; *NT,* 4 December 1884, p. 3; *NT,* 21 May 1891, p. 3; Todd et al., *American Military Equipage, 1851–1872,* 2:340, 348; *NT,* 23 April 1891, p. 3; Kilpatrick, *The Irish Soldier in the War of the Rebellion,* pp. 3–4 (quoting Rebel gunner); Jones's Report, p. 247, vol. 20/28, 39, CCMDM, RG 393; *OR,* 38, pt. 2, pp. 826–27; *CDC,* 31 August 1864, p. 1; *NYTB,* 5 September 1864, p. 1; *NT,* 22 January 1903, p. 6; *NT,* 3 December 1891, p. 4; *NT,* 26 July 1894, p. 3. Lieutenant George W. Clark of the 4th Michigan said Bailey "charged into the gunners and blew the Captain's brains out." Bob Minty, Captain Robert Burns, Robert M. Wilson of the 4th U.S. Cavalry, and the *Cincinnati Daily Commercial*'s correspondent agreed. The *New York Tribune*'s correspondent credited Bailey not only with "killing the Captain of the battery," but also with "severing the head of a Lieutenant," while Sergeant Coleman H. Watts of the 7th Pennsylvania said Bailey dismounted after shooting the Rebel captain and stripped him of his saber, belt, and pistols. Another eyewitness, Sergeant Garner Stimsen, did not specifically mention Bailey, but he did

assert, "As we neared the cannon the enemy broke and ran, except one officer, who foolishly refused to surrender and therefore was cut down." Lieutenant Will Curry of the 1st Ohio added the Rebel lieutenant commanding the artillery "gave his name as Young" and was "mortally wounded . . . as he was attempting to fire one of his pieces after all his men had deserted their posts." The howitzer was indeed commanded by Lieutenant George B. Young, but according to all the Confederate accounts, he survived the battle and was the only officer of the battery present. See *DAT*, 8 September 1864, p. 4; *OR*, 38, pt. 2, pp. 826–27; *NT*, 22 January 1903, p. 6; Burns to "My Dear Davidson," 28 August 1864; Barron, *Lone Star Defenders*, p. 224; *CDC*, 31 August 1864, p. 1; *NYTB*, 5 September 1864, p. 1; *NT*, 3 December 1891, p. 4; *NT*, 15 October 1891, p. 3; Curry, "Raid around Atlanta," p. 616; *DCE*, 27 August 1864, p. 2; *CT*, 26 August 1864, p. 2; Record of Events, July–August 1864, Croft's Battery, reel 13, M-861, RG 109; *OR*, 52, pt. 2, p. 725.

28. *HT*, 15 September 1864, p. 1; Regimental Returns, July and August 1864, 8th Indiana Cavalry, reel 35, M-594, RG 94; Morning Reports, 20 August 1864, Company D, 8th Indiana Cavalry, RG 94; Oblinger Diary, 20 August 1864; Ward Diary, 20 August 1864; *NT*, 24 March 1887, p. 4; "List of Casualties in the 10th Ohio," 10th Ohio Papers, RG 94; Compiled Service Records, RG 94; Ohio Roster Commission, *Official Roster*, 11:514; Pension Records, RG 15; *LDJ*, 23 September 1864, p. 1; Robinson, "With Kilpatrick," pp. 589–90; Fleming to "My Dear Parents," 13 September 1864; Nourse Diary, 20 August 1864; *LDJ*, 15 September 1864, p. 1; *NT*, 22 May 1890, p. 3; Chicago Board of Trade Battery, *Historical Sketch*, p. 29; *OR*, 38, pt. 2, pp. 852, 859, 861, 880, 897; *DCE*, 27 August 1864, p. 2; *92nd Illinois*, p. 152; *NT*, 1 March 1894, p. 3; *NT*, 15 December 1910, p. 7; "Report of Casualties 3rd Brig 3rd Div," RG 94; Tomlinson, ed., *Sergeant Cort*, p. 155.

29. Wulsin, *4th Ohio*, pp. 59–60; *OR*, 38, pt. 2, pp. 814, 826, 831, 834, 835, 840, 843, 845, 847, 859, 864, 897; Burns to "My Dear Davidson," 28 August 1864; *DFP*, 6 September 1864, p. 4; Vale, *Minty and the Cavalry*, p. 350; *CDC*, 31 August 1864, p. 1; Crane, "Bugle Blasts," p. 249; Curry, "Raid around Atlanta," p. 616; Rea, "Kilpatrick's Raid," p. 657; *NR*, 13 September 1864, p. 3; *DTB*, 6 September 1864, p. 2; Robinson, "With Kilpatrick," p. 591; *92nd Illinois*, pp. 152–53; Brown Notebook, [20] [August] 1864; *NT*, 21 May 1891, p. 3 (Major Frank Mix's account); *NT*, 22 January 1903, p. 6; "Rebel Prisoners of War," vol. 50/108, CCMDM, RG 393; "List of Prisoners of War Captured by 2d Brigade 2d Division Cavalry," pp. 6–7, vol. 57/140, CCMDM, RG 393.

30. *OR*, 38, pt. 2, p. 840; Long, *Synopsis of the Military Career of Brevet Maj.-Gen. Eli Long*, p. 1; Reid, *Ohio in the War*, 1:861; Warner, *Generals in Blue*, p. 283; *Catalogue of the Officers and Cadets of the Kentucky Military Institute*, pp. 25, 31; "Statement of the Services of Col. Eli Long Comdg. 2d Brig. 2d Division of Cavalry Army of the Cumberland," Eli Long Papers; Eli Long File, Letters Received by the Appointment, Commission, and Personnel Branch, Adjutant General's Office, 1871–1894, M-1395 (hereafter cited as M-1395), RG 94; Larson, *Sergeant Larson*, pp. 85–86; *NT*, 8 December 1887, p. 3; Wilson, *Under the Old Flag*, 2:170–71.

31. *OR*, 38, pt. 2, pp. 814, 826, 840, 843, 847; *NR*, 13 September 1864, p. 3; *NT*, 15 October 1891, p. 3.

32. The *Griffin Rebel*'s correspondent, quoted in the *Daily Columbus Enquirer*, 27 August 1864, p. 2, said Armstrong's brigade was "delayed about 2 hours by having to build a couple of bridges," but none of Armstrong's men made any mention of this.

33. Private W. C. Smith remembered Armstrong's brigade dismounting behind the Macon railroad, apparently on the left flank of Reynolds's infantry, and watching while Kilpatrick's column rode over Ross's brigade, but his recollection does not square with other Confederate accounts.

34. *DCE*, 27 August 1864, p. 2; Dixon Diary, 20 August 1864; Dixon, "Recollections of a Rebel Private," p. 218; Champion to "My Precious Wife," 22 August 1864; Barron, *Lone Star Defenders*, p. 214; Montgomery, *Reminiscences*, p. 195; Deupree, "The Noxubee Squadron,"

p. 104; Record of Events, July–August 1864, Company F, 1st Mississippi Cavalry, reel 27, M-861, RG 109; Record of Events, July–August 1864, Captain Farris's Battery (Clark Artillery, King's Battery), reel 34, M-861, RG 109; Smith, *Private in Gray,* p. 120.

35. *NT,* 15 October 1891, p. 3 (Sergeant Garner Stimsen's account); *CDC,* 31 August 1864, p. 1; *NR,* 13 September 1864, p. 3; *NT,* 8 December 1887, p. 3; *OR,* 38, pt. 2, pp. 826, 840, 843; Montgomery, *Reminiscences,* p. 195; Smith, *Private in Gray,* pp. 121–23; Long, *Eli Long,* p. 7; Crane, "Bugle Blasts," pp. 249–50; *DTB,* 6 September 1864, p. 2; Long, "Letter from General Long," p. 429 (quoting Colonel Seidel); *NR,* 20 September 1864, p. 1; "List of Casualties in the 2d Brigade 2d Division Cavalry," pp. 70–71, vol. 57/140, CCMDM, RG 393; *OR,* 38, pt. 2, pp. 840, 844, 847; Wulsin, *4th Ohio,* p. 60. Lieutenant Garfield was mortally wounded according to the *Norwalk Reflector* and the *Toledo Daily Blade,* but Private Grabach nursed him back to health. See Crofts, comp., *3rd Ohio,* p. 165.

36. Curry, "Raid around Atlanta," p. 617; Curry, comp., *Four Years in the Saddle,* pp. 374–75; Crofts, comp., *3rd Ohio,* p. 164; *OR,* 38, pt. 2, pp. 815, 826, 831, 834, 835, 840, 844; *NT,* 22 January 1903, p. 6; *NT,* 26 February 1891, p. 3; *CDC,* 31 August 1864, p. 1; *NYTB,* 5 September 1864, p. 1; Burns to "My Dear Davidson," 28 August 1864; Regimental Return, August 1864, 4th Michigan Cavalry, reel 83, M-594, RG 94; McLain Diary, 20 August 1864; *DAT,* 8 September 1864, p. 4; *DFP,* 6 September 1864, p. 4; Dornblaser, *Sabre Strokes,* p. 181. The Regulars later borrowed some ammunition from the 92nd Illinois near McDonough. See Barron, *Lone Star Defenders,* p. 225.

37. Lieutenant Will Curry of the 1st Ohio remembered twelve or fifteen women and children gathered on the front porch of the house. Private W. C. Smith of the 1st Mississippi recalled seeing only two women and three small children.

38. Long, "Letter from General Long," pp. 429–30; *OR,* 38, pt. 2, pp. 815, 826, 831 (quote by Major Frank Mix), 834, 852–53; *NT,* 22 January 1903, p. 6; *NT,* 26 February 1891, p. 3; Burns to "My Dear Davidson," 28 August 1864; Vale, *Minty and the Cavalry,* pp. 350–51; Crofts, comp., *3rd Ohio,* p. 164; Curry, "Raid around Atlanta," pp. 616–17, 620; Curry, comp., *Four Years in the Saddle,* pp. 183–84; Rea, "Kilpatrick's Raid," p. 657; Record of Events, July–August 1864, Captain Farris's Battery (Clark Artillery, King's Battery), reel 34, M-861, RG 109; *DCE,* 27 August 1864, p. 2; Smith, *Private in Gray,* p. 123; *CDC,* 31 August 1864, p. 1; *DFP,* 6 September 1864, p. 4 (quote by Captain Van Antwerp); *DAT,* 8 September 1864, p. 4; Nourse Diary, 20 August 1864; Fleming to "My Dear Parents," 13 September 1864; Nourse to Minty, 3 February 1903, Minty Papers; Nourse, "Kilpatrick's Raid," p. 7; *NT,* 10 April 1890, p. 4; *NT,* 22 May 1890, p. 3; *NT,* 4 September 1890, p. 3; Robinson, "With Kilpatrick," p. 591. Lieutenant Curry asserted in "Raid around Atlanta," p. 617, and again in *Four Years in the Saddle,* p. 183, that the explosion injured two of the gunners, while Captain Rea recalled in "Kilpatrick's Raid," p. 657, that several men were killed and wounded. However, artillerymen John Nourse and John Fleming, the *Cincinnati Daily Commercial,* and the *Detroit Advertiser and Tribune* all marveled that *no one* was hurt.

39. Robinson, "With Kilpatrick," pp. 591–92; *OR,* 38, pt. 2, pp. 815, 826, 831, 834, 859; *NT,* 22 January 1903, p. 6; *DCE,* 27 August 1864, p. 2; *NYTB,* 5 September 1864, p. 1; Curry, "Raid around Atlanta," pp. 617–18; Rea, "Kilpatrick's Raid," p. 658; Vale, *Minty and the Cavalry,* p. 351; *DAT,* 8 September 1864, p. 4; *DFP,* 6 September 1864, p. 4; Regimental Return, August 1864, 4th Michigan Cavalry, reel 83, M-594, RG 94; McLain Diary, 20 August 1864; *MJPGA,* 10 September 1864, p. 3; Paisley Diary, 20 August 1864; Burns to "My Dear Davidson," 28 August 1864.

40. *OR,* 38, pt. 2, p. 897; *92nd Illinois,* p. 153; Brown Notebook, [20] [August] 1864; Morning Reports, 20 August 1864, Company I, 92nd Illinois Mounted Infantry, RG 94; Rainer, *Henry County Georgia,* pp. 280–81; Tomlinson, ed., *Sergeant Cort,* p. 155; *NT,* 1 March 1894, p. 3. The regimental history, *92nd Illinois,* p. 153, says the bridge over South River was on fire when Van Buskirk's detachment arrived but he and his men quickly routed a squad of Rebel cavalry and put out the flames. Neither Sergeant Cort nor Major Woodcock

mention anything like this in their accounts of the hurried dash to South River, and given that it was pouring down rain on the night of August 20–21, any attempt to burn the bridge seems unlikely.

41. *OR,* 38, pt. 2, p. 897; Burns to "My Dear Davidson," 28 August 1864; *92nd Illinois,* p. 153; Ninety-Second Illinois, *5th Reunion,* p. 17.

42. Unless otherwise noted, the movements of Kilpatrick's column described in the rest of this chapter are based on the following sources: *OR,* 38, pt. 1, pp. 924–25 (weather); pt. 2, pp. 815, 826, 831, 834, 835, 840, 844, 845, 847, 848, 853, 856, 859, 864, 887, 897, 903; *DCE,* 27 August 1864, p. 2; *CDC,* 31 August 1864, p. 1; *NYTB,* 5 September 1864, p. 1; *LDJ,* 15 September 1864, p. 1; Burns to "My Dear Davidson," 28 August 1864; *NT,* 22 January 1903, p. 6 (Minty's account); Vale, *Minty and the Cavalry,* pp. 351–52; McLain Diary, 20–22 August 1864; Potter Diary, 21–22 August 1864; Potter to "Dear Father," 24 August 1864; *DFP,* 6 September 1864, p. 4; *DAT,* 8 September 1864, p. 4; *AJ,* 26 September 1864, p. 2; Regimental Return, August 1864, 4th Michigan Cavalry, reel 83, M-594, RG 94; *MJPGA,* 10 September 1864, p. 3; *MJPGA,* 17 September 1864, p. 1; *TWA,* 5 October 1864, p. 4; Dornblaser, *My Life-Story,* p. 64; Dornblaser, *Sabre Strokes,* pp. 182–83; Webb, "Kilpatrick's Great Raid," p. 733; Barron, *Lone Star Defenders,* p. 226 (quoting Robert M. Wilson, 4th U.S. Cavalry); Record of Events, July–August 1864, Muster Roll, Companies E and G, 4th U.S. Cavalry, RG 94; Regimental Return, August 1864, 4th U.S. Cavalry, reel 41, M-744, RG 94; *SOG,* 13 September 1864, p. 4; Crane, "Bugle Blasts," p. 250; Curry, comp., *Four Years in the Saddle,* pp. 185–86; Curry, "Raid around Atlanta," pp. 618–19; Rea, "Kilpatrick's Raid," pp. 658–61; *NT,* 15 October 1891, p. 3 (Sergeant Garner Stimsen's account); Crofts, comp., *3rd Ohio,* pp. 164–65; Morning Reports, 21–22 August 1864, Company G, 4th Ohio Cavalry, RG 94; Wulsin, *4th Ohio,* pp. 60–61; Fleming to "My Dear Parents," 13 September 1864; Lester Diary, 22 August 1864; Nourse Diary, 21–22 August 1864; Nourse, "Kilpatrick's Raid," pp. 7–9; *NT,* 10 April 1890, p. 4; Robinson, "With Kilpatrick," pp. 592–94; Chicago Board of Trade Battery, *Historical Sketch,* p. 29; Oblinger Diary, 21–22 August 1864; Ward Diary, 21–22 August 1864; Morning Reports, 21–22 August 1864, Company D, 8th Indiana Cavalry, RG 94; Paisley Diary, 22 August 1864; Morning Reports, 21 August 1864, Companies E and G, 10th Ohio Cavalry, RG 94; Record of Events, July–August 1864, Companies A and B, 10th Ohio Cavalry, reel 141, M-594, RG 94; Brown Diary, 21–22 August 1864; Brown Notebook, [20], 22 [August] 1864; Dawson to "Dear family and friends in General," 24 August 1864; Tomlinson, ed., *Sergeant Cort,* pp. 155–56; Morning Reports, 21–22 August 1864, Companies A, B, and I, 92nd Illinois Mounted Infantry, RG 94; *NT,* 1 March 1894, p. 3; Ninety-Second Illinois Reunion Association, *4th Triennial Reunion,* pp. 33–34; Ninety-Second Illinois, *5th Reunion,* p. 17; *92nd Illinois,* pp. 153–55; *NT,* 17 July 1924, p. 7; Rainer, *Henry County,* pp. 64, 281.

43. According to Mrs. Rainer's valuable history of *Henry County,* pp. 32, 64, 283, Kilpatrick's raiders burned the Timberridge Presbyterian Church on "September 16, 1864," at the same time they destroyed the Little Sharon Primitive Baptist Church during Sherman's March to the Sea. "They demolished these churches for firewood," she wrote, "as it was raining and turned cold when they camped there." While the right wing of Sherman's army did pass through McDonough during the March to the Sea on November (not September) 16, 1864, it continued south toward Locust Grove, not east toward Peachstone Shoals. Kilpatrick was several miles west of McDonough that day, moving down the east side of the Flint River, and according to a foot soldier marching with the right wing, the weather was "warm & cloudy," not raining and cold. Undoubtedly, Kilpatrick's men destroyed the two churches, but on the wet and miserable night of August 20, 1864. The oral history Mrs. Rainer had to rely on, handed down from one generation to the next, simply confused the events of Kilpatrick's raid with Sherman's subsequent March to the Sea. See *OR,* 44, pp. 66, 81, 147, 362–63; Black, ed., "Marching with Sherman through Georgia and the Carolinas: Civil War Diary of Jesse L. Dozier, Part II," p. 454.

44. G. Lamar Russell, McDonough, Ga., telephone interview with author; *OR,* 38, pt. 1, p.

172; pt. 2, p. 826; *NYTB,* 5 September 1864, p. 1; *NT,* 22 January 1903, p. 6; Vale, *Minty and the Cavalry,* p. 350; Madaus and Needham, *Battle Flags,* pp. cover, 120, 121, 126n.40; Rainer, *Henry County,* pp. 65, 245, 253, 268–70. The *New York Tribune*'s correspondent erroneously credited the 4th U.S. Cavalry with capturing the flag of Zachry's Rangers.

45. *DAT,* 8 September 1864, p. 4.

46. Captain Burns, Captain Vale, the correspondents of the *Cincinnati Daily Commercial* and the *New York Tribune,* and some of the other officers believed the previous night's heavy rains had swept away the bridge. However, in her study of Henry County records, Mrs. Rainer does not mention a bridge over this stretch of Cotton Indian Creek. The road apparently forded this stream. See Rainer, *Henry County,* pp. 61–63.

47. *NT,* 15 October 1891, p. 3; Dornblaser, *Sabre Strokes,* p. 183; *DAT,* 8 September 1864, p. 4; Wulsin, *4th Ohio,* pp. 60–61; *92nd Illinois,* p. 153; Rea, "Kilpatrick's Raid," p. 661.

48. "List of Casualties in the 2d Brigade 2d Division Cavalry," pp. 72–73, vol. 57/140, CCMDM, RG 393; Compiled Service Records, RG 94; Ohio Roster Commission, *Official Roster,* 11:40.

49. According to General David S. Stanley, "Kilpatrick rode in a family carriage of old style which he looted. It was overloaded with silver plunder, and, in crossing Yellow River [Cotton Indian Creek], which was up, the carriage upset and nearly drowned Kilpatrick." This fanciful tale is found in Stanley, *Personal Memoirs,* p. 179.

50. Robinson, "With Kilpatrick," p. 593. In his official report and all his postwar accounts, Lieutenant Robinson steadfastly maintained the disabled gun was thrown into the creek. Kilpatrick concurred in a brief report in *OR,* 38, pt. 2, p. 856, but on pp. 815 and 826, Bob Minty said the disabled gun was buried on the west bank of Cotton Indian Creek. Captain Joseph Vale added, in *Minty and the Cavalry,* p. 351, the site was marked as the graves of two 4th U.S. Cavalrymen. Robert M. Wilson of the 4th Regulars repeated this story in Barron, *Lone Star Defenders,* p. 226, as did artilleryman John Nourse in "Kilpatrick's Raid," p. 8. Minty, however, apparently was not at the scene, and Nourse, in an article he had previously written for the *National Tribune,* 10 April 1890, p. 4, said the gun was indeed thrown into the creek.

51. *92nd Illinois,* p. 154. There are no definitive figures enumerating Kilpatrick's losses at Cotton Indian Creek. Writing to his father on 24 August 1864, Captain Henry Albert Potter of the 4th Michigan Cavalry said, "two of our men were drowned there and some negroes." In a letter appearing in the *Detroit Free Press,* 6 September 1864, p. 4, Captain William W. Van Antwerp of the 4th Michigan said three men drowned. Another 4th Michigan cavalryman, Lieutenant George W. Clark, concurred in a letter to the *Detroit Advertiser and Tribune,* 8 September 1864, p. 4. Joe Malott, a trooper assigned to headquarters of the 3rd Brigade, 3rd Cavalry Division, told the *Louisville Daily Journal,* 23 September 1864, p. 1, that six men and twenty horses drowned attempting to cross the creek, while the *New York Tribune,* 5 September 1864, p. 1, reported sixty or seventy horses were lost. Postwar estimates tended to be vague. Private Lucien Wulsin, *4th Ohio,* p. 60, said "a few men and a number of horses and mules" were lost. In "Raid around Atlanta," p. 619, Lieutenant Will Curry recalled "a number of soldiers were drowned," and in a speech before the *5th Triennial Reunion* of the 92nd Illinois, p. 17, Lieutenant P. R. Walker noted, "We lost several men while crossing that river." Artilleryman John Nourse asserted in "Kilpatrick's Raid," p. 8, "All pack mules, all mess outfits, fifty-two horses and one man were lost at this crossing." This author has examined dozens of muster rolls and casualty lists for the regiments with Kilpatrick, and Private Francis Jones of the 1st Ohio Cavalry is the only trooper listed as drowned at Cotton Indian Creek.

52. *NT,* 1 March 1894, p. 3; *92nd Illinois,* p. 154.

53. Robert S. Stanton, Case Number 1,265, RG 233.

54. *NT,* 15 December 1892, p. 4.

55. Ninety-Second Illinois, *5th Reunion,* p. 17; Paisley Diary, 22 August 1864; *NT,* 17 July 1924, p. 7.

56. *OR,* 38, pt. 5, p. 353; Stanley, *Memoirs,* p. 179; Sturges Diary, 22 August 1864.

57. *NT,* 1 March 1894, p. 3. This hospitality did not extend to the rest of Kilpatrick's men. Fielder Jones's brigade, bringing up the rear of the column, bivouacked two miles east of General Thomas's headquarters that night with no supper and nothing to feed their horses. See *HT,* 15 September 1864, p. 1; Morning Reports, 22 August 1864, Company D, 8th Indiana Cavalry, RG 94; Oblinger Diary, 22 August 1864; Ward Diary, 22–23 August 1864; Paisley Diary, 22 August 1864.

58. Magee, *72nd Indiana,* p. 371; Rea, "Kilpatrick's Raid," p. 664.

59. *OR,* 38, pt. 2, pp. 827, 831, 834, 841, 844, 845, 848, 853, 854, 859, 897; *CDC,* 31 August 1864; *DFP,* 6 September 1864, p. 4; *DAT,* 27 September 1864, p. 4; *MJPGA,* 17 September 1864, p. 1; *MJPGA,* 1 October 1864, p. 2; *NR,* 13 September 1864, p. 3; *NR,* 20 September 1864, p. 1; Nourse Diary, 20, 22 August 1864; Lester Diary, 19, 20 August 1864; Fleming to "My Dear Parents," 13 September 1864; Chicago Board of Trade Battery, *Historical Sketch,* pp. 29, 46, 61, 70, 71, 72, 74, 76, 80; *HT,* 15 September 1864, p. 1; Regimental Returns and Muster Rolls, 4th Michigan Cavalry, 4th U.S. Cavalry, 1st Ohio Cavalry, 3rd Ohio Cavalry, 4th Ohio Cavalry, 8th Indiana Cavalry, 2nd Kentucky Cavalry, 10th Ohio Cavalry, 92nd Illinois Mounted Infantry, 3rd Kentucky Cavalry, 5th Kentucky Cavalry, 10th Wisconsin Battery, RG 94; "Casualties on the Macon Railroad Expedition," 7th Pennsylvania Cavalry Papers, RG 94; "List of Casualties in the 10th Ohio," 10th Ohio Papers, RG 94; "List of Casualties in the 2d Brigade 2d Division Cavalry," pp. 68–73, vol. 57/140, CCMDM, RG 393; "List of Casualties 2d Brig 3d Div," RG 94; "Report of Casualties 3rd Brig 3rd Div," RG 94; *NYTB,* 5 September 1864, p. 1. A Tennessee soldier asserted some of the twenty-three Yankees Dan Reynolds's brigade captured at Lovejoy's Station were "so drunk that we had to lift them on the train." See Lindsley, ed., *Military Annals of Tennessee,* p. 548.

60. *OR,* 38, pt. 5, pp. 628, 629, 630, 631, 639; pt. 1, p. 80; Sherman, *Memoirs,* 2:104. In his *Memoirs,* p. 179, General David S. Stanley recalled, "Kilpatrick on his return telegraphed from my headquarters: 'I have destroyed thirty miles of their railroads.' Sherman who was six miles off, replied: 'I know that is true, for I hear their trains coming in over the destroyed road this very minute,' adding the wickedest kind of an oath." Kilpatrick never claimed he had destroyed thirty miles of track, nor is there any record of the telegram Sherman supposedly sent in reply. However, the damage to the railroad at Jonesboro was repaired by 2:00 P.M., August 21. Trains began running an hour later, and regularly scheduled traffic between Macon and Atlanta resumed the next day. At 5:30 P.M. on August 22, just about the same time Sherman learned of Kilpatrick's return, a Yankee signal officer perched in a treetop west of Atlanta watched through his field glasses as an engine pulled five boxcars, two flatcars, a baggage car, and three passenger coaches into the city. See *ACS,* 25 August 1864, p. 2; *DCE,* 27 August 1864, p. 2; *ADI,* 23 August 1864, p. 3; *CDS,* 25 August 1864, p. 2; *OR,* 38, pt. 3, p. 692; pt. 5, pp. 629, 630, 631.

EPILOGUE

1. *OR,* 38, pt. 2, pp. 639, 642; Sherman, *Memoirs,* 2:104.

2. *OR,* 38, pt. 5, p. 688.

3. Sherman, *Memoirs,* 2:105.

4. *OR,* 38, pt. 5, p. 1008.

5. Warner, *Generals in Blue,* pp. 115–16; *OR,* 38, pt. 5, pp. 369–70, 391–93, 446.

6. Connelly, *Three Years in the Army of the Cumberland,* pp. 257–58.

7. McDonough and Jones, *War So Terrible,* p. 306; Sherman, *Memoirs,* 2:107–8.

8. Except where noted, the narrative describing Sherman's move to the south side of Atlanta and the battles at Jonesboro is based on *OR,* 38, pt. 1, pp. 80–931 passim; pt. 2, pp. 16–

490 passim, 518, 574–888 passim; pt. 3, pp. 43–929 passim; pt. 5, pp. 664–752, 990–1021 passim; Hoehling, *Last Train from Atlanta*, pp. 366–74; Howard, *Autobiography*, 2:37–39; Hood, *Advance and Retreat*, pp. 202–5; Roy, "General Hardee," pp. 371–72; Kerr, ed., *Ross' Texas Cavalry*, pp. 167–68; Manigault, *A Carolinian Goes to War*, pp. 245–48; Buck, *Cleburne and His Command*, pp. 250–58; Brown, ed., *One of Cleburne's Command*, pp. 126–28; Thompson, *The Orphan Brigade*, pp. 265–68; Kirwan, ed., *Johnny Green*, pp. 154–60; *MAR*, 20 September 1864, p. 1. The best and most recent scholarship concerning the controversial last days of the Atlanta campaign is found in Connelly, *Autumn of Glory*, pp. 458–67, and Castel's excellent *Decision in the West*, pp. 485–522.

9. Sherman, *Memoirs*, 2:108–9; *OR*, 38, pt. 1, p. 82; pt. 5, pp. 307, 670, 678, 683–84, 764, 768, 772, 1011–14; pt. 2, pp. 17, 20–21, 35, 145, 330–467 passim; pt. 3, pp. 633, 694–95, 765, 992; Hood, *Advance and Retreat*, p. 205; Sanford, *14th Illinois*, pp. 209–10; *CDC*, 13 September 1864, p. 1; *WBB*, 24 September 1864, p. 1; *AT*, 4 January 1889, p. 1; *NT*, 22 December 1887, p. 3; *NT*, 18 October 1888, p. 3; *NT*, 6 December 1888, p. 5; *NT*, 27 July 1893, p. 3; *NT*, 27 July 1893, p. 3; *NT*, 12 April 1923, p. 2; *NT*, 26 April 1923, p. 3; *NT*, 2 October 1924, p. 2; *NT*, 15 January 1925, p. 2; Hartsfield, "Document in Handwriting of Atlanta's War-Time Mayor Describes Formal Surrender of the City to Federal Army," pp. 12–13; Kurtz, "Surrender of Atlanta—Evacuation of Its Citizens," pp. 10–11; Garrett, *Atlanta and Environs*, 1:635–36. Some 7th Pennsylvania cavalrymen, who led a detachment of about 400 men from the 2nd Division of the XX Corps on a reconnaissance from Pace's Ferry to Howell Mill and across Peachtree Creek, also claimed to be the first Union soldiers to enter Atlanta. However, these troopers caught up with Coburn's column after Mayor Calhoun had surrendered the city. See *NT*, 2 November 1893, p. 3; *NT*, 9 August 1923, p. 8; *NT*, 13 November 1924, p. 7; *OR*, 38, pt. 2, pp. 145–46, 274, 286, 292, 318–20.

10. Hosea, "Side Lights on the War," pp. 42–43; Society of the Army of the Tennessee, *22nd Meeting*, p. 349. Captain Hosea recollected he delivered his message to Sherman, Thomas, and Howard at Lovejoy's Station about 9:00 A.M., on September 2, but this seems much too early. The actual hour must have been much later in the day. Early on September 2, Kenner Garrard had received orders to "feel up in the direction of Atlanta," and "Let us know the exact state of affairs." His patrols had not yet returned when Schofield wrote to Sherman at 10:25 A.M., "A negro who has just come in from Atlanta says our troops attacked the place about dark last night. The enemy immediately retreated on the McDonough road in great confusion and disorder, all the citizens joining the flight." Sherman was at a house in Jonesboro with Thomas and his staff when Schofield's note arrived a little before noon. This probably prompted the message the IV Corps' David Stanley received from Thomas at 1:45 P.M., announcing, "We have Atlanta." Lieutenant Eben Sturges, an aide to Thomas's chief of artillery, noted in his diary that Sherman and Thomas left Jonesboro about midafternoon and followed the railroad south. Stopping at a house on the east side of the track, about a mile and a half above Lovejoy's Station, they were joined by Generals Howard and Logan, who were marshalling an assault on the new Rebel line in front of them. Garrard, in the meantime, had completed his reconnaissance toward Atlanta, and this was almost certainly what sent Captain Hosea galloping toward Lovejoy's Station. Hosea said he overtook Sherman, Thomas, and Howard while the infantry columns of the Army of the Tennessee were "deploying and advancing in unbroken lines to the front." Howard reported this assault took place just before 4:00 P.M., when "I was instructed to stand on the defensive for the present." If Hosea's message prompted these instructions, and it apparently did, it must have been delivered shortly before 4:00 P.M. Although Sherman had what he called "strong evidence that the enemy blew up his magazines and abandoned Atlanta," he was still anxious to hear directly from Slocum. "You know that General Garrard reports General Slocum in possession of Atlanta," he wrote to Howard at 8:00 P.M. "I have sent couriers to learn the exact truth." At 11:20 P.M., he wrote Schofield, "Nothing positive from Atlanta, and that bothers me." Official confirmation of Atlanta's surrender did not arrive until

sometime later that night and was promulgated about 6:00 A.M., September 3. See Hosea, "Side Lights on the War," pp. 42–43; Sturges Diary, 2–3 September 1864; *OR,* 38, pt. 1, pp. 82, 166, 933–34; pt. 3, pp. 46, 328, 339–40; pt. 5, pp. 770, 771, 773, 774, 784, 789.

11. *OR,* 38, pt. 5, pp. 777, 792.

12. *OR,* 32, pt. 3, p. 246; *OR,* 38, pt. 5, p. 143; Sherman, *Memoirs,* 2:104.

13. Cate, ed., *Two Soldiers,* pp. 106–7.

14. Black, *Railroads of the Confederacy,* p. 270.

15. *OR,* 38, pt. 1, p. 75.

16. Sylvester, ed., "'Gone for a Soldier,'" p. 213; *ND,* 4 August 1864, p. 2; *DSH,* 5 August 1864, p. 2; *CDC,* 6 August 1864, pp. 1, 2; *LDJ,* 6 August 1864, p. 1; *WES,* 6 August 1864, p. 1; *KDGC,* 6 August 1864, p. 4; *RIU,* 10 August 1864, p. 4; *Harper's Weekly,* 20 August 1864, p. 531; *MDS,* 6 August 1864, p. 1; *NYT,* 31 August 1864, p. 5; *DDT,* 21 August 1864, p. 1; *DDT,* 21 October 1864, p. 2; *MDS,* 29 August 1864, p. 1; *OR,* 38, pt. 2, pp. 763–64.

17. *OR,* 38, pt. 2, pp. 748, 762–63, 774–75, 776, 783–84, 787, 790, 802, 917; *CDC,* 9 August 1864, p. 1; *NYT,* 31 August 1864, p. 5; Monlux, *To My Comrades,* p. 41; *NT,* 25 April 1889, p. 4; West, "McCook's Raid," pp. 22–24; *NT,* 21 January 1915, p. 5; *NT,* 15 July 1926, p. 5; Vaughter, *Prison Life,* p. 28; *NT,* 16 January 1890, p. 3; Carter, *1st Tennessee,* pp. 180–81; *NT,* 2 September 1909, p. 7; Hall Diary, 30 July 1864; Winkler Diary, 30 July 1864; *EDJ,* 15 August 1864, p. 1; *NT,* 31 October 1895, p. 3; *WF,* 23 August 1864, p. 1; *NT,* 3 November 1927, p. 5; Crouse, "18th Indiana Battery," p. 21; Campbell Diary, 5 August 1864; Ward Diary, 30 July 1864; *HT,* 18 August 1864, p. 1; *NT,* 6 June 1889, p. 3; *NT,* May 31, 1894, p. 3; *NT,* 5 April 1900, p. 7; *DDT,* 12 August 1864, p. 1; *DDT,* 21 August 1864, p. 1; Oscar A. Langworthy to "Dear Father," 8 August 1864, Langworthy Papers; *NT,* 22 July 1909, p. 7; Eckel, "The Rousseau and McCook Raids," p. 10; Eckel, *4th Tennessee,* p. 61; Capron, "Stoneman's Raid," pp. 680, 682; Sanford, *14th Illinois,* p. 196; *DAT,* 12 August 1864, p. 1; *DAT,* 22 August 1864, p. 1; *DAT,* 2 September 1864, p. 4; *DFP,* 16 August 1864, p. 1; *NT,* 28 February 1924, p. 7; *NT,* 8 February 1923, p. 2; *PRB,* 18 August 1864, p. 2; *LDJ,* 14 September 1864, p. 1.

18. *OR,* 38, pt. 2, p. 859; Burns to "My Dear Davidson," 28 August 1864; *NR,* 13 September 1864, p. 3; Vale, *Minty and the Cavalry,* p. 346; *NT,* 10 July 1890, p. 1; Curry, "Raid around Atlanta," pp. 620–21; Nourse, "Kilpatrick's Raid," pp. 9–10; Curry, *Four Years in the Saddle,* p. 182; Crofts, comp., *3rd Ohio,* pp. 165–66; Sipes, *7th Pennsylvania,* p. 135; *NT,* 22 January 1903, p. 6.

19. Sanford, *14th Illinois,* p. 193; Reynolds's Report, Reynolds Papers.

20. Magee, *72nd Indiana,* pp. 410, 422; Robert Burns to "My Dear Davidson," 2 August 1864.

21. *OR,* 38, pt. 2, p. 914; *NT,* 31 May 1894, p. 2. Minty attributed this remark to Judson Kilpatrick shortly after the 2nd Cavalry Division returned from Flat Shoals on July 31. At that time, however, Kilpatrick was still at Cartersville, some forty miles to the rear. What Minty actually may have remembered was a conversation with officers of Major General David Stanley's IV Corps. On August 1, Minty's brigade was assigned to the trenches northeast of Atlanta, almost within sight of Stanley's headquarters. The army was still waiting anxiously to hear the results of Stoneman's raid and on August 1, Stanley, formerly the chief of cavalry of the Army of the Cumberland, told William Salter of the U.S. Christian Commission that Stoneman was "not competent to command a company." See Jordan, ed., "Forty Days with the Christian Commission: A Diary by William Salter," p. 147. A more likely source of the remark Minty recalled may have been Brigadier General John Newton, commanding the 2nd Division of Stanley's corps. Newton had served with Stoneman in the Army of the Potomac and might have remembered camp gossip about the cavalryman's analogy to a bursting shell during his Richmond raid.

22. Tomlinson, ed., *Sergeant Cort,* p. 151.

23. *MAR,* 26 July 1864, p. 1; *ACS,* 23 July 1864, p. 3; *MM,* 23 July 1864, p. 2; *MM,* 24 July 1864, p. 2; *MM,* 26 July 1864, p. 1; *MM,* 21 July 1864, p. 1; *OR,* 38, pt. 5, pp. 904–5. Repairs

on Georgia railroads prevented Captain Grant from leaving his post in Atlanta to assist in reconstructing the Montgomery & West Point route. See L. P. Grant Papers.

24. *MM,* 30 July 1864, p. 1; *MM,* 31 July 1864, p. 2; *MM,* 24 July 1864, p. 1; *MM,* 26 July 1864, p. 1; *SMR,* 4 August 1864, quoted in Harper, "Rousseau's Alabama Raid," p. 62; *CDS,* 6 August 1864, p. 2; *MDA,* 26 July 1864, p. 2; *CDS,* 30 July 1864, p. 2; *ACS,* 13 August 1864, p. 1; George Whitfield to B. F. Jones, 9 September 1864, George Whitfield, Confederate Engineer Bureau, Compiled Service Records, RG 109; *OR,* 39, pt. 1, p. 430; pt. 2, pp. 737–38, 798; *CDS,* 27 August 1864, p. 2.

25. *OR,* 38, pt. 2, p. 762; pt. 3, pp. 688–89; *CT,* 3 August 1864, p. 2; *ACS,* 2 August 1864, p. 3; *ADC,* 2 August 1864, p. 3; *CDS,* 2 August 1864, p. 2; *CDS,* 3 August 1864, p. 2; *MDT,* 4 August 1864, pp. 1, 2; Vaughter, *Prison Life,* p. 35; *AT,* 2 January 1893, p. 2. The small break McCook made in the railroad just below Newnan posed a seemingly minor problem, but Private J. P. Cannon of the 27th Alabama Infantry noted in *Inside of Rebeldom: the Daily Life of a Private in the Confederate Army,* p. 245, he had to get out and walk when the southbound train he was riding reached the torn-up track at that point on August 4. When he returned on August 6, the damage had been repaired.

26. *OR,* 38, pt. 2, pp. 915–16, 920–21, 926; *CT,* 4 August 1864, p. 1; *ADI,* 5 August 1864, p. 3; *CT,* 8 August 1864, p. 1; *MM,* 11 August 1864, p. 2; *MDC,* 9 August 1864, p. 1; *ACS,* 10 August 1864, p. 1; Central Railroad and Banking Company of Georgia, *Reports,* p. 277; *MDT,* 20 August 1864, pp. 1, 2.

27. *OR,* 38, pt. 2, pp. 858, 861–62; pt. 3, p. 692; pt. 5, pp. 630, 631; *CT,* 23 August 1864, p. 1; *ACS,* 25 August 1864, p. 2; *DCE,* 27 August 1864, p. 2; *ADI,* 23 August 1864, p. 3; *CDS,* 25 August 1864, p. 2.

28. *OR,* 38, pt. 1, pp. 16–17; pt. 2, pp. 815, 924.

29. *OR,* 38, pt. 1, p. 83; *OR,* 39, pt. 2, pp. 414–22, 517; Sherman, *Memoirs,* 2:110–12, 118–27, 514–15, 516–23; Hood, *Advance and Retreat,* pp. 229–39; *OR,* series II, vol. 7, pp. 784, 791–92, 797, 799, 804, 808, 817–18, 822, 837, 846–47, 851–52, 879, 907–8, 1178; *MDT,* 2 October 1864, p. 2; *BDH,* 24 October 1864, p. 2; Belfield, "Sixty Days in Hades," pp. 461–63; *CDC,* 24 October 1864, p. 1; *KDGC,* 28 October 1864; Biddle, *Reminiscences,* pp. 250–57. Biddle remembered having this conversation with a major, but the Federal officer actually in charge of the exchange was Sherman's inspector general, Lieutenant Colonel Willard Warner.

BIBLIOGRAPHY

ABBREVIATIONS

A-Ar	Alabama Department of Archives and History, Montgomery
ArU	Special Collections Division, University Libraries, University of Arkansas, Fayetteville
CSmH	Henry E. Huntington Library, San Marino, California
CtRBD	Richard B. Dickson, Old Lyme, Connecticut
DLC	Library of Congress, Washington, D.C.
DNA	National Archives, Washington, D.C.
G-Ar	Georgia Department of Archives and History, Atlanta
GAFC	Fulton County Superior Court, Atlanta, Georgia
GAHi	Atlanta Historical Society, Atlanta, Georgia
GCMP	Chickamauga-Chattanooga National Military Park, Chickamauga, Georgia
GDE	Author's Collection
GEpFAR	Federal Archives and Records Center, East Point, Georgia
GEU	Robert W. Woodruff Library, Emory University, Atlanta, Georgia
GJPT	Juliet Powell Turner, Avondale Estates, Georgia
GJTC	Judge Jack T. Camp, Newnan, Georgia
GMcB	Willard B. McBurney, Atlanta, Georgia
GU	Hargrett Rare Book and Manuscript Library, University of Georgia Libraries, Athens
ICHi	Chicago Historical Society, Chicago, Illinois
ICN	Newberry Library, Chicago, Illinois
IHi	Illinois State Historical Library, Springfield
IU-HS	Illinois Historical Survey, University of Illinois Library, Urbana-Champaign
Ia-HA	State Historical Society of Iowa, Des Moines
IaHi	State Historical Society of Iowa, Iowa City
IaU	University of Iowa Libraries, Iowa City
In	Indiana State Library, Indianapolis
InBCD	Barbara Carruth Dickey, Upland, Indiana
InColu	Bartholomew County Public Library, Columbus, Indiana
InCW	Robert T. Ramsey Archival Center, Lilly Library, Wabash College, Crawfordsville, Indiana
InHAN	Duggan Library, Hanover College, Hanover, Indiana
InHHS	Howard County Historical Society, Kokomo, Indiana
InHi	William Henry Smith Memorial Library, Indiana Historical Society, Indianapolis
InNd	Archives of the University of Notre Dame, Notre Dame, Indiana
InU-Li	Lilly Library, Indiana University, Bloomington
KyBnG	Boone National Guard Center, Military Library, Frankfort, Kentucky
KyLoF	Filson Club, Louisville, Kentucky
MH-Ar	Harvard University Archives, Cambridge, Massachusetts
MH-H	Houghton Library, Harvard University, Cambridge, Massachusetts
MSBC	Stanley Butcher, Andover, Massachusetts
Mi-HC	Michigan State Archives, Lansing

MiD-B	Burton Historical Collection, Detroit Public Library, Detroit, Michigan
MiEM	Historical Collections, University Archives, Michigan State University, East Lansing
MiU-H	Michigan Historical Collections, Bentley Historical Library, University of Michigan, Ann Arbor
MnHi	Minnesota Historical Society, St. Paul
Ms-Ar	Mississippi Department of Archives and History, Jackson
NbHi	Nebraska State Historical Society, Lincoln
NcD	Perkins Library, Duke University, Durham, North Carolina
NcU	Southern Historical Collection, University of North Carolina, Chapel Hill
Nj-E	State Library, New Jersey Department of Education, Trenton
NyM	Archives, United States Military Academy, West Point, New York
OBgU-C	Center for Archival Collections, Bowling Green State University, Bowling Green, Ohio
OClWHi	Western Reserve Historical Society, Cleveland, Ohio
OHi	Ohio Historical Society, Columbus
OrU	University of Oregon Library, Eugene
PC	Private Collection
PCarlMH	U.S. Army Military History Institute, Carlisle, Pennsylvania
T	Tennessee State Library and Archives, Nashville
TxArU	University of Texas at Arlington, Arlington
TxU	The Center for American History, University of Texas, Austin
TxWB	Texas Collection, Baylor University, Waco
UkLPR	Public Record Office, London
ViW	Special Collections, Earl Gregg Swem Library, College of William and Mary, Williamsburg, Virginia.
WHi	State Historical Society of Wisconsin, Madison
WvBeC	Business Office, Bethany College, Bethany, West Virginia

PRIMARY SOURCES

Manuscripts

Allen, William Gibbs, "War Reminiscence," The Confederate Collection. T

Applegate, John J., Letters in John Sickles Collection. PCarlMH

Ash, John H., Diary. GEU

Atkinson, A. S., and Others, Executor of Charles J. McDonald vs. A. V. Brumby. GAFC

Avery, Isaac W., Letters and Papers in Lewis Leigh Collection. PCarlMH

Barnard, John M., Letters. InHi

Bigger, J. A., Diary. Ms-Ar

Biographical File. MH-Ar

Bishard, Daniel C., "A [*sic*] Abstract of My Life." Ia-HA

Black, James Conquest Cross, Diary. NcU

Boardman, Arthur E., Papers. GJPT

Bradley, David C., "Recollections of the Autumn and Winter of 1864." ICHi

Bragg, Braxton, Papers. OClWHi

Brown, William Henry, Diary. IHi

———, Notebook, *Civil War Times Illustrated* Collection. PCarlMH

Browne, William M., Papers. GU

Burns, Robert, Papers, microfilm copies. MnHi

Camp Family Papers. GJTC

Campbell, Henry, Diary. InCW

Capron, Horace, Papers. DLC

———, "A Brief Record of the Military Services of General Horace Capron and the 14th Regiment of Illinois Cavalry Volunteers." Horace Capron Papers, microfilm copies. WHi.

Carruth, Christine Parkhurst, Papers. InBCD

Champion, Sydney S., Papers, microfilm copies. NcD

Chase, George, Papers. MiU-H

Cobb, Howell, Papers. GU

Cobb-Erwin-Lamar Papers. GU

Conzett, Josiah, "Memoirs." IaHi

Crouse, William O., "History of the Eighteenth Indiana Battery." InHi

Dawson, James, Papers. GAHi

Dixon, Harry St. John, Diary. NcU

Dodge, Grenville M., Diary. Ia-HA

———, "Personal Biography of Major General Grenville Mellon Dodge, 1831–1870." 2 vols. Ia-HA

DuBose, John W., "51st Ala. Cavalry, CSA." 51st Alabama Cavalry Papers. A-Ar

———, "History of the 1st Alabama Cavalry, CSA." 1st Alabama Cavalry Papers. A-Ar

———, "Twelfth Alabama Cavalry 1863–1865." 12th Alabama Cavalry Papers. A-Ar

Ewing, Thomas, Papers. DLC

Ferguson, Samuel Wragg, "Memoirs of S. W. Ferguson," Heyward-Ferguson Papers. NcU

51st Alabama Cavalry Papers. A-Ar

Fleming, John C., Papers. ICN

Fleming, William Augustus, "Records and Reminiscences of the Liberty Independent Troop," *Civil War Times Illustrated* Collection. PCarlMH

Forbes, James Munro, Papers. CSmH

Fulkerson, Isaac, Letters. PC

Gaines, R. R. "Reminiscences of the 3rd Alabama Cavalry." 3rd Alabama Cavalry Papers. A-Ar

Georgia Adjutant General's Letter Book, 1861–1864 (typescript), 18 vols. G-Ar

Gibbs, Thomas Preston, Papers, Civil War Miscellany. G-Ar

Gooding, Othniel, Papers. MiEM

Governor's Letter Book, 1860–1865. G-Ar

Grant, L. P., Papers. GAHi

Griest, Alva C., Diary. GCMP

Hall, Stanley A., Diary. InHi

Harris, James Henry, Diary. InHi

Harrison, Thomas Joshua, Papers. InHHS

Haskell, Oliver C., Diary. InHi

Healey, George W., Papers. Ia-HA

Hill, John W., Papers. TxU

"History of Company F, 5th Indiana Cavalry." Regimental Correspondence of the 90th Regiment. In

Holliday, A. T., Papers. GAHi

Holmes, Erastus, Diary. InHAN

Homsher, Charles W., "A Few Notes While in Andersonville Prison, Ga.," *Civil War Times Illustrated* Collection. PCarlMH

Iverson, Alfred, Jr., Letters. Civil War Miscellaneous Collection. PCarlMH

———, Papers. MSBC

Iverson-Branham Family Papers. GEU

Jackson, Thomas, Diary. In

Jackson, William Hicks, Papers. T

Jenkins, David P., Letter. GDE
Jordan, Stephen A., Diary. T
Kemper, William H., Diary. OHi
Kentucky Adjutant General's Records. KyBnG
King, William, Diary. NcU
Kryder, George, Papers. OBgU-C
Kurtz, Wilbur, Papers. GAHi
Langworthy, Oscar A., Letters, Langworthy Papers. IaHi
Lanman, Charles, Papers. KyLoF
Lathrop, Stanley, Papers. WHi
Lee, Stephen D., Papers. NcU
Lemmon, John G., Diary. CSmH
Lester, A. W., Diary. IHi
Livingston's 8th Alabama Cavalry Papers. A-Ar
Logan, John A., Papers. DLC
Long, Eli, Papers. PCarlMH
Mackall, Thomas B., Diary, Joseph E. Johnston Papers. ViW
Maguire, Thomas, Diary. GAHi
Martin, William T., Papers. TxU
"Matriculation List 1841–1881." WvBeC
McBride, Andrew J., Papers. NcD
McBurney Family Bible. GMcB
McBurney Family Papers. GMcB
McBurney, James C., Papers. CtRBD
McLain, John C., Diary. MiEM
McPherson, Benjamin F. "I Must Tell." PC
Milam, George Scott, Diary. McKinney Family Papers. TxArU
Miller, George Knox, Papers. NcU
———, "Eighth Confederate Cavalry." Ms-Ar
Minty, Robert H. G., Papers. PCarlMH
Montgomery, Seaborn, Jr., Papers. NcD
Montgomery, Vincent, Papers, microfilm copies. GEU
Moore, J. George, "Biography of Our Grandfather—James George Moore." WHi
Nash, Wiley, "Harvey's Scouts," J. F. H. Claiborne Papers. NcU
Nickel, Levi, Diary. WHi
Nourse, John A., Diary. NcD
———, Letters. ICHi
———, Untitled typescript account of Kilpatrick's Raid in Robert H. G. Minty Papers. PCarlMH
Numerical Returns of Wheeler's Cavalry Corps, January 1864–April 20, 1865. GDE
Nutt, Leroy Moncure, Papers. NcU
Oblinger, Uriah W., Diary. NbHi
Paine, Edward L., Family Papers. WHi
Paisley, John, Diary. IaU
Pepper, William Allen, Diary. IU-HS
Persons, Horace T., Papers. WHi
Poe, Orlando M., Diary and Papers. DLC
Potter, Henry Albert, Diary and Letters. MiU-H
Rainey, I. N., "Experiences of I. N. Rainey in the Confederate Army." Civil War Collection. T
Record Group 15, Records of the Veterans Administration. DNA
Record Group 21, Records of the District Courts of the United States. GEpFAR
Record Group 56, General Records of the Department of the Treasury. DNA

Record Group 59–14, Records of the Michigan Military Establishment. Mi-HC

Record Group 76, Records of the Department of State. DNA

Record Group 77, Records of the Office of the Chief of Engineers. DNA

Record Group 94, Records of the Adjutant General's Office. DNA

Record Group 107, Records of the Office of the Secretary of War. DNA

Record Group 109, War Department Collection of Confederate Records. DNA

Record Group 123, Records of the United States Court of Claims. DNA

Record Group 153, Records of the Judge Advocate General's Office. DNA

Record Group 156, Records of the Chief of Ordnance. DNA

Record Group 217, Records of the General Accounting Office. DNA

Record Group 233, Records of the Southern Claims Commission. DNA

Record Group 393, Records of U.S. Army Continental Commands, 1821–1920. DNA

Record Group 404, Records of the United States Military Academy. NyM

Records, William H., Diary. In

Remley, Ambrose, Papers. InU-Li

Reniker, Samuel D., Diary. Civil War Miscellaneous Collection. PCarlMH

Reynolds, Daniel H., Papers. ArU

Roddey, Philip D., Papers. MH-H

Ross Family Papers. TxWB

Ross, Lawrence Sullivan, Papers. TxU

Shacklette, Isabelle Wood Johnston, Narrative. KyLoF

Sherman Family Papers. InNd

Sherman Map Collection. DLC

Sherman, William T., Papers. DLC

Sherman, William Tecumseh, Papers. CSmH

Sloane, William E., Diary. T

Stanley, Marcellus, Papers. GU

Stephens, Alexander H., Papers. DLC

Stevens, Silas Curtis, Papers. ICHi

Stevens, William C., Papers. MiU-H

Stout, Samuel H., Papers. GEU

————, Papers. TxU

Sturges, Eben P., Diary, *Civil War Times Illustrated* Collection. PCarlMH

Superior Court, Bibb County, Georgia, Deeds and Mortgages. G-Ar

Superior Court, Hudson County, New Jersey, Deeds and Mortgages. Nj-E

Thompson, Heber S., Diary. Wilbur Kurtz Papers. GAHi

Thompson, James S., Diary. InHi

Thomson, James, Diary. G-Ar

"To the Citizens of Macon." 30 July 1864. Crandall Number 1574–1. GU

Trask, William L., Journal, microfilm copies. GEU

United Daughters of the Confederacy, Georgia Division. "U.D.C. Bound Typescripts." 14 vols. G-Ar

Vernor, James, Family Correspondence and Papers. MiD-B

Walls, Albert Milton, Papers, *Civil War Times Illustrated* Collection. PCarlMH

Walthall, William T., Papers. Ms-Ar

Ward, J. W., Letter, Confederate States of America Records. TxU.

Ward, Williamson D., Diary. InHi

Warner, Ezra J., Papers. ICHi

War Office Series 12, General Muster Books and Pay Lists, 1732–1878. UkLPR

War Office Series 31, Commander in Chief, Memoranda Papers, 1793–1870. UkLPR

Weaver, Putnam, Letters. Confederate Miscellany. GEU

Webb, John, "Memoirs, 1861–1870." G-Ar

Weir, Andrew N., Diary. Edward A. Weir Collection. OrU
West, Martin, Diary. IHi
Wheeler, Joseph, Papers. A-Ar
————, Scrapbook. PC
Willoughby, Aurelius M., Diary. In
Wiltsee, David, Diary. InHi
Winkler, William M., Diary. InColu
Worthington Family Papers. Ms-Ar
Wynn, J. A., Papers, Civil War Miscellany. G-Ar

Newspapers

The (Wellsboro, Pa.) *Agitator*
Albany (Ga.) *Patriot*
Allegan (Mich.) *Journal*
American Tribune
Athens (Ga.) *Daily Banner*
Athens (Ga.) *Southern Banner*
Athens (Ga.) *Southern Watchman*
Atlanta Daily Appeal
Atlanta Daily Intelligencer
Atlanta Georgian
Atlanta Journal
Atlanta Southern Confederacy
Augusta (Ga.) *Daily Constitutionalist*
Augusta (Ga.) *Daily Chronicle & Sentinel*
Bellefonte (Pa.) *Democratic Watchman*
Birmingham (Ala.) *Age-Herald*
Brownlow's Knoxville (Tenn.) *Whig and Rebel Ventilator*
Burlington (Iowa) *Daily Hawk-Eye*
Christian (Macon, Ga.) *Index*
Cincinnati Daily Commercial
Cincinnati Enquirer
Clinton (Pa.) *Republican*
Columbus (Ga.) *Daily Sun*
Columbus (Ind.) *Republican*
Columbus (Ga.) *Times*
The (Turnwold, Ga.) *Countryman*
Covington (Ga.) *News*
Daily Columbus (Ga.) *Enquirer*
Daily Steubenville (Ohio) *Herald*
Daily Toledo (Ohio) *Blade*
Daily Zanesville (Ohio) *Courier*
Detroit Advertiser and Tribune
Detroit Free Press
Dubuque Daily Times
Early County (Blakely, Ga.) *News*
Evansville (Ind.) *Daily Journal*
Harper's Weekly
Houston (Tex.) *Daily Telegraph*
Howard (Kokomo, Ind.) *Tribune*
Indianapolis Daily Journal

Janesville (Wis.) *Daily Gazette*
Jersey City Evening News
Jersey Journal
Kennesaw (Ga.) *Gazette*
Keokuk (Iowa) *Daily Gate City*
Lebanon (Ind.) *Patriot*
Louisville Daily Journal
Macon (Ga.) *Daily Confederate*
Macon (Ga.) *Daily Telegraph*
Marietta (Ga.) *Daily Journal*
Milledgeville (Ga.) *Confederate Union*
Milledgeville (Ga.) *Southern Recorder*
Milwaukee Daily Sentinel
The Miners' Journal and Pottsville (Pa.) *General Advertiser*
Mobile Advertiser and Register
Montgomery Daily Advertiser
Montgomery Daily Mail
Montgomery Weekly Advertiser
Nashville Dispatch
National Tribune
Newnan (Ga.) *Times-Herald*
New York Herald
New York Times
New York Tribune
Norwalk (Ohio) *Reflector*
Ohio (Columbus) *State Journal*
Philadelphia Inquirer
Pittsburgh Commercial
Portage County (Ravenna, Ohio) *Democrat*
Port Huron (Mich.) *Press*
Portland Oregonian
Putnam (Ind.) *Republican Banner*
Ripon (Wis.) *Commonwealth*
Rock Island (Ill.) *Union*
Sandusky (Ohio) *Daily Commercial Register*
Savannah (Ga.) *Republican*
Scioto (Ohio) *Gazette*
Selma (Ala.) *Morning Reporter*
Semi-Weekly (Milwaukee) *Wisconsin*
Washington (D.C.) *Evening Star*
Waukesha (Wis.) *Freeman*
West Branch (Williamsport, Pa.) *Bulletin*
Wisconsin (Madison) *State Journal*
Wolverine (Flint, Mich.) *Citizen*

Public Documents

A List of the Officers of the Army and of the Corps of Royal Marines, on Full, Retired, and Half-Pay; with an Index. 1848–9. London: W. Clowes & Sons, [1849?].
A List of the Officers of the Army and of the Corps of Royal Marines, on Full, Retired, and Half-Pay; with an Index. Corrected Throughout to the 31st of March, 1849. 1849–50. London: W. Clowes & Sons, 1849.

A List of the Officers of the Army and of the Corps of Royal Marines, on Full, Retired, and Half-Pay; with an Index. Corrected Throughout to the 31st of March, 1850. 1850–51. London: W. Clowes & Sons, 1850.

A List of the Officers of the Army and of the Corps of Royal Marines, on Full, Retired, and Half-Pay; with an Index. Corrected Throughout to the 31st of March, 1851. 1851–52. London: W. Clowes & Sons, 1851.

A List of the Officers of the Army and of the Corps of Royal Marines, on Full, Retired, and Half-Pay; with an Index. Corrected Throughout to the 31st of March, 1852. 1852–53. London: William Clowes & Sons, 1852.

Bates, Samuel P. *History of Pennsylvania Volunteers 1861–5, Prepared in Compliance with Acts of the Legislature.* 5 vols. Harrisburg, Pa.: B. Singerly, 1869–1871.

Illinois Adjutant General. *Report of the Adjutant General of the State of Illinois.* 8 vols. Springfield: Phillips Brothers and Journal Printing Company, 1900–1902.

Indiana Adjutant General. *Report of the Adjutant General of the State of Indiana.* 8 vols. Indianapolis: Alexander H. Conner, W. R. Holloway, Samuel M. Douglass, State Printers, 1865–1869.

Iowa Adjutant General. *Report of the Adjutant General and Acting Quartermaster General of the State of Iowa. January 11, 1864, To January 1, 1865.* Des Moines: F. W. Palmer, State Printer, 1865.

Iowa Adjutant General. *Roster and Record of Iowa Soldiers in the War of the Rebellion Together with Historical Sketches of Volunteer Organizations 1861–1866.* 6 vols. Des Moines: Emory H. English, State Printer, 1908–1911.

Kentucky Adjutant General. *Report of the Adjutant General of the State of Kentucky.* 2 vols. Frankfort: Kentucky Yeoman Office, 1866–1867.

Kentucky Adjutant General. *Report of the Adjutant General of the State of Kentucky: Confederate Kentucky Volunteers, War 1861–65.* 2 vols. Frankfort: State Journal Company, [1915–1918].

Michigan Adjutant General. *Record of Service of Michigan Volunteers in the Civil War 1861–1865.* 46 vols. Kalamazoo: Ihling Bros. & Everard, 1905.

Ohio Roster Commission, *Official Roster of the Soldiers of the State of Ohio in the War of the Rebellion, 1861–1866.* 12 vols. Akron: Werner Printing & Lithograph Company; Cincinnati: Wilstach, Baldwin & Company; Cincinnati: Ohio Valley Company; Norwalk: Laning Company, 1886–1895.

Quartermaster General's Office. *Roll of Honor.* 27 vols. Washington, D.C.: U.S. Government Printing Office, 1865–1872.

Quartermaster General's Office. *Statement of the Disposition of Some of the Bodies of Deceased Union Soldiers and Prisoners of War Whose Remains Have Been Removed to National Cemeteries in the Southern and Western States.* 4 vols. Washington, D.C.: U.S. Government Printing Office, 1868.

Tennessee Adjutant General. *Report of the Adjutant General of the State of Tennessee, of the Military Forces of the State, From 1861 to 1866.* Nashville: S. C. Mercer, 1866.

U.S. Congress. House. *Troubles on Texas Frontier.* H. Exec. Doc. 81, 36th Cong., 1st sess., 1860.

U.S. Congress. Joint Committee on the Conduct of the War. *Supplemental Report of the Joint Committee on the Conduct of the War.* 2 vols. Washington, D.C.: U.S. Government Printing Office, 1866.

U.S. Congress. Senate. Committee on Veterans' Affairs. *Medal of Honor Recipients 1863–1973.* Committee Print No. 15. 93rd Cong., 1st sess., 1973.

U.S. Congress. Senate. *Reports and Subreports of the Battle of Buena Vista.* Senate Executive Documents, vol. 1, 30th Cong., 1st sess., 1847.

U.S. Department of the Interior, Census Office. Eighth Census of the United States, 1860: Population.

U.S. Department of the Interior, Census Office. Twelfth Census of the United States, 1900: Population.

U.S. Military Academy. *Official Register of the Officers and Cadets of the U.S. Military Academy, West Point, New York.* N.p., n.d.

U.S. War Department. *The Ordnance Manual for the Use of the Officers of the United States Army.* 3rd ed. Philadelphia: J. B. Lippincott, 1861. Facsimile ed., Grand Junction, Colo.: Ordnance Park Corporation, 1970.

U.S. War Department. *Revised United States Army Regulations of 1861. With an Appendix Containing the Changes and Laws Affecting Army Regulations and Articles of War to June 25, 1863.* Washington, D.C.: U.S. Government Printing Office, 1863. Facsimile ed., Yuma, Az.: Fort Yuma Press, 1980.

U.S. War Department. *U.S. Department of War, Adjutant General's Office, General Orders, 1863.* 3 vols. Washington, D.C.: U.S. Government Printing Office, 1864.

U.S. War Department. *U.S. Department of War, Adjutant General's Office, General Orders, 1864.* 3 vols. Washington, D.C.: U.S. Government Printing Office, 1865.

U.S. War Department. *The War of the Rebellion: A Compilation of the Official Records of the Union and Confederate Armies.* 70 vols. in 130. Washington, D.C.: U.S. Government Printing Office, 1880–1901.

Wisconsin Adjutant General. *Annual Report of the Adjutant General of the State of Wisconsin for the Year Ending December 30th, 1865.* Edited by Charles E. Estabrook. Madison: William J. Park & Company, 1866. Reprint ed., 1912.

Wisconsin Adjutant General. *Roster of Wisconsin Volunteers, War of the Rebellion, 1861–1865.* 2 vols. Madison: Democrat Printing Company, 1886.

Military and Civilian Memoirs, Published Letters and Diaries, Unit Histories and Reunions by Participants

Abbott, A. O. *Prison Life in the South: At Richmond, Macon, Savannah, Charleston, Columbia, Charlotte, Raleigh, Goldsborough, and Andersonville, during the Years 1864 and 1865.* New York: Harper & Brothers, 1865.

Akin, M. F., Mrs. "Faithful Slave, 'Col. Robert.'" *Confederate Veteran* 11 (October 1903):470.

Akin, Sally May. "Refugees of 1863." *Georgia Historical Quarterly* 31 (June 1947):112–17.

Angel, W. W. "To Secretary 5th Ind. Cav. Assn." In *Report of the Thirty-first Annual Reunion Fifth Indiana Cavalry Association Held at Indianapolis, Indiana, October 15–16, 1913.* N.p., n.d., pp. 28–29.

Ashford, Louisa Booth. *Mother's Letters.* Edited by Kate Ashford Maness. [Decatur, Ga.: n.p., 1925?].

Association of the Graduates of the United States Military Academy. *Tenth Annual Reunion of the Association of the Graduates of the United States Military Academy, at West Point, New York. June 12 1879.* New York: D. Van Nostrand, 1879.

———. *13th Annual Reunion of the Association of the Graduates of the United States Military Academy, at West Point, New York, June 12, 1882.* Philadelphia: Times Printing House, [1882].

———. *Twenty-Sixth Annual Reunion of the Association of the Graduates of the United States Military Academy, at West Point, New York, June 10th, 1895.* Saginaw, Mich.: Seeman & Peters, 1895.

———. *Forty-Eighth Annual Report of the Association of the Graduates of the United States Military Academy, at West Point, New York, June 12th, 1917.* Saginaw, Mich.: Seeman & Peters, Inc., 1917.

Atkins, Smith D. "With Sherman's Cavalry." In *The Atlanta Papers,* pp. 623–40. Compiled by Sydney C. Kerksis. Dayton: Morningside Bookshop, 1980.

Austin, J. P. *The Blue and the Gray: Sketches of a Portion of the Unwritten History of the Great*

American Civil War, A Truthful Narrative of Adventure with Thrilling Reminiscences of the Great Struggle on Land and Sea. Atlanta: Franklin Printing and Publishing, 1899.

Averell, William Woods. *Ten Years in the Saddle: The Memoir of William Woods Averell.* Edited by Edward K. Eckert and Nicholas J. Amato. San Rafael, Cal.: Presidio Press, 1978.

————. "With the Cavalry on the Peninsula." In *Battles and Leaders of the Civil War.* 2:429–33. 4 vols. Edited by Robert Underwood Johnson and Clarence Clough Buel. New York: Century, 1884–1888.

Barclay, Hugh G. "Reminiscences of Rousseau's Raid." *Confederate Veteran* 30 (June 1922):208–9.

Barron, S. B. *The Lone Star Defenders: A Chronicle of the Third Texas Cavalry, Ross' Brigade.* New York and Washington, D.C.: Neale, 1908.

————. "Wheeler's Cavalry in Georgia Campaign." *Confederate Veteran* 14 (February 1906):70.

Basler, Roy P., ed. *The Collected Works of Abraham Lincoln.* 8 vols. New Brunswick, N.J.: Rutgers University Press, 1953.

Beall, John B. *In Barrack and Field: Poems and Sketches of Army Life.* Nashville and Dallas: Publishing House of the Methodist Episcopal Church, South, 1906.

Beatty, John. *The Citizen-Soldier; or Memoirs of a Volunteer.* Cincinnati: Wilstach, Baldwin, 1879.

Beers, Fannie A. *Memories: A Record of Personal Experience and Adventure During Four Years of War.* Philadelphia: J. B. Lippincott, 1888.

Belfield, Henry H. "My Sixty Days in Hades. In Hades, Not in Hell,—Andersonville was Hell." In *Military Essays and Recollections: Papers Read before the Commandery of the State of Illinois, Military Order of the Loyal Legion of the United States.* 3:447–64. 4 vols. Chicago: A. C. McClurg, 1891, 1894; Dial Press, 1899; Cozzens & Beaton, 1907.

Biddle, Ellen McGowan. *Reminiscences of a Soldier's Wife.* Philadelphia: J. B. Lippincott, 1907.

Bigelow, John, Jr., *The Campaign of Chancellorsville: A Strategic and Tactical Study.* New Haven, Conn.: Yale University Press, 1910.

Bird, Hiram Thornton. *Memories of the Civil War.* N.p.: [1925?].

Black, Wilfred W. ed. "Marching with Sherman through Georgia and the Carolinas: Civil War Diary of Jesse L. Dozier, Part II." *Georgia Historical Quarterly* 52 (December 1968):451–74.

Brainard, Mary Genevie Green, comp. *Campaigns of the One Hundred and Forty-Sixth Regiment New York State Volunteers.* New York: Putnam's, 1915.

Brown, C. O. *Battle-Fields Revisited. Grant's Chattanooga Campaign. Horseback Ride from Chattanooga to Atlanta.* Kalamazoo, Mich.: Eaton & Anderson, 1886.

Brown, J. Willard. *The Signal Corps, U.S.A. in the War of the Rebellion.* Boston: United States Veteran Signal Corps Association [Press of B. Wilkins], 1896. Reprint ed., New York: Arno Press, 1974.

Brown, Norman D., ed. *One of Cleburne's Command: The Civil War Reminiscences and Diary of Capt. Samuel T. Foster, Granbury's Texas Brigade, CSA.* Austin: University of Texas Press, 1980.

Bruner, L. J. "A Seven Day's Ride In Rebeldom." In *Sixth Annual Re-Union of the Fifth Indiana Cavalry Association, Held at Noblesville, Indiana, October 10th and 11th, 1888.* [Portland, Ind.]: Portland Commercial Job Office, 1889, p. 8–15.

Buck, Irving A. *Cleburne and His Command, and Pat Cleburne: Stonewall Jackson of the West.* Edited by Thomas Robson Hay. [Jackson, Tenn.]: McCowat-Mercer Press, 1957.

Burge, Dolly Sumner Lunt. *A Woman's Wartime Journal: An Account of the Passage Over a Georgia Plantation of Sherman's Army on the March to the Sea, as Recorded in the Diary of Dolly Sumner Lunt.* Introduction and Notes by Julian Street. New York: Century, 1918.

Butler, Thomas H. "The Stoneman Raid and Why It Was a Failure." In *Report of the Reunion of the Fifth Indiana Cavalry, Held at Indianapolis, Ind., October 10th and 11th 1883.* pp. 9–12. Indianapolis: Central Printing, [1884].

Calef, B. S. "Prison Life." *Harper's New Monthly Magazine,* July 1864, pp. 137–150.

Cannon, J. P. *Inside of Rebeldom: The Daily Life of a Private in the Confederate Army.* Washington, D.C.: National Tribune, 1900.

Carmony, Donald F., ed. "Jacob W. Bartmess Civil War Letters." *Indiana Magazine of History* 52 (June 1956):157–86.

Capron, Albert Banfield. "Stoneman Raid to Macon, Georgia, in 1864." In *The Atlanta Papers,* pp. 707–20. Compiled by Sydney C. Kerksis. Dayton: Morningside Bookshop, 1980.

Capron, Horace. "Stoneman's Raid to the South of Atlanta." In *The Atlanta Papers,* pp. 667–705. Compiled by Sydney C. Kerksis. Dayton: Morningside Bookshop, 1980.

Carter, William R. *History of the First Regiment of Tennessee Volunteer Cavalry in the Great War of the Rebellion, with the Armies of the Ohio and Cumberland, under Generals Morgan, Rosecrans, Thomas, Stanley and Wilson. 1862–1865.* Knoxville: Gaut-Ogden, 1902.

Cash, William M., and Lucy Somerville Howorth, eds. *My Dear Nellie: The Civil War Letters of William L. Nugent to Eleanor Smith Nugent.* Jackson: University Press of Mississippi, 1977.

Cate, Wirt Armistead, ed. *Two Soldiers: The Campaign Diaries of Thomas J. Key, C.S.A. December 7, 1863–May 17 1865 and Robert J. Campbell, U.S.A. January 1, 1864–July 21 1864.* Chapel Hill: University of North Carolina Press, 1938.

Chadick, Mrs. W. D. "Civil War Days in Huntsville, A Diary by Mrs. W. D. Chadick." *Alabama Historical Quarterly* 9 (Summer 1947):199–333.

Chamberlin, William H. "Recollections of the Battle of Atlanta." In *The Atlanta Papers,* pp. 451–63. Compiled by Sydney C. Kerksis. Dayton: Morningside Bookshop, 1980.

Chicago Board of Trade Battery Memorial Association. *Historical Sketch of the Chicago Board of Trade Battery, Horse Artillery, Illinois Volunteers.* Chicago: Henneberry, 1902.

Clark, Walter, ed. *Histories of the Several Regiments and Battalions from North Carolina in the Great War 1861-'65: Written by Members of the Respective Commands.* 5 vols. Goldsboro, N.C.: E. M. Uzzell (vol. 1); Raleigh, N.C.: Nash Brothers, 1901.

Clark, Walter A. *Under the Stars and Bars: or, Memories of Four Years Service with the Oglethorpes, of Augusta, Georgia.* Augusta, Ga.: Chronicle Printing, 1900.

Clifton, William B. *Libby and Andersonville Prisons: A True Sketch.* Indianapolis: n.p., 1910.

Cobb, John A. "Civil War Incidents in Macon." *Georgia Historical Quarterly* 7 (September 1923):282–83.

Coleman, Samuel. "Master and His Faithful Slave." *Confederate Veteran* 20 (September 1912):410.

Compton, James. "The Second Division of the 16th Army Corps, in the Atlanta Campaign." In *The Atlanta Papers,* pp. 235–57. Compiled by Sydney C. Kerksis. Dayton: Morningside Bookshop, 1980.

Confederate Veteran 10 (April 1902):161.

Connelly, Henry C. "Recollections of the War between the States." *Journal of the Illinois Historical Society* 5 (January 1913):458–74.

Connolly, James A. *Three Years in the Army of the Cumberland: The Letters and Diary of Major James A. Connolly.* Edited by Paul M. Angle. Bloomington: Indiana University Press, 1959.

Conyngham, David P. *Sherman's March through the South: With Sketches and Incidents of the Campaign.* New York: Sheldon, 1865.

Cooper, Alonzo. *In and Out of Rebel Prisons.* Oswego, N.Y.: R. J. Oliphant, 1888.

Cox, Jacob D. *Military Reminiscences of the Civil War.* 2 vols. New York: Scribner's, 1900.

Cox, Rowland. "Snake Creek Gap, and Atlanta." In *The Atlanta Papers,* pp. 327–51. Compiled by Sydney C. Kerksis. Dayton: Morningside Bookshop, 1980.

Crane, William E. "Bugle Blasts." In *Sketches of War History 1861–1865: Papers Read before the Ohio Commandery of the Military Order of the Loyal Legion of the United States 1883–1886.* 1:233–51. 6 vols. Cincinnati: Robert Clarke, 1888, 1890, 1896, 1903; Cincinnati: Monfort, 1908.

Crofts, Thomas C., comp. *History of the Service of the Third Ohio Veteran Volunteer Cavalry in the War for the Preservation of the Union from 1861–1865 Compiled from the Official Records and from Diaries of Members of the Regiment by Serg't. Thos. Crofts, Company C, Regimental Historian.* Toledo: Stoneman Press, 1910.

Cumming, Kate. *Kate: The Journal of a Confederate Nurse.* Edited by Richard Barksdale Harwell. Baton Rouge: Louisiana State University Press, 1959.

Curry, William L., comp. *Four Years in the Saddle: History of the First Regiment Ohio Volunteer Cavalry. War of the Rebellion—1861–1865.* Columbus: Champlin Printing, 1898.

————. "Raid of the Union Cavalry, Commanded by General Judson Kilpatrick, around the Confederate Army in Atlanta, August, 1864." In *The Atlanta Papers,* pp. 597–622. Compiled by Sydney C. Kerksis. Dayton: Morningside Bookshop, 1980.

Dacus, Robert H. *Reminiscences of Company "H," First Arkansas Mounted Rifles.* [Dardanelle, Ark.: Post-Despatch Print, 1897]. Reprint ed., Dayton, Ohio: Morningside Bookshop, 1972.

Dana, Charles A. *Recollections of the Civil War with the Leaders at Washington and in the Field in the Sixties.* New York: D. Appleton, 1902.

Davis, Theodore R. "With Sherman in His Army Home." *The Cosmopolitan,* December 1891, pp. 195–205.

Davis, W. H. "Cavalry Expeditions in Georgia." *Confederate Veteran* 16 (June 1908):261.

————. "Cavalry Service Under Gen. Wheeler." *Confederate Veteran* 11 (August 1903):353–54.

Davis, William C., ed. *Diary of A Confederate Soldier: John S. Jackman of the Orphan Brigade.* Columbia: University of South Carolina Press, 1990.

Deupree, J. G. "The Noxubee Squadron of the First Mississippi Cavalry, C.S.A., 1861–1865." *Publications of the Mississippi Historical Society* 2 (1918):12–143.

Dixon, Harry St. John. "Recollections of a Rebel Private." *The Sigma Chi Quarterly* 6 (February 1887):141–49; (May 1887):218–23.

Dodge, Grenville M. "The Battle of Atlanta." In *The Atlanta Papers,* pp. 487–503. Compiled by Sydney C. Kerkis. Dayton: Morningside Bookshop, 1980.

————. *Personal Recollections of President Abraham Lincoln, General Ulysses S. Grant and General William T. Sherman.* Council Bluffs, Iowa: Monarch Printing, 1914.

Dodson, William C., ed. *Campaigns of Wheeler and His Cavalry 1862–1865 from Material Furnished by Gen. Joseph Wheeler to Which Is Added His Concise and Graphic Account of the Santiago Campaign of 1898.* Atlanta: Hudgins, 1899.

————. "Stampede of Federal Cavalry." *Confederate Veteran* 19 (March 1911):123–24.

Dornblaser, Thomas Franklin. *My Life-Story for Young and Old.* [Chicago]: n.p., 1930.

————. *Sabre Strokes of the Pennsylvania Dragoons, in the War of 1861–1865. Interspersed with Personal Reminiscences.* Philadelphia: Lutheran Publication Society, 1884.

Doyle, William E. *A History of the Seventeenth Indiana, from Its Organization to the End of the War; Giving Each Day's Action, Lists of Killed and Wounded, Descriptions of Battles, Etc. Also, Lists of All the Officers and the Roll of the Regiment on February 28, 1865.* Indianapolis: Holloway, Douglass, 1865.

Drake, Edwin L., ed. *The Annals of the Army of Tennessee and Early Western History, Including a Chronological Summary of Battles and Engagements in the Western Armies of the Confederacy.* Nashville: A. D. Haynes, 1878.

Drake, J. Madison. *Fast and Loose in Dixie. An Unprejudiced Narrative of Personal Experience as a Prisoner of War at Libby, Macon, Savannah, and Charleston, with an Account of a Desperate Leap from a Moving Train of Cars, a Weary Tramp of Forty-Five Days Through Swamps and Mountains, Places and People Visited, Etc., Etc.* New York: Authors' Publishing, 1880.

Dufur, S. M. *Over the Dead Line or Tracked by Blood Hounds: Giving the Author's Personal Experiences during Eleven Months That He Was Confined in Pemberton, Libby, Belle Isle, Andersonville, Ga., and Florence, S.C., as a Prisoner of War. Describing Plans of Escape, Arrival of Prisoners, His Escape and Recapture; with Numerous and Varied Incidents and Anecdotes of his Prison Life.* Burlington, Vt.: Free Press Association, 1902.

Duke, Basil W. *Morgan's Cavalry.* New York and Washington: Neale, 1906.

Dupree, T. C. *The War-Time Letters of Captain T. C. Dupree, C.S.A. 1864–1865.* Edited by W. J. Lemke. Fayetteville, Ark.: Washington County Historical Society, 1953.

Durand, Calvin. *Calvin Durand–Sarah Gould Downs Durand, A Memorial.* Chicago: privately printed, 1912.

Dyer, John Will. *Reminiscences; or Four Years in the Confederate Army. A History of the Experiences of the Private Soldier in Camp, Hospital, Prison, on the March, and on the Battlefield. 1861–1865.* Evansville, Ind.: Keller Printing and Publishing, 1898.

Eckel, Alexander. *History of the Fourth Tennessee Cavalry U.S.A. War of the Rebellion 1861–65.* Knoxville: n.p., 1929.

———. "The Rousseau and McCook Raids: Thrilling Adventures, Desperate Chances, Much Hard Fighting and Narrow Escapes." In *The National Tribune Scrap Book: Stories of the Camp, March, Battle, Hospital and Prison Told by Comrades.* 3:3–12. 3 vols. Washington, D.C.: National Tribune, [1909?].

Fanning, Thomas W. *The Hairbreadth Escapes and Humerous* [sic] *Adventures of a Volunteer in the Cavalry Service. By One of Them Who Has Been under Generals Grant, Lew. Wallace, Sherman, Halleck, Rousseau, Thomas, and Kilpatrick.* Cincinnati: P. C. Browne, 1865.

Felton, Rebecca Latimer. "Mrs. Felton's War Memories." *Atlanta Journal Magazine,* 14 October 1928, pp. 5, 24.

Ferguson, Joseph. *Life-Struggles in Rebel Prisons; A Record of the Sufferings, Escapes, Adventures and Starvation of the Union Prisoners.* Philadelphia: James M. Ferguson, 1865.

Fifth Indiana Cavalry Association. *Reports of the Second and Third Re-Unions of the Fifth Indiana Cavalry.* Indianapolis: Sexton & Jacques, [1886], pp. 13–15.

———. *Official Report Seventeenth Annual Reunion Held at Lafayette, Ind., Oct. 4–5, 1899.* Logansport, Ind.: Longwell & Cummings, [1900].

Finney, R. P. "The 5th Ind. Cavalry in the War and in Civil Life." In *Twenty-Sixth Annual Reunion of the Fifth Indiana Cavalry Association Held at Rushville, Ind. October 14–15, 1908,* pp. 7–23. Carmel, Ind.: Star Printers, 1909.

Finney, Russell P. "A Digest History of the Fifth Indiana Cavalry during the War of the Rebellion." In *Thirteenth Annual Reunion of the Fifth Indiana Cavalry Association, Held at DePauw College, New Albany, Ind., September 9th and 10th 1895,* pp. 36–47. N.p., n.d.

Fitch, John. *Annals of the Army of the Cumberland: Comprising Biographies, Descriptions of Departments, Accounts of Expeditions, Skirmishes, and Battles; Also Its Police Record of Spies, Smugglers, and Prominent Rebel Emissaries. Together with Anecdotes, Incidents, Poetry, Reminiscences, etc. and Official Reports of the Battle of Stone River. By an Officer.* Philadelphia: J. B. Lippincott, 1864.

Forbes, Eugene. *Diary of a Soldier, and Prisoner of War in the Rebel Prisons.* Trenton: Murphy & Bechtel, 1865.

Ford, John Salmon. *Rip Ford's Texas.* Edited by Stephen B. Oates. Austin: University of Texas Press, 1963.

Fowler, L. "Army Chaplains in Battle." *Confederate Veteran* 23 (May 1915):205.

Gates, Arnold, ed. *The Rough Side of War: The Civil War Journal of Chesley A. Mosman 1st Lieutenant, Company D 59th Illinois Volunteer Infantry Regiment.* Garden City, N.Y.: Basin Publishing, 1987.

Gay, Mary A. H. *Life in Dixie during the War.* 4th ed. Atlanta: Foote & Davies, 1901.

Gibbons, A. R. *The Recollections of an Old Confederate Soldier.* Shelbina, Mo.: Herald Print, [193-].

Giles, L. B. *Terry's Texas Rangers.* [Austin, Tex.: Von Boeckmann-Jones], 1911.

Glazier, Willard W. *The Capture, the Prison Pen, and the Escape: Giving a Complete History of Prison Life in the South, Principally at Richmond, Danville, Macon, Savannah, Charleston, Columbia, Belle Isle, Millin [sic], Salisbury, and Andersonville: Describing the Arrival of Prisoners, Plans of Escape, with Numerous and Varied Incidents and Anecdotes of Prison Life: Embracing, Also, The Adventures of the Author's Escape from Columbia, South Carolina, His Recapture, Subsequent Escape, Recapture, Trial as Spy, and Final Escape from Sylvania, Georgia.* New York: United States Publishing, 1868.

Goodloe, Albert Theodore. *Some Rebel Relics from the Seat of the War.* Nashville: Publishing House of the Methodist Episcopal Church, South, 1893.

Grant, Ulysses S. *Personal Memoirs of U. S. Grant.* 2 vols. New York: Charles L. Webster, 1885.

Gray, John Chipman, and John Codman Ropes. *War Letters, 1862–1865 of John Chipman Gray and John Codman Ropes.* Boston: Houghton Mifflin, 1927.

Grayson, A. J. *"The Spirit of 1861." History of the Sixth Indiana Regiment in the Three Months' Campaign in Western Virginia. Full of Humor and Originality, Depicting Battles, Skirmishes, Forced Marches, Incidents of Camp Life, Etc., with the Names of Every Officer and Private in the Sixth Regiment.* Madison, Ind.: Courier Print, [1875].

Grimsley, Mark, ed. "'We Prepare to Receive the Enemy Where We Stand.'" Translated by Bernatello Glod. *Civil War Times Illustrated,* May 1985, pp. 18–30.

Guild, George B. *A Brief Narrative of the Fourth Tennessee Cavalry Regiment, Wheeler's Corps, Army of Tennessee.* Nashville, n.p., 1913.

Guthrey, D. M. "Wheeler's Cavalry around Atlanta," *Confederate Veteran* 13 (June 1905):267.

Hadley, J. V. *Seven Months a Prisoner.* New York: Scribner's, 1898.

Hamilton, William Douglas. *Recollections of a Cavalryman of the Civil War after Fifty Years 1861–1865.* Columbus, Ohio: F. J. Heer Printing, 1915.

Hancock, Richard R. *Hancock's Diary: or, A History of the Second Tennessee Confederate Cavalry, with Sketches of First and Seventh Battalions; Also Portraits and Biographical Sketches.* Nashville: Brandon Printing, 1887.

Hargis, O. P. *Thrilling Experiences of a First Georgia Cavalryman in the Civil War.* Atlanta: n.p., n.d.

Harwell, Richard, and Philip N. Racine, eds. *The Fiery Trail: A Union Officer's Account of Sherman's Last Campaigns.* Knoxville: University of Tennessee Press, 1986.

Heaton, Eli. "The Rousseau Raid." In *Report of the Proceedings of the 16th Annual Re-Union of the Eighth Indiana Veteran Cavalry. 39th Regiment Indiana Volunteers, Held at Cicero, Indiana, on the 12th and 13th days of October 1899,* pp. 11–17. Kokomo, Ind.: Tribune Printing, 1900.

Hinman, Wilbur F. *The Story of the Sherman Brigade. The Camp, the March, the Bivouac, the Battle; and How "The Boys" Lived and Died during Four Years of Active Field Service.* Alliance, Ohio: Press of Daily Review, 1897.

Hitchcock, Henry. *Marching with Sherman: Passages from the Letters and Campaign Diaries of Henry Hitchcock, Major and Assistant Adjutant General of Volunteers, November 1864–May 1865.* Edited by M. A. DeWolfe Howe. New Haven, Conn.: Yale University Press, 1927.

Holmes, Erastus. "Andersonville and How We Got There." In *Reports of the Second and Third*

Re-Unions of the Fifth Indiana Cavalry Held at Indianapolis, Indiana, October 8–9, 1884, and October 14–15, 1885. Indianapolis: Sexton & Jacques [1886], pp. 2–8.

Holzhueter, John O., ed. "William Wallace's Civil War Letters: The Atlanta Campaign." *Wisconsin Magazine of History* 57 (Winter 1973–1974):91–116.

Hood, John Bell. *Advance and Retreat: Personal Experiences in the United States and Confederate Armies.* Published for the Hood Orphan Memorial Fund, G. T. Beauregard. New Orleans. [Philadelphia: Press of Burke & M'Fetridge], 1880.

Hosea, Lewis M. "Some Side Lights on the War for the Union." In *Sketches of War History 1861–1865: A Compilation of Miscellaneous Papers Read Before the Ohio Commandery of the Loyal Legion.* vol. 9:35–55 of *Military Order of the Loyal Legion of the United States.* 63 vols. Wilmington, N.C.: Broadfoot Publishing, 1991–1996.

Howard, Oliver Otis. *Autobiography of Oliver Otis Howard, Major General United States Army.* 2 vols. New York: Baker & Taylor, 1907.

———. "The Battles about Atlanta." *Atlantic Monthly,* October 1876, pp. 385–99.

Howe, M. A. DeWolfe, ed. *Home Letters of General Sherman.* New York: Scribner's, 1909.

Hull, Augustus Longstreet. *Annals of Athens, Georgia 1801–1901.* Athens, Ga.: Banner Job Office, 1906.

Isham, Asa B., Henry M. Davidson, and Henry B. Furness. *Prisoners of War and Military Prisons: Personal Narratives of Experience in the Prisons at Richmond, Danville, Macon, Andersonville, Savannah, Millen, Charleston, and Columbia with a General Account of Prison Life and Prisons in the South during the War of the Rebellion, Including Statistical Information Pertaining to Prisoners of War; Together with a List of Officers Who Were Prisoners of War from January 1, 1864.* Cincinnati: Lyman & Cushing, 1890.

James, Frank B. "McCook's Brigade at the Assault Upon Kenesaw Mountain." In *The Atlanta Papers,* pp. 365–89. Compiled by Sydney C. Kerksis. Dayton: Morningside Bookshop, 1980.

John, Samuel Will. "Alabama Corps of Cadets, 1860–65," *Confederate Veteran* 25 (January 1917):12–14.

Johnston, Joseph E. *Narrative of Military Operations, Directed, during the Late War between the States.* New York: D. Appleton, 1874.

Jones, Mary Miles, and Leslie Jones Martin, eds. *The Gentle Rebel: The Civil War Letters of 1st Lt. William Harvey Berryhill Co. D, 43rd Regiment, Mississippi Volunteers.* Yazoo City, Miss.: Sassafras Press, 1982.

Jones, William B. "The Late Maj. Gen. William Wirt Allen." *Confederate Veteran* 2 (November 1894):324.

Jordan, Philip D., ed. "Forty Days with the Christian Commission: A Diary by William Salter." *Iowa Journal of History and Politics* 33 (April 1935):123–54.

Keen, Newton A. *Living & Fighting with the Texas 6th Cavalry.* Gaithersburg, Md.: Butternut Press, 1986.

Kelley, Daniel G. *What I Saw and Suffered in Rebel Prisons.* Buffalo: Matthews & Warren, 1866.

Kendrick, J. R. "A Non-Combatant's War Reminiscences." *Atlantic Monthly,* October 1889, pp. 449–63.

Kerr, Homer L., ed. *Fighting with Ross' Texas Cavalry Brigade, C.S.A., The Diary of George L. Griscom, Adjutant, 9th Texas Cavalry Regiment.* Hillsboro, Texas: Hill Junior College Press, 1976.

Kilpatrick, Hugh Judson. *The Irish Soldier in the War of the Rebellion.* Deckertown, N.J.: Independent Steam Print, [1880].

King, B. H. "The Stoneman and McCook Raid." *Confederate Veteran* 34 (July 1926):262.

King, W. C., and W. P. Derby, comps. *Camp-Fire Sketches and Battlefield Echoes of the Rebellion.* Springfield, Mass.: King, Richardson, 1888.

Kirwan, A. D., ed. *Johnny Green of the Orphan Brigade: The Journal of a Confederate Soldier.* [Lexington]: University of Kentucky Press, 1956.

Larson, James. *Sergeant Larson 4th Cav.* San Antonio, Tex.: Southern Literary Institute, 1935.

Lathrop, Edward S. "Gossipy Letter from Georgia." *Confederate Veteran* 20 (November 1912):520.

Lavender, John W. *The Civil War Memoirs of Captain John W. Lavender, C.S.A.* Edited by Ted R. Worley. Pine Bluff, Ark.: Southern Press, [1956].

Letteer[?], Alfred W. "Andersonville: Diary of a Prisoner." *The Historical Magazine,* January 1871, pp. 1–7.

Lightcap, W. H. *The Horrors of Southern Prisons during the War of the Rebellion from 1861 to 1865.* Platteville, Wis.: Journal Job Rooms, 1902.

Lindsley, John Berrien, ed. *The Military Annals of Tennessee. Confederate. First Series: Embracing a Review of Military Operations, with Regimental Histories and Memorial Rolls.* Nashville: J. M. Lindsley, 1886.

Long, Eli. "Letter from General Long." *Journal of the United States Cavalry Association* 3 (December 1890):428–30.

Love, S. B. "Sharing Credit with General Wheeler." *Confederate Veteran* 16 (July 1908):343–44.

Love, William DeLoss. *Wisconsin in the War of the Rebellion; A History of All Regiments and Batteries the State Has Sent to the Field, and Deeds of her Citizens, Governors and Other Military Officers, and State and National Legislators to Suppress the Rebellion.* Chicago: Church and Goodman; Milwaukee: A. Whittemore; New York: Sheldon, 1866.

Lovett, Howard Meriwether. "Airy Mount—In Sherman's Track." *Confederate Veteran* 26 (May 1918):193–97.

Lyon, Adelia C., comp. *Reminiscences of the Civil War: Compiled from the War Correspondence of Colonel William P. Lyon and from Personal Letters and Diary by Mrs. Adelia C. Lyon.* San Jose, Calif.: Press of Muirson & Wright, 1907.

Mackall, William W. *A Son's Recollections of His Father.* New York: E. P. Dutton, 1930.

Magee, Benjamin F. *History of the 72d Indiana Volunteer Infantry of the Mounted Lightning Brigade. A Faithful Record of the Life, Service, and Suffering, of the Rank and File of the Regiment, on the March, in Camp, in Battle, and in Prison. Especially Devoted to Giving the Reader a Definite Knowledge of the Service of the Common Soldier. With an Appendix Containing a Complete Roster of Officers and Men.* Edited by William R. Jewell. LaFayette, Ind.: S. Vater, 1882.

Mallet, J. W. "Work of the Ordnance Bureau of the War Department of the Confederate States, 1861–65." *Southern Historical Society Papers* 37 (1909):1–20.

Manigault, Arthur Middleton. *A Carolinian Goes to War: The Civil War Narrative of Arthur Middleton Manigault Brigadier General, C.S.A.* Edited by R. Lockwood Tower. Columbia: University of South Carolina Press, 1983.

Maury, Dabney H. *Recollections of a Virginian in the Mexican, Indian, and Civil Wars.* New York: Scribner's, 1894.

McCain, General Warren. *A Soldier's Diary; or The History of Company "L," Third Indiana Cavalry.* Indianapolis: William A. Patton, 1885.

McCrory, William. "Early Life and Personal Reminiscences of General William T. Sherman." In *Glimpses of the Nation's Struggle, A Series of Papers Read before the Minnesota Commandery of the Military Order of the Loyal Legion of the United States.* 3:310–46. 6 vols. Edited by Military Order of the Loyal Legion of the United States, Minnesota Commandery. St. Paul: St. Paul Book and Stationery, 1887, 1890; New York, St. Paul, Minneapolis: D. D. Merrill, 1893; St. Paul: H. L. Collins, 1898; St. Paul: Review Publishing, 1903; Minneapolis: Aug. Davis Publisher, 1909.

McKeever, Elliott Bushfield. *He Rode with Sherman from Atlanta to the Sea.* Aberdeen, S.D.: McKeever Press, 1947.

Mead, Homer. *The Eighth Iowa Cavalry in the Civil War: Autobiography and Personal Recollections of Homer Mead, M.D.* Carthage, Ill.: S. C. Davidson, [1925].

Merrill, Samuel. *The Seventieth Indiana Volunteer Infantry in the War of the Rebellion.* Indianapolis: Bowen-Merrill, 1900.

Mims, Wilbur F. comp. *War History of the Prattville Dragoons.* [Thurber, Tex.]: n.p., n.d.

Monlux, George. *To My Comrades of Company "I" Eighth Iowa Cavalry, Living, and to the Memory of Those Who Are Dead, I Dedicate These Lines.* [Rock Rapids, Iowa: n.p., 193?].

Montgomery, Frank A. *Reminiscences of a Mississippian in Peace and War.* Cincinnati: Robert Clarke, 1901.

Moore, James. *Kilpatrick and Our Cavalry: Comprising a Sketch of the Life of General Kilpatrick, with an Account of the Cavalry Raids, Engagements, and Operations under His Command, from the Beginning of the Rebellion to the Surrender of Johnston.* New York: W. J. Widdleton, 1865.

Morrison, James L., Jr., ed. "Getting through West Point: The Cadet Memoirs of John C. Tidball, Class of 1848." *Civil War History* 26 (December 1980):304–25.

Moses, Daniel S. "Prison Life during the Civil War." In *The National Tribune Scrapbook: Stories of the Camp, March, Battle, Hospital and Prison Told by Comrades.* 2:22–25. 3 vols. Washington, D.C.: National Tribune, [1909?].

Munson, Gilbert D. "Battle of Atlanta." In *The Atlanta Papers,* pp. 409–29. Compiled by Sydney C. Kerksis. Dayton: Morningside Bookshop, 1980.

Newsome, Edmund. *Experience in the War of the Great Rebellion. By a Soldier of the Eighty-first Regiment Illinois Volunteer Infantry. From August 1862, to August 1865. Including Nearly Nine Months of Life in Southern Prisons, at Macon, Savannah, Charleston, Columbia and Other Places.* Carbondale, Ill.: E. Newsome, 1879.

Newton, George A. "Battle of Peach Tree Creek." In *The Atlanta Papers,* pp. 391–408. Compiled by Sydney C. Kerksis. Dayton: Morningside Bookshop, 1980.

Nichols, George Ward. *The Story of the Great March from the Diary of a Staff Officer.* 26th ed. New York: Harper & Brothers, 1866.

Ninety-Second Illinois Reunion Association. *Ninety-Second Illinois Volunteers.* Freeport, Ill.: Journal Steam Publishing, 1875.

———. *Proceedings of the Fourth Triennial Reunion of the 92 Ill. Volunteers Held at Oregon, Ogle Co., Illinois, September 4th, 1876.* Oregon, Ill.: Courier Book and Job Printing, [1876].

———. *Proceedings of the Fifth Triennial Reunion of the 92d Illinois Volunteers, Held at Lena, Stephenson County, Ill., September 4, 1879.* Freeport, Ill.: Journal Printing, 1879.

———. *The Seventh Tri-ennial Re-Union of the 92 Illinois Mounted Infantry at Oregon, Ogle County, Illinois. September 3–4, 1885.* Mt. Carroll, Ill.: Herald, 1888.

———. *Ninth Triennial Re-Union of the Ninety-Second Illinois Mounted Infantry, Held at Polo, Illinois, September 3 and 4, 1891.* Polo, Ill.: Press Print, [1891].

Nisbet, James Cooper. *Four Years on the Firing Line.* Edited by Bell I. Wiley. [Jackson, Tenn.]: McCowat-Mercer Press, 1963.

Nutt, Laetitia Lafon Ashmore. *Courageous Journey: The Civil War Journal of Laetitia Lafon Ashmore Nutt.* Edited by Florence Ashmore Cowles Hamlett Martin. Miami: E. A. Seeman, 1975.

Otey, Mercer. "Story of Our Great War," *Confederate Veteran* 9 (March 1901):107–10.

Otto, John. *History of the 11th Indiana Battery, Connected with an Outline History of the Army of the Cumberland during the War of the Rebellion, 1861–1865.* Auburn, Ind. [Fort Wayne, Ind.: W. D. Page], 1891.

Overley, Milford. "'Williams's Kentucky Brigade,' C.S.A." *Confederate Veteran* 13 (October 1905): 460–62.

Owens, John Algernon. *Sword and Pen; or, Ventures and Adventures of Willard Glazier, (The Soldier-Author,) in War and Literature: Comprising Incidents and Reminiscences of His Childhood; His Chequered Life as a Student and Teacher; and His Remarkable Career as a Soldier and Author; Embracing Also the Story of His Unprecedented Journey from Ocean to Ocean on Horseback; and an Account of His Discovery of the True Source of the Mississippi River, and Canoe Voyage Thence to the Gulf of Mexico.* Philadelphia: P. W. Ziegler, 1890.

Page, James Madison, and M. J. Haley. *The True Story of Andersonville Prison: A Defense of Major Henry Wirz.* New York and Washington: Neale, 1908.

Payne, Edwin W. *History of the Thirty-Fourth Regiment of Illinois Volunteer Infantry, September 7, 1861–July 12, 1865.* Clinton, Iowa: Allen Printing, [1902].

Pickerill, W. N. *History of the Third Indiana Cavalry.* Indianapolis: Aetna Printing, 1906.

Price, George F. comp., *Across the Continent with the Fifth Cavalry.* New York: D. Van Nostrand, 1883. Reprint ed., New York: Antiquarian Press, 1959.

Prutsman, C. M. *A Soldier's Experience in Southern Prisons, by C. M. Prutsman, Lieut. in Seventh Regiment, Wisconsin Volunteers, A Graphic Description of the Author's Experiences in Various Southern Prisons.* New York: Andrew H. Kellogg, 1901.

Quiner, E. B. *The Military History of Wisconsin: A Record of the Civil and Military Patriotism of the State, in the War for the Union, with a History of the Campaigns in Which Wisconsin Soldiers Have Been Conspicuous—Regimental Histories—Sketches of Distinguished Officers—The Roll of the Illustrious Dead—Movements of the Legislature and State Officers, Etc.* Chicago: Clarke, 1866.

Quisenberry, A. C. "The First Kentucky Cavalry, U.S.A." *Register of the Kentucky Historical Society* 18 (May 1920):15–20.

Rankin, R. C. *History of the Seventh Ohio Volunteer Cavalry.* Ripley, Ohio: J. C. Newcomb, 1881.

Ray, Lavender R. "Career of Gen. Iverson during Days of Sixties." *Atlanta Constitution Magazine,* 16 April 1911, p. 4.

Rea, John P. "Kilpatrick's Raid around Atlanta." In *The Atlanta Papers,* pp. 641–65. Compiled by Sydney C. Kerksis. Dayton: Morningside Bookshop, 1980.

Richardson, Albert D. *The Secret Service, The Field, The Dungeon, and The Escape.* Hartford, Conn.: American Publishing; Philadelphia and Cincinnati: Jones Bros.; Chicago: R. C. Treat, 1865.

Roach, A. C. *The Prisoner of War, and How Treated. Containing a History of Colonel Streight's Expedition to the Rear of Bragg's Army, in the Spring of 1863, and a Correct Account of the Treatment and Condition of the Union Prisoners of War in the Rebel Prisons of the South, in 1863–4. Being the Actual Experience of a Union Officer During Twenty-Two Months' Imprisonment in Rebeldom. With Personal Adventure, Biographical Sketches and History of Andersonville Prison Pen.* Indianapolis: Robert Douglass, 1887.

Robinson, George I. "With Kilpatrick around Atlanta." In *The Atlanta Papers,* pp. 567–95. Compiled by Sydney C. Kerksis. Dayton: Morningside Bookshop, 1980.

Robinson, William J. *Civil War Diary of Capt. William J. Robinson.* N.p.: 1975.

Roland, Charles P., and Richard C. Robbins, eds. "The Diary of Eliza (Mrs. Albert Sidney) Johnston: The Second Cavalry Comes to Texas." *Southwestern Historical Quarterly* 60 (April 1957):463–500.

Rose, Victor M. *Ross' Texas Brigade. Being a Narrative of Events Connected with Its Service in the Late War between the States.* Louisville: Courier Journal Book and Job Rooms, 1881.

Rosenberger, H. E., ed. "Ohiowa Soldier." *Annals of Iowa* 36 (Fall 1961):111–48.

Roy, T. B. "General Hardee and the Military Operations around Atlanta." *Southern Historical Society Papers* 8 (1880):337–87.

Rusling, James F. *Men and Things I Saw in Civil War Days.* New York: Eaton & Mains; Cincinnati: Curts & Jennings, 1899.

Sammons, John H. *Personal Recollections of the Civil War by John H. Sammons, A Private in the 5th Ind. Cav. Vol.* Greensburg, Ind.: Montgomery & Son, [188–].

Sanford, W. L. *History of the Fourteenth Illinois Cavalry and the Brigades to Which It Belonged Compiled from Manuscript History by Sanford, West and Featherson, and From Notes of Comrades; Carefully Compared with and Corrected by Government Published Official Reports and Statistics Furnished by Union and Confederate Officers. With Biographies of Officers and Rolls of the Men, and Embellished with Portraits.* Chicago: R. R. Donnelley & Sons, 1898.

Schofield, John M. *Forty-Six Years in the Army.* New York: Century, 1897.

Scribner, Benjamin F. *How Soldiers Were Made; or The War as I Saw It under Buell, Rosecrans, Thomas, Grant, and Sherman.* New Albany, Ind.: Donohue & Henneberry, 1887.

Shanks, William F. G. *Personal Recollections of Distinguished Generals.* New York: Harper & Brothers, 1866.

————. "Recollections of General Rousseau." *Harper's New Monthly Magazine,* November 1865, pp. 762–68.

————. "Recollections of Sherman." *Harper's New Monthly Magazine,* April 1865, pp. 640–46.

Sherman, William T. *Memoirs of General William T. Sherman.* 2 vols. 2nd ed. New York: D. Appleton, 1886.

Shoup, Francis A. "Dalton Campaign-Works at Chattahoochee River—Interesting History." *Confederate Veteran* 3 (September 1895):262–65.

Simon, John Y., et al., eds. *The Papers of Ulysses S. Grant.* 18 vols. Carbondale: Southern Illinois University Press, 1967–1991.

Sipes, William B. *The Seventh Pennsylvania Veteran Volunteer Cavalry: Its Record, Reminiscences and Roster with an Appendix.* Pottsville, Pa.: Miners' Journal Print, [1906].

Small, William. *Camp-Fire Talk on the Life and Military Services of Maj. Gen. Judson Kilpatrick.* Washington, D.C.: [1887].

Smith, David M., ed. "The Civil War Diary of Colonel John Henry Smith." *Iowa Journal of History* 47 (April 1949):140–70.

Smith, Gustavus W. "The Georgia Militia about Atlanta." In *Battles and Leaders of the Civil War.* 4:331–35. 4 vols. Edited by Robert Underwood Johnson and Clarence Clough Buel. New York: Century, 1884–1888.

Smith, Mrs. S. E. D. *The Soldier's Friend; Being a Thrilling Narrative of Grandma Smith's Four Years' Experience and Observation, as Matron, in the Hospitals of the South, during the Late Disastrous Conflict in America.* Memphis: Bulletin Publishing, 1867.

Smith, W. C. *The Private in Gray, Written by a Private. "Not an Officer, only one of the men."* N.p., n.d.

Snetsinger, Robert J. ed., *Kiss Clara for Me: The Story of Joseph Whitney and His Family, Early Days in the Midwest, and Soldiering in the American Civil War.* State College, Pa.: Carnation Press, 1969.

Society of the Army of the Cumberland. *Society of the Army of the Cumberland, Fourth Re-Union, Cleveland, 1870.* Cincinnati: Robert Clarke, 1870.

————. *Society of the Army of the Cumberland, Fifth Re-Union, Detroit, 1871.* Cincinnati: Robert Clarke, 1872.

————. *Society of the Army of the Cumberland, Eighth Reunion, Columbus, 1874.* Cincinnati: Robert Clarke, 1875.

Society of the Army of the Tennessee. *Report of the Proceedings of the Society of the Army of the Tennessee, at the Fourteenth Annual Meeting, Held at Cincinnati, Ohio. April 6th and 7th, 1881.* Cincinnati: By the Society, 1885.

————. *Report of the Proceedings of the Society of the Army of the Tennessee, at the Sixteenth Meeting, Held at Cleveland, Ohio. October 17th and 18th, 1883.* Cincinnati: By the Society, 1885.

————. *Report of the Proceedings of the Society of the Army of the Tennessee, at the Twenty-*

Second Meeting, Held at Cincinnati, Ohio. September 25th and 26th, 1889. Cincinnati: By the Society, 1893.

———. *Report of the Proceedings of the Society of the Army of the Tennessee, at the Twenty-Third Meeting, Held at Chicago, Ill. October 7th and 8th, 1891.* Cincinnati: By the Society, 1893.

———. *Report of the Proceedings of the Society of the Army of the Tennessee at the Twenty-Sixth Meeting, Held at Council Bluffs, Iowa, October 3rd and 4th, 1894.* Cincinnati: Press of F. W. Freeman, 1895.

Sparks, A. W. *The War between the States, as I Saw It. Reminiscent, Historical and Personal.* Tyler, Tex.: Lee & Burnett, 1901.

Spencer, Ambrose. *A Narrative of Andersonville, Drawn from the Evidence Elicited on the Trial of Henry Wirz, the Jailer. With the Argument of Col. N. P. Chapman, Judge Advocate.* New York: Harper & Brothers, 1866.

Stanley, David S. *Personal Memoirs of Major-General D. S. Stanley, U.S.A.* Cambridge, Mass.: Harvard University Press, 1917.

Stephenson, Eudora Weaver. "Refugeeing in War Time." *Confederate Veteran* 39 (April 1931):136–38.

Stewart, Edgar A., ed. "The Journal of James Mallory, 1834–1877." *Alabama Review* 14 (July 1961):219–32.

Stone, Henry. "The Atlanta Campaign." In *Papers of the Military Historical Society of Massachusetts,* 8:341–492. 14 vols. Boston: Military Historical Society of Massachusetts, 1895–1918.

Stormont, Gilbert R., comp. *History of the Fifty-Eighth Regiment of Indiana Volunteer Infantry. Its Organization, Campaigns and Battles from 1861 to 1865. From the Manuscript Prepared by the Late Chaplain John H. Hight, during His Service with the Regiment in the Field.* Princeton, Ind.: Press of the Clarion, 1895.

Strong, William E. "The Death of General James B. McPherson." In *The Atlanta Papers,* pp. 505–39. Compiled by Sydney C. Kerksis. Dayton: Morningside Bookshop, 1980.

Swint, Henry Lee, ed. "With the First Wisconsin Cavalry 1862–1865 (II): The Letters of Peter J. Williamson." *Wisconsin Magazine of History* 26 (June 1943):433–49.

Sykes, E. T. "Error in the Harris-Adair Article." *Confederate Veteran* 5 (September 1897):452–54.

Sylvester, Lorna Lutes, ed. "'Gone for a Soldier': The Civil War Letters of Charles Harding Cox." *Indiana Magazine of History* 68 (September 1972):181–239.

Synopsis of the Military Career of Gen. Joseph Wheeler Commander of the Cavalry Corps Army of the West. Revised ed. New York: n.p. 1865.

Tarrant, Eastham. *The Wild Riders of the First Kentucky Cavalry. A History of the Regiment, in the Great War of the Rebellion 1861–1865, Telling of Its Origin and Organization; A Description of the Material of Which It Was Composed; Its Rapid and Severe Marches, Hard Service, and Fierce Conflicts on Many a Bloody Field.* Louisville: Press of R. H. Carothers, 1894.

Taylor, John T. "Reminiscences of Services as an Aide-de-Camp with General William Tecumseh Sherman." In *War Talks in Kansas: A Series of Papers Read before the Kansas Commandery of the Military Order of the Loyal Legion of the United States,* pp. 127–42. Edited by Military Order of the Loyal Legion of the United States, Kansas Commandery. Kansas City, Mo.: Franklin Hudson Publishing, 1906.

Thatcher, Marshall P. *A Hundred Battles in the West. St. Louis to Atlanta, 1861–65. The Second Michigan Cavalry with the Armies of the Mississippi, Ohio, Kentucky and Cumberland, under Generals Halleck, Sherman, Pope, Rosecrans, Thomas and Others; With Mention of a Few of the Famous Regiments and Brigades of the West.* Detroit: L. F. Kilroy, 1884.

Thompson, Ed Porter. *History of the Orphan Brigade.* Louisville: Lewis N. Thompson, 1898.

Thorndike, Rachel Sherman, ed. *The Sherman Letters: Correspondence between General and Senator Sherman from 1837 to 1891.* New York: Scribner's, 1894.

Tomlinson, Helyn W., ed. *"Dear Friends," The Civil War Letters and Diary of Charles Edwin Cort.* [Minneapolis: n.p., 1962].

Travis, Allie, Mrs. "Heroism at Home." In *"Our Women in the War." The Lives They Lived; The Deaths They Died,* pp. 389–94. Edited by Charleston Weekly News and Courier. Charleston, S.C.: News and Courier Book Presses, 1885.

Tuthill, Richard S. "An Artilleryman's Recollections of the Battle of Atlanta." In *The Atlanta Papers,* pp. 431–49. Compiled by Sydney C. Kerksis. Dayton: Morningside Bookshop, 1980.

Upson, Theodore F. *With Sherman to the Sea: The Civil War Letters, Diaries & Reminiscences of Theodore F. Upson.* Edited by Oscar Osburn Winther. Bloomington: Indiana University Press, 1958.

Urban, John W. *Battle Field and Prison Pen, or Through the War and Thrice a Prisoner in Rebel Dungeons. A Graphic Recital of Personal Experiences throughout the Whole Period of the Late War for the Union—During Which the Author Was Actively Engaged in 25 Battles and Skirmishes, Was Three Times Taken Prisoner of War, and Incarcerated in the Notorious Rebel Dungeons, Libby, Pemberton, Andersonville, Savannah, and Others. An Inside View of Those Dens of Death, Atrocities Practiced, Etc., Etc.; in Fact, a Recital of Possibly as Varied and Thrilling Experiences as Were Known during All the Wild Vicissitudes of That Terrible Four Years of Internecine Strife.* Philadelphia: Hubbard Brothers, 1882.

Vale, Joseph G. *Minty and the Cavalry: A History of the Cavalry Campaigns in the Western Armies.* Harrisburg, Pa.: Edwin K. Meyers, 1886.

Vaughter, John B. [Sergeant Oats]. *Prison Life in Dixie. Giving a Short History of the Inhuman and Barbarous Treatment of Our Soldiers by Rebel Authorities.* Chicago: Central Book Concern, 1880.

Villard, Henry. *Memoirs of Henry Villard: Journalist and Financier, 1835–1900.* 2 vols. Boston: Houghton Mifflin, 1904.

Watkins, S. R. "The 'Fighting' Forty-Eighth Tennessee Regiment." *The Southern Bivouac* 2 (February 1884):246–51.

———. *"Co. Aytch," Maury Grays, First Tennessee Regiment; or, A Side Show of the Big Show.* Chattanooga: Times Print Company, 1900. Reprint ed., Wilmington, N.C.: Broadfoot Publishing, 1987.

Webb, William W. "Kilpatrick's Great Raid." *Frank Leslie's Popular Monthly,* December 1889, pp. 728–33.

Wells, James M. *"With Touch of Elbow" or Death Before Dishonor: A Thrilling Narrative of Adventure on Land and Sea.* Philadelphia, Chicago, Toronto: John C. Winston Company, 1909.

West, Granville C. "McCook's Raid in the Rear of Atlanta and Hood's Army, August, 1864." In *The Atlanta Papers,* pp. 541–66. Compiled by Sydney C. Kerksis. Dayton: Morningside Bookshop, 1980.

Whitenack, David S. "Reminiscences of Army Life." In *Report of the Twenty-ninth Annual Reunion Fifth Indiana Cavalry Association Held at Greenwood, Indiana, Oct. 11–12, 1911,* pp. 35–53. N.p., n.d.

———. "Reminiscences of the Civil War: Andersonville." *Indiana Magazine of History* 11 (July 1915):128–43.

Williams, T. J. "Captain Williams' Escape." In *Anecdotes, Poetry, and Incidents of the War: North and South. 1860–1865,* pp. 183–86. Compiled by Frank Moore. New York: Publication Office, Bible House, 1867.

Wilson, James Harrison. *Under the Old Flag: Recollections of Military Operations in the War for the Union, the Spanish War, the Boxer Rebellion, Etc.* 2 vols. New York: D. Appleton, 1912.

Wilson, Thomas B. *Reminiscences of Thomas B. Wilson.* N.p.: [1939].

Witt, W. P. "After M'Cook's Raid below Atlanta." *Confederate Veteran* 20 (March 1912):115–16.

Wulsin, Lucien. *Roster of Surviving Members of the Fourth Regiment Ohio Volunteer Cavalry 1861–1865 with a Brief Historical Sketch of the Regiment.* Cincinnati: Chas. H. Thomson, 1891.

———. *The Story of the Fourth Regiment Ohio Veteran Volunteer Cavalry from the Organization of the Regiment, August, 1861, to Its 50th Anniversary, August, 1911. Based on the Book of 1890.* Revised, corrected and edited by Eleanor N. Adams. Cincinnati: n.p., 1912.

Atlases and Miscellaneous Works

Catalogue of the Officers and Cadets of the Kentucky Military Institute, Six Miles from Frankfort, Kentucky; From Sept. 8, 1856, to June 9, 1857. Cincinnati: Moore, Wilstach, Keys, 1857.

U.S. War Department. *The Official Military Atlas of the Civil War,* with an introduction by Richard Sommers. New York: Arno Press and Crown, 1978. Reprint of *Atlas to Accompany the Official Records of the Union and Confederate Armies,* Washington, D.C.: U.S. Government Printing Office, 1891–1895.

SECONDARY SOURCES

Books and Articles

Agee, Rucker. "Highway Markers in Alabama." *Alabama Review* 14 (January 1961):61–75.

Albaugh, William A. III, and Edward N. Simmons. *Confederate Arms.* New York: Bonanza Books, 1957.

Alexander, Lee G., and James G. Bogle. "George Hewitt Daniel (1817–1864)." *Atlanta Historical Bulletin* 13 (September 1968):19–53.

Anderson, C. C. *A Preliminary Report on a Part of the Water-Powers of Georgia Compiled from the Notes of C. C. Anderson, Late Assistant Geologist, and from Other Sources.* Compiled by B. M. Hall. Atlanta: Franklin Printing and Publishing, 1896.

Anderson, Charles C. *Fighting by Southern Federals.* New York: Neale, 1912.

Appletons' Annual Cyclopaedia and Register of Important Events . . . Embracing Political, Civil, Military, and Social Affairs; Public Documents; Biography, Statistics, Commerce, Finance, Literature, Science, Agriculture, and Mechanical Industry, 1869 ed.

Athens Historical Society. *Newsletter,* May 1969.

Avary, J. Arch, Jr., and Marshall L. Bowie. *The West Point Route: A Story of the Atlanta and West Point Rail Road—The Western Railway of Alabama.* N.p., 1954.

"B. F. White." *Confederate Veteran* 7 (December 1899):561–62.

Bancroft, Hubert Howe. *The Works of Hubert Howe Bancroft.* Vol. 24: *History of California.* San Francisco: History Company, 1890.

Barnett, James. "Forty for the Union: Civil War Generals Buried in Spring Grove Cemetery." *The Cincinnati Historical Society Bulletin* 30 (Summer 1972):91–121.

Batts, Henry Lewis. *History of the First Baptist Church of Christ at Macon 1826–1968.* Macon: Southern Press, 1968–1969.

Benner, Judith Ann. *Sul Ross: Soldier, Statesman, Educator.* College Station: Texas A&M University Press, 1983.

Bigelow, John, Jr. *The Campaign of Chancellorsville: A Strategic and Tactical Study.* New Haven, Conn.: Yale University Press, 1910.

Black, Robert C. III. *The Railroads of the Confederacy.* Chapel Hill: University of North Carolina Press, 1952.

Blanchard, Charles, ed. *Counties of Howard and Tipton, Indiana. Historical and Biographical*. Chicago: F. A. Battey, 1883.

Bogle, James G. "George Hewitt Daniel (1816–1864) Part II." *Atlanta Historical Bulletin* 17 (Spring–Summer 1972):31–38.

Bonner, James C. *Milledgeville: Georgia's Antebellum Capital*. Athens: University of Georgia Press, 1978.

Boynton, H. V. *Sherman's Historical Raid. The Memoirs in the Light of the Record. A Review Based upon Compilations from the Files of the War Office*. Cincinnati: Wilstach, Baldwin, 1875.

Bradford, Gamaliel. *Union Portraits*. Boston: Houghton Mifflin, 1916.

Bragg, William Harris. "The Union General Lost in Georgia." *Civil War Times Illustrated*. June 1985, pp. 16–23.

Brewer, George E. "History of Coosa County." *Alabama Historical Quarterly* 4 (Spring-Summer 1942):7–300.

Brewer, W. *Alabama: Her History, Resources, War Record, and Public Men. From 1540 to 1872*. Montgomery: Barrett & Brown, 1872.

Brockett, Linus Pierpont. "Brevet Major-General Hugh Judson Kilpatrick." *United States Service Magazine*, November 1865, pp. 419–30.

Burne, Alfred H. *Lee, Grant and Sherman: A Study in Leadership in the 1864–65 Campaign*. New York: Scribner's, 1939.

Butler, John C. *Historical Record of Macon and Central Georgia, Containing Many Interesting and Valuable Reminiscences Connected with the Whole State, Including Numerous Incidents and Facts Never Before Published and of Great Historic Value*. Macon: J. W. Burke, 1879.

Camak, James W. "The Double-Barreled Cannon." *Confederate Veteran* 23 (July 1915): 310.

Candler, Allen D., and Clement A. Evans, eds. *Georgia: Comprising Sketches of Counties, Towns, Events, Institutions, and Persons, Arranged in Cyclopedic Form*. 3 vols. Atlanta: State Historical Association, 1906. Reprint ed., Spartanburg, S.C.: Reprint Company, 1972.

Carter, Samuel, III. *The Siege of Atlanta, 1864*. New York: St. Martin's Press, 1973.

Castel, Albert. *Decision in the West: The Atlanta Campaign of 1864*. Lawrence: University Press of Kansas, 1992.

———. "The Life of a Rising Son, Part I: The Failure." *Civil War Times Illustrated*, July 1979, pp. 4–7, 42–46.

———. "The Life of a Rising Son, Part II: The Subordinate." *Civil War Times Illustrated*, August 1979, pp. 12–22.

———. "Union Fizzle at Atlanta: The Battle of Utoy Creek." *Civil War Times Illustrated*, February 1978, pp. 26–32.

Central Railroad and Banking Company of Georgia. *Reports of the Presidents and Superintendents of the Central Railroad and Banking Co. of Georgia, from No. 20 to 32 Inclusive, and the Amended Charter of the Company*. Savannah: G. N. Nichols, 1868.

Cherry, F. L. "The History of Opelika and Her Agricultural Tributary Territory, Embracing More Particularly Lee and Russell Counties, from the Earliest Settlement to the Present Date." *Alabama Historical Quarterly* 15 (Summer 1953):175–339.

Clarke, Dwight L. *William Tecumseh Sherman: Gold Rush Banker*. San Francisco: California Historical Society, 1969.

Clendenen, Clarence C. *Blood on the Border: The United States Army and the Mexican Irregulars*. London: Macmillan, 1969.

Coleman, Kenneth. *Confederate Athens*. Athens: University of Georgia Press, 1967.

Coleman, Richard G. *A Short History of the Roswell Manufacturing Company of Roswell, Georgia Home of "Roswell Grey."* N.p., 1982.

Collier, Calvin L. *The War Child's Children: The Story of the Third Regiment, Arkansas Cavalry, Confederate States Army*. Little Rock: Pioneer Press, 1965.

Collier, Grace. "Yankees Raid Watkinsville." *North Georgia Life,* magazine section of *The Walton* (Monroe, Ga.) *Tribune,* August 1964, pp. 7, 18.

Confederate Veteran 6 (November 1898):533; 17 (June 1909):302.

Connelly, Thomas L. *Autumn of Glory: The Army of Tennessee, 1862–1865.* Baton Rouge: Louisiana State University Press, 1971.

Convis, Charles L. *The Honor of Arms: A Biography of Myles W. Keogh.* Tucson: Westernlore Press, 1990.

Cooke, Philip St. George. *Cavalry Tactics: or, Regulations for the Instruction, Formations, and Movements of the Cavalry of the Army and Volunteers of the United States.* 1862 ed. New York: D. Van Nostrand, 1872.

Coulter, Harold S. *"A People Courageous": A History of Phenix City, Alabama.* Columbus, Ga.: Howard Printing, 1976.

Cox, Jacob D. *Atlanta.* Vol. 9 of *Campaigns of the Civil War.* New York: Scribner's, 1882.

Cullum, George W. *Biographical Register of the Officers and Graduates of the U.S. Military Academy at West Point, N.Y., from Its Establishment, in 1802, to 1890, with the Early History of the United States Military Academy.* 3rd ed. 3 vols. Boston: Houghton Mifflin, 1891.

Daniel Larry J., and Riley W. Gunter. *Confederate Cannon Foundries.* Union City, Tenn.: Pioneer Press, 1977.

Dary, David. "Lincoln's Frontier Guard." *Civil War Times Illustrated,* August 1972, pp. 12–14.

Davidson, Victor. *History of Wilkinson County.* Macon, Ga.: J. W. Burke, 1930.

Davis, Stephen. "The Death of Bishop Polk." *Blue & Gray,* June 1989, pp. 13–14.

Dawson, George Francis. *Life and Services of Gen. John A. Logan as Soldier and Statesman.* Chicago and New York: Belford, Clarke, 1887.

DeLeon, T. C. *Joseph Wheeler, the Man, the Statesman, the Soldier, Seen in Semi-Biographical Sketches.* Atlanta: Byrd Printing, 1899.

Densmore, Frances. "The Garrard Family in Frontenac." *Minnesota History* 14 (March 1933):31–43.

Des Cognets, Anna Russell. *Governor Garrard, of Kentucky, His Descendants and Relatives.* Lexington, Ky.: James M. Byrnes, 1898.

Dictionary of American Biography, 1928 ed.

Donald, W. J. "Alabama Confederate Hospitals (Part II)." *Alabama Review* 16 (January 1963):65–78.

Drewry, Jones M. "The Double-Barrelled Cannon of Athens, Georgia." *Georgia Historical Quarterly* 48 (December 1964):442–50.

DuBose, John Witherspoon. *General Joseph Wheeler and the Army of Tennessee.* New York: Neale, 1912.

Dyer, John P. *"Fightin' Joe" Wheeler.* Baton Rouge: Louisiana State University Press, 1941.

Edwards, William B. "A Pedigreed Smith and Wesson." *Hobbies,* June 1952, pp. 142, 149.

Estes, Claud, comp. *List of Field Officers, Regiments and Battalions in the Confederate States Army 1861–1865.* Macon, Ga.: J. W. Burke, 1912.

Evans, Clement A., ed. *Confederate Military History Extended Edition: A Library of Confederate States History in Seventeen Volumes, Written by Distinguished Men of the South, and Edited by Gen. Clement A. Evans of Georgia.* 17 vols. Atlanta: Confederate Publishing, 1899. Reprint ed., Wilmington, N.C.: Broadfoot Publishing, 1987–1989.

Favorite Songs of the People: School, Home, and Community Songs and Choruses Old and New for All Occasions. Philadelphia: Theodore Presser, 1927.

Fayette County Historical Society. *The History of Fayette County 1821–1971.* N.p.: Fayette County Historical Society, 1977.

Flanigan, James C. *History of Gwinnett County Georgia 1818–1960.* 2 vols. Hapeville, Ga.: Tyler, 1943; Longino & Porter, 1959.

Fleming, Walter L., ed. *General W. T. Sherman as College President: A Collection of Letters,*

Documents, and Other Material, Chiefly from Private Sources, Relating to the Life and Activities of General William Tecumseh Sherman, to the Early Years of Louisiana State University, and to the Stirring Conditions Existing in the South on the Eve of the Civil War; 1859–1861. Cleveland: Arthur H. Clark, 1912.

———. "William Tecumseh Sherman as College President." *South Atlantic Quarterly* 11 (January 1912):33–54.

Forbes, William II. "The Old Bronze Gentleman of Lovejoy's Station." *Confederate Veteran,* November–December 1989, pp. 28–30.

Foreman, Carolyn Thomas. "The Armstrongs of Indian Territory, Part III: General Frank Crawford Armstrong." *Chronicles of Oklahoma* 31 (Spring 1953):56–65.

Freeman, Douglas Southall. *Lee's Lieutenants: A Study in Command.* 3 vols. New York: Scribner's, 1942–1944.

———. *R. E. Lee: A Biography.* 4 vols. New York: Scribner's, 1934–1935.

Fretwell, Mark E. "Rousseau's Alabama Raid." *Alabama Historical Quarterly* 18 (Winter 1956):526–51.

Fuller, Claud E., and Richard D. Steuart. *Firearms of the Confederacy: The Shoulder Arms, Pistols and Revolvers of the Confederate Soldier, Including the Regular United States Models, the Imported Arms and Those Manufactured within the Confederacy.* Huntington, W.Va.: Standard Publications, 1944.

Garrard, Kenner D., ed. *Nolan's System for Training Cavalry Horses.* New York: D. Van Nostrand, 1862.

Garrett, Franklin M. *Atlanta and Environs: A Chronicle of Its People and Events.* 3 vols. New York: Lewis Historical Publishing, 1954.

Garrett, William. *Reminiscences of Public Men in Alabama, for Thirty Years.* Atlanta: Plantation Publishing, 1872.

"Gen. William H. Jackson." *Confederate Veteran* 2 (June 1894):176–77.

"Generals in the Saddle." *Southern Historical Society Papers* 19 (1891):167–75.

Gist, W. W. "The Ages of the Soldiers in the Civil War." *Iowa Journal of History and Politics* 16 (July 1918):387–99.

Going, Allen J. "A Shooting Affray in Knoxville with Interstate Repercussions: The Killing of James H. Clanton by David M. Nelson, 1871." *East Tennessee Historical Society's Publications* 27 (1955): 39–48.

Gower, Calvin W. "Kansas Territory and the Pike's Peak Gold Rush: Governing the Gold Region." *Kansas Historical Quarterly* 32 (Autumn 1966):289–313.

Griffin, Richard W. "Cobb County: The Roswell Manufacturing Company 1838." Typescript in the possession of Katharine Simpson, Roswell, Georgia.

Harris, Julia Collier. *The Life and Letters of Joel Chandler Harris.* Boston: Houghton Mifflin, 1918.

Harris, W. Stuart. *Dead Towns of Alabama.* Tuscaloosa: University of Alabama Press, 1977.

Hartsfield, William B. "Document in Handwriting of Atlanta's War-Time Mayor Describes Formal Surrender of the City to Federal Army." *Atlanta Constitution Magazine,* 31 May 1931, pp. 12–13, 18.

Hay, Thomas Robson. "The Davis-Hood-Johnston Controversy of 1864." *Mississippi Valley Historical Review* 11 (June 1924):54–84.

Henderson, G. F. R. *The Science of War: A Collection of Essays and Lectures 1892–1903.* Edited by Neill Malcolm. London: Longmans, Green, 1905.

Henderson, Lillian, comp. *Roster of the Confederate Soldiers of Georgia, 1861–1865.* 6 vols. Hapeville, Ga.: Longino & Porter, 1959–1964.

Hickman, John P. "Confederate Generals of Tennessee." *Confederate Veteran* 18 (April 1910):170–72.

Hicky, Louise McHenry. *Rambles through Morgan County: Her History, Century Old Houses and Churches, and Tales to Remember.* N.p.: Morgan County Historical Society, 1971.

"High Shoals." Typewritten page. Vertical files, Hargrett Rare Book and Manuscript Library, University of Georgia, Athens, n.d.

Hitt, Michael D. *Charged with Treason: Ordeal of 400 mill workers during military operations in Roswell, Georgia, 1864–1865.* Monroe, N.Y.: Library Research Associates, 1992.

Hoehling, A. A. *Last Train from Atlanta.* New York: Thomas Yoseloff, 1958.

Holland, Lynwood M. "Georgia Military Institute, the West Point of Georgia: 1851–1864." *Georgia Historical Quarterly* 43 (September 1959):225–47.

Hoole, W. Stanley. "John W. Mallet and the Confederate Ordnance Laboratories, 1862–1865." *Alabama Review* 26 (January 1973):33–72.

Hunt, Roger D., and Jack R. Brown. *Brevet Brigadier Generals in Blue.* Gaithersburg, Md.: Olde Soldier Books, 1990.

Hurd, Charles, ed. *A Treasury of Great American Quotations: Our Country's Life & History in the Thoughts of Its Men and Women.* New York: Hawthorn Books, 1964.

Irons, George Vernon. "River Ferries in Alabama Before 1861." *Alabama Review* 4 (January 1951):22–37.

Jarrell, Charles C. *Oxford Echoes.* N.p., 1967.

Jasper County Historical Foundation, Inc., comp. *History of Jasper County, Georgia.* Roswell, Ga.: W. H. Wolfe, 1984.

Jemison, E. Grace. *Historic Tales of Talladega.* Montgomery, Ala.: Paragon Press, 1959.

Johnson, Sid S. *Texans Who Wore the Gray.* Austin: Texas State Library, [1907].

Jones, Charles C., Jr. "A Roster of General Officers, Heads of Departments, Senators, Representatives, Military Organizations, &c., &c., in Confederate Service during the War between the States." *Southern Historical Society Papers* 2 (1876):A5–A130.

Jones, J. William, comp. "The Treatment of Prisoners during the War between the States." *Southern Historical Society Papers* 1 (March 1876):113–221.

Jones, Mary Callaway, comp. "Holt Genealogy." Typewritten volume in Washington Memorial Library, Macon, Ga., 1938.

Katz, Mark. "The Mysterious Prisoner: Assassination Suspect J. G. Ryan." *Civil War Times Illustrated,* November 1982, pp. 40–43.

Kelly, Dennis. "The Atlanta Campaign: Mountains to Pass, A River to Cross. The Battle of Kennesaw Mountain and Related Actions from June 10 to July 9 1864." *Blue & Gray,* June 1989, pp. 8–12, 15–18, 20–28, 30, 46, 48–50, 52–56.

———. "Back in the Saddle." *Civil War Times Illustrated,* December 1988, pp. 26–33.

King, G. Wayne. "General Judson Kilpatrick." *New Jersey History* 91 (Spring 1973):35–52.

King, Monroe M. *Destruction of New Manchester, Georgia: The Story behind the Ruins at Sweetwater Creek State Park.* Douglasville, Ga.: Monroe M. King, 1982.

Krakow, Kenneth K. *Georgia Place-Names.* Macon, Ga.: Winship Press, 1975.

Kross, Gary. "That One Error Fills Him with Faults: Gen. Alfred Iverson and His Brigade at Gettysburg." *Blue & Gray,* February 1995, pp. 22–24, 48–53.

Kurtz, Annie Laurie Fuller. "Surrender of Atlanta—Evacuation of Its Citizens." *Atlanta Journal Magazine,* 12 January 1936, pp. 10–11.

Kurtz, Wilbur G. "Civil War Days in Georgia, No. 6: The Augustus F. Hurt House." *Atlanta Constitution Magazine,* 22 June 1930, pp. 5–6.

———. "Civil War Days in Georgia: At the Dexter Niles House." *Atlanta Constitution Magazine,* 28 September 1930, pp. 5–6, 20.

———. "Civil War Days in Georgia: On the Powder Springs Road." *Atlanta Constitution Magazine,* 12 October 1930, pp. 8–9, 16, 21.

Lanman, Charles. *The Red Book of Michigan; A Civil, Military and Biographical History.* Detroit: E. B. Smith, 1871.

"The Last Roll: Gen. B. M. Thomas." *Confederate Veteran* 13 (September 1905):424–25.

"The Last Roll: J. I. Cannon." *Confederate Veteran* 17 (March 1909):130.

Lawson, Lewis A. *Wheeler's Last Raid.* Greenwood, Fla.: Penkevill Publishing, 1986.

Lee, Mary Welch. "Old Homes of Talladega County. (Kingston, Mt. Ida, Selwood, Thornhill, Alpine.)" *Alabama Historical Quarterly* 10 (1948):81–93.

Leech, Margaret. *Reveille in Washington 1860–1865.* New York: Harper & Brothers, 1941.

Leeper, Wesley Thurman. *Rebels Valiant: Second Arkansas Mounted Rifles (Dismounted).* Little Rock: Pioneer Press, 1964.

Lewis, Lloyd. *Sherman: Fighting Prophet.* New York: Harcourt Brace, 1932.

Liddell Hart, B. H. *Sherman: Soldier – Realist – American.* New York: Dodd Mead, 1929.

Long, Sara L. *Synopsis of the Military Career of Brevet Maj. Gen. Eli Long, U.S.V.* N.p., n.d.

Longacre, Edward G. "Judson Kilpatrick." *Civil War Times Illustrated,* April 1971, pp. 25–33.

Lonn, Ella. *Foreigners in the Union Army and Navy.* Baton Rouge: Louisiana State University Press, 1951.

Lowry, Thomas P. *The Story the Soldiers Wouldn't Tell: Sex in the Civil War.* Mechanicsburg, Pa.: Stackpole Books, 1994.

Madaus, Howard Michael, and Robert D. Needham. *The Battle Flags of the Confederate Army of Tennessee.* Milwaukee: Milwaukee Public Museum, 1976.

"Major Gen. Joseph Wheeler, Jr." *The Literary Messenger* 38 (April 1864):222–32.

Marcot, Roy M. *Spencer Repeating Arms.* Irvine, Calif.: Northwood Heritage Press, 1983.

Marszalek, John F. *Sherman: A Soldier's Passion for Order.* New York: Free Press, 1993.

———. *Sherman's Other War: The General and the Civil War Press.* Memphis: Memphis State University Press, 1981.

Martin, John H., comp. *Columbus, Geo., from Its Selection as a "Trading Town" in 1827, to Its Partial Destruction by Wilson's Raid, in 1865.* Columbus, Ga.: Thomas Gilbert, 1874.

McAllister, Anna. *Ellen Ewing: Wife of General Sherman.* New York: Benziger Brothers, 1936.

McDonough, James Lee, and James Pickett Jones. *War So Terrible: Sherman and Atlanta.* New York: Norton, 1987.

McKinney, Francis F. *Education in Violence: The Life of George H. Thomas and the History of the Army of the Cumberland.* Detroit: Wayne State University Press, 1961.

McMurry, Richard M. "The Atlanta Campaign: Rocky Face to the Dallas Line, the Battles of May 1864." *Blue & Gray,* May 1989, pp. 10–18, 20–21, 23, 46, 48–60, 62.

———. "Cassville." *Civil War Times Illustrated,* December 1971, pp. 4–9, 45–48.

———. "'The Hell Hole': New Hope Church." *Civil War Times Illustrated,* February 1973, pp. 32–43.

———. *John Bell Hood and the War for Southern Independence.* Lexington: University Press of Kentucky, 1982.

———. "Kennesaw Mountain." *Civil War Times Illustrated,* January 1970, pp. 19–34.

———, ed. "More On 'Raw Courage.'" *Civil War Times Illustrated,* October 1975, pp. 36–38.

———. "Resaca: 'A Heap of Hard Fiten.'" *Civil War Times Illustrated,* November 1970, pp. 4–12, 44–48.

Memorial Record of Alabama: A Concise Account of the State's Political, Military, Professional and Industrial Progress, Together with the Personal Memoirs of Many of Its People. 2 vols. Madison, Wis.: Brant & Fuller, 1893. Reprint ed., Spartanburg, S.C.: Reprint Company, 1976.

Merrill, James M. *William Tecumseh Sherman.* Chicago: Rand McNally, 1971.

Miller, Rex. "John Thomas Croxton: Scholar, Lawyer, Soldier, Military Governor, Newspaperman, Diplomat and Mason." *Register of the Kentucky Historical Society* 74 (October 1976):281–99.

———. *Wheeler's Favorites: A Regimental History of the 51st Alabama Cavalry Regiment.* Depew, N.Y.: Patrex Press, 1991.

Mitchell, Frances Letcher. *Georgia Land and People.* Atlanta: Franklin Printing and Publishing, 1893.

Montgomery, Horace. *Johnny Cobb: Confederate Aristocrat.* Athens: University of Georgia Press, 1964.

Moore, Joseph Henry Hightower. *A History of Clayton County, Georgia 1821–1983.* Edited by Alice Copeland Kilgore, Edith Hanes Smith, and Frances Partridge Tuck. Roswell, Ga.: W. H. Wolfe, 1983.

The National Cyclopaedia of American Biography Being the History of the United States Illustrated in the Lives of the Founders, Builders, and Defenders of the Republic, and of the Men and Women Who Are Doing the Work and Moulding the Thoughts of the Present Time, 1904 ed.

Newton County Historical Society, comp. *History of Newton County Georgia.* N.p., 1988.

Northen, William J., ed. *Men of Mark in Georgia: A Complete and Elaborate History of the State from Its Settlement to the Present Time, Chiefly Told in Biographies of the Most Eminent Men of Each Period of Georgia's Progress and Development.* 7 vols. Atlanta: A. B. Caldwell, 1907–1912.

Nunn, Alexander. *Yesterdays in Loachapoka and Communities Nearby: Roxana, Rocky Mount, Macon's Hill, Beehive, Pine Knot, Armstrong, Crossroads, Concord.* Alexander City, Ala.: Outlook Publishing, 1968.

O'Connor, Richard. *Hood: Cavalier General.* New York: Prentice-Hall, 1949.

Orr, Dorothy. "Gustavus John Orr: Georgia Educator, 1819–1887." *Atlanta Historical Bulletin* 16 (Fall-Winter 1971):9–269.

———. "Life of Edgar Harold Orr as Revealed in Family Letters." Typewritten volume. Georgia Department of Archives and History, Atlanta, n.d.

Owen, Thomas McAdory. *History of Alabama and Dictionary of Alabama Biography.* 4 vols. Chicago: S. J. Clarke Publishing, 1921.

Patterson, Caroline. "Places of Historic Interest in Macon." *Confederate Veteran* 20 (May 1912):252–53.

Patterson, Gerard A. "The Death of Iverson's Brigade." *Gettysburg Magazine,* July 1991, pp. 13–18.

Perkerson, Medora Field. *White Columns in Georgia.* New York: Rinehart, 1952.

Perkins, Jacob Randolph. *Trails, Rails and War: The Life of General G. M. Dodge.* Indianapolis: Bobbs-Merrill, 1929.

Pohanka, Brian. "Myles Keogh from the Vatican to the Little Big Horn." *Military Images* 8 (Sept.-Oct. 1986):15–24.

Polk, William L. *Leonidas Polk: Bishop and General.* 2 vols. New ed. New York: Longmans, Green, 1915.

Powell, William H., comp. *List of Officers of the Army of the United States from 1779 to 1900 Embracing a Register of All Appointments by the President of the United States in the Volunteer Service during the Civil War and of Volunteer Officers in the Service of the United States June 1, 1900.* New York: L. R. Hamersly, 1900. Reprint ed., Detroit: Gale, 1967.

Power, Virginia W. "Bulloch Hall, I Love You." *Atlanta Journal and Constitution Magazine,* 15 August 1971, pp. 14, 24–28.

Prather, Susan Verdery. "When Sherman Marched through Georgia." *Confederate Veteran* 30 (September 1922):339.

Pratt, Isabel. "Captain Thomas E. King." *Southern Bivouac* 2 (July 1884):511–14.

Rainer, Vessie Thrasher. *Henry County, Georgia: The Mother of Counties.* N.p., 1971.

"Raw Courage." *Civil War Times Illustrated,* July 1974, p. 46.

Reedstrom, Ernest L. *Bugles, Banners and War Bonnets.* Caldwell, Idaho: Caxton, 1977.

Reid, Whitelaw. *Ohio in the War: Her Statesmen, Her Generals, and Soldiers.* 2 vols. Cincinnati: Moore, Wilstach & Baldwin, 1868.

Ripley, Warren. *Artillery and Ammunition of the Civil War.* New York: Promontory Press, 1970.

Robertson, John, comp. *Michigan in the War.* Revised ed. Lansing: W. S. George, 1882.

Rowell, John W. *Yankee Artillerymen: Through the Civil War with Eli Lilly's Indiana Battery.* Knoxville: University of Tennessee Press, 1975.

————. *Yankee Cavalrymen: Through the Civil War with the Ninth Pennsylvania Cavalry.* Knoxville: University of Tennessee Press, 1971.

Russell, Lewis C. "Georgia Towns Moved in War." *Atlanta Journal Magazine,* 28 February 1932, p. 6.

Sams, Anita B. *Wayfarers in Walton: A History of Walton County Georgia 1818–1967.* Monroe, Ga.: General Charitable Foundation, 1967.

Scaife, William. *The Campaign for Atlanta.* Atlanta: n.p., 1985.

Scott, W. S. "Kilpatrick's Raid around Atlanta, August 18th to 22d, 1864." *Journal of the United States Cavalry Association* 3 (September 1890):263–70.

Scruggs, Carroll Proctor, ed. *Georgia Historical Markers.* Valdosta, Ga.: Bay Tree Grove Publishers, 1973.

Secrist, Philip. "Resaca: For Sherman a Moment of Truth." *Atlanta Historical Journal* 22 (Spring 1978):8–41.

Sergent, Mary Elizabeth. *They Lie Forgotten: The United States Military Academy 1856– 1861 Together with a Class Album for the Class of May, 1861.* Middletown, N.Y: Prior King Press, 1986.

Sherwood, Adiel. *A Gazetteer of Georgia; Containing a Particular Description of the State; Its Resources, Counties, Towns, Villages, and Whatever Is Usual in Statistical Works.* 4th ed. Macon: S. Boykin; Griffin: Brawner & Putnam; Atlanta: J. Richards, 1860.

"Sketch of Major-General Joseph Wheeler." *Southern Review* 4 (November 1898):5–9.

"Sketch of Lieutenant-General Joseph Wheeler." *Southern Bivouac* 2 (February 1884):241– 46.

Smalley, E. V. "General Sherman." *Century Magazine,* January 1884, pp. 450–62.

Smedes, Susan Dabney. *Memorials of a Southern Planter.* Edited by Fletcher M. Green. New York: Knopf, 1965.

Smith, Gerald J. "The Battle of Brown's Mill." *Brown's Guide to Georgia* 2 (Winter 1973– 74):24–28.

————. "The Faded Coat of Blue." *Columbus* (Ga.) *Sunday Ledger-Enquirer Magazine,* 18 June 1972, pp. 14–15, 25.

Smith, J. Harmon, comp. "Organizational Summary of Military Organizations from Georgia in the Confederate States of America." Typewritten volume. Georgia Department of Archives and History, Atlanta, 1961.

"The Soldiers of Kansas. The Frontier Guard at the White House, Washington, 1861." *Transactions of the Kansas State Historical Society, 1907–1908. Embracing Addresses at Annual Meetings; The Centennial of Zebulon Montgomery Pike's Visit, Including a Review of One Hundred Years Under the Flag; Fiftieth Anniversary of the First Free-State Territorial Legislature, 1857; Also the First State Legislature, and the Session of 1868; The Disappearing Indians; The Soldiers of Kansas; Floods in the Missouri River; and Interesting Personal Narrative* 10 (1908):418–21.

Speed, Thomas, Robert M. Kelly, and Alfred Pirtle. *The Union Regiments of Kentucky.* Louisville: Courier-Journal Job Printing, 1897.

Standard, Diffee William. *Columbus, Georgia, in the Confederacy: The Social and Industrial Life of the Chattahoochee River Port.* New York: William-Frederick Press, 1954.

Starr, Merritt. "General Horace Capron, 1804–1885." *Journal of the Illinois State Historical Society* 18 (April–June 1925):259–349.

Starr, Stephen Z. *The Union Cavalry in the Civil War.* 3 vols. Baton Rouge: Louisiana State University Press, 1979–1985.

Steffen, Randy. *The Horse Soldier 1776–1943. The United States Cavalryman: His Uniforms, Arms, Accoutrements, and Equipments.* 4 vols. Norman: University of Oklahoma Press, 1977–1979.

Stegeman, John F. *These Men She Gave: Civil War Diary of Athens, Georgia.* Athens: University of Georgia Press, 1964.

Steiner, Paul E. *Medical-Military Portraits of Union and Confederate Generals.* Philadelphia: Whitmore Publishing, 1968.

———. *Physician-Generals in the Civil War: A Study in Nineteenth Mid-Century American Medicine.* Springfield, Ill.: Charles C. Thomas, 1966.

Stuart, A. A. *Iowa Colonels and Regiments: Being a History of Iowa Regiments in the War of the Rebellion; and Containing a Description of the Battles in Which They Have Fought.* Des Moines: Mills, 1865.

"Student Historian Researches McAfee-Holcombe Bridge." *Gwinnett Historical Society Newsletter,* Spring 1975, p. 2.

Suarez, Annette McDonald. *A Source Book on the Early History of Cuthbert and Randolph County, Georgia.* Edited by William Bailey Williford. Atlanta: Cherokee Publishing, 1982.

Sunderland, Glenn W. *Lightning at Hoover's Gap: The Story of Wilder's Lightning Brigade.* New York: Thomas Yoseloff, 1969.

Suppiger, Joseph E. "'In Defense of Washington.'" *Civil War Times Illustrated,* August 1976, pp. 38–45.

Telfair, Nancy. *A History of Columbus, Georgia, 1828–1928.* Columbus, Ga.: Historical Publishing, 1929.

Temple, Sarah Blackwell Gober. *The First Hundred Years: A History of Cobb County, in Georgia.* Atlanta: Walter W. Brown Publishing, 1935.

Tennessee Civil War Centennial Commission. *Tennesseans in the Civil War: A Military History of Confederate and Union Units with Available Rosters of Personnel.* 2 vols. Nashville: Civil War Centennial Commission, 1964–1965.

Throckmorton, A. B. "Major-General Kilpatrick." *Northern Monthly Magazine,* April 1868, pp. 590–605.

Todd, Frederick P., George Woodbridge, Lee A. Wallace, Jr., and Michael J. McAfee. *American Military Equipage, 1851–1872: A Description by Word and Picture of What the American Soldier, Sailor and Marine of These Years Wore and Carried, With Emphasis on the American Civil War.* 3 vols. Providence, R.I.: Company of Military Historians, 1974, 1977, 1978. Reprint ed., New York: Scribner's, 1980.

Tucker, Glenn. *High Tide at Gettysburg: The Campaign in Pennsylvania.* Indianapolis: Bobbs-Merrill, 1958.

Upham, Warren, and Rose Barteau Dunlap, comps. *Collections of the Minnesota Historical Society.* Vol. 14: *Minnesota Biographies 1655–1912.* St. Paul: Volkszeitung, 1912.

Utley, Francis Lee, and Marion R. Hemperly, eds. *Placenames of Georgia: Essays of John H. Goff.* Athens: University of Georgia Press, 1975.

Vandiver, Wellington. "Pioneer Talladega, Its Minutes and Memories." *Alabama Historical Quarterly* 16 (Summer 1954):163–297.

Van Horne, Thomas B. *History of the Army of the Cumberland: Its Organization, Campaigns, and Battles Written at the Request of Major-General George H. Thomas Chiefly from his Private Military Journal and Official and Other Documents Furnished by Him.* 2 vols. and atlas. Cincinnati: Robert Clarke, 1875.

Waters, John B. *Merchant of Terror: General Sherman and Total War.* Indianapolis and New York: Bobbs-Merrill, 1973.

Warner, Ezra J. *Generals in Blue: Lives of the Union Commanders.* Baton Rouge: Louisiana State University Press, 1964.

———. *Generals in Gray: Lives of the Confederate Commanders.* Baton Rouge: Louisiana State University Press, 1959.

White, George. *Historical Collections of Georgia: Containing the Most Interesting Facts, Traditions, Biographical Sketches, Anecdotes, Etc. Relating to Its History and Antiquities, from Its First Settlement to the Present Time.* New York: Pudney & Russell, 1854.

———. *Statistics of the State of Georgia: Including an Account of Its Natural, Civil, and*

Ecclesiastical History; Together with a Particular Description of Each County, Notices of the Manners and Customs of Its Aboriginal Tribes, and a Correct Map of the State. Savannah: W. Thorne Williams, 1849.

White, Goodrich C. "Emory in the Civil War Era." *Emory Alumnus* 36 (November 1960):7–15, 50–51.

Wiley, Bell Irvin, and Hirst D. Milhollen. *Embattled Confederates: An Illustrated History of Southerners at War.* New York: Bonanza Books, 1954.

Williams, Carolyn White. *History of Jones County Georgia for One Hundred Years, Specifically 1807–1907.* Macon, Ga.: J. W. Burke, 1957.

Williams, T. Harry. *McClellan, Sherman and Grant.* New Brunswick, N.J.: Rutgers University Press, 1962.

———. "The Military Leadership of North and South." In *Why the North Won the Civil War,* pp. 23–47. Edited by David Donald. Baton Rouge: Louisiana State University Press, 1960.

Williford, William Bailey. *The Glory of Covington.* Atlanta: Cherokee Publishing, 1973.

Worsley, Etta Blanchard. *Columbus on the Chattahoochee.* Columbus, Ga.: Columbus Office Supply, 1951.

Wright, Marcus J. *Arkansas in the War 1861–1865.* Batesville, Ark.: Independence County Historical Society, 1963.

Wyeth, John A. *Life of Lieutenant-General Nathan Bedford Forrest.* New York: Harper & Brothers, 1899.

Young, Bennett H. *Confederate Wizards of the Saddle: Being Reminiscences and Observations of One Who Rode with Morgan.* Boston: Chapple Publishing, 1914.

Young, Ida, Julius Gholson, and Clara Nell Hargrove. *History of Macon, Georgia.* Macon: Lyon, Marshall and Brooks. 1950.

Theses and Dissertations

Harper, John W. "Rousseau's Alabama Raid." M.A. thesis, Auburn University, 1965.

Pierce, John Edward. "General Hugh Judson Kilpatrick in the American Civil War: A New Appraisal." Ph.D. diss., Pennsylvania State University, 1983.

Sewell, Toxey H. "Rousseau's Raid through Northern-Eastern Alabama, July 10–22, 1864, Which Culminated in the Battle of Chehaw or Beasley's Farm." M.A. thesis, University of Alabama, 1914.

Shelton, Perry Wayne. "Personal Letters Written by Lawrence Sullivan Ross." M.A. thesis, Baylor University, 1938.

Thiele, Thomas F. "The Evolution of Cavalry in the American Civil War; 1861–1863." Ph.D. diss., University of Michigan, 1951.

Interviews

Elliott, Dr. W. Kerry. Newnan, Ga. Telephone interview with the author, November 1991.

Hutchins, Travis. Curator of Exhibits, Georgia State Museum of Science and Industry, Atlanta, Ga. Telephone interview with the author, January 1994.

Philpot, John. Franklin, Ga. Interview with the author, December 1973.

Russell, G. Lamar. McDonough, Ga. Telephone interview with the author, November 1993.

Wilson, James O., Sr. Glenn, Ga. Interview with the author, August 1973.

INDEX

DAVID EVANS, a native Georgian with a Ph.D. in military history, is the author of numerous articles on the Atlanta campaign and has appeared on the Arts & Entertainment Network's highly acclaimed television series *Civil War Journal*. He is an avid horseman and bugler, and his research for this book included three days in the saddle during a seventy-mile reenactment of a Union cavalry raid.